D0764221

# The Ways of Federalism in Western Countries and the Horizons of Territorial Autonomy in Spain

Alberto López-Basaguren • Leire Escajedo
San Epifanio

Editors

# The Ways of Federalism in Western Countries and the Horizons of Territorial Autonomy in Spain

Volume 2

FUNDACIÓN
CANADÁ

 Springer

*Editors*
Alberto López-Basaguren
Leire Escajedo San Epifanio
Fac. Social Sciences and Communication
University of the Basque Country
Leioa - Bizkaia
Spain

ISBN 978-3-642-27716-0      ISBN 978-3-642-27717-7 (eBook)
DOI 10.1007/978-3-642-27717-7
Springer Heidelberg New York Dordrecht London

Library of Congress Control Number: 2013938613

Printed on acid-free paper

Springer is part of Springer Science+Business Media (www.springer.com)

# Contents

# Contributors

**M. Agudo Zamora** Derecho Constitucional, Universidad de Córdoba, Córdoba, Spain

**Ignacio Álvarez Rodríguez** Universidad de Valladolid, Valladolid, Spain

**Xavier Arbós Marín** Universitat de Barcelona, Barcelona, Spain

**Esteban Arlucea Ruíz** University of the Basque Country, Bilbao, Spain

**Rainer Arnold** University of Regensburg, Regensburg, Germany

**Sebastian D. Baglioni** University of Toronto, Toronto, Canada

**Rémi Barrué-Belou** Université Toulouse 1, Toulouse, France

Université Laval, Quebec City, QC, Canada

**Francisco J. Bastida Freijedo** Universidad de Oviedo, Oviedo, Spain

**Nathalie Behnke** Konstanz University, Konstanz, Germany

**Iñigo Bullain** University of the Basque Country, Bilbao, Spain

**Ana M. Carmona Contreras** University of Seville, Seville, Spain

**Josep Ma. Castellà Andreu** University of Barcelona, Barcelona, Spain

**Eleonora Ceccherini** University of Genoa, Genova, Italy

**César Colino** UNED, Madrid, Spain

**Víctor Cuesta-López** Universidad de Las Palmas de Gran Canaria, Las Palmas de Gran Canaria, Spain

**Régis Dandoy** Université Libre de Bruxelles, Bruxelles, Belgium

**Luis Delgado del Rincón** Universidad de Burgos, Burgos, Spain

**Ignacio Durbán Martin** University of Valencia, Valencia, Spain

**Leire Escajedo San Epifanio** University of the Basque Country (UPV/EHU), Bilbao, Spain

**Bonnie N. Field** Bentley University, Waltham, USA

**Igor Filibi** University of the Basque Country (UPV/EHU), Bilbao, Spain

**María Jesús García Morales** Universidad Autónoma de Barcelona, Barcelona, Spain

**L.A. Gálvez Muñoz** Universidad de Murcia, Murcia, Spain

**Elena García-Cuevas Roque** San Pablo CEU University, Madrid, Spain

**Jule Goikoetxea** St Edmund's College, University of Cambridge, Cambridge, UK

**Eric Guntermann** Canada Research Chair in Electoral Studies, Université de Montréal, Montréal, Canada

**M.S. Ilchenko** Institute of Philosophy and Law, the Russian Academy of Sciences, Ural Branch, Ekaterinburg, Russia

**Jordi Jaria i Manzano** Universitat Rovira i Virgili, Tarragona, Spain

**Guy Laforest** Université Laval, Québec City, QC, Canada

**Antonio López Castillo** Universidad Autónoma de Madrid, Ciudad Universitaria de Cantoblanco, Madrid, Spain

**Luzius Mader** Ministry of Justice, Bern, Switzerland

**Joaquín Martín Cubas** Universidad de Valencia, Valencia, Spain

**Francisco J. Matia Portilla** Facultad de Ciencias Sociales, Jurídicas y de la Comunicación, University of Valladolid, Palacio de Mansilla, Segovia, Spain

**Anna Mastromarino** Centro Studi sul Federalismo, University of Turin, Torino, Italy

**Simon Meisch** University of Tübingen, Internationales Zentrum für Ethik in den Wissenschaften (IZEW), Tübingen, Germany

**Josu de Miguel Bárcena** Facultad de Derecho, Universidad Autónoma de Barcelona, Campus de Bellaterra, Barcelona, Spain

**C. Milione** Facultad de Derecho, Universidad de Córdoba (Españaa), Córdoba, Spain

**Michael Morden** University of Toronto, Toronto, Canada

**Alain Noël** Université de Montréal, Montréal, Canada

**Amelia Pascual Medrano** Universidad de La Rioja, Logroño, Spain

**Ian Peach** University of New Brunswick, Fredericton, NB, Canada

**Alexander Pelletier** University of Toronto, Toronto, Canada

**Benôit Pelletier** University of Ottawa, Ottawa, Canada

**Andoni Perez Ayala** University of the Basque Country, Bilbao, Spain

**M. Pérez Gabaldón** Universidad CEU Cardenal Herrera, Alfara del Patriarca, Spain

**Zulima Pérez i Seguí** Universitat de València, Valencia, Spain

**José M. Porras Ramírez** Universidad de Granada, Granada, Spain

**Cecilia Rosado Villaverde** Rey Juan Carlos University, Madrid, Spain

**Santiago Roura Gómez** Universidade da Coruña, Coruña, Spain

**J.G. Ruiz González** Universidad de Murcia, Murcia, Spain

**Eva Sáenz Royo** Universidad de Zaragoza, Zaragoza, Spain

**María Salvador Martínez** Facultad de Derecho, UNED, Madrid, Spain

**Remedio Sánchez Ferriz** University of Valencia, Valencia, Spain

**M. Soledad Santana Herrera** University of Las Palmas de Gran Canaria, Las Palmas de Gran Canaria, Spain

**José A. Sanz Moreno** Universidad Complutense, Madrid, Spain

**Esther Seijas Villadangos** Universidad de León, León, Spain

**Richard Simeon** University of Toronto, Toronto, Canada

**Juan J. Solozábal Echavarría** Universidad Autónoma de Madrid, Ciudad Universitaria de Cantoblanco, Madrid, Spain

**Javier Tajadura Tejada** University of the Basque Country, Bilbao, Spain

**Jorge Tuñón** Universidad Carlos III de Madrid, Getafe, Spain

**Eduardo Vírgala Foruria** University of the Basque Country (UPV/EHU), Bilbao, Spain

**Jennifer Wallner** University of Ottawa, Ottawa, Canada

**Carol S. Weissert** Florida State University, Tallahassee, FL, USA

**Cristina Zoco Zabala** Universidad Pública de Navarra, Pamplona, Spain

# Part I
# Intergovernmental Relations:
# The Experience in Federal Countries
# and in Spain

# Intergovernmental Relations in the Architecture of Federal System: The United States

Carol S. Weissert

The term intergovernmental relations originated in the United States in the 1930s and was motivated by a strong concern for the effective delivery of public services to clients. The term has come to mean the activities and interactions among governmental units within a federation and includes local general purpose and special governments and nongovernmental units (Agranoff 2004)—often working in intergovernmental networks. For comparativists, intergovernmental relations are the workings of governmental representatives at various levels usually in institutional settings.

Comparative federalism scholars have embraced the notion of multilevel governance or MLG (Hooghe and Marks 1996, 2001, 2003) in analyzing the EU, but now it is used widely outside this domain. The touchstone of MLG is flexibility where governance is disbursed across multiple jurisdictions, often in overlapping and task-driven capacity. U.S. network scholarship may be viewed as a first cousin to this work, although it is often conducted at the local level (Feiock and Scholz 2010; Peterson and O'Toole 2001). Earlier work by Ostrom and Ostrom and others also highlighted flexible governance arrangements and overlapping jurisdictions (see for example, Ostrom et al. 1988).

In U.S. scholarship, the focus has been primarily on state–federal relationships, and it is those relationships that I wish to speak to today, for in the United States, those relationships are prickly if not downright contentious today.

Minutes after President Obama signed the Patient Protection and Affordable Care Act, the major health reform measure that has become known derisively as "Obama Care," a handful of state attorneys general, led by my own attorney general in Florida, filed suit in federal court arguing that the measure was unconstitutional. This is clearly a federalism issue. As the Virginia Attorney General put it, his state's challenge to the PPCA "is not about health care, it's about our freedom and about

C.S. Weissert (✉)
Department of Political Science, Florida State University, 226 Bellamy Building, Tallahassee, FL 32306-2230, USA
e-mail: cweissert@fsu.edu

A. López-Basaguren and L. Escajedo San Epifanio (eds.), *The Ways of Federalism in Western Countries and the Horizons of Territorial Autonomy in Spain*, Vol. 2, DOI 10.1007/978-3-642-27717-7_1, © Springer-Verlag Berlin Heidelberg 2013

standing up and calling on the federal government to follow the ultimate law of the land—the Constitution" (cited in Joondepth 2011, p. 449). The focus of the states' complaint is the provision in the PPACA that calls for all citizens to have health coverage by January 1, 2014. Anyone failing to do so would pay a penalty. At issue was the clause in our constitution giving the Congress (the federal government) the responsibility to regulate interstate commerce.

The states contend that the provision is not interstate commerce because health care insurance is not an economic activity covered by interstate commerce. They note that the provision penalizes inactivity—not activity. The federal government, in contrast, argues that anyone choosing to not buy insurance is making an economic decision made more important by the fact that in the aggregate these individual decisions could result in billions of dollars in costs to others, including the federal government through our safety net programs. A 2005 Supreme Court decision finding that growing marijuana for personal use medically affected interstate commerce would tend to have us predict that the Court would support the broader definition of interstate commerce (*Raich v. Gonzales*). However, we also know that the court is not immune to public opinion and political statements (witness *Bush v. Gore* in 2000 that essentially decided the presidential race for George W. Bush).

There was a great deal of uncertainty until recently when the Supreme Court would consider the PPACA case. The Obama Administration could have delayed the decision through appeals until after the 2012 election but chose not to do so. It will now be decided in this term that ends in June 2012—prior to our November 2012 election. One might say that this means that the Obama Administration thinks the decision of the court will be positive for its case. Perhaps they know something we don't. Nonetheless, the case will be decided in the next few months and the decision will be a pivotal one for federalism and intergovernmental relations.

The states are also fighting in court over environmental protection, specifically against federal regulations issued by the Environmental Protection Agency on air pollution, mercury and air toxics standards for power plants, water pollution controls, and greenhouse gas regulations. Of course, these suits are not new—Democratic governors sued the EPA during the Bush Administration to get the agency to adopt regulations prescribed in law. Now Republican governors are fighting against the regulations that have been promulgated from the law. However, it is striking that many of these suits include a majority of the states in the effort.

Other cases include the following:

- Arizona is suing the federal government "to force the federal government" to do its job on immigration.
- Arizona and Florida are suing over the federal Voting Rights Act of 1965, which requires those states to seek prior approval from the Justice Department before making any changes in the state's election laws, saying that the law exceeds Constitutional authority.

The Republican Party—which hopes to take the White House in 2012—espouses states' rights and pretty much thinks that the federal government can do no right, although they are desperate to control that federal government. They are piling on the states' concerns—whether it is to embarrass the White House or be really in sympathy with the states is not clear. For example, a few months ago, the House passed a bill that would bar the EPA from overruling state decisions on water quality (Cappiello 2011).

Nevertheless, apart from the court case, the states—including my own—have pushed back in ways other than the courts. My state governor has refused to accept any federal dollars offered to it by the PPAC, something like cutting off your nose to spite your face. He also refused other federal grants—anything that represents a commitment that the state might be "stuck" with after the federal dollars end.

As I write this, the governor has said that he will not accept any of the president's proposed new job program—we don't call it a stimulus anymore—even though it amounts to over $6 billion for a state very much needing the money.

Other examples include:

- Texas has refused to participate in a federal permitting system on greenhouse gas regulation that every other state now follows (Broder and Galbraith 2011).
- Three states have refused to participate in a fingerprint-sharing program that the Obama Administration wants to impose nationwide. The proposal would send fingerprints of every person booked by state or local police to federal databases to be checked for immigration violations.
- In 2011, six states adopted 10th Amendment Resolutions asking the federal government to "cease and desist any and all activities outside the scope of their constitutionally-delegated powers."

States have pushed back on the implementation of the No Child Left Behind law—a George W. Bush-era education reform. It is very prescriptive, and this year—the ninth year of the law—called for 100 % of students in a state to be proficient in English and Math by 2014. Essentially, states have refused to meet the standards in the law. What happened? Nothing. The Feds blinked, saying that the states don't have to implement the controversial parts of the law.

The feds similarly "blinked" over a 2005 law that would have imposed tough requirements for driver's licenses. The law provided that if states did not comply, their citizens would not be able to board airplanes or enter federal buildings. None of the states had complied with the law by 2009, and 13 states had enacted laws prohibiting compliance with the act. A compromise measure was proposed but stalled. Real ID is in limbo and not likely to be resuscitated.

What's going on here, and how is it important to our discussion of intergovernmental relations? These relationships might best be understood by a simple causal model:

State preferences -> Federal actions (political safeguard)
State preferences <- Federal actions (compliance)

The first stage is the states successfully obtaining the federal public policies they desire. I've labeled this political safeguard since the notion that states can impact national policy through institutional means is very limited in the United States.

Rather, as summarized by a U.S. Supreme Court justice, states must rely on political safeguards—basically a means of lobbying the Congress for their desired policy.

The second stage kicks in after the policies have been put into law. Most domestic policies require intergovernmental cooperation in implementation. In short, the federal government simply cannot put the programs in place on its own but must get the states and localities to comply with their wishes. The literature here—largely called implementation research—is vast and useful.

## Political Safeguards

The first relationship might be called political safeguards. The framers of the U.S. Constitution thought that the states could be a check on federal power. In the earliest years of the United States, states were represented in the upper house— our Senate—and were selected by their state legislatures. This changed with the 17th amendment (we only have 27) adopted in 1913, which provided for popular election of the U.S. Senate. Thus, senators are elected statewide but are politicians in their own right—not delegates of the state legislature or the state. It seems amazing that 3/4 of the states would vote to take away this linkage, but their choices were so poor that even they voted to take the power away. So we have few institutional safeguards.

Rather, what we have today are political safeguards. According to the U.S. Supreme Court in *Garcia v. San Antonio Metropolitan Transit Authority* in 1985, the courts should not use the 10th amendment to limit congressional power to regulate state and local government. Rather, the court should trust that state interests will be protected by political safeguards of federalism (Pittenger 1992). It is the states working through the political process that protects federalism. It is the states as lobbyists. States have a collective interest in protecting their autonomy, but they don't do such a good job in this area, for often the states have a parochial interest as well—and a political interest (i.e., Republican governors may see an issue such as health care reform as very differently from Democratic governors).

How do the states obtain their preferences at the national level? We don't have the institutional components of an upper house representing states. We don't have the nice cooperative executive federalism of Canada. We don't have intergovernmental entities identifying problems and coming up with solutions. There was once a group called the Advisory Commission on Intergovernmental Relations, set up by statute and made up of federal, state, and local elected and appointed officials, which did just that. However, it was abolished in a money-saving effort (interesting since it was quite cheap) and was not replaced. Congress once had committees assigned the tasks of overseeing intergovernmental relations but no longer. Federal agencies and the Government Accountability office no longer have intergovernmental units. The White House maintains an office with intergovernmental in the title, but it is largely a political and favor-dispensing office (Kincaid 2012).

What we have left are associations representing states and localities that try to get their policies enacted in the U.S. Congress. How well do they do that?

Most researchers will say not so well. One reason might be institutional—or lack of institutions. A second reason is that collective action is a difficult one for the states. Smith (2008) and Dinan (2011) found that this individual state vs. collective action is a thorny one where the collective does not generally work well because state officials from the most populous states are tempted to "go it alone" in lobbying Congress, weakening the states' collective interests represented by groups like the National Governors Association. There are also political and ideological divides that make bipartisan organizations of states less effective in highly salient issues. The case in point is the Patient Protection and Affordable Care Act mentioned earlier. There was much at stake intergovernmentally in this bill. This was also an area where there was much state innovation—including the well-known Massachusetts health reform bill adopted when now presidential hopeful Mitt Romney was governor. The National Governors Association and National Conference of State Legislatures had much at stake but simply were not players in the discussions. As Dinan (2011) notes, the NGA and NCSL were unable to reach consensus on a state position, and partisan groups such as the Republican Governors Association were able to step in their place. Individual states stepped up their efforts. Dinan documents that individual states advanced universal state interests, as well as their own particularistic concerns largely to their own delegations. He also demonstrates that state officials attempted to mobilize public opinion and concludes that this mechanism was influential when states elevated state concerns in public consciousness to the point that congressional leaders had to take account of these concerns. The states' influence was most likely to succeed when the Members think it is in their interest to support states' preferences.

Nevertheless, it is not simply the problem of the states. There is also a lack of interest on the part of the Congress in federalism and intergovernmental issues. Kincaid (2012) quotes one senator—Carl Levin from Michigan—as saying, "there is no political capital in intergovernmental relations." So the politics aren't there and neither is much sympathy for states' problems. Ray Scheppach, long-time director of the National Governors Association, summarized his experience with the Congress by noting that it 'had few concerns' regarding financial burdens on the states." Indeed, recent scholarship supports this claim (Scheppach 2012).

Scheller and Weissert (2011) examined the potency of "state roots" or the value of state experience on the policymaking tendencies of Members of Congress. They posit that Members of Congress who have served in state legislatures will be more positively attuned to state interests. The rationale is that these state legislative veterans will sponsor state-friendly legislation because they have both political and policy knowledge that will lead them to recognize the importance of intergovernmental relations and state capacity. Weissert and Scheller examined major health legislation over six congressional sessions and whether Members with state experience were more likely to support state-friendly legislation, state-unfriendly legislation, or no mention of states. Surprisingly, they found that state legislative veterans were equally likely to sponsor state-friendly and state-unfriendly legislation.

They were not likely to sponsor legislation ignoring states. The authors concluded that there is evidence of state roots, but the roots can work both for and against states. One possible explanation is that their state legislative experience told them that the states are limited in what they can do and the federal government needs to provide considerable guidance—even preemption—to obtain desirable policy. A second possible explanation is that in coming to the Congress, the state legislative veterans build on their past experience but look forward to the rest of their career in Congress, so they sponsor legislation dealing with states but may be just as inclined to promote their new political home—the federal level—compared to their old one—the state.

These findings help explain the difficulty in tracing what has been called "vertical diffusion" where the federal government learns from the states. Researchers have generally found no support or modest support for the idea that the federal government uses state experiences in drafting federal legislation in similar policy areas (Mossberger 1999; Rabe 2007; Thompson and Burke 2007; Esterling 2009; Lowery et al. 2011). For example, Esterling found that the vast experience of state officials in implementing Medicaid programs was not being tapped in congressional hearings in what he called "a failure of federalism." The Members valued the views of lobbyists and academics more in this key intergovernmental program administered by state officials.

So we have problems with interest groups representing the states, with the states undercutting those collective interests and with the lack of receptivity from Members of Congress. A final problem, recognized by Bolleyer (2009) and not studied among U.S. scholars, is the tendency of the federal government to pick and choose whom to deal with. So this linkage isn't very strong.

## Compliance/Implementation

While political safeguards are highly political and involve largely elected officials, compliance relates to both politics and non-partisan administration or, as Kincaid (2012) calls it, policymaking and implementation. On the policymaking side, the usual analogy is carrots and sticks. Carrots are in the form of grants in aid to encourage states to act in the way desired by the federal government.

Federal grants totaled a whopping $624 billion in FY 2011. This amount was boosted by the 2009 stimulus package known as the American Recovery and Reinvestment Act, which provided enormous assistance to states—totaling some $275 billion in grants to states and localities. Much of this funding was intended to help states and local governments finance their own policy agendas (Conlan and Posner 2011). However, the AARA was an aberration—both in the number of dollars and the lack of restrictions. Moreover, in FY 2012, federal grants were expected to fall to $584 billion—much of this dominated by one program— Medicaid—the federal-state program providing health insurance for the poor and elderly.

The sticks are penalties or punishment for not acting in the way so desired. Unfunded mandates, cross-over sanctions, partial preemptions, and preemptions have been documented and analyzed to chart centralization trends in intergovernmental relations (Conlan 1991; Kincaid 1993; Posner 1997, 2007; Zimmerman 1991, 1993, 2007).

Once the carrots and sticks are proffered, the policy component is over and the implementation part begins. The implementation is generally undertaken by administrators and staff who are not ideological or political and is often cooperative in nature. Implementation often involves close working relationships among levels (Deil Wright called this picket fence federalism). As one example, a recent article in the New York Times about Texas Governor Rick Perry and his ongoing antagonism to the EPA contains a brief mention that "EPA officials work cooperatively with lower-level Texas officials, who often seek federal technical guidance and money to address environmental problems" (Broder and Galbraith 2011, A14).

However, in today's highly party-polarized politics, even the cooperation is often at a premium. That leads us to the pushback we are seeing now that I discussed at the beginning. Why is it that states are not "biting" on the federal dollars? The short answer is ideology or, in political science terms, goal congruence—you don't find too many Democratic governors and legislatures turning back federal dollars. Nicholson-Crotty (2004) documented that the level of congruence between states and the federal grant administrators was an important predictor of fund diversion. When the states shared the grant program's goals, the program was more successful at stimulating the desired spending. When the goals were not shared, more grant funding was diverted away from the desired areas.

In tough economic times, the federal government has more incentive to shift costs to state and local governments (Kincaid 2012), and it appears that this is the case today. The Congress today is not so generous. We have a special committee working to "find" $1.3 trillion in cuts or revenues over the next 10 years. One can be sure that these cuts will come in large part from federal grants to states and localities.

We haven't seen this pushback since the 1960s when we had governors standing at doors of schools to prevent federal officials from walking young African American students into classrooms. Frankly, it was what gave States' rights in the United States a bad name—but I'm wondering if we're about to see more of the same. There remains some racial animosity (much toward our president), and it seems—at least in the Republican debates—as though the animosity is becoming more accepted—at least in some political circles.

## Conclusion

Do all these weaken or strengthen intergovernmental relationships? What about our scholarship understanding these relationships?

There are few reasons to think that highly partisan, non-cooperative, lack of concern for intergovernmental issues on the part of the Congress environment coupled with extremely toxic economic times can be positive for intergovernmental relations in the United States. I can't think of any except that the system will survive as it has for over 300 years. Some scholars have called for a new "blueprint" of intergovernmental relations, taking into account the impacts of globalization and technology shifts and demographic trends (Scheppach and Shafroth 2008). These scholars suggest a better sorting out of intergovernmental responsibilities, especially in health policy, collapsing categorical grants, and a rethinking of how the three levels of revenue systems interact. What are the chances of this rather systematic rethinking occurring? Next to zero. The national government has its hands full with its massive deficit problem, and states have their own fiscal problems as well. Collaboration and far-reaching thinking simply isn't realistic.

There are more reasons to be optimistic on the scholarship side, however. We have moved beyond descriptive accounts of intergovernmental conflict and cooperation and are now looking at the dynamic relationship between the federal and state governments in terms of intergovernmental political competition. Hill and Weissert (1994) looked at the impact the possibility of federal action on the likelihood states would cooperate with each other in interstate compacts on low-level nuclear wastes. Volden (2005, 2007) and Nicholson-Crotty (2011) look at intergovernmental competition as expressed through credit taking. At issue in this work is understanding allocation of responsibilities in terms of efficiency. Volden finds that when one level of government is in a much better position to efficiently provide the service, that government does provide that services. However, when the capacities of the two levels are closer, the quest for political credit entices the less efficient government to join in the provision—thus overproviding the service and overtaxing in doing so. When he expands the work to federal grants in aid, he concludes that the impact of an increase in grant money will be larger when the state has limited ability to raise money through revenue and can claim credit for the production of the goods through the grant. Nicholson-Crotty is not convinced that the assumptions are accurate—particularly relating to credit taking or blame casting. He argues that confusion over proper credit assignment allows state legislators to claim credit for federal production, whether they increase or reduce spending and find empirical support for this "free-rider" notion of credit.

Intergovernmental relations can be informed by this game theoretical work (followed by empirical tests). I think we'll be seeing more theoretical and empirical work, testing some of the activities of pushback and blame casting.

So the conclusion is mixed. There are contextual stresses on intergovernmental relations in the United States that involve serious fiscal difficulties at the federal and state levels. The slow economic recovery has had a huge negative effect on most states, compounded by the fact that they must balance their budgets annually. The federal government does not have to balance its budget and is living with the excess spending that ensued in the past decade. While some optimists think that tough times can lead to meaningful reforms, I don't see it. Intergovernmental relations are in no danger in the United States in terms of survival. Unfortunately, the dysfunctions of that system are also likely to survive and perhaps even thrive in these tough times. The good news is in intergovernmental scholarship. Scholars are examining systematically and theoretically the dynamic and shifting nature of the system. We can understand how one governmental level's actions affect another. The scholarship may catch up with the actors and their actions. At least we can hope so.

# References

Agranoff, Robert. 2004. Autonomy, Devolution and Intergovernmental Relations. Regional and Federal Studies 14: 26–65.

Bolleyer, Nicole. 2009. Intergovernmental Cooperation: Rational Choices in Federal Systems and Beyond. New York: Oxford University Press.

Broder, John M. and Kate Galbraith. 2011. E.P.A. is Longtime Favorite Target for Perry. The New York Times. Sept. 30, A13–14.

Cappiello, Dina. 2011. Clean Water: House Bars EPA From Overruling States on Pollution. Huffington Post. July 13.

Conlan, Timothy. 1991. And the Beat Goes On: Intergovernmental Mandates and Preemption in an Era of Deregulation. Publius: The Journal of Federalism 21: 43–57.

Conlan, Timothy and Paul Posner. 2011. Inflection Point? Federalism and the Obama Administration. **Publius: The Journal of Federalism** 41,3, 421–446.

Dinan, John. 2011. Shaping Health Reform: Understanding the States' Challenges to the Patient Protection and Affordable Care Act. **Publius: The Journal of Federalism** 41,3: 395–420.

Esterling, Kevin. 2009. Does the Federal Government Learn from the States? Medicaid and the Limits of Expertise in the Intergovernmental Lobby. **Publius: The Journal of Federalism** 39,1: 1–21.

Feiock, Richard and John Scholz. 2010. Self-Organizing Federalism. New York: Cambridge University Press.

Hill, Jeffrey and Carol Weissert. 1995. Implementation and the Irony of Delegation: The Politics of Low-Level Radioactive Waste Disposal. Journal of Politics 57,2: 344–369.

Hooghe, Liesbet and Gary Marks. 1996. Europe With Regions? Regioanl Representation in the European Union. Publius: The Journal of Federalism 26: 73–91.

Hooghe, Liesbet and Gary Marks. 2001. Multi-Level Governance and European Integration. Lanham, MD: Rowman and Littlefield.

Hooghe, Liesbet and Gary Marks. 2003. Unraveling the Central State but How? Types of Multi-Level Governance, American Political Science Review 97: 233–243.

Joondepth, Bradley. 2011. Federalism and Health Care Reform: Understanding the States' Challenges to the Patient Protection and Affordable Care Act. **Publius: The Journal of Federalism** 41,3: 447–470.

Kincaid, John. 1993. From Cooperation to Coercion in American Federalism: Housing, Fragmentation and Preemption. Journal of Law and Politics 9: 333–433.

Kincaid, John, 2012. The Rise of Social Welfare and Onward March of Coercive Federalism. In Networked Governance: The Future of Intergovernmental Management. Jack W. Meek and Kurt Thurmaier, eds. Washington D.C. CQ Press, 8–33.

Lowery, David, Virginia Gray and Frank Baumgartner. 2011. Policy Attention in State and Nation: Is Anyone Listening to the Laboratories of Democracy? "Publius: the Journal of Federalism 41,2: 286–310.

Mossberger, Karen. 1999. State-Federal Diffusion and Policy Learning: From Enterprise Zones to Empowerment Zones. Publius: The Journal of Federalism. 29: 31–50.

Nicholson-Crotty, Sean. 2004. Goal Conflict and Fund Diversion in Federal Grants to the States. American Journal of Political Science 48,1: 110–122.

Nicholson-Crotty, Sean. 2011. Claiming Credit in the U.S. Federal System: Testing a Model of Competitive Federalism. Publius: The Journal of Federalism 41,2: 232–256.

Ostrom, Vincent, Robert Bish and Elinor Ostrom. 1988. Local Government in the United States. New York: ICS Press.

Peterson, John and Laurence J. O'Toole Jr. 2001. Federal Governance in the United States and the European Union: A Policy Network Perspective. In The Federal Vision, Kalypso Nicolaidis and Robert Howse, eds. New York: Oxford University Press. 300–334.

Pittenger, John C. 1992. Garcia and the Political Safeguards of Federalism: Is There a Better Solution to the Conundrum of the Tenth Amendment? Publius: The Journal of Federalism 22,1: 1–19.

Posner, Paul. 1997. Unfunded Mandate Reform Act: 1996 and Beyond. Publius: The Journal of Federalism 27: 53–71.

Posner, Paul. 2007. The Politics of Coercive Federalism in the Bush Era. Publius: The Journal of Federalism 37: 390–412.

Rabe, Barry. 2007. Can Congress Govern the Climate? Research Brief no. 1. John Brademas Center for the Study of Congress. Wagner Graduate School of Public Service, New York University.

Scheppach, Raymond C. and Frank Shafroth. 2008. Intergovernmental Finance in a New Global Economy. In Intergovernmental Management for the 21st Century. Timothy J. Conlan and Paul L. Posner, eds. Washington D.C.: Brookings Institution, 42–74.

Scheppach, Ray. 2012. Social Welfare Spending Dominates. In Networked Governance: The Future of Intergovernmental Management. Jack W. Meek and Kurt Thurmaier, eds. Washington D.C. CQ Press, 34–38.

Scheller, Daniel and Carol Weissert. 2011. State Roots and Policy Learning in the U.S. Congress. Unpublished manuscript.

Smith, Troy. 2008. Intergovernmental Lobbying: How Opportunistic Actors Create a Less Structured and Balanced Federal System. In Intergovernmental Management in the 21st Century. Timothy J. Conlan and Paul L. Posner, editors. Washington D.C: Brookings Institution Press. 310–337.

Thompson, Frank J., and Courtney Burke. 2007. Executive Federalism and Medicaid Demonstration Waivers: Implications for Policy and Democratic Process. Journal of Health Politics, Policy, and Law. 32: 971–1004.

Volden, Craig. 2005. Intergovernmental Political Competition in American Federalism. American Journal of Political Science 49,2: 327–342.

Volden, Craig. 2007. Intergovernmental Grants: A Formal Model of Interrelated National and Subnational Political Decisions. Publius: The Journal of Federalism 37,2: 209–243.

Zimmerman, Joseph P. 1991. Federal Preemption Under Reagan's New Federalism. Publius: the Journal of Federalism 21: 7–28.

Zimmerman, Joseph P. 1993. Preemption in the U.S. Federal System. Publius: the Journal of Federalism 23: 1–14.

Zimmerman, Joseph P. 2007. Congressional Preemption During the George W. Bush Administration 37: 432–452.

# Intergovernmental Relations in Canada: A Horizontal Perspective

**Benoît Pelletier**

**Abstract** Canada consists of two orders of government, each sovereign in its exercise of legislative powers, which stem from the Constitution. Canada is hence a federation, and as in any such state, the division of legislative powers is characterized by a certain constitutional rigidity. It cannot be formally modified except by means of a relatively complex procedure requiring the participation of both orders of government. The particular complexity of the procedure for amending the Constitution of Canada explains, in part, why intergovernmental relations focus essentially on ways to improve the Canadian federation through non-constitutional means.

**Note to the Reader** This text was presented in October 2011, long before a sovereignist government was elected in Quebec following the general elections held on September 4, 2012. Needless to say, this election should modify substantially the government of Quebec's position on Canadian intergovernmental affairs. The current text was also presented before the Supreme Court of Canada's decision

International Conference *The Ways of Federalism and the Horizons of the Spanish State of Autonomies*, Bilbao, Spain, October 2011.

This text is a modified and enriched version of a conference given at an International Seminar held in Zaragoza, Spain, in March 2009. The seminar's theme was *The Federalization of Spain: Deficits of Intergovernmental Co-operation*. The paper then prepared by the author has been published as: Benoît Pelletier, "Las relaciones intergubernamentales en Canadá desde una perspectiva horizontal" in José Tudela & Felix Knuepling (eds.) *España y modelos de federalismo* (Madrid: Centro de Estudios Políticos y Constitucionales: Fundación Manuel Giménez Abad de Estudios Parlamentarios y del Estado Autonómico, 2010), p. 301.

This text results from 10 years of active political life during which the author had the responsibility of intergovernmental affairs as official opposition critic (1998–2003) and as minister (2003–2008) in Quebec. The reader should therefore not be surprised if practical (rather than theoretical) aspects of intergovernmental relations are covered without scientific claim, nor should he or she be surprised if they are presented from a Quebec perspective.

B. Pelletier (✉)
Faculty of Law, University of Ottawa, 57 Louis-Pasteur, Room 213, Ottawa, ON,
Canada K1N 6N5
e-mail: Benoit.Pelletier@uottawa.ca

A. López-Basaguren and L. Escajedo San Epifanio (eds.), *The Ways of Federalism in Western Countries and the Horizons of Territorial Autonomy in Spain*, Vol. 2, DOI 10.1007/978-3-642-27717-7_2, © Springer-Verlag Berlin Heidelberg 2013

in *Reference re* Securities Act, [2011] 3 SCR 837, which was favourable for the government of Quebec (and Alberta). This decision is linked to note 51 of this text.

# Introduction

Canada consists of two orders of government, each sovereign in its exercise of legislative powers, which stem from the Constitution. Canada is hence a federation,[1] and as in any such state, the division of legislative powers is characterized by a certain constitutional rigidity: It cannot be formally modified except by means of a relatively complex procedure requiring the participation of both orders of government.[2]

In a federation, the first order of government is called central, as its jurisdictions extend throughout the State's territory. In Canada, this order of government is composed of the Canadian (or federal) Parliament and government and of the institutions or organizations they have duly created. It exercises its powers over the entire Canadian territory.

The second order of government composing a federation—any federation—is labelled decentralized because it holds jurisdictions only over a limited part of the State. In Canada, it consists of ten provincial parliaments (legislatures) and governments and of the institutions and organizations they have duly created. The institutions pertaining to each province only hold jurisdictions within that province's territory.

In any federation, intergovernmental relations can be examined from a vertical or a horizontal perspective. A vertical perspective studies the relationships between the centralized (or federal) government and the decentralized (or provincial[3]) governments. Intergovernmental relations can also be studied from the angle of the relationships between the entities of decentralized governments. In this case, the analysis is from a horizontal perspective.

In this essay, horizontal federalism in Canada—i.e., relations between provinces—will be discussed. The disparities that exist between Canadian provinces in socioeconomic, demographic, and political terms will be covered. Intergovernmental collaboration as a value in itself will be examined. Some comments on the bicommunal or multinational character of Canada will be

---

[1] A federation is composed of at least two orders of government. See Anderson (2008) at 3.

[2] In Canada, the division of legislative powers cannot be modified except by agreement of the Parliament of Canada and at least two-thirds of the provinces (meaning seven of them) representing at least 50 % of the total population of the provinces (the *7/50 procedure*). In all federations, the division of legislative powers is relatively rigid as it can only be modified through a complex process; this process nonetheless varies between countries.

[3] In Canada, the federated states are called *provinces*. In other federations, these decentralized entities may be designated under different terms, such as states, regions, communities, länder, cantons, etc.

included, which will naturally lead to discussing the place of Quebec within Canada, as well as the role of Aboriginal peoples in intergovernmental relations. The Canadian system's key players, as well as the forms and modalities of intergovernmental relations, will be highlighted. The institutions and mechanisms that are allowing "interprovincialism"[4] to develop in Canada will be presented, and lastly, the future of horizontal intergovernmental cooperation in this country will be explored. First, the very particular situation of the three Canadian territories (the Northwest Territories, Yukon, and Nunavut) will be introduced. These territories play a significant role in the realm of intergovernmental relations, even though their legal status is highly ambiguous.

## The Three Canadian Territories: An Imprecise Status

Canada's federation was created in 1867 with the adoption of the *British North America Act* (later renamed *Constitution Act, 1867*[5] following the patriation of the Canadian Constitution), which united the four original provinces of Ontario, Quebec, New Brunswick, and Nova Scotia into Canada and laid down the rules to admit other North American British colonies and lands in the newly created Dominion.[6] More precisely, section 146 of the *Constitution Act, 1867*, targeted what was known as the Northwest Territories (which was a Crown possession) and the Hudson's Bay Company's Rupert's Land acquired in 1870 by the British authorities for the Dominion of Canada.[7] These vast lands spread across most of today's Canada and became the provinces of Alberta, Saskatchewan, Manitoba, part of Quebec, and Ontario and, of course, the three territories: the Northwest Territories, Yukon, and Nunavut.

Between 1870 and 1905, the southern part of this land was fractioned into three provinces while the northern part was divided into two territories: Yukon and the Northwest Territories.[8] The creation of Nunavut occurred in 1999 following the 1993 *Nunavut Land Claims Agreement Act.*[9] The principle behind this agreement is to create a land where the majority of the population is Inuit, thus allowing the

---

[4] The concept of *interprovincialism* does not exist in dictionaries; it has been invented to describe the intensification of relations between provinces.

[5] *Constitution Act, 1867* (UK), 30 & 31 Vict, c 3, reprinted in RSC 1985, App II, No 5.

[6] *Ibid*, s 146.

[7] *Rupert's Land Act, 1868* (UK, 31 & 32 Vict, c 105, reprinted in RSC 1985, App II, No 6; *An Act for the temporary Government of Rupert's Land and the North-Western Territory when united with Canada*, SC 1869, c 3, reprinted in RSC 1985, App II, No 7, and *Rupert's Land and North-Western Territory Order (1870)*, RSC 1985, App II, No 9.

[8] *Manitoba Act, 1870*, 33 Vict, c 3 (Can); *Yukon Act*, SC 2002, c 7; *Saskatchewan Act, 1905*, 4–5 Edw VII, c 42 (Can); *Alberta Act, 1905*, 4–5 Edw VII, c 3 (Can); *Northwest Territories Act*, RSC 1985, c N-27.

[9] *Nunavut Land Claims Agreement Act*, SC 1993, c 29.

promotion of Inuit culture and values.[10] There was a hope that federal involvement in Inuit affairs would decrease, giving Inuit people greater autonomy and control over eastern Arctic policies.[11]

Although the territory's desire to control local affairs (instead of relying solely on federal goodwill) is best illustrated with Nunavut's quest for an Inuit land, its reality mirrors changes occurring in territories' role in intergovernmental relations. Territories, unlike provinces, are not granted legislative powers by the Constitution, but rather these powers are delegated by the Canadian Parliament. Lands that are not included in provinces, such as the territories and coastal waters, fall under the legislative powers of the Parliament of Canada.[12]

The three territories are ruled by similar acts giving them the same powers and political institutions. Each of them has a Commissioner, a legislative assembly, and tribunals.[13] They are under the responsibility of the Minister of Aboriginal Affairs and Northern Development Canada.[14] The Commissioner is appointed by the Governor General,[15] and his role is to be the link between the Minister and the population of the territory. His functions are similar to those of a provincial Lieutenant-Governor,[16] being the chief executive authority.[17]

Territories have virtually the same scope of legislative powers as provinces. The three territories' acts "empower the legislature to make laws for the government of its territory in relation to a long list of subjects roughly corresponding to the list of subjects allocated to the provincial legislature by s. 92 of the Constitution Act, 1867."[18] The difference lies in the fact that provinces are given these powers by the Constitution, whereas territories acts are federal legislation, thus subject to be amended by the Parliament of Canada.[19]

Provinces are created by the Constitution itself; they do not depend on central authorities. However, the federal order of government holds possession of the territories. It is *de jure* entitled to delegate powers to territorial authorities, amend

---

[10] Légaré (2008).

[11] *Ibid.*

[12] *Constitution Act, 1871* (UK), 34 & 35 Vict, c 28, s 4, reprinted in RCS 1985, App II, No 11.

[13] *Yukon Act, supra* note 8; *Northwest Territories Act, supra* note 8; *Nunavut Act*, SC 1993, c 28.

[14] See the website of Aboriginal affairs and Northern Development Canada for the list of acts for which the Minister has sole responsibility to Parliament: <www.aandc-aadnc.gc.ca>.

[15] Although the Governor General is the official representative of the head of State, the Queen, he always acts under the advice of the Prime Minister. Legally, the Governor General holds every executive powers, but *de facto* these powers belong to the Prime Minister and his cabinet.

[16] Lieutenant-Governors, much like the Governor General, hold every executive powers but always act under the advice of premiers and their cabinets.

[17] See the Commissioner of Nunavut's website: <http://www.commissioner.gov.nu.ca/english/commissioner/role_commiss.html>, the Commissioner of Yukon's website: <http://www.commissioner.gov.yk.ca/about/role.html>, and the Commissioner of the Northwest Territories' website: <http://www.commissioner.gov.nt.ca/role/>.

[18] Hogg (2008) at 332.

[19] See *Yukon Act, supra* note 8; *Northwest Territories Act, supra* note 8; *Nunavut Act, supra* note 13.

their constitutive acts, or reorganize them geographically. Provinces could even be created from these lands (which would obtain the same level of autonomy as other provinces) or be annexed to existing provinces. In order to do so, the consent of at least seven provinces representing at least 50 % of the total population of the provinces would be required, in accordance with what is called the *7/50 procedure*.[20] Still, such an amendment is unlikely to be considered any time soon as there is no appetite in Canada for reopening constitutional negotiations.[21]

Delegation of powers by the central Parliament to the territories is basically the same principle as delegating powers to municipalities or governmental commissions for example. Such delegation is therefore not deemed permanent in essence because it can, theoretically, be revoked by the Parliament at any time.[22] Although amendments to acts creating the territories are usually supported by the legislative assembly of said territories, by law such support is not mandatory.

Even though territories' governments arise from a delegation of powers, it is recognized that, *de facto*, it has become almost impossible to decrease the powers already held by territories. In fact, they have become quasi provinces, and it would be unthinkable for any federal government to alter this status. On this topic, authors David Cameron and Richard Simeon wrote that "the [...] territories [...] are now integrated with the provinces. Meetings are Federal/Provincial/Territorial or Provincial/Territorial despite the fact that the territories remain constitutional offspring of the federal government."[23] In this case, their constitutional status of federal protectorates becomes superfluous and much more theoretical than practical. "This evolution toward provincial status has evoked remarkably little comment, even though it has the potential for changing the dynamic of intergovernmental relations because three more voices are added to the six smaller and poorer provinces."[24] Obviously, this challenges the way intergovernmental relations used to be, for there are three extra entities engaging in intergovernmental discussions with the federal government or joining collaborative interprovincial relations.

This reality further characterizes the ambiguous status of the territories. Their participation in intergovernmental relations greatly departs from their constitutional status. They are said to be acting more like provinces than like federal protectorates, which redefines intergovernmental relations, parting away from the traditional federal–provincial–municipal framework.[25]

---

[20] *Constitution Act, 1982*, ss 42(1)e) and 42(1)f), being Schedule B to the *Canada Act 1982* (UK), 1982, c 11. For the *7/50 procedure*, see *supra* note 2. In addition, other laws complement this procedure, see *An Act respecting constitutional amendments*, SC 1996, c 1. On this topic, see Pelletier (1998), p. 271.

[21] The constitutional amendment procedure is such a heavy undertaking that it makes even the slightest constitutional reform very difficult (see *supra* notes 2 and 20).

[22] *Supra* note 10 at 348.

[23] Cameron and Simeon (2002) at 63.

[24] *Ibid.*

[25] *Ibid* at 70.

The Council of the Federation will be covered further in this text, but it is worth noting that the territories are members of this institution fuelling interprovincial relations. The inclusion of territories in the Council illustrates how they have come to play an important role in intergovernmental relations. In the long run, results can be twofold; it, on the one hand, will shift the dynamics of interprovincial relations and, on the other hand, will cement this view of the territories as quasi provinces. It will then become harder for the federal to mingle in territorial affairs. Moreover, because Nunavut represents *de facto* the first model of Aboriginal self-government, it influences other Aboriginal peoples to claim self-government rights and reinforces their will to be represented in intergovernmental relations.[26]

In the Constitution, territories were given a different status than provinces, a status that subjugates them to the federal Parliament and government and gives them very little self-determination power. The situation has changed since the creation of Canada, whereas that status has remained untouched constitution-wise, territories have *de facto* become very similar to provinces. As we have seen in this section, territories are only territories in the eye of the law; they are much more emancipated otherwise. This form of political leeway they have acquired over time is unlikely to be altered or to return to its former dependency position, even though it would be legally and constitutionally feasible.

## Disparities Between Canadian Provinces

While Canada's provinces are all equal in legal theory, profound differences set them apart from one another. Some are significantly more populated than others. This is the case for Ontario and Quebec, while Atlantic provinces are home to small populations.

Financially speaking, Alberta has seemingly limitless wealth because of its natural resources (mainly oil), which are only expected to be exhausted over a century from now. Its neighbor, Saskatchewan, also benefits (albeit less than Alberta) from the financial strength that comes from oil extraction. British Columbia is in the midst of major demographic and economic progress. Manitoba, located west of the still powerful Ontario,[27] is having a more difficult time. In the East, the four Atlantic provinces remain economically vulnerable. However, Newfoundland and Labrador and Nova Scotia have seen their revenues and fiscal capacity improve given the generous agreements reached with the federal government concerning the

---

[26] *Ibid.*

[27] Ontario recently entered the equalization payment program as a "have-not" province and is therefore entitled to receive transfer payments. One reason at the source of this change is that Ontario's manufacturing industry, especially the automobile industry, is suffering from high gasoline prices, low U.S. demand, and a strong Canadian dollar. Ontario remains, however, a financial hub in Canada. For the constitutional principle of equalization payments, see *Constitution Act, 1867, supra* note 5, s. 36(2).

distribution of royalty payments for the exploitation of offshore natural resources. In Quebec, although the economic situation has improved somewhat over the last few years, the public debt remains colossal.

The disparities between Canadian provinces are very real. They must be kept in mind when examining intergovernmental relations in Canada. These disparities have an influence on the relations that each province individually maintains with the federal government. For instance, the poorer a province is, the more dependent it becomes to money transfers from the federal government. These provinces are therefore less inclined than the others, in principle, to encourage the limitation of federal spending power in provincial jurisdictions.[28]

Of course, equalization payments make it possible to redistribute wealth throughout Canada in order to reduce inequities and financial gaps between provinces. As can be expected, provinces not receiving equalization payments take a dimmer view of the increase of those payments than provinces that do receive them. It is therefore markedly difficult for Canadian provinces to agree on certain contentious matters such as the solution to fiscal imbalance,[29] in which the question of reviewing equalization payments inevitably comes up. The same is true, as mentioned earlier, for the limitation of federal powers to spend in provincial jurisdictions.

In sum, the disparities between Canadian provinces make it more difficult for them to reach consensus on various subjects, a strain that comes out within the very heart of the Council of the Federation, an institution covered later.

## *The Values Inherent to Intergovernmental Collaboration*

It is common knowledge that we live in an era of interdependence. The world is flattening.[30] This is not a time of withdrawal but of collaboration. In this context, any community that is not open to the world will asphyxiate in the long term.

---

[28] No province, other than Quebec, is really insisting on limiting federal spending powers in provincial jurisdictions. The Government of Quebec has taken the habit of referring to the "presumed federal spending power" as the Supreme Court of Canada has not yet fully acknowledged this power. It has only done so in *obiter dicta*.

[29] Fiscal imbalance is a concept that refers to the difference that exists between provincial and federal revenues, taking into account their constitutional responsibilities. The Government of Quebec estimates that this matter is not yet solved in Canada, despite the revision of equalization that was carried out in the frenzy of the 2007 federal budget and even despite the fact that the financial crisis currently affecting the entire world has transformed the Canadian government's budget surpluses into deficits. According to Quebec, the solution to fiscal imbalance depends not only on increased equalization but also on an increase in federal transfers for postsecondary education and social programs and on a federal transfer to the provinces of tax points or tax room. Basically, this would mean revising equalization, federal transfers, and the tax base in a way that would provide provinces with a certain financial stability, an acceptable fiscal capacity considering their responsibilities, and predictability in their budget planning.

[30] The flattening of the world refers to the bestseller by Friedman (2005).

The Canadian provinces and territories must also learn to better work together. They must get to know one another and show stronger mutual acceptance. Their efforts to attain certain common goals must be planned and coordinated.

Dialogue is a value in itself. It needs to be reinforced among the provinces and territories. This dialogue must pursue a certain number of purposes. It must create the possibility of information and expertise exchange. Such sharing can address comparisons between provinces in order to increase their efficiency in a given area of activity. This is the case for discussions about best practices for example.

Canada is sometimes seen as being composed of four major regions (Quebec, Ontario, the Atlantic, and the West) or perhaps five (Quebec, Ontario, the Atlantic, the Prairies, and British Columbia). This vision of the Canadian federation is not without a valid basis, as Canada is certainly marked by strong regional trends, which show up even in partisan politics.[31] However, a conception of Canada that relies on four or five major regions must not overlook the fact that provinces, not regions, hold legislative and executive powers and make up—along with the federal Parliament—the constituent power (i.e., the power to change the Constitution) in Canada.

At any rate, provinces very much like to share expertise with one another on a regional basis. With that in mind, we note that Quebec and Ontario have recently shown a desire to work more closely together[32] in order to reinforce their influence compared to Alberta and British Columbia, which are increasingly threatening in terms of economic competition and political power.[33] Quebec and New Brunswick have also shown a desire to collaborate. As an example, a deal had been reached where Hydro-Québec, a crown corporation in Quebec, was to buy New Brunswick Power.[34] Although the deal ultimately failed because of lack of popular support, the point remains that cooperation between both provinces is increasing. Other deals

---

[31] To illustrate this tendency, let us ponder over the Bloc Québécois, which elects members of Parliament only among Quebec ridings, and the Canadian Alliance (previously known as the Reform Party), a Western political group that has merged with the Conservative Party of Canada in 2003.

[32] On September 11, 2009, Ontario and Quebec premiers and their respective cabinets held their second joint meeting, at which they signed the *Ontario-Quebec Trade and Cooperation Agreement* to reduce trade barriers, improve labor mobility, and make the two provinces more competitive in the global economy. See Office of the Premier, News Release, "Le Québec et l'Ontario continuent de renforcer leur partenariat" (11 September 2009) online: <http://www.premier-ministre.gouv. qc.ca/actualites>. A third joint meeting was held on June 16, 2010, where both "cabinets expressed their desire to develop and broaden their relations" and suggested an annual Ontario–Quebec meeting. See Office of the Premier, News Release, "Cooperation between Ontario and Québec is yielding tangible results" (16 June 2010) online: <http://www.premier-ministre.gouv.qc.ca/actualites>.

[33] There is currently an agreement between Alberta and British Columbia, the *Trade, Investment and Labour Mobility Agreement*, which makes the partnership very competitive, see <http://www.tilma.ca/>.

[34] See Hydro Québec, Press Release "New Brunswick and Québec conclude negotiations following energy agreement" (20 January 2010) online: <http://www.hydroquebec.com/communiques/>.

have been reached between Quebec and New Brunswick notably on workforce mobility in the construction business.[35]

## Canada's Bicommunal and Multinational Character

In addition to being made up of ten provinces, three territories, and—from a certain perspective—four or five major regions, Canada can be seen as a bicommunal and multinational federation.[36]

On the one hand, Canada is bicommunal because it is home to two major societies most easily distinguished by their language: French and English. Each of them constitutes a majority—the first in Canada as a whole, the second in Quebec. Canada's bicommunal character is not, however, expressed in the country's political institutions. *A fortiori*, this character is not recognized by the Canadian Constitution, aside of course for official bilingualism[37] and for a few constitutional measures that bespeak a certain consideration of the identity-related specificity of Quebec.[38]

On the other hand, Canada is not only bicommunal; it is also multinational. This is true because Quebec forms a nation within Canada.[39] It is also true because of the existence of Aboriginal nations.[40]

Canada has never really embraced its multinational dimension. It seems to deny it in the interest of a common identity construction (nation building) that leaves little space for other national realities than the Canadian nation *per se*.[41]

---

[35] See Office of the Premier, News Release, "Coopération accrue entre le Nouveau-Brunswick et le Québec en matière d'approvisionnement, de mobilité de la main-d'œuvre et de francophonie" (3 October 2008) online: <http://www.premier-ministre.gouv.qc.ca/actualites>.

[36] It is important not to confuse multiculturalism and multinationalism. Multiculturalism reflects the existence of many cultures, whereas multinationalism refers to more than one nation in a given area. A single nation can be deemed multicultural.

[37] The Canadian State recognizes two official languages: English and French. However, this applies only to the federal order of government. Among the Canadian provinces, only New Brunswick is officially (and constitutionally) bilingual.

[38] The *Constitution Act, 1867, supra* note 5, s 94, recognizes *a contrario* the civilian tradition in Quebec private law. The *Constitution Act, 1982, supra* note 20, s 59, stipulates that subsection 23 (1)a) (concerning some rights relating to education in the official minority's language, for instance English in Quebec) will apply only to Quebec should it decide so. However, every other stipulation laid down in section 23 applies to Quebec.

[39] By a motion approved by a very strong majority on November 27, 2006, the Canadian House of Commons recognized that the Québécois form a nation within a united Canada. However, this resolution has no constitutional value. See the House of Commons of Canada, 39th Parliament, 1st Session, Journal no. 87, November 27, 2006, at <http://www2.parl.gc.ca/HousePublications/Publication.aspx?Language=E&Mode=1&Parl=39&Ses=1&DocId=2539924>.

[40] The Aboriginals are recognized as peoples in the *Constitution Act, 1982, supra* note 20, ss 35 and 35.1. S 35(2), specifies that the term *Aboriginal peoples* designates the Indians, the Inuit, and the Métis.

[41] For many Canadians, there can be only one nation in Canada: the Canadian nation. For most Quebecers, Quebec forms a nation, in the sociological and political sense, within another nation: Canada. Canada's multinational character has never really been admitted by federal authorities, and there is no explicit mention of it in the Canadian Constitution.

Quebec and Aboriginal peoples will be discussed further on; at this stage, note that nothing indicates that intergovernmental relations in Canada are engaged in a bicommunal or multinational dynamic. They rather rest on the principle of equality among provinces. This does not mean that the presence of a majority Francophone society such as Quebec and of numerous Aboriginal peoples has no impact on intergovernmental relations in Canada. It has an impact. However, this influence is neither institutionalized nor formalized in any way, save the bilingualism mentioned earlier and the recognition of certain collective rights of a constitutional nature in favor of Aboriginal peoples.[42]

The Canadian federation is, like many other societies in the world, marked by numerous paradigms. Among them, note the following: collaboration *versus* autonomy, unity *versus* diversity, flexibility *versus* constitutionalism, Canadian identity construction (nation building) *versus* multinationalism, Canadian nation *versus* Quebec nation, continuity *versus* innovation, provincial equality *versus* specificity of Quebec, convergence *versus* the right to difference, formalization *versus* adaptability, harmonization *versus* asymmetry, and so forth. While these concepts are placed in opposition here, they are not always contradictory or incompatible. For example, collaboration between federative partners can be carried out with great respect for their autonomy. As for Canadian identity, it can be constructed while taking into account the multinational character of Canada. Likewise, the Quebec nation is contained within the Canadian nation; the two can very well cohabit.

## *The Institutions and Mechanisms upon Which "Interprovincialism" Is Founded*

Intergovernmental agreements (also called administrative agreements) are the primary instrument of relations between governments. These agreements can be global or general, sector-based or *ad hoc*. Through them, collaboration is built between provinces and also between provinces, territories, and the federal government.

When they concern the relations between the federal government and one or several provinces, administrative agreements allow a certain form of asymmetry to develop in the Canadian federal system. Even though this asymmetry is desirable, it should be limited, as otherwise it would quickly imperil the very survival of the Canadian federation. In essence, asymmetrical federalism can only authorize asymmetry of a finite scope if it wishes to remain federalism.

---

[42] Beyond ss. 35 and 35.1 of the *Constitution Act, 1982, supra* note 20, it is noteworthy that s. 25 lays down measures to ensure that the already existing rights—ancestral or treaty based—of Aboriginal peoples shall not be affected, construed, or derogated to under the *Canadian Charter of Rights and Freedoms* (being Part I of the *Constitution Act, 1982, supra* note 20).

Of course, when intergovernmental agreements apply to relations between provinces, they essentially reinforce provincial collaboration. They then rely on the free consent of the signing provinces and thus respect their autonomy and priorities in every way. This is not always the case for agreements between provinces and the federal government since in its negotiations with the provinces, the Canadian government usually attempts to impose various conditions, even when the subject at hand is in the province's exclusive jurisdictions. It also attempts to subject the provinces to various forms of accountability reporting. Most of the time, Quebec considers that these conditions and accountability go against the principle of provincial autonomy, which is essential to federalism.

As for institutions in service of intergovernmental relations, a few exist in Canada. Among them, the Council of Ministers of Education, the Canadian Council of Ministers of the Environment, and the Council of the Federation are particularly noteworthy. While the first two have targeted functions, as their names indicate, the latter has a wider vocation. It merits attention as do the events that led to its foundation.

A revitalization of Canadian federalism was launched in July 2003, on the occasion of an annual conference of provincial premiers and heads of territorial governments.[43] A few months later, on December 5, 2003, in Charlottetown, the provinces and territories signed the founding agreement of the Council of the Federation.[44]

Although the premiers conference was already an annual tradition dating back to 1960, the Council of the Federation gave an institutional basis to this practice and demonstrated the provinces' and territories' desire to move forward with this interprovincial dynamic set in motion 40 years prior.

Premiers take turns acting as chairpersons with 1-year terms. Although territories are members of the Council, head of territories cannot act as the Council chairperson.

The Council of the Federation facilitates the adoption of common, coherent, and concerted positions among provinces and territories. By managing to develop a true partnership, provincial governments can thus ensure better control of their own jurisdictions and engage more vigorously in areas of shared jurisdictions between provincial legislatures and the federal Parliament. This can only contribute to a better balance in the relationships between provinces and territories and also with the federal government. Consequently, the general climate of intergovernmental relations should improve.

One of the objectives of the Council of the Federation is to promote relations based on the respect of the Constitution and on acceptation of diversity within the

---

[43] The Government of Quebec is behind the creation of the Council of the Federation. For its inspiration, see Pelletier (2001), at 91–96.

[44] Council of the Federation Founding Agreement, December 5 2003. The agreement can be found at <http://www.councilofthefederation.ca/pdfs/COF_agreement.pdf>.

federation.[45] In the preamble to the founding agreement, it is stated that the recognition of the existence of differences between the provinces and the territories implies that governments may have different priorities and choices in their policies. The Council defines itself not only as a place for dialogue, consultation, and common action but also as a place for mutual appreciation and respect of differences.

In February 2004, the Council of the Federation adopted a work plan[46] in which it set out a certain number of priorities still valid today, including the reorganization of financial federalism or, more precisely, the solution to the problem of fiscal imbalance.[47] The work plan also included the reinforcement of the Canadian economic union and the participation of provinces (and territories) in the appointment of members of certain central institutions, such as the Senate and the Supreme Court of Canada—appointments that currently fall under the unilateral power of the federal government. Lastly, the work plan covered the provinces' (and the territories') participation in the negotiation of international agreements when their jurisdictions are affected, as well as their role in relations between Canada and the United States. Clearly, the Council's work deals with matters of major importance.

In sum, the Council of the Federation is an institution that encourages cooperation among provinces and territories. While it has demonstrated its effectiveness so far in certain matters,[48] the Council deserves to be reinforced in the future. Among others, it would be helpful if its Secretariat had more human and physical resources at its disposal than it currently does.[49] This would allow it to better fulfill its threefold mission, which consists in helping provinces fully take charge of their own constitutional jurisdictions in the context of common concerns, strengthening the provinces (and territories) in their dealings with the federal government and pushing for the provinces' greater participation in the definition and construction of Canada's tomorrow.

---

[45] *Ibid.*

[46] Council of the Federation Web site, *Report and Desisions*, 23–24 February 2004, available at <http://www.councilofthefederation.ca/pdfs/cof_report_e.pdf>.

[47] See *supra* note 29.

[48] The Council of the Federation proved itself in September 2004 during the negotiations between the provinces, the territories, and the federal government for an increase in federal transfer payments for health care. The results obtained by the provinces and territories were conclusive. See Council of the Federation, News Release, "Premiers Propose Alternative to Prime Minister's Offer" (14 September 2004) online: <http://www.councilofthefederation.ca/pdfs/premiersrelease_sept14.pdf>.

[49] For further reading on the Council of the Federation assessment, see, e.g., Pelletier (2008), at 203–223. See also *Constructive and Co-operative Federalism? A Series of Commentaries on the Council of the Federation* (Montreal: Institute for Research on Public Policy, 2003) online: <http://www.irpp.org/pubs/council_federation.php> and Bakvis et al. (2009) at 108–111 and 132.

## The Place of Quebec and Aboriginal Peoples in Canada, Seen from the Perspective of Intergovernmental Relations

Quebec is not a homogeneous society. Politically, Quebecers can be divided into two main categories: federalists and sovereignists. A certain consensus emerges from these political options: the defence of provincial autonomy and of constitutional jurisdictions. Some wonder if there is—and others hope for—a third option between federalism and sovereignism. It remains doubtful that such an option exists.

It is curious to note that some people in Canada believe that the Quebec society is hostile to the country, when in fact it is an ardent defender of the Canadian Constitution, the sharing of the powers it lays out, and the provincial autonomy it stipulates. In the same vein, people sometimes think that Quebec likes to be isolated, to keep to itself, whereas in reality it invests much energy into the improvement of intergovernmental relations. For instance, it was on Quebec's initiative that the Council of the Federation was created.[50]

In fact, since the election of a clearly federalist government in 2003, Quebec has tried to work positively, along with its federative partners, to revitalize Canadian federalism. Quebec is the province that is pushing the hardest for the reinforcement of the Canadian economic union, mainly through the elimination of trade barriers between the provinces and territories.[51] In short, it is Quebec that, of all the Canadian provinces, insists the most on the respect of federative principles and spirit.

This is no surprise because the need to preserve the special identity of Quebec was one of the reasons the federal model was chosen, instead of the unitary model,

---

[50] See *supra* note 43.

[51] The Government of Quebec is very supportive of strengthening an economic union in Canada through a better cooperation between the two orders of government. Much can be done by the provinces themselves in their own jurisdictions in terms of eliminating trade barriers. However, Quebec (and Alberta) is opposed to the initiative of the federal government aiming to create a unique securities commission in Canada. Quebec sustains that the creation of such an institution does not belong to the competence of the Canadian Parliament. Quebec is also against, for the same reason, the instauration by the Government of Canada of a single securities regulation that would be applicable to the whole country. For Quebec, if a common securities commission is to be created, it should be by virtue of an agreement between the provinces. In this regard, on October 16, 2009, Minister of Justice and Attorney General of Canada Rob Nicholson announced the intention of the Canadian Government to seek the opinion of the Supreme Court on the constitutionality of the enactment and implementation of a single Canadian common securities regulator. See Department of Justice Canada, News Release, "Government of Canada intends to seek opinion of Supreme Court of Canada on constitutionality of proposed Canadian securities legislation" (16 October 2009) online: <http://www.justice.gc.ca/eng/news-nouv/>. Decisions by the Alberta Court of Appeal and the Court of Appeal of Quebec have already declared the project unconstitutional. See *Reference Re Securities Act (Canada)*, 2011 ABCA 77 and *Quebec (Procureur géné ral) c Canada (Procureur général)* 2011 QCCA 591, [2011] RJQ 598. During the Supreme Court hearings, Ontario was the only province to totally agree with the position of the Government of Canada.

at the time of Canada's founding.[52] The Supreme Court of Canada itself recognized
it in the following terms:

> Federalism was a legal response to the underlying political and cultural realities that existed
> at Confederation and continue to exist today.
>
> [...]
>
> The social and demographic reality of Quebec explains the existence of the Province of
> Quebec as a political unit and indeed, was one of the essential reasons for establishing a
> federal structure for the Canadian union in 1867.[53]

As mentioned above, the ambition of the Quebec Government is to revitalize the
Canadian federation in collaboration with its federative partners. This ambition is in
line with Quebec's pursuit of a certain number of precise goals that could be
summarized as follows:

1) Develop stronger and more sustained solidarity among the Canadian provinces
   and territories, enabling them to work together harmoniously;
2) Increase the influence of the provinces and territories such that they have more
   impact on the evolution of the Canadian federation and take part more actively
   in the elaboration of the major orientations and decisions regarding the country,
   in part through the Council of the Federation;
3) Lead the Canadian Government to better respect the fundamental principles of
   federalism, including the autonomy of the provinces in the exercise of powers
   within their jurisdictions. This will be accomplished, among other things, by
   limiting federal spending power in the provincial jurisdictions;
4) Create a new synergy among Canadian provinces and territories, founded on
   mutual understanding, open-mindedness, and the search for compromise;
5) Encourage a better balance between the two orders of government in Canada.

Of course, Quebec hopes that a future reform of Canadian federalism will finally
allow its specificity, founded on its national characteristics, to be recognized in the
Canadian Constitution. This recognition has been the prime objective of the Quebec
governments in recent years, regardless of their political affiliation. It is worth
noting that Quebec's desire for a greater respect of its unique identity within
Canada is highly legitimate. If Quebec is enriched in its profound identity by its
adherence to the Canadian federation, the reverse is also true. Not fostering the
unique identity of Quebec would impoverish Canada's identity.

As for the Aboriginals, their rights were recognized in the Canadian Constitution, and the Supreme Court of Canada gave them great weight. Until now, the

---

[52] The choice to become a federation, which was made in 1867 with regard to Canada, resulted
among other things from a consideration of the identity-related needs of Lower Canada (today,
Quebec). The legislative union (or unitary State), so very much wanted by Sir John A. Macdonald,
one of the main architects of the political compromise that led to the birth of Canada, was not only
against the aspirations of Quebec above all but also against the Atlantic provinces' thirst for
autonomy.

[53] *Reference re Secession of Quebec,* [1998] 2 SCR 217, at para 244, 251–252.

recognition of those rights in the *Constitution Act, 1982*,[54] constitutes without a doubt the biggest victory obtained in Canada by Aboriginals. Another major victory should not be ignored: the creation of Nunavut, the only territory whose government is elected by an Aboriginal majority in Canada, the Inuit.[55] Like Quebec, the majority of its population speaks a language other than English.[56]

When it comes to Aboriginal participation in constitutional power, it must be mentioned that the *Constitution Act, 1982*,[57] was amended in 1983 to recognize that federal and provincial governments are bound by a commitment to principle. According to this, prior to any constitutional amendment concerning the Aboriginals being made, the Prime Minister of Canada must convene a conference with the provincial premiers, place the question of the proposed amendment on the agenda, and invite the representatives of Aboriginal peoples in Canada to participate in the works relating to the proposed amendment.[58] However, the political practices that have been applied since 1983 in Canada go even further than the stipulations of the *Constitution Act, 1982*,[59] by suggesting that, politically speaking, the Aboriginals have a veto on any constitutional amendment affecting their status or rights.[60]

The ultimate goal of Canada's Aboriginal peoples is to increase their political autonomy to the point of forming a third order of government. This was effectively what they were offered by the Charlottetown Accord of 1992, but there was no follow-up since the accord was defeated in referendums.[61]

The Aboriginals seek to improve their relations with all the governments in Canada, that is to say, with the Canadian Government itself—which holds the obligation to act as their fiduciary[62]—as well as with the provincial and territorial governments. For several years now, the main organizations representing Aboriginals have been meeting the provincial premiers and the territories' heads

---

[54] *Supra* note 20.

[55] In 2006, the population of Nunavut was 29,325, of whom 24,640 were Inuit. On this point, see Statistics Canada, Aboriginal peoples, 2006 Census, available online at <http://www.statcan.gc.ca/>.

[56] In 2006, more than 25 % of Nunavut residents declared an Inuit language, either Inuktitut or Inuinnaqtun, as their first language. More than 60 % identified this language as being the language most often spoken at home. On this point, see Statistics Canada, Languages, 2006 Census, available online at <http://www.statcan.gc.ca/>.

[57] *Supra* note 20.

[58] *Ibid*, s.35.1, added by the *Constitution Amendment Proclamation, 1983* (see SI/84–102).

[59] *Supra* note 20.

[60] See Benoît Pelletier *supra* note 20. In this text, the author noted that the consent of the Aboriginal peoples for constitutional amendments affecting their rights is not required, legally speaking, but that such a consent is certainly necessary from a political point of view.

[61] *Consensus Report on the Constitution: Final Text*, Charlottetown, August 28, 1992 (*Charlottetown Accord*), at <http://www.saic.gouv.qc.ca/publications/Positions/Part3/Document27_en.pdf>. Two separate referendums were held on the same day on the Charlottetown Accord: one in Quebec, the other in the rest of Canada.

[62] See, for example, *Wewaykum Indian Band v Canada*, [2002] 4 SCR 245.

of government on an annual basis, just before the summer meeting of the Council of the Federation. This meeting with the Aboriginals has become a sort of tradition. It offers the clear advantage of raising further awareness among the provincial premiers and territories' heads of government regarding the problems Aboriginals face and of creating closer relationships between them. All these meetings between first ministers (i.e., the Prime Minister of Canada and the premiers of the ten provinces), the three territories' heads of government, and the Aboriginal leaders are highly useful because, after all, the quality of interpersonal relations between them plays a key role with regards to intergovernmental relations in Canada. Truth be told, the quality of such interpersonal relationships sometimes makes all the difference in the success or failure of intergovernmental relations themselves.

## The Players, Forms and Modalities of Intergovernmental Relations in Canada

The players in Canadian intergovernmental relations are essentially the governments rather than the parliaments. The expression *executive federalism* is frequently used to explain this reality, which is not unique to Canada. In general, parliaments work to crystallize agreements reached between governments in legislative or constitutional form or to change domestic law based on those agreements. It is worth mentioning that the Canadian Senate does not play any role whatsoever in terms of intergovernmental relations.

Judicial bodies, in particular the Supreme Court of Canada, play a fundamental role in the interpretation and application of the Constitution and of laws, quasi constitutional[63] or otherwise. The courts are not players in intergovernmental relations as such, except for the fact that in the past some courts have prompted governments or political players in general to engage in or pursue negotiations. This is the case in Aboriginal matters, where the Supreme Court of Canada and other courts did not hesitate to pressure governments and Aboriginals to take the route of negotiation instead of pursuing legal proceedings.[64] This was also the case in 1981, in the context of discussions about the patriation of the Canadian

---

[63] Quasi constitutional laws take primacy over laws of the same order of government either because the legislator itself stipulated so or because jurisprudence recognizes such primacy.

[64] See for instance *Mikisew Cree First Nation v Canada (Minister of Canadian Heritage)*, [2005] 3 SCR 388; *Haida Nation v British Columbia (Minister of Forests)*, [2004] 3 SCR 511; *Taku River Tlingit First Nation v British Columbia (Project Assessment Director)*, [2004] 3 SCR 550; *R v Marshall*, [1999] 3 SCR 533; *Delgamuukw v British Columbia*, [1997] 3 SCR 1010; and *R v Sparrow*, [1990] 1 SCR 1075.

Constitution.[65] It could happen again if, one day, Quebec were to seek to secede from Canada.[66]

Aboriginals are taking an increasingly stronger place as full partners in Canadian intergovernmental relations. Nonetheless, what about municipalities, nongovernmental organizations (NGOs), interest groups, and social movements?

Strictly speaking, municipalities do not currently have a role in intergovernmental relations. They are the creatures of the provinces.[67] Their powers are delegated to them by provincial legislatures. Over the last 10 years, however, we have seen the Canadian Government showing a greater interest in municipalities, to the point of wishing to invite them to sit at negotiating tables where major national decisions are made.[68] The federal government's goal in municipal affairs remains rather nebulous. Presumably, it only wants to recognize the major role that municipalities play in the lives of Canadians and in Canada's social and economic evolution. The Government of Quebec suspects the federal government of aiming to dilute the provinces' influence in discussions and negotiations by adding other partners and seeking to place the interests of municipalities in opposition with those of the provinces. In short, the Quebec Government believes that the federal government, in flirting with the municipalities, is only using the well-known "divide and conquer" strategy. Regardless of the true motivation behind the Canadian government's interest in municipalities, it can be supposed that, when prosperity

---

[65] In 1981, in a highly significant decision, the Supreme Court of Canada declared that the patriation project of the Canadian Constitution, which at the time was supported only by the Canadian Parliament and government and by two of the ten provinces, was legal but broke with constitutional conventions. This had the effect, no doubt desired by the Court without being said outright, of bringing the political players back to the constitutional negotiation table. That is what happened in November 1981. This federal–provincial conference, spoken of as a last chance, resulted in an agreement between the federal government and all the provinces, except Quebec, and led to the patriation of the Canadian Constitution. See *Reference re a Resolution to Amend the Constitution*, [1981] 1 SCR 753.

[66] In 1998, the Supreme Court of Canada made a statement about the legality of a process for the unilateral secession of Quebec. It concluded that, when it comes to Canadian constitutional law, a clear vote on the part of Quebecers on a clear question would lead, in the case of a secessionist victory, to an obligation on the part of political players in Canada to negotiate the terms of the secession on the basis of a certain number of principles inherent to the Canadian Constitution. The constitutional amendment procedure would then apply to constitutionalize the result of such negotiation, in particular to render official the secession of Quebec. See *Reference re Secession of Quebec*, *supra* note 53.

[67] The provinces hold exclusive jurisdictions when it comes to municipal affairs, see *Constitution Act, 1867*, *supra* note 5, s 92(8).

[68] See, for example, the address by then Prime Minister Paul Martin in reply to the speech from the throne at <http://www.pco-bcp.gc.ca/index.asp?lang=eng&page=information&sub=publications&doc=aarchives/sft-ddt/2004_1_reply-eng.htm>: "That is why we have made a new deal for Canada's municipalities one of our highest priorities. That is why we created a new Secretariat. We want the voice of our municipalities to be heard nationally". See also the speech from the throne to open the 37th Parliament of Canada at <http://pco-bcp.gc.ca/index.asp?lang=eng&page=information&sub=publications&doc=aarchives/sft-ddt/2004_1-eng.htm>.

returns, it will not hesitate to use its spending power or intervene in other ways in municipal affairs.

As for NGOs, interest groups, and social movements, they have no more voice than municipalities when it comes to intergovernmental relations. As can be imagined, they may have a certain influence over decision-makers, meaning, for current purposes, over the federative partners themselves.

Essentially, the federal and provincial governments are masters of the game when it comes to intergovernmental relations. However, this so-called executive federalism is subject to much criticism. Among other things, some accuse it of lacking transparency and call for a democratization of intergovernmental relations.[69]

It is true that intergovernmental meetings are usually held behind closed doors. Live television coverage of such discussions is relatively rare. So far, they have never been open to the public. This is why some citizens accuse the first ministers and other political players involved in such conferences of making important decisions regarding the country's future on the sly, without informing the population.

However, criticism aimed at executive federalism seems to be greatly exaggerated. Federal–provincial and federal–provincial–territorial conferences, meetings of the Council of the Federation, and other meetings attended by first ministers or ministers always come to a close with a press conference and are given plenty of media coverage before, during, and after they are held. Moreover, the fact that these meetings usually take place behind closed doors encourages honest discussion and reciprocal concessions.

The opening of intergovernmental relations to other players, such as municipalities and NGOs, should be done only with great care. It risks weighing down these relations and making it even more difficult to reach conclusive results. While transparency and democratization are trendy concepts, we must not seek to apply them to intergovernmental relations without carefully measuring the impact they may have on those relations, for instance, when it comes to reaching consensus and making decisions.

The constitutional amendment procedure is already heavy in Canada, to the point that many have lost all hope of ever seeing a reform of Canadian federalism from a constitutional standpoint. If intergovernmental relations were to be overburdened by questions of any nature—constitutional or not—then it would become even more delicate to reach a political compromise, thus slowing down the country's progress. In addition, while executive federalism is the object of criticism in Canada, it has rarely been accused of lacking political legitimacy or of failing to respect the elementary rules of justice and equity.[70]

---

[69] See for example: Smiley (1970). See also Brown (2003).

[70] See *supra* note 69 and accompanying text.

There is no mechanism in Canada to "constitutionally entrench"[71] administrative agreements. It remains that the idea of creating a global entrenchment mechanism is valid and deserves being considered. The Meech Lake Accord, which failed finally, did not go that far. It only stipulated the "constitutionalization" of a single agreement in the country's Constitution: the Ottawa-Quebec agreement on immigration.[72]

Intergovernmental relations may take diverse forms. They are sometimes bilateral, sometimes multilateral; at times, they focus on simple exchange of information or expertise, other times on the implementation of policies. Sometimes they aim to develop common positions on a subject, other times to prevent conflicts between federative partners. They can be federal–provincial–territorial or simply provincial-territorial or purely regional.[73] They sometimes bring together first ministers, sometimes ministers, and at other times only civil servants. Of course, the further down in the hierarchy of public administration, the less formal the intergovernmental relations are. Still, these relations are becoming more formal, no matter the hierarchical authority of the people involved.

In most cases, decisions are made unanimously. Otherwise, they are made on the basis of a large consensus, and it is not unusual to see dissident partners insist that their concerns, reservations, or nuances be formally noted. For a certain time, Quebec made extensive use of the so-called asterisk method to express its concerns regarding agreements with the federal government to which other provinces consented more easily.

The Canadian Intergovernmental Conference Secretariat provides support to a large number of conferences, as well as simultaneous interpretation services.[74] It was created in 1973 by an accord between the federal and the provinces, and although it was later designated as a department of the federal government, the federal and the provinces participate in its direction. Its mission is to provide the administrative services required for intergovernmental conferences.

The agenda for intergovernmental meetings is developed either among all the participants or by the political entity chairing the meeting. As for the decisions that are made, they are usually detailed in communiqués. They may be set out in political agreements in due form; this has happened in the past for decisions regarding constitutional matters.

When it comes to settling differences between the two orders of government, there is no Canada-wide mechanism, i.e., there is no single mechanism that is applicable regardless of the circumstances and the subject at hand. Certain

---

[71] The term *constitutional entrenchment* refers to the insertion of a measure into the Constitution.

[72] The 1987 Constitutional Accord, June 3, 1987 (The Meech Lake Accord), at <http://www.saic.gouv.qc.ca/publications/Positions/Part3/Document22_en.pdf>.

[73] Regional in this context refers to the regions (British Columbia, Prairies, Ontario, Quebec, and Atlantic) of Canada.

[74] See the website of the Canadian Intergovernmental Conference Secratariat at <http://www.scics.gc.ca/>.

intergovernmental agreements include procedures for settling differences in precise situations. This is true for the agreement on internal trade[75] and for the agreement on social union.[76] For the latter, the mechanism has never been implemented, as the agreement itself has never been enforced either.

While it is good when political players agree on methods for settling differences applicable to certain agreements, there is no need to create a general-scope mechanism. Rather, a *moral* obligation of federative partners to respect a certain code of conduct in their relationships with one another should be insisted upon. This is related to the concepts of conviviality, loyalty, or federal courtesy, found in the constitutions of some countries.[77] These concepts are based on a certain number of rules or principles that political players commit to respect in order to ensure a practice of federalism aligned with the federative principle and inspired by a federalist mindset. In 2005, the Prime Minister of Canada, Mr. Stephen Harper, suggested a charter of federalism, the nature of which has not been fully explained but which could very well contain a code of conduct similar to the one mentioned before.[78] It would be a good thing to reiterate to Canadians, in the form of a charter if necessary, that federalism is important for the country and that political players must conduct themselves in a way that is fully compatible with the federal principle and spirit. Unfortunately, the current Harper government is apparently not including this charter as one of its priorities, and the project has seemingly been dropped.

When it comes to intergovernmental relations, useless conflicts between the two orders of government should be avoided. This does not mean that everything should always be harmonious; conflicts are inherent to federalism and are not necessarily negative. Nevertheless, they must not be allowed to become bitter or systematic.

The fact that provinces hold their ground in their areas of jurisdictions should not be perceived as a threat or as a declaration of war against the federal government. On the contrary, such affirmation by the provinces is perfectly normal in a federal system.

The Council of the Federation was founded in 2003 precisely on the principle that provinces should show renewed and strengthened leadership in their own areas of jurisdictions. It was based on the premise that by developing more common

---

[75] *Agreement on Internal Trade (AIT)*, 1994, available online at <http://www.ait-aci.ca/>.

[76] *Social Union Framework Agreement (SUFA)*, 1999, available online at <http://www.socialunion.gc.ca/>.

[77] For further discussions on the concept of federal loyalty, see Jean-François Gaudreault-Desbiens, "The Challenge of Maintaining a Federal (or Quasi-Federal) Culture: Canadians Musings on the Legal and Political Dynamic of the European Constitutional Project" from the Conference *Towards A European Constitution: from the Convention to the IGC and beyond*, organized by the Federal Trust and the University Association for Contemporary European Studies, Goodenough College, London, July 2004, 9–10, online: <http://www.fedtrust.co.uk/default.asp?groupid=0&search=desbiens>.

[78] See "Building Stronger Institutions" in the *Speech from the Throne 2008: Protecting Canada's Future*, 2008, online: <http://www.sft-ddt.gc.ca/eng/media.asp?id=1364>; see also Robert Dutrisac, "Harper courtise le Québec," *Le Devoir (20* December 2005) online: <http://www.ledevoir.com/>.

positions in their own jurisdictions, provinces would end up acting on those positions with greater effectiveness, thus avoiding federal interference. Another Council of the Federation goal was to strengthen provinces (and territories) vis-à-vis the federal government in order to encourage a better balance in relations between the two orders of government. Truly, if the provinces hold their positions in their own jurisdictions, it can only have positive effects on Canadian federalism from both the horizontal and vertical perspectives.

In general, French-speaking Quebecers and Canadian Anglophones see the Constitution in a much different way.[79] The former tend to see the Constitution as a virtually sacred contract between federative partners founded on a political compromise, historical or contemporary. It must not be changed or modified except by due constitutional process, which implies prior political negotiations. Anglophones in general have a more pragmatic way of seeing the Canadian constitutional framework. For them, the Constitution is not an absolute but only a guide. It is only the result of a political agreement reached at one precise moment and must be allowed to evolve and adapt to changes in society. It is up to both the courts and the political players to steer this evolution. Above all, the Constitution, as seen by Anglophones, should never be an impediment to the country's progress. This leads them to favor infra and paraconstitutional solutions to work around the Constitution and solve the particular problems that come up.

In other words, while French-speaking Quebecers hold a more global, contractual, and structural view of the Constitution, Anglophones take a more pragmatic, time-bound, and flexible approach. This leads the former to favor a historical approach with regard to the interpretation and application of the Constitution, while the latter favor an evolutionary approach. The historical approach has the downside of freezing the Constitution in time, but the evolutionary approach poses the inconvenience of dismissing political compromises, leaving too much space for judges as opposed to elected officials and opening doors to arbitrary decisions.

Identity and culture have a lot to do with the way individuals understand the Constitution and federal relations. These components explain in good part the attitude differences between Francophones and Anglophones when it comes to intergovernmental relations. Legal traditions—civil law and common law—reinforce these differences.

## Future Paths for Intergovernmental Relations in Canada

The reform of Canadian federalism will continue to be the most fundamental issue in intergovernmental relations in the future. However, contrary to what some may

---

[79] See Pelletier (2010), p. 251.

believe, such a reform does not necessarily require constitutional amendment. On the contrary, much can be accomplished in Canada in terms of remodeling the federal system without modifying the Constitution. In fact, many issues can be solved in a nonconstitutional manner without engaging in the constitutional amendment procedure. Administrative agreements are one of the means that political players have at their disposal for rearranging Canadian federalism and helping it progress without recourse to the delicate and laborious process of constitutional amendment.

Other major issues, more tightly framed than the general reform of federalism, are also appearing on the horizon of intergovernmental relations. These include the solution to fiscal imbalance, the limitation of federal spending power, and the provinces' participation in the negotiation of major international agreements or treaties and their participation in certain international fora. All the aforementioned questions can be dealt with easily and to great satisfaction by nonconstitutional means. While intergovernmental relations in Canada were substantially absorbed by the constitutional question until 1992—the year that the Charlottetown Accord failed[80]—since then they have been focused on subjects of a nonconstitutional nature.

Intergovernmental relations have served in the past, and could again serve in the future, to tackle major goals, such as a better distribution of wealth throughout Canada for a greater social justice, environmental protection and the reduction of greenhouse gases emissions, the reduction of overlaps and duplications within the two orders of government, and the development of national standards or goals in strategic areas. Intergovernmental relations could also make it possible to develop a certain form of asymmetry in Canada. Such asymmetry, if properly framed, could better suit the diversity inherent to Canadian federalism in general and better adapt to the specificity of Quebec in particular.

---

[80] After having said that the Meech Lake Accord was "the popular code name of a federal–provincial heads-of-government agreement," Edward McWhinney, concerning the Charlottetown Agreement, said: "But this also meant the incidental political horse-trading necessary to secure its preliminary adoption—again by a heads-of-government consensus—was exposed much more clearly to public view, and consequent criticism. Mulroney, to counter charges of *elitism* leveled against the essentially oligarchic, intergovernmental process that had been followed throughout the Meech Lake exercise, made a symbolic gesture to Trudeau-style participatory democracy. In a 'gambler's throw,' he submitted the Charlottetown Agreement to a nation-wide referendum. Public support thus enlisted, he believed, would compel a prompt across-the-board ratification of the Agreement by the provincial legislatures as a constitutional amendment. This was a bold move. It reflected Mulroney's confidence in direct democracy and its impact on political decision-makers. Certainly, his position contrasted sharply with the arcane process and behind-the-scenes negotiation and bargaining effectively enjoined by the new constitutional amending machinery established under the Trudeau government's Constitution Act of 1982". See McWhinney 2003), at 18–20.

Intergovernmental relations in Canada contribute to the constitutional distribution of legislative powers, which was initially established by the *Constitution Act, 1867*.[81] By arbitrating and clarifying that distribution, they help solve the many questions surrounding the sharing of legislative powers that touch on the detailed management of the jurisdictions and responsibilities of the two orders of government and on the relationships between these levels: fiscal relations and the distribution of financial resources, the development of public policies, trade and investment, infrastructure, and so forth. Moreover, the distribution of powers is not and cannot be absolutely watertight. Not only do lines get crossed here and there—as when the federal Parliament steps into provincial jurisdictions—but in addition, there are grey zones: situations for which it is extremely difficult to precisely determine which order of government holds jurisdictions.

The Aboriginals are currently playing a stronger role with regard to intergovernmental relations in Canada; nonetheless, this is not the case for another major group: Francophone minority communities. They are often left aside from these relations; they are never invited to discuss with all the first ministers about the problems they are facing and their potential solutions.[82] The first ministers would gain great advantage from listening more closely to them.

# Conclusion

In Canada, intergovernmental relations are relatively formalized, in the sense that they are recurrent, fairly solemn, and well structured; they are taken seriously and rest on well-established traditions and practices. These relations are numerous, occur through different fora,[83] and touch on a long list of topics at times in provincial jurisdictions, at times in federal jurisdictions, and at times in shared jurisdictions. Should Canada lean towards greater formalization, stronger institutionalization of intergovernmental relations? This could be a good thing, but relations between the governments should not be complicated or weighted down. Canada is a complex enough country already.

The Aboriginals will be called upon in the future to play an even stronger role in intergovernmental relations. This is entirely inevitable, as they constitute a growing

---

[81] *Supra* note 5.

[82] Francophones in Canada are a well-organized minority. They are represented by different organizations across the country. As an example, consider the *Fédération des communautés francophones et acadienne du Canada*, which has become a nationwide as well as an international voice and representation of French-Canadian communities. Although francophone groups sometimes meet individual premiers, they do not meet premiers in the context of provincial or federal–provincial conferences. Francophone organizations are not invited to meet all the Canadian premiers at the same time.

[83] Some of these fora have been mentioned before: the Council of the Federation, the Council of Ministers of Education, the Canadian Council of Ministers of the Environment.

dimension of Canadian federalism. Ways to arrange the presence of Aboriginals in intergovernmental relations without weakening the influence of the provinces along the way must be found. A theory of federalism that better includes the Aboriginal reality as part of Canada has to be developed.

Overall, intergovernmental relations in Canada are of high quality, although they lack creativity, and provide tangible results, although incomplete ones.[84] Among other things, these relations have a true emulation effect. They stimulate healthy competition between governments. Also, they usually reduce tensions between governments and in society in general, rather than stoke them or create new ones. In short, despite their weaknesses and imperfections, intergovernmental relations have a positive effect on the evolution of Canadian federalism.

When exploring the future paths for intergovernmental relations in Canada, the question of the provinces' role within the Canadian federation immediately arises. In Canada, like in any other federal State, the existence of the federated entities tangibly manifests the principle of federalism. In the case of Canada, the provinces are at the origin of the federal project; they, in October 1864 at the Quebec Conference, chose this form of government. They constituted the Canadian federation and brought it to life. If only for that, the provinces are and should remain at the heart of Canadian federalism.

It is important for Canadian federalism to evolve in a way that is more respectful of the provinces' autonomy. The provinces have every interest in taking more charge as full partners in Canadian federalism. Unfortunately, they too often have the habit of eclipsing themselves, disappearing behind the federal government, to which they generally attribute hierarchical superiority despite the fact that the federal principle, classically, places them on an equal footing, at least in legal theory.

The definition of the common good and of national interest must not be left in the hands of the federal government alone. Rather, they must be defined collaboratively between both orders of government, via institutions and mechanisms encouraging intergovernmental cooperation.

The vast majority of Quebecers are ready to make positive contributions to the construction of Canada's future, as long as they feel that their identity is better respected and valued in the Canadian union. It would be unfortunate if, because they feel a lack of respect for who they are, Quebecers were to end up refusing to

---

[84] Kumanan Wilson explained the pros and cons of intergovernmental collaboration while addressing the issue of the implementation of a Canadian Agency for Public Health in the following terms: "The collaborative approach offers many advantages, including consideration of the interests of all orders of government, minimizing conflict and reducing the likelihood of violating jurisdictional sovereignty. [...] The primary difficulty with collaborative approaches is the potential for the decision-making process to lack transparency and for accountability to become blurred. This permits each order of government to blame the other when agreements do not succeed". See Wilson (2004), p. 222.

influence Canada's evolution, failing to recognize themselves as part of it, and digging the chasm between the "two solitudes"[85] even deeper.

The Canadian Constitution is a work in progress because, among other things, Quebec's National Assembly and the Quebec Government have still not endorsed the *Constitution Act, 1982*.[86] For now, Intergovernmental relations will without doubt help the country progress by nonconstitutional means using political agreements. In a certain way, these relations already show Canadians' political maturity because they work via dialogue, collaboration, and compromise. They have demonstrated their value in the past in many ways. Let us put them to the service of a much-desired reconciliation between Quebecers and other Canadians.

# References

André Légaré, "Canada's Experiment with Aboriginal Self-Determination in Nunavut: from Vision to illusion" (2008) 15 International Journal on Minority and Group Rights 336.

Benoît Pelletier, "Les modalités de la modification de la Constitution du Canada" in Gérald-A. Beaudoin, Joseph E. Magnet, Benoît Pelletier, Gordon Robertson and John Trent, eds, *Le Fédéralisme de demain: réformes essentielles - Federalism for the future: Essential Reforms* (Montreal: Wilson & Lafleur Ltd, 1998) 271.

Benoît Pelletier, ed., *A project for Quebec: Affirmation, Autonomy and Leadership*, final report, Special Committee of the Quebec Liberal Party on the Political and Constitutional Future of Quebec Society (Montreal: Quebec Liberal Party, 2001).

Benoît Pelletier, "Le bijuridisme au Canada et son impact sur le droit constitutionnel et sur les relations intergouvernementales" (2010) 40 RGD 251.

David Cameron & Richard Simeon, "Intergovernmental Relations in Canada: The Emergence of Collaborative Federalism" (2002) 32:2 Publius 49.

Donald V. Smiley, *Constitutional adaptation and Canadian federalism since 1945*, Documents of the Royal Commission on Bilingualism and Biculturalism 4 (Ottawa: Queen's Printer, 1970).

Douglas M Brown, "Getting Things Done in the Federation: Do We Need New Rules for an Old Game?" in *Constructive and Co-operative Federalism? A Series of Commentaries on the Council of the Federation* (Montreal: Institute for Research on Public Policy, 2003).

Edward McWhinney, *Chrétien and Canadian Federalism: Politics and the Constitution, 1993–2003* (Vancouver: Ronsdale Press, 2003).

George Anderson, *Federalism: An Introduction* (Toronto: Oxford University Press, 2008) at 3.

Herman Bakvis, Gerald Baier & Doublas M Brown, *Contested federalism: certainty an ambiguity in the Canadian federation* (Don Mills, Ont: Oxford University Press, 2009).

Kumanan Wilson, "A Canadian Agency for Public Health: Could it work?" (2004) 170:2 CMAJ 222.

Peter Hogg, *Constitutional Law of Canada*, student ed (Toronto: Thomson Carswell, 2008) at 332.

Réjean Pelletier, *Le Québec et le fédéralisme canadien: Un regard critique*, (Quebec: Les Presses de l'Université Laval, 2008).

Thomas L. Friedman, *The World is Flat: A Brief History of the Twenty-first Century* (New York: Farrar, Straus and Giroux, 2005).

---

[85] The expression *two solitudes* is often used to describe the differences that separate Quebec from the rest of Canada, whether due to identity clashes or different perceptions of Canadian federalism and its future.

[86] *Supra* note 20.

# The Intergovernmental Relations in Federal Systems: The Model of Germany

Rainer Arnold

**Abstract** The German system of "cooperative federalism" is characterised by a multiplicity of vertical and horizontal intergovernmental relations. Of particular significance are the relations of the Federal Council with the Federal Parliament in the legislative process. External intergovernmental relations take place, in particular, in EU matters. The autonomy of the members of the German Federation, the Länder, is considerably relativated by the intergovernmental cooperation.

## The Notion of Intergovernmental Relations

In the present context, intergovernmental relations are divided into (a) *institutional* and (b) *functional* relations:

a) The *institutional type* of intergovernmental relations refers to the relations of the members of a federal or regional system with the central government or with the governments of the other members of such a system (if they are self governed as in Germany) or even with the government of a foreign State or the government of a supranational organisation such as the European Union, meaning *in concreto* with the Commission and/or with the Council of Ministers of the European Union.

   In Germany, the intergovernmental relations of the members of the Federation exist with all these types of government, of course on different levels.

b) The intergovernmental relations in a *functional* sense do not refer to institutions but to the governmental *function* as such, which can be exercised not only by the government in the institutional sense but also and, in particular, by the *legislator* because legislation is the most significant expression of political orientations and has decisive normative impact on living conditions.

R. Arnold (✉)
University of Regensburg, Universitätsstraße 31, 93053 Regensburg, Germany
e-mail: jean.monnet@gmx.de; rainer.arnold@jura.uni-regensburg.de

A. López-Basaguren and L. Escajedo San Epifanio (eds.), *The Ways of Federalism in Western Countries and the Horizons of Territorial Autonomy in Spain*, Vol. 2, DOI 10.1007/978-3-642-27717-7_3, © Springer-Verlag Berlin Heidelberg 2013

It seems therefore important to consider the relations between the Federal Council, composed of members of the governments of the 16 member states of the German Federation, and the Federal Parliament in the context of the legislative process. Furthermore, the member states' relations with foreign governments and with the political actors in the European Union, in particular, with reference to their participation in the supranational lawmaking process must be looked at.

The following study combines the institutional and the functional aspects of the issue in question and tries to make concise explanations.

## The Realisation of the Intergovernmental Relations

The intergovernmental relations of the members of the German Federation, that is of the *Länder*, are characterised by the fact that the *Länder* have the characteristics of *states*[1] with their own political life, independent from other member states and the Federation as such. The *Länder* have their own constitutions created by themselves and not by the Federation. All have constitutional courts, which apply their Constitutions, reviewing the actions and omissions of their legislative, executive, and jurisdictional institutions. Their political institutions, Parliament and Government, have been established in conformity with the constitution of the *Land* and have their own margin of action. Politics of a *Land* are developed in the framework of its own particular constitutional order. In principle, the politics of the *Land* are independent from the politics of the Federation. However, many interactions exist between law and politics of the *Land* and the Federation.

The fact that the *Länder* are autonomous with regard to their legal orders and political process clearly results from their statehood.[2]

The Federation has only those competences that have been transferred to it from the *Länder* by the Basic Law (BL), the German Constitution. Article 28 (1) BL confirms this autonomy by requiring conformity between the constitutional orders of the *Land* and the Federation only for certain general principles: democracy, republicanism, rule of law, and social orientation of the State. Rule of law also includes the protection of fundamental rights by the *Land*, as well as by the Federation, but it is left open by the Federal Constitution in which way and with which contents the Länder Constitutions will recognise them. Thus, the *Länder* can guarantee specific fundamental rights or make reference to those guaranteed by the Federal Constitution, are free to establish social rights and to provide an individual constitutional complaint, etc.[3] The only requirement is that the protection of the fundamental rights would be efficient.

---

[1] Federal Constitutional Court (FCC), Off. Rep., vol. 1, 34.

[2] FCC vol. 102, 234; vol. 103, 332, 347, 349–350.

[3] Arnold (2002), pp. 1029–1037.

In summary, the governmental function is in principle up to the *Land* and its political institutions. In this perspective, the politics and the governmental functions of the *Land* are separated from those of the Federation.

## The Indispensability of "Co-operative Federalism"

In the modern social state, the members of the Federation have to co-operate between themselves and the Federation; they cannot exist in isolation and with total autonomy. Many forms of co-operation exist in the German federal system, both formal and informal ones.[4] Conferences of the member states' ministers, together with the Federal Minister, in a variety of matters aim to obtain solutions that are adequate for the whole Federation but that, at the same time, leave the member states' autonomy intact. Furthermore, the member states can conclude formal treaties between themselves, as well as with the Federation, a competence that results from their quality of statehood.[5] These treaties, for example in the field of radiodiffusion and universities, cover matters that fall into the exclusive competence of the Länder and have to be ratified by the Länder Prime Ministers in conformity with the consent of the Länder Parliaments. It can be said that *horizontal* intergovernmental relations exist between the governments of the Länder in the case of treaties concluded between them, and *vertical* relations exist in the case of treaties concluded by them with the Federation. Both types are common in Germany.

The co-operative federalism[6] as a phenomenon of intergovernmental relations is also an expression used in the so-called common tasks (*Gemeinschaftsaufgaben*, articles 91 a–91 d BL, as modified by the federalism reform I of 2006). These tasks demonstrate the need for cooperation in representing an intergovernmental matter between a particular Land and the Federation, using as a basis a mechanism corresponding to the traditional structures of the German federal system: the separation of the political, constitutional, legislative, administrative, financial, etc. "spaces" (*Räume*) of the singular *Länder* from another, as well as of the Länder from those of the Federation.[7] In this context, the Basic Law establishes the obligation of *Land* and Federation to cooperate, despite the mentioned separation, and to finance these tasks, which are important not only for one *Land* but also for the State as a whole, in order to better the living conditions of the population. These tasks aim at ameliorating the regional economic structure, the agrarian structure, and the protection of the coast. Financing is also in common, the part of the Federation being determined by the Basic Law and ordinary laws. More precise

---

[4] FCC vol. 42, 103; vol. 90, 60; Kisker (2010), pp. 700–711.

[5] FCC vol. 90, 60.

[6] See Kisker (1971).

[7] FCC vol. 96, 345, 368.

details on the common tasks and on the coordination between the participants, the *Land* and the Federation, are laid down in laws that require the explicit consent of the Federal Council. It seems important that the *Land* does not lose its autonomy through these mechanisms of coordination.

For a long time, this cooperation, meaning the interactive and interconnected relation between the different governments and parliaments in the German Federation, has been subject to criticism. In particular, the political influence of the Federation exercised on the *Land* in the context of these common tasks has often been considered a financial pressure restricting the *Land*'s autonomy. It was declared that a voluntary cooperation would be more desirable as it is more protective of this autonomy. In the field of universities and research, there is also a common task of corporation in accordance with article 90 b BL, which is effectuated, since the federalism reform I of 2006, by a treaty through which the details of coordination and financing are to be negotiated. This modality seems more flexible and more adequate to the requirements of the German federalism. Furthermore, cooperation based on treaties has been introduced in the field of information technology (Art. 91 c BL). In this way, the intergovernmental relations are flexible and take account of the will of all participants by negotiating a treaty.[8] This seems to conform more to the fundamental requirements of the Constitution.

## The Federal Council: Where the Länder Governments Collaborate with the Central Parliament

The Federal Council is the centre of the intergovernmental relations in Germany. As is well known, this political institution of the Federation is composed of the Prime Ministers and Ministers of all the 16 *Länder*, which cooperate in the fields of legislation, administration, and jurisdiction of the Federation. The most important cooperation is in the field of legislation.

The legislator exercises a governmental function by adopting laws that are the expression of political orientations. Thus, intergovernmental relations are also comprised of the legislative function, as has already been mentioned.

This function is distributed to both the Federation and the *Länder*. Two small parts of these legislative competences are competences exclusive to the Federation and *Länder* alone. The largest category is comprised of the concurring competences between *Länder* and Federation; the so-called framework competences of the Federation have been considered superfluous and have been abolished by the federalism reform I in 2006.

The concurring competence comprises three subtypes[9]:

---

[8] See Chr. Gröpl (note 4), marg. notes 692–697.
[9] Art. 72 BL.

a. The traditional type that authorises the Federation to use this competence, permitting it to adopt a federal law, but only if this federal law is indispensable either for upholding legal unity or economic unity in Germany or in order to create equal life conditions in the entire German territory.

b. The second subtype covers the largest quantity of competences, which authorise the Federal Parliament to federalise the matters without fulfilling the mentioned conditions. In other words, the federal Parliament can adopt the federal law whenever it considers it adequate, without the necessity of fulfilling the specific conditions mentioned above.

c. Finally, the third subtype permits the Federal legislator to act without fulfilling the conditions but attributes to the *Länder* divergence in their own legislation from the federal law.[10] This is the new possibility of diverging legislation, introduced by the Federalism Reform I in certain matters that had been before of the former framework competence matters.

The cooperation of the Federal Council in all fields of exclusive competences of the Federation, in addition to concurring competences, goes as such: Normally, Federal law is transmitted to the Federal Council after the vote in Federal Parliament. The Council then has the right to make objections after trying to reach a compromise through the deliberations of the Mediation Committee, composed of members of the Federal Parliament and of the same number of members of the Federal Council. Objections made by the Federal Council can be rejected by an absolute majority of the Federal Parliament (though if these objections have been made by a two-thirds majority of the Federal Council, the same majority is necessary in the Federal Parliament to reject them).[11]

In certain cases, enumerated by Basic Law, the explicit consent of the Federal Council is necessary. In these cases, governments of the *Länder* are in a strong position because their definite refusal to consent is an absolute obstacle for the realisation of the law in question. Before the 2006 reform of Federalism, this second type of cooperation of the Federal Council was frequent due to the fact that article 84 of the Basic Law required the consent of the Federal Council in all the cases in which the federal law has regulated a question concerning the execution of this law, even in one provision.[12] The reason for this was that matters of this type (for example, the question of which authority will execute this law or in which procedure this will be done) are matters of administrative law, a branch of law that falls within the competence of the *Länder*. If the Federation regulated such a question, it needed, what was a certain form of compensation, the consent of the Federal Council. Many Federal laws regulated such questions and therefore required the consent of the Federal Council. As a consequence, this type of cooperation between Federal Parliament and Federal Council increased significantly, complicating the

---

[10] See Beck (2008).

[11] Art. 77 (2), (3) and (4) BL.

[12] FCC vol. 8, 274.

relations between the two institutions in times of diverging political orientation. The Federal Council blocked important laws voted by the Parliament that had a different political majority. In order to normalise the situation, article 84 of the Basic Law was reformed in 2006 by abolishing the requirement of a consent of the Federal Council transforming such laws into laws of the normal type of cooperation as described above. As a result, the legislative procedure in such cases has been simplified. As compensation for the *Länder*, the new version of article 84 gives the *Länder* the right to adopt divergent provisions insofar as the procedural rules regulated in the federal law are concerned.

## The Politics in the Federation and in the *Länder* as a Process Reflecting Autonomy as Well as Interaction

Both the governments of the *Länder* and the government of the Federation are elected by their Parliaments. Decisive for politics is the contribution of political parties to the formation of the political will of the people, as stated by article 21 of the Basic Law. The definition of what a political party is has been laid down by Federal law—the Act on the Political Parties[13]—which is also valid for the definition of political parties in the *Länder*. This definition requires that an association will only be recognised as a political party if it participates during a certain time period in federal elections or in *Länder* elections.

The electoral system is laid down not in the Constitution but in an ordinary Federal law, for the Federation,[14] and in *Länder* laws, for the *Länder* elections. The German system is, in principle, a proportionality election system. It combines with this certain elements of the direct election of a candidate (in the Federation, the elector has two votes, one to elect a candidate and the second one to vote for a list of a party; the number of mandates corresponds to the number of the second votes). Each Land can establish its own electoral system, but it must respect the principles of electoral law, which are the same for the Federation and the *Länder*.[15]

While the normative framework for elections and political parties is to a great extent federal, the political process itself, seen from a juridical standpoint, takes place separately in the Federation and in the *Länder*. Politically, the political process in Germany is strongly interconnected on both of these levels. The elections in a Land are significantly influenced by federal politics. It is also a tradition that the politicians of the Federation are present in the electoral campaign in a *Land*. Furthermore, the Prime Ministers of the *Länder* often are candidates for the Chancellor of the Federation. In politics, the political parties are the most important connecting elements between the different levels (Federation and *Länder*), with the

---

[13] BGBl. 1994 I S. 149 with modif.

[14] Bundeswahlgesetz, BGBl. 1993 I S. 1288 with modif.

[15] Art. 38 (1) BL.

exception of Bavaria where the CSU exists, a party only active in this *Land*. In principle, the orientation of a political party is the same in the whole country. This means that the parties represent centralising elements, which leads to the homogeneity of the political process. Of course, there are important differences in the regions as to the preferences of the electorate.

The political process, decisive for the institutionalisation of the governments on the federal and *Länder* levels is, on the one hand, uniform (with respect to the orientation of the political parties) and, on the other hand, divergent (with respect to the preferences of the electorate). The existence of various political processes, in the 16 *Länder* and in the Federation, represents, despite the aforementioned interconnection, an important aspect of a vertical separation of power. This is the case because the elections in the *Länder* take place in different periods, which permits to know the reaction of the electorate in a determined moment. During a period of four or five years, 17 elections take place in Germany, 16 in the *Länder* and one in the Federation. It is evident that the composition of the Federal Council, which has an important impact on the federal legislation, can undergo polical changes during this period. This has a great impact on the federal politics and the position of the federal government. The interconnection of the political process in Germany is therefore of high importance for the intergovernmental relations between the Federation and *Länder*.

## The Governments of the *Länder* and Foreign Countries

Foreign affairs are the matter of the Federation. Article 32 (3) BL, however, provides the possibility for a *Land* to conclude international treaties in fields of its own competences, but with the previous consent of the federal government. The Land, which is juridically a State, has maintained this competence, which is seldom used in practice. With respect to cultural matters that fall into the exclusive competence of the *Länder*, it must be noted that, by the agreement of Lindau (1957), the *Länder* have authorised the Federation to conclude such treaties with third states despite the internal competence of the *Länder*. The *Länder* can influence the contents of the treaty through a specific Commission; the position of the Federation in this context has to follow the wishes of the *Länder* during the negotiations of the treaty. In the other fields of exclusive competence of the *Länder*, such as police law, international agreements are made by certain *Länder* themselves.

Furthermore, the *Länder* observe the external politics of the Federation and maintain many informal contacts with the governments of foreign countries exercising consultative activities, in particular, for the benefit of the economy. From a constitutional standpoint, such activities are possible, but they must never interfere with the foreign relations competences of the Federation.

## The Intergovernmental Relations with the European Union

There are three levels of participation of the German *Länder* in the legislative process of the European Union: participation in a weak, in a strong, and in an intermediate form.[16]

It should first be mentioned that the Federal minister negotiates in the EU Council of ministers, except in the case of a strong participation. In this latter case, a minister of one of the *Länder* chosen by the Federal Council represents Germany as a member state in the EU Council.

If the Council of ministers is concerned with the matter that falls into the competence of the Federation on the German internal level but is of interest for the Länder, the Federal Council can vote a position that has to be taken into account (berücksichtigen) by the Minister negotiating in Brussels. If the Minister has good reasons not to follow this position, he is allowed to do so. Therefore, this possibility is a weak one.

Strong participation takes place when the Council of ministers is concerned with a matter that falls into the exclusive competence of the *Länder* on the internal level: culture, education, or radiodiffusion programmes. In such a case, the Federal government has to send, as a representative of Germany, a *Land* minister to Brussels chosen by the Federal Council. This minister has to discuss his/her opinion with the federal government but is not really obliged to follow the line of the Federation. Otherwise, the participation of a *Land* Minister would be superfluous. It is the opinion of the Land Minister that counts in the Council. It is not completely clear whether he/she can present the view of the government of this *Land* or the view of the *Länder* as predetermined by a vote within the Federal Council.

The intermediate form of participation takes place if, for example, administrative law questions are treated by the Council of ministers. These questions are closely connected, on an internal level, with *Länder* competences. If a European legal act intends to regulate questions of administrative procedure, this form of participation is relevant. The Federal minister has to follow the position of the Federal Council as an obligatory orientation (maßgeblich berücksichtigen) in such cases. If the resolution of the Federal Council shall be binding on the Federal minister in this manner, the Federal Council has to confirm its position by a two-thirds majority vote (a so-called confirmation resolution).[17]

This participation system reflects a precisely determined system of intergovernmental relations between the federal government, the *Länder* governments, and the supranational legislative power.

---

[16] Art. 23 (5) and (6) BL.

[17] See for further details Art. 5 of the Act on the Cooperation of Federation and Länder in EU matters, BGBl.1993 I S.313 with modif.

## Conclusions

The German *Länder* have autonomy but take part in a Social State that is based on cooperation. The "cooperative federalism" is embedded in a multiplicity of intergovernmental relations, in particular, in the field of legislation. Horizontal intergovernmental relations take place between the governments of the *Länder*; vertical relations exist with respect to the federal government and the European Union.

As a conclusion, it can be said that the autonomy of the German *Länder* is manifest in the existence of numerous intergovernmental relations both on the national and on the supranational levels.

## References

R. Arnold, La tutela dei diritti fondamentali nelle Costituzioni dei Länder tedeschi, in: Diritto pubblico comparato ed europeo, Torino, 2002, 1029–1037.

L. Beck, Die Abweichungsgesetzgebung der Länder aus staatsrechtlicher, rechtsvergleichender und dogmatischer Sicht, 2008.

G. Kisker, Kooperation im Bundesstaat: eine Untersuchung zum kooperativen Foderalismus in der Bundesrepublik Deutschland, 1971.

Chr. Gröpl, Staatsarecht I, 2nd. ed. 2010, marg. notes 700–711.

# The Intergovernmental Relations in Switzerland

Luzius Mader

## Introduction

Intergovernmental relations are extremely manifold and of vital importance for the practical functioning of the federal system in Switzerland. They are deeply rooted in the history of this country, in its political culture, and in its institutional and constitutional framework. Although the Swiss Constitution is not very explicit about them, Swiss federalism is indeed unconceivable without intense intergovernmental relations and a large variety of intergovernmental institutions. It would not be wrong, indeed, to say that the Swiss federal state even owns its existence to intergovernmental relations because the governments of the member states of the former Swiss Confederation played a major role in 1846–1848, when the Swiss federal State was created. The intergovernmental institutions and relations are closely linked to or even derive from one of the distinctive features of Swiss federalism, namely the close co-operation existing between the sub-national entities (the cantons) and also between the cantons and the centre (the Confederation).[1]

   In this contribution, I first outline the general constitutional framework within which the intergovernmental relations have to be seen. I then give an overview of the various types of intergovernmental institutions and briefly present the most important of them. Next, I try to enlarge the perspective and to show that intergovernmental relations are not limited to the existence of intergovernmental institutions or organs; they may have other forms too. I also address the multiple functions of intergovernmental relations and institutions. Finally, I shall make some comments on their strengths and weaknesses.

---

[1] For the main features of Swiss federalism today, see, e.g., Mader (2002), pp. 155 ss.

L. Mader (✉)
Ministry of Justice, Bundesrain 20, 3003 Bern, Switzerland
e-mail: Luzius.Mader@BJ.admin.ch

A. López-Basaguren and L. Escajedo San Epifanio (eds.), *The Ways of Federalism in Western Countries and the Horizons of Territorial Autonomy in Spain*, Vol. 2, DOI 10.1007/978-3-642-27717-7_4, © Springer-Verlag Berlin Heidelberg 2013

# The General Constitutional Framework

I am not going to outline main features of Swiss federalism or—in an even wider sense—the main elements of the Swiss institutional set-up. This is done in the contribution made by Regula Kägi-Diener.[2] It may be useful, however, to briefly mention some of the constitutional aspects that are relevant with regard to inter-governmental relations or institutions.[3]

First, it is important to be aware of the fact that the cantons are—together with the people—the constituent units of the Swiss Confederation.[4] More than that: they are, as I have said already, the founding fathers of the Swiss federal State. Article 1 of the Swiss Constitution clearly states that "the people and the cantons . . . form the Swiss Confederation". Implicitly, this provision also embodies the principle of the equality of the cantons. In other words, regardless of their population and size, all cantons are placed on the same footing and have equal rights and obligations.[5] It is not surprising, therefore, that ever since its origins in 1848, the cantons played a decisive role in the functioning of the Swiss federal State. The importance and intensity of intergovernmental relations partly reflect this particular situation.

Second, the principle of co-operation is essential to Swiss federalism. It is now explicitly laid down in the Federal Constitution. Article 44 states that the Confederation and the cantons shall support each other in the fulfilment of their tasks and shall generally cooperate with each other. They owe each other a duty of consideration and support. Thus, Swiss federalism is more orientated towards partnership and solidarity rather than to competition.[6] Partnership includes also the idea that disputes between cantons or between cantons and the Confederation should be resolved by negotiation and mediation rather than by litigation in courts (Article 44 paragraph 3).

Third, the cantons participate in the federal decision-making process, as Article 45 of the Federal Constitution states it in general terms. According to Article 45 paragraph 1, the cantons shall participate in the federal decision-making process and, in particular, in the legislative process. According to paragraph 2 of the same provision, the Confederation shall inform the cantons of its intentions fully and in good time, and it shall consult the cantons where their interests are affected. I am not talking here about the bicameral system with the Second Chamber (the Council of States) being of completely equal standing with the National Council (the House

---

[2] See her contribution in this volume.

[3] See, in particular, Abderhalden (1999) and Zehnder (2007).

[4] In spite of its official name (Swiss Confederation), Switzerland is, since 1848, a federal State and not any more a confederation of States. The official name is a reminiscence of the confederal past.

[5] There are only two exceptions: According to Article 142 paragraph 4, six cantons have only half a cantonal vote as regards the mandatory referendum, and according to Article 150 paragraph 2, the same six cantons have only one (instead of two) representative in the Council of States.

[6] With one notable exception perhaps, namely when it is about practising fiscal dumping with the aim of attracting interesting taxpayers and enterprises.

of Representatives),[7] about the majority of cantons necessary for constitutional amendments,[8] or about the fact that eight cantons may make use of the optional referendum and request that a law enacted by parliament (the National Assembly) be submitted to the vote of the people.[9] I am talking especially about the fact that, according to Article 147 of the Federal Constitution, the cantons—as well as political parties and interested organisations of civil society—must be consulted whenever the Confederation prepares important legislation or other projects of substantial impact or when it concludes significant international treaties.[10] In the field of foreign policy, the cantons must be consulted whenever foreign policy decisions affect their powers or their essential interests, and the views expressed by the cantons are of particular importance if their powers are affected[11]; in this case, they shall even participate in international negotiations in an appropriate manner.

The fourth reason intergovernmental relations are particularly important in Switzerland is due to the fact that, according to Article 46 of the Federal Constitution, the cantons bear the main responsibility for the implementation of federal legislation. This is a right as well as a duty of the cantons, and implementation must be understood in this context in a broad sense, including not only the application of federal legislation in concrete cases but also the necessary legislative activities at the cantonal level. Cantonal legislations implementing federal legislation comprehend, on the one hand, the necessary organisational and procedural measures and, on the other hand, substantial legislation whenever, as it is often the case, federal legislation does not fix all the details or is limited to laying down principles.[12] Although from the point of view of international law the Swiss Confederation is responsible for the implementation of international treaties, from the point of view of internal law the responsibility of the cantons exists also with regard to the implementation of international treaties. The fact that federal legislation and international treaties are only exceptionally implemented by federal authorities, in other words that the implementation of the law is mainly left to the sub-national level of government, is a major justification for the participation of the cantons in federal decision-making.

A final point is that the Federal Constitution also clearly holds, in Article 48, that the cantons may enter into agreements with each other and establish common

---

[7] See Article 148 paragraph 2 of the Federal Constitution.

[8] See Article 142 paragraph 2 of the Federal Constitution.

[9] See Article 141 paragraph 1 of the Federal Constitution. This right has been used only once but successfully, in the history of the Swiss Confederation (in 2003, regarding an amendment of the fiscal legislation that would have led to a substantial reduction of fiscal revenues for the cantons). It is, in a certain sense, sometimes considered as a substitute for the lack of judicial control of the constitutionality of federal legislation, a view that may be questioned of course.

[10] For more details regarding the consultation procedure, see the Consultation Procedure Act of 18 March 2005.

[11] See Article 55 paragraphs 1 and 3 of the Federal Constitution. See also Sturny (1998).

[12] See, e.g., Article 75 (spatial planning) or 79 (fishing and hunting) of the Federal Constitution.

organisations and institutions.[13] The Confederation may participate in such organisations or institutions within the scope of its powers. According to Art. 48a, the Confederation even may, at the request of interested cantons, declare such agreements between cantons to be generally binding for all cantons or it may oblige reluctant cantons to join regional agreements. I have to admit that this rather new constitutional provision—it was introduced in 2004 only—has never been used yet, and I strongly doubt that it will ever be used as it is hardly compatible with the idea that the cooperation between the cantons should, in principle, work on a voluntary basis.[14]

## Intergovernmental Institutions

If we have a look now at the intergovernmental institutions in Switzerland today, I would like to emphasise that there is a very large variety of such institutions. We can indeed distinguish different types of intergovernmental institutions based on a multitude of criteria:

A first distinction may be made between intergovernmental bodies aimed at favouring the vertical cooperation between the Swiss Confederation and the subnational entities, on the one hand, and intergovernmental bodies dealing mainly with horizontal cooperation between entities of the same State level, in particular between the cantons. The so-called Federalist Dialogue, a regular meeting (at least twice a year) of three to five representatives of the Conference of cantonal governments (CCG) with a delegation of the federal government, is an example of the first type, whereas regional conferences of the cantonal governments are a typical example of the second type. Most national conferences of cantonal ministers responsible for specific policy fields have vertical as well as horizontal functions because, at least for some of the items on the agenda, the responsible federal minister is usually invited and takes part in these meetings.

According to the status of the members or participants, we then may distinguish between political or technical-administrative institutions. Political organs are, in particular, those composed of members of cantonal governments. As we shall see, such political conferences exist in nearly all policy fields. However, in most fields where a political conference exists, there is also a technical-administrative conference usually composed of high-ranking civil servants. To give an example: in the field of police (internal security), we have the Conference of cantonal ministers responsible for justice and police (political level), and the Conference of the Heads of the cantonal police corps (technical level).

---

[13] With the constitutional amendments of 2006 concerning the Swiss education area (in particular, Articles 61a, 62, 63, and 63a of the Federal Constitution), a further step has been made with regard to intergovernmental institutions and relations. See, in this context, Biaggini (2008), pp. 449 ss.

[14] Mader (2005), pp. 103 ss; Mader (2009), pp. 133 ss.

Furthermore, intergovernmental institutions may exist nationwide and include all the cantons, or they have a regional character. Some of the regional conferences even include entities outside of the Swiss territory; they are in other words cross-border conferences.

To give some examples:

- The Conferences of cantonal ministers or civil servants responsible for specific policy fields include all the cantons and are, in this sense, national conferences.
- Regarding the regional conferences, some of them are based on a purely geographic criterion (cantons of the central part of Switzerland, of the East, of the North-west, of the West).[15] Others are based on topographic or sociographic criteria (e. g., Conference of the alpine—and mainly rural—cantons, Conference of the so-called metropolitanian area Zürich). Thus, regional intergovernmental institutions are in various senses "à géometrie variable".
- Cross-border conferences exist, in particular, for the region around the lake of Geneva, for the region around the lake of Constance, for the Jura region, for Basel, and for the canton of Ticino and its neighbouring Italian regions (regione insubrica).

Intergovernmental institutions may have sectional or cross-sectional (comprehensive) responsibilities or fields of interest. Examples for the first case are again the conferences of cantonal ministers responsible for a specific policy field. The main example for the second case is the CCG, which I'll present more in detail later because it is probably the most important intergovernmental conference in Switzerland today.

Intergovernmental bodies may exist permanently and hold regular meetings (once, twice, or more times a year), or they may be set up for specific tasks or projects limited in time. Examples for the second case are "round tables", joint working parties, or joint task forces organised to deal with specific questions or problems. There are many of them. To mention just one example: after some conflicts between federal and cantonal authorities regarding the entry into force of federal legislation (the cantons were complaining about the short terms fixed for implementing federal legislation), a joint working party with public officials from the federal level, from the CCG, and from the cantons was established to examine the problem and to propose solutions. Quite often, such joint working parties (at the technical-administrative level but sometimes also at the political level) are established to prepare new federal legislation or its implementation. A recent example of this practice is the joint working party preparing the new federal legislation in the field of gaming (casinos, lotteries, and betting). It is based on an agreement between the responsible federal ministry and the inter-cantonal conference responsible in the field of lotteries and betting.

---

[15] For regional co-operation, see in particular Brunner (2000). It may be interesting to note that the most important Swiss canton, the canton of Zurich, is not member of one of the regional conferences. However, it has an observer status in several of them.

Some of the intergovernmental institutions have permanent secretariats and staff; others do without. Among the conferences of cantonal ministers responsible for specific policy fields, we find examples for both solutions mainly according to the practical importance of each conference. However, there seems to be a certain trend to set up permanent secretariats engaging their own staff. The most important inter-cantonal conferences have nowadays permanent secretariats (e.g., CCG and conferences in the fields of police and justice, of education, of health and social policy). Others still practice a rotation system (the secretarial tasks are accomplished by the canton exercising the annual lead or presidency).

Most bodies are multilateral in the sense that they include several cantons or even all of them. Others, like the so-called Federalist Dialogue, are bilateral in the sense that they bring together cantonal authorities, on the one hand, and federal authorities, on the other. A special case is tripartite bodies such as the so-called Tripartite Agglomeration Conference (TAC), comprising federal, cantonal, and municipal representatives. The communes or municipalities are represented in this body, in particular, by the presidents of the national umbrella organisations for the communes and for the cities. In this context, it may be added that, at the local level, intergovernmental cooperation between communes (in particular cities) or municipalities is very important too. It may take the form of inter-communal agreements—some of them setting up inter-communal bodies in various fields such as school education, hospitals, fire brigades, etc.—or of membership in the national umbrella organisations for the communes and, in particular, the cities. These organisations take also part in the consultation procedure at the national level.

Last but not least, institutional co-operation exists not only between executive or administrative authorities but also between cantonal parliaments, which may create inter-parliamentary committees, for example, to examine together draft inter-cantonal agreements submitted for parliamentary approval in the cantonal parliaments.

Of course, these examples based on a certain number of criteria are in no way meant to be exhaustive. We could distinguish also between bodies having purely consultative functions and others having decision-making—and even legislative—powers. We could further distinguish between formal and informal bodies. However, what does "formal" or "informal" mean in this context? If "formal" is supposed to mean bodies created on the basis of explicit constitutional or legal provisions (be it at the federal or at the cantonal level), most such intergovernmental institutions would be of an informal character indeed.

Let me now add some complementary information regarding three important and recently created intergovernmental institutions.[16]

---

[16] For the intergovernmental conferences in general and these three examples in particular, see Meyer (2006) and Affolter (2008). The following information is mainly based on these two publications.

## The Conferences of Cantonal Ministers Responsible for Specific Policy Fields

The most important examples to be mentioned are undoubtedly the conferences of cantonal ministers responsible for specific policy fields. There are at least 12 of them. The oldest and at the same time the most important one is the conference in the field of school education. It has been founded in 1897. Others, such as the Conference of the cantonal ministers responsible for justice and police established in 1905, date from the beginning of the twentieth century. Others, still, were created in the middle of the last century. This is the case, for example, for the Conference of cantonal ministers responsible for public economy (1944) or the Conference for social affairs (1945). One of the youngest sectional conferences is the Conference in the field of energy policy, founded in 1979. Most of these intergovernmental conferences meet between two and four times a year, and they usually invite the responsible federal minister for at least a part of the meeting. The most important issues addressed by these conferences are the development of policies, the preparation of cantonal and federal legislation, or inter-cantonal agreements and implementation problems.

## The Conference of Cantonal Governments

The CCG is the youngest intergovernmental conference at the political level. It was set up in 1993 in the context of the Swiss political debate about the European Economic Area and in view of the upcoming total revision of the Federal Constitution and the reform of Swiss federalism. Unlike the other cantonal conferences at the political level, the CCG has a cross-sectional, comprehensive perspective. Its members represent the cantonal governments, not the ministers responsible for certain policy fields. Every canton has one vote. Decisions taken by a majority of 18 cantons are considered to express the consolidated view of the cantons. Members of the federal government are usually invited to participate in the meetings at least for certain items on the agenda, but in most cases they renounce to do so.

Since its creation, the CCG has mainly dealt with general institutional questions and with the Swiss European policy. It also tries to coordinate the activities of the sectional conferences, but these efforts are not always and not unanimously welcomed by the sectional conferences. Indeed, some of them sometimes do not seem to be very keen on giving too much weight to the CCG. The same is true for some cantons. A certain scepticism or reservation exists also in the National Assembly, in particular in the Council of States, which has also the mission to give special attention to the interests of the cantons. Nevertheless, there is no doubt that the CCG has become, in less than two decades, a key player regarding horizontal and vertical intergovernmental cooperation in the Swiss federal system. In particular, for cross-sectional issues such as institutional reforms or problems, foreign policy and especially European policy the CCG is nowadays a crucial interlocutor and partner of the federal authorities.


## *The Federalist Dialogue*

At least twice a year, the meetings of the CCG are followed by a meeting of three to five representatives of this Conference with a delegation of the federal government (Federal Council). This is the so-called Federalist Dialogue created nearly 20 years ago when the CCG replaced the former contact group, Confederation/cantons, set up a decade earlier to deal with a project aiming at reforming the allocation of powers between the Confederation and the cantons.[17] The Federalist Dialogue permits the cantons to give voice to their common concerns and to their expectations regarding the policies and practices of the federal authorities. The dialogue within a reduced circle of persons allows to openly address misunderstandings, tensions, diverging views, problems, or even conflicts that may arise between the different levels of government and to agree upon how to proceed for preparing decisions to be taken by the formally responsible authorities. In other words, the Federalist Dialogue is a purely deliberative body and has no decision-making powers.


## *The Tripartite Agglomeration Conference*

The last intergovernmental conference I would like to mention is the so-called TAC, created in 2001. It is the only institutionalised forum of co-operation between the three State levels. The TAC usually meets twice a year and deals with questions of interest to not only the Confederation and the cantons but also the communes and, in particular, the cities: cross-sectional institutional questions, spatial planning, social problems in urban agglomerations crossing cantonal borders, etc. Each party has a maximal number of eight representatives, and the chair is usually held by a representative of the cantons. The creation of this tripartite body was, to some extent, a way of implementing the new constitutional provision relating to the communes (Art. 50 introduced by the Federal Constitution of 1999). In the same time, it was also aimed at stopping direct contacts between federal and communal authorities, respectively, at making sure that these contacts took place in a setting where the cantons had the lead.

---

[17] This contact group was chaired by the federal minister responsible for justice and police.

## Other Forms of Intergovernmental Relations

Of course, intergovernmental relations are not limited to intergovernmental conferences or institutions in a narrow sense. There are many other forms that have to be mentioned too.

There are, in particular, numerous inter-cantonal—and also inter-communal—agreements. Indeed, in Switzerland, we have a very intense network of inter-cantonal agreements. We can count more than 800 of them covering a large variety of subject matters. They are of various types: some of them with the participation of the Confederation, some of them dealing with administrative matters, and some of them being of legislative character, i.e., containing legal norms that are binding for the cantons having ratified the agreements. To mention just four recent examples of this type of intergovernmental relations: the agreement on measures against hooliganism; the agreement regulating the activities of private security enterprises and, in particular, the delegation of cantonal police tasks to such enterprises; the—quite controversial—agreement on the harmonisation of cantonal legislations in the field of school education (Harmos); and the agreement in the field of lotteries and betting. In order to avoid democratic deficits that may result from them, intergovernmental agreements authorising inter-cantonal bodies to issue legislative provisions have to be approved under the same procedure that applies to other (cantonal) legislation and must determine the basic content of the provisions to be issued.[18]

Another form is the numerous—more or less informal and ad hoc—round tables, working parties, and task forces. Some of them are joint bodies equally composed of federal and cantonal representatives, set up in particular to prepare federal legislation. Examples exist in many fields, such as financial equalization, lotteries and betting, language law, etc.

Also very important is the so-called consultation procedure giving the cantons the possibility to react to legislative proposals prepared by the federal authorities before the federal government submits a bill to parliament or before the federal government issues secondary legislation. As already mentioned before, the cantons—individually or via intergovernmental conferences—are in this way closely associated to the federal decision-making process.

Sometimes, parliamentary committees organise hearings with cantonal representatives when they are debating bills.[19] This is important, in particular, when they amend bills in a way that could affect the implementation of federal legislation by the cantons. Today, we can observe a clear trend to use this possibility more often. Intergovernmental institutions having permanent secretariats play a major role in this context.

A rather new form of intergovernmental relations is the cantonal representatives working in the federal administration as a sort of "liaison officers" between

---

[18] See Article 48 paragraph 4 of the Federal Constitution.

[19] See Article 45 paragraph 1 of the Federal Parliament Act.

cantonal and federal authorities. Such "liaison officers" exist, in particular, in the field of European policy (bilateral treaties between Switzerland and the European Union).

Sometimes, when matters falling within the scope of cantonal competences are concerned (e.g., in the fields of education or internal security), cantonal representatives are members of Swiss delegations involved in international negotiations. They may even head such delegations.

Finally, to mention a last particular form of intergovernmental relations, there is the House of the cantons. Since 2008, the cantons have their proper building in the Swiss capital in Berne. Many intergovernmental conferences hold their meetings in this building. Most permanent secretariats of intergovernmental conferences are now located there. Quite often, joint working groups or task forces composed of cantonal and federal representatives use the premises for their meetings. In other words: for intergovernmental meetings, the cantons are no longer the guests of federal authorities; they sometimes are the hosts. Besides these meetings, a lot of training activities for the staff of cantonal administrations are organised in the House of the cantons. Thus, the House of the cantons has become the tangible sign of the increasing importance and vitality of intergovernmental relations and the growing intensity of the co-operation between the cantons themselves (horizontal co-operation), as well as between the Confederation and the cantons (vertical co-operation). It is a symbol of the growing self-confidence and self-assertion of the cantons in the Swiss federal system. Indeed, after decades of transfers of legislative powers to the Confederation, the cantons have now organised themselves in order to have a stronger voice and more weight in the federal decision-making process.

## Functions of Intergovernmental Relations and Institutions

The presentation of the different types and forms of intergovernmental relations and of the main institutions, in particular the cantonal conferences, clearly illustrates also their principal functions:

They are mechanisms for horizontal as well as vertical co-operation: horizontal in the sense that the cantons (or the communes) co-operate among each other, vertical in the sense that the different State levels co-operate. Horizontal and vertical co-operation are, of course, closely linked. Indeed, in many intergovernmental conferences, the cantons first try to develop consolidated views or positions before they communicate them to the federal authorities or before they enter into negotiations with the federal authorities.

In questions of vital importance to the cantons, intergovernmental conferences serve as lobby mechanisms with regard to the federal level. They voice demands and proposals by various ways (meetings with federal authorities, statements approved by the members of these conferences, information to the media, public actions, etc.

In most cases, intergovernmental conferences serve to exchange information and experiences or views. Usually, the results of these exchanges are not formally binding; they are mainly consultative. Nonetheless, they have particular weight in the shaping of federal decisions and in the preparation for the implementation of federal legislation.

Exceptionally, intergovernmental institutions may take binding decisions. An example is now explicitly mentioned in the Federal Constitution. Indeed, according to Article 63a of the Federal Constitution, the Confederation and the cantons may delegate certain tasks to joint administrative authorities having decision-making powers in the field of higher education.

Besides, intergovernmental bodies may also play a role in mediation processes. The best example for this particular function is the so-called Tripartite Jura, composed of the federal minister of justice and police and representatives of the governments of the cantons of Berne and Jura. This tripartite body regularly meets to discuss questions related to the status of the francophone districts remaining in the canton of Berne after the creation of the new canton of Jura more than 30 years ago.

## Strengths and Weaknesses

In Switzerland, the growing importance and intensity of intergovernmental relations and institutions are a necessary and, to some extent, unavoidable process, a process that offers opportunities, contributes to the strength of Swiss federalism, but includes also weaknesses and threats. It is a chance and a challenge for the functioning of the Swiss institutions.[20] We can try to assess its negative and its positive aspects.

Among the negative aspects, I would emphasise in particular the following:

- The process may lead to a certain over-institutionalisation and, consequently, to inefficiencies. Indeed, we have now not only three but also five tiers of government, if we add the inter-cantonal and the inter-communal levels (without talking about the international level). This seems to me to be clearly too much for a small country such as Switzerland.
- Many intergovernmental institutions and procedures are very complex and lack transparency.
- Dense intergovernmental relations considerably slow down the decision-making process and may even lead to stalemates or, at least, risk to create stalemates.
- They also include a high risk of blurred responsibilities. Indeed, they may be considered as a form of "institutionalised irresponsibility" and are hardly compatible with the efforts that have been made in the last few decades to delineate

---

[20] See also Waldmann (2010), pp. 3 ss.

more clearly the responsibilities and powers of the cantons and of the Confederation in the Swiss federal system. There is an ever-growing gap between formal responsibilities and factual or practical powers in the decision-making process. This gives also rise to a lack of legitimacy.

- Intergovernmental relations and institutions are very executive driven and suffer from "democratic deficits".
- Last but not least, they may be an obstacle to more fundamental, in particular territorial, reforms of the federal system. Indeed, nowadays, many small cantons are unable to accomplish their tasks without co-operating with and relaying more and more on other cantons.

Nevertheless, without any doubt, there are many important positive aspects too:

- Intense intergovernmental relations and institutions permit to coordinate services provided to the citizens (such as education, health, welfare, waste removal, water purification) and thus help to overcome shortcomings due to territorial fragmentation. In this way, they help avoid further centralisation and, in this sense, contribute to implement the principle of subsidiarity.
- They facilitate the development of political consensus and compromise.
- They guarantee a wide acceptance of federal decisions and, in this sense, favour the legitimacy of political decisions.
- They help to assure good practicability and effective implementation of federal legislation by taking into account the particular situations at the cantonal and communal levels.
- In particular, the informal intergovernmental relations are more flexible than formal institutions and permit to respond more easily and more rapidly to momentary needs and concerns.
- Finally, they help to better cope with the territorial heterogeneity and smallness of most of the cantons, with unclear or outdated allocations of powers and with certain shortcomings of the traditional institutions.


## Conclusion

Intergovernmental relations and institutions are of paramount importance for the functioning of the Swiss federal system. Although intergovernmental relations and institutions are only scarcely mentioned in the Swiss Constitution and in federal or cantonal legislation, they play a vital role in practice. Formal and informal mechanisms of co-operation between the cantons and between the cantons and the Confederation are the indispensable lubricant of Swiss federalism.

We, however, may ask the question whether the intensification of intergovernmental relations, as well as the growing number of intergovernmental institutions, is just a transitional phenomenon or if it is a process that is bound to continue and to last. In other words: we may ask whether the developments that occurred, in particular, in the last two decades are in fact a dead end road or the panacea for the shortcomings and weaknesses of the Swiss federal system. I am not quite sure about the answer to this question. My feeling is that they are both: they are part of the problem, as well as part of the solution. The practical conclusion I would draw from this diagnosis is that we have to accommodate these developments, but at the same time we should try to eliminate deficits in terms of inefficiencies, lack of transparency, lack of democratic (popular and parliamentary) participation, and political legitimacy. Perhaps, more intense horizontal co-operation between the cantons will also sharpen the willingness of federal authorities to better co-operate among each other and to overcome their sectional approach to federal policies. Strong intergovernmental relations between the cantons indeed also call for better inter-ministerial coordination at the federal level if the Confederation wants to maintain its leading role in the Swiss political system.

# References

Bernhard Waldmann, Föderalismus unter Druck – Eine Skizze von Problemfeldern und Herausforderungen für den Föderalismus in der Schweiz, in Markus Gredig et al. (ed.), Peters Dreiblatt: Föderalismus – Grundrechte – Verwaltung, 2010, pp. 3 ss.

Giovanni Biaggini, Kooperativer Föderalismus zwischen Freiwilligkeit und Zwang: Die neue schweizerische "Bildungsverfassung" als Experimentierfeld, in Europäisches Zentrum für Föderalismus-Forschung Tübingen (ed.), Jahrbuch des Föderalismus 2007, 2008, pp. 449 ss.

Luzius Mader, The participation of subnational units in the foreign policy of a federation: the Swiss case, in: Manuel Calvo-Garcia and William L. F. Felstiner (ed.), Federalism, 2002, pp. 155 ss.

Luzius Mader, Erfahrungen und Erwartungen auf dem Gebiet des kooperativen Föderalismus, in Bernhard Waldmann (ed.), 1. Nationale Föderalismuskonferenz, 2005, pp. 103 ss.

Luzius Mader, Die Föderalismusreform – ein Reformvorhaben in mehreren Schritten, in Georg Kreis (ed.), Erprobt und entwicklungsfähig – Zehn Jahre neue Bundesverfassung, 2009, pp. 133 ss.

Markus Meyer, Die interkantonale Konferenz – ein Mittel der Kantone zur Zusammenarbeit auf Regierungsebene, 2006.

Simon Affolter, La participation des conférences intercantonales au processus de décision sur le plan fédéral, 2008.

Stephan C. Brunner, Möglichkeiten und Grenzen regionaler interkantonaler Zusammenarbeit, untersucht am Beispiel der Ostschweiz, 2000.

Thiemo Sturny, Mitwirkungsrechte der Kantone an der Aussenpolitik des Bundes. 1998.

Ursula Abderhalden, Möglichkeiten und Grenzen der interkantonalen Zusammenarbeit, 1999.

Vital Zehnder, Die interkantonale öffentlich-rechtliche Körperschaft alsd Modellform für die gemeinsame Zusammenarbeit – Rechtsgrundlagen der interkantonalen Zusammenarbeit und des interkantonalen Vertrags, 2007.

# The Participation of Autonomous Communities in the Central Bodies of State

Eduardo Vírgala Foruria

## Participation in Central Bodies, Federalism and Autonomous State

The participation of local authorities in the central bodies of the State, or relations of inordination, according to M. García Pelayo, is the legal expression of the dialectical synthesis between central authority and local authorities, evidenced in a federal State by "the participation of States as autonomous personalities in the shaping of federal will and in the reform of the federal Constitution".[1]

Following this definition, the doubt that might arise is whether or not Spain is a federal State and the consequences this might have for the participation of Autonomous Communities in the central bodies of the State. However, I think it is pointless to be arguing in the year 2010 over whether or not Spain is a federal State. It is an autonomous State with particular characteristics but that shared many features with federal Status, one of which is that of establishing certain mechanisms for the participation of Autonomous Communities in the central bodies of the State. The problem arises to a great degree from the confusion between federalism as a value concept or ideology based on the idea of divided political power and Federation or federal State as a specific institutional form in which the idea of federalism may manifest itself in different ways,[2] with this levelling of the two terms giving rise to serious misunderstandings in Spain.[3] For this reason, there may be federalism without the federal constitutional form (Spain, Belgium before 1993), just as a State may be federal without establishing authentic federalism (as in Austria, where

---

[1] García-Pelayo (1984, p. 239).

[2] Erk (2004, p. 3).

[3] Moreno (2008, p. 31).

E. Vírgala Foruria (✉)
Department of Constitutional Law and History of the Political Thought, University of the Basque Country (UPV/EHU), Campus of Sarriena, Post Box 644, Bilbao 48080, Spain
e-mail: eduardo.virgala@ehu.es

A. López-Basaguren and L. Escajedo San Epifanio (eds.), *The Ways of Federalism in Western Countries and the Horizons of Territorial Autonomy in Spain*, Vol. 2, DOI 10.1007/978-3-642-27717-7_5, © Springer-Verlag Berlin Heidelberg 2013

social homogeneity and the predominance of national parties transform member States into weak local authorities).[4]

An additional fact that supports the above argument is the diversity of institutional forms adopted by the self-styled federal States. In terms of its federal constitutional structure, the USA has little in common with Australia and neither of these two with, for instance, Belgium. If we proceed to analyse each of their fundamental characteristics, we also see that what predominates is diversity rather than uniformity.[5] Focussing upon the participation of Autonomous Communities in the central bodies of the State, the most important means of involvement in the formation of federal will, to which M. García Pelayo referred, is the composition of the Senate and one could almost say that each federal Senate responds to a different conception, in the same way that there are federal States elements of which participate in constitutional reform in different ways or do not even participate at all. Without now going into what I will later attempt to develop, the federal Senate may be elective (USA, Switzerland, Australia), appointed by the federal Parliaments (Austria), formed by governmental delegates (Germany), appointed by the federal Government (Canada: formally the Governor General), or mixed (as in Belgium where there are those appointed by the Parliaments of the Communities, elected by the citizens, and co-opted by the former). If we take into account constitutional reform, there are cases of parliamentary approval, plus ratification by the federated Parliaments (USA, Canada), of simple parliamentary approval

---

[4] The patronage of a formally federal structure in Spain tends to overlook the fact that, in practice, we possess a greater degree of territorial decentralisation than most federal States in the world, that the federal State favours uniformisation between its territorial bodies and is hostile to excessive differences between the latter because its objective is the construction of a common nation and not the disaggregation of one that already exists, whilst in Spain the leading advocates of the introduction of federalism are champions of difference and of confederal solutions in which part and whole are related as equals.

[5] At the time (Vírgala 2006, pp. 405–407) I pointed out, on the subject of judicial power in federal States, that what is striking is disparity in the area. For instance, it might be said that the model of dual structure of judicial power as in the USA is the exception. In its federal judicial system, there are courts of first instance (the District Courts, an average of two per State) and of second instance or appeal (the 13 Appeal Courts, 11 combining various States, one in Washington D.C., and the *Court of Appeals for the Federal Circuit*, which encompasses the entire national territory and only deals with questions of customs and patents), whilst in the state judicial system are the Courts of demarcation and a state Supreme Court, both networks unified by the federal Supreme Court. On the other hand, in Germany, Switzerland, or Australia the system is that of first instance served by state or cantonal Courts, crowned by federal high courts appointed by the federation. There are some hybrid systems, like in Canada, in which, in a dual system, at a local level the Courts of first instance are appointed by the Provinces, whilst the provincial High Courts of first instance and the provincial Courts of Appeal are appointed by the federal Government, which, in addition, appoints the federal Courts (first instance, appeal, and federal Supreme Court). Finally, there are unitary federal judicial systems, which have, in other words, as in Spain, only one common judicial structure in which territorial bodies do not participate as they do in Belgium (Courts of first instance, appeal, or cassation) or in Austria (district courts; regional courts; courts of first instance, appeal, or second instance; Supreme Court).

(Germany, Austria, Belgium), of parliamentary approval, of the member states and of the electors (Australia, Switzerland).

Having said this, and returning to García Pelayo's definition, in this work I shall restrict myself to analysing the participation of the Autonomous Communities in the formation of the will of the central bodies of the State, not existing in our case, more participation of the Autonomous Communities in constitutional reform than that of ordinary autonomous initiative in the legislative procedure, which is one more of the former that I shall aim to highlight. This would not pose a problem were the Senate genuinely a territorial Chamber, as in those European states self-styled as federal, constitutional reform does not include participation in local institutions, except in the case of Switzerland. However, in Spain the route for channelling territorial representation, understood in the sense that will subsequently be explained, is not materialised in the Senate so that, in fact, there is no autonomous participation in constitutional reform, even indirectly.

The Constitution only envisages as mechanisms for the participation of the Autonomous Communities in central bodies of the State[6] the "autonomous" designation of part of the Senate and the legislative initiative of the autonomous Assemblies. To the former have been added in previous years the autonomous proposal to the Senate of candidates as Constitutional Court magistrates (since 2007 and conditional upon the provision of the Catalan Statute of 2006) and following the statutory reforms.[7] Approved in 2006 and 2007 was the provision, constitutionally questionable, of new forms of participation by the Autonomous Communities in the central bodies of the State, which, for reasons of space, cannot be considered in this work.[8]

## The Participation of the Autonomous Communities in the Senate

Autonomous participation in constitutional reform having been ruled out, it is the Senate that remains as maximum expression of the participation of the Autonomous Communities in the central bodies of the autonomous Spanish State. The Upper House is usually regarded as the most crucial element of these relations or of the so-called "infra-state federalism", which does not render superfluous other mechanisms of relationship between regional authorities and central or federal bodies such as intergovernmental conferences of various types. However, it is the Senate that enables regional institutions to participate in the national process of political decision-making,[9] though it is true that in the member states the territorial

---

[6] Amongst which do not feature, logically, inter-governmental relations of cooperation and coordination as these are not forms of participation by Autonomous Communities in an organ of the State but merely a system of composition of diverse interests (Central State-Autonomous Communities).

[7] This is more a case of preparing new Statutes.

[8] On this question, see Virgala (2011).

[9] Bolleyer (2006, p. 388).

Chamber has lost influence to the organs of collaboration of an executive nature,[10] even to such a degree as to ponder its suppression as in Australia.[11]

In any case, it is a well-known fact that our upper house is not that Chamber of territorial representation referred to in art. 69.1 CE[12] but a chamber elected by 78 % of the citizens (208 out of 264) in constituencies not adjusted to the territorial division of political power, leaving only 21.22 % (56) of the Senators appointed by the autonomous Assemblies. The former was probably the result of the uncertainty regarding the development of the autonomous State, but it should be pointed out that the widespread notion that the constitutional Senate is born of the indefinition of the territorial model established in Title VIII is contradicted by the original version of the Preliminary Draft of the Constitution, art. 60 of which establishes the appointment of Senators by the autonomous Assemblies (ten each plus one more per half million or fraction higher than 250,000, without any assembly able to more than double in number those of another) pursuant to a proportional system and with the Senate having suspensive vote only. Neither does its role in parliamentary functions affects to a particular dedication to autonomous issue, despite the "botch jobs" attempted in the last 20 years, so that, as the detailed analysis of E. Albertí shows, the Spanish Senate occupies the lower ranks of democratic member states in terms of both autonomous participation in legislation and the specific representation of territories.[13] In short, it is an elected Chamber dedicated to slowing down decisions taken in the House of Deputies without contributing the territorial content necessary in order to consider it an ideal mechanism for the participation of the Autonomous Communities, especially as a forum for channelling the territorial tensions that, after 1979, shifted quickly towards the conflict model making a protagonist of the TC.[14]

In this sense, I believe that the focus upon the Senate within the participation of the Autonomous Communities in the central bodies of the State should be redirected towards constitutional reform, as its current situation contributes little towards this participation. For this reason, this work will only seek to establish certain points regarding the present situation and its hypothetical reform rather than to attempt a reconstruction of the debate over the position, composition, and functions of the Senate.[15]

---

[10] Aja (1994, p. 212).

[11] Albertí (2004, p. 287).

[12] During this debate, the Senate underwent multiple phases. In the Drafts it was defined as autonomous Chamber with representation in the different territories, then it became a Chamber of representation of territorial institutions with remission as regards its finalisation as an organic Law, to become a provincial Chamber in the Congress Commission and, in the Senate debate, finally turning into a mixed chamber with provincially elected senators and others appointed by the autonomous Assemblies: González-Trevijano (2006, pp. 828–829).

[13] Albertí (2004, pp. 314 and 321).

[14] Da Silva (1994, pp. 18–19).

[15] The bibliography with reference to the Senate is enormous and, and this work focuses not only upon the Upper House. I would refer to http://www.senado.es/docynot/index.html, which provides exhaustive and updated details of this bibliography. For a clear and penetrating vision of the Senate and its evolution since 1978, see Morales (2008).

The definition of the Senate as "Chamber of territorial representation" should be framed within the form of the State established by the Constitution of 1978. The only possible conclusion is that of understanding that in a State which that is not federal but has a federalist structure, in the sense outlined initially, what is needed is a territorial State which that allows for the integration within itself of the political momentum of each of the 17 Autonomous Communities. It is clear, as Santaolalla[16] points out, that the concept of "territorial representation" taken literally makes no sense, as the members of a House will always represent citizens and not territories, which can be neither subject to laws nor object of representation. Admittedly, as the same author also indicates, it would be more correct to speak of representation of territorial institutions, but all of this in no way prevents us from considering the present Senate to be the Chamber of territorial representation or, rather, representation of territorial institutions or, as Albertí says, of the bodies attributed with entity and political power.[17] Certainly, the final result will be influenced by the political parties, and those appointed will struggle to act as loyal representatives of their territorial institution, but the problem is not this but rather that of creating a Chamber or Council that gives an idea of the diverse political formulae directed towards the Autonomous Communities, in particular, if these political formulae do not respond to the designs of the two major parties. I even believe that a formula for translating the majority will of each Autonomous Community directly to the Senate would result in a more complex coordination between these delegates and their peers from the same party in other Autonomies or in the Government of the Nation.

On the basis of the aforementioned definition, one could scarcely describe as a territorial Chamber a Senate which that is elected via universal suffrage in constituencies that do not coincide with the global territorial ambit of the Autonomous Communities (except, of course, in the case of single-province Communities). Senators are elected by their province, in representation of the electorate thereof and identifiable only as belonging to their political party. Once elected, their legitimacy is born of popular will, the only difference from MPs being the use of a different electoral system. The so-called autonomous Senators (less than one quarter part) are indeed appointed by autonomous bodies but with a proportional system (ex art. 69.5 and constitutional case law) that does not faithfully follow the formula of government of each Autonomous Community. Basically, a Senate to a large degree elected independently of the autonomous political map and with a minute quota of members stemming from the Autonomous Communities and failing strictly to represent autonomous interests.

As regards its functions, one might say that the Senate is a reviewing Chamber but with little capacity for autonomous decision-making or decisive participation in decisions made by Parliament. It only enjoys an exclusive intervention in the

---

[16] Santaolalla (2007, p. 48 ss.)

[17] Albertí (2004, p. 282).

approval of the measures of state coercion in art. 155 CE and only has decision-making authority in the constitutional reform of art. 168 CE, in the authorisation of international Treaties of art. 94.1 CE, in the appointment of members of some constitutional bodies (like the TT or the CGPJ), in recognition of the need to harmonise the exercise of autonomous competences (art. 150.3 CE), and in the relationship with the Crown (due to end of the Royal line, denial of the marriage of a member of the Royal Family, or appointment of a regency). Neither does it intervene at politically decisive moments, such as investiture, question of confidence, motion of censure, convalidation of decree laws, the authorisation of states of emergency, or the authorisation of a referendum being held. It is glaringly absent from autonomous issues, with the exception of the aforementioned state coercion and need for harmonisation, especially in the legislative process. The Senate does not present any autonomous speciality in the ordinary legislative process, neither does it initiate procedures; it has no option of specific veto and can always be superseded by Congress. Its irrelevance may even attain the perverse effect of distorting the normal functioning of institutions, as E. Albertí shrewdly pointed out with reference to the introduction in the Senate of amendments that substantially modify the text approved in Congress, so that they are returned to Congress for a simple vote with a far more limited and watered-down debate.[18]

The solution is to be found not in well-meant but barely effective measures, such as the General Commission of the Autonomous Regions, but in constitutional reform resulting in the territorial definition of the Senate. This reform is necessary in order to tailor our State to its federalist nature but not in the belief that this will resolve the problems of integration posed by some Autonomous Communities. The drive for independence or, at least, confederacy and detachment from Spain of political parties that have governed (PNV, EA, BNG, CiU, ERC) and will presumably do so again will not be modified with a Senate as a genuine Chamber of territorial representation, of a federal or integrating type.[19] On the contrary, they will always be impervious to a Senate which that equates or puts them on a par with "ordinary" Autonomous Communities and will tend to belittle them, unless it acknowledges their special status (for example, specific vetoes), which asserts their blocking and blackmailing capacity. Neither does it appear to appeal much to the national parties, which can far better control, with the electoral system, a Senate like the current one

Therefore, reform of the Senate has to be seen in a structural and functional sense and not as the path to the insertion of the Spanish political "special nature", which is the existence of independentist parties governing in various Autonomous Communities.

---

[18] By 2003, the situation had reached such a point that a new Act was introduced to modify The Criminal Code via Senate amendment of the draft Bill on arbitration: Albertí (2004, pp. 326–328).

[19] As J.C. Da Silva pointed out over 15 years ago (1994, p. 34), the existence of territorial party subsystems means that their majority parties do not regard it as natural to act in a framework shared with the remaining Communities.

Reform of the Senate has been contemplated on several occasions, and this seeks not to be an exhaustive account but rather a highlighting of most significant moments. Constitutional reform apart, noteworthy in this sense was the creation in 1994 of the General Commission of the Autonomous Communities.[20] This Commission, formed by double the members in the ordinary Commission, allows for the intervention both of the central Government and of the Presidents and ministers of autonomous Governments and must, amongst other functions, report as to the autonomous content of any initiative to be processed in the Senate; be informed as to agreements that Autonomous Communities reach amongst themselves regarding the management and provision of services within their competence; pronounce upon the authorisation the Spanish Parliament may grant for the conclusion of cooperation between Autonomous Communities; be informed by the Government of agreements between the latter and the Autonomous Communities; report upon initiatives of allocation by the Spanish Parliament, in areas of state competence, to all or some of the Autonomous Communities of the capacity to enact, by themselves, laws within the framework of the principles, rules, and guidelines established by state Law; report upon initiatives by means of which the State agrees to transfer or delegate to the Autonomous Communities powers corresponding to questions of state ownership, as well as upon the State's methods of controlling these; report upon draft bills in which are established the principles needed in order to harmonise the regulatory provisions of the Autonomous Communities, under the terms provided for in art. 153 CE; report upon Government initiatives directed towards requesting Senate authorisation in order to take measures necessary to oblige an Autonomous Community into forced compliance with its constitutional and legal obligations or prevent any action that seriously undermines the general interest of Spain, in accordance with art. 155 CE; inform upon the provision, distribution, and regulation of the Interregional Compensation Fund, control and monitor investment projects included in the latter, and assess its joint impact in the correction of interregional imbalances; and take legislative initiative via legislative proposals. The General Commission of the Autonomous Communities is, in addition, the forum for the so-called Annual Debate on the State of the Autonomies.

The General Commission of the Autonomous Communities, although created to compensate for the absence of constitutional reform, has neither the composition nor the functions required in order to meet the needs of the Senate as territorial Chamber. Its existence has been listless and weak. As at April 2010, it has issued reports on only eight legislative texts (art 56.b Senate Rules) and six statutory reforms and has undertaken not one single legislative initiative.

Turning to the attempts at constitutional reform in recent years, it should be pointed out that in 1995, following the first debate on the State of the Autonomies, President F. González proposed the creation of a parliamentary body to study a limited constitutional reform. Nineteen meetings were held, and 35 interested

---

[20] Regarding this Commission, see Ripollés (2007).

parties attended prior to Parliament being dissolved in 1996. The conclusions favoured a Senate elected by the citizens or by Parliaments but not by Governments, which is permanent in character, and has functions linked to "territorial laws" although without fully clarifying who would determine the speciality and which laws it would affect, acting as an organ of territorial cooperation (Conference of Presidents), of participation in relations with the EU, there being no agreement with regard to differentiating elements (increase in Senators or suspensive veto).[21]

The subsequent legislature saw the constitution of a Commission to study the constitutional reform of the Senate (December 6, 1996), which was unable to complete its work prior to the dissolution of January 2000. After the elections, on June 21, 2000 a Paper was commissioned for the study of the constitutional reform of Senate within the General Commission of the Autonomous Communities, but this also failed to bear fruit.[22]

The most serious attempt appeared to be that initiated in his investiture address, given on April 15, 2004 by the new Socialist President, José Luís Rodríguez Zapatero, who proposed the implementation of a "specific and limited reform of the Constitution", which would affect four areas: (I) the Senate, to underline its role as Chamber of territorial representation; (II) the laws that regulated the order of succession to the Throne in order to adapt them to the principle of non-discrimination against women; (III) the incorporation into the constitutional text of the official title of the seventeen Autonomous Communities and the two Autonomous Cities and finally, (IV) the European Union, incorporating a reference to the future European Constitution as formal evidence of our commitment to Europe and the real value we attach to our status as European citizens. For this, he requested a preliminary report from the Council of State, which would serve as the basis for the project. The Council was not asked to draft the texts in which the reform would be specified but to report on the proposed constitutional modifications, bearing in mind that it was not a question of rectifying the nucleus of the decisions adopted by the drafter but of adapting to the present the regulatory framework of 1978. The President's proposal necessitated the reform of the Organic Act of the Council of State, Organic Act 3/2004.[23] The report was finally requested via Council of Ministers Approval on March 4, 2005 so that the Council of State could report on the four modifications of the Constitution announced by the President almost a year earlier. The Council of State approved an extensive and very interesting Report on February 16, 2006, with four dissenting votes.[24] However, to date, the reform is at a standstill without the existence even of an official project.

---

[21] Ripollés (2007, pp. 119–120).

[22] Alonso de Antonio (2008, pp. 312–313).

[23] In its new drafting, article 2.3 of the Act establishes that "the Council of State will produce alone or under supervision the studies and reports commissioned by the Government and will draw up the legislative proposals or proposals for constitutional reform assigned it by the Government. It will also be able to prepare the studies and reports deemed necessary for the better execution of its functions".

[24] Council of State (2006). I described the latter in Vírgala (2008).

At this point, I will now outline my ideas with regard to how the Senate ought to be reformed in order to turn it into a genuine Chamber of territorial representation, aware as I am of the scant political likelihood of this occurring and of its uselessness as a means of integrating the most unrepentant nationalisms.

In keeping with the idea put forward in this work that the territorial Chamber should express the majority political will of the autonomous institutions rather than be a direct voice of the people, a role reserved for the House of Deputies, it would make sense for the composition of the Senate to tend towards equality in terms of the number of components representing each Autonomous Community. This would be counterbalanced by the situation actually created by the present Senate in which each Autonomous Community already has a different number of seats depending on the number of provinces (in the "provincial" ones) and inhabitants (in the "autonomous" ones) that would make an equal distribution hard to accept.

In any case, without attaining the original federal idea of equal representation as in the USA, Switzerland, or Australia, I agree with the conclusion of the Council of State Report that a proportion of seats should be established not exceeding 1–3 or 1–4,[25] starting with a fixed quantity that would have to be increased, taking into account, on the one hand, population and, on the other, size or internal diversity.

As regards the form of election or appointment of Senators in a hypothetical new territorial Senate, the literature, as everyone knows, has fluctuated between three models, which would be direct election by the citizens, appointment by autonomous Parliaments, and representation of autonomous Governments.

Direct election, typical of the "old" federalisms (USA,[26] Switzerland, Australia), would seem to me to be superfluous in our case[27] as it would mean a repetition of the popular will expressed in the House of Deputies, even if the constituency is

---

[25] Council of State (2006, p. 286). There are several formulae, and at this point I do not see much need to go any further. In any case, I think it is interesting to note A. Garrorena's suggestion (1995, pp. 32–33) regarding the inclusion of the autonomous Presidents, followed by the designation of six Senators per Autonomous Community, plus one for each Community with historical status, one for 2–5 million inhabitants and one more for over 5 million, 2 for Ceuta and 2 for Melilla, making a total of 136 seats.

[26] In the USA, this has been a direct election since 1913 with Senators assuming the role of defenders of their State, not only in their representative function but also as decisive actors in the designation of federal offices in their territory.

[27] The Council of State Report (2006, p. 306) also suggested the possibility of a second method that entailed leaving to the legislative Assemblies the election of the majority of Senators (the set number assigned to each Community and those corresponding to the latter according to population), electing by popular vote in provincial constituency and majority vote the additional Senators assigned to the Community by virtue of number of provinces. The basic aspects of the electoral system should be established in the Constitution, which could refer in some issues to the Statutes. The Council believed that a majority system would facilitate unity of argument of the representatives of each community elected by the Assemblies, although this should not be a formula of simple majority, as this would leave political parties significantly powerful political parties with no representation. For this reason, it raised the possibility of maintaining the present system, which requires "adequate proportional representation", a term that, as the Constitutional Court has indicated, is liable to interpretations correcting proportionality in a majority direction.

autonomous, although it should be borne in mind that, even in this case, there could be resistance in certain Autonomous Communities, like the Basque Country, where the historical influence of the provinces (Historical Territories) is very strong. This will never be territorial representation in the sense referred to in this work. It will be no more than a duplication that will more or less faithfully reproduce the will of the people of Spain, depending on the electoral system employed,[28] but which will struggle to express the territorial component of the autonomous State.

A second option, very popular in certain sectors of the literature, enjoying the early support of G. Trujillo and brilliantly defended by E. Aja, has been that of configuring the Senate as a Council formed by a delegation of autonomous Governments, in the style of what exists in Germany. Aja has proposed a Council in which 85 votes could be used, in such a way that each autonomous Government would send its representatives who would have 3 votes per Autonomous Community and 1 more per million inhabitants, so that Andalusia would have 10 votes, and the less-populated single-province Communities 3 votes.[29]

Although I believe that this proposal is on the right track in that the upper House would be a genuine territorial Chamber reflecting the particular political interests of each Autonomous Community and would allow for Autonomous participation in legislation that directly affects them, it poses various problems within our constitutional rule.[30] In the first place, it would be necessary to modify what is established by art. 67 CE with respect to the binding mandate if government delegates are to comply with the instructions of their Executive. In the second place, it introduces clearly confederal elements derived from their German model (representation of member States, free designation of delegate, *ad hoc* delegation, relative consideration of the population factor to determine the importance of each *Land*),[31] toned down in present-day Germany by the levels of inter-territorial cohesion, without distinguishing elements.[32] In the third place, neither would the political result be very different from now because in 2010 it would mean, applying the Aja model, that the Socialist representatives would have 38 votes (including 5 of the PSC and 2 of PS-IB) and the PP would have 36 votes (including 3 of UPN), in other words,

---

[28] The Council of State Report (2006, p. 306) declared "a moderate preference" for the election of all Senators by universal suffrage, free, equal, direct, and secret, in elections held simultaneously with the autonomous legislative Assemblies via the procedure regulated in the Organic Law on the general electoral system, which could establish some renvoi to the Statutes.

[29] Aja (2004, 2006, p. 713 and pp. 726–727).

[30] To those I mention in the text has usually been added that of qualitatively modifying the principle of separation of powers when members of the autonomous Governments become embedded in legislative power (Solozábal 2006, pp. 389–390), but I regard these as powers that are not on the same horizontal level, and it is not a case of the central Government being introduced into the Senate but rather of Senate representing territorial institutions finding expression through their governments, provided, of course, it does not participate in the function of controlling the national Executive.

[31] Fernández-Miranda (2005, p. 354).

[32] Fernández Manjón (2003, p. 19).

74 out of 85, which would not be very much to the liking of the nationalists, unless it is accompanied by the option of veto in certain issues (for instance, in distinguishing elements), which would again introduce a markedly confederal element,[33] hard to accept in a federalising autonomous State model. In any case, if established it would mean the disappearance of the Senate as Chamber of control of the Government and as determining factor in the decisions constitutionally attributed to the Government or Congress.[34]

Finally, the option most compatible with our autonomous State is, from my point of view, appointment by the autonomous Parliaments. Although it is a system that has been criticised in Austria where it is in place, I believe it to be a system that is more federal in name than in reality, as national political homogeneity dominates and the distribution between parties is a reflection of what occurs in the Lower House, with federal States possessing little will to differentiate. Parliamentary designation allows for politically similar results to those of governmental representation but without turning the Senate into a Chamber elected by regional governments or violating the prohibition of the binding mandate of art. 67 CE.

For this reason, I believe that this method should be established in the Spanish case, in keeping with the suggestion that Senate should reflect majority political momentum in each Autonomous Community or, as R. Punset has said, "what is truly important—and genuinely territorial—is that Senators should represent the dominant political direction in their Autonomous Community", with this method providing, in comparison with the Government one, "an additional bonus of legitimacy, bearing in mind the directly popular origin of the designating body and the greater openness of the electoral process, subject moreover to the rules of parliamentary dialectic".[35] In my opinion, the appointment should not respond merely to criteria of proportional distribution but reflect the prevailing political momentum in each Autonomous Community. An acceptable proposal in this sense might be that made almost 15 years ago by A. Garrorena,[36] which entailed the application of a majority system corrected with a Senator for the second party, although I prefer the formula recommended by J.J. Solozábal of assigning 80 % to the Autonomous Parliament majority and 20 % to the opposition, achieving a level of representation of the political majority similar to that of the Council system, but without its complications.[37]

Another question is whether the political landscape in the Senate would differ from the present one or from the representation of autonomous governments seen previously, as the PSOE and PP would monopolise the seats, and parties like CiU or the PNV might have one seat or even none, appointees acting as mere terminals of their political parties, as criticised by Fernández-Miranda (2005, p. 357).

---

[33] Fernández-Miranda (2005, p. 356).

[34] Ortega (2005, pp. 43–44) and Pauner (2006, p. 277).

[35] Punset (2006, p. 877).

[36] Garrorena (1995, p. 31). Santaolalla (2007, p. 68) also advocates this model.

[37] Solozábal (2006, p. 390).

Nonetheless, this is more an issue of political culture that legal regulation can little influence.

As has been noted, the current Senate has scant relevance in terms of its "autonomous" functions, a situation that would inevitably change in a genuine territorial Chamber of the future.[38] This new Senate role would be particularly evident in the legislative procedure but would also have to encompass other areas.

In the legislative procedure, there exists a doctrinal trend towards a reduction in the future of decisive Senate intervention in laws of "particular autonomous relevance" (Statutes of Autonomy, LOFCA, FCI, laws of art. 150),[39] which has the advantage of being based upon objective elements that clearly identify the type of law, rejecting the use of less easily interpreted terms such as "competence-delimiting acts" or "basic acts". This reduction, however, would contribute little since, as P. Biglino indicates, in the case of the Statutes the Autonomous Community participates significantly with the elaboration of the proposed reform; the acts of art. 150 are very few and far between, and the LOFCA and the FCI Act are specific acts.[40]

Therefore, I relieve that the new Senate would need to play a prominent role in most central legislation, both in basic acts and in those whose enforcement might correspond to the Autonomous Communities. In this way, the delimitation of competences would be facilitated, and there would be a better connection between the lawmaker and its subsequent development.[41] It is true that this solution poses two problems, namely, the drafting of acts, in the words of E. Aja, "susceptible to development or enforcement by the Auonomous Communities" and the establishment of a legislative procedure that reappraises the role of the Senate.

Laws "susceptible to development or enforcement by Autonomous Communities" would be those that are to be developed and applied by the Autonomous Communities (shared and concurrent competences), and whether or not this was the case would depend upon the decision taken by the Bureau[42] upon initiating processing.[43] With regard to legislative procedure in these acts, I think one could begin, with some slight change, with what is proposed by E. Aja in the sense of distinguishing between acts that do not affect the Autonomous Communities or, in any case, do so incidentally, in which the current procedure could be maintained,[44] acts in which the Autonomous Communities would only be responsible for

---

[38] Against this, see Punset (2006, 888 ss.).

[39] Summary by García-Escudero (2006, pp. 217–218) of proposals by various authors.

[40] Biglino (2006, p. 740).

[41] Aja (1994, p. 215).

[42] With the resulting possibility of an application for protection being submitted by the MP who believes that the decision affects the applicable legislative procedure.

[43] Aja (1994, p. 218).

[44] For Aja, it would be sufficient in the former if the Senate could deliver merely a non-binding ruling and for the latter to establish a Senate veto by simple majority that Congress could also overcome via simple majority.

enforcement, so that State intervention could become a procedure similar to that of organic acts in such a way that the Senate veto could only be avoided via absolute majority in Congress and, finally, acts in shared competences (basic acts), FCI Act, LOFCA, and Statutes in which the procedure would begin in the Senate[45] itself and its veto by absolute majority would lead to the formation of a joint committee whose proposal would have to be approved by both Houses with Congress holding sway only via a qualified majority of 3/5.[46] Whichever route is used, it would be necessary to modify the current time limit of 2 months, which the Senate has in order to issue a legislative opinion, as this prevents its meaningful participation, and should be extended, as proposed by the Council of State, to 4 months.[47]

The Senate would also have to play a more significant role in all affairs related to the European Union since, although the internal distribution of competences is not formally affected by European Law, in practice the fact is that the absence of the autonomies in European organs and their minimal intervention in European issues has produced, in the words of E. Aja, a kind of constitutional mutation.[48] In the upward phase, it might have an influence upon the position of the Government (binding negotiation mandates as in Sweden or Denmark) or issue a report regarding issues of particular importance (as in France).[49] Sensible in this context are the reflections of the Council of State with regard to seeking to combine the activity of sector-based conferences and, in particular, of the Conference on Affairs Related to European Communities, with the Senate, which would host the debate on fundamental issues in both the ascendant and descendent phases of Community law. The Senate might thus appear to be a forum for the participation of the Autonomous Communities in determining the position of the State in European affairs.[50]

---

[45] For the Council of State (2006, p. 251), a list should be submitted to Congress of the votes of the Senators with reference to their respective autonomous Communities, to strengthen the position of the Senate, making more difficult the opposition of Congress.

[46] Aja (2006, pp. 715–719).

[47] Council of State (2006, p. 247).

[48] Aja (2006, pp. 721–722).

[49] Biglino (2006, pp. 743–744).

[50] It should not be forgotten that the Treaty of Lisbon offers national parliaments more opportunities to participate with European institutions in the work of the EU. The rights and obligations (right to information, control of subsidiarity, evaluation mechanisms in areas of freedom, security and justice, revision of Treaties, etc.) of national parliaments within the EU are established, and in particular, if a national parliament believes that a Community proposal is not in accordance with the principle of subsidiarity, it may initiate a procedure to be developed in two phases: If one-third of the national parliaments believe that the proposal contravenes the principle of subsidiarity, the Commission must re-examine it and can decide to maintain, modify, or withdraw it; if a majority of national parliaments share this point of view but the Commission decides in the end to maintain its proposal, it will have to explain its reasons and its will to the European Parliament, and the Council will correspond the decision to decide whether or not the legislative procedure continues.

In questions of autonomous coordination and cooperation, the Council of State declares in its report on constitutional reform that member States have, through constitutional or legal provision, various mechanisms that permit either horizontal cooperation or collaboration between institutions possessed of political autonomy and vertical relations with the State.[51] The absence or inadequacy of these instruments in our autonomous State has been noted by most of the literature, which has criticised the regulation effected by 145 CE of the conventions and agreements of cooperation between Autonomous Communities and has highlighted the shortcomings observed in the functioning of the Sector-based Conferences as well as the previously indicated general Commission for the Autonomous Communities of the Senate, which has also failed to promote consultation or cooperation. Nonetheless, I concur with the Council of State in that relations between the different Administrations, central and autonomous, have to be conducted by intergovernmental bodies (Sector-based conferences, Conferences of Presidents, Commission for Fiscal and Financial Policy).[52] It is here, and not in a legislative Chamber, where dialogue and negotiation should take place, without prejudice to the possible convenience of, if not need for, some kind of connection between the institutionalised organs of cooperation and the Senate, so the latter might have the discretion to convene it. To this end, the Senate might request the presence of members of the autonomous executives or allow these to appear before the Chamber, in both cases via the procedure established via the Regulation.

To conclude with the Senate, it should be noted that if it opted for the system advocated in this work it would need to become a permanent Chamber, as occurs in all the cases when the Senate does not participate in the relationship of trust (Switzerland, Belgium, Germany, Austria), in such a way that the Senate would not be dissolved either as a result of it being impossible to swear in the President of the Government in the space of two months (art. 99.5 CE) or at the President's discretion (art. 115 CE).[53] However, what seems reasonable is the position of the Council of State with regard to maintaining dissolution in the more complicated procedures of constitutional reform of art. 168 CE, so the Autonomous Communities can assume a new stance vis-à-vis such a crucial question as constitutional revision. In any case, following the dissolution of the Congress of Deputies, the Senate would have to be suspended until the constitution of the new lower Chamber, at which point new governing bodies would be elected.

---

[51] Council of State (251 ss.).

[52] Regarding this type of organ, see García Morales et al. 2006).

[53] The Report of the Council of State (2006, p. 314) left the door open for a possible dissolution "in case, in a particular instance, circumstances deemed it advisable" (a possibility that, however, was not included in the proposal for constitutional reform produced).

# Autonomous Legislative Initiative Before Parliament

The legislative initiative of territorial bodies before the central or federal government is relatively infrequent in comparative Law,[54] as territorial participation is
channelled, at least in theory, according to what has been seen in this work, via the
presence of territorial representatives in the Upper House. In our constitutional
history, it was not anticipated in the federal project of 1873 or the Constitution of
1931, although it did feature in art. 92.3 of the provisional Rules of Congress of
1977 for pre-autonomous institutions.[55]

Art. 87.2 of the Constitution establishes two possibilities for this autonomous
legislative initiative: requesting of the Government the adoption of a draft bill and
the direct presentation in the House of Deputies of a legislative proposal. The
former, in any case, is not really an initiative since the adoption of the project is
subject to the decision of the Government and even if that possibility had not
existed in the Constitution, nothing would have prevented an autonomous Parliament from requesting of the Government the presentation of a draft bill. What
might cause surprise in the second case is its non-presentation before the Senate.[56]
However, this brings us once again to the subordinate position of the Upper House
and its limited functionality as territorial Chamber. In any case, the only difference
with respect to the regular procedure is that the autonomous Chamber may delegate
up to three autonomous MPs to defend the legislative proposal.

In practice, we may encounter not only legislative proposals by an autonomous
Parliament but also a single joint legislative proposal by several autonomous
Assemblies or various proposals of identical content by different Assemblies.[57]

# References

AJA, E., ALBERTI ROVIRA, E. y RUIZ RUIZ, J. J., 2005. La reforma constitucional del Senado.
Madrid: CEPC.
AJA, E. y VIVER, C., 2003. Valoración de 25 años de autonomía. Revista Española de Derecho
Constitucional 69: 69–113.
AJA, E., 1994. Perspectivas de la reforma constitucional del Senado. AA. VV. La reforma del
Senate. Madrid: Senado-Centro de Estudios Constitucionales 211–223.
- 2004. De los Gobiernos autonómicos. El País 2 de mayo.

---

[54] Mexican, Soviet 1977, Italian, Portuguese, Swiss, Yugoslav, and German constitutions,
although in this case the true author is the *Bundesrat*, as upon arrival of an initiative from a
*Land* there simply exists the obligation to transfer it to the competent Commission, which may
adopt it or not: Lavilla (1990, pp. 11–12),

[55] Lavilla (1990, pp. 11–12).

[56] Lavilla (1990, p. 21) points out that although some Italian academics usually denies this
possibility, there is neither positive dogmatic nor legal reasons in our system to deny it.

[57] Lavilla (1990, p. 21).

- 2006. La reforma constitucional del Senado: hacia una Cámara autonómica designada por los Gobiernos. F. Rubio Llorente y J. Álvarez Junco (eds.). El informe del Consejo de Estado sobre la reforma constitucional. Texto del informe y debates académicos. Madrid: Consejo de Estado-Centro de Estudios Políticos y Constitucionales 709–731.

AGUIAR DE LUQUE, L., 2005. Poder Judicial y reforma de los Estatutos de Autonomía. La justicia ante la reforma de los Estatutos de Autonomía. Centro de Estudios Jurídicos. Cizur Menor: Centro de Estudios Jurídicos-Aranzadi 21–50.

AGUILO LUCIA, L., 1981. La presencia de las nacionalidades y regiones en el Tribunal Constitucional. AA. VV. El Tribunal Constitucional. Madrid: Instituto de Estudios Fiscales I: 349–367.

ALBERTI ROVIRA, E., 2004. La representación territorial. Fundamentos 3: 279–330.

ALONSO DE ANTONIO, J. A., 2008. La función legislativa del nuevo Senado (apuntes para una constitutional reform). AA. VV. Estudios sobre la Constitución española. Homenaje al Profesor Jordi Solé Tura. Madrid: Cortes Generales I: 311–326.

ARAGON REYES, M., 2009. La reforma de la Ley Orgánica del Tribunal Constitucional. Revista Española de Derecho Constitucional 85: 11–43.

ARNOLD, Rainer, 2007. Modelo de Estado en el Derecho comparado: el caso alemán. V. Garrido Mayol (dtor.). Modelo de Estado y reforma de los Estatutos. Valencia: Fundación Profesor Manuel Broseta 455–463.

ARROYO GIL, A., 2009. La reforma del Estado federal alemán: un primer balance. J. Tudela Aranda y Mario Kölling (eds.). La reforma del Estado autonómico español y del Estado federal alemán. Madrid: CEPC-Fundación Manuel Giménez Abad 127–162.

BALAGUER CALLEJON, F., 2000. Poder Judicial y Comunidades Autonomas. Revista de Derecho Político 47: 53–67.

BELDA PEREZ-PEDRERO, E., 2008. Las Comunidades Autonomas en el Tribunal Constitucional a través del Senado. Dudas razonables de constitucionalidad y eficacia política para Castilla-La Mancha. Parlamento y Constitución 11: 275–284.

BIGLINO CAMPO, P., 2006. El Senado, Cámara de conexión entre las Comunidades Autónomas y la Unión Europea. F. Rubio Llorente y J. Álvarez Junco (eds.). El informe del Consejo de Estado sobre la reforma constitucional. Texto del informe y debates académicos. Madrid: Consejo de Estado-Centro de Estudios Políticos y Constitucionales 733–750.

BILBAO UBILLOS, J. M., 2003. Construyendo el ámbito vasco de confusión. Cuadernos de Alzate. Revista vasca de la cultura y las ideas 28: 83–95.

BOLLEYER, Nicole y BYTZEK, Evelyn, 2009. Government Congruence and Intergovernmental Relations in Federal Systems. Regional and Federal Studies 3: 371–397.

BOLLEYER, Nicole, 2006. Intergovernmental Arrangements in Spanish and Swiss Federalism. Regional & Federal Studies 4: 385–408.

BIFULCO, Raffaele, 2009. La reforma costituzionale del Titolo V tra inattuazione legislativa e supplenza giurisprudenziale. J. M. Castellà Andreu y Marco Olivetti (coords.). Nuevos Estatutos y reforma del Estado. Las experiencias de España e Italia a debate. Barcelona: Atelier 37–46.

CAMARA VILLAR, G., 2002. El principio de colaboración entre el Estado y las Comunidades Autonomas. Siena. Disponible en http://www.unisi.it/ricerca/dip/dir_eco/COMPARATO/camara.doc (última visita 17-12-2009).

CARRERAS SERRA, F. de, 2009. Reformar la Constitución para estabilizar el modelo territorial. AA. VV. La reforma constitucional: ¿hacia un nuevo pacto constituyente?. Madrid: CEPC-Asociación de Letrados del Tribunal Constitucional 47–112.

CARRILLO, M., 2008. El Senado de las autonomías. El País 17 de julio de 2008.

CONSEJO DE ESTADO, 2006. Informe sobre modificaciones de la Constitución española (disponible en http://www.consejo-estado.es/pdf/MODIFICACIONES%20CONSTITUCION%20ESP.pdf, última visita 20 de mayo de 2010).

CONSEJO GENERAL DEL PODER JUDICIAL, 2005. Informe de 5 de octubre de 2005 sobre el anteproyecto de ley orgánica de modificación de la ley 6/1985, de 1 de julio, del poder judicial, en materia de organización de la administración de justicia (fuente: www.poderjudicial.es/ eversuite/GetRecords?Template=cgpj/cgpj/principal.htm).

ERK, Jan y GAGNON, Alain-G., 2000. Constitutional Ambiguity and Federal Trust: Codification of Federalism in Canada, Spain and Belgium. Regional & Federal Studies 1: 92–111.

ERK, Jan, 2004. Austria: A Federation without Federalism. Publius: The Journal of Federalism 1: 1–20.

FERNANDEZ FARRERES, G., 2007. La reforma de la Ley Orgánica del Tribunal Constitucional. Revista Española de Derecho Constitucional 81: 11–62.

FERNANDEZ MANJON, D., 2003. El Senado y la configuración de una diversidad territorial. Apuntes históricos y situación actual. Boletín de la Facultad de Derecho de la UNED 21: 15–49.

FERNANDEZ SEGADO, F., 2007. La reforma del régimen jurídico-procesal del recurso de amparo. Madrid: Dykinson.

FERNANDEZ-CARNICERO, C. J., 2008. La STC 49/2008, una sentencia desfalleciente. Repertorio Aranzadi del Tribunal Constitucional 10.

FERNANDEZ-MIRANDA CAMPOAMOR, A., 2005. Sobre la reforma del Senado en el contexto de la reforma de los Estatutos de Autonomía. Revista Jurídica de Castilla y León Nº especial "Reforma de los Estatutos de Autonomía" 317–359.

FERRANDO BADIA, J., 1976. El federalismo. Revista de Estudios Políticos 206–207: 23–76.

GARCIA MORALES, M. J.; MONTILLA MARTOS, J. A.; y ARBOS MARIN, X., 2006. Las relaciones intergubernamentales en el Estado autonómico. Madrid: Centro de Estudios Políticos y Constitucionales.

GARCIA-ESCUDERO MARQUEZ, P., 2006. A vueltas con la reforma constitucional del Senado: de las opciones a las decisiones. Teoría y Realidad Constitucional 17: 195–221.

- 2009. Las funciones de un futuro Senado: cuestiones resueltas en el Informe del Consejo de Estado. Revista Española de Derecho Constitucional 87: 157–182.

GARCIA-PELAYO, M., 1984 (reimp. de la 7ª ed. de 1961). Derecho Constitucional Comparado. Madrid: Alianza.

GARRORENA MORALES, A., 1995. Una propuesta para la reforma constitucional del Senado. Revista de las Cortes Generales 34: 7–49.

- 2009. Nuevas condiciones desde las que replantear el cometido de la doctrina respecto de la reforma del Senado. Revista de Estudios Políticos 145: 11–31.

GOMEZ-FERRER MORANT, R., 2007. La reforma del Tribunal Constitucional. Revista de Administración Pública 174: 75–111.

GONZALEZ-TREVIJANO, P., 2006. Una reforma constitucional del Senado o una Cámara en busca de autor. F. Rubio Llorente y J. Álvarez Junco (eds.). El informe del Consejo de Estado sobre la reforma constitucional. Texto del informe y debates académicos. Madrid: Consejo de Estado-Centro de Estudios Políticos y Constitucionales 825–841.

JIMENA QUESADA, L., 2000. El principio de unidad del Poder Judicial y sus peculiaridades autonómicas. Madrid: Centro de Estudios Políticos y Constitucionales.

LAVILLA RUBIRA, J. J., 1990. Las proposiciones de ley remitidas por las Comunidades Autónomas al Congreso de los Diputados. Revista Española de Derecho Constitucional 28: 9–73.

LLERA RAMOS, F., 2006. Escenarios para una reforma en la composición y elección del Senado español. F. Rubio Llorente y J. Álvarez Junco (eds.). El informe del Consejo de Estado sobre la reforma constitucional. Texto del informe y debates académicos. Madrid: Consejo de Estado-Centro de Estudios Políticos y Constitucionales 843–855.

MANGIAMELLI, Stelio, 2009. Il Senato federale nella prospectiva italiana. Istituto di Studi sui Sistemi Regionali Federali e sulle Autonomie"Massimo Severo Giannini"-Studi e Interventi (http://www.issirfa.cnr.it/download/Mangiameli_Senato%20federale_2010.pdf última visita 18-2-2010).

MORALES ARROYO, J. M., 2008. El Senado perseguido. AA. VV. Estudios sobre la Constitución española. Homenaje al Profesor Jordi Solé Tura. Madrid: Cortes Generales I: 741–758.

MORENO, L., 2000. El futuro de la federalización en España. V. Navajas Zubeldia (coord.). Actas del II Simposio de Historia Actual (http://dialnet.unirioja.es/servlet/fichero_articulo? codigo=1321434&orden=0 última visita 24 de febrero de 2010) 211–238.

- 2008 (2ª ed.). La federalización de Spain. Madrid: Siglko XXI.

ORTEGA, L., 2005. Reforma constitucional y reforma estatutaria. Cizur Menor: Thomson-Civitas.

PAUNER CHULVI, C., 2006. La reforma constitucional del Senado en su función de Cámara designante. Teoría y Realidad Constitucional 17: 261–284.

PENDAS, B., 2003. Fragmentos del Poder Judicial. ABC 30 de julio.

PORTERO MOLINA, J. A., 2001. El principio democrático ordenador de las relaciones entre los principios de unidad y autonomía. F. García de Cortázar (coord.). El Estado de las autonomías en el siglo XXI: cierre o apertura indefinida. Madrid: FAES 67–116.

PULIDO QUECEDO, M., 2004. ¿magistrados constitucionales de designación autonómica?. Repertorio Aranzadi del Tribunal Constitucional 15.

- 2007. La reforma del Reglamento del Senado y el nombramiento de magistrados constitucionales. Repertorio Aranzadi del Tribunal Constitucional 16.

- 2008. El fin de un conflicto: El Senado elige a los magistrados constitucionales y los parlamentos territoriales proponen. Repertorio Aranzadi del Tribunal Constitucional 11.

PUNSET, R., 2006. De un Senado a otro. Reflexiones y propuestas para la reforma constitucional. F. Rubio Llorente y J. Álvarez Junco (eds.). El informe del Consejo de Estado sobre la reforma constitucional. Texto del informe y debates académicos. Madrid: Consejo de Estado-Centro de Estudios Políticos y Constitucionales 857–896.

REQUEJO PAGES, J. L., 2007. Doctrina del Tribunal Constitucional durante el segundo cuatrimestre de 2007. Revista Española de Derecho Constitucional 83: 209–242.

- 2008a. Doctrina del Tribunal Constitucional durante el primer cuatrimestre de 2008. Revista Española de Derecho Constitucional 83: 209–242.

- 2008b. Doctrina del Tribunal Constitucional durante el segundo cuatrimestre de 2008. Revista Española de Derecho Constitucional 84: 225–250.

RIPOLLES SERRANO, R., 2007. La reforma del Senado (Senado y Estado autonómico 1978–2004). V. Garrido Mayol (dtor.). Modelo de Estado y reforma de los Estatutos. Valencia: Fundación Profesor Manuel Broseta 65–122.

RODRIGUEZ-PATRON, P., 2010. El Tribunal Constitucional ante la reciente reforma de los artículos 16 de su Ley Orgánica y 184 del Reglamento del Senado. Revista de Derecho Político 77: 107–140.

ROLLER, Elisa, 2002. Reforming the Spanish Senate: Mission Impossible? West European Politics 4: 69–92.

SAIZ GARITAONANDIA, A., 2009. La Administración de justicia en las Comunidades Autónomas. Valencia: Tirant lo Blanch-IVAP.

SANCHEZ BARRILAO, J. F., 2009. La participación de las Comunidades Autónomas en la elección por el Senado de los magistrados constitucionales. Teoría y Realidad Constitucional 23: 387–424.

SANTAOLALLA LOPEZ, F., 2007. La representación territorial y el Senado. En torno a la propuesta del Consejo de Estado. Revista Española de Derecho Constitucional.

SANZ PEREZ, A. L., 2008. STC 101/2008: La nueva relación entre el Senate y los Parlamentos autonómicos. Repertorio Aranzadi del Tribunal Constitucional 13.

SILVA OCHOA, J. C. Da, 1994. El Senado en la encrucijada: la reforma reglamentaria de 11 de enero de 1994. AA. VV. La reforma del Senado. Madrid: Senado-Centro de Estudios Constitucionales 17–38.

SOLOZABAL ECHAVARRIA, J. J., 2003. Algunos problemas constitucionales del Plan Ibarretxe. Cuadernos de Alzate. Revista vasca de la cultura y las ideas 28: 111–121.

2006. Nuevas perspectivas sobre la reforma del Senado. Revista Aragonesa de Administración Pública 28: 373–395.

SORIANO HERNANDEZ, E., 2008. Los magistrados de las CCAA y del Senado. Repertorio Aranzadi del Tribunal Constitucional 16.

VIRGALA FORURIA, E., 2006. El poder judicial en las Comunidades Autónomas. Estudios de Derecho Judicial 90: 397–447.

2008 El Informe de 2006 del Consejo de Estado sobre modificaciones de la Constitución española. Revista Española de Derecho Constitucional, 82: 211–260.

2011 Las relaciones de inordinación en el Estado autonómico. Revista de Estudios Políticos 151: 109–152.

# Intergovernmental Relations in Spain and the Constitutional Court Ruling on the Statute of Autonomy of Catalonia: What's Next?

María Jesús García Morales

## Introduction

The Spanish Constitution (SC) of 1978 represents the advent of democracy in Spain after a long dictatorship and also the construction of a politically decentralised state, the so-called State of Autonomies, formed by the central government, 17 autonomous communities (ACs), and 2 autonomous cities. The territorial decentralisation process in Spain has dismantled a traditionally centralist state, has occurred in parallel with the consolidation of democracy, and moreover has coincided with the integration of Spain in 1986 in the European Union.

Cooperation relations between the two levels of self-government have helped build a system with a considerable degree of political decentralisation. These relationships emerged in the early 1980s without any prior experience. Their instruments have been platforms for encounter, dialogue, discussion, and where appropriate, agreement between the central government and the ACs. For this reason, intergovernmental relations have a significant symbolic and pedagogic value in Spain: they display a new form of distribution of power in democracy and have prompted a dialogue between the central government and the ACs aimed at different ends, such as completing the decentralisation process, exchanging information, distributing financial transfers, participating in Europe, or undertaking programmes of common interest.

This work is part of the research project of the R+D+I National Plan funded by the Spanish Ministry of Science and Innovation: "Statutory Reforms and New Instruments of Relationship between the State and the Autonomous Communities" (DER 2008-04108/JURI).

M.J. García Morales (✉)
Facultad de Derecho, Universidad Autónoma de Barcelona, Campus de la UAB, Bellaterra, 08193 Barcelona, Spain
e-mail: mariajesus.garcia@uab.es

A. López-Basaguren and L. Escajedo San Epifanio (eds.), *The Ways of Federalism in Western Countries and the Horizons of Territorial Autonomy in Spain*, Vol. 2, DOI 10.1007/978-3-642-27717-7_6, © Springer-Verlag Berlin Heidelberg 2013

In Spain, intergovernmental relations have had a new regulatory framework since 2006, both in their vertical form (central government–ACs) and in their horizontal form (between ACs). This new legal framework was not the result of a change in the Constitution but rather was brought about through a process of reforms in several statutes of autonomy (the equivalent, with many exceptions, to the constitutions of the constituent units in a federal system). Among them, the new Statute of Autonomy of Catalonia, of 19 July 2006, proposed a comprehensive attention to intergovernmental relations that has notably influenced the rest of the new statutes, to the point that some contain similar or identical provisions.

However, the new Statute of Catalonia was also a very controversial legal reform. It was challenged before the Constitutional Court, which ruled on the issue in a landmark decision in Spain, the ruling on the Statute of Autonomy of Catalonia of 28 June 2010. It should not be ignored that Catalonia is one of the so-called historical ACs (along with the Basque Country and Galicia), and one of the characteristics of the State of Autonomies is the existence of ACs with special attributes, with a feeling of nation based on their own identity and with nationalist parties established in these ACs.

In this context, the existence of a new regulatory scenario in Spain has generated expectations of change in cooperation. However, have there really been changes? To answer this question, I shall first examine the new legal setting of intergovernmental relations. Second, I shall consider the impact of this new legal framework on vertical relations, which are the most developed relations in Spain. Third, I shall explore the effect of the new framework on horizontal relations, which are barely institutionalised in the State of Autonomies. Furthermore, one cannot forget that Spain's integration in the European Union has been an important stimulus for cooperation. Therefore, fourth, I will examine the new regulation of the European dimension of domestic intergovernmental relations. Last, in this new legal context, I shall conclude with some prospects for the future of cooperation in the State of Autonomies.[1]

# The Regulatory Framework of Intergovernmental Relations and the Role of the Constitutional Court

## The Spanish Constitution of 1978

The first significant issue is the importance in Spain of trying to regulate cooperation by means of legislation. The regulatory framework of these regulations has

---

[1] In this text, the terms 'intergovernmental relations' and 'cooperation relations' are used interchangeably. It should be noted that, in the State of Autonomies, the expression 'intergovernmental relations' is used in academic circles. In laws, in institutional documents, and between the *practitioners* themselves, reference is made to 'cooperation relations'.

been built gradually. Moreover, this regulation has often been controversial and, on several occasions, has been challenged in the Constitutional Court. As a result, the High Court has had to rule on the laws governing instruments of cooperation (formal mechanisms and structures) and has thus helped define the boundaries of the regulatory ground rules and the physiognomy of these relations. It is unusual for a Constitutional Court to be an actor in intergovernmental relations, but in Spain this body has played an important role in this area.

The interest in providing cooperation with a regulatory framework is perhaps surprising, given that the Spanish Constitution of 1978 makes little provision with regard to intergovernmental relations. The constitutional text prefigured a system of political decentralisation and regulated the competences of the central government and the potential competences of the ACs, but cooperation was not contemplated.

The Spanish Constitution did not address vertical intergovernmental relations. It only focused on horizontal agreements that were regulated immediately after the prohibition of federation between ACs (Art. 145 SC). At that time, this instrument was perceived as a potential mechanism of union between ACs that might jeopardise the unity of the state. This defensive attitude made sense in 1978 but has been transcended after over 30 years of the State of Autonomies. Horizontal cooperation began to be developed in Spain only recently. As we shall see, it cannot be claimed that the constitutional framework is solely to blame for this situation; however, it is clear that it has not been ideally suited to the signing of agreements between ACs.

As in other countries, the Spanish Constitutional Court has recognised a principle of cooperation or institutional loyalty in vertical and horizontal relations. This is an unwritten constitutional principle inherent in the decentralised structure of the State of Autonomies. In theory, this principle is materialised in duties to refrain from harming the other party, to consider and take into account the interests of the whole, and to provide reciprocal assistance, and in the obligation to exchange information. However, unlike other systems, the Spanish Constitutional Court does not normally employ this principle to declare a law unconstitutional, so it acts more as a kind of *soft law*.[2]

## *Legal Regulation of Cooperation: Instruments and Joint Actions*

Despite that fact that they are not specifically recognised by the Constitution, intergovernmental relations between the central government and the ACs shortly began to develop in a spontaneous manner. The first Sectorial Conference between the central government and the ACs was created on 1 July 1981, the Fiscal and Financial Policy Council. Not long afterwards, in November 1981, for the first time

---

[2] Cruz Villalón (1990), pp. 119–134.

ever the government of Spain considered regulating vertical multilateral cooperation by law; specifically, it considered regulating Sectorial Conferences between the central government and the ACs. It should be noted that this draft bill was challenged in the Constitutional Court by Catalonia and the Basque Country, two historical ACs with 'special traits' and clear identity-related claims. Both ACs protested that the vertical Sectorial Conferences were mechanisms that enabled the central government to impose decisions and removal of all autonomy from the new ACs.

The Constitutional Court ruled that the Sectorial Conferences between the central government and the ACs were constitutional as 'fora of discussion for examining common problems and for discussing appropriate courses of action'.[3] Following this ruling, Law 12/1983, on the Autonomous Process, was passed. This law is a central government law[4] that regulates Sectorial Conferences in order to 'exchange points of view and jointly examine the problems of each sector and the actions proposed to address and resolve them'.[5]

Ten years later, Law 30/1992, on the Legal Regime of Public Administrations and Common Administrative Procedure (also a central government law), once again addressed vertical cooperation in the State of Autonomies. This law enshrines the principle of institutional loyalty and, above all, regulates instruments of vertical cooperation: Sectorial Conferences between the central government and all the ACs, the so-called Bilateral Commissions between the central government and each Autonomous Community, agreements, consortia, as well as joint plans and programmes.[6]

The next step was to legislate multilateral vertical cooperation in specific sectors. In 2006 and 2007, two central government laws, the Law on Dependent Care and the Law on Sustainable Rural Development, provided for very intense cooperation between the central government and ACs in these two sectors: social assistance for people requiring dependent care and regional agricultural policy. These cases represent what could be seen as 'common tasks'—areas of co-decision and co-funding—between the central government and the ACs in sectors in which the ACs have competence. This is a situation that is not provided for by the Constitution, that was reached without constitutional reform, and that is consented by all ACs that have not challenged these laws in the Constitutional Court.[7]

---

[3] STC 76/1982, FJ 13.

[4] Central government law (*ley del poder central o ley estatal*) in this paper is used to refer to any law governing the country of Spain as a whole.

[5] Ley 12/1983 (Art. 4).

[6] Ley 30/1992 (arts. 4–10). Alberti Rovira (1993), pp. 41–70.

[7] Specifically, on dependence, Sáez Royo (2010), pp. 361–386.

## The New Statutes of Autonomy and the Constitutional Court Ruling on the Statute of Catalonia

The Spanish Constitution of 1978 has only been reformed twice: in 1992, on the occasion of the ratification of the Maastricht Treaty to give the citizens of EU member countries the right not only to vote but also to be elected in local elections (Art. 13.2 SC), and in 2011, to include the principle of budgetary stability as a consequence of the economic crisis (Art. 135 SC).

A reform of the Constitution that includes territorial reform has not been possible yet. The alternative has been to reform the statutes of autonomy, the equivalent—with many exceptions—to the constitutions of the constituent units in a federal system. Statutes of autonomy are special laws negotiated between the central government and each AC. Their territorial effectiveness is limited to the sphere of the corresponding Autonomous Community. Along with the Constitution, the statutes of autonomy constitute the so-called territorial constitution in Spain. The first statutes of autonomy were adopted during the period 1979–1983. The new statutes, also called 'second-generation statutes', were approved between 2006 and 2011. It should be noted that not all ACs have opted to reform their statute of autonomy. Of the 17 ACs, eight have a new statute or have partially reformed their previous one.[8]

How cooperation and cooperation instruments are handled is one of the most significant new elements of the new statutes. Through this, the new statutes have sought to supplement the scant treatment of this question in the Constitution—and in the first statutes of autonomy—and provide regulatory visibility to this type of cooperation. The statutory reforms are heterogeneous. However, all the new statutes devote particular attention to cooperation in its vertical, horizontal, and European dimensions.[9]

As we will see, in the vertical dimension, the most notable addition has been the strengthening of bilateralism with the central government and of bilateral instruments, especially through the new Bilateral Commissions. To the contrary, horizontal cooperation has not been a priority for the new statutes, nor have there been important legal developments in this area. Nevertheless, there is evidence of change in cooperative practice. The new statutes also regulate both vertical and horizontal domestic cooperation in so-called European clauses. The participation of regional institutions in the integration process has increased the need for cooperation with the central government in all decentralised systems in Europe, and Spain has not been an exception.

---

[8] Valencian Community (2006), Catalonia (2006), Balearic Islands (2007), Andalusia (2007), Aragon (2007), Castilla y León (2007), Navarra (2010), Extremadura (2011). The new Statutes are available on the web page of the Ministry of Territorial Policy: http://www.mpt.gob.es/es/areas/politica_autonomica/Estatutos_Autonomia.html.

[9] García Morales (2009a).

Amongst the new statutes of autonomy, the Statute of Catalonia of 2006 contains the most extensive regulation of intergovernmental relations. It has served as a reference for all subsequent statutes, and the regulation of the Statute of Catalonia of 2006 was also very controversial. The controversy lies not only in this area but also in practically the entire Catalan text. The Statute of Catalonia has left nobody indifferent.

As mentioned, Catalonia is a historical Autonomous Community that, along with the Basque Country in particular, has constantly pursued a greater level of self-government and even a new territorial organisation. The objectives of the reform of the Statute of Catalonia included an enhanced recognition of Catalan identity, increased competences for Catalonia, and a new funding system. As far as cooperation was concerned, the most controversial aspect of the Statute of Catalonia was bilateralism between the central government and Catalonia. Other statutes contain similar or even identical provisions; however, only the regulation of the Statute of Catalonia was challenged in the Constitutional Court.[10]

In June 2010, the High Court upheld that the way cooperation is regulated in the Statute of Catalonia was constitutional, with certain qualifications. No article in this area was declared unconstitutional. Constitutional Court ruling 31/2010, of 28 June, affects not only the regulation of intergovernmental relations in the Statute of Catalonia but also the regulation provided for in other statutes, in particular in those drafted in a similar or identical fashion to that of the Statute of Catalonia. The Constitutional Court once again became an actor in cooperation relations through a legal decision regarding the compliance of this regulation with the Constitution and through the political impact of this decision on cooperative practice. Let us consider the impact of this new legal regulation and this ruling on cooperation relations.

## Vertical Cooperation: Multilateralism and ... More Bilateralism?

### The Culture of Cooperation with the Central Government: As Always, the Multilateralism Plus Bilateralism Approaches

Intergovernmental relations in Spain have been and continue to be predominantly vertical. The culture of cooperation in the State of Autonomies has been developed with the central government. The historical circumstances of the Spanish decentralisation process and the constitutional architecture have aided vertical development of intergovernmental relations.

---

[10] The Statute of Andalusia is the most similar. The Statute of Catalonia was contested in the High Court by 50 MPs from the Popular Party parliamentary group in the Spanish Parliament, the *Defensor del Pueblo* (the Spanish Ombudsman), and the government of the Autonomous Community of La Rioja.

Autonomous Communities need the central government to realise their objectives: transfer of competences (from the central government to the ACs), attainment of financial resources (the central government has the *spending power*, and the ACs are heavily dependent upon state revenue), and participation in the European Union (the central government is the main interlocutor for Brussels). However, the central government does not need the Autonomous Communities to pass its laws or to approve constitutional reform. Furthermore, in Spain, there is no senate serving as a chamber of regional representation where Autonomous Communities can participate in central government legislation. Moreover, ACs do not have the right to veto central government initiatives.

Vertical cooperation relations in Spain are formalised multilaterally, primarily through the Sectorial Conferences, and in bilateral structures, the so-called Bilateral Commissions for Cooperation. This multilateralism–bilateralism combination in formal structures of cooperation is a peculiarity of the State of Autonomies.

In Spain, there are ACs with differentiating elements acknowledged in the Constitution and in the statutes of autonomy. Such elements are historically well-founded characteristics that endow them with a special 'personality' in comparison to other regions (in particular, a language, a private law, and a funding system unique to certain regions).

The legal expression of differentiating elements should not be confused with the existence of nationalist ideologies or parties in these ACs. Such parties have government duties in these Autonomous Communities and, in addition, provide parliamentary support to the central government vested in the two major parties statewide, the conservative Popular Party (PP) and the Socialist Party (PSOE). Nationalist parties established in an Autonomous Community also participate in state institutions based on results obtained in their Autonomous Community and support the central government in power on state governance.[11] Most nationalist parties primarily seek to defend the interests of their Autonomous Community and have given political backing to the bilateral approach in order to negotiate 'one-on-one' with the central government. In the State of Autonomies, there is an informal bilateralism that normally exists between parliamentarians and politicians in central government institutions and a formalised bilateralism in *ad hoc* structures, the Bilateral Commissions for Cooperation.

The driving force behind the creation of these Bilateral Commissions has been technical rather than political. Bilateral Commissions as formal structures of cooperation came into being in order to negotiate the transfer of competences from the central government to the ACs. Political decentralisation in Spain has entailed a gradual process of transfers from the central government to the ACs. This has been a bilateral process with each Autonomous Community. In addition, bilateralism has been necessary because this process has not been simultaneous in all ACs. The journey of the Autonomous Communities towards self-government has occurred at 'two speeds': some, the so-called fast lane ACs (which include the

---

[11] Aja (2003), pp. 169–199. Viver Pi-Sunyer (2010), pp. 213–234.

historical Autonomous Communities), assumed *ab initio* more competences than the other 'slow lane' ACs. This difference in speed has favoured bilateral negotiation with each Autonomous Community individually.

## Multilateralism: The Conference of Presidents and the Sectorial Conferences, How Do Their Accords Bind?

Formal structures of vertical cooperation in Spain are multilateral and bilateral, but the most important are the former.

The Conference of Presidents should be the most important instrument of cooperation. It was created in 2004 to annually convene the president of the government (the prime minister of Spain) and the presidents of the Autonomous Communities. It has been held at the Senate. The constitution of this Conference was one of the items on the agenda of the Socialist Party that won the general election that year.[12] All ACs have attended the meetings of this Conference. Its rules give it an important function: to discuss broad guidelines for public policies and matters of great importance for the State of Autonomies. In practice, the Conference of Presidents has reached a situation of impasse: Four meetings have been held in seven years, and it has not been convened since December 2009. In such a short period, the results have been limited: basically, an agreement on health funding and a map of investment in science and technology infrastructure. For the time being, its impact on the cooperative landscape has been non-existent and its future is uncertain.

In the absence of a Conference of Presidents, the most important instrument of cooperation in Spain has been the Sectorial Conferences, which are multilateral cooperation bodies characterised by their subject speciality by area. Sectorial Conferences were the first instruments of cooperation in the State of Autonomies. It should not be forgotten that in Spain, these conferences are vertical. They have existed for years not only without a vertical Conference of Presidents but also without horizontal coordination, as there is no Conference of Presidents only for ACs, nor are there horizontal Sectorial Conferences.

Vertical Sectorial Conferences are addressed not in the new statutes but in Law 30/1992. This law gives the minister from the central government the power to convene the Conference and to set the agenda. This power was ruled to be constitutional by the Spanish Constitutional Court, interpreting that it does not necessarily vest a hierarchical power in the central government.[13] The law also refers to the composition of the Sectorial Conferences, made up of members from

---

[12] The creation of the Conference of Presidents became one of the items on the regional agenda of the president of the government, Mr Rodríguez Zapatero. Further details, Tajadura Tejada (2010), pp. 134–172.

[13] STC 76/1983, FJ 13.

the central government and from the governments of the ACs. Typically, the members of the Sectorial Conferences are the minister from the central government and the regional ministers from the ACs of the subject area in question. The main products stemming from the Sectorial Conferences are *accords* (*acuerdos*), which have a political value, and *intergovernmental agreements (convenios de colaboración)*,[14] which are legally binding.

The new statutes recognise 'multilateralism' but do not mention the expression 'Sectorial Conference'. To be precise, the Statute of Autonomy of Catalonia refers to multilateralism as a principle governing relations between Catalonia and the central government, along with the principle of bilateralism.[15] This Statute pays particular attention to the effects of multilateralism. It has been the only statute of autonomy to include the provision that the Autonomous Community should not be bound by agreements adopted in multilateral forums and should be able to express reservations regarding those agreements adopted without its approval.[16]

The Constitutional Court ruled that both aspects are constitutional. According to the High Court, participation in multilateral mechanisms is voluntary. For this reason, decisions adopted there cannot be imposed upon those who attend these forums. As a consequence of this voluntary nature, it is possible for the Autonomous Community to express its disagreement with multilaterally adopted accords. This disagreement in the form of reservations in no case represents a veto by the Autonomous Community.[17]

From a legal standpoint, this ruling contributes nothing new. The Constitutional Court reiterates its jurisprudence regarding the voluntary nature of cooperation and the impossibility of an Autonomous Community to waive its own powers in the framework of cooperative instruments. By contrast, the provisions in the Statute of Catalonia evidence Catalonia's historical mistrust of vertical multilateral instruments. Once again, there is the underlying Autonomous Community perception of multilateralism as a central government strategy to impose its points of view and attempt to equalise the ACs by means of the so-called coffee-for-all (or one-size-fits-all) approach, an expression often used in the State of Autonomies to illustrate the central government's strategy of trying to appease all ACs and use multilateralism to dilute identity-related and unique demands that call for a different solution.

---

[14] In Spain, vertical agreements are usually referred to as *agreements* (*convenios*) if they are legally binding and simply as *accords* (*acuerdos*) if they are political commitments that are not legally binding. To underline this difference, in this text I have used accord as a translation for *acuerdo* (agreements that are not legally binding) and agreement as a translation for *convenio* (agreements that are legally binding).

[15] Multilateralism appears in the Statute of Catalonia as a principle (Art. 3), a means of cooperation with the central government (Art. 175), and a means of participation in European affairs (Art. 186) and in funding issues (Art. 210).

[16] Art. 176 of the Statute of Catalonia.

[17] STC 31/2010, FJ 112.

In this context, the new statutes and the ruling on the Statute of Catalonia do not change the legal framework of vertical multilateral instruments. Moreover, the practical activity of the Sectorial Conferences in Spain has not changed with the new statutes.

There are currently 15 Sectorial Conferences that operate regularly with meetings at least twice a year. The activity of the Conferences varies considerably (the most active are agriculture and education). The decision rule in the Sectorial Conferences tends to be unanimity.[18] The most routine function in these fora is to set criteria that the central government uses, employing its *spending power*, to assign financial transfers to ACs that are then formalised via vertical agreements. Through this financial cooperation, the central government promotes programmes in the ACs and achieves considerably homogeneous actions in sectors like social issues and education. Regulatory cooperation between the central government and the ACs is not very institutionalised. The central government decides which draft legislation to bring to the attention of a Sectorial Conference. In European affairs, the Sectorial Conferences are the fora where the ACs are involved in forming the state's position with regard to the European Union, a very important function in 'Europeanised' sectors (in particular, agriculture and fisheries).

This practical operation of the Sectorial Conferences has led to criticism of multilateralism. The problem is not technical, cannot be solved with laws, and does not lie in its instruments. The major stumbling block is political. ACs do not always share the central government's concern for multilateralism. In many cases, ACs give priority to their own demands. Moreover, ACs perceive an initiative of a minister from the central government in a Sectorial Conference (which is vertical) as a political initiative of the ruling party. The absence of ACs at meetings of the Sectorial Conferences and their scant interest in including issues on the agenda show the lack of involvement of the ACs in the actual functioning of the Sectorial Conferences. In this context, it is not always easy to define common goals between ACs and the central government in these fora.[19]

## Bilateralism: The New Bilateral Commissions as a Potentially Confederal Element and the New Rights of Participation

The so-called Bilateral Commissions between each Autonomous Community and the central government have been the most significant and controversial addition in

---

[18] García Morales and Arbós Marín (2012). Institutional information about existing conferences, available on the web page of the Ministry of Territorial Policy (Autonomous Policy): http://www. mpt.gob.es/es/areas/politica_autonomica/coop_multilateral_ccaa_ue/cooperacion_multilateral/ Conf_Sectoriales.html.

[19] Pérez Medina (2009), p. 350. The existence of diverse interests hinders cooperation even in countries that are a model of cooperative federalism, Jeffery (1999), pp. 50–63.

the statutory reforms. However, bilateralism is nothing new in the State of Autonomies. The Bilateral Commissions were created to negotiate the transfer of competences from the central government to each AC and to address specific problems with an Autonomous Community. The first Bilateral Commission was set up in 1983 between the central government and Navarra. The extension of this structure, which today exists with each AC, has been a gradual process that concluded in 2000.[20]

Law 30/1992 defines Bilateral Commissions as cooperation bodies designed to address general issues as opposed to the sectorial initiatives of the multilateral Conferences. Bilateral Commissions bring together members of the central government and of the Autonomous Community governments but not their presidents. The government representation from the central government is usually headed by the minister of Territorial Policy, and the delegation from the ACs is comprised of regional ministers. In the Bilateral Commission, each government has equal representation and either side may request that a meeting be convened. In 2000, the reform of the Organic Law on the Constitutional Court gave the Bilateral Commissions a significant impetus to try and use negotiation in these fora to resolve the considerable number of disputes between the central government and the ACs brought before the Spanish Constitutional Court.[21] This is bilateralism with all ACs. Furthermore, this 'pacifying' function is the most routine activity of the Bilateral Commissions.

The Bilateral Commissions of the new statutes are known as 'new Bilateral Commissions' or 'statutory Bilateral Commissions', so as to differentiate them from the first 'non-statutory Bilateral Commissions' that are not in the statutes of autonomy. The first change is how they are regulated in the text of the statutes.

The Statute of Catalonia of 2006 was the first to extensively regulate this instrument. The regulation of bilateralism and of bilateral instruments in the Statute responds to a technical question. Statutes of autonomy are a special kind of law: these special laws are developed through a procedure involving the institutions of the relevant Autonomous Community and the institutions of the central government. The statutes of autonomy are laws passed by the respective Autonomous Community parliament and also laws ultimately passed by the Spanish Parliament (they may occasionally be ratified through a positive referendum of the people of

---

[20] The Bilateral Commissions were established in this order: with Navarra (1983); with Catalonia, the Basque Country, and Galicia (1987); with Murcia and La Rioja (1988); with the Balearic Islands (1989); with the Canary Islands and Aragon (1990); with Cantabria (1991); with Castilla y León and Extremadura (1992); with Asturias (1993); with Castilla-La Mancha (1996); and with the Valencian Community and the Community of Madrid (2000). The Bilateral Commissions with the Autonomous Cities of Ceuta and Melilla (1995).

[21] According to the Organic Law on the Constitutional Court (Art. 33.2), if the parties choose to resolve a dispute through negotiation, the deadline for lodging an appeal in the Constitutional Court is extended by 6 months with regard to the three initially provided. In terms of efficiency, results vary between Bilateral Commissions. In general, it may be said that these instruments have helped to reduce the number of disputes in the Constitutional Court.

the AC in question). As a result, a statute of autonomy may regulate relations between an Autonomous Community and the central government (and are therefore bilateral), but they are not instruments in which all ACs participate. Furthermore, the regulation of bilateralism also indicates an attempt to encourage the bilateral relationship demanded by governments of this Autonomous Community, in view of the problems and dissatisfaction generated by the relationship in multilateral fora. The provision for a Bilateral Commission in the Statute of Catalonia was repeated in most new statutes adopted later and in ACs where identity-related demands are not as strong or non-existent.[22]

In the Statute of Catalonia, bilateralism is recognised as one of the principles determining the Autonomous Community's relationship with the central government, along with multilateralism. The Bilateral Commission is a materialisation of this principle. It is regulated extensively and assigned functions in multiple policy areas.[23] The breadth of this regulation contrasts with the frugality with which multilateral relations are regulated. The Bilateral Commission was challenged in the Constitutional Court on the grounds that it represented a clear movement towards a confederal state model that would introduce a radical change and even a severing in the territorial system in Spain.

The Constitutional Court held that the principle of bilateralism and bilateral instruments may be regulated in the Statute of Autonomy. It also ruled that the Bilateral Commission between Catalonia and the central government (officially called the *Comisión Bilateral Generalitat-Estado*) is constitutional, but with certain nuances that point to prevention rather than bilateralism as a means of expressing special status for Catalonia.

First, the Constitutional Court has insisted on recalling who the *subjects* of this bilateral relationship are: Catalonia as an Autonomous Community and the central government, 'that is, between two constitutive elements of the Spanish state', under no circumstances between Catalonia and the Spanish state. This precision is a consequence of the polysemy of the term state (*Estado*) in Spanish. Unlike in other countries, where the words *Bund* or Federation refer to the central government, in Spain there is no specific expression, so the term state (*Estado*) is used to refer to both the central government (*Estado central*) and to the State as a whole. Second, the Bilateral Commission is *another instrument of cooperation* between the Autonomous Community and the state, which means denying its exclusiveness as a form of relationship. Third, the Bilateral Commission is a mechanism of *voluntary cooperation* that, like other cooperative instruments, can neither alter the distribution of competences nor condition nor limit the exercise of competences by either

---

[22] The statutes of the Valencian Community and the Balearic Islands are the only ones that do not provide for a Bilateral Commission. The Statute of Andalusia follows the Catalan regulation in almost identical terms. Ridaura Martínez (2010), pp. 256–274.

[23] The Bilateral Commission may deliberate, make proposals, and pass resolutions with regard to the following areas: draft laws, economic policy agendas, promotion of measures to improve cooperation, assessment of such measures, power disputes and subsequent resolution, monitoring of European policy, monitoring of overseas activity, and any issue of common interest (Art. 183).

institution. The High Court thus denies the possibility of the Bilateral Commission serving as a co-decision body.[24]

In cooperative practice, there is no evidence that the new Bilateral Commissions perform actions or have dynamics different from those of previous Bilateral Commissions or other non-statutory Bilateral Commissions. The Bilateral Commissions of Catalonia and Andalusia were the most active ones during the period 2007–2011.[25] As in their previous phase, these new Bilateral Commissions are primarily responsible for negotiating outstanding transfers from the central government to an Autonomous Community and for addressing specific problems between both sides. The new Bilateral Commissions continue to prevent jurisdictional disputes, thus maintaining this pacifying function. Consequently, for the time being, the new Bilateral Commissions have not led to changes in the cooperative or institutional landscape.[26]

Bilateral Commissions are the most visible manifestation of bilateralism in the Statute of Catalonia and in those following it. However, the commitment to bilateralism is also evident in the new procedures for Autonomous Community participation in decisions taken at a national level. The new statutes provide for two types of participation: first, participation in appointing members of state institutions (including the Constitutional Court) and second, participation in exercising competences of the central government. While the former has to be carried out via central government laws, the latter represents a new form of cooperation.

An Autonomous Community's participation in exercising central government competences shows its particular interest in influencing central government activity affecting its region. This trend had been apparent for years and was formalised with the adoption of the new statutes. This was an attempt to offset the lack of participation by ACs in the central government's decision-making processes, as the latter was under no legal obligation to consult the Autonomous Communities in these cases.

This participation is materialised bilaterally through consultation with the Autonomous Community, the issuing by the AC of mandatory (non-binding) reports, or the Bilateral Commission's intervention in certain cases. In the Catalan Statute, there are numerous instances of the Autonomous Community's participation. For example, the Autonomous Community should voice its opinion if action is proposed in the area of public works, infrastructures, or transport within its region.

---

[24] STC 31/2010, FFJJ 115, 116. Along with the general Bilateral Commission, the Statute of Catalonia provides for two specific Bilateral Commissions: the Joint Economic and Fiscal Affairs Commission (Art. 210) and a Bilateral Commission on Investments in Infrastructures (third additional provision). The Constitutional Court has also upheld their constitutionality.

[25] The Bilateral Commission with Catalonia: eight meetings; the Bilateral Commission with Andalusia: seven meetings; the Commission with Aragon: three meetings; the Commission with Castilla y León (two meetings) (source: prepared by the author).

[26] García Morales (2009b), pp. 383–394. Institutional Information about the Bilateral Commissions: http://www.mpt.gob.es/es/areas/politica_autonomica/coop_bilateral_CCAA/comisiones_bilaterales. html.

Only some of the new statutes contain examples of participation similar to those of the Statute of Catalonia.[27]

The Constitutional Court ruled that the projected participation is a new form of cooperation. It cannot change who holds the competence or condition the decision to be adopted by the central government. For this reason, this participation cannot be manifested in decision-making bodies but only 'in consultative and advisory bodies'.[28] The central government is thus required to listen to the Autonomous Community, but it is not bound to follow the opinion expressed by the latter.

The new projected participation in central government competences may produce asymmetries between ACs. From a legal standpoint, such projected participation is a right available only to those ACs providing for it in their statute. However, there is nothing to prevent a political decision by the central government from unilaterally extending that participation to all Autonomous Communities. Nevertheless, this new projected participation for Autonomous Communities represents a major step forward towards cooperation in the exercise of competences.[29] The rights of ACs to participate in central government decision-making processes have not yet been put into practice.

## Horizontal Cooperation: Signs of Change . . . Greater Cooperation Between Autonomous Communities?

### *The Scant Development of Cooperation Between Autonomous Communities, Until the New Statutes?*

Since the adoption of the Spanish Constitution of 1978 and for almost 30 years, formalised and institutionalised horizontal cooperation in the State of Autonomies has been very rare. The clearest indicator of this situation has been the number of agreements between ACs: Some 20 horizontal agreements were officially recorded between 1985 and the adoption of the first new statutes in 2006.[30] Beyond the actual number of agreements, this cooperation has normally been initiated between neighbouring ACs in order to resolve problems arising from their relations as neighbours, in particular firefighting and health care between bordering ACs. During this time, no agreement has been signed involving most Autonomous

---

[27] In particular, the Statute of Andalusia and partially the Statute of Aragon.

[28] STC 31/2010, FJ 111.

[29] Corretja et al. (2011), pp. 403–446; Montilla Martos (2011), pp.184–195.

[30] The official number of agreements between ACs is calculated on the basis of agreements communicated to the Spanish Parliament, which may be viewed on the Senate web page: http://www.senado.es. See also, García Morales (annual).

Communities, which shows that for nearly 30 years of the State of Autonomies, ACs have been unable to find an area of interest common to all of them.

This state of cooperation between Autonomous Communities is not only a particularity of the State of Autonomies but also a great anomaly.[31] The state of horizontal cooperation contrasts with the development and institutionalisation of vertical relations. In contrast with cooperation with the central government, there are neither horizontal conferences nor structures where ACs have been able to meet, discuss, and agree upon the results of their cooperation without the central government.

As noted, the constitutional structure and political dynamics have favoured the development of vertical cooperation. The relationship with the central government provides ACs with more money, more competences, influence in Europe, and indeed more prestige than cooperation with other ACs. Autonomous Communities have not perceived the advantages of establishing strong horizontal relations. Moreover, the construction of the State of Autonomies has not encouraged a culture of cooperation between ACs. Until 1992, there were Autonomous Communities with a different number of competences. The way self-government is felt has also differed considerably among ACs that base their political autonomy upon a prior historical tradition and other Autonomous Communities that, in the absence of such historical tradition, have had a far more administrative conception of their auton-omy. ACs have primarily defended their own interests before the central govern-ment on an individual basis without seeking consensus with other ACs.

To what extent is the law to blame in this situation? As mentioned, the Spanish Constitution regulates agreements between ACs. Article 145 SC prohibits federa-tion between ACs. Having established this prohibition, it sets forth conditions for adopting these agreements to ensure that this prohibition is not violated using this instrument. Article 145.2 SC differentiates between two types of pacts between ACs: collaboration agreements (*convenios de colaboración*), which must be communicated to the Spanish Parliament, and cooperation agreements (*acuerdos de cooperación*), which must be authorised by the latter. This article has not been amended since 1978, although it is on the 'agenda' of aspects in need of reform in the Spanish Constitution.[32]

The text of the current Constitution makes it impossible to know what a collaboration agreement is and what a cooperation agreement is. The Constitution does not define them, and neither has the Constitutional Court. Nevertheless, each pact must fulfil different requirements in order to be validly approved. In practice, nearly all horizontal agreements are collaboration agreements between ACs.[33]

The first statutes in the late 1970s and 1980s further complicated the already complex nature of the Spanish Constitution. The first statutes included additional

---

[31] García Morales (2009b), pp. 116.

[32] Rubio Llorente and Álvarez Junco (2006), pp. 163–165.

[33] Only one cooperation agreement has been signed: the so-called Mediterranean Arc Agreement signed in 1994 by Andalusia, Murcia, the Balearic Islands, and the Valencian Community.

requirements for signing an agreement between ACs; specifically, the parliament of the Autonomous Community needed to be involved in the formalisation of an agreement between ACs by granting its approval or authorisation, something that only applied to agreements between ACs and not to agreements between an Autonomous Community and the central government. Furthermore, most of the early statutes of autonomy have enabled the Spanish Parliament to reclassify a text that the ACs announced as a collaboration agreement (which only needs to be reported to the Spanish Parliament) or as a cooperation agreement (which requires greater control by central government institutions). It is no exaggeration to say that ACs wishing to sign agreements with one another have to undergo a genuine legal ordeal. In Spain, it is easier to sign a vertical agreement or even a cross-border cooperation agreement (with regions of another country) than an agreement between ACs.

Nonetheless, the law is neither solely nor most directly responsible for this situation. Until recently, there was no more cooperation between ACs because the necessary political will was lacking. The regulatory framework for horizontal cooperation has not been optimal, but it cannot be pinpointed as the cause of the limited development of horizontal cooperation. Since the entry into force of the first new statutes, beginning in 2006, the number of agreements between ACs reported to the Senate has grown significantly. The figures on the number of agreements reported to the Senate speak for themselves: Some 20 horizontal agreements were recorded during the period 1978–2005, while in the period 2006–2011, there were over 40 agreements between ACs. Are the new statutes responsible for this major change? Does the law have the power to change cooperative practice in this way?

## The Constitutional Court's Appeal for Horizontal Cooperation vs. a Deficient Legal Design

The first point to note is that horizontal cooperation was not a priority when the new statutes were drafted. Cooperation between ACs was a secondary goal for most second-generation statutes.

The Statute of Catalonia has been one of the new statutes inclined to include appeals for cooperation between ACs. Thus, several provisions provide for cooperation between Catalonia and other ACs in matters like emergency actions, natural areas, and protection of the Catalan language. These are appeals for sectorial cooperation with neighbouring ACs. Specifically, the promotion of the Catalan language, a differential factor that Catalonia shares with other ACs (in particular, the Balearic Islands), is one of the most fertile areas for bilateral horizontal cooperation in the State of Autonomies.

The Statute of Catalonia also promotes cooperation between all or most ACs. In generic terms, this text provides that Catalonia can establish cooperation relations with other ACs in order to set common policies, to effectively exercise its competences, and to address issues of common interest, especially when their impact extends beyond the region. Indeed, in cases of supra-regional impact, cooperation between ACs is a way of avoiding central government intervention. Only a few of the new statutes have also included this provision.[34]

The Constitutional Court has confirmed their constitutionality. These statutory provisions are not exactly innovative, as they reflect the jurisprudence of the Court itself, which has repeatedly stated that a supra-regional reach cannot be an excuse for the central government to 'seize' Autonomous Community competences 'but that what is constitutionally applicable should be the establishment of mechanisms for cooperation between affected Autonomous Communities without modifying competences'.[35] These declarations call for cooperation between ACs to avoid re-centralisation, but they have not served to stimulate this cooperation except in very specific cases, like the creation of a consortium between three ACs in the north of Spain in order to manage a national park.

The new statutes seek to promote bilateral and multilateral cooperation between ACs. They reflect constitutional jurisprudence that is *pro* horizontal cooperation. However, there are hardly any reforms in the legal design of the agreements between ACs, which are the instruments that should materialise the desire to cooperate. Most of the new statutes have again included requirements that do not make it easier to formalise an agreement between ACs. Because of this, the process of statutory reform has been an (incomprehensibly) missed opportunity to facilitate the signing of agreements between ACs in Spain. Unlike vertical instruments, the regulatory framework for horizontal agreements in the Statute of Catalonia has not generated controversy. It is one of the few articles that have not been challenged in the Constitutional Court.

## Meetings Between Autonomous Communities, the Conference of Autonomous Community Governments, and Multilateralism Between Autonomous Communities: Has the Time for Horizontal Cooperation Arrived?

The new statutes make few legal changes to horizontal cooperation. Nevertheless, approval of the statutes has represented *de facto* the emergence of a climate of cooperation and the political will to activate it. As mentioned, in a period of 5 years (between 2006 and 2011), the number of agreements between ACs tripled the number of horizontal agreements signed during the preceding 25 years (between 1978 and 2005). This increase in agreements between ACs is mainly due to the emergence of the so-called Meetings between ACs with new statutes. It is

---

[34] Art. 115 Catalan Statute. The equivalent in the Statute of Andalusia: Art. 43.

[35] STC 329/1993, FJ 3; STC 194/2004, FJ 8.

interesting to note how the same cooperation between Autonomous Communities that was a secondary aim during the drafting of the new statutes became a political priority once it was approved.

The decentralisation process in Spain began in order to satisfy political demands, i.e., to respond to the self-governing aspirations of the historic ACs. However, the State of Autonomies is also legitimised by efficiency. There are areas where the absence of horizontal relations may cause citizens problems. The best known case has been that of hunting and fishing licences; in Spain, individuals who hunt must request a licence for this activity in each Autonomous Community where they wish to engage in their hobby. There is no procedure for validating licences across ACs. Validation of hunting and fishing licences across ACs was one of the first issues these Meetings sought to address. ACs seem to have discovered areas where they perceive the advantages of collaboration. After 30 years of the State of Autonomies, ACs may be mature enough to implement horizontal cooperation and horizontal cooperation instruments.

The Meetings between Autonomous Communities to develop the new statutes began in 2008, at the request of the government of the Autonomous Community of Aragon. They brought together the first six ACs with new statutes.[36] It should be stressed that these were ACs governed by different political parties (PP, PSOE, and nationalist party coalition governments). These fora were normally meetings between regional ministers from Departments of Presidency or Autonomous Community vice-presidents. The Meetings between ACs have not been attended by Autonomous Community presidents. These Meetings have been the first stable structure of multilateral horizontal cooperation in the State of Autonomies.

Between 2008 and 2010, eight Meetings were held between ACs, and the frequency of these meetings has been constant (at least two per year). Moreover, the number of members from Autonomous Community governments has grown steadily, to the point where nearly all ACs (with or without a new statute) have participated in these Meetings.

The Meetings between ACs have advanced in two directions so far. First of all, there is a more political facet: An 'early warning' system has been developed within this group to detect if there is draft legislation by the central government that might encroach upon AC competences. Second of all, these Meetings have also served to agree on joint statements with a political value that express a point of view or make a request to the central government. In addition, in these fora, ACs have been able to identify areas for joint actions in order to increase efficiency and benefit citizens. As a result, multiple horizontal agreements have been reached, and these are the results of the Meetings between ACs that have most media impact.[37]

---

[36] The Valencian Community, Catalonia, the Balearic Islands, Andalusia, Aragon, and Castilla y León.

[37] The ACs have created a website to make the work of these Meetings more visible: http://www.comunidadesautonomas.org.

These Meetings have not only been the main 'producer' of agreements in recent years; they have also changed the quality of horizontal relations in Spain. Until the Meetings were created, cooperation between Autonomous Communities was scarce, barely formalised, and normally bilateral between neighbouring ACs. With the Meetings, multilateral cooperation between Autonomous Communities has also emerged in Spain. It should not be forgotten that the Meetings began with a small group of ACs (the first six to adopt new statutes). The number of participants has risen steadily and now includes most ACs. Thus, if this cooperation is confirmed, agreements may potentially be signed by all ACs.

The emergence of horizontal multilateralism is of crucial importance in the State of Autonomies. Previously, ACs had been unable to identify common areas of action or formalise the cooperation necessary to perform such action. The agreements between ACs resulting from these Meetings address 'domestic' issues focused on the recognition of licences and qualifications and on mutual assistance (e.g., validation across ACs of hunting and fishing licences and health-care products, aid for battered women, etc.). In Spain, agreements between ACs are not legal provisions. Agreements do not create rights for third parties directly for, as indicated, they are not a source of law in Spain. These agreements contain commitments to exchange information, coordination of criteria, rules on allocating financial costs, and occasional commitments to amend the laws of each Autonomous Community in the manner agreed. Harmonisation of legislation of regional institutions directly under a horizontal agreement does not exist in the State of Autonomies.

Compared to the development of this emerging multilateral cooperation between ACs occurring in 'domestic' affairs, the formal instruments of cooperation between them are still barely 'Europeanised', as will be seen later.

In December 2011, participants in the Meetings between ACs decided to continue with their activity but with the format of a Conference of Autonomous Community governments.[38] The first meeting was in March 2011. It should be noted that the Conference was not attended by Autonomous Community presidents, as it normally brings together regional ministers from the Departments of Presidency or Autonomous Community vice-presidents. All ACs, with the exception of the Basque Country, took part in the first meeting. It is important to stress that this Conference is still only a political project. Horizontal cooperation is not easy in Spain. Horizontal relations require a learning period between the ACs themselves, and this type of structure requires strong political will and a consolidation period that only the future can confirm.

---

[38] De Pedro Bonet (2011), pp. 94–113.

# Internal Cooperation in European Affairs: More Vertical Cooperation and More Horizontal Cooperation?

## *The Emergence of the European Dimension of Internal Cooperation in the New Statutes*

The European Union is one of the main factors behind cooperation in all politically decentralised states, in particular, in its vertical dimension. The central government represents the state's position in EU institutions in Brussels and is responsible for any breaches of the obligations of European law.

Spain joined the European Community in 1986. The Spanish Constitution of 1978 did not provide for the participation of ACs in European affairs. Unlike what has happened in other countries, European integration has not resulted in constitutional reform to regulate the participation of ACs in the integration process. This process was negotiated between the central government and the ACs within an *ad hoc* Conference, the Conference for European Union Affairs, created in 1988 and regulated by law in 1997.[39] This Conference is comprised of the minister of Public Administration (from the central government), who presides over it, and the regional ministers responsible for European affairs (from the ACs).

The instruments employed to formalise Autonomous Community participation in European affairs have been successive political accords between the central government and the ACs.

With regard to AC involvement in establishing the position defended by the central government in Brussels, in 1994, the Conference for European Union Affairs passed the political Accord on Internal Participation of the ACs in European affairs via the Sectorial Conferences. It should be remembered that the Sectorial Conferences in Spain are vertical. As noted, there are neither horizontal Sectorial Conferences nor a Conference of Autonomous Community presidents. Apart from the Sectorial Conferences, it is possible to create Bilateral Commissions between the central government and an Autonomous Community in European affairs to address issues exclusively relating to that Autonomous Community.

In 2004, and once again within the Conference for European Union Affairs, political Accords were approved allowing for direct participation of ACs in some formations of the Council of Ministers of the European Union.[40] The Sectorial Conferences must appoint an Autonomous Community representative who participates in the Spanish delegation before the Council of Ministers. Autonomous Community participation in state delegations in the Council represents a major

---

[39] Central government Law 4/1997, of 13 March, creating the Conference for European Union Affairs.

[40] On direct participation, one may consult the web page of the Ministry of Territorial Policy (ACs and European Union): http://www.mpt.gob.es/es/areas/politica_autonomica/coop_multilateral_ccaa_ue/ccaa_y_ue.html.

advance. They have an important symbolic value because this is a door that, for a long time, was closed to Autonomous Communities.

Since 2006, the statutes of autonomy have included European clauses that reflect Constitutional Court jurisprudence regarding Autonomous Community participation in European affairs and the contents of the political Accords of the Conference for European Union Affairs, but now in a legal provision. The new statutes regulate the internal decision-making process, the direct participation of ACs in European institutions, and the phase of implementation of European law. The peculiarity and the problem lie in the fact that the statutes can only regulate the participation of an Autonomous Community in European affairs (these are laws with limited territorial effectiveness), whilst the model of participation of the ACs is a multilateral procedure that must be regulated in the Constitution or in a central government law that does not yet exist.

## Autonomous Community Participation in Decision-Making: Once Again, the Emergence of Bilateralism–Multilateralism

The most controversial aspect of the Statute of Catalonia of 2006 was Catalonia's involvement in deciding the Spanish state's positions with regard to the institutions in Brussels. In particular, two aspects have been especially controversial. First is the manners in which the Autonomous Community participates: bilateral in European issues that affect it exclusively and multilateral in other circumstances. Second, the Statute sets out the nature and effects of this participation. Catalonia's stance is 'decisive' in forming Spain's position if the proposal affects exclusive competences or if there are potential financial or administrative consequences of special significance for Catalonia. If the central government opts not to share the view taken by the Autonomous Community, this must be explained before the Bilateral Commission. This option was reflected in the new statutes.[41]

The bilateralism–multilateralism tandem, a characteristic feature of Spanish cooperation relations, is also evident in relations between the central government and ACs in European matters. The bilateral route again appeals to the defence of one's own interests, and the European Union serves as one of the principal stimuli for promoting multilateral cooperation in Spain.[42] The dialectic between the quest for participation with all and the defence of regional interests is a characteristic feature of the system of Autonomous Community participation.

The Constitutional Court upheld that the forms of Catalonia's participation in European affairs were constitutional, with certain qualifications, as were the effects of such participation. According to the Court, the Statute of Catalonia limits

---

[41] Art. 186 and additional provision 2 of the Statute of Catalonia. In almost identical terms, the Statute of Andalusia (Art. 231).

[42] Pérez Medina (2009), pp. 353–354. Börzel (2000), pp. 17–42.

bilateralism to particular situations and does not exclude multilateralism. The Constitutional Court also confirmed the constitutionality of the 'decisive' nature of the stance expressed by Catalonia in the abovementioned cases but qualifies this by saying that this stance is not 'binding'. Similarly, the duty to provide explanations before the Bilateral Commission only constitutes 'a mechanism of collaboration in cases when the interests of the Autonomous Community are especially affected'. In no event is the central government bound by the opinion of the Autonomous Community.[43]

In practice, the participation of ACs in forming the positions of the Spanish state with regard to the European Union is achieved through the Sectorial Conferences, a mechanism of intergovernmental, multilateral, sectorial, and vertical cooperation. The model of participation hinges upon an instrument that presents certain problems of practical functionality. The Sectorial Conferences are not true bodies for participation of ACs in internal state affairs or in European affairs. The central government voluntarily informs ACs about European projects. In the absence of formal structures of horizontal coordination between ACs, the central government meets with 17 ACs, each with its own agenda. The central government's presence in this format prevents the Sectorial Conferences from being the appropriate forum in Spain to discuss a common position of the ACs—which only they should decide upon—which might subsequently be communicated to the central government.

With regard to the Bilateral Commissions in European affairs, experience suggests that their role has been minimal. In the State of Autonomies, there have been three *ad hoc* Bilateral Commissions in the area of European affairs (with the Basque Country in 1995, with Catalonia in 1998, and with the Canary Islands in 2001).[44] In practice, these structures have been fairly inactive. Rather than the Autonomous Community's own issues, these fora have often addressed general questions of interest to an Autonomous Community. With the new statutes, the new Bilateral Commissions have also assumed the functions of monitoring European policy to ensure the effectiveness of the Autonomous Community's participation. For the time being, the activity of the new Bilateral Commissions in European issues has not been significant.

## And the European Union as a Factor in Developing Horizontal Cooperation

European law is implemented and applied by ACs in those cases where they have competence. This was ruled by the Constitutional Court and is reflected in most of the new statutes. In practice, implementation of most European laws is undertaken

---

[43] STC 31/2010, FJ 210.

[44] Roig Molés (1999), pp. 203–207. Cordal Rodríguez (2010), pp. 293–301.

by the central government by virtue of its so called horizontal competences (e.g., general legislation regulating the economy).

The Statute of Catalonia has been the only one to provide for the possibility of using multilateral cooperation between ACs to execute European law. If implementation corresponds to the ACs and requires measures extending across more than one AC, an attempt must be made at horizontal cooperation 'via mechanisms of coordination or collaboration'.[45] This provision reflects the jurisprudence of the Constitutional Court, mentioned above, according to which the central government may seize Autonomous Community competences for the simple reason that an action may affect various ACs.

The execution of European law through mechanisms of cooperation between Autonomous Communities might be an alternative to unilateral regulation by the central government. However, in practice, this option is not yet viable in Spain. Multilateral horizontal cooperation must be consolidated further in order to contemplate in the State of Autonomies a transposition of directives via cooperation between ACs.[46]

Prior to the new statutes, the integration process fostered significant development of cooperation between ACs. Since 2004, ACs have had direct representation in the institutions of Brussels. Autonomous Community representation is carried out by including in the Spanish delegation a member, with the rank of regional minister, or a member of a Ministry of an Autonomous Community, who represents all Autonomous Communities in matters affecting their competences. The Sectorial Conferences between the central government and the ACs must appoint an Autonomous Community representative who forms part of the Spanish delegation before the Council of Ministers. This is boosting cooperation between Autonomous Communities in order to appoint the Autonomous Community representative.

The participation of Autonomous Communities through their offices in Brussels is strategic and has led to a great deal of informal cooperation between Autonomous Communities. In their offices, ACs are in much closer physical proximity, work together quite effectively, and have prompted meetings that later take place in Spain to agree upon positions vis-à-vis the Council of Ministers of the European Union. In the same vein, it is also important to note the cooperation between ACs in the Committee of the Regions. In Spain, a meeting of Autonomous Community presidents has not (yet) been possible. However, these informal meetings are possible in the Committee of the Regions because the Autonomous Community presidents are part of the Spanish delegation in the Committee.

Intergovernmental relations between ACs in projects involving cross-border cooperation with neighbouring regions of other states are an interesting phenomenon. There is hardly any institutionalised cooperation between ACs within Spain; however, ACs do meet up and cooperate in a stable manner with other European regions using cross-border cooperation programmes and instruments. This is the

---

[45] Art. 189 of the Statute of Catalonia.
[46] García Morales (2011), pp. 42–45.

case of the Midi-Pyrenees Euroregion, where Catalonia, Aragon, and the Balearic Islands meet on a permanent basis. Similarly, September 2010 saw the official creation of the Macroregion 'Regions of South-west Europe', comprised of Castilla y León, Galicia, and North Portugal, the first Macroregion to be established on the Iberian Peninsula. This is an instrument of cooperation with a dual profile—inter-Autonomous Community and cross-border—which represents an attempt to create competitive spaces that transcend borders.[47] Most of the new statutes contemplate cross-border cooperation as a kind of relation that lends prestige to the ACs and is easier to legally formalise than horizontal cooperation.


## Future Perspectives: A New Legal Framework, a Landmark Ruling ... and What Next?

The new statutes and the Constitutional Court have proposed some legal ground rules for cooperation relations in Spain. In 2006, a reform of the statutes of autonomy addressed these relations. The Constitutional Court's ruling regarding the Statute of Catalonia of 2010 is a landmark ruling, as it examines not only a statute but also a proposed revision of the State of Autonomies. This ruling confirms the constitutionality of how the Statute regulates cooperation relations with legal and political consequences that go beyond the Catalan legislation. The intended innovations in the area of cooperation are the result of second-generation statutes, not of the Constitutional Court ruling. These innovations are few and far between, are mainly to be found in the vertical dimension of cooperation, and basically serve to reinforce bilateralism through the Bilateral Commission and the new rights of Autonomous Community participation.

This new legal setting has generated expectations of change for cooperation in Spain. However, law plays a minor role. Experience has shown that legal regulation of instruments of cooperation in the State of Autonomies guarantees neither changes nor their effectiveness. The responsibility for change lies with the participants of intergovernmental relations, governments, and senior officials. At the moment, cooperation in the State of Autonomies is at a crossroads: there are differing opinions that may lead to different results, depending on the path chosen.

As far as the vertical dimension is concerned, the new statutes do not regulate multilateral cooperation. Its regulatory framework is in a central government law that grants the central government considerable power to direct multilateral instruments, power which has been confirmed by the Constitutional Court, but also agreed to and requested by the ACs. With regard to the specific instruments, the Conference of Presidents is currently an instrument with an uncertain future. On 20 November 2011, there was a general election won by the conservative Popular

---

[47] Benz (2007), pp. 421–436.

Party. The future president of the government, along with the presidents of the ACs, will have to decide the fate of this instrument.

Most decentralised countries around us have a Conference of Presidents that works closely with the Sectorial Conferences. For this reason, one of the peculiarities of cooperation in Spain is the existence of Sectorial Conferences without a cooperation body at the highest level. The Sectorial Conferences are the most consolidated instruments of cooperation in the State of Autonomies. However, in many cases, the ACs attend out of institutional duty and with limited conviction as to the usefulness of the Conferences, as they are platforms where the central government outlines its projects or distributes money to the ACs. The challenge is for these Conferences to become genuine instruments for participation of ACs in state politics.

The big question posed by the new legal setting is whether bilateralism will be reinforced in Spanish intergovernmental relations. To date, regulation of the Bilateral Commissions in the new statutes has not resulted in different activity or dynamics in the non-statutory Bilateral Commissions. Previous experience shows that the Bilateral Commissions have not been an instrument of the State of Autonomies that has replaced multilateralism. On the contrary, many Bilateral Commissions have been formal structures that have rarely met, and those that have met have played a complementary and secondary role with regard to multilateral instruments. Experience also shows that it is not easy to find issues to be dealt with exclusively in a bilateral manner in these Commissions. In many cases, bilateral demands are made that are likely to be addressed in multilateral fora with all Autonomous Communities.

The Bilateral Commissions and the agreements reached in them do not rule out possible asymmetries between ACs. This possibility is counterbalanced by the tendency towards emulation in the State of Autonomies, emulation between Autonomous Communities occurring in the creation of the instrument, in its regulation in the statute and even in the dynamics of each Commission. All ACs have a Bilateral Commission with the central government, while the Statute of Catalonia of 2006 provides for a Bilateral Commission with the central government that has been imported into other statutes. Moreover, the Bilateral Commissions have a similar practical activity. Regulation of the Bilateral Commissions in a statute of autonomy has made them more visible, but it has not ensured their success. The new Bilateral Commissions may run the risk of becoming, as occurred in their earlier phase, a merely formal structure that is little more than symbolic.

In matters of horizontal cooperation, the new statutes of autonomy represent a major paradox. They seek to stimulate cooperation between Autonomous Communities, but the legal design of horizontal instruments (in particular, the agreements between ACs) in the new statutes has scarcely been modified and reproduces old problems. The new statutes have introduced few legal changes but have generated a political will that has placed multilateral cooperation between the ACs on the agenda of Autonomous Community governments. For the time being, there are signs of change that only time will confirm as having been merely an attempt to change things or a very real and significant change in cooperation relations.

The most noticeable changes in Spanish intergovernmental relations may arise from a clear and sustained promotion of horizontal cooperation. The absence in Spain of solid horizontal cooperation strengthens the central government and allows it to clearly lead cooperation in Spain. Horizontal cooperation requires the creation and consolidation of cooperation bodies that provide stability and institutionalise this kind of relationship between ACs. The experience of other European countries shows that horizontal relations can help increase efficiency in the State of Autonomies, prevent the re-centralisation of competences, and achieve effective participation of the ACs in state and EU policies. Indeed, the European Union has been and presumably will continue to be an important stimulus for the development of multilateral cooperation between ACs and also between ACs and the central government.

In these pages, I have analysed the role of law and, in particular, the role of the new statutes and of the Constitutional Court in how cooperation is shaped in Spain. Intergovernmental relations are obviously much more than formal instruments with a specific legal regulation. Informal cooperation in Spain exists and could be as important as its formal counterpart. The process of statutory reforms has finished for now in a political and economic context that is totally different from that in which it began. General elections and Autonomous Community elections in most ACs were held in 2011, with victories for the Popular Party. Furthermore, the global economic crisis that began 3 years ago has been especially severe in Spain. The impact of this almost total political homogeneity between the central government and the governments of the ACs remains to be seen, as does the impact of an international economic crisis on domestic cooperative relations. Politics and economics will undoubtedly be fundamental in any discussion in coming years of continuity or changes in cooperation in the State of Autonomies.

# References

Aja, E. (2003), El Estado autonómico. Federalismo y hechos diferenciales. Alianza, Madrid, pp. 169–199.

Alberti Rovira, E. (1993). Relaciones entre Administraciones Pública. In: Leguina Villa, J., Sánchez Morón, M. (dirs.). *Comentarios a la Ley 30/1992, de 26 de noviembre, de Régimen Jurídico de las Administraciones Públicas y del Procedimiento Administrativo Común*. Tecnos. Madrid, pp. 41–70.

Benz, A. (2007). Inter-Regional Competition in Co-operative Federalism: New Modes of Multi-level Governance in Germany. Regional & Federal Studies, No. 4, pp. 421–436.

Börzel, T.A. (2000). From Competitive Regionalism to Cooperative Federalism: The Europeanization of the Spanish State of the Autonomies. Publius 30:2, pp. 17–42.

Cordal Rodríguez, C. (2010). Regiones, Länder y Comunidades Autónomas en la Unión Europea. Torculo Ed. Santiago, pp. 293–301.

Corretja, M., Vintró J., Bernadí, X. (2011). Bilateralitat i multilateralitat. La participació de la Generalitat en polítiques i organismes estatals i la Comissió Bilateral. Revista d' Estudis Autonòmics i Federals, No. 12, pp. 403–446.

Cruz Villalón, P. (1990). La doctrina constitucional sobre el principio de cooperación. In: Cano Bueso, J. (ed.,). Comunidades Autónomas e instrumentos de cooperación interterritorial. Parlamento de Andalucía. Madrid. Tecnos, 1990, pp. 119–134.

De Pedro Bonet, X. (2011). La Conferencia de Gobiernos de las Comunidades Autónomas. In: Tornos Mas, J. (dir.), Informe Comunidades Autónomas 2011. Instituto de Derecho Público. Barcelona, pp. 94–113.

García Morales, M.J. (2009a), Los nuevos Estatutos de Autonomía y las relaciones de colaboración. Un nuevo escenario, ¿una nueva etapa? Revista Jurídica de Castilla y León, No. 19 [número monográfico], pp. 383–394.

García Morales, M.J. (2009b). La colaboración a examen. Retos y riesgos de las relaciones intergubernamentales en el Estado autonómico. Revista Española de Derecho Constitucional, No. 86, pp. 116.

García Morales, M.J. (2011). La prevención del incumplimiento del Derecho europeo en el Estado autonómico: instrumentos, posibilidades y límites. In: Biglino Campos, P., Delgado del Rincón, L. (dirs.). El incumplimiento del Derecho comunitario en el Estado autonómico. Prevención y responsabilidad. CEPC. Madrid, pp. 42–45.

García Morales, M.J. (since 2001, annual). Convenios de colaboración entre el Estado y las Comunidades Autónomas y entre Comunidades Autónomas. In: Tornos Mas, J. (dir.), Informe Comunidades Autónomas. Instituto de Derecho Público. Barcelona.

García Morales, M.J., Arbós Marín, X. (2013). "Intergovernmental Relations in Spain". In: Saunders, Ch., Poirier, J. (eds.), Intergovernmental Relations in Federal Systems. A Global Dialogue on Federalism, vol. 8, McGill/Queen's University Press, Montréal/Kingston (in press).

García Morales, M.J. (coord.) (2009). Las relaciones de colaboración en los nuevos Estatutos de autonomía. Revista Jurídica de Castilla y León, No. 19 [número monográfico].

Jeffery, Ch. Vom kooperativen Föderalimus zu einer Sinatra-Doktrin der Länder. In: Meiner-Walser, R.C., Hirscher, G. (Hg.). Krise un Reform des Föderalismus. Olzog, München, 1999, pp. 50–63.

Montilla Martos, J. A. (2011). Las relaciones de colaboración en el nuevo marco estatutario: bilateralidad y participación. Revista de Estudios Políticos, No. 151, pp.184–195.

Pérez Medina, J.M. (2009). Las relaciones de colaboración entre el Estado y las Comunidades Autónomas desde la perspectiva de la Administración General del Estado. Revista Jurídica de Castilla y León, No. 19 [número monográfico], p. 350.

Pérez Medina, J.M. (2009). Las relaciones de colaboración entre el Estado y las Comunidades Autónomas desde la perspectiva de la Administración General del Estado. Revista Jurídica de Castilla y León, No. 19 [número monográfico], pp. 353–354.

Ridaura Martínez, M. J. (2010). Comisiones Bilaterales de Cooperación y nuevos Estatutos de Autonomía. In: García Roca, J., Albertí Rovira, E. (coords.). Treinta años de Constitución. Tirant lo Blanch. Valencia, pp. 256–274.

Roig Molés, E. (1999). Asimetría y participación autonómica en la formación de la voluntad española en asuntos de la UE: ¿participación a dos velocidades? Revista Vasca de Administración Pública. No 55, pp. 203–207.

Rubio Llorente, F., Álvarez Junco, J. (eds.) (2006). Informe del Consejo de Estado sobre la reforma constitucional. Texto del informe y debates académicos. CEPC, Consejo de Estado. Madrid, pp. 163–165.

Sáez Royo, E. (2010). "Las relaciones intergubernamentales en España: Las relaciones de cooperación intergubernamental en la Ley de Dependencia: un paso sustantivo". In: Tudela Aranda, J., Knüpling, F. (eds.). España y modelos de federalismo. CEPC. Madrid, pp. 361–386.

Tajadura Tejada, J. (2010). El principio de cooperación en el Estado autonómico. Comares. Granada, pp. 134–172.

Viver Pi-Sunyer, C. (2010). El reconeixement de la plurinacionalitat de l'Estat en l'ordenament jurídic espanyol. In: Requejo, F., Gagnon, A.-G. (eds.), Nacions a la recerca de reconeixement. Institut d'Estudis Autonòmics, Barcelona, pp. 213–234 [In French in: Requejo, F., Gagnon, A.-G. (2011). Nations en quête de reconnaissance. Peter Lang, Brussels].

# Intergovernmental Relations in the Spanish Federal System: In Search of a Model

César Colino

## Introduction: Is Spain So Different?

When taking stock of the Spanish version of federalism, the "*Estado autonómico*", it seems of utmost importance to address not just the distribution of powers and resources or its diversity but also its complex machinery of government and its everyday workings, that is, its intergovernmental relations (hereafter IGR) and the way its strengths and weaknesses have been evolving and treated by both political science, public administration, and public law. The academic study of IGR may serve primarily to identify patterns of functioning and its evolution and thus to pinpoint possible problems and pathologies. Only then can institutional design solutions have a chance of success. This, in turn, can only be done by comparing the Spanish system with other similar ones, i.e., by understanding its historical evolution and workings in comparative perspective.

Consequently, this chapter seeks to establish which characteristics of the Spanish IGR actually reflect peculiar and/or pathological features and which are usual features in other federations. In general terms, the main argument of this chapter is that intergovernmental relations in the "autonomic" state are not that different from other systems as it is frequently asserted. Spanish IGR have had, for many years, a much worse reputation than they deserve, if examined empirically and compared to those in several other countries with territorial structures similar to Spain. This does not mean that IGR in Spain are flawless or do not suffer from various problems. My point is, and the claim will be certainly controversial, that for various reasons of different nature, the conventional wisdom about the Spanish IGR in traditional public law and much of the political science literature has gradually ceased to be valid and should be reconsidered for the most part.

C. Colino (✉)
Facultad de Ciencias Políticas, Dpto. de Ciencia Politica y de la Administración, UNED,
C/ Obispo Trejo s/n, 28040 Madrid, Spain
e-mail: ccolino@poli.uned.es

A. López-Basaguren and L. Escajedo San Epifanio (eds.), *The Ways of Federalism in Western Countries and the Horizons of Territorial Autonomy in Spain*, Vol. 2, DOI 10.1007/978-3-642-27717-7_7, © Springer-Verlag Berlin Heidelberg 2013

In general, these reasons have to do both with the lack, until recently, of systematic, empirical, and sector-specific studies on IGR and with the inadequate choice of the reference models or benchmarks for assessing our IGR, for example, through an almost exclusive fixation of Spanish IGR experts in the central European federations. For these reasons and also determined by the different normative or ideological models espoused by academics on the desirable territorial model, existing work on IGR in Spain has had an overly pessimistic bias that has tended to emphasize the negative aspects against the positive ones. This pessimistic bias, either responding to lack of comparative knowledge or to ideological preferences against the model, has sometimes generated a series of stereotypes that have been transmitted through academic citation both inside Spain and in the international literature. If these stereotypes may have had some basis in reality at the outset of the Spanish territorial model in the 1980s, they are no longer consistent with their daily workings and its developments since several years ago.

In account of this, the recent availability of new research and increasing knowledge of other models should lead us to reconsider these stereotypes. It is clear, however, that we cannot prevent the circulation of some of them in the ideological clash against our territorial model, but at least this chapter aims to modestly contribute to this rethinking and debate by, at the same time, taking stock of what we already know about the Spanish IGR and its similarities with other countries.

## The Academic Study of IGR Institutions and Practices in Spain

Although it would be problematic to try to present here an exhaustive overview of all the literature produced on the Spanish IGR system in the last 30 years, one can try to identify some major areas of discussion that have preoccupied lawyers, economists, and political scientists in the past three decades. Five major issues could be singled out that have traditionally been the subject of debate and five emerging topics and research programs that have yet to develop fully.

If we look at the first, most of the studies and debates have revolved around

- The historical and political peculiarities of IGR, especially their weaknesses and difficulties for institutionalization in a context of asymmetric and conflictive development despite some attempts by the central government to import some features of other established models;
- The analysis of the constitutional and legal framework and the formal institutionalization of the principles, bodies and instruments of vertical IGR. More recently, the amendments of several regional statutes of autonomy and their inclusion and formalization of certain existing mechanisms have led to the study of new forms of collaboration and participation;
- The mechanisms for horizontal cooperation between regional governments and their shortcomings. Some studies have addressed the constitutional distrust, the poor design of the instruments and the practical difficulties of intergovernmental actors to undertake horizontal cooperation, the explanations of its weaknesses, and the need

to improve horizontal instruments and mechanisms (García Morales 2009a; 2009b; Colino 2010; 2011).

- The vertical and horizontal intergovernmental aspects of finance and fiscal and budgetary coordination. It has been debated on the shortcomings of the funding system and the "limits" of solidarity and financial equalization. Some political scientists and economists have tried to explain the instability of the funding system or the political determinants of intergovernmental fiscal relations (Gordin 2004, León 2007).
- The consequences of EU membership, Europeanization of IGR, and the participation of autonomous communities in the EU decision-making process.

In addition to these five areas, one could mention five new issues or areas of research that, despite having been traditionally present in public debate, have only recently started to develop due to the increasing incorporation of new disciplines to the study of the IGR, such as political science and public administration, or to the impact of foreign scholars interested in the Spanish IGR system. These are:

- The role of political parties and their decentralized organizations in IGR (Grau i Creus 2000; Fabre and Méndez 2009).
- The study of sectoral differences in the degree and success of intergovernmental cooperation (Bolleyer 2006; León and Ferrín 2011).
- The new role of the central government after the consolidation of a highly decentralized model (Parrado 2010).
- The public policy implications of existing intergovernmental relations;
- Comparisons with other countries and the assessment of the relevance of foreign experiences and best practices.

Finally, one could mention a series of new research fields to explore in the Spanish case that have so far not been dealt with by the territorial politics or institutions scholarship. Some of them could build on, or replicate, some studies that have been made in other parliamentary federal countries such as Canada, Australia, or Germany (see Cameron and Simeon 2002; Johns et al. 2007; Inwood et al. 2011; Painter 2001; Scheller and Schmid 2008; Kropp 2010). These are, for instance, the development, configuration, and real influence of new intergovernmental management units at both levels of government, the concentration of intergovernmental activity in the hands of regional premiers, the role of parliaments as fora of IGR and the scrutiny of executives, the role of the Senate's Standing Legislative Committee for the Autonomous Communities, or specific sectoral studies, focused on understanding the mechanisms and consequences of cooperation in sectors such as health, education, research and innovation, long-term care, environment, etc.

## A Diagnosis in Comparative Perspective. IGR in Spain: A Peculiar Model or a Model Still in the Making?

This section seeks to briefly present and discuss some of the defining features of the Spanish IGR that are comparable to those of similar parliamentary federations and those that appear to be unique features determined by its mode of emergence and its sociopolitical basis. This is done by contrasting the traditional diagnoses of the system in various aspects with the most recent empirical findings. Broadly speaking, in simplified terms, the Spanish system of intergovernmental relations, determined by its history and its specific constitutional provisions, could be characterized in general by twelve key characteristics that are also found in greater or lesser extent in other similar systems (vid. Meekison 2001; Stein and Turkewitsch 2009). However, these twelve features are routinely presented in Spanish academic or political discourse as deficiencies or pathologies of our system. Obviously, this means that they are only peculiar or pathological if compared with a non-existent ideal model but not when compared with the norm in other federal systems.

Many traditional diagnoses on the Spanish IGR have almost always been marked with a sense of deficiency or imperfection, and often associated with a presumption of incomparability with other systems, due in part to the difficulty of identifying the model that was emerging in Spain in comparative terms. However, with the consolidation of the system during the nineties, the model attained recognizable features present in other federal countries that increasingly questioned the notion of radical uniqueness and incomparability of Spanish IGR. This gave rise to the impression that, rather than a unique system, it was a system that was going through several phases also typical of other federal systems previously. Undoubtedly, its particular origin and evolution have produced structural features that other systems do not show. It is expected, however, that many other of its traits will evolve to resemble those of other federal countries.

These characteristics are

1. *Non-constitutionalization of IGR* but increasing regulation in recently amended regional statutes. As in other federations, indeed in the majority, the constitutional framework is silent or restrictive (in the case of horizontal collaboration) regarding intergovernmental cooperation. The regulation of some of the intergovernmental bodies and instruments occurs in subsequent legislation on administrative procedure (Trench 2006).

2. *Ineffectiveness of the second chamber for IGR.* As in the case of Canada, Australia, Austria or other federations, in the Spanish case there is also a lack of mechanisms for cooperation or intrastate participation through the second chamber, which does not possess real participation or veto rights for regional representatives in central institutions. With the recent round of reforms of the regional statutes of autonomy, however, an increase in participation rights of the ACs in central government bodies and the ability to participate in the appointment of members of certain constitutional bodies (advisory councils, public companies, the appointment of some judges of the Constitutional Court by the Senate, etc.) have been recognized.

3. *Lack of formalization and consultative character* of most intergovernmental bodies. As in most federal countries (the exception here would be Germany, but only in a minority of intergovernmental bodies), the intergovernmental bodies of the executive are consultative and rarely take collective binding decisions.

In almost all cases (also in Germany and the EU), the principles of unanimity and consensus dominate for making decisions in these bodies. In Spain, there is also a preference among intergovernmental actors at regional level for informal, non-institutionalized relationships, and a certain distrust of formal cooperation by most regional governments, concerned about the risks of centralization or interference. Traditionally, some critical observers have used the purely consultative and voluntary nature of most multilateral cooperation bodies to disdain the Spanish system of IGR, not realizing that the situation is identical in most federal systems. According to those critics, from this condition it would derive a certain lack of effectiveness in terms of concrete decisions shaping public policies. Some have advocated more joint decision-making mechanisms. These criticisms, as well as the proposals that arise from them, can be also found in other systems.

4. *Lack of transparency and dominance of executives in IGR*, alongside a certain lack of coordination within them. The prevalence of executives in the IGR and the relative independence of the line departments in intergovernmental relations with other levels, despite the gradual emergence of internal coordination units or units of intergovernmental affairs in many regional administrations, are another typical feature of the Spanish system that it shares with most federal systems. In others, however, coordinating bodies of intergovernmental affairs have emerged (vid. Dupré 1985; Pollard 1986; Warhurst 1987). In Spain, they are still rudimentary but growing.

5. *Coexistence between multilateralism and bilateralism* at the political level but predominance of multilateralism. Despite some stereotypes disseminated by Spanish and foreign scholars on the prevalence of modes of bilateral cooperation and interaction in our territorial model, a detailed study of intergovernmental meetings indicates that bilateral cooperation bodies have not been widely used and, in any case, have been much less used than multilateral ones. In fact, they have been consistently utilized only with six or seven of the regions. For example, half of the 178 bilateral meetings held in the last 20 years have been with Navarre, Canary Islands, and Catalonia. There has been a parallel growth of both types of bodies, multilateral and bilateral, but the proportion remained clearly in favor of multilateral bodies (A. González 2006; Ramos 2006; Colino and Parrado 2009).

6. *Predominant role of central government in IGR*, mostly unopposed or tolerated by most regional governments and even in sectors in which regional jurisdiction is exclusive, either through the deployment of its concurrent powers or its role as intermediary with the EU institutions, and the use of its spending power. As in other federations such as Canada, USA, Austria, and Australia, intergovernmental agreements are often used as a vehicle for federal grants and shared-cost programs in areas like education, health, and social services. The central government maintains its own enforcement agencies operating at subnational level in some sectors of public policy, such as unemployment and social security benefits, order and security, infrastructures, and tax collection. At the same time, in the Spanish case there is a clear willingness among regional

governments to recognize a role for the central government in most sectors of public activity and to renounce the exercise of certain powers in exchange for central funds, situation that is usually found in other federations, usually also accompanied by the insistent criticism of lawyers and most regionalist scholars.

7. *Funding system based primarily on the sharing of central government tax revenues*, some regional own sources, and mostly unconditional equalizing grants. Regional governments have consistently preferred to increase their share in central government revenues rather than use their discretion to increase revenue by taxing their own citizens. This has led to a tacit agreement where regional governments have been able to relinquish the responsibility to tax their citizens in exchange for letting the central government retain some capacity to decide on several key policies and continue to bear the fiscal responsibility before citizens. The spending power of the central government has been exercised in many areas of regional jurisdiction through the use of conditional grants or joint programs, which account for much of the activity of intergovernmental bodies.

8. *Party politicization of IGR at the level of "high politics" and increasingly in the implementation of central legislation*, alongside cooperation and problem-solving orientations at the level of public officials. The politicization of cooperation bodies by the opposition parties is not peculiar to the Spanish case (Canada, Germany, and USA). At the same time, there is a relatively high degree of jurisdictional conflict at the political level, together with cooperation and problem-solving orientation at the level of public officials, in part driven by high mobility of senior officials and politicians between the two levels of government. Also noteworthy is the importance of political parties as alternative mechanisms of intergovernmental relations. The growing influence of regional organizations and party leaders in the major Spanish statewide parties and the spread of coalition governments in many autonomous communities have made IGR more complex to manage, both internally and externally. Moreover, in recent times, vertical IGR and implementation of central public policies have been increasingly politicized by the main opposition party, which has utilized intergovernmental bodies and regional governments to block or impede the implementation of some central or shared policies out of ideological or simply electoral reasons. This has occurred with long-term care programs, anti-tobacco laws, the introduction of civic education in schools, or some central regulations on abortion. This phenomenon of politicization of IGR and boycott of central policies by regional governments in areas of shared competence is a phenomenon commonly observed in federations like the USA and Switzerland (Bednar 2009; Nugent 2009; Kissling-Näf and Walti 1999).

9. *Predominance of vertical cooperation vis-à-vis horizontal cooperation.* Similar to Canada, Australia, or the U.S., but unlike in Germany and Switzerland, there has been little use of horizontal collaboration between the component units in the Spanish system (vid. Zimmerman 2002; O'M Bowman 2004; Poirier 2004; Bochsler 2009). Distrust of horizontal collaboration in the Constitution and in practice has been offset, however, by informal collaboration practices, in many

cases difficult to detect. The absence of formal horizontal multilateral bodies and initiatives between the autonomous communities has thus been replaced by some informal agreements between neighboring autonomous communities and everyday informal cooperation. In any case, the EU membership and other factors are promoting cooperation between regions through various formal and informal mechanisms that make the autonomic State go down the same path as other federations (Colino 2010).

10. *No voting within intergovernmental bodies and predominance of unanimity* as decision-making rule. This does not mean that there is no deliberation and coalition formation in these bodies but is usually dominated by the search for consensus and a shared legitimacy for the agreements, so that in practice they deliberate until a consensus is reached. It seems that rather than ideological confrontation, what predominates within intergovernmental bodies, particularly in the second level ones composed by politicians, who in many cases are also sectoral or policy professionals, are pragmatic problem-solving strategies. In all these cases, there has been a predominance of professional comradeship or sector interests above partisan ones, as happens in other federations.

11. *Still no clear role, and party-politicization, of the newly created and increasingly formalized Conference of Presidents.* The lack of clear role and the dependence on the will of the Spanish Prime Minister of the newly formed and incipiently formalized Conference of Presidents is a feature that the Spanish system shares with other federal systems that have apex intergovernmental bodies such as the First Ministers Conference in Canada (vid. Meekison et al. 2004; Bakvis, Baier and Brown 2009; Painter 1996; Watts 2003). The recently adopted standing orders for the Conference of Presidents, due to the criticisms that had been directed to their lack of formalization, have established a fixed schedule, and reinforced a preparatory secretariat and established clear rules for the adoption of agreements, although it still leaves the power to convoke it in the hands of the central prime minister. Due to its party politicization by the main opposition party, it has not been convoked in the last 3 years. This is not unheard of in other federations, and similar criticisms of the lack of formalization or the arbitrariness of its partisan use by the prime ministers have often been heard in Canada or in Australia, for example.

12. *Weak internal coordination of IGR within individual regional governments' machinery.* In recent times, this weak coordination has produced some attempts of institutional design consisting of the emergence of specialized bodies, with different names and powers, which have had the task of "analysis, promotion and monitoring" of intergovernmental affairs within different generalist departments or line ministries. In the case of the Spanish central government, these bodies have had a longer tradition and considerable experience from the 1980s, as reflected by the existence of the DG for Territorial Cooperation in the Ministry for Public Administrations or the DG for Financial Coordination with the Autonomous Communities in the Ministry of Finance. In the Autonomous Communities, EU membership and the growing activity of many intergovernmental ministers'

conferences alongside the recent reform initiatives of regional statutes of autonomy have promoted, in recent years, the need for the establishment of specialized
bodies to perform tasks of coordination, negotiation with other governments,
giving of advice to other organs, and so on. Until then, this was made from
different units in the presidency or the ministries of finance. In this trend, the
Spanish case now goes before a path followed by parliamentary federations
such as Germany, Australia, or Canada.

## What Is Then Really Peculiar to Spanish IGR?

To define what is really peculiar of the Spanish case, one should distinguish
between those features that are unique because of the parliamentary system and
the type of legislative-executive relations that it shares with other parliamentary
federations (such as the dominance of the executives or the effects of the party
system) and those elements that are derived from the particular history of the model
institutions, the asymmetric devolution process, and the mode and sequence of
decentralization in a context of different impulses and capacities of self-
government. Even among the latter, one could still distinguish those features that
over time are expected to converge with other federations and those who appear
more structural and more impervious to change. These structural features that are
really "unique" are those that require further attention regarding its consequences
and possible reform. At first glance, we might speak of five possible structural or
systemic unique features:

1. A relatively high level of jurisdictional conflict before the Constitutional Court,
   produced by the constitutional flexibility and the role assigned to the regional
   statutes of autonomy in the constitutional jurisprudence. This naturally entails an
   intense Constitutional Court TC intervention in the system, with the problems
   this can bring;
2. Persistence of some bilateral modes of interaction for some issues that, in other
   countries, are dealt with multilaterally. This situation, which has the potential to
   cause some inefficiency, or inequity and untransparency at times, does not
   encounter, however, and for various reasons, much resistance among central
   government or regional governments;
3. The particular role of central government, its ubiquity, and interventionist
   stance. Although one could argue that this is a feature that will tend to fade
   and can be also found in other federations, both parliamentary or presidential, it
   seems that in Spain, as long as this role is recognized and accepted by most of the
   autonomous communities, the central government will maintain a certain
   *auctoritas* that exceeds their own constitutional powers and that comes probably
   from the inertia of history and the mode of decentralization, i.e., from the initial
   asymmetry, the flexibility of interpretation of competencies, the gradual transfer
   of powers and resources, the funding arrangements, etc. As in other federations,

this feature will remain as long as the weakest autonomous communities do not renounce a strong role of the central government in order to guarantee a certain level of cohesion in the system and as long as horizontal collaboration does not develop to a much larger extent;
4. The existence of IGR bodies not utilized and the tendency toward excessive regulation of cooperation. This feature seems more like a cultural-administrative peculiarity shared with other European legal systems such as France, Italy, or even Germany. It is also determined in part by a sociological condition such as the predominance of the legal training and the legal profession at all levels of public administration as is the case in other states of the Napoleonic tradition;
5. The regional preference for funding through shared and devolved taxes rather than for the utilization of their own source taxes.

Although not unique to Spain, there are also some peculiar features already mentioned that make a change in this features seem difficult. First is the high mobility of top officials and politicians between the two governmental levels. Second is the importance of political parties as alternative mechanisms of intergovernmental relations. We can also mention some practical problems peculiar to the Spanish model of IGR, which are not strictly pathologies or structural features but are derived from the immaturity or lack of system capacity and inertia of certain governmental units in central government. These negative traits in the workings of the system, which have a clear impact on its effectiveness, joint decision-making capacity, and transparency, could be overcome over time and with some focused institutional redesign and reallocation of resources. Being as schematic as above, these practical features can also be summarized in five points:

1. Lack of regular meetings in some intergovernmental ministerial councils or conferences and dependence on the minister's will. There are meetings where the component units do not play a clear or significant role in the calling or chairing thereof. Oftentimes, the dependence on the will of the minister may lead to the opposite evil, an excessive number of intergovernmental extraordinary meetings in some areas without clear goals.
2. Agenda and organizational problems and meeting overload in some first-level or second-level bodies. This often leads to the delegation of attendance duties by regional ministers in their ministerial high officials that must attend numerous committees and councils at different levels, which detracts value and legitimacy from the decisions made in the intergovernmental bodies and sometimes is a clear reflection of regional ministerial overload and lack of staff.
3. Attitudes of lack of commitment and responsiveness by central government representatives. In some sectors when the regional representatives have to be legally consulted within those intergovernmental councils, and they express their views, the central government may not take them seriously enough. Some consultative meetings are used as part of the formal consultation procedure but without appreciable effect on the central government position. In many cases, there is a lack of discussion and deliberation on central government's initiatives that are highly relevant to the autonomous

communities. A perpetuation of some hierarchical relations between spheres in some bodies has been observed.

4. Some practical and procedural problems of operation and organization of inter-governmental bodies. One could mention some procedural shortcomings (concerning issues such as insufficient sharing of information, the meetings' agenda preparation, and lack of minutes, non-attendance or lack of mandate of participants) with possible legal consequences in case of conflicts before the courts. There are also deficiencies in the distribution of previous materials for the meetings and occasional lack of monitoring of regional proposals and critical positions.

5. Problems in monitoring the agreements. The lack of a culture of evaluation of results in Spain is also extended to intergovernmental bodies, which may in some cases jeopardize the effectiveness of some intergovernmental agreements. There is also a lack of focus in cross-cutting issues that should be coordinated with other intergovernmental bodies.

## Recent Developments and Trends: Towards Convergence with Other Federations?

After this rough overview of the academic discussions regarding Spanish IGR and a brief analysis of the unique and not so unique features of the Spanish federal model, one may reflect upon its prospects and eventual convergence with other similar systems. As Roig has pointed out, recent years have seen several important developments that would be producing a new phase in the evolution of the Spanish model, largely characterized by new mechanisms of intergovernmental relationships, increasingly effective, both for collaboration in sectors with concurrent jurisdiction and for participation in joint decisions or central government policies by the autonomous communities (Roig 2008).

The most recent findings of the legal and political science research show how sectoral conferences have overcome, in practice, many of the limitations of constitutional design and within some sectors of public policy have actually become decision-making bodies that increasingly, through intergovernmental agreements, for example, and shared-cost programs between the two levels of government, have become shapers of common and coordinated policies in various sectors, although the central government may retain a role slightly more prominent than in other comparable systems.

Some trends towards sectoral differentiation of cooperation are also noticeable in the system, which seem to be determined in part by the distribution of powers in each of them and by the type of functional activity that is required of public authorities in each case (regulation, distribution of funds, information sharing, consultation on draft EU, or central government, legislation, etc.).

We can also note new trends in joint decision-making and the establishment of collaborative joint bodies, such as the intergovernmental council for adult long-term care, whose standing orders provide for the issuance of agreements that become automatically royal decrees of the central government, through an articulation of both multilateral joint decisions and bilateral agreements between the central government and the autonomous communities or, within the agriculture sector, the new instrument of collaboration called the Rural Development Plan, provided for in the Sustainable Rural Development Act, which binds the central government in policy and financial terms, in its subsequent bilateral agreements with each autonomous community.

Also very important in this new situation is the aforementioned Conference of Presidents, which has produced general agreements in the areas of research or health policy funding but has failed to reach agreements on anti-crisis policy. Its mere existence, however, which makes the Spanish system closer to other well-established federations, represents a qualitative change in the system, which should be carefully monitored in the coming years.

Finally, we can see many activities leading in the direction of increasing horizontal collaboration and coordination between the autonomous communities. In recent years, more and more policy areas have been subject to cooperation between regions through some kind of horizontal agreements. A recent initiative, originally known in 2008 as the regular meetings of the six regions with recently amended statutes of autonomy (Balearic Islands, Catalonia, Andalusia, Castile-Leon, Valencia, Aragon) has turned into a Conference of Regional Governments similar to the Swiss one. Until this conference was finally established in 2011, autonomous communities have met and reached agreements to boost cooperation or make political statements on current and institutional affairs. It is also expected that soon a conference of regional presidents may be established. All these trends do increasingly equate the situation of the Spanish IGR with that in other more established federations.

## Conclusions: An Interim Evaluation and an Agenda for Research

Overall, and despite the large number of issues dealt with by the Spanish, and some foreign, literature on IGR, relevant to understanding the practice of cooperation in the autonomic State, there are arguably many more avenues to explore in addition to strengthening the emerging ones noted above. As this chapters has pointed out, among the topics that are still awaiting further systematic and empirical study both from juridical and political science, one could mention, without being exhaustive: the development, configuration and real power of the new intergovernmental management units at both levels of government, the concentration in the hands of the regional premiers of intergovernmental activity, the role of parliaments as arenas of IGR, the particular intergovernmental role of the Senate Committee of the Autonomous Communities, as well as specific sectoral studies, aimed at understanding the mechanisms and consequences of cooperation in sectors such as long-term care, health, education, research and innovation, environment, etc.

It is true that the study of IGR necessitates many resources, a costly methodology and information that is not always available to individual researchers and increasingly requires collective and more ambitious research projects. In any case, we should welcome the recent interest for IGR in Spain shown by various social scientific disciplines that join the traditional interest of public law and can thus complement their particular view sometimes limited to the legal definition of IGR institutions and instruments, which is usually not the most important component in the study of IGR. One should also be grateful to the growing support of certain public research institutions that have supported ambitious research projects (Arbós et al. 2009; Leon and Ferrin 2009) and have represented a significant advance on the previous situation and reflect a growing interest in the governments they represent to know the actual operation of intergovernmental collaboration and try to improve it.

# References

Arbós, X.; C. Colino, M. García Morales, S. Parrado (2009). Las relaciones Intergubernamentales en el Estado autonómico: la posición de los actores, Barcelona: Institut d'Estudis Autonòmics.

Bakvis, H. G. Baier y D. Brown (2009). Contested Federalism. Certainty and Ambiguity in the Canadian Federation, Toronto: Oxford University Press.

Bednar, J. (2009). The robust federation. Principles of Design. Cambridge: Cambridge University Press.

Bochsler, D. (2009). "Neighbours or Friends? When Swiss Cantonal Governments Co-operate with Each Other", Regional & Federal Studies, 19: 3, 349–370.

Bolleyer, N. (2006). "Federal Dynamics un Canada, the United States and Switzerland: How Substates' Internal Organization Affects Intergovernmental Relations." Publius: The Journal of Federalism: 1–32.

Cameron, D. y Simeon, R. (2002). "Intergovernmental Relations in Canada: The Emergence of Collaborative Federalism", Publius: The Journal of Federalism, Vol.32, No.2, pp.49–71.

Colino, C. (2010). "¿Hacia la normalidad federal? La existencia y el surgimiento reciente de nuevos mecanismos para la cooperación horizontal entre CCAA", en J. Tudela y F. Knüpling (eds.) España y modelos de federalismo, Madrid CEPC/Fundación Manuel Giménez Abad.

Colino, C. (2011) "Federalismo horizontal en el Estado autonómico. La evolución de los mecanismos de cooperación horizontal en España", Cuadernos Manuel Giménez Abad, num. 2, 43–55.

Colino, C. y S. Parrado (2009). "Análisis de la práctica y la dinámica de los procesos formales e informales de las relaciones intergubernamentales", en X. Arbós, C. Colino, M. García Morales, S. Parrado Relaciones Intergubernamentales en el Estado autonómico: la posición de los actores, Barcelona: Institut d'Estudis Autonòmics, 135–296.

Dupré, J. S. (1985). "Reflections on the Workability of Executive Federalism," in Richard Simeon ed. Intergovernmental Relations, Toronto: University of Toronto Press.

Fabre, E. and M. Méndez Lago (2009). "Decentralization and Party Organizational Change: The British and Spanish Statewide Parties Compared", en Wilfried Swenden y Bart Maddens Eds. Territorial Party Politics in Western Europe, London: Palgrave.

García Morales, M. J. (2009a). "La colaboración a examen. Retos y riesgos de las relaciones intergubernamentales en el Estado autonómico", *Revista Española de Derecho Constitucional*, núm. 86, mayo-agosto, 65–117.

García Morales, M. J. (2009b). "Los nuevos estatutos de autonomía y las relaciones de colaboración, Un nuevo escenario, ¿una nueva etapa?", *Revista Jurídica de Castilla y León*, 19.

González, A. (2006). "La cooperación multilateral institucionalizada: las Conferencias Sectoriales", en Lourdes López Nieto (coord.) Relaciones intergubernamentales en la España democrática. Interdependencia, autonomía, conflicto y cooperación, Madrid: Dykinson, 97–114.

Gordin, J. P. (2004). Unraveling the politics of decentralization: Argentina and Spain in comparative perspective, PhD Thesis, University of Pittsburgh.

Grau i Creus, M. (2000). "Spain: Incomplete Federalism", en Ute Wachendorfer-Schmidt (eds.), *Federalism and Political Performance*, London/New York: Routledge.

Inwood, G. J., C. M. Johns, and P. L. O' Reilly (2011). *Intergovernmental policy capacity in Canada. Inside the Worlds of Finance, Environment, Trade, and Health*, Montreal: McGill-Queen's University Press.

Johns, C. M., P. L. O' Reilly y G. J. Inwood, (2007). "Formal and informal dimensions of intergovernmental administrative relations in Canada", *Canadian Public Administration*, Volume 50 Issue 1, 21–41.

Kissling-Näf, I. Y S. Wälti (1999). "Der Vollzug öffentlicher Politiken", en U. Klöti, P. Knoepfel, H. Kriesi, W. Linder y Y. Papaopoulos (eds.) *Handbuch der Schweizer Politik - Manuel de la politique suisse*. Zürich: NZZ Verlag, 651–689.

Kropp, S. (2010). *Kooperativer Föderalismus und Politikverflechtung*, Wiesbaden: WS verlag für Sozialwissenschaften.

León, S. (2007). *The Political Economy of Fiscal Decentralization. Bringing Politics to the Study of Intergovernmental Transfers*, Barcelona: Institut d'Estudis Autonòmics.

León, S. and M. Ferrín (2009). *La cooperación intergubernamental en el Estado autonómico*, Santiago de Compostela, Escola Galega de Administración Pública.

León, S. and M. Ferrín (2011). "Intergovernmental cooperation in a decentralised system: the Sectoral Conferences in Spain", *South European Society and Politics*, 16(4), 513–32.

Meekison, J. P. ed. (2001). *Las relaciones intergubernamentales en los países federales*, Otawa. Forum of Federations.

Meekison, J. P.; H. Telford y H. Lazar (2004). "The Institutions of Executive Federalism: Myths and Realities", en J. P. Meekison, H. Telford and H. Lazar (eds) *Reconsidering the Institutions of Canadian Federalism. The State of the Federation 2002*, Montreal & Kingston: McGill-Queen's University Press, 3–31.

Nugent, J. D. (2009). *Safeguarding Federalism. How States protect their Interests in national Policymaking*, Norman: University of Oklahoma Press.

O' M. Bowman, A. (2004). "Horizontal Federalism: Exploring Interstate Interactions", *Journal of Public Administration Research and Theory*, Vol. 14, (4), 535–546.

Painter, M. (1996). "The Council of Australian Governments and Intergovernmental Relations: A Case of Cooperative Federalism", *Publius: The Journal of Federalism*, Vol.26, No.2, pp.101–120.

Painter, M. (2001). "Multi-level governance and the emergence of collaborative federal institutions in Australia", *Policy and Politics* 29(2): 137–150.

Parrado, S. (2010). "The role of Spanish Central Government in a Multi-level State", *International Review of Administrative Sciences* 76(3), 469–488.

Poirier, J. (2004). "Intergovernmental Agreements in Canada: At the Crossroads between Law and Politics", en H. Lazar, J. P. Meekison, H. Telford eds. *The State of the Federation 2002: Reconsidering the Institutions of Canadian Federalism*, McGill-Queen's University, 425–462.

Pollard, B. G. (1986). *Managing the Interface: Intergovernmental Affairs Agencies in Canada*, Kingston: Institute of Intergovernmental Relations.

Ramos, J. A., (2006). "Las Comisiones Bilaterales de Cooperación en el sistema español de relaciones intergubernamentales", en Lourdes López Nieto (coord.) Relaciones intergubernamentales en la España democrática. Interdependencia, autonomía, conflicto y cooperación, Madrid: Dykinson, 115–132.

Roig, E. (2008). "La regulació de les relacions de la Generalitat amb l'Estat en el nou Estatut d'Autonomia de Catalunya", *Activitat Parlamentària*, N°. 15, 63–77.

Scheller, H. and J. Schmid eds. (2008). *Föderale Politikgestaltung im deutschen Bundesstaat. Variable Verflechtungsmusterin Politikfeldern*, Baden-Baden: Nomos.

Stein, M. y L. Turkewitsch (2009). "Similarities and Differences in Patterns of Intergovernmental Relations in Parliamentary and Presidential Federations: A Comparative Analysis", Paper Presented to the International Political Science Association (IPSA) 21st World Congress of Political Science, Santiago de Chile, July 14.

Trench, A. (2006). "Intergovernmental Relations: In Search of a Theory", en: Scott L. Greer (ed.). *Territory, Democracy and Justice. Regionalism and Federalism in Western Democracies.* Nueva York: Palgrave Mac-Millan.

Warhurst, J., (1987). "Managing Intergovernmental Relations", in H. Bakvis y W. M. Chandler eds. *Federalism and the Role of the State*, Toronto: University of Toronto Press,

Watts, R. L. (2003). "Intergovernmental Councils in Federations, Constructive or Co-operative Federalism?", Working Paper No.2, IIGR Montreal: Queen's University.

Zimmerman, J. F. (2002), *Interstate Cooperation: Compacts and Administrative Agreements*, Wesport: Praeger.

# The Principle of Separation of Powers in Crisis: Intergovernmental Relations in Comparative Perspective

Eleonora Ceccherini

**Abstract** Every decentralized state has got the problems about the relationships between the different institutional levels. One kind of relationships can be expressed by the Senate, but in some decentralized States the Second Chamber is no longer perceived as an effective mechanism of representation of the regional (or federated) entities.

Therefore, interstate federalism can be preferred to intrastate federalism, increasing the role of government branch as to legislative assemblies.

The co-operation among institutional levels gives birth to a tight network of relation between the different levels of government and is substantiated with a variety of involved actors and concrete procedures. To have a classification of these relations, the doctrine referred to institutional and functional cooperation. The first drove to the creation of some organs that gather both state bodies and regional and local ones. The "State–Regions" Conference is a significant example, together with the Conferencias sectoriales in Spain or the Joint committee in the U.K. Hereafter, our attention will move to the co-operation forms between government levels from which acts and procedures arise. Such acts and procedures are a result of the meeting between the different representatives of the administrations. This helps to speed up the administrative process and to improve, then, the public performance quality. For instance, we can cite the Austrian *öffentlich-rechtliche Verträge*

In conclusion, I'd like to underline two points: One, there is an increase of intergovernmental relationships in the decentralized States. This trend can be explained with the reason to give the regional level a collective voice in the national policy process, especially, where no regional second chambers exist. The second point is: the institutions of intergovernmental relationships are clearly important for the development of coherent policy, but they can reduce the legislative role. The intergovernmental institutions operate in a space between the region and the Member state levels, and as the decisions reached are a compromise between

E. Ceccherini (✉)
University of Genoa, Via Balbi 22, 16126 Genova, Italy
e-mail: eleonora.ceccherini@unige.it

A. López-Basaguren and L. Escajedo San Epifanio (eds.), *The Ways of Federalism in Western Countries and the Horizons of Territorial Autonomy in Spain*, Vol. 2, DOI 10.1007/978-3-642-27717-7_8, © Springer-Verlag Berlin Heidelberg 2013

executives, neither the member state parliament nor the regional legislature will be responsible for the decisions taken. Despite this, they may be obliged to follow these decisions.

**Keywords**  Judiciary power • Legislative power • Multilevel state

## Federal States–Regional States: Different Origin, Common Destiny?

From the point of view of the relationship between sovereignty and territory, states can be divided into centralized and composite ones, with the latter being formed, in turn, by regional or federal states.

The assignment of competences between the central government and the centralized units is usually carried out through a normative act that determines a list of subjects. This technique provides legal certainty and guarantees the autonomy of the territorial communities. However, while bearing in mind that it is not possible to completely put aside the necessary existence of lists of competences, history compels us to realize that these lists represent inadequate tools since the boundaries of the areas of competences are necessarily mobile. Firstly, notwithstanding the comprehensive vocation of these lists, the economic, social, and technological developments create new areas that challenge traditional classifications. Secondly, it is worth bearing in mind that these lists identify subject matters using linguistic expressions not consistent or in tune with their legal meaning, especially in light of the fact that, from a normative standpoint, it is not possible to define a single subject matter but only to identify a group of norms that connect different functions, activities, and institutions. Thirdly, notwithstanding the tendency to draft these lists in a comprehensive way, the Constitution at the same time hosts general definitions that work as safety clauses for the crystallization of the division of competences.

Therefore, the competences can be effectively implemented only through a joint and coordinated action of the multiple institutional levels that share common profiles in the various areas. This cooperative action is increasingly often carried out by means of intergovernmental relations conducted through relations between representatives of the executive branch, which can be either horizontal (if the members of the executive branch belong to the same institutional category) or vertical (if the relation involves government members of different territorial areas) (Rolla 2011).

The emergence of this tendency has two consequences: the first affects the legislature, while the second affects the judiciary.

With regard to the first aspect, a phenomenon of competition/subsidiarity in the intergovernmental relations with the territorial Senate has emerged. Indeed, historically, at the beginning cooperation between the center and the periphery was established through the creation of a legislative assembly representative of the territorial communities. This solution was consistent with the liberal view that looked at legislative power as the center of the whole system, built around the concept of statutory law as the main source of law. However, the development of composite States has shown some critical profiles connected to the functioning of the High Chamber of territorial inspiration. Firstly, it has been underlined how the Senate cannot be any longer identified with a Chamber of the States since the representatives elected therein are now more responsive to party logics than to territorial interests; secondly, since modern States perform a higher number of functions, they also need that the competences pertaining either to the central State or to the decentralized entities be clearly spelled out; this process of identification, however, would not be completely compatible with the characters of generality and abstractness typical of legislation.

Indeed, it is possible to be a witness to the consolidation of interstate federalism dynamics, according to which the relation between center and periphery is declined through the action of the executive and is based on negotiation processes (Ruggiu 2006).

However, this tendency upsets the balance between the executive and legislative powers to the advantage of the executive powers (both State and Regional) and to the detriment of the role of the legislative assemblies.

This phenomenon is usually associated to a more recent one, according to which members of the executive powers are also vested with the power to solve the conflicts of competence in which they happen to be involved. Indeed, the parties to the conflict would be inclined to find mechanisms to solve the conflict among themselves in order to avoid recourse to a jurisdictional procedure, traditionally considered a safeguard for the autonomies. This tendency shows at least two elements: The first concerns the role of Courts and the downgrading of the parameters of judicial legitimacy in solving controversies; the second element concerns the general approach to controversies, which brings about the disappearance of an impartial—or at least equally distant from the parties—subject, to rely exclusively on the parties themselves.

## Examples of Cooperation in Comparative Law

After addressing this tendency, it is now necessary to classify the intergovernmental relations, whose manifestation may give raise to the form of institutional cooperation and to the establishment of bodies or functional forms of cooperation, that is, the improvement of acts and procedures. Furthermore, the cooperation can be either horizontal or vertical.

Composite systems have not developed final choices within this area, being drawn mainly towards the establishment of various types of intergovernmental relations, whose outcome is dependent more upon the peculiarities of the single countries than on the quality of one type against another. What is worth emphasizing is that this is a tendency that is absolutely shared by all composite systems.

Outside of Europe, the Australian and Canadian experiences are worth mentioning. In the former, the example is represented by the Council of Australian Governments, established in 1992 and composed of the Prime Minister, by States Premiers, by Territory Chief Ministers, and by the President of the Australian Local Government Association. Its functions consist in carrying out joint actions and politics between the different levels of government within the defined areas: health, education and training, Indian reform, early childhood development, housing, microeconomic reform, climate change and energy water reform, natural disaster arrangements. With regard to Canada, the negotiation between the two institutional levels that finalized the solution and clarification of the exercise of each level's competences appears to have become a dominant methodology, so much that it has been said that "[m]ore than other federations, Canada relies on intergovernmental negotiation to help resolve political differences" (Magnet 1993).

The negotiation is articulated on different levels, in which not only the Prime Ministers of the provinces and the federation are involved—that is, the subjects in charge of the Ministries of the territorial entities and of the central State—but also, and mainly, provincial and federal public officials with overlapping responsibilities. The agreements emerging from this process usually represent a complex series of compromises that cannot be changed without completely falling apart. Consequently, these agreements are presented to the federal Parliament and the provincial legislative bodies exclusively for ratification, reducing therefore the possibility of detailed examination and robust public debate.

Among the most relevant areas in which intergovernmental relations have played a primary role, it is possible to identify that of the international relations pertaining to foreign commerce, an area of competence assigned to the federation. Indeed, before ratifying international agreements, whose implementation would bring about consequences in areas falling within the exclusive competence of the provinces, the territorial communities actively participated to the signing of the international agreements through a series of meetings between the members of their own executive bodies and the federal negotiators. This process has become an example of a system of core-periphery relationship suitable to safeguard the autonomy of the decentralized instances and in a way qualitatively equivalent to a centralized representative body (Feldman and Gardner Feldman 1984).

It is mostly due to worldwide processes of economic globalization that the division of competences between the central State and the autonomies is affected, since it is the increasing tendency to establish international organizations operating in areas falling within the purview of the sub-national units' reserved competences that can create a "centripetal" movement. It is worth noting, for instance, that this phenomenon upsets the systems of divisions of competences as established by Constitutions and shifts the attention from the owner of the competence to the articulation of the decisional processes. The decentralized States of the European continent face a process of supranational integration that, on one hand, appears to be centripetal with regard to the EU institutional bodies and, on the other hand, puts under strain the division of competences between the core and the periphery codified in the Constitutions.

It is not by chance, therefore, that the intergovernmental relations focus part of their efforts in the attempt to find a forum for consultative policies between central and local authorities within the EU area.

In this respect, it is possible to refer, as examples, to three different systems: the Italian, the British, and the Spanish ones.

Italy, by way of Legislative Decree no. 281/1997, attempted to the rationalize the activity of as many as three intergovernmental Conferences: the State–Regions and Autonomous Provinces Conference, the State–Cities Local Autonomies Conference, and the one resulting from the unification of the two previously mentioned ones – the State–Regions–Autonomous Provinces–Cities Local Autonomies Conference. The liaison activity is mainly conducted by the State–Regions and Autonomous Provinces Conference, which can promote and sign understandings and agreements to further the harmonization of State and Regional legislation, the achievement of shared positions, and the achievement of goals common to the central Government and the Regions (D'Atena 2007).

All the more so, it is within this very Conference that the governmental actions of guidance and coordination abolished by a 2001 constitutional reform have resurfaced and are currently conducted in a consultative manner within the Conferences. The various institutional levels are therefore jointly responsible for the integrated and functional exercise of their respective competences and must act consistently with the principle of loyal cooperation. In addition to the function of connection and coordination, the State–Regions Conference carries out important tasks with regard to the relationship with the European Union. More specifically, when a draft Community normative act falls within the area of competence reserved to the Regions, the Government convenes the State–Regions Conference in order to reach an agreement; at the same time, it is possible to request the Government to make mandatory a review by the Council of Ministers. Furthermore, a Communitarian session of the Conference is foreseen, devoted to the analysis of those aspects of the Community policies that are of Regional interest. Finally, Law no. 131/2003 and Law no. 11/2005 have left some room for an intervention both in the rising and in the descending phases of the Community's normative acts addressing horizontal cooperation through the Conference of the Presidents of the Regions (Parodi and Puoti 2007).

This European Community-related aspects enjoy primary importance also in the United Kingdom, where the institutional and functional cooperation is regulated by the Memorandum of Understanding and Supplementary Agreements, an agreement entered into on 1 October 1999 by the British, the Scottish, and Welsh Governments and, in 2000, agreed to also by the Northern Ireland Government, whose aim is to clarify "the principles which underlie relations" between the different institutional levels. The Memorandum expressly establishes that the Memorandum itself and the agreements based upon it are not binding. However, it is worth pointing out that the clauses of the Memorandum have been complied with, given the general perception of these tools as useful in making more flexible the functioning and implementation of the processes of decentralization.

This is consistent with a recurring factor in the British legal system, that is, the central role played by so-called "soft-law". The mandatory character of the Memorandum is therefore conditioned upon the willingness of the parties to abide by it, in a view that can be likened to compliance with the principle of loyal cooperation.

The Memorandum has foreseen the establishment of the Joint Ministerial Committee, a body composed of the Prime Minister (or his representatives), the Scottish and Welsh First Ministers, the Northern Ireland First Minister and Deputy First Minister, and the Secretaries of State for Scotland, Wales, and North Ireland.

The Committee is assigned the task to monitor the implementation of the concordats and of the Memorandum and has jurisdiction over issues that may arise with regard to both matters delegated and not delegated to the regions and, most importantly, with regard to those areas where these matters overlap. This collegial body may also represent a place to establish and keep under review liaison arrangements between the UK Government and the territorial autonomies and exchange information between the administrations. Furthermore, it is worth highlighting that the UK position within the EU Council of Ministers is formulated within the Committee, a circumstance of special interest for the devolved administrations.

The Memorandum also addresses forms of functional cooperation through concordats. These arrangements are instrumental to a uniform application of the law in certain given areas and further administrative cooperation and exchange of information and represent the mechanisms through which the UK system has tried to address problems in the cooperation between various institutional levels at a post-devolutionary stage. In a most effective way, these arrangements have been defined as the "glue of a reinvented Union State" (Rawlings 2000). The Memorandum identifies the need to adopt four main concordats in as many areas where the need for coordinate action and consistency is deemed of primary importance, which are the coordination of EU policy and implementation, financial assistance to industry, international relations touching on the responsibilities of the devolved administrations, and statistical surveys.

Other specifying arrangements, holding a hierarchically subordinate status, can join the abovementioned typologies and can be entered into bilaterally (Poirer 2001).

A further element of significant importance for regional autonomies is provided by the common attachment to the concordat on international relationships, which establishes the general prerequisites for the international activity of the decentralized institutional levels in the areas falling under their competence, in cooperation with the Foreign Common Office. The Office must be consulted before taking actions from which an international responsibility could arise. In those cases in which, conversely, the negotiation between States falls within the area of competence of the Regions, the concordat foresees the possibility that representatives from the Regions can join the national delegation.

The theme of intergovernmental relationships is also present in the Spanish system, which currently foresees mechanisms of institutional cooperation like the Conference of the Presidents, composed of the Presidents of the Government and of the Autonomous Communities; or like the Multilateral *Sectoriales Conferencias* where the heads of the executive bodies with subject-matter competence participate in the meetings and those of functional cooperation declined through *convenios* (Ridaura Martínez 2009).

The rationale underlining the existence of the *convenios* is opposite to the one at the basis of the conferences; indeed, the latter are multilateral bodies to which all the Autonomous Communities participate equally. The establishment of *convenios*, conversely, is inspired by the principle of bilateralism, according to which each Autonomous Community negotiates directly with the central State, without the need or concern to find a common position with the other Communities. The most immediate and positive consequences of the multilateral bodies with regard to the *convenios* are represented by the establishment of a unified place for debate, where the most "autonomous" positions are moderated during the phases of negotiation to the advantage of the general safeguard of the system (García Morales 2009).

With more specific regard to the theme of the participation of the intra-State entities to the supranational process of integration, it is worth underlining the establishment in 1992 of the *conferencia sectorial para los asuntos relacionados con la Union Europea* and, most importantly, the more recent creation of *consejos consultivos* within the respective sectional conferences, whose activity is finalized to the determination of the Spanish position within the Council of Ministers of the European Unión (*consejo consultivo de política agricola*, de política medioambiental, de política pesquera). These latter bodies have recorded the highest number of meetings in the past year, compared to all the other conferencias sectoriales: a testimony, of the rising sensibility devoted to this matter.

## The Para-Jurisdictional Negotiation

Another function carried out by these cooperative bodies is the subsidiarity function conducted with regard to the traditional jurisdictional bodies competent to address controversies.

A forerunner system, in this respect, is the Belgian one, which, with the Law of institutional reform of 9 August 1980, has established a consultative committee. This body is composed of the President and five representatives of the federal Government, the President and a member of the Flemish government, the President of the francophone community, the President of the Walloon community, the President (normally a francophone) and the first member of the other linguistic community of the Bruxelles region. The committee is vested with the task to prevent the conflicts of competence and interests between the different institutional levels. In the first case, whenever a draft statute or decree is deemed to encroach on the competences, the Council of States submits the controversy to the committee that, within forty days, must address the conflict; in the event the conflict is not solved by the committee, the draft statute or decree can again be considered for approval. In case of conflicts of interest, if an assembly deems that a draft statute or decree is vitiated in the merits, 3/4 of the members can ask that consideration of the draft be suspended in order to seek a compromise with the other assembly. If these attempts prove unsuccessful, the Senate will invite the consultative committee to an attempt of mediation, which must conclude within 30 days; in this case as well, in the event an agreement is not reached, the draft statute or decree can again be considered for approval. In the exercise of this function, the Committee must reach its decisions unanimously, and therefore each member is vested wtih veto power. The analysis of this procedure furthers a few reflections. It should be underlined that the subjects that enter into a State–Region and Communities agreement are formally on an equal footing; that is, there is not hierarchical relationship between the various institutional levels involved in the process, especially since each subject has veto power.

With regard to the controversies on the implementation of close cooperative agreements among the various institutional levels, the *loi spéciale de réformes institutionnelles* of 8 August 1990 introduces the possibility to establish an arbitration board, where each of the parties to the agreement elects a board member and the board has competence over the interpretation and abidance to the agreement's provisions by the contracting parties. The decision of the board is final, and its content is enforceable. These bodies with a clear intergovernmental origin are assigned the task to decide conflicts of competences on a political basis in order to limit jurisdictional recourses. This also appears to be the purpose of the bilateral commissions of cooperation between the State and the autonomous communities in Spain, on the basis of Organic Law no. 1 of 2000 of the Constitutional tribunal, which established that in case of conflict between the State and the Autonomous Communities over a law or an act with the force of law, the term within which a recourse must be filed is extended from three to nine months in case a conciliatory procedure before the bilateral Commission of cooperation is activated by the parties (Tornos Mas 2002). In analogy with the Belgian consultative committee, the members of the bilateral Commission are the representatives of the executive bodies of the respective institutional levels, and analogously, the Spanish body has the task to activate a conciliatory procedure between the parties in order to avoid a controversy before the Constitutional Tribunal. However, in the Spanish case, in analogy to the Belgian one, if the bilateral Commission of cooperation is not able to adequately solve the conflict, the parties can always resort to the possibility to activate the procedure before the constitutional court. In the United Kingdom as well, the Joint Ministerial Committee has taken on extrajudicial competences, thanks to the Protocol for avoidance and resolution disputes attached to the Memorandum of Understanding. More specifically, it is worth highlighting an aspect that emphasizes the difference between recourse to the classic jurisdictional avenues and recourse to intergovernmental bodies. While the former provides a motivated decision on the legitimacy of the act or action, the latter, conversely, takes into account also the merits of these acts; indeed, the Protocol establishes that the application can be filed whenever "circumstances, particularly those arising from differences in political outlook" are deemed to be present.

The Protocol details a six-step procedure, ranging from bureaucratic consultations to an exam by the heads of the various governments in a plenum meeting of the Committee. In case an agreement is not reached, the jurisdictional avenue remains available.

Therefore, the Committee has a complementing-subsidiary function that applies to conflicts among different powers, with the purpose to avoid or limiting disputes.


## Conclusions

The expansion of the intergovernmental relations as operative units of decentralized States, beyond the actual methods through which they are carried out (multilateral, bilateral, functional, institutional), highlights the progressive establishment of a relational—as opposed to hierarchical—system. This undoubtedly contrasts with the established and traditional core-periphery relationships previously conducted in a manner consistent with the principle of supremacy, with the State at the higher level of the hierarchy. This process has two corollaries: The first concerns the role of soft-law sources of law, while the second addresses the preservation of the constitutional rigidity.

With regard to the former aspect, it is possible to witness the progressive permeation of soft-law sources into the system, that is, acts that increasingly affect the division of competences established in full-fledged normative acts. Therefore, it is not just the hierarchical setting of the institutions that is abandoned but that of the sources of law as well.

This statement leads therefore to reconsideration of both the civil law principle mandating tipicity of legal acts and—especially—of the principle of legality. In the end, civil law systems should reconsider the role of those conventional sources of law that, in common law systems, significantly contribute to the fluidity of the relations between different territorial levels.

With regard to the latter aspect, it is worth pointing out how the higher degree of deliberation involved in co-decisional procedures contributes to the blurring of the legal parameters of the division of competences defined in normative sources. Indeed, composite legal systems try to supplement the jurisdictional avenues with merit-based (rather than legitimacy-based) mechanisms of composition of conflicts. Indeed, when a competence-based conflict is solved within consultative bodies, it cannot be excluded that the final outcome may actually be in violation of constitutional provisions, therefore mitigating the rigidity of the constitution. Figuratively, this new face in the prism of intergovernmental relations appears to represent a further declination and development of the subsidiarity principle, no longer limited to administrative functions but now applying also to the jurisdictional ones (Ruggeri 2011).

The constitutional division of functions between the State or and the territorial communities, on the other hand, has already been put under strain by the EU process of supranational integration that, in eroding the sovereignty of the, also affects devolved entities (D'Ignazio 2011). This centripetal process is able to explain in part the reason for the vocation of the intergovernmental relations with the international-communitarian landscape. Indeed undoubtedly, Community law exerts a perilous re-modulation of the areas of decentralized autonomy connected to the international responsibility of the central State. In conclusion, we would like to emphasize how inter-institutional cooperation downsizes the role of the legislative power, which, through an efficient system of bicameral representation of the communities, could represent an element of cohesion of the whole federal system (Allegretti 1996). However, it is undeniable that we are witnessing, in the majority of the democratic systems, the predominance of the executive bodies in the determination of the general policy; within this landscape, the intergovernmental relations represent the tangible aspect of this alteration in the relations between different State powers. In order to overcome the abovementioned critics, it appears more useful to modify a few aspects pertaining to the implementation of the intergovernmental relations, trying to engage more significantly the representative bodies and enhancing transparency of the collective body.

In this view, it is worth mentioning the experience of the German *Bundesrat* that, like a two-faced Janus, on one hand, is part of the legislative power and, on the other, is composed of members of the executives of the Landers and that, therefore, can represent—at least theoretically—a well-designed synthesis of these two different profiles.

# References

Allegretti, U. (1996) Per una camera "territoriale": problemi e scelte. Quaderni dell'associazione di studi e ricerche parlamentari 7: 75.

D'Atena, A. (2007) Regionalismo e integrazione sovranazionale in prospettiva europea e comparata. In: Floridia, G. and Orrù, R. (eds) Meccanismi e tecniche di normazione fra livello comunitario e livello nazionale e subnazionale. Giappichelli, Torino, Italy, pp. 148–159.

D'Ignazio, G. (2011) Le sfide del costituzionalismo multilivello tra il trattato di Lisbona e le riforme degli ordinamenti decentrati. In: D'Ignazio, G. (ed.) Multilevel Constitutionalism tra integrazione europea e riforme degli ordinamenti decentrati. Giuffrè, Milano, Italy, 6–11.

Feldman E. J., Gardner Feldman L. (1984) The Impact of Federalism on the Organization of Canadian Foreign Policy. Publius 4: 40 ff.

García Morales M.J. (2009) La colaboración a examen. Retos y riesgos de las relaciones interguber-namentales en el Estado Autonómico. Revista española de derecho constitutional: 65.

Magnet J.E. (1993) Constitutional Law of Canada. Juriliber, Edmonton, Canada, 107.

Parodi G., Puoti M.E. (2007) L'attuazione del diritto comunitario nelle materie di competenza regionale dopo la legge n. 11 del 2005. In: Floridia G. and Orrù, R. (eds) Meccanismi e tecniche di normazione fra livello comunitario e livello nazionale e subnazionale. Giappichelli, Torino, Italy, pp. 89–116.

Poirer J. (2001) The Functions of Intergovernmental Agreements: Post-Devolution Concordats in A Comparative Perspectives. Public Law: 148.

Rawlings, R. (2000) *Concordats of the Constitution*. Law Quarterly Review 116: 261.

Ridaura Martínez, J. (2009), Relaciones intergubernamentales: Estado-Comunidades Autónomas. Tirant lo Blanch.

Rolla, G. (2011), Lineamenti del regionalismo nei sistemi costituzionali multilivello. Un approccio di diritto comparato. In: D'Ignazio, G. (ed.) Multilevel Constitutionalism tra integrazione europea e riforme degli ordinamenti decentrati. Giuffrè, Milano, Italy, 157–170.

Ruggeri, A. (2011), Dinamiche della normazione e valori, nella prospettiva di una ricomposizione "multilivello" del sistema delle fonti. In: D'Ignazio, G. (ed.) Multilevel Constitutionalism tra integrazione europea e riforme degli ordinamenti decentrati. Giuffrè, Milano, Italy, 30–46.

Ruggiu, I. (2006) Contro la Camera delle Regioni, Jovene, Napoli, Italy.

Tornos Mas, J. (2002), Órganos mixtos de colaboración y reducción de la conflictividad. Revista de estudios autonomicos 1: 201.

# Roads to Rome: Alternative Intergovernmental Routes to Policy Frameworks in Federations

Jennifer Wallner

**Abstract** All federations must find ways to create and maintain policy frameworks to guide the decisions of authoritative actors within specific sectors. The division of powers, however, profoundly complicates the formulation of policy frameworks, and achieving them requires intergovernmental processes that breathe life into the formal division of powers to allow actors from the various constituent units to develop and install shared directives to guide policy choices within the pertinent sectors. This paper examines the alternative intergovernmental roads that authoritative actors use to develop policy frameworks creating a typology of vertical and horizontal. Drawing on the work of Smiley (1987), who demonstrated the salience of *intragovernmental* relations for the organization and execution of *intergovernmental* relations, we can begin to systematically anticipate the types of intergovernmental processes that will tend to dominate within a federal system. Following Radin and Boase (2000), this paper also considers how the configuration of intergovernmental relations and the workability of certain processes are also affected by the underlying logic of the broader political system. Factors beyond institutions must nevertheless be added into the mix, as norms and culture influence the workability of certain interactions and the crystallization of policy frameworks (Wallner 2012). Correctly anticipating the configuration and subsequent results of intergovernmental relations to install frameworks thus requires careful identification of internal groupings and cultural synergies at work within a particular federation.

J. Wallner (✉)
Faculty of Social Sciences, University of Ottawa, 55 Laurier Avenue East, Desmarais Building, Room 9109, 120 University, Ottawa, ON, Canada K1N 6N5
e-mail: jennifer.wallner@uottawa.ca

A. López-Basaguren and L. Escajedo San Epifanio (eds.), *The Ways of Federalism in Western Countries and the Horizons of Territorial Autonomy in Spain*, Vol. 2, DOI 10.1007/978-3-642-27717-7_9, © Springer-Verlag Berlin Heidelberg 2013

All federations must find ways to create and maintain policy frameworks to guide the decisions of actors within specific sectors. The division of powers, however, profoundly complicates the formulation of policy frameworks. By constitutionally allocating policy competencies between at least two orders of government, policy capacity and authority is not maintained by a single sovereign entity. The achievement of policy frameworks thus requires intergovernmental processes that breathe life into the formal division of powers to allow actors from the various constituent units to develop and install shared directives to guide policy choices within pertinent sectors.

This paper examines the alternative intergovernmental roads that authoritative actors use to develop policy frameworks creating a typology divided between vertical and horizontal processes. In so doing, I map out the characteristics of the various processes and the conditions that make certain types of intergovernmental interactions more likely. Drawing on the work of Smiley (1987), who demonstrated the salience of *intragovernmental relations* for the organization and execution of *intergovernmental* relations, we can begin to systematically anticipate the types of intergovernmental processes that will tend to dominate within a federal system. Following Radin and Boase (2000), moreover, I also consider how the configuration of intergovernmental relations and the workability of certain processes are also affected by the underlying logic of the broader political system. Factors beyond institutions must nevertheless be added into the mix, as norms and culture influence the workability of certain interactions and the crystallization of policy frameworks (Wallner 2012). Correctly anticipating the configuration and subsequent results of intergovernmental relations to install frameworks thus requires careful identification of internal groupings and cultural synergies at work within a particular federation.

To help illuminate the alternative roads to policy frameworks, I draw on material from Canada and the United States focusing on the field of education. These two federations were initially designed according to the principles of dual federalism where large numbers of competencies—including education—were constitutionally assigned to afford the two orders of government considerable autonomy to exercise their respective powers (Bolleyer 2006a: 475). Furthermore, in contrast to a number of other federations, both countries have only loosely institutionalized their respective intergovernmental infrastructures—suggesting that the formulation of policy frameworks should be a considerable challenge. Despite these obstacles, both countries have worked to establish overarching frameworks but have taken noticeably different routes with considerably different results.

I advance the argument in four stages. It opens by defining policy frameworks, articulating some benefits that can be derived from them, and the challenges that federations face in formulating them. The second section maps out the alternative roads to framework formulation, distinguishing between vertical and horizontal processes. The third section compares the emergence of K-12 policy frameworks in Canada and the United States. The evidence reveals that horizontal processes have dominated in Canada, with the national government completely excluded, while vertical processes that have prevailed in the US carried on the back of increasing federal intervention into the field. Interestingly, however, the framework in Canada demonstrates more subnational consistency than the one at work in the US. I argue that these differences in intergovernmental processes and the subsequent outcomes stem from institutional and cultural factors of these two federations. I conclude with a brief discussion of these findings and consider the lessons that can be applied to emerging federations, like Spain.

## Policy Frameworks and Federations

Policy frameworks are the scaffolding that guides the actions and choices of decision-makers. While frameworks vary in the level of details included within them, hallmarks include defined objectives and goals of a particular sector or for a specific initiative, definitions of programs that can be used by the various jurisdictions, specification of certain instruments and methods of administration, and monitoring and enforcement mechanisms to track whether or not the framework is being respected. Policy frameworks thus structure activity by installing a particular logic for policymakers to use as a marker informing choices as they develop and deploy the individual practices within a broader sector.

Frameworks can provide three benefits addressing, in turn, the ideas of equality, efficiency, and effectiveness. By establishing a baseline, frameworks can help nurture the realization of equality by encouraging subnational decision-makers to invest at comparable levels, establish similar entitlements, and introduce common regulations on various activities such that all citizens of a federation enjoy the benefits that the country as a whole can provide (Simeon 2006a). Moreover, frameworks contribute to efficiency in a federation by sharing the task of policy-making across multiple jurisdictions, potentially elevating the capacity of smaller governments to act in their spheres of competency while simultaneously smoothing out interjurisdictional inconsistencies that may disrupt public activity. The scaffolding also helps ensure that the quality of products is reasonably consonant across the constituent jurisdictions, which should promote economic growth and minimize internal transaction costs. Finally, frameworks can also elevate policy effectiveness. Simply put, if the activities of the constituent governments are not somewhat coordinated, with major variations demarcating the individual jurisdictions, policy outcomes as a whole may suffer.

The obstacles to framework formulation start with constitutional division of powers. Because more than one authority enjoys jurisdictional authority over designated policy areas, intergovernmental collaboration is required to construct the scaffolding. This challenge is particularly acute in dual federations, like Canada and the United States, while likely somewhat more muted in cooperative ones where many of the spheres of competency are held concurrently such as Germany and Austria (Thorlakson 2003). Beyond this institutional factor, economics and geography can weigh heavily on these processes. Smaller federations with less variation between the constituent units may be better able to maintain cohesive frameworks to structure particular policy sectors. Divergent economic interests can also act as a powerful countervailing force impeding the abilities for political actors to work together and agree to common arrangements. Indeed, even variations in the relative size of the constituent units can deter collaboration. Economically strong governments, for example, "quite regularly find it more beneficial to 'fend for themselves' and strive for special deals" (Bolleyer 2009: 9) further eroding the installation of viable frameworks.

At this point, some caveats must be made. Not all frameworks are beneficial, and there are a number of negative consequences that can accompany their installation. Most obviously, the advantages of frameworks are heavily dependent on the suitability of their design and execution. Overly broad, frameworks will be too vague to provide meaningful guidance; overly specific, the frameworks will be unsuitable given the various needs and conditions within each of the subnational jurisdictions. Furthermore, coercive instruments—particularly from the national to the subnational governments—are likely to breed resentment among the various players. However, without such mechanisms, compliance becomes less assured and the effectiveness of the framework is put in doubt. The crafting and installation of policy frameworks thus require a high degree of sensitivity and awareness from all those engaged to formulate a workable and viable arrangement to provide a meaningful beacon for decision-makers. Finally, overarching standards, mandates, and the prescriptions that frameworks imply all have the potential to stymie creativity and innovation or inappropriately impose the priorities of one government onto others. Consequently, the techniques and strategies that are used to generate and maintain policy frameworks are of critical import to their long-term success.

## Intergovernmental Roads to Policy Frameworks

For students of federalism, the most familiar paths to policy frameworks are the vertical interactions between the national and subnational governments, also known as cooperative or collaborative federalism (Cameron and Simeon 2002; Simeon 2006b). Vertical intergovernmental processes can manifest in three ways: universally, bilaterally, and unilaterally. Under vertical universal processes, all members of the federation are involved in the intergovernmental interactions. Such multilateral engagements require considerable time, ongoing negotiations, and stable, institutionalized support to reap meaningful benefits (Bolleyer 2009). In Australia, for example, key policy reforms that are of national significance are jointly negotiated through the Council of Australian Governments (COAG), comprised of the Prime Minister, State Premiers, Territory Chief Ministers, and the President of the Australian Local Government Association.

Vertical bilateral negotiations see the deployment of one-on-one processes between the national and one subnational government that, when added together, ideally manifest in a coherent framework. Such processes are more likely in

federations with salient internal diversity, either social or economic, that differentiate the various subnational jurisdictions. In federations such as these, gaining the
unanimous consent of every jurisdiction will present major difficulties, thus encouraging the deployment of bilateral processes. This road to framework formulations
has become the preferred route for the Canadian federal government, traversed with
increasing frequency over the past decade, as federal politicians have largely
abandoned the multilateral route choosing instead to engage the provinces
individually.

Fully exerting a sense of hierarchy, national governments can also do it alone,
developing frameworks unilaterally without engaging the subnational governments
directly. Here, national decision-makers take firm control to sketch out the
parameters of the blueprints, identify key priorities and targets, and then encourage
subnational decision-makers to adopt the protocol. Here, federal funds in the form
of conditional grants can act as a powerful carrot to garner the necessary
endorsements of the other intergovernmental players. This type of process is most
likely in federations with stronger forms of *intragovernmental* representation as
national institutions enjoy greater legitimacy to legislate on behalf of the country as
a whole.

Horizontal processes are less familiar to students of federalism. As Bolleyer
(2009: 2) opines: "Interstate relations, the horizontal relations between lower level
governments, have received astonishingly little attention so far". Similar to the
vertical processes, horizontal interactions can manifest bilaterally, multilaterally,
and universally. Like vertical universalism, horizontal universalism can be a challenge particularly in federations with considerable internal diversity, leading some
jurisdictions to pursue undertakings either bilaterally or multilaterally, in the hopes
that others join in later. Institutionalized organizations also facilitate horizontal
coordination by providing historical memory, regularizing their interactions, and
generally strengthening the capacity for subnational governments to collaborate
(Bolleyer 2009). Key instruments in these horizontal processes include pacts,
mutual recognition clauses, and shared policy initiatives. Mechanisms familiar in
vertical interactions, such as conditional grants and unilaterally developed
mandates, however, do not appear in horizontal relations as the crucial attribute
of hierarchy does not prevail. Instead, adherence to the frameworks relies on the
voluntary commitments of participating governments. Horizontal processes are
more likely to emerge when the national government is disengaged from a particular area or as a defensive posture to resist incursions from the national government
(Bolleyer 2009; Rabe 2007).

Building from Smiley (1987), the processes of framework formulation are
influenced by other institutions—specifically those designed to build subnational
representation *within* the central government, known as *intragovernmental
relations*. As mentioned above, in federations that have developed strong forms
of intragovernmental relations where the interests of the constituent members are
represented within the institutions of the national government, the processes of
negotiating and defining the terms for the various sectors will likely occur within
that arena. For those federations that only weakly represent the interests of the

constituent governments within the national chambers, vertical bilateral and universal processes are more likely to prevail. What is more, where intragovernmental representation is stronger, the national government is better equipped to stake a role in policy areas that fall outside of its constitutional authority more frequently deploying vertical unilateralism. Radin and Boase (2000) also implicate institutional factors suggesting that the underlying logic of the political structures is a significant determinant of intergovernmental relations. Due to the logic of centralization and executive dominance, in parliamentary federations, greater consistency across the subnational governance arrangements is likely to appear, facilitating horizontal collaboration reducing the transaction costs of exchanges. For those deploying alternative political structure that privilege fragmentation, inconsistencies in subnational governing arrangements are likely to hinder horizontal coordination. Finally, all undertakings are influenced by the prevailing cultural and normative climate that pervades a given federation. Looking at national and subnational processes, following Erk (2007), multilingual federations are more likely to resist national incursions in areas of subnational responsibility. Drawing on the work of sociological institutionalists, moreover, subnational interactions are more likely to occur within internal regional subgroups that share common ideas, historical memories, and a tradition of collaboration.

## Framework Development: Education in Canada and the US

The Canadian provinces have jealously guarded their authority in the field of K-12 education, choosing to work together to fashion a fairly integrated and coherent policy framework to oversee programs, regulations, and activities in the field (Wallner 2012). To be sure, provinces employ their own unique strategies and educational programs, but in the main, the elementary and secondary education systems are similarly configured across the country.

Every time the federal government tried to infiltrate the sector, typically through conditional grants, the ensuing results failed to install a lasting legacy of federal engagement. Developments in vocational training are illustrative. In the 1960s, Ottawa unilaterally wanted to encourage the provinces to expand vocational training within the secondary system and offered a series of lucrative conditional grants. All of the provinces accepted the funds and used the federal monies to build new schools, ostensibly promising to dedicate space exclusively for vocational training. However, once the funds were turned over, the provinces deviated from the federal mandates and deployed the money to support comprehensive schooling, an alternative form of high school programming, rather than the exclusive vocational training desired by the federal government. Federal funds offered unilaterally thus failed to gain a permanent foothold in the crafting of the Canadian education policy framework.

Actions from the federal government nevertheless encouraged a crucial development in the sector. In the 1950s, officials from Ottawa started circumventing the provinces and tried to establish a leadership position as the formal representative for Canadian education on the international stage. In response, the provinces established the Council of Ministers of Education Canada (CMEC), an organization dedicated to strengthening provincial leadership in the field, facilitating interprovincial learning, and nurturing collaborative initiatives. Unlike other sectoral tables, the federal government is excluded from the K-12 table, leaving it entirely in the hands of provincial (and territorial) leaders. Voluntary coordination and cooperation among the subnational governments are goals of the Council, and the institutionalization of this coordinative body has increased horizontal engagements in the sector. While undeniably a provincial initiative, it was nevertheless motivated by a fear of federal intervention in the field.

Over the past 20 years, interprovincial undertakings have markedly increased, with formal collaborations emerging in universal assessments, teacher mobility, and curriculum. These collaborations have advanced under the auspices of a series of intergovernmental organizations, including the CMEC, with noticeably different results that reveal the influence of both institutional and cultural factors on horizontal intergovernmental relations for policy frameworks. Transformations in curriculum policy neatly encapsulate these realities.

Under the Atlantic Provinces Education Foundation (APEF), in 1993, the four provinces of Atlantic Canada ratified a common statement on essential graduation learnings, followed by foundation documents across six curriculum areas that led to the complete harmonization of curriculum across the jurisdictions in 2000. At the same time, British Columbia, Alberta, Saskatchewan, and Manitoba signed the Western Canadian Protocol for Collaboration in Basic Education (WCP). The WCP led to the articulation of common learning outcomes across a wide array of subject areas. However, unlike Atlantic Canada, full harmonization was not achieved. Finally, the CMEC adopted the Pan-Canadian Protocol for Collaboration on School Curriculum in 1995. The Pan-Canadian process led to the formulation of common learning outcomes in science, released in 1997, with no further advancements in other areas.

Looking at the CMEC undertaking, the impact of the horizontal universal process has been limited at best. According to one official: "The Pan-Canadian framework on science has way too many outcomes because of the number of provinces believing what is important and insisting on their priorities—so you need to filter from what's there to shrink it to a doable size". Another official affirmed: "Working through the CMEC is often an unwieldy process. Getting all the governments to agree is a real challenge and results are frequently watered down". Regional curriculum collaborations thus demonstrated noticeably more success than the one shepherded by the CMEC. Nevertheless, contrasting outcomes emerged here with Atlantic Canada fully harmonizing, while western Canada still maintains separate curricula. The explanation for this variation turns on differences in the institutional and cultural connections of the regions.

The APEF (which later evolved in the Council for Atlantic Ministers of Education and Training) provided crucial support throughout the various stages of harmonization, with the permanent secretariat offering vital administrative assistance. One respondent from Nova Scotia put it most succinctly: "Without the CAMET, the harmonized curriculum would not have been achieved". Such well-institutionalized organized supports are not a reality in Western Canada. A former minister of education from Saskatchewan acknowledged: "In Western Canada, the relations among the ministers are more like an informal working group with irregular meetings and haphazard efforts. Our relations are simply not as formalized as those in Atlantic Canada". A respondent from Alberta similarly noted: "There is not even a separate caucus dedicated exclusively to the education ministers of Western Canada". Provincial education officials in Western Canada thus lack the critical organizational support that is necessary for comprehensive harmonization.

The greater institutionalization of intergovernmental relations in Atlantic Canada is also reflective of cultural ties. In particular, the three Maritime Provinces have long demonstrated close affinities with each other that frequently manifest in similar policy choices and a general proclivity to look to one another when formulating educational reforms. The provinces of Western Canada have never exhibited a comparable degree of cultural synergy. Sources involved in the WCP also reported that ideological differences in the governing parties, particularly between Alberta and the other provinces, further undermined the potential for comprehensive harmonization. At the time, the Alberta government was pursuing an agenda for radical change in education with one prominent proposal involving strengthening choice by creating public-private partnerships and charter schools. These ideas became lightning rods in heated debates that stretched beyond Alberta's borders, and the impulse towards privatization clashed with many of the ideas held by other signatories of the Protocol, particularly in Saskatchewan and Manitoba. Ideological distance among the affected parties thus reinforced the barriers to curriculum harmonization in Western Canada.

Like Canada, K-12 education in the United States falls to the states. However, unlike Canada whereby the provinces established clear roles and centralized the governance of schooling under the respective ministries of education, the authority and management of American K-12 schooling involves the national, state, and local levels of government. What is more, marked variations continue to demarcate the American educational landscape from governance and administration to finance and curriculum. In the words of Paul Manna (2011: 12): "State and local power over education has created a diverse patchwork quilt of approaches and institutions across the United States. Saying that the country has a 'system' of elementary and secondary education overstates the degree of coherence that actually exists". The roots of these variations lie in certain institutional and cultural conditions of the American federation.

Washington's influence in American education has intensified over the last 50 years. The first major step was taken in 1965, when President Lyndon B. Johnson secured the passage of the Elementary and Secondary Education Act (1965). While initially targeting the needs of disadvantaged students, this act is the foundation for most federal activity in the field, having witnessed a host of major revisions through a series of Congressional reauthorizations. Throughout these authorizations, three goals have stood out: improving access and outcomes for impoverished children;

hastening the development of state standards, tests, and accountability; and, finally, holding schools and districts accountable for results. Under the most recent iteration, Congress reauthorized the ESEA as the No Child Left Behind Act (NCLB), signed into law on 8 January 2002, where under its many features states are compelled to develop adequate yearly progress (AYP) statements and increase student testing and accountability regimes in exchange for funds from the capital. What are the factors that led to such a concerted national engagement in an area of state responsibility?

Due to the stronger institutionalization of intragovernmental representation, these federal undertakings were fashioned within the Congressional arena rather than in direct negotiations with state and local actors themselves. As a result, the formulation of a policy framework was fashioned through vertical unilateral processes, as federal decision-makers crafted the scaffolding for states and local decision-makers to implement in their areas of authority. Where Canada is a multilingual federation, moreover, the US has a linguistically unified public space, enabling the emergence of a national policy discourse. However, Washington's ability to install a comprehensive and lasting framework through this strategy has been stymied by the persistent desire for state and local control, described as a "hallowed principle" of the American system.

Zeroing in on the administrative policies at the substate level, the configuration of education in Canada is remarkably centralized. Each provincial department of education, with the political minister of education supported by the permanent staff of the public service, maintains strong control over the vast schooling enterprise. There has been no comparable standardization of administrative practices in the US, and interstate differences extend up to the peak of the governance structure. Simply put, where parliamentary government requires strong and fairly consistent executive leadership, the American political structure does not encourage such standardization. State-level inconsistencies in educational administration stymie subnational coordination, impeding horizontal collaborations.

Nevertheless, recently, states have shown some initiative in the area of curriculum perhaps as a reaction to the increasing prominence of the federal government in an effort to regain control of the sector. Mobilized by the National Governors Association and the Council of Chief State School Officers in 2009, all the states are participating in a series of working groups composed of individuals representing multiple stakeholders and a range of expertise in curriculum design. According to Dane Linn, director of the NGA Center's Education Division: "The Common Core State Standards Initiative allows states to work together to develop common standards that will ensure our students are prepared for the future". Consequently, there are some indications that horizontal processes among the states themselves may help smooth out the existing inconsistencies among the various systems. Despite the glimmer of horizontal relations, however, the outlook for lasting change in K-12 education remains remote. Until the governance and administrative practices are somewhat standardized, with greater authority and policy capacity maintained by the states, an overarching education framework is unlikely to emerge.

Evidence from the two cases thus supports the hypotheses that institutional features beyond the division of powers shape the configuration and execution of intergovernmental relations. The configuration of intragovernmental representation in the United States is markedly stronger than Canada, which expedited Washington's infiltration into the education sector. However, the logic of centralization and executive dominance embedded within the Canadian parliamentary structures contrasts with the logic of fragmentation encapsulated in Madisonian tradition of checks and balances, contributing to subnational collaborations in Canada while hindering coordination in America. Finally, the influence of culture looms large in both countries, enabling Washington interventions while Ottawa remains outside, while simultaneously assisting regional collaborations in Canada while delaying the emergence of a cohesive framework in the US.

## Conclusion

What insights from this discussion can be applied to Spain? Due to a number of salient shared characteristics, there are likely to be strong parallels appearing in Spain with the dynamics and processes that have featured prominently in Canada. Already, the national government has demonstrated a clear preference for bilateral interactions. The majority of policy framework formulation occurs through one-on-one negotiations, which are dominating the Spanish landscape likely related to the historical process of internal devolution that advanced progressively with individual regions negotiating separately with the central government to establish the Autonomous Communities. Bilateral interactions have been institutionalized with the creation of joint commissions to somewhat regularize the interactions between the national and pertinent subnational governments. Vertical universal processes nevertheless are gradually emerging, nested beneath a series of sectoral conferences organized according to functional areas, including health, education, and transportation. However, like those in Canada, these sectoral councils are underdeveloped with irregular meetings and lack permanent secretarial support, translating into underwhelming results overall.

Presently, some researchers report that there is a perception across the ACs that intergovernmental institutions are instruments for national control (Bolleyer 2006b).

For horizontal processes to flourish in Spain, allowing the ACs to contribute to the crafting of policy frameworks, the Autonomous Communities need to establish intergovernmental tables that do not directly involve the national government similar to the CMEC. To be sure, asymmetries between the ACs could undermine the viable institutionalization of such forums as regions such as the Basque Country and Catalonia have negotiated more autonomy than others, but common ground across a variety of policy areas could be nurtured under the auspices of intergovernmental organizations, elevating the capacity of the ACs to work together.

While furthering our understanding of intergovernmental processes and policy development, there are a plethora of questions that remain unanswered. It seems clear from the results in Canadian and American education, that policy decisions *within* each of the respective subnational sectors also influence the crafting and institutionalization of a meaningful framework. Further research is thus required to determine the ways in which meso-level policy choices can act as a grillwork of gears furthering the emergence of a cohesive framework in a federation. Finally, another aspect that remained unaddressed here was the role of nongovernmental actors in policy development. The federalism literature often struggles to integrate the engagement and influence of members of the wider policy networks in the processes of policy framework formulation. The position of nonstate actors within the decision-making processes and the influence they exert can greatly influence the degree to which subnational governments can work together. Interactive effects of policy choices and the autonomy of state actors from members of the policy community are two new avenues of research that will further contribute to our understanding of the dynamics of policymaking in federations.

**Acknowledgements** This paper is part of a broader research project on intergovernmental relations in federal systems generously funded by the Mowat Centre for Policy Innovation.

# References

Bolleyer, N. (2009) Intergovernmental cooperation: rational choices in federal systems and beyond. Oxford University Press, Oxford, 251 pp. 251.

Bolleyer, N. (2006a). Federal dynamics in Canada, the United States, and Switzerland: how substates' internal organization affects intergovernmental relations. Publius: The Journal of Federalism 36: 471–502.

Bolleyer, N. (2006b) Intergovernmental arrangements in Spanish and Swiss federalism: the impact of power-concentrating and power-sharing executives on intergovernmental institutionalization. Regional and Federal Studies. 16: 385–408.

Cameron, D. and Simeon, R. (2002) Intergovernmental relations in Canada: the emergence of collaborative federalism" Publius: The Journal of Federalism. 27: 377–409.

Erk, J. (2007) Explaining federalism: state, society and congruence in Austria, Belgium, Canada, Germany, and Switzerland. London, Routledge, 168 pp.

Manna, P. (2011) Collision course: federal education policy meets state and local realities. CQ Press, Washington DC, 206 pp.

Rabe, B. (2007) Beyond Kyoto: climate change policy in multilevel governance systems. Governance. 20: 423–444.

Radin, B., and Joan B. (2000) Federalism, political structure, and public policy in the United States and Canada. Journal of Comparative Policy Analysis. 2: 65–89.

Simeon, R. (2006a) Social justice: does federalism make a difference? Choudhry, S., Gaudreault-DesBiens, JF., and Sossin, L., (eds.) Dilemmas of solidarity: rethinking redistribution in the Canadian federations. University of Toronto Press, Toronto, 31–44.

Simeon, R. (2006b) Federal-provincial diplomacy: the making of recent policy in Canada. Toronto, University of Toronto Press, 342 pp.

Smiley, D. (1987) The federal condition in Canada. McGraw-Hill Ryerson Limited, Toronto, 202 pp.

Thorlakson, L. (2003) Comparing federal institutions: power and representation in six federations. West European Politics. 26: 1–22.

Wallner, J. (2012) Political structures, social diversity, and public policy: comparing mandatory education in Canada and the United States. Comparative Political Studies. (July) 45(7): 850–847.

# Evolution of Intergovernmental Relations and the Strengthening of Autonomy

Rémi Barrué-Belou

**Abstract** Intergovernmental relations can have a new voice in the federalism. Dualistic federalism has given way to Cooperative federalism. As a consequence, constitutional distribution of legislative responsibilities has become unclear. This evolution, over time, has amounted to an overrun of responsibilities amongst the different government orders. One such overrun has occurred in the legislative area of government. That is, the consequence of this change in federalism, particularly in federalism's cooperations and responsibilities, has spread to the financial sectors of society. Cooperation with respect to financial policies is an important step in the evolution of federalism, as it has given power to some state governments to get financial help, such as grants, and to realize projects. This cooperation has given autonomy to many states, thanks to block grants from various federal governments. Such cooperation has occurred in many federations, including but not limited to the United States, Canada, and Brazil. Spain is a European example. With regard to Spain, this cooperation took place both with the central government and with the European Union, as well as with the subsidiarity principle. Today, the overrun of responsibilities from the legislative point of view seems to be an outdated problem, and especially as it concerns the issue of defending state autonomy. The actual power to focus on, when attempting to defend a state's autonomy, is the states' financial power. Strengthening of autonomy must be organized from a financial point of view. If legislative powers are not allocated to one specific order of government, then the legislature is given the discretion to act in financial matters, concerning all areas that are not otherwise prohibited.

R. Barrué-Belou (✉)
Université Toulouse 1, Toulouse, France

Université Laval, Quebec, Canada
e-mail: remi.barrue@wanadoo.fr

A. López-Basaguren and L. Escajedo San Epifanio (eds.), *The Ways of Federalism in Western Countries and the Horizons of Territorial Autonomy in Spain*, Vol. 2, DOI 10.1007/978-3-642-27717-7_10, © Springer-Verlag Berlin Heidelberg 2013

Intergovernmental relations are a main feature of federalism. This is an evolutionary part of a dynamic system. Considering this, intergovernmental relations will depend on various factors and can be modified given any extraordinary circumstance, i.e., crisis, war, peace, etc. Other factors may include national public policy, national and international economic conditions, or the will of member states and/or the will of the nation. For example, a nation might consider centralization or decentralization. This is precisely why many federal-type countries have an evolutionary intergovernmental relations system.

Intergovernmental relations can be studied from the legislative power point of view, i.e., under the distribution of authorities. From this vantage point, the legislative branch, as well as the power of administration in every level of government, will be important for intergovernmental relations. This in turn will determine the condition of relations between state and federal government. As a consequence, it will also be an indication of the balance of power between the respective branches. However, intergovernmental relations can also be studied from the point of view of fiscal authorities. In fact, the degree of fiscal power in every order of government will have a crucial and determinant impact on the autonomy of the respective state. Thus, fiscal power will dictate relations with the other governments.

In considering the challenges of federalism and the future of member states, especially the autonomy of the respective states, it is imperative to analyse the distribution of powers (legislative and fiscal), the evolution of the respective states, and the cooperative relations between regional and federal governments in those states.

The creation of a new framework such as the European Union instils a will of regional identity and respect. It reflects the trend of globalization. It promotes conduct that will reinforce regional identity and will therefore reinforce the autonomy of local and/or state governments.

In light of the foregoing, horizontal relations between the individual states and the regional governments will be fortified and will develop further, so as to increase cooperation. As a consequence, the role of regional government power will evolve into greater prominence.

The evolution of power and responsibility in federalism can be observed and monitored in other countries as well, including but not limited to the United States or Brazil. Indeed, it may be observed that this evolution leads to more cooperative relations between the various governments in the respective federations and, in particular, cooperation concerning financial and legislative issues. Viewing federations through this lens may enable us to assess the positive attributes that may flow from the newly formed Spanish federation.

Thus, in the first section, I will analyse the dynamism of intergovernmental relations in some federal systems, that is, legislative and financial (I). In a second part, I will analyse the strengthening of autonomy amongst the member states in various federal systems; as well, I will try to find elements of solution to the ongoing Spanish issue (II).

# I) Dynamism of Intergovernmental Relations from the Distribution of Powers Point of View

The dynamism of intergovernmental relations will be analyzed from the legislative point of view (A) and from the financial point of view (B).

## A) *Evolution of Legislative Power: The Overrun of Responsibilities in Canadian and American Federations*

The twentieth century has shown that federalism was not a static framework but was a dynamic system. Indeed, coordination and cooperation were developed in all levels of the federation, both vertically and horizontally.

From the horizontal point of view, member states increased relations between themselves in various areas such as trade, justice, and public policy ... Nevertheless, cooperation and coordination were developed from a vertical standpoint too. This is particularly evident in the policies that have been implemented since 1930 and the ensuing economic crisis.

In several cases, the federal government decided to help their respective populations overcome the serious difficulties that they were faced with and to survive. This *help* took on the form of the *Welfare State* in different countries, most famously the United States, Canada, and then Brazil ... However, the federal governments, in the latter experiments, were not used to having a leading role in these social sectors. This role was generally a mission for the individual member state, especially considering the delegation of authority in the federation and the distribution of power between the federation and the state. Jenna Bednar confirms this idea of separation of responsibilities and powers writing "any distribution of authority implies compromise. Not all objectives are complementary" (Bednar 2009, p. 7). From this moment, dualistic federalism was replaced by dynamic federalism; in the latter system, the distribution of powers cannot be readily observed, and particularly because of the increasing role of federal government. This period fostered cooperation between the federal, state, and local governments and eventually led to an interdependence amongst the states. From the legislative point of view, the consequence was a decompartmentalizing of powers and responsibilities amongst the respective states. The distribution of powers was not respected anymore. Certain powers were allocated to a particular government, or certain federations were granted an overlapping of powers. As a consequence, this change had, and still has, the possibility of a government (generally the federal government) acting and legislating in the respective member states' legislative areas. It is important to point out not only that cooperation does not only exist between channels of formal government but also that cooperation occurs in informal form through commissions and/or organizations composed by ministers or public officials.

So, the overlap of responsibilities has had a negative influence on states and local autonomy. This has enabled the federal government to act in areas that have not traditionally been its responsibility and to cut or reduce the power of the states that comprise the federation.

To illustrate this evolution of federalism, we will first consider the Canadian example and its evolution of responsibilities (1) and then the American one (2).

## 1) Evolution of Responsibilities in the Canadian Federation

As an evolutive system, federalism is not confined within a fixed framework. Thereby, the capacity of a state's members can be stronger or weaker according to different periods or circumstances. Canadian federalism is a typical example of the evolution of responsibilities associated with federalism. When the Canadian federation was built, a strong federal government was required. They were tasked with exercising terminal authority over the provincial governments. This was necessary for two main reasons: First, the federal government had to usurp the role of the Crown. This would avoid popular uprising. Also, this would maintain unity in a vastly wide territory. Under these circumstances, it was important that the federal government show its domination. Second, this strict federal authority was necessary because the French Canadian population was reticent to be stripped of their culture, and more importantly, they wanted to be autonomous and self-governed.

However, various factors changed the federal domination in Canada. A first factor was that a reactionary period during the end of nineteenth century weakened the legitimacy of the federal government (Simeon and Papillon 2006, p. 101). A second factor was that important provincial political leaders were able to wield substantial influence in the federal Parliament. These leaders, such as Honoré Mercier, who was Primier of Quebec, or Oliver Mowat, Premier of Ontario, were the initial founders of interprovincial conferences. The first conference, in 1887, was commenced by strong critics of the federal government. A third factor effecting the erosion of federal dominance was that some of the resources governed by the provinces, like hydroelectric and/or mining energy, became an important sector of industrial activities and income for Canada as a whole. Thus, it strengthened the power of provinces. A fourth factor in the weakening of the federal role was that the judgments of the courts were often in favour of provincial independence, thereby strengthening their responsibilities. This, therefore, weakened federal power. For example, Canada's federal authority on trade or international relations was interpreted restrictively by the Canadian judiciary.

Nevertheless, the Great Depression, in the 1930s, reversed this tendency. The Canadian federal government had to pursue a policy of assistance for the entire country. This tended to unify Canada, thereby strengthening the influence and power of their federal government. This was particularly due to a centralization of decisions in the federal infrastructure. This inclination toward federalism carried on after the Second World War, as is evinced by Canada's pursuit of a Keynesian policy in economic and social fields. A new era began in the 1970s, however. Several Canadian provinces voiced opposition to the federal establishment, eventually leading to the *Quiet Revolution* in Quebec. This fanned the flame of decentralization and fuelled the cries for reduction of federal authority in the provincial regions. Of notable concern to the provinces were conditional grants.

## 2) Evolution of Responsibilities in the United States

The autonomy of states is measured by their ability to act in areas of exclusive competence. Consequently, the ability of the federal government and its financial powers to act on states affects the autonomy granted to those respective states. The role of the states has always been very important in the American federation. As an illustration, we can observe that the states are mentioned fifty times in the American Constitution. As in the quasi totality of federal systems, states have their own constitution and citizens elect their own public and government officials. The state constitutions allow modifications of their institutions and self-powers. An example illustrates this idea: the states' governors' status, which were weakly developed in the first drafting of the respective states constitutions, have since been modified to reinforce their public and legislative powers in the states. This has allowed governors to be leaders of public policies in different areas such as education, health, economic development, and criminal justice. If local governments, like cities, towns, or counties, are not specifically set forth in the Constitution, their creation has been relegated to the various states that house those entities. The power of these municipal authorities (like the power to levy taxes) has also been delineated by the states. Even if the power of local governments derives from the states that give them that authority, local governments are left with a lot of independence and autonomy in their day-to-day operations. This independence is ensured both by the representation of local governments in state legislatures and by the important role played by local governments in the development of intergovernmental relations. This feature of government has been especially prominent from the 1960s forward. According to Elis Katz, "under Pennsylvania's constitutional provision concerning home rule, local government 'may exercise any power or perform any function not denied by this Constitution, by its home rule charter, or by the General Assembly'" (Katz 2006, p. 306). However, the individual American states have lost a part of their autonomy from a financial point of view. The federal government has notoriously used its fiscal power to influence the individual states' policies. For example, many grants were conditional ones, and state governments had to follow strict federal instructions in order to receive those grants, even in areas that had been traditionally allocated to state government.

The U.S. federal system is "symmetric" inasmuch as all states are supposed to enjoy equal constitutional status. Indeed, the U.S. Constitution recognizes broad powers to states but gives exclusive jurisdiction to the federation. In fact, the Constitution specifically sets forth the powers conferred to the federal government, leaving the remaining powers to the states and then to the people. This was originally intended to limit the powers of the federation and its invasion upon the rights of the individual states. Nonetheless, the autonomy of states is significantly protected in the text of the U.S. Constitution. For example, each state has control over the organization and implementation of its state legislative, executive, and judicial branches according to each respective states' constitution. This is a clear indication that the individual states in the United States' federation retain a high degree of state autonomy. That is, the federal entity cannot act in member state areas, unless it is specifically provided for in the U.S. Constitution. Thus, the areas left to federal jurisdiction are limited by the federal Constitution and the States possess a significant amount of autonomy and independence.

The United States, like Canada discussed earlier, also went through a period of centralization. After the Great Depression, the federal government was able to centralize and increase its authority, often at the expense of state autonomy. As a consequence, state and local governments developed cooperatives to reinforce their constitutionally allocated powers and to avoid submission to the unbridled reign of the federal government.

In conclusion, it should be noted that cooperation has been a very important theme in the story of American federalism; indeed, this cooperation is what fostered the evolution of American federalism as it exists today. This new federalism innovated the traditional constitutional notions of distribution of responsibilities. The cooperation of governments facilitating American federalism has been realized in the legislative context, but more importantly, this cooperation has been realized in the financial realm of government.

## B) Evolution of Financial Power: The Development of Cooperation and the Three Solutions of Public Finance Integration

In studying cooperation amongst governments in the financial context, integration of public finances in federations is a crucial key for consideration. Indeed, cooperation has a positive effect for state governments as they can receive grants and other benefits from the federal government. What's more, cooperation can allow for resolution of more global or international problems that may be faced by the individual states. For example, this would be the case when many local or state governments are faced with a common problem(s) and are not able to reach a solution alone, which may most commonly be the result of a shortage of funds or other resources. In this context, cooperation with the federal government permits the allocation of grants and other resources, even if the federal government will impose conditions upon receipt of those resources, and may thus be given a hand in controlling areas of government traditionally left to the states. From the federal point of view, cooperation can be a valuable tool for observing the state or local experience and particularly for observing their ability to implement nationally sponsored programs that depend on local conditions that may vary amongst each state. There are currently three major categories of integration in public finance: firstly, conditional and unconditional grants-in-aids,; secondly, coordination of financial policies; and thirdly, fiscal harmonization.

## 1) Conditional and Unconditional Grants

From a financial point of view, cooperation can take two forms. The first is the transfer of grants from one government to another. Most of the time, the national government transfers a part of its income to a state or local government. The second form of cooperation is fiscal revenue sharing. In the latter case, certain designated fiscal revenues are shared by different governments on the state and federal levels.

In various federations, intergovernmental fiscal transfers are an important check to insure the balance of powers. Grants can also be a good means for allowing states to act with more autonomy in their respective fields of authority. In the logic of vertical cooperation, federal governments can decide to help states by initiating development programs within the fields of state authority. However, in order to respect the autonomy and independence of the various states, financial aid should not take the form of conditional grants or require mandatory programs.

In Canada, for example, two kinds of fiscal transfers can be observed. Both are based on the federal spending power. A program of equalization payments has existed since 1957 and is protected by Section 36 of the 1982 Canadian Constitution. This program is based on the principle of equality of chances amongst the regions. According to this principle, each province must have "comparable levels of services, with comparable levels of taxation". Unconditional grants from the federal government to provincial programs have been set up in order to equalize the respective provinces' revenues and thus to protect their autonomy. The second kind of redistribution revenue from the federal government is the payment of federal grants in certain policy areas that have traditionally been left to the governance of the provinces. This type of program, styled a "shared cost program", is less interesting for the individual provinces because, as a conditional grant, it threatens the provinces' autonomy. Effectively, in this case, the federal government acts in provincial areas. It participates financially and sometimes even politically. Moreover, it imposes conditions on the respective provinces' receipt of financial aid, which in turn forces the provincial government to act in accordance with the wishes of the federal government.

In the United States, the Constitution does not specifically provide for transfers from the federal government to the states, but case law through the years has allowed such financial transfers in the form of grants-in-aids. The courts have cited the *General Welfare Clause* (art. 1 section 8) and the *Spending Clause in justifying these transfers.*

## 2) Coordination of Financial Policies

Coordination of Financial policies is a characteristic element of federal systems. Coordination enables a federation to develop unified trade policies. Coordination takes the form of intergovernmental meetings that organize and plan financial agreements. In Canada, for example, there are interprovincial meetings and federal-state meetings with provincial ministers and the Premier Minister of each of the respective provinces and the federal government.

Two types of coordination exist: a concerted cooperation and a hierarchical one. Hierarchical cooperation means that one of the governments involved is more powerful than the others involved and, hence, drives the negotiations. It means that the dominant government—generally the federal government—imposes its will in the form of conditions upon the states. In this case, autonomy and independence of the states are not truly respected. However, in the second kind of coordination, contrary to the first, state governments are more free and their autonomy tends to be better served. Notably, concerted cooperation lends more possibility to state or local governments in terms of their influence on the process of decision-making and in having their opinions form the basis of the ultimate choices and solutions adopted. In this case, states are not subjected to a upper entity and are free to invoke their autonomy.

## 3) Fiscal Harmonization in the United States and Canada

The basis of cooperation in a federalist system depends on the financial dimension in each level of government. Without financial powers, it is impossible to carry out a collaboration amongst governments (Brasileiro 1974, p. 122). Financial cooperation can be realized in various ways. It can be carried out by constitutional mechanisms that organize the cooperation process. It can also be reached by grants, unscheduled by the respective constitutions. Coordination of financial policies amongst state and federal governments functions to harmonize fiscal laws overall. Fiscal vertical harmonization must necessarily include the harmonization of state and federal taxes that are of the same or similar nature. A partial and moderate disinvestment of proceeds from the federal government in local and state fiscal revenues will function such that local and regional taxes will take the place of what was once reliant upon federal grants. Harmonization, in this sense, may be achieved by including a tax credit or tax relief. That's what has happened in the United States since the 1930s and in Canada since 1962. However, when the federal government has a weak influence in fiscal matters, harmonization can only be made by the states, themselves, horizontally. This was the case in Canada as it concerns income tax.

There is no specific financial cooperation model, but such a model could be generally summarized as consisting of budgetary harmonization and corresponding fiscal rules (a) and/or fiscal and financial coordination amongst governments (b).

## a) Harmonization of Budgetary Rules

The coordination of practices has resulted from the harmonization of budgetary documents, more precisely accounting presentation. This accounting presentation coordination was the consequence of a standardization of budgetary law. In Canada, harmonization began in the 1960s because of problems associated with intergovernmental coordination, as well as budgetary policies in general. Difficulties of coordination resulted from the diversity of institutions in the various provinces. The problem also derived from the use of different budgetary methods, depending on the state and/or local administration implementing those methods.

## b) Harmonization of Fiscal Rules

Fiscal harmonization can be realized in both the vertical and horizontal planes. Vertical harmonization is a harmonization of state and federal taxes that share a common nature, while horizontal harmonization aims to harmonize different special taxes or tax systems amongst member states. Vertical harmonization is mostly catalyzed by federal government withdrawal. Then, to compensate for this withdrawal, the regional government gives an incentive for further catalyzation. Thus, prospective means for harmonization may be via tax credits or by other fiscal deductions. Canada and the United States have both used these techniques.[1] Tax credit techniques for harmonization are most commonly used when the federal government collects an income tax and a death tax. When the basis of state and federal taxes is the same, the federal government can deduct a part of the state tax from its own tax in order to reduce the cost on the taxpayer to the federal government. In other words, states and federal governments can each collect a part of the same tax.

Horizontal taxing coordination is only possible when member states have close relations and work together in unison. Canada is a good example of horizontal harmonization with interprovincial agreements on income tax.

The defence of state autonomy in federalism is a complicated road. From the legislative point of view, autonomy of states depends on the capacity to legislate and carry out administrative actions in the areas of state authority and responsibility. From the financial point of view, different objectives can be reached. Financial cooperation is the first step in defending state and local autonomy. Coordination is the second step. Coordination, however, should be a hierarchical coordination and not a concerted coordination. These efforts may be facilitated through intergovernmental meetings in which each government is allowed to participate, debate, and receive due consideration for its respective concerns. Harmonization is the third step. In this step, the states are able to collect their own taxes and do not depend on federal grants or other assistance from the federation. Block grants are, of course,

---

[1] United States, since 1930s and Canada, since 1970s.

the best way to provide for more autonomy to state and local governments. The state and local governments can use these grants as they choose and are not subject to federal mandates that impose obligations and limit the actions of states. In the second part of this study, we are going to consider the role that cooperation plays in strengthening state autonomy.

# II) Strengthening of Autonomy of the Member State in Federal Systems

The evolution of responsibilities has some consequences on autonomy and cooperation (A) and shows a strengthening of member states and regions autonomy (B).

## A) *Consequences of Legislative and Financial Balance on Autonomy and Cooperation*

### 1) State and Local Autonomy

Initially, cooperation in the United States took the form of horizontal cooperation. Indeed, the U.S. constitution allows each state to conclude agreements with other States, if approval is given by Congress. This follows from the Constitution, Article 1 paragraph 10. However, the U.S. culture has given a lot of independence to the states, and those have organized themselves autonomously. Cooperation was not a natural attitude for the states because they had an opposite vision of independence. If this cooperation is in theory possible since 1787, it had no real practical existence until the late nineteenth century and especially in the 1920s. It is actually in the 1960s that agreements between states (interstate compacts) have assumed great importance in key areas such as education and regional development. Agreements are the result of cooperative federalism and are driven by commissions composed of members appointed by the governors of the states concerned. However, it is often difficult to establish a clear division of responsibilities. In addition, by specifying precise needs, they cannot see in a comprehensive manner the problems that arise and only occasionally solve narrow problems instead of acting on the overall issue. Most of the time, it was the central power that solved the problems by itself, going beyond the state, instead of two bodies cooperating in unison. From a vertical perspective, even if the federal share of public spending has increased extensively, states have maintained broad decision-making responsibilities, including cases where the federal government provides most funding. This is the case for road or urban development and education. This observation is also true regarding cooperation between administrations. However, cooperative federalism, because of centralized development, took progressively the form of a coercive federalism.

In addition, states also have a substantial fiscal autonomy and can determine their tax system rather freely. The United States fundamental principle of autonomy of states and economic culture decrees that horizontal equalization is not considered as a main objective of federal policy. The results of reducing financial inequalities have been, in this country, much less positive than in most federations. The autonomy is therefore a barrier to any desire to reduce inequalities between states, except for the financially weaker states, which cannot accept this aid in order to provide the minimum services to its residents.

In conclusion to these financial developments, it's possible to consider that federal grants have been a good way for the American states to improve their autonomy. The federal grants have permitted the states to act in more policies because of a more significant financial capacity. States can act with more easiness in their areas of competences, thanks to federal grants.

## 2) Autonomy of Brazilian Entities

Autonomy is the power of self-determination "exercised independently inside the boundaries of a superior rule" (Mortati 1967, p. 694). Self-determination implies self-organization, according to Anna Cândida da Cunha Ferraz, and auto-organization logic is a characteristic of the Brazilian federation (da Cunha Ferraz 1979, p. 53). The 1988 Brazilian constitution admits a real autonomy to the member states of federation and to municipalities. Thus, articles 25 and 18 of the federal Constitution allow states to have their own constitution.[2] Three levels can be observed in the Brazilian organization (union, states, and municipalities), and union and states have legislative, executive, and judiciary powers.

The union shall have jurisdiction in matters relating to the sovereignty of the Brazilian Federation and in the fields of legislative, executive, and judicial within its jurisdiction. States also exercise the powers in three regional interests. Executive power is held by the governor, who is elected by the people. He leads the state policy as a whole and is not subjected to the policy of the Union. Legislative power is vested in an assembly composed of deputies, also elected by the people. The unicameral assembly may legislate in all areas except those having jurisdiction of another entity.[3] States also organize their own judicial system according to their own constitution and have a taxing jurisdiction to ensure their financial independence. The areas in which states may levy taxes are targeted under section 155 of the 1988 Constitution. They can create taxes in some areas and receive a share of tax revenues collected by the federal entity.

Municipalities, in turn, have a legislative authority to enable them to make laws that apply in their areas of expertise. They hold an executive power for their

---

[2] Article 25: "Os Estados organizam-se e regem-se pelas Constituições e leis que adotarem, observados os princípios desta Constituição".

[3] Article 25 of the Federal Constitution provides fields in which federated legislatures cannot act.

implementation and also to ensure their fiscal powers and, thus, genuine autonomy. Municipalities can set their own taxes in specific areas. The autonomy of the entities of the Federation is carried out by several elements. First, they have a capacity for self-organization as each state has a Constitution, according to the 1988 Federal Constitution[4]; the municipalities are organized by organic laws.[5] The autonomy of these entities is further reinforced by the fact that they are elected by the people, members of their executive, and because their legislative power suffers no subordination on the part of the Union. Municipalities were granted by a very favorable status in the Constitution of 1988. They can take any kind of act in their jurisdiction, and theses acts are not subjected to any control. They hold a legislative power, exercised by the council acting in the affairs of local interest, and an executive power held by the mayor. However, they hold no judicial power. From a tax and financial perspective, municipalities enjoy a degree of autonomy since they can create taxes[6] and receive a share of federal revenues and state.[7]

## B) *Strengthening of Member States and Regions Autonomy*

In some federations, like the American or Canadian federations, each government order has equivalent responsibilities in the executive and legislative branches. This has several advantages. Firstly, it reinforces the autonomy of the regional and sometimes local order, when local orders have legislative authority. Secondly, each order can properly implement its own legislation and make adjustments if necessary.

In Spain, the Constitution lists the exclusive powers of the federal government. The constitutional text transfers the determination of the powers of Autonomous Communities to States Autonomy. In spite of the rules determined in the constitution and the assignment of authority, the reality of Spanish federalism shows the gap between theory and practice. A lot of areas require the cooperation of various governments. That's a good omen for the states and their capacity to have influence on matters that belong generally to the federal authority. Otherwise, concerning residual powers, the Constitution gives to federal government the capacity to act. This has important consequences on the communities' autonomy. It limits their autonomy because they cannot act in areas that are not explicitly assigned to federal government. Residual areas are, usually, areas with no national interest (most of the time), and so those are areas interesting to states or local governments.

---

[4] Article 25 of the Constitution of 1988.

[5] Article 29 of the Constitution of 1988.

[6] Articles 156 and 145 of the Constitution of 1988.

[7] Articles 158 and 159 of the Constitution of 1988.

## 1) Cooperation and Collaborative Federalism: A Key to Strengthen States Autonomy

Cooperation can be a very good way for states to keep a part of autonomy. More precisely, if cooperation creates the participation of several political institutions, the establishment of public policies of each state can be autonomous through the realization of politics that could not be achieved by the state itself. However, cooperation can also represent a danger for state autonomy as in the negotiation process; one level of governance can take the ascendance on the others and, as a consequence, restrict the others' government autonomy. Furthermore, cooperation can take a form of interdependence or sometimes centralization if the federal government is too powerful. Then, each government order must be on equal foot in the cooperation process.

Collaborative federalism is the process that realizes national objectives in collaboration with federal government and with all or several member states of the federation. Collaborative federalism is quite different from cooperative federalism because there is no influence from the federal government by means of conditional grants. Collaborative federalism can take two forms. The first one consists in collaboration with all levels of government in order to share and find a balance of power and responsibilities. Nevertheless, an assumption must be made: Each level of government must have fiscal and administrative powers as coordination of public policies depend on interdependence and interdependence presumes that every actor has power to act (Cameron and Simeon 2002, p. 55). The second kind of collaboration is the one between state and local governments. In this case, federal government has a secondary role. It is not the principal but the second actor.

Collaborative federalism is also a way to find a solution to authority overlap when an area is under federal and regional ability. Main advantages of collaboration are to let one level act, to avoid changes and amendments of the federal Constitution. Canada is a good illustration of collaborative federalism. Federal-provincial Premier Ministers Conferences have been created as the Annual Conference of Provincial Premier Ministers. This Annual Conference prepares plans and writes statements to the federal government offering him solutions to solve a problem. Local or regional administrations analyze problems they meet and propose plans to resolve at the federal government level, when this problem concerns a shared area.

## 2) Influence of European and International Relations

Internationalization of relations, borders opening, conducted regions to protect their identity and their autonomy. European Union also had an influence on the protection of regions. The European Regional Development Fund is a general program that gives grants to regions and many others. More specific programs also exist, like economic and social cohesion programs or programs for the development of rural territories. These programs have been created in the logic of subsidiarity principle.

This well-known fundamental principle gives priority to the closest authorities to act in local areas. This principle gives more power to regions delivering grants in order to reinforce economic and social policies. Furthermore, regions could protect their identity and their culture, thanks to European grants allowing development and emphasizing regional culture. Concerning the allocation of resources, the Council for Financial and Fiscal Policy is in charge of allocating these resources to regions and brings them important support.

The European integration process of EU has extensively changed the center-periphery relations. Transfers of some decision-making authority have made the European Commission a significant actor to development of regional governments. Then, communities cooperate also with the European Commission without the federal Spanish government. Regional governments have gained more power as they are represented in some European institutions like the European parliament or the Assembly of European Regions.

# Conclusion

For Spanish communities, coordination is a crucial issue in the Spanish system due to the overlap between regional and national areas. As a consequence, coordination is executed by sectoral committees, composed by regional and national ministers.

Concerning the sources and the allocation of resources, Spanish systems do not really seem like a federal system. Except the Basque country and Navarra, none of the communities collect their own resources[8]. All taxes are levied by the federal government and allocated to communities after a negotiation process. In the Basque country, the situation is the total opposite as the regional government collects all the taxes and gives a part of its revenues to federal government after negotiation. A specific fund also exists for the poorer regions. In respect of article 2 of the Spanish Constitution, which recognizes the right of autonomy to the regions and solidarity, an Interterritorial Compensation Fund has been created to help regions with economic difficulties. This fund has been reinforced by the European Union by regional development programs. Political and financial relations with other governments like Spanish or European entities are a good solution to maintaining some autonomy for Spanish communities. Spanish or European grants give to Spanish communities the capacity to act in more policies regarding the financial increase of the state governments. Thus, financial and fiscal cooperation are good mechanisms to solve solutions related to state or local problems as cooperation promotes the mutual expressions of view and organizes helping relations, in particular in matters of financial difficulties. The distribution of powers and its respect is not anymore an important key to defend state autonomy. The federalism evolution,

---

[8] Richard Gunther and José Ramon Montero, The Politics of Spain, Cambridge, Cambridge University Press, 2009, p.83.

in various countries, has showed that overruns of responsibilities are very frequents and do not secure state powers. However, the financial capacity is a fundamental key to keep and protect autonomy. Grants without federal mandates enable state to act the way they want their home rule and so preserve their autonomy.

# References

## *Books*

Bednar J. (2009), The Robust Federation, Cambridge University Press, New York, USA, 242 p.
Katz E. (2006), United States of America, in Majeed A., Watts R. L. and Brown D. M., A Global dialogue on Federalism – Distribution of Powers and Responsibilities in Federal Countries, vol.2, McGill – Queen's University Press, pp. 296–321.
Mortati C., Istituzioni di Diritto Pubblico, 1967, 7a ed., Pádua, CEDAM, v.2.

## *Periodicals*

Brasileiro A. M. (1974), O Federalismo Cooperativo , Revista Brasileira de Estudos Politicos, Julho, n°39, pp. 83–128.
Cameron D. and Simeon R. (2002), Intergovernmental Relations in Canada: The Emergence of Collaborative Federalism, Publius, Vol. 32, No. 2, The Global Review of Federalism (Spring), pp. 92–122.
Ferraz da Cunha A. C. (1979), Poder Constituinte do Estado-membro, Revista dos Tribunais, São Paulo, pp. 7–49.- Gonçalves Ferreira Filho M. (1991), O Estado Federal Brasileiro à Luz da Constituição de 1988, Revista da faculdade de direito, Universidade de São Paulo, vol.86, pp. 116–129.
Simeon R. and Papillon M. (2006), Canada, in Majeed A., Watts R. L. and Brown D M., A Global dialogue on Federalism – Distribution of Powers and Responsibilities in Federal Countries, vol.2, McGill – Queen's University Press, pp. 92–122.

# The Present and Future Nature of Intergovernmental Relations: A Comparative Vision of the Model in the USA and in Spain

Eva Sáenz Royo

## Introduction

Intergovernmental relations of co-operation exist as an inherent part of every system of political decentralisation. Even in those systems traditionally referred to as dual federalism, the essence of which is a radical separation of competences and functions between the different levels in such a way that each level of government manages its laws via its own administration. To this model corresponds the federal model of the USA, where "paradoxically" intergovernmental relations have been developing since the nineteenth century, as evidenced by Elazar in 1962.[1]

This experience in intergovernmental relations of other federal systems much older than ours will be of great help to us in order to understand the nature of relations of co-operation within the framework of our Autonomous State and to analyse the opportunities that these relations may generate in the future.

This paper places in the Project of Research (DER2009-14235) on "The Reforms of the Descentralized Systems", financed by the Department of Science and Innovation, D. Tomás de la Cuadra-Salcedo Janini being the main investigator.

[1] Elazar (1962). The construction of this theory is fundamentally based upon two other works: Corwin (1950, pp. 1–24), which employs the term "co-operative federalism" and Grodzins (1966).

E.S. Royo (✉)
Facultad de Derecho, Departamento de Derecho Público, University of Zaragoza, C/ Pedro Cerbuna 12, 50009 Zaragoza, Spain
e-mail: evasaenz@unizar.es

A. López-Basaguren and L. Escajedo San Epifanio (eds.), *The Ways of Federalism in Western Countries and the Horizons of Territorial Autonomy in Spain*, Vol. 2, DOI 10.1007/978-3-642-27717-7_11, © Springer-Verlag Berlin Heidelberg 2013

## How Did Relations of Co-operation Contribute to the Origins of Our Autonomous State?

Intergovernmental relations in Spain were originally strengthened as a result of the process of transfer of competences, and the objective of their—essentially—financial content is the transfer to the AC of most of the resources required in order to exercise their competences.[2] This is explained by the fact that the political priority in our Autonomous State was the devolution of numerous areas to the AC, whilst the transfer of tax revenues was slower and more limited. IGRs have been employed as a means of maintaining the financial insufficiency of the AC. Indeed, more than a third of the agreements concluded between the State and the AC have been in Social Services, a competence transferred exclusively to the AC, and have basically consisted of establishing the State's contribution to the AC.[3]

Absolutely essential to this end was the recognition by constitutional case law of the scope of state expenditure beyond its competences, and given that this was a question of compensating for an autonomous financial insufficiency, the State ought not to attempt to influence the exercise of the said autonomous competence, denying that autonomous consent legitimised an encroachment of competences on the part of the State. This was decreed by STC 13/1992 of February 6.

> One might think that the State can hardly damage the political and financial autonomy of the Communities when the latter are under no circumstances obliged to accept the subsidy established in the General State Budgets for actions to promote areas or services that are exclusively of their own competence. Thus, the Autonomous Community would always be able to avoid the damage to its political autonomy or encroachment of competences rejecting the subsidy as formulated in the General State Budgets, and if it accepts it of its own free will, agreeing to the conditions and form of the subsidy, this eliminates the basis for any protest regarding competence in this sense, as this would be tantamount to being in conflict with its own acts. However, reasoning of this type would be constitutionally unacceptable because autonomy and one's own competences are unavailable to both the State and the Autonomous Communities and because, as was stated in STC 201/1988, legal basis 4, the financial autonomy of the Autonomous Communities recognised in articles 156.1 of the Constitution and 1.1 of the LOFCA requires the full availability of financial means in order to exercise, without undue conditions and to their full extent, the relevant competences and, in particular, those configured as exclusive (FJ 7).

This sentence denies that autonomous consent may legitimise state encroachment of competences, employing two basic arguments: the unavailability of the autonomy and of the competences themselves and—I believe this to be

---

[2] Vid. Cicuéndez Santamaría/Ramos Gallarín (2006) and Cicuéndez Santamaría (2006).

[3] García Morales (2004, pp. 71 and 72), which indicates that during 2003, 35 % of the total number of agreements dealt with social services, 258 agreements in total. In 2005, the number of agreements in social services was 252 out of 580, in other words, over 43 %, in García Morales (2006a, p. 83). This trend continues in 2006, with 287 agreements in social services (García Morales (2007, pp. 86–87) and in 2007 (García Morales 2008, p. 179). Vid. also García Morales (2006b, p. 26).

fundamental—the need for financial sufficiency for the exercise of one's own competences.

Based specifically on the doctrine of our TC, provisions are approved with reference to reinforcement activities during the final process of statutory reforms (*vid.* art. 114 EAC).

# The Current Objective of Intergovernmental Relations in Spain: State Influence on Autonomous Policies

During the last decade in particular, in Spain we have witnessed a gradual process of financial decentralisation. The fact that today the financing the autonomous regions is effected largely via wholly or partially assigned taxes, with regulatory capacity included, means that the resources available to the Autonomous Community depend, to a great extent, upon the fiscal capacity of the Autonomous Community itself. Therefore, on the issue of whether the ACs possess sufficient resources for the exercise of their competences, what could be said is that what the ACs do have today are sufficient funding mechanisms to freely decide whether or not to accept a conditional subsidy from the State.

If the **current objective** of IGRs in Spain were to compensate for the financial insufficiency of the autonomies, the trend would clearly have been towards their reduction, in parallel with the reduction in financial transfers from the State to the AC. Paradoxically, the number of agreements between the State and the AC, just like the amount of transfers from the State, has gradually increased.[4]

The process of financial decentralisation and the parallel increase in the number of intergovernmental agreements and state transfers rule out any notion today that these seek to make up for the financial insufficiency of the autonomous regions. What else could be the justification for IGRs and, in particular, the financial transfers resulting from these in federal models where the objective is not to compensate for financial insufficiency? In short, in a context of financial autonomy, what might be the objective of these transfers from the Centre to the autonomous regions?

If we take as a model the first of the Federal States, the USA, a model of so-called dual federalism, we can see that in the nineteenth century, it was already developing intergovernmental relations between the Federation and the member States. These relations were and still are based upon financial concessions from the Federation to the States (the *grants-in-aid*, technically termed "federal intergovernmental transfers").[5] However, the aim of these financial concessions was not to

---

[4] *Vid. Informe sobre los Convenios de colaboración Estado-CCAA suscritos durante 2009*, p. 23: http://www.mpt.gob.es/dms/es/publicaciones/centro_de_publicaciones_de_la_sgt/Periodicas/parrafo/0111116/text_es_files/Informe-convenios-Estado-CCAA-2009-INTERNET.pdf.

[5] Elazar (1962). For the concept of grants-in-aid and specific cases of the development of intergovernmental relations in the USA during the nineteenth century, see Sáenz Royo (2011, p. 3) et seq.

make up for a financial insufficiency of the States, as State revenues were dependent upon their own fiscal capacity upon adopting the principles of a multiple fiscal system or system of separation. The purpose of these financial concessions and, in essence, of intergovernmental relations between the Federation and the States is that the States, in the exercise of their competences, observe federally established priorities. With the adoption of the Sixteenth Amendment in 1913, granting federal government the right to tax incomes, financial concessions from the federation to the States increased,[6] and so, in parallel fashion, did conditions imposed by the Federation in intergovernmental relations, as well as its capacity to influence state politics.[7]

Meanwhile, in Spanish political practice, there have been a multitude of agreements related to questions of autonomous competence directed towards financing measures considered by the State to be of national interest and, thus, associated with conditional subsidies. Amongst these are the agreements regarding the National Plan for Transition to Digital Terrestrial Television (TDT), the Development of the Advanced Plan for the Information Society, those related to hydrologic and forest restoration, those directed towards funding for books and teaching materials during compulsory education, those concerned with the development of incentive programmes for research activity, or those that finance programmes aimed at specific collectives, such as dependent persons, young people, women, female victims of gender violence, immigrants, unaccompanied immigrant minors, etc.[8]

For this reason, in Spain, as in the USA and in comparative law in general, the present nature of relations of co-operation between the State and the CA is, by and large, the orientation and promotion from the centre of specific autonomous policies. A good example of this is the ever-increasing demand for co-financing by the CA.[9] In return, the CA receive funds without having to raise their taxes.

Ultimately, it is neither a peculiarity of our Autonomous State for intergovernmental relations to be closely connected with conditional subsidies nor for them to direct, to a great extent, the exercise of autonomous policies.

---

[6] On the increase of *grants*, see Dilger (2000, pp. 98–107) and Vines (1976, pp. 3–48).

[7] Zimmerman (2001, p. 20).

[8] *Informe sobre los convenios de colaboración Estado-Comunidades Autónomas suscritos durante 2009*, p. 14 *in* http://www.mpt.gob.es/publicaciones/centro_de_publicaciones_de_la_sgt/Periodicas/parrafo/0111116/text_es_files/file/Informe_convenios_Estado-CCAA_2009-INTERNET.pdf.

[9] Specifically, of the 1,059 agreements signed in 2009, in 542 cases, i.e., 51 %, there is an autonomous financial contribution: *Informe sobre los Convenios de colaboración Estado-CCAA suscritos durante 2009, p. 17:* http://www.mpt.gob.es/dms/es/publicaciones/centro_de_publicaciones_de_la_sgt/Periodicas/parrafo/0111116/text_es_files/Informe-convenios-Estado-CCAA-2009-INTERNET.pdf.

## The Future Objective of Intergovernmental Relations in Spain: Regional Influence on State Decisions

Intergovernmental relations in federal models not only serve to influence from the centre towards the regions but also act as an instrument by means of which autonomous territories bring influence to bear upon State decisions. This goal of intergovernmental relations in Spain had previously been little in evidence, so a novelty in this respect was Law 39/2006, of April 14, on Promotion of Personal Autonomy and Care for Dependent People (LPPACDPP).[10]

Article 1.2 of the LPPACDPP establishes that the System for the Autonomy and Care of Dependent Adults will respond to coordinated and co-operative action by the Central Government Administration and the Autonomous Communities, which will contemplate measures in all the areas that affect people in a situation of dependency, with participation, when appropriate, of Local Institutions. In article 3 (ñ) also, co-operation features as one of the fundamental principles behind the law. The SACDA is thus configured as "a common ground for the collaboration and participation of the Public Administrations, in the exercise of their respective competences, on the subject of the promotion of personal autonomy and protection for dependent persons" (art. 6.1 LPPACDP).

The method of structuring this co-operation is through the Territorial Council of the System for the Autonomy and Care of Dependent Adults. According to Final Provision 2 of the LPPACDP, "Within the maximum timeframe of 3 months after the entry into force of this Act, the Territorial Council of the System for Autonomy and Care for Dependency regulated in article 8 shall be formed". Its effective establishment took place on January 22, 2007.

This is an organ of multilateral co-operation, similar to the classical Sectorial Conferences, with the participation of the State, the AC, and if appropriate, Local Institutions (article 12 LD) but with powers previously unknown within our Sectorial Conferences. This is now a question not only of agreeing upon criteria for the distribution of funds (which is included—article 8.2.a LPPACDP) but also of agreeing upon the content of the Royal Decrees and other provisions developed by the law and even informing the Government with regard to the minimum level of protection for which it is exclusively responsible. In this sense, the following are indicated as competences of the Territorial Council:

a. *Agreeing on the framework of inter-administrative cooperation for implementing the Act, as foreseen in article 10;*
b. *Establishing the criteria for determining the intensity of protection of the services foreseen in accordance with articles 10.3 and 15;*
c. *Agreeing on the conditions and amount of the financial benefits foreseen in article 20 and in the first additional provision;*

---

[10] On this subject, see also Sáenz Royo (2010, p. 372) et seq.

d. *Adopting the criteria for the beneficiary's participation in the cost of the services;*
e. *Agreeing on the scale referred to in article 27, with the basic criteria of the assessment procedure and of the characteristics of the assessment bodies;*
f. *Agreeing on joint plans, projects, and programmes, where applicable;*
g. *Adopting common criteria for action and assessment of the System;*
h. *Facilitating the availability of common documents, data, and statistics;*
i. *Establishing the coordination for the case of displaced dependent population;*
j. *Informing on the state implementing rules on the subject of dependency and, in particular, the rules foreseen in article 9.1;*
k. *Serving as a common ground for cooperation, communication, and information between public administrations (Art. 8. 2 LPPACDP).*

Thus, with the ratification of the LPPACDP, co-operation between the State and the CA is confirmed not only as a vehicle for financing the system—via the bilateral collaboration agreements with each Autonomous Community, article 10.4 LPPACDP, but also—and this is what is politically relevant—as a form of legislative development of the law by means of the agreements reached by the Territorial Council of the SACDA.

With the LPPACDP, the State opts to participate in a traditionally autonomous sphere by means of a **horizontal title**, but not to make extensive use of this horizontal title, unilaterally approving the implementing regulations of the law and using the collaboration agreements with the AC to involve and point autonomous policies in that direction via co-financing; instead of that, the central legislator indicates those areas where homogeneity is considered necessary (competences assigned to the Territorial Council), but the finalisation of this is left in the hands of the Territorial Council. Thus, the orientation of autonomous policies with regard to dependence in order to achieve a degree of homogeneity is not in the hands of the State but is decided multilaterally

a.1. *Composition of and decision taking within the Territorial Council*

The decision-making importance of the Territorial Council for the development of the whole System for the Autonomy and Care of Dependent Adults attributes particular relevance with regard to assessing the real contribution of each of the Administrations to the composition of the Council and its method of decision taking. This will reveal to us the degree of involvement of the AC in the definition of "supracommunity general interest".

The Council is constituted by the Minister for Social Policies, the Government representatives in the AC, relevant authorities, and eleven representatives of the Central Government Administration. There is also participation with the right to vote of a representative of each of the autonomous Cities of Ceuta and Melilla, responsible for social issues, and of two representatives of Local Institutions, appointed by the Spanish Federation of Municipalities and Provinces. In total, there are 33 members, of whom 12 represent the State, 2 the local authorities, and

19 the CA and Autonomous Cities. This guarantees the majority of representatives of the Autonomous Communities required by article 8.1 LPPACDP.

The role of the AC is safeguarded in the call for the Plenary Session of the Council, at the request of the President or of one-third of the members or half of the AC. In the latter cases, reasons shall be given for the application, indicating the issue or issues to be considered (article 10.1 Regulation).

Agreements and proposals will be adopted via the approval of those present; failing this, adoption of agreements and proposals will be made by virtue of the majority vote of the representatives of the Central Government Administration and the majority of the Autonomous Communities (art. 12.2 Regulation). This guarantees that it is not sufficient for the Central Government Administration to add to its 12 votes 5 more from Local Institutions, Autonomous Cities, or CA in order to reach an agreement but that it is necessary for the majority of the AC to be in agreement. This is in contradiction with the doctrinal provisions according to which central government would preserve its leading role in the regulatory development of the system.[11]

a.2. *Binding effect of the agreements adopted by the Territorial Council*

One of the problems arising within the SACDA is the very fact that the regulatory development of the law is assigned to an organ of an operational character, given the voluntary nature and the lack of legal force of decisions taken by organs of this kind (STC 31/2010, FJ 112).

It is difficult to deny the legal force of decisions adopted within the Territorial Council and subsequently reflected in a state regulatory provision.

Nevertheless, according to the wording of the LPPACDP, not all the agreements adopted within the Territorial Council have to be reflected in a state regulatory provision. In fact, such important aspects as determining the beneficiary's financial circumstances and the criteria for his or her eligibility for benefiting from the System for the Autonomy and Care of Dependent Adults or the common accreditation criteria to guarantee the quality of centres and services within the System for the Autonomy and Care of Dependent Adults are not included in a Government-approved Royal Decree but are simply published by means of a Resolution issued by the Secretary of State for Social Policy, Families and Care for the Dependent and Disabled. The non-inclusion within legislation has led legal practitioners and literature to question the legal effectiveness of these agreements and the state legislator's reasons for establishing this differentiation depending upon the framework agreed within the Territorial Council. In fact, it has been claimed that Council agreements that do not require the incorporation of a government Royal Decree "will not be binding for the Autonomous Communities that have not expressed their agreement, so that these may depart from them", these agreements merely having

---

[11] Thus is indicated the likelihood that "the representation of the Central Administration in collaboration with that of the Autonomous Communities in which the party in power governs will, in fact, impose its criteria within the Council" (Pérez de Los Cobos (2007, p. 121).

the value of "recommendation".[12] To my mind, this is an incorrect interpretation, as competence in these matters is conferred upon the Territorial Council for the purposes of a homogenous development of the law and cannot be unknown to the AC.

In any case, in the event of the Autonomous Communities opposing the agreement reached within the Territorial Council and then raising problems when it comes to signing the corresponding bilateral Agreement, what appears unacceptable is the possibility of reaching a bilateral agreement that differs from the guidelines established at a multilateral level. Blocking the signature of a bilateral agreement would imply the State's commitment to only the minimum guaranteed level of financing, preventing execution of the loan facility in the Budgets intended for the financing of the bilateral agreement (Transitional Provision 1ª LPPACDP).

## b. *The activities of the AC outside the co-operative framework*

Beyond their involvement and participation within the framework of the Territorial Council and, thus, in the legislative development of the LPPACDP, the work of the ACs is practically reduced to managing the system for dependency previously agreed upon in the Territorial Council and, when appropriate, the possible improvements that might be incorporated through their own Budgets (article 11 LPPACDP).

In the end, it will be the AC who will determine the status of dependence by virtue of the place of residence of the applicant for the benefit, this recognition being valid throughout the national territory. It will also be the social services of the AC who will decide upon, following consultation with and taking into account the opinion of the beneficiary and, when appropriate, of his or her family or legal guardians, an Individual Care Programme (ICP) that will determine the modes of intervention that are most suitable to their needs from among the services and financial benefits established in the Law. Currently, as developed by Royal Decree 727/2007, the AC will also determine the intensity of the services, except in the case of home help (arts. 5–10), the system of compatibilities and compatibilities of the services (art. 11) and the criteria for accessing financial aid (art. 12), and the amount of benefits respecting the maximum figure established (for the year 2010, Royal Decree 374/2010 of March 26).

Meanwhile, the possibility of the AC funding improved care for dependent persons via their own Budgets has been specifically anticipated by the state legislator in paragraph 2 of article 11. This dispels any possible doubts regarding any autonomous intervention outside the State system of care for dependent persons; doubts that have arisen in connection with other areas of health care regulated by central government.[13]

---

[12] Roqueta Buj (2009, p. 87, 101).

[13] On this subject, Sáenz Royo (2009, p. 57) et seq.

# Conclusion

In Spain, there is a fairly widely held perception that the relations of intergovernmental co-operation are not as they should be and that they constitute rather a form of State intervention in autonomous affairs. In this paper, I have attempted to demonstrate that vertical relations of intergovernmental co-operation in Spain largely served as a means by which the State financed the CA so that these might exercise the transferred competences. **This original picture** has changed as advances have been made in financial decentralisation. In a context like today's, with extensive financial decentralisation, financial transfers from the State via intergovernmental relations—which contrary to appearances may actually have increased—are aimed less at compensating for a financial insufficiency than towards directing and fomenting certain autonomous policies. The nature of these intergovernmental relations then is similar to that which has always characterised these relations in other countries like the USA and, therefore, is not unique to our Autonomous State.

With regard to the future, the relations of co-operation established between the State and the AC in the LPPACDP constitute a complete novelty within our history of autonomy in terms of the way in which each of the territorial administrations involved exercises its competences. Up until now, the different Territorial Administrations involved have basically striven to defend and establish their respective sphere of actions so as to exercise it unilaterally, something that, as we have seen, has proved particularly difficult and conflictive in the area of shared competences. The participation of the AC within the Territorial Council in determining the "basic conditions" for the care of dependent adults undoubtedly represents a qualitative step in the development of our Autonomous State and an attempt to reduce conflict not so much through legal channels (as has been attempted with the statutory reforms) as by political means.

While the intention deserves nothing but praise, there is no doubt that this route has been complex in its development and limited in terms of its efficiency, according to the *Informe sobre* "La participación de la Administración General del Estado en el sistema para la autonomía y atención a la dependencia", published by the Government of Spain/ministry of the Presidency, State Agency for the Assessment of Public Policy and Service Quality in 2009. This report indicates that even when the subjects that are competence of the Territorial Council "include such fundamental questions for the development of the SACDA as common criteria for the participation of beneficiaries in the cost of services (copayment), common accreditation criteria for centres or minimum objectives and contents for the necessary establishment of the information system, the Territorial Council has not regulated, or has done so with considerable delay, almost 2 years after the adoption of the law, many of these questions". Another criticism refers to the monitoring and analysis of the regional regulatory development performed by the State.[14]

---

[14] *Informe sobre* "La participación de la Administración General del Estado en el sistema para la autonomía y atención a la dependencia", Government of Spain/Ministry of the Presidency, State

The lack of efficiency, blocking, difficulty in decision-making, and the blurring of responsibilities are the main criticism of the SACDA and of co-operative federalism in general. In fact, these deficiencies have carried recent reforms of German co-operative federalism.[15]

Money is indeed in the very origins of intergovernmental relations in Spain, and without money it would be impossible to understand the present development of most of these relations in our country, where the State uses its spending power to shape autonomous policies. Today's debate revolves around determining whether it is appropriate for that directing of autonomous policies/politics to continue to occur unilaterally at the centre or in a concerted, multilateral manner. It is probable that a commitment to this co-operative federalism and greater decision-making capacity on behalf of the AC would inevitably lead to a reduction in state transfers and an increased financial commitment on the part of the AC: less state decision, less state financing. Is the State prepared? More importantly, are the ACs prepared?

# References

ARROYO GIL, A. (2009), *La reforma constitucional del federalismo alemán: Estudio crítico de la 52ª Ley de modificación de la Ley Fundamental de Bonn, de 28 de agosto de 2006*, Generalitat de Catalunya/Institut d'Estudis Autonòmics
- (2010): "La reforma constitucional de 2009 de las relaciones financieras entre la Federación y los Länder en la República Federal de Alemania", *REAF*, núm. 10
CICUÉNDEZ SANTAMARÍA, R. (2006): "Las transferencias y subvenciones como instrumentos de las relaciones intergubernamentales en España", en LÓPEZ NIETO, *Intergovernmental relations en la España Democrática: interdependencia, autonomía, conflicto y cooperación*, Dykinson
CICUÉNDEZ SANTAMARÍA/RAMOS GALLARÍN (2006): "La dimensión intergubernamental del sistema de financiación autonómico", en LÓPEZ NIETO, *Intergovernmental relations en la España Democrática: interdependencia, autonomía, conflicto y cooperación*, Dykinson
Edward S. Corwin, "The Passing of Dual Federalism," Virginia Law Review 36 (February 1950): 1–24
DILGER, R. J. (2000): "The Study of American Federalism at the Turn of the Century", *State and Local Government Review*, 32
ELAZAR (1962): *The American Partnership: Intergovernmental Cooperation in the Nineteenth-Century United States*, University of Chicago Press
GARCÍA MORALES, M. J. (2004): "Relaciones de colaboración con las Comunidades Autónomas", en *Informe Comunidades Autónomas 2003*, Barcelona, Instituto de Derecho Público
- (2006a): "Relaciones de colaboración con las Comunidades Autónomas" en *Informe Comunidades Autónomas 2005*, Barcelona, Instituto de Derecho Público
- (2006b): "Las relaciones intergubernamentales en el Estado Autonómico: Estado de la cuestión y problemas pendientes", en *Las relaciones intergubernamentales en el Estado Autonómico*, CEPC

---

Agency for the Assessment of Public Policy and Service Quality, 2009, p. VI. A table of the areas still subject to negotiation when the report was written on p. 26 (http://www.imserso.es/InterPresent2/groups/imserso/documents/binario/informesaadageneval.pdf).

[15] Arroyo Gil (2009, pp. 88–92, 122–125) and Arroyo Gil (2010, p. 44).

- (2007): "Relaciones de colaboración con las Comunidades Autónomas" en *Informe Comunidades Autónomas 2006*, Barcelona, Instituto de Derecho Público
- (2008): "Relaciones de colaboración con las Comunidades Autónomas" en *Informe Comunidades Autónomas 2007*, Barcelona, Instituto de Derecho Público
Morton Grodzins, The American System: A New View of Government in the United States (Chicago: Rand McNally & Company, 1966
PÉREZ DE LOS COBOS, F. (2007): "La distribución de competencias entre el Estado y las Comunidades Autónomas en la Ley de Dependencia", en MONTOYA MELGAR (dir), *La protección de las personas dependientes. Comentario a la Ley 39/2006, de promoción de la autonomía personal y atención a las personas en situación de dependencia*, Thomson/Civitas
ROQUETA BUJ, R. (2009): "El sistema para la Autonomía y Atención a la Dependencia", ROQUETA BUJ (coord.), *La situación de dependencia. Régimen jurídico aplicable tras el desarrollo estatal y autonómico de la Ley de Dependencia*, Valencia, Tirant lo blanch
SÁENZ ROYO, E. (2009), "Derechos de protección social y Estado Autonómico: los márgenes constitucionales de actuación del Estado y de las Comunidades Autónomas", EMBID IRUJO (coord.), *Derechos económicos y sociales*, Iustel
- (2010): "Las Relaciones de cooperación intergubernamental en la Ley de Dependencia: un paso sustantivo hacia el federalismo cooperativo", en TUDELA ARANDA/KNÜPLING (eds.), *España y modelos de federalismo*, Madrid, CEPC/Fundación Manuel Giménez Abad
- (2011): "La reforma sanitaria de Obama en el marco del federalismo americano", *Revista General de Derecho Constitucional*, núm. 11
VINES, K. (1976): "The Federal Setting of State Politics", en Jacob/Vines, *Politics in the American States,* 3 ed., Boston, Little, Brown
ZIMMERMAN, J. F. (2001): "National-state relations: Cooperative federalism in the twentieth century", *Publius*, 31

# The Principle of Bilateralism in the Statutory Reforms Following Constitutional Court Ruling: STC 31/2010. Desire and Reality

Ana M. Carmona-Contreras

## Preliminary Considerations

In the wake of events in Catalonia, the various processes of statutory reform that have taken place in Spain in recent years have focused particular attention on regulating institutional relations between Autonomous Communities. Accordingly, it can be stated that including legal sections specifically devoted to said question in the revised basic institutional norms of the Autonomies, in which the various spatial expressions of autonomous community relations are set out,[1] emerges as one of the main features[2] characterising the major changes to the content concerning relations. In this vein, we should remember that, although institutional relations do not figure in the list of necessary contents that Article 147.2 of the Spanish Constitution (SC) assigns to the statutory norm, such relations' direct link to self-government entirely justifies their inclusion in the basic institutional norm of the Autonomous Community.[3] What needs to be clarified, therefore, is not the question of whether they should be included in the statute but rather the constitutional limits to which they should be subject.

In this unprecedented statutory context dominated by the emergence of regulation addressing the previously referred to matter of institutional relations, the present study seeks to explore the key role that the principle of bilateralism plays

---

[1] In the first-generation Statutes, regulation of autonomous community relations with other entities was restricted to those of a horizontal nature: that is to say, to those with other autonomous bodies. Leaving aside said area, however, the general guideline places us in a regulatory context dominated by the absence of statutory references to other spatial expressions regarding relations.

[2] García Morales (2009), p. 363.

[3] Albertí Rovira (2006), p. 716.

A.M. Carmona-Contreras (✉)
Facultad de Derecho, University of Seville, Campus Ramón y Cajal, C/ Enramadilla 18-20, 41018 Seville, Spain
e-mail: anacarmona@us.es

A. López-Basaguren and L. Escajedo San Epifanio (eds.), *The Ways of Federalism in Western Countries and the Horizons of Territorial Autonomy in Spain*, Vol. 2, DOI 10.1007/978-3-642-27717-7_12, © Springer-Verlag Berlin Heidelberg 2013

in the New Statute of Autonomy of Catalonia vis-à-vis vertical cooperation. Likewise, as the institutional forum that plays the leading role[4] through which said principle is channelled (defining itself as a "general and permanent framework for relations" between the governments of the Autonomous Community of Catalonia and central power), special attention is given to the role assigned to the Generalitat-State Bilateral Commission [Article 182, Statute of Autonomy of Catalonia (SAC)].

In this respect, it should be highlighted that both the firm commitment of the reformed Catalan Statute in favour of this principle and its expression in regulatory terms through the previously mentioned Commission,[5] as well as the assessment that in terms of constitutionality it has merited from the Constitutional Court in its groundbreaking Ruling 31/2010, emerge as fundamental analytical referents for our proposed task and provide the framework within which the interpretative dialectic that determines its effective configuration is incorporated. Indeed, only by starting from the interplay between the normative information present in the statutory provisions and the Constitutional Court's interpretation of this is it possible to obtain the full picture of how bilateralism should be understood in our legal code.

Nevertheless, in order to obtain a contextualised picture of the innovations that are concurring at the present time, we deem it essential to apply a diachronic methodological approach that, as a starting point, draws on the concept of bilateralism as it was initially set out in the statute (Thesis: Where have we come from?) and demonstrating its characteristic outlines. Such a genealogical analysis is a key to undertaking an accurate appraisal and, likewise, an effective comparison with the defining features adopted by bilateralism in statutory reform (Antithesis: Where were we heading?), enabling us to understand the changes that have taken place. The finishing point of our analytical journey is inevitably dominated by the interpretation that Constitutional Court Ruling 31/2010 has made of the said principle (Synthesis: Where do we stand now?). Such a comparison will, by way of a conclusion, allow us to determine how much actually remains of the reformed

---

[4] Regulatory expression of bilateralism, however, is not confined solely to the previously cited Commission. Adopting a clearly specific genetic code from a material point of view, the Generalitat-State Joint Commission for Economic and Fiscal Affairs (Article 210.1, SAC) assumes significant competences in the field of Autonomous Community financing, forming a privileged forum for dialogue and harmonisation with central power.

[5] A further point to remember is that the underlying tone of the Catalan commitment to bilateralism was adopted by the reformed text of the Statute of Andalusia as regards its expression in regulatory terms, a Bilateral Commission being set up between the Andalusian Government and the State with a list of functions that was practically identical to its counterpart in Catalonia. Nevertheless, compared to the concept of the relations with the State envisaged under Article 3.1, SAC (The Generalitat's relations with the State are founded on the principle of mutual institutional loyalty and are governed by the principle of autonomy, bilateralism, and multilateralism), the Andalusian norm (Article 219.1, Statute of Autonomy of Andalusia) introduced significant differences, stipulating that said Autonomous Community's relations with the State were to be conducted "within the framework of the principle of solidarity" and based on "collaboration, cooperation, loyalty and mutual help".

SAC's keen desire[6] to place bilateralism in the front line of the region's relations with the State.

## Bilateralism in the Early Stages of Autonomy (Thesis: Where Have We Come From?)

By way of a premise, it is essential to remember that, as a channel for two-way relations between State and Autonomous Community, bilateralism is in no way an innovation that is attributable to recent statutory reforms. On the contrary, since Spain's early involvement in autonomy, said principle has been evident in a wide range of areas through Cross-party Commissions on Transfer of Competences[7] and has emerged as an intrinsic feature of the incipient Autonomous State.[8] The introduction of self-government in the Autonomous Communities in Spain entailed a complex process of transfer of competences from the central State to the new peripheral territorial structures, a process that has basically followed a dual, equal path taken by the two leading parties: the State and each Autonomous Community considered separately.[9]

As regards the activities carried out by said commissions, these mainly involve having been assigned legislative power in the matter of transfer of competences, their decisions being taken as binding.[10] This is clearly evidenced by the fact that the State's power in this regard was restricted to formalising such agreements, the Council of Ministers approving them as Royal Decrees without being able to introduce changes in their content. Thus, in material terms, these were norms that were agreed on and were the result of bilateral agreements and the assertion of diversity.[11]

Once this initial and essential phase of the autonomic process had concluded, the preference for said relational mechanism did not disappear but remained part of

---

[6] Cruz Villalón (2006), p. 84, refers to the presence in the text of the new Catalan Statute of an "unmistakeable spirit of bilateralism as a strategic criterion for relations with the State".

[7] In this respect, the provision contained in Article 147.2 d) of the Spanish Constitution should be placed first, indicating as "necessary" content of the Statute of Autonomy not only "the competences assumed within the framework established in the Constitution" but also (with regard to our argument) "the rules for transferring the services corresponding to said competences". Thus, be it only tacitly, it is in the constitutional provision itself where the existence and justification of this expression of bilateralism is anchored.

[8] Aja Fernández (2003), p. 215.

[9] Said commissions were set up in all the Autonomous Communities, thereby leading to a spread of bilateralism that, in the words of Corretja et al. (2011), p. 32, gave rise to a situation of "multi-bilateralism".

[10] It should be recalled that Constitutional Court Ruling 76/1983, Legal basis 28, expressly underlines the existence of a "competence reserve" in favour of said commissions.

[11] Corretja et al. (2011), p. 31, *op. cit.*

vertical cooperation in the Spanish autonomic system, undergoing deep-rooted changes that mainly involved adopting renewed functions. Compared to the previous stage, this was reflected in a more low-key approach in legal terms, countered by increased cooperation. Indeed, although once matters related to the transfer of services from centralised power to the autonomies had been dealt with, and the sectorial conferences (multilateral forums of an intergovernmental nature) had taken centre stage in the vertical relations, at the same time it could also be seen that bilateralism and its new organic bodies (the Bilateral Cooperation Commissions)[12] asserted not only a determined desire to survive but also a considerable ability to adapt to the new context. However, in this new stage in the development of autonomies, the Commissions were now stripped of their former capacity to regulate over Autonomous Community matters and took on a role that was conceived in general terms[13] and based on political cooperation and the prevention of conflicts.

In this regard, although these commissions were not standardised until the approval of Law 4/1999, through which Law 30/1992 governing the legal system for public administration and common administrative procedure (Article 5[14]) was reformed, it should be stressed that said authorities did enjoy explicit political support, thanks to the Autonomous Pacts endorsed by the two main national parties (PSOE and PP) in 1992. By formulating bilateralism as a complement to multilateral cooperation relations, said Commissions are also perceived as "the most effective means for continuous exchange of information, negotiations and agreements in order to respond to needs resulting from geographical, cultural and linguistic peculiarities, or from the statutory content of each Autonomous

---

[12] Ridaura Martínez (2009), p. 106, reminds us of the chronology in the process of creating said Commissions: the series commenced in 1983 with the creation of the Cooperation Board of the Autonomous Community of Navarre. By 1987, those corresponding to Catalonia, Galicia, the Basque Country, and Andalusia had already been set up. In 1988, the Commissions corresponding to the Regions of Murcia and La Rioja held their first meetings. Those corresponding to the Balearic Islands (1989), the Canary Islands and Aragon (1990), Cantabria (1991), Castilla-Leon and Extremadura (1992), Asturias (1993), Castilla-La Mancha (1996), the Valencian Community and Madrid (2000) were subsequently constituted. Those corresponding to the cities of Ceuta and Melilla held their constituent meetings in 1995.

[13] García Morales (2009), p. 369, *op. cit.*, interprets this intense generalist character, which is typical of Bilateral Commissions, as reflecting their nature as "non-specific platforms".

[14] Section 1 of said precept establishes the generic foundation for two-way collaboration when stating that "The General Administration of the State and the Administration of the Autonomous Communities can create organisations for cooperation between both of a bilateral or multilateral composition, of a general or sectorial scope, in those subject-matters where an interrelation of competences exists, exercising coordination and cooperation, as may be required". Section 2 confers explicit approval of Bilateral Commissions, outlining their main defining features as (a) non-specific nature or general character ("cooperation bodies ... of the general sphere"), (b) intergovernmental nature ("members of the Government, in representation of the General Administration of the State and members of the Government Council, in representation of the respective Autonomous Community"), (c) voluntary constitution and power of self-regulation ("its creation is carried out by agreement which determines the essential elements of its rules").

Community". It is clear, therefore, that the predominant feature in this concept of bilateralism is its necessary link to the specific and singular realities that, as such, require particular treatment in a framework that is suited to channelling such demands.

The low-key nature that, in practice, the tasks undertaken by the various Bilateral Commissions evidenced[15] was to change substantially following reform of the Organic Law of the Constitutional Court in 2000 (Organic Law 1/2000). It should be remembered that, by virtue of the new section 2 of Article 33 of Constitutional Court Organic Law,[16] said authorities assumed the role of determinant arbitrators vis-à-vis conflicts that arose subsequent to the approval of laws or norms that enjoyed the status of Law. In this regard, extending the deadline for lodging an appeal of unconstitutionality was envisaged (from 3 months in general terms, it was extended to a maximum of nine), provided the corresponding Bilateral Commission adopted an agreement to initiate negotiations regarding the interpretation of the norm that was subject to dispute.[17]

Quite a different (and certainly not irrelevant) matter concerns instances in which, should intergovernmental dialogue lead to an agreement indicating the need to modify any legal precept (assuming the commitment to revise the content), its effectiveness must perforce be subordinate to the receptive will manifested by the corresponding assembly vis-à-vis the legislative initiative presented by the Government in question. Assuming the constitutionality of the norm that is the subject of dissent, cases in which agreements reached in the Bilateral Commission and that concern future regulatory implementation, the content of which the

---

[15] García Morales (2009), p. 368, *op. cit.*, draws attention to the fact that these commissions "have proved far less important than multilateral mechanisms, to the point that they have been symbolic in many cases".

[16] "Notwithstanding the stipulations set out in the previous section, the President of the Government, together with the official executive bodies of the Autonomous Communities, may lodge an appeal of unconstitutionality within a period of 9 months against laws, provisions or acts which have the status of Law, in regard to which, and in an effort to avoid said appeal from being lodged, the following requirements are met:

a. That the Bilateral Cooperation Commission involving the General Administration and State and the respective Autonomous Community meet, either of the two authorities having the power to request said meeting be convened.

b. That an agreement be adopted by the above-mentioned Bilateral Commission concerning the commencement of negotiations to solve discrepancies. Should it prove necessary, a requirement may be put forward for the regulatory text to be changed. Such an agreement may or may not call for the norm to be suspended should the appeal be lodged within the period stipulated in the present section.

c. That the Constitutional Court be notified of the agreement by the above-mentioned bodies within a period of 3 months subsequent to the Law, provision, or act which has the status of Law being published in the *Official State Bulletin* and in the *Official Gazette* of the corresponding Autonomous Community".

[17] For comprehensive information regarding the activities undertaken in this area by the various Bilateral Commissions, see García Morales (2009), pp. 386–389, *op. cit.*

exercise of executive power must assume,[18] appear to be less problematic. Without obviating such difficulties, the fundamental idea to highlight is that by exercising this faculty, the Bilateral Commissions assume an important role in such an important field as that of the creation of norms.


## Bilateralism in Statutory Reform (Antithesis: Where Were We Heading?)

Having established bilateralism as a principle and described the areas in which it has operated throughout the long experience of constructing and establishing the Autonomous State, it is evident that the changes in nuance set out under statutory reforms should be embraced not in the field of *ex novo* creation but, on the contrary, in that of the assumption of a renewed functionality. In this respect, the intention of statutory reformers is not confined to ratifying the previous model but goes further and evidences a keen desire for change. It is not, therefore, a question of changing bilateralism so that it remains the same.[19] The "strong winds of change in bilateralism"[20] that impregnate the reform of the SAC reflect nothing more than the determined expression of a will to introduce fundamental changes in said principle, leading it to establish a new *modus operandi* in relations between Autonomous Community and State. An unmistakeable pointer in this respect is the tendency towards asymmetry that the multilateralism-bilateralism binomial displays: an asymmetrical relation that is manifested in an unbalanced relation of forces that is committed to strengthening bilateral rather than multilateral channels. All of this takes place in a constitutional context dominated by the absence of normative precautions in this regard and in which the statutory norm arrogates a regulatory prominence that, strictly speaking, should not correspond to it.[21]

   The content of Article 3.1 of the SAC clearly evidences the reinforcing approach when, in the task of delimiting the political framework of the relations between the Generalitat (after stating that these "are founded on the principle of mutual institutional loyalty"), it stipulates that "they are governed by the general principle according to which the Generalitat is a State, by the principle of autonomy, bilateralism and multilateralism". Against such a background of relational frameworks, bilateralism would tend to operate as the rule, while multilateralism

---

[18] A detailed reflection regarding the problem posed in the text can be found in González Beilfuss (2008), p. 33.

[19] París Domenech (2006), p. 399 expressly states that "the SAC seeks to go beyond the framework of relations which has naturally been established".

[20] See note 5.

[21] In this regard, we fully concur with the view of Cruz Villalón (2006), p. 84, *op. cit.,*: "The essential problem of this process is the *order of factors,* which is important since it is clear they should have begun with the Constitution and then continued with the Statutes".

would be seen as the exception: that is, as a secondary or residual channel of Autonomous Community relations with the State.[22] The constitutionality of conceiving institutional relations in such a manner has been questioned by the appeals lodged by the Partido Popular (PP), the Ombudsman, and the Regional Government of La Rioja, considering that this would confer on the Generalitat a status of equality with the State to the detriment of the other Autonomous Communities and that it would eventually generate asymmetries that were not acceptable under the constitutional text. It was left to the Constitutional Court to determine whether or not it agreed with such an interpretation of the statutory precept.

In this relational landscape dominated by the idea of duality, it is logical and inevitable that the Generalitat-State Bilateral Commission for Cooperation should assume the leading role, taking on an undoubted relevance and prominence, resulting from it being considered under Article 183.1 SAC as a "general and permanent framework for relations between the Governments of the Generalitat and the State for the following purposes:

a) The participation and collaboration of the Generalitat in exercising competences which affect the autonomy of Catalonia.
b) Exchanging information and establishing, when appropriate, collaboration mechanisms in the respective public policies and matters of common interest".

Compared to the previous stage, the interpretation of this first section heralds a major shift, displaying an "emphasis, ambition and detail in statutory regulation", which *per se* reflects a significant development.[23] From a strictly semantic point of view, although with an undoubted political intention, the change in name given to the participants involved in the forum referred to is striking, its previous administrative character (Article 5 of Law 4/1999 referred to representatives of the respective Administrations) now giving way to one that is essentially connected to the political sphere of executive power (governments).

As regards the main underlying issues that the commission addresses, fundamental change seems to be related to the fact that, whilst maintaining the criterion of "interrelation of competences" (sic: "competences that affect the autonomy of Catalonia"), not only are the traditional "functions of coordination and cooperation depending on each case in question" envisaged but also the power of the Autonomous Communities to participate. With this, said principle, which is set out in general terms under Article 174.3 SAC[24] and which is subject to subsequent

---

[22] This idea is not neutralised by resorting to the otherwise unquestionable argument that the Statute is not the ideal normative framework for regulating multilateralism, as it goes beyond its area of competences. The determinant point in this respect is that, beyond the literal tone of Article 3.1 SAC, a complete and systematic reading of the reformed basic institutional norm of Catalonia clearly shows an unequivocal preference for the bilateral option, a direct dialogue being established between central power and the Generalitat.

[23] Corretja, Vintró, Bernadí (2011), p. 36, *op. cit.*

[24] "In matters which affect its competences, the Generalitat participates in national decision-making institutions, organisations and procedures, in application of the stipulations set out in the present Statute and Laws".

specification throughout the statutory text,[25] is later reinforced, specified through mandates to the central legislator and thus emerging as a powerful instrument for penetrating central power, thereby opening up important areas for greater interrelation between the various levels of government.[26]

In this respect, where the Catalan text broke new ground was not so much in affirming the previously referred to power to participate, which, to all intents and purposes, already existed in our code at the legislative scale, but rather by actually including it in the highest level of regional legislation and redirecting it towards the bilateral framework. It was precisely these two aspects that gave rise to further reservations concerning the issue of constitutionality, the argument being that, should this be the case, the Generalitat would be given the power of co-decision in areas under State competence.

Having established the structural foundations on which the principle of bilateralism rests, the Statute subsequently sets out the functions attributed to the Commission ("to deliberate, make proposals and, where appropriate, to adopt agreements in the cases laid down" in the Statute), thanks to which the Statute begins to take shape and is able to engage in a number of activities linked to a wide range of areas, as reflected in Article 183.2 SAC:[27]

a. Drafting laws, particularly those affecting the distribution of competences between State and Generalitat;
b. Planning the general economic policy of the national government in all matters specifically affecting the interests and competences of the Generalitat and regarding the application and implementation of said policy;
c. Promoting appropriate measures to improve cooperation between State and Generalitat and to ensure a more effective exercise of the respective competences in areas of common interest;
d. Dealing with any conflicts that may arise between the two parts concerning competences and, where necessary, proposing measures to resolve them;
e. Evaluating the effectiveness of collaboration mechanisms established between State and Generalitat and proposing measures for the improvement thereof;

---

[25] Thus, the Generalitat's capacity to participate in appointing members of state organisations is envisaged. This is affirmed in relation to the General Council of the Judiciary and the Constitutional Court "in the terms which the laws establish or, where appropriate, the parliamentary code" (Article 180, SAC). A similar provision can be found in Article 182, devoted to the "appointment (by the Generalitat) of representatives in financial and social organisations". In such instances, Autonomous Community participation will also always be bound by "the terms set out in the relevant legislation".

[26] Roig Molés (2006), p. 169, maintains that autonomic participation in decisional processes included in the state sphere is "an implicit element of our system".

[27] Other functions assigned to the Bilateral Commission concern the following matters: gaming and betting (Article 141.2, SAC) and infrastructures and equipment under State ownership in Catalonia (Article 149.2).

f. Proposing a list of national financial organisations, institutions, and public enterprises in which the Generalitat may appoint representatives, as well as forms of representation;

g. Monitoring European policy to ensure the effectiveness of the Generalitat's participation in European Union affairs;

h. Monitoring any foreign activity of the State that may affect the specific competences of the Generalitat;

i. Any matters of common interest that may be established by law or proposed by the parties.

Attention should be drawn to the fact that Sections a, b, and f, namely those provisions entailing greater functional innovation and enhancing regional powers vis-à-vis the central State, were challenged by the Constitutional Court, either directly, when pointing to the unconstitutionality of the Bilateral Commission's assumption of certain functions, or indirectly, when questioning the constitutional viability of the Generalitat's assumption of specific faculties set out under other Articles of the Statute, jurisdiction over which corresponds to the Bilateral Commission, according to Article 183.2 SAC.

To conclude our analysis of the statutory configuration of this body, reference should be made to the provision contained in the Second Additional Provision of the SAC, by virtue of which the Commission's position as the main forum for meetings between the Autonomous Communities and the State is strengthened. Indeed, said precept stipulates that "should the Statute establish that the position of the Generalitat is determinant when establishing an agreement with the national government and should the latter fail to take such a position into account, then the national government must provide sufficient justification before the Generalitat-State Bilateral Commission". The cases referred to by the norm envisage activities related to a wide range of matters:

1) Authorising new forms of betting and gaming at the State level (Article 141.2, SAC);

2) Determining the location of infrastructure and facilities under State ownership in Catalonia (Article 149.2, SAC);

3) Establishing the State's position with regard to European initiatives or proposals that affect its "exclusive competences" and determining whether "financial or administrative consequences of a special relevance to Catalonia" may derive from the latter.

In view of the intergovernmental disagreement arising out of national government discrepancy concerning the determinant position formulated by the Generalitat, the Commission emerges as the framework in which central power is obliged to justify its decision. Nevertheless, how such a duty should be fulfilled is left totally undecided by the Statute without, however, any legal consequences arising. Leaving for the following section an appraisal of what this provision merits from the Constitutional Court in terms of constitutionality, the key element that deserves to be highlighted is that, thanks to this obligation, establishing a channel of communication between the two political authorities is not left to political fate or to the climate of collaboration prevailing at any given moment. From the standpoint of consolidating an environment of cooperation, such an obligation should be viewed in positive terms.

# Constitutional Court Ruling 31/2010: Where Do We Stand? (Summary)

Having established the existential outlines of the principle of bilateralism and of the main forum on which it is based—the Generalitat-State Bilateral Commission—in the Statute of Catalonia, we now analyse the interpretation that the Constitutional Court has made thereof through Ruling 31/2010. As stated above, understanding the interpretative approach adopted by the Constitutional Court is essential towards determining the real image that both the previously mentioned principle and the areas in which it is applied have in our legal system. Comparing the norm and the interpretation thereof made by the Constitutional Court will provide us with a précis of the acceptable constitutional framework for dealing with the issues posited.

## *General Considerations Concerning the Principle of Bilateralism*

Addressing the preliminary question of whether the Statute of Autonomy can regulate relations with the State, as a basis the Court claims that said regulatory framework is not "inappropriate" for such a purpose.[28] However, the regulatory capacity of said norm is confined to an eminently general structure, namely to setting out the principles that govern the previously mentioned vertical relations. In this sense, the Court is conclusive when highlighting that "beyond these principles, laying down any specific rules that govern such a system must respond to structural demands of a constitutional nature which, as with the principle of each Autonomous Community's cooperation with the State and of all Autonomous Communities' cooperation with one another, *can clearly only be derived from the Constitution itself*".[29] Therefore, a yardstick for assigning competences is being applied which leaves no room for doubt and which reserves a major role for the Constitution, reflected in its "laying down any specific rules" governing cooperation.[30] If such a criterion is applied, the room for manoeuvre left to the statute is clearly predetermined and must comply with constitutional provisions and, consequently, be confined to dealing with content of a general nature.

---

[28] Constitutional Court Ruling 31/2010, Legal basis 13.

[29] *Ibidem* (our italics).

[30] *Ibidem*.

Analysing the statutory reference to the principle of bilateralism as the channel for the Generalitat's relation with the State, which, as Article 3.1 of the Statute of Catalonia sets out, does not exclude multilateral relations, the Constitutional Court states that it is "constitutionally acceptable (...) since it merely indicates that, because both are the 'Spanish State', the respective position will in each instance be imposed depending on what emerges from the constitutional system of distributing competencies".[31] Following on from its initial considerations, the Court goes on to give further reasoning, stressing that statutory bilateralism is posited "in terms of integration and not differentiation",[32] such that when it claims that "the Generalitat is the State" (Article 3.1 of the SAC) it is merely stating that the Generalitat as a unit or integrating part of the overall structure of the State has the capacity to undertake direct relations with the latter, whether it be the central State or the general State. No objection may be raised to the Constitutional Court's interpretation, which merely confines itself to evidencing a principle of regulatory preference that favours the Constitution and in which the scope of action corresponding to statutory norms must perforce accommodate itself.

Having come to this point, however, the Constitutional Court has not yet concluded its interpretation since, in an "unusual divergence",[33] it goes on to state that

1) Bilateralism cannot be understood "as expressing a relation between political bodies which are on an equal footing and are able to negotiate such a condition with one another, since (...) the State always holds a position of superiority over the Autonomous Communities (Constitutional Court Ruling 4/1981, Legal basis 3)".

    How inaccurate such an interpretation is has been highlighted by a number of scholars, who concur[34] in the belief that, within their respective areas of competences, relations between the various national and regional entities can in no way be governed by the principle of hierarchy but should rather be governed by the principle of competences. In such a relational context, therefore, there is no doubt that both entities are on an equal standing and not in a position of dominance and subordination.[35]

---

[31] *Ibidem.*

[32] *Ibidem.*

[33] Balaguer Callejón (2011), p. 461.

[34] Corretja, Vintró, Bernadí (2011), p. 3, *op. cit.*

[35] F. Balaguer Callejón (2011), pp. 462–463, *op. cit.*, draws attention to one key concept that the Court has overlooked in its approach, namely, "Superiority of the State over the Autonomous Communities is reflected in certain constitutional techniques, but may not be resorted to with regard to bilateral cooperation mechanisms, which must be based on a scrupulous respect for respective competences". For their part, Corretja, Vintró, Bernadí (2011), p. 4, *op. cit.* consider that the Constitutional Court's argument "reflects its mistrust of the principle of bilateralism and the possibility that such a principle may allow Catalonia to adopt a unique position within the State concerning a range of matters".

2) Said principle, "should only be considered within the sphere of relations between bodies as an expression of the general principle of cooperation, implicit in the territorial organisation of our State (Constitutional Court Ruling 194/2004, Legal basis 9)".

When making this second statement, the Court seems to be offering an indication of what its position will be vis-à-vis the scope of functions defined under a bilateral relation, restricting such a relation to what is solely of a cooperative nature. Such an interpretation thus already excludes the area of participation which, as already highlighted, has, thanks to statutory reform, come to form part of the list of powers that run along a dual track.

## The Participative Aspect of Bilateral Relations

### A General Approach

Even though, as we have just seen, the Ruling restricts the scope of bilateralism to tasks concerning cooperation, the provision regarding the Generalitat's involvement in national decision-making procedures "affecting its competences in application of the stipulations set out in the present Statute and Laws" (Article 174.3 SAC) was not ruled unconstitutional. The Constitutional Court's strategy concerning not only this general provision but also vis-à-vis the various specific expressions to emerge from it was to subject them to intense change. One key mechanism for achieving this is by systematically applying the interpretative guideline that refers to the preference of the constitutional framework as the legal system that is to regulate specific aspects of institutional relations and that condemns the Statutes to merely affirming the general principle. As a result of applying such an interpretative precept, the Court goes on to state that "the precept in question is sufficiently *general and unclear* to make it impossible to determine the meaning thereof unless it is through the link to the rules (...) to which the precise definition of each one of its terms refers".[36]

Together with this preliminary interpretation, it should not be forgotten that, since "the precept deals with organic and functional involvement in national matters", reference to the laws that such a precept has laid down should be understood as favouring those emanating from the State as the holder of the competences in question. Having established such premises, the immediate consequence is that statutory provisions "must perforce *leave untouched the control over any state competences involved as well as total freedom* which exercise thereof entails in the hands of national bodies and institutions".[37] In this way, both the content of Article 174.3 of the SAC and the remaining precepts in which this is specifically expressed with regard to particular national bodies and institutions are

---

[36] Constitutional Court Ruling 31/2010, Legal basis 111 (our italics).

[37] *Ibidem* (our italics).

changed significantly since they are all stripped of the prescriptive value to regulate over any matters that concern key or programme-related content.[38]

## Involvement in the Bilateral Commission

Analysis of participation based on the consideration of the Generalitat-State Bilateral Commission as the setting in which this was to be developed came through Legal basis 115 of the Ruling. Said Legal basis supports the constitutionality of the statutory definition as a "general and permanent framework for relations" between the two governments, although in order to achieve this, a profound reshaping of what interpretation should be made of said provision needed to be carried out. When undertaking this task, the Constitutional Court chose to adopt a negative or exclusionary approach since it set out said body's existential and functional guidelines based on the following observations: "it does not exclude other areas of relations, nor confers on said Commission any other function than that of voluntary cooperation in the area of the unalterable competences of the two governments".[39]

Such an approach should have been adopted as a basic criterion for rejecting the constitutionality of Article 183.1(a) of the SAC, which attributes to the Bilateral Commission "the participation and cooperation of the Generalitat in exercising the competences which affect the autonomy of Catalonia". However, this was not to be the case since, once again, the Court resorted to the previously applied criterion that this is "a faculty of political action which only entails commitment in the political sphere related to it and to which it is necessarily confined".[40] Contained within these limits, regional involvement and cooperation when exercising national competences "do not violate the Constitution, since they do not prevent or undermine the State's free and full exercise of its own competences".[41]

An identical conclusion is reached with regard to assigning to the Bilateral Commission the following powers contained in Article 183.2 of the SAC:

a) Draft laws that specifically affect the distribution of competences between State and Generalitat;
b) Plans for the national government's general economic policy in all matters that particularly affect the interests and competences of the Generalitat and concerning the application and implementation of said policy;

---

[38] One view that is openly critical in this regard is held by París Domenech (2006), p. 403, *op. cit.*, who states that the Constitutional Court's interpretation "strips of all content the idea of participation that is set out in the statutory text, it now being forced to depend on political will and not on the concept of the Autonomous State, and denies a practice which is widespread and already envisaged in various legal systems".

[39] Constitutional Court Ruling 31/2010, Legal basis 115.

[40] Constitutional Court Ruling 31/2010, Legal basis 115.

[41] *Ibidem.*

c) Proposals for any financial bodies or institutions and national public companies in which the Generalitat may appoint representatives, as well as the various forms that said representation may take.

In this regard, by applying the same well-worn argument, it reiterates that "any decisions or agreements which the Bilateral Commission may adopt, as a cooperation body" lack any binding force as such, since they may not "in any way prevent the free and full exercise by the State of its competences nor, as a result, replace, bind or annul the decisions which it is charged with adopting".[42] Special mention should be made of the provision contained in section a) of the precept analysed, which goes beyond the Commission's functional sphere by referring to the "legislative competences of the national parliament and the parliament of Catalonia".[43] The reason given by the Court is that because the matter concerns relations between governments, "the competences affected can only be, in a strict sense and in terms of voluntary cooperation, those which correspond to one executive power and to another", excluding those of a legislative nature, exercised by the national parliament and by the parliament of Catalonia, "bodies which are outside the Bilateral Commission".[44]

At this point, it should be stated that these arguments prove clearly questionable not only because they fail to take account of the literal tone of the precept analysed, since at no time is the Commission endowed with the faculty to exercise legislative functions concerning the draft laws in question, but also, and more importantly, because what seems to have been ignored is the fact that the legislative initiative that corresponds to the two executives—central and regional—emerges as a key government mechanism and thus falls within the sphere of their competences. In addition, it overlooks the main virtue that, thanks to the provision set out under Article 33.2 of the Organic Law on the Constitutional Court, has been put into practice by Bilateral Commissions, namely the task of preventing regulatory and legislative conflicts.[45]

## The State's Duty to Provide Justification as Set Out in the Second Additional Provision

As the Constitutional Court itself highlights, challenging the Additional Provision—that "should the Statute set out that the position of the Generalitat is determinant when establishing an agreement with the national government and should the latter fail to take such a position into account, then it must provide

---

[42] Constitutional Court Ruling 31/2010, Legal basis 116.

[43] *Ibidem.*

[44] *Ibidem.*

[45] Corretja, Vintró, Bernadí (2011), p. 38 *op. cit.*, level their criticism at the Constitutional Court, feeling that the arguments put forward evidence "echoes of the nineteenth century, far removed from the dynamics of parliamentary systems of government".

sufficient justification before the Generalitat-State Bilateral Commission"—is of a "clearly rhetorical nature"[46] since circumstances indicate that the challenge lodged "fails to indicate the constitutional precept being infringed".[47]

In light of such a pronouncement, it is clear throughout Legal basis 117 that the constitutionality of the obligation foreseen is in no doubt, although no material link on the part of the State may be assumed to exist,[48] "given the general terms of the provision challenged, as a cooperation mechanism in cases in which the interests of the Autonomous Community are or may be particularly affected, without the State in any way being bound by the decision which it must adopt when exercising its competences".[49] In light of such observations, the Constitutional Court concludes its reasoning by stating that the Statute is not "an inappropriate framework for envisaging such mechanisms in the general terms in which they are set out in the provision challenged".[50]

The Court adopted a similar criterion when discarding the constitutionality of the specific statutory provisions that particularly envisaged a national duty to provide justification, namely:

a) The preliminary report to be issued by the Generalitat for authorising new types of gaming and betting at a national scale (Article 141.2 of the SAC). It is felt that, since it is not binding, it "in no way affects the decision to be adopted by the State". As regards the obligation to provide justification should a different position to that of the Generalitat be held, this does not "interfere with national competence".[51]

b) The same conclusion is reached regarding the report issued by the Bilateral Commission to determine the location of nationally owned infrastructure and facilities in Catalonia (Article 149.2 of the SAC).[52] The fact that said report is not issued exclusively by the regional government but by the Commission does not alter the sense of the interpretation generally applied in other cases.

c) A more detailed argument is provided by the Court with regard to the provision contained in Article 186.3 of the SAC—national discrepancy concerning the position formulated by the Generalitat with regard to European initiatives that affect its exclusive competences and arising from which there may be financial

---

[46] F. Balaguer Callejón (2011), p. 464, *op. cit.*, is critical of the position adopted by the Constitutional Court on this matter: "The statutory precept is so clear that it specifically contemplates the instance in which the State, as a result of not being bound by the decision it must adopt, opts to take the contrary position to that held by the Generalitat (which it could not do if it were bound). It is therefore difficult to understand why there is such insistence on repeating something which is so obvious".

[47] Constitutional Court Ruling 31/2010, Legal basis 117.

[48] Balaguer Callejón (2011), p. 463, *op. cit.*

[49] *Ibidem.*

[50] *Ibidem.*

[51] Constitutional Court Ruling 31/2010, Legal basis 86.

[52] Constitutional Court Ruling 31/2010, Legal basis 92.

or administrative implications. Indeed, rejecting a maximalist approach to the term "determinant", which would allow it to be considered equivalent to "binding", an alternative interpretation is proposed that would not affect the possibility that "the State might establish and assert its position should, this statutory provision having become generally established, two or more Autonomous Communities maintain differing positions".[53] The State's duty to provide justification is thus embraced within the concept of cooperation and is considered as a means to externalise discrepancy "in cases in which the competences and interests of the Autonomous Community are particularly affected".[54] Interpreted thus, the conclusion is that the Statute is not "an inappropriate framework" to describe the position of the Autonomous Community as determinant, provided the latter "does not refer to European initiatives of a general nature but only to those contained under Article 186.3 of the SAC".[55]

## Final Thoughts: Desire and Reality

Having concluded the analysis of the regulatory framework that marks out bilateralism in the reformed SAC, as well as the interpretation thereof made through Constitutional Court Ruling 31/2010, some final thoughts concerning the current status of the question from an empirical standpoint need to be addressed. Legal commentators are faced with a series of unresolved issues that must be dealt with such as; what remains of statutory will, of that desire to open up new horizons to the principle of bilateralism? After the highest authority (the Constitutional Court) has applied its corrective filter to the Constitution, what is the reality now facing said principle of bilateralism? Bearing in mind the context that defines bilateralism, according to the Constitutional Court's interpretation, has the principle taken a step backwards vis-à-vis its original configuration? Are fresh winds blowing for bilateralism in our legal system?

An overall appraisal of the pronouncements contained in Constitutional Court Ruling 31/2010 in the matter of institutional relations with particular regard to the dual nature thereof clearly evidences the Constitutional Court's profound mistrust in the matter. This is clearly reflected in the Court's tendency to adopt interpretative criteria that seek to deactivate the regulatory mandate included in the statutory provisions analysed. As we have seen, acting in such a manner maintains constitutionality but at the expense of sacrificing the prescriptive nature of the rules over which control is exercised.

The positive consequences arising from the understandable interpretation of bilateralism as an integrating mechanism and not one that causes disruption are

---

[53] Constitutional Court Ruling 31/2010, Legal basis 120.

[54] *Ibidem.*

[55] *Ibidem.*

quickly overshadowed by declaring the State to be in a position of hierarchical superiority, ignoring the criterion of competence and immediately resulting in the Autonomous Communities being relegated to a position of subordination.

Despite the fact that most of the provisions challenged are expressed in general terms that leave central legislative power intact, and are therefore not unconstitutional, Autonomous Community power to take part in decision-making processes at a national scale is stripped of prescriptive content in light of the total freedom that national legislation has to act by applying its own criteria.

Finally, the renewed list of functions assigned by the Statute to the Bilateral Commission, the key institutional reference embracing the main expressions of the dual relationship between governments, has also been subject to a profound reinterpretation. The constitutionality of the provisions analysed is linked directly to an interpretation in which the core aspect is the voluntary nature of the functions set out. Strictly confined to inter-governmental relations, the effects relate to the area of political cooperation and coordination.

Corseted within these constitutional constraints, the potential of this predominantly consultative bilateralism remains undeniable. It should be remembered that formalised and institutionalised bilateralism is "easier to force"[56] and leads to a system that necessarily tends towards cooperation. Having established the required regulatory basis, however, we must remember that the success of institutional relations (of any kind) inevitably entails a spirit of cooperation in which political will emerges as an "essential structural requirement".[57]

# References

E. Aja Fernández, *El Estado Autonómico. Federalismo y Hechos Diferenciales*, Alianza Editorial, Madrid, 2003, page 215.

E. Albertí Rovira; "¿Pueden los Estatutos suplir el déficit constitucional relativo a la previsión de relaciones intergubernamentales? (Las relaciones de las Comunidades Autónomas con el Estado, las demás Comunidades y la Unión Europea en las reformas actuales de los Estatutos de Autonomía)", in G. Ruiz-Rico (coord.), *La reforma de los Estatutos de Autonomia*, University of Jaen/Tirant lo blanch, Valencia, 2006, page 716.

F. Balaguer Callejón, "La incidencia de la STC 31/2010 en la formulación estatutaria de las relaciones entre la Generalitat de Cataluña y el Estado", *Revista de Estudios Federales y Autonómicos*, issue 12, 2011, page 461.

G. Cámara Villar, "El principio y las relaciones de colaboración entre el Estado y las CCAA", *Revista de Derecho Constitucional Europeo*, issue 1, 2004, page 207.

P. Cruz Villalón, "La reforma del Estado de las Autonomías", *Revista Estudios Autonómicos y Federales*, issue 2, 2006, page 84.

M. Corretja-J. Vintró-X. Bernadí, "Bilateralidad y multilateralidad. La participación de la Generalitat en políticas y organismos estatales, y la Comisión Bilateral,", *Revista de Estudios Autonómicos y Federales*, issue 12, 2011, page 32.

---

[56] Roig Molés (2006), p. 172, *op. cit.*

[57] Cámara Villar (2004), p. 207.

M. J. García Morales: "Los nuevos Estatutos de Autonomía y las relaciones de colaboración. Un nuevo escenario, ¿una nueva etapa?" *Revista Jurídica de Castilla y León,* issue 19, 2009, page 363.

M. González Beilfuss, "La resolución judicial de las discrepancias competenciales entre el Estado y las Comunidades Autónomas: el mecanismo del artículo 33.2 LOTC", in J. Tornos Mas (dir.): *Informe Comunidades Autónomas 2007,* Instituto de Derecho Público, Barcelona, 2008, page 33.

N. París Domenech, "Las relaciones institucionales de la Generalitat en la Sentencia sobre el Estatuto de Autonomía de Cataluña", *Revista catalana de dret públic,* Special edition on Ruling 31/2010, regarding the 2006 Statute of Autonomy of Catalonia, page 399.

M. J. Ridaura Martínez, *Relaciones intergubernamentales: Estado-Comunidad Autónoma,* Tirant lo Blanch, Valencia, 2009, note 128, page 106.

E. Roig Molés, "La reforma del Estado de las Autonomías: ¿ruptura o consolidación del modelo constitucional de 1978?" *Revista de Estudios Autonómicos y Federales,* issue 3, 2006, page 169.

# Cooperation Between Autonomous Communities: An Opportunity to Rationalise the Autonomous State in Times of Crisis

Josep M. Castellà Andreu

## Uneasy Constitutional Regulation Towards Cooperation Between Autonomous Communities: Article 145.2 of the Spanish Constitution

Autonomous Communities involvement in national decision-making and cooperation between State and Autonomous Communities tend to be cited as one of the
major weaknesses of the Autonomous State. Within this particular situation, horizontal relations between the various Autonomous Communities pose somewhat of a
paradox. On the one hand, they are the only kind of relations set out in the
Constitution, albeit from a standpoint of cautious unease towards the Autonomous
Communities, through express mention of the legal mechanisms on which such
relations are based: cooperation accords and agreements (Art. 145.2 of the Spanish
Constitution: hereinafter "SC"). On the other hand, a look at the past 30 years of the
Autonomous State reveals how little such relations have been used by the Autonomous Communities. The Council of State has highlighted the "clearly inadequate
nature [of the constitutional precept], which focuses more on restricting Autonomous Community initiative to cooperate or collaborate with one another and with
the State than on imposing on them the need to act in accordance with such

The current work forms part of the activities involved in the research project "Estado autonómico y
democracia: los derechos de participación en los estatutos de autonomía" (MCI, DER2009-12921).

J.M. Castellà Andreu (✉)
University of Barcelona, Av. Diagonal 684, 08034 Barcelona, Spain
e-mail: castella@ub.edu

principles...".[1] Autonomous Communities have tended to deal with the central administration individually regardless of the fact that the Constitution makes no mention of any such vertical relations.

Specifically, the Constitution confines itself to referring to two kinds of mechanism: agreements and accords, without clarifying how they differ, except for the nature of parliamentary intervention—communication in the former case and authorisation in the latter. With regard to agreements, the Constitution merely adds that they are for the "management and provision of services inherent to the Autonomous Communities", although what purpose accords serve is not made clear.[2] With regard to the parliamentary procedure for authorising accords, Art. 74.2 of the SC specifies that said procedure is to commence in the Senate (Upper House) and requires the agreement of both Houses. Should such an agreement fail to be reached, a mixed parliamentary commission comprising members from both the Upper and Lower Houses would need to be set up. The key lies in knowing what criterion Parliament would apply when deciding whether to deem it an agreement and the type of parliamentary control to be exercised.

In order to determine the difference between agreements and accords, it is not enough to apply formal or literal criteria, which in any case fail to clarify the issue ("management and provision of services" in the case of agreements). Rather, we are forced to draw on material criteria or content. In this vein, José María Rodríguez de Santiago points to a grading or scaling system, ranging from greater to lower intensity, and to the types of link that Autonomous Communities forge with one another through agreements. These range from (1) forbidding the federation of Autonomous Communities (Art. 145.1 of the SC), as would be the case of an agreement between Autonomous Communities that endowed themselves with a common, shared organization, to (2) signing cooperation accords with the authorisation of Parliament, such as agreeing upon the text of a law between two Autonomous Communities that would be approved by each of them, concluding with (3) entering into agreements that would be notified to Parliament, such as setting up a joint commission for consultation and deliberation.[3] Although not referred to by the author, mention should also be made of (4) protocols or informal agreements (widely used) that reflect political commitments or statements of intent and that do not need to be set down in formal terms (these will be dealt with later

---

[1] *El Informe del Consejo de Estado sobre la reforma constitucional*, published by Rubio Llorente et al. (2006), pp. 163–164. The Council of State refers to the "vagueness and lack of flexibility" of this constitutional regulation as being responsible for such a small number of agreements between Autonomous Communities and urges other informal means of cooperation to be sought (p. 164).

[2] Many authours have criticised the impreciseness of this particular constitutional provision. See the recent work of Tajadura et al. (2010a), p. 218 et seq.

[3] Rodríguez de Santiago (2009), p. 2184. The author feels that, in legal terms, the 1996 accord between the Basque Country and Navarre should have been treated merely as an agreement and not as a cooperation accord since it was confined to setting up a standing body for meetings, which was consultative in nature and whose decisions were not binding. However, the author recognises that in political terms it was not perceived as such.

when examining Constitutional Court Ruling 44/1986 and autonomous legislation concerning agreements).

One problematic issue concerns the kind of control exercised by Parliament, in other words, whether it would be of a legal nature (Rodríguez de Santiago) or, rather, a reflection of political opportunity, since it stems from a political body. Any appeal by the Autonomous Communities against Parliament's decision not to authorise an accord would also seem to be unlikely since such appeals do not appear to have found a place in the various procedures dealt with by the Constitutional Court.

The Statutes of Autonomy, the ordinary state legislator, and the Constitutional Court have all attempted to solve the problem of how the principles and mechanisms concerning relations between State and Autonomous Communities should be handled. To a lesser degree, Statutes and autonomous legislation have sought to regulate the mechanisms governing horizontal cooperation between Autonomous Communities based on the stipulations set out under Art. 145.2 of the SC. The legal system has tended to concern itself with agreements and not with the recently created bodies for horizontal cooperation that have begun to emerge as a result of political agreements between autonomous governments.

## Changes to the Statutes Since 2006: An Attempt to Relax Horizontal Relations

Art. 145.2 of the Spanish Constitution urges the Statutes to implement inter-regional cooperation mechanisms: "Statutes may establish instances, requirements and terms ... as well as the nature and effects of the corresponding notification to Parliament". The early Statutes (approved between 1979 and 1983), as well as those approved since 2006, have included provisions that addressed cooperation accords and agreements. Horizontal relations between Autonomous Communities are cited as content, which may be added to the Statute, according to Constitutional Court Ruling 247/2007, 11. This content springs from "specific [constitutional] provisions" (such as Art. 145.2 of the SC) and not from the clauses contained in Art. 147 of the Spanish Constitution, which represents the Statute's minimum or necessary content.

In Constitutional Court Ruling 31/2010, the Court reaffirms its belief that the Statute "is not an inappropriate legal framework in which to proclaim the principles that are to inspire the system of relations between the central administration and the institutions of the Autonomous Community of Catalonia" (Legal basis 13, reiterated in Legal basis 110), although this may be interpreted as meaning that it falls to such rules to determine mainly general principles.[4] However, it goes on to specify the (implicit) constitutional nature of cooperation and underpins the role of

---

[4] Montilla Martos (2011), p. 160.

the Court itself in the interpretation thereof: "the specific regulatory organisation of this system of rules should reflect the structural constitutional demands which, as the grounding principle for cooperation between each Autonomous Community and the State as well as the relations between all of these bodies, can clearly only be derived through the Constitution itself and, consequently, through the jurisdiction which interprets it . . .".

The theoretical doctrine that has explored the issue has shown how the problem of specifically regulating horizontal relations between Autonomous Communities is largely due to the way in which said regulation has been implemented in the Statutes. Without having been forced to do so by the Constitution, it is the Statutes themselves that from the outset (a) anticipated the required approval of the respective autonomous Parliament; (b) endowed Parliament with the power to change agreements to accords, and (c) in some instances, limited certain agreements to areas that were the exclusive competence of the Autonomous Communities.

The inflexibility of statutory regulation has led the Autonomous Communities to try to circumvent these formal requirements and to sign "protocols" rather than agreements so as to avoid having to inform Parliament. As a result, an informal relationship has prevailed over the relation formed through agreements and accords. As mentioned earlier, experience has, in my view, evidenced that the virtual lack of horizontal relations is not merely a problem of an inflexible system of rules. In general terms, the Autonomous Communities have tended to neglect one another and have focused their attention on the central administration (vertical relations). Moreover, regional governments have shown a greater concern for political considerations and party affinity rather than for institutionalising relations. Finally, regional governments that are in the hands of nationalist parties have shown no desire to form part of multilateral bodies and mechanisms or at least those of a more political or higher ranking nature. Agreements tend to affect the territorialisation of subsidies and financial support and tend to be bilateral in nature, such that the State signs agreements on certain matters with the Autonomous Communities one by one. Horizontal relations have tended to confine themselves to bilateral relations between neighbouring Autonomous Communities concerning matters of mutual interest, and there have been very few multilateral horizontal relations involving all Autonomous Communities or groups of them.[5]

The new Statutes have, however, broadened their attention to include inter-institutional relations. Particularly, (1) they have embraced certain general principles of said relations (bilateral and multilateral cooperation, institutional loyalty), (2) they have regulated bilateral relations (bilateral commissions), and (3) they have concerned themselves with Autonomous Community involvement in certain bodies or have used procedural or functional mechanisms of involvement (opinions, reports) regarding State competences, in which the Autonomous Communities may have an interest (due to their being related to their own competences). Less attention has focused on

---

[5] For an overview of the current situation, see Arbós Marín (2009). Also in García Morales (2010), p. 163 et seq.

multilateral relations, whether vertical (which is understandable since regulation over any such matters should be general) or horizontal (which is not quite so understandable since the Constitution calls on the Statutes to regulate thereon).

With regard to the latter relations, the revised statutory provisions have in part amended certain features of previous regulation that had been the focus of criticism from scholars, except for the case of Andalusia (Art. 226), which has remained virtually the same as before.[6] In general:

a) There is no need to seek approval or authorisation from the regional Parliament, it being sufficient to inform said body (as well as the national Parliament: Aragon Statute Art. 91.2). If approval is required, it is confined to cases in which the agreement affects legislative functions (Catalonia, Art. 178; Balearic Islands, Art. 118)[7];

b) Any mention of the exclusive nature of the competences that the agreements deal with is removed (although it does remain in the Statute of the Valencian Community). Regarding this, we feel that it might be considered that the Statute is not adopting a hard and fast interpretation of exclusive competence but is referring rather to the part of the competence over which the Autonomous Community holds exclusive power (commonplace in many post-1979 Statutes).

However, in the new statutory regulation, there is no change to Parliament's power and authority to redefine agreements as accords.[8]

The case of Extremadura, the latest Autonomous Statute approved to date, is significant due to the detailed nature of its provisions (Organic Law 1/2011).[9] With regard to agreements, a mechanism for notifying the Regional Assembly has been put into place (and for notifying the national Parliament, which may issue a "non-binding recommendation") should there be any clash of statutory competences. The Assembly may require authorisation through an absolute majority vote (Art. 65.3), applying in this instance the mechanism established for solving conflicts between governing institutions (Art. 44). Prior to their being signed by the President, cooperation accord, must be subject to "authorisation without amendments". In other words, they must be ratified by the Assembly, in addition to national Parliament (Art. 66.2). Finally, the Statute of Extremadura establishes that institutions shall promote and take part in horizontal cooperation forums. In this context, reference is made to "purely programme-related or political commitments", apart from agreements and accords (Art. 67).

---

[6] A detailed analysis of recent changes included in the new Statutes may be found in the special issue of the *Revista Jurídica de Castilla y León,* issue 19, 2009.

[7] This is not the case in the Valencian Community, where an overall majority in the Regional Parliament of Valencia is always required (Art. 59).

[8] Concerning the issue of redefinition by Parliament, see the recent favourable considerations thereon (a minority opinion amongst scholars), González García (2011), p. 103 et seq.

[9] In the 2010 reform, no changes were made to this reform in the Organic Law on the Re-integration and Improvement of Charter-granted rights (Spanish acronym—LORAF) in Navarre.

## The Absence of State Legislation: Failed Attempts at Regulating Regional Cooperation in 2001 and 2006: Adopting a Conventional Approach

Parliament first regulated vertical cooperation through Law 12/1983, governing the process of autonomy, and subsequently through Law 30/1992, amended in 1999, focusing particular attention on the system of (multilateral) sectorial conferences. However, this was not the case for horizontal cooperation since it would initially correspond to the Autonomous Communities to establish the legal system for mechanisms governing mutual relations. Yet, it has often been quite rightly pointed out that further horizontal cooperation is key to improving vertical cooperation.[10] As regards cooperation between Autonomous Communities, the standing orders of the Senate (Upper House) set out the parliamentary procedure (Arts. 137–139) as do the standing orders of the Congress (Lower House) (Art. 166). The standing orders of the Senate establish that, at the request of a parliamentary group or of 25 Senators, the agreement may require authorisation, concerning which the General Commission of the Autonomous Communities and the Plenary must issue an opinion. Through an agreement of the Bureau of the Senate in 2008, it was decided to streamline the procedure by disposing of any intervention from the General Commission of the Autonomous Communities, such that now only the Senate Plenary intervenes. In truth, however, the Senate has changed the definition of very few of the agreements brought before it.

Faced with disparities in the Statutes, shortcomings in Law 30/1992 concerning the matter of vertical cooperation, and the problems of implementing vertical and horizontal cooperation in practical terms in the Autonomies, the Minister for Public Administration, Jesús Posada (Popular Party cabinet), put forward a proposal in 2001 for a General Law on Cooperation to the Senate General Commission of the Autonomous Communities. To date, this is the most detailed attempt at setting out in a single national law the systematic regulation of cooperation, lacking in Law 30/1992.[11] The government sought to establish formal, adaptable, flexible, and efficient means for ensuring cooperation between Autonomous Communities; eliminate disputes concerning competences and enhance extrajudicial means of dealing with conflicts; set up or strengthen regional or national cooperation procedures in areas related to competences over which said authorities may not

---

[10] García Morales (2009), p. 396. For said author, enhancing multilateral horizontal cooperation may serve to offset the politicisation of certain sectorial conferences.

[11] In 2002, the Ministry for Public Administration website published five volumes of the *Informe sobre le proyecto de Ley General de Cooperación Autonómica*. A summary and appraisal thereof may be found in Corcuera (2002), pp. 202–211. I follow the above cited author on this point.

have power, but in which cooperation is advised, and without their power over such competences being affected.[12]

In order to achieve these goals, the proper mechanisms and bodies are required. Reference is made of the need to review the sectorial conferences and bilateral commissions (through already existing multilateral and bilateral cooperation, respectively), the setting up of a "sectorial conference for regional cooperation", vertical and horizontal agreements (concerning which it is stated that they are not playing the role that they could and should be playing), joint consortia and bodies set up by the State and by one or more Autonomous Community or by several so as to accomplish certain goals. Also envisaged is the creation of a "Conference for General Cooperation" or "Conference of Autonomous Community Presidents". Regarding this particular matter, a series of general and open questions are raised that said law should address: holding such meetings with or without representation from national government, with or without all the Autonomous Communities should any refuse to take part, with or without a permanent secretary; the rotational nature of the presidency; convening ordinary meetings once or twice a year and convening extraordinary meetings at the request of a specific number of members; whether agreements need to be passed unanimously or by a majority depending on the case in hand.

The proposal was given a cool reception by the opposition socialist party (PSOE), which stressed the need to reform the Senate rather than strengthen inter-governmental relations, and particularly by nationalist parties and governments, who described it as updating the spirit of the LOAPA (Organic Law on the Harmonisation of the Autonomy Process) or who saw it as an attempt by the State to oversee and control the Autonomous Communities, proposing instead bilateral relations between the State and the individual Autonomous Community in question. The proposal was eventually forgotten, and in July 2002 the Minister was replaced. The issue was never raised again.

Four years later, the Minister for Public Administration, Jordi Sevilla (PSOE), prepared a draft law for cooperation between State and Autonomous Communities, which sought to strengthen multilateral bodies and regulate the workings of the Presidents' Conference.[13] Said draft law never went before the Lower House. In its role as the highest body for vertical cooperation, the Presidents' Conference had been working somewhat intermittently since 2004 and had had very few matters to deal with in its later years.[14] Its own internal rules date from 2009, although thus far there is no legislation governing it. It remains to be seen whether its creation will

---

[12] The Minister called for broad political consensus, recognising that "whilst the principle of cooperation remains mandatory, as we are reminded by the Constitutional Court ... such an obligation to cooperate can only be achieved voluntarily, since it is extremely difficult, if not impossible, to force cooperation", see Cortes Generales (2001), p. 3.

[13] http://www.elpais.com/articulo/espana/Gobierno/ultima/ley/coordinar/competencias/autonomicas/elpepiesp/20060116elpepinac_4/Tes (consulted 12 November 2011).

[14] On the same issue, see Tajadura (2010b), p. 134 et seq.

give rise to a Conference of Regional Presidents without the presence of the President of the National Government.

Meanwhile, the governments of the six Autonomous Communities that had approved reforms of the Statutes of Autonomy[15] began to meet in 2008, setting up a forum called "Meetings between Autonomous Communities for the Development of Statutes of Autonomy", with a view to increasing cooperation on matters of common interest. Other Autonomous Communities gradually joined this forum, until finally in 2010 an agreement was signed to set up the "Conference of Governments of Autonomous Communities".[16] This is the only body for horizontal cooperation formally set up to date without the presence of the central government. Thus far, they have only approved declarations on certain issues and have adopted a limited number of relevant agreements, with a further three agreements and one cooperation protocol currently in force.[17] The body was created through an agreement between Autonomous Community governments, without it having required the approval of any national law. This particular mechanism's consolidation and recognition will depend on the extent to which it is perceived by its members as proving useful for securing and disseminating information, conveying proposals, and so on. In light of experience to date, it cannot be said that this has been achieved. Fostering horizontal relations between Autonomous Communities has to a large extent proved possible, thanks to the implementation of the accords adopted by the 2004 Conference on Issues Related to the European Communities (CARCE), which allow for Autonomous Community government involvement in the Spanish Delegation of certain formations in the European Union Council of Ministers and its preparatory bodies. Ensuring the presence of one representative from all the Autonomous Communities has enhanced communication between governments and has boosted the creation of cooperation mechanisms.

## Constitutional Court Doctrine regarding Cooperation Relations and Its Application to Horizontal Cooperation

Based on the constitutional systems of (cooperative) federal and regional states, Constitutional Court jurisprudence stated early on the implicit principle of collaboration (sometimes also referred to as cooperation, added to which was the principle

---

[15] Valencian Community, Catalonia, Balearic Islands, Andalusia, Aragon and Castilla y León.

[16] The Santiago de Compostela agreement of 25 October 2010 signed by all the Autonomous Communities with the exception of the Basque Country, Castilla-La Mancha, the Canary Islands, Madrid, and Asturias. With the exception of the Basque Country, all of these Autonomous Communities subsequently signed the agreement. The autonomous cities of Ceuta and Melilla were not included. In 2011, a meeting was held in Santander of what was the first (and to date, only) conference. After the victory of the nationalist CiU federation in Catalonia in the November 2010 elections, the Catalonian government withdrew. President Mas's government opting for bilateral relations with the State.

[17] http://www.comunidadesautonomas.org/ (consulted on 12 November 2011).

of institutional loyalty), "which does not need to be justified in specific precepts" since "it is implicit in the very essence of the State's organisation, set out in the Constitution".[18]

At the same time, the Court has declared with regard to vertical relations that "national competences may not be extended. Nor is it possible thereby to restrict or limit the exercise of Autonomous Community powers in this matter to merely entering into or complying with any agreement between regional administrations" (Constitutional Court Ruling 96/1986).[19] At another point, it also stated that "the duty to cooperate ... involves facilitating the competences of the other body as much as possible" (Constitutional Court Ruling 11/1986).

By contrast, the Court makes scant reference to horizontal relations, although the guiding principles previously stated may be applied to them. Constitutional Court Ruling 44/1986 addresses one very specific agreement between Catalonia (*Generalitat*) and the region of Murcia prior to its autonomy. On that occasion, the Constitutional Court stated that "point 2 of Art. 145 is not, therefore, a precept which enables Autonomous Communities to establish agreements with one another, but rather, assuming such a capacity, delimits through its content the requirements which said regulation in the matter must adhere to in the Statutes, and sets out national parliament control over cooperation agreements and accords" (Legal basis 2). However, as we have seen, there is very little delimitation of content between agreement and accord, the Court clarifying very little else on the matter.

The Court has clearly set out in Constitutional Court Ruling 194/2004 that the inter-regional nature of a matter does not necessarily entail transfer to the State over said matter or State involvement in the handling thereof.[20] Quite the opposite: it provides a favourable opening for horizontal cooperation between Autonomous Communities. This occurred in the case of the composition of the management bodies running the natural parks (based on the competence set out under Art. 149.1.23 of the SC), in which the Law governing the conservation of natural

---

[18] For instance, Constitutional Court Ruling 18/1982 refers to the duty to cooperate "arising from the general obligation of national and regional authorities to provide mutual help". The Constitutional Court stresses this idea literally, or almost, in subsequent rulings, in which it adds certain features of cooperation: a duty on the part of national and regional authorities to provide mutual information (Constitutional Court Ruling 76/1983) and mutual aid (Constitutional Court Ruling 80/1985), the duty to provide mutual support, and mutual loyalty (Constitutional Court Ruling 96/1986).

[19] In a similar vein, it has also stated that "since this duty does not involve any extension of national competences, the State cannot impose such a duty by adopting coercive measures but, for those which are to be adopted, should seek to do so through the prior agreement of the competent Autonomous Communities, which will thereby participate in shaping the will of the State" (Constitutional Court Ruling 80/1985).

[20] This would only be true when specifically indicated by the SC when competences were shared out. When distinguishing between ports and airports of general interest, water supply works, and communication networks spreading over more than one Autonomous Community, the SC assigns competence to the State, under Art. 149.1 of the SC.

areas and flora and wildlife reserved participation therein for the State. According to the Court, since the Autonomous Communities held exclusive competence over the management of natural areas (executive competence), State administration had no reason to be present in the managerial body. In this instance, an agreement is an appropriate mechanism for providing coordinated management. An agreement is also an appropriate mechanism for the composition of the managerial bodies, which may be made up of representatives from the Autonomous Communities involved.

Constitutional Court Ruling 31/2010 on the constitutionality of the Statute of Catalonia addresses certain issues concerning inter-institutional relations that, whilst not dealing directly with horizontal relations, establish general criteria to be applied thereto, and that may prove to be of interest when envisaging a legal framework for such relations. The Court responds to the challenge lodged against Art. 176.2 and 3 of the Statute of Catalonia concerning involvement in voluntary multilateral cooperation mechanisms between State and Autonomous Communities, and between Autonomous Communities with one another, recalling the basic tenets of multilateral cooperation (valid for horizontal cooperation): the voluntary nature of cooperation and consequent lack of any legal obligation regarding the decisions adopted by such multilateral bodies and mechanisms "which may not impose themselves on those participating therein", non-alteration of control over a competence, and the inability of any Autonomous Community to veto an agreement involving the other Autonomous Communities (either with one another or with the State) (Legal basis 112).

Another aspect that the Ruling deals with is Autonomous Community involvement in national decision-making bodies or procedures, the importance of which in terms of horizontal cooperation cannot be overlooked since one of its principal objectives concerns participation in decision-making at a national scale. One issue to address would be joint action on the part of the Autonomous Communities or action undertaken by some of them against the State in defence of their common interests, as is commonplace in comparative law. This matter is dealt with as a result of the challenge lodged against Article 174.3 (Catalonian regional involvement in decisions made at a national level concerning institutions, bodies, and procedures that affect its competences) and Article 182 of the Statute of Catalonia (Catalonian regional involvement in appointing members of a range of bodies belonging to or related to national administration).[21] The Ruling states that cases concerning involvement in organic and functional terms (1) are contained in general and imprecise precepts, which may be implemented in a number of ways; (2) should be specified by national laws; (3) should safeguard national control over the competence in question; (4) should ensure the "absolute freedom" that in the exercise thereof corresponds to national bodies and institutions (specific scope and specific implementation). From this, it emerges that once it has been set out in the

---

[21] Due to its particular nature, involvement in appointing judges to the Constitutional Court and members to the General Council of the Judiciary set out under Art. 180 Statute of Catalonia (Legal basis 113) is excluded from the analysis for the moment.

corresponding national legislation, said involvement cannot be of a decision-making nature but must take place in consultative or advisory bodies and within the procedures themselves in the form of non-binding reports (Legal basis 111, reiterated in 114).

## Recent Autonomous Legislation: The Cases of Aragon and Catalonia

The new Statutes normally remit the establishment of the legal provisions concerning agreements to autonomous laws. Aragon (in application of Art. 91 of the Statute) and Catalonia (Art. 177.2) were the first to legislate, although they have followed different paths. Whereas Aragon approved a specific law, Catalonia included it in the legal system governing public administration. To date, laws governing agreements at a regional level have been spread over a number of differing rules of a more general nature (standing orders, the law on the government that included the signing of the agreement by the President, such as the 2008 Catalonian Law on the President and the Government, or the law on the consultative council).

The first contribution of Law 1/2011 concerning agreements undertaken by the Autonomous Community of Aragon is the systematic and specific handling of the region's inter-institutional relations through accords (with the central administration, with other Autonomous Communities, within the scope of the European Union, and foreign action, as well as agreements with public law institutions). The Law describes the principles on which accords should be based: institutional loyalty, coordination, and mutual support; the purpose thereof—"to provide citizens with a better service and to ensure rational use of public resources"—together with the limits—non-intervention in control over competences (Art. 5); as well as the possible content of the agreements, such as signatory bodies, the competence that enables the action to be undertaken, the kind of agreement in question, the goal, funding, the duration and period of application, reasons for termination, mechanisms for filing complaints and grievances and for dealing with disputes (Art. 6). With regard to horizontal cooperation relations (Chapter III), the scope of application is described, both for multilateral relations with other Autonomous Communities and for specific relations with neighbouring Autonomous Communities.

The Law draws a distinction between and regulates over three kinds of agreement: (a) protocols or cooperation accords (Art. 16), (b) cooperation agreements (Art. 17), and (c) cooperation accords (Art. 18).

A. Protocols or cooperation accords. These are mission statements or declarations of political intent, exchange of information, or accords setting up joint collaboration or coordination bodies. Whatever the case, the defining characteristics are that they do not entail legal obligations for the parties involved and that neither the regional Parliament of Aragon nor the national Parliament is informed. How other issues are dealt with is less clear; however, a report issued by the person or centre promoting the accord needs to be included, setting out the goals, background, and commitments, as well as the financial implications for the Autonomous Community (Art. 26 refers it to the "agreement projects", although it is assumed that it should be extended to cover all kinds of "agreement", in the general sense as is used in Art. 15, of which protocols are just one "type"); it is not clear who may sign such protocols; mention is made of regional government of Aragon representatives in the cooperation bodies (Art. 27.2), in this case, seemingly without it being necessary for them to obtain authorisation through a regional government of Aragon agreement in order to sign; by way of a general consideration, at another point it is indicated that entering into "accords and agreements" requires authorisation through a regional government of Aragon agreement (Art. 28.1) or whoever the latter may authorise to do so through a regulation (Art. 28.2).

This is a particularly interesting case due to its simplicity and lack of any requirement to inform Parliament. Its drawback is that it may not entail legal obligations.[22] As we have seen, Autonomous Communities have resorted to such mechanisms on many occasions in an effort to circumvent the need to inform Parliament.

B. Cooperation agreements. With regard to the purpose thereof, the Constitution refers to "the management and provision of their own services", adding, "which result from regional competences" and which are no longer required to be exclusive. The need to inform the regional Parliament of Aragon, as well as the national Parliament within the space of 1 month, is set out, although the consequences take effect immediately subsequent to signing.

C. Cooperation accords. These are used residually, when the action envisaged is not covered by the other mechanisms. They need to be authorised by the national Parliament and "ratified" (voted on in their entirety, without amendments) by the regional Parliament of Aragon.

With regard to cooperation accords and agreements, the stipulations mentioned in point A for protocols are also applicable. In other words, a report describing the agreement project must be included, and authorisation for signing must be sought from the regional government of Aragon with the possibility of delegating the capacity to sign. The authorisation accord must stipulate who the designated signatory will be.

Changes to accords or agreements may involve the following: (a) minor changes made through "addenda" by the legitimate authority or signatory representative, subsequent notification to the government being required; (b) fresh authorisation required in the case of "substantial changes" (one example cited of a substantial

---

[22] Constitutional Court Ruling 44/1986 had referred to such protocols as "mere statements of cooperation or proclamations of aspirations and reciprocal intentions" different to accords and agreements (Legal basis 3). At that moment, the Court noted the difficulty involved in clarifying the contents of an agreement and defended the need to apply a joint legal system, which would move towards the concept of a cooperation accord or agreement requiring parliamentary intervention.

change being greater financial cooperation on the part of the Autonomous Community), Art. 30.

Finally, for the purpose of public notification, all the agreements, as well as any amendments thereto, must be registered with the Autonomous Community Register of Agreements within 2 months of being signed (Art. 31) and will be published in the Aragon official regional bulletin (Art. 32).

In Catalonia, Law 26/2010, governing the legal and procedural system for public administration in Catalonia, devotes Title IX to inter-administrative relations and deals with administration authorities in Catalonia. Said Law's application to relations with other Autonomous Communities, the State, and public bodies in other States and international bodies is set out under the Fourth Additional Provision, which remits to Arts. 110 and 111, devoted respectively to the form and content of agreements and protocols and to the procedures and particular file in question. This regulation is, therefore, far less ambitious, as it is less direct and does not address head-on the matters dealt with in our study.


## Conclusions

As we have seen, there are a variety of reasons that have hindered horizontal relations between Autonomous Communities, which pose a threat to the future of said relations and which need to be dealt with: (a) lack of flexibility in constitutional and statutory norms, which has led to the informal practice of using "protocols"; said lack of flexibility has an effect on regional Parliament intervention and on the national Parliament's capacity to change the status of protocols; (b) lack of transparency or public dissemination of the agreements signed, hindering awareness and understanding thereof, as well as access to them; and particularly (c) lack of political will on the part of the Autonomous Communities when dealing with one another. Without such a will, legislative reform is unlikely to be able to solve the problems that have arisen.

Over the last few years, a shift has been in evidence, although this has been due more to direct Autonomous Community involvement in European Union institutions than to reform of the Statutes of Autonomy. Even though horizontal relations were not a priority for those who drafted the Statutes in 2008, said Autonomous Communities did begin to engage in a practice that has spread and has led to the creation of the Conference of Autonomous Community Governments.

There is a legal framework (which, in large measure, has emerged from the Statutes and from Constitutional Court jurisprudence) that acts as a restriction to be taken into account when addressing regulation of the issue of horizontal cooperation relations: (a) the inalterability of control over competences; cooperation relations affect the exercise of competences, in addition to which national competences may not be extended at the expense of Autonomous Community competences, nor may any Autonomous Community exercise its own competences at the expense of another Autonomous Community; and (b) the voluntary nature of cooperation that is reflected in the inability to force anyone to cooperate and also by one party not being able to veto or prevent another from cooperating.

In basic terms, the legal challenges that must be faced if horizontal relations are to improve are (a) setting up bodies for cooperation relations (conferences of Autonomous Community Presidents, sectorial conferences to deal with specific matters) and their link with existing relations at the vertical scale; (b) regulating the legal system governing agreements in terms of flexibility and avoiding disputes on this point between Autonomous Communities. This involves creating mechanisms to enhance public knowledge and awareness of existing agreements; and (c) restricting parliamentary intervention in agreements to a minimum. Rather than having to ratify or authorise agreements, parliaments should receive information concerning those that have already been signed.

Faced with these challenges, the question concerns what the most appropriate legal mechanisms for regulating cooperation between Autonomous Communities might be. If we are to heed the Constitution and the Constitutional Court, the Statutes provide *one* (but not *the*) suitable mechanism, although at the same time it tends to be accepted that not everything can be regulated by the Statutes: firstly, because norms are general and based on principles such that it corresponds to the Statutes to determine the general basic framework; secondly, because the effectiveness of these rules at a territorial scale is limited such that regulations of a general scope are required. Faced with such a situation, several possibilities emerge, complementary to the statutory provision. Firstly, approval of autonomous laws governing agreements, laws to which some of the reformed Statutes, such as the one recently approved by Aragon, have remittance. This would be an appropriate regulatory mechanism for directing the legal system covering agreements in each Autonomous Community.

Regulating horizontal cooperation relations through a national law would prove more problematic. Indeed, certain authors have already proposed that this should be effected by reforming Law 30/1992 or by approving a Law of Regional Cooperation (organic or ordinary).[23] The latter option is justified due to the need to provide one standard legal mechanism that is common to all Autonomous Communities. However, I do not feel this latter option to be the most suitable legal mechanism in political terms; previous attempts at approving such a law having been viewed by nationalist governments as interference from the State. By contrast, from a legal standpoint, merging under a single law all of the regulation governing cooperation would give rise to a systematic and coherent regulation that would embrace all mechanisms and bodies. The same basic legal objective could also certainly be reached by reforming Law 30/1992, governing the legal system for public administration, and without arousing the same sentiments. Regulating horizontal relations

---

[23] This latter view is held by Tajadura (2010a), *op. cit.*, pp. 231 and 247 et seq. In our view, unless foreseen in constitutional reform, there is no reason to consider that for the moment the normative category of the organic law should be used since it is not a matter reserved to said category by the Constitution.

through a national law, whatever this law may happen to be, does raise certain reasonable doubts concerning respect towards Autonomous Communities self government (Why should the State legislate over cooperation between Autonomous Communities?) and should always respect the voluntary nature of cooperation between Autonomous Communities (except in instances where the State holds specific competences over coordination, as is the case of health).

Constitutional reform of Art. 145.2 of the SC, which sets out in more cautious and realistic terms relations between Autonomous Communities, is seen by many as the culmination required to consolidate cooperation relations. The advisory opinion issued by the Council of State in February 2006 on constitutional reform specifically refers to two areas of any possible reform: (a) including the duty of all entities with territorial autonomy to cooperate and (b) making relations more flexible, such that the need for any authorisation from Parliament would be removed, "to the extent in which such action corresponds to competences of the Autonomous Communities themselves", whilst maintaining, however, the duty to inform Parliament "and even the Government", as a consequence of the "duty to ensure mutual loyalty".[24] One point that should be remembered, nevertheless, is that in many federal and regional states, such horizontal relations are para-constitutional, which has not, however, prevented them from being implemented.

Without wishing to detract from the merits of the other alternatives, at this particular point in time perhaps the most important thing is achieving a legal-political solution that merges institutionalisation and flexibility, regulating the legal system of cooperation through regional laws, and fostering its implementation in all Autonomous Communities or certain groups thereof via agreements between them. It is the responsibility of the Autonomous Communities involved to draw up their internal rules for the horizontal cooperation bodies that are set up, laying down the procedure for convening meetings and drafting the agenda, alternating the presidency, debating, and taking decisions.

There is nothing to prevent any Autonomous Communities that wish to do so from signing agreements with one another concerning exercise of their competences or accords expressing a commitment to legislate or establish common laws (education, a single market, health services, etc.). Adopting such a bottom-up approach would surely have a knock-on effect amongst other Autonomous Communities and would herald a major step forward in the effort to rationalise the Autonomous State at a time of deep crisis like the present. All that is required is the political will of the Autonomous Communities.

---

[24] *El Informe del Consejo de Estado* (2006), p. 165, *op. cit.* For the Council of State, ensuring the constitutional and legal appropriateness of said cooperation agreements should fall to judicial and not political bodies.

# References

X. Arbós Marín (coordinator), *Las relaciones intergubernamentales en el Estado autonómico. La posición de los actores,* IEA, Barcelona, 2009.

J. Corcuera Stienza, "Colaboración y cooperación en el sistema autonómico español. Reflexiones tras el fracaso de la propuesta de ley general de cooperación autonómica", *Anuario Jurídico de La Rioja*, issue 8, 2002.

Cortes Generals, *Diario de Sesiones del Senado,* VII Legislature, Commissions, issue 147, 12 June 2001.

M.J. García Morales, "Los nuevos estatutos de autonomía y las relaciones de colaboración. Un nuevo escenario, una nueva etapa?", *Revista Jurídica de Castilla y León*, issue 19, 2009.

M.J. García Morales, "Las relaciones de colaboración en el Estado autonómico a los treinta años de la Constitución", in J. García Roca and E. Albertí (coordinators), *Treinta años de Constitución*, Tirant lo Blanch, Valencia, 2010.

I. González García, "La facultad de recalificación de las Cortes Generales ex artículo 145.2 CE: una tesis personal", *Revista Española de Derecho Constitucional*, issue 91, 2011.

J.M. Rodríguez de Santiago, "Artículo 145. Convenios y acuerdos entre Comunidades Autónomas", in M.E. Casas and M. Rodríguez-Piñero (directors), *Comentarios a la Constitución Española. XXX Aniversario*, Wolters Kluwer Foundation, Madrid, 2009.

J.A. Montilla Martos, "Las relaciones de colaboración en el nuevo marco estatutario: bilateralidad y participación", *Revista de Estudios Políticos*, issue 151, 2011.

F. Rubio Llorente and J. Alvarez Junco, (ed), *El Informe del Consejo de Estado* sobre la reforma constitucional Council of State and Centre for Political and Constitutional Studies, Madrid, 2006.

J. Tajadura Tejada, "Los convenios de cooperación ente comunidades autónomas: marco normativo y propuestas de reforma", *Revista d'Estudis Autonòmics i Federals*, issue 11, 2010.

J. Tajadura Tejada, *El principio de cooperación en el Estado autonómico*, 3rd ed, Comares, Granada, 2010.

# Horizontal Cooperation: Unfinished Business for the Spanish Autonomic State Framework

Javier Tajadura Tejada

## Introduction

Leaving to one side the controversy as to whether Spain's regional state system, the *estado autonómico*, constitutes a federal state or not (in light of the clear confluence between federalisms and regionalisms in devising organisational formulae that are so similar that it is difficult to distinguish between them), a study of the federal model is essential in order to address the problems of the Spanish *autonomic*[1] state. It is not, therefore, our intention to establish the differences between classic federalism and other forms of decentralised state. Moreover, we need to recognise that there are several variants of federalism. What we are interested in examining here is the distinction between two essential models: dual and cooperative federalism.

Classic federalism (*dual federalism*) involves a rigid vertical separation of powers. Underlying it is a political philosophy of "sealed compartments". There are two clearly delimited fields of action without any type of link between them: the central government and the state governments. Cooperative federalism (*new federalism*), on the other hand, seeks to overcome the formal and absolute separation of competences, avoiding focusing its attention on the constitutional division of authority between the central government and state governments and highlighting instead the interdependence that exists and the mutual influence that each tier of government is capable of exercising over the other. In short, dual federalism is

---

[1] Translator's Note: In order to avoid confusion of terminology, throughout the text, *autonómico* has been translated as "autonomic" (rather than regional) when it refers to the framework of devolution but as "regional" when it refers to the specific administrations of the various autonomous communities. Hence, "autonomic state" (*estado autonómico*) but regional parliament (*parlamento autonómico*).

J.T. Tejada (✉)
Department of Constitutional Law and History of the Political Thought, University of the Basque Country, Campus of Sarriena, Post Box 644, Bilbao 48080, Spain
e-mail: javier.tajadura@ehu.es

A. López-Basaguren and L. Escajedo San Epifanio (eds.), *The Ways of Federalism in Western Countries and the Horizons of Territorial Autonomy in Spain*, Vol. 2, DOI 10.1007/978-3-642-27717-7_14, © Springer-Verlag Berlin Heidelberg 2013

based on the idea of independence and cooperative federalism is based on that of interdependence.

This cooperative federalism has two essential manifestations: (a) a vertical dimension: cooperative vertical federalism; this formula involves the system of relations that can occur between the federal state, on the one hand, and the member states, on the other; this system can be institutionalised, even constitutionalised, or can lack formal legal supports and be based on mere political praxis and (b) a horizontal dimension: cooperative horizontal federalism. This formula refers to the system of relations that occurs between member states. The essential issue for this system lies in whether the federal power can intervene in this system or not, and, if so, what degree of intervention it should exercise. As a general rule, it is usually accepted that the federal government assumes the role of guarantor of this type of relation. Here, too, we can distinguish between informal and institutionalised relations.

The common opinion is that dual federalism constitutes the first moment in the evolutionary process of the federal state. In both the USA and in the Federal Republic of Germany (to cite two paradigmatic cases), the techniques of cooperative federalism prevail over the philosophy of dual federalism because the former responds to current issues better than the latter. The cooperative federalism operating in Germany and the United States is characterised by the cross-over of the competences of the central and territorial authorities, leading federation and states *increasingly to act in a joint fashion* by way of agreements in which they design a model of common action, which will later be executed by acts of the federation or of the states depending on the ownership of the specific competence being exercised in each case. The advantages of cooperative federalism for the functioning of any composite state are clear.

From this perspective, the legal and political instruments through which cooperative federalism is structured can and must be seen as guarantors of territorial pluralism. Unfortunately, this view is not shared by those who have simply identified cooperation with centralisation. Correcting this mistake requires us to examine the relationship between the principle of cooperation and the principle of autonomy.

The progressive penetration of the central power to be observed in all composite states is a logical response to the successive transferral to the area of general interest of questions that were previously strictly regional or local. In recent years, many issues have drawn intense public scrutiny (environment, energy, food), causing them to emerge out of the sphere of local interest (at which the few public decisions required were taken) to become part of the general interest. The transition from the liberal state to the social state has undoubtedly reinforced central power. However, this phenomenon has not been accompanied by an exclusive appropriation on the part of the central authorities of all competences related to the aforementioned problems, yet it has made it necessary for them to participate in resolving them. Otherwise, the requirements of the general interest will not be satisfied. It is they that demand co-operation.

There are essentially three reasons cooperation and autonomy should not be viewed as being in opposition to one another:

a) Firstly, because this is a false opposition since co-operation arises simply from the need to articulate the exercise of the powers and make the distribution of competences operative. In this sense, autonomy is the first presupposition of cooperation;

b) Secondly, because autonomy, as the Spanish Constitutional Court has repeatedly ruled, can only be explained in the context of unity and unity requires participation by the central authorities in resolving problems of general interest; when a problem becomes general, the intervention of the central power is inevitable.

c) Thirdly—and this is the most important reason autonomy and cooperation should not be viewed as incompatible—*because co-operation strengthens autonomy and on many occasions enables regional authorities[2] to continue to have responsibilities in areas in which they would otherwise be deprived.*

Without recourse to the principle of cooperation and the different techniques whereby it is manifested, the process of centralisation required by the necessary increase in state intervention would have resulted in a notable loss of power for the regional authorities. The shift to the field of general interest of previously local problems could have resulted in the central authority's assuming a monopoly over political decision-making on these issues. What has prevented this from happening has been the implementation of cooperative techniques. These techniques exclude unilateral decision-making and allow responsibility for the regional authorities to be extended to fields that would otherwise be monopolised by the central power. In some cases, certain cooperative techniques are even used directly by the regional bodies to agree joint actions that prevent intervention by the central power. Horizontal co-operation—one of the two manifestations of cooperative federalism referred to in Article 145 of the Spanish constitution—can even end up preventing certain issues from being taken from the regional sphere; were it not for the actions undertaken in the exercise of that inter-regional cooperation, such issues would pass to the sphere of action of the central power.

In short, the principle of cooperation turns the general interest into an object of the concurrent attention of all levels of power. This means that more than one theoretical principle is needed by any composite state—and in the case that concerns us, by the autonomic state.

The essential instruments through which the horizontal and vertical dimensions of cooperative federalism are structured are sector conferences [*conferencias sectoriales*] and conventions on cooperation. Whereas the former have no express basis in the constitution, the same is not true of horizontal agreements, which are expressly provided for in Article 145. The purpose of this paper is to analyse their legal regulation and put forward some proposals for reform.

---

[2] See Translator's Note 1 above.

## Regulation of Horizontal Cooperation in the Constitution and in the Statutes of Autonomy

Any analysis of the legal framework of inter-regional conventions and agreements on cooperation must necessarily start from Article 145 of the constitution. The unfortunate wording of this article is an indication of the mistrust with which the framers of the constitution—the constituent assembly—always viewed horizontal co-operation between autonomous communities.

The definitive wording was adopted by the joint committee of the congress and senate. Article 145 reads as follows:[3] "(1) Under no circumstances shall the federation of Autonomous Communities be allowed. (2) The Statutes [of Autonomy] may provide for the circumstances, requirements and terms under which the Autonomous Communities may enter into conventions [*convenios*][4] amongst themselves for management and the rendering of services in matters pertaining to them, as well as the nature and effects of the consequent communication to the Cortes Generales. In all other cases, cooperation agreements [*acuerdos de cooperación*] between the Autonomous Communities shall require the authorisation of the Cortes Generales".

Thus, two types of inter-regional agreements are allowed for: *convenios* [conventions] and *acuerdos de cooperación* [cooperation agreements], the difference being that the former do not require authorisation from the Cortes Generales and the latter do. The only material difference is that the former must involve the "management and rendering of services in matters pertaining to them". This does not clarify matters very much. In practice, the fact is that Article 145 does not allow us to determine what type of cooperative actions should be considered conventions and what should be considered agreements or, to put it another way, what we should understand by "management and rendering of services in matters pertaining to them". This is an issue of capital importance since on this distinction hinges the requirement of approval from the central parliament.

This failure adequately to address certain technical/legal aspects of one of the main instruments for achieving the techniques of cooperation is censurable. The reasons for this insufficiency and for this constitutional vagueness can be found in the proceedings for the sessions dealing with this precept. In the constitutional debates, an erroneous belief prevailed that any type of cooperation between the regions necessarily involved centrifugal tendencies, thus ignoring the important integrating function that such cooperation played.

---

[3] Translator's Note: There are a number of different "official" translations of the Spanish Constitution. I have used that provided by the Tribunal Constitucional, available at http://www.tribunal-constitucional.es/es/constitucion/Paginas/ConstitucionIngles.aspx.

[4] Translator's Note: The two Spanish terms, "convenio" and "acuerdo", whose precise distinction is discussed here, are generally both translated in English as "agreement". To avoid confusion, I have used the alternative translation "convention" for "convenio", limiting "agreement" exclusively to "acuerdo".

Technically speaking, the wording of Article 145.2 is flawed in that it does not allow us to differentiate between conventions and cooperation agreements. Nonetheless, it allows that shortfall to be resolved by leaving it up to the statutes of autonomy to regulate the circumstances, requirements, and terms under which autonomous communities may reach agreements [*convenios*] amongst themselves, as well as the nature and effects of the consequent communication to the Cortes Generales.

The Constitution speaks of *convenios* for the "management and rendering of services in matters pertaining to them" and of other cooperation agreements. We should start by noting that this is not a distinction *imposed* by the Constitution itself, which limits itself to leaving the possibility open to the statutes of the various autonomous communities to differentiate between "conventions" and "agreements". In actual fact, the concept of "management and rendering of services in matters pertaining to them" is so broad that practically all agreements could, if the statutes so provided, be subsumed into it, thus obviating the need for authorisation from the Cortes. It is therefore up to the statutes to establish the distinction between the two. It is worth insisting on the importance of this distinction, which determines whether the intervention of the Cortes Generales takes the form of an authorisation or a mere communication.

However, as we shall see, far from clarifying the issue, the statutes have only served to further muddy the waters. This is a very serious failing since it shows that the framers of the statutes—like most of the framers of the constitution—were unaware of the importance of relations of horizontal cooperation. We shall first examine the way the different original statutes address the issue of horizontal cooperation. We shall then go on to examine the regulations established in autonomous communities that have enacted new statutes of autonomy as and from the eighth parliamentary session (2004–2008).

Two statutes of autonomy (those of Aragon and Andalusia) did not sufficiently develop Article 145 of the Constitution. The statute of Aragon contained only a short reference to the subject. Article 16, Section f) states that:

> It is also the competence of the Cortes of Aragon: f) To ratify any agreements and conventions of cooperation of which the autonomous community of Aragon is part.

The consequences of this insufficient regulation are abundantly clear. Article 145.2 of the Constitution designates *acuerdos* [agreements] as a residual category, i.e., it covers anything not defined as *convenios* by the statute. By failing to define *convenios*, therefore, the statute of Aragon, in practice determined that all interregional relations of Aragon must be categorised as *acuerdos*, requiring explicit authorisation from the Cortes Generales.

For its part, the statute of Andalusia establishes, in Article 72: 1:

> In the circumstances, conditions and requirements determined by the (regional) parliament, the autonomous community may enter into conventions with other autonomous communities for the management and joint rendering of services in matters pertaining to them.

The constitution leaves regulation of the conventions up to the statute, which in turn attributes this function to a regional law, in a clear example of transferral. The referral contained in the statutes could be considered to be a breach of Article 145.2 in that it illicitly de-constitutionalises the subject. However, it appears more logical to think that the Cortes's approval of the statute, by way of an organic law, implies that the Cortes have considered this remittal to be valid.

Having noted the shortfalls in the statutes of Aragon and Andalusia, let us now turn to the other statutes. We need to ascertain what is meant by "management and rendering of services in matters pertaining to them" since this is this the only datum provided by the Constitution to distinguish between agreements and conventions. We shall first analyse the meaning of the expression "management and rendering of services". Given that it will not provide us with any criterion of distinction, we shall seek such a distinction in the term *propios*.[5] We shall then go on to examine the scope given by the statutes to the term "communication", the second distinguishing feature of "conventions" as opposed to "agreements", since the latter do not have to be merely notified to but authorised by the Cortes Generales.

The purpose of the conventions may be the exercise of certain competences but never their ownership. This is merely a requirement of the reiterated principle of non-transferability of ownership [*indisponibilidad*] of the competences. This is the meaning of the term "management and rendering of services". However, this meaning is evidently of no use as a criterion for distinguishing between "conventions" and "agreements", given that the latter, which are also subject to the general principle of non-transferability of ownership of competences, must refer to the "management and rendering of services". In other words, the Cortes may never authorise an agreement that, in broad terms, does not involve management and rendering; if it does, it would be sanctioning a transferral of the ownership of the competences, an operation it is not entitled to perform as a constituted power.

In short, all matters falling within the competences of the autonomous communities may form the subject of an inter-regional convention. Any classification *ratione materiae* is therefore of no use.

The interpretation of the adjective *propios* [in matters pertaining to them] accompanying the aforementioned term has been widely debated.

It is important to stress that *propios* need not be identified with exclusive competences, for two reasons: firstly, because this criterion for distinction was expressly rejected during the framing of Article 145, and secondly, because given that, despite what is stated by many statutes, very few competences are "exclusive", this interpretation reduces the scope of cooperative activity of the autonomous communities.

Given that the constitution limits itself to requiring that the competences be *propias*, one should understand that *propias* includes not only exclusive but also

---

[5] Translator's Note: In the official translation of the Constitution, the term "propios" is rendered accurately but somewhat cumbersomely as "in matters pertaining to them". Given that the discussion here relates to the meaning of the Spanish term, I have mostly left the term untranslated.

shared or concurrent competences. Moreover, in its first ruling of 2 February 1981, the Constitutional Court distinguished between own competences and exclusive competences [*competencias propias* and *competencias exclusivas*].

In reality and given that all the interpretations are possible and valid, one needs to refer once more to the provisions of the statutes of autonomy. Here, the various solutions adopted can basically be grouped into two blocks:

a) On the one hand, those that consider that the term *propias* refers in all cases to "exclusive competences of the autonomous communities covered by the convention": statutes of Catalonia (Article 27.1), Galicia (Article 35.1), Asturias (Article 21), Valencia (Article 42), Castile-La Mancha (Article 40), Canary Islands (Article 38), Extremadura (Article 14), and Castile-Leon (Article 30);

b) On the other hand, those that establish the possibility of entering into conventions on "the management and rendering of services in matters pertaining to their competence": statutes of Cantabria (Article 30), La Rioja (Article 15), Murcia (Article 19), Balearic Islands (Article 17), and Madrid (Article 14).

All of these arrangements are constitutional; however, the decision on which to adopt has important practical consequences, in that it determines whether the capacity of the autonomous communities to enter into conventions without the need for authorisation from the Cortes is limited. However, obvious this may seem, it was overlooked by the framers of the various statutes. If *propios* is taken to be a synonym of "exclusive competences", all conventions on matters that are not part of an exclusive competence, i.e., the majority, will be considered to be "cooperation agreements" and will therefore require the prior authorisation of the Cortes. On the contrary, a broad interpretation of the term *propios* allows a greater number of inter-regional agreements to be included in the category of conventions, therefore making any authorisation from the Cortes unnecessary.

The purpose, in short, was to take advantage of a constitutional referral to the statutes made in terms so broad that it is difficult to imagine that cooperation agreements could be entered into that do not fit into the category of "conventions". Incomprehensibly, however, many statutes failed to see the issue in these terms.

The failings in the statutes also extend to the definition of the concept of "communication" to the Cortes Generales.

Just as Article 145.2 leaves it up to the statutes to establish the "circumstances, requirements and terms" under which the autonomous communities may enter into conventions for the management and rendering of services in matters pertaining to them, this precept also leaves it up to the statutes to regulate the "character and effects of the corresponding communication to the Cortes Generales".

The statutes can regulate, therefore, the nature and effects of the communication, but necessarily have to retain the regime of communication, deemed to consist of advising another authority of certain facts.

The "communication" can take the form of a simple notification. What it can never become is a request for an explicit authorisation from the central parliament, since that would involve departing from the framework of what is to be understood by "communication".

As in the case of the interpretation of the term *propios*, the issue is dealt with in many ways in the various statutes. It is worth noting from the outset that many statutes have denaturalised the "communication", providing the Cortes with real decision-making powers as to the nature of the act.

The various statutes of autonomy may be divided into two main groups, by distinguishing between two different types of "communication":

a) On the one hand, the statute of Valencia, for all types of convention, and the statutes of the Basque Country, only for conventions with historical territories,[6] and of Navarra (LORAFNA), only for conventions with adjoining territories, limit themselves to giving a period for the entry into force of the convention in order for the Cortes Generales to be made aware of its implementation within that time. Only in these three circumstances is a real "communication" *per se* provided for. This is the legal regime that most closely matches the requirements of the constitution.

b) All other statutes (except for the statute of Aragon, which does not regulate the issue), i.e., Catalonia, Cantabria, Canary Islands, Navarra (with the exception set out above), Balearic Islands, Murcia, the Basque Country (with the exception set out above), Galicia, Asturias, Castile La Mancha, Extremadura, Madrid, Castile-Leon, Andalusia, and La Rioja, essentially relinquish to the Cortes the faculty to classify the text as an agreement or as a convention.

From the above, we can draw the following conclusion: statutes in which the communication simply produces a *vacatio legis* as to the validity of the convention are the exception. In the immense majority of cases, the effect of this communication is to authorise the Cortes in the event of "manifest misgivings" to ensure that any "convention" be processed as an "agreement". Thus, in most of the cases, there occurs a relinquishment of the statutory ownership to the Cortes Generales, meaning that in practice the central parliament is entrusted with classifying each specific case as one of the two types. This allows for an additional control by the Cortes over the autonomous communities that is not provided for in the Constitution. In accordance with Article 145.2 of the Constitution, one may argue that the Cortes can in no way "reclassify" the convention. The only admissible form of control of the constitutionality of the convention is that provided for in Article 162 of the Constitution and performed by the Constitutional Court. However, most of the statutes of autonomy, paradoxically, have not interpreted it in this way.

In short, in the light of the cooperative exercise of the regional competences, it is difficult to understand why it is necessary to establish additional systems of control that do not exist when the autonomous communities exercise those same competences in isolation.

By establishing that additional control by the Cortes, the statutes have entirely vitiated the regime of the "communication" and have practically unified the

---

[6] Translator's Note: The three component territories or provinces of the autonomous community of the Basque Country are governed by a special regime. These are the "historical territories".

instruments of "convention" and "agreement". The statutory regulations restrict the faculties of the autonomous communities in a way that is difficult to reconcile with the spirit and letter of Article 145.2. The purpose of the regime of "communication" of "conventions", as opposed to "authorisation" of "agreements", was to establish an inter-regional field of activity outside the control of the Cortes Generales. As we have seen, however, the statutes of autonomy have renounced this field of regional cooperative activity.

One final problem related to the issues under discussion is to determine what happens when a convention is entered into between two communities that provide for a different regime of intervention by the Cortes. In such cases, the only possible solution would appear to be to apply the more restrictive statutory regime. In other words, if one community interprets *propio* as meaning "exclusive" and another interprets it as "not unrelated", it shall be necessary to consider that a convention is not possible and that an agreement of cooperation is needed. Likewise, if a community establishes a regime of authentic "communication" and another allows the Cortes to reclassify the convention as an agreement, the latter will have to be considered to be possible.

To address this, in the last section of this paper we advocate a reform that would establish a homogenous regulation of these instruments in the body of constitutional law. Given that leaving this regulation up to the statutes cannot guarantee the necessary uniformity, it should instead be left to a General Organic Law of Cooperation. Moreover, to settle any dogmatic debate as to its legitimacy, the wisest course of action would be to include an explicit reference to it in the text of the constitution itself.

The competence to approve inter-regional conventions and agreements is a matter of the internal organisation of each autonomous community. The issue of the definitive approval of the convention by the organ of government or by the legislative assembly of the autonomous community depends entirely on the statutory regulation of the issue, by virtue of the remission made under Article 145.2.

Examining the way that the issue is dealt with in the statutes, the first thing that strikes one is that the statutes of Galicia, Extremadura, and the Basque Country contain no rule whatsoever in this regard. The statute of Andalusia has no such rule either, although Article 72 states that the regulation is to be made by means of an act of the Andalusian Parliament. The other regulations can be classified into three blocks:

a) The most intense intervention by the legislative assembly in this area is provided for in the statute of La Rioja, Article 17. The parliament is responsible not only for approving but also for authorising the regional government to enter into any convention or agreement.

b) On the other hand, the statutes of Catalonia (Article 27), Cantabria (Article 9.1.d), Valencia (Article 42), Castile-La Mancha (Article 9.2), the Canary Islands (Article 38), and the Balearic Islands (Article 17) simply establish that their respective parliaments should approve the conventions and agreements. Similarly, the statutes of Aragon (Article 16 f. Madrid (Article 14, Paragraphs 13 and 14) and Castile-Leon (Article 14, Paragraphs 13 and 14) attribute to the parliament the faculty of "ratifying" the conventions and agreements.

c) Finally, the statutes of Asturias (Article 24.7), Murcia (Article 23.7), and Navarra (Article 26 b, relating exclusively to the conventions, not to the agreements, although the rules of the regional parliament [*parlamento foral*] have unified the regime of the two) contain a different formula. In general terms, they establish the need for prior authorisation from the regional legislative assemblies for entering into agreements and conventions. However, they do not establish who is responsible for approving them.

If we examine how approval of the cooperative instruments is regulated in the different statutes of autonomy, we see that the great majority (the Basque Country, Catalonia, Galicia, Asturias, Cantabria, Murcia, Castile-Leon, Castile-La Mancha, Canary Islands, Balearic Islands, Extremadura, Madrid and Ceuta, and Melilla) address the issue not as if dealing with a form of exercise of their own competences but as if it were a substantive competence of its own that requires a specific regulation.

The fact of having adopted this material approach to cooperation (as if drawing up conventions were a substantive competence), rather than a merely formal one, has led to an extraordinary complication of the issue. It would have been possible simply to have done without regulation of the "approval" of the conventions, given that the logic of the system would in itself have attributed this competence: wherever the isolated exercise of the competence corresponds to the government, it is the government that approves it; wherever the individual exercise of the competence corresponds to parliament, it is the parliament that approves it. This continues to be perfectly valid as a criterion for interpretation and a subsidiary of the statutory regulations.

In any event, the result has been an extraordinary reinforcement of the positions of autonomous parliaments in this area. This parliamentary control, which initially reinforces the democratic nature of the system, also has a less favourable dimension in that it introduces a degree of rigidity that is incompatible with the flexibility required of this type of instrument. In this regard, the doctrine stresses that the conventions must necessarily be instruments that are flexible in their action because of the very needs that they seek to satisfy. From this perspective, it is evident that some statutes have taken the requirements of parliamentary control too far. For all of these reasons, Article 145 has very seldom been put to use. The rigidity of the procedure for approving the conventions, combined with the regional governments' desire to avoid both parliamentary intervention and control by the central bodies of the state, has impeded the development of inter-regional relations and has transferred them from the area of juridified and formalised public relations towards that of informal and uninstitutionalised relations. The net result is that horizontal co-operation has been channelled through different mechanisms to those envisaged in Article 145.2 of the Constitution, essentially by means of queries, protocols, or informal agreements between the governments or the respective administrations.

From all of the above, we may conclude that there is clear room for improvement in the regulation of the conventions of cooperation. The defects we have discussed could have been remedied during the process of statutory reforms in the eighth session of parliament (2004–2008), but unfortunately, in practice, the chance was missed. An examination of the provisions of the six new statutes of autonomy dealing with this issue confirms that with a few meritorious exceptions, the framers did not pay the necessary attention to the matter. It is for this reason that I refer to horizontal cooperation in the title of this paper as "unfinished business".

A) Valencia. Article 59 of the new statute regulates the conventions of collaboration under the same terms as Article 42 of the 1982 statute. It thus continues to restrict the material area regarding which conventions can be entered into in matters over which the community has exclusive competence, and it requires that the conventions be approved by an absolute majority of the Parliament of Valencia.

B) Catalonia. The new statute devotes Article 178 to regulating the conventions and cooperation agreements with other communities. Firstly, it establishes certain contents of the conventions of cooperation: the creation of joint bodies and the establishment of joint projects, plans, and programmes. Secondly—and this should be judged as being positive—it regulates parliamentary intervention in the following terms: "Entry into conventions and agreements requires prior approval of Parliament only in cases that affect its legislative powers. In other cases, the Government shall inform Parliament of the signing of conventions and agreements within 1 month of the date of signature". This speeds up the procedure for signing up to this type of instrument. Thirdly, and this is less positive, it retains the Cortes Generales's power to reclassify the convention: "Collaboration conventions signed by the Generalitat with other autonomous communities shall be notified to the Cortes Generales and shall come into effect 60 days after notification, unless the Cortes Generales decide that these are to be classified as cooperation agreements requiring the prior authorisation referred to in Article 145.2 of the Constitution". In short, the statute of Catalonia rectifies the issue of intervention by the regional parliament, but incomprehensibly, it does not remove that reclassifying power of the Cortes that, as we have seen, is in no way imposed by the Constitution.

C) Balearic Islands. The conventions and cooperation agreements are regulated in Article 118 of the new statute. Two changes are made with regard to Article 17 of the first statute. According to the premises of this study, one may be viewed as positive and the other not. The first novelty is the omission of the intervention of Balearic parliament in the procedure. This will clearly help speed matters up, and in all cases, when the contents of the agreement requires that it be translated into a legal rule, the intervention of the parliament will continue to be obligatory. What the change means is that no decision is now required from the parliament in cases in which the validity of the convention requires only the approval of regulatory rules. The second change is that, in retaining the reclassificatory powers of the Cortes, the period required for entry into force following communication to the Cortes is raised to 60 days. This increase benefits the Cortes but in no way favours the autonomous community.

D) Andalusia. The new statute simply reproduces the wording of Article 72 of the original statute, deficiencies and all. Firstly, the statute continues to leave regulation of the subject to an act of the parliament. Secondly, it expressly retains the Cortes' power of reclassification in Art. 226.2. The only new feature consists of the provision contained in Article 226.1 *in fine*, according to which power over "control and monitoring" of the conventions lies with the parliament of the autonomous community.

E) Aragon. Article 91 of the statute of Aragon includes some interesting amendments. Firstly, it attributes to the regional government the faculty to enter into conventions. This no longer requires the authorisation of the Aragon parliament; a mere communication of the convention in question is sufficient. Secondly, with regard to the effects of the communication to the Cortes, the statute indicates that it must be notified within a period of 1 month, but unlike others, it does not limit its validity to any period, from which we may deduce that the conventions take effect from the moment of their signing. Finally, the new statute leaves regulation of the legal procedure of the agreements to an act of the Aragon parliament. One may therefore conclude that some progress has been made in making the issue more flexible.

F) Castile and Leon. The new statute of Castile and Leon incorporates a specific chapter (Heading IV, Chapter I) devoted to the autonomous community's relations with the state and with other communities. Article 30 of the initial statute phrased regulation of the conventions and cooperation agreements in very unfortunate terms. On the one hand, it restricted the scope of the conventions to subjects of the exclusive competence of the community, and on the other, it attributed to the Cortes the power to reclassify such conventions as agreements. The article was amended by Organic Law 4/1999 and became Article 38. This amendment notably disimproved the article; not only did it retain the two existing errors but it also added the requirement that all conventions must be approved by the parliament of Castile and Leon. The subject is regulated by Article 60 of the new statute. Incomprehensibly, it retains the requirement for approval by the regional parliament in all cases and the central parliament's power of reclassification. The only change that should be rated positively is the extension of the material scope of the conventions to encompass the management and rendering of services that are the competence of the autonomous community, removing the term "exclusive".

G) Conclusions. Based on this analysis of the regulation of cooperation that conventions contained in the six new statutes of autonomy, we can draw three partial conclusions and one general one. The first partial conclusion refers to approval of the conventions: Whereas Catalonia, Balearic Islands, and Aragon have made the procedure more flexible by making approval from the regional assemblies unnecessary, Valencia, Andalusia, and Castile-Leon retain that requirement. The second conclusion is that most of the statutes (Andalusia, Catalonia, Balearic Islands, and Castile-Leon) continue to confer on the Cortes

Generales the power to reclassify the conventions—a faculty that is no way required by the Spanish Constitution. Third—and this is indeed astonishing—one of the new statutes (Valencia) continues to limit the scope of the conventions to matters that are the exclusive competence of the autonomous community. Based on these three partial conclusions, we have to give a generally negative rating to the reforms studied in that they do not solve the problems we have discussed.

# A Proposal for Reform of Horizontal Cooperation in the Body of Constitutional law

Some of the aspects of the Spanish state model that could be improved upon include excessive bilateralism in the construction of the autonomic state, the relative lack of participation of the autonomous communities in state decisions that largely affect them (such as European politics), excessive territorial conflict, and the practical non-existence of horizontal cooperation.

Over the preceding pages, we have sought to show some of the reasons for the last of these shortfalls: the practical absence of horizontal inter-governmental cooperation. However, the causes run deeper.

Sector Conferences [*conferencias sectoriales*]—undoubtedly the most representative institution of what we call cooperative federalism—have been exclusively devised as organs of vertical cooperation. This is logical insofar as they were created and are regulated by the state parliament. However, the autonomous communities have shown a surprising lack of initiative in establishing caucuses of horizontal cooperation, which could be achieved by creating conferences of regional ministers [*consejeros*] by convention.

Given that the subject has been inexplicably excluded from the agenda of the current debate on the development of the autonomic state, we should note that co-operation among the autonomous communities is fated to be one of the great axes of their development; to a certain extent, too, it will be the test that they will have to pass to prove their organisational maturity. Unfortunately, 30 years since the system was first established, this test of maturity is still a long way from being passed.

All of the above show that the principle of cooperation requires fresh impetus. In one of the best studies written on territorial reforms, the eminent professor of administrative law, Luis Ortega, accurately discusses the need to go beyond Heading VIII of the constitution as currently worded: "We must go from a Heading VIII governing the creation of the model to a Heading VIII that will address the working of the model". The principle of cooperation must have a central place in this new heading because the effective working of the State will only be achieved if mechanisms and procedures are designed that will channel co-operation between the different territorial authorities and in which there exists a real desire for cooperation between them.

The consolidation and fine-tuning of our autonomic state requires modernising reforms: "One of the keys to this necessary modernisation which is slowly being introduced—writes Prof. Ortega—is the prospect of a joint result of the action of all the political authorities involved in an issue. The social result of the public policies in a decentralised model is always the product of a plural action. For this reason, the new reform must essentially affect, not so much the body of the competences as the forms of this exercise of competences. The principles of a cooperative and solidarity-led way of acting must be instilled in the Constitution".[7]

From this point of view—and it is one that I fully share—the purpose of the necessary territorial reform (constitutional and statutory) should essentially be not so much to reopen the issue of the distribution of power through an increase in the competences of the territorial authorities at the expense of the central authorities (as occurred during the eighth session of parliament) but to develop the constitutional principle of cooperation, i.e., the creation and fine-tuning of instruments and procedures that serve as a channel for cooperative relations between the various territorial authorities. To put it more simply, the debate should centre not solely on the assumption of new competences but also, and primarily, on the form of exercising better the competences that are already held.

That constitutional reform would enable a better legal manifestation of cooperative instruments such as the one discussed here. Without a proper constitutional design of a cooperative federal model, one may foresee serious problems in the working of the autonomic state.[8] I therefore think it is appropriate to conclude this paper by setting out the outlines of that design.

Horizontal co-operation is expressly provided for by the Constitution, but the regime very vaguely specified, including control by the Senate, and its formalisation through conventions in which the different statutes have generally included participation by the parliaments of their respective autonomous communities, suffers from excessive rigidity and dissuades the regional governments from taking this path.

Legal authorities are practically unanimous in recognising that the existing regulation of horizontal cooperation hinders the use of conventions and agreements as a medium for promoting and consolidating a cooperative autonomic state in Spain.

This shortfall and deficiency in constitutional regulation was rooted in political reasons. The constitutional assembly was haunted by the phantom of the "Catalan countries" and was on the verge of making any inter-regional convention dependent on authorisation under an organic law. The final formula could have determined a flexible solution, but, and this is the most surprising thing, the statutes—both the original ones and the new ones approved during the eighth session of parliament—reduced the scope of action of the respective communities by extending the possibilities of control by the Cortes and, in general, made the system more rigid.

---

[7] Ortega (2005), pp. 49–50.

[8] On the meaning and overall scope of that reform, see Tajadura Tejada (2010).

We believe it is clear that that it is essential to remove those elements that give the system this excessive rigidity—in other words, to make our model of horizontal cooperation more flexible—in order to promote smooth and flexible inter-regional relations, capable of tackling the challenges of the twenty-first century state. Regulation of the subject in the body of constitutional law must be made more flexible. This would require an amendment to Article 145 of the Constitution to this end. Any such amendment would contain three elements:

a) The amendment should consist of removing Section 1 from Article 145, given that it adds nothing to the implicit and explicit limits that the text of the Constitution imposes on cooperation: non-transferability of ownership of the competences themselves, respect for the internal balance of powers in each autonomous community, and principle of solidarity.

b) The distinction between conventions and agreements should be definitively removed; the distinction offers no benefits and many disadvantages. One could argue that it is necessary, since in certain circumstances it is advisable for the Cortes—through the mechanism of the authorisation—to exercise control over the cooperative activity of the autonomous communities. However, I believe that this additional control, intended to verify whether the aforementioned limits are being respected, is unnecessary.

By removing Section 1 and doing away with the distinction between conventions and agreements, one might ask whether it ultimately makes any sense to retain the precept at all. The answer can be found at the beginning of this paper: An article of this kind avoids the disadvantages of having to seek an implicit constitutional basis for horizontal cooperation. It should therefore be retained.

c) The referral to the statutes should also be removed; if there is no possible distinction between conventions and agreements, it is no longer necessary. Moreover, in this paper we have explained the technical difficulties arising from varied regulation of the subject. Insofar as this is an instrument whose effectiveness and functionality requires a uniform regulation, it seems advisable to attribute it to an Organic Law of Cooperation, applying to all communities. Given that there has been discussion at times as to whether the Cortes are qualified to enact such a law, the purpose of introducing this referral is to settle that discussion. Consequently, the new wording of Article 145 of the Constitution might be as follows: "The autonomous communities may enter into conventions amongst themselves in order to co-operate in matters of common interest. An Organic Law of Cooperation shall establish the legal regime of the conventions".

d) This constitutional precept, which would replace Article 145, should be placed in the context of a new chapter of Heading VIII devoted expressly to the principle of cooperation, constitutionalising the basic instruments of cooperative federalism: the Conferences of Presidents, the Sectoral Conferences, and the vertical and horizontal conventions. The chapter in question would establish the basic design thereof and would leave development of the regulations to the Organic Law of Cooperation.

Any objections that might be raised to the very existence of such a law, with the argument that regulation of the cooperative instruments should be a power of the statutes, would be groundless for two reasons: firstly, because in 30 years the framers of the statutes have failed to concern themselves with it—or when they have, it has been with the unfortunate results that we have set out here, and secondly, because the functionality of these instruments requires their uniform regulation. We have already seen the problems caused by the diversity of legal regimes on the conventions.

However, it is clear that this law must be the result of consensus among the political forces and between the state and the autonomous communities. Although I consider the proposed constitutional reform timely and I also believe it is advisable to enact a General Organic Law of Cooperation, I must recognise that they would be of little use if they are not a legal reflection of a political desire for cooperation.

# References

ORTEGA, L.: Reforma Constitucional y Reforma Estatutaria, Civitas, Madrid, 2005, pp. 49 and 50.
TAJADURA TEJADA, J.: El principio de cooperación en el Estado Autonómico. El Estado Autonómico como Estado Federal Cooperativo, (3rd edition) Comares, Granada, 2010.

# New Cooperation Mechanisms Within the State of Autonomies

L.A. Gálvez and J.G. Ruiz

**Abstract** The absence of a system of intergovernmental relations within the State of Autonomies has resulted in limited multilateral cooperation. However, in recent years, there has been a consistent tendency to incorporate into the Spanish political practice new cooperation mechanisms characteristic of cooperative federalism, both in the relations between central State and Autonomous Communities (vertical dimension) and among the Autonomous Communities themselves (horizontal dimension).

Thus, in the field of vertical cooperation, the Conference of Presidents was constituted in 2004 for the Head of the Spanish Government and the presidents of all the regional governments to discuss problems that concern the State in general. On the other hand, in 2008, the Autonomous Communities which that had passed statutory reforms created the forum *Meetings between Autonomous Communities for the development of the Statutes of Autonomy*, with a view to implementing harmonically their new powers. After seven meetings and the inclusion of the governments of other Autonomous Communities which that had not reformed their Statutes of Autonomy, the Conference of the Autonomous-Community Governments was constituted in 2010, with the aim of promoting collaboration and cooperation among Autonomous Communities, as well as improving the functioning of the so called State of Autonomies.

This paper focuses on studying these new bodies and analysing the results achieved by them until present.

L.A. Gálvez (✉)
Facultad de Derecho, Universidad de Murcia, C/ Santo Cristo 1, 30001 Murcia, Spain
e-mail: lgalvez@um.es

J.G. Ruiz
Facultad de Derecho, Universidad de Murcia, C/ Santo Cristo 1, 30001 Murcia, Spain
e-mail: jgabriel.ruiz@carm.es

A. López-Basaguren and L. Escajedo San Epifanio (eds.), *The Ways of Federalism in Western Countries and the Horizons of Territorial Autonomy in Spain*, Vol. 2, DOI 10.1007/978-3-642-27717-7_15, © Springer-Verlag Berlin Heidelberg 2013

# Intergovernmental Cooperation Within the State of Autonomies

After recognising the right to autonomy of the nationalities and regions making up the Spanish nation, the Spanish Constitution (hereafter referred to as SC) designed an open and flexible territorial model with regard to both access to self-governance and distribution of powers. The latter is based on the willingness of each Autonomous Community to take on competences, limited by the matters and competences allotted to the State by Article 149 of the SC. This process of political decentralisation has brought about the creation of seventeen Autonomous Communities of similar nature, which, by way of their Statutes of Autonomy, are legally entitled to broad legislative, administrative, and financial powers.

The complexity of the State of Autonomies contrasts with the lack of constitutional provision of a system of collaboration between the Autonomous Communities and the State—vertical cooperation—even though the model for the distribution of powers, as laid down in the SC, stems from the need for cooperation between the various territorial bodies, given that the most part of the powers are allocated on a shared power basis.

The only specific mention that the Constitutional Text makes of cooperation refers to horizontal cooperation, that is, collaboration among Autonomous Communities. In particular, Article 145 envisages the possibility of the Autonomous Communities establishing agreements with one another for cooperatively implementing their powers, though the wording does not specially favour cooperation and instead strengthens the prominence of the *Cortes Generales* (Parliament). In particular, this provision states that

> The Statutes may provide for the circumstances, requirements, and terms under which the Autonomous Communities may reach agreements amongst themselves for management and the rendering of services in matters pertaining to them, as well as the nature and effects of the consequent communication to the Cortes Generales. In all other cases, cooperation agreements between the Autonomous Communities shall require the authorisation of the Cortes Generales.

Cooperative relations are inherent in any model of political decentralisation. That is the reason the Constitutional Court has repeatedly proclaimed that the principle of partnership, though not explicitly spelled out in the SC, is an essential part of the State of Autonomies. Thus, as is clear from the Constitutional Court ruling STC 106/1987, of 25 June, there is a reciprocal and general duty within the State of Autonomies—both at the vertical and horizontal level—made manifest in the non-abusive exercise of each body's powers, which should not hinder the exercise of the other bodies' powers. This duty derives from the fact that every public authority is bound to the Constitution and the legal system, as laid down in Article 9.1 of the SC.

This normative framework, which does not particularly promote cooperation, along with a non-existent cooperative tradition, has brought about scarce cooperative relations within the State of Autonomies, unlike in other federally organised countries in our setting. For a long time, the Sectoral Conferences have been the sole mechanisms for multilateral cooperation, while no other systems—legally regulated or not—govern institutional relations.

However, there appears to be a change of trend after the last statutory reforms. The new Statutes of Autonomy include, without exception, the principle of mutual institutional loyalty, as well as the principles of collaboration, partnership, solidarity, and mutual assistance. Furthermore, they formalise bilateralism in the relations with the State and recognise multilateralism, though in the latter case not pointing at any particular means of formalisation.

In the same vein, and coinciding with the new reform drive of the State of Autonomies we have pointed at, new cooperation mechanisms have been introduced by way of the political praxis, both between the central State and the Autonomous Communities and amongst the latter. We are referring to the Conference of Presidents and the Conference of the Autonomous-Community Governments.

The main purpose of this paper is to describe the main characteristics of these new cooperation instruments and examine the results obtained through them.

## The Conference of Presidents: A New Mechanism for Vertical Cooperation

One of the most significant weaknesses of the institutional model of vertical cooperation within the State of Autonomies has been the absence of a mechanism that allows for political dialogue at the highest level between the various public authorities, enabling the coherent functioning of the State. This situation is compounded by the fact that the current Senate, though defined by Article 69 of the SC as the House of territorial representation, does not fulfil this role in its composition or in its powers. Rather, it is a replica of the Congress of Deputies, with its legislative powers limited to second reading and supervision of the Government, but with no specific powers regarding regional organisation.

Therefore, in line with the onset of the process of statutory reforms, and with the aim of establishing a new channel for cooperation within the State of Autonomies, the First Conference of Presidents of regional governments was convened on 28 October 2004, at the initiative of the Head of the Spanish Government. This institution, though not typical of the Spanish legal and political traditions, plays an important role in federal states. The Conference of Presidents, recently created and with an uncertain future, includes among its members the Head of the Spanish Government and the Presidents of the Autonomous Communities. It was intended to create a new forum for discussion and decision-making with regard to major issues concerning the Spanish system of regional autonomies, as well as guarantee equality, solidarity, and a smooth functioning of the State.

Since then and until the present day, the Conference has been held four times, during the last of which the Internal Rules were adopted.[1] We will now examine the main characteristics of this body as laid out in the latter.

The key feature of the Conference of Presidents is its eminently political orientation; its objective is not making legally binding decisions. Rather, Article 1 of the Internal Rules defines the Conference as the highest body for political cooperation between the Spanish Government and the governments of the Autonomous Communities, subject to the principle of mutual institutional loyalty.

The political orientation of the Conference of Presidents results in a number of legal consequences, the first of which being that its implementation does not require a Constitutional reform. Second, its functioning does not require strict regulation, given that there are no legal consequences attached to its actions. Last, its functioning must rely on consensus.

As for its scope, according to its Internal Rules, the Conference of Presidents has the following purposes:

1. Discussing the broad public, sectoral, and territorial State policy guidelines, joint actions of a strategic nature, as well as relevant issues for the State of Autonomies which that may affect both the State and the Autonomous Communities' areas of responsibility;
2. Fostering partnership between the State and the Autonomous Communities.
3. Encouraging and guiding the activity of the Sectoral Conferences and other multilateral cooperation bodies.

In keeping with its political nature, every act that the Conference of Presidents adopts is considered a political agreement that does not give rise to direct legal consequences. To that effect, Article 6 of its Internal Rules establishes that, based on the degree of consensus achieved, the Conference of Presidents may adopt two kinds of acts: agreements and recommendations. Agreements are political decisions supported by the consensus of all the members present at the Conference, provided that two-thirds of the Presidents of the Autonomous Communities attend. Recommendations, on the other hand, are political statements that may be adopted by the Head of the Spanish Government and two-thirds of the Presidents of the Autonomous Communities attending the conference, committing only those members who endorse it.

Regarding its membership, the Conference of Presidents is composed of the Head of the Spanish Government, who presides over it, and the Presidents of the Autonomous Communities and the Cities of Ceuta and Melilla. The minister responsible in the field of territorial cooperation will attend the meetings as Secretary.

In its almost 7 years of existence, the Conference of Presidents has been held four times. The issues discussed have been of varied nature, and in the course of the

---

[1] Decree TER/3409/2009, of 18 December, establishing the publication of the Internal Rules of the Conference of Presidents.

first two meetings, important agreements were reached in the fields of health funding as well as research, technological development, and innovation. However, no agreements were reached in the last meeting, held in December 2009, where the discussion focused on employment, sustainable economy, agriculture, livestock, fisheries, and water.[2] Since then, no other meeting has been convened.

# The Commitment of the Autonomous Communities to Horizontal Multilateral Cooperation

Upon reading the recently reformed Statutes of Autonomy, it may be concluded that inter-regional cooperation must still be addressed within the State of Autonomies, for there has been no significant progress in the establishment of cooperative relations when compared with the previous Statutes. In practice, we observe that there has been a change of trend in the field of horizontal cooperation in Spain, which coincides in time with the process of statutory reforms.

On the one hand, the agreements between Autonomous Communities, almost unheard of in the Spanish political praxis, have significantly grown in number since 2006. On the other hand, a particularly relevant and novel event in the field of horizontal cooperation took place in 2008: We are referring to the meeting held in Saragossa among those Autonomous Communities which that had reformed their Statutes, and that resulted in the initiative *Meetings between the Autonomous Communities for the Development of the Statutes of Autonomy*, the origin of the current Conference of the Autonomous-Community Governments.[3]

## *The Autonomous-Community Meetings*

On 9 July 2008, following an initiative of the Government of Aragon, the highest representatives of the Governments of Valencian Community, Catalonia, Balearic Islands, Andalusia, Castile and León, and of course Aragon, the host community, gathered in Zaragoza with the aim of expanding the relations among the Autonomous Communities and deepening the process of transfer of new autonomous powers. In this gathering, it was agreed to continue holding such Meetings, in order to move ahead with regional development. Thus, the State of Autonomies

---

[2] The issues dealt with during the meetings of the Conference of Presidents can be accessed on the website http://www.mpt.gob.es/areas/politica_autonomica/coop_multilateral_ccaa_ue/ Confer_Presidentes.

[3] The Conference of Autonomous-Community Governments has a comprehensive Internet website from which we have gathered a significant part of the information included in this paper. Available at http://comunidadesautonomas.org.

is provided with an institution for multilateral horizontal cooperation similar to the existing ones in other decentralised States in our sociopolitical environment, such as the *Ministerpräsidentenkonferenz*, or meeting of the Presidents of the *Länder*, in Germany, or the National Governors Association, in the United States.

Surprisingly for many, it did not take long for the Meetings to give their first results. In the 3rd Autonomous-Community Meeting, held in Valladolid on 23 February 2009, the first two agreements, as well as the Operating Rules, were adopted.

According to the aforesaid Operating Rules, the Meetings are shaped as a political instrument, just as the Conference of Presidents is. This is the reason the agreements, which have to be adopted unanimously, are not legally binding. They only commit the corresponding Autonomous Communities to start the procedures, by the means determined by the applicable rules, until, once they are over, they may be signed by all of the regions. In addition to the agreements, the possibility is envisaged of political statements being adopted in the Meetings.

Since their creation in 2008, eight Meetings have been held, during which six statements have been adopted and eleven agreements or protocols have been signed. By means of these instruments, a result of the voluntary horizontal cooperation among Autonomous Communities, it has been possible to reach joint positions in such important matters as the effects of setting a State basis in the system of distribution of powers, the participation of the Autonomous Communities in shaping the positions of the State towards European Union issues, the function of the Senate, or the impact of the State subsidies in the system of distribution of powers. Likewise, with the aim of improving the provision of Public Services to its citizens, protocols and agreements in several areas have been promoted.

Although the Meetings between the Autonomous Communities arise at the initiative of the six Communities with new Statutes of Autonomy, their members expressed from the outset their will of all of the regions progressively joining the Meetings. Once sixteen Autonomous Communities were part of them and having reached, in a record time, stability as an inter-regional cooperation mechanism, the member regions agreed in the 7th Meeting, held in Santiago de Compostela on 25 October 2010, to give the Meetings greater institutional representation by creating the Conference of Autonomous-Community Governments.


## The Conference of Autonomous-Community Governments

The Communities taking part in the Meetings agreed to establish in 2010 the Conference of Autonomous-Community Governments, with a view to holding a Conference of Presidents of the Autonomous Communities. This was done with the aim of consolidating an institutional and regulatory framework that would promote political and administrative cooperation and collaboration among the Autonomous Communities. In its constitutive meeting, its Organization and Operation Rules were adopted.

The Conference was created as an instrument for voluntary political and administrative cooperation in the field of regional powers, and as a forum for dialogue among the autonomous regions, in order to improve the functioning of the State of Autonomies for the benefit of the citizens. To this end, the main objectives of the Conference were set as follows:

1. Promoting the collaboration among the Autonomous Communities in their respective areas of responsibility;
2. Promoting the collaboration between the Autonomous-Community Governments and the Government of Spain;
3. Promoting political actions concerning State affairs;
4. Expediting the celebration of a Conference of Presidents of the Autonomous Communities.

According to this duality, as forum for dialogue and cooperation instrument, the Conference of Autonomous-Community Governments allows for Communities to both discuss political questions of general interest and adopt agreements. Such agreements may, in turn, consist of political statements or aim at encouraging the conclusion of agreements or collaboration protocols. Political statements need to be endorsed by at least fifteen Autonomous Communities, whereas the promotion of agreements and protocols generally requires unanimity; these may also be approved by a majority agreement, although in this case they will only be effective for the Communities involved.

In any case, given their political nature, the agreements adopted at the Conference of Autonomous-Community Governments have no legal implications; they merely constitute political engagements for each region to carry out—according to each Autonomous Community regional Law—the appropriate actions in order for the agreements to be effective.

As for the relations of the Conference of the Autonomous-Community Governments with the State, the Organization and Operation Rules envisage the possibility of inviting the Government of Spain to the Meetings, and commit to duly inform the latter of the results. Furthermore, they clearly express the will of the Conference to promote partnership through vertical cooperation mechanisms. This is an essential aspect since it denotes the willingness of the Autonomous Communities to promote a real intergovernmental cooperation system within the State of Autonomies.

The Conference of Autonomous-Community Governments held its constitutive meeting on 21 March 2011 in Santander. An Institutional Statement was then approved, which defended the soundness of the model of regional autonomy as a forward-looking instrument, highlighting its co-starring role, along with the State, in the Spanish social and economic development. Also, in this first meeting of the Conference of Autonomous-Community Governments, its members expressed their will to continue with the line of inter-regional cooperation that had characterised the Autonomous-Community Meetings, and several collaboration agreements and protocols on the subject of fisheries, industry, research, and transport, among others, were approved.

## By Way of Summary, Has a New Stage for Cooperation Within the State of Autonomies Been Launched?

As a consequence of the absence of an efficient system for multilateral cooperation in a highly decentralised State as Spain, real cooperation has been developed in practice in an informal way, bilaterally articulated through meetings between the Head of the Spanish Government and the Presidents of the Autonomous Communities, or by way of negotiations between the leadership of the two major national parties. Thus, institutionalised cooperation—especially that of a multilateral nature developed through Sectoral Conferences—is circumscribed to matters of lesser importance and, in any case, sectorial.

Although very useful to consolidate the model of regional autonomies, this system does not favour at all an appropriate and coherent functioning of the State: in many cases, it elicits a feeling of infringement of the principles of equality and partnership among the different Autonomous Communities which constitute the foundation of the constitutional loyalty that should govern the actions of the regional authorities in any complex State.

There is no doubt that both the Conference of Presidents and the Conference of Autonomous-Community Governments have covered a gap in the Spanish system for institutional cooperation. In matters of collaboration between the central State and the Autonomous Communities, and among the latter, the first step has been taken with their institutionalisation, maybe the most difficult and important one.

As mentioned before, the Conference of Presidents has been held only four times in its almost 7 years of existence, and the agreements reached in its last gatherings were few. The consolidation of the Conference of Presidents is, in our view, remarkably difficult due to the fact that it is a vertical initiative and not an instrument arising from a need on the part of the Autonomous Communities—as it happened originally in Germany or the United States—as well as the temptation of infusing the Conference with partisan positions.

The situation of the Conference of Autonomous-Community Governments is different. This institution arose from the wish of cooperation of the Autonomous Communities which that had reformed their Statutes of Autonomy in 2008, deriving in the initiative known as the Autonomous-Community Meeting. Since its creation, there has been a progressive increase in the number of member regions, as well as in the number and importance of the agreements and protocols signed and the issues dealt with in the meetings.

Thus, the State of Autonomies now relies on two new cooperation instruments that begin to take their first steps, although at a different pace. There is no doubt that a new stage for intergovernmental cooperation in Spain has been launched. Nonetheless, what is necessary for the consolidation of these new cooperative mechanisms?

Said newly introduced cooperation instruments, both on their horizontal and vertical dimensions, prove that, although regulations—constitutional, statutory, and legal—could be significantly improved in order to promote intergovernmental collaboration, this is not an essential obstacle to encouraging cooperation within the State of Autonomies, especially that of a multilateral nature.

Doubtless, to have a constitutional framework that enshrines the principle of partnership and removes the obstacles for the collaboration among the different territorial powers would help to consolidate these new cooperation mechanisms, especially in a country like Spain, where a culture of political cooperation has yet to take root. It might also be useful to have a Law regulating the coordination among the different territorial powers. It is also true that the recent reforms of the Statutes of Autonomy have been a missed opportunity for giving multilateral cooperation an unprecedented impetus.

Nevertheless, though all of these circumstances, upon occurring, would promote the consolidation of these new cooperation mechanisms, it is truly essential for their strengthening that both the central State and the Autonomous Communities overcome their historical distrust and understand the duty of cooperation as a product of the principle of constitutional loyalty that, far from limiting their powers, may allow them to implement them with greater efficiency for the benefit of their citizens. This aspect is currently of paramount importance since, as a consequence of the economical crisis in which Spain is immersed, there is a widespread public debate on the inefficiencies of the State of Autonomies. In our view, cooperation needs nowadays more support than ever in order to avoid gaps between the different territorial authorities, which may provoke duplication of functions, squandering, and ultimately, social discredit of the territorial model of the State itself.

The statement of support for the State of Autonomies, adopted at the 1st Conference of the Autonomous-Community Governments, is a step in the right direction. The soundness of the State of Autonomies as a forward-looking instrument was defended there, although specific emphasis was placed on the need for acting in the name of constitutional loyalty and cooperation among Autonomous Communities, as well as between the latter and the Government of the Spanish nation.

# Horizontal Cooperation in the Autonomous State: The Conference of Autonomous Presidents

Zulima Pérez i Seguí

**Abstract** One of the most important constitutional problems in our country, and one that has not yet been solved, is precisely the territorial distribution and organisation of power. Our Constitution defined a State that could be territorially decentralised, leaving it to the Autonomy Statutes and other laws on development to give it its final shape. The State has now reached decentralisation levels that were unthinkable at the time when the Constitution was adopted. The Autonomous Communities have a consolidated institutional organisation, and they have undertaken numerous powers successfully. However, important deficiencies still exist in vertical cooperation relations—between the State and the Autonomous Communities, but, more importantly, in horizontal cooperation relations, i.e., among the Autonomous Communities themselves.

The recently created Conference of Governments of the Autonomous Communities, following the Meeting of the Autonomous Communities for the development of the Autonomy Statutes, is preparing the first Conference of Autonomous Presidents, which has been scheduled after the May elections. Horizontal cooperation has proven to be a powerful tool against centralisation as the Autonomous Communities can exercise their common powers jointly, even those that are outside their territorial scope, in such a manner that there is no need of intervention from the State. Furthermore, making use of mechanisms of horizontal cooperation allows a better and stronger working of vertical cooperation, which makes it possible for the Autonomous Communities to coordinate their stances and be in a stronger position to negotiate with the State. In recent years, a claim for a Conference of Presidents on the horizontal level has gained followers. This would serve as

Translated by *Ana Luisa Nuño de la Rosa*.

Z. Pérez i Seguí (✉)
Facultat de Dret, Departament de Dret Constitucional Ciència Política i de l' Administració, Universitat de València, Edifici Departamental Occidental, Av. Tarongers s/n, 46022 València, Spain
e-mail: Zulima.Perez@uv.es

A. López-Basaguren and L. Escajedo San Epifanio (eds.), *The Ways of Federalism in Western Countries and the Horizons of Territorial Autonomy in Spain*, Vol. 2, DOI 10.1007/978-3-642-27717-7_16, © Springer-Verlag Berlin Heidelberg 2013

forum for the Presidents of the Autonomous Communities, without the participation of the President of the Government.

This paper analyses, firstly, the need to improve the existing cooperation mechanisms, especially those working on a horizontal level, and secondly, the potentiality of a Conference of Autonomous Presidents from a comparative law approach. Proposals on the configuration of the Conference and its relation to other powers will also be discussed in this paper.

## Introduction

After more than three decades of the autonomous State, even though the global evaluation is positive, there are still unresolved constitutional issues in our country. One of the most significant of these is the territorial distribution and organisation of power.

Our Constitution set up a territorially decentralised State, leaving its final configuration to the Statutes of Autonomy and other laws of development. Our model of State has therefore an indefinite and open nature, and some have even stated that it is de-constitutionalised (Cruz 1981). It has been argued in scholarly writings that this "open" character does not entail an absence of a constitutional model in relation to this matter but the existence of a model with flexibility so great that it results in fundamentally negative limits (Tomás y Valiente 1993, p. 186). The Constitution left some freedom to the public powers to shape the State. This freedom is not absolute as the Constitution establishes very clearly a set of principles about territorial distribution that must be taken into account by the legislator. Our State has even been labelled as "autonomous judicial State" (Aragón 1986) due to the fact that the de-constitutionalisation of the model allowed for flexible interpretations by the constitutional case law. However, the realisation of the constitutional model is a task for the legislator by means of the Statutes of Autonomy and other competence-limiting regulations, without forgetting the work done by the Constitutional Court, which kept in mind from the outset some general traits of what the Autonomous State ought to be (Tomás y Valiente 1993).

Despite the lack of concretion of the State model, our Constitution includes a series of principles that have allowed for the doctrine and the case law to build a concept of the Autonomous State. In this regard, Article 2 of the Constitution includes three fundamental principles concerning the territorial distribution of power: the principles of unity, autonomy, and solidarity. Even though the principle of cooperation is not among them, this principle is presented as an inevitable consequence of the articulation of the former. It is present (albeit implicitly) in our system, as it is in all compound States.

There are two dimensions to cooperation. One is vertical, and it refers to relations between the State and the Autonomous Communities. The other is horizontal, and it deals with relations of the Autonomous Communities with each other.

## The Benefits of Horizontal Cooperation: Towards a Collaborative Autonomy

The cooperation relations in Spain are markedly vertical, and still today cooperation among Autonomous Communities is regarded as unreliable.

False beliefs are still quite widespread that horizontal cooperation can create strong autonomic blocs at a regional level, which could pose a risk to the unity of the State; there is also the belief that these relations lessen the autonomy of the Autonomous Communities. These assumptions have caused that, while the vertical intergovernmental relations have developed normally, cooperation between the Autonomous Communities is still scarce. The situation is compounded when considering that there has been no forum where regional governments could carry out such cooperation (Montilla 2005).

Another setback for establishing horizontal relations is the extreme rigidity for the signature of cooperation agreements among Autonomous Communities which derives from the regulation that Article 145 of the Constitution made of cooperation agreements, which require approval by the Cortes Generales (Parliament), and of the agreements among the Autonomous Communities for management and services provision, for which the Constitution leaves it to the Statutes of Autonomy to define the cases when the aforementioned agreements shall be adopted, the requirement under which they may be adopted, and the effects of communication thereof to the Cortes Generales. As far as the Statutes of Autonomy go, the issue remains unclear. They make no distinction between agreements and conventions; they do not describe the requirements for passing agreements. In this respect, several regulations in the Statutes have added rigidity. Some Statutes, such as Valencia's (Article 42) and Catalonia's (Article 27), attributed to the Parliament the power to ratify conventions and agreements. Others, like La Rioja's (Article 17), much more rigid, establish the need for Parliament not only to ratify the agreements and conventions but also to authorise the regional government to implement them. In the case of Asturias (Article 24.7), Murcia (Article 23.7), and Navarre (Article 26.b), the Statutes establish the need for prior authorisation, but they do not mention adoption of the agreements and conventions.

Parliamentary scrutiny, which is always positive in democracies, in the case of horizontal cooperation, is exceedingly stiff and often incompatible with the dynamism and agility that the conventions should have (Tajadura 2010). All this has greatly affected the development of relations between regional governments. Thus, while vertical agreements are not included in constitutional provisions, they are abundant in the Autonomous Communities—State relations; further, while horizontal agreements are recognised under Article 145 of the Constitution, they have had a very limited use (Alberti 2002; Tajadura 2010).

The Autonomous Communities should be aware of the benefits of cooperation among themselves. The truth is that strong relations between the Autonomous Communities favor an effective and harmonious working of the State. Such relations allow, among other things, that the regional governments be able to address common problems beyond the scope of the Community itself without interference from the central power in matters assigned to them. The fact that several Autonomous communities are affected by the same thing has served as pretext for the State to regulate and exercise powers conferred to them.

Intergovernmental relations allow for horizontal competencies to be exercised by their legal holder, i.e., by the Autonomous Communities. It also constitutes an alternative to re-centralisation of powers. This issue, which has surfaced in the political debate in recent months, could be tackled if the Autonomous Communities cooperated among them. Cooperation enables more effective management of the powers held by the Autonomous Communities; it can reduce costs and efforts. However, cooperation makes it possible to address not only common interests but also conflicting interests, and it may be a tool for conflict resolution among Communities.

Yet another advantage of cooperation is the possibility that the Autonomous Communities reach a common stance on certain issues, improving their negotiation position with the State. The existence of forums for dialogue among regional governments, in turn, allows for the implementation of multilateral mechanisms, avoiding bilateralism as the only resource. Therefore, the existence of both common interests (tackling common interests) and conflicting interests (conflict resolution) and the formation of a common stance (strength and pressure against the State) and putting a halt to intervention from the central power make cooperation among Autonomous Communities an essential tool for a proper articulation of the Autonomous State and a greater cohesion of it (Montilla 2006).

It seems that, so far, the Autonomous Communities were not aware of their need for collaboration. The celebration of the Meetings among Autonomous Communities has led to the Conference of Governments of the Autonomous Communities, which is a critical step in the promotion and development of horizontal cooperation. It has been created at the initiative of the Communities themselves, as a framework for cooperation, and it has been institutionalised by a Regulation. It has promoted a number of agreements and proposed the creation of a horizontal Conference of Autonomous Presidents.

## The Conference of Presidents

The conference of Presidents is the highest political body of cooperation between the State and the Autonomous Communities, and it is at the top of the multilateral cooperation bodies in Spain. The Conference is composed of the President of the Government, who chairs the meetings, and of the Presidents of the seventeen Autonomous Communities, and of the Autonomous Cities of Ceuta and Melilla.

The creation of the Conference of Presidents in Spain was announced by the President of the Government at the investiture debate, and it was constituted on 28th October 2004. Its existence represents an element of constitutional normality; it creates a space for intergovernmental debate and dialogue, which had been inexistent thus far. All the autonomous presidents met for the first time at the Conference, making a visual image that the autonomous communities are part of the State too.

In the outset, it was decided that this body should not be institutionalised in favour of informality and flexibility. However, the strong pressure exerted by different sectors concluded in the fourth meeting of the Conference, held on 14 December 2009, where the Internal Regulations of the Conference were passed. Regulation was quite clearly a good decision. Although in many countries around us there is no institutionalisation of this body, a state like ours, with no culture of cooperation, would have been doomed to failure without it. AJA pointed out in relation to the possibility of regulation that it would "erase suspicions of opportunism when Conference meetings were called, enable better participation of the Autonomous Communities, and the experience can be used to stay away from improvisation" (Aja 2005). Therefore, regulation is necessary in a state that lacks a cooperative tradition, where partisan political debate far outweighs the territorial debate, as was seen in the Second Conference of Presidents, where the meeting was divided into two major political blocs.

Unlike other compound states, the Conference of Presidents in the Autonomous State springs from and is driven by the central government, and it has a unique vertical nature. In surrounding countries, the Conference of Presidents shows a horizontal nature. In Germany, the *Ministerpräsidentenkonferenz* (MPK) is the meeting place for the presidents of the *Länder* without the presence of the Federal Chancellor. The MPK was born of the need for the different territories to adopt joint positions for negotiations with the State, and although it is horizontal in nature, it uses a double-shift system. Of the four meetings held each year, in at least two it is scheduled that the Länder meet with the Federal Chancellor without prejudice that the former meet together previously. It is also a body that lacks regulation, except for the recognition made by the Federal Government Regulation on the Federal Chancellor's invitation to participate in meetings (Bocanegra and Huergo 2005).

In Austria, it is also a body of horizontal and non-institutionalised character, and it has a great moral weight (Pernthaler 2004). In Switzerland, the Cantonal Governments Conference is a new body because, unlike the Conference of Presidents of Germany and Austria, which appeared in the forties to deal with a post-war context, it was created in 1993 by an administrative agreement signed by the cantons, with the aim to provide a platform for coordination between them for the possible accession of Switzerland to the European Economic Area (Garcia 2004). Furthermore, this body, which is also horizontal, is not strictly a Conference of Presidents but of representatives of the different cantons elected by the Cantonal Government.

In Italy, the *Conferenza delle Regioni e delle Province Autonome* was established in January 1981 and became a mechanism of policy coordination between the Presidents of the Regional Boards and the Autonomous Provinces. It meant an improvement in the relations between them and an increase of their force against the Central State through the production of documents shared by all regions, the ongoing exchange of good practices, the need to represent the system of regional governments abroad as in institutional relations, as well as highlighting of the role of the Regions in the construction of the European Union.

This Conference is composed of the 20 regional presidents and the 2 presidents of the Autonomous Provinces, without the presence of the Central Government, and it is the official home for inter-regional institutional dialogue. In this forum, the Regions discuss and then prepare the documents that will be presented and discussed at the *ConferenzaStato-Regioni*. This horizontal conference serves as a preparation for a subsequent vertical one. On 9 June 2005, the Conference adopted a Regulation which that rules its operation. So far, it had worked without any kind of institutionalisation, based solely on the praxis. The President and Vice President of the Conference are elected by the members of the Conference. This Conference is organised into 11 Working Committees (*Determinazione* of 9 June 2005).

As noted above, the Conference of Presidents in Spain is vertical in nature, but in recent years increasingly strong demands have called out for a conference of Presidents of a horizontal character, which serves as meeting place for the Presidents of the Autonomous Communities without the participation of the President of the Government.

On 9 July 2008, the first meeting between Autonomous Communities, for the development of their Statutes of Autonomy, was held in Zaragoza. It was attended by the Autonomous Communities of Catalonia, Andalusia, Valencia, Aragon, Balearic Islands, and Castilla y León. All had reformed their statutes in the wave of reforms that accompanied the Eighth Legislature. These meetings, devised as an instrument of horizontal cooperation to coordinate the development of new statutes and greater cohesion of the Autonomous State, soon saw new additions; from the seventh meeting on, the rest of Autonomous Communities joined in, with the exception of Asturias.

These meetings were provided with basic operating rules, which are far from rigid and which establish, among other things, the nature and purpose of the meetings, their composition, their convening, the conduct of the meetings, the agreements in them adopted, and the organisation thereof. The rules established that the objective was to pool together the issues that affect or interest them, to exchange information, and to set up lines of action that can lead to the signature of cooperation agreements or the creation of collaborative tools for a better performance of their powers in the interests of citizens.

It was agreed, at the VIIth Meeting held in Santiago de Compostela on 25 October 2010, to transform the meeting model that was being applied to the "Conference of the Governments of the Autonomous Communities". It was also agreed that the autonomous community of Aragón should host the Permanent Secretariat of the Conference. This conference, which was institutionalised by virtue of an agreement signed by the Autonomous Communities, faces the upcoming challenge of organising a Conference of Autonomic Presidents, which may constitute a prior step to the existence of a body of political relations among the presidents.

On 21 March 2011, the Conference of Governments of the Autonomous Communities was held in Santander. The Conference constitutes a means of collaboration and cooperation between regions within the scope of their powers, and it is the forum for permanent dialogue among them. It aims to promote collaboration and political and administrative cooperation between the different Autonomous Communities in order to consolidate and improve the political and administrative decentralisation of the State. The Conference has set as its objectives the promotion of cooperation both among the Autonomous Communities and between them and the State, as well as the promotion of political actions in State affairs and the facilitation of the celebration of the Conference of Autonomous Presidents.

It is composed of the Plenary Session, the Presidency, and the Permanent Secretariat. The Plenary Session, which is the highest governing body of the Conference, shall meet in ordinary session twice a year, on the first week of March and November. An extraordinary session can be called at the request of at least nine members. The Plenary Session has a Technical Commission composed of representatives of each Autonomous Community with a minimum rank of Director General, which is in charge of preparing the meetings of the Conference. It also can create specific commissions or working groups. The representatives of the Autonomous Communities in the Plenary Session and the Commissions may be accompanied by experts in the subjects that will be discussed.

The Presidency is rotational, and it is exercised by the representative of the Autonomous Community where the meeting is scheduled to be held for a period of 6 months, either from 1 January to 30 June or from 1 July to 31 December. The Secretariat of each meeting is held by the Community holding the Presidency. The Secretariat calls for preparatory meetings when deemed necessary, and it calls for the Conference itself. There is also a Permanent Secretary, who is based in an Autonomous Community to be agreed upon and who is in charge of the tracking, the communications, the preparation, and the custody of the documents of the Conference.

It is expected that the President of the Government of Spain will be invited to participate in the Conference meetings. Furthermore, the Government of Spain will be given report on the agreements adopted in every meeting, thus contributing to a collaborative relation between the two instances.

The Conference has the power to deliberate on political matters of common interest such as agreements. Agreements may include declarations and other political actions; they may intend to promote the adoption of collaboration agreements, the execution and signature of which shall create legal obligations, or they may focus on the creation of collaboration protocols for the establishment of principles or guidelines for common action, which do not create legal obligations.

The agreements consisting of declarations and other political actions, which are not legally binding, are adopted by unanimity. However, if a proposal is supported by at least 15 Governments, this proposal automatically becomes the Conference's official stance. Agreements oriented to promoting cooperation conventions or protocols are adopted unanimously and exceptionally by a majority. To this end, when unanimity is not reached at a meeting, the Autonomous Community or Communities that promote the agreement seek a compromise with the others to pass the agreement at the next meeting. If not possible, the agreement may be adopted should it obtain the support of most of the Autonomous Communities and if none of them expresses opposition to the signing of it by the other Communities.

The creation of the Meetings and recently of the Conference of Governments has proven highly positive. For the first time, the Autonomous Communities have a forum to collaborate and exchange information, and it represents a great impulse for multilateral horizontal cooperation. In fact, since the meetings were constituted, two cooperation conventions have been passed, one for the coordination of networks of domestic violence shelters for women and another one for the mutual recognition of licenses for hunting and recreational freshwater fishing. Furthermore, a Protocol of collaboration has been signed for drafting common strategies aimed at promoting joint actions regarding the tourism industry. Another 8 conventions and 6 protocols have been promoted, as well as various Agreements and Declarations. The figure does not seem too high, and yet it is if we take into consideration the small number of agreements among the Autonomous Communities that were adopted to date. The figure is even lower for horizontal multilateral agreements.

## Conclusion

Horizontal cooperation is one of the unfinished businesses in the autonomous State. Autonomous Communities, with the creation of the Conference of regional governments and the provision of a conference without the presence of Presidents of Central State, have taken a big step forward in horizontal relations. This drive has already begun to bear fruit and has been promoted and signed several agreements. The proper functioning of both the conferences as a possible autonomic Conference of Presidents can greatly enhance horizontal relationships in our state.

The wide dispersion laws of intergovernmental relations stimulate an inadequate and complex regulatory system frequently misunderstood and therefore is infrequently used. Streamlining the system is essential for creating coherent policy, as noted Fernandez Alles, building an "inclusive and realistic constitutional system of intergovernmental relations, conceptually well defined and limited in nature and legal" (Fernández Alles 2004, p. 52). The need exists for the adoption and implementation of a law containing the basis for the development of intergovernmental relations. Providing framework for joint cooperation in the autonomous State can serve to eliminate the shortcomings and deficiencies of the current regulatory system, considering the lack of culture of cooperation that exists in our state.

## References

Aja, E. (2005) "La Conferencia de Presidentes en el Estado Autonómicos" en Informe Comunidades Autónoma. TORNOS, J (Dir.) 2005, Instituto de Derecho Público, Barcelona 2006.

Alberti Rovira, E. (2002) Los convenios de colaboración. Anuario Jurídico de la Rioja, 8: 149–160.

Aragón Reyes, M. (1986) "Estado jurisdiccional autonómico", RVAP, n°16.

Bocanegra Sierra, R; Huergo Lora, A. (2005) La Conferencia de Presidentes, Madrid, 152 pp.

Cruz Villalón, P. (1981) "La estructura del Estado o la curiosidad del jurista persa". Revista de la Facultad de Derecho de la Universidad Complutense, n° 4, monográfico.

Fernández Alles, J.J. (2004) "Bases para una teoría constitucional española sobre las relaciones intergubernamentales". REDC, n° 74. 2004.

García Morales, M.J. (2004) La conferencia de los gobiernos cantonales en Suiza http://www. idpbarcelona.net/docs/actual/act_morales.pdf

Montilla Martos, JA, (2005) Apuntes sobre colaboración y participación en el Estado Autonómico. A propósito de la propuesta de reforma del Estatuto de Autonomía de Cataluña, Revista d' Estudis Autonòmics i Federals, n° 1.

Montilla Martos, J.A. (2006) El marco normativo de las relaciones intergubernamentales, in Las Relaciones intergubernamentales en el Estado Autonómico, Centro de Estudios Políticos y Constitucionales, Madrid.

Pernthaler, P. (2004) La Conferencia de Presidentes de los Länder en Austria en AJA, Eliseo, Informe sobre la Conferencia de Presidentes (resultados del Seminario celebrado en Barcelona el 21 de julio de 2004), IDP, Barcelona, 2004.

Tajadura, J. (2010). Los convenios de cooperación entre comunidades autónomas: marco normativo y propuestas de reforma. Revista d' Estudis Autonòmics i Federals 11: 207–255.

Tomás y Valiente, F. (1993) Escritos sobre y desde el Tribunal Constitucional, Centro de Estudios Constitucionales, Madrid.

# Vertical Cooperation in Horizontal Subjects: Immigration as an Issue for All

Ignacio Álvarez Rodríguez

**Abstract** The aim of this article is to present, in summary form, the main mechanisms adopted within the Spanish system of Autonomous Regions in order to implement the cooperation principle in a field of utmost importance: immigration. For this purpose, the article is structured as follows: firstly, it sets out the rationale for cooperation; secondly, it discusses the criteria that define the subject matter; thirdly, it explains cooperative mechanisms; and, finally, it concludes with some brief remarks.

**Keywords** Cooperation • Immigration • Spanish autonomous regions

## Shared Competence in Immigration as the Main Rationale for the Inter-administrative Cooperation

The legal–political framework set out in the Spanish Constitution of 1978 is characterised, among other things, for recognising the territorial decentralisation of powers. A quick reading of the Spanish Constitution combined with an analysis of how our Institutions work show three clearly specified levels: National, Regional, and Local. For the matter at hand, International Law is especially relevant (and more precisely, European Community Law). For this reason, it will be highlighted that inter-administrative cooperation will become more necessary as a systematic and coherent operational model is adopted.

As regards immigration, it seems that the majority part of the doctrine observes a shared competence, although the State has the main role in the regulation of immigration (Aja Fernández 2006, p. 153). According to art.149.1.2nd of the

I.Á. Rodríguez (✉)
Departamento de Derecho Constitucional, Universidad de Valladolid, Plaza de la Universidad 1, 47002 Valladolid, Spain
e-mail: ignacio.alvarez@sjc.uva.es

A. López-Basaguren and L. Escajedo San Epifanio (eds.), *The Ways of Federalism in Western Countries and the Horizons of Territorial Autonomy in Spain*, Vol. 2, DOI 10.1007/978-3-642-27717-7_17, © Springer-Verlag Berlin Heidelberg 2013

Spanish Constitution, the State holds competence over the regulation of the legal status of immigrants, the conditions of their entry, and their stay and expulsion from the country. For those Autonomous Regions that have jurisdiction pursuant to different sectorial competences—most of them derive such powers from their Statutes of Regional Autonomy—immigration is a matter under their competence in each of the areas they cover, such as health, education, or housing (Montilla Martos 2007, pp. 11 & ff.; Vidal Fueyo 2007, pp. 68 & ff.). As a consequence, it would not make sense to require transferring those sectorial competences in favour of the generic power of the Central Government as stated in the abovementioned article (Santolaya Machetti 2007, *pássim*).

Therefore, one can argue that the possible success of public policies on the matter would thus depend on how the two levels cooperate, without forgetting the local level, whose first response and acceptance services involve strenuous efforts that probably deserve more attention from the regulator (García Roca 2008, p. 70).

All this leads to conclude that immigration is a matter that traverses many areas of government and law and that for the fulfilment of the main mandate under the relevant regulation—i.e., the social integration of immigrants—the appropriate collaborative mechanisms should be put in place (art. 2. *ter* Organic Law 4/2000, in its version of 2009. Moya Malapeira and Donaire Villa 2011, pp. 321 & ff.), aiming at the consolidation of a model that somehow is still under construction (Roig Moles 2006, p. 89).

# Criteria That Define Cooperation: The Principle of Participation and the Organic Structure Principle

The most important basic principle is the principle of collaboration, also translated into its corresponding duty of allegiance to the Spanish Constitution. The Spanish Constitutional Court provides, as established doctrine, an important parameter: it cannot be used to distort or alter the competence regime, but it must be considered in the exercise of such competences (in this regard, see for instance: Ruling of the Spanish Constitutional Court 152/1988, 20th July). In turn, that principle will involve three internal separate areas: assistance (the provision of assistance among administrations), coordination (the development of mechanisms to achieve a common perspective, even when each of them exercises its respective powers), and cooperation itself, based on the co-exercise of the powers (Albertí Rovira 2011, pp. 395 & ff.).

We should not forget that the *new* Statutes of Regional Autonomy have played, and still play, an important role in this regard. There are several rules that call for a collaboration among administrations, both at general and at immigration-specific levels. These include Aragon (art. 75), Catalonia (art. 138), Andalusia (art. 62), Castile-Leon (art. 76), and Extremadura (art. 9), which is the last Autonomous

Region that has undertaken the amendment of its Statute (in 2011). Exploring the idea further, the model that appears to be opened by these innovations rests on the *principle of participation*, by those Regions involved in the decision-making processes of the State in related areas in which there are specific autonomic interests, despite being competences of the State (Montilla Martos 2011, pp. 184 & ff.).

Furthermore, administrative legislation has addressed individuals at a general level, regulating the *organic structure principle*. Art. 5.1 of Law 30/1992 sets out that the State and the Autonomous Regions may set up cooperation bodies, bilateral or multilateral, general or sectorial. Pursuant to this article, it shall not be considered that such bodies, created by the Central State Administration, exercise their powers and that the composition of which is foreseen as involving autonomous representatives for purely advisory purposes. Thus, a narrow cooperation among bodies shall require the agreement in creating those entities involved in sectors where a power interrelationship exists, as we believe occurs with immigration, although obviously it is not the only case (on those issues from a general view, Arévalo Gutiérrez 2002, p. 470).


## Cooperative Mechanism Based on the Principle of Participation

The principle of participation is linked to several areas that involve many other tasks. Schematically, it comprises actions on information, actions on the field of labour, actions on matters of planning, and finally, some actions in terms of funding.


### *Actions on Information*

Two wide areas with the participation of regional governments can be distinguished; both of them are set out in art.68 of Organic Law 4/2000, as amended by Organic Law 2/2009. The first one is that any root-based labour authorization shall observe what the regional government—or local authority—has established regarding social roots recognition (art. 68.3). The roots report thus becomes a crucial instrument for granting permits since the negative judgement—be it regional or local—shall not provide sufficient basis to take effect in that regard (Delgado del Rincón 2011). The second one empowers Autonomous Regions that have assumed competences on citizen security and public order to draft impact assessments of the processes for residence permits (and their renewal). Those finally drafted are included in the file made by the State law enforcement agencies (Cuerpos y Fuerzas de Seguridad del Estado) (art. 68.4).

## Actions on the Field of Labour

There are several regional actions on labour, although they have different intensity levels (Parra Rodríguez 2011, pp. 205 & ff.). Pursuant to the competences assumed under their respective Statutes, Regional Authorities grant the initial work permits for self-employed individuals. Since the State is responsible for authorising residence permits (arts. 36 and 37 of the Organic Law 4/2000), a regulatory procedure is provided with the simultaneous participation of both administrations, so their actions are duly coordinated, when refusing or granting the abovementioned permits (art. 107 of Regulation of 2011). Autonomous Regions also participate in the granting of work permits for employed individuals, although in a less clear way. This kind of permit is obtained in accordance with the data contained in the State public employment service from information provided by the Autonomous Regions. Once the list of open occupations has been created—i.e., those jobs that can be taken by foreign workers—the national employment situation is determined, which serves as a parameter for granting or denying those permits. The regulatory procedure also determines that efforts must be co-ordinately channelled: under the framework established by the Spanish Ministry of Labour and Immigration, on the basis of a report by the Tripartite Labour Commission (Comisión Laboral Tripartita, a body comprising of the Central State Government and trade unions' and employers' organisations most representative at a national level), the public employment services of the Autonomous Regions are the bodies commissioned to undertake this task (art. 65 of Regulation of 2011).

Another area with autonomic voice is recruitment in the countries of origin. What is commonly referred to as "quota" refers to the number of foreign citizens that may be needed in order to occupy certain national jobs. The contracts are made according to the national employment situation and, as its name states, in the citizen's country of origin. Spanish Ministry of Labour and Immigration approves an annual estimate of the jobs according to the data provided by, among others, the Autonomous Regions. The legislation on the matter aims at making this procedure co-ordinately (art. 39 of Organic Law 4/2000). According to the regulation, it seems that the scheme has favoured the State in this matter, especially due to the importance of the abovementioned Commission. This, together with other factors—such as the subsequent non-participation in the quota management—has led some parts of the doctrine to claim that there is less room for collaboration than what it seemed at first glance (Roig Moles 2006, p. 38).

To conclude this section, we would like to mention seasonal recruitment or, what is the same and in the words of the Organic Law 4/2000, the regime of the foreign "seasonal" workers (temporeros). Autonomous Regions directly participate—together with the social agents and municipalities—providing the information the State needs to set their legal framework. The approach of the provisions in force sets a model that allows seasonal workers to subsequently dovetail different jobs (art. 42 of Organic Law 4/2000, as amended by Organic Law 2/2009). Indirectly, we could also refer to certain regional activity since, by law, it is required that these people develop their activity with a guarantee of dignity, sufficient hygiene, and safety (art. 42 of Organic Law 4/2000, as amended by Organic Law 2/2009); thus, those Autonomous Regions that have assumed competence regarding the sectors related to the abovementioned subjects would be able to regulate some issues related thereto, including health care.

## Actions on Matters of Planning

There is a double participation of the Autonomous Regions in the setting up of schemes on the multiple tasks that the immigration phenomenon involves. On the one hand, those schemes developed solely by each of them, which are valid through certain periods of time and which were largely created from 2001 onward. These schemes contain many calls to inter-administrative cooperation, and their principal link is the integration of immigrants (Bonino Covas et al. 2003, pp.18 & ff.), a planning reality that also concerns many municipalities since similar mechanisms are at their disposal (in this regard, see for instance: Aragón Medina et al. 2009, pp. 52 & ff.; Pajares Alonso 2005, pp. 151 & ff.; Vidal Fueyo 2011).

On the other hand, Autonomous Regions took part previously in what has become, from the perspective of the state, the reference framework for managing immigration in Spain: the Strategic Plan on Citizenship and Integration 2007–2010 (PECI). This was done following a two-stage process. Before the plan was passed, a consultation period was launched where stakeholders were able to express their opinions, thus contributing to the final draft of the Plan. Then some of the bodies, where Regions were represented, issued corresponding reports in a similar manner (such as the Forum for the Social Integration of Immigrants and the High Council for Immigration Policy—which no longer exists). So, we can conclude that somehow the aim was to promote the visibility of all those involved in the Plan and under its scope. Constant references to the need for collaboration among all of them are also made in the text itself. However, it is not disguised that its scope is nationwide, and it is made explicit that the implementation of the regional policies on the matter shall be an option, not a prescription (PECI: 2007, pp. 8 and 9; and 27 & ff. http://www.tt.mtas.es/periodico/inmigracion/200702/plan.pdf).

Despite this, the Spanish legal system has not developed the potential of art.7 of Law 30/1992, at least in this regard. According to this article, both the state and regional administration may *jointly* subscribe plans and schemes in order to achieve common goals regarding concurrent competences (Roig Moles 2006, p. 134).

## Actions in Terms of Funding

There are mainly two ways of funding immigration-related issues with budget lines assigned to Autonomous Regions. One is at state level and is called Fund for

Immigrant Reception and Integration and Educational Support (FAIRE). The other one is at European level and is known as European Fund for the Integration of Third-Country Nationals.

The FAIRE was established in the State General Budgets of 2005 and, at present, is consolidated by the current legislation on this matter. The details of its specific budget allocations have suffered a severe reduction due to the financial crisis that we are still facing. In 2009, it had a budget of 141 million euro and in 2010, 71 million euro. [Resolution of the Technical Secretary-General of the Spanish Ministry of Labour and Immigration of 24 March (Spanish Official Gazette no. 80, of 2 April 2009); and Resolution of the same body of 18 May 2010 (Spanish Official Gazette no. 127, of 25 May 2010)]. The Fund is based on three principles (subsidiarity, complementarity, and institutional cooperation), which regulate the allocation of the Fund according to some objective allocation criteria. All of the Autonomous Regions are provided with a basic allocation, in order to guarantee inter-regional solidarity, taking into consideration the geographical situation of the region, the proportion of immigrant population, non-EU foreigners registered as residents, and workers affiliated to the Spanish Social Security system, to both its general and its special scheme for agricultural workers. Finally, another aspect to be highlighted is that regional involvement is reinforced since the reporting, analysis, and monitoring of the budget allocations are made within the bodies (analysed below) where Regions have the right to vote, especially within the Autonomous Region Conference for Immigration, since the extinct High Council for Immigration Policy was formerly responsible for these tasks (Roig Moles 2006, p. 92 & ff.).

The European Fund for the Integration of Third-Country Nationals was established by the European Union in 2007. Three features shall be highlighted above the rest. Firstly, its duration is temporary since it was established for the period 2007 to 2013. Secondly, resources are distributed annually beforehand. Thus, out of the overall resources reserved for Spain (123 million euro), the Plan establishes the usage of resources in 8.5, 11.5, 14, 15, 20, 25, and 28 million for 2007, 2008, 2009, 2010, 2011, 2012, and 2013, respectively. Thirdly, the Plan highlights the cooperation among all those involved in the matter and not only inter-administrations. Therefore, a system has been established based on call for proposals to access the fund. The call for proposals is open not only to the relevant public administrations but also to any non-governmental organisation, immigrants' associations, and private bodies (*Plan Plurianual que establece el Fondo Europeo para la Integración de Nacionales de Terceros Países*, 2007: pp. 70 & ff.).

How has all this been translated into our legal system? Through what is considered to be one of the main privileged instruments in this regard: the Bilateral Conventions on Cooperation (Montilla Martos 2007, pp. 36 & ff.). In 2008, around 1,011 conventions and agreements were signed. The Spanish Ministry of Labour and Social Affairs (which, as we all know, by that time held immigration powers) played a very important role since it signed 115. Eighteen of them were on immigrant integration, being the state's contribution to the "great groups of conventions" (those signed by at least five Regions), one of the most significant, amounting to almost 198 million euro. In 2009, 1,059 conventions and agreements were signed. With regard to immigration, 16 out of the abovementioned 18 have been updated, and the budget to cope with this situation is once again one of the highest: around 200 million euro (largely aimed at these people's integration). (Ministerio de Política Territorial 2009, 2010, *Informe sobre los Convenios de Colaboración Estado-Comunidades Autónomas suscritos durante 2008*, and *Informe sobre los Convenios de Colaboración Estado-Comunidades Autónomas suscritos durante 2009*.)

To conclude this section, it is worth noting that the latter form of inter-administrative cooperation, although nominally called "bilateral", has been developed in practice as a sort of implicit multilateralism, as it is argued by some part of the doctrine (García Morales 2006, p. 18). The reason for this asseveration is that, despite that formally they are agreements between one Autonomous Region and the State, the content of the texts proposed to the Regions are so similar, if not equal, that sometimes no unique features are included, regardless of who the signatories are (Duque Villanueva 2007, p.134).

## Cooperative Mechanisms Based on the Organic Structure Principle

We shall now proceed to take a brief look at the bodies involved in the area of immigration that exist in our legal system. For presentation purposes, we will take into consideration the difference between bodies in a broad sense and bodies in a narrow sense, discussed above.

### Bodies in a Broad Sense: The Immigration Permanent Observatory (Observatorio Permanente de la Inmigración) and the Forum for the Social Integration of Immigrants (Foro para la Integración Social de los Inmigrantes)

Established by the Plan for the Social Integration of Immigrants of 1994 and currently regulated by Royal Decree 345/2001, of 4 April, the Immigration Permanent Observatory (OPI) is a collegiate body whose main task is to carry out studies and analysis on immigration, thus giving support and assistance to the rest of the involved agents and bodies. It is under the Ministry of Labour and Immigration, and it consists of a President, a Secretary and 16 members: 10 representing the State, 4 representing the Autonomous Regions and the autonomous cities, and 2 representing local authorities. Probably from the cooperative perspective, this is its main weakness because its composition favours obviously the State representation, not only due to the members distribution but also because the Central Government Representative for Aliens Affairs and Immigration holds the Presidency and the Secretary is appointed by the President from the permanent officials of his own cabinet. Commendably, the transparency and publicity of its activity should be noted, which are easily accessible in their entireties on its website (http://extranjeros.mtin.es/es/ObservatorioPermanenteInmigracion/).

The Forum for the Social Integration of Immigrants (FISI) was created by article 70 of the Organic Law 4/200, as amended by Organic Law 2/2009 modifying its first paragraph. The article envisages that it is a balanced body, whose composition follows a tripartite model with representatives of the Public Administrations, immigrants' associations, and organisations with interests and involvement in the area of migration (including trade unions'/employers' organisations). Its legal nature is also explained, establishing that it is the main body for consultation, information, and advice on immigration. The Royal Decree 3/2006, of 16 January, regulates its legal framework: its composition, competences, and functions.

From the perspective of this subject matter, it is worth noting three aspects: The first one refers to the lack of balance in favour of the State in the composition of the body. It is composed of a President, two Vice-presidents, a Secretary and 30 members. The President is appointed by the Minister of Labour and Immigration at the proposal of the State Secretary of Immigration and Emigration. The first vice-president is chosen from the members representing the immigrants' associations and social organisations. The regulation establishes that the second vice-president shall be the Director General for the Integration of Immigrants of the ministerial department, while the Secretariat shall be exercised by the Sub-director for Institutional Relations of the same Ministry (arts. 6 and 7 Royal Decree 3/2006). Regarding membership, the aim has been to give greater importance to the presence of social agents and associations of immigrants than to the public administrations. Ten members correspond to the first ones and 10 to the latter; furthermore, of the remaining 10, two represent the Autonomous Regions, two represent the local authorities, and six represent other Ministries. The second aspect to be considered is that this point is demonstrable with regard to certain functioning guidelines of the body. For example, Autonomous Regions do not have the possibility to call for an extraordinary Plenary meeting, since to do so, the agreement of the majority of members would be necessary: Another piece of evidence supporting this idea, at least to some extent, is that it is understood that the Plenary shall be deemed validly constituted at the first call with the sole presence of the Secretary and the President, a condition that becomes relevant if it is considered who it is that holds these positions.

There are, however, some signs of hope for the collaboration within this body, maybe by giving a second thought to the abovementioned questions. On the one hand, the FISI has made efforts to achieve a comprehensive compendium of rules applicable to its internal organisation and functioning—and also to make it public—which guarantees transparency and legal certainty of its activities. Furthermore, it has duly developed its activities, completing its mandate (2006–2009), and currently is midway through the second mandate (scheduled to cover the period 2010–2013).

## Bodies in a Narrow Sense: Sectorial Immigration Conference (Conferencia Sectorial de Inmigración) and the Conference of Presidents (Conferencia de Presidentes)

Now is the moment to present two bodies that are considered to play a leading role in intergovernmental relations concerning immigration matters (the first of them has a more important role). There are others, such as the Subcommittees on cooperation, but they are not very well regarded concerning their efficiency (Roig Moles 2006, pp. 115 & ff.).

The Sectorial Immigration Conference (CSI) is a little-known recently created body, although it is one of the privileged consultation and participation bodies between the State and the Autonomous Regions (Moya Malapeira and Donaire Villa 2011, p. 343). It is ruled by arts. 5, 7, and 8 of Law 30/1992, provided that art. 4 of Law 12/1983, on the autonomous process, which was subject to interpretation by the Spanish Constitutional Court in its famous ruling STC 76/1983, of 5 of August (which, in addition, endorsed the set-up envisaged by the law as regards sectorial conferences, Duque Villanueva 2007, p. 115) shall likewise apply. In short, we have here a multilateral body comprising Central Government and Regional Government members, generally acclaimed but with some weaknesses to overcome (in this regard, see for instance: González Gómez 2006, pp. 111 & ff.). To date, and according to data from the Spanish Ministry for Regional Policy, there are 35 Conferences, 25 of which are regularly functioning. Several conferences were set up during the period 2004–2007, among them the one to which we are referring, which in turn was promoted by the Conference of President held on 11 January 2007.

Its legal provisions are contained in article 68.1 of the Organic Law 4/2000, as amended by the Organic Law 2/2009, where it is set forth that it is a body that shall guarantee the necessary coordination of the actions developed by those administrations concerning immigration matters. According to official information, to date four CSIs have been held: in 2008—where its internal rules were approved but not made public—ones in 2009, in 2010, and finally, on 22 February 2011. During these meetings, issues of the highest importance were addressed, including financing aspects and the analysis of the new Aliens Regulation draft (Royal Decree 557/2011, of 20 April).

The Conference of Presidents (CP) does not have a long tradition in our country. In 2004, and with clear echoes from Germany, Switzerland, and Austria, a body was set up whose aim is to promote the cooperation and coordination between the State and the Autonomous Regions, bringing together the Prime Minister of Spain and the presidents of the Autonomous Regions. This fact suggests that its structure could be deemed vertical (in this regard, see for instance: García Morales 2006, pp. 43 & ff.), but some areas of the doctrine have wanted to see in it certain horizontal nuances since some of the functions of the Conference do not require the (compulsory) presence of the State representative (Bocanegra Sierra and Huergo Lora 2005, pp. 7 & ff.). Its first meeting took place in 2004, and three more have been held in 2005, 2007, and 2009. As is known, in the third meeting the creation of the CSI was promoted, and in the fourth one (the most recent) its internal ruling was passed, in which it seems that an attempt to balance those involved in establishing the functions and composition of the Conference of Presidents was made (Order TER/3409/2009, of 18 December, establishing the publication of the internal ruling of the Conference of Presidents, published in the Spanish Official Gazette no. 305, of 19 December 2009).

Against this background, the coordination and communication between the CP and the Conference of Regional Governments would be necessary and advisable, which is a horizontal instrument that was held for the first time on 21 March 2011, replacing the meetings that had been taking place since 2008. Thus, this could serve as a discussion forum on some issues of regional interest, contributing to establishing common positions on specific areas. In addition, and with the exception known, it does not appear that the CP has devoted special efforts to channel the phenomenon of immigration so far. However, due to the importance of the body itself and of its members, it will probably prove to be more than adequate for this purpose.

## Final Comments

I would like, at this point, to make two final comments. Many of the mechanisms for cooperation between the State and the Autonomous Regions surveyed work reasonably well, at least as far as immigration issues are concerned, both at participative and institutional levels. However, the poor efficiency of some of them has a negative impact on the creation of a reasonable and reliable management model. The attempts to rationalise it are encouraging since this implies real concern on how to solve the problems and conflicts that are unavoidable when dealing with these matters. Moreover, this undoubtedly enhances the credibility of collaborative policies between the State and Autonomous Regions. We will have to wait for future developments, and obviously for future works, to see how the system described in the present article evolves.

## References

Aja Fernández, E. (2006). "La política inmigratoria del Estado como marco de la actividad de las Comunidades Autónomas", in Aja Fernández, E; Montilla Martos, J.A; and Roig Moles, E. (Coords.); *Las Comunidades Autónomas y la Inmigración*, Tirant lo Blanch, Valencia, pp. 153–182.
Albertí Rovira, E. (2011). "Cooperación interterritorial", in Aragón Reyes, M. (Dir.); and Aguado Renedo, C. (Coord.); *Organización General y Territorial del Estado. Temas Básicos de Derecho Constitucional. Tomo II*; Civitas-Aranzadi-Thomson Reuters, Cizur Menor (Navarra), pp. 394–398.

Aragón Medina, J.; Artiaga Leiras, A.; Haidour, M. A.; Martínez Poza, A.; Rocha Sánchez, F. (2009). *Las políticas locales para la integración de los immigrantes y la participación de los agentes sociales*; Los Libros de La Catarata, Madrid, 232 pp.

Arévalo Gutiérrez, A. (2002). "Las relaciones entre la administración estatal, autonómica y local en el marco constitucional", in Rodríguez-Arana Muñoz, J. (Dir.); y Calvo Charro, M. (Coord.); *La Administración Pública Española*, Instituto Nacional de Administración Pública, Madrid, pp. 435–506.

Bocanegra Sierra, R; y Huergo Lora, A. (2005). *La Conferencia de Presidentes*, Iustel, Madrid, 152 pp.

Bonino Covas, C.; Aragón Medina, J.; y Rocha Sánchez, F. (2003). *Los planes de las Comunidades Autónomas para la integración social de las personas immigrantes*. Confederación Sindical de Comisiones Obreras-Fundación 1º de mayo. Madrid, 196 pp.

Consejo de Ministros-Gobierno de España (2007). *Plan Estratégico de Ciudadanía e Integración 2007–2010*. Available at: (http://www.mtin.es/es/sec_emi/IntegraImmigrantes/PlanEstrategico/ Docs/PECIDEF180407.pdf).

Delgado del Rincón, L. E. (2011). "Los derechos sociales de los extranjeros", in Matia Portilla, F.J. (Dir); *Crisis e inmigración en España: reflexiones interdisciplinares sobre la inmigración en España*, Tirant lo blanch, Valencia, 2012, pp. 301–344.

Duque Villanueva, J.C. (2007); "Las Conferencias Sectoriales", *Revista Española de Derecho Constitucional* 79: 113–153.

García Roca, J. (2008). "Inmigración, integración social de los extranjeros y concurrencia de competencias territoriales", in VVAA; *Derecho, inmigración e integración*, Ministerio de Justicia, Madrid, pp. 53–80.

García Morales, Mª.J (2006). "Las relaciones intergubernamentales en el Estado Autonómico: estado de la cuestión y problemas pendientes", in García Morales, Mª.J; Montilla Martos, J.A; y Arbós Marín, X; *Las relaciones intergubernamentales en el Estado Autonómico*, Centro de Estudios Políticos y Constitucionales, Madrid, pp. 9–72.

González Gómez, A. (2006). "La cooperación multilateral institucionalizada: las Conferencias Sectoriales", in López Nieto, L. (Coord.); *Relaciones Intergubernamentales en la España Democrática. Interdepedencia, autonomía, conflicto y cooperación*, Dykinson, Madrid, pp. 97–114.

Ministerio de Trabajo e Inmigración-Gobierno de España (2007); *Plan Plurianual que establece el Fondo Europeo para la Integración de Nacionales de Terceros Países*. Available at:(http://www. mtin.es/es/sec_emi/IntegraImmigrantes/Fondo_Solidaridad/pdf/FEI_PLAN_PLURIANUAL_ 2007_2013.pdf).

Ministerio de Política Territorial-Gobierno de España (2009); *Informe sobre los Convenios de Colaboración Estado-Comunidades Autónomas suscritos durante 2008*. Available at: (http:// www.mpt.gob.es/publicaciones/centro_de_publicaciones_de_la_sgt/Periodicas/parrafo/0111116/ text_es_files/file2/Informe_convenios_Estado-CCAA_2008-INTERNET.pdf).

Ministerio de Política Territorial-Gobierno de España (2010); *Informe sobre los Convenios de Colaboración Estado-Comunidades Autónomas suscritos durante 2009*. Available at: (http:// www.mpt.gob.es/publicaciones/centro_de_publicaciones_de_la_sgt/Periodicas/parrafo/0111116/ text_es_files/file/Informe_convenios_Estado-CCAA_2009-INTERNET.pdf).

Montilla Martos, J.A. (2007). "La distribución de competencias en inmigración entre el Estado y las Comunidades Autónomas en la reforma del Estado autonómico", in Montilla Martos, J. A; y Vidal Fueyo, C; *Las competencias en inmigración del Estado y de las Comunidades Autónomas*, Centro de Estudios Políticos y Constitucionales, Madrid, pp. 9–57.

Montilla Martos, J.A. (2011). "Las relaciones de colaboración en el nuevo marco estatutario: bilateralidad y participación", *Revista de Estudios Políticos* 151: 153–199.

Moya Malapeira, D; and Donaire Villa, F.J. (2011). "El nuevo marco competencial y organizativo de la inmigración", in Boza Martínez, D; Donaire Villa, F.J; y Moya Malapeira, D. (Coords.); *Comentarios a la Reforma de la Ley de Extranjería (LO 2/2009)*, Tirant lo Blanch, Valencia, pp. 321–350.

Pajares Alonso, M. (2005). *La integración ciudadana. Una perspectiva para la inmigración.* Icaria, Barcelona, 247 pp.

Parra Rodríguez, C. (2011). "El nuevo marco de las autorizaciones de trabajo", in Boza Martínez, D; Donaire Villa, F.J; y Moya Malapeira, D. (Coords.); *Comentarios a la Reforma de la Ley de Extranjería (LO 2/2009)*, Tirant lo Blanch, Valencia, pp. 205–218.

Roig Moles, E. (2006). "Relaciones intergubernamentales en materia de inmigración: desarrollo de un modelo en construcción", in Aja Fernández, E; Montilla Martos, J.A; y Roig Moles, E. (Coords.); *Las Comunidades Autónomas y la Inmigración*, Tirant lo Blanch, Valencia, pp. 77–152.

Santolaya Machetti, P. (2007). "Extranjería y nuevos Estatutos de Autonomía", *Revista d´ Estudis Autonómics y Federals* 4: 159–183.

Vidal Fueyo, C. (2007). "Breve aproximación a las políticas autonómicas en materia de inmigración", in Montilla Martos, J.A; y Vidal Fueyo, C; *Las competencias en materia de inmigración del Estado y de las Comunidades Autónomas*, Centro de Estudios Políticos y Constitucionales, Madrid, pp. 59–79.

Vidal Fueyo, C. (2011). "Políticas públicas e integración", in Matia Portilla, F.J. (Dir.); *Crisis e Inmigración: reflexiones interdisciplinares sobre la inmigración en España*, Tirant lo Blanch, Valencia, 2012, pp. 377–400.

# Intergovernmental Cooperation and Social Policies in the State of the Autonomies: The Institutional Framework for the Governance of the Dependent Care

Víctor Cuesta-López

**Abstract** Over the recent years, we have assisted to the progressive consolidation of the intergovernmental cooperative relations between the Spanish Government and the Autonomous Communities. In fact, the institutional arrangements allowing multilateral interactions, particularly the Sectoral Conferences, have gained political significance. In order to assess the recent evolution of the multilateral relations in the State of the Autonomies, our research shifts to a case study: the governance of the long-term care services granted by the System for the Autonomy and Care for Dependency (SAAD). A first approach to the institutional framework envisaged for the implementation of the SAAD evidences the strengthening of the cooperative relations in this social policy domain. The functioning of the Territorial Council of the SAAD, where the General State Administration and the ACs can jointly reach binding decisions by majority rule, clearly exemplifies the change of the traditional pattern of multilateral cooperation.

## Introduction: Institutional Arrangements for Intergovernmental Cooperation in Spain

The large list of shared and concurrent competencies enunciated in the Spanish Constitution (SC) and the Statutes of Autonomy has irremediably fostered the interdependence between the State and the Autonomous Communities (ACs). However, the institutional arrangements allowing cooperation and joint action for the implementation of shared policies were not properly envisaged in the SC. It is a well-known fact, for instance, that the Spanish second chamber, the Senate, does not serve to integrate regional interests in the national decision-making. Besides,

V. Cuesta-López (✉)
Facultad de Ciencias Jurídicas, Universidad de Las Palmas de Gran Canaria, Campus
Universitario de Tafira, Módulo B - despacho 156, CP 35017 Las Palmas de Gran Canaria, Spain
e-mail: vcuesta@ddp.ulpgc.es

A. López-Basaguren and L. Escajedo San Epifanio (eds.), *The Ways of Federalism in Western Countries and the Horizons of Territorial Autonomy in Spain*, Vol. 2, DOI 10.1007/978-3-642-27717-7_18, © Springer-Verlag Berlin Heidelberg 2013

the asymmetrical character of the State of the Autonomies and the political significance of the Catalan and Basque nationalisms favored the bilateral negotiations
between the historical nationalities and the central government. As a result, the
traditional pattern of intergovernmental relations in Spain was mainly limited to
informal, irregular, and bilateral interactions among the central-state administration
and individual ACs.

Following the political agreements of 1981 and 1992 between the two major
national parties (*Acuerdos Autonómicos*), clearly inspired by the rationale of territorial harmonization, the Spanish legislation tried to overcome the constitutional
shortcomings establishing an institutional framework for multilateral cooperation.
A very significant step in this direction was the creation of the sectoral conferences
that were conceived as multilateral forums where "high ranked officials and political representatives of both central government and *Comunidades Autónomas* meet
to discuss sectoral matters in order to maximize intergovernmental cooperation and
avoid conflicts" (Moreno 2001). Even if we find the first reference to the sectoral
conferences in Law 12/1983 on the Autonomic Process (art. 4), the scarce rules
governing their composition and functioning are established in Law 30/1992 on the
Legal System of Public Administrations and Common Administrative Procedure
(art. 5). This very basic legal framework has allowed a high degree of autonomy to
the sectoral conferences when establishing its own rules of procedures.

At first, the sectoral conferences were perceived by some CAs as a way to
control and to confine their self-government. In fact, the Basque and the Catalan
ACs argued before the Constitutional Court that the institutionalization of the
sectoral conferences had to be considered as an unconstitutional intervention in
their sphere of autonomy. The Constitutional Court confirmed the constitutionality
of the sectoral conferences but, at the same time, ruled that the sectoral conferences
could not replace the decision-making powers of the ACs over its own
competencies (Constitutional Court Judgment 76/1983 5 August). Consequently,
the functions of the sectoral conferences were mainly restricted to the exchange of
information and the joint examination of problems concerning their shared policies.
The political distrust from CAs towards the sectoral conferences—a strong direction from the national government, their limited functions, and the irregularity of
the meetings— determined their inefficiency as forums for real cooperation. Nevertheless, this situation gradually changed during the 1990s. As Börzel has clearly
argued, the progressive Europeanization of the domestic competences created
considerable incentives for both the Spanish government and the ACs to strengthen
its cooperative relationships: The ACs depended on the Spanish Government for
direct access to EU decision-making, and the central-state administration relied on
the ACs for the effective implementation of EU policies. The institutionalization
of the cross-sectoral Conference on European Affairs (1992) and the Agreement on
the Participation of the CAs on European Matters through the Sectoral Conferences
(1994), which provided a framework for regular information and participation
of the ACs in the formulation and the implementation of EU policies, favored
significantly the cooperative interactions between the two layers of government
(Börzel 2000).

Progressively, the sectoral conferences have gained political relevance, and even though the regularity and the outcome of the meetings strongly vary from one conference to another, many of them have a prominent role in drafting legislation on shared competencies or adopting common criteria for the implementation of joint plans and programs, as well as their funding regime. Up to now, a network of 37 sectoral conferences that covers practically all the policy domains has been set up, and it normally relies on the work of committees where national and subnational officials deal with technical matters. The trend towards multilateral cooperation seems to be confirmed by the ever-growing amount of joint agreements (*convenios*) between the central and the autonomic administrations and other initiatives at the highest political level such as the Conference of Presidents. This forum, convened for the first time in October 2004 by the Spanish Prime Minister Zapatero, brings together the Presidents of the ACs and the cities of Ceuta and Melilla and has been conceived to reach consensus and adopt political resolutions on matters of particular relevance to the autonomic system. The adoption of the rules of procedure in its last meeting held on December 2009 confirmed the institutionalization of the Conference of Presidents, which should be convened by the Prime Minister at least once a year.

The progressive consolidation of the multilateral cooperation in the State of the Autonomies does not mean, however, that bilateral relations are no longer significant. Particularly if we consider that, the Statutes of Autonomy amended during the last decade have institutionalized the bilateral commissions, which are intended to enable permanent collaboration between the individual ACs and the Spanish government. For instance, the Statute of Autonomy of Catalonia adopted in 2006 (which has clearly inspired the successive statutory reforms) entrusts the *Generalitat*—State Bilateral Commission—with the deliberation and the adoption of joint agreements regarding a long list of matters that could affect the interests and powers of the *Generalitat* (art. 183). This legislative strategy enhancing the bilateral relations, and consequently the asymmetry of the State of the Autonomies, is supported by another provision of the Catalan Statute, which declares that "the *Generalitat* is not bound by decisions taken within the framework of multilateral voluntary collaboration mechanisms with the State and with other autonomous communities with regard to which it has not manifested its agreement" (art. 176.2).

# Enhanced Multilateral Cooperation on Social Policies: The Case of the System for Autonomy and Care for Dependency

## *The System for Autonomy and Care for Dependency*

In order to assess the recent evolution of the multilateral relations in the State of the Autonomies, let us now pay particular attention to the social policy domain of public assistance for dependent citizens, more commonly known as long-term care services. National Law 39/2006, of 14 December, on the Promotion of Personal Autonomy and Care for Dependent Persons proposes an intricate model of governance, the System for Autonomy and Care for Dependency (SAAD), that has been categorized as the "fourth pillar" of the Spanish welfare system (together with the Social Security, the Educational System, and the National Health System). According to the Explanatory Memorandum of Law 39/2006, "the very nature of the purpose of the Law requires the commitment and combined action of all of the public powers and institutions, which means that coordination and cooperation with the Autonomous Communities is a fundamental element". The progressive implementation of the SAAD represents a major challenge for the Spanish intergovernmental relations, considering that it demands enhanced cooperation and shared efforts that go beyond the traditional pattern of policy coordination through the sectoral conferences.

Before going specifically into the issue of the intergovernmental relations envisaged by the SAAD, we will briefly refer to the context in which Law 39/2006 has been enacted, to its constitutional foundations, and to its major developments. Following the traditional Mediterranean pattern of social assistance, the care for dependent citizens in Spain has been mainly provided by the families. As Costa-Font and Patxot noticed, "nearly 70 % of the Spanish older people with dependency receive exclusively family care, mainly provided by women and children, In fact, nearly 5 % of the population—83 % of which are female—are caregivers, while scarcely 3 % older people receive social services" (Costa-Font and Patxot 2003). On the other hand, the provision of formal care for dependency, a policy framed within the broad competence of "Social Assistance", has been assumed by the ACs on the basis of article 148.1.20 of the Spanish Constitution. Even if the regulation of the formal care services corresponded to the CAs, its provision has been mainly undertaken at the local level. In addition, an extensive network of third sector organizations has been, for years, providing assistance to dependent people complementing the effort of families and administrations. The role of the central-state administration through the Institute for Older Persons and Social Services (IMSERSO) had been mainly limited to the coordination of social assistance through guidelines and action plans (gerontology plans). This central planning tool, however, "has had a remarkably weak impact in the coordination of services" (Costa-Font and Patxot 2003).

The dispersion of dependent care policies and the lack of an efficient national coordination led to a situation where the opportunities for public assistance strongly varied among CAs. Law 39/2006 should be considered, thus, as a legislative intervention of the State in order to ensure a nationwide "stable framework of resources and services for the dependent population" (Explanatory Memorandum of the Law 39/2006). Even if the "Social Assistance" is an exclusive competence of the ACs, we can easily find a constitutional ground for the State's legislative intervention: Article 149.1.1 SC assigns the State the exclusive (crosscutting) competence for regulating the basic conditions that guarantee the equality of all Spaniards in the exercise of their constitutional rights. In particular, the dependent people's constitutional rights are implicitly enounced as principles governing social policies addressed to all the public authorities. Article 49 SC refers to the specialized care required by the physically and mentally handicapped and the consequent obligation of all the Spanish administrations to "carry out a policy of preventive care, treatment, rehabilitation and integration". Regarding the public assistance for the elderly, article 50 SC declares that public authorities shall promote "their welfare through a system of social services that provides for their specific problems of health, housing, culture and leisure".

Law 39/2006 proposes the reorganization of social services for dependent people on the basis of three basic principles: universality, high quality, and sustainability. Actually, these principles correspond to the common objectives established at the EU level for the "long-term care" policies in the framework of the Open Method of Coordination on Social Protection and Social Inclusion. Article 4.1 of Law 39/2006 declares the subjective enforceable right of the dependent persons, "regardless of where in Spanish State Territory they reside", to have access under equal conditions to the benefits and services foreseen in the Law. As a matter of fact, "the recognition of the social right has entailed the commitment by all level of Spanish public administration to ensure an universal coverage of this right, in accordance with the principle of safeguard of regional governments autonomy" (Izzo 2010).

The situation of dependency is clearly defined in article 2.2 as the "permanent state in which persons that for reasons derived from age, illness or disability and linked to the lack or loss of physical, mental, intellectual or sensorial autonomy require the care of another person/other people or significant help in order to perform basic activities of daily living or, in the case of people with mental disabilities or illness, other support for personal autonomy". The acknowledgement of the situation of dependency corresponds to the Autonomous administrations (art. 28.2). The citizens who have been formally declared dependent persons are then entitled to receive from the Social Services Network of the respective AC the appropriate services (services for the prevention of situations of dependency and for the promotion of personal autonomy, personal alert system, home care services, day and night center service, and/or residential care service) that correspond to their degree (moderate, severe, and major dependency) and level (each degree is classified into two levels, depending on the person's autonomy and on the intensity of the required care) of dependency.

Regarding the public funding of the SAAD, the General State Administration must finance a minimum level of protection to each of the beneficiaries of the system according to his degree and level of dependency. A second level of protection is financed between the General State Administration and the ACs by means of joint agreements. In addition, the ACs could offer to the dependent citizens who reside in its territory an additional third level of protection that must be financed by the autonomic budget. The beneficiaries of the SAAD could also make a financial contribution to the funding of the services, depending on the type and cost of the service and on their personal economic ability (art. 33.1). In case the Social Services Network cannot provide adequate assistance, Law 39/2006 also foresees financial benefits intended to cover the expenses of the accredited private care centers (art. 17). Dependent citizens could also receive, "on an exceptional basis", financial benefits that would allow them to get the services of non-professional caregivers in their homes, whenever their home "meets adequate standards of inhabitability and co-existence" (art. 14.2). Non-professional caregivers must then comply "with the rules on affiliation, registration and contribution to the Social Security" (art. 18.3). Law 39/2006 also foresees financial support for severely dependent persons to hire a personal assistant, which support provides the beneficiary with access to education and employment and, consequently, more autonomy in daily living (art. 19).

As regards the power sharing between the State and the CAs, Law 39/2006 establishes a clear division of functions: On one hand, the General State Administration determines the minimum level of protection that is guaranteed to each of the beneficiaries of the System and provides public funding for this level of protection (art. 9); on the other hand, the ACS are responsible, among other functions, for planning, ordering, coordinating, and managing the dependent care services and resources; establishing the procedures and bodies for the coordination between the care services and the health system; creating and updating the Registry of Centres and Services, facilitating the necessary accreditation in order to guarantee compliance with the quality requirements and standards; inspecting and, where applicable, applying sanctions for noncompliance with the quality requirements and standards of centers and services; and carrying out regular evaluations on the functioning of the System in their respective territories (art. 10).

## *Institutional Framework for Shared Governance: The Territorial Council of the System for Autonomy and Care for Dependency*

The SAAD does not limit the interactions between the central-state administration and the ACs to a mere coordination of their respective functions. The major contribution of Law 39/2006 to the enhancement of the intergovernmental relations is the establishment of specific mechanism allowing the shared governance of the SAAD and, particularly, the creation of Territorial Council of the SAAD. According to Izzo, "one of the more significant innovations introduced by the 2006 law has established an effective "drive belt" among the different administrative layers: the SAAD territorial council. This institutional mechanism has permitted the establishment of a continuous policy dialogue among the different administrative bodies involved in elderly care governance, thus facilitating coordination and monitoring" (Izzo 2010).

The Territorial Council is formed by the Minister in charge of social affairs, who chairs the meetings; the political representatives from each of the autonomic Governments, also in charge of social affairs; and, according to the internal rules of procedure adopted in the constitutive session of the Territorial Council held on 22 January 2007, eleven representatives from different departments of the Central State Administration, two representatives of the Autonomous Cities of Ceuta and

Melilla, and two representatives from the Spanish Federation of Local Governments (FEMP). In any case, the representatives from the Autonomous Communities must always be in the majority (art. 8.1 of Law 39/2006). The Territorial Council meets in plenary sessions, at least twice a year, and is supported by the work of an executive committee formed by second-level representatives of the public administrations.

The list of important functions regarding the implementation of the SAAD reserved to the Territorial Conference confirms that this intergovernmental body is much more than an arena for political deliberations. In fact, the Territorial Council is responsible for establishing the criteria that determine the intensity of protection of the care services; agreeing on the framework of inter-administrative cooperation for the implementation of the aforementioned Law; agreeing on the conditions and amount of the financial benefits for dependent person; adopting the criteria for the beneficiary's participation in the cost of the services; agreeing on the scale that determine the degree and level of dependency; agreeing on joint plans, projects, and programs; adopting common criteria for action and assessment of the System; facilitating the availability of common documents, data, and statistics; establishing the coordination mechanisms for the case of displaced dependent population; informing about the implementation of rules regarding dependency; and, finally, serving as a common ground for cooperation, communication, and information between the Public Administrations.

A particularly significant function assigned to the Territorial Council is the establishment of the criteria determining the intensity of protection that must be guaranteed to each of the beneficiary of the SAAD (according to his degree and level of dependency). In order to guarantee a minimum level of protection across the country, the binding decision adopted by the Territorial Council about these criteria will be finally enacted by the Spanish Government by means of a Royal Decree. Following the agreement of the Territorial Council held on 23 March 2007, Royal Decree 504/2007 incorporates the International Classification of Functioning, Disability and Health adopted by the World Health Organization. Even if the hard-law resolution formally corresponds to the Spanish Government, it is also clear that Law 36/2009 has conferred, for the very first time, an actual decision-making power to this kind of intergovernmental bodies. We could argue, however, that the *sui generis* normative power of the Territorial Council of the SAAD could contradict the Constitutional Court decision that confined the sectoral conferences functions to the exchange of information and the joint examination of problems concerning their shared policies (Constitutional Court Judgment 76/1983 of 5 August). Another important difference between the Territorial Council of the SAAD and the multilateral sectoral conferences, where decisions are always reached by consensus, is that the formal agreements and the political proposals could be finally adopted by the affirmative vote of a majority of the representatives of the General State Administration and a majority of the representatives of the ACs (article 12.2 of the Rules of Process). The majority rule dramatically alters the traditional consensual character of the multilateral relationships.

Within the Territorial Council of the SAAD, the General State Administration and each of the ACs must also agree on the "framework of interadministrative cooperation" by means of joint agreements (*convenios*). These joint agreements determine the objectives, means, and resources for the application of the dependent care services and, particularly, the public funding assigned to each Administration in order to guarantee the services and financial benefits that correspond to the second level of protection. The *convenios* must include the funding distribution criteria (considering factors as the amount of dependent citizens, geographical dispersion, insularity, the amount of returned emigrants) and, according to article 33.2 of Law 39/2006, equal contribution from the General State Administration and the AC. We could argue that the joint funding of the services reinforces the shared character of the SAAD governance. In any case, we must remember that the General State Administration guarantees funding to the Autonomous Communities for developing the minimum level of protection for the dependent population.

Despite the fact that the two main layers of government involved in the governance of the SAAD are the General State Administration and the ACs, we should mention that local governments also participate in the management of dependent care services in accordance with the regulations of their respective ACs. Consequently, the Rules of Process of the Territorial Conference foresees the inclusion of two representatives from the local governments associated to FEMP. The participation of civil society organizations in the SAAD, however, takes place outside the Territorial Council. The institutional framework of the SAAD incorporates other consultative bodies, whose functions are limited to inform, advise, or formulate general proposal, that integrate the interest of the trade unions and employers' organization (the Consultative Committee of the SAAD), the elderly (State Council for Older Persons), the handicapped people (National Council for the Persons with Disabilities), and the third sector organizations (State Council of Non-Governmental Social Work Organizations).

## Conclusions

It is undeniably true that the establishment of the SAAD represents a significant progress of the Spanish welfare system. In addition, the functioning of its institutional framework has also changed the traditional patterns of the intergovernmental cooperative relations. As we have seen, the provision of the long-term care services for the dependent citizens requires a strong commitment between multiple institutional actors, including national, subnational, and local administrations, and other non-institutional collective actors representing the civil society. As a matter of fact, the concept of multilevel governance "can be fruitfully applied in order to explain the current arrangement of elderly home care in Spain" (Izzo 2010). Moreno has also argued that the model of governance of the SAAD "would not be one of centralized "command-and-control", but one which should be worked out gradually by intergovernmental agreement with respect to practicalities and, more importantly, funding by the three main layers of government" (Moreno 2008).

However, the implementation of the SAAD highly depends on the financial resources of the ACs. Considering the difficult situation of the public finances, the problems regarding the funding of the dependent care assistance has already arise. According to the report on the implementation of Law 39/2006 from the *Observatorio de la Dependencia* (January 2011), 234,463 dependent citizens are still in the "limbo of dependency", which means that they do not receive any public assistance despite the fact that they are formally accredited by the ACs (Barriga Martín et al. 2011). In addition, "services with a more inclusive approach, such as personal assistant services, are insufficient in terms of the financial support available" (Verdugo et al. 2009). Although Law 39/2006 tried to overcome regional inequalities regarding the provision of public assistance to dependent citizens, the implementation of the SAAD evidences strong differences among the ACs. For instance, in the Autonomous Community of La Rioja, the public administrations spent 183 € per capita in dependency care last year, while in the Canaries, the expense is more than five times smaller (32 €). Another significant fact is that the proportion of the accredited dependent citizens who still do not have access to public assistance varies from 60 % in the Canary Islands to 11 % in Navarre (Barriga et al. 2011).

# References

Barriga Martín, L.A., Brezmes Nieto, M.J., García Herrero, G.A. and Ramírez Navarro (2011). Desarrollo e implantación territorial de la Ley de promoción de la autonomía personal y atención a las personas en situación de dependencia: Informe de evolución de la Ley cuatro años después. VI Dictamen del Observatorio para el desarrollo de la Ley de promoción de la autonomía personal y atención a la dependencia, 238 pp. Available at: http://www.imsersomayores.csic.es/documentos/documentos/barriga-dictamen-05.pdf

Börzel, T.A. (2000), From Competitive Regionalism to Cooperative Federalism: The Europeanization of the Spanish State of the Autonomies. The Journal of Federalism 30: 18–42.

Costa-Font, J. and Patxot, C. (2003). Long-term care for older people in Spain. In: Comas-Herrea, A. and Wittenberg, R (ed.) European Study of Long-Term Care Expenditure, Study Series 2003, European Commission Employment and Social Affairs, pp. 43–57. Available at: http://ec.europa.eu/employment_social/social_situation/docs/european_study_long_term_care_en.pdf

Izzo, M. (2010). The governance of home care for the elderly in Spain and in Italy, Working paper 4/2010, Centro Studi di Politica Internazionale. Availabrle at: http://www.cespi.it/WP/DOC4-10%20Izzo.pdf

Moreno, L. (2001) Decentralisation in Spain. Regional Studies 36, 399–408.

Moreno, L. (2008). The Nordic Path of Spain's Mediterranean Welfare, Center for European Studies Working Paper Series 163. Avaliable at: http://aei.pitt.edu/9000/1/CES_163.pdf

Verdugo, A., Jenano, C. and Campo, M. (2009). Spain: ANED country report on the implementation of policies supporting independent living for disabled people. Academic Network of European Disability experts (ANED), 18 pp. Available at: http://www.disability-europe.net/content/aned/media/ANED%20Independent%20Living%20report%20-%20Spain.pdf

# The Commission Co-ordinating Climate Change Policies: About the Complexity of Vertical and Horizontal Mainstreaming of Climate Change Policy and the Intergovernmental Relations

M. Pérez Gabaldón

**Abstract** This paper is aimed to explain the positive elements of the Commission Co-ordinating Climate Change Policies as an instrument of intergovernmental relations in the frame of a shared competence. Also, it is directed to show the main causes of its lack of effectiveness and efficacy and propose some changes in the system of intergovernmental relations regarding climate change policies, as well as of being pertinent in environmental policies too.

When Climate Change came into the Spanish public agenda, it followed the imprecise system of distribution of competences established for the environmental matter, and this way, it has been seen as a shared competence between the State and Autonomous Communities. In fact, after reviewing Article 45.2 of the Spanish Constitution, which gives public authorities *in general* a duty to protect, restore, and promote the environment and paying attention to sections 149.1.23 and 148.1.9, it is necessary to turn our attention to the provisions set out by Autonomous Statutes and the jurisprudence of the Constitutional Court. Anyway, even after that, there are no well-drawn borders between their spheres of competence. The lack of clarity in the distribution of competence shows how indispensable the existence of instruments is to guarantee the normal functioning of the environmental policies.

The complexity of the matter and its peculiar mainstreaming—horizontal and vertical—showed the necessity to establish new instruments in order to avoid the overlapping and duplicity of measures and efforts designed to achieve the same objective and to construct a common policy to fight against a global problem. This is the panorama where the Commission Co-ordinating Climate Change Policies was created by the law 1/2005 of 9th of March, establishing a scheme for greenhouse gas emission allowance trading—transposition of directive 2003/87/EC. It was created as an instrument for the cooperation and coordination of the measures developed by the central power and the Autonomous Communities.

M. Pérez Gabaldón (✉)
Universidad CEU Cardenal Herrera, Luis Vives 1, 46115 Alfara del Patriarca, Valencia, Spain
e-mail: marta.perez@uch.ceu.es

A. López-Basaguren and L. Escajedo San Epifanio (eds.), *The Ways of Federalism in Western Countries and the Horizons of Territorial Autonomy in Spain*, Vol. 2, DOI 10.1007/978-3-642-27717-7_19, © Springer-Verlag Berlin Heidelberg 2013

In order to analyze this instrument, it is necessary to start with the complex distribution of competences and the special situation of climate change issues. This will lead us to the study of the Spanish intergovernmental relations system as a possible way to solve the problems between competent authorities and, concretely, the paper of the Commission Co-ordinating Climate Change policies.

# Introduction: An Approach to the Complexity of Climate Change as a Matter

Although the urgency of action against the human impact on climate change and its effects are now well documented, there are still some doctrinal positions reluctant to affirm the incidence of industrialization processes and economic development on climate change. In fact, without going into detail, the Intergovernmental Panel on Climate Change (hereinafter IPCC) accepted the unequivocal warming of climate system in its Fourth Assessment Report in 2007, affirming that most of the observed increase in globally averaged temperatures since mid-twentieth century is very likely (more than 90 %) due to the observed increase in anthropogenic greenhouse gas concentrations. It evidences that, if the international community adopts the position of no mitigation and adaptation to its effects, it will develop in irreversible consequences for the planet and human life. The IPCC scenarios have a percentage of failure but are the clearest evidence of situations that international society does not want to make real.

Facing the global problem of Climate Change is one of the most important and complicated twenty-first century challenges, even more when we observe the particular elements that characterize the activity that all levels of government can implement. We would like to focus our attention on two elements of climate change policies that mark the development of the Spanish competent administrations' action:

a. *Multidimensionality and horizontal mainstreaming of environmental issues*

The assumption of the environmental multidimensionality promotes the integration of environmental considerations into public policies (Alda Fernández and Ramos Gallarín 2006). We have to note that environmental mainstreaming was introduced as a principle that must guide the activity of governments in Article 6 of the Maastricht Treaty of 1992. It leads to understanding the environment as something else than the mere sum of its elements; it must also take into account the social, political, and economic conditions in which human activities take place. This creates an inevitable systematic set of relations (Leff 2003). This is especially evident when the interests of the competent authorities are not always related on environmental protection and they are in collision against each other (the relation between environmental protection and economic development is especially tense), showing how long the tentacles are of climate change issues.

Definitely, this character of the matter that is the object of our study makes the delimitation of its limits more difficult. Even law 1/2005—which is referred in this document later on—has really presented this relation between economic progress and environmental protection—in relation to the principle of sustainable development—in the explanatory memorandum, trying to take into account the distribution of competences in both areas.

b. *Vertical mainstreaming and plurality of instruments*

Climate change is faced with several perspectives trough legal, economic, fiscal, penal, and administrative instruments trying to impact on human behavior. They are coming together to achieve the main goal of preventing and mitigating the negative impact of climate change, as well as to support adaptation to inevitable changes. However, competent authorities shall also take into account simultaneous implementation of several instruments over the same territory and specific cases that can have unintended consequences, even when they are negative for the consecution of the goal for which they were established.

Authorities must keep in mind that climate change is a transnational problem, and its consequences cannot be limited or circumscribed to the legal frontiers between States or borders inside the State. That's the reason we can find several levels of governments developing policies in this area. Even in Spain, environmental and climate change policies are developed, in more or less degree, by the European Union (hereinafter EU), State, Autonomous Communities (hereinafter AC), and municipalities; we will focus our attention on the activity of State and AC, starting from the distribution of competences that must delineate the borders within which both authorities can develop their activity. It is established by the residual character of environmental distribution of powers (which only operates when there is no specific title to a concrete area related to environment, for example, protection of the atmosphere), which can never give us the all-encompassing concept of environment that is only fragmented in order to give some order to its protection. The problem that is the starting point is then the unclear distribution of competences.

# The Origin of the Problem: The Distribution of Competences Between State and Autonomous Communities for Environmental Issues as the System Employed for Climate Change Policies

In fact, the vague wording contained in Article 45.2 of the Spanish Constitution (hereinafter SC), which gives public authorities *in genere* a duty to protect, restore, and promote the environment but does not show the actual distribution of powers between the central power and the peripheral or regional entities, is the beginning of the controversy. Thus, it was insufficient to place any enabling competence in any particular administration. For more clarity, we must turn our attention to sections

149.1.23°SC, which includes the exclusive jurisdiction of the State to set "basic legislation on environmental protection, without prejudice the Autonomous Communities' faculties to establish additional standards of protection," and 148.1.9°SC, which expresses that ACs may assume "the management in protecting the environment".

The reading of both provisions can only lead us to the conclusion that there is a nonexclusive jurisdiction for this matter between the state and the regional government. Then this writing is generating a "shared" competence and making it necessary to address the provisions set out by Autonomous Statutes (hereinafter AS)— (Arlucea Ruíz 2005; Ortega Álvarez 2008) and their interpretation through the jurisprudence of the CC (Terol Becerra 2000; Lozano Cutanda et al. 1999) to try to define more precisely the limits of their areas of competence.

In short, and very generally, before continuing with this paper, we have to describe the competence distribution on climate change issues in Spain as follows:

a. The State must establish the basic legislation (the question is up to what extent the State interprets it as "basic") and some implementation task when it is necessary for the nature of the subject—especially when it is about protection of public domain goods or a problem that needs supra-autonomic actions—or to save irreparable damages to the environment. Also, the State can develop some execution task to ensure the achievement of the aim connected to the central competence (CCS 48/1988), even when it is forcing the Constitution to introduce the possibility of execution acts within a concept of normative nature as "basic legislation" is (Jaria i Manzano 2005) concretely, about climate change issues, not only to provide legal basis but also to establish the basis of the legal regime of the greenhouse emission rights and its trade, the authorization to form pool (grouping of installations concerned), the elaboration and approval of the State's National Allocation Plan (NAP), the treatment of and decision on the process of allocation of emission rights, and the regulation and management of the National Emission Allowances Registry. Those competences were given by law 1/2005 of 9th of March establishing a scheme for greenhouse gas emission allowance trading.

b. Autonomous Communities are able to develop basic legislation, establish additional laws for protection, and execute the environmental policy according to what is provided in its own AS. We must take into account that the initial level of competences established in each AC depends on the interpretation of whether they understand "development laws" as a synonym or an antonym of the possibility of developing the state "basic legislation" and if they understand "development laws" and "additional protection laws" as something different and complementary from each other. It generated several problems between regions, but finally, due to reform processes, all of them have more or less a similar level assumed.

Regarding climate change matters, ACs are specially focused on the following: first, on adaptation policies because of the principle of proximity; second, on no directive sectors due to the fact that their level of competence is higher in areas related to them and to the special faculties—which we referred before—that law 1/2005 gives to central power; and third, on the implementation and execution task that the mentioned law gives them because of the competences in environmental issues that ACs assumed by virtue of their AS.

Nevertheless, the different interpretations of constitutional provisions made by the 17 Statutes of Autonomy and the Constitutional Court have led to a difficult situation trying to delineate those areas, generating numerous policy failures and the lack of coordination and administrative conflicts between the different entities with jurisdiction over environmental issues, caused by the concurrence of the State and the AC in the development of environmental public policies (Marco Marco and Pérez Gabaldón 2010).

## The Commission Co-ordinating Climate Change Policies: The Reason for Its Creation and Its Main Elements

Within federal or quasi federal States, the inevitable overlapping of policies coming from different competent authorities and their interdependence—as a consequence of the exercise of the shared powers between those governments—has generally required the different orders of government to treat each other as partners (Watts 2008). In fact, the correct functioning of the *Estado de las Autonomías* requires "from one side, of structures guaranteeing the participation of autonomic entities in the formation of the common volition; and from other side, the existence of enough mechanisms to allow the coordination, cooperation, and mutual information and help between different governments; as well as for the resolution of conflicts which can appear. Participation is a way for channeling and increasing collaboration, which at same time makes possible the efficacy of adopted decisions for the common and autonomic benefit, re-feeding participation" (González Ayala 2008, p. 8). Then it is obvious that the system is in need of an extensive consultation, cooperation, and coordination between governments.

In Spain, previous to the legal recognition of bilateral and multilateral organic instruments of intergovernmental relations, CC had stated that "the necessity of making compatible principles of unity and autonomy which support the State territorial organization constitutionally established, involves the creation of instruments that will enable to build the action of various public administrations" (CC judgment 76/1983 of 5th August), as other States organized attempts to decentralized principles already created.

Law 30/1992 of Legal Regime of public Administration and Ordinary Administrative Procedure and Regulatory Law 7/1985 on the Foundations of the Local Governments System are creating an intergovernmental relations' system based on principles of institutional loyalty—which implies taking into consideration all the public interests involved and, therefore, respecting the sphere of competence of other governments—and collaboration—concept that we understand in a

comprehensive way that includes cooperation, coordination, and mutual information (Pérez Gabaldón 2011). Nevertheless, its implementation has given a scheme
full of gaps, failures, and inconsistencies that are diminishing the capacity of the
instruments. In fact, intergovernmental relations in Spain in the best possible
situation presents some important deficiencies, while in the worst the relation
between different competent authorities is inexistent in practice (Aja 2003).

In any case, we have to note that instruments created by Law 30/1992 are not
running out all the possible tools for intergovernmental relations because some
sector laws have created specific organs to make possible the collaboration between
competent authorities. That is the case for Climate Change because of its special
elements and its complexity as a subject in which several levels of governments
have the faculty to act, but they cannot delimitate the problem and the effects of
their policies to national frontiers or autonomic borders.

The Commission was set up by Law 1/2005 of 9th of March, regulating the
greenhouse gas emissions allowances trading scheme—transposition of directive
2003/87/EC—as a mechanism of "coordination and collaboration between General
Administration of the State and Autonomous Communities to implement the
provisions of the regime of emission trading and the compliance with international
and community obligations of information".[1]

It is composed of the General Secretary on Climate Change, who is the chairman
of the Commission; five members in representation of the General Administration
of State; one member representing each AC; one member from each one of the
Autonomous Cities of Ceuta and Melilla; and a variable number of local authority
representatives.

Its activity should be specifically focused on the following functions:

a. Monitoring of climate change and adaptation of policies to its effects. In this
   area, we have to highlight the special coordinative action developed by the
   central government. Attending to the principle of proximity, adaptation policies
   are specially developed by ACs and municipalities, and this was clear during the
   process of elaboration of the Spanish Strategy of Adaptation to Climate Change.
b. Making of policies to prevent and reduce emissions of greenhouse gases. The
   most important work developed in this area is related to the European Union's
   system, and essentially, the Commission has been the point where central power
   has notified the AC the final transposition of directives and the implementation
   of European guidelines. For example, we can note the discussion about law
   13/2010 of 5th of July, modifying law 1/2005, further to improve and refine the

---

[1] It is necessary to highlight that coordination is obligatory only on economic planning, scientific
and technical researching, and health (Article 149.1 SC), in such way that facultative coordination
is coming into scene as a result of its necessity or political volition. Climate change question is
midway between both possible reasons for a facultative coordination. Anyhow, it is necessary to
emphasize that CC considers that although it is not constitutionally recognized, in environmental
issues we cannot deny the coordination faculty of central power (judgment 102/1995 of 26th June,
legal basis 31).

scheme of greenhouse gas emissions' rights market, including aviation, as transposition of Directive 2008/101/EC.

c. Fostering of carbon absorption capacity by plant formations. Forest policy is guided by strategies at national and, especially, at regional levels. State power tries to establish some common elements even when it is the competence of AC, which is the reason its main work in this area is to support regions in the protection of their forest areas and to create special tools to face threats and fires.

d. Establishment of general guidelines of the National Authority Designated by Spain and the criteria for approval of compulsory reports on voluntary participation in the projects of Clean Development Mechanism (CDM) and Joint Implementation (JI). This will be done by bearing in mind the criteria established by the National Climate Council.

e. Promotion of programs and actions aimed at reducing emissions from sectors not included in the area of application of the Directive. The so-called diffuse sectors are usually related to autonomic spheres of competence and the Spanish Strategy on Climate Change and Clean Energy. Horizon 2007–2012–2020—which was evaluated by the Commission—is giving a vast space to regional strategies to act on those areas to work in the fight against climate change using several instruments (taxation, forest policy, education and sensitization, sustainable edification, etc.).

We have to point out that, even when law refers to cooperation and coordination, as well as to the provision of information in their possession to each other, the real working system is more coherent with the name of the instrument. This way, it is really more focused on the coordinative aspect than on the cooperative element of the principle of collaboration we expressed *ut supra*. It means that, strictly speaking, there is no cooperation as long as there is no co-decision and joint action, but there is a coordination of AC and State activities against climate change because of the effective hierarchical role assumed by central government trying to give some coherency to the system in the whole Spanish territory—without losing sight the evidence of climate change's transnationality.

By all events, it does not mean that when a subject is to "submit to their consideration", AC's position was not taken into account, but it is not the usual way of working. It is related to the moment when this instrument becomes prominent because the work of the Commission starts when the national decision is made—not during the decision-making process—but the process about Strategies has given some hope for change because documents are exposed to lower levels of governments to claim for their "approval". The question is that even when AC and municipalities disagree, the prevalent opinion is that of the central power. From our point of view, including a real cooperation in which regional positions are taken into account can help make them a part of the unity, within the diversity of the State, as part of this common interest and common goal that climate change challenge must involve.

In any case, even when there are important failures that we have been insinuating until now, and that we will expose in the next point of this paper, the Commission is developing a very important and necessary work for the implementation of this complicated shared competence. As the report called "Recommendations of the Commission Co-ordinating Climate Change Policies for the coordinated application of the scheme of greenhouse gas emissions' rights market in Spain" of February 13th 2007, the system implementing the European Union directive in the multilevel system has a lot of elements needed for harmonization between the seventeen ACs. During the first year of its execution, ACs utilized different techniques to face the same situation, giving as a result the disparity of treatment to installations. That is the evidence upon which the central government supports its argument on the necessity of higher levels of coordination among the Spanish territory. However, we doubt whether this type of collaboration is the only one that can be developed to improve the operability, efficacy, and efficiency of the system, attending to a common structure.

## The Functioning of the Instrument of Intergovernmental Relations: Positive and Negative Aspects of Its Working System

Consequently, in the *Estado de las Autonomías*, the satisfaction of the goal of collaboration and political integration that *de facto* would follow depends, from the structural viewpoint, on mechanisms created for channeling the regional participation in the creation of the State's position. However, from a functional point of view, it depends on the assumption and maintenance of a political will of loyalty and political integration. This is the reason technical and legal instruments for coordinating and cooperating between different levels of government are needed (Cámara Villar 2004).

The intergovernmental relations in Spain are marked by some axioms, premises, and rules. This way, "first, two axioms related to the Spanish case, although they are generally applicable to most of the contemporary world's decentralized and federal-like systems: (a) conflicting intergovernmental relations; and (b) politicizing of ethno territorial institutions. Second, two premises dating from the pre-"*Estado de las Autonomías*" era will be analyzed: (c) differential fact; and (d) centralist inertia. Third, three principles will be identified as fundamental pillars upon which the organizational rationale of the 1978 Constitution rests (explicitly or implicitly); and (g) inter-territorial solidarity. And finally, three rules will be shown to play a most important role in the social and political structuring of the progressive process of federalization in Spain: (h) spatial centrifugal pressure; (i) ethno territorial mimesis; and (j) inductive allocation of powers" (Moreno 2000, p. 91). Those elements are showing some of the best and the worst characteristics of Spanish intergovernmental relationship's system are more or less present in climate change subject as a shared matter.

Anyhow, we have to note some positive aspects of the Spanish intergovernmental relations' system established for climate change policies. First, we have to congratulate our politicians as the creation of this instrument is an important step, and it seems to have sprung from a volition to work together for the benefit of the State and of men and the environment. In addition, it supposes the intent of the authorities to intensify the fight against climate change, recognizing that its special complexity makes necessary the creation of a specific instrument. Unfortunately, we cannot affirm all the areas of shared competences, but the one that is occupying us is in a better position.

Second, and linked to the positive aspect we have just mentioned, the Commission has achieved to set up a system against climate change more or less coherent in the whole territory. We cannot forget about the special work that law 1/2005 is leaving in AC's hands, as well as the initial problems and diversity. The Commission has worked, and is still working, in order to harmonize the minimum that is common in the Spanish system—according to the European Union's guidelines and taken into account the faculty of AC for establishing a higher level of environmental protection—and to eliminate disparities that were hampering some of them; moreover, it is helping to avoid the increase in figure of environmental free-riders within the national territory. From the initial insecurity that ACs can feel about the legality of their means of implementing the scheme of greenhouse gas emissions' rights market, regions actually have reached a system of working more efficiently as results of the approximation of techniques that the Commission supposes. Then coordinative competence of the State has given some successes in this area.

Third, through a reading of the present dissertation, it is obvious that we have organized our critique over the lack of cooperation, but we have to advise the reader that it is taking place within other instruments where climate change issues are exposed, discussed, and negotiated and where AC has a bit bigger space for acting.

Also, there are some important elements that show a negative side of the system established for the intergovernmental relations in Climate Change issues. First, it is evident that questions related to this subject are studied, discussed, and agreed within other instruments as Sector Conference on Environment, Conference on Issues Related with the European Union, or Advisory Committee on Environmental Policy for Community issues for multilateral relationships and every Bilateral Commission for bilateral relations between the State and each one of ACs. From one part, it is linked to the complexity of the subject—its mainstreaming, its transnationality, and its constantly changing character—because it makes climate change a multifaceted problem incomprehensive for only one instrument; also, it can help introduce more cooperation. From the other part, the mentioned dispersion of its treatment can confuse ACs in determining where they can expose their position; what can be taken into account is where they are present, for the purpose of being informed of their national policies, or where they can demand and claim for their interests—in that case, we are referring to their interests in accordance with their special necessities because they are not the same for the most industrialized regions, the most rural ACs, or the regions where there are important forest areas, for example.

Second, as we have noted through this document, the system gives an excess of protagonist character to coordinative techniques. It supposes that there are nonsymmetric participation of the State and ACs in the process of discussion and negotiation because coordinating tools are given a hierarchical superiority to central power as coordinating body. Then ACs become disjunctive or claim for Constitutional justice or claim that their voices are not heard. However, we have to note that, Commission Co-ordinating Climate Change Policies is a really workable system in which specialized permanent work groups are generating important results. Maybe the interest for intergovernmental collaboration seems more evident within this instrument than within others, but it is really limited to coordination even when the law that created the Commission refers to its cooperative faculties.

As a result, nationalist political parties of some regions do not want to have a competence level equal to other ACs, and an advantaged bilateral negotiation can bring them to a better situation—that is the reason new ASs have emphasized the presence of those instruments. Canarias employed the instrument in relation to law 13/2010 of 5th July because of its insular condition to "develop a cooperation regime to fulfill legal provisions and avoid negative impact of the system", but if cooperation was really possible within the Commission, the problem can be treated and they would have come to a common position in which all the ACs affected (Canarias, Baleares, Ceuta and Melilla) can show their opinion and discuss about it to achieve an agreement where the general interest of the State can be reflected.

Third, it is important to note the mix of regional and political interests within a system based on coordination. Even when we affirmed the excessive protagonist role of the central power, it is in contrast with reality where some ACs are trying to extend their level of competences. In fact, this fact is aiding to the incongruence of the system. In this context, it is important to consider that the operational and effective role of the valid instruments of inter-administrative connection depends on the attitude of bodies and Administrations present in it. The will to collaborate and an atmosphere of understanding are what really determines and makes possible their existence, getting over the possible deficiencies so it could be overcome in a context of agreement. The semipolitical composition of this tool of intergovernmental relations gives a higher level of conflict to it and makes it very difficult to find the common goal and the common interest when it is covered and hidden by the stubborn defense of their political ideology, their hunger for power, or some regional interests. Then the inexistence of a Federalist Culture of cooperative relations is to be blamed for the lack of concern about common interest and common will in the entire State. This strange situation is evident at the core of intergovernmental relationships in Spain. Misgivings between the AC, the absence of sense of State union that some ACs present, and the desire of having a preeminent role in the State are clear when the State tried to coordinate a common position.

## Conclusion: Some Propositions to Improve This Instrument of the Spanish System of Intergovernmental Relations in Climate Change

According to what has been exposed, we must note the presence of four authorities with capacity or expertise to decide, execute, and implement in climate change policies. The mentioned vertical environmental mainstreaming involves the development of the projects, strategies, and specific actions concerning several government levels. Thus, the optimal way to develop their competence should result in each one of them acting exclusively within the scope of its powers, coordinating and cooperating, to reach the common objective of the so-called sustainable development. This way, authorities are not losing the anthropocentric perspective of the guiding principle of Article 45 SC.

From our point of view, intergovernmental relations in climate change issues would be better if authorities take into account the next elements. First, it is essential, in order to achieve a more workable and fluid system of relations between State and ACs regarding Climate Change, to give more weight to cooperation within the system in order to facilitate the AC's participation in national decision-making processes as they are the authorities that finally must implement those decisions. This way, it is more probably that special problems or specific situations of the AC facing the challenge of fighting against climate change can be taken into account. Nonetheless, maybe it supposes that the participation of instruments of intergovernmental relations must appear before and not at the final the process, when decision has been made and it is exposed to the regional entities. If it worked this way, including ACs at the first steps of the decision-making process, CC would be free of solving a countless number of conflicts between the State and ACs and our organizational system would be closer to being characterized completely as a Federal system.

Second, and linked to the proposition we have just exposed, ACs use to employ Bilateral Commissions to try to solve problems of competence with central power, following Article 33.2 of Organic Law of Constitutional Court, but in a beneficial way, and it is generating some disparities between ACs—disparities that obviously are increasing misgivings between regions. Although bilateral relations are useful and necessary—to approach national law to the particularities and specific situation of each AC, as an instrument where they can solve concrete conflicts or temper some legal provisions for implementing law to the particular region—it is a priority to give an impulse to multilateral collaboration.

It leads us to consider that it is urgent to display horizontal collaboration—between ACs—because it is the unfinished and unresolved system of intergovernmental relations. The meeting of ACs must be established as a prior step to the meeting with national government, as a point of agreement between them, where ACs can expose their own position and concerns and, finally, where they can arrive at a common position to be exposed to the central power. Therefore, as a common element to instruments for multilateral horizontal relations, "the constitutional jurisprudence (co-management as a way to answer supra-territorial divisions), new ASs (explicit and implicit provisions of collaboration) or the process of integration (top-down and bottom-up phases) open ways to consultation between the ACs; but they are the ones which should appreciate the incentives of this relation and the benefits that it reports to them" (García Morales 2009, p. 127) because their unity, acting as a block, can help them defend their interests. However, the high level of politicization is not helpful.

Third, it is necessary to consider how to stop the high level of "regionalinalization"—understanding this concept as a movement that is giving priority to regional interest in opposition to national interests, offending against principle of interterritorial solidarity directly—and politicization—understanding it, in climate change issues, as the political attitude based on the utilization of environmental policies as a tool of confrontation. In those cases, we can see that probably the main problem is that the political system in Spain is not really close to the Federalist Culture; the coexistence of several levels of government acting over the same subject requires a sense of State that is not present in our country. Moreover, environmental issues are needed with a political agreement in which they give priority to the common challenge that climate change supposes, even to the detriment of their own interests—specially political or economic interests. Then the interest of the party that governs, the interest of concentrating higher levels of competences—or whatever it could be—will not matter.

The environmental protection, from the vertical and horizontal transversal, should be characterized by the need to be the guide of their acts in this area, even breaking intergovernmental formal relations, because they are taking care of a bigger question. Obviously, horizontal and vertical interdependence between different government levels requires increasing efforts to reach consensus, and this tends to make the decisions and their implementation difficult, but they have to *act in dubio pro natura*.

# References

Aja, E. (2003). El Estado Autonómico. Federalismo y hechos diferenciales. Alianza. Madrid.

Arlucea Ruíz, E. (2005). Las competencias medioambientales estatutarias: entre la legislación básica estatal y la normativa local. In Vidal Beltrán, J.M. and García Herrera, M. A. Estado Autonómico: integración, solidaridad y diversidad, Instituto Nacional de Administración Pública. COLEX. Madrid. 453-585 pp.

Alda Fernández, M. and Ramos Gallarín, F. (2006). Relaciones intergubernamentales y políticas públicas: el caso de la política de medio ambiente. In López Nieto, L. (coord.) Relaciones intergubernamentales en la España Democrática: interdependencia, autonomía, conflicto y cooperación. Dykinson. Madrid.

Cámara Villar, G. (2004). El principio y las relaciones de colaboración entre el Estado y las Comunidades Autónomas. Revista de Derecho Constitucional Español 1: 197-240 pp.

García Morales, M.J. (2009). Instrumentos y vías de institucionalización de las relaciones intergubernamentales. In Arbós Martín, X., Colino Cámara, C., García Morales, M.J. and

Parrado Díez, S. Las relaciones intergubernamentales en el Estado autonómico. La posición de los autores. Generalitat de Catalunya. Institut d'Estudis Autonòmics. Barcelona.

González Ayala, M.D. (2008). Las relaciones intergubernamentales en el nuevo marco de las reformas estatutarias: la diferente conciliación de la bilateralidad-multilateralidad en las relaciones Estado-Comunidad Autónoma. INDRET. Revista para el análisis del derecho. Barcelona.

Jaria I Manzano, J. (2005). Problemas competenciales fundamentales en material de protección del medio ambiente. Revista Vasca de Administración Pública 73: 117-134 pp.

Lozano Cutanda, B.; Alonso García, R. and Plaza Martín, C. (1999). El medio ambiente ante el Tribunal Constitucional: problemas competenciales y ultraeficacia protectora. Revista de administración pública 148: 99-132 pp.

Leff, E. (2003) La complejidad ambiental. Siglo XXI editores. México. 29 p. (3$^{rd}$ ed.)

Marco Marco, J. J and Pérez Gabaldón, M. Constitución y medio ambiente: una cuestión todavía por definir. In Martínez Sospedra, M. La Constitución Española después de su trigésimo aniversario. Tirant-Lo Blanc. Valencia. 2010. 179-210 pp.

Moreno, L. (2000), Federalization of Spain. Frank Cass. London.

Ortega Álvarez, L. (2008). El medio ambiente y los nuevos Estatutos de Autonomía. Noticias de la Unión Europea 182: 55-62 pp.

Pérez Gabaldón, M. Los problemas competenciales en materia medioambiental y las relaciones intergubernamentales como posible vía de solución. Corts Valencianes. Col.lecció Temes de Les Corts. Valencia. 2012.

Terol Becerra, M. J. (2000). Acerca del carácter más razonable que racional de la jurisprudencia constitucional relativa al medio ambiente. Revista Española de Derecho Constitucional 59: 331-344 pp.

Watts, R.L. (2008). Comparasing Federal Sytems. Institute of Intergovernmental Relations. 117-191 pp.

# The Relations of the Autonomous Community of the Canary Islands in the European Integration Process

M. Soledad Santana Herrera

**Abstract** From the point of view of the European political decentralisation process, the relations system between the Government of the Canary Islands and the National Government in both phases of the Community Law, primary and secondary phases, are analysed. The chances of participating in the Community rulemaking process that the Government of the Canary Islands has also been evaluated.

As a consequence of the silence of the SC of 1978, the analysis starts from sections 37 and 38 of the SACI and focuses especially on the legislative proposal of the reform project of the aforementioned Statute in 2006. The latter was never passed because it filled the void of the SC. In particular, we shall consider the innovations that the passing of this reform would have meant regarding the new faculties conceded to the Canary public powers in both phases of the Community Law—the primary and secondary phases. In the last section, whether the reform project specifies much more than the Statute of Autonomy, in force today, is considered, in addition to the presence of the Canary public powers before the Community Institutions.

In essence, it is concluded that the reform project fits the political decentralisation process characteristic of the European Union. However, until the power territorial organisation model in Part VIII of the SC is redefined and the State of Autonomies is integrated into one of the federal models classifications, passing these reform project of the Statute of Autonomies is, obviously, going to be a difficult task.

M.S.S. Herrera (✉)
Ph. D. Candidate in Constitutional Law at the, University of Las Palmas de Gran Canaria, de Gran Canaria, Spain
e-mail: santanasoledadm@hotmail.com

A. López-Basaguren and L. Escajedo San Epifanio (eds.), *The Ways of Federalism in Western Countries and the Horizons of Territorial Autonomy in Spain*, Vol. 2, DOI 10.1007/978-3-642-27717-7_20, © Springer-Verlag Berlin Heidelberg 2013

## Introduction: The Influence of the European Political Decentralisation Process on the State of Autonomies

The Lisbon Treaty intensifies the European political decentralisation process more than any previous Treaty enacted by the European Community, defining "political decentralisation" as the participation of central authorities, local or regional bodies in the decision-making or advisory bodies of the Community Institutions.

The reason for this choice is that the exposing of social-economic problems by European regional or local public authorities belonging to the European Union (EU) leads to much more efficient solutions. This is because regional or local public authorities acknowledge and feel a greater sensitivity towards their citizens' concerns that affect the region or municipality they represent.

However, the success of the European integration process is based on its respect towards the principle of institutional autonomy of the Member States. Therefore, the EU does not interfere in the decision of whether the power territorial organisation—provided in each national Constitution—is a Unitary State or a Federal State.

In this case, the silence of the Spanish Constitution (SC), due to the political, social, and cultural conflicts germane to previous years, was overcome, thanks to the commendable contribution of the constitutional doctrine concerning the precepts of the SC that are directly or indirectly linked to Part VIII thereof. This concerns itself with the territorial organisation of the State: the development of the Organic Laws (OL) on the matter, as well as the enactment of and, sometimes, the adoption of reforms on the Statutes of Autonomy (SA). Thus, the State of Autonomies has been defined as an "asymmetrical State" (López Aguilar 1998), based on the classification of the federal models.

Consequently, the Spanish Constitutional Court have, since 1989, permitted the Governments of the Autonomous Communities (ACs) to exert a certain influence on the position that the National Government adopts with regard to the negotiation and conclusion of the International Treaties. It also consents to the presence of the Community Institutions before the decision-making or advisory bodies, providing that the matter affects the competences that are exclusive to the ACs and are included in their respective SA. Nevertheless, the core of section 149.1.3 of the SC "international relations", which is the obligation to make international or community commitments and the power to negotiate and conclude International Treaties is an exclusive competence of the State, in accordance with sections 93 and 94 of the SC.

However, the constitutional doctrine does not specify the extent of the participation of the ACs on the relation between the National Government together with the Autonomous Governments and the Community Institutions. It is not even specified in the constitutional text, which has obviously no part or chapter concerning this matter. This silence is usually overcome by the SA, which often determines the possibilities of action of the autonomies abroad. This applies to the Statute of Autonomy of the Canary Islands (SACI), in its sections 37 and 38, after the reform passed by OL 4/96, and it is further specified in the draft bill of the reform proposal of the SACI submitted by the Parliament of the Canary Islands on 22nd September 2006, and which dedicates Part V in Chapter II to the "relations with the European Union and external actions", as will be described below.

## The Participation of the Government of the Autonomous Community of the Canary Islands in the European Integration Process

### Regulatory Framework

As is well known, the particularity of the "Canary particular situation" is based on the condition of islands as part of an archipelago, significant because of its distance from the Spanish mainland, from the rest of Europe, and from other foreign States. This, together with its geographic relief, which is notable for having a warm climate and little rain, creates a large demand for importation. A wide range of products must be imported to avoid the Canaries encountering themselves in a situation of economic dependence. Therefore, the Canary Islands have a special economic and fiscal regime (EFR) in order to make its income *per capita* reach the Community's average levels.

The "Canary particular situation" is recognised in section 138.1 of the SC in accordance with section 2 of the SC, and specifically the additional disposition 3 of the SC considers a number of specific provisions regarding the EFR.

Consequently, the entry of Spain into the European Economic Community (EEC) entailed that the Autonomous Community of the Canary Islands (ACCI) was exempted from certain economic and custom policies and was permitted to participate in the EU structural funds. This is illustrated in section 25 of the Act of Accession of Spain to the EEC and in Protocol 2 concerning the Canary Islands, Ceuta, and Melilla and was updated in 1991–1994.

With the enactment of the Single European Act, the establishment of an internal market involved the integration of the ACCI in the Community trade and customs policies. Thanks to the proposals made by the Inter-services Group, a special unity for community action, during the years 1987–1989, the ACCI gets the ultra-peripheral region status. As a result of the Treaty of Amsterdam, this status changed from secondary Law into primary Law through section 227.2 or 299.2 of the ECT, today section 349 of the TFEU. Therefore, the Canary archipelago's status of ultra-peripheral region is described in section 46 of the SACI of 1996 and in section 130 of the proposal of reform of the SACI, regarding the EFR of the Canary Islands, and in section 2 related to the "distance, insularity and ultra- periphery".

The interests the ACCI is related to the position the National Government adopts during the negotiations and conclusions of the Treaties establishing the EU and the presence of the ACCI before the Community Institutions mainly focus on all the matters that concern their EFR and its status as an ultra-peripheral region.

Henceforward, the faculties at the disposal of the Government of the Canary Islands related to the position the National Government adopts in the negotiation and conclusion of Community Treaties and the participation of the ACCI before the Community Institutions will be analysed, whenever it affects the competences that are exclusive of the ACCI provided in sections 30 and 31 of the SACI. With regard to this, an analysis of sections 37 and 38 of the SACI will first be conducted, and special attention will be paid to the innovations that the approval of sections 157 and 151 of the reform proposal would have resulted in—despite the fact that this proposal was never passed. It is very likely that the main problem arose in section 157.1 since it granted the Government of the Canary Islands the authority to exert its own external action in the range of its competences and in the defence of the general interest constitutionally conferred, with no detriment to the function of representation and the competences that belong to the State. This is simply because the core of these rules, concerning the international relations, is an exclusive competence of the State, in accordance with section 149.1 of the SC.

## The Faculties of the Government of the Autonomous Community of the Canary Islands to Participate in the Adoption of the Disposition of the State Government in Accordance with the Negotiation and Ratification of the Community Treaties

We shall now focus on the primary phase of the Community Law. According to sections 37 and 38 of the SACI, the Government of the Canary Islands has the authority to do the following:

a. *The right to request:* It is understood as the power to request that the National Government the negotiate certain provisions of the Community Treaties, which affect the insular interests and, specifically, its EFR or geographical location as an ultra-peripheral region, as considered in section 38.3 of the SACI.

 Likewise, section 160.3 of the reform project concerns itself with this same matter, though placing greater emphasis on it. Nevertheless, it stands out because it considers the possibility to request the celebration of International Treaties or Agreements within the framework of the development cooperation policies, with neighbouring countries and countries or territories where Canary communities or descendants of Canaries can be found, so as to strengthen cultural bonds. Of course, this can be extended to all the peoples that make up the EU.

 The aforementioned precept was updated in line with the European neighbourhood policies and was also confirmed in section 158.2 of the reform project, and today it is vaguely considered in section 38.2 of the SACI. In this sense, section 157.2 of the reform project stands out because it granted the

Government of the Canary Islands the right of initiative regarding all the aforementioned actions, and above all, it added the possibility to promote initiatives aimed at the cooperation with the other ultra-peripheral regions in the framework of the European territorial cooperation programs.

Finally, section 161.2 of the reform project stands out because it considers the possibility of the Government of the Canary Islands to urge the Government of Spain to interpose the Action for Annulment before the Court of Justice of the European Communities (CJEC), as considered in section 230 of the ECT, today section 263 of the TFEU, in the cases where the community act, subject to challenge, affects the competences that are exclusive to the ACCI, specially its EFR or its status as an ultra-peripheral region.

b.  *The right to information*: The interpretation of section 38.1 of the SACI in accordance with section 19.h) of Law 1/83 of the Government and Public Administration of the ACCI means that the Government of the Canary Islands has the right to receive information from the State and has the competence to announce its autonomous opinion. Should the Community Treaties consider the customs legislation policies and affect those matters that are exclusive to the ACCI whenever there is a direct or indirect link? The ACCI's autonomous opinion is not binding on the National Government, since the negotiation and conclusion of the Treaties are an exclusive competence of the State, in accordance with section 149.1.3 of the SC. Therefore, if the Treaty is negotiated or concluded by the National Government, without taking into consideration the autonomous opinion, the implementation of the Community Treaty will still affect the ACCI since the latter has no faculty to challenge the subject matter.

Section 160.2 of the reform project asserted the same. However, it adds the possibility to inform the Government of the Canary Islands about the conditions for the implementation of the community regulations on the matter.

c.  *The right of consultation*: This has only been considered in section 159.4 of the reform project, with regard to the participation of the national parliaments concerning the control of the principles of subsidiarity and proportionality during the procedure for adopting Community legislation. Through this, the Parliament of the Canary Islands can be consulted regarding the European legislative proposals that are affecting the insular interests, prior to the issue of the Spanish General Courts' expert opinion.

As for the secondary phase of the Community Law, section 38.2 of the SACI bestows the right of implementation on the ACCI, in accordance with the constitutional doctrine: It has the obligation to implement the Community regulation in the legal system, within the subject matters that affect its competences. Otherwise, it becomes the State's responsibility for breaching the Community Law, as considered in sections 226–228 of the ECT, today sections 258–260 of the TFEU.

Indeed, part 3 of section 159.1 of the reform project stands out because it grants the ACCI the faculty to directly apply and implement the Community Law in the autonomous legal system within the range of its competences, committing it to informing the National Government about the dispositions and resolutions adopted.

In short, during the primary phase of the Community Law, the Government of the Canary Islands has the right to request and the right to be informed by the National Government. On the contrary, it lacks the right to request the interposition of the Action for Annulment before CJEC and also lacks the right of initiative. Least significant is that the Parliament of the Canary Islands has the right of consultation, just as it was considered in the reform project. According to the secondary phase of the Community Law, it has the right of implementation, which constitutes an obligation too, but it lacks the faculty to directly apply or implement the Community Law in the autonomous legal system in line with the reform project.

The extent to which the Canary regional representatives are conferred the power of participation before the Community Institutions shall now be analysed.

## The Government of the Canary Islands' Participation in the Community Institutions

The silence of the SC and the lack of consolidation of the constitutional doctrine on behalf of section 37.2 of the SACI determine that it only expresses that "the Government of the Canary Islands may participate within the Spanish delegations before European Community bodies provided that subjects with an specific interest for the Canaries are being discussed, according to what the Spanish Nation legislation establishes". Despite section 158 of the reform project concerning "the relations with the European Union", in reality it does not specify much more: it clarifies that "the ACCI participates in the Community Institutions and in the different international bodies, in accordance with the terms established in the SC, the SA, the valid legislation, the international treaties or agreements and the agreements endorsed between the State and the Canaries, whenever the subject matters affect the "Canary particular situation" and, in particular its status as an ultra-peripheral region".

Due to the fact that the Canary's regional representatives' authority to stand before the Community Institutions is not specified, attention must be paid to the way the Community regulation development process works.

Very briefly, in the aforementioned text, the Commission must be in permanent contact with the regions and municipalities and has the obligation to consult the Committee of the Regions—provided in section 265 of the ECT, today section 307 of the TFEU—whenever the subject of debate, in conformity with the Community legislation, affects their interests. This is done in order to achieve effective Community rules that can solve problems that involve the people of Europe. It is simply because the regional and local authorities are very much aware of the needs and concerns of the citizens they represent.

On this matter, and because the Spanish Conference for European Community Affairs agreement was reached in 1997, the ACCI regional representatives have the chance to participate in the Committees and working groups of the Commission if the subject matter affects the insular interests. Moreover, there is an ACCI representative in the Committee of the Regions. From this point of view, it is important to remark on section 160.4 of the reform project as it fills the legal void of the SC, planning that the ACCI would participate in those international organisations that admitted the presence of the European regions and the non-State political entities.

Finally, the ACCI, working with regional entrepreneurs and bodies in charge of commercial promotion, has been given the chance to offer all the necessary information about its products to the representation offices of the Autonomous Communities in Brussels in order to intensify the economic activity and promote tourism in the islands.

In essence, the age gap of the SC in this field can only be overcome partly, thanks to the dynamic of the European political decentralisation process. This way, the ACCI has certain degrees of participation in the Community rulemaking process.

## Conclusions

As a general rule, the SA reform processes precede the reforms, in which it is compulsory to tackle the national public powers in relation to the constitutional text of 1978.

Indeed, Chapter II of Part V of the proposal of the SACI, which refers to the relations between the Autonomous Community and the EU, is in tune with the European political decentralisation process.

Nonetheless, the SA reform proposals, which comply with the territorial power organisation model of the State of Autonomies and consider the relation systems having to mediate between the State and the ACs, will usually fail unless the will to raise the 1978 constitutional text reform does not deeply affect the conscience of the state public authorities, in other words, until there is a set target to reach a consensus on integrating the State of Autonomies in the classification of the federal models, more specifically as an "asymmetrical federalism." Therefore, the recognition of the "particular situations" of each of the ACs is emphasised much more in order to obtain the constitutional recognition with regard to its participation in the process of negotiation and conclusion of the Community Treaties with the Nation's Government, plus the constitutional recognition related to the presence of the ACs before the Community Institutions.

It is submitted that the constitutional reform could reach a satisfactory solution regarding the territorial power organisation if it is approached from the perspective of the political decentralisation processes, which not only are activated by the EU but also represent the dynamic of many other European countries. Only this way can a citizen from the Canary Islands, Madrid, or Extremadura, amongst others, be guaranteed and be confident that their interests and concerns will be considered within the context of the Community Institutions.

In conclusion, problems could potentially be solved by adopting the European integration process as a reference parameter based on the premise "unity in diversity." This way, a harmonious coexistence with no fissures could take place, provided that the national public powers and the citizens consciously assume respect for the different cultures, languages, and traditions that characterise each of the 17 ACs that are part of Spain as a Member State of the EU.

## References

Carballo Armas, P. (2003). Canarias ante la Unión Europea: integración comunitaria y hechos diferenciales. Revista del Foro Canario 98: 77–95.

García Otero, C.J. (1996). Comentario. In: Varona Gómez-Acedo, J. (ed.). Comentarios al Estatuto de Autonomía de Canarias, Instituto Canario de Administración Pública, Marcial Pons, Madrid, pp. 841–866.

López Aguilar, J.F. (1998). Estado autonómico y hechos diferenciales: una aproximación al "hecho diferencial" en el Estado de la Constitución de 1978: el caso de la autonomía canaria. Centro de Estudios Políticos y Constitucionales, Madrid, 277 pp.

López Aguilar, J.F., Carballo Armas, P., García Andrade, D. (2006). La posición de la Comunidad Autónoma Canaria ante la Unión Europea In: López Aguilar, J. F., Rodríguez Drincourt, J. R. (eds.). Derecho público de Canarias, Thonsom- Civitas, Cizur Menor, Navarra, pp. 409–425.

Rodríguez Drincourt, J.R. (2006). La organización territorial del Estado, Estado autonómico y Estatuto de Autonomía. In: López Aguilar, J. F., Rodríguez Drincourt, J. R. (eds.). Derecho público de Canarias, Thonsom- Civitas, Cizur Menor, Navarra, pp. 55–88.

# Institutionalization of Intergovernmental Relations in a Federal State: Bilateral Treaties Under "New Centralism" in Russia

M.S. Ilchenko

**Abstract** This article examines institutional dynamics of Russian federalism with the focus on the analysis of intergovernmental interaction practices. It argues that although the Russian federal system passed through serious centralized reforms in the last decade, the general mode of relations between the Center and regions has not changed drastically if it is to compare with the 1990s. Certain elements of the bilateral negotiation system still continue to function in the form of a backdoor "individual" dialogue between the federal and regional elites. Taking into account that the Center is striving to implement new "technological" principles in regional governance, it appears that one of the basic contradictions of Russian federalism lies in reproducing the two different types of intergovernmental interaction practices within one institutional frame.

The last decade in Russian federative policy is generally viewed as a period of centralization that resulted in a highly subordinative system of relations between the Center and regions. However, although the strength of centralizing tendencies in Russian federalism does not give rise to doubts, it would be overrating to affirm that the Center managed to gain total control over regional space. Federal reform implementation and building the vertical governance did not signify disappearance of a dialogue between federal and regional elites. Moreover, the process of their interaction in the recent years proved to be even more intensive than earlier. Trying to set the unified rules in regional policy, the Center failed to avoid "personified" contacts with elite groups in the regions. As a result, at the present time federal elite has to follow a highly controversial policy, on the one hand, relying on the new "technological" principles of governance and, on the other, using entrenched

M.S. Ilchenko (✉)
Institute of Philosophy and Law, the Russian Academy of Sciences, Ural Branch, Kalinina Str. 8-50, Ekaterinburg 620012, Russia
e-mail: msilchenko@mail.ru

A. López-Basaguren and L. Escajedo San Epifanio (eds.), *The Ways of Federalism in Western Countries and the Horizons of Territorial Autonomy in Spain*, Vol. 2, DOI 10.1007/978-3-642-27717-7_21, © Springer-Verlag Berlin Heidelberg 2013

mechanisms of bilateral "individual" agreements that actually still continue to function despite the formal abolishment in the beginning of the 2000s.

In such conditions, the dynamics of Russian federalism is primarily determined by the set of practices and institutions steadily reproduced in the interactions between the Center and subunits rather than by simple aggregate of their strategies. Dominant traditions of the analysis of the Russian federal system seriously neglected the examination of its institutional dynamics. Structural-institutional approaches are mostly normatively oriented and, thus, concentrated on large-scale processes of the system development (Kempton 2001; Koniyhova 2004; Ross 2002), whereas actors-oriented models are mainly focused on the transformation of certain "rules of the game" configuration and therefore usually overlook a broad institutional context of changes (Gelman 2009; Heinemann-Grueder 2002; Pascal 2003).

This paper will explore how and to what degree the set of institutional practices of intergovernmental relations in Russia changed for the period of "new centralism" in the 2000s. According to that, the general conceptual framework for the analysis will be suggested in the first section of the paper. Then the process of federal practices institutionalization will be examined regarding the two main fields of Russian regional politics—governor appointment system and relations of federal elite with the regions of a "special status."

## Intergovernmental Interaction Practices in a Federal State: General Framework for the Analysis

One of the key questions in federal studies is usually formulated in the following way: How does federalism affect policy outcomes? (Riker 1964; Volden 2004). The most serious contribution to the analysis on this direction was made within the rational choice theory. Due to its theoretical framework, the main research focus was put on the federal structures' ability to affect actors' behavior while federalism itself was viewed from the perspective of the "rules of the game" setting or, in other words, as a situational phenomena. If to assume that such effect has continuing character and federalism is capable to acquire certain stability characteristics, then the question mentioned above can be specified and formulated in the following manner: How does federalism "structure" politics? (Gibson 2004). This "structuring" effect means that federal institutions appear to be capable of shaping certain models of behavior subsequently reproduced in the interaction practices. As a result, federalism manifests itself not just in a structural aspect (constitutional legal norms, system of government) or strategic aspect (activity of the main political actors—federal and regional elite groups) but also in the reproduction of such models and the level of their stability.

The most useful way to observe how these models are functioning is to examine the elements of federal system's stability themselves—namely intergovernmental interaction practices. Their analysis enables to cover those areas and tendencies in federal relations that are traditionally neglected by rational choice and normative approaches. Among them, in particular, there are "fragmentary" establishment of federal institutions taken in various forms, the rise of informal relations as one of the basic factors of federal system development, gradual "dovetailing" of federal practices with other political institutions (electoral practices, clientelist practices, party system), etc.

Generally, the analysis of intergovernmental interaction practices can be based on the exploration of the main parameters—first, the level and intensity of their institutionalization (which ultimately determine the level of their reproduction) and, second, the correlation between the different types of such practices (which determines the degree of congruence/divergence between them). Therefore, these parameters allow to determine to what degree a certain set of institutional practices is stable, cohesive, and reproducible.

This conceptual framework seems to be highly applicable to the Russian experience of federalism. The dynamics of intergovernmental relations in Russia can hardly be explained in terms of rational choice or structural transformation. Today, the relationships between the Center and subunits are regulated by a complicated set of practices being resilient enough to the changes of actors' preferences and of the actors themselves. The role of institutional inertia in contemporary Russian politics is even much more significant than it may seem at first glance.

The bilateral negotiation system between the Federal Center and subunits was considered to be a key instrument for regional politics in the 1990s. Although it was formally rejected with the Putin's coming to power, the main principles of this system are still reproduced today in the intergovernmental relations. The changes and modifications of these principles in the last decade deserve a special analysis, as well as the reconsideration of the whole bilateral negotiation system in the institutional perspective.

The system of bilateral agreements in the Russian federalism has two main traditions of conceptual interpretation. The first one focuses on the legal nature of agreements, viewing the treaties in normative terms (Khakimov 2001; Koniyhova 2004), while the second is concentrated on the rational choice aspects of the practice trying to reveal its strategic sense (Solnick 2000; Stoner-Weiss 2006). Both traditions emphasize essential facets of the bilateral negotiation system but nevertheless remain unable to explain its "continuing" effect on the contemporary regional politics in Russia. Thus, it seems to be more useful to view the bilateral agreement system as a compound institutional setting containing legal norms, informal regulators and symbolic practices.

Of course, it would be a rough oversimplification to examine bilateral practices only from the "path dependence" perspective. The main goal here is to show how these practices changed and were modified in the current context and also how compatible they turned out to be with the new mechanisms of governance. Therefore, we'll pay a special attention, first, to the institutionalization process of the new governor recruitment practices and, second, to the changes in the "individual approach" strategy of the Center in relation to the most significant regional partners.

## Institutional Peculiarities of the Governor Appointment System in Russia

Cancellation of the direct election of regional governors in 2004 with a good reason can be considered as the most radical and rapid change in the whole complex of measures undertaken by the Russian government at the beginning of 2000s which used to be known as a "federal reform". If, moreover, the federal reform appeared to be a sort of "declaration of intentions" for the new authorities, then the implementation of the governor appointment system became a core element of the reform itself—both in institutional and symbolical aspects. Along with the abolition of the governor election, the process of the "vertical of power" construction seemed to be almost completed. The central government gained, in fact, total control over the regional political process, and federal system took its final configuration in the period of the "new centralism".

At the same time, although the appointment system affirmed principles of centralization and rigid subordination in federal relations, it did not mean a dissolution of the negotiating process between Center and regions at all. Moreover, in some cases, this process turned out to be even more intensive than earlier. In general, that can be explained by the two main factors.

First, elite interaction and possible conflicts among the interest groups concerning the choice of the governor candidate did not vanish but just shifted from the sphere of public policy to the "shadow" sector with numerous informal channels of communication. Second, the implementation of the appointment practice essentially modified the configuration of the relations between federal and regional elites by itself due primarily to serious changes in the both political and institutional roles of a governor in the new system.

The process of institutionalization of the established recruitment system was highly complicated and contradictory. Despite a practice of the governors' appointment has been lasting nearly for 7 years passing through different phases (Turovskii 2010); its setting up is still underway. During that time, the Kremlin managed to employ various strategies of appointment from the "mass" reconfirmation of the incumbent acting governors to the appointment of "outsiders" as the heads of the regions (candidates who actually have no any strong ties with regional elites and who are usually called "varangians", on the analogy with the historical experience of vikings who ventured the territories of Eastern Europe from the ninth to eleventh centuries).

Analysis of the Kremlin's main steps on this direction reveals the twofold character of the "new centralism" regional policy. On the one hand, the Center proclaimed a movement towards the doctrine of universalism in relations with the regions, thus adopting new principles in the personnel appointments. On the other, the federal elite could hardly overcome the effect of the personalized regional networks developed into the interaction practices acquired a sufficient level of stability in the previous decade of the "Yeltsin era". As a result, order of gubernatorial appointment has become regulated by the complex set of rules in which legal norms are usually supplemented or even substituted by the practices of "individual" approach or "back door" dialogue.

It is interesting that while building relationships with "strong" regions, the Center has been keeping rather cautious behavior trying to prevent any rapid move capable to cause tension or open contradiction. In most such cases, the choice was made in favor of either the incumbent acting governor or the candidate put forward by the dominant elite group. According to Nicolay Petrov, in case of existence of political machine functioning at the regional level, "federal elite was ready to be unaware either of 'incorrect' ideological preferences or previous and present declarations and actions made against the Kremlin's will and also of the wrong-doing concerning legislation" (Petrov 2007).

Even the Kremlin's course on gradual replacement of the "heavyweight" governors has not changed the situation drastically. In those cases where the candidature of a new governor was lacking strong ties with the regional elite, it nevertheless was approved by the main political actors of the region. As a consequence, system of relations between the Center and a definite region could be partially modified on the surface but remained the same in fact, maintaining all fundamental features unchanged.

Gradual reconfiguration process of the Center–regions relations seems to be the main result of the elections' cancellation viewed from institutional perspective. An evident dependence of the appointed governor on federal elite found expression not so much in a new position of the region in relation to the Center but mostly in a new position of regional elite in relation to the appointed governor itself. Appointment of "outsiders" as the heads of regions, along with the formation of the new policy maker teams coming into power at the regional level, seriously altered the institutional role of a governor in the current political system. Actually, the governor turned into a sort of intermediary in the relationships between regional and federal elite groups. In the perception of regional elite, he was stated as a protege and "conductor" of the federal interests. Therefore, to build up relations with a "newcomer" first of all meant to keep concealed dialogue with the Center. As one of the regional managers notes, "if earlier governor positioned himself as a regional leader possessing his own resource, now the both elites and ordinary people perceive a governor as a man embedded in the vertical of power" (Chirikova 2010). So, on one side, the local elite groups are found to be distanced from the Center being under the control of the governor who is, in its turn, accountable to the Kremlin. While on the other, the governor itself remains dependent on the balance of forces formed in the region.

Such situation stimulates the rise of different strategies that are used by regional political actors involved in the implicit negotiating process with federal elite. The fact that the governor's candidature is unquestionably approved by local elite groups does not necessary mean that all initiatives of the new head of the region will be fully accepted. If a policy of a new governor comes into collision with the interests of local elite groups, they can choose at least two possible ways of behavior. Thus, for instance, regional elite can take a course on the open conflict with the new governor striving for his resignation (e.g., Alexandr Tishanin in the

Irkutsk region or Nikolay Kolesov in the Amursk region) or, in the other case, local elite groups can be oriented on maintaining permanent tension in relations with the governor being aimed at the loss of his authority in the Center (Ilya Michalchuk in the Arkhangelsk region).

Moreover, appointment of the Kremlin's protege to the position of a governor can be considered as a tool for getting special economic preferences by the region. In this sense, approval of suggested candidature by the regional elite can be viewed from the perspective of rationale strategy. In particular, it is interesting to pay a special focus of attention to statistics of the inter-budget transfer distribution in those regions where appointments of the governors—"varangians"—have taken place in the recent years. Relying on the most rigid criteria of the governor— "varangian" as a man who never lived and worked in the region in which he is appointed—it is possible to mark 15 assignments of such a kind. Analysis shows that, almost in all cases, the total amount of uncompensated receipts in the region's budget essentially increased in the first year after the appointment (Budget Monitoring Center 2011). Thus, the first year after Valery Shantsev's coming to power in Nizhegorodsky region in 2005 was distinguished by the five times increase in the total inter-budget transfer amount in the consolidated budget of the region. Increase of the same indicator in Kaliningrad region after Georgiy Boos's appointment in 2005 was found by two times, meanwhile after Mikhail Men's coming in economically weak Ivanovskaya region amounted to 1.7.

Evidently, all those indicators could hardly be explained by the economic achievements gained by new governors in such a short period. In fact, they prove to be the result of rewarding policy conducted by the Center in relation to certain regions as a form of support of their new leaders.

The process of a new recruitment system institutionalization demonstrates all those contradictions characterizing Russian regional politics in the recent years. Settlement of the new formal rules caused actual coexistence of the "technical" practices of appointment and "personalized" practices of individual dialogue within the same institutional frame. However, if in the case of the governors' assignments we can distinguish only certain elements of bilateral agreements—such as the possible strategies of federal and regional elite, expected preferences, and the subject of bargaining—then in the other spheres of federal relations the effect of bilateral practices seems to be getting even stronger.

# A "Special Status" of Region Under "New Centralism": Mode of Reproduction

The use of individual approach in the relation with the regions turned out to be a necessary and, to a large extent, unavoidable measure for the Center in the recent years. In some cases, "individual" agreements acquired new "technological" features interfusing with the "manual control" practices as it was shown on the example of the governor appointment system. In other cases—such agreements were reproduced by customary mechanisms of bilateral exchange based on the special benefits and preferences. Thus, being abolished legally as a set of formal rules, the system of bilateral treaties, nevertheless, has not lost institutional significance. It continued to function in the form of stable models of behavior deeply rooted in the relationships between the Center and regions and various mechanisms of their informal negotiating. Especially that can be observed clearly in the relations between the Kremlin and regions of a "special status."

It is important to note that reinforcement of asymmetry tendencies in the Russian federalism appeared to be one of the most serious consequences of the "new centralism" reforms. Such a "by effect" of the Kremlin's politics can be explained by the change of a "special status" itself. In the 1990s, to a greater or lesser degree, region's "special status" was assumed by accepted rules of the game—primarily, by the system of bilateral treaties in its both formal and informal dimensions. As a result, a "special status" of a certain region was institutionalized and partially legitimated. Today, on the contrary, regions are getting their preferences out of any stable rules and established principles. In such situation, every region that benefited from the Center immediately stands out against others, making its position even more privileged. On the background of the declarations about "universal standards", a real asymmetry in Russian federal system is in a way increasing. That can be distinctly seen on the mode of Kremlin's relationships with "strong" ethnic regions and, in particular, with the Republic of Tatarstan.

In the 1990s, "the Tatarstan model" meant the existence of a permanent informal backdoor dialogue between elites of ethnic regions and the Center. According to Jeffrey Kahn, the Russia–Tatarstan Ttreaty of 1994 "set the standard for bilateral treaties that followed" (Kahn 2002).

The signing of the treaty between Moscow and Kazan in 1994 brought the Republic a number of serious preferences in different spheres of social and economic development, which provided maintaining a special status in Federation. The division of powers in that case was realized through a series of individual agreements on such basis that was far from any common rules. That gave Tatarstan's elite strong and favorable platform in the negotiating process. Stoner-Weiss remarks: "This effectively established Tatarstan's association with Russia as distinctive from other regions in that it reserved for the republic a special set of rights that other regions did not share—in particular, control over key social and educational programs that enabled the preservation of Tatar ethnicity" (Stoner-Weiss 2004). Moreover, the treaty allowed the Republic to gain "increased jurisdictional control over the mineral resources located in its territory" (Stoner-Weiss 2004).

Actually, the character of such agreements evidently proved that the most of the key decisions in the field of power division had been built up much earlier than the document was signed. The treaty with Tatarstan turned out to be a kind of compromise achieved by the central and regional elites as the result of a long-standing bargain that was still underway even after documents' adoption. Thus, according to Raviot: "Russia–Tatarstan treaty showed that the relations between Moscow and Kazan were characterized not only by intention but also by the permanent and constructive backdoor dialogue taking place from the very beginning of the Post-Soviet era" (Gaida and Rudenko 1998). Along with solving out the problems, the treaty at the same time revealed new condradictions also needed to be resolved. In particular, Moukhariamov suggests that the treaty did not have the direct juridical force and did not abolish constitutional collisions between the Russian Federation and the Republic of Tatarstan (Moukhariamov 1997).

In this context, Russia–Tatarstan treaty should be viewed as a complicated institutional setting that combines the legal norms, informal rules, and even discourse practices. To a great extent, its political significance was determined by the public resonance that the treaty had after signing. The effect of that resonance was even stronger than the treaty's conclusion. For instance, the expression "the Tatarstan model" itself was widespread after being mentioned in a number of official speeches. In such a way, the adviser of President Yeltsin for the relations with the subjects of Federation Nikolay Medvedev declared: "The treaty signed with Tatarstan is a model for construction of federalism in our country" (Anonymous 1994). The rhetoric of such kind also meant regulative function of the treaty in a strict way.

To a large extent, core principles of the bilateral system relations with Tatarstan are still working today. Moreover, under new conditions, the informal practices of negotiations between the Center and ethnic elites proved to become stronger than in the previous decade. In the beginning of the 2000s—period of "political will" demonstration—the Kremlin was nevertheless highly cautious in relationships with the republican elite. Every serious decision concerning the reconciling of federal and regional legislation was accompanied by a variety of informal meetings and agreements. If any tension occurred, the Center followed a proven method of negotiation. While demonstrating equanimity, it refrained from making public declarations relying on the discourse of "trust relationship". At the same time, all the problems had been solving in the course of closed negotiations and individual meetings of the federal and regional elite representatives. The existence of these problems could be publicly articulated and recognized, but only after formal announcements about "strengthening relations". In such a manner, during the visit to Tatarstan in March of 2000, V. Putin declared: "Today President Shaimiev has proposed an absolutely acceptable variant of interbudgetary and federal relations. They are in the framework of Russian nationhood. I have already told and I repeat again that President of Tatarstan appears to be one of the founders of contemporary Russian state. He was one of the originators of the Federation" (Anonymous 2000).

However actually, it is not a "special status" itself to deserve close attention but primarily the mechanisms causing this status to be reproduced. Recent years, experience shows that practices of bilateral changes in relations between Moscow and Kazan are successfully complying with the new "technological" mechanisms of regional governance. Maintenance of economic privileges by Tatarstan in the 2000s brightly demonstrated that.

In the 1990s, the tax and financial preferences of the Republic were generally the result of shadow and "closed" agreements. Today, such preferences are in various forms confirmed by quite open and legitimate mechanisms of federal politics assuming unified standards of governance. In such a way, a practice of granting preferences to the Republic is successfully adjusted by means of development institutions and, as a result, by "different channels for realization of numerous investment programs" (Zubarevich 2010). Almost every large-scale federal project seems to have a good basis for that. In particular, under initiative on the creation of special economic zones (SEZ), Alabuga was created (which is located on the territory of Tatarstan), which is the largest special economic industrial zone in the country and one of the first SEZ established in 2005. Besides, the Republic of Tatarstan turned out to be one of the leaders in crediting within the national priority project on agricultural development. In the beginning of 2011, a special agreement between the Republic and "Rosselkhozbank" was signed approving the order of investment credits accommodation for preferable branches of agriculture up to the end of 2012 (Anonymous 2011).

Finally, the distribution of federal funds directed to the development of technoparks seems to be indicative of the general tendency. Here, the volume of investments channeled to technopark creation in Kazan amounted to almost 20 % of the total investments volume, which are channeled to financing of all ten technopark creation projects in the different regions of the Russian Federation. At that, the total amount of financing of the project in Tatarstan exceeds the level of similar projects financing in other regions by 8–10 times (Kuznecova 2009).

Along with the new methods of economic stimulation, the Center continued to employ old mechanisms of political encouragement. Signing of a new power delimitation treaty in 2007 proved their availability. This document can be considered as a rather ceremonial one and "hugely modest" (Sidorenko 2010). Nevertheless, even the very fact of its emergence in the period of the unification policy confirms, once again, the existence of special mutual obligations between Moscow and Kazan. Moreover, treaty contains essential item. Article 2 of the document designates the requirement for the candidatures for the Republic's President post to know the official languages of the Republic. Taking into account that according to the same article the Tatar language, along with the Russian, is approved as an official one in the Republic, knowing this language became a sort of supplementary guarantee for ethnic elite to prevent governor-outsider appearance in the region. That legal norm was already used in the beginning of 2010, when republican elite enabled to realize successor scenario by supporting the candidature of the former prime minister of the Republic, Rustam Minnikhanov, to the post of President. His further election proved that possible replacement in the leadership of the Republic could hardly cause any significant changes in its relationships with the Center.

Thus, the use of the term "the Tatarstan model" is actually of no significance today. In the 1990s, that term meant two major principles: firstly, a certain pattern of building relationships with the concrete region and, secondly, the rules of the game that made that strategy possible. Today, a "special status" of the region is determined not by any set of rules or interaction order but, primarily, by the individual choice of the Center, which is realized out of any norms and settings. Regarding republics, this tendency is precisely characterized by Zubarevich: "There are no more special privileges of republics according to their status, there are only special privileges of certain republics in relation to which a special policy of the Center is implemented" (Zubarevich 2010).

Therefore, a "special" position of the region can be stipulated either by the region's permanently high political status and significance (Tatarstan, Dagestan, Chechnya) or by situational interest to a certain region due to the concrete political circumstances (Krasnodarskiy kray, Primorskiy kray). As a result, favoritism in federal relations seems to be seriously reinforcing: The Center gives privileges to certain regions but at the same time is not bound by any obligations—whether they are the rules of the game "for all" or "narrow" secret agreements. In such a way, "individual" approach is losing its significance as a basic principle of regional politics but is only strengthening as a strategy used in concrete cases.

Institutional analysis of intergovernmental interaction practices enables to reveal probably the basic contradiction of the current federal policy in Russia. Despite the declarations about the new principles in regional politics, the Center in fact is following a twofold strategy, relying on both "technological" and "personified" mechanisms of interaction with regions. Such ambiguity leads to a serious institutional divergence in federal system being marked by coexistence of the two different types of regulators within the same institutional frame. As a result, today federal system development is accompanied by the increase of uncertainty and unpredictability.

Of course, Russian regional politics in the 1990s was also quite controversial. At the same time, however, it was consistent enough. In particular, it was clear who gets what and why in rewards distribution or granting the benefits among the regions. Now a considerable part of decisions is accepted due to casual circumstances without any visible logic. Therefore, it is not surprising that many of those tendencies that characterized the Russian federalism development in the 1990s are just aggravating today. Strengthening of favoritism policy by the Center, reinforcement of a privileged status of "special" regions, and restoration of a highly centralized management style in the most of regional political systems demonstrate that brightly.

In this way, despite the Kremlin's aspiration to show the ability of keeping absolute control over all political processes, the trajectory of a further federal system development seems to be uncertain even in a short-term perspective.

# References

Anonymous (1994). Nezavisimaia gazeta. March 17, 1994. Cit. ex: Gaida, A.V., Rudenko, V.N. (eds.) (1998). Federalism i decentralizacia. UrO RAN, Ekaterinburg, Russia, 1998, p.260.

Anonymous (2000). Respublika Tatarstan. March 23, 2000. Cit ex: Moukhariamov, N.M. and Moukhariamova, L.M. (2004). Tatarstan v usloviyah recentralizacii po-putinski. In: Macuzato, K. (ed.) Fenomen Vladimira Putina i rossiiskie regiony: pobeda neozhidannaia ili zakonomernaia? Moskva, Russia, p. 323.

Anonymous (2011). Rosselkhozbank i Respublika Tatarstan podpisali Soglashenie o vzaimodeistvii v ramkah Gosprogrammy razvitia selskogo hoziaistva. Available at: http://president.tatarstan.ru/news/view/99253

Budget Monitoring Center (2011). Open Budget. Regions of Russia. Budget and inter-budgetary relations. Available at: http://openbudget.karelia.ru/en/index.php

Chirikova, A.E. (2010). Regionalnye elity Rossii. Aspekt Press, Moskva, Russia, p. 199.

Gaida, A.V., Rudenko, V.N. (eds.) (1998). Federalism i decentralizacia. UrO RAN, Ekaterinburg, Russia, 1998, p. 273.

Gelman, V. (2009) The return of the Leviathan? The policy of recentralization in contemporary Russia. In: Ross, C. and Campbell, A. (eds.) Federalism and local politics in Russia. Routledge, London and New York, pp. 1–24.

Gibson, E.L. (2004). Federalism and democracy: theoretical connections and cautionary insights. In: Gibson, E.L. (ed.) Federalism and democracy in Latin America. Baltimore and London, pp. 1–28.

Heinemann-Grueder, A.(2002). Is Russia's federalism sustainable? Perspectives on European Politics and Society 3 (1): 67–91.

Kahn, J. (2002). Federalism, democratization, and the rule of law in Russia. Oxford University Press, Oxford, p 150.

Kempton, D.R. (2001). Russian federalism: continuing myth or political salvation? Democratizatsiya 9(2): 201–242.

Khakimov, R. (2001). On the bases of asymmetry of Russian Federation. In: Khakimov R. (ed.) Federalism in Russia. Institute of History, Tatarstan Academy of Sciences, Kazan Institute of Federalism, Kazan, Russia, pp. 212–218.

Koniyhova, I.A. (2004). Sovremennyi rossiiskii federalism i mirovoi opyt: Itogi stanovlenia i perspektivy razvitia. Publishing House "Gorodec", Moskva, Russia, 592 pp.

Kuznecova, O.V. (2009). Regionalnye aspekty deiatelnosti federalnyh institutov razvitia. Problemnyi Analiz i Gosudarstvenno-upravlencheskoe Proektirovanie 2(4): 17.

Moukhariamov, N.M. (1997). The Tatarstan Model: a situational dynamics. In: Stavrakis, B.J., DeBardeleben, J., Black, L.(eds.) Beyond the monolith. The emergence of regionalism in Post-Soviet Russia. Washington, Baltimore, London, pp.213-323.

Pascal E. (2003). Defining Russian federalism. Praeger, Westport, Connecticut, London, 203 pp.

Petrov, N. (2007). Korporativizm vs regionalizm. Moskovskii Centr Karnegi, Moskva, Russia. Pro et Contra 11(4–5): 85.

Riker, W.H. (1964). Federalism: origin, operation, significance. Little, Brown & Company, Boston, 169 pp.

Ross, C. (2002). Federalism and democratisation in Russia. Manchester University Press, Manchester, 193 pp.

Sidorenko, A. (2010). Politicheskaya vlast v etnicheskih regionah. In: Busygina, I. and Hainemann-Gruder, A. (eds.) Federalism i etnicheskoe raznoobrazie v Rossii. Rossiiskaya Politicheskaya Enciklopedia, Moskva, Russia, p. 97.

Solnick, S.L. (2000). Is the center too weak or too strong in the Russian Federation? In: Sperling, V. (ed.) Building the Russian state: institutional crisis and the quest for democratic governance. Westview Press, Boulder, pp. 137–156.

Stoner-Weiss, K. (2004). Russia: managing territorial cleavages under dual transitions. In: Amoretti, U.M. and Bermeo, N. (eds.) Federalism and territorial cleavages. The Johns Hopkins University Press, Baltimore and London, 2004, p. 303.

Stoner-Weiss, K. (2006). Resisting the state: reform and retrenchment in Post-Soviet Russia. Cambridge University Press, Cambridge, 182 pp.

Turovskii, R.F. (2010). How Russian governors are appointed: inertia and radicalism in central policy. Russian Politics and Law 48(1): 58–79.

Volden, C. (2004). Origin, operation, and significance: the federalism of William H. Riker. Publius : Journal of Federalism 34(4): 89–107.

Zubarevich, N. (2010). Socio-ekonomicheskie razlichia mezhdu etnicheskimi regionami i politika pereraspredelenia. In: Busygina, I. and Hainemann-Gruder, A. (eds.) Federalism i etnicheskoe raznoobrazie v Rossii. Rossiiskaya Politicheskaya Enciklopedia, Moskva, Russia, p. 91.

# Sub-state Entity Participation During the 2010 Presidencies of the EU Council

Jorge Tuñón and Régis Dandoy

**Abstract** The theoretical development in several social disciplines identifies a transformation of the functionality of sub-state governments. It has been argued that regions progressively acquire functions of representation, legitimacy, and governability within the state, not only at national but also at international scales. Furthermore, it has been claimed that the European Union (EU) rotating presidencies (which still coexists even with the entry into force of the Treaty of Lisbon) constitute such an interesting opportunity for the Member States to—during a 6-month period—highlight their own interests, at European scale, thus influencing the EU political agenda. Within this context, we will seek to underline how the Member States regional participation affects the different EU presidencies.

Hence, the objective of this research will be to assess the influence of the regional institutional actors (regional parliaments, cabinets, and representation offices in Brussels) on the main priorities and policies of the countries' presidency of the EU. Very little scientific research has been done on the study of the rotating presidency of the Council of the EU, and to our knowledge; nothing has ever been done around the involvement of the regional actors in such process. Our aim is therefore to fill in this gap in the political science literature by identifying the key regional actors in the Presidency of the EU and drawing conclusions from the comparison of the recent experiences of two highly regionalised countries, i.e., the Spanish (January–June 2010) and Belgian (July–December 2010) presidencies. This attempt constitutes an innovative and unique opportunity to fully study the

J. Tuñón (✉)
Faculty of Social Sciences (Office 17.02.05), Department of Journalism and Communication, Universidad Carlos III de Madrid, C/ Madrid 133, 28903 Getafe, Madrid, Spain
e-mail: jorgetn@gmail.com

R. Dandoy
Université Libre de Bruxelles, CEVIPOL – CP 124 (Office S11.230), Avenue Jeanne 44, 1050 Bruxelles, Belgium
e-mail: rdandoy@ulb.ac.be

A. López-Basaguren and L. Escajedo San Epifanio (eds.), *The Ways of Federalism in Western Countries and the Horizons of Territorial Autonomy in Spain*, Vol. 2, DOI 10.1007/978-3-642-27717-7_22, © Springer-Verlag Berlin Heidelberg 2013

impact of the regions on the presidency of the Council of the EU (the next presidencies of the EU for Spain and Belgium are scheduled in 2023).

## Introduction

Much has been said around the introduction of the position of the president of the EU council once the Lisbon treaty has been ratified. The creation of this position and its mediatisation shadowed the fact that the system of the rotating presidency of the council will remain present and part of the institutional structures. Globally, the regions have a significant impact on the policies of the EU: directly and formally through the committee of the regions or due to their participation in the council or in the committees of the European commission, directly and informally through their representation offices in Brussels and their lobbying activities alone or joining and cooperating with other regions, or indirectly through the official mechanism and representation of their national state. The rotating presidencies are, in this regard, another opportunity for the regions to exert some influence on the European (and in some extent, national) policies.

This research intends to analyse the contributions of the regions to the various tasks and issues related to the presidencies of the European Union. The presidency constitutes for some regions a unique opportunity to give some light on their presence, main characteristics, and assets and to put their specific issues high on the political agenda. Regions from federal or highly decentralised states take the opportunity to emphasise during the presidency particular policies such as regional development, structural funds, culture and language, trade and education.

This article aims at analysing the factors that trigger or block the sub-national entities' participation within the rotating presidencies of the countries they belong to. Particularly, we will analyse the regional influence (and also the factors that promoted it) exerted by the 17 Spanish *Comunidades Autónomas* and the three regions and three communities in Belgium during the Spanish and Belgian presidencies in 2010. The comparative analysis will be used to identify the different organisational adaptations of the regional framework.

Indeed, our initial main hypotheses are twofold since the presidency constitutes for some regions a unique opportunity to give publicity on their presence, main characteristics, and assets and to put their specific issues high on the European political agenda: (1) the involvement of the sub-national entities is not equal, and thus some of them would be more directly and more importantly involved in the presidency process than others, depending on their autonomy, their size, or their wealth and (2) due to the high centralisation of the main political events in Brussels or in the capital city, regions should compensate the lack of visibility for their region and be more active in the organisation of so-called para-events (cultural events, conferences, seminars, etc.).

Through mainly an exhaustive events, codification and data collection (and also some interviews and key policy documents analysis), we will identify some common patterns of regional influence on the decision-making process in the Council of the European Union, on other institutions and bodies, and on the overall priorities of the EU. Furthermore, we will be able to compare across countries and across different types of regions. Indeed, all analysed regions are not equal in autonomy, demographic weight, specific culture and language, wealth, or even geographic location. All these variables will be included in a global explanatory model in order to fully grasp the sometimes diverging characteristics of each region of Belgium and Spain and their influence of the EU through the rotating presidency of the Council.

## Sub-state Mobilisation Within the Europeanisation Process

The regional phenomenon can be grasped through two different logics. We may distinguish the bottom-up one, on the one hand, and the top-down one, on the other hand. The first logic relational direction goes from the regional or sub-state level towards the state (regionalism); while the second logic goes, on the contrary, from the state towards the regional level (regionalisation). Both the *Third Level* and the *Multilevel Governance* theories should be also pointed out. Following the *Third Level* theory, the sub-national authorities enjoy a growing influence within the European model. In fact, their possibility not only to develop some of the capacities but also to reach a legal and political status within the EU institutional architecture has been recognised. Indeed, the *Third Level* concept refers to the sub-national entities' action and linkage within the EU framework, together with not only the first level (the European institutions) but also the second level (member states) (Tuñón 2009, p. 19). It is consequently not possible to deny the existence of this regional/third governance level and its influence, just below the member states and the EU. This level is often closer to the citizens and, most of the times, also more useful and efficient to carry out European policies. Therefore, the interaction between the *Third Level* and the (so-called) *Multilevel Governance* (MLG) leads to the fact that the European Governance is shared among different but interconnected levels and that the sub-national is the third one of them.

Hence, the EU appears as a new political dimension characterised by authority dispersion and competences shared among the different government levels. However, member states still play a predominant role in the European process. Nevertheless, they are obliged to confront with other actors that limit their action (Tuñón 2009, p. 21). The emergence of this MLG model (pioneered by Gary Marks 1993) is due to an extensive institutional building and decision-making (UE regions) reallocation process.

A well-known phenomenon within the comparative politics literature (since the 1990s) has also been the regional European activation. Hooghe (1995) first used the "sub-national mobilisation" concept, which has been regularly adopted by many other academics (for example, Claeys et al. 1998; Négrier and Jouve 1998; Keating 2004). It aimed to describe the performances of sub-national entities within the

European decision-making process. It was apprehended not only in its descendant dimension as mere "arenas" of European policies, but also its ascendant perspective seeking to become influential actors within the European process. Finally, Leonardo Morlino (Fargion et al. 2006), among others, contested this concept of sub-national mobilisation and proposed another concept: activation.

Through initiatives, actions, or decisions, the European regions seek to assure an active and visible presence at the EU level. It is impossible to deny that regions develop a vast European activation through different paths or mechanisms (Caciagli 2006, p. 220). The development of formal channels to involve the sub-national governments within the European decision-making process, the cooperation activities implemented within the interregional organisations framework (even outside the EU programmes), or the European regional offices set up in Brussels prove the European regional activation. These patterns constitute the sub-State reaction towards the new possibilities provided by the European framework: regional participation not only in the Committee of the Regions but also (to some extent) in the European Commission (through the *Comitology* system) and the Council of Ministers (Dandoy and Massart-Piérard 2005; Tuñón 2009).

Since the 1990s, the European sub-national entities have become conscious of the advantages offered by the increase of the access channels to the European Institutions. Regions realised the amount of influence they would be able to obtain within the design of European policies. Hence, regions have gradually established direct formulas to deal with Brussels, while they also have promoted non-direct or mediated—through their own states—mechanisms (Tuñón and Dandoy 2009; Tuñón 2010, 2011). Within the described framework, European regions cannot waste the growing participation opportunities offered by rotating presidencies to benefit from this mechanism. Regions are additionally allowed to give some light on their presence and to put their specific issues high on the European political agenda. Their member states are often being assisted in their tasks of organising the Council presidency, while many of them are perfectly ready to benefit from it and thus influence the EU decision-making process.

## The Rotating Presidencies of the Council of the European Union During 2010

One of the major changes introduced by the Treaty of Lisbon has affected the rotating presidencies model. From the political perspective, many have pointed out the loss of influencing and lobbying opportunities due to the Lisbon reform (Beke 2011; Bunse et al. 2011). Some analyst even stated that the rotating presidency lost relevance and visibility (Molina 2010, 2011). Indeed, the nominations of the Council President and the High Representative for Foreign Affairs and Security Policy and the setting up of the TRIO model threats at least erode the visibility and influence of the country holding the rotating presidency. Although a period of coordination and cohabitation between the rotating and the "permanent" presidencies might be needed, holding the rotating presidency still means "the possibility of exerting influence through, among other things, agenda-setting and external representation" (Bursens and Van Hecke 2011).

Traditionally, the rotating presidency of the Council of Ministers and the European Council never constituted an important issue among the European Union study literature. Among those who have dealt with the rotating presidencies, some have focussed on roles and functions attached to it (Schalk et al. 2007; Tallberg 2003, 2004, 2006, 2007) and others on influence or success from a multiple or single case-oriented perspective (Beach and Mazzucelli 2007; Bunse 2009; Elgström 2003; or Quaglia and Moxon Browne 2007). However, to date, there are no analyses of the participation, opportunities, visibility, or influence exerted by the sub-national entities within the rotating presidencies framework.

As it has been already been pointed out, the rotating presidencies constitute (also for the regions) an opportunity to set and manipulate the agenda, display initiatives, make broker agreements, show leadership, and/or represent the decision body vis-à-vis third parties (Bursens and Van Hecke 2011). Following the so-called Power of the chair theory (Tallberg 2006, 2007), "negotiation chairs generally benefit from privileged access to a set of important power resources, notably information and procedural control" (Tallberg 2007, p. 23).

Different analyses have pointed out from different perspectives many opportunities given by the rotating presidencies of the Council to exert—to some extent—some kind of influence; no hints have been found (to date) about the role of the sub-national entities. Within this context, the 2010 rotating presidencies of the Council have been held by both countries with federal or quasi-federal structures. The regional involvement in this process can be compared and contrasted. In addition, Spain and Belgium have been similarly affected by the implementation of the Treaty of Lisbon, on the one hand, and the worldwide economic crisis, on the other hand. Moreover, both countries have had to deal with relatively uncomfortable internal contexts. Indeed, the international economical crisis impact was harder in Spain where financial cuttings (even affecting the wages of the civil servants) in order to reduce the public debt were decided during the presidency. Nevertheless, internal situation in Belgium was not much better. The whole presidency had to be managed by a caretaker government since Belgian internal politics have prevented the formation of a federal government since June 2010 (Beke 2011).

Since visibility and political influence could be (more easily than usual) achieved, the sub-State entities of both Belgium and Spain have been involved in the process of the presidency of their State. Therefore, the next sections will analyse the degree of dynamism (exhibited by Spanish and Belgian regions and communities) in the organisation of presidency events: official political meetings, conferences organised by pressure groups, or cultural events, to name a few.

# Sub-state Participation During the 2010 Rotating Presidency

The rotating presidency of the European Union does not only mean exercising the formal presidency of ministers' meetings, but plenty of other events, activities, manifestations, etc., are also associated to this phenomenon. During the Spanish and Belgian presidencies (respectively January–June and July–December 2010), no less than 1,480 events specifically related to each individual presidency have been recorded.[1] These events were unequally spread over the two presidencies and covered various types of meetings (from European Council meetings to cultural events), various types of actors (from the UN representatives to local citizens associations or even individuals), and various issues (from foreign affairs to purely technical industrial processes).

Each event has therefore been coded into a category according to its type or its nature. Different categories have been distinguished. The three encompassing categories are the political meetings, the so-called non-political events and the cultural events. The first category consists in all political meetings organised by institutionalised actors and coded in subcategories, i.e., Council of Ministers meetings, European Council meetings, European parliament meetings, Permanent Representatives meetings, Officials and experts meetings, meetings with Third Countries, as well as informal meetings at the ministerial level. The second category of events regroups—under the label "Seminars and Conferences"— includes, mainly, the events organised by non-institutional actors (i.e., companies, lobbies, pressure groups, NGOs, universities, etc.) even in the presence of institutional or political actors, as well as scientific or vulgarisation conferences, workshops, seminars, forums, or congresses regarding specific aspects of the presidency and of the EU policies. The last category consists in various cultural events, such as exhibitions, museum collections, theatre, movies, concerts, dance performances, parties, etc.

In Table 1, we observe that the Spanish and the Belgian presidencies can be distinguished in terms of the amount of political meetings they organised. This type of meetings represents significantly more than the half of the Spanish presidency events, while it only accounts for 44.15 % of the total amount of events organised during the Belgian presidency. Variation is also observed as far as the number of seminars and conferences is concerned, but the country differences go into the opposite direction.

In Fig. 1, we observe a large variation of the absolute number of events organised per month. As expected, the months of January, July, and August witness fewer events than the other months due to the holidays at both EU and national levels. The same logic explains the small amount of events organised in December as the very last official meeting occurred on the 22 December 2010 (Coreper II

---

[1] The criteria for the event selection was either whether the event was organised directly in the framework of the presidency's activities, either whether it received the presidency "label" and was included in the official presidency calendar.

**Table 1** Number of Presidency events (per category)

|  | Spanish presidency | Belgian presidency | Total |
|---|---|---|---|
| Political meetings | 428 | 332 | 760 |
|  | 58.79 % | 44.15 % | 51.62 % |
| Seminars and conferences | 112 | 206 | 318 |
|  | 15.38 % | 27.39 % | 21.22 % |
| Cultural events | 156 | 166 | 322 |
|  | 21.43 % | 22.07 % | 21.76 % |
| Others | 32 | 48 | 80 |
|  | 4.40 % | 6.38 % | 5.41 % |
| Total | 728 | 752 | 1480 |
|  | 100.00 % | 100.00 % | 100.00 % |

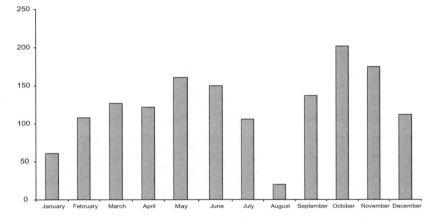

**Fig. 1** Number of Presidency events (per month)

meeting). The core moment of the Spanish presidency is therefore rather evenly spread over 5 months, while the Belgian one occurred for 3 months (from September to November), with a peak on October 2010 with no less than 202 events organised in the framework of the Belgian presidency.

Finally, the location of the events was included in the database (city–region–country), allowing us to investigate the degree of activism of the regional actors, compared to the one of the federal actors. In other words, we grasp the capacity of a political entity to organise presidency events by assessing the amount of events organised on its territory. We observe that the large majority of the events are taking place on the Belgian territory: 880 events, i.e., 59.5 % of all presidency events in 2010. No less than 600 events took place in other countries, among which 464 were in Spain (31.4 %). Surprisingly, only six events have been organised in Hungary, the partner country of both Spain and Belgium in the framework of the Trio Presidency.

**Table 2** Number of Presidency events organised in Spain and Belgium, per region

| Spain | N | Percentage (%) | Belgium | N | Percentage (%) |
|---|---|---|---|---|---|
| Andalucía | 56 | 12.10 | Bruxelles | 476 | 70.62 |
| Aragón | 11 | 2.38 | German-speaking community | 8 | 1.19 |
| Asturias | 11 | 2.38 | Vlaanderen | 107 | 15.88 |
| Balearic Islands | 11 | 2.38 | Wallonie | 83 | 12.31 |
| Basque Country | 7 | 1.51 | | | |
| C. Valenciana | 12 | 2.59 | | | |
| Canary Islands | 7 | 1.51 | | | |
| Cantabria | 3 | 0.65 | | | |
| Castilla la Mancha | 10 | 2.16 | | | |
| Castilla y León | 23 | 4.97 | | | |
| Catalonia | 37 | 7.99 | | | |
| Extremadura | 8 | 1.73 | | | |
| Galicia | 15 | 3.24 | | | |
| La Rioja | 1 | 0.22 | | | |
| Madrid | 245 | 52.92 | | | |
| Murcia | 3 | 0.65 | | | |
| Navarre | 3 | 0.65 | | | |

Among the 464 events organised in Spain and the 880 events in Belgium, no less than 1,138 of them could be related to a specific region. Missing data is due to the lack of specification on the exact location of the event or to the fact that events are sometimes simultaneously organised in more than one region. Distributing the events per region unsurprisingly confirms that the two capital regions attract the majority of the events: 476 events in Brussels and 245 in Madrid. As previously stated, the status of capitals of, respectively, Spain and Belgium and, in the latter case, of the seat of the European Union, explain to a larger extent why these events are organised in such regions. As shown in Table 2, the events organised outside these two regions mostly take place in Flanders (107 events), followed by Wallonia (83 events) and Andalusia (56 events).

In order to take into account the bias introduced by the events organised in the normal working of the EU institutions (Coreper meetings, plenary sessions of the European Parliament, etc.), as well as international events whose organisation does not rely on the rotating presidency, such as UN meetings, these events were removed from our database. This will help us not only to focus on purely Presidency events but also to potentially reduce the "capital region" bias, i.e., the fact that most of the events take place in Madrid and Brussels just because they are the capitals of each country. Assessing the relative role of the sub-national entities in the framework of the EU presidencies can therefore be done by limiting the analysis to such events.

Among these 1,231 non-institutionalised and non-routine events, the proportion of events organised outside the Spanish and Belgian territories is slightly larger even if cultural and economic events were poorly organised outside these two countries in the framework of the EU presidency. However, more interesting is the fact the share of events organised in the two capital regions (Madrid and Brussels) is smaller, with respectively 40.4 % and 61.1 % of all Spanish and Belgian events. The focus on solely non-institutionalised and non-routine events thus reinforces the presence and impact of the regions on the Presidency process.

Indeed, if we now want to test our hypothesis concerning the organisation of so-called para-events, we focus in this section only on the cultural events and on the "Conferences and Seminars" category. Results indicate that the two capital regions are still the most active during the Presidency in the organisation of such events: 42.8 % of all Spanish cultural and conference-like events were organised in Madrid, while 69.6 % were organized in Brussels in the Belgian case. The hierarchy of the most active regions is also not modified, as the two most active regions—after Madrid—are still Andalusia (13.19 %) and Catalonia (11.54 %). In Belgium, Flanders and Wallonia are relatively active in the organisation of such events with, respectively, 15.5 % and 12.8 % of all Belgian cultural and conference-like events. Differences with figures concerning the total number of events are not striking, and in this case, one cannot conclude that regions use cultural events and conferences and seminars as a way to balance the amount of political events organised in the capital regions.

In this last section, we integrate the different variables in a larger model in order to confirm our main hypothesis regarding the fact that stronger/larger regions use the Presidency as an opportunity and a tool for recognition. We operationalised the strength/size of a region in different ways: in terms of population (number of inhabitants), territorial size (number of square kilometres), density of population, wealth (GDP per capita), and constitutional autonomy (following the regional authority index built by Hooghe et al 2010). Among these size variables, only the population variable is proven to be significant with all Presidency events (correlation of 0.692**), with only non-institutionalised and non-routine events (0.689**) and with only cultural and conference-like events (0.667**). No other variable is significant, meaning that the size of a region, its wealth, or even its status of "special region" (as in the case of Catalonia, Basque Country, Galicia or Andalucía) does not play a role in the presidency process.

Finally, negative binomial regression models (Table 3) indicate that only one independent variable explains the number of Presidency events organised in one region. Confirming correlation figures, the population variable is significantly (and positively) related to the number of Presidency events. More events will be organised in more populated regions, independently of their size, their wealth, their degree of autonomy, or their constitutional status.

# Conclusions

Presidencies of the EU are unique opportunities for a country to demonstrate its capacity and skills chairing and organising the European arena. Besides this formal task of articulating the European debate, presidencies also allow various actors

**Table 3** Negative binomial
regression of the amount of
events

|  |  | Model |
|---|---|---|
| Regional variables | Status | 0.176 (0.122) |
|  | Size | 1.294 (5.054) |
|  | Population | 1.996** (4.857) |
|  | Density | −0.82 (0.114) |
|  | PIB | −1.416 (2.623) |
| Control variables | Country | 1.094 (0.4739) |
|  | Capital | 2.816** (2.816) |
|  | Constant | −0.723 (1.588) |
|  | Negative binomial | 0.041 (0.037) |
|  | Pearson Chi$^2$ | 25.575 |
|  | Log likelihood | −68.899 |
|  | Observations | 21 |

*Note*: *Significant at 0.05 level; **significant at 0.01 level

(political, socio-economic, academic, civil society, etc.) to express their voice and opinion or merely their existence. This article analysed the occurrence of the so-called presidency events by taking into account different variables. The collected data allowed us to evaluate the presence and dynamism of each political actor and policy level in the framework of the 12-month Spanish and Belgian presidencies. The conclusions are threefold.

First of all, this article intended to assess the involvement of sub-national actors during the presidency of the EU, compared to the one of national actors. The obtained results confirmed that the presidency still remains strongly on the hands of the national government and that the majority of the events are organised in the capital of the country. Even if Spain and Belgium witness a strong policy decentralisation and if their regions and communities enjoy a direct access to the EU decision-making level, these entities do not manage to strongly influence the presidency agenda, neither directly via the organisation of formal and informal political meetings nor indirectly via cultural and societal events.

Still, regions and communities form Spain and Belgium are relatively active during the presidency. Nevertheless, our results demonstrated that this degree of involvement varies according to the different sub-national entities. Some regions are much more active than others. Unsurprisingly, small entities such as the German-speaking community or La Rioja are relatively less active than others. Overall, large regions, such as Flanders, Wallonia, Andalucía, or Catalonia, hosted many presidency events. Besides country differences, the key variable allowing to differentiate the degree of activities between each region has been identified. Large regions in terms of population host more Presidency activities than other regions, independently of their wealth, status, degree of autonomy, etc.

Finally, EU presidencies are composed of a variety of organised events. These events can take the form of various formal and institutional political meetings such as Council meetings or European Parliament plenary sessions, as well as many other activities from seminar and conferences to numerous cultural events, such as exhibitions or concerts. Our results demonstrate that regions do not use these two latter types of events in order to compensate the lack of political visibility for their region. Strong regions manage, at the same time, to attract political meetings to be held in their region (for example, an informal meeting of the council of ministers), as well as a larger amount of cultural events and conferences, meetings, seminars, etc.

# References

Beach, D. & Mazzucelli, C. (eds.) (2007). *Leadership in the big bangs of European integration.* New York: Palgrave-Macmillan.

Beke, M. (2011). Review of the Belgian Rotating Presidency: From Political to Administrative Leadership. *ARI Working Papers*, 16/2011.

Bunse, S. (2009). *Small States and EU Governance. Leadership through the Council Presidency.* Basingstoke: Palgrave/Macmillan.

Bunse, S., Rittelmeyer, Y. –S. & Van Hecke, S. (2011). The Rotating Presidency under the Lisbon Treaty: From Political Leader to Middle Manager?. In S. Van Hecke & P. Bursens (eds.). *Readjusting the Council Presidency. Belgian Leadership in the EU.* Brussels: Academic and Scientific Publishers.

Bursens, P. & Van Hecke, S. (2011). The 2010 Belgian Presidency of the Council of the European Union: A framework for analysis. In S. Van Hecke & P. Bursens (eds.). *Readjusting the Council Presidency. Belgian Leadership in the EU.* Brussels: Academic and Scientific Publishers.

Caciagli, M. (2006). *Regioni d'Europa: Devoluzione, regionalismi, integrazione europea.* Bolonia: Il Mulino, 2nd edition.

Claeys, P. H., Gobin, C., Smets, I. & Winand, P. (eds.) (1998). *Lobbysme, pluralisme et intégration européenne.* Bruxelles: Presses Interuniversitaires Européennes.

Dandoy, R. & Massart-Piérard, F. (2005). The external action of autonomous regions in Europe, *ECPR Joint Sessions*, Granada, 14–19 April.

Elgström, Ole (ed.) (2003). *European Union Council Presidencies. A Comparative Analysis.* London and New York: Routledge,

Fargion, V., Morlino, L. & Profeti, S. (eds.) (2006). *Europeizzazione e rappresentanza territoriale. Il caso italiano.* Bologna: Il Mulino.

Hooghe, L. (1995). Subnational Mobilisation in the European Union. *Working Paper*, n° 95/6, Florence, European University Institute.

Hooghe, L., Marks, G., Schakel, AH. (2010): *The rise of regional authority. A comparative Study of 42 Democracies*, Oxford, Routledge.

Keating, M. (ed.) (2004). *Regions and Regionalism in Europe.* Cheltenham: The International Library of Comparative Public Policy. An Elgar Reference Collection.

Marks, G. (1993): *Structural Policy and Multilevel Governance in the EC.* In Cafruny, A. and Rosenthal, G. (coord): The State of the European Community. Boulder/Harlow.

Molina, I. (2010). Innovating Europe in troubles times: A first assessment of Spain's EU Presidency in 2010. *ARI Working Paper*, ARI 115/2010.

Molina, I. (2011). The Role of the General Affairs Council Revisited in Light of the Experience of 18 Months with the Lisbon Treaty. *ARI Working Paper*, 105/2011.

Négrier, E. & Jouve, B. (eds) (1998). *Que gouvernent les régions d'Europe.* Paris: L'Harmattan.

Quaglia, L. & Moxon Browne, E. (2007). What makes a Good EU Presidency? Italy and Ireland Compared. *Journal of Common Market Studies*, vol. 44 (2), 349–368.

Schalk, J., Torenvlied, R., Weesie, J. & Stokman, F. (2007). The Power of the Presidency in EU Council Decision Making. *European Union Politics*, vol. 8 (2), 229–250.

Tallberg, J. (2003). The Agenda-Shaping Powers of the EU Council Presidency. *Journal of European Public Policy*, vol. 10 (1), 1–19.

Tallberg, J. (2004). The Power of the Presidency: Brokerage, Efficiency, and Distribution in EU Negotiations, *Journal of Common Market Studies*, vol. 42 (5), 999–1022.

Tallberg, J. (2006). Leadership and Negotiation in the European Union. Cambridge: Cambridge University Press.

Tallberg, J. (2007). Bargaining power in the European Council, *Report n.1/2007*, Stockholm, Swedish Institute for European Policy Studies.

Tuñón, J. & Dandoy, R. (2009). El papel de las regiones en la actual Unión Europea. *Actualidad*, n.47, Fundación del Centro de Estudios Andaluces.

Tuñón, J. (2009). *La activación europea de las regiones legislativas. Análisis comparado de las estrategias de Canarias, Escocia, Toscana y Valonia*, Doctoral dissertation, Universidad Complutense, Madrid.

Tuñón, J. (2010). Regions. In I. Barlinska, B. Klandermans, K. Kosaka & M. Wieviorka (Eds), *Sociopedia*, International Sociology Association (ISA) and SAGE Publications.

Tuñón, J. (ed) (2011). *Escenarios presentes y futuros de las Regiones en la Unión Europea/ Current and Future Developments of the Regions within the European Union*. Sevilla: Fundación del Centro de Estudios Andaluces.

# Devolution in Scotland: A Historical Institutionalist Approach for the Explanation of Anglo-Scottish Relations

Simon Meisch

**Abstract** There is an implicit historical institutionalist agreement within academic literature on Scottish devolution: Institutions and history are relevant for explaining how the Scottish institutions evolved and how they shaped politics. However, there is disagreement on the question to what extent the devolution reforms, which started in 1997 and transferred powers from UK institutions to newly created Scottish institutions, form a real break with the previous institutional settlement. It is also criticised that studies on devolution highlighted the explanatory power of history, but without elaborating what they actually mean by history matters and without theorising on the issue.

My paper will address this criticism by discussing three different conceptual approaches and by suggesting an explicit historical institutional approach for the study of devolution. It provides a dynamic understanding of institution and combines the concept of path dependency and the theory of gradual change.

## Introduction

Within academic literature on Scottish devolution, i.e., the transfer of powers from UK institutions (Westminister Parliament, Whitehall) to newly created Scottish institutions (Scottish Parliament, Scottish Executive), it is warned that scholars of Scottish politics should take history seriously. It comes almost as a truism that today's political institutions are shaped by legacies from previous developments. In the case of devolution of Scotland, the establishment of the Scottish Parliament owes much to the evolution of the Scottish Office and the Scottish committee

S. Meisch (✉)
University of Tübingen, Internationales Zentrum für Ethik in den Wissenschaften (IZEW),
Wilhelmstraße 19, 72074 Tübingen, Germany
e-mail: simon.meisch@uni-tuebingen.de

A. López-Basaguren and L. Escajedo San Epifanio (eds.), *The Ways of Federalism in Western Countries and the Horizons of Territorial Autonomy in Spain*, Vol. 2, DOI 10.1007/978-3-642-27717-7_23, © Springer-Verlag Berlin Heidelberg 2013

system in Westminster, which themselves followed an institutional path (Mitchell 2003; McGarvey and Cairney 2008).

This paper argues that the claim that history matters in explaining institutional development has not been sufficiently elaborated theoretically. This observation can build on the academic literature itself. It was criticised that research avoided theorising and that the big post-devolution research projects did not advance the theoretical debate on the historicity of regionalism and multilevel governance in the UK (e.g., Bradbury 2003, 2006). At the same time, historians saw it as insufficient that political scientists highlighted the explanatory importance of history without elaborating this claim analytically and without finding appropriate methods to capture the dynamic nature of social processes such as devolution (Finlay 2001).

In my paper, I will address this criticism and suggest an explicit historical institutionalist approach. I will firstly use 'snapshots' from 1997 to 2012 in order to illustrate the multifaceted character of Scottish devolution that oscillated between institutional stability and change. A discussion of different approaches and schools within the academic literature (UCL Constitution Unit, 'Edinburgh school', 'Strathclyde school') will secondly reveal that the degree of institutional change and transformation is disputed. The 'Strathclyde school' also criticised that most studies on devolution do not spell out what they understand by 'History matters!' and that they lack a theory-driven approach. I will thirdly address this criticism and suggest a historical institutional approach that provides a dynamic understanding of institution and combines the concept of path dependency and the theory of gradual change. This paper aligns itself with the 'Strathclyde school' and aims to add to its analytical tools. Finally, I will give a short sketch on how political science studies on Scottish devolution could use this approach.

## Scotland and the Union: 'Snapshots' from 1997 to 2012

With regard to the Anglo-Scottish relations, the year 2007 was remarkable in many respects. First of all, it saw the 300th anniversary of the Union of Parliaments: The previously independent states of England and Scotland merged into an incorporating union and formed ever since the United Kingdom of Great Britain. Although this merger layed the foundation of today's UK, birthday celebrations were rather reserved. The Union that started with great expectations and was grounded on common and unifying projects such as the Empire, defending Protestantism against continental Catholicism, industrialisation and the welfare state seemed to have run into an identity crisis (Keating 2009: 45/6; Mitchell 2009; Devine 2004; Paterson 2000).

In 2007, the Labour landslide victory had its tenth anniversary. By introducing the devolution legislation in its first year, the Blair government started one of its great constitutional reform projects. For Labour, devolution was one of the core elements in modernising the British state and society and was meant to put the Anglo-Scottish union on a new and more legitimate ground. Retrospectively, the different devolution reforms (Scotland, Wales, Greater London) were characterised as 'the most radical constitutional change this country has seen since the Great Reform Act of 1832' (Bogdanor 1999: 1).

The 1997 devolution legislation gave Scotland its own parliament elected by an electoral system (Additional Member System) different to that used for UK general elections and a government accountable to this new parliament. With some matters reserved to Westminster, the Scottish parliament basically deals with all Scottish home affairs. Before 1997, Scotland was governed for more than a century by specific institutions within the British machinery of government. The executive in Scotland was exercised by a Cabinet member, the legislative by special parliamentary committees that dealt with Scottish matters. Departing from the UK norm, responsibilities within this system were defined along regional and not functional lines. Since the 1930s, this system was called 'Administrative Devolution'.

During the 1997 election campaign, George Robertson, Labour's Shadow Secretary of State for Scotland, famously stated that 'devolution will kill nationalism stone dead'. A Scottish parliament was intended to solve the so-called democratic deficit. Subsequent Conservative governments under Thatcher and Major progressively lost seats and votes in Scotland while winning the UK general elections. Being the party in government, the Conservatives appointed the Secretary of State for Scotland and pursued policies that were increasingly unpopular in Scotland. It was Labour's strategy to contain the arising national sentiment by devolution and channel it into support for a Scottish parliament. This was seen to be the unionist alternative to the SNP's 'Independence in Europe' (Stolz 2010; Finlay 2001).

In May 2007, however, George Robertson and those supporting his judgement were proven wrong. The SNP did not die. The party under its leader Alex Salmond won the third Scottish parliament election and formed a SNP minority government. For the first time within 50 years, Labour lost its position as the strongest party in Scotland. In the following years, the Nationalists succeeded in keeping Scotland's constitutional place in the UK on the political agenda. Shortly after forming a government, the SNP started its 'National Conversation' with the Scottish people on their constitutional preferences. It was clear from the outset that the SNP government favoured Scottish independence (Scottish Executive 2007: 38). The other parties (Labour, Conservatives and Liberal Democrats) responded to this challenge by setting up the 'Commission on Scottish Devolution'. Rejecting Scottish independence, the commission's remit was to

> review the provisions of the Scotland Act 1998 in the light of experience and to recommend any changes to the present constitutional arrangements that would enable the Scottish Parliament to serve the people of Scotland better, improve the financial accountability of the Scottish Parliament, and continue to secure the position of Scotland within the United Kingdom (Commission on Scottish Devolution 2009: 20).

In 2012, based on the recommendations of the 'Commission on Scottish Devolution', Westminster Parliament passed the Scotland Act 2012, transferring substantial fiscal powers from London to Edinburgh. Although this act again can be regarded as another milestone in the Anglo-Scottish relationship, it is eclipsed by other events: negotiations between the Scottish and UK government on a Scottish independence referendum. The 2011 Scottish Parliament elections produced a result that, according to the constitutional fathers and mothers of the 1997 devolution legislation, should have never happened. The SNP won a landslide victory, formed a single party majority government, and started legislating on an independence referendum held in 2014.

The 1997–2012 'snapshots' show many different aspects of Anglo-Scottish relations. On the one hand, there is much institutional stability. Kastendieck (2000: 82) once described the United Kingdom as the paradigm of a state whose constitutional development is characterised by continuity. Since the Union of Parliaments, the UK constitution witnessed organic growth and change. As special as it might have been, administrative devolution, the institutional settlement that determined Scottish politics for more than a century, grows out of British institutions.

On the other hand, the 'snapshots' also show a high degree of constitutional dynamics. The 1997 devolution legislation was seen as a constitutional milestone, and again the 2012 Scotland Act was described as yet another major constitutional reform (The Herald 2011). Still, only about 15 years after the devolution legislation that was meant to strengthen the Union, there might be a referendum on Scottish independence. While former unionist adversaries of devolution might feel confirmed in their view that devolution will actually prove a slippery slope to the break up of Britain, unionist resistance in 2012 seems to be quite mute (Stolz 2010: 7; Keating 2010; Hazell 2008).

Against the background of the multifaceted picture provided by the 1997–2012 'snapshots', my paper asks whether the 1997 reforms can be understood as the beginning of a new institutional path. As will be demonstrated in the next section, academic literature is divided on the question of continuity or discontinuity in the Anglo-Scottish relations. It is agreed that institutions play an important role in politics and that history in a specific sense matters. There is disagreement on the degree of autonomy of Scottish politics within administrative devolution and on the degree of change after 1997. It is also criticised that theory-driven analysis of devolution is lacking.

## Literature on Scottish Devolution

Academic literature on Scottish devolution can broadly be divided into three strands. There are two Scottish groups named after the home universities of most of its researchers, the 'Edinburgh school' and the 'Strathclyde school', and an English research group that is located at the Constitution Unit of the University College London (UCL) (McGarvey and Shepard 2002; Mitchell 2001).

The research focus of the London group on Scottish devolution is one from outside. It is interested in the whole of constitutional reforms initiated by British governments since 1997. Their main disciplinary background is political science and constitutional law. The London group continuously reviews, comments, and documents political events in public lectures and seminars, in reports and (edited) volumes. In the quarterly published 'Devolution monitoring reports' (1999–2005), they produced a rich and timely collection of material on political and legal aspects of devolution. As most research is done by a think tank (UCL Constitution Unit), the main focus does not lie on social science basic research but on policy advice. Its specific approach, however, resulted in works that stay close to politics of the day and that lack an explicit theory-led analysis of devolution. By focussing on potential conflict in the UK multilayer polity, it also tends to underestimate the degree of actual cooperation between Scottish and British actors.

The Scottish schools can basically be differentiated in two aspects. They disagree on (1) the degree of autonomy that Scotland had within the UK and (2) the degree of novelty that devolution brought about. Both schools also have a different disciplinary background. While the 'Edinburgh school' is more sociological in focus, the 'Strathclyde school' is based on the political sciences (McGarvey and Shepard 2002: 6; Mitchell 2001: 218).

The 'Edinburgh school' stresses both the large degree of autonomy enjoyed by Scotland within the UK political system pre-devolution and the successful political change post-devolution. As this school employs a wide understanding of politics, it analyses Scottish political institutions (Scottish Office, regional parliamentary committees, and related Scottish policy networks) within the wider context of Scottish civil society. The emerging picture is a 'world of dense Scottishness, which creates a feeling of natural allegiance in nearly everyone who has been brought up here, or who has lived here for an appreciable length of time' (Paterson 1994: 181). The Scottish institutions serve as evidence for Scotland's special place within the Union. Their role is seen to safeguard Scotland's national identity. The 'Edinburgh school' also highlights the degree of policy change that resulted from the post-devolution Scottish institutions. Special focus was given to (a) the intentions of the institutional reformers in the Scottish Constitutional Convention, which prepared the blueprint for the subsequent devolution legislation and (b) the degree to which these intentions materialised and thereby led to a more consensual style of politics and new policies.

The 'Strathclyde school' assesses Scottish pre-devolution autonomy and post-devolution change more sceptically. It acknowledges the importance of Scottish pre-devolution institutions within the political life in Scotland. However, it doubts that Scottish institutions really enjoyed autonomy in policy terms as politics was dominated by Westminster's and Whitehall's rules and procedures that did not allow for substantial deviation. Midwinter et al. (1991:82) graphically comment that the Scottish Office's scope of action consisted in 'persuading Cabinet or Cabinet committees to let it pursue a slightly different line tangential to, but not in conflict with, overall policy'. Adopting a historical institutionalist perspective, the 'Strathclyde school' analyses Scotland's post-devolution order with regard to institutional legacies and incremental change. In contrast to the 'Edinburgh school', it stresses political continuity with regard to institutions, politics, and policies.

Within the scope of this paper, a more detailed literature review cannot be provided. This short sketch intends to demonstrate that the academic literature intensely discussed the matter of institutional (dis-)continuity. All three research schools did focus on institutions and discussed their impact on policies or inter-institutional relations. While research related to Edinburgh and London tends to stress institutional change and novelty, those related to Strathclyde focussed on institutional continuity and incremental change:

> The post-devolution literature on Scottish politics has been predominantly focussed on change and difference. In doing so it has tended to neglect the significant degree of continuity and conformity that exists.' (McGarvey and Shepard 2002: 29) or 'From a research perspective the interesting question becomes not an explanation of change in Scottish politics but rather what explains continuity (McGarvey 2001: 432).

The 'Strathclyde school' criticises not only the focus on stability but also the lack of theory-driven political science research. According to McGarvey (2001: 428), 'students of Scottish politics are lacking a political-science-informed analysis of Scottish politics'. Building on and extending beyond that observation, Bradbury (2006: 559/60) calls for more theory-driven research: 'The challenge for UK political science is how to theorise the origins and development of these reforms. [. . .] Indeed, there is reluctance among many scholars to theorise the subject at all'. Mitchell (2001: 222) criticises that '[r]eference in many works is made, for example, to new institutional or multilevel governance but there is little effort to really engage with debate'. Studies of devolution should expand its search for analytical tools (Mitchell 2001: 222) and causal mechanisms (Bradbury 2003).

Over many years, social science literature has acknowledged the importance of history for understanding devolution (e.g., McCrone et al. 1992: 9; Mitchell 2003: 207; McGarvey and Cairney 2008: 16). Yet, a debate on the theoretical implications of this insight has not taken place. Bradbury (2006: 566) regrets that the great post-devolution research projects failed to advance theoretical debate on the historicity of the UK's regionalism and multilevel system. Historians also criticise social science studies on devolution for continuously referring to the explanatory power of history but without elaborating an appropriate methodology. According to Finlay (2001: 244/5), the (statistical) methods used are insufficient and explanations are too static to capture causal mechanisms for dynamic processes.

This paper shares the criticism of the Strathclyde school. I therefore want to suggest a way of capturing devolution as a process. Within the scope of this short paper, I will present a historical institutionalist research project that combines the concept of path dependency with the theory of gradual change. This approach will meet several challenges: (a) it analyses devolution as a process and (b) identifies causal mechanisms with the help of which it is possible to explain continuity and discontinuity.

# A Historical Institutionalist Approach to Devolution

By suggesting a historical institutionalist approach to devolution, the following section follows Streeck's (2009: 30) programmatic approach that a

> dynamic perspective on institutions and on the social world in general seems vastly preferable to a static one. A dynamic theory of society locates its objects in an irreversible flow of time, thereby recognizing their historical nature and uniqueness. Change appears both permanent and incremental, with the most important changes in human conditions related to or caused by the passage of time.

From this point of departure, a historical institutional approach shall provide a dynamic understanding of institution and combines the concept of path dependency with the theory of gradual change.

## *Institutions*

Generally, institutions are described as 'rules of the game in a society' (North 1990: 3) or as 'building-bock of social order' (Streeck and Thelen 2005b: 9). They represent socially sanctioned, i.e., collectively enforced expectations to the behaviour of social actors. By defining mutual rights and obligations, they define what is possible or impossible, appropriate or inappropriate, and good or bad. Thereby, social action becomes predictable and reliable. Institutions enable and restrict social action alike. They can be formal (constitutions, laws) or informal (conventions). Rules can be newly created in order to solve collective action problems or they are adopted from the past. In order to organise social action according to predictable and reliable patters, institutions have to be stable and formalised. However, they also have a dynamic side as their stability is the result of reproduction processes (Streeck and Thelen 2005b; North 1990; Mayntz and Scharpf 1995; Hall and Taylor 1996).

There has been a huge debate on the general issue of how stable institutions are and to what extent they influence behaviour. Streeck and Thelen (2005b) suggest an understanding of institution that is based on Max Weber's concept of 'political ruling organisation'. Defining institutions in this way solves many problems that emerge when applying the idea of institution to empirical cases: it becomes possible to integrate purposive-rational action, cultural influences, and power (asymmetries) into the description of institution.

According to Weber, an organisation has a defined membership, a set of rules, and a specific group of individuals who have the legitimate task of rule enforcement. Organisations can be distinguished by its ability to set its own rules and to choose its own leadership. In autonomous organisations, its members are able to establish the organisation's governing order, while in heteronomous organisation, the order is imposed from outside. The same applies to the selection of an organisation's leadership. If the membership is able to select its own leader and his staff, we speak of an autocephalous organisation; if the leadership is imposed from outside, it is a heterocephalous organisation. An organisation can be described as a ruling organisation 'insofar as its members are subject to domination by virtue of the existing order' (Weber 1978: 53). Three other terms from sociology of domination are relevant in this context: domination, discipline and obedience. Weber defines domination 'as the probability that certain specific commands (or all commands) will be obeyed by a given group of persons' and discipline as 'the probability that by virtue of habituation a command will receive prompt and automatic obedience in stereotyped forms, on the part of a given group of persons' (Weber 1978: 53). By obedience, Weber understands

> that the actions of the person obeying follows in essentials such a course that the content of the command may be taken to have become the basis of action for its own sake. Further-more, the fact that it is so take referable only to the formal obligation, without regard to the actors own attitude to the value or lack of value of the content of the command as such (Weber 1978: 215).

Beyond that, a *political* ruling organisation safeguards its existence and its order continuously 'within a given territorial area by the treat and application of physical force on the part of its administrative staff' (Weber 1978: 254). Weber admits that the use of physical force is neither the sole nor the most usual administrative method. However, he sees no chance to define a political ruling organisation by its ends, as organisations can serve all kinds of ends.

With regard to the ruling organisations, Weber distinguishes two social actions: political action and politically oriented action. The first type of action refers to actions of the ruling organisation itself, while the second one attempts 'to influence the activities of the political organization' (Weber 1978: 55). The character of a ruling organisation is hence determined by 'the mode in which the administration is carried out, the character of the personnel, the objects over which it exercises control, and the extent of effective jurisdiction' (Weber 1978: 54).

Methodologically, I follow Streeck and Thelen (2005b: 14/15) that defining an institution as a ruling organisation offers advantages for empirical research. First, the term institution becomes analytically more accessible because institutional relations can be captured as interaction between an organisation's leaders and members. Within a ruling organisation, there are different groups that try to influence the activities of the political organisation, to take over control, and to set those rules other members have to comply to. Second, interaction between different groups, as well as between members and leaders, determine the institution's content and development. Third, it can be distinguished between a rule and its enforcement. In this respect, membership discipline and the way of enforcing rules by the leadership becomes relevant. Fourth, an institution is embedded in a wider social context: being part of a wider (hierarchical) institutional web, it is also influenced by its own environment. Fifth, as ruling organisations are not defined by its ends, this definition is wide enough to include all types of possible institutions such as policies, political organisations, or corporations.

By defining institutions as ruling organisations, the tension between structure and strategic action can be reduced. Institutions are formalised rules that will be enforced (Streeck and Thelen 2005b: 10). Institutions are neither voluntarily agreed conventions to facilitate social action as long as actors take profit from it, nor are they mental or cognitive scripts that actors follow unconsciously. An organisation's leadership and staff will enforce rules when violated. Rule enforcement might then become the source of institutional stability and instability at the same time, as for many reasons there might always open up gaps between (the meaning of) a rule and its enactment. First, rules are never self-evident. They need to be interpreted, and a common understanding of a rule has to be continuously further developed. Second, rule setters can never predict all eventualities. Therefore, rules have to be adjusted. A reinterpretation can be facilitated if a rule possesses a certain degree of flexibility and ambiguity. Sometimes, rules are ambiguous as rule setters pursued multiple (and sometimes conflicting) ends. Furthermore, rule enforcement needs feedback about a rule's real effects. Third, membership discipline might decline due to incomplete socialisation, increasing costs of rule obedience, or decreasing legitimacy. Members might try to find loopholes or to change the effects of a rule in the course of its enactment. Organisation leadership then has to contain institutional border crossing. Fourth, rule enforcers might accept deviant behaviour in order to keep the rule flexible or to protect the institution. Thereby, different institutional interpretations might become accepted and legitimate.

In discussing the term institution with reference to Max Weber's concept of political ruling organisation, the foundations were laid for a dynamic understanding of institutions. In the next section, I will briefly elaborate that the notion of 'history matters' should be understood as taking institutional historicity and processuality seriously. Subsequently, both terms will be explained within the context of current theory debate.

## History Matters

An approach that claims that history plays an important role in explaining political phenomena such as Scottish devolution has to clarify how it uses the term history in the first place. I follow the historical institutionalist literature that highlights two aspects in particular: context and process. Historical explanations deal with real cases that can be located in time and space (Mayntz 2002: 9). According to Pierson, dealing with history in political science studies means 'recognizing that any particular moment is situated in some sort of temporal context – it is part of an unfolding social process' (Pierson 2004: 167). Placing social phenomena in a spatial and temporal context, and treating them analytically as processes (Mayntz 2009) can be regarded as a return to classical social science studies:

> Classical social science explored how the modern way of life grew out of the past, and what this might imply for the future. [...] In the writings of Marx, Durkheim and Weber – even in Adam Smith, and certainly in Schumpeter – static and dynamic analyses were inseparable: The way modern institutions worked was explained in terms of their location in a

historical process, while the way that process would continue was assumed to be driven by institutions' present functions and dysfunctions (Streeck 2009: 5)

In historical institutionalism, the term history neither implies that an object of studies is located in the past nor implies that social science studies use historical cases to illustrate abstract statements on politics or to generate more cases (Pierson 2004: 4/5; Pierson and Skocpol 2002). When we claim that history matters, we refer to two characteristics of social processes: historicity and processuality (Mayntz 2002). By historicity, it is expressed that past decisions influence present ones. In theoretical terms, we capture this by the concept of path dependency (Mayntz 2002: 27/28; Thelen 1999: 369; Pierson 2004: 153). Processuality refers to the dynamic character of social macro-phenomena such as institutions. Explanations that deal with that dynamics are interested in how and by what intermediate steps social processes evolve. While some processes might be unique, recurrent processes that link specified initial conditions, and a specific outcome can be described as social mechanisms (Mayntz 2004: 241). They are the kind of theoretical statements with regard to processuality.

As path dependency has become a well-known and often employed concept, I will keep its discussion to a minimum. Usually, an institutional path follows a specific analytical structure (Mahoney 2001: 5; Pierson 2004: 17–53). At the beginning, contingent factors determine available options that shape selection processes. During the so-called critical juncture, a particular institutional option is selected among multiple options. It is commonly assumed that the critical juncture is a moment of relatively low determination. While the selected option is subsequently reproduced, the alternative selection of a previously available option becomes less and less likely. Path reproduction is ensured by social mechanisms. Early concepts of path dependency assumed path stability to be so great that it could not be altered even if an alternative would have been better (lock-in). Change was thought possible only by an exogenous event. This view has been modified, and incremental change has been accepted as cause for path change or transformation.

In his work on path dependency, Deeg dealt with the question what a path actually is and concluded that a path is not identical with its constituting institutions. A path can be characterised by its special logic that is generated by the interplay of this constituents, i.e., 'typical *strategies*, *routine* approaches to problems, and *shared decision rules* that produce predictable patterns of behavior by actors within the system' (Deeg 2005: 172). Based on this definition, Streeck and Thelen describe a path as a meta-rule, 'governing the interpretation of a given structure of institutional constraints and opportunities – whose meaning [...] is never self-evident and therefore needs to be continuously constituted in practice' (Streeck and Thelen 2005b: 18).

This definition of a path fits to the dynamic understanding of institution and copes with some of the shortcomings in the early literature on path dependency. It was firstly criticised that the concept assumed enormous institutional stability and needed exogenous shocks to bring about path change. Secondly, the relationship between mechanisms that reproduce a path and those that result institutional change also remained unclear (Thelen 1999; Thelen 2003).

Reviewing the literature on path dependency, Beyer (2010) identifies social mechanism associated with path stability (increasing returns, sequences, function, complementarity, power, legitimacy, and conformity). He shows that in the course of reproduction, the same mechanisms can also effect path instability. Hence, institutional paths can become susceptible to path destabilisation by strategic action. This brings us back to our understanding of institution. The reproduction of an institution is never stable but the result of dynamic processes of rule enforcement. Depending on the type of reproduction, destabilisation of an institutional path is possible. Therefore, institutional change cannot solely be assumed to be a rare event triggered by external causes. However, knowing about possible ways of path destabilisation tells us neither when to find the right time for an intervention nor whether the intentions behind an intervention will materialise (Beyer 2010: 9).

Criticism of path dependency was not only directed to the (as we have just seen) wrongly assumed hyperstability but also to the open relationship of mechanisms of reproduction, on the one hand, and change, on the other. Within the theory of gradual change, many scholars tried to link mechanisms of path reproduction to specific mechanisms of institutional change (Streeck and Thelen 2005a; Mahoney and Thelen 2010a). They elaborated an analytical framework with the help of which it becomes possible to identify and explain types of institutional change. Within this framework

> the characteristics of both the political context and the institutions in question together drive the type of institutional change we can expect. Political context and institutional form have these effects because they shape the type of dominant change agent that is likely to emerge and flourish in any specific institutional context, and the kinds of strategies this agent is likely to pursue to effect change (Mahoney and Thelen 2010b: 15).

So far, the literature on gradual institutional change has identified five types of gradual institutional change: displacement, layering, drift, conversion, exhaustion (Streeck and Thelen 2005b: 31). Again, this framework is built on a dynamic understanding of institution: Institutional rules have to be enforced, and there might open up a gap between a rule and its enforcement. Depending on the political context and institutional characteristics, different types of institutional change will be likely. Expected change depends, for instance, on the veto possibilities available to defenders of the status quo or on the level of discretion in the interpretation or enforcement of an institutional rule. Finally, different types of actors can be distinguished according to their strategic interest (long term and short term) in an institution (Mahoney and Thelen 2010b).

In the previous section, it was sketched both how I understand the term history and how I analytically use the historical institutionalist claim and catchphrase 'History matters!'. A historical social science study locates its object of study in a specific temporal and spatial context. History effects institutions in two ways: (a) present political decisions are influenced by past ones, and (b) (even apparently stable) institutions are reproduced by social processes. Built on these observations, causes of institutional stability were linked to causes of institutional change, types of institutional change, and change agents. In the last section, I will sketch how to study devolution within this framework.

## Adopting the Historical Institutionalist Approach: Placing Devolution in Time

So far, I illustrated with the help of the 1997–2012 'snapshots' that devolution has been a process with long periods of stability that came to an end in 1997, when the Blair government introduced its devolution legislation. It was also shown that (a) the academic literature is divided over this issue whether devolution really marked an institutional change and that (b) the 'Strathclyde school' criticised the reluctance to engage in theory-driven studies of devolution. This paper aligns itself with the 'Strathclyde school' and aims to contribute to its methodology by suggesting a historical institutional approach that allows theorising on devolution and unfolding how history matters within this process.

The first step would be to identify the institutional setting in question. One would therefore have to describe the political ruling organisation pre- and post-devolution. In the academic literature, they are called administrative (pre-1997) and legislative (post-1997) devolution (Münter 2005: 31–35). However, both have to be treated as dynamic orders as both faced (from time to time) considerable change. One can argue about the extent to which the Scottish ruling organisation has become more autonomous. However, it is obvious that it became autocephalous in the sense that it is able to select the organisation's (executive and legislative) leadership. In an approach that deliberately puts emphasis on strategic action, this will be an important aspect.

The second step would place devolution in a dynamic context. Analytically, this means that we have to identify the logic of an institutional path and the social mechanisms that the production is based on. From this, we can deduce ways of institutional destabilisation, types of change, and change agents.

Many studies on devolution agree that there has been a Scottish institutional path called 'Administrative Devolution' and that the creation of the Scottish Office can be seen as an important critical juncture (e.g., Mitchell 2003; Bulpitt 1983). Some studies focus on other critical junctures (e.g., Münter 2005). However, path dependency was more used as a metaphor than as an analytical concept. A historical-institutionalist research project identifies the logic of the institutional path and those mechanisms responsible for path reproduction. By applying the theory of gradual change, it assesses whether transformative moments on the way (e.g., creation of the modern Scottish Office in the 1930s) can be explained with the same social mechanisms. Such a project also links mechanisms of reproduction to mechanisms of change. The analysis aims to give a dynamic picture of devolution that places Scottish institutions within a wider context (e.g., development of Westminister and

Whitehall systems) and within other social processes (e.g., socialisation of political elites, nationalism). Though I agree with the 'Strathclyde school' that the 1997 institutional settlement can be traced back to the pre-devolution settlement, I argue that 1997 can be understood as a critical juncture.

Analysing Scottish devolution with the suggested approach takes up and addresses criticism and proposals for improvement voiced within the UK literature. However, it can also be transferred to the study of other multilevel systems.

# References

Beyer, Jürgen: The Same or not the Same – On the Variety of Mechanisms of Path Dependence. In: International Journal of Social Sciences 5 (2010), pp. 1–11.

Bogdanor, Vernon: Devolution in the United Kingdom. Oxford 1999.

Bradbury, Jonathan: Territory and Power Revisited: Theorising Territorial Politics in the United Kingdom after Devolution. In: Political Studies 54 (2006), pp. 559–582.

Bradbury, Jonathan: The political dynamics of sub-state regionalisation. A neo-functionalist perspective and the case of devolution in the UK. In: British Journal of Politics and International Relations 5 (2003), pp. 543–575.

Bulpitt, Jim: Territory and Power. An Interpretation. Manchester 1983.

Commission on the Scottish Constitution: Serving Scotland Better: Scotland and the United Kingdom in the 21st Century. Final Report (June 2009). Edinburgh 2009.

Deeg, Richard: Change from Within: German and Italian Finance in the 1990s. In: Beyond Continuity. Institutional Change in Advanced Political Economies, ed. by Streeck, Wolfgang; Thelen, Kathleen. Oxford 2005, pp. 169–203.

Devine, Thomas: Scotland's Empire, 1600–1815. London 2004.

Finlay, Richard: Does History Matter? Political Scientists, Welsh and Scottish Devolution. In: Journal of 20th Century British History 12 (2001), pp. 243–250.

Hall, Peter A.; Taylor, Rosemary C. : Political Science and the Three New Institutionalisms. In: Political Studies 44 (1996), pp. 936–957.

Hazell, Robert: The Acts of Union – the next Thirty Years. Sunningdale Accountability Lecture (29.1.2008). Online: http://www.ucl.ac.uk/spp/people/robert-hazell/Accountability_Lecture. pdf (13.5.2012).

Kastendieck, Hans: Verfassungskritik und Verfassungsreform in Großbritannien. In: Politische Studien 51 (2000), pp. 82–97.

Keating, Michael: Scottish independence. In: Ten Years of Devolution in the United Kingdom. Snapshots at a Moving Target, ed. by Stolz, Klaus. Augsburg 2010, pp. 110–128.

Keating, Michael: The Independence of Scotland. Self-governing and the Shifting Politics of Union, Oxford 2009.

Mahoney, James: Path Dependence and Political Regimes in Central America. Baltimore; London 2001.

Mahoney, James; Thelen, Kathleen: Explaining Institutional Change. Ambiguity, Agency, and Power. Cambridge 2010a.

Mahoney, James; Thelen, Kathleen: A Theory of Gradual Institutional Change. In: Explaining Institutional Change. Ambiguity, Agency, and Power, ed. by Mahoney, James; Thelen, Kathleen. Cambridge 2010b, pp. 1–37.

Mayntz, Renate: Kausale Rekonstruktion: Theoretische Aussagen im akteurzentrierten Institutionalismus. In: R.M.: Sozialwissenschaftliches Erklären. Probleme der Theoriebildung und Methodologie. Frankfurt/Main; New York 2009, pp. 83–97.

Mayntz, Renate: Mechanisms in the Analysis of Social Macro-Phenomena. In: Philosophy of the Social Sciences 34 (2004), pp. 237–259.

Mayntz, Renate: Zur Theoriefähigkeit makro-sozialer Analysen. In: Akteure – Mechanismen – Modelle. Zur Theoriefähigkeit makro-sozialer Analysen, ed. by Mayntz, Renate. Frankfurt/ Main; New York 2002, pp. 7–43.

Mayntz, Renate; Scharpf, Fritz W.: Der Ansatz des akteurszentrierten Institutionalismus. In: Gesellschaftliche Selbstregulierung und politische Steuerung, ed. by Mayntz, Renate; Scharpf, Fritz W. Köln 1995, pp. 39–72.

McCrone, David; Kendrick, Steve; Straw, Pete: Introduction: Understanding Scotland. In: The Making of Scotland. Nation, Culture and Social Change, ed. by McCrone, David; Kendrick, Steve; Straw, Pete. Edinburgh 1992, pp. 13–30.

McGarvey, Neil: New Scottish politics, new texts required. In: British Journal of Politics and International Relations 3 (2001), pp. 427–444.

McGarvey, Neil; Cairney, Paul: Scottish Politics. An Introduction. Basingstoke 2008.

McGarvey, Neil; Shephard, Mark: Policy Outputs in Scotland: Devolution or Duplication? Paper presented to the Political Studies Association Annual Conference, University of Aberdeen, 5–7 April 2002. Online: http://www.psa.ac.uk/journals/pdf/5/2002/mcgarvey.pdf (13.5.2012).

Midwinter, Arthur; Keating, Michael; Mitchell, James: Politics and Public Policy in Scotland. Basingstoke 1991.

Mitchell, James: Devolution in the UK. Manchester 2009.

Mitchell, James: Governing Scotland. The invention of Administrative Devolution. Basingstoke 2003.

Mitchell, James: The Study of Scottish Politics Post-Devolution: New Evidence, New Analysis and New Methods? In: West European Politics 24 (2001), pp. 216–223.

Münter, Michael: Verfassungsreform im Einheitsstaat. Die Politik der Dezentralisierung in Großbritannien. Wiesbaden 2005.

North, Douglass C.: Institutions, Institutional Change and Economic Performance. Cambridge 1990.

Paterson, Lindsay, Scottish Democracy and Scottish Utopias: The First Year of the Scottish Parliament. In: Scottish Affairs 33 (2000), pp. 45–61.

Paterson, Lindsay: The Autonomy of Modern Scotland. Edinburgh 1994.

Pierson, Paul; Skocpol, Theda: Historical Institutionalism in Contemporary Political Science. In: Political Science. The State of the Discipline, ed. by Katznelson, Ira; Milner, Helen. Washington, DC 2002, pp. 693–721.

Pierson, Paul: Politics in Time. History, Institutions, and Social Analysis. Princeton; Oxford 2004.

Scottish Executive: Choosing Scotland's Future. A National Conversation. Edinburgh 2007.

Stolz, Klaus: Devolution – A Balance after Ten Years. In: Ten Years of Devolution in the United Kingdom. Snapshots at a Moving Target, ed. by Stolz, Klaus. Augsburg 2010, pp. 6–11.

Streeck, Wolfgang: Institutions in History. Bringing Capitalism Back In: MPIfG Discussion Paper 09/8, Köln 2009.

Streeck, Wolfgang; Thelen, Kathleen (ed.): Beyond Continuity. Institutional Change in Advanced Political Economies. Oxford 2005a.

Streeck, Wolfgang; Thelen, Kathleen: Introduction: Institutional Change in Advanced Political Economies. In: Beyond Continuity. Institutional Change in Advanced Political Economies, ed. by Streeck, Wolfgang; Thelen, Kathleen. Oxford 2005b, pp. 1–39.

The Herald: Commons clears transfer of powers (28.1.2012).

Thelen, Kathleen: Historical Institutionalism in Comparative Politics. In: Annual Review of Political Science 2 (1999), pp. 369–404.

Thelen, Kathleen: How Institutions Evolve. Insights from Comparative Historical Analysis. In: Comparative Historical Analysis in the Social Sciences, ed. by Mahoney, James; Rueschemeyer, Dietrich. Cambridge 2003, pp. 208–240.

Weber, Max: Economy and Society. An Outline of Interpretive Sociology. Berkeley 1978.

# Part II
# The Management of Diversity: Canada and Spain

# Reflections on Diversity in Canada: Competing Models

**Richard Simeon**

Canada and Spain, along with just a few others such as the UK and Scotland, are perhaps pioneering new models of the post-Westphalian state.

We are two binational, multinational, or plurinational polities (Gagnon and Tully) seeking both independence and autonomy for minority nations and for effective relations between them and their surrounding majorities.

Relations between Canada and Quebec have been the dominant division in Canada since its inception. However, several other dimensions of difference are also critical for understanding Canadian politics and the management of diversity. First, Canada is a settler society, and relations between the majority and the Aboriginal peoples remain a central concern. Second, regional differences from East to West play out continually in differing political economies, party politics, elections, and adversarial intergovernmental relations. Third, while Canada has always been an immigrant society, recent waves of immigration have made recognition and integration of newcomers of central concern. Each of these dimensions of difference raises somewhat different concerns and is played out in different institutions, policies, and practices.

This chapter outlines how Canadians have recognized, accommodated, and managed these multiple diversities.

Then I want to turn to what is a common theme in divided societies like ours—the differing understandings, interpretations, and evaluations of institutions and processes that are manifested by the different constituent groups. There is no single narrative to tell for Canada and Quebec—or for the United Kingdom and Scotland or for Spain and Catalonia or the Basque country. Majorities and minorities often interpret the same set of facts in quite different ways.

In the Canadian case, the majority often thinks of itself as generous, tolerant, and accommodating to minority nations and groups, even as they emphasize the need

R. Simeon (✉)
Department of Political Science, University of Toronto, Smith Hall, 100 St. George Street,
Toronto, ON, Canada M5S 3G3,
e-mail: richard.simeon@utoronto.ca

A. López-Basaguren and L. Escajedo San Epifanio (eds.), *The Ways of Federalism in Western Countries and the Horizons of Territorial Autonomy in Spain*, Vol. 2, DOI 10.1007/978-3-642-27717-7_24, © Springer-Verlag Berlin Heidelberg 2013

for unity. Nevertheless, the minorities often feel that the majority's responses are grudging, reluctant, condescending, and insufficient. I want to explore this tension as it plays out in Canada.

A number of colleagues, on both ides of the linguistic divide, have joined this discussion, including two who are represented in this volume, Alain Noel and Guy Laforest. (See also Gagnon, Rocher.)

## Plurinational Canada: French and English

First, Canada is a multinational federation: Quebec and English Canada.

Both these are socially constructed concepts. Indeed, Canada would simply not exist without a bargain between French and English, which was embodied in the Constitution Act, 1867 (originally the British North America Act, which was an Act of the British Parliament rather than a formal constitution). Not until 1982 was Canada fully and unequivocally sovereign.

Nonetheless, there were competing conceptions of Confederation from the start. Was it a confederal 'compact' between formerly autonomous nations, a true federation of equal partners, or a vehicle for central government dominance? Each interpretation had support in the text of the BNAA—and in the views of different participants.

Today's binational Canada had its origins in the European wars between France and Britain that resulted in the British capture of France's North American possessions, including most of what is now Canada, in 1749. The British agreed[1] that Quebec was to be permitted to keep its French language, its Catholic religion, and its civil law legal tradition, setting a pattern of compromise that remains an important legacy.[2]

Nevertheless, tensions remained high, and following abortive rebellions in both French and English Canada, a British Commissioner, Lord Durham, was sent to investigate. Finding 'two nations warring in the bosom of a single state', his solution was assimilationist: the two colonies would be merged into one, where the British majority and British values and practices of parliamentary government were expected to prevail, along with responsible government on the British parliamentary model. Instead, the United Province of Canada, created in 1840, quickly became a classic consociational system, with equal representation of the two linguistic communities, dual ministries and bureaucracies, and mutual vetoes on key matters. Nonetheless, soon the rapid growth of the English-speaking population in Canada West made the equal representation of the two groups in a single unit unworkable. English-speaking Canada West now called for 'representation by

---

[1] Partly because they were worried that the French Canadians might support the increasingly rebellious American colonies to the south.

[2] Catholicism was outlawed in Britain at the time.

population', while Francophones in Canada East worried about being outnumbered and voted by the Anglais.

The answer, led by strong leaders on both sides—Sir John A. Macdonald and Georges-Etienne Cartier—was to follow the US model and to reconstitute the relationship as a federation that would eventually incorporate the remaining British colonies in North America.

John A. Macdonald was confident that Canada would soon evolve into close to a unitary state—and indeed, the BNAA contained important provisions (such as the federal power to 'disallow' any provincial legislation) that implied federal dominance. However, political resistance from Quebec and other provinces in Canada and a series of judicial decisions changed the direction, and by the 1920s Canada looked like a classical federation.

The Great Depression of the 1930s and the Second World War altered the direction once again. Several provinces were unable to cope with the financial crisis and looked to Ottawa for help. Then the conduct of war further concentrated power in Ottawa. In the postwar period, it was federal financial resources and political leadership that underpinned the development of the modern welfare state. Most of the constitutional authority for social policy lay with the provinces. Nevertheless, through a combination of transfers of power to the federal government (unemployment insurance and pensions) and the use of federal funds (the 'spending power'), the basic building blocks were put in place. These developments had broad support in English Canada but were bitterly resisted by the conservative, Catholic government of Quebec, both on cultural and religious grounds and because of its undermining of Quebec autonomy.

However, powerful forces driving modernization, democratization, and secularization were at work in Quebec, fundamentally challenging the conservative, Catholic, rural and antimodern ideology that had dominated the province for decades. In the 1950s and 1960s, the 'Quiet Revolution' led to the emergence of a progressive, secular, Quebec nationalism and to the call for greater political autonomy—a movement strongly reminiscent of events in other conservative and Catholic countries such as Spain and Ireland at much the same time. Nationalism was now less a matter of preserving a Catholic Quebec than preserving the predominance of the French language. Quebec embraced the modern welfare state, but now it would be *maîtres chez nous*.

From the late 1960s, Quebec nationalism took an increasingly independantiste turn. The *Parti Quebecois* was formed in 1968. It was dedicated to independence for Quebec, along with an 'association' or 'partnership', with the remaining Canada. It won its first provincial election in 1976 and has alternated in power with the provincial Liberals since then. Its orientation has been social democratic, unlike earlier manifestations of Quebec nationalism. It was joined by the *Bloc Quebecois*, promoting the same program at the federal level, in 1990. In 1993, the BQ won 54 of Quebec's 75 parliamentary seats and briefly formed the Official Opposition in the central government. It continued to hold the majority of Quebec's federal seats until it was decimated in the 2011 federal election.

From 1979 until 1992, Canadians engaged in an intense process of constitutional negotiation seeking a new accommodation between Quebec and the rest of Canada. Virtually, all Quebec participants in the debates sought greater autonomy for the province—the PQ calling for independence, the Liberals calling for more powers and constitutional recognition of Quebec as a 'distinct society' in which the government of Quebec had a special role beyond that of other provinces to preserve and protect the province. They also called for a greater share of the fiscal pie and for strict limits on the federal power to use its power to spend to shape areas of provincial jurisdiction. Quebec's 'traditional demands' also included formal representation from the Quebec bar on the Supreme Court of Canada and a voice in Canadian immigration policy and in the affairs of the international *francophonie*.

Responses to these demands took two main forms. The first was *accommodation*. In the 1960s, the federal Liberal government went a long way towards meeting Quebec's autonomist aspirations, accepting a large measure of de facto asymmetry (through not according it formal constitutional recognition) and transferring significant taxing powers. This approach was followed by that of Prime Minister Pierre Trudeau, a francophone Quebecer with a deep aversion to Quebec nationalism. His project was integrationist—recognizing the duality of French and English from coast to coast, strengthening Francophone representation in the central government and extending French language rights and services across the country. The argument was provincial equality, not special status for Quebec. His primary achievement was the 'patriation' of the Canadian constitution from Great Britain and enactment of the Canadian Charter of Rights and Freedoms in 1982.

This was widely supported outside Quebec but unanimously rejected by the National Assembly and government of Quebec because it provided so little in terms of powers and autonomy for the province and provided no recognition of Quebec's distinctiveness. The Charter also included affirmation of the 'multicultural' character of Canada, seen by some Quebecers as an attempt to shift the discourse from Quebec as a 'founding nation' to Quebecers as just another ethnic group in the Canadian mosaic. The accommodationist approach resurfaced when, in 1984, a new Progressive Conservative government, led by Brian Mulroney, came to power, promising to bring Quebec back into the constitutional family, 'with honour and enthusiasm'. The result was the 'Meech Lake Accord', an agreement among governments that did recognize Quebec's distinct role and responded to several other Quebec concerns. However, according to the rules for constitutional amendment adopted in 1882, the governmental agreement had to be passed in all the provincial legislatures. Massive opposition to the accord developed across Canada, in part because of the perceived special treatment for Quebec and also in response to public hostility at the elitist, closed-door nature of the intergovernmental process and the failure to respond to the constitutional concerns that had developed elsewhere, including recognition of the aboriginal right to self-government, and reform of the Senate to give greater weight to the smaller provinces, a matter of particular concern to western provinces.

Yet another attempt at finding constitutional agreement, the 'Charlottetown Accord', failed in 1992. It sought to build consensus by bringing Aboriginal representatives to the table, by discussing constitutional change such as Senate reform of interest to other parts of the country, and by seeking ratification through a national referendum. It too was defeated.

Thus, what Peter Russell describes as the 'constitutional odyssey' ended with a result satisfactory to no one. However, it was now clear that, given the rules for constitutional amendment requiring unanimity and given the deep divisions, formal constitutional change to resolve the issue was impossible. Perhaps more fundamentally, managing and balancing Canada's multiple differences were becoming increasingly difficult, and in a more democratic age, elite bargaining to deal with them was no longer legitimate.

Events then moved in rapid succession. The PQ in Quebec called a referendum on sovereignty, now linked to 'partnership', for November 1995. It came within a hairsbreadth of passage, losing by a mere 44,000 votes, from a turnout of almost five million voters. The result showed how unprepared both sides were to manage a secession or to deal with the multitude of complex questions that would follow. The federal government responded with a reference to the Supreme Court of Canada. It asked whether under the current constitution a Canadian province has a unilateral right to secession, under either Canadian or international law. The Court said 'no'. The constitution was silent on the matter and Quebec's claim for independence would not pass the international test because Canada was a functioning democracy and Quebecers were not an oppressed people. Nonetheless, the court added a critical proviso—that were a province to vote with a *clear majority* on a *clear question* for sovereignty, then the other governments would have a 'constitutional' obligation to negotiate the matter. In effect, the court had written a secession clause into the Canadian constitution.

The federal parliament then sought to preempt future discussion by passing the 'Clarity Act', which asserted that it would be the federal parliament that would determine if any future question was clear and if the majority (undefined) was clear. Quebec responded with its own legislation: It was for Quebec to decide the question, and 50 % plus one was a sufficient majority in a democracy.

Canadians now stepped back from the constitutional brink. They realized that major constitutional change was unattainable; attention now turned to a few incremental, non-constitutional reforms. In the 'Calgary Declaration' (1997) provincial governments recognized Quebec as a 'distinct society'; though this declaration had no political or legal consequences. In 2003, parliament recognized that 'Quebec constitutes a nation within a united Canada', an important statement but again without legal implications. Neither of this resulted from a national constitutional conversation, and few paid much attention.

Following the 1995 referendum, parliament also recognized 'regional vetoes', including Quebec, over any future constitutional amendments. More generally, the interest in constitutional change appears to have fallen sharply since the 1995 referendum. A significant proportion of Quebec society continues to support some form of sovereignty, but the passion and urgency have faded. More than ever, Quebec and the rest of Canada seem less interested in forging a consensus than in each living its own culture and society, with relatively little interchange between them. Even sovereignist Quebecers continue to retain a limited identification with Canada, as do most of their counterparts in Scotland.

## Regionalism

Canada is a highly regional federation. Many outside observers tend to see the fundamental Canadian debate as that between Quebec and Canada. Indeed, many Quebecers see it this way as well. They tend to think that Canadians outside Quebec see the federal government as the most important and identify with 'Canada', not their provinces.

The evidence simply does not support this.

There are nine other provinces and three territories. They vary hugely in size, wealth, economic structures, historical backgrounds, cultures, and even identities.

While not as strong as in Quebec, provincial identities and loyalties are strong. Provincial governments are powerful political actors, which see themselves as equal partners with the federal government, not as subordinate in any way.

Differences between the booming, resource-rich west of Canada, the declining industrial and manufacturing base of Ontario; and so on are fundamental to understanding Canadian federalism as it is currently developing.

There are fascinating links between the idea of a two-nation Canada and a ten-province Canada, with Quebec and the other provinces not only sometimes in tension but also often allies in their dealings with Ottawa.

Quebec's demands for more autonomy have provided a model for other provinces to follow. Their refusal to kowtow to Ottawa has, in turn, helped reinforce Quebec's bargaining power in the federation.

So, Canada is a profoundly federal society, and this fact has deeply shaped federal institutions and practices. Regional tensions have been constant in Canadian history, from the nineteenth century 'National Policy', which subordinated western resource producers to manufacturing, financial, and transportation interests based in Central Canada, to the present day. Indeed, economic pressures have recently greatly intensified regional tensions. With the global rise in commodity prices, especially for oil, gas, and potash, the provinces where these resources are concentrated (Alberta, Saskatchewan, and to a lesser extent Newfoundland and Labrador) have boomed. Ontario and Quebec, once the leading provinces economically, have seen their traditional manufacturing industries badly eroded, in part due to the rise in the value of the Canadian dollar, which results from the energy boom. In the westward shift, incomes are higher, unemployment is lower, and government revenues have dramatically increased. These provinces have virtually eliminated public debt and can impose lower taxes while maintaining services.

It is a different story in central Canada, faced with higher unemployment, higher taxes, and large debts, and deficits. The Canadian Equalization program, designed, as the Constitution says, to ensure each province the resources to provide comparable levels of public services at comparable levels of taxation, is now under serious strain, with no easy solutions in sight—especially as Ontario, once the largest and wealthiest province, is now itself a recipient of equalization.

Managing these tensions is made more difficult because of some larger features of the Canadian federal system. The first-past-the-post electoral system rewards political parties with regionally concentrated support. The result is a regionalized party system, in which important sections of the country can feel excluded from influence in Ottawa. This effect is accentuated by one-party rather than coalition government and by cabinet dominance combined with very strict party discipline that limits the ability of MPs to speak for their local constituents.

## Aboriginal Canadians

The territorially based divisions of region and language, inscribed in our institutions, are still not the whole Canadian story. Two other lines of diversity are critical. The first is deeply embedded in our history—the division between Europeans and native or Aboriginal peoples.

These peoples—most of them now living in the cities—are also scattered among many small 'first nations' across the country. They are a classic subordinated group, resonant of indigenous peoples in other settler societies, like the US, Australia, New Zealand, and some Latin American countries.

Some progress has been made recently with respect to recognizing traditional land rights and self-government, but the integration and accommodation of Aboriginal peoples remain perhaps Canada's greatest failure of accommodation. Rates of poverty, disease, poor housing, educational achievement, and suicide are much greater in aboriginal communities than among other Canadians.

## Multiculturalism

The final dimension of diversity to address is Canada's tradition of multiculturalism. Canada has, of course, been a country of immigrants from its first days. Since the 1970s, the country has embraced 'multiculturalism' as a fundamental defining feature of the country enshrined in the law and the constitution.

In proportion to the population, Canada accepts more immigrants than any other advanced country, close to one per cent of the population each year. These immigrants, once mainly European, now come from a wide variety of countries—China, South Asia, Africa, and others. The overwhelming majority settle in a few metropolitan areas—Toronto, Vancouver, and Montreal, though there is now movement to other cities like Calgary as well. A majority of the residents of Toronto, Canada's largest city are now foreign born.

Perhaps the most striking fact about all this is how little political tension has resulted.

Unlike the US and Europe, there is simply no organized political opposition to immigrants and immigration. Any politician who expressed such views would be condemned at once.

So we can argue that this is a huge Canadian success story. It is not that there are no tensions. In recent years, immigrants have been doing less well economically. Some worry that immigrant communities are living too much in isolated societies, with little exchange with the majority, or other groups.

Furthermore, there has been some debate about what we call 'reasonable accommodation'. To what extent are immigrants expected to adopt 'Canadian' attitudes and values? To what extent are they permitted and accepted to retain their previous cultures and practices?

This has expressed itself most forcefully in Quebec, where there has been nervousness about immigration. Multiculturalism, as espoused by Pierre Trudeau, was seen by some as an attempt to define Francophones as 'just another ethnic group'. Moreover, as the minority language, Quebec worried that migrants were more likely to assimilate to the Anglophone majority. It has therefore worked hard through its language and other policies to encourage them to integrate into the French language community, with some success, arguing that Quebec nationalism is language based and is a civic rather than an ethnic nationalism.

However, Quebec too retains a liberal attitude and has a major voice in national immigration policy, in order to ensure that a large proportion of newcomers to Quebec are from francophone countries in Africa and elsewhere.

Thus, perhaps more than most other countries, Canada manages multiple diversities and does so through a wide variety of policies and practices.

Nevertheless, it is the language division that has historically been the dominant cleavage, fundamentally shaping Canadian politics, from the start.

So let me turn to my other main theme. This is the difference between francophone and Anglophone interpretations and understandings of Canadian federalism, the chief means through which the language dimension is institutionalized. The broad understanding in English Canada would make some of the following points about the accomodation of linguistic difference in Canada:

- That since the Conquest—with many important exceptions—the rest of Canada has, in general, responded positively to Quebec's distinctiveness;
- That Quebec has been the primary driver of the exceptional degree of decentralization in Canada;
- That while it has not been achieved constitutionally, Quebec benefits from a very high degree of distinctiveness and non-constitutional asymmetry;
- That Quebec has continued to exert a high degree of influence in central government institutions—in the postwar period, Prime Ministers St Laurent, Trudeau, Mulroney, Martin, and Chretien were all Quebecers;
- That the underrepresentation of Quebecers in senior positions in the federal cabinet and civil service documented in the 1960s has been corrected;

- That the economic disadvantages of Francophones in business and incomes, again fully documented by a Royal Commission in the 1960s, have also been reversed;
- That English Canadians—contrary to the views of some Quebec scholars who believe that they identify most strongly with the federal government—are highly committed federalists, with deep national and provincial identities. They may define Elazar's shared rule and self-rule a little differently from Quebecers, but they believe it deeply.

More generally, some would argue that far from being a failure, membership of Quebec in the federation has not been the straitjacket that former Premier Rene Levesque called it. What is most remarkable is the success of the Quiet Revolution and of the Quebec nation-building project since the 1960s:

- Quebec has been free to develop a powerful set of policies to protect and enhance the Francophone character of the state.
- It has been free to develop a set of highly progressive social policies that should be the model for Canada.
- It has been free to develop a distinctive set of economic and industrial policies, sometimes known as 'Quebec Inc'.

Even deeper than that, in culture high and low, in civil society and other nongovernmental areas, Quebec and Quebecers demonstrate dynamism, a confidence, a liveliness, and sense of control of their lives that is powerful testimony to the virtues of provincial autonomy and decentralized federalism.

In this context, an Anglophone observer like this writer might wish to say that the Quebec nation-building project has been a huge success.

Quebecers argue a different interpretation. For them, the Conquest of 1749, followed by the largely Anglophone development of Canada, remains a historical legacy not to be ignored. In the present, despite all the demands, the rest of Canada has failed to recognize the distinctive character of Quebec and the role of the provincial government in preserving and promoting that distinctiveness in the constitution. That Quebec remains a French-speaking minority in an Anglophone ocean, moreover a province with a declining proportion of the total Canadian population, and this of influence in Ottawa. Indeed some argue that the result of the 2011 election, in which a majority Conservative federal government was elected with only a few seats from Quebec, is an omen for the future. If Canadian politics from 1960 to 1990 was dominated by the search for accommodation with Quebec, it can be argued that the next decades will be dominated by the search for accommodation between eastern and western Canada and between native-born and immigrant Canadians.

In conclusion, I have concentrated on the tensions and conflicts in French–English relations.

This should not obscure the successes we have made together. First among these is our mutual tolerance. We have managed to debate secession—breakup of the country in the eyes of English-Canadians—peacefully and democratically over a long period. With one important exception, in 1980, there has been only one outbreak of violence and one instance of state repression in this period.

Second, one could argue that the alliance between Quebec and the rest of Canada is a central factor in Canada's ability to remain independent of the United States.

Third, one can argue that Canada has been exemplary in integrating a multicultural society.

Fourth, one can argue that justice and equality for Aboriginal peoples have been our greatest weakness.

Alain Gagnon, a Quebec scholar with whom I do not always agree, were able to jointly write a history of Canadian federalism, in which we could find agreement that what distinguished Canada is that it is deeply committed to negotiating difference; we are a 'negotiated country' from its very beginnings in the encounter between French fur traders and fishermen. Balancing and negotiating difference and diversity are never easy.

We will still come to different conclusions. It is unclear whether such differences—normative and empirical—can be resolved by evidence and analysis or whether they are matters of a priori belief, not subject to evidence, and rooted in the historical legacies that both groups have inherited.

First, outside observers, and perhaps many Quebec nationalists, appear to believe that the Canada story is a French–English story.

That is not true. Canada is a highly regionalized country.

# Trust and Mistrust Between Harper and Québec

**Guy Laforest**

## Introduction

I will explore in this paper the complex and evolving relationship of trust and mistrust between Stephen Harper, the current federal Prime Minister of Canada, first elected in 2004 and reconducted in power with a majority government on 2 May 2011, and Québec. Trust and mistrust are already complex affairs for contemporary Political Science and federalism studies. I will make them even more complex by considering qualitatively and quantitatively different partners in the relationship: one human being, who happens to be the most important political leader of a sophisticated federal democracy, and a geographical entity, which happens to be a distinct national society in this federation. Québec here, for the purposes of this paper, will encompass the following realities: the province of Québec, Québec francophones, Québec nationalism and Québec nationalists, and finally, the political leaders of Québec—I will essentially refer here to the current Premier of Québec, Mr. Jean Charest, in power since 2003. Although trust is relational, and requires levels of reciprocity, I shall look at this phenomenon mostly from the perspective of Mr. Harper himself, exploring his political and intellectual trajectory. I will altogether not completely ignore the other perspective, which can be glimpsed for instance by the electoral fortunes of Mr. Harper in Québec at federal elections since 2004, but my focus will remain on the factual, historical, and perceptual elements that, taken together, have shaped Mr. Harper's cognitive perspective on Québec, leading over time to various degrees of trust and mistrust.

The paper will start with an exploration of these two primary concepts, trust and mistrust, in contemporary Political Science literature. It will then proceed to critically assess Mr. Harper's intellectual and political trajectories, concentrating with the dimensions that relate to Québec, as previously and broadly characterized.

G. Laforest (✉)
Department of Political Sciences, Université Laval, Québec City, QC, Canada G1K 7P4
e-mail: Guy.Laforest@pol.ulaval.ca

A. López-Basaguren and L. Escajedo San Epifanio (eds.), *The Ways of Federalism in Western Countries and the Horizons of Territorial Autonomy in Spain*, Vol. 2, DOI 10.1007/978-3-642-27717-7_25, © Springer-Verlag Berlin Heidelberg 2013

This part will be further divided in three subsections: 1986–2005, 2005–2008, and 2008–2012. In the conclusion of the paper, I wish to explore some alternatives for the future concerning the relationship between Harper and Québec, and I may try to adventure myself in comparative waters, particularly those of Spain, in the aftermath of the Spanish general elections of 20 November 2011, which led to the formation of a new majority Partido Popular government led by Mariano Rajoy.

## Some Reflections on Trust and Its Derivatives

Until recently, Political Theorists have been rather neglectful of the concept of trust, although this very idea is quite central in John Locke's liberal philosophy of sovereignty, explaining the relationship between the people and their elected representatives. Trust, following Locke, is always a limited affair; it can never be blind; it is revisable and consequentialist, depending on how our representatives behave when we "entrust" them with power. Before exploring in greater detail the cognitive dimension of trust, I will show its relevance for my topic—Harper and Québec—by quoting two Canadian academics, Ronald Watts and Wayne Norman, who have respectively analyzed the role of trust in the political culture of federal regimes and its place in the context of multinational societies:

> The necessary conditions for a federal solution: A first precondition is the existence of a will to federate. Federal political systems depend on consensual support and therefore are unlikely to succeed as imposed solutions. Second, since federal systems involve both self-rule and shared-rule, without some basic underlying shared values and objectives, the basis for long-run shared rule will in the end be impossible to achieve. Third, trust is necessary to make federal arrangements work. An essential condition is the development of mutual faith and trust among the different groups within a federation and an emphasis upon the spirit of mutual respect, tolerance and compromise (Watts 2010: 339).

> From the point of view of the majority, the collective assent of federal partners cuts both ways: it constitutes a form of commitment and loyalty to the federal project by the national minorities and the majority alike, one that cannot be easily shirked. If minorities want assurances that the fundamental terms of partnership will not be violated without their consent, majorities will expect no less from minorities. The language of loyalty or solidarity is also likely to figure in the wording of a fair multinational constitution...There are tremendous benefits to trust in a federal partnership and a demonstrated commitment to anti-assimilationism is essential to secure the trust of minorities (Norman 2006: 164–165).

Watts and Norman's combined perspectives provide us with insights about the complexity of trust and mistrust in multinational regimes. François Rocher, Alexandre Pelletier, and Richard Simeon have attempted to build on these insights without neglecting the more general literature on trust in political sociology. The following remarks attempt to synthesize their main contributions. Rocher builds on the work of Russell Hardin and attempts to go beyond the confusion between trust and trustworthiness. He considers that trust is relational, whereas trustworthiness deals with the quality of the person, or group, to whom trust has been granted (Rocher 2012: 2). Trust comes from the positive evaluation that one makes of the trustworthiness of the other. Trust, for Rocher, is the result of a calculation of an evaluation. I believe that this is very important to keep in mind when dealing with such a Cartesian political figure as Stephen Harper. If trust is about calculating and evaluating, it is endowed with a major cognitive dimension. This involves a stable relationship between partners, tested by experience and basing itself on a substantial knowledge of the other or others. Enriched by his survey of the political sociology literature, Rocher wonders about the challenges at hand whenever scholars attempt to apply to the dynamics of trust/mistrust in multinational contexts the insights of most of the work on trust that concentrates its emphasis on interpersonal dyadic relationships. In multinational contexts, social relations will involve a variety of actors, majority and minority national groups, political parties wishing to represent them, political leaders, intellectual communities, governments, state institutions. These various entities not only deal with those of the same social "family" (parties with parties, governments with governments, etc.) but also interact with other groups or entities in a crosscutting way. Stephen Harper, for instance, as a political leader, has dealt and is currently dealing with the Province of Québec, with the Government of Québec, with Jean Charest as the Premier of Québec and key political interlocutor, and also, if less systematically, with Québec nationalism and Québec's intellectual community.

Trust, however, is not exclusively a cognitive affair. It has to translate into reality in a political space, which happens to involve in multinational federations asymmetrical power relationships between majorities and minorities. Alain Noël has written intelligently about this dimension, inviting scholars of multinational regimes, particularly political theorists, to integrate in their reflections "the arguments of power as well as the power of arguments" (Noël 2006: 438). The existence of a power disequilibrium means that generally, as Rocher suggests, the most important or influential group does not require the same degree of trust in its relation with minorities than vice versa, because its interests are more easily preserved or safeguarded. The cognitive and power dimensions of trust, as well as some others, are summarized in Table 1, reproduced at the end of this paper (taken directly from Rocher 2012).

In their own work on trust relations in civil society associations in multinational contexts, Pelletier and Simeon provide a nice supplement to Rocher's typology and reflections. With regard to types of trust, they also suggest four variations.

| Rocher | Pelletier and Simeon |
| --- | --- |
| Unconditional trust | Substantial trust |
| Moderate trust | Instrumental trust |
| Moderate mistrust | Cooperation without trust |
| Radical mistrust | Absence of cooperation |

Pelletier and Simeon also insist, like Rocher, on the need in such complex federal contexts for an equilibrium between autonomy and interdependence. They suggest that trust always involves a combination of strategic (instrumental) and moral dimensions requiring good faith and reciprocity (Pelletier and Simeon 2012: 4).

**Table 1** Trust–mistrust—dynamics in a plurinational context marked by the asymmetry of communities

| Type of trust | Power relation | Institutional characteristics | Cognitive dimension | Normative dimension |
|---|---|---|---|---|
| Unconditional trust | Symmetrical | Double majority | Fusion of interests | Trustworthiness predictability and general interest |
| Moderate trust | Asymmetrical | Conventional/ constitutional veto | Divergent interests and common goals | Dialogue, compromise and general interest |
| Moderate mistrust | Asymmetrical | Political capacity to bloc | Divergent interests and disagreements concerning goals | Pressure, compromise and particular interests |
| Radical mistrust | Domination | Majoritarian unilateralism | Antagonical interests | Treason, treachery and particular interests |

Reproduced from Rocher (2012), with the permission of François Rocher

The domain of trust is of course always, or almost always, the realm of uncertainty. Reflecting on the two typologies of trust offered by Rocher, on the one hand, and Pelletier and Simeon, on the other hand, I wonder if it is at all theoretically or empirically possible to find such a thing as unconditional trust in a multinational context. Therefore, I prefer, prima facie, a political sociology that places substantial trust at the apex. I doubt, however, that substantial trust, in multinational contexts, can be devoid of instrumental dimensions. The logic of interest, both Rocher and Noël have insisted on it, cannot be discarded. Therefore, I believe that Rocher's notion of moderate trust is, prima facie, more helpful than Pelletier and Simeon's category of instrumental trust. I now move to the consideration of the evolving relationships concerning trust and mistrust between Harper and Québec.

# Harper and Québec

## *The Contours of Deep Mistrust Between 1986 and 2005*

Stephen Harper is, arguably, the most important figure in Canadian politics since the advent of the new millennium. In the Canadian federal elections of 2000, the Liberal Party, led by Mr. Jean Chrétien, won its third consecutive majority government. In the aftermath of the election, Mr. Stockwell Day, leader of the Canadian Alliance Party, resigned. Alongside the Canadian Alliance, another right-wing party, the Progressive Conservative Party of Canada, was roundly defeated. Consider the achievements of Stephen Harper since these events: in 2002, he became leader of the Canadian Alliance Party; in 2003, he was instrumental in the fusion of the two right-wing parties and he became leader of the New Conservative Party of Canada; in 2004, his party was successful in reducing the Liberal Party, now led by Paul Martin, to the status of a minority government following the federal elections held in June; in January 2006, Mr. Harper became Prime Minister of Canada in the wake of the triumph of his party, which formed a minority government; in October 2008, Mr. Harper was reconducted as Prime Minister, winning a second mandate at the helm of a minority government. In May 2011, the day of his greatest triumph so far, Mr. Harper and his party won the Canadian federal election and formed their first majority government while altogether thoroughly demolishing two opposition parties, the Liberals led by Michael Ignatieff and the Bloc Québécois led by Gilles Duceppe. Both of these leaders were defeated in their own ridings. As matters stand in the Spring of 2012, the Bloc Québécois has a new leader, Daniel Paillé, but is relegated to the margins of Parliament without the status and the resources of a parliamentary group. The Liberals have an interim leader in the person of Bob Rae. The New Democrats, fresh from taking most seats in Québec for the first time ever, are in the process of selecting a new leader following the death of the previous one, the much-esteemed Jack Layton. Stephen Harper, in this context, reigns supreme at the top of the sphere of power in Canadian politics.

Born in Ontario in 1959, Mr. Harper moved to Alberta and Western Canada in his early twenties. He got involved into federal politics at that time, supporting Jim Hawkes, his local Conservative candidate who got elected in 1984 when Brian Mulroney became Prime Minister of Canada. He became estranged with Mr. Mulroney's government and with the Progressive Conservative Party of Canada, becoming disappointed with their treatment of Western Canada, their conduct of federal–provincial relations and constitutional politics during the Meech Lake sage (1987–1990), and their support of interventionist, statist economic and social policies, over such matters as unemployment insurance. He sided with Preston Manning's Western populist movement, made a major speech at the founding congress of the Reform Party in late October 1987, and became soon thereafter senior policy advisor to Manning as the first leader. The contours of Mr. Harper's deep mistrust and suspicion of Québec were already well established at that time. I insisted in the previous section on the fact that trust is endowed with a major cognitive dimension. This is created over time in a multiplicity of experiences. In the case of Mr. Harper, many of these experiences were shared with one major significant other, John Weissenberger, with whom he developed a deep personal relationship in his first years in the West.

Weissenberger had spent the first part of his life in Québec, as part of the Anglophone minority in Montréal, during the eventful years between the October Crisis in 1970, the language laws of 1974 and 1977, culminating with the victory of René Lévesque's sovereigntist Parti Québécois in the elections of 1976. With Weissenberger, Harper came to develop a vision of Québec's language régime as curtailing freedom of expression and the primacy of individual rights. As William Johnson, Harper's biographer, argues, both developed a profoundly conservative understanding of Canada and of the world (Johnson 2005: 43). With regard to the philosophical understanding of modernity, they came to support a strongly individualistic liberal vision, considering the state as a mere instrument to support the goals and projects of individuals. Owing much to Friedrich Hayek's vision of spontaneous order, they sided with the free market and remained immensely suspicious of the State's interventions in economic and social affairs. This played a role in Harper's vision of Québec. Ever since the Quiet Revolution of the early 1960s, the state had been used in Québec by an upper middle-class academic and intellectual political elite to serve the interests of the French-speaking majority. René Lévesque's Parti Québécois could be seen as pursuing this project. Ever since that time, Harper has sided with at least a soft libertarian approach in economic and social policies, attempting to limit as much as possible the interventions of the state (Johnson 2005: 47). Weissenberger and Harper were also, at that time, self-proclaimed conservatives in the Burkean sense, placing greater value on traditions and conventions following the British experience, emphasizing reformist gradualism and deeply suspicious of radical, revolutionary change. This dimension heightened Harper's distrust of Québec. During the Quiet Revolution, statist Québec elitism had opted for radical change, and in the mid-1970s, it appeared to become even more revolutionary with the Parti Québécois' sovereigntist project aimed at securing Québec's secession from Canada. On language matters, Weissenberger and Harper considered Québec profoundly disloyal.

On the one hand, according to them, Québec and francophones from Canada benefited from Pierre-Elliott Trudeau's symmetrical pan-Canadian language regime of official bilingualism, whereas Québec enforced within its borders a regime of official unilingualism detrimental to the rights of Anglophone Québecers. To make matters worse, Québec's political culture of interventionist statism was considered by them thoroughly entrenched in Canada, with the domination of the Liberal Party in general and with the vision of Pierre-Elliott Trudeau in particular. To make matters even worse, in the late 1970s, Trudeau's federal government appeared embarked on a collision course with Alberta and other Western provinces over the control of natural resources. With his friend Weissenberger, Harper was profoundly ill at ease with Québec's perceived attacks on Hayekian economic and epistemological conservatism, on Burkean's political conservatism, on a principled conservative defence of the rule of law in the British tradition of which Canada is considered to be one of the most important heirs in the world. According to his biographer, Stephen Harper has always shown a lot of respect for Mr. Trudeau's 1982 vision of patriating the Canadian constitution, enriching it with a Charter of Rights and Nations and attempting to consolidate Canada as one nation. At the same time, philosophically, he was profoundly opposed to Mr. Trudeau's policies, over such issues as languages and resources, to impose to the whole of Canada Québec's culture of nationalistic statism. Mr. Trudeau and his Liberal Party, according to Stephen Harper in the mid-1980s, were obsessed with the question of Québec and neglected the higher purposes of individual and regional justice for all Canadians.

Beyond Hayek and Burke, Weissenberger and Harper were also quite influenced in the 1980s by a book by Peter Brimelow, which looked strategically at the future of Canada in North America and in the world, from a rather Churchillian perspective strongly prejudiced in favour of the English-speaking peoples and their contribution to the history of humanity. Brimelow offered a view of Québec's importance and role in the history of Canada. Weissenberger and Harper read the following passage about a decade after Lévesque's first victory, 5 years after the failed sovereignty referendum of 1980, and just as Brian Mulroney, Robert Bourassa, and other Canadian politicians were about to agree on the terms of the Meech Lake Accord, recognizing Québec as a distinct society within Canada and granting the government and the National Assembly of Québec—the STATE of Québec, from Harper's perspective—constitutional authority to legislate to protect and promote Québec as a distinct society

> The history and politics of Québec are dominated by a single great reality: the emergence of the French-speaking nation. The process has been slow, complex and agonizing. There have been false starts, reversals and long periods of quiescence. But for over two hundred years its ultimate direction has been the same: towards ever greater self-expression, as the growing plant seeks the light (Brimelow 1986: 180).

From the first signing of the Meech Lake Accord in 1987 to its demise in 1990 and to the Canadian and Québec referendums of 1992 over the Charlottetown Accord, Stephen Harper, in solidarity with Preston Manning and the Reform Party or by himself, acted on his principled conservatism and on the cognitive and normative dimensions of his mistrust of Québec to strongly oppose the constitutional transformations that these projects offered for Canada. In essence, Harper was strongly opposed to real or perceived special status for Québec, adhering to a vision of individual, provincial, and regional equality under the umbrella of the Canadian rule of law. As a Westerner and as a Canadian historical conservative, he did develop an understanding of federalism that allowed for strong provinces and substantial decentralization. Meech Lake and its distinct society provisions not only were at odds with his vision of provincial equality but also meant that the state of Québec could become even more interventionist, endowed with the constitutional authority to preserve and promote such a distinct society. Moreover, by granting Québec a right of veto, Meech Lake meant that the Reform Party's cherished project of a Triple-E Senate (equal, effective, and elected) would probably never see the light of day because Québec would oppose it. Interestingly, it seems relevant while discussing trust and mistrust in multinational contexts to remark that Harper, during the Meech Lake era, thought that Québec was not asked or did not propose to grant a significant concession of its own, which could have been "surrendering a clean option to secede" (Johnson 2005: 83). Obviously, from opposite perspectives developed at the time in the Québec government or in Québec's political and intellectual circles, the Meech Lake Accord was of course interpreted in a substantially different light, linked to the substantial transformation of the Canadian constitution in 1982 without the consent of Québec, thus seen as necessary to reestablish trust in the Canadian federal project. However, my focus in this paper remains insisting on the significance of Harper's trajectory and of his perspective. His angle on the matters of trust and mistrust remains my primary concern.

From the Charlottetown Accord to the end of the decade, including the fateful months before, and after, the 1995 Québec referendum, Stephen Harper was steadfast in attempting to maintain, coldly, analytically, precisely, the coherence of his vision of politics and of his vision of Canada. Harper had epistemological and philosophical misgivings about the conduct of politics in Québec—too much statism. From Brimelow, he carried strong prejudices about the historical inevitability of Québec's quest for ever greater forms of political self-expression—too much Québec nationalism; moreover, he did not like the ambiguities surrounding Québec's struggles for sovereignty and self-determination and their relationships with the rule of law in Canada, in other words, with the primacy of the Canadian constitution. With Manning and the Reform Party, and also acting on his own, he sought a greater commitment to Canada as one nation on the part of Québec, and he sought greater clarity with regard to the legality of any secessionist enterprise. After the 1995 Québec Referendum, the 1998 Supreme Court of Canada Reference Case on the Secession of Québec and the law passed by the Canadian Parliament in early 2000 under the initiative of Jean Chrétien and Stéphane Dion, known as the Clarity Act, can together be regarded as offering substantial satisfaction to Harper, to his actions and vision of the early 1990s. Taken together, the Supreme Court judgment and the Clarity Act reiterated the underlying principles of the Canadian constitution—federalism, democracy, constitutionalism and the rule of law, respect for the rights of minorities—and established a legal framework for the secession of a Canadian province within the categories of the constitution—following a referendum on a clear question translated into a clear answer leading to negotiations where all parties should show good faith and respect for the principles of the constitution, and specified under which conditions the Canadian federal Parliament would consider the question clear, as well as the answer. The two excerpts that I am about to quote come from a motion submitted at a Reform Party Congress during the Charlottetown saga and from an individual Member's Bill that Stephen Harper submitted to the Canadian House of Commons in 1996, in the aftermath of the second Québec referendum. These two excerpts reveal a lot about the context of the times, which was using the terms of Rocher's typology, characterized by radical mistrust (absence of cooperation according to Pelletier and Simeon), of Québec nationalists and secessionists from the perspective of Harper and a broad section of Canadian opinion. Taken together, these two excerpts are, for me, the intellectual predecessors of the Canadian central government "Plan B" in the Chrétien-Dion years of the Supreme Court's Reference on Secession and of the Clarity Act itself. They contributed, possibly, to a transformation of the climate of politics in Canada in the late 1990s, from radical mistrust to moderate mistrust (Rocher) or from absence of cooperation to cooperation without trust (Pelletier and Simeon). This move from radical mistrust to moderate mistrust obviously characterizes here, if I am not mistaken, public opinion in the majority nation of a multinational federation. Beyond these excerpts, however, I believe nothing had really changed about Stephen Harper's deep mistrust of Québec.

Whereas concessions made on account of this separatist threat are, for many, proving to be costly, ineffective, a source of deepening friction between Quebec and the rest of Canada, and a barrier to the development of national purpose for the country as a whole... Be it resolved that the Reform Party state clearly its belief that Confederation should be maintained, but that it can only be maintained by a clear commitment to Canada as one nation, in which the demands and aspirations of all regions are entitled to equal status in constitutional negotiations and political debate, and in which freedom of expression is fully accepted as the basis for language policy across the country (as quoted by Johnson 2005: 147).

A unilateral declaration of independence by the government of Quebec or the legislature of Quebec, or the refusal of either to submit to any Canadian law that applies in Quebec is unlawful and of no force and effect with respect to the Constitution of Canada and the general laws of Canada and does not affect: (a) the jurisdiction of Parliament to pass laws that have effect in Québec; (b) the ability of the Government of Canada to govern Quebec as a province of Canada; (c) the jurisdiction of the courts to apply the law of Canada in Quebec; or (d) the continuance of Quebec as a part of Canada under Canadian law (quoted by Johnson 2005: 255).

Evaluating Harper's relationship with Quebec, I believe nothing of substance really changed between 1996, the year Harper submitted this Member Bill to Parliament, and late 2004, some time after his first federal electoral campaign as leader of the reunited forces of the right and of the new Conservative Party of Canada. In 2004, struggling against the Liberal Party led by Paul Martin, Harper's Conservatives elected 99 members of Parliament and reduced the Liberals to the status of minority government. However, their performance was dismal in Québec, with less than 9 % of votes and no elected representatives. From 1996 to 2004, Harper remained adamant that Québec needed no form of special status, no new substantial or symbolic recognition, that it was legally fully integrated in Canada. In essence, the only fundamental difference between his group and their Liberal adversaries was that the Conservatives espoused a form of federalism that appeared more respectful of the powers of provinces. If nothing of substance really changed, some signs indicated that Harper could reconsider, at least in part, his own vision, his approach to his understanding of Québec and of Canada. I shall consider these signs in the introduction of the next section, which deals with the period 2005–2008.

## The Promises of Thin Trust 2005–2008

Stephen Harper's conservative vision privileges market libertarian values over the Welfare State and the political culture that supports it, it promotes individual rights and family values against the hedonism and nihilism of much of Late Modernity in the West, it nurtures a politics of conflict that favors taxpayers from the private sector over welfare recipients, it harbors huge suspicions as we have seen vis-à-vis the nationalistic statism of Québec and its perceived absence of commitment vis-à-vis Canada, and it promotes an understanding of Canadian federalism that grants at least equal value to federalism and the founding of 1867 than to the refounding accomplished by Pierre Trudeau with Patriation and the Charter of Rights and Freedoms in 1982. Harper's mind fully integrates a vision of politics that sees it as primarily conflictual. In order, therefore, to secure a lasting presence for his vision with all its elements in twenty-first century Canada, he believes that the Conservative Party must attempt the Herculean task of displacing the Liberal Party as the dominant party in the political system. From 1996 onwards, ever so gradually, Harper acted on the premise that in order to secure a stable anchoring for his vision, in order to displace the Liberals, the Conservatives had in a way to make their peace with Québec. I use the expression thin trust to characterize the shift that occurred in Harper's approach and that can be clearly seen at work in speeches he made in Québec City in Montréal in December 2005 and January 2006 in the midst of the federal electoral campaign that led to the formation of a Conservative minority government. In these speeches, and in some pronouncements thereafter, Harper coined a new doctrine, "fédéralisme d'ouverture", which can be translated as "open federalism" or "federalism of openness" (Pelletier 2008; Hébert 2007). It is clear in my mind that "fédéralisme d'ouverture" as a form of thin trust towards Québec corresponded to what Pelletier and Simeon called instrumental trust. Once again, this is not necessarily negative or pejorative. Everybody has interests: political leaders, governments, nations. Thin or instrumental trust is a progress from the two inferior categories in our two typologies, moderate mistrust (Rocher), or cooperation without trust (Pelletier and Simeon). Over time, because trust is endowed with a cognitive dimension that integrates the meaning and consequences of experiences, thin or instrumental trust can stabilize as moderate trust. I wish to argue that however we interpret the promises of "fédéralisme d'ouverture" between 2005 and 2008, they did not stabilize themselves as moderate trust, therefore leading to our last and possibly current moment in the relations between Harper and Québec, characterized by renewed mistrust from 2008 to 2012.

The seeds of thin or instrumental trust between Harper and Québec were already planted in 1996, when Harper evoked at a philosophically conservative policy convention in Calgary the conditions that would allow the Canadian political right to reestablish itself as a major force in order to compete with, and eventually to displace, the Liberal Party as the primary partisan group in the country. At that time, Harper believed that whenever conservative forces had coalesced to win an election, they included people from three groups: people from Ontario and Atlantic Canada who had traditionally supported the old Conservative Party; people from Western Canada who had supported historically various populist parties stemming from the West, in the late 1990s the Reform Party; and finally, people linked with the nationalist tradition in Québec who had not completely abandoned the idea of a federal Canada as a political project (Johnson 2005: 264). In 1996, Harper had precious little to say about the ways in which such a coalition could be formed again in the future. In the ensuing years, events unfolded to create some preconditions for the realization of this project. Following three consecutive majority governments obtained by Jean Chrétien, the Liberal Party was becoming more and more engulfed in a fratricidal conflict involving the supporters of Mr. Chrétien and those of his internal arch-rival, Paul Martin. The latter would ultimately prevail and replace

Mr. Chrétien in the Winter of 2004. In Québec, things began to change in 2003, when the Québec Liberal Party under the leadership of Mr. Jean Charest won the April 14 election and propelled the sovereigntist Parti Québécois in the Opposition.

Mr. Charest and his Liberals were committed federalists and sympathetic to Canadian nationalism while remaining autonomist nationalistic Québecers. They developed a coherent approach towards Canadian federalism, wishing to improve the quality of horizontal intergovernmental relations through the creation of a new institution of cooperation between provinces and territories, which rapidly saw the light of day as the Council of the Federation in late 2003. Rapidly, Mr. Charest and the Canadian Prime Minister were successful in changing the climate of federal–provincial relations by agreeing, with other provincial leaders, in the Fall of 2004, about a new ten-year deal to jointly finance the health system in Canada, completing this agreement with a parallel, asymmetrical accord between the central government and Québec. Mr. Martin and his government were less successful in Québec with the creation of a Commission of Enquiry, led by Mr. Justice John Gomery, which explored the ways in which regulations of many federal administrative departments were disrespected, while irregular means were employed to finance the federal Liberal Party, in a vast scheme to try to reinforce a sense of Canadian allegiance in Québec in the aftermath of the 1995 referendum. The electoral fortunes of the Liberal Party in Québec, already weakened in 2004, could be fatally wounded if the situation was to be properly exploited by their adversaries. All in all, these events provided Mr. Harper with an opportunity that he began to seize during the early weeks of the federal electoral campaign in December 2005 and January 2006, when he expounded the major aspects of his new doctrine—"fédéralisme d'ouverture":

a) Beyond domineering and paternalistic federalism, show greater respect toward constitutional provincial jurisdiction and division of powers;
b) Foster better collaboration and coordination with provinces and circumscribe Ottawa's spending power;
c) Recognize the existence of a vertical fiscal imbalance between Ottawa and the provinces and willingness to act on this problem;
d) Recognize the special cultural and institutional responsibilities of Québec and attribute a significant role to the government of Québec in the Canadian delegation at Unesco;
e) In Canada-Québec relations, offer a noticeable change of tone: "we shall change the debate, change the programme and change the federation" (Harper's federalism of openness is discussed in Pelletier 2008, as well as in Caron and Laforest 2009).

It can be argued that Mr. Harper's surprising new flirt with Québec was the key element that led to the Conservative's victory in 2006, thus enabling Mr. Harper to become Prime Minister of Canada (Hébert 2007: 10). In 2006, Mr. Harper and his party made more than a modest breakthrough in Québec. They won ten seats in the province, whereas they had taken none in 2004 and garnered 24.6 % of the votes, compared with 8.8 % in 2004. Between Harper and Québec, between 2005 and

2007–2008, things were far from perfect. Mr. Harper was, and remains, far too conservative and anti-statist for Québec's left-of center mainstream public opinion and for its political elites. In the circumstances, it would have been totally unseemly to expect unconditional or substantial trust between Harper and Québec. However, for a while, at least for 2 years, it looked as if Harper and Québec were jointly navigating the waters of instrumental and moderate trust.

Although the Harper-led Conservative minority government has failed to deliver on its promise to elaborate a so-called "Charte du fédéralisme d'ouverture", I believe there is some consensus in Québec that Mr. Harper has made significant progress on most items of this agenda between 2006 and 2008. Considering, moreover, that Mr. Harper moved through the House of Commons in late 2006, a resolution recognizing that the Québécois form a nation in a united Canada, that he has shown tremendous respect for the French language, that he has highlighted here and abroad the role of Québec in general and of Québec City in particular, in the founding of Canada, it is somewhat surprising that he did not make substantial gains in Québec in the 2008 Fall federal election. In October 2008, Mr. Harper's Conservative won the election yet again, once more forming a minority government, once more with ten seats in Québec, but with a reduced voter support of 21.7 %. Any analysis of these matters must be careful. In truth, the engine of "fédéralisme d'ouverture" had been losing part of its energy from the start of 2007 on a variety of issues: Statements about the need to circumscribe the spending power have been timid at best; some ambiguities remain concerning what Mr. Harper really meant in the nation resolution, senate reform projects, coupled with the desire to establish more provincial equality in the House of Commons by giving more seats to Ontario, Alberta, and British Columbia (reform ideas met with resistance in Québec), and the idea of an Ottawa-based national securities regulator have met strong resistance in federalist Québec City. Moreover, Mr. Harper, between 2006 and 2008 has shown no enthusiasm towards streamlining coordination through regular and more rational First Ministers Conferences, and he has generally stayed away from the idea of reopening the constitutional file in order, among other matters, to formally recognize Québec's national identity. Add to this the rift between Mr. Harper and Québec Premier Jean Charest dating back to the latter's decision to reduce income taxes in the aftermath of a 2007 federal budget addressing the fiscal imbalance issue and you get a more realistic portrait of the relationship between Mr. Harper's government and Québec. Somewhere between 2007 and 2008, the engine of thin or instrumental trust between Mr. Harper and Québec were derailed. I shall explore the psychological dimensions of this reality in the next section.

## Renewed Mistrust 2008–2012

In the Canadian federal elections of 2 May 2011, Stephen Harper saw his Conservative Party comfortably win the election, garnering 166 of 308 seats with 39.6 %

of voter support—see Table 2—and in the days thereafter, he formed the Cabinet of his first majority government. However, he did this with considerably reduced support in Québec, moving from ten to five seats from 21.7 % to 16.5 % of voter support—see Table 3. During this election, seismic political changes did occur in Québec, with the New Democratic Party led by Jack Layton moving from 1 to 58 seats, garnering 42 % of voter support, and with the collapse of both the sovereigntist Bloc Québécois led by Gilles Duceppe and the Liberal Party led by Michael Ignatieff. In the campaign leading to the election, it became clear that Mr. Harper and the Conservatives applied a different strategy than the one they had used in 2006 and 2008, placing much less emphasis on everything related to "fédéralisme d'ouverture". Creating jobs, supporting families, eliminating the deficit, providing increased security to Canadians, protecting Canada here and abroad by strengthening the Armed Forces and investing in the development and security of the North were the Conservative priorities in 2011, and they had nothing particular to offer to Québec. Clearly, the richest and best organized political party in Canada, the Harper-led Conservatives, attempted to secure a majority by making gains in Ontario, the Maritimes, and British Columbia, strategically selecting potential seats and cleverly segmenting the electorate. In the months following the election, the new majority government made good of Mr. Harper's campaign promises.

The government's blueprint, as it appeared in the Throne Speech delivered by the Governor-General on 3 June 2011, included the following priorities: supporting growth and employment, eliminating the deficit, supporting hardworking families, protecting Canada, helping law-abiding Canadians, helping communities and industries, promoting integrity and responsibility. The latter priority included ideas such as a reform of the senate, more equitable representation in the House of Commons by granting more seats to Ontario, Alberta, and British Columbia; and eliminating of state support for the financing of political parties. All these elements bring Mr. Harper on a collision course with Mr. Charest's Liberal government in Québec and with mainstream public opinion in the province. Cooperation does exist between the governments of Mr. Harper and of Mr. Charest, as was demonstrated by the agreement on sales tax harmonization devolving two billion dollars to Québec on 30 September 2011, but I would argue that this is an example of cooperation without trust. Moreover, Mr. Harper was forced after the election to reshuffle personnel in the Prime Minister's Office with the resignation of his Press Secretary, Dimitri Soudas, who also happened to be his top Québec advisor. He replaced him with Angelo Persichillli, a veteran of the ethnic media in Toronto who does not speak French and made disparaging comments about Québec's role in Canada in the recent past. Considering all these events, the following question needs to be asked: What really went wrong between Mr. Harper and Québec in 2007–2008 to explain this change of course, this move from instrumental or thin trust to renewed mistrust?

Whenever partners in a relationship move from deep mistrust (radical mistrust, absence of cooperation, cooperation without trust, in the typologies I have used here) to instrumental or thin trust, the whole matter remains quite fragile. I believe

**Table 2** Results of Canadian general elections, 2000–2011

| Year | | Alliance-Reform | Bloc Québécois | Liberal | New Democratic Party | Conservative Party[a] | Green Party | Independent | Other parties | Total[b] |
|---|---|---|---|---|---|---|---|---|---|---|
| 2000 | % of valid votes | 25.51 | 10.71 | 40.8 | 8.5 | 12.2 | | | 2.2 | |
| 2000 | Number of seats | 66 | 38 | 172 | 13 | 12 | | | 0 | 301 |
| 2004 | % of valid votes | | 12.4 | 36.7 | 15.7 | 29.6 | 4.3 | 0.3 | 1 | |
| 2004 | Number of seats | | 54 | 135 | 19 | 99 | 0 | 1 | 0 | 308 |
| 2006 | % of valid votes | | 10.5 | 30.2 | 17.5 | 36.3 | 4.5 | 0.5 | 0.5 | |
| 2006 | Number of seats | | 51 | 103 | 29 | 124 | 0 | 1 | 0 | 308 |
| 2008 | % of valid votes | | 10 | 26.3 | 18.2 | 37.7 | 6.8 | 0.6 | 0.4 | |
| 2008 | Number of seats | | 49 | 77 | 37 | 143 | 0 | 2 | | 308 |
| 2011 | % of valid votes | | 6.1 | 18.9 | 30.6 | 39.6 | 3.9 | 0.4 | 0.5 | |
| 2011 | Number of seats | | 4 | 34 | 103 | 166 | 1 | | | 308 |

[a]The Reform-Alliance Party fused with the Progressive-Conservative Party to form the new Conservative Party of Canada in 2003
[b]In 2003 as well, the number of seats in the Canadian House of Commons, the Lower House of Parliament, moved from 301 to 308

**Table 3** Votes obtained by the Alliance-Reform-Progressive Conservatives and later by the Conservative Party in Québec, 2000–2011

| Year of the election | % of votes | No. of seats |
|---|---|---|
| 2000 | 5.6 | 1 |
| 2004 | 8.8 | 0 |
| 2006 | 24.6 | 10 |
| 2008 | 21.7 | 10 |
| 2011 | 16.5 | 5 |

that in the era of "fédéralisme d'ouverture" and thin trust, Mr. Harper's stance towards Québec started to change in the Spring of 2007, in the context of the Québec electoral campaign that ultimately saw Mr. Charest's Liberals reduced to the status of a minority government, with Mario Dumont's ADQ replacing the Parti Québécois as the Official Opposition. Prior to the election, Mr. Harper's government in Ottawa announced that in the settlement of the issue of the existence of a fiscal imbalance between the central government and the provinces, which had been for years a priority of Québec and of Mr. Charest's government, Québec would receive over one billion dollars. Mr. Charest had always said that Québec needed this money in order to face rising costs in its two most important jurisdictions, health and education. However, at the end of a difficult first mandate in government, Mr. Charest chose instead to use these subsidies to offer Québec voters substantial income tax reductions. Obviously, the Québec government is perfectly entitled to do whatever it wants, within the rule of law and within its jurisdictional ground in the federations, with its revenues. Mr. Harper, however, who had spent some political capital in the rest of Canada to recognize the legitimacy of the issue of a fiscal imbalance, must have been quite surprised and deeply disappointed by the move. Mr. Charest made matters worse, in 2007–2008, not only by disagreeing with Mr. Harper's government policy on environmental issues such as climate change but also by vigorously expressing himself about this disagreement in a number of important international forums. "Fédéralisme d'ouverture" remained an important theme for the Conservative electoral platform leading to the elections of October 2008, and it figured among the elements that were mentioned in the Throne Speech that followed this election reconducting Mr. Harper's Conservatives with a minority government. Although the words remained there, the spirit did not happen to be. Mr. Harper's Conservatives did not lose seats in Québec in 2008, but they did not gain ground either. In levels of voter support, they suffered a marked loss, moving from 24.6 % to 21.7 % after a lackluster campaign where they were cleverly attacked by the Bloc Québécois for intended federal reductions of governmental support for culture. By the end of 2008, in the weeks following the reelection of Mr. Charest with his third government and second majority one, with the electoral disaster suffered by the ADQ and Mario Dumont, with whom Mr. Harper had established good personal relations and with whom he shared some ideological traits—suspicion vis-à-vis Welfare statism, broad support for greater individual responsibility—the window of opportunity for "fédéralisme d'ouverture", for instrumental or thin trust between Mr. Harper and Québec appeared to be closing.

# Conclusion

Trust and mistrust are cognitive affairs. They are experience-based, dynamic, fluid, evolving with changing historical and political circumstances. In multinational federations, between majorities and minorities at the level of civil societies, between political leaders and governmental representatives, trust will always be something fragile, inherently unstable. Majorities and minorities, and their respective leaders, do not exclusively seek the same objectives. Some objectives will be commonly shared: security, social peace, economic prosperity, the crafting and preserving of a liberal polity enhancing individual rights, the normal functioning of representative and deliberative institutions of democracy, the establishment of a pluralistic public sphere. Still, in a multinational democracy, the majority nation, as Simeon coherently showed, will put greater priority at national integration at the level of the state, at securing solidarity and interdependence for all individuals and groups throughout the state. On the other hand, minority nations will put greater focus on national empowerment for minorities, through increased powers, through expressions of distinctiveness and asymmetry, through securing forms of symbolic and substantial recognition by the majority nation and by the state.

In this general context, to come back to the categories explored in this paper, unconditional trust is unimaginable. At best, majorities, minorities, and their leaders will reach a reasonably stabilized order hovering between what Rocher has called moderate trust and moderate mistrust, between the broader spectrum suggested by Pelletier and Simeon from cooperation without trust to instrumental trust to substantial trust. As I have suggested in this paper, I believe an element of instrumentality will always exists.

In order to stabilize a form of moderate trust, I believe that two lessons can be learnt from an examination of the relationship between Harper and Québec. Harper's trajectory helps us understand that, when moderate or instrumental trust has been achieved, in a personal context steeped in historic mistrust and deeply held prejudices, top-elected leaders must act coherently and respect their promises. Jean Charest failed to do this in the Spring of 2007, when he used the money Québec had received as a form of compensation for vertical fiscal imbalance in the federation to reduce the income taxes of its citizens. Moreover, although they may have substantial policy differences, leaders of majorities and minorities should not act at the international level as if to widen these policy differences, without any appearance of communication on the matter with each other. On environmental issues, the Premier of Québec, Mr. Charest, showed a kind of lack of respect for Mr. Harper in a variety of international forums. What can be the meaning of all this for Spain and particularly for the relationship between Mariano Rajoy, the freshly elected President of the Spanish government, and Artur Mas, the leader of CIU and President of the Catalan government? Rajoy and Mas talked to each other at least twice between the November 20 Spanish elections and the Christmas recess. They met formally at La Moncloa in Madrid for a formal work session on February 3rd. I believe the categories explored in this paper can be useful to understand the relationship between these two leaders, their respective governments, and the peoples-societies they represent. Unconditional trust should not be seeked. Discussions should be frequent. Each side should understand the hierarchy of each other's objectives. Whenever possible, common speeches and deeds should be pronounced and accomplished to build up the edifice of relative trust. Promises, whenever expressed, should be kept at all costs. Whenever conflicts will be unavoidable—and considering the essence of politics in a multinational federation, this is bound to happen—channels of communication should be maintained, and interpersonal respect should be observed. The rest, as ever, will be cognitive, experience based and revisable.

# References

Brimelow, Peter (1986). The Patriot Game: National Dreams & Political Realities. Toronto: Key Porter Books.

Caron, Jean-François and Guy Laforest (2009). Canada and Multinational Federalism: From the Spirit of 1982 to Stephen Harper's Open Federalism. Nationalism and Ethnic Politics 15(1): 27–55.

Hébert, Chantal (2007). French Kiss: Stephen Harper's Blind Date with Québec. Toronto: A. Knopf Canada.

Johnson, William (2005), Stephen Harper and the Future of Canada. Toronto: McClelland & Stewart.

Noël, Alain (2006). Democratic Deliberation in a Multinational Federation. Critical Review of International Social and Political Philosophy 9(3): 410–444.

Norman, Wayne (2006), Negotiating Nationalism: Nation-Building, Federalism and Secession in the Multinational State. Toronto: Oxford University Press.

Pelletier, Alexandre and Richard Simeon (2012). Groupes linguistiques et société civile: confiance, coopération et accommodements au sein des associations volontaires au Canada, in Dimitrios Karmis and François Rocher. La dynamique confiance-méfiance dans les démocraties multinationales, Québec: Presses de l'Université Laval.

Pelletier, Réjean (2008). Le Québec et le fédéralisme canadien: un regard critique. Québec: Presses de l'Université Laval.

Rocher, François (2012). La construction du Canada en perspective historique: de la méfiance comme élément consubstantiel des débats constitutionnels, in Dimitrios Karmis and François Rocher. La dynamique confiance-méfiance dans les démocraties multinationales. Québec: Presses de l'Université Laval.

Watts, Ronald (2010), Comparative Reflections on Federalism and Democracy. In Michael Burgess and Alain-G. Gagnon, Federal Democracies. London: Routledge, 325–346.

## *Ressources électroniques d'intérêt général pour étudier la politique canadienne et québécoise/Web resources of general interest to study Canadian and Québec Politics*

Gouvernement du Canada, Bureau du Conseil privé, Affaires intergouvernementales du Canada, http://www.pco-bcp.gc.ca/aia

Gouvernement du Québec, Ministère du Conseil exécutif, Secrétariat aux Affaires Intergouvernementales canadiennes, http://www.saic.mce.gouv.qc.ca

Premier Ministre du Canada, http://www.pm.gc.ca

Premier Ministre du Québec, http://www.premier.gouv.qc.ca

Institut de recherches sur les politiques publiques, http://www.irpp.org/fr/index.htm

Institute of Intergovernmental Relations, http://www.queensu.ca/iigr/

Institute for Research on Public Policy/ Institut de recherches en politiques publiques, http://www.irpp.org

Parlement du Canada, Sénat et Chambre des Communes, http://www.parl.gc.ca

Parti conservateur du Canada, http://www.conservateur.ca

Parti libéral du Canada, http://www.liberal.ca

Nouveau parti démocratique du Canada, http://www.npd.ca

Bloc québécois, http://blocquebecois.org

Parti vert du Canada, http://www.greenparty.ca

Parti libéral du Québec, http://www.plq.org

Parti Québécois, http://www.pq.org

Parti de l'Action démocratique du Québec, http://www.adq.qc.ca/

Québec Solidaire, http://quebecsolidaire.net/

Principaux journaux québécois et canadiens, en français http://www.cyberpresse.ca

Et http://www.ledevoir.com

En anglais, http://www.nationalpost.ca et http://www.globeandmail.ca En anglais http://www.cbc.ca et Réseau public canadien de télévision, en français http://www.radio-canada.ca

Association québécoise de droit constitutionnel, http://www.aqdc.org/public/main.php?s=1&l=fr

Assemblée nationale du Québec, http://www.assnat.qc.ca

Association internationale des études québécoises, http://www.aieq.qc.ca/

Bibliothèque de l'Université de Toronto, http://content.library.utoronto.ca/

Bibliothèque de l'Université Laval, http://www.bibl.ulaval.ca/mieux

Bulletin électronique trimestriel sur la citoyenneté, la démocratie et la diversité ethnoculturelle, http://www.queensu.ca/cded/news.html

Centre de recherche interdisciplinaire sur la diversité au Québec (CRIDAQ), http://www.cridaq.uqam.ca/

Chaire de recherche du Canada en études québécoises et canadiennes, http://www.creqc.uqam.qc.ca/

Commission de consultation sur les pratiques d'accommodement reliées aux différences culturelles, ou Commission Bouchard-Taylor, http://www.ccpardc.qc.ca/

Conseil international des études canadiennes, http://www.iccs-ciec.ca/

Cour suprême du Canada, http://www.scc-csc.gc.ca

Directeur général des élections du Québec, http://wwwdgeq.qc.ca/

Elections Canada, http://www.elections.ca/

Jurisprudence de la Cour suprême du Canada sur les questions relatives aux Chartes des droits et au fédéralisme, http://www.lexum.umontreal.ca/csc-scc/fr/

Forum des Fédérations : un réseau international sur le fédéralisme, http://www.ciff.on.ca

Gouvernance démocratique et ethnicité, grands travaux de recherche concertée du Conseil de Recherches en sciences humaines du Canada, http://www.edg-gde.ca/

# ¿Café para todos? Homogeneity, Difference, and Canadian Federalism

Alain Noël

"Café para todos" was the expression used in Spain to characterize a certain way of reconciling homogeneity and difference. The expression described the process whereby accommodations granted to the "historic nationalities" were gradually extended to all, in the name of unity and national identity or in that of solidarity and citizenship, usually against the will of the "historic nationalities" (initially, the Basque country, Catalonia, and Galicia; Moreno and Colino 2010: 291; Balfour and Quiroga 2007: 61–62). Café para todos; what was good for one was good for all.

I am not sure what it is exactly that we serve to all in Canada (hopefully not coffee), but we certainly can relate to this call for uniformity, which has been made again and again either in the name of presumably equal provinces (think Meech Lake and Charlottetown Accords) or in that of necessarily equal citizens (think national standards). Over the years, political scientists have proposed numerous accounts of this North American version of "café para todos" politics. Guy Laforest, for instance, has written eloquently about the recurrent and powerful pull, in our political life, in favor of what he called a "monochrome" Canada (2004: 70–79). Earlier, Alan Cairns and many others used the term "province-building" to describe a process of institutional development and ambition that, they thought, ran across most provinces, with similar effects (Black and Cairns 1966; Young, Faucher and Blais 1984). Later, Peter Russell coined the terms "mega-constitutional politics" to capture the broad reach of a multifaceted debate that rapidly involved much more than "two nations." This was the hour of the "Canada Round," a game where all governments and social actors were claiming a place, on par with all others (Russell 2004).

There is much to be said about these perspectives on federalism, which concur in indicating how, paradoxically, conflicts about difference often turn into multilateral quests for homogeneity. I will not dwell, however, on such accounts. I wish to

A. Noël (✉)
Département de science politique, Université de Montréal, C.P. 6128, succ. Centre-ville, Montréal, QC, Canada H3C 3J7
e-mail: alain.noel@umontreal.ca

A. López-Basaguren and L. Escajedo San Epifanio (eds.), *The Ways of Federalism in Western Countries and the Horizons of Territorial Autonomy in Spain*, Vol. 2, DOI 10.1007/978-3-642-27717-7_26, © Springer-Verlag Berlin Heidelberg 2013

emphasize instead that, however important, this multilateral politics of difference and homogeneity—our own brand of "café para todos" politics—has not been the main driver of Canadian federalism. The scramble for a "monochrome" Canada was undeniably important. Indeed, in the 1990s, the country almost disintegrated in the wake of constitutional debates over homogeneity and difference. Still, for most of the country's history, such oppositions over distinctiveness and uniformity constituted a second order line of conflict, behind a more fundamental one, over autonomy and unity.

It is easy to conflate the two conflicts because they are connected. In a federation, those who emphasize difference are likely to favor decentralized solutions and those who vie for homogeneity often speak the language of solidarity and unity, which justifies the guidance of a strong central government. However, the questions at stake are different. Debates over homogeneity and difference have to do with the nature of public intervention and the possibilities of more or less symmetric or asymmetric arrangements in a federation. Debates over autonomy and unity concern more explicitly the division of powers and of financial resources among orders of government, and they call into question the proper balance between self-rule and shared rule. Such debates, then, are not primarily about difference; they concern the realization of the core federal idea, which makes it possible for peoples to live at once together and separately (Noël 1998).

To take one example, Yves Vaillancourt explained in a survey of social policies in the 1960s and 1970s that the reforms implemented by the Quebec government in these two decades were not all that different from those accepted and adapted elsewhere in Canada. At the time, wrote Vaillancourt, Quebec's social vision "was fundamentally the same" as that favored elsewhere in Canada, but it nevertheless stood out because it was to "be implemented not by Ottawa but by Quebec" (2003: 160). The issue was not difference as such but the exercise of autonomy.

In this chapter, I broaden this argument to contend that over time, the politics of Canadian federalism has been defined less by the politics of homogeneity and difference or by the issues of symmetry and asymmetry than by the more classically federal politics of autonomy and unity. This distinction is not merely semantic. Established early, the precedence of autonomy and unity over homogeneity and difference fashioned durably the politics of Canadian federalism, and it yielded important lessons both for our understanding of Canada and for the comparative study of federalism in multinational settings. Canada's evolution pointed, in particular, to the lasting importance of the federal principle in a multinational arrangement and to the inherently political and situated—here and there, now and then—nature of federalism.

This chapter first explains, briefly, how the debate was initiated in Canada. From the outset, Canadian federalism was defined by the tension between autonomy and unity, notably as an outcome of the dualist politics that prevailed prior to 1867. Then, the chapter moves forward in time to discuss how, in recent decades, the politics of autonomy usually trumped the politics of difference, leaving asymmetric arrangements as minor, almost accidental by-products of Quebec's relentless search for autonomy. Finally, the third part draws out a few comparative implications to underline, in particular, the political significance of the federal principle in the development of multinational societies.

## How Did Canada Get There?
## The Dualist Origins of the *British North America Act of 1867*

I do not wish to go at length over a well-known history, but it is important to keep in mind that in its early days Canada was much more dualist than it is today. In 2006, the year of the last available census, French was the mother tongue of 21.8 % of Canadians, compared to 57.2 % for English and 19.7 % for other languages (Statistics Canada 2007). The proportion of francophones was not much above a fifth of the country's population. As for Quebec, it had fallen below a quarter of the total. In 2012, the province's population was estimated to be slightly above eight million, out of more than thirty four million Canadians, for a proportion of 23.1 % (Statistics Canada 2012: 16). In 1871, by contrast, in the early days of the federation, French Canadians formed almost a third of the country's population (31.1 %), and so did the province of Quebec (32.3 %; Linteau et al. 1983: 38). At the time, with 1.2 million inhabitants, Quebec still appeared roughly on par with its former partner in the United Province of Canada, Ontario, which had a population of 1.6 million (Basavarajappa and Ram 1983; Series A2–A14). Everyday politics reflected this social dualism.

The *British North America Act of 1867*, the law that gave birth to the Canadian federation, was indeed a response to the dualist politics that had fashioned practically every debate in the previous decades. In 1840, the British government had brought Quebec (then Lower Canada) and Ontario (then Upper Canada) into a single entity, the United Province of Canada, to amalgamate French Canadians within a broader colony, where they would be underrepresented and eventually assimilated. The new province, however, further entrenched the existing dualism. In fact, it gave rise to an even more elaborate pattern of dual arrangements, where most political positions and advantages were shared and where practically every decision had to be approved by a double majority. French Canadians were not dissatisfied with this complicated but balanced state of affairs, which gave them an effective veto on virtually all decisions, but their English counterparts grew impatient, especially once the population of Canada West (Ontario) became not less but more numerous than that of Canada East (Quebec). In some respects, the situation was akin to that of contemporary Belgium, with two relatively equal partners constantly having to compromise to govern together. For many Canada West politicians, this requirement appeared increasingly burdensome: "We have two races," declared George Brown in 1864, "two languages, two systems of religious belief, two systems of everything, so that it has become impossible that, without sacrificing their principles, the public men of both sections could come together in the same government. The difficulties have gone on increasing every year" (quoted in McRoberts 1997: 9). Brown advocated a federal alternative, where most powers would be devolved to separate provincial legislatures, so as to let each side govern itself as it wished. In the end, in 1867, the adopted solution was indeed federal but with two additional provinces (New Brunswick and Nova Scotia) and a relatively strong federal government. Beyond the specifics of this history, what is important to see here is that the search for a working solution led the founders less to asymmetry—which made little sense in a dualist context—than to the federal principle, the idea of letting different societies make their own autonomous choices on matters not associated directly to the common purpose. This solution, which combined elements of self-rule and shared rule, emerged as a working compromise between those who would have favored a unitary government and counted on the inclusion of additional provinces to dilute the existing dualism and those who wanted to establish autonomous provinces with their own legislatures, the majority view in Quebec, and also in New Brunswick and Nova Scotia (McRoberts 1997: 10).

The *BNA Act of 1867* constitutionalized both types of aspirations: it created the new country that the majority wanted, with a relatively strong federal government endowed with well-delineated powers and adequate financial resources and also maintained autonomous provinces with their own powers and resources. In English Canada, many celebrated the emergence of a new "nation" with "a common vision and sense of purpose," embodied in the new federal government (Silver 1997: 250–251). In Quebec, by contrast, most saw in the new federation the consolidation of "an autonomous French-Canadian country under the control of French Canadians" (Silver 1997: 218–219). Still, French Canadians also kept a stake in Canada as a whole, just as many in English Canada appreciated as well the benefits of provincial autonomy.

In the beginning of the twentieth century, Quebec politician Henri Bourassa proposed the image of a "double compact" to explain how the federation was meant both to seal a "pact" between English and French Canadians and to bring together the different colonies of North America (McRoberts 1997: 20–21). This idea of a dualist pact fitted better the French Canadian than the English Canadian vision of the federation, but it nevertheless indicated that, even among French Canadian nationalists, a preoccupation remained for the imperatives of unity. Autonomy and unity, shared rule and self-rule: Everywhere in Canada, these two aspirations coexisted, albeit with different weights. Together, they made Canada a federation.

Over time, there were numerous attempts by the Quebec government to gain some form of recognition for its people's distinct, national status, in line with the dualist origins of the federation, but these attempts remained relatively rare and usually quite modest. In fact, there were hardly any attempt to achieve national recognition in the first century of the federation when constitutional conflicts concerned mostly the respect of the initial division of powers and the sharing of financial resources. During the "Quiet Revolution" in the 1960s, Quebec governments began to speak in terms of recognition, equality, and a possible "statut particulier," but concretely, the main political discussions continued to concern the distribution of powers and of resources, questions where tangible gains appeared more likely. Even in the negotiations leading to the adoption of the *Constitution Act of 1982*, the government of René Lévesque did not insist all that much on recognition and sought to make gains on powers and resources through an agreement with other dissident provinces. Having lost its bid for sovereignty, the Quebec government seemed once again ready to play the conventional game of federal–provincial negotiations, defined by the antinomy between autonomy and unity.

The situation changed dramatically after 1982, following the adoption of a new constitutional law without the consent of Quebec's National Assembly. The negotiations that ensued over the Meech Lake and Charlottetown accords, to bring the Quebec government to agree on the new constitution, did include recognition clauses. They failed, however, and for all practical purposes, they sealed the fate of constitutional reforms in Canada. After the 1992 referendum on the Charlottetown Accord, changing the constitution became highly unlikely and in fact more difficult than pursuing Quebec's sovereignty.

All this to say that, throughout Canadian history, the main object of contention between governments concerned less homogeneity and difference as such than autonomy and unity, which is the balance to establish between self-rule and shared rule. In a number of occasions, Quebec governments sought explicit forms of national recognition from other governments in the federation, but in almost every instance, when confronted to a choice, they privileged the enhancement of provincial autonomy over the formal acknowledgement of difference. In 2004, for instance, a federal–provincial–territorial agreement over health financing provided a modicum of asymmetry for the Quebec government, but this asymmetry meant essentially that, in a domain of provincial jurisdiction, the Quebec government would build and collect its own indicators for health care delivery, probably with an approach similar to that adopted elsewhere (Noël 2004). Then as before, autonomy proved more significant than difference. All in all, in Canadian federalism, difference and asymmetry have rarely been the name of the game.

Without ever renouncing to the search for some form of national recognition, the Quebec government—and probably Quebec voters, parties, and groups—usually focused on the more immediate and tangible objective of enhanced autonomy and self-rule, combining it with a lasting preoccupation for fair and balanced shared rule arrangements. The idea was to establish and consolidate a strong and autonomous Quebec state, while making sure that shared rule in federal governance was, indeed, shared. Hence, again and again the Quebec government insisted on the respect of the constitutional division of powers established in 1867 and on a sharing of financial resources more or less on par with this division of powers. When change was sought, it was always with the objective of enhancing, not reducing, Quebec's autonomy. At the same time, Quebeckers expected shared rule to reflect the making of the country and, in particular, to give them and their language an adequate standing in federal affairs. Self-rule and shared rule always weighted more than homogeneity and difference. In this context, when asymmetry emerged, it was usually by accident, as a by-product of conflicts over autonomy and unity.

## Asymmetry as a By-Product

In the first decades of the federation, the politics of autonomy and unity remained muted because state intervention itself was limited. The federal government intervened little beyond its core functions associated to security, trade, and economic development, and the situation corresponded rather well to the classical federal image of the division of powers as a set of "watertight compartments" (Simeon and Robinson 1990: 49). All across Canada, politics remained largely defined by places and territories, and provincial and federal politicians saw themselves primarily as representatives of their own community. Organized support for an interventionist federal state acting in the name of an overlapping national vision simply did not exist. Social actors, political elites, and court decisions tended to reinforce provincial autonomy in a rather symmetric fashion (Simeon and Robinson 1990: 53–54). The most heated conflicts, then, had to do not so much with the pursuit of autonomy but with the demands of unity and shared rule and, in particular, with the place of French Canadians in a federal order where they no longer stood on par with English Canadians. The abolition of French schools in Ontario and Manitoba and debates over Canada's participation in British imperial wars, for instance, polarized public opinion and further convinced French Canadians that their rights were protected strongly only within Quebec. These intense conflicts did not bring, however, a profound transformation of the federation as it was created in 1867.

This transformation came after the 1930s, with the development of the contemporary welfare state. The first important federal initiative in this respect was undertaken during the Great Depression, when the government of R.B. Bennett introduced an *Employment and Social Insurance Act* to create a federal unemployment insurance program. Both the Supreme Court and the Judicial Committee of the Privy Council, Canada's court of last instance at the time, struck down this law because it went beyond federal jurisdiction. Other avenues had to be taken, and from that moment, the politics of the welfare state in Canada became an object of contention in intergovernmental relations (Banting 2005: 101). In the subsequent years, two opposite visions were articulated: One, best advocated by the Rowell-Sirois federal inquiry commission, proposed a stronger federal role in social policy, anchored in a new division of powers and financial resources; the other, defended by Quebec's own Tremblay commission, reaffirmed the primacy of the established division of powers and the importance of providing adequate financial resources to each order of government in a federation created to preserve the autonomy of its constituent entities (Rocher 2009).

For those who favored a strong federal role, two options seemed available: The federal government could either seek constitutional amendments to alter the division of powers or use the financial resources it controlled to do indirectly what it could not do directly. Given Quebec's entrenched reluctance to concede powers to the federal government, the constitutional avenue proved unsuccessful; only two constitutional amendments were adopted in this respect, one to allow for a federal unemployment insurance program in 1940 and the other to make federal old age pensions possible in 1951. Hence, Ottawa rapidly turned to its considerable financial resources to intervene indirectly in areas of provincial jurisdiction either by providing financial support to individual Canadians or by introducing conditional transfers to the provinces, which in effect allowed the federal government to dictate "national standards" in social policy matters. Politically and financially, the federal government was then dominant, and it largely won what in effect had become a "struggle for control over the Canadian welfare state" (Banting 2005: 102).

Once again, however, this struggle was about autonomy and unity. Provincial governments, including the post-1960 Quebec government, were less in opposition to the model of social protection propounded by the federal government than vying for the leeway and capacity to manage autonomously their own programs in areas over which they had constitutional jurisdiction. The federal government, on the other hand, saw itself as the guarantor of a new, more ambitious understanding of Canadian citizenship and, at the same time, as the primary, and indeed sole, instrument of national unity. This was a confrontation between nation-building and province-building in a competitive but relatively progressive process.

In this evolution, no provincial government pushed as hard for autonomy as the Quebec government, and this unique determination led to some de facto asymmetry in the federation. In 1954, for instance, Quebec introduced its own income taxes, a step that would never be taken by any other provincial government. This decision forced the federal government to make special arrangements to leave additional fiscal room to the Quebec government. In 1963 and 1964, Quebec was again the only province to take advantage of the "contracting out" formula it had sought, whereby a provincial government could opt out of a federal shared-cost arrangement and receive financial compensation to finance and run its own equivalent program. The Quebec pension plan, in particular, which was created alongside the Canada Pension Plan, was born out of this opting out logic (Simeon and Robinson 1990: 198–199; McRoberts 1997: 41).

There is no denial that the politics of homogeneity and difference informed and sustained this evolution. Canadian Prime Minister Lester Pearson acknowledged explicitly this reality when he admitted in a 1964 interview that Quebec was "in some vital respects not a province like the others but the homeland of a people" (quoted in McRoberts 1997: 40), and so did Quebec Premier Jean Lesage, who underlined the same year that the creation of Quebec's own pension plan assured that it "would be recognized as a province with special status in Confederation" (quoted in McRoberts 1997: 42). At the same time, the Quebec government rarely sought asymmetry as a good in itself. Opting out usually stood more as an affirmation of autonomy than as one of difference. Once again, for instance, in the negotiations that preceded the 1999 Social Union Framework Agreement, which it did not sign, the Quebec government pushed for the opting out with compensation logic, willingly making autonomy available to all governments wishing to go along (Noël 2000). The same was true later with the 1998 Canada-Quebec Labour Market Development Agreement and the 2005 Canada-Quebec Final Agreement on the Quebec Parental Insurance Plan (Noël 2011). In this perspective, which also suited a federal government wary of asymmetry, it was all the best if other provincial governments availed themselves of the opportunities created by Quebec's initiatives. ¿Café para todos? ¿Por qué no?

What can we conclude from these developments? First, in Canada the core federal principle, whereby autonomy coexisted with unity, always had precedence over the real tension between homogeneity and difference. The recognition of difference did matter, for Quebec in particular, but it was mostly sought and achieved through the preservation and enhancement of autonomy. In fact, for Quebec, a maximum of autonomy for all provinces often appeared as a potentially useful safeguard, as a sort of firewall to protect existing differences. Second, the Canadian example suggests as well that different roads lead to asymmetric arrangements, which may come without a formal recognition of difference, often as by-products of the search for autonomy. This is what happened, for instance, with the Quebec pension plan in 1964 or with the Quebec parental insurance plan in 2005. Third, and most importantly, the ever-debated question of autonomy and unity points to the always-contested nature of federalism, a mode of government that, in a sense, is less a set institutional form than a way of doing politics. In this light, for instance, Spain is indeed a federal country.

## The Real Politics of Real Federalism

Before getting to the mechanisms through which federalism is debated and contested, I wish to open a rather long parenthesis on the academic and political use of comparisons. In a conference such as this one on the ways of federalism, it is normally and rightly assumed that much can be learned from comparing federations. Indeed, the conference program is constructed to make comparisons possible. More than this, in international meetings on federalism, it is often assumed that much can be learned, in particular, from the Canadian experience, that of a rather well-working, long-running, prosperous, and democratic multinational federation. Canadians, of course, have been active in this respect, to promote an aspect of politics that is existential for them, and one of the main organizations in doing so—the Forum of Federations—is Canadian. Canadian scholars and practitioners are indeed convinced—naturally I suppose—that their own federal experience has relevance for others. As Richard Simeon noted with satisfaction in a recent state of the art on the study of federalism, the "Canadian experience with a multinational, regionalized federalism, simultaneously managing other dimensions of diversity has become relevant around the world" (2002: 45).

It is not my intention, here, to deny the importance of comparative scholarship and of enlightened deliberation in the understanding and transformation of federalism. We cannot know too much about the politics of federal countries. I wish to question, however, the role and deployment of expertise on such matters and reaffirm the necessarily political character of federal governance.

Three recent warnings about the politics of expertise—from Will Kymlicka, François Rocher, and Jan Erk—can help us understand the issues at stake. They concern the close connection between Canada's own domestic politics and the construction of international expertise, the illusion of a consensual terrain on federal matters in Canada, and the perils of a too narrow focus on rules and institutions.

Consider, first, the construction of international expertise. In a clear-sighted essay, Will Kymlicka, himself a highly successful partner in the enterprise, acknowledges that the international promotion of the Canadian model of federalism constitutes a core feature of his country's foreign policy (2008: 99). Selling its own brand of multiculturalism and federalism abroad, explains Kymlicka, allows the Canadian government to express the humanitarian dimension of its foreign policy and to present the country as an attractive location for investors, visitors, students, and immigrants. More importantly, these international conversations reverberate inside Canada: "if the rest of the world declares Canadian federalism as a success in accommodating diversity, then Quebec separatists (...) appear as radical ideologues, living in a nationalist myth disconnected from reality" (2008: 101). Likewise, the sought-after international praise for Canadian multiculturalism "serves to disarm right-wing critics of multiculturalism in Canada" (102). Realist assessments are thus warranted. One should keep in mind, in particular, the limits of the lessons that can be drawn from the Canadian experience, which is at once unique and not radically different from that of other democratic multinational federations. One should also remember that words of advice are also expressions of domestic political stances.

Indeed, the politics of expertise tends to downplay the profound divergences that remain within the country. François Rocher has amply documented the gap that persists between the understanding of Quebec scholars—focused on the initial division of sovereignty and on provincial autonomy—and that of their English-Canadians colleagues—more concerned by governmental legitimacy and performance (Rocher 2009). These divergent readings, Rocher notes, are produced and conveyed not only by scholars and experts but also by political actors, journalists, and bureaucrats (2009: 121). They can, in fact, be found among the general public as well, where the same antinomies tend to be expressed (Fafard, Rocher, and Côté 2010). The same could be said of divergences between mainstream conceptions of self-government and more ambitious and transformative Aboriginal visions of self-determination (Irlbacher-Fox 2009). When the Canadian model is promoted abroad, such disagreements are acknowledged and sometimes deplored, but they tend to be minimized or brushed aside in the name of workable solutions. In many ways, however, these lasting differences constitute the heart of the matter (Papillon 2008: 137–139).

Finally, the politics of expertise on federalism is also, well, a politics of expertise. Like all expert or technocratic discourse about social and political affairs, the comparative message on federalism tends to focus on technical or institutional solutions, and, in the international arena, on solutions that can travel. This pragmatic bias, common in the social sciences, is fuelled by a misplaced aspiration to authoritativeness, which encourages the search for apparently uncontroversial, scientific responses (Lindblom and Cohen 1979; Dryzek 1994). It is also encouraged, as Jan Erk noted in a paper presented at the Toronto conference in honor of Richard Simeon, by the neo-institutional turn in the study of federalism, which tends to draw the light on explicit rules and institutions, at the expense of culture, political dynamics, or uncodified aspects of federalism (2011).

The self-conscious politics behind the promotion of the Canadian model, the unwarranted focus on the consensual dimensions of Canadian federalism that accompany this politics, and the technocratic and neo-institutionalist preference for workable and exportable rules and institutions over less palatable social norms and codes all concur to downplay the real politics that animate Canadian federalism, a politics defined by true power relations and conflicts. It is this federal politics that I want to address here, to draw more realist comparative lessons from the Canadian case. My point is not simply to reaffirm that Canadian politics remains stuck in a constitutional impasse. We all know this, and most Canadians, at least outside Quebec, seem happy to accommodate with this unfortunate circumstance. Canadians, writes Peter Russell, have tried and failed to sign a formal, Lockean social contract, but they can nevertheless pursue their informal, Burkean arrangement, which has not served them all that badly (2004). More critical, my friend Guy Laforest would rather speak of a persistent "federative deficit" in our country, thus coming closer to the perspective I want to present here, but he would suggest that this is a Canadian anomaly more than a standard feature of federations (Caron et al. 2009). The argument I want to submit here is more general: As scholars, and at times practitioners, of federalism, we have not always appreciated fully the political tensions inherent to the working of federalism, especially in a multinational context. When we compare, we tend to focus on rules designed to share power and financial resources at the expense of the politics that brought these rules in the first place. Hence, we have not often drawn generalizations on the comparative *politics* of federalism.

Given this limited attention to politics, it would be foolhardy to propose strong theoretical and empirical claims at this stage. A few lines of argument nevertheless seem plausible in light of the Canadian case:

1. In a multinational context, federalism rarely works against the majority. Federal arrangements may be conducive to what could be called enlightened majority rule, but they are rarely contramajoritarian. Alain Gagnon's work, here, is very instructive (2010).
2. Although this is a widely neglected aspect of the question, the politics of federalism is never detached from the broader politics of left and right, the most enduring and universal political opposition (Noël and Thérien 2008). Indeed, the left and the right hold strong views about any country's politics of federalism.
3. Because they generate uncertainty, economic and political crises tend to strengthen majoritarian impulses in federations and they usually lead to a centralization of powers and resources. Autonomous governments can then see

their sovereignty "slip away," and when this happens, "the trend is difficult to reverse" (Rodden 2006: 250–252 and 267).
4. In democratic federations, however, politics is never simply majoritarian, and it is never driven solely by power relations. Legitimacy matters, and so do claims and arguments from minorities (Noël 2006). At times, windows of opportunity open, and these claims are acknowledged. When this happens, the federative imbalance may be corrected up to a point.

Consider, first, the idea that in a federation, as in a unitary regime, majorities rule. In a multinational federation, in particular, at the heart of debates over shared rule and self-rule there is usually a long-standing opposition between the majority and one, or a few, national minorities. In such a context, when one asks rhetorically to privilege not what is good for governments but what is best for citizens, it really means that the standard should be the preferences of the majority. In modern-day Canada, such a majoritarian bias has regularly been justified in the name of the equality of citizens but, as the title of this conference suggests, the ways of federalism are multiple. In her study of Supreme Court decisions, for instance, Andrée Lajoie demonstrates how the court often grants recognition to minorities, and sometimes financial resources, but never goes so far as hurting frontally the values of the majority and, when it came to national minorities, rarely with the consequence of enhancing substantially their autonomous, sovereign power (2002).

In 2006, when the Conservatives came to power in Canada, they promised a new form of "open federalism," in principle more favorable to provincial autonomy. Many would argue, as does Gerald Baier in this book (?), that the Harper government did move in this direction, being more careful than its predecessors not to intervene in areas of provincial jurisdiction and continuing the revision in federal–provincial transfers that was initiated by the previous Prime Minister, Liberal Paul Martin. Nevertheless, as Benoit Pelletier explains elsewhere in this volume (?), the Canadian federation remains plagued by fiscal imbalance at the expense of the provinces. In this respect, the recent federal decision to limit the future growth of the Canada Health Transfer will only make matters worse. While the federal government will be able to reduce revenue or raise spending without worsening the debt, provincial governments will need to increase revenue, reduce spending, or incur growing deficits, just to maintain existing services (Matier 2012). More broadly, as Jean-François Caron and Guy Laforest explained in a recent article, the Harper government has not moved substantially away from a "monist" or majoritarian perspective (2009). On many fronts, one could in fact speak of a regression. When this government canceled the federal–provincial bilateral agreements on Early Learning and Child Care Agreements signed by Paul Martin in 2005 to replace them with a unilateral, ill-conceived, and basically useless Universal Child Care Benefit, it respected neither the principle of self-rule nor the spirit of shared rule (Cool 2007; Prince and Teghtsoonian 2007). Likewise, and more dramatically, when they took power in 2006, the Conservatives simply abandoned the recent federal commitment to take concrete steps to close the gap in living standards between aboriginal peoples and the rest of the population. The agreement reached in November 2005, in Kelowna, British Columbia, was truly unprecedented. It involved the federal government, all the provinces and territories, and representatives from all the major aboriginal organizations, and initiated a consensual and collaborative 10-year process that would finally address a dismal situation (Patterson 2006). The new Indian Affairs Minister, Jim Prentice, reneged on this agreement and stated that his government would not be bound by a pre-election deal that no one had signed and that amounted to little more than "a one-page press release" (Webster 2006). The majority ruled, alone.

After they obtained a new mandate and a majority government, in May 2011, the Harper Conservatives became even more unabashedly majoritarian. Unilingual anglophones were chosen to occupy top official positions in the Supreme Court or in government; British imperial symbols were reintroduced and celebrated in Canadian public affairs; and a host of decisions were taken with little regard for the consequences in the provinces (on criminal justice, health care transfers, or old age security in particular). Thus, one should take with a grain of salt diagnostics suggesting that Canada has become more committed to autonomy and more decentralized. The center still holds.

Aside from the ever-present power of majorities, the politics of real federalism is also profoundly determined by the politics of left and right. There is perhaps no better location than Spain to underline the deep and consequential interaction that exists between federalism and left and right politics. In this country, indeed, debates over autonomy and unity were very much debates between the left and the right (Balfour and Quiroga 2007). Although this is not always acknowledged, this was also the case in Canada. The politics of equal citizenship that, under the Liberals, led Ottawa to intervene massively in areas of provincial jurisdiction was indeed a center-left project, and in contrast, the center-right often appeared more favorable to provincial autonomy. It was a Conservative government, for instance, that attempted in the 1980s to bring the Quebec government to accept the *Constitution Act of 1982*. Note, by the way, that the positions in this case were opposed to those the parties defined in Spain. In Canada, the left stood for unity and the right for autonomy. Within Quebec, by contrast, autonomist forces were mostly on the left and the right supported the federal status quo. Quebec politics was akin to that of Catalonia or Scotland, but Canadian politics was not quite that of Spain or the United Kingdom, where the right tended to carry the flag of unity against a more accommodative left. What is left and what is right in a given place at a given time may vary, according to the alignment of social forces and to the construction of public debates. The conflict between the left and the right, however, always matters for federalism, just as do tensions between majorities and minorities.

Times may also be good or bad. Speaking in Spain and in Europe, today, I cannot say too much about the paramount importance of the fiscal and economic context for the pursuit of debates about federalism and democracy. In *Hamilton's Paradox*, Jonathan Rodden argues that economic crises are usually favorable to federal authorities and to centralization (2006). Historically, this was certainly the case in Canada. The Great Depression of the 1930s prepared the ground for the concentration of most financial resources in the hands of the federal government, the introduction of new federal transfers aimed at individual citizens, and the deployment of a host of shared-cost programs that, in effect, made social protection comparable across provinces. Likewise, in the mid-1990s, Ottawa eliminated its budget deficit largely by cutting transfers to the provinces, leaving them to scramble with the consequences (Noël 2009: 285). Today, in Canada, the situation appears relatively favorable. The Harper government remains committed, however, for ideological reasons, to austerity policies, and the recent evolution of federal transfers and expenditures suggests a move toward an arrangement that will become both less generous and more centralized in favor, in particular, of oil-producing provinces, which also happen to support massively the current government. Context matters.

This being said, majorities do not always prevail and windows of opportunity are sometimes open, allowing for contra-majoritarian innovations. This was the case, most recently, with the signature in 2005 of the Agreement on the Quebec Parental Insurance Plan. Largely unnoticed by scholars and practitioners interested in federalism, this agreement was perhaps the most important since the creation of Quebec's pension plan in 1964. Indeed, it allowed the Quebec government to recuperate from Ottawa a jurisdiction that practice and court judgments had associated to the federal competence on unemployment insurance, duly accepted by the provinces in 1940. The Quebec government put this agreement to good use and created its own parental insurance program, which is unique in Canada and far superior to what is offered by the federal employment insurance program (Noël 2011). Quebec social actors and political parties had built a strong consensus on the question, and the reform proposed by the Quebec government was sound and in line with its broader family policy. Change, however, would never have taken place without a window of opportunity, which came when Paul Martin replaced Jean Chrétien as Prime Minister. While Chrétien was adamant in its opposition to Quebec's demand, Martin proved more flexible and, also, more in need to consolidate the relatively fragile position of a minority government mired in the scandals left by his predecessor. At this time, it is hard to see any comparable opportunity on the horizon. It remains important to note that, at times, federations do change.

# Conclusion

Comparing multinational countries is less useful to pinpoint recurrent features or to find established recipes or models than to take a distance from immediate concerns and get a better grasp of the real politics of federations. This chapter can only begin to address this broad topic, but it nevertheless suggests a few factors and dimensions that scholars and practitioners should keep in mind in this respect.

First, in the Canadian case at least, the politics of autonomy and unity mattered more than that of homogeneity and difference. The dualist origins of the country explain, to a large extent, the primacy given to autonomy; indeed, in a dual relationship, asymmetry simply does not make sense. This observation, drawn from the Canadian case, serves as a useful reminder that, where it matters most, federalism is more about the sharing of power—self-rule and shared rule—than about the expression of distinct social preferences or orientations. In other words, the core debates of multinational societies concern less homogeneity and difference as such than the political expression and institutionalization of distinct national identities.

Second, in such a multinational context, asymmetry may well come as a by-product of the evolution of power-sharing arrangements. In Canadian history, for instance, the Quebec government certainly sought some form of national recognition, but it was generally more bent on preserving and enhancing autonomy than on negotiating distinctiveness. To the "café para todos" intimation, the answer was, most of the times: ¿por qué no? These Canadian developments underline as well the always-contested nature of federalism, which in the end constitutes less an established and well-defined institutional form than a constantly renewed pattern of conflicts, an ever debated way of doing politics. In this respect, Spain, like Canada, is truly federal.

Third, given such recurring debates and conflicts, the expertise that can be derived from comparisons must be informed by prudence and modesty. The Canadian experience illustrates very well that the production and diffusion of knowledge about federalism is itself a political undertaking. This intellectual enterprise constitutes an integral part of the country's ongoing multinational debates. Some political lessons nevertheless can be drawn, at least tentatively, from the Canadian experience. Four such lessons were proposed above, to suggest that, usually, majorities rule; that conflicts over federalism are also very much conflicts between a country's left and right; that economic and social crises tend to favor the center at the expense of autonomous units; and, finally, that windows of opportunity may sometimes open to facilitate reforms favorable to autonomy.

Because power relations matter and because majorities usually have the upper hand, especially in difficult times, strong, explicit, constitutional or institutional rules appear critical for national minorities (on this question, see Gagnon 2011). A well-established federal principle, in particular, that is the entrenchment of a balance between autonomy and unity appears important and more so than the pursuit of difference or asymmetry captured indirectly in the "café para todos" idea. Then again, no matter what the rules are, they always work in context, and the context we also construct together.

# References

Balfour, Sebastian and Alejandro Quiroga (2007). *The Reinvention of Spain: Nation and Identity since Democracy*, Oxford, Oxford University Press.
Banting, Keith (2005). "Canada: Nation-Building in a Federal Welfare State," in Herbert Obinger, Stephan Leibfried, and Francis G. Castles (eds.), *Federalism and the Welfare State: New World and European Experiences*, Cambridge, Cambridge University Press, pp. 89–137.

Basavarajappa, K. G. and Bali Ram (1983). "Section A: Population and Migration," in Statistics Canada, *Historical Statistics of Canada*, Ottawa, Statistics Canada (11-511-XIE).

Black, Edwin R. and Alan C. Cairns (1966). "A Different Perspective on Canadian Federalism," *Canadian Public Administration*, 9, 1, March: 27–44.

Caron, Jean-François and Guy Laforest (2009). "Canada and Multinational Federalism: From the Spirit of 1982 to Stephen Harper's Open Federalism, *Nationalism and Ethnic Politics*, 15: 27–55.

Caron, Jean-François, Guy Laforest and Catherine Vallières-Roland (2009). "Canada's Federative Deficit," in Alain G. Gagnon (ed.), *Contemporary Canadian Federalism: Foundations, Traditions, Institutions*, Toronto, University of Toronto Press, pp. 132–62.

Cool, Julie (2007). *Child Care in Canada: The Federal Role*, Ottawa, Library of Parliament, PRB 04-20E, April.

Dryzek, John S. (1994). *Discursive Democracy: Politics, Policy, and Political Science*, Cambridge, Cambridge University Press.

Erk, Jan (2011). "Theorists of Federalism, Practitioners of Federalism: Engagé Intellectuals, Technocratic Experts, and Scholars," Paper presented at the *Global Promise of Federalism* workshop, Toronto, University of Toronto, 23 September.

Fafard, Patrick, François Rocher and Catherine Côté (2010). "The Presence (or Lack Thereof) of a Federal Culture in Canada: The Views of Canadians," *Federal and Regional Studies*, 20, 1, March: 19–43.

Gagnon, Alain-G. (2010). *The Case for Multinational Federalism: Beyond the All-Encompassing Nation*, New York, Routledge.

Gagnon, Alain-G. (2011). *L'âge des incertitudes: essais sur le fédéralisme et la diversité nationale*, Québec, Presses de l'Université Laval.

Irlbacher-Fox, Stephanie (2009). *Finding Dahshaa: Self-Government, Social Suffering, and Aboriginal Policy in Canada*, Vancouver, UBC Press.

Kymlicka, Will (2008). "Marketing Canadian Pluralism in the International Arena," in Linda A. White, Richard Simeon, Robert Vipond, and Jennifer Wallner (eds.), *The Comparative Turn in Canadian Political Science*, Vancouver, UBC Press, pp. 99–120.

Laforest, Guy (2004). *Pour la liberté d'une société distincte: parcours d'un intellectuel engagé*, Québec, Presses de l'Université Laval.

Lajoie, Andrée (2002). *Quand les minorités font la loi*, Paris, PUF.

Lindblom, Charles and David K. Cohen (1979). *Usable Knowledge: Social Science and Social Problem Solving*, New Haven, Yale University Press.

Linteau, Paul-André, René Durocher, and Jean-Claude Robert (1983). *Quebec : A History, 1867–1929*, Toronto, Lorimer.

Matier, Chris (2012). *Renewing the Canada Health Transfer: Implications for Federal and Provincial-Territorial Fiscal Sustainability*, Ottawa, Office of the Parliamentary Budget Officer, January 12.

McRoberts, Kenneth (1997). *Misconceiving Canada : The Struggle for National Unity*, Toronto, Oxford University Press.

Moreno, Luis and César Colino (2010). "Kingdom of Spain," in Luis Moreno and César Colino (eds.), *Diversity and Unity in Federal Countries,* Montreal and Kingston, McGill-Queen's University Press, pp. 288–319.

Noël, Alain (1998). "The Federal Principle, Solidarity and Partnership," in Roger Gibbins and Guy Laforest (eds.), *Beyond the Impasse: Toward Reconciliation*, Montréal, Institute for Research on Public Policy, pp. 241–72.

Noël, Alain (2000). "General Study of the Framework Agreement," in Alain G. Gagnon and Hugh Segal (eds.), *The Canadian Social Union Without Quebec: Eight Critical Analyses*, Montreal, Institute for Research on Public Policy, pp. 9–35.

Noël, Alain (2004). "Déblocages?," *Policy Options*, 25, 10, November: 48.

Noël, Alain (2006). "Democratic Deliberation in a Multinational Federation," *Critical Review of International Social and Political Philosophy*, 9, 3, September, pp. 419–44.

Noël, Alain (2009). "Balance and Imbalance in the Division of Financial Resources," in Gagnon (ed.), *Contemporary Canadian Federalism*, pp. 273–302.

Noël, Alain (2011). "Asymmetry at Work: Quebec's Distinct Implementation of Programs for the Unemployed," Background Paper, Mowat Centre Employment Insurance Task Force, Toronto, Mowat Centre for Policy Innovation (http://mowateitaskforce.ca/sites/default/files/Noel.pdf).

Noël, Alain and Jean-Philippe Thérien (2008). *Left and Right in Global Politics*, Cambridge, Cambridge University Press.

Papillon, Martin (2008). "Is the Secret to Have a Good Dentist? Canadian Contributions to the Study of Federalism in Divided Societies," in White, Simeon, Vipond, and Wallner (eds.), *The Comparative Turn in Canadian Political Science*, pp. 123–39.

Patterson, Lisa L. (2006). *Aboriginal Roundtable to Kelowna Accord: Aboriginal Policy Negotiations, 2004–2005*, Ottawa, Library of Parliament, PRB 06-04E, May.

Prince, Michael J. and Katherine Teghtsoonian (2007). "The Harper Government's Universal Child Care Plan: Paradoxical or Purposeful Social Policy?," in G. Bruce Doern (ed.), *How Ottawa Spends 2007–2008; The Harper Conservatives — Climate of Change*, Montreal and Kingston, McGill-Queen's University Press, pp. 180–99.

Rocher, François (2009). "The Quebec-Canada Dynamic or the Negation of the Ideal of Federalism," in Gagnon (ed.), *Contemporary Canadian Federalism*, pp. 81–131.

Rodden, Jonathan A. (2006). *Hamilton's Paradox: The Promise and Peril of Fiscal Federalism*, Cambridge, Cambridge University Press.

Russell, Peter H. (2004). *Constitutional Odyssey: Can Canadians Become a Sovereign People?*, Third Edition, Toronto, University of Toronto Press.

Silver, Arthur I. (1997). *The French-Canadian Idea of Confederation, 1864–1900*, Second edition, Toronto, University of Toronto Press.

Simeon, Richard and Ian Robinson (1990). *State, Society, and the Development of Canadian Federalism*, Volume 71, Studies for the Royal Commission on the Economic Union and Development Prospects for Canada, Toronto, University of Toronto Press.

Simeon, Richard (2002). *Political Science and Federalism: Seven Decades of Scholarly Engagement*, Kingston, Institute of Intergovernmental Relations.

Statistics Canada (2007). *Language Highlight Tables, 2006 Census*, Ottawa, Statistics Canada (97-555-XWE2006002).

Statistics Canada (2012). *Quarterly Demographic Estimates, October to December 2011*, Ottawa, Statistics Canada, (91-002-X, vol. 25, no. 4).

Vaillancourt, Yves (2003). "The Quebec Model in Social Policy and Its Interface with Canada's Social Union," in Sarah Fortin, Alain Noël and France St-Hilaire (eds.), *Forging the Canadian Social Union: SUFA and Beyond*, Montréal, Institute for Research on Public Policy, pp. 157–95.

Webster, Paul (2006). "Canadian Aboriginal People's Health and the Kelowna Deal," *The Lancet*, 368, 9532, July 22: 275–76.

Young, Robert A., Philippe Faucher and André Blais (1984). "The Concept of Province-Building: A Critique," *Canadian Journal of Political Science*, 17, 4: December: 783–818.

# The Federal Option and Constitutional Management of Diversity in Spain

Xavier Arbós Marín

## Introduction

In this work, I propose to share some ideas regarding the federal development of our political system. I fear they will not augur well for federalists: I do not think our territorial system will evolve towards a federal model—quite the contrary. As far as it *does* evolve, I believe it will incline more towards homogeneity than diversity. These are the initial impressions that I will later seek to verify and that may orient this work. However, confirming these subjective impressions is not the primary aim of this article. The fundamental idea is that the relationship between federalism and diversity is based more on interest than inevitable attraction. I will explain this subsequently in the introductory section, but it may also prove useful in the general discussion. Although diversity has fitted in very little and indeed badly with constitutionalism, I believe that a federation without federalism is not necessarily the solution to Spain's territorial problems. Neither is it the solution in the version of federalism promoted by significant sectors of doctrine. Perhaps the constitutional formula of the so-called Autonomous State, due precisely to the peculiarities that distinguish it from the canonical federal state, is more suited to accommodating diversity. I will deal with this in the following section. I will now refer to the ideas regarding federalism present in discussions concerning the Autonomous State. I have the impression that if, in the birth of the Autonomous State, there are political demands based on diversity, in a large part of doctrinal federalism re-centralisation is justified and the irrelevance of diversity is postulated. I finish not with a conclusion as such but rather with some final thoughts. The Spanish territorial model does not enable us to reach definite conclusions regarding the issue under study since it lacks the necessary stability. Such a conclusion might prove feasible if

X. Arbós Marín (✉)
Facultat de Dret., Universitat de Barcelona, Av. Diagonal 684, 08034 Barcelona, Spain
e-mail: xavier.arbos@ub.edu

A. López-Basaguren and L. Escajedo San Epifanio (eds.), *The Ways of Federalism in Western Countries and the Horizons of Territorial Autonomy in Spain*, Vol. 2, DOI 10.1007/978-3-642-27717-7_27, © Springer-Verlag Berlin Heidelberg 2013

the model were enshrined in the Constitution, which would enable it to attain the maximum possible legal safety.

We should begin with a brief terminological clarification. It seems necessary to me to distinguish between "federalism" and "federal state", drawing on the classical approach of Preston King.[1] If federalism is a normative theory[2] that postulates territorial distribution of power, the federal state, or federation, is a type of State that may be the object of a descriptive theory. It so happens, however, that we also use the word "federalism" descriptively to deal with that related to distribution of competences and to organs and actors that participate in this distribution in specific federal states. Thus, we refer to "Federalism of the United States" or "German Federalism" to describe processes that may prove contrary to that normative postulate of territorial division of power. This is neither serious nor necessarily erroneous but, as I hope to explain, presents the more centralising versions of the federal states as "federalism" may have seriously encumbered the possible attraction of the federalist doctrine in our country.

Whatever the case, the federal state is set out as an option *vis-à-vis* the crisis of the Autonomous State. In recent times, some reports have highlighted the inefficiencies of our territorial structure,[3] without the factor that causes it appearing, which in my opinion is nothing other than the diversity of feelings of belonging to the political community. Without Catalan, Galician, and Basque nationalism, there would not have been Constitutions such as those of 1978 or 1931. Based on feelings, that diversity is subjective, even though it may be based on objective elements such as language or religious belief. It might be held to be a private matter, but frequently it is not only private. What defines it, whether it be physical appearance, language, or religion, is in keeping with individual personality. Nonetheless, when it does not coincide with those who surround us, our particular human condition is also defined by difference. The empires of the past maintained the differences between individuals: Some, who had the position of citizens, could accede to the institutions and project their culture, their religion, and their language onto public life. Those who did not hold the position of citizen, and were different, lived out their diversity on another level, often as a private matter: between tolerance and respect in good times and under persecution in bad times. However, diversity between inhabitants of an empire is not incompatible with its existence. In fact, those who defend empires *vis-à-vis* national states argue that they have allowed peaceful coexistence between different nations.[4]

---

[1] King (1982), pp. 74–76.

[2] Hueglin (1987), pp. 38–545 (p. 35); LaCroix (2010), p. 10; Riker (2001), pp. 508–514 (p. 509); Scott (2011), p. 1.

[3] For example, in Otero and Hernández (2010), pp. 76–77: The opinions of various experts from civil society are synthesised and, in that which refers to the autonomous model, calls to avoid inefficiencies abound. http://fundacion.everis.com/FUListRepositoryFiles/TransformaEspa%C3%B1a.pdf, consultation: 06/10/2011.

[4] Dalberg Acton (1985a), pp. 409–433 (pp. 425–426). See also his aphorisms regarding federalism and nationality, including Dalberg Acton (1985b), pp. 558–560 (p. 560).

However, at present, when it is frequently taken for granted that each state is the political organisation that corresponds to one nation, diversity may become a relevant question for public life. The fundament of the legitimacy of supreme power is attributed to the nation, and insofar as this is defined with cultural criteria, diversity acquires public significance. There are versions of constitutionalism that promote policies of diversity recognition. A significant example is that of Francisco Caamaño, Professor of constitutional law and Minister of Justice, who stated: "In plural democracy, power which is *blind* to differences is a power which ignores humiliation, its statute of neutrality being an excuse for mockery. The equal dignity with which early liberalism dressed man/citizen is only fulfilled in the hypothesis of a non-existent panorama of homogeneity, as a policy of domination and cultural imposition".[5]

The social aspect of diversity has taken on a political dimension. When what makes us diverse forges feelings of belonging, the human group thus delimited may be imagined as a political subject. It is well known that we argue about what is spontaneous or imposed concerning the connection between that feeling and a political project of self-government, but I believe we can agree that, as regards this work, it does not make sense to posit the debate in absolute terms. Borrowing the categories of "community" (*Gemeinshaft*) and "association" (*Gesselshaft*) from Ferdinand Tönnies,[6] it could be highlighted that, in community, emotional bonds predominate among individuals, whereas in association, those bonds have an essentially abstract, rational and legal nature. The specific reality is located somewhere between these two ideal types, whilst the inherent identity of the group, which is its diversity in relation to another, may embrace emotional or legal aspects. The group becomes a political subject when its distinct existence is invoked as a fundament of an inherent power, and it passes from being a political subject to a legal one when it is recognised by a legal code: either international public law, as a sovereign State, or the state code, as an entity endowed with the right to self-government.

Politically relevant diversity gives us a key for presenting the framework in whose interior federalism appears. In the Declaration of Independence (1776) of the future United States of America, the "nation" is presented as an entity that breaks its bonds with another in order to occupy the place corresponding to it, separate and equal, between all nations on Earth: "When in the Course of human events, it becomes necessary for one people to dissolve the political bands which have connected them with another, and to assume among the powers of the earth, the separate and equal station to which the Laws of Nature and of Nature's God entitle them, a decent respect to the opinions of mankind requires that they should declare the causes which impel them to the separation". There is therefore a specific

---

[5] Caamaño (2004), pp. 353–378 (p. 356).

[6] I have used Tönnies (1979). Tönnies says that the nation "can only exist thanks to its (of the citizens) united rational will, even when that may be a necessary and involuntary product of those wills. Not only is it founded on a present accidental unity, but also on the essential unity which outlives the generations" (p. 254).

differentiation in order to be affirmed as a political subject, which later, and also as a "nation", the Constitution that founded the United States of America establishes: "We the people of the United States, in order to form a more perfect union, establish justice, insure domestic tranquillity, provide for the common defence, promote the general welfare, and secure the blessings of liberty to ourselves and our posterity, do ordain and establish this Constitution for the United States of America".

In the American case, diversity today seems obvious in view of the cohesion fostered by the feeling of financial grievance shared by the American colonists of the time and by the great distance that separated the metropolis from the colonies. In the same cultural context of liberalism generated by the Enlightenment, diversity also delimits the idea of nation. It seems clear in the well-known text of Sieyès: *Qu'est-ce que le tiers État?* The Third Estate is the complete nation insofar as it excludes the privileged, a different category from that of the citizens. If the nation is "Un corps d'associés vivant sous une loi commune et représentés par la même législature", such a definition is preceded by considerations by which the idle and the privileged are excluded from the nation.[7] The nation is later transformed into the human group to which sovereignty is attributed: that is, the ownership of the supreme political power of the State in which its inhabitants have gone from being subjects to citizens.

The nation thus enters the front line of political ideas as a subject of sovereignty. Nevertheless, federalism and national sovereignty are not a good match. If there is a constitution that delimits both spheres of differentiated competences, it is very difficult to maintain the unique and indivisible nature that is normally attributed to national sovereignty. This idea rather favours the principle of nationalities and justifies the right to self-determination. We can insist that national sovereignty belongs to the citizens who form the nation: The citizenry generates the nation. However, this vision does not satisfy everybody: There are those who think that the *demos* of the citizens should coincide with the *ethnos* – with the nation configured by culture or some of its elements. Since Romanticism, cultural diversity has been invoked as a distinctive element of the nation, giving rise to the "principle of the nationalities" formulated by Mancini,[8] endorsed by Stuart Mill,[9] and accepted, among others, although not by ourselves, by Cánovas del Castillo.[10] This principle comes down to the fact that each "nationality" must have its sovereign State.

---

[7] Sieyès (2002). From the first chapter it is stated that the third state is the complete nation. The definition is on p. 5.

[8] Mancini (1873), pp. 1–64.

[9] Mill (1980), pp. 359–366.

[10] Cánovas del Castillo (1884), pp. 11–97. On p. 51, he mentions the principle of nationalities and states: "The existence of the current States distributed around the learned world, surely highly worthy of respect may, and in general *must,* subsist for centuries: but to deny that it is better constructed where there is a single nation, or race or a single language, or, let alone dialects fundamentally linked to the common language, and where all the population is full of equal memories and who love identical traditions, imbued, in sum, by a common spirit, seems like denying the day its light".

The diversity of a group that is perceived as a political subject may mean that those who hope to assume their representation define it as "nationality" or "nation". Whether it really is or not is of little importance. What is most important is that its existence is believed in and that this belief may give or deny legitimacy. Given the unpopularity of foreign domination, the feeling that both governors and governed belong to the same group seems to be a condition for legitimising the former's power. There, we can recognise a dimension of nationalism, insofar as it is postulated that national identity must be common to both governors and governed alike. Taken to the extreme of the principle of nationalities, a State corresponds to each nation, and a State can only have one nation. In a less radical version, and adapted to the shared identities that people can adopt, federalism and nationalism may be compatible. This is the approach of Brendan O'Leary: In a multinational federation, nations can be represented and self-governed.[11] Self-government is not sovereignty, and in a multinational federation, competences reserved for federal institutions do not correspond to a nation. A federation is characterised by combining self-government of the federated entities and shared government in the federation: *self-rule and shared rule*, in the words of Daniel Elazar.[12] That is to say, what is not self-government is not exactly an alien government from which member states are excluded: It is government that is shared, normally in one of the two chambers of the federal legislative power. In this way, and although federalism historically precedes nationalism, the federal state may become a formula that embraces national diversity.

It will not be a magic formula because national diversity can be asymmetrical. In a multinational federation, not all the nations are equal in population or in wealth, and what defines each of them (language or religion, for example) does not have the same dimension or international bonds. Therefore, certain normative features of federalism that characterise the organisation and functioning of the federations stand out. It is the essence of the rule of law and does not require much more explanation. The second can be seen as a limit on democracy that proposes a procedure by which the majority governs. However, in the federations, there are diverse demoi: that which corresponds to the nation of the federation and those inherent to each of the member states that comprise it. For this reason, a double majority is desirable to reform the organisational rules of political power[13]: one that can be attributed to the majority of the population in the whole of the federal state and another in which what counts are the wishes of the member states that comprise it. If a population that is in a minority in the whole of the federation is in a majority in one or more of the member states, their vote as a member state may check any proposals for change that are detrimental to them. Obviously, for these types of clauses to function, the minorities must have a territory in which they are not in

---

[11] O'Leary (2001), pp. 273–296 (p. 278).

[12] Elazar (1987), p. 12.

minority and from where they can promote the essential decisions to activate the safeguards that can protect them in the event of constitutional reform: a safeguard that, from another perspective, may be seen as an intolerable limitation for the majorities.[13] In addition to the formal clauses that we find in some constitutions, federalism has a tradition of taking decisions that are characterised by multilateralism. In that tradition, we can recognise a third federalist recommendation. Just as at the formal level there is diversity of governments, in informal practice it can be easily assumed that there is a diversity of political and social actors. Further, the effort to find agreed solutions reminds the minorities that they are part of the political community and that their opinion may be taken into account. There is no federalism without diversity, and multilateral dialogue seems not only a method but also a value of coexistence.[14] The internal logic of federalism excludes unilateralism in questions that are crucial for a political community.

Whatever the case, (with or without minorities) federalism leads to diversity. It promotes the federal state model, distributing normative competences that, when implemented with autonomy, can engender normative diversity. There is, therefore, a complex legal code, the result of multiple sources.[15] This structure of government and the dynamic of intergovernmental relationships that arise are not merely mechanisms for drawing up public policies: They express the principle of respect for diversity that emerges from the structure and working of the federations. It is true that, by invoking this principle, the problems derived from diversity are not resolved, given that the principles *per se* do not resolve the problems. What they do, importantly, is to give a grounding of legitimacy to the solutions that will always be complex.[16]

Legitimacy in the rule of law is based on constitutional structures: on the principles that are affirmed and the rules for organising power. Solutions can be implemented via public policies, and we have to assume in the contemporary world that reticence towards the actions of governments predominates. Due to the influence of social democracy, twentieth century European constitutionalism opted to include social rights in the constitutional texts. When cultural or collective rights appear in the constitution, a new stage is initiated when all the dimensions of existence, both cultural and material, are taken into account. A circle is thus closed since constitutionalism finally embraces the human condition in its entirety.

---

[13] Simeon and Conway (2001), pp. 338–365 (pp. 340–341).

[14] Friedrich (1968), p. 39: "Federalism, by providing channels for intergroup communication, by delaying precipitate action and offering a stage for intergroup compromise, seems to be one of the political instrumentalities for negotiating the problem of a divided loyalty, by affording both integrative and differentiating forces some room to operate in"; Burgess (2009), pp. 428–440 (pp. 430–431).

[15] Pizzorrusso (1986), pp. 217–235.

[16] De Tocqueville (1837), p. 20.

## The Constitutional Formula

The 1978 Spanish Constitution (SC) established a particular model for territorial distribution of power, inspired by the precedent of the 1931 Constitution. Our fundamental norm establishes a "social and democratic rule of law" (Article 1, SC), without including in this political formula any of the normal descriptions relating to territorial distribution of power. No "regional" or "federal" aspect is mentioned: What is more, if the word "federation" *does* appear, it is to preclude it. Article 145.1 (SC) stipulates that "in no case shall federation of the Autonomous Communities be admitted". Yet, despite its indecisiveness, the constitutional text has been implemented in such a way that, in many respects, Spain can be compared to countries that are undeniably federal.

In an effort to explain this, we can suggest three features that would define the federal constitutional model, partially inspired by the well-known manual of García-Pelayo.[17] The first would be the distribution of competences, carried out by the Constitution itself. From this constitutional origin, the normative faculties of the legislative organs of the federation and those of the federated states are not related according to the hierarchical principle but rather to the hierarchy of competence.[18] Exercising these normative faculties of the legislative bodies may give rise to conflicts if the federation or a member state considers that the sphere of its competences has been invaded. The characteristic feature of federal constitutions is that they foresee a jurisdictional body to resolve conflicts over competences in accordance with the law. This may be considered the second defining element of a federal constitutional order. The third is provided by the compound nature of the formation of federal state will. On the one hand, its laws are drawn up in a bicameral parliament, in which one chamber represents federation member states and the other the population of the federation as a whole. On the other hand, the federal constitution can only be modified with the participation of the federated states: the favourable vote of the majority of the citizens of the whole federation or their representatives in the corresponding chamber is not sufficient.

After these observations, we can now consider our constitutional formula. Article 2 (SC) recognises the right to autonomy "of the nationalities and regions". Self-government is a right, although it is not inherent in the Constitution. For self-government to exist, an Autonomous Statute has to be approved by the National Parliament in the form of an Organic Law in which the competences assigned to each Autonomous Community are specified. In the same Statute, the features of diversity will be reflected depending on each case: a local language that may be official alongside Spanish in the autonomous territory and the description as "nationality" or "region". Recognition of the diversity of collective identities as

---

[17] García-Pelayo (1984), pp. 233–234.

[18] In the contemporary world, it is difficult to find codes that are at the same time homogeneous and closed *per se*. Therefore, I believe that the competence principle is more useful than the hierarchical principle for explaining contemporary public law. See, Modugno (2002), pp. 11–12.

"nationalities" or "regions" is attributed in accordance with the content of each Statute. The Statutes and autonomous laws will also depend on the development of the local language that is different to Spanish, one of the defining elements of diversity. Once autonomy is established, guaranteeing the competence of each level of government is in the hands of the Constitutional Court, which resolves any conflicts. This is laid out in Article 161.1.c of the Constitution. We, thus, see that if general self-government is not established by the Constitution itself, the latter *does* allow it, and its guarantee via a court corresponds to the federal model. However, Autonomous Community participation in legislation is minimal, given that in the second Spanish legislative chamber only a small number of its members have been elected by the Autonomous Assemblies. If the Constitution does not immediately distribute competences, the Spanish political system fits badly into the federal state model. In reality, it rests on what is referred to as the "dispositive principle",[19] which endows political will with a key role. For there to be self-government, it must be requested: The initiative of the Autonomous Communities on the part of Parliament is presented as an exception justified in the "national interest" (Article 144.c, SC). Further, the content of self-government will be specified in a Statute of Autonomy that, like an Organic Law, will be approved by the Spanish Parliament. The constitutional formula transfers regulation of the territorial division of power to legislation: an open formula, moreover, because it is always possible to alter it by extending the extra-statutory competences set out under Article 150 of the Constitution, again via an Organic Law. The initiation, content, and reform of self-government depend on the political will of the representative political parties.

In the Constitution, we find formulae that ensure respect for the distinct identity that each Statute of Autonomy manifests. The Statutes witnessed the "nationality" or "region" that each Autonomous Community wished to give itself, together with the joint official character of their own language, should that be the case, as well as the competence to establish the legal regime thereof. The plurality of "nationalities" and "regions" can be considered one integrative element of the "Spanish Nation"; in the terms of Article 2: "The Constitution is founded on the indissoluble unity of the Spanish nation, common and indivisible homeland of all Spaniards, and recognises and guarantees the right to autonomy of the nationalities and regions which comprise it and the solidarity between all of them". Diversity appears as a defining element of the Spanish nation. It is not homogeneous but rather made up of nationalities and regions. That diversity, however, is irrelevant. There is no legal difference linked to their nationality that makes it different from that which may characterise a region. The official nature of languages other than Spanish remains, for the Constitution, confined to the territorial sphere of the Autonomous Communities (Article 3, SC). It does not prevent their use outside these areas, but it does create a State with diverse official languages in the common institutions. The Constitution takes into account the "circumstances of the insular reality" (Article 138.1, SC) as regards geography. With respect to history, "it protects and

---

[19] Fossas Espadaler (2007). See also Aranda (2011), pp. 231–279, especially p. 250.

respects the historical rights of the "foral" (charter-granted) territories" (First additional provision) and offers a shortcut for access to autonomy to the "territories which in the past had affirmatively decided the Statute of Autonomy projects by plebiscite and have, when promulgating this Constitution, provisional autonomous regimes" (Second transitory provision). The Constitution takes into account factors that explain that there are human groups that consider themselves distinct, but it does not merge them in order to turn geography and history into configurative features of specific political subjects. It could be said that geography and history are more important than their result.

The parties that agreed the 1978 Constitution belonged to the right and left of the Spanish political spectrum and, together with them, the Catalan nationalists. That plurality of the constituent assembly was not to be repeated when essential decisions for distribution of territorial power were taken. The first was taken in July 1981: The centre-right Government (Unión de Centro Democrático: UCD) of Calvo-Sotelo and the main opposition party, the PSOE, agreed[20] to generalise self-government. Until then, a certain correlation between self-government and diversity could be established. The Basque Country, Catalonia, and Galicia were awarded a Statute of Autonomy. To these three territories, whose particular identity has served historically as a base for demanding political power, we have to add Andalusia. In the 1980 referendum, the Andalusians showed clear support for the initiative to attain the highest possible degree of self-government, comparable to that of the three previously mentioned regions. The path foreseen in Article 143 (SC) was to be used, which determined a lower ceiling of competences.

The second decision was taken in 1992 by the Government and the main opposition party.[21] The PSOE and Partido Popular (PP) agreed to extend the competences of the Autonomous Communities driven by the autonomous pacts of 1981. In this way, a further element of diversity was reduced: asymmetry in the degree of self-government. As in 1981, this was achieved with a more reduced base than that on which the 1978 Constitution was founded, with only the two main parties, while the nationalists remained on the sidelines.

The third decision refers to the pact regarding the Catalan Statute of Autonomy (CSA) in 2006. In this case, the decision sprang from a majority wish of the Catalan Parliament to initiate reform of the 1979 Statute. The process began in 2003 in Catalonia, and in 2004, after the elections, the National Government in Madrid changed. After pushing for changes in the procedures through the National Parliament, the new socialist government ended up supporting reform. However, the main opposition party, the PP, opposed the new Autonomous text, challenging it in the Constitutional Court, which gave its ruling (31/2010).

As with the Organic Law on the National Parliament, the Catalan Statute heralded two changes. First, it sought to widen the sphere of competences by

---

[20] Autonomous Agreements signed by the Government of the Nation and the PSOE, 31st July, 1981, Madrid: Presidency of the Government, 1981.

[21] Autonomous Agreements of 28th February, 1992, Madrid: Ministry for Public Administration, 1992.

imposing limits on basic state legislation.[22] The second change entailed extending the identity of Catalonia in its characterisation and language. Thus, in the Preamble, it stated in a roundabout way that Catalonia is a nation, consisting of evoking a prior declaration that, with this content, the Catalan Parliament had formulated. The adjective "national" was added to refer to the symbols of Catalonia.[23]

Finally, it was hoped to strengthen the position of the Catalan language: Among the diverse precepts that refer to the language of Catalonia, Article 6.1 (CSA) stipulates that Catalan should be "the normal and preferential language of the public authorities and the public media of Catalonia" and "also the language normally used as a vehicle for learning in schools". The Constitutional Court declared that the phrase "and preferential" was unconstitutional and that in schools "Catalan must, therefore, be a vehicle for learning in schools, yet not the only language to enjoy said condition, since Spanish must also have equal rights as an official language in Catalonia".[24]

The three agreements mentioned can be considered essential references for understanding the Spanish variant of the composite state. We see in them how territorial distribution of power and diversity contained therein derive essentially from the will of the political actors: the parties, which in turn are the expressions of the popular will in their ideological and territorial variants. The content of the agreements may be considered materially constitutional given that in the Statutes of Autonomy which specify the competences, a territorial division of power is made effective, which the 1978 Constitution allows but does not establish as such.[25] Whatever the case, in none do we find the same consensus that lay behind the

---

[22] Article 110 and onwards of the Statute of Catalonia. According to Constitutional Court Ruling 31/2010, of 28 June, regarding the Catalan Statute, Article 110 should be interpreted in terms of Legal Basis 59. In Article 111 (CSA), it was hoped to limit the capacity of basic legislation of the State by stipulating that it had to contain "principles or minimum common norms with the status of a law, except in the suppositions which are determined in accordance with the Constitution and the present Statute". This observation was declared unconstitutional due to the arguments contained in Legal Basis 60.

[23] Preamble to the CSA: "The Catalan Parliament, embracing the feeling and will of the citizens of Catalonia, has defined Catalonia, by a wide majority, as a nation. The Spanish Constitution, in its second Article, recognises the national reality of Catalonia as a nationality". Article 8.1, CSA: "Catalonia, defined as a nationality in Article 1, has as its national symbols the flag, public holidays and anthem". Constitutional Court Ruling 31/2010 establishes that those expressions should be interpreted in terms of the Legal Basis 12: "For all these reasons, the terms "nation" and "national reality" with respect to Catalonia, used in the preamble, lack legal interpretative effectiveness which, given the special significance of a statutory preamble, would thus stipulate in the Ruling; and the term "national" in Article 8.1, CSA, is in accordance with the Constitution interpreted in the sense that said term refers exclusively, in meaning and use, to the symbols of Catalonia, "defined as a nationality" (Article 1 CSA) and integrated in the "indissoluble unity of the Spanish nation" as Article 2, SC, establishes and would thus be stipulated in the Ruling".

[24] Constitutional Court Ruling 31/2010, Legal Basis 14.

[25] The Statutes of Autonomy complete the Constitution, according to Constitutional Court Ruling 247/2007, of 12th December Legal Basis 6. Ruling 31/2010, Legal Basis 3, with which I disagree, understands that considering the Statutes as "materially constitutional norms (. . .) has no scope beyond the purely doctrinal or academic".

Constitution. In the first two agreements, the Catalan nationalists were absent: from the second, the Spanish centre-right represented by the Partido Popular (PP) was missing. Nevertheless, if the first two cases had no direct consequences on the legitimacy of the system, from the third arises a serious difficulty. The system for territorial distribution of power and diversity is specified in the legislative sphere: that of Organic Laws which that are the Statutes of Autonomy and that of the Organic Laws for transfer and delegation that, under Article 150.2 SC, allow the area of autonomous self-government to be extended without a very precise limit— that of the competences of the State that, "because of their inherent nature, can be transferred or delegated". Everything depends on the legislators: that is to say, the political parties. Yet, norms with the status of law are subject to the Constitution and to the interpretation thereof that the Constitutional Court enforces, parties being able to use the constitutionality control procedure as part of their strategy.[26]

The Spanish Constitution has transferred territorial distribution, together with recognition and management of the different collective identities, to norms with the status of law: the Statutes of Autonomy and the laws foreseen in Article 150 SC, which allow the sphere of competences set out in the Statute of Autonomy to be extended. The Spanish formula makes it possible to attain results comparable to those that federalism proposes and, moreover, to achieve flexibly: It does not have the rigidity of constitutions because it is specified in Organic Laws. However, the deployment of self-government that the Constitution allows lacks the symbolic legitimacy of the constituent agreements of 1978. The Autonomous State thus evolves within another framework that does not bring together the same ideological sectors that imbued the 1978 Constitution. On the other hand, reaction to the Catalan Statute represents a problem of specific legitimacy. The Statute had been approved by 73.9 % of the votes cast but with a very high abstention rate of 50.59 % in the referendum of the Catalan citizens on 18th June 2006. On being contested, the Constitutional Court challenged the legitimacy that resulted from the referendum, in addition to the legitimacy that lay behind the author of the Statute: the Spanish legislator. Further, the ruling resulted in the declaration of unconstitutionality of precepts of the Catalan Statute, the same as others in force in other Statutes, yet which had gone unchallenged by the PP.[27] For example, Article 144 of the Statute

---

[26] Constitutional Court Ruling 31/2010, Legal Basis 2, admitted that the challenge—in this case, the Catalan Statute of Autonomy—could "legitimately correspond to political reasons or opportunism". It should be pointed out that the Autonomous Community Process Bill, derived from the Agreements of 1981, was challenged before the Constitutional Court by, among others, 50 Members of Parliament, including Catalan Nationalists. The challenge gave rise to Ruling 76/1983, of 5th August.

[27] A comparative summary is contained in *El Mundo*, 14/07/2010, p. 7. On the previous page, Luis Ángel Sanz echoed the stupefaction of Carles Bonet, then Senator for Esquerra Republicana de Catalunya, when verifying how the Grupo Popular copied a precept, which it challenged, of the Catalan Statute and presented it as an amendment in the proposal for a Statute for the Balearic Islands.

of Andalusia refers to the Andalusian Board of Justice, based on Article 97 of the Catalan Statute. However, the Catalan precept was declared unconstitutional but not the Andalusian one, since it had remained unchallenged. Another case is that of Article 206.3 of the Catalan Statute, which contains a section declared unconstitutional. This same section appears in Article 123.2 of the Balearic Islands Statute, which has not been challenged either. Setting aside the intentions of all and sundry, a new diversity now appears: What for Catalans is not constitutional *is* constitutional in Andalusia or the Balearic Islands.

From the point of view of our recent constitutional history, the situation is unprecedented. After the pacts of 1978, the Spanish Parliament tried to pass an Organic Law on the Autonomous Community Process (LOAPA), which was challenged by nationalist and communist parliamentarians. The Constitutional Court announced Ruling 76/1983, which substantially altered what the parliamentary representatives of the two main Spanish political parties sought. A combination of political minorities obtained from a court something that it had not been able to achieve by vote: This is similar to what followed the Catalan Statute of 2006. The relevant difference resides in the fact that while in 1983 the supporters of self-government obtained partial satisfaction, their hopes were frustrated by the 2010 Ruling. What is more, as an institution, the Constitutional Court lost credibility on announcing its decision after almost 4 years' deliberation and with some of its members' terms of office prorogated.[28]

The constitutional structure was intended to be flexible, capable of embracing diversity in different forms: when defining the community as a nationality or region (Article 2, SC), when adopting its own co-official language for the Autonomous Community (Article 3, SC), and in the level of self-government by means of the dispositive principle that makes it possible, in the last resort, to include competences not reserved exclusively for the State (Article 149.1, SC). Yet this latter limit can be overturned by an Organic Law for transferring or delegating the competences foreseen in Article 150.2, SC. With these elements, the formula seems ideal for the different aspirations for self-government to be accommodated in both scope and content. However, flexibility is subject to the decisions of the political parties, which are in a position to transfer their initiatives as regards autonomy to the code, legislating or appealing to the Constitutional Court. The agreements of the major parties in Spain have tended to reduce diversity in the levels of self-government. When, through reform of a Statute of Autonomy, an Autonomous

---

[28] To which we have to add that the President of the Constitutional Court was recorded in a conversation with a lawyer who was investigated by the police. The Supreme Court shelved the proceedings regarding this matter: "The Supreme Court closes the file on the proceedings regarding the conversation of Casas with a lawyer", *Público*, 05/06/2008, consultation: 27/10/2010, http://bit.ly/hxAk8h. *El Periódico de Catalunya* on the 2 July, 2010, published the legal grounds of the Constitutional Court's Ruling (31/2010) and the President of the Court ordered an investigation into the leak (*El Periódico de Catalunya*, 03/07/2010, http://bit.ly/d0DED6, consultation: 18/12/2010. She had not ordered an investigation after *El País* (17/04/2010, p. 14) gave advanced notice of the ruling.

Community seeks to enlarge its self-government and does so with the opposition of a national political party, the process leads to a situation in which the self-government of those who aspired to obtain more is reduced while that of some who had followed their example remains unchanged. As a consequence, the majority of Catalan political forces, with the exception of the PP and Ciutadans-Ciudadanos, reject the current autonomous model.

# Federal discourse and diversity

The evolution of the Autonomous Communities has frustrated the expectations of those considered to be their promoters. In these circumstances, constitutional reform in a federal sense seems a viable alternative, although it poses a problem of credibility.[29] From the moment that self-government spread in 1981, an important part of the doctrine of Spanish public law proposed that the Autonomous State should advance towards cooperative federalism. Almost 30 years later, it still seems to be the model sought by Rodríguez Zapatero, President of the Socialist Government between 2004 and 2011.[30] With respect to diversity, political efforts to recognise so-called "differential facts" proved to be in vain.[31] In the first investiture debate of Rodríguez Zapatero, in 2004, the candidate for the Presidency of the Government presented a programme that included certain proposals for constitutional reform such as reforming the Senate (Upper House) so as to convert it into a federal-like second chamber and including the name of the Autonomous

---

[29] I developed this idea in Marín (2006).

[30] José Luis Rodríguez Zapatero: "I have launched what we could call a federal programme. It is a model typical of the Federal States, a programme of financial coordination where the central Government provides resources for an objective – in this case an objective which everybody can consider reasonable – to which the Autonomous Communities contribute and shared action is agreed. Its aim is not to invade the territory of any competence, but rather to agree the areas where the obligations pertain to both State and Autonomous Communities, because logically there are competence rules for positing the perspective in terms of the responsibility of the central Government or the Autonomous Communities". *Diary of the sessions of Congress*, number 82, 2009, IX Legislature, p. 11, 13/05/2009. See also the speech of Jordi Sevilla, Minister for Public Administration in 2004, before the Senate: "Cooperation is the essence of the process which we want to set up and we are sure that its logic – which has an enormous power – will eventually be introduced in all the territories. The dynamic of cooperation in search of an effective joint ruling of an Autonomous Spain demands the widest possible agreements in which all the political forces with parliamentary representation can participate. To integrate plurality is, in sum, the meaning of what we have to do. It is a question, therefore, of initiating a new stage, leaving behind the mechanics of confrontation and laying new foundations for a new shared management of public matters within a framework of cooperation". A speech, at his own request, to explain the general outlines of the autonomy policy of the new Government: Autonomous Community General Commission, *Diary of the sessions of the Senate, number* 25, 2004, VIII Legislature, p. 4, 3/06/2004.

[31] I dealt with this matter in Marín (2008), pp. 1543–1562. The classical text of reference is that of Aja (1999).

Communities.[32] In a political context marked by the debates surrounding the 2006 Catalan Statute, these reforms were not even initiated although they did appear to evidence a keen desire to reflect the evolution of the Autonomous State in the Constitution.

Federalism hovers over the history of the Spanish territorial formula of 1978, but with a centralising proposal that leaves diversity to one side. The Autonomous Community pacts of 1981 assumed the immediate generalisation of self-government as a rule[33] and not as a temporary exception to benefit the people of Catalonia, Galicia, and the Basque Country. Eduardo García de Enterría remarked upon this orientation towards federalism: "The declared federal formula remits the entire configuration of the system to the Constitution without detriment to its complements remitted to member states. There are more and more of us who consider it rather superior to that adopted by our Constitution and to be the inevitable conclusion for the system in the not too distant future".[34] In particular, it opts for a version of federalism that displays its contempt for the legal rules that guarantee the distribution of competences and the Autonomous Communities:

> Federalism - old style - is dead. Yet federalism - new style - is alive and well and living in the United States. Its name is *intergovernmental relations*.
>
> Old-style federalism is a legal concept, emphasizing a constitutional division of authority and functions between a national government and state governments, with both levels having received their powers independently of each other from a third source - the people. New-style federalism is a political and pragmatic concept, stressing the actual interdependence and sharing of functions between Washington and the states and focusing the leverage that each actor is able to exert on the other.[35]

The centralising sense of federalism promoted by García de Enterría has been evident ever since, in the United States, this new orientation was first studied.[36] In Spain, although without much repercussion, it was brought to our attention by González Encinar:

> Whatever the judgement which cooperative federalism deserves, the fact is – and, as such, it is worth remembering – that the majority political parties believe they have discovered a panacea in the techniques of cooperative federalism, the solution to many of the problems inherent in our system of decentralisation. That cooperative federalism, as well as a "modern" type of decentralisation, may also be the form that decentralisation takes in some modern federal states is something that the majority opinion in Spanish doctrine chooses or hopes to ignore.[37]

---

[32] *Diary of sessions of Congress*, number 2, 2004, VIII Legislature, p. 19, 15/04/2004.

[33] A critical point of view regarding the generalisation of self-government was expressed by someone who presided over an Autonomous Community for 20 years. Bono (2011). In the article it is also said that "This was done, as I have explained, to please the Army at the end of the dictatorship which threatened to rebel if the Constitution recognised the right to self-government of the Basque Country and Catalonia". José Bono was Minister of Defence.

[34] De Enterría (1985), pp. 411–416 (p. 411).

[35] Reagan and Sanzone (1981), p. 3. Italics by the authors.

[36] . See, Benson (1941), p. 21.

[37] González Encinar (1991), pp. 49–62 (p. 60).

In the cooperative federalism approach, the notion of exclusive competences appears to lose all sense. In a relatively rudimentary way in regard to intergovernmental relations, Richard Rose stated that "policy unites what constitutions divide".[38] In the development of Spanish constitutional doctrine, the division of power inherent in federalism becomes blurred at the level of concepts and, specifically, that of exclusive competences that is considered typical of an "old mythology" vis-à-vis the social realities in which the problems include competences both of the State and the Autonomous Communities. Our Constitution succumbed to that mythology:

> The drafters of the two Statutes approved up to now [Basque Country and Catalonia] have fought their entire battle around this key concept which in the mind of the local political forces would be the scale of autonomy, in the same way that, in the spirit of those who have believed themselves to be fighting against the dissolution of the State, certain exclusive competences in favour of this would be the essential guarantee of its maintenance.[39]

This pragmatism, which is opposed to the rigour of legal norms, however, is not always maintained. It vanishes when it is a question of the exclusive competences of the State: They are intangible.

> In conclusion, in the entire set of exclusive State competences, which are set forth in Article 149.1 of the Constitution, the specificity of the common nucleus of the Spanish nation that Article 2 formulates as a basic constitutional principle must be seen, of those that dominate this interpretation of the supreme norm. The intangibility and inseparability of those competences from the hands of the State, which is the intention of its constitutional description as exclusive, is thus presented as a derivation of the clause of indissolubility and indivisibility of the Nation contained in Article 2.[40]

The federalism that the dominant doctrine in Spain proposes loses its normative dimension. It rejects territorial division of power, as well as the notion of exclusive competences. In other words, it seems to defend a federation in which there are no legal guarantees for self-government or a sphere in which autonomy can be exercised. Under the hegemony of certain exclusive competences of the State, to which all legal force *is* given, cooperation as a coordinated exercise of competences is emphatically proposed. It has its repercussion in the Constitutional Court, which has invented the existence of a principle of cooperation, which does not appear in the Constitution. Obviously, it states it differently, with the complacency of someone who does not have to give explanations. Constitutional Court Ruling 194/2004, of 4th of November (Legal Basis 19), states that said principle, "which need not be justified in specific precepts, is implicit in the very essence of the type of territorial

---

[38] Rose (1985), pp. 13–32 (p. 21).

[39] De Enterría (1980), pp. 13–23 (p. 26).

[40] De Enterría (1982), pp. 63–94 (pp. 76–77).

organisation of the State which is established in the Constitution" (Ruling 18/1982, 4th May, Legal Basis 14) since it is linked to "the need to make the principles of unity and autonomy compatible" [Ruling 214/1989, Legal Basis 20.e].[41]

On the other hand, empirical studies show that in cooperation the hegemonic position is that of the State. Although it does not always have a clear jurisdiction as regards competence,[42] the State has the political resources and initiative to implement programmes that usually rely on the consensus of Autonomous Communities.[43] When national policy affects the competences of the Autonomous Communities, we should ask ourselves why the latter fail to react.

Probably, invasion of competences is not perceived or the advantages gained are deemed to outweigh the temporary erosion of self-government. Certain data allow us to illustrate the lack of respect for the distribution of competences. The norm that, in practice, regulates cooperation in Spain is Law 30/1992 (26th November), concerning the Legal System for Public Authorities and the Common Administrative Procedure (LRJAP in Spanish). In its present draft, Paragraph 1 of Article 6 states that "The General Administration [of the State] and the Public Organisations linked to or dependent on the latter may sign agreements with the corresponding bodies of the Authorities of the Autonomous Communities in the area of their respective competences". In Paragraph 2 of the LRJAP, an ambiguous expression is used. It lists the requirements of the collaboration agreements between the State and any Autonomous Community, stating that they should specify "when thus appropriate: (B.) the competence which each Authority exercises". It is very difficult to imagine any case in which mention of its title of competence is "not appropriate": The principle of legality and legal safety (Article 9.3, SC) appears to dictate that the source of the competence by which each party acts is explicitly mentioned.[44] Until 2009, the Official State Gazette (the BOE) published cooperation agreements in

---

[41] The Constitutional Court does not justify the existence of that principle at all. Constitutional Court Ruling 18/1982, of 4 May, Legal Basis 14, states: "As the State Lawyer alleges, the obligation to remit the "Official Gazettes" is explained as a duty of collaboration stemming from the general *duty of reciprocal aid* between State and Autonomous Authorities. *This duty, which it is not necessary to justify in specific precepts,* is found to be implicit in the essence *per se* of the type of territorial organisation of the State which is implanted in the Constitution, although we should recall that that the principle of coordination, in relation to Autonomous Communities, is elevated by the fundamental norm to the consideration of one of the principles of action (Articles. 103.1 and 152)". What "is not necessary to justify in specific concepts" is the "duty of reciprocal aid" and not the principle of cooperation. The italics are ours.

[42] The reference of the Council of Ministers of 13th February, 2009, regarding a programme of aid to victims of domestic violence stated: "Although we are dealing with a competence of the Autonomous Communities, the Ministry for Equality distributes this fund, within the programmes to be implemented regarding comprehensive social assistance for victims, to strengthen and prioritise those devoted to assisting foreign women and minors exposed to this type of violence". http://bit.ly/sobWLQ, consultation: 29/12/2011.

[43] León-Alfonso and Mónica Ferrín (2009), pp. 253–275. See also: García Morales (2009), pp. 41–122 (pp. 52–53).

[44] Montalvo (2000), pp. 55–56.

which precepts of Autonomous Statutes repealed 2 years previously were cited as competence titles.[45] It seems more serious that transfers of competences are carried out almost 30 years after an Autonomous Statute has come into force and that the transfers appear as compensation for an agreement on parliamentary stability. This is what occurred on 14th October 2010, when transfers to the Basque Country were signed after the agreement between the governing PSOE and the Basque Nationalist Party (PNV) and the Canary Islands Coalition (CC).[46] What is more contradictory in relation to the cooperative federalist discourse is the rigour with which party discipline is enforced on the autonomy of the authorities. At times it can be observed with extraordinary clarity. During a Fiscal and Financial Policy Meeting in 2009, which brought together the economic heads of the Autonomous Communities with the Finance Minister of the central government, the Regional Minister for the Community of Madrid declared to the press: "The Madrid PP would have voted against if it had not been ordered to abstain. I can say it louder but not more clearly".[47] We note that he spoke in the name of a political party and not the institution that he represented. On the other hand, it is not difficult to imagine that same discipline may govern in other parties whose sphere reaches beyond an Autonomous Community. The federalism that is most frequently manifested is hostile to the exclusivity of normative competences. It is described as cooperative while the hegemony of the political initiative of the State is in fact maintained *vis-à-vis* the Autonomous Communities, cooperation seemingly proving a continual alternative to self-government. "We have culminated the self-government phase and we must develop a phase of cooperation", stated Rodríguez Zapatero when appearing as President of the Government before the Senate in 2010.[48]

If references to self-government have been subsumed in cooperation, the reflection of diversity has been maintained as expressed in the constitutional text of 1978.

---

[45] For 2009, see the agreements of the Ministry of Health and Consumer Affairs with Aragon in the BOE 22/01/2009; of the Ministry of Industry, Commerce and Tourism with Andalusia in the BOE 01/10/2009; of the Ministry of Education, Social Policy and Sport with the Valencian Community in the BOE 09/02/2009; of the Ministry of Industry, Commerce and Tourism with the Valencian Community in the BOE 30/03/2009; of the Ministry of Work and Immigration with Andalusia in the BOE 24/02/2009; of the Ministry of Industry, Commerce and Tourism with the Balearic Islands in the BOE 28/03/2009; and of the Ministry of Equality, also with the Balearic Islands, in the BOE 23/10/2009.

[46] *El País*, 15/10/2010, http://bit.ly/9gNA9K, consultation: 16/10/2010.

[47] Beteta (2009), p. 12.

[48] *Diary of sessions of the Senate*, number 80. IX Legislature, 2010, p. 4213, 25/05/2010. On 30th August 2003, the PSOE had approved a document entitled: "Plural Spain: constitutional Spain, Spain united, Spain positive", http://bit.ly/sPHcbf, consultation: 30/12/2012. It is curious to recall what Javier Arenas said in 1999, when he gave a talk about Autonomous Communities at the XIII National Congress of the PP ("Plural Spain [*sic*], a common future project"): "[I find it] necessary that after the natural phase of claiming competences there will be a new phase in which the shared assumption of responsibilities, proposals for cohesion and improvement of the common model predominate according to the efficacy and efficiency of the service to citizens". *El País*, 09/09/1999, http://bit.ly/tTMdzF, consultation: 30/12/2012.

In the 1990s and since nationalist governments have been in power in Catalonia, recognition of so-called differential facts has been sought in an attempt to justify greater levels of self-government. The President of the Catalan Parliament, Jordi Pujol, addressed a conference at the Carlos III University in Madrid in which he stated:

> The existence of differential facts should be borne in mind. When it is said, and I quote: "we have to close Title 8" or "we have to move on from the period of ambiguities" or "we have to reach a pact on the Autonomous Communities", then things have to be called by their name. For 10 years we have been moving in a kind of calculated and perhaps positive ambiguity, although at times, after what I have just said, one has doubts about it. But if we now have to close the chapter, things have to be that way, and we have to call them by their name which means that there is a reality which President González calls the "differential fact" and which I do, too.[49]

We must remember that in 1992 the autonomous agreements were signed by which the competences between Autonomous Communities were homogenised upwardly. Seeking to recognise diversity, understood in this context, was not limited to a nominal question. Recognition was confined to mentioning whether the only thing posited was the explicit binding of the concept of "nationality" or "region" (terms from Article 2 of the Constitution) to each Autonomous Community explicitly mentioned in the constitutional text.[50] Demanding peripheral nationalism poses more than just a question of names: It seems to aspire to recognition of national diversity being linked to a greater level of self-government and to the nationalities being recognised as playing a specific role in Spanish institutions. From this sector, no formal proposal is presented for reform of the Constitution. In fact, as has been said, in 2004 a reform of the Constitution was announced, which included specific mention of the names of the Autonomous Communities and reform of the Senate, and a report was requested from the Council of State regarding all the modifications proposed. That report echoes the debate regarding the "differential facts", given that the Council of State wondered whether such facts "have to be the basis for a distinct constitutional status in the Senate as regards a chamber of territorial representation". After enumerating what in the constitution are considered differential facts, the Council of State declares: "One thing is to recognise difference and its need for safeguards and protection, yet it is quite another to transform it into a system dominated by the will of the state. Given that the majority of the differential facts are built or specified in competences assumed by the Statutes of Autonomy, that will be the sphere for developing their

---

[49] Pujol (1991), p. 33. The person who first used the expression "differential fact", referring to the language of Catalonia, was Francesc Cambó in his: *Per la concòrdia* of 1929; cited in Cambó (1984), pp. 467–515 (p. 473).

[50] It was the demand of the Catalan nationalist Member of Parliament Duran i Lleida in the investiture debate of Rodríguez Zapatero in 2004: *Diary of sessions of the Congress of Deputies,* number, 2, 2004, VIII Legislature, p. 44, 15/04/2004. There (p. 73), the Basque Nationalist Member of Parliament Erkoreka directly demanded recognition of the multinational nature of the State.

authority and implementation".[51] In other words: for the Spanish Constitution, the difference is politically irrelevant at the state level.

## An uncertain future

The future of the Autonomous State is constitutionally unpredictable, almost by definition. Because of constitutional rigidity, it is not a settled model. Distribution of competences, which is inherent in any federal formula, does not appear in the Constitution. It is carried out through organic laws, leaving self-government of the Autonomous Communities in the hands of National Parliament legislators (not of the constituent members). The primary mechanism is the Statute of Autonomy, which has the list of exclusive competences of the state from Article 149.1 SC, as the maximum ceiling. Furthermore, the sphere of competences of each Statute can be discretionally extended through competences set out in Article 150.2 SC: In that case, the limit is as indeterminate as the expression it uses. They can only be transferred or delegated via organic law, the "faculties corresponding to that regarded as state matters which by their own nature can be transferred or delegated". The flexible nature of the Autonomous State is perhaps the facet that least fits into the theoretical pattern of the federal state. It comes close when the distribution of competences reaches a materially constitutional level: Article 28.1 of the Organic Law of the Constitutional Court empowers it to declare the unconstitutionality of laws that "within the constitutional framework, had been passed to delimit the competences of the State and the various Autonomous Communities". Nevertheless, if the constituent process did not create a federal Constitution as such, it did seem to show attitudes close to federalism: firstly, a positive view of self-government—that autonomy is a right (Article 2, SC), and secondly, the multilaterality that is shown in taking into consideration the political will of those affected when the legal framework of its autonomy is established and when it is reformed. The system of access to self-government via the statutes, and that of their reform, appears to protect it.[52] With regard to the diversity of collective identities, the Constitution accepts it without awarding it political importance. As has been said, it does not link greater or lesser degrees of autonomy to the aspect of "nationality" or "region" (Article 2, SC). Nor does it give a general dimension, for all Spain, to linguistic diversity, which may be regulated by the Autonomous Statutes.

Based on this brief background summary, we can consider what federalism may mean for the future of the Autonomous State, and the importance that diversity may have in its evolution. The final consideration of this work is inevitably marked by a political climate in which self-government is associated with inefficiency. One fairly clear example is a paragraph taken from a speech that the President of the Community of Madrid, Esperanza Aguirre (PP), gave at a summer course for a foundation linked to the Partido Popular:

---

[51] Council of State (2006), pp. 329–332 (p. 331).

[52] Castellà Andreu (2004). Lasagabaster Herrarte (2005), pp. 15–56.

If the two parties restore consensus and forget their own personal interests, agreements could be reached to reduce bureaucracies. The state, autonomous and municipal competences could be defined and delimited once and for all to avoid duplication. The functioning of the Sectorial Conferences could be truly strengthened. Certain competences could be returned to the State so that some services might work better and more cheaply. Those regiments of national functionaries which have disappeared could be restored and even constitutional reforms could be addressed in order to conclude the decentralisation process which at the moment remains open.[53]

It is no exaggeration to assign preference for a change of model to this point of view in which decentralisation is reduced and the opportunity to augment self-government is brought to a conclusion. Naturally, this point of view is entirely legitimate yet represents a political stance that should be taken into account. We must remember that the Autonomous State, in its establishment and development, depends on the influence of the political parties with parliamentary representation. Direct influence is obvious because it is the legislators who approve the Statutes of Autonomy and laws of transfer and delegation that increase their competences. Indirect influence is exerted through the Constitutional Court. Its composition depends on party decisions and some of the rulings that most affect the Autonomous State stem from appeals that are lodged due to decisions of this type. This is the case of two that we already mentioned: Constitutional Court Ruling 76/1983, regarding the LOAPA, and Ruling 31/2010, concerning the Catalan Statute of Autonomy.

The political parties are the main actors in the Autonomous State. They have the democratic legitimacy given by the citizens at each election, and their behaviour is influenced by the electoral costs and benefits that can be derived from each decision. However, not all parties address the same electorate: There are parties that seek votes throughout Spain and others that are limited to one or various Autonomous Communities. The stance that a party adopts in relation to self-government or diversity may have electoral repercussions. The popularity of the leaders and the votes obtained may vary if the demands for increasing self-government or recognising diversity by means of "national" terminology are admitted or opposed. Moreover, no party that hopes to govern will insist on any ideological position that might lose its votes. Neither the PP nor the PSOE appears to have, among their future proposals, an increase in self-government of the Autonomous Communities and recognition of diversity, whereas these topics are ever present in the programmes of the nationalist parties of Catalonia, Galicia, and the Basque Country. They may also be present in the territorial organisations corresponding to the PP or the socialists. Tension is thus inevitable.

This could be considered a feature inherent to democratic life, which is characterised by plurality of opinions. The problem is that the tension may lead to a generalised conflict of legitimacies. For some, in accordance with the Spanish Constitution, the relevant *demos* in decision-taking is the Spanish nation as a

---

[53] Aguirre (2011), p. 16.

homogeneous and sovereign political subject (Article 1.2, SC). In the last resort, it is the representation of that nation in Parliament (Article 66, AC) that decides the laws that approve or reform the Statutes of Autonomy and, in extraordinary cases, suspension of self-government (Article 155, SC). If the Constitution has to be reformed (Articles 166–168, SC), only the Spanish nation or its representatives may decide. However, there is an opposite point of view, which is present in those who consider that there is another political subject, different to the Spanish nation, that gives legitimacy to the decisions. The framework of democratic action is also a nation, but not the Spanish one. That nation also has its democratically representative institutions that express aspirations regarding self-government or recognition. When the decision of the National Parliament dilutes them or when a ruling of the Constitutional Court frustrates them, the interpretations of both sectors differ. For some, it is the normal working of a democratic state subject to a Constitution in terms that the Constitutional Court decides. For others, it is an imposition on the democratic decision of the nation that has the legitimacy to take that decision, whatever the Constitution might say.

The flexibility of the Spanish Autonomous Community formula, based on the dispositive principle, may at the same time prove to be both the solution and the problem. It has certain clear limits: The right to self-determination is impossible since the indivisibility of Spain is proclaimed and does not allow Spain to be denied its definition as a nation (Article 2, SC). It allows a wide margin for embracing differing aspirations, both regarding levels of self-government and recognition of collective identities. As a technique for the territorial distribution of power and for adapting to diversity, its virtue is its very capacity to adapt. The quality of the outcome, however, is by no means ensured. Everything depends on the political actors involved reaching acceptable arrangements, a very difficult task, since they operate depending on electoral strategy or whether, when taking decisions, some relevant point of view is marginalised. Those excluded can then go to the Constitutional Court, hoping that the political veto of the minority is achieved through a ruling that declares it unconstitutional.

The autonomous state appears to have come full circle, with reproaches from all sides. According to some, it has not gone far enough and has failed to satisfy their aspirations for improved self-government. For others it has gone too far, fostering administrative inefficiency or reprehensible linguistic policies. In view of the crisis, the federal option seems to be an alternative. Following the well-known model, we would have to begin by including distribution of competences in the Constitution, thus removing it from the legislators. The composition of the Senate would correspond to the federal formula as a chamber for exclusive representation of the Autonomous Communities and a federal change minimally recognisable would thus be set in place. Nothing guarantees, however, that a more integrative solution than the present Autonomous State may thus be attained. A constitution could not be drawn up that would satisfy both those favouring greater centralisation and less diversity, on the one hand, and opponents thereof, on the other. The resulting constitution would be based on a less plural foundation than that which has maintained the 1978 Constitution and would reopen a serious internal wound, much deeper of course than the one caused by the reform of Article 135 of the Constitution in 2011, with only the votes of the PSOE and PP. In the history of Spain, tensions between the centre and the periphery are associated with violent civil conflicts, which is not the case of the limits on public debt contemplated under revised Article 135.

The federal option requires a constitutional change with a potentially conflictive outcome. On the other hand, a credible federalism that sustains it cannot be discerned. What is being promoted is cooperative federalism, which leaves aside or is opposed to the idea of exclusive competence, which is what motivates those who aspire to self-government. Administrative criteria predominate, thereby avoiding deep-seated questions. The problems not only concern public policy but also "politeia" or polity. The core of the question was summarised and highlighted by Juan Linz in 1973: "Spain today is a state for all Spaniards, a nation-state for much of the population, and only a state but not a nation for important minorities".[54] Five years later, a Constitution was approved, which embraced diversities reasonably well. Consecrating the national character of Spain, it was accepted that Autonomous Communities were established as "nationalities". This peculiar recognition of diversity, however, remained at the internal level of each Community. The most striking case is that of languages other than Spanish whose formal use outside the Autonomous territory is limited to certain sessions in the Senate, but neither in those terms is it generally accepted. In these conditions, nothing guarantees that constitutional reform (federal or otherwise) would have the plural basis of consensus that the 1978 Constitution had. A new distribution of competences would probably move in a centralising direction. If, instead of transferring it to the Autonomous Statutes, the area of competences of the Autonomous Communities were fixed in the Constitution, the frustration of those in favour of greater levels of self-government would be considerable. Centralisation will be seen to be irreversible if, moreover, the possibility of correcting it by extending competences via Article 150.2 SC disappears.

The panorama here presented stems from the hypothetical agreement on constitutional reform limited to the Partido Popular and the PSOE. It could be enforced in the National Parliament without problems and, if submitted for approval by referendum, would probably obtain a majority that was popular with the electorate of both. From the legal point of view, there would be little to say regarding the democratic nature of the procedure. Nonetheless, it should be remembered that, politically, it would be more dubious, according to our concept of *demos*. If it is believed that only the Spanish nation is a constituent political subject, everything is correct. If it is believed that the determining democratic legitimacy is given by another different nation, the political dimension of the internal diversity of Spain will flourish. The strictly legal dimension of the citizen has been unable to dilute the political strength of the differences of identity. It matters little whether it exists or not or whether its manifestations are imagined or genuine: They account for

---

[54] Linz (1973) pp. 33–116 (p. 99).

political behaviour and its being channelled through political parties. On all of them, and especially those represented in the National Parliament, has fallen the weight of the Autonomous State. The crisis facing the unique Spanish formula is the result of their inability to agree and to convey to the citizens an example of harmony in important questions. However, there have also been episodes in which specific agreements have been reached with those excluded from the general Autonomous pacts. They could be repeated. If we like: federalism without federation rather than federation without federalism.

# References

ALESSANDRO PIZZORRUSSO: "Sistema delle fonti e forma di Stato e di governo", *Quaderni constituzionali*, number 2, 1986, pages 217–235.

ALEXIS DE TOCQUEVILLE: "Le système fédératif repose donc, quoi qu'on fasse, sur une théorie compliquée, dont l'application exige, dans les gouvernés, un usage journalier des lumières de leur raison", *De la démocratie en Amérique I*, Tome II. Bruxelles: Société belge de libraire, 1837 [1st edition, 1835], p. 20.

ALISON LACROIX: *The Ideological Origins of American Federalism*, Cambridge: Harvard University Press, 2010, p. 10.

ANTONIO BETETA, Regional Finance Minister for the Madrid Community, in *La Vanguardia*, 16/07/2009, p. 12.

ANTONIO CÁNOVAS DEL CASTILLO: "Discurso pronunciado el 6 de noviembre de 1882 [in the Ateneo of Madrid]", in his work: *Problemas contemporáneos*, Madrid: printed by A. Pérez Dubrull, 1884, 2 vols. Vol. II, pages 11–97.

BRENDAN O'LEARY: "An iron law of nationalism and federation? A (neo-Diceyan) theory of the necessity of a federal *Staatsvolk* and of consociational rescue", *Nations and nationalism*, vol. 7, num. 3, 2001, pages 273–296 (p. 278).

CARL. J. FRIEDRICH: *Trends of Federalism in Theory and Practice*, New York: Federick A. Praeger, 1968, p. 39.

J.M. CASTELLÀ ANDREU: *La función constitucional del Estatuto de Cataluña*, Barcelona: Institut d'Estudis Autonòmics, 2004.

COUNCIL OF STATE: "Report on the modifications to the Spanish Constitution", number E 1/2005, 16th February, 2006, p. 329–332 (p. 331).

DANIEL J. ELAZAR: *Exploring Federalism*, Tuscaloosa: The University of Alabama Press, 1987, p. 12.

EDUARDO GARCÍA DE ENTERRÍA, "Estudio preliminar", in his: *La distribución de las competencias económicas entre el poder central y las autonomías territoriales en el derecho comparado y en la Constitución española*, Madrid: Instituto de Estudios Económicos, 1980, pages 13–23 (p. 26).

EDUARDO GARCÍA DE ENTERRÍA: "La significación de las competencias exclusivas del Estado en el sistema autonómico", *Revista Española de Derecho Constitucional*, number. 5, 1982, pages 63–94 (pages 76–77).

EDUARDO GARCÍA DE ENTERRÍA: "Prologue to: *Les autonomies régionales dans la constitution espagnole*, París: Economica, 1981", in his studies: *Estudios sobre autonomías territoriales*, Madrid: Civitas, 1985, pages 411–416 (p. 411).

ELISEO AJA: *"El Estado autonómico. Federalismo y hechos diferenciales"*, Madrid: Alianza, 1999.

EMMANUEL-JOSEPH SIEYÈS: *Qu'est-ce que le tiers État?* París: Éditions du Boucher, 2002 [1st edition, 1789].

ESPERANZA AGUIRRE: "Speech by Esperanza Aguirre in the FAES Campus", Navacerrada, 08/07/2011, p. 16, http://bit.ly/wPKyge, consultation: 30/12/2011.

FERDINAND TÖNNIES: *Comunidad y asociación: el comunismo y el socialismo como formas de vida social*, Barcelona: Península, 1979 translation by J.F. Ivars [1st edition, 1887].

E. FOSSAS ESPADALER: *"El principio dispositivo en el Estado autonomic"*, Madrid: Marcial Pons, 2007.

FRANCESC CAMBÓ: *Obres*, vol. 4, Barcelona: Alpha, 1984, 467–515 (p. 473).

FRANCISCO CAAMAÑO: "Representación o participación de las minorías: sobre la determinación de algunos espacios útiles a las políticas del reconocimiento", *Fundamentos. Cuadernos monográ ficos de teoría del Estado, derecho público e historia constitucional*, num. 3, 2004, pages 353–378 (p. 356).

FRANCO MODUGNO: *Diritto pubblico generale*, Bari: Laterza, 2002, p. 11–12.

GEORGE C. S. BENSON: *The New Centralization. A Study of Intergovernmental Relationships in the United States*, New York: Farrar & Rinehart, 1941. We have used the New York edition: Arno Press, 1978 (p. 21).

JOHN E. E. DALBERG ACTON [Lord Acton]: "Nationality" [1862]: "The combination of different nations in one State is as necessary a condition of civilised life as the combination of men in society." in *Selected writings of Lord Acton. Volume I: Essays in the history of liberty*, Indianapolis: Liberty Fund, 1985, pages 409–433 (p. 425–426).

JOHN E. E. DALBERG ACTON "Nationality: Originally a truly liberal idea. It made Austria a federation. It produced the federal idea." *Selected writings of Lord Acton. Volume III: Essays in religion, politics and morality*, Indianapolis: Liberty Fund, 1985, pages 558–560, (p. 560).

JOHN STUART MILL: "On nationality, as connected with representative government", chapter XVI of *Considerations on Represesentative Government* [1861]. I quote *Utilitarism, On Liberty and Considerations on Representative Government*, London: Dent & Sons, 1980, pages 359–366.

JORDI PUJOL: *La personalidad diferenciada de Cataluña. Historia y presente*, Barcelona: Generalitat de Catalunya, 1991, p. 33. Conference speech given at the Carlos III University, 14th May, 1991.

JOSÉ BONO: *"Bono says that "drinks all round" was a mistake which should be corrected" Público*, 25/01/2011, http://bit.ly/f5HxTg, consultation: 30/12/2011.

JOSÉ JUAN GONZÁLEZ ENCINAR: "El Estado federal asimétrico y el fin del Estado", in ANTONI MONREAL (ed.): *El Estado de las autonomías*, Madrid: Tecnos, 1991, pages 49–62 (p. 60).

JUAN LINZ: "Early State-Building and Late Peripheral Nationalisms against the State: the case of Spain", in S.N. EISENSTADT and STEIN ROKKAN (eds.): *Building States and Nations*, Beverly Hills/London: Sage Publications 1973, vol. 2, pages 33–116 (p. 99).

KYLE SCOTT: *Federalism. A Normative Theory and its Practical Relevance*, New York: Continuum, 2011, p. 1.

I. LASAGABASTER HERRARTE: "La reforma de los estatutos de autonomía: una reflexión sobre su teoría y práctica actuales", *Revista catalana de dret públic*, number 31, 2005, pages 15–56.

J. TUDELA ARANDA: "¿Reforma constitucional en clave federal? (Sistematización de problemas generados por las reformas y posibles soluciones)", *Revista de Estudios Políticos*, number 151, 2011, pages 231–279.

MANUEL GARCÍA-PELAYO: *Derecho constitucional comparado*, Madrid: Alianza Editorial, 1984 [1959], pages 233–234.

MARC ALBA OTERO; DAVID GARCÍA HERNÁNDEZ (coords.): *Un momento clave para construir entre todos la España admirada del futuro*, 2010, p. 76–77.

MARÍA JESÚS GARCÍA MORALES: "Instrumentos y vías de institucionalización de las relaciones intergubernamentales", in XAVIER ARBÓS MARÍN (COORD.); CÉSAR COLINO CÁMARA; MARÍA JESÚS GARCÍA MORALES; SALVADOR PARRADO DÍEZ: *Las relaciones intergubernamentales en el Estado autonómico. La posición de los actores*, Barcelona: Institut d'Estudis Autonòmics, 2009, pages 41–122 (pages 52–53).

MICHAEL BURGESS: "Managing Diversity in Federal States: Conceptual Lenses and Comparative Perspectives", in ALAIN-G. GAGNON (ed.): *Contemporary Canadian Federalism. Foundations,*

*Traditions, Institutions*, Toronto: University of Toronto Press, 2009, pages 428-440 (pages 430-431).

MICHAEL D. REAGAN and JOHN G. SANZONE: *The New Federalism*, New York/Oxford: Oxford University Press, 1981 (2nd edition, from which we cite 1st edition, 1972), p. 3.

PASQUALE STANISLAO MANCINI: "Della nazionalità come fondamento del diritto delle genti. Prelezione al corso di Diritto internazionale pronunziata nella R. Università di Torino nel dì 22 gennaio 1851", in his *Diritto internazionale*, Nápoles: G. Margheri, 1873, pages 1-64.

PRESTON KING: *Federalism and Federation*, London: Croom Helm, 1982, pages 74-76.

RAFAEL FERNÁNDEZ MONTALVO: *Relaciones interadministrativas de colaboración y cooperación*, Madrid: Marcial Pons, 2000, pages 55-56.

RICHARD ROSE: "From government at the centre to nationwide government", in YVES MÉNY; VINCENT WRIGHT (eds.): *Centre-periphery relations in Western Europe*, London: George Allen and Unwin, 1985, pages 13-32 (p. 21).

RICHARD SIMEON; DANIEL-PATRICK CONWAY: "Federalism and the management of conflict in multi-national societies", in ALAIN-G. GAGNON; JAMES TULLY (eds.): *Multinational Democracies*, Cambridge: Cambridge University Press, 2001, pages 338-365 (pages 340-341).

SANDRA LEÓN-ALFONSO; MÓNICA FERRÍN: *A cooperación intergobernamental no Estado autónomico*, Santiago de Compostela: Escola Galega de Administración Pública, 2009, pages 253-275.

THOMAS HUEGLIN: "Legitimacy, democracy and federalism", in HERMAN BAKVIS; WILLAM M. CHANDLER: *Federalism and the Role of the State*, Toronto: Toronto University Press, 1987, pages 38-545 (p. 35).

WILLIAM H. RIKER: "Federalism", in ROBERT E. GOODIN; PHILIP PETIT (eds.): *A Companion to Political Philosophy*, Oxford: Blackwell, 2001, pages 508-514 (p. 509).

XAVIER ARBÓS MARÍN: "Doctrinas constitucionales y federalismo en España", *Working Papers. Institut de Ciències Polítiques i Socials*, 245, 2006.

XAVIER ARBÓS Marín: "Hecho diferencial, hecho referencial. La política en la Constitución", in *Estudios sobre la Consitución española. Libro homenaje a Jordi Solé Tura*, Madrid: Centro de Estudios Políticos y Constitucionales, 2008, vol. II, pages 1543-1562.

# Political Autonomy, Federalisation and Statutary Declaration of Rights

Francisco J. Bastida Freijedo

## Heterogeneity of Declarations and Homogeneity of Rights

There exists today a considerable output of declarations of rights in terms both of quantity and territorial extension. Along with general declarations of rights, the most relevant in recent times being the *Charter of Fundamental Rights of the European Union* (Nice, 2000), there has been a proliferation of declarations of a sectorial type, amongst others, the *Universal Declaration on Bioethics and Human Rights* (Oviedo, 2005) or the *International Convention on the Rights of Persons with Disabilities* (New York, 2006), which join a long list of others regarding the widest possible variety of subjects (childhood, gender, mental health, amongst others). On a territorial level, to the classic declarations of rights contained in the Constitutions have been added not only those with an international or European scope but also those of a regional or internal nature, within a federal or autonomous State, creating a multilevel system of guarantee of rights. This phenomenon of heterogeneity of rights and guarantees has been offset by an increasingly intense homogenisation of the contents of rights, via their interpretation by international courts, especially the European Court for Human Rights, and the constitutional courts. Further contributing to this confluence is an element of emulation amongst the advocates of declarations of rights. In short, globalisation cohabits with decentralisation and equality with difference. In this context, the new Statutes of some Autonomous Communities incorporate a specific declaration of rights for the territory in question, and the question posed is both legal and political, with regard not only to the possibility of its existence and its constitutional compatibility but also to its appropriateness insofar as it may be a factor of confrontation and inequality between citizens instead of an instrument of integration.

F.J. Bastida Freijedo (✉)
Facultad de Derecho de la, Departamento de Derecho Público, Universidad de Oviedo, C/ Valentín Andrés Álvarez s/n, 33006 Oviedo, Spain
e-mail: fbastida@uniovi.es

A. López-Basaguren and L. Escajedo San Epifanio (eds.), *The Ways of Federalism in Western Countries and the Horizons of Territorial Autonomy in Spain*, Vol. 2, DOI 10.1007/978-3-642-27717-7_28, © Springer-Verlag Berlin Heidelberg 2013

The aim of this paper is not a legal analysis of the declarations of rights contained in the Statutes of Autonomy. From this perspective, there already exists an extensive bibliography to which to refer. Here, it is simply a case of setting out, inevitably in rather a broad sense, the political considerations that underlie the legal content of these declarations because, to a large extent, the legal arguments upon which they are based and that determine their scope express a prior conception of the decentralised territorial structure that permits the autonomous constitutional principle.

## The Controversy Over the Inclusion of a Declaration of Rights in the Statutes: The Legal and Political Dimensions of the Debate

As we know, no Statute of Autonomy was initially passed as a declaration of rights. The constitutional function of the Statute is to serve as a basic institutional law for each Autonomous Community, defining its territory, creating its institutional organisation, and establishing its competences (art. 147, 1 and 2 of our Constitution, henceforth SC). The reference to the rights of the citizens of the Autonomous Community consisted in a renvoi to "those established in the Constitution" and a mention of the special attention that the public authorities would pay to the effectiveness of these and to specific social and economic policies in favour of justice, equality, participation, and employment. All of these are expressed in very general terms and with a set of principles or directives to be followed by the autonomous authorities.

More than 25 years after its ratification, the Statute of Catalonia and other more recent ones were reformed in order to, amongst other things, include a catalogue of rights, which has given rise to an abundance of legal writing regarding the nature and the scope of this measure. The controversy intensified when the Constitutional Court (CC) issued rulings 347/2007 and 31/2010, in relation to the Valencian and Catalan statutes, respectively, providing arguments that were not shared by all.

The intensity of the debate is due to the fact that the inclusion of a catalogue of rights in the Statutes involves two different but very closely related questions. One refers to the capacity or potential of the political autonomy of the Autonomous Communities to regulate laws and freedoms in the Statutes. The other asks whether what is truly regulated by the Statutes in terms of rights is compatible with the constitutional text in that it can be interpreted as the development of fundamental rights acknowledged in the SC. Clearly, the negative answer to the first question stops the second in its tracks. However, it is not easy to reach an agreement when one is speaking of the same thing but with different names and when one seeks to give the same name to different things. This is apparent in the terminology employed to refer to the same declarations of rights: "statutory declaration of rights" according to some, "declaration of statutory rights" says others, and of course with differing objectives. The initial debate amongst jurists relates to whether or not these catalogues of rights are constitutional. The classic works of Picazo (2006), "Pueden los Estatutos de Autonomía declarar derechos, deberes y principios" (1), and Francisco Caamaño, *Sí pueden (Declaraciones de derechos y Estatutos de Autonomy)* (2), offer contrasting answers to the question, partly because they do not refer to the same thing and partly too because there are political assumptions that, in the one case, are attributed with a legal significance and, in the other, not.

One might say that in these declarations of rights, there is tension between the *lyrics*, apparently correct, and the *music*, which recalls a melody of federal or even sovereignist tone, tending to drown out the notes that the Constitution establishes both for fundamental rights and for the definition of competences. Some academic writers have judged the lyrics whilst ignoring the music, and others have judged the lyrics according to the music. Meanwhile, the CC has declared in its rulings that the lyrics are not unacceptable, provided the music is played (interpreted) in accordance with its own rules—an interpretation met by a division of opinions.

## The Declaration of Rights in the New Statutes of Autonomy and Their Basis in Assumed Competences

The possibility of a declaration of rights forming part of the contents of a Statute of Autonomy cannot be negated by the fact that the Constitution does not include it in the contents of the basic institutional regulations of the Autonomous Community. What seems clear, and more so since the STC 247/2007, is "the constitutional legitimacy of a statutory content configured "within the terms of the Constitution" (art.147.1 CE), provided it is linked to the specific constitutional previsions related to the *purpose* of the Statutes" (FJ 11). The minimum or necessary content of the Statutes provided for in art. 147.2 CE may be complemented, then, with an additional element that, "whilst not specifically indicated by the Constitution, is a complement rendered suitable by the aforementioned constitutional previsions, a suitability to be understood with reference to the function that, strictly speaking, the Constitution attributes to the Statutes, as a basic institutional regulation responsible for la regulations of the functions, institutions and competences of each Autonomous Community" (FJ 12). The problem lies in knowing whether the statutory declarations of rights are constitutionally suitable.

The way of justifying the existence of a declaration of rights in the Statutes has consisted in situating it within the field of competences. In other words, the self-government of the Autonomous Communities is achieved via the exercise of the competences assumed within their territorial scope, and the inclusion of a catalogue of rights in the Statutes is dovetailed into the system of competences via different channels. A first one involves the specification of rights and of socioeconomic guiding principles deduced from the range of *material competences* provided for in the Statute. A second route is the specification of rights linked to the institutional organisation of the autonomy (*institutional competences*), that is, the political Rights of the autonomous citizenry: the right to vote and other rights of political participation, linguistic rights. The third path, and the most controversial, is a specific increase in competences in the sphere of rights. Unlike the previous two, this is not a case of recognising on a statutory level Rights resulting from the exercise of material or institutional competences but of establishing rights that could involve an *increase* in competences, by including rights not easily included within the area of assumed competences.

The polemic over whether there can be a *statutory declaration of rights*, containing rights that are not necessarily born of institutional and material competences assumed within the Statute, is resolved by interpreting that what the Statute establishes is a *declaration of statuary rights*, as all these rights originate from assumed competences, be they of an institutional or a material type, of an **iusfundamental** nature that does not affect the contents of fundamental rights. The questions are whether or not these latter competences are acceptable; whether or not they affect this content or the regulation of basic conditions in the exercise of the constitutional rights and duties of the Spanish people; whether, although they may be administered by the Autonomous Communities, they can appear in the Statute of Autonomy or whether, on the contrary, their regulation corresponds to an autonomous law.

Art. 37.4 of the Catalan Statute (EAC), introduced during its processing in the Congress of Deputies (and also art. 13 of the Andalusian Statute, EAA), waters down to a considerable extent the legal controversy. This provision states that "The Rights and principles of this Title will not involve an alteration of the regime of distribution of competences, nor the creation of new enabling provisions or the modification of existing ones. None of the provisions of these Titles may be developed, applied or interpreted in a manner that reduces or limits the fundamental rights recognised by the Constitution and by the international treaties and conventions ratified by Spain". Thus, there is a lessening of the tension that might initially exist between the statutory declaration and the legal system of fundamental rights.

## Political Reasons for the Inclusion of the Declaration of Rights in the Statutes of Autonomy and for Their Exclusion

The declaration of rights is clearly not a required content of the Statute of Autonomy, their inclusion responds to purely political reasons; and these reasons are not the same in the different processes of statutory revision. The first reform that really **promotes** this new content of the Statute, the Catalan reform (2006), has a *sovereignist and federal vocation*, with the objective of providing Catalonia with legislation that, under the name of Statute, is equivalent to what is meant by the Constitution of a member State of a federation. This will be discussed in the next section. The reform of the Andalusian Statute (2007), on the other hand, gives the impression of including the declaration of rights with the aim of upholding the generosity established by the Statute. A kind of *autonomous goodness*—if you will pardon the expression—or, if one prefers, of *benign autonomy* that, in the interest of legitimating the autonomy itself, includes in the Statute a long list of basic objectives of the Autonomous Community, of rights and guiding principles of public policies, of advantages and benefits that citizens may obtain from their territorial autonomy. In other words, the declaration of rights in the Andalusian Statute does not seek to serve a mutation of the nature of the Statute, to give it the appearance of a Constitution, but is intended rather to introduce a new level (the autonomous) within a multilevel system of guarantees of rights. In both cases, the result is an inflationary declaration of rights, much more evident from a quantitative than a qualitative point of view.

The reforms of the other subsequent Statutes of Autonomy largely respond to this latter idea, producing the effect of emulating the Catalan and Andalusian Statutes, though in some cases incorporating specific rights used as a particular autonomous demand; for example, "the rights with regard to water", which, with opposing intentions, are acknowledged in the Valencian Statute (reform of 2006, which, though approved before that of the Catalan Statute, draws its inspiration from the preparation of the latter) and in the Aragonese Statute (2007).

The political background to the debate over the incorporation of a declaration of rights within the Statutes de Autonomy resulted in an exaggeration of its legal relevance. Of far greater political and legal significance in the decentralisation of power is the list of competences assumed by an Autonomous Community through its Statute. However, its potential effect of an increased degree of self-government, for some, or the breaking-up of territorial homogeneity, for others, does not arouse such passion and sense of grievance as that of the Statutes with different declarations of rights. This is so because the diversity of autonomous legal systems is rationalised within the more technical and complex idea of "decentralization of State competences". The inequality between *territorial entities*, between subjects of public law within the same State, will always be questioned, but is always more acceptable than the possible inequality *between Spaniards* in different Autonomous Communities according to the application of these systems. There is acceptance of Autonomies "of two speeds" but total rejection of "first- and second-class" citizens, when, in reality, the very exercise of the competences assumed may mean that in some Autonomous Communities citizens have different benefits and duties from those of other Communities. In essence, it must be said, what underlies the polemic regarding the affirmation or negation of a statutory declaration of rights is not so much a legal-constitutional question as a question of national or territorial identity, that is, politics and ideology. The interpretation or pre-comprehension of the Statute as legislation with a sovereignist or federalising vocation lies not only with the advocates of the reform of the Catalan Statute but also with its detractors. For the former, the statutory declaration of rights is an expression of their self-government as a people, whilst for the latter it is an unacceptable and condemnable affirmation of nationalism, which explains why there are substantially similar provisions in the

Catalan Statute and in the Andalusian Statute, but the former have been appealed against in the CC, whilst the latter have not.

## The Sovereignist and Federal Vocation of the Declaration of Rights of the Catalan Statute: The Declaration as an Exhibition of Self-Government in a Statute with a Constitutional Soul

This vocation is coherent with the spirit accompanying the birth of the reform of the Statute and that inspired its processing in the Catalan Parliament. A reading of its Preamble and of the Preliminary Title highlights the affirmation of Catalonia as "nation", of "the Catalan national reality", and of the "undeniable right of Catalonia to its self-government", "which is also based on the fundamental rights of the Catalan people, its secular institutions and on the Catalan legal tradition". This self-referentiality of the origin and basis of power is specified in art. 2.4 of the Statute, which establishes that "The powers of the Generalitat emanate from the people of Catalonia". A typical expression in a Constitution that proclaims national or popular sovereignty, however much it qualifies its scope by declaring that the exercise of these Powers will be "in accordance with what is established by the current Statute and the Constitution", as one thing is the ownership or source of power and another its exercise. Very different is the Andalusian Statute; art 1.3 of which states that "The Powers of the Autonomous Community of Andalusia emanate *from the Constitution* and from the Andalusian people, *in the terms of the current Statute of Autonomy*, which is its basic institutional law"). Nevertheless, the CC has **salvaged** the constitutionality of this provision of the *EAC*, interpreting that it does not refer to the extra-constitutional origin of the powers of the Generalitat but to the democratic legitimacy that has to govern the exercise of these powers by the Autonomous Community (STC 31/2010, FJ 9). Whatever the case, the fact is that the drafting of the Catalan Statute is full of replacement circumlocutions of an irrevocable sovereignty, in other words, indisputable for those who support the idea of original and inalienable indigenous power but, at the same time, unnameable in the statutory text, in their opposition to the only sovereignty recognised by the Constitution, that of the Spanish nation.

This process of federalising the autonomous State via the reform of the Statute of Autonomy is apparent in the evolution of academic writing regarding the legal nature of the Statutes. Initially, the debate revolves around whether the Statute was not only a *double-faced organic law*, as an organic State law, but also a basic institutional law of the Autonomous Community—*a thesis defended by the central State*—or a *ley paccionada*, that is, formally an organic law, but materially a law born of a pact between the State and the nationality or region forming an Autonomous Community—*a thesis defended from autonomous positions*. The paradigm of this conception is Organic Law 13/1982, of August 10, on the Reintegration and Enhancement of the Foral Regime (of Navarra). However, the *paccionado* (pacted) character of the Statutes is defended by the State (the expression is even employed by the CC in STC 247/2007, FJ 6, though it disappears in STC 31/2010), whilst from a position tending towards sovereignty the argument is that the Statute, once approved by the autonomous parliament, must be "ratified" by Parliament. In the Catalan Statute, the reform of its Titles I and II can only be via autonomous initiative, not through Parliament, and it envisages as ordinary the ratification process of reform by the latter (art. 222). The very degree of regulation in the Statute, with 223 articles and numerous additional provisions, illustrates the desire of its advocates to create as self-sufficient a body of legislation as possible, which some authors (amongst others, Juan José Solozábal, in El País (30-06-2010)) described as "An ambiguous Statute, with a Constitutional soul and a regulatory body".

The inclusion of a declaration of rights in the Statute has its own value, irrespective of the actual range of rights established within. This is acknowledged by Marc Carrillo, when he comments that "It is, essentially, a specific expression of self-government, if not of an increase in self-government" (Carrillo 2006, p. 72). In fact, the statutory denomination of "rights" provides shelter for diverse legal realities (subjective rights, mandates for public powers, and guiding principles). Nevertheless, what is most relevant is the very presence of that declaration in the Statute because it fulfills an important political and symbolic function, which consists in seeking to equate the Statute to a Constitution. The classic Declaration of the Rights of Man and of the Citizen (France, 1789) formulated a material concept of Constitution, still in valid, according to which "Any society in which the guarantee of rights is not assured, nor the separation of powers determined, has no Constitution" (art. 16). Consequently, from this perspective the Statute, introduced in its preamble and initial form as the fruit of a *quasi constituent* power, acquires a quasi *constitutional* sense, by adding to the regulation of an autonomous institutional organisation—articulated on the basis of a separation of legislative and governmental powers—a declaration of rights the guarantee of which appears specifically to be ensured in the basic institutional regulations of the Autonomous Community. Furthermore, in the drafting of some rights there is a quest for 'iusfundamental' content, in other words, a projection within the Statute of fundamental rights recognised in the Constitution. This effect, this transfer to the Statute of the dogmatic part of the Constitution, is apparent in the confusing assignation of the ownership of rights (sometimes pertaining to the citizens of Catalonia and, on other occasions, to everybody) and also in the provisions regarding the statutory guarantees of rights, some of which are drafted in a manner that reflects the CC's interpretation of art. 81.1 CE. Thus, art. 37.3 EAC establishes that "The *essential regulation* and the *direct development* of the rights acknowledged by sections I, II and III of the present Title must be via Parliamentary law".

From a vision of the Statute as a symbolic expression of a *quasi constituent* power, it is logical that the inclusion of rights in the Statute is presented by its advocates as a *statutory declaration of rights* rather than a declaration *of statutory rights*, defined at the root by the Spanish Constitution. The declaration acquires importance as a "symbolic statutory right" (Comella 2006, p. 34). As the CC has often reiterated, autonomy is not sovereignty; however, it is a question of exercising it in the hope of attaining, or at least appearing to, a political self—referentiality and its legal positivisation. The statutory declaration of rights is not only a "specific expression of self-government"; it is, above all, an *exhibition or show* of self-government, as a means of affirmation of the national identity of Catalonia. That is why it is conceived as an instrument to "institutionalise the difference" (Carrillo 2010, pp. 338 and 345) and even as a "challenge" or an *"act of defiance"* that the Statute presents to the CC (Carrillo 2010, p. 347) and, thus, to the Constitution. In other words, it seems to go hand in hand with that idea of symbolisation of self-government, not only the Community's capacity to decide autonomously but also the need to be able to show oneself as different from the rest.

This conception is also present in the sponsors of the declaration of rights as an autonomous level of guarantee of rights within a multilevel system. These authors emphasise that "the recognition of rights contributes to the formation or development of one's own identity articulated upon legal-political references" and "the important dimension of symbolic integration that is intrinsic to rights" (Balaguer 2008, p. 177). Hence the consideration as healthy of the differentiating function that can be performed by a declaration of rights in comparison with others and even the perception as undesirable "that constitutional jurisprudence play a homogenising role, in a similar fashion to in the area of competences" (Balaguer 2008, p. 195). The problem lies in knowing whether that differentiating function is integrating or not and whether it fits within the Constitution. It is noteworthy that a right like that of access to a dignified death is regarded by the CC as a logical consequence of the right to life and, therefore, a manifestation of a fundamental right enjoyed by all (STC 31/2010, FJ 19), whilst some sectors consider it to be susceptible to diverse and contradictory autonomous qualification. Caamaño states that "In a politically decentralised State like ours it is perfectly rational that there should coexist one legislator who maintains the rightness of self-determination before death and another who argues that it is wrong; what is truly important is that neither of them violates the right to life contained in art. 15 CE" (Caamaño 2007, p. 45). The question is: Is it possible to respect the fundamental right to life in both cases?

The vision that the statutory declaration of rights seeks to be, first and foremost, an exhibition of self-government is corroborated by the mandate of art. 37.2 EAC, which, despite the numerous "rights, duties and guiding principles" established in Title I (arts. 15–54 EAC), declares that the Catalan parliament "must approve by law the Charter of the rights and duties of the citizens of Catalonia". Another question is whether symbolic character is also detected by the CC when it notes that in the declaration of rights of the Statutes there is, apparently, an acknowledgement of subjective rights but that, regardless of the *nomen iuris* employed, "in the new Catalan Statute there is evidence above all, as we will see, the presence of proclamations of subjective rights stricto sensu not withstanding, of the second type of rights, that is, mandates for the action of public powers, be they specifically termed "guiding principles", be they literally declared as rights that the autonomous legislator has to make a reality and the other autonomous public powers have to respect (. . .). These kinds of statutory declarations, which are not subjective rights but mandates for public powers (STC 247/2007, FFJJ 13–15), technically function as guidelines (prescriptive or directive, as is the case) for the exercise of autonomous competences" (STC 31/2004, FJ 16).

Part of the literature considers that the declaration of rights, beyond the judgement of intentions with regard to the objective of its inclusion in the Statute, performs a function of limiting public powers themselves, and indeed this is so. However, without denying this guaranteeing function, it can be interpreted as secondary. One cannot seriously claim that the statutory declaration creates subjective rights that were not previously in existence via the constitution or through autonomous or State legal channels or that it fills a gap in the guarantee of citizens'rights by creating an autonomous level in the multilevel system of guarantees. This new multilevel is more fictitious than real as it is largely covered by existing levels. Even when additional guarantees are established, like the creation of a Council of Statutory Guarantees of Catalonia and its competence to issue binding rulings in the area of rights (art. 76 EAC), this has more to do with the aforementioned attempt to present the Statute as a *quasi Constitution*, in which the said Council would appear as a *cuasi jurisdictional* organ. This was the CC's interpretation in Ruling 31/2010, FJ 32, when considering that "the differences between Council and Constitutional Court—fundamentally based on the value of the thing judged to be **privative of** jurisdictional pronouncements—are considerably diluted, however, bearing in mind the binding character that section 4 of art. 76 EAC attributes to the rulings of the Council of Statutory Guarantees 'in relation to the draft bills and draft laws in parliament which develop or affect rights acknowledged by the present Statute'". It adds that this function "would configure the control exercised by the Council hat were too close (materially equivalent, certainly) to a jurisdictional control of legal norms absolutely perfect in their content, thus damaging the monopoly of rejection of norms with force of law reserved for this Court by art. 161 CE". The CC concludes that this leads to the "declaration of unconstitutionality and nullity" of the provision. The same occurs with the statutory petition that the Síndic de Greugues supervise "with exclusive character" the activity of the Administration of the Generalitat, preventing the state Ombudsman from developing his constitutional functions in this area.

In reality, the limiting function of the statutory declaration of rights does not contradict the sovereignist idea that inspires the sponsors of the Statute and that corresponds to the principles of the Declaration of Rights of Man and of the Citizen of 1789, that is, the affirmation of a quasi-constituent Catalan power and how it differs from the powers constituted in the Statute. The declaration of rights would operate as a limit to these, in the name of the nation (Catalan) and to the benefit of the citizens. However, it is worthwhile qualifying the scope of this limiting function. The classic declarations of rights are born as brakes or resistance to constituted powers, but, in the territorial dialect of Autonomous Communities versus State, rights are not interpreted as limitations to public powers themselves because the **statute-maker** does not regard these powers as enemies or opponents of the citizens of the Autonomous Community. On the contrary, they are instruments for improving the legal position of the people who live in that Autonomous

Community compared with the citizens of other Communities or with the benefits that, in general, the State provides for individuals. In all of these, what prevails is the symbolic sense of the declaration of rights as an exhibition or manifestation of self-government before its citizens and in comparison or contrast with the power of the State or of other Autonomous Communities. Moreover, the actual principal structure of the statutory rights means that they are more guidelines for public authorities, objectives to be pursued, than limits to their activity. It will be the autonomous legislator who specifies the sense in which rights are appropriate for citizens. The aforementioned mandate to Parliament so it approves the "Charter of the rights and duties of the citizens of Catalonia" (art. 37.2 CE) is a good example of this.

## The Position of the Constitutional Court: The Declaration of Rights of the Statutes as a Declaration of Statutory Rights

The CC salvages the constitutionality of the inclusion of declarations in the Statutes, insofar as this is not a prohibited content but implies that it considers them neither appropriate nor convenient. According to its doctrine, provided there is respect for the clauses of equality (art. 139 CE) and homogeneity of the basic conditions for the exercise of constitutional rights, there is room for diversity in the exercise of autonomous competences and subject to these specific rights arise in each territory (149.1.1$^a$ CE) (SSTC 247/2010, FFJJ 11 and 13, and 31/2010, FJ 16).

For the CC, the declaration of rights in a Statute can only be a *declaration of statutory rights*. This means that the declaration cannot be open to rights not resulting from the competences assumed by the Autonomous Community in its Statute. "The Statute has not created fundamental rights different from those announced in the Constitution or contradictory to these, nor can it have affected the system of these rights with regard to their ownership, regulation and conditions of exercise. Meanwhile, with regard to the rights and principles declared in the Statute, their proclamation cannot imply any alteration whatsoever of the scope of the autonomous competences defined on the basis of the constitutional regime of distribution of competences; in other words, this proclamation must operate always, and exclusively, on the assumption of the specific competences attributed to the Generalitat of Catalonia in accordance with constitutional provisions" (STC 31/2010, FJ 18).

Statutory rights cannot be territorialised fundamental rights, assigned to the citizens of the Autonomous Community or persons subject to its legal system. In its early STC 25/1981, it declared that "as a fundamental element of an objective legal system, fundamental rights give that system its basic contents, in our case social and democratic rule of law, and apply to the entire state. In this function, fundamental rights are not affected by the federal, regional or autonomous structure of the State. One might say that fundamental rights, as they establish the basis of a unitary legal-constitutional status for all Spaniards and are equally decisive in the configuration of the democratic order in the central State and in the Autonomous Communities, are a unifying element, all the more so when the task of ensuring this unification, according to art. 155 of the Constitution, corresponds to the State. Fundamental rights are thus a common heritage of citizens both individually and collectively, constitutive of the legal system the enforcement of which applies to us all in equal measure. It might be said that they establish a direct link between individuals and the State and act as a basis of political unity without any mediation whatsoever" (FJ 5). Almost 30 years later, the CC makes the same claim and concludes that "the rights recognised in Statutes of Autonomy must be, therefore, something different (from fundamental rights). Specifically, Rights that only *bind the* autonomous legislator (. . .) and rights, moreover, materially linked to the range of competences pertaining to the Autonomous Community" (STC 31/2010, FJ 16).

Consequently, "as constitutional rights are such as a result of their enshrinement in the Constitution, they clearly cannot be the object of regulation by the Statutes of Autonomy" (STC 247/2007, FJ 15, d). In this regard, the CC understands as fundamental rights "genuine constitutional rights, that is, those that the Constitution reflects in Title I, Chapter II, which, for this reason, may be described as fundamental rights" (STC 247/2007, FJ 13, a). In other words, it uses a wider concept than that which itself applies to define the scope of the organic law with regard to legislative development of fundamental rights, which is restricted to the rights of section 1 of chapter II, title I, of the Constitution (for all see STC 160/1987, FJ 2). The CC adds in the same legal basis that its reproduction in the Statute is technically incorrect, but the cancellation of the provision will depend upon the scope of this reproduction.

Nevertheless, it should be borne in mind that one thing is the regulation of the object and contents of these Rights from chapter II (direct development) and another the regulation of their exercise, which could be undertaken by the Autonomous Community as this falls within the scope of its competences. According to the CC "nothing decrees that the legal regime of constitutional rights should be *subject* to the rules of the distribution of competences, as we know that neither art. 53 nor 81, both CE, are provisions that allocate competences, so that, the aforementioned guarantees of unity intact (art. 81.1 CE), it is possible, as we indicated in legal basis 4 c), for the autonomous legislation, issued within its own areas of competences, to affect the regulation of the legal regime of those rights, always respecting, naturally, the resolutions that could arise from state competences (art. 149.1 CE). This occurs, for instance, with regard to education (arts. 27 y 149.1.30 CE) and, similarly, with rights of association (art. 22 CE and correlative statutory provisions attributing competence in the field), foundation, or the right to receive and broadcast information, etc. (this has been declared recently, amongst others, in SSTC 341/2005, of December 21, FJ 4, and 135/2006, of April 29, FJ 2) (STC 247/2007, FJ 13)" (STC 247/2007, FJ 13, a).

The CC does not have a clear theory regarding the structure of statutory rights. It admits the possibility that true subjective rights can be those rights derived from the capacity of the Statutes as acknowledged by the Constitution to organise their institutions of self-government (for example, the right to active and passive suffrage) (STC 247/2007, FJ 15, b) but denies that the same can be said of statutory rights linked to competences assumed in the Statute. According to the CC, under the *nomen iuris* of rights, there can only be guidelines, objectives, or mandates for autonomous public authorities. Mandates "which will have to be connected with an area attributed as a competence by the Statute and which, although in effect they bind the public authorities of the Autonomous Community, will require in order to attain full efficiency the autonomous legislator's exercise of the legislative competence belonging to them, so that the principle or right in question will lack direct justiciability until effective clarification of their legal regime, as only then will be determined the corresponding subjective rights of citizens, with the said legislator integrating the **constitutional requirements** that must be safeguarded (arts. 81.1 y 149.1 CE)" (STC 247/2007, FJ 15, c). This differentiating criterion between genuine subjective statutory rights, if of an **institutional competence** nature, and statutory Rights as mere principles and directives for autonomous authorities, if of a **material competence** type, does not appear in STC 31/2010.

In this ruling, the CC recognises that in the Catalan Statute there is no absence of "proclamations of subjective rights stricto sensu" but does not clarify which they are and focuses its attention on what are "mandates of action for public authorities, be they specifically termed "guiding principles", or be they literally described as rights which the autonomous legislator implements and the other autonomous public authorities respect" (FJ 16). On this issue, the CC declares three extremely important questions. The first, that the rights acknowledged in Statutes of Autonomy must be "Rights that only bind the autonomous legislator (...) and rights, moreover, materially linked to the range of competences of the Autonomous Community" (FJ 16). The second, that most statutory rights are mandates for autonomous public authorities to be fulfilled in the field of assumed competences, "from which results, naturally, a principle of differentiation not to be confused with the inequality or privileges prohibited by arts. 138.2 and 139.1 CE, as this only highlights the diversity inherent to the autonomous state [STC 76/1983, of August 5, FJ 2 a)] in that it is implicit in the plurality of regulations which, based and reduced to unity in the Constitution, operate in diverse areas of competences in which are active legislative and governmental powers the exercise of which may legitimately be conditioned by the same law that defines, **along with the** Constitution, each of these privative areas" (FJ 16). The third, that the Statute is not a law that may regulate the exercise of fundamental rights. The autonomous law can do this provided that regulation corresponds to the Community **terms of material** (mention has been made of education, association, foundation), but not the Statute. Although the Statute is an organic law, it is not the type of organic law reserved by the Constitution for the *direct* development of fundamental rights (art. 81 CE), and with regard to *indirect* development or regulation of its exercise, art. 53.1 CE refers this to the ordinary legislator, be he state or autonomous, but not to the statute-making legislator: "The divisory organic law/ordinary law in the field of fundamental rights (development/regulation: arts. 81.1 y 53.1 CE) means that the Statute, as an organic law, can neither declare or develop fundamental rights or affect these, nor even regulate the exercise of these rights. This can be done, when appropriate, by the autonomous legislator, being the ordinary legislator and in accordance with the constitutional division of competences, but not the (organic) statute-making legislator. Hence the absence of any paradox in the fact that a simple autonomous law (ordinary law) can affect what is not possible via a Statute (a superior law to an autonomous one). In reality, it is not that more can be achieved via autonomous law; it is that something different is achieved, as corresponds in a set of laws ordered according to the criterion of competence" (FJ 17). Here, the CC contradicts the contents of STC 247/2007, regarding the possibility of true statutory subjective rights, derived from the regulation of the institutions of self-government that the Constitution, art. 147, confers upon the Statutes.

With respect to statutory rights referred directly to other fundamental rights, such as the "the right to receive adequate treatment for pain and *comprehensive palliative care* and to live through the process of death with dignity" (art. 20.1 EAC), the CC considers that this is a specification of the fundamental right (to life) and in that sense "an obligatory, as implicit, consequence of the guarantee of that fundamental right, which, thus, it neither contradicts nor impinges upon (. . .), it is simply a manifestation of the right to a dignified life and with a similar scope to that which for this concept may be deduced from arts. 10.1 and 15 CE" (STC 31/2010, FJ 19). In other words, it forms a part of what one might judge to be like a decantation or reproduction of the aforementioned fundamental right. The same occurs with the right guaranteed to parents by art. 21.2 EAC so that their children "receive the religious and moral education that is in accordance with their convictions in schools of a public nature, in which teaching is lay" (STC 31/2010, FJ 20). However, this solution provided by the CC does not cover every eventuality. There are statutory rights that are not an obligatory consequence of a fundamental right but that have an unequivocal structure of subjective rights, as rules and not as principles. For instance, the Andalusian Statute states that "In the field of competences of the Autonomous Community, unmarried couples listed in the register will enjoy the same rights as married couples" (art. 17.2). "Free text books are guaranteed during compulsory education in schools supported by public funds" (art. 25.1). Similarly, art. 26 declares that "In the exercise of the constitutional right to work, all persons are guaranteed: a) free access to public employment services".

In short, the CC preserves the constitutionality of the declarations of rights established in the Statutes of Autonomy and, therefore, maintains their symbolic character but reduces their legal significance, denying them direct efficiency and attributing them the value of principles and guidelines that bind autonomous authorities and are only citable as subjective rights in accordance with that established by the autonomous legislator. Moreover, as was said at the beginning of this paper, the EAC itself deactivates the apparent legal significance of this declaration and its potential territorial heterogeneity of rights with the inclusion in art. 37.4 (and similarly EAA, art. 13) of an agreement clause, according to which "The rights and principles of the present Title will not imply any alteration of the system of distribution of competences, nor the creation of new enabling provisions or the modification of those already existing. None of the provisions of this Title may be developed, applied or interpreted in such a manner as to reduce or limit the fundamental rights recognised by the la Constitution and by the international treaties and agreements ratified by Spain".

This deactivation via legal channels and through interpretation of the scope of the declaration of rights is completed by the CC dismantling the basic aspects of the novelties in the guarantee of these rights. In this case, it does this by declaring the unconstitutionality and nullity of the provision (art. 76.4 EAC) that attributes a binding nature to the rulings of the Council of Statutory Guarantees "relating to Parliamentary draft bills and laws that develop or affect rights acknowledged by the present Statute", interpreting that it might interfere in the legal function of the Constitutional Court itself (STC 31/2010, FJ 32). The same fate was met by the provision (art. 78.1 EAC) assigning the Síndic de Greugues the function of supervising autonomous administrative activity, in all orders, "of an exclusive nature", as this exclusivity would render impossible the Ombudsman's action with regard to the Catalan administration, violating art. 54 CE (FJ 33).

## Declaration of Rights and Ownership: Statutes with a Federal Vocation and Feet of Clay

The Statutes of Autonomy are not always clear with regard to the attribution of the ownership of the rights that they acknowledge. For example, the Catalan Statute entitles *section of its* art. 15 "Rights of persons". However, the first section establishes that "*the citizens of Catalonia* are the holders of rights and duties recognised by the laws referred to in art. 4.1". This article refers to freedoms and Rights of a general character, proclaimed in "the Constitution, the European Union, the Universal Declaration of Human Rights, The European Convention for the Protection of Human Rights and other international treaties and conventions signed by Spain that recognise and guarantee fundamental rights and freedoms". Consequently, they are applicable to all persons who reside in Catalonia and not only to its citizens. Section 3 of art. 15 states that "The rights which the present Statute recognises as pertaining to the citizens of Catalonia may be extended to other persons, in the terms established by the laws". However, it is the Statute and not the laws that imposes this extension, as all rights, except those that are "political" (art. 7.2) or of "political participation" (art. 29) and some of a linguistic nature (art. 33), are expressly acknowledged as being enjoyed by "all people". There is a sort of tension between the wish to make a "universal" declaration of rights and the desire to limit this recognition of rights to the "citizens of Catalonia". The Catalan Parliament's mandate to pass by law the "Charter of the Rights and Duties of the Citizens of Catalonia" *fuels* the confusion arising from this tension.

Clearer without a doubt is the Statute of Andalucía, declaring that "*The recipients* of public policies and holders of the Rights and duties contained in this

Title are all persons with administrative residence in Andalusia, without prejudice to the provisions for the right of participation in public matters in Article 30 and in accordance with the regulatory laws of Fundamental Rights and Public Liberties". Nevertheless, many of the rights, being merely a clarification of fundamental rights, are recognised in the wording of the Statute as pertaining to all persons, with or without administrative residence in Andalusia.

The CC states with regard to the Statute of Catalonia, but applicable to any other, that "the Rights recognised in the Statute can only bind Catalan public authorities and have as holders the citizens of Catalonia, as faithfully stated by art. 15.1 EAC. This without prejudice to the fact that, in accordance with art. 15.3 EAC, that ownership may be extended to other Spaniards or, when appropriate, to foreigners, provided this is "in the terms established by the laws", which must obviously be, in every case, the relevant laws; in other words, also, eventually, the laws of the State" (STC 31/2010, FJ 18). The CC errs in this consideration because the Statute has a territorial value and may attribute rights to other persons who do not have the status of citizens of the Autonomous Community. Moreover, for some rights, the recognition must be general to all persons, not as a result of the generosity of the *statute-maker* but due to the constitutional imperative of the principle of equality.

However, what is of interest is to examine the basis for establishing the ownership of rights and, more specifically, political Rights or Rights of political participation, which are the clearest expression of self-government; in other words, it is interesting to know who holds autonomous citizenship. This paper has highlighted the federalising and even sovereignist vocation of the reform of the Statute of Catalonia and, in general, the symbolic aim of the inclusion of a declaration of rights in the Statutes, which is none other than the affirmation of the autonomous identity of the nationality or region. Nevertheless, that vocation and aim only make sense if there is a prior autonomous decision regarding who belongs to the Community. If the powers of the Autonomous Community emanate from the people (Catalan, Andalusian, etc.), it will be necessary for the Statute to define who legally embodies that people, who express their will via the channels of political participation and, particularly, via elections and referenda.

The criterion chosen in all the Statutes breaks with the supposed self-referentiality sought through the self-government of the nationality or region. The configuration of autonomous citizenship is based on two laws that are not autonomous but of the state. According to art. 7 EAC, "1.The political condition of Catalans or citizens of Catalonia is enjoyed by Spanish citizens who have administrative residence in Catalonia. 2. The political Rights defined by the present Statute are enjoyed, as by Catalans, by Spaniards resident abroad whose last administrative residence was in Catalonia, as well as their descendants who maintain this citizenship, if requested, as determined by the law". According to art. 5 EAA, "1. According to the present Statute, the political condition of being Andalusian is enjoyed by Spanish citizens who, in accordance with the general laws of the State, have administrative residence in any of the municipalities of Andalusia. 2. Like Andalusians, the political Rights defined in this Statute are enjoyed by Spanish citizens resident abroad whose last administrative residence was in Andalusia and who verify this condition in the corresponding Consulate in Spain. These Rights will also be enjoyed by their descendants registered as Spanish, if they so request, in the manner determined by State law". Art. 147.2 CE obliges a definition in the Statute of the territory of the Autonomous Community, but it says nothing about the delimitation of its people. However, it seems consistent with the autonomous principle that this be done, and in fact all the Statutes do this by establishing who has the political status of citizen of the Community. What is unusual is that the political status lies beyond the control of the basic institutional legislation of the Autonomous Community, as it refers to two requirements defined in State laws: *nationality*, regulated in the civil code, and *administrative residence*, regulated in the local Government Regulatory Law. A legislative change in the conditions of access to Spanish nationality or administrative residence involves a change in the composition of autonomous citizenry.

If autonomy is not sovereignty, the requirement for Spanish would not have to be essential to be a citizen of an Autonomous Community. The Andalusian Statute states that "the recipients of public policies and the holders of statutory Rights and duties are all persons with administrative residences in Andalusia" (art. 12), consequently, also the foreigners who fulfil this condition. Nothing would prevent this from being a criterion to determine the political status of Andalusian. Even thus, this would mean depending upon what State law considers to be administrative residence. Nonetheless, the Statute could also substitute this criterion with another more appropriate and more in keeping with what is meant by an Autonomous Community. It is not coherent in democratic terms for autonomous citizenship to depend upon so volatile a condition as administrative residence, and this is also the case for municipal citizenship. The Statutes should insist upon a certain continued temporal rooting, a sort of political or autonomous stability, for example, 4 years of residence, to accede to the status of citizen of an Autonomous Community. In a similar sense, the recognition of autonomous citizenship could be limited to "Spaniards resident abroad whose last administrative residence was in the Autonomous Community, as well as their descendants who maintain this citizenship, if they so request, in the manner determined by the law". This is a hybrid criterion, which appears in all the Statutes, which mixes nationality, residence abroad, administrative residence and descent, which is distant from the democratic self-referentiality sought via autonomous government.

To sum up, the exhibition of self-government sought via the inclusion of an extensive declaration of rights in the Statutes is revealed to have feet of clay when one observes the lack of concern of the ***statute-making power*** when it comes to defining autonomous citizenship, renouncing its power of self-government, which would allow it to establish, without referral to external legislation, the conditions for the acquisition or loss of that citizenship.

# References[1]

Luis María Diez Picazo, *¿Pueden los Estatutos de Autonomía declarar derechos, deberes y principios?*, REDC 78/2006, pp. 63–75.

Francisco Caamaño, *Sí pueden (Declaraciones de derechos y Estatutos de Autonomía)*, REDC 79/2007, pp. 33–45.

Marc Carrillo, *La declaración de derechos en el nuevo Estatuto de Autonomía de Cataluña: expresión de autogobierno y límites de los poderes públicos*, in Derechos, deberes y principios en el nuevo Estatuto de Autonomía de Cataluña, CEPC, Foro, 8, 2006, pp. 63–88.

Víctor Fererres Comella, *Derechos deberes y principios en el nuevo Estatuto de Autonomía de Cataluña*, in Derechos, deberes y principios en el nuevo Estatuto de Autonomía de Cataluña, CEPC, Foro, 8, 2006, pp. 9–37.

Marc Carrillo, *Los derechos estatutarios y sus garantías en la sentencia 31/2010, de 28 de junio, sobre la reforma del Estatuto de Autonomía de Cataluña*, REDC, n° 91, 2010, pp. 331–354.

Francisco Balaguer Callejón, *Derechos estatutarios y constitucionalismo multinivel*, in Derechos, deberes y principios en el nuevo Estatuto de Autonomía para Andalucía. Perspectiva comparada, Obra colectiva, Fundación Centro de Estudios Andaluces, 2008, pp. 170–206.

---

[1] The quotations in the text correspond to the following authors and works. A wide bibliographical reference on the subject may be seen in Mar Carrillo 5, 353–4.

# Special Civil Law as a Sign of Political Identity: A Constitutional Approach to the Case of the Valencian Community

Remedio Sánchez Ferriz

**Abstract** We seek to clarify the political terminology and meaning of what is contained in the Valencian Statute in the light of the (far more developed and diverse) doctrinal and jurisprudential contributions to arise from the demands of other autonomous communities. This is necessary after the 2006 reform of the Valencian Statute, due to the tendency towards historical law evident therein, and is also essential if progress is to be made towards the constitutional reform that will bring to a close the evolution of the Autonomous State into an ordered Federal State.

When positing such a federalist position, perhaps the first step towards evaluating its viability in each state should be to determine the specificities of each of the territories involved, together with the constituent elements thereof. Only on such solid foundations can we thus hope to establish the common as well as particular rules that federation will contribute towards consolidation and respect.

Aside from the specific roads to autonomy initially adopted, two major territorial groups have clearly stood out in the Spanish autonomous state, one consisting of territories that, even before the Constitution and throughout their 33 years of existence, have consistently challenged the structure of the constitutional state which has not always been readily accepted, and a second group comprising autonomous communities that merely through emulation, and/or a sense of grievance, have demanded greater legislative powers than those assigned to them at each stage.

This second group doubtlessly includes the Valencian Community; however, much statutory reform of 2006 may have been seen to be seeking the claims and aspirations to which I will subsequently refer. In my view, it should be made clear that the pretensions of the Valencian Community cannot (and thus far have not)

R.S. Ferriz (✉)
Campus dels Tarongers, Edificio Departamental Occidental, University of Valencia,
Av. dels Tarongers s/n, 46022 Valencia, Spain
e-mail: Remedio.Sanchez@uv.es

A. López-Basaguren and L. Escajedo San Epifanio (eds.), *The Ways of Federalism in Western Countries and the Horizons of Territorial Autonomy in Spain*, Vol. 2, DOI 10.1007/978-3-642-27717-7_29, © Springer-Verlag Berlin Heidelberg 2013

proved to be an obstacle to the federalisation of the Spanish state. Quite the opposite, should such a constitutional situation arise, Valencia is a region that, together with certain others, may well aspire to a fairer treatment from the standpoint of the equal consideration that presides over any federal approach.


## Clarifications Concerning the Title and Purpose of This Commentary

My aim is to show that the statutory system in the Valencian Community is perfectly consistent with the structure of the autonomous state set out in the Constitution, any references to historical law proving no more than a claim to historical identity, devoid of the political connotations evident in other autonomous communities.[1]

The controversial application of its powers in the area of civil law (expressly recognised in the 1982 Statute) and the understandable tension arising from the general questioning of such a power account for the concern of those who were at the head of statutory reform in 2006 in consolidating and strengthening such a recognition of power. This was understood to be the case by the repeated references to the historical nature of the law being claimed. Yet, neither this nor the failed attempt to mention the First Additional Provision of the Constitution may, in my view, be interpreted as a political strategy aimed at forcing any constitutional interpretation, however much it may have been criticised and compared to the case of Catalonia at the height of the controversy sparked by such reforms in 2006. Rather, I feel that even if we focus our attention on the period surrounding the 2006 Statute, which heralded the moment of greatest activism in this regard, it is difficult to conclude that there has been any attempt to impose on the constitutional system the federal considerations that are, by contrast, to be found in other second (or third[2]) generation statutes.

As I highlighted on another occasion, the scarcity of any studies addressing the issue from the standpoint of constitutional law[3] is striking (contrary to what has been the case in civil law and history of law). This leads me to a simple reflection concerning the vacuity of a controversy that, sometimes in an excessively critical fashion,[4] has surrounded any attempt to implement and apply Valencian civil law in legislative terms, which is usually greeted with appeals contesting its constitutionality. Said appeals stem more from the inappropriate (and we shall later see whether

---

[1] For all of these, and the Valencian perspective, Vivancos Comes (2005).

[2] Vivancos Comes (2005), p. 229 et seq.

[3] With very few exceptions: see Mayol (2003), pp. 291–295.

[4] Izquierdo Tolsada (2007), pp. 331–381.

unnecessary) use of historical-legal[5] language in the Statute and in the corresponding laws through which it is applied than perhaps from any actual intention to extend the competences of the Regional Government beyond the constitutional framework.

## The Civil Law Debate and Its Approach to a Plausible and Useful Constitutional Interpretation

In contrast to those of us concerned with Constitutional Law, those immersed in civil law in Valencia have not shied away from the matter and from adopting conflicting opinions concerning the issue.

From the negationist stance (which in the case of Montes I feel to be more a case of scepticism), mention must be made of Montes Penades,[6] who affords us an invaluable historical overview of how our historical laws (*fueros*) were lost in the annals of time, for which purpose he resorts to the most illustrious historians in the region and at this university.[7] A similarly negative viewpoint is expressed by Montes Rodríguez[8] and Ballarin Hernandez,[9] whose constitutional approach I feel should be highlighted when stating that however warranted it may be to reclaim historical law in political terms, "...this is something which under the Rule of Law, such as in Spain, can only possibly be achieved legitimately by respecting the legal system, the maximum expression of which is the 1978 Constitution...".

Yet, together with positions that staunchly defend the legitimacy of legislative power, either from the political standpoint of claims based on historical injustice or detailed legal studies,[10] we should not overlook other less controversial positions[11] since in the Constitution itself (and in the Statute) elements may be found that support such a recognition of legislative power in Valencia in the matter of civil law and that are perfectly constitutional, provided they are based not on "reclaiming

---

[5] Ragel Sanchez (2005) (p. 13) expressly refers to the text of the Valencian Statute in the following terms: "The aim is now to include a reference to historical law (*Derecho Foral*) and to remove the word "civil". Yet, when regulating the exclusive legislative power of the Catalonian Regional Government, the Statute of Catalonia makes clear reference to the "preservation, modification and implementation of Catalonian civil law", without restricting itself to what it is considered Catalonian civil historical law. We feel the term "civil" to be more appropriate than "historical" (*foral*), although we also feel the best expression to be "own civil" or "special civil".

[6] Montes Penades (2007), pp. 261 et seq.

[7] Thus, and in various notes, reference is made to Peset Reig (1972, p. 657 et seq.) or in note 20 to Simo Santonja (1979).

[8] Montes Rodríguez (2008).

[9] Ballarin Hernandez (2010), pp. 18–19.

[10] Domínguez Calatayud (2004); Blasco Gasco and Clemente Meoro (1989), p. 117 et seq.

[11] Blasco Gascó (2011), p. 22 or López Beltrán de Heredia (2000), p. 64.

historical law" but rather on powers foreseen in the Constitution and embraced by
the Statute.

Bataller provides one example when positing the idea[12] that he refers to as
"inductive autonomous civil law" and concerning which he concludes: "we may no
longer speak of "historical law", but rather to it being replaced by a more comprehensive "regional law", since it refers both to the former historical law inherited by
the those autonomous communities set up on the basis of territories in which said
law remained in force when the 1978 Constitution was drawn up, as well as to the
new civil law which each and every one of the autonomous communities, without
exception, may put into force in application of the general legislative powers
assigned to them".[13] We shall later examine in greater depth this position, which
may well today provide us with a solution to the conflicts brought before the
constitutional court.


## Specifying Problems from a Constitutional Perspective

The debate amongst civil law jurists and historians should perforce be far more
wide-ranging and diverse than that which concerns us since, doubtlessly, what will
prove most difficult will be to determine what civil law is available to the autonomous communities in the terms set out under article 149.1.8 of the Spanish
Constitution and, if the historical connection is to be maintained, when applicable,
its links to the old historical laws.

From the standpoint of constitutional law, however, the issue may focus on two
specific aspects that those involved in civil law have in some way provided us with.
I will particularly focus on the second.

The first is the matter of the constitutional legitimacy and/or basis of the powers
of certain autonomous communities and/or regions governed under historical law,
the widespread impact and general nature of which (in no way confined solely to the
Valencian Community) account for the extent to which constitutionalist doctrine
has devoted itself to the matter.

The second issue, and the one that specifically needs to be dealt with in the case
of Valencia, involves determining the degree to which the Constitution allows the
Valencian Community to legislate in the matter of civil law. It is true that an
affirmative ruling has already been issued concerning this second matter by the
constitutional court through ruling 121/1992, dated 28 September, on the historical
lease act (*Ley de arrendamientos históricos*). Yet, it is also true that by linking said
legislative power to *surviving* customs, the highly restrictive interpretation thereof
rekindled the question of competence, in my view leaving it open to constitutional

---

[12] Also put forward in other areas, such as Arechederra Aranzadi (1992), pp. 491–511, particularly
p. 498.

[13] Bataller Ruiz, p. 7.

interpretation. It is precisely in this area where I now attempt to approach the question once more, focusing on the present situation to which the evolution of such an interpretation has brought us.

In light of the profound changes to Section VIII of the Constitution in the three decades it has been in force, and of the interpretation thereof being made by the Statute of Catalonia (not without the collusion of important legal figures), I pointed to the possibility that should we fail to undertake the necessary constitutional reform that would once again frame the territorial problem in the terms constitutional values demand, then we should not rule out the possibility that with the Constitution having changed in such key areas as the structure of the autonomous state, we might be faced with a more flexible interpretation of the Constitution or one less "akin" to the political concerns with which the founding text was drawn up 33 years ago and that might, whether we like it or not, have played such a part in its subsequent confusion–interpretation.[14]

Naturally, the most logical solution is constitutional reform that would clarify the possibilities afforded by the constitution,[15] as indeed some, following the civil law approach, have so brilliantly defended.[16] The political situation would not, however, appear to favour such an ideal and suitable solution (which Herrero would judge to be *geometric*[17]), as a result of which, as I said, our only option at the moment is a constitutional interpretation that, although not openly expressed by the main exponent of the Constitution, might well be the case since that is the direction that its constitutional jurisprudence seems to be taking.[18]

In the case of the Valencian Community, this would also require such a position to be previously accepted by those involved at a legal level in defending the competence in their future respective action, shifting the focus of the argument that the authorities in Valencia have put forward when having to defend and exercise the legislative power in question. From the civil perspective, quite another matter would be whether any efforts to legislate were successful and whether the right technical approach had been adopted.

---

[14] Sanchez Ferriz (2008), pp. 14–35.

[15] By everybody, Ortega, Luis, Reforma constitucional y..., already cited. In the same critical sense with the "centrifuge" method used in Spain, most of the doctrine may be cited. One example that may be cited is Corcuera Atienza (2009), p. 70.

[16] Cf. Ragel Sanchez (2005) p. 3 et seq, Blasco Gasco (2011, p. 23), or Moliner Navarro (2007), p. 364.

[17] Herrero de Miñon (1998), p. 54 et seq.

[18] Montes Penades (2007), pp. 281–82.

## *Status Questionis* in Constitutional Doctrine Prior to Statutory Reform: The First Additional Provision of the Spanish Constitution and Valencian Autonomy

The undeniable reference in the defence of historical rights, not only through full application of the First Additional Provision for those to whom it is addressed but also with a view to the future[19] and of the potential of such historical rights, is Herrero de Miñón, whose theories may in no way be applied to the Valencian Community and who has not indeed expressed himself in such terms. We are therefore forced to resort to the majority constitutionalist doctrine, which has always been the interpretation of the exceptional nature of the Constitution's First Additional Provision and which, moreover, coincides with the constitutional court's recently confirmed ruling (STC 31/2010).

From this standpoint, the most eminent opinion concerning the constitutional text even prior to its final approval was that of Prof. García Pelayo,[20] who warned not only of the risks and contradictions inherent in including historical elements in a rational constitution but also of the confusing and unclear manner in which it was expressed in the famous First Additional Provision of the constitutional text.[21] No less concerned with the historical references was Tomás y Valiente[22] or Clavero,[23] as indeed have been all of those who have impartially undertaken an analysis of the Constitution with regard to nationalist demands.[24]

Corcuera[25] alerted early on to the difficulties that would emerge from the First Additional Provision, beginning with how inefficient it could prove in legal terms, even before the only political effect that its inclusion in the Constitution might have justified had yet to come about,[26] as well as the contradictions to arise from the twin historical-autonomous community approach and the various and conflicting interests that the two positions represented.[27] Yet, though already complex in itself, the problem was confined to the historical regions, Basque autonomy maintaining its particular recognition set out under the Constitution.

The subsequent attempt to apply it to other territories-autonomous communities led to a radical rejection from both constitutional law and doctrine, such that the

---

[19] Herrero de Miñón (2009), pp. 4–12.

[20] García Pelayo (1991), p. 3171 et seq.

[21] Cf. Tajadura Tejada (2009), pp. 147–174, particularly 168, et seq.

[22] Tomás y Valiente (1995).

[23] Clavero Salvador (1982).

[24] Thus expressed by Solozábal Echavarria (1998), Corcuera Atienza and García Herrera (2002). A well-rounded summary of the varying doctrinal positions concerning the famous First Additional Provision may be consulted in Tudela Aranda (2009), p. 63 et seq.

[25] Corcuera Atienza (1985), pp. 55–89.

[26] Ibidem, p. 56.

[27] Ibidem, p. 76: "la autonomía aparece como superación de la foralidad y la foralidad como resistencia –o, al menos, reticencia- ante la autonomía. . ."

only instance in which the reference to the First Additional Provision was successfully included in the Statute has had scarcely any legal effect whatsoever[28] as commentators on the Statute of Aragon have concurred in pointing out.

However, the attempt made when reforming[29] the Statutes of Autonomy in 2006[30] was far more controversial, an attempt whose political paths in the cases of Valencia and Catalonia have proved quite different.[31] Even though, as was immediately evident in the doctrine, the main discussions centred on the Statute of Catalonia, it was clear that whatever was to be established therein would eventually have an impact on the territorial organisation of the State as a whole.[32]

## The First Additional Provision of the Spanish Constitution Today

Assuming that in no way should it be called upon in the case of Valencia, in the light of recent doctrinal declarations it may well also be considered more of a hurdle to the removal of certain injustices and/or unjustified differences in the way Valencia is treated. There is no doubt that its survival in the constitutional text has not only led to a malfunctioning thereof but that its removal from the fundamental text is being advocated. Tudela is clear as to its dysfunctionality: "I think it is safe to say that today the First Additional Provision has had a negative effect. It has failed to resolve the issue of Basque Country inclusion in the constitutional system and has served to fire other conflicts... in a fresh version of the statutes of autonomy, historical rights have reached beyond their natural borders".[33]

Torres also criticises the spurious use of the First Additional Provision, regarding which he maintains that, as the level of powers has increased, it may be deemed obsolete since it serves to differentiate only a minority of autonomous communities, leading him to recommend constitutional reform to remove it.[34]

Such a negative description is today fairly commonplace to the extent that it has been deemed by Tajadura to be unconstitutional (based on the theory of unconstitutional constitutional norms),[35] leading him to advocate much needed constitutional (depurative) reform to bring to an end the dysfunctions it causes and to

---

[28] Sainz Arnaiz (2004), p. 53, or Tudela Aranda (2009) p. 78.

[29] Tudela Aranda (2009), p. 72 et seq.

[30] Sevilla et al. (2009), p. 184 et seq. and pp. 209–210.

[31] Today, quite a number of Catalonian jurists continue to defend the application of the First Additional Provision of the Spanish Constitution. For instance, Vernet i Llobet et al. (2011), p. 125 et seq.

[32] López Basaguren (2007), p. 5 et seq., in which he develops the "overflowing of the dispositive principle".

[33] Tudela Aranda (2009), p. 589, cit.

[34] Torres del Moral (2007–2008), pp. 55–79.

[35] Cf. Tajadura Tejada (2008), pp. 137–192.

conclude that said provision is an insurmountable obstacle to establishing a federal state.[36]

Yet, striking is the previously mentioned position that is expressed by one sector of Catalonian doctrine that not only defends its functionality but also the legitimacy of its application to Catalonia, for which reason they express their "grievance", criticising ruling 31/2010 in which, they state,[37] the constitutional court fails to clarify or justify the restrictive interpretations set out in legal basis no. 10, which we cite in part regarding the impossibility of applying the First Additional Provision to Catalonia.

# The Use of Civil Law Terminology in the Valencian Statute: Civil Law, Special Civil Law, or Historical Law?

A comparison between the former (1982) and latter (2006) Statutes of the Valencian Community reveals not only how much greater attention is paid to the issue with which we are concerned but also the firm decision to opt for the use of the term historical (*foral*), either by itself (historical law) or together with the expression civil law to refer in both instances to special (private) law.

Article 31 of the 1982 Statute read: "the Valencian Regional Government has exclusive legislative power in the following matters: . . .2. Preservation, amendment and application of Valencian civil law". What should not be overlooked here is that this is a specific power that, as a result, as also occurs in the new Statute, is directly applicable unlike other references contained in rules of a programmatic nature.

The new Statute of 2006 introduced certain changes in terminology with regard to the 1982 text, which might have sparked some mistrust amongst those charged with ensuring adherence to the constitutional framework, as indeed proved to be the case on its passage through the Lower House where it had to be amended. We should attempt to see whether, aside from the mistrust, there really has been a substantial change reflecting a shift in the political perspective of the Valencian Community within the heart of Spanish unity. What cannot in principle be denied is the insistence with which recourse is made to the term historical (*foral*), indicating that autonomous concerns (*autonomismo*) have been abandoned in favour of historical ones (*foralismo*).[38]

The key issue from the constitutional standpoint is to find an answer to the question of why. Have the constitutional basis of the whole system and the indissoluble unity of the Spanish nation been called into doubt? In my view, absolutely not.

---

[36] Tajadura Tejada (2009), p. 172, cit.

[37] For all, Vernet (2011), p. 127, op. cit.

[38] Blasco Gascó (2011), p. 22.

What simply happened was that the term *foralismo* was used in the belief that it would thus prove easier to consolidate a legislative power that, up to that point, had been called into question. Was this overzealousness? I do not think it was a question of that either. The Valencian Community has found itself reeling in the confusion[39] that political considerations (of every persuasion) tend to bring into legal norms when the latter are forced to regulate "hot" issues, as was doubtlessly the case with the norm that the constituent assembly sought to "cool down" through a First Additional Provision that has never since ceased to generate expectations, disenchantment, and injustice.

The present situation and certain interpretations thereof have, in my view, been accurately described as a muddle: "These positions are a clear reflection of the tangle caused by a procedure such as the one set out in our Constitution, once an autonomous state has been generally consolidated in which all autonomous communities assume the maximum possible degree of autonomy in the Constitution".[40]

Returning to the Valencian Statute of 2006, we remain well aware of the introduction (and repetition) of the term *foral*, which is to be found in the numerous references in the Statute to the problem that said text has introduced. Such are those contained in the following precepts transcribed below:

1. Without doubt, the full force of reform in the matter immediately appears in the Preamble without any delay, yet also without the slightest friction with the legal system, as we shall see later when it states that: "Likewise, this reform seeks to provide recognition of the Valencian Community as a historical nation due to its historical roots, its separate identity, its language and culture and its *civil historical law*". "...This reform also seeks to promote and develop applicable *Valencian civil historical law*, an understanding and use of the Valencian language, the individual and unique culture of our people, their customs and traditions. Legislative implementation of Regional Government powers, in full harmony with the Spanish Constitution, will seek restitution of what was set out under the Historical Law of the Kingdom of Valencia, abolished by Decree on 29 June, 1707." It is difficult to see any legislation in what is written, not because it is the preamble but simply because what is expressed therein is the statement of a historical fact and no more.

2. With regard to Section I, under the paragraph "The Valencian Community" (this being the appropriate place to contain a special reference to identity or political demands), there are two precepts in which the mention of the historical nature (*foralidad*) of the Community stands out.

Article 3.4: "*Historical civil law in Valencia* shall be applied regardless of place of residence, on all those born in Valencia in application of the rules set out under the preliminary section of the civil code, which shall also be applied to resolve any conflicts involving laws".

---

[39] Aparicio Perez (2002) (pp. 29–57).

[40] López Basaguren (2007), p. 16, cit.

Article 7.2: "The rules and provisions of the Regional Government as well as those which constitute *historical law in Valencia* shall be applicable throughout the whole of the territory except in those cases in which the personal statute and other extraterritorial rules are applicable".

3. A further group of precepts that again mention historical law are to be found in the following Articles which that make indirect reference thereto:

Art. 35.1: "At the request of the Regional Government, the competent body shall call public examinations to fill vacancies for the positions of magistrates, judges, court secretaries and other personnel working for the justice administration, in accordance with the stipulations set out under the organic law governing the judiciary. Account will be taken of their specialisation in *historical civil law in Valencia* and command of the Valencian language".

Concerning a different area and adopting a different literal tone, Article 58.2 also makes reference to knowledge of the language and special civil law and reads: "When filling the position of public notary, applicants shall be accepted under equal conditions, irrespective of whether they exercise their profession in the Valencian Community or in any other part of Spain. Under no circumstances may any exception be established on the grounds of nature or residence. Public notaries should ensure a use of the Valencian language when exercising their profession within the Valencian Community in application of the rules set out in the present Statute. They should also ensure application of *historical civil law in Valencia,* with which they should be familiar".

Art. 37.1: "Competence in jurisdictional bodies in the Valencian Community comprises: ... 2) In the matter of historical civil law[41] in Valencia, knowledge of *appeals and reviews, as the exclusive competence of the supreme court of* justice in the Valencian Community, as well as appeals for unification of doctrine and appeals in the interest of the law within the area of administrative justice when only affecting laws issued by the Valencian Community".

Amongst these references that we might deem indirect, final mention should also be made of Article 71.1., in which, when listing the assets that make up the possessions held by the Regional Government of Valencia, reference is made to .... c) assets, as well as any other, whatever their nature, deriving from persons dying intestate, as set out under Valencian *historical civil legislation*, when, in application of state legislation, the deceased was born in Valencia.

4. No doubt clearer, as indeed it was in the corresponding precept of the 1982 Statute already mentioned, is the precept contained in and defined as a competence of the Regional Government of Valencia, namely article 49 of the Statute of 2006: "1. The Regional Government of Valencia has exclusive competence over the following matters: ... 2) Preservation, implementation and amendment of *histori-cal civil law in Valencia*".[42] Indeed, in this precept and overall in those just

---

[41] The term *civil*, which appeared in the final text, did not form part of the proposal.

[42] We should also perhaps recall that, on this occasion, the proposal stressed more the term historical (*foral*) when referring to "historical and Valencian Law".

mentioned, there are no qualitative differences with regard to the 1982 text, only terminological differences arising from the use of the adjective "*foral*", an attempt now being made to use it on every possible occasion.

With regard to the changes introduced in the reform, its insistence on underlining the historical nature (*foralismo*) of the Valencian Community is the most notable conclusion to be drawn, although from the constitutional standpoint it is striking to note that legislative power in Valencia has ultimately been incorporated through what Blasco refers to as *agroconsuetudinaria* (agro-common law): in other words, that deriving from constitutional court ruling 121/92 (concerning the historical lease act [(*Ley de arrendamientos históricos*)]) and notably reinforced by the subsequent flexibility put into practice by the constitutional court in its interpretation of Article 149.1.8, for autonomous communities as a whole, and consequently for Valencia as well, to the extent that the scope of the idea of "application"[43] ultimately becomes a gold mine enabling "application" to institutions even if they did not exist when the 1978 constitution came into being. This is somewhat curious since, as Blasco[44] himself points out, what has in fact proved to be the spearhead pointing the way for Valencia is a custom, the historical lease act, that dates not from historical rights (*fueros*) but from the nineteenth century.

## Historical Civil Law in Valencia and Its Constitutional Legitimacy (Which in No Way Can Be Deemed Historical)

Without doubt, the most controversial of the statutory provisions was the Third Transitory Provision of the Statute of Autonomy reform proposal, whose final text scarcely, if indeed at all, resembles that which it sought to approve, although it has to be said that the final text is much improved in terms of style and coherence. The third transitory provision read as follows:

> Exclusive legislative power over historical civil law in Valencia will be exercised by the Regional Government of Valencia, based on the historical laws repealed under the Decree of 29 June, 1707, having then been reintroduced and implemented by updating the contents of the historical legislative system in force in the Kingdom of Valencia, in accordance with the First Additional Provision set out under the Spanish Constitution.

Leaving aside how poorly the text was able to reflect the aim thereof at the time, it is clear that express reference to the First Additional Provision of the Constitution burdened it with such constitutional doubts as could scarcely be overcome, not because it sought to reach beyond the limits of the constitutional framework (which, as I have already said, is beyond all doubt) but because, ultimately, neither the

---

[43] An interesting remark concerning constitutional court ruling 88/93 with the doctrine on the term "implementation" and its eventual application to the Region of Valencia, in Montes Penades (2007), p. 294 cit., et seq.

[44] Blasco Gascó (2011), p. 24.

Valencian Community nor the other communities that had direct recourse to the First Additional Provision are historical regions and it is precisely on them that said additional provision focuses (according to an authentic, verifiable interpretation consulted in the parliamentary work of the constituent assembly, already conducted by the constitutional court).

Why was such an "attempt" made to hide behind said Additional Provision of the Constitution? Even though Valencia has not stood out for the doctrinal (constitutional) interest that this particular question has aroused, the latter has been the subject of consideration by all the schools or groups in our constitutional area, allowing us at this point to attempt to synthesise the "constitutional and not so constitutional life" of the Additional Provision with the sole aim of reflecting on the text vis-à-vis the Valencian Community and on an appropriate interpretation of the historical nature (*foralismo*) of the Valencian Community that we today find in many written precepts.

The heated controversy that said (first additional) constitutional provision gave rise to is no doubt what has led certain writers and/or promoters of reform in Valencia to propose the *unborn* text of the above-mentioned Third Transitory Provision, which could evidently not be accepted (unless use had subsequently been made of the awful legal technique employed by the constitutional court which consisted of leaving the text as it was and describing it as irrelevant).[45]

The questions now, however, are even if the Valencian Statute contains no reference to the First Additional Provision of the Spanish Constitution, whether repeatedly describing the special civil law as historical (*foral*) enhances the efficiency of the statutory provisions or whether they prove unnecessary vis-à-vis consolidation of the legislative power in question and, should this be the case, whether they may be deemed claims related to identity, stressing the historical uniqueness of the Kingdom of Valencia in an attempt to recall that it once enjoyed its own charters.

When drafting Valencian statutory reform, two perfectly clear and contradictory positions had already been consolidated: the legal question concerning the meaning of the First Additional Provision, which had come down firmly on the side of the restrictive interpretation of its application, from which the true constitutional interpretation could be derived and the political interpretation (or with ulterior political motives), the ambiguity of which served to provide grounds both for exaggerating its effects in the regions for which it was originally devised and for subsequent application to any regions wishing to enter the fray. When proposing reform, legislators in Valencia thought that, if accepted, such a proposal would have meant an end to so many unjust rejections, thus joining forces with the effort made by other autonomous communities.

---

[45] It has, however, been justified as one of the many ways of avoiding open confrontation between Constitution and Statutes. Cf. López Basaguren (2007), p. 4 cit.

## The First Additional Provision of the Spanish Constitution and Valencian Autonomy

In order to avoid any misunderstanding, what should first be pointed out in this section is that the two terms contained in the statement cannot coexist. However much during the reform of the Statute of Catalonia an effort was again made to try to extend the First Additional Provision, there seems to be no doubt that at no point during the drafting of the Constitution was said provision ever considered for application anywhere other than in the "historical territories (*forales*)", as expressed in the text itself,[46] however much its ambiguity may have led to considerable error and confusion, not only for the autonomous communities for which it was not intended (but which expressed a wish to benefit from it) but also in the territories for which it was devised (which have made further use of the historical clause than originally expected).

Valencia is obviously amongst those regions that, although not intended as recipients/beneficiaries of the provision, have however expressed a desire to be considered under it, as can clearly be deduced from the above-mentioned Third Transitory Provision whose text was rejected. Yet, unlike Catalonia, I think it is safe to say that the Valencian parliament sought to use it without the political pretension that could have been drawn from it and with no intention other than to affirm legislative power in civil law.

This in no way appears to be the view of Fernando Rey,[47] who not only points a critical finger at Valencia and Catalonia (which they no doubt equally deserved "in formal terms") but also continues to mistrust the way the Third Transitory Provision has been written in the Statute's final text, in which he feels, "all of the doubts referred to concerning constitutionality remain, since the reference to the First Additional is clear, even though it is not explicitly cited (since it is the only clause in the Constitution which allows historical rights in the historical (*foral*) territories to be reinstated)".[48]

I find myself disagreeing with what for me is clearly an exaggerated interpretation since however much it may surprise Rey Martínez that Valencia does not refer to itself or attempt to make mention of the notion of historical region, it is clear that the Valencian Community has in no way sought any such thing or consequently attempted to compare itself to other autonomous communities that have pursued an application of the First Additional Provision similar to that of historical regions. Had any invocation of the Additional Provision been in evidence in the final text, then a comparison may indeed have been drawn with that made in the first Statute of Aragon, which has in fact ultimately proved to be totally harmless,[49] not because

---

[46] Logendio Irure (1985).

[47] Rey Martinez (2006), pp. 69–102.

[48] Ibid, p. 91.

[49] For all of them, see Tudela Aranda (2009), p. 91, cit.

we are dealing with second or third class autonomous communities, or with those that do not value their own history and political identity, but rather for two far simpler reasons.

Firstly, regardless of how accurate or inaccurate any mention may be, no benefit could have been derived from said transitory provision had it survived since it is not provided for in the Constitution. Secondly, neither has there been any public "interpretation" of the *historical rights* nor indeed are they mentioned in the Statute. Attempting to draw any comparison between the two cases of Valencia and Catalonia in the following terms is therefore excessive: "Valencia and Catalonia have come to use the concept of historical rights in an effort to establish their uniqueness as autonomous communities in something we might term a residual, anterior, superior and latent sovereign consociation with regard to the State (Article 2 of the Spanish Constitution).[50]

Indeed, this second reason runs parallel with the other constitutional profile of the problem, which is the important one, namely that which refers to the establishment of power and of each autonomy and which, for the case of Aragon and Valencia, is undoubtedly contained within the Constitution and not outside it, however much they strive to evoke the wealth of their own history.

The question has recently been clarified by the constitutional court under ruling 31/2010, which resolves the appeal of unconstitutionality filed against Organic Law 6/2006, of 19 July, concerning the reform of the Statute of Autonomy of Catalonia. The high court makes it clear through Legal Basis no. 10 that there are no historical rights enabling the Statute of Catalonia[51] to claim any base other than a constitutional one, not even when "added" to that of the Constitution. In other words, neither wholly nor in part can any base be found that does not emanate exclusively from the Constitution, as the Constitutional court makes clear regarding Article 5 of the new Statute of Catalonia[52]:

> It would be improper to interpret such historical rights as also providing a legal basis for the self-government of Catalonia, since their constitutional scope only allows for the statutory assumption of certain legislative powers within the framework of the Constitution, but never the basis for the existence in law of the autonomous community of Catalonia and its

---

[50] Rey Martinez (2006), p. 85, cit.

[51] The idea had also been defended with regard to the Basque Country by, amongst others, Tomás y Valiente (1979), p. 28. The author referred to the second part of the First Additional Provision of the Spanish Constitution in the following terms: "This clarification underlines the principle of constitutional supremacy; such that updating both historical rights inherited from the past and in force today as well as the drafting of completely new rules, valid in "historical territories" or even in potential future autonomous communities which may not have enjoyed a special or historical legal system ... shall always be carried out by applying the stipulations laid down in the corresponding Statutes of Autonomy, which in turn should always be understood within the terms of the present Constitution".

[52] It sets out the following: "self-government in Catalonia is also based on the historical rights of the Catalonian people, its secular institutions and on Catalonian legal tradition, which the present Statute incorporates and updates under article 2, the second transitory provision and other precepts of the Constitution".

constitutional right to self-government. Far from providing in the true sense the basis for the self-government of Catalonia, the rights, institutions and traditions referred to in the precept derive their constitutional relevance from the fact that they are assumed in the Constitution, from which in constitutional terms, they provide the basis for the institutional and legislative system inducted through the Statute of Autonomy.

In sum, Article 5 of the Statute of Autonomy of Catalonia is not contrary to the Constitution interpreted in the sense that its inclusion of "the historical rights of the Catalonian people" does not refer to the content of the First Additional Provision of the Constitution nor provides the legal basis for the self-government of Catalonia outside of the Constitution itself, and will thus be set out in the ruling...

Seen thus, I feel that there is no doubt concerning the obvious difference between the political intention of those writing the Catalonian statutes and those who drew up the Valencian statutes, in the sense that any efforts that the latter make to strengthen their positions may be seen as a defence of legislative powers in private law. Having thus ruled out any possible application of the First Additional Provision contained in the Constitution either to Aragon, Valencia, or Catalonia, the following final question is posed.

# Is It Necessary to Hold a Historical Nationality or to Be a Historical Territory to Enjoy the Right to Special Law?

Clearly it is not. Moreover, what is also clear is that when considering such a question we find ourselves in a completely different situation to the one so far discussed with regard to the application or otherwise of the First Additional Provision of the Spanish Constitution.

Legislative powers in the matter of civil law need not call into question the constitutional legitimisation of power. Such powers are perfectly compatible in constitutional terms with article 149.1, 8, of the Spanish Constitution, which Saiz Arnaiz,[53] amongst others, has affirmed when expressing his position concerning the possibility of the Regional Government of Catalonia legislating on the matter here under debate. For such a purpose, recourse to the legal framework of the First Additional Provision of the Constitution proves unnecessary since reference need only be made to Article 149. 1, 8, of the Constitution. For the remaining, in the matter of civil law studies, I concur with the view put forward and, in particular, with Ragel.[54]

Such should be the position of the Valencian Community, namely to focus its efforts on maximising the possibilities available to it under Article 149.1, 8, and through the *supra*-constitutional jurisprudence referred to regarding the full scope of the possibilities afforded by the term "application". Notwithstanding any mention in the Statute of the matter of the historical nature of these regions, should the

---

[53] Sainz Arnaiz (2004), p. 53 et seq.

[54] Ragel Sanchez (2005), p. 3.

latter be deemed merely as a reference to identity from which no attempt is being made to enhance legislative efficiency in any future laws that the region may draw up, no major problems should be expected to arise for the constitutional court providing, of course, that the statutory legislative power being implemented in each case is duly debated and that there is no invasion of the civil legislative powers attributed to the state under Article 149.1, 8.

# References

APARICIO PEREZ, Miguel Ángel, "Aproximación a la regulación contenida en el texto de la constitución española de 1978 sobre la distribución territorial del poder político", in M.A. Aparicio, La descentralización y el Federalismo. Nuevos modelos de Autonomía Política (España, Bélgica, Canadá, Italia y Reino Unido). Barcelona, Cedecs, 2002 (pages 29–57).

ARECHEDERRA ARANZADI, Luis Ignacio, Art. 48, in Comentarios al Estatuto de Autonomía de la Comunidad Autónoma de Navarra. Madrid, MAP, 1992, pp. 491–511.

BALLARIN HERNANDEZ, Rafael, Prologue to MAS BADIA, Mª Dolores (coordinator) El Régimen Económico Matrimonial de la Comunidad Valencia, Madrid, Tecnos, 2010.

BATALLER RUIZ, Enric, Derecho Civil Autonómico en España: Génesis y perspectivas, en Revista de Derecho civil valenciano, available on the Internet: http://derechocivilvalenciano. com/index.php?option=com_content&task=view&id=66&Itemid=29.

BLASCO GASCO, Francisco y CLEMENTE MEORO, Mario, "La sucesión intestada en favor de la Generalitat Valenciana y la condición jurídica de valenciano", en Libro en recuerdo a la Profesora Silvia Romeu. Valencia, 1989, vol. I, pages 117.

BLASCO GASCÓ, Francisco, "La competencia legislativa de la Generalitat Valenciana en materia de Derecho Civil", Revista Jurídica de la Comunidad Valenciana (RJCV), issue 33 (2011), pages 7–30.

CLAVERO SALVERO, Bartolomé, El Código y el Fuero: de la cuestión regional en la España contemporánea, Madrid, Siglo XXI de España, 1982.

CORCUERA ATIENZA, Javier, Notas sobre el debate de los derechos históricos de los territorios forales, en R.E.P. (nueva época) 46–47, 1985, pages 55–89.

CORCUERA ATIENZA, Javier y GARCÍA HERRERA, Miguel Ángel, La constitucionalización de los derechos históricos. Madrid, CEPC, 2002.

CORCUERA ATIENZA, Javier, Las reformas del modelo territorial en Alemania y en España: dos lógicas diferentes, in TUDELA ARANDA, José y KÖLLING, Mario (eds.), La reforma del Estado Autonómico español y el Estado Federal Alemán. Madrid, CEPC, 2009, page 70.

DOMÍNGUEZ CALATAYUD Vicente, Posibilidades constitucionales de una plena recuperación de nuestro Derecho Foral Civil, Valencia, Corts Valencianes, 2004.

GARCÍA PELAYO, in El País 24 September, 1978, in Obras Completas. Madrid, 1991, III, p. 3171 et seq.

IZQUIERDO TOLSADA, Mariano, Nuevos Estatutos de Autonomía y legiferación civil, in Derecho Privado y Constitución, issue 21, CEPC, 2007, pages 331–381.

LOGENDIO IRURE, Ignacio María, "La disposición Adicional Primera y los derechos históricos", in RVAP, 1985, issue 12, pages 95–122.

LÓPEZ BELTRÁN DE HEREDIA, Carmen, "El Derecho civil valenciano en el momento presente: vías de creación y desarrollo", in Carmen López Beltrán de Heredia (coord.), Curso de Derecho civil valenciano, Valencia, RGD, 2000.

LÓPEZ BASAGUREN, Alberto, El Contenido Constitucional de los Estatutos de Autonomía en Web Fundación Giménez Abad, 2007. Available at http://www.fundacionmgimenezabad.es/images/Documentos/2009/20091218_ot_lopez_basaguren_a_es_o.pdf.

HERRERO DE MIÑON, Miguel, Derechos Históricos y Constitución. Madrid, Taurus, 1998.

HERRERO DE MIÑÓN, Miguel, Los derechos históricos cara al siglo XXI, in Revista de pensamiento e historia, 2009, issue 32, pages 4–12.

MOLINER NAVARRO, Rosa, "Las competencias en materia de Derecho civil foral a la luz del artículo 49.1.2ª del nuevo Estatuto de Autonomía de la Comunidad Valenciana", in Corts. Anuario de Derecho Parlamentario, 2007, issue 18, pages 345–365.

MONTES RODRÍGUEZ, Mª Pilar, Competencia legislativa de la Comunidad Autónoma Valenciana en materia de Derecho civil, in Revista Jurídica de la Comunidad Valenciana. Valencia, Tirant, issue 25/2008, pages 530.

MONTES PENADES, Vicente L. "El Derecho Foral valenciano. Un estudio sobre la competencia legislativa de la Generalitat en materia de Derecho Civil", in BAÑO LEON, José María, Comentario al Estatuto de Autonomía de la Comunidad Valenciana. Madrid, Civitas, 2007, pages 261–322.

PESET REIG, Mariano (amongst other works, "Notas sobre la abolición de los Fueros de Valencia", AHDE, XLII, 1972, pages 657 et seq.).

RAGEL SANCHEZ, Luis Felipe, (Las competencias legislativas en materia de Derecho civil y su deseable reforma constitucional, in Revista de Derecho Privado, 2005, issues 7–8, pages 3–17).

REY MARTINEZ, Fernando "El concepto de "derechos históricos" en la reforma de los Estatutos de Autonomía", in *Cuadernos de Alzate*, issue 34, 2006, pages 69-102.

SAINZ ARNAIZ, Alejandro "Hecho diferencial y reconocimiento nacional en el Estatuto de Autonomía", in VV. AA. Estudios sobre la reforma del Estatuto. Barcelona, Institut d' Estudis Autonòmics, 2004, pages 47–91.

SANCHEZ FERRIZ, Remedio, El Estado de las Autonomías antes y después de 2006, in Revista Valenciana de Estudis Autonomics, 2008, issue 51, pages 14–35.

SEVILLA, Jordi, VIDAL BELTRAN, José Mª y ELIAS MENDEZ, Cristina, Vertebrando España. El Estado Autonómico. Madrid, Biblioteca Nueva, 2009, pages 184 et seq. and pages 209–210.

SIMO SANTONJA, Vicente, Derecho histórico valenciano (Pasado, presente y futuro) Valencia, 1979.

SOLOZÁBAL ECHAVARRIA, Juan José, amongst whose works it is suffice to cite: *Las bases constitucionales del Estado autonómico*. Madrid, Mc Graw Hill, 1998.

TAJADURA TEJADA, Javier, "Legitimidad democrática frente a legitimidad histórica", in *Teoria y Realidad*, 2008, issue 22, pages 137–192.

TAJADURA TEJADA, Javier "Manuel García Pelayo y los Derechos Históricos", in Revista de Derecho Político UNED, issues 75–76, 2009, pages 147–174.

TOMÁS Y VALIENTE, Francisco, "Los derechos históricos de Euskadi", in Sistema. Revista de Ciencias Sociales, 1979, issue 31, pages 3–28.

TOMÁS Y VALIENTE, Francisco "Uniformidad y diversidad en las Comunidades Autónomas, en la legislación estatal y en la doctrina del Tribunal Constitucional", *Uniformidad o diversidad de las Comunidades Autónomas*, Barcelona, Institut d'Estudis Autonómics, 1995, pages 19–40.

TORRES DEL MORAL, Antonio, "¿Qué son los derechos históricos?", in *Ius Fugit*, 15, 2007–2008, pages 55–79.

TUDELA ARANDA, José, El Estado desconcertado y la necesidad federal. Pamplona, Civitas, 2009.

VERNET i LLOBET, Jaume, Drets Historics, MONTAGUT ESTRAGUES, Tomas, Ruptura i transició a la democracia com a fonts de dos tipus de drets historics compatibles per a Catalunya, or FERRER JACAS, Joaquim, Els drets Historics, todos ellos en Revista Catalana de Dret Public, 2011, issue devoted to the STC 31/2010.

Vicente GARRIDO MAYOL, "Las Competencias de la Generalitat Valenciana en materia de Derecho Civil: perspectivas de futuro", *Revista Valenciana d'Estudis Autonòmics (RVEA)*, issue 41/42 (2003), pages 291–395.

VIVANCOS COMES, Mariano, La propuesta de Estatuto político de la Comunidad de Euskadi ("Ibarretxe Plan"), in Revista Española de la Función Consultiva, 2005, issue 4, pages 227–274.

# "Fragmentation" of the Fundamental Right to Life: Between Territorial Decentralization and the Knowledge-Based Economy

Leire Escajedo San Epifanio

## Human Life, Multilevel Governance and the "Ductile" Constitution: Definition of a Scenario Based on the Spanish Case

In October 2003, the Parliament of the Autonomous Community of Andalusia passed a law[1] authorising the use of human embryos that were biologically viable in biomedical research. At that time, the use of such embryos was banned for other researchers in Spain. The national government lodged an appeal of unconstitutionality, claiming, among other things, State competence *in the definition of the legal status of the human embryo*. For its part, the government of Andalusia alleged that the law had been created under the protection of its competences in the matter of *scientific and technical research*. The Socialist Party victory in the 2004 national elections led, however, to the appeal being withdrawn[2] and deprived us of knowing the ruling of the Constitutional Court (hereinafter CC) vis-à-vis a growing phenomenon: the fragmentation of multilevel governance, linked to scientific-technological progress and the knowledge-based economy, is favouring the protection of the right to life. The present research seeks to address this phenomenon.

---

The present research work is framed within the Project: *The Federal System: between integration of diversity and stability,* financed by the Ministry of Science and Innovation (DER 2010-20850) and within the work of the Consolidated Research Group: Legal mechanisms for the integration of difference (Basque Government, IT509-10).

[1] The 7/2003 Law, which regulates research in Andalusia with "inviable" human embryos for *in vitro* fertilisation: BOE (Official State Gazette) no. 279/2003, 21st November, 2003. Among "inviable" embryos, the Law includes those that are biologically viable but have exceeded the time period during which the law allows their cryopreservation.

[2] For more details, see Escajedo San-Epifanio (2005), pp. 345–366.

L. Escajedo San Epifanio (✉)
Department of Constitutional Law and History of the Political Thought, University of the Basque Country/Euskal Herriko Unibertsitatea, Post Box 644, Bilbao 48080, Spain
e-mail: leire.escajedo@ehu.es

A. López-Basaguren and L. Escajedo San Epifanio (eds.), *The Ways of Federalism in Western Countries and the Horizons of Territorial Autonomy in Spain*, Vol. 2, DOI 10.1007/978-3-642-27717-7_30, © Springer-Verlag Berlin Heidelberg 2013

Until the 1990s, human life and its value had been defined by European constitutional doctrine as *a legal principle* or *ontological prius* without which remaining fundamental rights could not possibly exist.[3] Since its specific inclusion in post-second world war constitutions, the right to life has frequently been referred to as an *integral element—together with others—of society's moral and ethical conscience,* a conscience that predates written law. In the words of Böckenförde,[4] preserving that conscience over the generations constitutes an important referent for constitutional law. In the case of the fundamental right to life, it gave rise for many decades to the construction of a categorical concept of human life.[5]

However, that referent for constitutional law, that *terra firma* to which Böckenförde refers, is breaking down. A series of factors, which we will indicate below, is favouring the gradual replacement of constitutional concepts such as those of life and person with what R. Alexy describes as *pluralism*[6] or, in other words, a space for diversity. The multilevel model of governance and the trend towards constitutional ductility are, together with important scientific-technological breakthroughs in the field of biomedicine, the keys to change in which "it is difficult to find a harmonious path between, on the one hand, absolute fundamentalism and, on the other, unprincipled arbitrariness".[7]

In this context, we seek to consider the reasons and consequences of the decentralisation and territorial differentiation in the Spanish system with regard to the fundamental right to human life. Federal doctrine justifies the autonomy of each of the territorial levels as a response to different needs, among them plural coexistence, although the decentralisation that the protection of the right to life has undergone seems to be due more to questions of opportunity/opportunism than necessity.

Prior to interpreting their consequences and drawing our conclusions and final observations, a detailed analysis of the reasons and process requires us to perform three previous tasks. In sum, we first refer to the process by which a jurisprudential construction was consolidated in Spain wherein the content of the right to human life easily transcends that expressly included in the Constitution. The fundamental right to human life could well be employed as a paradigm from which to explain the *irradiation or expansion* of the phenomenon of fundamental rights[8] characteristic of recent decades: of a paradigm in a dual sense, both as regards an analysis of the positive aspects of the said irradiation phenomenon of the fundamental rights,

---

[3] See, for all, the Spanish Constitutional Court Ruling, 53/1985, and references to Comparative Law in González Moran (2006), p. 53 onwards.

[4] Böckenförde (2003), pp. 810–813.

[5] Isensee (2002), pp. 11–12. Bastida Freijedo employs the same expression in Bastida Freijedo (2011), p. 21.

[6] Alexy (1994), p. 322.

[7] Eser (2002), p. 139.

[8] Volkmann (2008) pp. 188–189. See also BVerfGE 7, 198 (Ruling of the German Constitutional Court in the Lüth case, 1958) and the CC Ruling of March, 1981.

as well as with respect to appreciating their negative dimension. In this latter sense, *the weakness* that this expansion has led to in terms of safeguards is significant.[9]

Second, attention should be drawn to how the emergence of new dimensions of human life, especially as a consequence of scientific-technological progress and in the scenario of a knowledge-based economy, has fostered the participation of infra-state (Autonomous Communities) and supra-state (European Union) levels of governance in the legal structuring of the fundamental right to human life. Finally, we will analyse the circumstances that have led to the participation of certain Autonomous Communities in the development of aspects related to the end of life and *death with dignity*.

## The "Expanded" Concept of the Right to Human Life in Spain: The Jurisprudential Construction of the Constitutional Court in the 1990s and Its Weakness

In the contemporary theory of Constitutional Law, normative Constitutions are metaphorically presented as a kind of bridge: a bridge between, on the one hand, *a system of essential values and principles* and, on the other, a *technical display* by means of which the previously mentioned system is *specified* in the legal code.[10] Coherently, when fundamental rights and their constitutional recognition are the object of theoretical reflection, it is also common to note not only that such rights imply recognising subjective positions but also that their recognition includes an objective dimension. This dimension is thus linked to the constitutional vocation of determining what the values are on which a specific political system is built.[11]

Recognising an axiological or valuational dimension to fundamental rights is not limited to our age. In fact, C. Hesse[12] traces its presence to the traditional origins of the theory of rights. To this effect, he establishes that an additional element has always existed in any recognition of the legal positions of the holders to the rights: a collective interest, whether it be express or merely *latent*.[13] The historical instances of this presence, however, are in no way comparable to the scale that they have attained in recent decades.

In addition to having a subjective nature and purpose, the inclusion of rights in revolutionary constitutions also had a *non-subjective dimension*, which was the

---

[9] Escajedo San-Epifanio (2012).

[10] G. Cámara Villar refers to a "setting", in Balaguer et al. (2011), p. 47. See CC Ruling of 31st March 1981.

[11] Ruiz Rico (1997), p. 1759.

[12] Hesse, p. 91.

[13] Hesse, ult loc cit, points to von Ihering and his reflection on the aims of Law as determinants in the initiation of theoretical reflection on said element.

"defining character of the political system as regards limiting power".[14] "A society in which the safeguarding of rights *is not ensured*, or the separation of powers defined" says that the Declaration of the Rights of Man and of the Citizen (1789)[15] *has no Constitution*. Without having lost sight of that objective (that of serving to limit power), an evaluative dimension that transcends that initial idea is associated with the current recognition of fundamental rights.

One example of such a projection can be seen in the jurisprudential construction that the Constitutional Court has developed regarding the normativity of the right to life (Article 15 of the 1978 Spanish Constitution: henceforth SC).[16] The SC is the first in Spanish constitutional history that expressly incorporates *the right to life*. The closest to this formulation that is possible to find in Spanish constitutional history is the *proscription of torment* contained in the Cadiz Constitution of 1812.[17] That proscription is also considered an antecedent to the present right to personal integrity and to the outlawing of torture, also included in the literalness of Article 15, SC. That absence may be considered striking in contrast to the references to life that can, for example, be found in the Declaration of Independence of 4th July, 1776, which refers to life as one of the *inalienable rights with which all men are endowed*. Yet, what is certain is that in continental European tradition, the protection of life tended to be seen as obvious and evident, and specific references to life were not included until virtually after the Second World War.[18]

According to the doctrine applied by the Spanish CC in the 1990s, a series of subjective positions or rights were given protection under Article 15 SC, as were legal rights that have no relation to a specific subject. We shall analyse them synthetically by grouping them into the following blocks: (a) the legal position of the holder of the right to life who *demands its defence*, (b) the protection of human life in the different subjective positions in which the holder to that life *desires its extinction*, (c) the constitutional situation of the *in vivo* embryo (or in a uterus), and (d) the constitutional situation of the extracorporeal embryo (whether *in vitro* or cryopreserved).

---

[14] De Cabo Martin, p. 245.

[15] Article XVI.

[16] In Title I of the 1978 Spanish Constitution, Article 15 opens the section that bears the heading: *De los derechos fundamentales y de las libertades públicas* with the following statement: "Everyone has the right to life and physical and moral integrity and cannot, under any circumstance, be subjected to torture or inhuman or degrading penalties or treatment. The death penalty is hereby abolished except that which may be stipulated in criminal military laws in times of war".

[17] The French Constitution of 1848 similarly included a rejection of the death penalty (Article 5) as, for its part, did the Tenth Declaration of the English Bill of Rights or the 8th Amendment of the 1787 American Constitution, introduced in 1791.

[18] Italian Constitution of 1947 (Articles 13.4 and sections 3 and 4 of Article 27), Article 2.2 of the Fundamental Law of Bonn (together with Articles 102 and 104.1), and years later, the Greek Constitution (Sections 2 and 3 of Article 7) and that of Portugal (25 and 26).

## Protection of Human Life When the Holder of the Fundamental Right Wishes to Defend It

The right to life, as regards a *subjective right*, gives holders the possibility of claiming the protection of the Judiciary or, where appropriate, of the Constitutional Court.[19] The European Court of Human Rights had declared itself along the same lines in the Ruling on the *Soering case*, repeating it years later in its Ruling in the *Jabari v. Turkey case*.[20] Thus, the ECHR declared that "in coherence with the absolute prohibition of torture and inhuman or degrading penalties and treatment, {. . .} the fundamental right to life allows the request of protection against any imminent threat to life itself".

Historically, two matters closely linked to the question of the *title to the right to life* have been clarified regarding the fundamental right to human life. First, there is the question of *who* (which holders) are included under the wide-ranging expression *everyone has the right to life*. González Moran describes in detail the debate that took place when the 1978 Spanish Constitution was being drawn up. This question confronted those who defended the use of the term *everyone* in the drafting of Article 15 (attempting thus to include those conceived and unborn) and those who proposed the expression *every person*. The latter sought to prevent interpretations of the article from impeding future decriminalisation of the termination of a pregnancy.

The Constitution eventually embraced the term *everyone,* although the doctrine continued to discuss whether that implied or not the inclusion of the *nasciturus*. The Constitutional Court settled the debate with its 53/1985 Ruling. It declared that the right to life, in the strict sense, can only have an *already born person* as a holder, regardless of whether or not the *nasciturus* deserves any type of protection, to which we shall refer later.[21] The protection of the right to life in the strict sense includes "the physical–biological existence of the individual",[22] namely from birth to death.

A second question concerns that of *the limits* within which human life is protected by the legal norm: that is to say, the beginning and end of the right to human life in a strict sense. At present, full detachment from the maternal womb continues to be considered a key criterion in the Spanish legal code and there are no significant changes with respect to the criteria for determining death.

Finally, jurisprudential doctrine is interesting regarding *when and in what situation the protection of this right can be requested.* Constitutional Court Ruling 120/1990 specifically drew attention to the fact that the legal position that allows

---

[19] Constitutional Court Ruling 120/1990 of 27th June, Legal Foundation (henceforth LF) 7, and CC Ruling 5/2002, of 14th January, in its LF, 4.

[20] See, especially, ECHR Ruling of 7th July, 1989, in the *Soering* case, § 88 and in ECHR Ruling of 11th July, 2000, *Jabari v. Turkey case*, § 39.

[21] See II.3 and II.4.

[22] For all, see Romeo Casabona (1991), pp. 42–44.

the protection of the right to life is a situation in which there is a threat of *special intensity*.[23] Such an interpretation prevented, among other things, developing content concerning the right to life, which included the right to *an adequate standard of living* or the *dignity or quality of life,* whether in its economic, social, cultural, or environmental condition, among others. In a very similar vein, in the 1990s it distinguished between the risks or damage to health, against which there is no legal position, giving the person the opportunity to request speedy protection, and those cases in which a person is really in a situation to request protection for their physical and moral integrity. The key to distinguishing between one and other supposition was established in the existence or not of a "serious and certain danger" to personal integrity.[24] It is important to recall that 20 years later, as a consequence of the appeal of unconstitutionality against the *Statute of Catalonia,* the Constitutional Court appears to have qualified this interpretation.[25]

## *Protection of the Fundamental Right to Human Life in Those Cases in Which the Holder* Wishes Its Extinction[26]

The way in which the right to life is reflected in legislative terms when the holder of the life wishes to extinguish it raises important question marks. In the expression of the CC, despite the "axiological importance of the problem",[27] it is essential to focus judgement on "the legal-constitutional criteria and with full awareness of the limits of the law". There are, therefore, certain difficulties in order, a priori, to find a legal reasoning regarding this matter. It is problematical to establish whether the legal position of the person who wishes to put an end to his life has to be protected or not and how the conflict between protection of life that may correspond to the State, should the answer be affirmative, has to be tackled.

Above and beyond the desire to put an end to life, which is characteristic of all forms of suicide, the truth is that the *situations or circumstances* that may lead a person to such a decision differ enormously.[28] Therefore, it is understandable that the legal code does not resolve all of them in the same terms. Although they are ways that, in the last resort, can fulfil the same desire (putting an end to life itself),

---

[23] See also CC Ruling 5/2002, of 14th January, in its LF, 4.

[24] CC Ruling 119/2001, of 14th May, in its 6th LF.

[25] See, IV.

[26] One small remark before continuing: In coherence with the heading of this section (the legal position of the holder who wishes to put an end to life), the cases of "charitable homicide" have not here been considered in which *there is no specific request by the person.* At present, these situations are punished by the Criminal Code, even in those cases in which the demonstration of the charitable component may be commuted to a lesser sentence than that of generic homicide.

[27] CC Ruling 120/1990. See also Chueca (2008), p. 1 onwards; from the same author: Chueca (2009), pp. 99–123.

[28] We coincide in this with González Moran (2006), pp. 348–350, cit.

the different situations and circumstances deserve a different consideration in the Spanish legal code. Thus, the case of a person who puts an end to his life by his own means is distinguished from that of the person who requests the aid of a third party or the State or that of a person who requests collaboration and that of a person who requests a third party to carry out a consenting homicide.

It should, nevertheless, be highlighted that in accordance with this jurisprudential interpretation, none of the suppositions allows the Spanish norm to deduce from the right to life a *right not to live, a right to death itself* or a *right to suicide* in the strict sense: namely, in the sense of rights from which can be derived duties or obligations for a third party or public authority. Neither does it seem that the right or freedom to *dispose of the right to life* is an adequate expression for referring to an act that includes *death itself,*[29] although a person is not *de facto* forbidden from putting an end to his own life.

The legal position of those who wish to end their right to life has, therefore, no protection under Article 15 SC but rather under a sovereignty over themselves whose constitutional protection must be sought elsewhere: namely, in the foundations of the political order and social peace established in Article 10.1 SC, particularly the dignity of the person and free development of the personality. That sovereignty has, moreover, connections with other fundamental freedoms, such as freedom of conscience (Article 16, SC). As Rodotá states, contemporary codes recognise for the person *sovereignty over oneself*, which prevents any intervention in one's corporeality and health that the person *does not desire.*[30] That right to refuse corporal interventions[31] also includes those that might be necessary *to maintain life*.

Said sovereignty over oneself does not, however, attain a legal position that allows one to ask for *help from third parties*. Nevertheless, there are certain circumstances in which third party intervention is not considered as *cooperation in suicide*. This is the case, for example, in which *refusing vital treatment* implies disconnecting a person from a life-support system that keeps them alive. This refusal is understood as an expression of the autonomy of the patient, and logically, the Spanish political code has even recognised the possibility that such a refusal is performed beforehand by drawing up a living will. The life-support system is considered the *longa manus* of the doctor[32]: that is, a type of permanent medical intervention, and consequently, disconnecting the life support is explained as an interruption of the initial consent given by said intervention.

---

[29] CC Ruling 120/1990, of 20th June 20, which ruled on the appeal for protection lodged by various prisoners belonging to the terrorist group, Grapo, against a Ruling by the Provincial Court of Madrid, which ordered their force-feeding. See also ECHR, case 2342/02, in the Ruling on *Pretty versus UK*, especially paragraphs 8 and 9.

[30] Rodotá (1999), p. 43.

[31] See also Ruling of the ECHR in the case of *Pretty versus UK*, of 29th April, 2002; see Canosa Usera (2006), p. 101.

[32] See González Moran (2006), p. 578, cit.

As regards implementing the living will in Spain, this has been entrusted to the Autonomous Communities,[33] which have determined the working rules of the so-called Register of Previous Instructions. In all the cases, these living wills obviously have limits. Thus, only instructions that do not involve either charitable homicide or the help or cooperation required to commit suicide, classified as a crime in the present Spanish penal code,[34] may be included. It basically covers, therefore, decisions that refer to a *limitation of therapeutic care*.

Cases in which the person who refuses essential lifesaving treatment or care (such as sustenance or liquids) is in a *special situation* deserve a mention apart. We refer, on the one hand, to adult persons who are serving a prison sentence and who refuse any type of treatment or care and, on the other, to minors who refuse essential lifesaving medical treatment.

Regarding those prisoners who are in special detention, the Spanish Constitutional Court made its decision known in 1990, in two rulings, and in 1991. These dealt with cases in which some prisoners went on hunger strike. It is important to note that they were not cases of refusing medical treatment in the strictest sense but rather the refusal of *necessary lifesaving care*, specifically sustenance. Rulings 120/1990 and 137/1990 of the Spanish Constitutional Court considered that in such cases, force-feeding could be applied. In Ruling 120/1990, the Constitutional Court understood that "coactive medical assistance would constitute a damaging limitation of the fundamental right to physical integrity unless it was constitutionally justified", and that justification was applicable in the case because the penitentiary situation "is the source of a framework of reciprocal rights and duties between the Authorities and the prisoner, among which we should stress the essential duty of the former to safeguard the life, integrity and health of the latter".[35] This criterion was qualified by Ruling 11/1991 to indicate that force-feeding was only legitimate in a situation where a prisoner was semi-conscious.

In the case of minors, the refusal of lifesaving treatment in general—or for religious reasons, specifically—is not protected by any of the suppositions in the present legislation because the minor cannot consent to the refusal of treatment or to the care on which their lives depend, nor is it possible for their parents or legal guardian to confirm their incapacity in order to give consent.

---

[33] Law 3/2001, of 28th May, of the Autonomous Community of Galicia, regulator of informed consent and of the medical records of the patients; Law 6/2002, of 15th April, on Health in Aragon or Law 7/2002, of 12th December, of the Basque Country, of anticipated wills in the field of health; Law 6/2005, of 7th July, of Castilla La-Mancha, regarding the Declaration of Anticipated Wills with respect to health; Law 1/2006, of 3rd March, of the Balearic Islands, of anticipated wills or Law 2/2010, of 8th April, of Andalusia, Rights and Safeguards of the Dignity of the Person in the Process of Death.

[34] De Montalvo Jääskeläinen (2009).

[35] Extracts from the 5th and 7th Legal Foundation of Ruling 120/1990.

## Constitutional Protection of In Utero Human Life (Conceived and Unborn or Nasciturus)

Constitutional protection of the life of an individual who has been conceived but has still not been born (the *nasciturus*) has been a central question in the legal treatment of the termination of pregnancy. Practically, all the cases in which consent of the expectant mother does not intercede are subject to criminal persecution, which is the reason it has been said that the best person to safeguard the protection of the *nasciturus* is not the state but precisely "the expectant woman herself".[36] The situation of the *nasciturus* is different when the expectant mother *does not wish to continue with the pregnancy*. As Constitutional Court Ruling 53/1985 makes clear (7th LF), the value of life of the embryo that has been recognised "does not mean that the said protection should be absolute". This is coherent with what is interpreted with regard to all constitutionally recognised rights: in some circumstances, their protection may and even must be subject to limitations. This approach to the conflict, which the German Constitutional Court situates between *the freedom of the expectant mother to terminate the pregnancy* and the life of the *nasciturus*, has been posited over the last 40 years in many European countries, including Spain.

In the initial reforms, Spain opted for decriminalisation of abortion in the case of the convergence of certain indications. The absence of consensus in a ruling regarding this question when drafting the penal code in 1995 (still in force) meant that Article 417 (of the Penal Code), introduced in the 1973[37] Penal Code in 1985,[38] remained in force until approval of the 2/2010[39] Organic Law on Sexual and Reproductive Health and Voluntary Termination of Pregnancy. That is to say, for 25 years a system was in force according to which abortion *was not criminally penalised* if it was by consent of the mother, was performed by a doctor in an authorised centre, and further, was accompanied by any of the special circumstances described in the law. The first of these circumstances or indications considered was that termination of the pregnancy was necessary to prevent serious danger to the life or physical or psychological health of the pregnant woman (such a situation having to be confirmed by a doctor other than the one performing the abortion). The second circumstance referred to the fact that the pregnancy was the consequence of rape that had been reported, in this case limiting the abortion to the first 12 weeks of gestation. The third indication included, finally, those cases in which it was presumed that the foetus would be born with *serious physical or*

---

[36] ECHR Ruling, 2007/20, 20th of May.

[37] Decree 3096/1973, by which the revised text of the Penal Code is published.

[38] The 9/1985 Organic Law introduced Article 417bis into the Penal Code of 1973, decriminalising abortion in certain situations.

[39] Organic Law 2/2010, of 3rd March, on Sexual and Reproductive Health and Voluntary Termination of Pregnancy (BOE, number 55, of 4th March, 2010).

*psychological defects.* The requirements in this regard were that a report should be prepared by two specialists and that the abortion should be performed within the first 22 weeks of gestation.

The system of indications, nevertheless, caused certain practical problems, some of which were brilliantly described by G. Jakobs in his work: *Geschriebenes Recht und wirkliches Recht beimSchwangerschaftsabbruch* (The Written Law and Real Law in the Termination of Pregnancy). Many of the unwanted pregnancies were terminated under the claim, not very rigorously applied, of risk to the psychological health of the mother. This discrepancy between legislation and reality was described as undesirable in the Council of State Report issued in 2009,[40] during the procedures of the recent 2/2010 Organic Law on Sexual and Reproductive Health. To a certain extent, this Law heralds a *constitutional mutation,* given that it opts for a mixed system (of time limits and indications), clashing somewhat with what the Constitutional Court expressed in Ruling 53/1985.[41] Said ruling hinted that a system of indications was more appropriate for the protection of the *nasciturus* than a system of time periods.

Understanding that the relationship between the expectant mother and the *nasciturus* forms part of her strictest intimacy and in that intimacy decisions relating to it also have to be taken,[42] the new law extends the faculty of terminating the pregnancy by the mother within the first 12–14 weeks. Nonetheless, in contrast, after the first 14 weeks the possibilities of terminating the pregnancy are limited to serious medical causes that, moreover, must be supported by the opinion of a medical committee.[43] The latter means that the new system, after the first months of gestation, is much more rigorous than the previous one.

## The Extracorporeal Embryo (In Vitro or Cryopreserved) as Regards a Protected Legal Right in Article 15 of the Spanish Constitution

Louise Brown was born in the United Kingdom in 1978. Known to posterity as the first "test-tube" baby, she was born in a hospital in Manchester, thanks to an experimental technique developed by Dr. Patrick Steptoe and Dr. Robert Edwards. Less famous was the birth of Zoe, the first baby born from a cryopreserved embryo (The Ice Baby) in Australia or the birth in 2010 in the USA of a healthy baby who had been cryopreserved for 20 years in an embryonic state. These births brought

---

[40] Council of State Report regarding the Bill for the Organic Law on Sexual and Reproductive Health and Voluntary Termination of Pregnancy, 2009.

[41] Ferreres Cornella (2011), p. 19 onwards.

[42] Paragraphs 106 and 107 of the ECHR Ruling 2007/20.

[43] Articles 14 and 15 of the OL 2/2010.

about a revolution and left the law perplexed[44] (Roca Trías). Until a few years ago, the desire to procreate was limited by numerous factors: two progenitors were necessary, a man and a woman, and the age or biology of these was determining aspects, not to mention other circumstances of a legal nature (such as marital status).

The first legal statute concerning extracorporeal embryos was drawn up in Spain through two laws: Law 35/1988 for Assisted Human Reproductive Techniques and Law 42/1988 on Donation and Use of Embryos and Human Foetuses. The legal statute on extracorporeal embryos was completed by the Rulings of the CC.[45] With the exception of clinically inviable embryos, the CC considered that all forms of antenatal human life—including, therefore, *in vitro* embryos—were deserving of constitutional protection, and it situated that protection in Article 15 SC (fundamental right to life), although it did not consider them holders of the right but rather legal rights protected by said Article. It argued in this respect that the precepts relating to fundamental rights and public freedoms, in this case especially Article 15 SC, do not exhaust its content in the recognition of the rights but can contain, above and beyond it, other requirements for the legislature,[46] such as institutional safeguards, guiding principles, or constitutionally protected legal rights, as is the case of the life of the *in vitro* human embryo. It has been said, and indeed validated by the CC, that the protection offered to these forms of antenatal life is *gradual*[47]: that is to say, the possibility that the foetus or embryo, which is not subject to rights, may *attain* such protection is considered the *foundation* of said protection and that, further, how near or how far that possibility may be is used as a criterion for *grading* the protection accorded.[48]

## Situation of the Extracorporeal Embryo in the Twenty-First Century: Consequences of the *Knowledge-Based Economy* and the Assumption of Competences by the Autonomous Communities—The Potential of Embryonic Stem Cells

The spread of fundamental rights implied the implicit understanding of the Constitution as a document *open to transformations and developments*.[49] Constitutional Law was thus explained as something positive and potentially revitalising.

---

[44] Roca Trias (1994), p. 121 onwards.

[45] CC Ruling 212/1998, of 19th December, regarding Law 42/1988 and the CC Ruling STC 116/1999 of 17th June, regarding Law 35/1988.

[46] Escajedo (2005), p. 345 onwards, cit.

[47] Gabaldón López, who was to develop his proposal in Gabaldón López (2001), p. 134, pp. 155–156; Romeo Casabona (2003), p. 30, pp. 40–42; Femenía López (1999), p. 101 onwards.

[48] Against this, Böckenförde considers it artificial to distinguish between person and human being, given that in the recognition of dignity, the German Constitution refers to *human being* (Mensch), in Böckenförde (2003), pp. 810–813, cit.

[49] Volkmann (2008), pp. 188–189.

Nevertheless, in the first decade of the twenty-first century it has been seen that this revitalisation, linked to other factors, has eventually weakened the constitutional safeguards.[50] In the case of the right to life, there have been two factors of greatest importance in that weakening. First is the fact that scientific-technological breakthroughs have questioned the *categorical concept of life*,[51] which no longer seems to be able to specify at what moment we have to protect a human life and, depending on the case, how.

Until relatively recently, developing the right to human life was fundamentally carried out by means of legal mechanisms that involved the use of the *jus puniendi* of the State. The classification of the different types of homicide and abortion was principally found in criminal law and around it was also formed the suppositions of *total or partial decriminalisation* of some of the voluntary terminations of pregnancy. Scientific-technological progress, and particularly the potential associated with embryonic stem cells, has modified that consideration. It has even been said, in this vein, that the concept of *nasciturus* no longer serves to refer to all situations in which the extracorporeal embryo is found,[52] insofar that some embryos must be destroyed at the blastocystic stage in order to obtain stem cells from them with an important therapeutic potential.

The appearance of dimensions to human life that are the subject of development in non-criminal matters has also been noteworthy, such as the regulation of assisted human reproductive techniques and of some of its consequences in administrative and civil laws. This has allowed a type of *decentralisation* of the protection of human life, giving participation to other levels of governance, both international as well as supra-state and infra-state: in the latter case, through both Autonomous Community laws and by means of statutory reforms to which we will refer below. This decentralisation complicates the application of the safeguard that is covered by Article 149-1.1, SC, according to which the State must regulate the *basic conditions* for the exercise of fundamental rights, including the right to life.

In the last decade, legislation applicable to the extracorporeal embryo has been modified so drastically that we wonder how it is possible that no appeal has yet reached CC to request the annulment of Ruling 116/1999 with reference to previous legislative application. Three laws approved by the National Parliament[53] and two passed by the Andalusian Parliament[54] have made Spain one of the most receptive countries to advances in assisted human reproductive techniques and the use of embryos for biomedical research. Thus, to give one example, it is one of the few

---

[50] Böckenförde (1992), p. 159 onwards.

[51] See, note 6.

[52] Cruz Villalón (2006), pp. 25–26.

[53] Law 45/2003, already cited; Law 14/2006, on Assisted Human Reproductive Techniques, of 26th May; and Law 14/2007, on Biomedical Research.

[54] Law 7/2003, of 20th October, cit. supra and Law 1/2007, of 16th March, regulating research into cell reprogramming for exclusively therapeutic purposes. BOE of 13th April, 2007.

countries in which the creation of embryos by means of cloning techniques identical to those which gave rise to the birth of the sheep, Dolly, is allowed[55] or where genetic selection of an embryo in order to become a *Saviour Sibling* is permitted, that is, a baby selected to save the life of a sick sibling.

In accordance with the regulation in force since 2006, the progenitor or progenitors of a cryopreserved embryo must specify the fate they envisage for the latter, choosing between the following four possibilities: (a) it can be used by the woman or (if she is married) by her spouse, (b) it can be donated for reproductive purposes, (c) it can be donated for research purposes, (d) its preservation can be terminated (after the end of the maximum preservation time). The consent establishing the corresponding use is taken before creating the embryo, and the law establishes that every 2 years the woman or the progenitorial partner will be requested to renew her consent, which they can modify.

Law 7/2003 of Andalusia and, in response, Law 45/2003, authorised research in Spain into assisted human reproductive techniques with *surplus* embryos that, for various reasons, had not been used in reproduction. The measure was countered by appeals before the Constitutional Court, which had to make a ruling regarding a question it had avoided in Ruling 116/1999, leaving in doubt whether future research with viable human embryos could be legalised or not. That possibility has been included in Law 14/2006 on Assisted Human Reproductive Techniques, but neither that Law nor Law 14/2007, which also envisages suppositions of the use of viable embryos in research, has however been subject to appeal.

The most problematic case, all the same, is the creation of human embryos by cloning. These are not referred to in the laws as embryos but rather with the terms *activated or reprogrammed ovocyte*, as can be seen in Law 14/2007 on Biomedical Research and Law 1/2007 of Andalusia. In a scenario with a lack of consensus concerning the concept of the embryo, Spain is one of the countries in which most terms are used to refer to the different conditions of the extracorporeal embryo. These are sub-concepts in which regulation, for its part, supports the existence of various sub-statutes of the human embryo. Thus, the term *pre-embryo* is employed to refer to the embryo created by assisted human reproductive techniques, *embryo* to refer to the post-implanted embryo (or already implanted in a uterus), and the term *activated or reprogrammed ovocyte* to refer to the ovule to which has been transplanted the nucleus of a somatic cell.[56] With respect to the latter, Article 2.e) of Law 1/2007 of Andalusia describes these ovules as *enucleated ovocytes* to which

---

[55] Andalusian Law 1/2007 includes the *transfer of the nucleus of a somatic cell to the cytoplasm of a previously nucleated ovocyte* as a nuclear reprogramming technique (Article 2.e). Law 14/2007, for its part, in Article 33, indicates that "the use of any technique for obtaining human stem cells for therapeutic or research purposes which does not involve the creation of an *in vitro* embryo or of an embryo exclusively for this purpose is permitted, in the terms defined by this law, including the activation of ovocytes via nuclear transfer".

[56] Cloning via nuclear transfer.

*the nucleus of a somatic cell* has been transferred. Law 14/2007, for its part, includes the *activation of ovocytes activated by nuclear transfer* among the possible sources for obtaining human stem cells, although it excludes this as a way of creating a pre-embryo in Article 33.[57]

There is no consensus regarding the reasons that led the Andalusian and State legislatures to employ distinct terms to refer to "entities" that the Court of Justice of the European Union (and other legal codes, such as the British) identifies within the category of embryo, although various reasons have been mentioned, including the commitments acquired by Spain with the ratification of the European Convention on Human Rights and Biomedicine (henceforth, ECHRB), of 1996.[58] Article 18.2 of the ECHRB "prohibits the construction of embryos for the purpose of experimentation". Recently, however, the ruling of the CJEU in the case of *Brüstle v. Greenpeace* (October 2011)[59] adopted at the EU level a broad concept of embryo, which specifically includes not only those embryos fertilised *in vitro* but also those human ovules that *have not been fertilised* but from which it would be possible to give rise to the birth of a person. The consequences of this ruling do not modify the legal status of embryos in Spain since the EU has no competences to decide on the use of embryos in research, although it will prevent patents resulting from research that is not only legal in Spain but has been the subject of major public investment, prominent amongst which is the *Andalusian Programme for Cell Therapy and Regenerative Medicine*. In the same situation are innovations that involve obtaining embryonic stem cells by destroying human embryos.

## Autonomous Community Competences in the Regulation of *Living Wills* and Recognition of Statutory Rights Relating to *Death with Dignity*

The Spanish Law, which was announced, regarding *death with dignity* was shelved by the National Parliament of the 9th Legislature (2008–2011) due to the announcement of early elections. Nevertheless, by then some interesting previsions had already been included in certain Organic Laws for reforming the Statutes of

---

[57] Article 33 of Law 14/2007 reads thus: "The use of any technique is permitted to obtain human stem cells for therapeutic or research purposes, but which does not involve the creation of a pre-embryo or of an embryo exclusively for this purpose, in the terms defined by this law, including the activation of ovocytes by means of nuclear transfer".

[58] Its full title is: "Protection of the Human Rights and Dignity of the Person with Regard to the Applications of Biology and Medicine: Convention on Human Rights and Biomedicine", in force in Spain since 1st January, 2000. See Escajedo San-Epifanio (2010), pp. 161–189.

[59] See Escajedo San-Epifanio (2010), pp. 161–189, cit.

Autonomy of the 8th Legislature, which were translated into Autonomous Community Laws in 2011 and 2012. The objective of the State Bill was to implement Basic Law 41/2002 for Patient Autonomy, defining a series of rights of the person in the final stages of life. Had it been approved, it would further have coordinated the three Autonomous Community laws that had already been published regarding this matter: Law 2/2012 of Andalusia on the rights and safeguards of the dignity of persons dying; the Navarre Law 8/2011 on the rights and safeguards of the dignity of persons dying, and the Aragonese Law 10/2011 on the rights and safeguards of the dignity of persons dying and regarding death. The Bill was presented in June, 2011, but months later the legislature came to an end with the calling of early elections.

With respect to the content of the Autonomous Community norms approved, we coincide with Bastida in that neither the Autonomous Laws previously mentioned nor the State Bill considers that the subject matter applies fundamental rights. That explains why at no time has the advisability of considering that it is a question of matters reserved for Organic Law been put forward. Nevertheless, where a state law is to be approved, the autonomous regulations should be adapted to this, given that the state norm would have the nature of basic legislation.[60]

This lack of references to that reserved for Organic Law seems coherent with the doctrine mentioned above, in the sense that we cannot deduce from the fundamental right to life (Article 15, SC) a right to *a dignified life* or a *right to death with dignity*, in the sense of subjective legal rights and positions from which it is possible to demand safeguards from the State or a third party in order to enforce the latter. Quite another matter is the fact that the right to life and free development of the personality implies recognition for the person of an area of *sovereignty over oneself*, as an autonomous person, which prevents the State or third parties from intervening in that sovereignty. Only a few authors, such as M. Palacios, include the right to a dignified life and the right to death with dignity in that sovereignty, doing so in a sense that is more moral than strictly legal.[61]

We shall now consider the reforms of the Statutes of Autonomy in the 8th Legislature (2004–2008), which include a series of rights related to death[62] and which form part of the legal category that Spanish constitutionalist doctrine refers to as *statutory rights*. In the 2006–2007 reforms, these types of rights were presented as integrants of, to a greater or lesser extent, systematic catalogues.[63]

---

[60] Bastida (2011), pp. 29–30, cit.

[61] Palacios (2008).

[62] Article 25 of Organic Law 1/2007, 28th February, of reform of the Statute of Autonomy of the Balearic Islands; Article 20 of Organic Law 2/2007, 19th March, of reform of the Statute of Autonomy of Andalusia; and Article 14 of Organic Law 5/2007, 20th April of reform of the Statute of Autonomy of Aragon.

[63] Rodríguez (2011), pp. 73–74, cit.

Castile and León, the Balearic Islands, Andalusia, Catalonia, and Aragon are the Autonomous Communities that included a prevision relating to the terminal stages of life, among which, nevertheless, different levels can be distinguished. Andalusia and Catalonia *do* literally refer to *a right to death with dignity*, while other statutes adopt formulas with references to palliative care, the treatment of pain, or mechanisms such as previous instructions (living will). The Statutes of Autonomy, especially the more recently reformed, include catalogues to a greater or less extent of statutory rights. However, in this regard, the CC has declared that the territorial diversity that these inclusions may bring about has a limit, namely that which is envisaged in the State Constitution.[64] They therefore bind the legislatures of their respective Communities but do not authorise new autonomous competences and cannot violate the constitutional previsions. In this way, when the statutory rights overlap subject matters in which the Autonomous Community has specific competences, they *can* affect the conditions for exercising said rights but always within the limits established in the 1978 Spanish Constitution.[65]

With respect to the doctrine that the CC maintained when interpreting the circumstances in which it is necessary to claim protection of life itself, it appears interesting to us to draw attention to a change. Specifically, this refers to a section of the Ruling which that it issued in response to the appeal of unconstitutionality of the Statute of Catalonia. The legal position of holders who claim protection of their life was contextualised by the CC and the ECHR in a situation in which a threat of *special intensity*[66] is present and decision-taking in the final stages of life was interpreted in relation to the free development of the personality (Article 10.1, SC) or the freedom of conscience (Article 16, SC), among others.[67]

This, it should be remembered, hampered application of the content of the right to life, which would include the right to an *adequate standard of living*, *dignity* or *quality of life*, whether economically, socially, culturally, or environmentally, among others. In its application to the final stages of life, it prevented the possibility of requesting a certain quality of terminal care. It seems, however, that we are at a time of change. Article 20.1 of the Statute of Autonomy of Catalonia (henceforth, SAC) left the Autonomous Parliament with the heading: *The right to die with dignity*. During its procedural stage in the National Parliament, seeing that certain interpretations linked said heading to euthanasia, it was subsequently changed to the "right to live in dignity during the process of death", proclaiming in its content

---

[64] See CC Ruling 247/2007, 5th LF, and subsequent ones and CC Ruling 2010, 16th LF and following ones. Likewise, Rodríguez, loc cit, pp. 73–73.

[65] See, in this respect, Ortega (2008), p. 113 and Agudo Zamora (2008), p. 301.

[66] See also CC Ruling 5/2002, of 14th January, in its 4th LF. See: II.1.

[67] As has been seen in II.2.

"a right to treatment for pain and palliative care". Even so, the Article was subject to an appeal of unconstitutionality.

In the 19th Legal Foundation of Ruling 31/2010, the Constitutional Court responded to the appellants, making a series of observations. Basically, the appellants considered that said Article, even with the new heading, contained a right to assisted death or euthanasia. Over and above the consideration that it was not the intention of the precept, the Ruling conspicuously went on to perform a series of considerations that bore no relation to the object of the appeal and that considerably modified the interpretation that it had previously given to the right to life when its holder requests protection from the State.[68]

Thus, *inter alia*, it says that Article 20.1, SAC, accords "perfectly naturally with the fundamental right to life and physical and moral integrity". Subsequently, it says further that "the right to treatment for pain and palliative care" is, implicitly, "an obligatory consequence" of the safeguard of that fundamental right, which therefore it neither contradicts nor impinges upon.

For that reason, the Ruling continues, "to live the process of death with dignity" is nothing more than a statement of the right "to life with dignity" and with the same scope that can be deduced for the concept from Article 10.1 and 15, SC. It considers, thus, that "it is not irrelevant nor is it an innocuous precept that the legislature (in this case the statutory one) has decided to give its own substantivity to the treatments which people in the final stage of their lives should receive, embracing them in the chapter on rights in the civil and social sphere of the Statute. It is an explicit mandate for the legislature which predetermines exercise of the subjective rights of freedom and the consequent obligations regarding health personnel which the competent legislators will have to specify". It refers to the health sector as an area in which "people's fundamental rights are present" and understands that it is the obligation of the legislators "to safeguard the last will of the patient".

What we have said herein poses a doubt as to whether or not demands can be made in order to improve medical attention for persons in the final stages of life,[69] not merely as an application of the right to health but based on the fundamental right to life established in Article 15, SC. This is not, it should be noted, a supposition of *imminent threat* to life but rather of a *threat to its quality*. However, it was the CC that broke a tradition that both it and the ECHR have traditionally applied when interpreting a situation in which a person can claim State protection of his right to life. It also remains to be seen whether similar provisions will be interpreted that other Statutes of Autonomy have included regarding the right to live the process of death with dignity and to formulate prior declarations of will with respect to medical interventions and treatment.

---

[68] Carrillo López (p. 162 onwards) on p. 156.

[69] The recent Andalusian Law 2/2010, regarding the rights and safeguards of the dignity of the person when dying, approved in Plenary Session of the Parliament on 17th and 18th March, 2010, would also enter into this refection.

## The Right to Human Life: Between Territorial Decentralisation and the Knowledge-Based Economy—Final Observations Regarding Current Fragmentation

The majority of the world population lives in multicultural societies fragmented into ethnic, cultural, linguistic, and/or religious groups.[70] This results in important internal conflicts and puts both the stability of the States and, in some cases, the entire international community at risk. Since the 1960s, that concern has resulted in comparative doctrine and in a growing interest in the search for formulas that *reconcile unity and diversity* and that allow a response to the challenges posed by globalisation and the local needs of plural societies. From different perspectives, contemporary studies regarding the different models of decentralised territorial organisation have taken part in that search.

To a certain extent, the phenomenon that is the focus of our study could be situated in such a framework of analysis: Autonomous Community diversity in the treatment of certain aspects of the right to life. It is true that the roots of this diversity present peculiarities with respect to other diversities to which accommodation has been sought through decentralised systems. There are also important differences in regard to the consequences that are posed regarding unity: in the case of the right to life, in that which refers to the state establishment of certain conditions of equality for the exercise of fundamental rights.

With their inclusion in the Constitutions, it has been understood that fundamental rights remain—at least in their essential content—aside from the ups and downs of the majority processes.[71] Modern constitutionalism has always aspired to placing limits on those who, in fact, have the monopoly of force[72] and to establishing and preserving the demands that stem from respect for dignity and freedom of the person.[73] What has been safeguarded through the rigidity of the constitutions has not of course prevented a prevision of flexibility, of a correlate of the social complexity.[74] As Judge Marshall said: the nature of the constitutions demands that *only their general lines* be established, leaving both room for action for the free political process[75] and a space for the interpreter to adapt the content of the Constitution at each historical moment. However, it is essential for rigidity and flexibility to find a reasonable balance.

That balance between rigidity and flexibility is not, however, easy to reach. Hesse states that when a Constitution is adapted, without reservations, to the circumstances of the moment, the circumstances (and not the normativity of the

---

[70] For all, with further references, see Fleiner (2009), p. 511 onwards.
[71] Rubio Llorente (2009), p. 19.
[72] Mateucci (1963), p. 1039, 1041.
[73] Lucas Verdú (1976), pp. 45–46.
[74] López Pina (2001) p. XXIII.
[75] Dahl (2001), p. 17.

text) act as its parameter[76] and the constitution is deprived of one of its primary functions, namely as a safeguard. In a scenario in which the ability to put constitutional commitments into writing is being lost,[77] the *fundamental right to life* serves as a paradigm for confirming two phenomena of constitutionalism in recent decades: on the one hand, the tendencies to expand and spread the fundamental rights towards the *social whole*, as we have seen in the construction of the Constitutional Court in the 1990s and, on the other, the evident ductility of that safeguard when forced to confront not only a scenario of multilevel governance but also a new conception of life derived from scientific and technological progress.

Medicine, warns Mainetti, acquires a capacity "to shape human nature" at an incredible pace, and some of its applications, still based on individual and apparently private decisions (such as the formation of the family), may impact on the habitability of the planet. This has placed *tragic choices* on the table (especially in view of the potential impact of the market arbiter),[78] posing the question as to whether such applications should remain the exclusive responsibility of individuals or not or, on the other hand, whether they should be submitted (and in what case and in what way) to some type of intervention on the part of the community and, therefore, of the political powers.

Isensee wondered whether, in view of scientific-technological progress, we can understand that *the categorical concept of "Life" described in the Constitution specifies, in sufficient detail, at what moment and in what conditions it is possible to speak of a human life which has to be protected and how.*[79] To his question, we would have to respond with another one today: Where is that categorical concept of life described in the Constitution? Applying Aristotle's thesis to the case, *life is more, much more than the sum of all the parts*, and from there the fundamental right to human life was only minimally included in the written Constitution.

It is our opinion that the worth and human dignity of the types of antenatal life have no solid statute at present. If, in Rulings 53/1985 and 116/1999, it seemed that the limits of the right to life were artificially inflated, now they appear to have been simply deflated. The warning given by Jiménez Campo is thus fulfilled, in the sense that when the outlines of a right are not easy to identify "there is a risk of extending its limits, of artificially inflating it and including too much".[80] That artificiality, however, in practice ends up weakening the Constitution and making it docile. Without doubt, the competences that, with regard to the provision of health services or of promotion of scientific-technological research, the Autonomous Communities have taken on have contributed to this, without having reached the position of

---

[76] Hesse, p. 9, cit.

[77] Ackermann (2011), pp. 21–22; Miguel Ángel (2005); Garcia Herrera (2011).

[78] Calabresi and Bobbitt (1978). We have only had access to those extracts mentioned by Coleman and Holahan (1979), p. 1379 onwards.

[79] For further detail, see note 6.

[80] This happens, states Jiménez Campo, when the outlines of a law are not clear: in Jiménez Campo (1999), p. 36.

questioning the effect that this has on the competence that, with respect to the right
to life, corresponds to the State: that is to say, as Article 149.1.1, SC, establishes, the
exclusive competence regarding "the regulation of the basic conditions which
safeguard the equality of all Spaniards in the exercise of the rights and the
fulfilment of constitutional duties".[81]

Nevertheless, in our opinion this evolution was, to a certain extent, within the
bounds of possibilities. Let us explain: Doctrine has for a long time been warning
that, despite important international declarations, it does not seem possible to
deduce, for legal practice in the restricted sense, an interpretation of what life
means, reaching a common universal denominator (or at least national) in this
respect.[82] In the scenario of present fragmentation, it might thus seem that it has
merely been possible to express in regulatory terms a situation that was previously
accepted *de facto* but was not adopted *de jus*. Pluralism affects not only current
decisions but also principles of a categorical nature, which were used because the
existence, among other things, of a *moral universe* is questioned, of a shared
conscience that serves as a reference for constitutional law.

Over and above the legal position that leads to the possibility of requesting
protection from imminent aggressions, the remaining legal rights that are understood to be protected in Article 15, SC, were already in a very weak position from
the 1990s onwards, a weakness that has ended up clashing with reality. The most
obvious case is that of the extracorporeal viable embryo. Current Spanish legislation no longer makes it possible to consider it as *nasciturus* in every case because it
accepts that it can be employed for different research purposes that rules out its
subsequent use for human reproduction. Perhaps it is time to reconstruct the right to
life based upon its fundamental function[83] and place special emphasis on those
problems that might truly be solved by means of the mechanisms that Constitutional
Law has at its disposal.[84]

# References

B. ACKERMANN, *La Constitución viviente*, 2011.
M. AGUDO ZAMORA, "Derechos Sociales. Deberes y Políticas Públicas", in S. MUÑOZ/M REBOLLO (eds),
    *Comentarios al Estatuto de Autonomía para Andalucía*, Civitas, Madrid, 2008, page 301.
R. ALEXY, *Teoría de los Derechos fundamentales*, 2nd edition, Frankfurt, 1994.
F. BALAGUER/G. CÁMARA VILLAR/ET ALTERE, *Manual de Derecho Constitucional*, 2011.

---

[81] Article 149.1.1 of the Spanish Constitution. An approach to its content and application can be
found in the Catalan journal of public law.

[82] Christian Byk (2008), pp. 175–176.

[83] Schlink (1984), p. 457 onwards, cited by Ignacio Gutiérrez, in "Teoría y Realidad", p. 200,
number 11.

[84] Cormick (1996), pp. 25–31.

F. J. Bastida Freijedo "El derecho fundamental a la vida y la autonomía del paciente", M. A. Presno (coord.), *Autonomía Personal, Cuidados Paliativos y Derecho a la Vida*, Procuradora General del Principado de Asturias, University of Oviedo, 2011, page 21.

E. W. Böckenförde, *Staat, Verfassung, Demokratie*, 2nd edition, Frankfurt a. M., 1992.

E.-W. Böckenförde, "Menschenwürde als normatives Prinzip. Die Grundrechte in der bioethischen Debatte", *Juristen Zeitung*, 2003, pages 810–813.

G. Calabresi/P. Bobbitt, *Tragic Choices*, Norton & Company, 1978.

R. Canosa Usera, *El derecho a la integridad personal*, Lex Nova, Valladolid, 2006.

M. Carrillo López "Derechos y Garantías Jurisdiccionales", Monográfico de la Rev Catalana de Dret Public, special edition, regarding the Ruling on the Statute (pages 162 onwards) on page 156.

C. BYK, in: *The Nexus of Law and Biology. New Ethical Challenges*, Ashgate, 2008.

R. Chueca, "Los derechos fundamentales a la vida y a la integridad física: el poder de disposición sobre el final de la propia vida", in *Derecho y Salud*, Vol. 16, 2008.

R. Chueca/J. Coleman/W. L. Holahan, "El marco constitucional del final de la propia vida", *REDC*, n°85/2009, pages 99–123.

J. Coleman and W. L. Holahan, in the *Californian Law Review* (67), 6 (1979), page 1379.

M. Cormick, "La Sentencia de Maastricht: soberanía ahora", in *Debats* 55, 1996, pages 25–31.

P. Cruz villalón, "Perspectivas Constitucionales ante los Avances de la Genética", AFDUAM, special edition 2006, *Derecho y Genética*, pages 25–26.

R. A. Dahl, *How Democratic is the American Constitution*, Yale University Press, 2001, page 17.

C. de Cabo Martin, *Teoría Histórica del Estado y del derecho Constitucional, Vol. II, Estado y Derecho en la transición al capitalismo y en su evolución: el desarrollo constitucional*.

F. de Montalvo Jääskeläinen, *Muerte Digna y Constitución: Límites del Testamento Vital*, Pontifical University of Comillas, 2009, *passim*.

L. Escajedo San-Epifanio, "Acerca de la investigación con preembriones y la incidencia autonómica en la determinación del contenido esencial de los derechos fundamentales", in *Estado autonómico: integración, solidaridad, diversidad*, Colex-Goberna, 2005, Volume II, pages 345 to 366.

L. Escajedo San-Epifanio, "Constitucionalismo transnacional y nuevos derechos. Sobre la validez del Corpus Iuris de los Derechos Humanos y la Biomedicina, como paradigma", in I. Filibi/ J. M. Belise (cordinators), *Constitucionalismo transnacional. Derecho, democracia y economía política en la Globalización*, University of Cordoba (Argentina), 2010, pages 161–189.

L. Escajedo San-Epifanio, "El inconsistente estatuto del embrión humano extracorpóreo en la Unión Europea. Proyecciones constitucionales de la Sentencia TJUE *Brüstle v. Greenpeace* (as. C-34/10)", ReDCE, 2012, in press.

A. Eser, "Auf der Suche nach dem mittleren Weg: Zwischen Fundamentalismus und Beliebigkeit?" in Langer, m./laschet, A. (eds), *Unterwegs mit Visionen, Festschrift für R-Süssmuth*, Freiburg, 2002, page 139.

J. Femenía López, *Status jurídico del embrión humano, con especial consideración al concebido "in vitro"*, Madrid, 1999.

V. Ferreres Cornella, "*El Tribunal Constitucional ante la objeción de conciencia*", in AAVV, *Jurisdicción constitucional y democracia*, CEPC, 2011.

Th. Fleiner, "The Multicultural State: the Challenge of the Future", in AA. VV., *Constitutional Democracy in a Multicultural Globalised World*, 2009.

J. Gabaldón López "Libre desarrollo de la personalidad y derecho a la vida.", *Persona y Derecho*, n° 44, 2001, p 134, 155–156.

M. A. Garcia Herrera, voz *Biopolítica, Enciclopedia de Bioderecho y Bioética*, Comares, 2011.

M. A. Garcia Herrera, "Derechos nuevos y nuevos derechos en la Unión Europea", Teoría del Diritto e dello stato, 2005/1, pages 27–55.

L. González Moran, *De la Bioética al Bioderecho. Libertad, Vida y Muerte*, Dykinson, 2006, pages 53.

C. Hesse, "Significado de los Derechos Fundamentales", Benda/Maihoffer, Vogel, Hesse, Heyde, *Manual de Derecho Constitucional*, 2nd Ed. Marcial Pons, page 91.

J. Isensee, *Wann beginnt das Recht auf Leben?* Akademie Journal 2002.

J. Jiménez Campo: in *Derechos fundamentales y Garantías,* Trotta, Madrid, 1999.

A. López Pina, "La Dogmática Alemana, punto de partida de una Teoría del Derecho Público", in Benda/et altere, Manual, 2001, page XXIII.

P. Lucas Verdú, *Curso de Derecho Político*, T.I., Técnos, Madrid, 1976.

N. Mateucci, "Positivismo giuridico e costituzionalismo", in *Rivista trimestrale di diritto e procedura civile*, 1963, page 1039 and page 1041.

L. Ortega, "Eficacia y garantía de los derechos", in F. Balaguer (ed), *Reformas Estatutarias y Declaraciones de Derechos*, IAAP, Seville, 2008, page 113.

M. Palacios, "Soy mi dignidad. Consideraciones y propuestas sobre la muerte digna", *Revista de Jurisprudencia de Buenos Aires*, 2008.

E. Roca Trias, "El Derecho perplejo: los misterios de los embriones". *Rev. Der. G H* 1/1994, pages 121.

S. Rodotá, in VVAA, *Libertad y Salud*, Cuadernos de la Fundación Grifols, no.1/1999, page 43.

A. Rodríguez, "Muerte digna y derechos en los Estatutos de Autonomía", in M. Presno (coord.), 2011, pages. 73–74.

C. Romeo Casabona, *El Derecho y la Bioética ante los límites de la vida humana*, 1991, pages 42–44.

C. M. Romeo Casabona, "El derecho a la vida: aspectos constitucionales de las nuevas biotecnologías", 2003, page 30, 40–42.

F. Rubio Llorente, "Rigidez y Apertura en la Constitución", in AAVV, *La Reforma Constitucional*, 2009, page 19.

J. J. Ruiz Rico, "Problemas de objetividad y neutralidad en el estudio contemporáneo de la política", *Estudios de Derecho Público en Homenaje a J. J. Ruiz Rico*, Tecnos, Madrid, 1997, page 1759.

B. Schlink, "Rekonstruktion der klassischen Grundrechtsfunktion", *Europäische Grundrechte Zeitschrift*, 1984, page 457.

U. Volkmann, "El Derecho Constitucional, entre pretensión normativa y realidad política", *Teoría y Realidad Constitucional*, 21/2008, pages 188–189.

# Federalization and Minority Accommodation

Nathalie Behnke

**Abstract** It is often assumed that federalization or decentralization reforms are the appropriate remedy for accommodating minority conflicts in multinational states. The underlying expectation is that by granting political competences and/or rights of cultural autonomy to regionally concentrated minorities, threats of secession, separation, or even civil war can be curbed, thereby securing plurality in unity. Based on this assumption, the establishment of federal institutions was (and still is) a common policy recommendation for transitional states. Even in established democracies, however, recent processes of competence devolution did not unequivocally confirm this assumption, let alone federal experiences in postcommunist states in Eastern Europe. Rather, it is still quite unclear whether those reforms did indeed contribute to conflict accommodation among regional groups or between regions and the central state. In Spain, as well as in the UK, recent developments seem to indicate that the fire of minority requests for more autonomy is 'fueled' further (Brancati, Int Org 60:651–685, 2006) in spite of recent reforms. In investigating selected processes of 'federalization' or 'decentralization' in Western democracies, which were initiated as reactions to minority requests for more autonomy, it is thus the purpose of the research project presented here to uncover relevant mechanisms that can help explain the success or failure of those measures. By taking an analytical perspective of reconstructing situational definitions, strategic decisions, and actions of regional as well as central-state actors in a long-term process marked by 'waves' of events (action and reaction), the dynamics at work can best be understood and explained. In this temporal stream of events, the individual perceptions of relevant actors are of course shaped by contextual factors. Therefore, the paper aims primarily at presenting the analytical framework combining the analysis of events, perceptions, and context. As the research project is still at the very beginning, I am not yet able to present empirical evidence.

N. Behnke (✉)
Lehrstuhl für Verwaltungswissenschaft, Fachbereich Politik- und Verwaltungswissenschaft,
Konstanz University, 78457 Konstanz, Germany
e-mail: nathalie.behnke@uni-konstanz.de

A. López-Basaguren and L. Escajedo San Epifanio (eds.), *The Ways of Federalism in Western Countries and the Horizons of Territorial Autonomy in Spain*, Vol. 2, DOI 10.1007/978-3-642-27717-7_31, © Springer-Verlag Berlin Heidelberg 2013

# Introduction

This paper aims at presenting a new research project, which is, however, still at the very beginning. Therefore, empirical results cannot be presented. Rather, in the paper the basic analytical framework is outlined that is to be applied to the cases, thereby hoping to open a discussion on basic concepts, relevant variables, and suggested causal relationships.

Recently, we can observe an increasing number of regionally concentrated minority groups that define their group identity based on ethnic, national, religious, ideological, or linguistic unity. Those groups live, however, on the territory of a larger nation state. Consequently, requests for autonomy or threats of separation generally accompany those group feelings and find their expression in acts of conflict, ranging from a lower intensity—such as declarations or demonstrations— to outright violence in the form of terrorist attacks, if not civil wars. How can such groups be successfully integrated without suppressing their group identity and without jeopardizing the integrity of the nation state? This development poses a major challenge for the Western-type nation-state (Benz 2008; Obinger et al. 2005), which seemed to have triumphed ultimately after the breakdown of communism 20 years ago.

As a possible remedy to appease intrastate conflicts of the kind described, it has often been proposed to introduce or enlarge federal institutions and to decentralize competencies from center to periphery, for it is hypothesized that by granting minority groups more rights of autonomy, they can be successfully integrated (Agranoff 1999; Bakke and Wibbels 2006; Bermeo 2002; Chapman and Roeder 2007; Elkins and Sides 2007). Most recently, similar proposals have been made with regard to conflicts in Nigeria and Iraq (Elkins and Sides 2007; Schrijver 2006) for, traditionally, it is regarded as one particular strength of federal arrangements to safeguard unity in diversity. On the other hand, this hypothesis is violently contradicted theoretically, as well as empirically. It is argued that more subnational autonomy provides more resources for the leaders of protesting groups who will consequently reinforce their protest (e.g. Hale 2008). Also, the knowledge that their protest has successfully induced the central government to devolve competencies may fuel their hopes to gain even more if they continue. Both hypotheses are plausible and have been proven empirically but contradict each other fundamentally (for a balanced discussion of the two hypotheses, see, e.g., Elkins and Sides 2007). In the light of those contradictions, which recommendations can be given to governments trying to deal with multinational conflicts?

This is the basic question guiding the research presented here. Obviously the straightforward recommendation that the introduction of power-sharing institutions and the devolution of competences appease group conflicts is not always true. In order to arrive at a better understanding of the dynamics of the policies of accommodating group conflicts, it is necessary

1. To enlarge the temporal perspective and take into account a longer period of time. Short-term reform processes and reactions to them are embedded in a long

historical stream of struggles for competences between center and periphery. In this long-term process, sequences or phases of group request, reforms initiated by the central state, and reactions by the protesting groups can be interpreted as waves of action and reaction following each other in shorter or longer distance.

2. To reconstruct the sequence of events, as well as the actor orientations and strategic decisions in great detail in single cases. A narrative of the things that happened, when they happened, and why they happened from the perspective of the actors involved is the most promising way for theory construction, for only based on this evidence is it possible to derive hypotheses about the causal mechanisms at work that represent at least distantly the real complexity of causal and temporal interrelationships.

It is thus the aim of the research project to come to an understanding of the dynamics and mechanisms at work guiding the interplay between regional and central actors in multinational states. The conditions under which requests are formulated, reform policies are selected and implemented, and the effects that these policies have on state-periphery relations are to be specified in greater detail.

Empirically, we proceed by conducting comparative case studies. Although variants of federal institutions are currently being discussed in real-life politics, especially in conflict-prone societies in Africa, in the Middle East, and in Eastern Europe, we start by limiting our research interest to established democracies in Western Europe. It is of course problematic to transfer results gained in one type of political system to another—the so-called travelling problem (Sartori 1970) is well known to all comparativists. But acknowledging that the processes under investigation are highly complex, by comparing cases within Western Europe, we can control at least some of the basic systemic variables. Cases are selected in Spain and in the UK. Spain is most interesting for investigating those dynamics of minority requests, decentralization reforms, an asymmetric distribution of competences, and renewed 'rounds' of conflict. While in the short run conflicts seem to be appeased by reforms, in the long run the autonomous communities formulate new and farther reaching requests, thus pushing the conflict between center and periphery further and jeopardizing the stability of the Spanish state (Agranoff 1996; Colino 2009; Grau i Creus 2000). In the UK, where contrasting cases are selected, conflicts are seen to be far less violent than in Spain, and the overall tendency of recent developments is less disintegrative (Bradbury 2006; Jeffery and Wincott 2006; Trench 2005). Thus, even if structural conditions are similar for regions in Spain and in the UK, there must be a reason for those differences, which deserves further investigation.

In the following, I will first outline our analytical framework ('Analytical Framework' section). In particular, I specify the temporal horizon of the analysis ('Sequences of Events' section), as well as the theoretical background for distinguishing reform approaches, namely the distinction between integration and accommodation ('Reform Options' section), which is basically rooted in the old dispute between liberalism and communitarism in political theory (Kymlicka 2005). The mechanisms at work that are to be reconstructed in our research are rather complex and cannot be adequately represented by bivariate causal relations. Thus, in order to understand the logic of those complex relationships, the sequences of events under investigation need to be embedded in broader historical, institutional, structural, and cultural contexts. Therefore, in 'Relevant Influences on the Reform Process' section, those sets of variables are explained that are deemed to be important in influencing the development of the sequences of events. 'Analytical Framework' and 'Relevant Influences on the Reform Process' sections outline together the theoretical conception and assumptions of our research, which however are still waiting for their empirical test and possible reformulation. The 'Case Selection' section explains briefly the rationale of case selection. Instead of providing a (necessarily premature) conclusion, the 'Research Agenda' section gives then a short overview of the future research agenda.

# Analytical Framework

## *Analytical Perspectives*

In approaching the cases under investigation, I take a certain analytical perspective in two respects:

1. The temporal perspective: The processes to be analyzed have a very long time horizon. Singular events are embedded in a long-lasting power struggle between center and periphery. It is thus necessary to take into account historical roots of minority groups, as well as long-term effects of single reform events. When talking about the 'process', this long-term perspective is intended. From this process, shorter periods of time can be distinguished. The term 'sequence of events' is used for describing the phases immediately before, during, and after a decentralization reform, which form in their whole a kind of 'wave' in the long-term process. The single events can be manifestations of protest, requests by minority groups, reactions of the central government, formal or informal rounds of negotiation and decision, and finally reform acts, agreements, or treaties. The sequence in which those events occur is likely to be of great importance for the results of those 'waves' (Falleti 2005).
2. The individualistic perspective: It is not intended to impose one 'objective' external perspective on strategic options of action or in evaluating the possible 'success' of reform measures. Rather, it serves our aim to reconstruct processes and dynamics that preferences, strategies, options for action, and situational definitions are seen through the lenses of relevant actors. Relevant actors are political decision-makers (elites) at the levels of the central state, as well as the region. Focusing on elite perceptions does not necessarily mean to neglect the influence of popular opinions. Rather, it is assumed that—although a broad mobilization of the population on autonomy issues is possible and possibly important for their success—the relevant actors are elite actors. This is plausible

because the subject matter is complex and relatively remote from everyday living experiences. Thus, elites are more likely to take a reasoned opinion and then to act as political entrepreneurs and opinion leaders. In this regard, the elite perceptions are more important for understanding the dynamics of the process.

## Sequences of Events

As was said, within the long-term process of conflict, reform, and (possible) appeasement, the focus of the case studies is on sequences of events around one or several specific reform measures. These reforms are usually the result of negotiations between a regional group and the central government. They may be more or less far-reaching, decentralizing many or few competences, or granting extended or limited rights of autonomy. The distinction between competences and rights of autonomy is meant to highlight the difference between political and fiscal competences on the one hand—rights of self-rule and rights of shared rule (Marks et al. 2008), as well as tax levying and spending powers—and rights of cultural autonomy on the other—e.g., official recognition of a native language, independent organization of schools, holidays, or religious services (e.g. Roach 2005). Furthermore, those reforms can aim at integration or rather at accommodation of the protesting groups (see the 'Reform Options' section).

From this analytical starting point, it is also taken into consideration how those measures are implemented and which effects they have—whether and how they influence subsequently the self-perception of the regional group, their requests, or potentially further protests. From the perspective of the regional actors, the success of the reform measure will be evaluated according to the degree to which their requests have been satisfied. From the perspective of the central actors, the success of the reform measures will be evaluated according to the degree of national stability and societal peace that they helped to (re-)establish. Indicators for the level of acceptance of reform measures can be, e.g., the results of subsequent regional elections (whether radical/separatist parties gained more votes than before), as well as acts of protest (political manifestoes, founding of new parties, demonstrations, or violent protest to a varying degree).

On the other hand, the focus is also directed 'backwards', trying to understand which actions or events lead to the reform measure. Generally, it can be assumed that such reforms did not come out of the blue sky but that they have a history of requests, protests, and negotiations. This history is most enlightening in trying to understand which things happened, how they happened, and which results they produced. It can be useful, e.g., to point out which requests were formulated by the minority groups and on which arguments they were founded. In this regard, the look backward includes an account of regional history, as well as a reconstruction of the mechanisms of minority mobilization; an analysis of the forms, frequency, intensity, and sequence of protest; a narrative of negotiations—between governments, party leaders, or individual politicians at the two levels of government—were they formalized or rather personalized? All those sets of variables are necessary to get a more complete picture and a better understanding of the mechanisms at work in this struggle between center and periphery.

## *Reform Options*

The choice for implementing any reform at all, as well as for selecting a particular type of measure depends on the 'framing' of the actors involved at both levels of government. A reaction to minority requests can range from suppression of the conflict in order to reinforce the status quo over more or less far-reaching changes in the territorial order to granting of rights and competences to the regional minority to outright secession of the protesting region. While the two extreme cases (suppression of protest and secession) are no dominant options in Western European States, the 'middle ground' of the dimension still encompasses various degrees of acceptance of group differences. Two major 'paradigms' are 'integration' and 'accommodation' (McGarry et al. 2008). In an integrationist approach, group differences are accepted but relegated to the private domain. Integration aims, thus, not at suppressing group differences but on a liberal ideology of guaranteeing individual equality of rights instead of granting collective rights to groups. In the framework of this ideology, it is the state's duty to protect individual rights, but not to secure the survival of groups.

In contrast to this, an accommodationist approach allows the manifestation and realization of group differences also in the public/political domain. 'Accommodation, minimally, requires the recognition of more than one ethnic, linguistic, national, or religious community in the state. It aims to secure the coexistence of different communities within the same state, though supporters of accommodation may support secession or partition if accommodation is impossible' (McGarry et al. 2008: 52).

In relation to the territorial dimension of group requests for reform, it can generally be assumed that a regional group aims at getting possibly far-reaching rights of autonomy, while actors of the central state tend to concentrate power at the central level. Based on this assumption, the distinction between an integrationist and an accommodationist attitude allows for the formulation of several hypotheses:

1. Regional actors will request accommodationist reforms, while central actors will rather offer integrationist measures.
2. Regional actors will request integrationist reforms only if they expect that accommodationist requests will have no chance of success.
3. Central actors will offer accommodationist measures only if they expect that integrationist offers will not be accepted.

Consequently, the requests that regional actors formulate, as well as the offers that central actors make, depend heavily on their relative assessments of the chances of success. Expected chances for success, again, depend on their relative bargaining power. The bargaining power of regional actors can be low, e.g. when they cannot make credible threats of secession, when they lack internal or external support, or when they are economically dependent on transfer payments by the central state. The bargaining power of central actors, on the other hand, can be low when the central government needs regional support in coalition building, when the central state is economically dependent from the region, or when they face an increased pressure for action due to credible secession threats or upcoming elections.

## Relevant Influences on the Reform Process

The perceptions of the actors involved, their estimates of their bargaining power, as well as the general climate between the conflicting groups are obviously influenced by several external factors. Those contextual factors need to be taken in particular consideration in understanding the dynamics of the process. Although empirically the distinction is sometimes hard to take, analytically it is useful to distinguish between institutional and cultural contextual factors.

Institutional factors serve to describe the situational environment in which the conflict takes place. The most important among them are:

- The initial level of rights and competences available to the group as compared to the aspirational level. It can be described by (a) the list of competences and rights of which they dispose and (b) the degree of asymmetry in the distribution of rights and competences between the regions. Furthermore, it makes a difference (c) whether those rights and competences extend to self-rule or include shared rule, i.e., whether the group has, e.g., veto power in subsequent rounds of institutional reforms (Petersohn 2011); asymmetry might also be seen by some actors as a value in and of itself that needs to be maintained, in a way that not the absolute extent of rights of autonomy and political competencies is relevant but the distance to other regions (Hombrado 2011), an attitude that is likely to generate a dynamic of its own;
- The degree to which power-sharing institutions (Lijphart 1969, 2004; Norris 2002) form an integral part of the institutional structure. Bicameral parliaments, proportional electoral systems, and a federal organization of the state are generally assumed to curb intragroup conflicts;
- The existence of a vertically integrated party system providing for cross-cutting cleavages (Goodin 1976) as compared to a regionalized party system that might reinforce separationist cleavages (Swenden 2009).

Cultural factors are not always easily distinguished from institutional factors. Among those are cognitive and behavioral patterns shaping the manner in which conflicting groups interact:

1. If a state has, for example, a long tradition of consensus democracy (Lehmbruch 1967) there is obviously an overlap to the power-sharing institutions mentioned above, and conflicts can be more easily accommodated by securing the

participation of all relevant groups in decision-making. Such consociational features can be more procedural than institutional. A perfect example is Switzerland, where the consociational culture is deeply engrained in politics and society.

2. Another important aspect of 'culture' is the degree of internal and external support that minority groups receive for their requests. First of all, the popular support within their own group is relevant for underpinning requests for more autonomy. In this regard, the distinction is useful whether the movement is only elite driven or whether there is a broad popular sense of belonging and of suppressed needs for autonomy. Second of all, external support is just as important. In this regard, the EU policy played a major role in the past 20 years. With its explicit regional policy, the normative basis for regional requests for more autonomy, as well as intraregional cooperation, was strongly enforced (Balme 2004; Börzel 2002).

## Case Selection

In trying to understand complex multivariate mechanisms, the appropriate number and selection of cases are always a tricky problem. Large-N-comparisons cannot be accomplished with the necessary depth, single case, or small-N-studies make it hard to generalize the results. Therefore, I opted for a middle road, choosing a design of a two-by-two comparison, that is, two regions in two states, thereby controlling for a maximum of third variables with a relatively small sample. In comparing Spain and the UK, two of the most interesting cases in Western Europe were selected: Both are traditionally described as unitary states but have a multinational character and have, in the past few years, initiated far-reaching reforms that resulted in altering fundamentally their institutional structure. Their regional units now dispose of a large number of competencies, which are, however, distributed asymmetrically among them. Therefore, Spain and the UK were also denominated as 'union states' (McGarry et al. 2008) or as 'hybrid states' (Loughlin 2009). This asymmetry is likely to spin the disintegrative dynamic further.

In the second step, two regions in each of the states were selected, making a sample of four regions altogether. One region in each state is commonly known to be a leading actor in the process of requesting more autonomous competences from the state—Catalonia in Spain and Scotland in the UK. Those are contrasted with another region in each state where the strive for autonomy is less expressed, which has a less pronounced autonomous tradition but which profits now from the general political climate of decentralization, enlarging its competences, so to say, by clutching the coattails of the leading regions. There are a number of regions for which this description is suitable. Among those, Wales in the UK and Andalusia in Spain were selected. Both have a relatively weak economy, and both can at least point to several origins of difference from the central state in terms of language and culture.

This way, different couples of cases can be formed that have different traits in common: In terms of historical experience, for example, the Spanish regions have lived a sustained period of massive suppression under the Franco regime, followed by a very liberal democratic constitution, which did not even define the number, borders, or names of the communities (Schrijver 2006). In the UK, the situation was fundamentally different because Wales and Scotland joined the Union voluntarily and Scotland always retained special rights. However, the conservative government from 1979 on, with its restrictive antiunionist politics, hitting the regional industries painfully and was perceived as a kind of siege. In terms of economic strength and concomitant bargaining power, as well as a history of autonomous rights, Scotland and Catalonia have lots in common in contrast to Wales and Andalusia.

One might ask why the Basque Country in Spain and Northern Ireland in the UK were not included in the sample: Both cases are highly insightful for investigating the dynamics of struggles for autonomy. Both regions, however, are populated by cross-border minorities, whose situation is so different from groups that are mainly concentrated within one country, that it seemed wise to reduce complexity and leave those cases out. It is, however, intended to do follow-up research enlarging the sample and including those cases (as well as possibly several others).

## Research Agenda

As was pointed out at the beginning of this paper, the research project is only about to get started, thus so far, there is no empirical evidence available. The agenda for the next 2 years' research will be to investigate those processes in the four selected regions by conducting in-depth comparative case studies. The case studies aim at reconstructing the different phases of the processes as described above and enriching the evidence by taking into account the possibly relevant context factors. The logic of the two-by-two-cases design makes it possible to distinguish idiographic from systematic evidence and to arrive at preliminary hypotheses about the dynamics of minority requests for competences and autonomy, on the one side, and federal politics of accommodation or integration, on the other.

## References

Agranoff, R. (1996). Federal Evolution in Spain. International Political Science Review 17: 385–401.

Agranoff, R. (1999). Accomodating Diversity: Asymmetry in Federal States. Nomos, Baden-Baden.

Bakke, K. M. and Wibbels, E. (2006). Diversity, Disparity, and Civil Conflict in Federal States. World Politics 59: 1–50.

Balme, R. (2004). Regional Policy and European Governance. In: Keating, M. and Loughlin, J. (ed.) The Political Economy of Regionalism. Routledge, London, pp. 63–76.

Benz, A. (2008). Der moderne Staat. Oldenbourg, München.

Bermeo, N. (2002). The Import of Institutions. Journal of Democracy 13: 96–110.

Börzel, T. A. (2002). States and regions in the European Union: institutional adaptation in Germany and Spain. Cambridge Univ Press,

Bradbury, J. (2006). Territory and Power Revisited: Theorising Territorial Politics in the United Kingdom after Devolution. Political Studies 559–582.

Brancati, D. (2006). Decentralization: Fueling the Fire or Dampening the Flames of Ethnic Conflict an Secessionism? International Organization 60: 651–685.

Chapman, T. and Roeder, P. G. (2007). Partition as a Solution to Wars of Nationalism: The Importance of Institutions. American Political Science Review 101: 677–691.

Colino, C. (2009). Constitutional Change without Constitutional Reform: Spanish Federalism and the Revision of Catalonia's Statute of Autonomy. Publius: The Journal of Federalism 39: 262–288.

Elkins, Z. and Sides, J. (2007). Can Institutions Build Unity in Multiethnic States? American Political Science Review 101: 693–708.

Falleti, T. G. (2005). A Sequential Theory of Decentralization: Latin American Cases in Comparative Perspective. American Political Science Review 99: 327–346.

Goodin, R. E. (1976). Cross-Cutting Cleavages and Social Conflict. British Journal of Political Science 5: 516–519.

Grau I Creus, M. (2000). Spain: Incomplete Federalism. In: Wachendorfer-Schmidt, U. (ed.) Federalism and Political Performance. Routledge, New York, NY, pp. 59–77.

Hale, H. E. (2008). The Double-Edged Sword of Ethnofederalism. Ukraine and the USSR in Comparative Perspective. Comparative Politics 40: 293–312.

Hombrado, A. (2011). Learning to catch the wave? Autonomy demands in contexts of asymmetrical power-sharing. Regional and Federal Studies 21: 579–501.

Jeffery, C. and Wincott, D. (2006). Devolution in the United Kingdom: Satehood and Citizenship in Transition. Publius: The Journal of Federalism 36: 3–18.

Kymlicka, W. (2005). Federalism, Nationalism, and Multiculturalism. In: Karmis, D. and Norman, W. (ed.) Theories of Federalism—A Reader. Palgrave MacMillan, New York, NY/ Houndmills, pp. 269–292.

Lehmbruch, G. (1967). Proporzdemokratie: Politisches System und politische Kultur in der Schweiz und in Österreich. Mohr, Tübingen.

Lijphart, A. (1969). Consociational Democracy. World Politics 21: 707–725.

Lijphart, A. (2004). Constitutional Design for Divided Societies. Journal of Democracy 15: 96–109.

Loughlin, J. (2009). Reconfiguring territorial governance in Western Europe. Perspectives on European Politics and Society 10: 49–66.

Marks, G., Hooghe, L. and Schakel, A. H. (2008). Measuring Regional Authority. Regional and Federal Studies 18: 111–121.

Mcgarry, J., O'leary, B. and Simeon, R. (2008). Integration or accommodation? The enduring debate in conflict regulation. In: Choudry, S. (ed.) Constitutional Design for Divided Societies. Oxford University Press, Oxford, pp. 41–88.

Norris, P. (2002). Ballots not Bullets: Testing Consociational Theories of Ethnic Conflict, Electoral Systems, and Democratization. In: Reynolds, A. (ed.) The Architecture of Democracy: Constitutional Design, Conflict Management, and Democracy. Oxford University Press, Oxford, pp. 206–247.

Obinger, H., Castles, F. G. and Leibfried, S. (2005). Introduction. Federalism and the Welfare State. In: Obinger, H., Leibfried, S. and Castles, F. G. (ed.) Federalism and the State. Cambridge Universitiy Press, Cambridge, pp. 1–48.

Petersohn, B. (2011). Konfliktakkommodierung bis zur Selbstaufgabe? Stabilität und Dynamik der Verfassungsentwicklung in Belgien. Politische Vierteljahresschrift 51: 195–219.

Roach, S. C. (2005). Cultural Autonomy, Minority Rights, and Globalization. Ashgate, Aldershot.

Sartori, G. (1970). Concept Misformation in Comparative Politics. American Political Science Review 64: 1033–1053.

Schrijver, F. J. (2006). Regionalism after Regionalisation Spain, France and the United Kingdom. Amsterdam University Press, Amsterdam.

Swenden, W. (2009). Territorial Party Politics in Western Europe. Palgrave Macmillan, Basingstoke.

Trench, A. (2005). The Dynamics of Devolution: The State of the Nations. Imprint Academic, Exeter.

# Spanish Languages and the Constitutional Order to Be Upheld (or How to Report on a *Continuous Present* Half-Way Through the Day)

A. López Castillo

## From the Spanish Constitution (SC) to the Statutes of Autonomy (SAs): Concerning the Flexible Regulatory Framework of the Spanish Linguistic Model

One of the characteristic features of the constitutional regeneration of Spain in the late 1970s was the constitutional recognition of the country's linguistic diversity. In strict compliance with the proclamation made in the preamble ("The Spanish Nation... proclaims its will to: [. . .] Protect all Spaniards and peoples of Spain in the exercise of human rights, of their cultures and traditions, and of their languages and institutions"), Article 3 SC sets out the guidelines for a linguistic model that, combined with the clause governing the gradual exercise of the right to autonomy of the nationalities and regions that compose the common and indivisible country of all Spaniards (Article 2 SC) and in the light of the parallels with the gradual planning, by means of a statutory enabling clause, of the political symbols of that complex unitary community (Article 4 SC), may be considered an open model but by no means an imprecise or incongruous one. Notwithstanding, therefore, the details of other constitutional provisions governing linguistic matters,[1] the cornerstone of possible constitutional order in this matter lies in the interpretation of the sense and scope of Article 3 SC.

---

A modified and extended version of this contribution will be brought out in an e-publication in Spanish in an upcoming monographic issue of the Revista general de derecho constitucional (RGDC) by *Iustel* dealing with STC 31/2010.

[1] A reference to the clauses of the constitution governing linguistic matters can be found in Castillo (2008), pp. 309–346.

A. López Castillo (✉)
Facultad de Derecho, Universidad Autónoma de Madrid, Ciudad Universitaria de Cantoblanco, 28049 Madrid, Spain
e-mail: antonio.lopez@uam.es

A. López-Basaguren and L. Escajedo San Epifanio (eds.), *The Ways of Federalism in Western Countries and the Horizons of Territorial Autonomy in Spain*, Vol. 2, DOI 10.1007/978-3-642-27717-7_32, © Springer-Verlag Berlin Heidelberg 2013

In correspondence with the agreed constitutional formula of the conjunction of the remaining political unity of the Spanish Nation and the gradual opening up through the exercise of the recognised right to autonomy of nationalities and regions to establish themselves as Autonomous Communities (ACs),[2] Article 3 SC, in general terms, declares the special respect and recognition, as part of its rich cultural heritage, afforded the different linguistic modalities of Spain (Article 3.3 SC). It also provides for the gradual establishment of territorial regimes of linguistic *co-official status* with Castilian, the official Spanish language of the state (Article 3.1 SC), of those other Spanish languages that, by express statutory declaration, might also constitute official languages in the respective ACs (Article 3.2 SC).[3]

This ultimate lack of definition of the model, in terms of any precise identification of its territorial scope, although it can be specified in a different way, based on the variables deriving from the specific legislative regulation of the corresponding autonomic clauses, could not reach the regulation of the status of the common Spanish language,[4] the official language of the state, or question its operability in the national territory as a whole without calling into question the immediate effectiveness of the constitutional clause declaring the official status of the language that "all Spaniards have the duty to know [...] and the right to use [...]".

As is well known, the co-official linguistic status arising from effective statutory implementation of the constitutional enabling clause "presupposes not only the coexistence (which, as such, requires no legislative intervention), but the 'cohabitation' [*convivencia*] of the two co-official languages to conserve the bilingualism

---

[2] A broad and graduateable process of opening up, but within an inclusive political framework, marked by structural demands of solidarity and unity, a consequence of their constitutional supposition, ex Article 2 SC (*see*, in synthesis, Solozábal Echavarría 2009, pp. 53–63), which are clearly set out in Articles 138 ("2. The differences between the statutes of the different Autonomous Communities may in no case imply economic or social privileges") and 145 ("1. Under no circumstances shall the federation of Autonomous Communities be allowed"). This constitutional channelling of the process of autonomy allows, if it does not impose, a restrained characterisation of the sense and scope of the *principium dispositivium* (*see*, in synthesis, López Guerra 2009, op cit., pp. 2067, 2069–2070) in light of the unequivocal import of Article 1.2 SC (*see*, in synthesis, Aragon Reyes op. cit., pp. 25, 36–43).

[3] This complementary statutory intervention, by application of the constitutional enabling clause, for the purpose of constituting the effective constitutional existence of "territories provided with a statute of linguistic *co-official status*" lies at the basis of constitutional jurisprudence, from STC 82/1986 (FJ 3) through STC 337/1994 (FJ 6) to the more recent STC 31/2010 (FJ 14).

[4] The operative reality of the social presence of that Spanish language, in general, used throughout Spain is denoted in the fact that, in common usage, the term "Castilian" is replaced by the identification "Spanish". This term is particularly expressive of that cultural dimension that, *ex* Article 3.1 SC, governs the national territory as a whole and that, *ex* Article 3.3 SC, is considered worthy of respect and recognition as an integrating part of a rich national heritage that, insofar as it contributes to apprehending and structuring the Latin American cultural area, unquestionably extends beyond merely national bounds.

Moreover, in terms of its genesis, it is clear that in the formation of the current Spanish language, Castilian has borrowed loan words of very diverse ranges from the other Iberian languages (to illustrate this point, see Hernández (2011).

existing in those Autonomous Communities that have their own language and which in itself, constitutes part of the cultural heritage..." (STC 337/1994, FJ 6).

The fact that, as the Constitutional Court has ruled in reference to the languages of Spain in the process of normalisation, the complementary statutory declaration of official status of a territorial language must be considered operative "independently of its real position and weight as a social phenomenon... as a normal means of communication in and between (the public authorities) and in their relationship with private individuals, with full validity and legal effects..." (STC 82/1986, FJ 2) does not in any substantial way change the applicable constitutional premises of the enabling clause of Article 3.2 SC.

Consequently, any attempt at a policy of restriction or deferment of uses and a defective presence in the public sphere of Castilian or Spanish, under the aegis of linguistic entitlements to intervention, whether or not they are classed as entitlements attributing powers in matters of language,[5] could not be justified merely on the grounds of a statutory safeguard of inescapable demands of public constitutional order, such as the prohibition on discrimination against Spaniards by reason of language.

The notion that the constitutional declaration of the official status of the common Spanish language practically throughout the national territory—and, by reason of its historical community, throughout the Hispano-American sphere—might be considered to be satisfied merely with a policy of tolerance and a reactive safeguard of the linguistic rights of citizens must be considered a distorted exercise of automatism and interpretative schematicism, not merely of the sense and scope of Article 3 SC.

The fact that between the potential expressed in the autonomic enabling clause of the Constitution, *ex* Article 3.2 SC, and the effective declaration of the official status of Spanish languages other than Castilian there must necessarily be a statutory declaration speaks volumes about its significance as a completive rule. As is the case in other issues, here too the *SAs* are a necessary regulatory complement to the SC. Precisely for that reason, because of their necessary intermediation, the constitutive effects of the statutory declaration of official status of another Spanish language must be recognised.

In this measure, as an instrument for the positive identification of constitutional potential, autonomic regulation of the effects relating to the scope of the declared official status of "own languages" would normally entail some form of reflex impact on the effective use of the common Spanish language.

However, as a consequence of its constitutionally derived legislative nature, that possible effect could never go to the extreme of questioning the uniform scope that the official status of the Spanish language, constitutionally declared the official language of the state, logically involves.

---

[5] Before the second wave of statutory reforms, such as those resulting in the renovated Statute of Autonomy of Catalonia *SACat*, some of whose provisions on linguistic matters we shall examine again in 2, in constitutional jurisprudence, when referring to interventions in this matter, mentions to linguistic competence alternated with references to mandates or authorisations, reflecting the regulation of the inherent content or scope of the co-official status (with regard to the jurisprudential detail regarding this lack of definition *see*, in particular, STC 87/1997, FFJJ 3–4).

Just as the constitutional nature derived from the statutory declaration does not impose a subsidiary character on the official status of that other own tongue of the territory, leaving the road open to policies of promotion and encouragement of social normalisation of its use, so does it not allow it to be afforded a preferential status, much less an exclusive alternative use.

Although the initial lack of definition in drawing up the autonomic map, which was to a large extent created in 1983, explains why in 1978 the constitution merely stated that "The other Spanish languages shall also be official in the respective Autonomous Communities in accordance with their Statutes", the fact is that the lack of definition of this formula left the door open to a potential diversification of the constitutional model of bilingualism outlined *ex* Article 3.2 SC.

A model of uncertain extension, in line with autonomic policies of linguistic normalisation (and acceptance of the standards of the European Charter for Regional and Minority Languages or *ECRML* has certainly contributed to promoting this), could lead to further statutory declarations on the official status of other regional languages less widely used than those already declared official, such as Bable or Aragonese, not to mention other hypothetical situations of processes being initiated for the differentiated normalisation of dialectical variants of [Castilian] Spanish or other Spanish languages.[6]

Like the process that has effectively taken place thus far, Article 3.2 SC might be considered also to provide for that hypothetical development, which, because of its open wording and dispositive regulatory structure and because it deals with cases related to "the other Spanish languages", will continue to be applicable.[7]

---

[6] The fact that such hypotheses are improbable in today's Spain should not prevent us from considering the long-term possibility that situations might arise of a hypertrophied configuration of identities, on similar drifts, through the invocation of that (collective) right to a language of their own that, in the process of territorial restructuring that followed the political break-up and dismembering of the state within the Soviet political space, was recognised in some of the constitutions of the political territories that were granted autonomy within the framework of the Russian Federation (on the complex linguistic structuring of that Euro-Asian space see Ruiz Vieytez 2004, (http://www.ciemen.org/mercator/pdf/simp-vieytez.pdf).

[7] In such a case (STC 31/2010, F 14), the own languages of residents (including EU citizens) and the languages of origin of naturalised Spaniards would remain outside this classification.

Another issue would be whether, looking to the future, it might be constitutionally viable to recognise the indigenous languages spoken in the autonomous cities of Ceuta and Melilla as "Spanish languages". Any doubt in this regard is due not so much to the failure to comply with the proviso of "Spanishness", if it is accredited that, because they are spoken normally in the basic political community, they can be characterised as Spanish languages but rather to the explicit wording of the condition *ex* Article 3. 2 SC that any recognition of official status must be by means of a statutory declaration "in the respective Autonomous Communities" (in this regard, see my Castillo (2008) op. cit.—Note 1—pp. 321–322). In such a case, there would be nothing in the constitution to obstruct, and indeed the conventional commitments of the ECRML would advise the regulation of the provision of the teaching of such languages and a deferential linguistic practice in the provision of public services (cf. Informe sobre la aplicación en España de la Carta europea de lenguas regionales y minoritarias, 2010; available at http://www.coe.int/t/dg4/education/minlang/report/Periodical/Reports/SpainPR3_es.pdf).

The ductility and malleability of the enabling clause *ex* Article 3.2 SC allows for a certain degree of bending (in this simile, this would be the result of a hypothetical increase in the number of "official" Spanish languages), provided that it does not exceed breaking point (in this hypothesis, a statutory declaration that limits the sense and scope of the official status of the commonly used Spanish language by means of an exclusive reading or even a reductive interpretation). Otherwise, just as with plastic materials, major deformation would begin to appear after the elastic limit was reached by striction or complete breakage.[8]

# A Comment on the Attempt to Amend the Model by Means of Statutory Reform, in the Light of Supreme Court Ruling STC 31/2010 on the Statute of Autonomy of Catalonia (SACat)

## *Preliminary Considerations*

With regard to the linguistic issue, the renewed *SACat* has been characterised by an unusual legislative density and a protracted regulatory "punctiliousness", all the more striking when compared to other regulatory texts of a similar nature and function or with its immediate predecessor, the first *SACat* of 1979.

The *SACat* contains a vast collection of linguistic provisions that, as if guided by a transverse scheme, is expressed in multifaceted form in the institutional or jurisdictional perspective or with regard to the guiding rights, duties, and principles or—particularly strikingly—by its clear constitutional pretensions, in the medullar (fundamental) Article 6, under the preliminary heading.

It is a medullar provision, in particular, because of its directive on the preferential normalised use of Catalan, which, as its "own" language, is declared to be the official language "of" Catalonia and whose status is formally reinforced by a generic right and duty of knowledge that is intended to parallel that established with regard to Castilian or Spanish *ex* Article 3.1 SC.

It may also be considered medullar, in a less immediate and intense fashion, in that the Aranese variant of the Occitan language, as the "own language" of the Aran

---

[8] On the precise meaning of the concepts used here to bring greater flexibility to the argument on the existence of a constitutional limit to the evolution of an open linguistic model, see, for example, Callister (1998).

Valley, is declared to be an official language "in" Catalonia, in a sense and with a scope to be determined by law.[9]

In addition to this type of provisions with constitutional pretensions, the *SACat* also contains a sort of statutory rewording of what might well be characterised as the regulatory heritage on the *own language* of Catalonia. Having thus fulfilled the strategy of anchoring in the higher regulatory tiers of the autonomic sub-legislation—where it would be secured against changing political majorities—what until then had been managed through the intensive application of a protracted regulatory scheme tending towards the measured and gradual implementation of the basic legislative provisions?[10]

The patent alteration of the previous legislative position on the language issue has met with two responses: politically, by People's Party (PP) MPs when the reform of the statute was debated in the Cortes (the Spanish national parliament) and, jurisdictionally, by the CC.

The parliamentary response can be said to have proved politically insufficient and constitutionally defective. Despite isolated improvements in the text submitted by the Catalonian Parliament, there has been no substantial modulation whatsoever of the radical leap in regulatory circumstance from the provisions of the 1979 Statute to the unrestrained *SACat* now in force or, to put it another way, from the effective operativity, *ex lege*, of a political directive tending towards the compensatory normalisation of language uses until such time as the final goals of that set of compensatory provisions were achieved, to its being set in stone as an unregressive structural principle by way of express provision in the statute.

This defective political intervention in the parliamentary processing of the statutory reform was followed by a referendum in the autonomous community and the subsequent entry into force of the renovated *SACat*.[11]

---

[9] A referring clause that in substance has been included by *Generalidad* [Catalan Government] Act 35/2010, of 1 October 2010, on Occitan, Aranese, in Aran (in reality, Aranese is a variation on the *Gascon* language, which is one of the forms of Occitan), pending a ruling in a *recurso de inconstitucionalidad* (cf. Dictamen del Consejo de Estado núm. 970/2011, of 7 July, majority ruling with the dissenting vote of Council-member Herrero Rodríguez-Miñón).

The *Aranese* Act develops and completes its legal system intensively. This is particularly evident in what might be considered to be a sort of central theme, variously and not always unequivocally formulated, a directive of preferential normalised use of *Aranese* (in this regard, see Dictamen num. 22/2010, of 5 August 2, of the *Consell de Garanties Estatutàries de Catalunya*, on the Bill on Occitan, Aranese in Aran [proyecto de ley del occitano, *aranés* en Arán], which unanimously concluded that "with the purpose of avoiding equivocation, it is proposed to abolish the term (preferential)", in Articles 3 a) of that bill).

[10] In 1979, the linguistic question had encountered a relatively synthetic commitment (outside Article 27.4 and Additional Provision Five), in Article 3 of the now repealed *Statute*, which was applied intensively in the course of a term that focused initially on the Linguistic Normalisation Act 7/1983, and later on the Linguistic Policy Act (1/1998) (on the Linguistic Policy Act (1/1998), see the various contributions and the documentation compiled in the journal Teoría y realidad constitucional, Issue 2, a monographic study on languages and constitution).

[11] Following endorsement in a referendum on 18 May, 2006, with 73.9 % of valid votes cast, the *SACat* (BOE—Official State Gazette, No. 172, of 20 July, 2006, pp. 27269–27310) came into force on 9 August, 2006.

From that moment on, the doubts with regard to the constitutional soundness of the updated *statutory treatment* of the linguistic heritage of Catalonia could only be resolved, where applicable, by means of a jurisdictional exercise of comparison by the CC. A number of appeals on the grounds of unconstitutionality [*recursos de inconstitucionalidad*—RIs] have been brought. Of these, given the scope of the jurisdictional response, one of the most interesting is that raised by a large number of Partido Popular [People's Party] MPs.[12]

STC 31/2010 gave a wide-ranging jurisdictional response.[13] The import and details of this response have been openly opposed within the full bench of the CC, basically, on the ground of the complexity of an aggregate of interpretative declarations of uncertain effect or more precisely, not always without a certain veil of uncertainty, for orthodox reasons of interpretative technique rather than for the failure to observe radical demands of a constitutional nature that, as the supreme interpreter of the Constitution, in the performance of its specific jurisdictional function a CC must always observe.[14]

These interpretations have, to some extent or other, managed to cast some doubt on the viability and effective implementation of constitutional demands that, because of the reactive nature of the judgements of constitutional comparison[15] in

---

[12] The appeal submitted on the grounds of unconstitutionality by ninety-nine congress members of the PP parliamentary party (RI No. 8045-2006) was ruled on in STC 31/2010, of 28 June; the ruling is referred to insofar as its subject is not discharged by extinction or with which STC 137/2010, of 16 December (Second and Third Ruling), is congruently issued at the behest of the Ombudsman (RI No. 8675-2006).

Likewise, although on a separate plane, the rulings of the Constitutional Court SSTC 46/2010 and 47/2010, both of 8 September 2010; STC 48/2010, of 9 September 2010; STC 49/2010 of 29 September 2010; and STC 138/2010 of 16 December 2010 must also be considered as rulings on the RIs submitted by the Government of Aragon (RI No. 9491-2006), Balearic Is. (RI No. 9568-2006), Valencia (RI No. 9501-2006), Murcia (RI No. 8829-2006), and La Rioja (RI No. 9330-2006).

[13] For a detailed analysis, see the monographic pieces offered by various periodicals, such as *El Cronista del Estado social*, 15 October, 2010, and the *Revista catalana de pret public*, 43, July 2010; similarly, for a more limited perspective, not without systematic pretensions, see the different contributions to REP., No. 151, monographic (coord.: A. López Castillo/J. Tajadura Tejada) on El Estado autonómico en cuestión. La organización territorial del Estado a la luz de las recientes reformas estatutarias (2006–2010).

[14] In this regard, for the synthesis it makes of the issue, Solozábal Echavarría *op. cit.* (Note 20), 2011, pp. 203–229 is of interest.

[15] Questioned almost in its entirety (except for Articles 12, 37.1, 44, 65, 143 and 146.3), the bulk of the decisions relating to statutory linguistic discipline are of an interpretative nature, which only in some of the cases (such as in relation to Articles 5, 6. 2, 33. 5, 34, 35. 1 and 2, 50. 5) are reproduced in the dispositive part, to which also the declarations of constitutionality (Article 50. 4) and unconstitutionality (Article 6. 1) lead.

Otherwise, independently of the matter relating to the perfectible legal certainty of those interpretative rulings that have yet to be issued (Articles 11, 33. 1–4, 36. 1 and 2, 101.3 and 102. 1, 3 and 4, and 147.1 a), of STC 31/2010, it is worthwhile highlighting a particularly expressive element of the jurisdictional nature of the control. This is the impossibility of ruling on the sense and scope of statutory provisions with regard to whose supposed—entirely

their positive detail, might only be clarified, at least in a systematic and integrated fashion, which given its state of evolution the constitutional model of territorial bilingualism requires, through the regulatory intervention of the national legislator.[16]


## From the Dense Constitutional Interpretation of Certain Linguistic Keys, ex *Article 6* SACat

Hereafter, we shall deal only with certain decision particularly worthy of note, either because of the equivocal or assertive nature of their import, because they were or were not taken to the dispositive part, or because they contained no ruling whatsoever. More specifically, we shall address the interpretation of the clauses relating to the diverse declaration of official status of the own languages "of" and "in" Catalonia:

a) *Concerning the own language "of" Catalonia.* Of all the matters dealt with *ex* Article 6 *SACat* on the statute of official status of the Catalan language, STC31/ 2010 addresses in particular intensity, by reason of their impact on the constitutional model of bilingualisms of a territorial base, the statutory clauses relating to the "right and duty (of citizens) to know (the official Catalan language)" (1) and to the characterisation of the own language "of" Catalonia as "the language of normal and preferential use" and as the "language of normal use for teaching and learning in the education system" (2).

1. In judging the constitutive statutory provision of a duty on the part of citizens to know the official language of Catalonia (which, judging by the generic nature of its formulation, appears to have been related to the rule *ex* Article 3.1 SC establishing a similar duty with regard to the official state Spanish language), the CC has faced an unresolved question.

   An attempt to establish a similar duty with regard to the Galician language by means of a regional law had already been declared unconstitutional. However, what was at stake here was whether, by means of a statutory provision substantially similar to the constitutional rule regarding Castilian, contained in Article 3.1 SC, a duty to know another official Spanish language might be established *ex novo* given that, in contrast with what we have already discussed with regard to the recognition of the right to use them, this duty "is not inherent to co-official status".

---

unfounded—unconstitutionality has been argued by the appealing parties that, in this point, ignoring a charge of process, required even within the objective framework of a process of direct control of constitutionality, consisting in providing a minimum foundation for the constitutional grounds for the appeal (Article 6.3 and 5).

[16] In this regard, see Heading III, 2°.

In order to give a congruent constitutional response to this new issue, STC 31/ 2010 FJ 14 b) makes a comparative study of the import and sense of Articles 3.1 SC and 6. 2 *SACat* in two interrelated steps:

Firstly, it clarifies the sense and scope of the constitutional duty to know Castilian, assuming that, "rather than being an 'individualised and demandable' duty (STC 82/1986, FJ 2)... it is in fact the counterpoint of the faculty of the public authority to use it as a medium of normal communication with citizens without their being able to demand the use of any other[17] so that acts of *imperium* which are the subject of communication regularly deploy their legal effects".[18]

Thus, once it is recognised that all citizens resident in any linguistic territory "have the right to use both (languages) in their relations with the authority and only the—constitutional—obligation to know Castilian. . .", it is concluded that in these areas of co-official status, the public authorities would lack an equivalent faculty. Therefore, no generic presumption of knowledge could be formalised in the manner of Article 3.1 SC; neither could citizens be obliged to a given linguistic usage nor can an attitude of tolerance be expected with the linguistic wishes of the public authorities.

---

[17] Without that reflexive understanding of the constitutional duty to know Castilian, a claim of ignorance of the language or a simple refusal to use it in relationships with the public authorities would be exposed to police surveillance and a sanctionary procedure.

An interpretation of the constitution which that is more in keeping with the principle of freedom of language has led the CC to rule that the duty to know Spanish must be considered to have been fulfilled in "the presumption that all Spaniards know it", a presumption *iuris tantum* that, presupposing a knowledge that is practically coextensive with the area of application of the constitutional order, lies in an expectation of public provision in matters of education and training and that, should the safeguard of guarantees be endangered or if the full exercise of the constitutional law be hindered, any person, even someone of Spanish nationality, could legitimately question *ad casum*. In short, this is a presumption that may be nullified in cases of ignorance or insufficient knowledge of the official Spanish language either because a person arrested or imprisoned credibly so claims or because it becomes clear in the course of police action (*cf.* STC 74/1987, *cit.*).

[18] For the purposes of maintaining as an effective reality that presumption of knowledge of the Spanish language of common use (*a language common to all Spaniards or a common official tongue of general scope* as CC jurisprudence has traditionally put it; *cf.*, among many others, SSTC 84/1986, 82/1986 and 56/1990). the clause, which is formally presented as a duty of all Spaniards, must be related to the various powers of intervention of the public authorities for the purposes of ensuring and fostering the ability of all Spaniards to deploy their capacities through participation in public life, whatever their respective linguistic systems and dialectical forms of speech, be they of Castilian or of other Spanish languages,or even of other languages native to their place of origin.

In any case, a deliberate refusal by Spanish nationals who manifestly know the Spanish language to use it goes beyond the specific field of safeguarding the guarantees of arrest and due process and should be considered to form part of an ideological liberty, in that it can be extended to positions of indemnity compatible with the safeguarding of public order that constitutionally limits its exercise and, in any case, as an intended statement of conscience instrumental to civil disobedience, with political pluralism.

Secondly, having established the distance between the two provisions, it notes that Article 6.2 *SACat* accompanies this reference with the qualification that "The public authorities of Catalonia shall establish the necessary measures to enable the exercise of these rights and the fulfilment of this duty. . .".

Moreover, it is in this addendum that the CC finds the possible sense of an interpretation compatible with the constitutional demands of a statutory provision, considering it "evident that this can only be an individualised and demandable duty to know Catalan, i.e. a duty of a different nature to that whose object is Castilian in Article 3.1 SC. . . an individual and binding duty that has its specific and own place in the area of education, as one can infer from Article 35. 2 SACat and from the special binding relations. . . in Article 33. 1 SACat. . .". Considered in these terms,[19] in the context of the constitutional model of territorially based linguistic conjunction, it would prove to be the expression of a mandate on the better observance of specific linguistic duties, expressly established in the *SACat*.[20]

It is politically unclear whether, following that intended imperative characterisation of a duty to know the Catalan language as the own language "of" Catalonia, an identitary tendency has been revealed, while there is no change in the legal framework of reference that has been constitutionally settled by a complex interpretation of terms that are either interpreted in accordance with the constitutional model outlined *ex* Article 3 SC or are included in an orthodox statement of unconstitutionality and nullity, *ex* Article 38 LOTC.

2. From the constitutional interpretation of the statutory clauses relating to the characterisation of the own language "of" Catalonia as "the language of normal and preferential use" and "the language of normal use for teaching and learning in the education system".

---

[19] It is within this line of reductive interpretation in then light of the constitutional framework that my Castillo (2008) *cit.* (Note 1) operates.

[20] It is true that the characterisation of this hermeneutic effort by the CC may invite criticism (thus, for example, Milian Massana (2010) cit. (Note 20), p. 133: "It is not a question. . . merely of an interpretation of the precept, but of a mutation"), but it seems equally true that a critical approach similar to the technique used by the CC might prove less convincing if, leaving aside any assessment of a hypothetical alternative of making a declaration of unconstitutionality, everything was limited to opposing an interpretation in line with the constitutive declaration of the CC with regard to the constitutional framework in which the constitutional model of territorially based linguistic conjunction should be developed in order not to exceed what might be called—to use our previous simile—the breaking point of Article 3 SC (it is only possible to reach that point of no return legitimately through an express reform of the Constitution that, as we have seen, cannot be limited to amending Article 3).

In any case, if, following abstraction of its consequent jurisprudential interpretation, it can be critically argued that Article 3.1 SC is "an unusual precept in comparative law" [thus, for example, Enric Fossas Espadaler, in his commentary on the jurisprudence relative to 3 SC, in Casas and Rodríguez-Piñero 2009, p. 65 and, likewise, Milian Massana 2010 *cit.* (Note 20), p. 133], what can one say of the intended structuring, through statutory clauses, as Article 6 *SACat*, appears to have sought to do on a similar duty with regard to the other official Spanish languages?

i) *Normality* and *preference* of use of the own language "of" Catalonia. STC 31/ 2010 clearly states something that had been somewhat obscured by the intricate politics of linguistic normalisation, viz. that "the definition of Catalan as 'the own language of Catalonia' cannot entail an imbalance of the constitutional regime of co-official status of the two languages in prejudice of Castilian. . ." (FJ 14 a).

With regard to the characterisation of Catalan as an own language, STC 31/ 2010 establishes a clear division between the normality of its use and its intended status of preference, following consideration of the suppositions of application of Article 3.2 SC.

The CC begins by making it clear that the existence of differentiated linguistic identities is the authentic enabling supposition of the clause of statutory remission *ex* Article 3. 2 SC; "the inescapable constitutional condition for its recognition as an official language by a Statute of Autonomy [given that] Article 3. 2 SC does not allow the Statutes of Autonomy to proclaim the official status of any Spanish language other than Castilian [. . . other than] the language of the "respective" autonomous community, that is, the characteristic, historical, exclusive language, in contrast to the language common to all autonomous communities, which is, in this regard, an 'own' language".

In consequence, based on the respective declaration of official status, an attempt shall be made to foster a regular or normal use of the own language, which, depending on the extension of its effective social presence, may be promoted by means of policies of normalisation.[21]

It thus concludes that to say that the own language declared to be official language of the *Autonomous Community of Catalonia* is the language of normal use in public administration bodies and in the public media is not equivalent to saying—if it is interpreted, as it should be, in the context of the constitutional model of territorially based linguistic conjunction—that said language must be the language of exclusive or preferential use, since that would result in a complete distortion of the sense and scope of the enabling clause of Article 3.2 SC.

Consequently, it declares the unconstitutionality and nullity of the interpolation "and preferential", insofar as it "involves the primacy of one language over another in the territory of an autonomous community... imposing... the prescriptions of a priority use of one of them, in this case, of Catalan over Castilian [which is] detrimental to the inescapable balance between two equally official languages, and which in no case may receive privileged treatment. . .".

From this synthetic extract from STC 31/2010, one can clearly see that one thing is the temporal and compensatory prescription of a preference of use, for the

---

[21] In actual fact, using a deliberately open formula, the CC ruled in favour of an open—if not undifferentiated (two-way?)—conception of the meaning of such compensatory measures to maintain "the legitimacy of the legislator's adopting, where applicable, proper and proportionate measures of linguistic policy intended to correct, where they exist, historical situations of imbalance of one of the official languages with regard to another, and thus rectify the secondary or deferential position one of them might hold".

purpose of making swift and ordered progress in the normalisation process, of a tongue-declared official, which begins from a position of clear imbalance, as a consequence of pre-democratic policies, and another quite different thing is that once that goal of normalisation has been achieved or is close to being achieved, by means of regulatory petrification of a sort of inverted imbalance, by virtue of explicit statutory structuring, one might defend a policy of deferment and preterition, if not of simple, systematic exclusion of the official Spanish language of the state that, as an appropriate language and one in normal use in that territory, is also an appropriate language and one in normal use in Catalonia.

So the CC has seen in the statutory regulation of a clause of preference for use of the own language "of" Catalonia an example of articulation that excessively pushes the point of maximum tension of the constitutional framework of reference and thus, were it not to be declared unconstitutional and null and void, could cause fractures in the constitutional model of territorially based linguistic conjunction that would be difficult to repair.

ii) *Language of teaching [vehicular language] and learning in the education system.* Paragraph VI of FJ 14 a) of STC 31/2010 addresses the sense and scope of the explicit statutory consideration of the own language of Catalonia as "the language of normal use for teaching and [for] learning in the education system" extremely synthetically.

Using a citation from its own jurisprudence, it stresses, as a basilar element in the matter, a pronouncement that has been repeated with greater or lesser explicitness with regard to co-official languages or the official language of the state (SSTC 6/1982, FJ 10; 137/1986, FJ 1; and 337/1994, FJ 9 and 10), the inseparability of the condition of official language from that of teaching language in education.

Having settled this point and following a detailed reference to the judgement of Article 35 SACat in relation to the specific regime of linguistic rights in the area of teaching dealt with later, in FJ 24 it categorically concludes: "that, on principle, Castilian cannot cease to be also a language of teaching and learning in the education system".

In consonance with this categorical statement, in ruling upon the sense and scope of the provision *ex* Article 35. 1 and 2 *SACat*, the CC directly addresses the issue of whether the statutory recognition of the right to receive teaching in Catalan is necessarily tied to a refusal to recognise Castilian as a language of teaching and learning in the education, which is expressly only attributed to the own language "of" Catalonia.

Within a respectful and manifest agreement with the demands arising from the constitutional model of territorially based linguistic conjunction (substantially outlined with regard to the recognition of the vehicular centrality of Catalan in the school education system in the relevant STC 337/1994, extracts of whose more significant paragraphs are reproduced in STC 31/2010), the answer to that question could not have been clearer. Just as "nothing prevents the Statute from recognising the right to receive education in Catalan, and that this should be the language of normal use for teaching and learning at all levels of the education system... there is nothing [either] that would allow Castilian not to enjoy an identical right as Catalan, to be a language of normal use for teaching and learning in the education system" (Paragraph Three).

Following a measured description of the imperative features of the constitutional model of territorially based linguistic conjunction, it proposes a completing interpretation of Article 35.1 and 2, Interpolation 1, *SACat*, in order to overcome the unconstitutionality that by means of a literal interpretation could have entailed by certain emphatic and omissive provisions that, in the CC's understanding, "allow for an interpretation in accordance with the Constitution in the sense of not preventing the free and efficient exercise of the right to receive an education in Spanish as a language of teaching of learning in the education system".

In a comprehensive formulation of its nuances, that line of case law, basically expressed on the occasion of the refusal to extract from the right of linguistic choice any pretensions of exclusive education in just one of the official languages (in this case, the Spanish Language), is now extended to the whole educational process and is also projected with regard to the official Spanish language.

Paragraph Seven of FJ 24 summarises that new projection in twin considerations and a conclusion before going on to interpret the constitutionality of Article 35. 1 and 2, Interpolation I, *SACat*.

The consideration is that "since it is opposed by the implicit constitutional mandate upon the state and regional public authorities to encourage knowledge and guarantee mutual respect and protection of both official languages of Catalonia (STC 337/1994, FJ 9)" and "because teaching in the official languages constitutes one of the inherent consequences... of co-official status (STC 87/1983, of 27 October, FJ 5)... both languages must not only be the object of teaching, but also a means of communication in the educational process as a whole... as teaching [vehicular] languages".

The conclusion is that if one presupposes the right to receive an education in either of the two languages, the centrality of Catalan as a teaching language, consequent with the aim of linguistic normalisation, always comes up against "the limitation that it should not determine the exclusion of Castilian as a teaching language so that its knowledge and use is guaranteed in the territory of the CA" (STC 337/1994, FJ 10).

Along these same lines, as well as the first interpolation of Article 35.1, Section 2. *SACat*, is said to be constitutional only if "interpreted in the sense in which the mention of Catalan does not deprive Castilian of the condition of a language of teaching and learning in the education system" (*Enunciado* 2) "it leads to the existence of that right to education in Spanish" (*Enunciado* 1).

Without prejudice to the criticism that, in technical terms related to the theory of constitutional interpretation, within the Constitutional Court itself and among theoretical commentators[22] one should not ignore the integrating effect of a hermeneutical trial that, by virtue of its determination of the sense and scope of those controversial clauses and its recognition of the complementary function that *ex* Article 3. 2 SC corresponds to the *SAs*, contributes to consolidating the characteristic features of the constitutional model of territorially based linguistic conjunction. This model, in its initial configuration with regard to the controversial possible confluence of the two official languages of Catalonia in the area of education, in STC 31/2010, now appears to stand, given its comprehensive potential, in a decisive criterion for the purposes of clarifying the sense and scope of a constitutional regime, *ex* Article 3 SC, on which, if not before, when the time comes to resolve the *recurso de inconstitutionalidad* (RI)[23] brought against the aforementioned Education Act of the Parliament of Catalonia (Act 12/2009, of 10 July 2009), of Education, the CC must return.[24]

In any case, whatever the criterion of case law and without prejudice to the political legitimacy of any opposing position, now that the constitutional case law has been established, the STC 31/2010 must be considered a turning point, inescapable whether the issue at stake is the settlement of conflicts in process of jurisdiction or its structuring in law.

Clearly, without prejudice to the reactive process of jurisprudence, proper and safe application of the constitutional regulations established in STC 31/2010 requires a regulatory intervention from the legislator.

---

[22] With regard to the external criticism, we refer the reader here to a somewhat nuanced Catalan theoretical perspective: see the commentaries by *Milian Massana, Pons Parera, Pla Boix* and *Muro Bas, in the special issue of Revista catalana de pret public* (*cit.* Note 20) on the Statute.

With regard to the criticisms raised within the CC itself, of varying tone and form, whose details it is not possible to address here, the dissenting votes of *Conde Martín de Hijas, Delgado Barrio, Rodríguez-Zapata Pérez* and *Rodríguez Arribas* are of interest.

[23] Translator's Note: "**recurso de inconstitucionalidad:** application for judicial review of proposed legislation; the ground of this application or appeal which can only be brought by MPs—*diputados*—elected members of the Senate or upper chamber—*senadores*—or members of the Cabinet—*Gobierno*—is always that the proposed act—*ley*—or bill—*proyecto de ley*—violates some constitutional principle; it is heard by the Constitutional Court—*Tribunal Constitucional*", Alcaraz Varó, Enrique and Hughes, Brian. Diccionario de Términos Jurídicos Ariel Derecho 7th edition 2003, p. 903].

[24] Granted leave to proceed by ruling of 27 October 2009, RI No. 8741-2009, moved by more than fifty members of congress from the PP parliamentary party, targets Paragraphs 7, 20, 22, 27, 28, and 36 of the Preamble; Articles 4.2, 8.1 and 3, 9.2, 10.2 and 4, 17, 51, 52, 53, 55.1, 52, 53, 55.1 and 6, 57.1, 58, 59, 61, 64.4 and 5, 68, 70.1, 104.3, 109, 111, 112, 114.1, 117.1 c), d) and f), 119, 120, 121, 125, 153, 154, 155, 158.1 and 2 a), I, II, and IV, and f), and 161; and Additional Provisions II and IX.

A good example of the expectations in the light of a punctilious and incisive regulation may be seen in the commentary by Milian Massana (2010) *loc. cit.*, p. 135: "This law, compared to the preceding legislation (Art. 21.2 and 2 LPL) and the legislation examined by the Constitutional Court in STC 337/1994, to a great extent restricts the sphere in which teaching in Spanish is guaranteed. In the light of the case law of STC 337/1994, this circumstance already called into question the constitutionality of some of its points when it was passed".

In effect, a close consideration of the complex jurisdictional framework in which the provision of the public service of education takes place allows one to understand clearly that only from a congruent regulatory intervention by the state, general and regional legislators, can the effective and full operativity of the constitutional standards outlined, if not detailed, in STC 31/2010 be expected.

Without seeking, on this occasion, to go beyond merely indicating the path to be followed, we can at least define the extremes of a segment that is broad enough to host relatively different linguistic policies to their limits.

Such limits would lead us, on the one hand, to definitively rule out the intention to return to the idea of schools separated by reason of language (whether that should entirely exclude a modulated variation, in concurrence with certain suppositions and not without certain requirements, of alternative classrooms to the approach of individualised reinforcement, is a question that we need not address here). And at the same time, to recognise the condition of the Spanish language as a teaching language, by definitively superseding the attempts to structurally downgrade it to a merely curricular condition, without obscuring the true issue with matters related to times (2 or 3 h) or the methodological argument on the language of learning (grammar in Spanish or not), which are certainly additional aspects to be considered.[25]

2. *Concerning the own language "in" Catalonia*. One particularly noteworthy element of the statutory reform, even if it may initially have gone somewhat unnoticed, given the lack of a ruling in STC 31/2020 faced with "the absence of an explicit grounds for the appeal" by the appellants, is the explicit recognition of the Aranese variant of the Occitan language, following its classification as the own language of the *comarca*, as an official language "in" Catalonia. This, it states, is "as established by this... Estatut and by the laws of linguistic normalisation" (Article 6.5 *SACat*).

---

[25] I made a similar call for compromise, without in any way demanding a radical abandonment of the normalisation policies, with my argument for an overarching need to return to normality, in my Castillo (2008) *op. cit.* (Note 2). In a very significant article published more recently in El País ("Evitar la guerra lingüística" [Avoiding a linguistic war?], El País, 30 April, 2011), one of the protagonists of the debate in Catalonia argued in similar terms for an inescapable renewal of the linguistic commitment, without prejudice to the possible maintenance of Catalonia as an educational centre of gravity.

If the development of this or other types of system of joint operation of the teaching languages in education were to be considered as a pro-Spanish attack on the Catalan school system, then the traditional exclusive Spanishism [*españolismo*] has been replaced by a newly forged Spanishism, emerging in a territory with its own language, which dressed up as consequent Catalanism might seem to have set its sights, just like the Spanishism of yore, on undervaluing and denying its position as a teaching instrument (without which a tongue loses its social presence and, in any case is undervalued, as Antonio Milian Massana rightly argues with regard to the Catalan Language, in *Los derechos lingüísticos en la enseñanza de acuerdo con la Constitución*, REDC 7, 1983), directed no longer towards Catalan but Castilian, which this movements seek to relegate to a mere subject on the curriculum of the educational system of Catalonia.

The issue with regard to the *SACat* is based on a triple reference regarding the rights of *Aranese* speakers to know and use this variation of Gascon (both in their dealings with the public authorities and in the provision of public services in the Aran Valley and, in general, in their dealings with the Catalan government): the public promotion of the use of the language, its dissemination and knowledge, and finally, the shared responsibility of the Catalan government and the *Conselh Generau d'Aran* in the process of normalisation, under the terms of Articles 36, 50.1, and 143.2 *SACat*. This *ion the contrary* means that, without prejudice to the scope that may be granted to it in law, *Aranese* could not avail of the statutory regime of guarantees that, *ex* Article 37.1, Paragraph 2, are applicable in the case of the own language "of" Catalonia.

Nonetheless, its explicit statutory recognition as an official language "in" Catalonia involves a clear advance on the previous situation in two regards: firstly, because the current declaration of official status goes beyond the legal range that existed previously, under Act 16/1990, of 13 July 1990, on the special regime for the Aran Valley and, secondly, since by virtue of its extensive personal projection to the whole of Catalonia, in keeping with its statutory declaration as an official language "in" Catalonia, that Gascon variant of the Occitan linguistic family achieves, by means of regional Act 35/2010, of 1 October 2010, a degree of development that is unique throughout the Occitan language area.

The Preamble to Act 35/2010, which by way of a repealing provision impacts on the linguistic heritage of Aranese, as a result of the confluent application of Acts 16/199 and 1/1998, establishes that, by virtue of its statutory recognition of official status, "in" Catalonia there are now not two but three official languages. On this point, it is worth making a preliminary note of caution and an additional consideration.

The caution consists of clarifying that the *Aranese Act* is awaiting resolution of an RI by the Prime Minister, basically, with regard to the recurring provision, in some of the provisions on the institutional area, of a rule of preference of usage or equivalent that, in the case of the Catalan language, has already been declared unconstitutional and null and void in STC 31/2010.

Whether this strict judgement may be unqualifiedly transferred to the control of the provision on rule of preference of the use of Aranese established not in Article 6.5 *SACat* but by means of an autonomic law requires further reflection. In this regard, without seeking in any way to second-guess the final ruling or to draw the attention of the supreme interpreter of the Constitution to the projection of its jurisprudence over that controversial issue,[26] it might not be entirely out of place to make a hermeneutic effort to take into consideration operative criteria in

---

[26] With regard to this detail, *cf.* Dictamen del Consejo de Estado núm. 970/2011, of 7 July (available at (http://www.consejo-estado.es). The RI has been granted leave to proceed by the CC, which, it is reported, in consonance with the government's invocation of Article 161.2 SC, suspends the validity and applicability of the contested precepts (Articles 2.3, 5.4 and 7, 6.5).

the matter of the normalisation of linguistic uses of minority regional languages in contexts of concurrence with other official languages, without losing sight of the commitments derived from the CELRM but in accordance with the demands of the Spanish constitutional model of territorially based linguistic conjunction. The additional consideration is already related not so much to the criteria that should govern the detailed constitutional judgement of the legal status of Aranese expressed in that controversial autonomic law (it is known to substantially involve provision for its uses in the areas of public institutions, education, media, etc., following the formulation of certain general principles, in which one can see the constitutional designs of the statutory clause) but to the very meaning of the declaration of official status of Aranese "in" Catalonia, as the own language, expressing the specific *national reality* of the Aran Valley.

Here, the issue to be elucidated, since it has not been prejudged in STC 31/2010, is whether by virtue of the identitary substratum expressing a political singularity, of which the own language is considered a very important instrument but which also projected in the recognition of the institutional singularity of a territory which, remaining outside the traditional local grouping in *vegueries*,[27] has a bilateral relationship with the *Generalitat*, that explicit statutory recognition should be compared by looking exclusively at the provisions of Article 3 SC or by extending the scope to interpret it in attendance upon its immediate constitutional context and, in any case, the provisions of Article 2 SC.[28]

## *And a Final Note on the Regulatory Framework to Be Developed by Law... and by Constitutional Reform? Or How to Map the Road Ahead Half-Way Through the Day*

In this final point of my article, I would like to refer, looking at the road still left to travel, to two possible ways of seeking to overcome the *impasse* created based on authorised pronouncements in STC 31/2010 that, as a turning point, leave around them a complex panorama of interpretations of constitutional conformity of statutory provisions, referring to legislative and regulatory standards, prior or subsequent to the reform of the *SACat*, pending the aforementioned interpretative

---

[27] See Act 30/2010, of 3 August 2010, on the *veguerias* (*cf.* Dictamen del Consejo de Estado núm. 2440/2010, of 2 December 1992; available at (http://www.consejo-estado.es), amended by Act 4/2011, of 8 June 2011, which postpones its full entry into force.

[28] The pertinence of this type of systematic constitutional interpretation is concisely referred to in the presentation (*El Estado autonómico en la encrucijada*) in Issue 151 (monographic) of the REP., *cit.*, pp. 9–24, which called into question the notion that by means of a mere statutory reform one might presuppose "that same condition of national reality (which in STC 31/2010 is expressly extended to a constitutional recognition of "nationalities" ex Article 2 SC) a propos of an internal region –in this case the Aran Valley–... lacking all coverage in the aforementioned Article 2..." (p. 22).

settlement that, however strange it might seem, is not always undertaken with the proper observance of a system of regulatory checks that, until such time as there is an alteration to the current regulatory framework, by means of constitutional reform (3) obviously binds all, both the jurisdictional (1) and the political organs, including national and autonomic legislatures (2).

1. On the jurisprudential assumption of the constitutional standards established with regard to the judgement of the *SACat*, the reference that imposes itself here over other possible ones is to a recent emerging line of jurisprudence in the Contentious-Administrative section of the Supreme Court in which, in process of the cassation of resolutions of the Higher Courts of Justice (Tribunales Superiores de Justicia or TSJ) of Catalonia (which, on the presumption of constitutionality of the Linguistic Policy Act (Act 1/1998), ignored claims related to the ignorance by the autonomic educational administration of the guarantee of education in Spanish), without raising, as was expressly demanded in some of the cases, any issue of unconstitutionality (IQ), that constitutional case law *ad casum* is being projected without hesitation.[29]

So the implementation of these rulings by the competent government is likely to be problematic, given the lack of an express declaration of unconstitutionality of the current LPL, a situation that the presentation of an IQ might help to resolve; likewise, the case law that might be set as a result of the ruling on the appeal of unconstitutionality (RI) pending against the Education Act of Catalonia (EAC) will be of interest.[30]

---

[29] For information purposes, there follows a partial reproduction of the ruling of STS, Court III, Section IV, of 10 May, 2011, issued in cassation (Appeal No. 1602/2009) against the sentence of the Contentious-Administrative Court (Section V) of the High Court [Tribunal Superior de Justicia] of Catalonia, of 30 September 2008 (Judge responsible for drafting the leading opinion: Antonio Martí García): "(...) we uphold the appellant's right for Castilian to be used also as a teaching language in the education system of the Autonomous Community of Catalonia, and in consequence and for this purpose the new situation created by the declaration of Ruling 31/2010 of the Constitutional Court which considers Castilian also to be a vehicular language of education in Catalonia together with Catalan including the right of children in infant education and in the first cycle of primary education to be schooled in the tongue petitioned by their parents...".

The case law, which is also reproduced in the STS, of 19 May, 2011, issued in the case of Appeal to the Supreme Court [*recurso de casación*] No. 395/10 (same judge), and which had already been applied on previous occasions, in the sentences of the same court and section, of 13 and 16 December 2010, issued in settlements of the Appeals to the Supreme Court No. 796/2009 (judge: Celsa Picó Lorenzo) and 1839/2009 (judge: Celsa Picó Lorenzo), comes from the ruling of the Supreme Court of that same court and section, of 9 December 2010, issued in the case of Supreme Court Appeal No. 793/2009 (judge: Santiago Martínez-Vares García).

[30] At the beginning of September 2011, the press (cf., for example, La Vanguardia, of 3 September 2011; El País, of 4 September 2011) reported on the controversy generated in the *CACat* as a result of the resistance to the educational administration of the government of Catalonia that, with political support from most of the parliamentary forces (*See* La Vanguardia cit.: Ultimátum del TSJ a la Generalidad para que el castellano sea lengua vehicular en la escuela; El PSC se alinea con la Generalidad en "la defensa del modelo lingüístico", etc.; at the same time a motion was announced by members of parliament from the People's Party in the Parliament of Catalonia to demand compliance with the jurisdictional rulings; *See* La Vanguardia cit.: "El PPC presentará una

2. If the issue is the critical consideration of the national and autonomic legislators, the first thing one notes is a clear comparison between the legislative voluntarism of the autonomic legislator, of which the aforementioned EAC might well be considered an example, and the defective assumption of its responsibilities by the national legislator as the body responsible for implementing the constitutional provisions by way of the corresponding regulation, thus, for example, staying within the area of education, with regard to the general status of the common Spanish language as a teaching language in a differentiated linguistic context of provision of public education service.

In this regard, it is necessary to advance the characterisation, on the recurring invocation of the different sections of Article 149.1 SC, of an implicit jurisdictional power inherent, in particular, in the medullar Article 3 SC.

Just as, in relation to the autonomic linguistic regime of the co-official languages, the jurisprudence of the CC has dealt in different, but recurring, ways with the autonomic powers of intervention in linguistic matters (before the *SACat* was amended to extensively and intensively identify the ownership of powers over linguistic matters and in relation to the general regulation of the status of the own language), in the current constitutional order there is nothing to prevent a congruent interpretation in that sense of provisions of a linguistic nature or content and, in particular, when it comes to regulating the constitutional regime, the sense and scope of the linguistic dimension of the constitutional rights and duties.

This said, without prejudice to other possible legislative interventions of a reactive nature, such as those which, with due political guarantees, following a political appreciation of a risk to the national interest, might be adopted to harmonise regulatory situations arising out of a legitimate autonomic intervention, through the establishment, *ex* Article 150.3 SC, of the precise principles in this regard.

---

propuesta en el Parlamento para forzar el cumplimiento del fallo"), appeared to indicate a clear desire not to comply.

Here it is worth differentiating between the logic of a political reaction that is not incompatible with the formulation and lodging of the corresponding appeals in process of jurisdiction and a possible derivation, in the form of defiant statements and attitudes, expressing disobedience with the mandates and obligations that might be imposed within the framework of the current constitutional order.

This episode, while evidencing a certain break-up of the Spanish political panorama, is also an example of the dysfunctional exercise of their respective powers by the constitutional organs with powers of linguistic matters: in the case of the jurisdictional bodies, because it is within their powers to raise questions of unconstitutionality and they have failed to do so (perhaps awaiting the ruling of the RI currently pending on the Education Act), even when constitutional reinterpretations of the statutory clauses show a clear incompatibility between the constitutional model of territorially based linguistic conjunction and provisions such as Article 21 LPL, and, in the case of the political bodies, because in neither house of the national parliament are other linguistic initiatives being proposed that are not related to the extra-territorial projection of the other Spanish languages and because they have not received from the Spanish government any initiative intended to provide some systematic and congruent structuring of this complex linguistic regime.

However much the experience of the Organic Law on Harmonisation of the Autonomic Process has marked its path, not only should it not be considered unusable, but in a context of asymmetric dispositive drive and a notable presence of differential facts, one can expect from a regulatory instrument such as the Harmonisation Act an integrating capacity which is particularly suitable in linguistic matters insofar as, on the more or less controversial invocation of attributions of power, there is a certain need to safeguard the general interest of the nation..[31]

3. Finally, one should make one last reference to the hypothesis of constitutional reform—or, rather, to the alternative hypotheses of reform comprising completion and fine-tuning or reform comprising superseding the constitutional model outlined in Article 3 SC.

The first, that is to say, a possible completive reform might largely be summarised in two notes:

One related to a (certain) determination of the other Spanish languages that might be declared official, thus demarcating a hypothetical trend of dispositive invocation of a kind of implicit collective right to the recognition of own languages, by means of intense processes of normativisation and normalisation of linguistic modalities, to which we have already referred in a simple reflection on the degree of openness of the enabling clause of Article 3.2 SC.

On a second note is intensive or *in extenso*, on the common status of the official Spanish language of the state. In this area, the greatest difficulty lies, not so much in the remnant but in the relative revival of those majorities and minorities present in the constituent process, to borrow an expression from Professor Rubio Llorente's well-known contribution.[32]

With regard to the hypothesis of supersedent reform or of a change in the constitutional model of territorially based asymmetric bilingualism, I will limit myself to pointing out that, in consonance with the constituent base on which the current constitutional order stands, this would be a highly speculative hypothesis.

But albeit only to conclude with a provocative paradox, one must accept as correct the opinion of those who maintain that, for practical purposes, a constitutional reform establishing the exclusive official status of the own language, for example of the *CACat*, in the curriculum of the public education system, could scarcely worsen the consideration of the common Spanish language as a curricular subject contained in the current Education Act of Catalonia, *EAC*.

---

[31] Merely for information purposes, one might consider, for example, the hypothesis of a renewal of external uses and in the framework of the EU of other Spanish languages that, without calling into question the respective qualifications of intervention, might seek to safeguard the national interest underlying the achievement for the common Spanish language of a (generic or specific) status as a working language.

With regard to this and other possible situations of harmonised intervention by the national legislator, see my lecture at the symposium on *Lenguas y Constitución española [Languages and the Spanish Constitution]*, UAM, 28 November 2011.

[32] Minorías y mayorías en el poder constituyente, in Rubio Llorente (1993), pp. 135–163.

# References

Antonio López Castillo, Aproximación al modelo lingüístico español: un apunte crítico, in RDPo 71-72, 2008, 309–346.

Antonio Milian Massana, *El régimen de las lenguas oficiales. Comentario a la sentencia del Tribunal Constitucional 31/2010, de 28 de junio*, in Revista catalana de dret public—Especial. . ., p. 133.

Casas/Rodríguez-Piñero (dirs.), Comentarios a la Constitución española, XXX aniversario, Wolters Kluwer, Madrid, 2009, page. 65).

Eduardo J. Ruiz Vieytez, 2004, Lenguas oficiales y lenguas minoritarias: cuestiones sobre su estatuto jurídico a través del derecho comparado, available at (http://www.ciemen.org/mercator/pdf/simp-vieytez.pdf).

Francisco Rubio Llorente, *La forma del poder (estudios sobre la Constitución)*, CEC, Madrid, 1993 (2nd ed., 1997), pp. 135–163.

Inés Fernández-Ordóñez Hernández, La lengua de Castilla y la formación del español, maiden speech at the Real Academia Española de La Lengua, given on 13 February 2011; available at (http://www.rae.es/rae/gestores/gespub000011.nsf/. . ./$FILE/Discurso.pdf).

Juan José Solozábal Echavarría, 2011, *La sentencia sobre el Estatuto de Cataluña: una visión de conjunto*, in López Castillo/Tajadura Tejada (coords.), Las reformas estatutarias. . ., pp. 203–229.

Juan José Solozábal Echavarría, *Artículo 2 CE*, in Casas/Rodríguez-Piñero -dirs.-, Comentarios a la Constitución española, XXX, FWK España, Madrid, 2009, pp. 53–63.

Luis López Guerra, 2009, *Título VIII CE*, Capítulo I, Principios generales, in Casas/Rodríguez-Piñero -dirs.-, Comentarios pp. 2067.

Manuel Aragon Reyes, *Artículo 1 CE*, in Casas/Rodríguez-Piñero -dirs.-, Comentarios pp. 25, 36–43.

William D. Callister, *Introducción a la ciencia e ingeniería de los materiales*, Ed. Reverté, 1998.

# Religious Freedom in School Dining Areas and Its Enemies

## Regulatory Consistency and Coordination of the Actions of the State and Autonomous Communities in School Canteens

Miren Gorrotxategi Azurmendi

## Diversity, Religion, Food and School

### The Age of Diversity

In the field of education in Spain, the term "addressing diversity issues" [*atención a la diversidad*] was first coined by the General Education Act (LOGSE)[1] in the 1990s. It is meant to refer to a new demand on the education system. Essentially, the underlying consideration is as follows: In order to guarantee the right to education,[2] it is no longer considered sufficient simply to afford access to the school system; in addition, in order to offset any inequalities that might otherwise arise, the system must adapt to the particular needs of pupils arising from their diversity (different concerns, cognitive qualities, aspirations, socio-economic contexts, etc.).

Today, all the basic instruments of action in the field of education in Spain seek to address diversity issues; it is one of the principles of the current Education Act, enacted in 2006.[3] The autonomous communities are required by basic state regulations to procure the necessary resources for adaptation; schools design strategies, etc.

---

This study was conducted as part of the research project "Federal System between Diversity Integration and Stability" 2011–2013, financed by the Ministry of Science and Innovation.

[1] Ley Orgánica General del Sistema Educativo of 3 October 1990 (published in the Official State Gazette (BOE) on 4 October 1990).

[2] Provided for in Article 27 of the Spanish Constitution.

[3] Ley Orgánica 2/2006 de Educación, 3 May 2006. Published in the *Official State Gazette (BOE) No. 106 of 4 May, 2006.*

M.G. Azurmendi (✉)
Facultad de Ciencias Sociales y de la Información, Universidad del País Vasco/ Euskal Herriko Unibertsitatea
e-mail: miren.gorrotxategi@ehu.es

A. López-Basaguren and L. Escajedo San Epifanio (eds.), *The Ways of Federalism in Western Countries and the Horizons of Territorial Autonomy in Spain*, Vol. 2, DOI 10.1007/978-3-642-27717-7_33, © Springer-Verlag Berlin Heidelberg 2013

Nonetheless, this concern is not exclusive to Spain. In 1990, the World Conference on Education for All discussed, *inter alia*,[4] the world community's endeavours to guarantee everyone—children and adults—the chance to avail of the educational opportunities on offer to satisfy their basic learning needs. UNESCO echoed this concern in the Salamanca Statement of 1995.[5] More recently, on 17 June 2010, the European Council approved the education objectives for the decade 2010–2020, one of which is *Inclusive education, diversity and interculturality: A right to difference without a difference in rights*.[6]

As the title suggests, this concern for diversity does not originate exclusively in the area of education. The rhetoric of "addressing [school] diversity issues" is full of terms such as integrating education, equality, inequality, compensatory measures, discrimination, interculturality, right to difference, etc., which are also characteristic—in use and intentionality—of other sectors. In the postmodernist discourse, renewed importance is given to the individual, his or her particularities, identity, personal development, etc. It is a common approach in all the social sciences to stress the diversity that characterises our society and the need to address it, looking for its positive side, highlighting and developing strategies that will serve it, encouraging values that respect it, etc. The cultural nature of the difference reflected in the title of this objective is an example of the central importance that cultural diversity has acquired in the debate on equality. Inequality is measured not solely in material terms but also in terms of the guarantee of living the difference offered to particular identities.[7]

Indeed, judging by the content of documents containing public policies at different levels, interculturalism has proved itself to be the best strategy for coping with the multicultural societies in which we live. The Council of Europe launched its

---

[4] Approved at the World Conference on Education for All, held in Jomtien, Thailand, 5–9 March, 1990. Naturally, diversity was not the only topic addressed; the conference concentrated particularly on universal access to education.

[5] Salamanca Statement and Framework for Action on Special Needs Education, passed on 10 June 1995 at the World Conference on Special Needs Education: Access and Quality, sponsored by UNESCO and organised by the Spanish government and held in Salamanca on 7–10 June 1995.

[6] Objective 12. On 25 June 2010, a cabinet meeting of the Spanish government approved the Action Plan 2010–2011, developing on these objectives. The plan includes measures for meeting each of the 12 benchmarks—although it is true that the target on diversity refers mainly to diversity resulting from disability.

[7] Political philosophy has studied in great detail the paradigm shifts that take place as a reaction to the homogenising trend of modernist liberalism, as well as the multicultural and communitarist alternatives and even the alternatives based on identitary liberalism that have been posed to combat this trend. Charles Taylor's Politics of Recognition and Will Kymlicka's Multicultural Citizenship (both authors are Canadian) are "globalised" discussions in this field. Various strands of feminism have analysed, to great effect, the conditions of discrimination in which social groups in a non-dominant position can live behind the facade of an inclusive regime because the universalism they posit is in no way neutral. Feminist writers have also shown better than anyone that by concealing the differences, by confining them to the private sphere, the weakest identities have been kept out of the public space—the space of political decision; here, Iris Young, whose work has been widely published, is a key reference.

*White Paper on Intercultural Dialogue "Living Together as Equals in Dignity"*.[8] The document defended the need to establish an intercultural dialogue for democratic management of a growing cultural diversity in Europe. Recently, the Council of Europe too has published its report *"Living Together": Combining diversity and freedom in 21st-century Europe*,[9] which advocates developing "intercultural competencies" in the curriculum, as a strategy for combatting a resurgence of intolerance and discrimination in Europe. In Spain, the interest in multiculturalism in the educational sphere has been reflected in the creation of the Centro de Recursos para la Atención a la Diversidad Cultural en Educación (CREADE) [Resource Centre for Addressing Issues of Cultural Diversity in Education][10] in 2006.

The commitment to interculturalism evokes the peaceful and enriching coexistence of different cultures within the same political and legal area and involves a certain degree of tolerance by the cultural majority towards minority practises in the conflictive context that can arise out of diversity. But what, specifically, does interculturalism consist of? And what about interculturalism in the school area?

## Religious Dietary Laws

If "we are what we eat", then it is equally true that "we eat what we are". Anthropologists use this new aphorism to highlight the fact that the way we eat is conditioned not only by our biological circumstances but also by our psycho-social ones.[11]

Why do we not eat certain foodstuffs that are biologically edible? Dogs, insects, pigs, etc. are consumed in some places and considered repugnant in others.[12]

The origin of different cultures' food taboos and whether or not they reflect rational criteria (ecological, technological, economic, etc.) are immaterial. The fact is that food taboos and rules are sometimes dictated by ideological and religious lines.[13] We learn good food choices from a collective knowledge forged over

---

[8] At the Ministerial Session of 7 May, 2008. Document available at http://www.coe.int/t/dg4/intercultural/Source/Livre%20blanc%20final%20FR%20020508.pdf.

[9] Report by the Council of Europe Group of Eminent Persons, 2011.

[10] The CREADE is a project of the *Instituto de Formación del Profesorado, Investigación e Innovación Educativa* (IFIIE) [Institute for Teacher Training, Educational Research and Innovation] and thus of the Ministry of Education. https://www.educacion.gob.es/creade/index.do.

[11] Contreras Hernández and Gracia Arnáiz (2005).

[12] Ibid. p. 38.

[13] It is often difficult to determine the origins of the prescriptions, among other reasons, due to their antiquity (some of the Jewish laws, for example, date back to the times of Noah). Anthropologists offer a number of possible reasons (the rules are an allegory of vice and virtue; they are arbitrary, and their only purpose is to discipline the faithful; they are intended to protect the faithful from external influence; they originated in food crises; they have a dietary basis, etc.), but there is no definitive consensus on the issue.

generations, and they go to form part of our belief set. Some are confirmed by experience; others, such as fasting, the quest for the sacred and religious prohibitions are entirely symbolic or magical. By following all these food prescriptions, we contribute to a food culture, giving food a profound symbolic value. Through certain food habits, the individual identifies with a given social group; sharing the same food customs strengthens the feeling of belonging to a community.[14]

Food prescriptions are a common feature of many religions. Whether as a way of communicating with God, of demonstrating faith through the acceptance of divine rulings on diet—in other words, to develop a disciplined, solidarity-led, reflective attitude, etc. (fasting, for example)—it is common for religions to concern themselves with our food and to issue edicts on what we can and cannot eat; they nearly all ban some form of food, either entirely or at certain times of year; they may also encourage the consumption of certain products at specific times.

In the case of Christianity, for example, which considers gluttony to be one of the Seven Deadly Sins, the strong anthropocentrism[15] of the faith makes food freedom the general rule, although there are certain rules, conceived mainly as acts of penitence, purification, and reinforcement of the faith. So, for example, eating meat is forbidden on Fridays during Lent and fasting is prescribed before receiving communion.

However, Judaism and Islam are much stricter in matters of food. They have explicit food codes in their holy texts that affect not only the consumption of certain foodstuffs but also the way in which they are obtained and prepared; these precepts draw a strict differentiation between food that is considered pure or acceptable and food that is classed as impure or unacceptable.

People of Islamic faith consider food to be *halal* or pure if it respects the prescriptions contained in the Qur'an. These include a prohibition on eating the fat or flesh of the pig and specific rites for slaughtering animals for food; among other things, these must ensure that the animal is fully bled. If these rules are not complied with, the food is considered to be *haraam* or impure. The reason for branding some food as impure is related to God's will to protect people and maintain the integrity and health not only of their bodies but also of their minds and spirits. The way one eats places a profound value on the relationship between the Creator's products and the human being.[16]

Islam also prescribes periods of fasting, most importantly the month of Ramadan. During this time, the faithful cannot eat or drink from dawn to dusk—although especially vulnerable people (the elderly, pregnant women, etc.) are exempt. During this period, Muslims are called upon to intensify their relationship with

---

[14] Ibid.

[15] In which nature is seen as being a context at the service of mankind, according to Bizzarri and Pelanda (2008), p. 26.

[16] Bizzarri and Pelanda (2008), pp. 33–34.

Islam; fasting is a way of rooting important values such as patience, determination, solidarity, discipline, etc.[17]

As for Judaism,[18] *Kashrut* is the body of religious law contained in the *Torah* dealing with food. It determines when a particular foodstuff is *kosher* or pure and when it is *treif* or impure. Judaism bans the consumption, among other things, of pork and shellfish. Meat and milk must be kept separate. It also prohibits the consumption of animal blood, necessitating specific rites of slaughter and culinary procedures.[19] For Jews, food rules are a way of bringing the sacred into their everyday lives; the more they live their lives in accordance with the dictates of the *Torah*, the holier their lives will become,[20] whatever the reasons for the imposition.[21] There are a number of special days when fasting is compulsory for Jews. The most solemn, most celebrated, and strictest of these is *Yom Kippur*, the Day of Atonement, when Jews gather in the synagogue to hold a special service and cannot eat, drink, labour, or indulge in entertainment.

## School Canteens

Values associated with food and healthy eating are increasingly being learnt outside the home and, to a large degree, at school. The importance of the school canteen has not escaped the attention of public authorities, who consider it to be a *complementary part of schooling*. With varying degrees of detail, the rules generally charge the school canteen with some important educational, compensatory, and integrational functions.

In the school canteen, children learn habits of hygiene, good behaviour, and notions of good nutrition. The existence of a school canteen means that children living at a distance from urban centres can spend the full day at school. Because of the policy of subsidising the canteen service, low-income families can be sure that their school-aged children are being well fed. The work-life balance would be much more complicated than it already is if this service did not exist; in some families, it would be impossible for both parents to work outside the home, with all the social and economic consequences that would entail. School is a basic area of socialisation, and within that framework, the dining room is a place of contact and social integration. Having all the children engaged in the same activity of the same quality allows for a degree of equality and encourages responsibility, solidarity, etc.

---

[17] On the functions of fasting, see www.sufi.it/islam/ramadan_focus.htm.

[18] According to the Federation of Jewish Communities in Spain, http://www.fcje.org/.

[19] The rules mentioned here are only some of those contained in the sacred texts of Jews and Muslims. There are many studies in the field of food anthropology that offer a more exhaustive description of the food precepts of these and others religions.

[20] Bizzarri and Pelanda (2008), p. 17.

[21] The website of the Federation of Jewish Communities in Spain offers a secularised perspective on food laws, claiming that they have been shown by modern science to be best for human health.

In other words, bear in mind that

> Education is a basic human right and we must therefore offer students at all levels of the
> education system an inclusive, intercultural, and plural education in which all pupils learn
> to relate to each other, from a position of respect, to coexist with those different to
> themselves,... to promote educational environments that stimulate the participation of all
> pupils, promote social relations and school success of all students. We must achieve
> effective educational inclusion, governed by the principles of addressing issues related to
> diversity of conditions, origins and cultures; guaranteeing effective equality of
> opportunities and reconciling quality with fairness in the resources and support provided
> to make up for individual inequalities; in particular, those arising out of disability.[22]

The school canteen can be seen as an ideal venue in which to address diversity in general and religious diversity in particular. It offers a test ground for the exercise of religious freedom[23] and a rare opportunity to try out interculturalism. From the perspective of addressing diversity issues, therefore, it seems consistent that the important symbolic value assigned to food should be taken into account when preparing school menus. As well as respecting essential dietary rules, it should be possible for all pupils to eat school meals without contravening their religious food rules.

## What Diversity?

Recent conflicts over the presence of elements of religious significance—such as the veil, the *burqa*, mosques, ritual slaughter, crucifixes, etc.—sits uneasily with our idea of an "intercultural" society. In a global context marked by a fear of religious fundamentalism, they appear to reflect the tension caused by proposals based on a social recognition of diversity.

Here, it is important not to lose sight of the fact that the increase in religious diversity has much to do with the number of immigrants. The fear of terrorist attacks carried out in the name of religion has become a fear of the consequences of the impossible integration of certain (Muslim) immigrants. This has led to the emergence in our societies of a sort of "coercive integration"[24] that is strongly culturalist in nature. The perception that immigrants are particularly religiously devout has often led to a shift in the debate on the exercise of religious freedom from the field of fundamental rights to the field of immigration.

The school sphere is no exception.

In effect, if we focus on food habits in relation to religious prescriptions, it is reasonable to deduce that the secularisation of our societies has made such norms more flexible, as has been the case with other religious rules. In addition, given that Christianity (the majority religion in Spain) has few rules, it is logical that the only

---

[22] Extract from the measures related to Spanish Government Objective 12, cited in Note 6.

[23] The notion of the canteen as an opportunity is reflected in the Guide to Managing Religious Diversity in Schools in Catalonia, 2010.

[24] Pajares Alonso (2009).

(civil) "religion" afforded any weight in regard to food is health. The result has been the development of what has been termed "food sectarianism"[25] associated with this creed. Often, when the issue of adapting school menus to religious prescriptions is raised, there are those who argue that immigrants should assimilate Spanish eating habits.

Yet this approach seems ill-suited to a position of interculturalism; however, it is defined. Immigrants have no choice but to adapt many of their eating habits; the reason is not only because they have difficulty finding particular products from their native cuisine (or because they prefer local products) but also because they are swept along by the social dynamic in terms of meal times, numbers of meals, etc. At the same time, migratory movements commonly result in assimilations of culinary culture. An example can be seen in the range of Jewish cuisines, which vary depending on the place in which they were developed by the diaspora.[26] However, requiring a renunciation of religious food laws as a sign of successful integration is far more adaptation than any interculturalist could ask.

Moreover, secularisation is a sociological not a legal issue. The fact that religion has been subjectivised, with each individual reconstructing it to his or her own criteria, or that religion has lost some of its ability to dictate the meaning of different conduct does not oblige us to make religious observance more flexible. From a perspective open to diversity, it seems more logical that whether one chooses to live a secularised religion[27] or a practising religion (or, indeed, an anti-religious practise) should be a personal and available option.

Nonetheless above all, school food compliant with religious precepts is not (only) an issue of integrating immigration; it is to a great degree a matter of exercising religious freedom. Despite the secularist trend towards considering religion as a form of culture,[28] it is important to remember that the issue at stake here is not one of (culinary) culture. Rather, it is a mandate derived from a religion that may be just as deeply rooted in "Spanish culture" as any that does not have such mandates (one should not forget that there was an Islamic and Jewish presence in Spain quite some time before Spain became a target country for immigrants).

Thus the issue can only be approached, in legal terms, from the perspective of the exercise of religious freedom. Do school canteens guarantee the provision of food that is in accordance with different religions? Is there any way pupils can use the school canteen service without renouncing their religious practice? Is it legally discriminatory that the menus served in school canteens do not take into account the beliefs of religious minorities?

---

[25] Contreras, p. 424, referring to veganism, vegetarianism, and other current trends.

[26] Specifically, one can distinguish between Sephardic, Ashkenazic, and Levantine culinary modes, according to Bizzarri and Pelanda (2008), op. cit.

[27] This is not the form preferred by Pope Benedict XVI. Addressing the World Youth Day events in Madrid (16–18 August 2011), he called on young people not to follow God "on their own".

[28] Secularisation always grows out of a given religion that has already contributed to modelling the customs of the society. Some of its dictates are assimilated—stripped of their religious connotations—and as a result, religion is seen as the value system of a given culture that does not involve strict compliance with the religious practice.

# Freedom and Food in Spain

The existence of various "profound beliefs" should not constitute a problem in a democracy; one of the pillars on which our societies and our states are founded is precisely the recognition that pluralism is a constitutive factor of society. When a democratic state addresses the religious issue legally, it must therefore do so from a secular perspective.

Secularity requires, on the one hand, that the state should be neutral with regard to religion. This means that it cannot favour any one religion and must allow civil society absolute freedom in its religious option; that choice is guaranteed the protection of the state through the recognition of religious freedom. At the same time, secularism requires the separation of church and state, in the sense that no religion's dogmas may become the bases for action or the parameters for validating the public authority.

However, once these necessary features are in place, secularism can take different forms. Depending on the level of public recognition it reserves for religion, the state may practise a more open secularism (recognising the importance of religion for society and accepting some of the consequent legal implications) or a more closed one (in which religion is viewed as something that should not occupy the public authorities or even as something from which society must be defended). Likewise, it may intervene, to a greater or lesser extent, in safeguarding the exercise of religious freedom for religious minorities.

Focusing on the menu of school canteens, the fact that it is not possible to provide food that conforms to the pupils' religious precepts represents a restriction on the exercise of their religious freedom. Yet as we know, rights are not absolute; in the case of religious freedom, the scope of the right depends, to a great extent, on how the concept of secularism has been constructed in law. In the case of Spain, would catering to specific food requirements mean violating the principle of state secularism? Or on the contrary, would it be discriminatory not to cater to specific food requirements in the school canteen?

## *Religious Freedom in the 1978 Spanish Constitution*

The first legal tier defining the characteristics of a state's secularism is its Constitution. Article 16 of the Spanish Constitution lists religious freedom, among the highest ranking of fundamental rights,[29] in the following terms:

---

[29] Rights for which the greatest level of legal guarantee is provided: the requirement that it must be developed by an Organic Law, which must respect the essential content of the right; the possibility of appealing against a law on the grounds of unconstitutionality to the Constitutional Court, which may invalidate a law even if it has been passed by a significant parliamentary majority; the possibility for anyone who considers their right to have been violated to make an application for defence of basic constitutional rights [*recurrir en amparo*] first to the ordinary courts and then also to the Constitutional Court.

1. Freedom of ideology, religion and worship of individuals and communities is guaranteed, with no other restriction on their expression than may be necessary to maintain public order as protected by law.
2. No one may be compelled to make statements regarding his religion, beliefs or ideologies.
3. There shall be no state religion. The public authorities shall take the religious beliefs of Spanish society into account and shall consequently maintain appropriate cooperation with the Catholic Church and the other confessions.

Constitutional jurisprudence has clarified the scope of this article in two directions. On the one hand, religious freedom contains an individual right that, in turn, has two manifestations, one internal and the other external. In its internal dimension, religious freedom involves the absolute freedom of the individual to adopt the religious beliefs he/she sees fit. As a consequence, nobody may be obliged to declare his beliefs. In its external dimension, it guarantees that people may adapt their behaviour to the imperative of their own convictions, without interference from the state or from private individuals, with no other limitation than a respect for public order protected by law, which is interpreted as a respect for others in the exercise of their public freedoms and fundamental rights, as well as the safeguarding of public safety, health, and morality.[30] Moreover, Article 16 guarantees that this right will be exercised collectively, with immunity from coercion and without hindrance or disruption of any kind.

At the same time, the Constitution requires the public authorities to take into account the religious beliefs of Spanish society and to enter into cooperation agreements with the different religious faiths and denominations (an example of open secularism). In addition, the Constitutional Court[31] has related this right to Article 9.2 of the Constitution, which makes it incumbent upon the public authorities to promote conditions that ensure that the freedom and equality of individuals and of the groups to which they belong may be real and effective and not merely empty formulae. In other words, the state's neutrality with regard to religion cannot consist of doing nothing but of acting to allow it to be developed effectively. Constitutional jurisprudence appears to back the interpretation that sees in religious freedom a certain duty of provision on the part of the state.[32]

---

[30] Nonetheless, the Constitutional Court has accepted other limitations on the right, insofar as its expression would require from third parties some considerable effort in order to adapt. This was the case of the employee of a business who had adopted a religion that prohibited her from working on Saturdays; she asked her employer to be exempted from working on that day and to be allowed to work some other day in lieu. Her dismissal for unauthorised leave, following a failure to reach agreement, was not deemed by the CC to be an infringement of her religious freedom (STC 19/1985 of 13 February 1985). However, in a similar case, the Supreme Court of Canada ruled just the opposite (STCS 17 December 1985).

[31] STC 46/2001 and 38/2007, for example.

[32] Albeit not an absolute one, for example, when CC was asked to rule on whether the state should require the public health-care service to provide alternative treatment in order to ensure compatibility with different religious faiths, it concluded that no such right to provision for individuals exists; by extension, it also determined that there was no requirement to reimburse patients for the medical expenses incurred in a private clinic in order to comply with these religious requirements (STC 166/1996).

# Organic Law 7/1980, of 5 July 1980, on Religious Freedom[33]

The fundamental rights recognised in the Constitution must be developed by an Organic Law. This law, while respecting the essential content of the right, must provide the legislature with the option of regulation within the framework of the possibilities admitted by the constitution. In Spain, the right to religious freedom has primarily been developed in Organic Law 7/1980 of 5 July 1980 on religious freedom.[34]

Article 1 of the law reiterates the state's non-denominationalism (open secularism) as established in the Constitution and adds that religious beliefs cannot constitute grounds for inequality or discrimination before or in the application of the law. The law goes on to specify the way in which the state must fulfil its duty to take into account the religious beliefs of Spanish society.

In the exercise of religious freedom in its internal dimension, the law specifies that any person has the right to profess the religious beliefs that they freely choose or to not profess any, to change faith or abandon that which they had, freely to manifest their own religious beliefs or absence thereof, or to refrain from manifesting them.

The external dimension of the exercise of religious freedom encompasses actions such as practising acts of worship and receiving religious assistance in their own faith, commemorating its feast days, celebrating its matrimonial rites, receiving appropriate burial without discrimination on religious grounds, and not being obliged to practise acts of worship or receive religious assistance that contravenes their personal convictions. It also establishes the right to receive and give religious teaching and information of all kinds and to choose religious and moral education in accordance with their personal convictions. It includes the right to gather or demonstrate publicly for religious purposes and to associate with others for the purposes of performing religious activities as a community. With regard to churches, faiths, and religious communities, the law recognises the right to establish places of worship or meeting for religious purposes, to appoint and train ministers, to disclose and promulgate the creed, to maintain relations with their own organisations or with other religious faiths in Spain or abroad.

As for the duty placed on the state by the Constitution to take an active role, the law establishes that for the real and effective application of these rights, the public authorities shall adopt the necessary measures to facilitate religious assistance in public, military, hospital, care, prison, and other establishments under their control, as well as religious education in public education centres.

---

[33] There are numerous monographic works on this Law in Spain. Recently, Navarro Valls et al. (2009).

[34] The law has remained on the books for over thirty years despite a significant evolution in the challenges faced by the state in religious matters. In 2008, the parliamentary *party Esquerra Republicana. Izquierda Unida-Iniciativa Cataluña Verts* unsuccessfully sought to table a motion to have the law amended. In 2010, the Spanish government announced that the Council of Ministers was seeking to approve an amendment bill to be tabled in parliament, but this never materialised.

In addition, the law establishes how the state should maintain relations of cooperation with religious faiths operating in Spain; by means of agreement with the churches, faiths and religious communities entered in the Register, which by their scope and number of members may be considered to be manifestly established in Spain. It adds that, in all cases, these agreements shall be approved by an act of the national parliament (*Cortes Generales*).

The provision for separate agreements with the faiths is clearly a way of allowing a special relationship between the state and the Catholic Church, although given the duty of secularism, it has to be extended to all religions with a manifest degree of establishment in Spain. The end result is that in addition to the protection afforded by the law to any individual in the exercise of their religious freedom, there are certain faiths (or members thereof) whose religious rights are to be established as specific obligations to be fulfilled by the state. The existence of agreements with certain faiths and not with others introduces an element of differentiation between religious groups in their relations with the state.

Regardless of whether this option is legitimate and consistent with the principle of secularism, one might argue that it at least offers a commitment by the state to the religious rights of certain persons, that setting down a religious practice in an agreement appears to reinforce the guarantees that ordinary law might provide.

## The Agreements Between the Spanish State and the Manifestly Established Religous Faiths in Spain[35]

The Spanish state has entered agreements with four faiths (all of which are still in force). The first was with the Catholic faith, the majority religion in Spain, and took the form of an International Agreement signed in 1979.[36] In 1992, following a lengthy negotiation process, it signed a further three agreements that obtained wide parliamentary backing with the three leading minority faiths in Spain: Evangelical,[37] Jewish,[38] and Islamic.[39]

For the state, the task of negotiation fell to the Under-Directorate-General for Religious Affairs, which forms part of the Directorate-General for Religious Affairs and Conscientious Objection of the Ministry of Justice.[40] As for the faiths, there were essentially two requirements for acting as interlocutors with the government. These related to the persons who could be the negotiators and the level of presence they should have in society to be accepted as interlocutors.

---

[35] With regard to the contents of the agreements, see *Acuerdos del Estado español con los judíos, musulmanes y protestantes*, Publicaciones Universidad Pontificia de Salamanca 1994.

[36] By means of cooperation agreements between Spain and the Holy See of 3 January, 1979.

[37] Act 24/1992, of 10 December 1992.

[38] Act 25/1992, of 10 December 1992.

[39] Act 26/1992, of 10 December 1992.

[40] However, in the case of the Catholic Church, given the interstate nature of the agreement, the Ministry for Foreign Affairs took charge.

They had to form a single entity representing the different trends existing within the faith, so that each faith was represented by a single interlocutor at the talks and could assume the same right and obligations for all of them. All communities belonging to a religion entered in the Ministry of Justice's Registry of Religious Organisations therefore had to agree on the composition of a representative committee, which was assigned a legal personality of its own (through registration) with the capacity to negotiate, agree, and monitor the agreements. These bodies are:

- The *Federación de Entidades Religiosas Evangélicas Españolas* (FEREDE) [Federation of Spanish Religious Evangelical Entities];[41]
- The body known since 2004 as the *Federación de Comunidades Judías de España* (FCJE) [Federation of Jewish Communities in Spain],[42] known at the time of signing the agreement as the *Federación de Comunidades Israelitas de España* [Federation of Israelite Communities of Spain];
- The *Comisión Islámica de España* (CIE) [Islamic Commission of Spain ],[43] made up of the two Islamic federations (which in turn comprise several different Islamic communities): the *Unión de Comunidades Islámicas de España* (UCIE) [Union of Islamic Communities of Spain][44] and the *Federación Española de Entidades Religiosas Islámicas* (FEERI) [Spanish Federation of Islamic Religious Entities].[45]

In addition, in order to be qualified to negotiate, the faiths had to be recognised by the Advisory Committee on Religious Freedom (an organ of the public administration created by the Religious Freedom Act and answerable to the Ministry of Justice) as religions manifestly established in Spain. This classification was awarded on the basis of their geographical extension and how long they had been operating in Spain. The classification of "manifest establishment" was awarded in 1985 to Evangelicals[46] and Jews[47] and in 1989 to Muslims.[48]

---

[41] http://www.redevangelica.es/.

[42] http://www.fcje.org/.

[43] The lack of a common source of information on this faith and the need to rely on two separate bodies (the UCIDE and the FEERI) are an example of the difficulty of integrating all the Islamic movements in Spain. As a result, the Spanish government issued *Royal Decree 1384/2011, of 14 October 2011, developing Article 1 of the cooperation agreement between the state and the Islamic Commission of Spain*, in order to overcome the difficulties faced by newly registered Islamic communities (30% of the total) in joining the common body.

[44] http://es.ucide.org.

[45] http://feeri.eu.

[46] According to FEREDE, there are currently approximately 1,200,000 Protestants, of whom 400,000 are Spanish and 800,000 non-nationals: Of the latter, the immense majority are EU citizens and a small percentage are Latin American. They are represented with places of worship in all towns of over 20,000 inhabitants and in the majority with over 15,000.

[47] According to the FCJE, there are currently around 40,000 in Spain. They have specific schools for infant, primary and secondary education, some of which—for example in Murcia—are state subsidised [*concertados*]. There are over 30 synagogues in Spain. The website of the faith also offers information on catering companies providing *kosher* food in Spain.

[48] According to information published by several Islamic media outlets, in 2010 there were approximately one and a half million Muslims in Spain (3% of the Spanish population), with 785 mosques and 14 *almacabras* (cemeteries).

The internal structure of the three agreements is very similar. They include a regulation that can be adjusted to each religion on places of worship and burial, ministers, regulation of marriage, religious assistance, education and teaching, economic and fiscal regime, and religious festivities. The differences in the issues addressed relate to references to questions of heritage conservation and food issues in the case of the agreements with the Jewish and Islamic religions.

The issue of food is regulated in Articles 14 of the respective agreements, although the content varies.

– Article 14 of the state agreement with the FCJE (FCI in the text of the Agreement) states that

> In accordance with the spiritual dimension and the specific particularities of the Jewish tradition, the names "casher" [kosher] and its variants, "kasher", "kosher", kashrut" and those associated with the terms "U", "K" or "parve", shall be used to distinguish food and cosmetic products prepared in accordance with Jewish Law.
>
> For the purpose of protecting the proper use of these terms, the F.C.I. must request and obtain from the Registry of Industrial Property the corresponding brand registrations, in accordance with current regulations.
>
> These requirements having been met, these products, for the purposes of marketing, importation and exportation shall be guaranteed to have been prepared in accordance with Jewish Law and tradition, when the packaging bears the corresponding sign of the F.C.I.
>
> The slaughter of animals in accordance with Jewish law must respect current health regulations.

– Article 4 of the state agreement with the CIE states:

1. In accordance with the spiritual dimension and specific particularities of Islamic law, the name "halal" shall be used to distinguish food products prepared in accordance therewith.
2. For the purpose of protecting the proper use of these terms, the "Comisión Islámica de España" must request and obtain from the Registry of Industrial Property the corresponding brand registrations, in accordance with current regulations.
3. These requirements having been met, these products, for the purposes of marketing, importation and exportation shall be guaranteed to have been prepared in accordance with Islamic Law and tradition, when the packaging bears the corresponding sign of the "Comisión Islámica de España".
4. The slaughter of animals in accordance with Islamic laws must respect current health regulations.
5. An attempt shall be made to ensure that the food of those interned in public centres or establishments and military facilities, and that of Muslim pupils attending public and private state-subsidised education centres who so request, is adapted to Islamic religious precepts and to meal times during the month of Ramadan.

As we can see, these two agreements contain references to the existence of brands and certificates of food quality, i.e., they provide legal backing for the appearance of a brand to avoid fraudulent practice with regard to the nature of these foodstuffs. This implicitly involves valuing a religious issue as a decisive factor in consumer information. Moreover, in the case of Muslim pupils, the agreements established an obligation to procure foodstuffs in keeping with religious beliefs in school canteens. Additional Provision One of the three Agreements establishes a requirement obliging the state to notify the religious communities of any legislative initiatives affecting the content of the agreements in order to enable them to make the relevant submissions. Additional Provision Two establishes the obligation to form joint committees (between the government and the religious entity) for monitoring and applying the agreement, and the Final Provision authorises the Ministry of Justice, together with other ministers concerned, where necessary, to develop and execute the agreements.

Therefore, at least in the case of Muslim pupils, the provision of food in accordance with religious precepts in school canteens is an obligation that must be guaranteed by the state, unless there should exist any higher reason preventing it. However, despite the rights and procedures described in these laws, it is important to bear in mind that the laws merely contain the general rules and outline the structure of the questions to be considered with regard to any given theme. They subsequently need to be developed in law, a function that is performed by areas of action, by means of sectoral laws or regulations, issued by public authorities in accordance with the distribution of powers between the state and the autonomous communities established by the Constitution and the Statutes of Autonomy. It is through this development that the law is made truly effective.

# Regulation of School Canteen Menus in Spain and Its Autonomous Communities

## Distribution of Powers between the State and the Autonomous Communities (ACs)

Following the enactment of the 1978 Constitution and with the development of the systems allowed for under Heading VIII, Spain has been structured along politically federal lines to form what is termed an "autonomic" (or regional) state. Under this constitutional arrangement, the distribution of political power follows a logic of territorial decentralisation, whereby the legislative and executive functions to act in certain matters are distributed in different jurisdictional powers that correspond exclusively, jointly or concurrently, to the autonomous communities and/or the state. Powers are distributed on the basis of the terms of the Constitution, the Statute of Autonomy of each community, establishing a regulatory framework that can, on occasions, be altered by delegation of powers in favour of the autonomy or by harmonisation of state provisions. Any dispute over the attribution of powers is resolved by the Spanish Constitutional Court.

In this system, jurisdiction over the composition of school menus depends largely on the general power for *education*, although some features are related to the area of *health*, as we shall see. Very recently, the state has begun to intervene through its powers in the area of *Relationships with Religious Faiths*, held by the Ministry of Justice.

If we look at the distribution of powers in the principal questions in which there has been regulatory intervention, we can see that

- For the development of the Basic Right to Education[49] the state reserves the power to establish the basic regulations guaranteeing fulfilment of the obligations of the public authorities in this matter.[50] In respect of these basic provisions, the Autonomous Communities, for their part, may assume powers in designing their own education policy by drafting, developing, and implementing laws. The regulation of school canteens has not been considered to a basic matter within the framework of education, hence the role of the autonomous communities.
- In matters of health care, the state reserves regulation of the bases and general coordination,[51] leaving it to the autonomous communities to develop regulations in law and to execute these bases within the framework of state coordination. The latest state law on food safety and nutrition[52] has largely been considered as basic. Insofar as it affects school canteens, its prescriptions must therefore be respected throughout the territory of the state.

By virtue of this distribution of powers, all territorial authorities have acted. The state has passed legislation, some basic and some in the form of an extension. In addition, practically all the autonomous communities[53] have issued their own regulations and strategies of action for regulating the operation of school canteens. If one analyses all of these regulations, one is struck by their diversity. Not only does the extent to which religious prescriptions are accepted or excluded as grounds for exceptions to the common menu vary, so too does the content of the different forms of regulation depending on the matter and source (regulatory or otherwise).

Certainly, if one combines these two extremes and based on the final result of a joint interpretation of all the rules and documents, one can "reduce" the diversity to four regulatory models. These consist of:

---

[49] Article 27 of the Spanish Constitution.

[50] Art. 140.1.30 of the Spanish Constitution.

[51] Art. 140.1.16 of the Spanish Constitution.

[52] Act 17/2011, of 5 July 2011, on food safety and nutrition. Official State Gazette [BOE] No. 160 of 6 July, 2011.

[53] Of the 17 Autonomous Communities in Spain, only Asturias has no regulations of its own. The two autonomous cities (Ceuta and Melilla) have both participated, together with other autonomous communities and the state in preparing the Food Guide for the PERSEO Programme, which we shall deal with separately.

- ACs that make no provisions from which one might infer a position on whether religion may be considered as grounds for an alternative menu;
- ACs that exclude religion as grounds for an alternative menu;
- ACs that leave the way open to the possibility of accepting religion as grounds for an alternative menu, though with no explicit recognition;
- ACs that expressly recognise religion as grounds for an alternative menu.

However, by looking at the combination process, one can draw important conclusions as to the way in which the public authorities consider that the food commitments acquired through the agreements with the faiths should be implemented.

## Regulatory Intervention through Jurisdictional Powers in Education

As we have already seen, the school canteen service is assigned, inter alia, important educational functions. In the school sphere, the meal is an educational act in which the uniqueness of the menu fulfils an educational function, and its preparation, independently of personal preferences, is based on a previously designed nutritional strategy. For this reason, the existence of alternative menus constitutes an exception that must be expressly regulated.

### State Intervention

The current basic regulation on education, which comes under the jurisdiction of the state, is set out in Organic Law 2/2006, of 3 May, on Education. As already mentioned, this law makes no reference to the functioning of school canteens. However, the non-basic nature of the regulation of this matter has not prevented regulatory intervention by the state.

In 1992, the state issued its *Directive regulating school canteens*. This directive, which was issued to be applied in provinces that were within the area of power of the central Spanish Ministry of Education and Science and which remains in force today as an additional regulation for autonomous communities that do not have their own regulations,[54] regulates the definition, users and management, financing and operating systems of school canteens.[55] Within this framework, the directive contains a reference to the school menu. Give that it was issued just 2 weeks after the signing of the agreements with the religious faiths, the absence of any mention of the food-related particularities for religious reasons is remarkable. The directive states that

---

[54] Asturias is the only autonomous community with no regulations in this regard, although it does have other instruments of intervention, such as the guide to *Healthy Eating and Consumer Habits*. Directorate-General of Academic Regulation and Innovation, 2005.

[55] The structure and content of this regulation have served as a general guide for drafting subsequent regional regulations on the same subject.

This menu shall be approved by the school board of the education centre in accordance with the dietary needs of the pupils.

Subsequent to the approval of the state directive, with the transfer of the corresponding functions and services, the autonomous communities have gradually assumed powers in matters of education. This includes not only responsibility for the regulation of school canteens but also the decision to implement religious freedom under the terms provided for in the agreements.

## Intervention by the Autonomous Communities

The governments of the autonomous communities have acted primarily through decrees and directives from the respective heads of the departments of education. At the same time, these regulations have been developed through circulars and instructions, intended to upgrade technical information, to adapt to the circumstances within the framework of a political strategy, or to incorporate other regulatory dictates, etc.

Analysing the general regulations of the ACs, we can see that

- No autonomous community expressly excludes religion as grounds for an alternative menu in its principal regulation.
- No autonomous community makes a direct mention to religion as grounds for justifying an alternative menu in its provisions on the school menu. Until very recently, Andalusia had a specific provision to this effect,[56] but this was removed from the 2010 directive.[57]
- There are autonomous communities whose principle regulations do not include any content on the quality of the menus from which one might infer exclusion or acceptance. This is the case of Aragon,[58] Extremadura,[59] Navarra,[60] and the Balearic Islands.[61]
- The most common situation is that religion is indirectly excluded as grounds for an alternative menu. This is the case when the list of causes, such as food allergies, intolerance to some foodstuff or other health problems and/or

---

[56] In the Directive of 27 March, 2003, which remained in force until 2010.

[57] Directive of 3 August, 2010, regulating the complementary services of morning class teaching, school canteens, and extracurricular activities in public education centres and the extension to school hours.

[58] Directive of 12 June, 2000, of the Department of Education and Science, establishing instructions for the organisation and operation of the school canteen service in public non-university education centres.

[59] Decree 192/2008, of 12 September, governing school canteen and morning class services in public centres in the Autonomous Community of Extremadura.

[60] Territorial Decree 246/1991, of 24 July 1991.

[61] Decision of 9 September 2003 of the Director of Education and Culture, regulating the organisation and operation of the school canteen service in the public non-university education centres.

requirements related to nutrition, is presented as a closed list of reasons. This is the model in the Autonomous Community of the Canary Islands,[62] Castile-Leon,[63] Galicia,[64] Cantabria,[65] Valencia,[66] La Rioja,[67] Catalonia,[68] Madrid,[69] and Murcia.[70]

– In contrast to the above case, sometimes the regulations are ambiguous and might be interpreted to allow religion to be viewed as grounds for alternative menus. This is the case when "other justified causes" are mentioned in addition to health-related causes, without explicitly stating what these might be,[71] as is the case in Andalusia[72] and the Basque Country[73] or as in the case of Castile La Mancha,[74] when a generic reference is made to other regulations and when "culture" is given as grounds for the provision of an alternative menu.

In principle, the secondary regulation contained in the Circular and Instructions might be presumed to contribute nothing new to the treatment of religious freedom. Yet, on occasions, through these regulations, the content of the principal regulation is nuanced, altering the consideration of the religious grounds. This happens when

---

[62] Directive of 25 February 2003, governing the organisation and operation of school canteens in public non-university education centres under the Ministry of Education, Culture and Sports and establishing the rules for convening posts and grants for pupils eating at school.

[63] Decree 20/2008 of 13 March 2008, governing the public school canteen service, and Directive edu/693/2008, of 29 April 2008, developing Decree 20/2008. See also the Food Guides for the school canteens of Castile and Leon, regional ministry of education, 2005.

[64] Decree 10/2007, of 25 January, governing the operation of school canteens in public non-university education centres under the Consellería of Education and University Regulation.

[65] Directive EDU/27/2007, of 10 May, 2007, governing operation of the complementary school canteen service in public non-university education centres under the regional ministry of education.

[66] Directive 47/2010, of 28 May, of the regional ministry of education, governing the school canteen service in non-university education centres owned by the regional government.

[67] Directive 27/2006, of 28 September, of the regional ministry of education, culture and sport, governing the organisation and operation of the school canteen service in public non-university education centres under the regional ministry of education, culture and sport of La Rioja.

[68] Decree 160/1996, of 14 May 1996 governing the school canteen service.

[69] Directive 917/2002 of 14 March, of the regional ministry of education, regulating the collective school canteens in public non-university education centres in the Community of Madrid, amended by Directive 4212/2006, of 26 July 2006. See also the *service of nutritional advice on the school menu* (http://www.madrid.org/menuescolar) provided by the community.

[70] Decree No. 97/2010, of 14 May 2010, establishing the nutritional characteristics of menus and the encouragement of healthy eating habits in non-university education centres.

[71] The decision is therefore left up to the individual school boards.

[72] As per the aforementioned Regulation of 2010.

[73] Directive of 22 March, 2000, of the Director of Education, Universities and Research, regulating school canteens in public non-university education centres in the Autonomous Community of the Basque Country at compulsory education and infant education stages (2nd cycle).

[74] Directive of 2 March, 2004, governing the organisation and operation of the school canteen service.

– The Instruction ring-fences an interpretation that could be deemed to be open to being interpreted on religious grounds, by developing the causes of exclusion of the common menu only in terms of health issues. This is the case in the Basque Country;[75]

– The Instruction indirectly opens the way to the consideration of religious grounds. This is the case in Extremadura,[76] which regulates the existence of alternative menus and, together with the exclusions on health grounds, makes mention of "other duly justified grounds". This is also the case in the Balearic Islands,[77] in referring back to the Consensus Document on School Food approved by the Inter-territorial Council of the National Health System,[78] in which, inter alia, religious and cultural reasons are given as grounds for allowing an alternative menu;

– The Instruction expressly includes "properly based reasons of a religious nature" as grounds for an alternative menu although there is no explanation of what the proper base consists of. This is the case in the Canary Islands.[79]

## Legislative Intervention Through Jurisdictional Powers in Health

The school canteen establishes eating habits that, whether they are correct or not, will be maintained throughout the rest of the pupil's life.[80] Given that nutrition is very closely related to health associated with good eating,[81] proper eating at school age will not only allow children to grow up healthily; if it encourages them to maintain these habits into adult life, it will also ensure that they remain in good health, hence the need for regulatory intervention in school canteens on health grounds.

Among the actions that the public authorities can develop in the field of health, there are two perspectives that have managed to permeate the matter of school food. Firstly, there is the perspective of food safety and hygiene and, subsequently, the

---

[75] Circular of the Regional Under-Ministry of Administration and Services, issuing instructions for the operation of school canteens under direct management, from academic year 2011/2012.

[76] Instruction 1/2011 of the public-sector body of complementary educational services of Extremadura, governing operation of the school canteen service in the public centres of the Autonomous Community of Extremadura for academic year 2011–2012.

[77] Ruling of 9 May, 2011 of the Director General for Planning and Centres with regard to the school canteen service in public non-university education centres and 'escoles matineres'.

[78] At the session of 21 July, 2010. We shall refer to the contents in a later section.

[79] Resolution of 5 July, 2011, issuing instructions for the management and operation of school canteens of public non-university school centres for academic year 2011–2012 and of planning for academic year 2012–2013.

[80] As recognised by the PERSEO Programme (Pilot School Reference Programme for Health and Exercise against Obesity), Ministry for Health and Consumer Affairs, 2008.

[81] As stated in Act 17/2011, of 5 July, on food safety and nutrition.

perspective of nutrition. Sometimes, through its impact on the content of the menus prepared, the authorities look beyond the perspective of health care and consider questions of a religious nature.

## The Draft Royal Decree on School Canteens of March 2005

In March 2005, the Ministry for Health and Consumer Affairs, in collaboration with the Ministry of Education and Science, drew up a *Draft Royal Decree establishing the sanitary conditions for the school canteen service of the public and private non-university education centres.* This Royal Decree was designed to complement regional regulations—given that the ACs had already drawn up their regulations on the subject—to incorporate the perspective of food safety and nutrition.

Article 4, referring to menus and a balanced diet, stated that

> Alternative menus shall be offered for pupils at the centre who for reasons of health, intolerance to certain foodstuffs, religious beliefs or other duly justified circumstances may require a special menu.
>
> (. . .) When this is not possible, suitable means of conservation shall be provided in order for the schoolchildren to store food prepared at home until such time as it is to be consumed. Likewise, schoolchildren shall be provided with the resources necessary for heating meals previously prepared at home.

This Royal Decree was issued under the aegis of the powers reserved to the state in Article 149. 1. 16. of the Spanish Constitution of 1978, from which it may be inferred that it was intended to act as basic legislation.

The Project was presented to the Inter-territorial Council of the Health System (CISNS)[82,83] on 2 March 2005 and the content was made public by the government's communication channels and by the media.

However, the project was never approved by the government. The next session of the Inter-territorial Council, held on 29 June 2005, approved the *draft agreement on the meal service in education centres (school canteens),* a document with no regulatory power, which set out the recommendations of the CISNS and from which any reference to the religious issue had been removed.

---

[82] The Inter-territorial Council of the National Health System was founded in April 1987. Since the passing of Act 16/2003 of 28 May, on cohesion and quality in the national health system, it has been the standing body for coordination and cooperation, notification, and information of the health services among all public authorities with powers in the area of health. The members of the council are one representative from each autonomous community and an equal number of representatives of the state, giving a total of 34 members. The council's agreements are given expression in recommendations that are approved by consensus.

[83] A report of the council's activities for 2005 is available online at http://www.msps.es/organizacion/consejoInterterri/docs/actividadCisns05.pdf.

### Act 17/2011, of 5 July 2011, on Food Safety and Nutrition

This law represents the culmination of the state's intervention in the matter of school canteens from a health perspective. Moreover, it was classified as basic legislation and therefore constitutes the compulsory framework for autonomic intervention in accordance with the distribution of powers referred to above.

As well as the classic perspectives of food safety, such as the detection and elimination of physical, chemical, and biological hazards, the act takes into account the growing importance of nutritional hazards, addresses issue considered to be of topical concern—obesity, particularly among children and young people. From this perspective, the law includes initiatives that the state government of the state had already been adopting in the area, such as the NAOS strategy and the Consensus Document on School Food.

Nutrition, Physical Activities, Prevention of Obesity and Health [Nutrición, Actividad Física, Prevención de la Obesidad y Salud] (NAOS)

This is the title of Article 36 of the act,[84] which incorporates into the law the strategy begun by the Ministry for Health and Consumer Affairs, through the Spanish Agency for Food Safety and Nutrition (AESAN) in 2005, and designed to raise awareness amongst the population of the problem posed by obesity for health.[85]

It should be said that this article makes no provisions as to the grounds for exclusion of the common menu, let alone any reference to religion as a conditioning factor in designing the menus. However, it merits a place in this text because it was within the framework of this strategy, in 2006, with the collaboration of the central government's departments of education and health and some regional governments,[86] that the PERSEO Plan was designed (*Pilot school programme of reference for health and exercise, to counter obesity*), still in operation today.[87]

As part of this programme, a *General Guide for the Preparation of School Menus* was published. It sets out in detail the general rules that need to be taken into account in designing, preparing, and consuming a healthy diet from the point of view of safety and hygiene and nutrition. The guide focuses on health issues and consequently pays particular attention to the needs of pupils with food incompatibilities and allergies. However, it also contains a reference to the existence of food prohibitions of a religious nature, and Appendix D gives a list of Jewish, Muslim, and Hindu dietary features.

---

[84] In Chapter VII on healthy eating, physical activities, and prevention of obesity.

[85] Full information on the programme was published by the Spanish Ministry of Health, Social Policy and Equality at www.naos.aesan.msps.es.

[86] Andalusia, Canary Islands, Castile and Leon, Extremadura, Galicia, Murcia, Ceuta, and Melilla.

[87] The contents are available at the NAOS strategy website and on its own site at http://www.perseo.aesan.msps.es/.

Consensus Document on School Food

Part of the document, which was approved by the CISNS on 21 July 2010, was included in Article 40.5. of the Law, when it established that if the organisational conditions and facilities so permit, pupils with medically certified food allergies or intolerances should be offered an alternative menu that will not harm their health; if this is not possible, they should be provided with appropriate means of refrigeration and heating, to be used exclusively for these foodstuffs, in order that the special menu provided by the family can be conserved and consumed.

However, one should not ignore the fact that the content of the Consensus Document—which included other possibilities for an alternative menu—have been excluded. Specifically, it excludes the section that stated that

> In the case of pupils who for cultural or religious reasons require the exclusion of some type of food, provided that the organizational conditions and facilities so permit and it is economically feasible, an alternative menu shall be provided considered sufficient to cover the nutritional needs of the schoolchildren.

## The Action of the ACs: Food Guides

Practically, all the orders and decrees of the Autonomous Communities regulating operation of school canteens have traditionally included precepts relating to food safety and hygiene. Today, more and more also contain precepts related to nutrition, thus affecting the content of the menus.

However, the instrument that has played the most important role in detailing school menus has been the guide, an information document containing recommendations on the composition of the menus. These guides are generally drawn up by the health departments, on occasions with the collaboration of the education departments, and they nearly always address the issue of food from a health and nutrition-related perspective. In some cases, they even contain an extensive list of recipes.

Naturally, from this perspective, the symbolic nature of the food is not given great importance. However, in some cases, the guides include a reference to religious food particularities as a circumstance to be taken into account.

For example, the *Food Guide for School Canteens* published by the Autonomous Community of Castile La Mancha in 2004[88] states that religious and ethnic particularities must be taken into account. To a certain extent, the same is true of the guide issued in Catalonia,[89] although no reference whatsoever is made to

---

[88] Guía de Alimentación para Comedores Escolares Dirección General de Salud Pública y Participación. 2004.

[89] The government of Catalonia has published other support materials for managing religious pluralism in public institutions that deal, amongst other matters, with the issue of food. One of these focuses on teaching institutions: "Guía per a la gestió de la diversitat religiosa als centres educatius"; another on hospitals: "Guia per el respecte a la pluralitat religiosa en l'àmbit hospitalari".

religion. In the 2005 Guide *L'alimentació saludable a l'etapa escolar*, it advises schools to adapt the basic menus in cases in which pupils do not eat pork. This is a clear reference to Muslim pupils or, to be precise, to Muslim immigrants, since the guide goes on to state that "given the increase in the immigrant population in recent years, the school canteen can be turned into an interesting instrument for inter-relating different food cultures".

## *Regulatory Intervention through Jurisdictional Powers in Justice*

Very recently, the state has begun a new form of intervention in school menus through the powers it assumes in matters related to religious organisations, an area controlled by the Sub-Directorate-General of Relations with Religious Faiths, which is answerable to the Ministry of Justice.[90]

Specifically, an Observatory of Religious Pluralism in Spain has been created.[91] The observatory's main objective is "to guide public authorities in the implementation of management models suited to constitutional principles and to the regulatory framework governing the exercise of the right to religious freedom in Spain". With the launching of the observatory, the government has sought to show its interest in standardising and developing the right to religious freedom and conscience. Indeed, the institution can be said to have set in motion a deliberation on how school canteens operate from the perspective of respect for religious freedom.

Specifically, in order to provide tools for managing religious diversity, in 2011 the Observatory of the Religious Pluralism in Spain prepared (among other documents[92]) a *Guide to the public management of religious diversity in the field of food*. The following aspects of this guide (which is for information purposes and not regulatory) are of interest to the issues discussed here:

– Food, as well as being nutritional, is a social, cultural, and identitary phenomenon, which is conditioned, inter alia, by ideological and religious criteria.
– There are two food-related issues that make adaptation necessary: the area of ritual slaughter of animals and the make-up of menus.
– When individuals are in the care of a public institution, they do not have entire freedom to choose the food they eat. In such cases, the public administrations

---

[90] The Ministry of Justice includes the Office of the Secretary of State for Justice, which in turn contains three Directorates-General, one of which is in charge of international legal co-operation and relations with religious faiths. In turn, this directorate general is subdivided into three Sub-Directorates-General, each of which is exclusively engaged with one of the areas of intervention, one of which involves relationships with religious faiths.

[91] An initiative of the Ministry of Justice, the Spanish Federation of Municipalities and Provinces and the Foundation for Pluralism and Coexistence. It was published on 5 July 2011. http://www.observatorioreligion.es/.

[92] The case of the guide to managing religious diversity in hospitals is also noteworthy.

and public institutions are responsible for establishing the necessary measures for adapting the menus to the religious prescriptions of their users.
–   No references are made to non-religious ideological food prescriptions. The guide refers to the Jewish, Muslim, and Adventist faiths as being the ones whose food rules involve the greatest number of special features.
–   The Guide sets out specific recommendations such as the following:

  •   When drawing up the technical specifications for calls for tender for food service providers, make the provision of menus suited to religious precepts one of the requirements.
  •   Record the demands for adapted menus on religious grounds. This will make it possible to quantify the volume and regularity of the demands and thus to plan adaptation of the service.
  •   Consider the possibility of enabling users who practise ritual fasting to receive their diet outside the normal distribution times.
  •   The volume and regularity of the recommended measures for adaptation depend on the specific circumstances of the place in which they are to be applied.

## *Summary*

The 1992 State Agreements with Religious Faiths clearly recognise the food rights, at least of Muslim pupils, in school canteens. The legislation containing these agreements is a specific law, i.e., one that has sufficient force to take precedence over regulatory standards and other laws of a non-specific nature; it is up to the state to ensure that its own regulations and those of the CAs arising from the distribution of powers respect the content of these agreements.

Under the distribution of powers in Spain, the regulation of school canteens, as a complementary service to education, lies within the jurisdiction of the autonomous communities. As for health-related aspects of the regulation of school canteens, the Autonomous Communities are responsible for issuing regulations developing the basic state legislation, which must be coordinated by the state itself, and also for implementing all the regulations.

Spain has a wide range of legislation and documents of action regulating school canteens. There are state regulations classified as basic law, ministerial directives, autonomic directives and decrees, circulars and instructions from Directorates-General, rulings from various bodies, action plans, programmes and guides. Analysing them all, one can draw a number of clear conclusions:

–   It is true that no general regulation expressly excludes any reference to the justification of an alternative menu on religious grounds. However—and more surprisingly, given the clarity of the agreement with the Islamic Commission— no regulation expressly includes it.

– Only the Autonomous Community of the Canary Islands has included an express reference to religion through its instructions for the development of the directive regulating school canteens issued for academic year 2011/12.
– References to religious grounds for alternative menus have largely been confined to the food guides issued at regional level as part of the school food plans. However, even in this case, they are not a majority; apart from the Canary Islands, only Castile La Mancha, Catalonia, and the Balearic Islands make such a mention. Moreover, the references are strikingly reticent. Any mention tends to be succinct and lacking in any great detail in contrast to the profusion of details provided on other health-related grounds for alternative menus.[93] Moreover, they commonly explain these grounds with references to "culture" or the "multicultural area". In other words, the possibility of offering exceptions to the menu is related not so much to religious freedom in general as to the cultural and religious diversity arising from immigration.

The Ministry of Justice's involvement led to a radical change in the way the religious grounds have been reflected. For the first time, food is viewed not only in terms of its educational and nutritional value but also in terms of its symbolic value. For the first time, too, adapting school menus to conform to religious prescriptions is viewed as an obligation deriving from the fundamental right to religious freedom as regulated in Spain. For the first time, there is an undisguised mention to religion, and food specialities are expressed in far more than just anecdotic terms.

This shift into a new field of activity is only natural, bearing in mind that the Under-Directorate-General of Relations with the Faiths is entrusted with functions related to the promotion and development of religious freedom,[94] some of which have been set out in the Organic Law on Religious Freedom and in the final provision of the aforementioned agreements.

Nonetheless, it is striking that the intervention in this regard comes in the form not of regulation but of guides, in which any obligation on the agents involved is replaced by facilitation, guidance, advice, etc. Moreover, the effectiveness of the recommendations depends on circumstances that lie outside legal control.

In 2008, a parliamentary initiative[95] proposed to reform the law to include the following reference: "An attempt shall be made to adapt the food and meal times and periods of fasting to the moral and religious precepts in public centres or establishments and military facilities, and in public and state-subsidised private education centres, when any of the interested parties expressly requests".

---

[93] For example, the guide drawn up within the framework of the PERSEO Programme offered 12 pages on allergies and food incompatibilities, 2 pages on cases requiring soft diets, and just one page for information purposes, on religiously related grounds.

[94] Specifically, "the analysis, monitoring, surveillance, promotion and development of religious freedom, in coordination with the competent bodies of other departments, as well as its development in collaboration with the institutions and organisations interested in it", as well as "the preparation of draft regulations on matters pertaining to the exercise of the rights of religious freedom, in coordination with the Technical Secretariat General, and the knowledge and, where applicable, report on any draft regulations that might affect such rights".

[95] By parliamentary party Esquerra Republicana. Izquierda Unida- Iniciativa Cataluña Verts.

The proposal was not accepted.

In 2009, the Government of Spain considered the possibility of reforming the Organic Law on Religious Freedom. The reform drawn up in this period took the opportunity to issue the basic legislation (the minimum level of guarantee that would have to be respected by any regulation of the matter) on the operation of school canteens, in regard to the compatibility of school menus with the different religious beliefs present in Spanish society. Indeed, the Minister of Justice referred to the government's view of this issue in a number of public declarations. Specifically, he said that it was based on the idea that, since the canteen is a public service for all, any menu apart from the shared one could not be guaranteed for all. However, given that Muslim children must be guaranteed the possibility of eating in accordance with the dictates of their religion, the following solution was proposed: Under the (health-related) responsibility of their parents, the children could take food prepared at home to school and share the dining room with the other pupils.

This reform, promised, announced, and postponed in the context of a government weakened by a major economic crisis, was never actually enacted.

## Conclusions

Food anthropologists are fond of saying that "food has been medicalised", in reference to a form of reductionism that has extended throughout the public discourse: The food issue is viewed from a health-related perspective with absolute pre-eminence being given to nutritionists and dieticians when it comes to taking decisions in this regard. In this context, the question of whether it is wise for school canteens to respect the "ideological needs" of the pupils in preparing the menus is certainly debatable.

In addition to that—rational—enemy of religiously adapted menus, there is also another opponent: a fear or aversion of the unintegrateable immigrant, whose most striking feature is his non-Christian religion.

With logic and mistrust as enemies, and if we accept that multiculturalism—as a means of managing a diversity policy—cannot be "decreed",[96] the law does not appear to be capacitated to be the best ally of the religious freedom interpreted in terms of "diversity". The best guarantee of an interpretation that is open to diversity is to persuade society; otherwise, any law promulgated behind the back of the real situation cannot but be ineffectual.

Paradoxically, despite the lax regulation on religious food diversity in school canteens in Spain described here, the fact is that at least the most basic elements of

---

[96] Sociologist Andrea Semprini explains that the individualist and socio-cultural mutation of the public space makes dirigisme impracticable, arguing that a multicultural space is borne and develops *in vivo* in the great laboratory of society. In Semprini (2000).

the demands of Muslim pupils[97] are often catered to. Again, one could say that, whatever the law may state, society has the capacity to adapt to real needs.

However, the purpose of the law is precisely to mediate in social and other conflicts, especially when fundamental rights are at stake. The defence of such rights constitutes "the law of the weakest",[98] constructed as powerful instruments to contain the majority.

Many Muslim families prefer their children to eat at home.[99] This is a statement often heard when the issue of school food is being discussed, and it reflects the insecurity that affects these families. Whether their demands are catered to depends on the good will of school boards and the business strategy of the school food service suppliers, and this conveys the impression that decisions are improvised way and that it is all a matter of luck. As a result, this group seeks refuge in the law, demanding compliance with the cooperation agreement signed between the CIE and the Spanish state in 1992.[100] From a legal perspective, based on the legal guarantee of fundamental rights, it is not acceptable that the exercise of religious freedom depends on the last private agent involved in the school canteen service and that the person whose rights might be violated has no legal instrument to turn to in order to defend their interests.

Food in school canteens might be said to be an example of the "multi-level governance", in which various questions related to a single issue come together, each of which is resolved at different jurisdictional tiers. This confluence of perspectives and players should allow different lines of action, but they must be compatible with common actions that make it possible to see a given political vision. In the case in question, for example, the community vision of food safety and nutrition cannot be evaded in Spanish law in this regard. At the same time, it is logical that this view has not generated an obligation on catering to religious demands in school canteens; in a Europe of diversity, there is no common defining position. However, in Spain, the common view of this issue has already been decided upon: in the Constitution, in the Law on Religious Freedom, and in the Agreements with the Faiths. A common vision is common insofar as it defines the extension of the religious freedom provided for in the constitution.

Multilevel governance requires coordination of all the subjects involved in the provision of the service, and that coordination gives the law its necessary

---

[97] The demand from Muslim pupils is to be served *halal* meat. Although this demand is not generally met, it appears to be common that when the menu contains forbidden meat (such as pork), other alternative menus are offered without the meat in question. This information has been taken from the documents and annual reports of the UCIDE (http://es.ucide.org) on the situation of Muslim citizens and Islamophobia in Spain.

[98] Ferrajoli (2004).

[99] Sí (online newspaper). Madrid, 24 June 2008. http://www.sisepuede.es/noticias-gastronomia/el-menu-del-inmigrante-230620082894.html.

[100] Ibid. The refusal to satisfy the requests for religiously permitted food is based on a lack of specific legislation regulating this matter, according to the UCIDE's 2010 report on the situation of Muslim citizens and Islamophobia in Spain, http://oban.multiplexor.es/isj10.pdf.

consistency. It is this aspect that is not being fulfilled in the case that concerns us here. It is not being fulfilled because the necessary link in the chain between the agreements with the faiths and the general state regulations and particular regional ones is missing. That link lies in the hands of the central state, one of whose exclusive powers, as established in Article 149.1.1 of the constitution, is the "regulation of the basic conditions guaranteeing the equality of all Spaniards in the exercise of their rights and in the fulfilment of their constitutional duties"; religious freedom is a fundamental right, and many Spaniards profess the religious beliefs contained in the agreements.

The notable lack of consistency in the provisions governing food in school canteens between the agreements and the laws regulating the operation of school dining areas seriously restricts the exercise of the constitutional right to religious freedom in Spain.

In order to prevent the law from becoming the enemy of religious freedom and if we take this freedom seriously, the state must accept its responsibility for coordination and ensuring consistency of law and action, with legal forms that allow a true regulatory guarantee of this fundamental right.

# References

Andrea Semprini *Le Multiculturalisme*, puf, 2000 (2nd ed.)

Jesús CONTRERAS HERNÁNDEZ/ Mabel GRACIA ARNÁIZ, *Alimentación y cultura. Perspectivas antropológicas*, Ariel 2005

Luigi FERRAJOLI, *Derechos y garantías. La ley del más débil*, Trotta, 2004 (4th ed.)

PAJARES ALONSO, Miguel,"Inmigración y políticas públicas", in DE LUCAS Javier and SOLANES, Ángeles (Ed.) Equal rights: keys to integration, Dykinson, 2009.

Paola BIZZARRI, Davide PELANDA in *La fede nel piatto. Saperi e sapori del cibo dei Boveri*, Paoline, 2008, p. 26

Rafael NAVARRO VALLS, Joaquín MANTECÓN SANCHO and Javier MARTÍNEZ TORRÓN (coordinators), *La Libertad religiosa y su regulación legal*, Iustel 2009

# Cultural Diversity, Human Rights, and Democratic Process: A Case of Limits

Jordi Jaria i Manzano

**Abstract** Recent concern about sustainability, biodiversity, and environmental protection and the vitality of indigenous movements, in places like Latin America, has changed the vision of the value of the non-Western cultures and the preservation of their law and institutions. That has led to constitutional comparative law seeking new ways of integrating these indigenous communities into broader institutional complexes (i.e., the nation-state). These processes pose various questions of interest about the limits of this integration and the possibility of change and evolution within these chthonic communities.

This presentation aims to focus on the main problems raised when a particular political system or legal tradition tries to integrate radical diversity (i.e., Western and non-Western cultures and communities). In short, these problems are how to make chthonic legal traditions compatible with the culture of human rights clearly dependent on Western assumptions, how to preserve minorities from assimilation once they have been integrated into the nation-state institutional system, how to manage radical diversity within a system, and the limits placed on democratic decision-making processes at different levels by the decisions taken in lower and higher spaces of consensus. Political evolution in places like Latin America makes these questions of clear interest in the present.

This paper has been written as a result of the work carried out by the author within the research project Estado autonómico y democracia: los derechos de participación en los Estatutos de Autonomía, funded by the Spanish Ministry of Education and Science for the period 2009–2012 (DER2009-12921/sub-programme JURI) and directed by Josep M. Castellà Andreu.

J. Jaria i Manzano (✉)
Centre d'Estudis de Dret Ambiental de Tarragona, Universitat Rovira i Virgili, Av. de Catalunya 35, 43002 Tarragona, Catalonia, Spain
e-mail: jordi.jaria@urv.cat

A. López-Basaguren and L. Escajedo San Epifanio (eds.), *The Ways of Federalism in Western Countries and the Horizons of Territorial Autonomy in Spain*, Vol. 2, DOI 10.1007/978-3-642-27717-7_34, © Springer-Verlag Berlin Heidelberg 2013

# Beyond the Negation of the Diverse

## *The Nation-State and the Oblivion of Non-Western Cultures*

To make the goals of this presentation clear, I should start by saying something about the cultural matrix of our institutional reality (i.e., the nation-state as a framework for the democratic decision-making process). Even in the European Union, the most advanced case of supranational (suprastate) integration, and despite the existence of the European Parliament, the institutional structure has no popular basis; there is no European people, so to say. Although there are different forms of informal and supranational decision-making processes at regional and global levels, the nation-state is the model on which fair and accountable processes for political decision-making can be inspired. I shall discuss how cultural diversity is taken into account in these processes at intra-state, state, and supra-state levels and offer an intercultural multilevel model of (democratic and sustainable) decision building.

To start, it is necessary to take into account that nation-state is modelled on modern Western culture, which clearly has pretensions of universality. Accordingly, the nation-states model, when implanted in non-Western (i.e., colonial) contexts, has ignored or even gone against non-Western (aboriginal) cultures and become an instrument for the universalization of the Western *Weltanschauung* (Sánchez 2010, p. 281). In fact, the implantation of nation-state—first, by subjection to colonial power and then by the foundation of the new "independent" states—in the non-Western world is the result of the Western world-system absorbing new territories that, in turn, involves the implantation of capitalism as the prevailing economic pattern and technoscience as the model of (legitimate) knowledge. Then a process of cultural homogenization starts at the global level, imposing the views and practices of Western culture and marginalizing, absorbing, or wiping out other cultures.

The nation-state appears here as a space of (cultural and legal) uniformity. It allows the process of capitalist accumulation and the consolidation of an internal market, creating a territory of (economic) rationality and equality in which non-Western realities have no place. This has obviously been the case of many states in Latin America, which we shall use as examples because of the transparency with which the issues we discuss appear in this area and recent constitutional developments on cultural diversity and integration of non-Western cultures.

In its two great traditions (American and French-Continental), modern constitutionalism developed on the basis of the idea of the free individual, citizen and proprietor—at first, white, male, and bourgeois—who interacts with other individuals on an equal footing and takes part in the decision-making process in which all votes are equal.[1] The search for a rational foundation for political power

---

[1] This individualist understanding of the human being has been considered "the most important artefact of European history, fundamental for self-understanding of most individuals in the Western world" (Von Bogdandy 2006, p. 7).

led to contractualism, the idea that power has to be established by the free will of individuals to submit themselves to an authority (supposed to be necessary to protect their freedom and property). This framework contains the modern idea of constitution, with the nation-state as the authority based on this original *contrat social* or constitution. So, when constitutionalism and nation-state are implanted in a (post)colonial context, local non-Western cultures are normally ignored, or even persecuted, by the institutional structure, which is built on Western cultural assumptions.

Modern Western culture (not just politics) has its origin in the individual, an abstract and rational subject, with no social or cultural features. The individual is homme—that is to say, the fundamental unit of social being—and citoyen—the very foundation of the political community—and is the basis of Western culture's claim to be universal, the characteristic way of life of the human condition. So Western culture embodies Reason (with a capital R) and is *the* Civilization (with a capital C as well). Therefore, other cultural expressions are marginalized because it is assumed that (Western) Reason conquers the wild (natural resources) and the savages (non-Western cultures) and dominates (civilizes) them in a process of scientific progress, as Condorcet conceived.[2] Therefore, the expansion of modern Western culture around the world is interpreted as the advance of civilization versus the other (old-fashioned and obsolete) cultures, threatening them all with disappearance. As a consequence, the foundation of new nation-states during the processes of (supposed) decolonization (i.e., in Latin America during the nineteenth century) was based on the oblivion/rejection of aboriginal cultures and the building of local elites on Western patterns.

In the framework of new independent nation-states, the citizenship is seen as the way to integrate individuals raised in a non-Western cultural context into Civilization and Modernity. Rights policies, which theoretically give all citizens equal status, provide uniformity and, consequently, lead to the loss of cultural diversity. Becoming part of the institutional nation-state system means losing the characteristics of (non-Western) cultural identity. The assimilation (a-culturation) of the other is the main means by which Western institutional complexes deal with cultural diversity through such biased ideas as civilization, (high) culture, freedom, and equality, as well as savagery, folklore, obscurantism, superstition, etc. This process, which has been developing for almost two centuries in the new Latin American states, has the ultimate aim of the *desindianización* (de-indianization) of the aboriginal population and the formal integration of its members as citizens of the nation-state.

In Ecuador, for example, Simón Bolívar went beyond the former colonial power and annulled the authority of the indigenous leaders, substituting them by local officers appointed by the state (Ortiz 2010, p. 464). The new state that was founded

---

[2] Conquest and colonization implied not only political and economic occupation by the West but also the expansion of its culture (science, Universities), as American colonization shows (Fornet-Betancourt 2004, p. 122).

after independence became an institutional structure designed to serve the *criollo* elites. It was based on the patterns of European Enlightenment and despised the autochthonous cultures. So modernization is understood to be a process of cultural assimilation that aims to suppress non-Western cultures in such extensive areas of the Earth as Latin America and Africa.[3]

## *Reassessing the Worth of Cultural Diversity*

Nevertheless, the effects on our environment of the capitalist world-system and Western technoscience, based as it is on a paradigm of dominion of nature (the wild) by the human individual (civilization), have led to a reassessment of Western culture's pretensions of universality and of the (alleged lack of) value of non-Western cultures. The worth of these traditions has been defended in many cases, and it has been suggested that the transition from (Western) monoculturalism to interculturalism in which the dialogue between different cultural traditions is possible, fruitful, and even necessary can happen.

Recent concern about sustainability, biodiversity and environmental protection, and the vitality of indigenous movements (in places like Latin America) has changed understanding of non-Western cultures and the preservation of their law and institutions. The so-called chthonic traditions—that is to say, those that belong to indigenous or aboriginal peoples—can be seen as an alternative source of knowledge that can be used to find solutions in the present day. These traditions are being reassessed in an attempt to find a way to integrate the cultural diversity of particular places into the corresponding political systems. This should lead to new solutions in constitutional comparative law so that these indigenous communities can be integrated into broader institutional complexes (i.e., the nation-state). Of course, this demands rethinking the nature of nation-state as well.

There are two main reasons the value of cultural diversity and, therefore, the need to integrate different cultures within particular systems of decision should be reconsidered. First, from a utilitarian point of view, the complexity, plurality, and richness of cultural forms and the diversity of understanding of life, both human and non-human, could be a way of responding to the present situation of environmental degradation and scarcity of resources. Second, the intrinsic value of this knowledge must also be taken into account: It is a manifestation of human communities and individuals, an expression of their creativeness. Therefore, the worth of this threatened knowledge must be considered from the perspective not only of its

---

[3] Continuing with the case of Ecuador, during the drafting of the Constitution of 1945, when issues such as the plurinationality of the state and incorporation of indigenous individuals to the nation-state were considered, it was the opinion of the majority that to complete such an incorporation, they had to assimilate the Western vision of the world (Tuaza 2010, p. 467).

usefulness for us but also of its link with human dignity as an expression of human forms of life that have developed for centuries.

This raises a variety of questions about the extent to which these cultures can be integrated and what possibilities there are of change and evolution within them. In any case, the institutional reality in most of the particular cases where these cultures exist is based on Western patterns (nation-state). Therefore, diversity needs to be integrated in a particular institutional reality in such a way that the community concerned can take and share decisions. It is particularly necessary to define the basis on which this integration is built, what the language of communication is, and the common values that allow dialogue between cultures in a particular system of integrated decision-making processes.


## Non-Western Traditions, Human Rights, and Shared Decisions

### *Cultures in a Museum: Isolationism and Folklorization*

To begin this section, I should point out that diversity was (allegedly) respected by a certain alternative approach to assimilationism in the same period when the latter was adopted. The way in which this was done had the flaw that it also assumed the cultural superiority of Western culture. I call it the "isolationist" approach: "other" cultures are confined to a separate territory to preserve their singularity, but they are isolated and prevented from taking significant part in the evolution of the whole. They are treated as if they were a remnant of the past. This was the case of the Indian reservations in the U.S., for example. For reasons of isolation and marginality, the reservations were conceived as "separate land" and became (vulnerable) islands of chthonic people, which threatened their real survival as robust and healthy socio-cultural spaces.

The reported point of view does not conceal a confidence in the superiority of Western culture and therefore a deep disdain of the value of other cultures, which are regarded as little more than museum pieces. Here too the intrinsic worth of these cultures is denied, people are isolated, and cultures are believed to be frozen, as if cultural traditions were absolutely stable. As a consequence, people (individually and collectively) belonging to communities that embody a cultural perspective other than the Western one are excluded from the decision-making process, and their perspective is marginalized, thus giving the Western-inspired institutional system the exclusive right to political decisions. The multicultural interpretation pattern that inspires this point of view does not allow non-Western cultures to have a real voice in regional and global political arenas. As has been shown for national parks in their role as reservoirs of biodiversity, isolation implies musealization and banalization. Nowadays, a more holistic point of view prevails: The isolation of protected areas is insufficient because the environment works as a unit. The same can be said about humankind.

So a way must be found to give people belonging to communities based on a non-Western cultural tradition the possibility not only of having their own space of decision but also of taking part in wider decision-making processes with other people, including those belonging to communities based on Western patterns. Isolation has to be overcome if different cultural perspectives are to influence the varying levels of decision because of their intrinsic value and their contribution to enriching transcultural dialogue at different levels, in an attempt to reach a multi-level decision-making system that participants with different perspectives can be part of.

Again, the example of Latin America can be used to illustrate my argumentation. In recent decades, the indigenous movement there (with significant "national" variations in different states) has stated that there is a need to go beyond the paternalistic attitudes of the *criollo*-based nation-states towards indigenous peoples (Indians), to establish the right to preserve their cultures, and to take part in the decision-making processes, starting from the idea of autonomy and self-determination to defend a particular space of decision for the indigenous communities. The ideology underlying the idea of *mestizo*, a person of mixed-blood, consists in the alleged overcoming of the differences between aboriginal peoples and colonial/*criollo* elites and conceals a belief in the superiority of the West and an effort for assimilation. The defence of the aboriginal point of view, holistically regarded as a cultural perspective that pervades economic, political, social, and environmental issues, therefore resists being made to disappear in a *mestizo* identity and accepting Western culture at the expense of the indigenous one.

## Intercultural Dialogue and Political Pluralism

To go beyond the assimilationist and the isolationist point of view, we can no longer assume Western superiority or separate humanity into "primitive" and "advanced" societies. We have to build a fair global and regional dialogue, which gives political density to the individuals and groups that preserve the cultural heritage of humanity beyond hegemonic (Western) culture (i.e., they should be allowed to participate in the relevant decision-making processes and in public political discussion). It is not a question of (supposed) preservation based on isolation but of communication and respect. I propose a political approach to the preservation (and enhancement) of cultural diversity through finding means of political participation, giving voice and say to points of view other than the hegemonic discourse of Western capitalism and science. If this "equality" of points of view in the political debate is not accepted, then it will probably be impossible to preserve this cultural heritage and it will be condemned to folklorization, banalization, and eventual disappearance.

This approach to cultural diversity is based on two main arguments. First, all human beings and groups are essentially equal. No point of view has more value than any other before a debate is over. So those who have different outlooks must be allowed to take part in the debates and decision-making processes that are relevant to them. This primary equality of human beings and cultures is a necessary condition if there is to be a real dialogue between human beings and human groups. So a way must be found to allow the individuals and groups of different cultures to take part in the political debate. They should not be treated simply as citizens in the context of a democratic state because, if they are, the result is concealed assimilation. It is not a question of arithmetic democracy but of seriously taking into account the diversity of perspectives that result from different conceptions of the world, all of which are of intrinsic value and of unquestionable interest for the rest of humanity.

The second argument is freedom, understood as the possibility that the groups and individuals within a framework of a system of rules that has been designed to take their points of view into account can have a real choice. If this possibility of choice does not exist, surely we are endorsing assimilation without saying so. Individuals and groups, then, must be allowed to take part in the multilevel dialogue that will result in decisions being taken on a variety of matters (local and global, individual and collective) that affect them as individuals.

It is important to underline that traditional forms of democracy (representative or direct) are insufficient to channel cultural diversity in a given context because an arithmetic conception of democracy cannot integrate the qualitative perspectives that are so necessary for dealing with cultural diversity and, more generally, with the complexity of contemporary societies. Nevertheless, how can a sound intercultural framework for taking decisions be established in contexts in which different communities from different cultural backgrounds come together? Well, if we rely on equality and freedom as a basis for promoting an integrationist approach to cultural diversity in the political arena, it seems clear that some assumptions provided by Western enlightened tradition can be useful as a starting point (but not as a point of arrival, as I will argue below).

It should seem obvious at this point that we have to avoid cultural chauvinism and introduce ideas belonging to other conceptions of the world if society is to be sufficiently inclusive. At first, it would seem that Western political tradition can be used as a sound basis on which to build intercultural dialogue aiming to design the strategies required for different communities of different cultural backgrounds to share a common space for (certain) decisions. The idea of human rights, in particular, in conjunction with respect for the equal dignity of all cultures, seems to be the right starting point.[4] In fact, the indigenous movement in Latin America can be interpreted within the wider paradigm of the defence of human rights (Burguete Cal y Mayor 2010, p. 64).

In this context, it would be interesting to rebuild the culture of human rights by taking into consideration the ideas of respect and responsibility. The Lockean conception of rights associated with a male, property-owning, white individual

---

[4] This seems to be the point of view of the UNESCO Convention on the Protection and Promotion of the Diversity of Cultural Expressions (particularly, article 2).

has to be overcome. At the same time, the belief in the dignity, equality, and freedom of human beings provided by the modern Western tradition has to be preserved. The idea of responsibility has been introduced in some modern constitutional texts (for example, the new Swiss Constitution of 1999) and developed by such authors as Hans Jonas (1995) in a Western context. It could be used to adapt human rights to cultural diversity, transforming them so that they become the basis for intercultural dialogue and decisions.

However, if cultural diversity is to be taken seriously in an institutional structure for political decision, in my opinion, there must be a common regulatory culture (based on human rights), which has to be open and evolutionary, and the communities representing the cultural diversity beyond Western hegemonic culture must be given the political density and capacity to take and share decisions. This involves the perspective of communities that are not based on Western cultural patterns in the political process and giving them their own spaces of autonomy and the chance to take part in a wider consensus. No attempts should be made to isolate them, and obviously they should not be assimilated (Pacari 2009, p. 36).

Therefore, flexible political structures need to be designed on a basis of pluralism and cooperation in order to respond to cultural diversity, on the one hand, and to the fact that humanity and its different cultural, social, and political groups share a common destiny, on the other. This suggests that it is necessary to renounce the homogeneity of the political spaces and the Cartesian political geometry of the community of equals, where pluralism is concealed by the arithmetic idea of democracy.[5]


## Building a Model of Management of Cultural Diversity in Decision-Making Processes

### *Limits of a Multilevel Decision-Making Process Designed to Cope with Cultural Diversity*

I would like to make three suggestions. Plans should be made to build (i) spaces of decision for communities with a singular cultural identity and (ii) higher spaces of consensus (of different ranges and levels) for different communities. I imagine a multispace shaped by different ranges of consensus (at community, state, regional, or global level). Value should be given to different cultures, not as museum pieces but as living evolutive sets of human practices. This involves current society taking

---

[5] These ideas have been hegemonic in the political thought of the West since the sixteenth century, as the case of *Politica* by Johannes Althusius shows. For this, it is probably not easy to go beyond this idea of the political space for Westerners.

on a certain responsibility towards future generations so that (iii) the flow of cultural diversity can be preserved.

Starting from these three points, we can set three different kinds of limit on decision-making processes:

- First, to preserve the space of decision of a particular cultural community, defined as a political subject, we have to prevent illegitimate interference by higher spheres of power that represent wider ranges of consensus of which the community affected is a part (i.e., "democratic" decisions taken at a higher level that pose a serious threat to the foundations of the smaller community).
- Second, the limits imposed by the general rules of decision-making also need to be imposed on the minor spaces of decision (i.e., respect for human rights at a global level in each space of political decision, regardless of its cultural singularity).
- Finally, it is necessary (but not easy) to set limits for lower and higher levels of decisions to preserve the flow of cultural diversity for future generations, as is done in the field of environmental law and policies through the precautionary principle.

To cope with the overlapping of limits at different levels/ranges of decision, we can use the rules that are applied to less acute levels of cultural diversity in Western culture. I am referring to the Western federal tradition. However, we have to be careful. At present, we are witnessing a new frontier for federalism, which is fluctuating in an attempt to answer complex questions and take into account the point of view of people who do not belong to Western hegemonic culture (and who are, therefore, alien to certain procedures and mechanisms). This requires an open attitude so that the rules can evolve with the flow of intercultural dialogue. Western federal culture may well be a good (procedural) way to start, as is the case with human rights in a substantive way.

In the federal tradition, the limits imposed by the federal constitution on member states define a common space of consensus and prevent disloyal attitudes at lower levels. This allows the federal ensemble to work, but at the same time member states have their own space of decision, protected from the illegitimate interference of the central government. From this basis, we have to be able to overcome cultural chauvinism, excessive rigidity, and institutional sclerosis and bring in previously marginalized communities. In this way, we will create overlapping circles of consensus to preserve (the flow of) cultural diversity.

Limits also need to be placed on all the present actors at their different levels of decision to protect future generations. As happens with the precautionary principle and the (controversial) idea of sustainable development, limits need to be set on present decisions for the benefit of future generations. The idea of responsibility that I have mentioned above seems to be a good justification for these limits, but it is always difficult to define procedures and empower actors to guarantee this kind of limit, given the fact that there are still no stakeholders.

## Circles of Consensus, Fragmented Democracies, and Aggregated Communities

The federal tradition is inspiring because it establishes upper and lower levels of government, which define concentric circles of consensus and mark successive borders for the decisions taken at lower levels and because it is concerned with allowing the lower levels of government to participate in the wider decision-making processes. From this starting point, we may be able to define more complex circles of consensus to cope with both cultural and political diversities.

The way to preserve cultural diversity could be to reinforce cultural federalism at different levels, overcome mechanical majorities as a source of legitimacy, and design legal frameworks to establish different circles of cultural, social, and political consensus. Whatever the case may be, it is crucial not to forget that isolated circles of consensus are not enough to guarantee cultural diversity; communities need to be allowed to take part in higher levels of decision-making. Moreover, the traditional idea of sovereignty based on the conception of nation-state as an absolute monad of homogeneous, independent, and isolated power has to be discarded in favour of a more flexible conception of political power and decision-making processes.

Therefore, if dialogue is to be fair and to include all the different cultural perspectives, circles of consensus need to be defined with different ranges, where partial consensus can be reached, inspired by the federalist tradition. For example, in a given nation-state, the rules of distribution of political decisions can be defined in such a way that some matters can be decided in cultural circles, others in territorial circles, and others only at the highest level through processes that allow different interests (cultural, economic, etc.) to participate. It is not easy to lay down the rules for such a dialogue, but it seems to me that it is the only real option if cultural diversity is to be preserved.

All higher levels define the possibilities of the lower ones. So the "national" decisions act as a limit on the decisions taken within groups or territories. For this reason, they have to be limited to issues of "national" interest and subject to even higher limits that aim to preserve diversity (perhaps imposed at international level). For example, higher circles of consensus should not leave minority groups unprotected against the powerful forces that overcome them, as happens with the recent, significant phenomenon of so-called biopiracy, in which market rules of global economy are harming small communities in America or Africa, for example.

These procedures would lead to fragmented democracies (within the state, at state level, and beyond the state) with attributions that depend on the cultural characteristics of each group, which can be mono- or multicultural. Each of these fragmented democracies would have its own political procedures, based on an open concept of democracy, which embody different ways of taking decisions with the condition that the members of the community reach a consensus. Given the democratic nature of this institutional system, all the communities would have political status, so they would not be left to depend on wider communities, and the line beyond which higher authorities (representing, so to say, the will of the majority in the wider circle of consensus) cannot go would be clearly marked.

This is extremely important for lightly populated communities that are part of wider political institutional systems, as is common for indigenous peoples in states populated by a Westernized majority (i.e., Indian minorities in the Latin American states, dominated by *criollo* or *mestizo* majorities). If there is a flexible flow of institutional relations and circles of consensus have been built, the possibility exists that an integrated community could voluntarily withdraw from the wider institutional system to which it belongs (right to self-determination) because some of its essential features are threatened—but always respecting the global consensus of human rights and democratic decision-making (or perhaps some local variation), which is the ultimate limit on diversity.

Finally, the basic (cultural-political) communities form wider circles of consensus, building bigger communities that can interact successively with another up to the global level. This level is defined by the prevailing conception of human rights and an open idea of democracy, conceived through the flow of intercultural dialogue. The combination of fragmented democracies and communities joined by the dynamics of evolutionary circles of consensus is intended to give political density, and therefore capacity to survive, to different cultures in an integrated world with common problems.

# References

Alder, J., Wilkinson, D. (1999). Environmental Law & Ethics. Macmillan, London, UK.

Arbòs, X., Vernet i Llobet, J. (1999). Los nuevos federalismos y el constitucionalismo del siglo XXI: In Aparicio, M. A. (ed.), La Descentralización y el Federalismo. Nuevos modelos de Autonomía Política (España, Bélgica, Canadá, Italia y Reino Unido), Cedecs, Barcelona, Spain, 261–271.

Ávila Santamaría, R. (2011). El neoconstitucionalismo transformador. El estado y el derecho en la Constitución de 2008, Abya-Yala - Universidad Andina Simón Bolívar, Quito, Ecuador.

Böckenförde, E.-W. (2006). Sviluppo storico e mutamento di significato della costituzione: In Böckenförde, E.-W., Stato, costituzione, democracia — Studi di teoria della costituzione e di diritto costituzionale, Giuffrè, Milan, Italy, 29–60.

Bravo, E. (2009). Conocimiento ecológico tradicional para la conservación: dinámicas y conflictos. Papeles de relaciones ecosociales y cambio global, 107: 69–76.

Burguete Cal y Mayor, A. (2010). Autonomía: la emergencia de un paradigma en las luchas por la descolonización en América Latina: In González, M., Burguete Cal y Mayor, A., Ortiz-T., P. (eds.), La autonomía a debate. Autogobierno indígena y Estado plurinacional en América Latina, FLACSO (Sede Ecuador) - Cooperación Técnica Alemana (GTZ) - Grupo Internacional de Trabajo sobre Asuntos Indígenas (IWGIA) - Centro de Investigaciones y Estudios Superiores en Antropología Social (CIESAS) - Universidad Intercultural de Chiapas (UNICH), Quito, Ecuador, 63–94.

Carrillo Salcedo, J. A. (1991). El Derecho internacional en perspectiva histórica. Tecnos, Madrid, Spain.

Chevallier, J. (1998). Vers un droit post-moderne? Les transformations de la régulation juridique. Revue de Droit Public, 3: 659–690.

Clarkson, S.; Wood, S. (2009). A Perilous Imbalance — The Globalization of Canadian Law and Governance. UBC Press, Vancouver-Toronto, Canada.

Estermann, J. (2004). Filosofía andina — Estudio intercultural de la sabiduría autóctona andina. Abya-Yala, Quito, Ecuador.

Fleiner-Gerster, T. (1990). Die Zukunft des schweizerisches Rechtstaates: In Festgabe Alfred Rötheli zum fünfundsechzigsten Geburstag. Staatskanzlei des Kantons Solothurns, Solothurn, Switzerland, 89–103.

Fornet-Betancourt, R. (2004). Ciència, tecnologia i política en la filosofia de Panikkar: In Boada, I. (ed.), La filosofia intercultural de Raimon Panikkar, CETC, Barcelona, Spain, 119–132.

García-Pelayo, M. (1984). Derecho constitucional comparado, Alianza, Madrid, Spain.

Glenn, H. P. (2007). Legal Traditions of the World. Oxford University Press, Oxford-New York, UK-USA.

Jagmetti, R. L. (1982). Der Bürger im Entscheidungsprozeß: In Staatsorganisation und Staatsfunktionen im Wandel. Festschrift für Kurt Eichenberger zum 60. Geburtstag, Helbing & Lichtenhahn, Basel-Frankfurt am Main, Switzerland-Germany, 363–373.

Jaria i Manzano (2011). La cuestión ambiental y la transformación de lo público. Tirant lo Blanch, Valencia, Spain.

Jiménez Asensio, R. (2003)[2]. El constitucionalismo — Proceso de formación y fundamentos del Derecho constitucional. Marcial Pons, Barcelona-Madrid, Spain.

Jonas, H. (1995). El principio de responsabilidad — Ensayo de una ética para la civilización tecnológica. Herder, Barcelona, Spain.

Martínez, E. (2009). Los Derechos de la Naturaleza en los países amazónicos: In Acosta, A., Martínez, E. (eds.) Derechos de la Naturaleza — El futuro es ahora. Abya-Yala, Quito, Ecuador, 85–98.

Mickelsen, K., Rees, W. (1993). The Environment: Ecological and Ethical Dimensions. In Hughes, E. L., Lucas, A. R., Tilleman, W. A. (eds.) Environmental Law and Policy. Emond Montgomery, Toronto, Canada, 1–29.

Mora, M. (2010). Las experiencias de la autonomía indígena zapatista frente al Estado neoliberal mexicano: In González, M., Burguete Cal y Mayor, A., Ortiz-T., P. (eds.), La autonomía a debate. Autogobierno indígena y Estado plurinacional en América Latina, FLACSO (Sede Ecuador) - Cooperación Técnica Alemana (GTZ) - Grupo Internacional de Trabajo sobre Asuntos Indígenas (IWGIA) - Centro de Investigaciones y Estudios Superiores en Antropología Social (CIESAS) - Universidad Intercultural de Chiapas (UNICH), Quito, Ecuador, 291–315.

Mora Rodríguez, A. (2008). La racionalidad de la economía capitalista y la vida digna de las personas. Papeles de Relacions Ecosociales y Cambio Global, 107: 9–23.

Moreno Navarro, I. (2000). Quiebra de los modelos de modernidad, globalización e identidades colectivas: In Alcina Franch, J., Calés Bourdet, M. (eds.) Hacia una ideología para el siglo XX — Ante la crisis civilizatoria de nuestro tiempo, Akal, Tres Cantos, Spain, 102–131.

Müller, J. P. (1982). Elemente einer schweizerischen Grundrechtstheorie, Stämpfli, Bern, Switzerland.

Ortiz-T., P. (2010). Entre la cooptación y la ruptura: la lucha por el derecho a la autodeterminación de las nacionalidades indígenas del centro sur amazónico del Ecuador: In González, M., Burguete Cal y Mayor, A., Ortiz-T., P. (eds.), La autonomía a debate. Autogobierno indígena y Estado plurinacional en América Latina, FLACSO (Sede Ecuador) - Cooperación Técnica Alemana (GTZ) - Grupo Internacional de Trabajo sobre Asuntos Indígenas (IWGIA) - Centro de Investigaciones y Estudios Superiores en Antropología Social (CIESAS) - Universidad Intercultural de Chiapas (UNICH), Quito, Ecuador, 455–508.

Pachano, S. (2010). Estado, ciudadanía y democracia: In Burbano de Lara, F. (ed.), Transiciones y rupturas. El Ecuador en la segunda mitad del siglo XX, Flacso Ecuador - Ministerio de Cultura, Quito, Ecuador, 43–74.

Pacari, N. (2009). Naturaleza y territorio desde la mirada de los pueblos indígenas: In Acosta, A., Martínez, E. (eds.), Derechos de la Naturaleza — El futuro es ahora, Abya-Yala, Quito, Ecuador, 31–37.

Salazar Benítez, O. (2005). El derecho a la identidad cultural como elemento esencial de una ciudadanía compleja. In Ruiz-Rico Ruiz, G., Pérez Sola, N. (eds.), Constitución y cultura — Retos del Derecho constitucional en el siglo XXI, Tirant lo Blanch, Valencia, Spain, 207–241.

Sánchez, C. (2010). Autonomía y pluralismo. Estados plurinacionales y pluriétnicos: In González, M., Burguete Cal y Mayor, A., Ortiz-T., P. (eds.), La autonomía a debate. Autogobierno indígena y Estado plurinacional en América Latina, FLACSO (Sede Ecuador) - Cooperación Técnica Alemana (GTZ) - Grupo Internacional de Trabajo sobre Asuntos Indígenas (IWGIA) - Centro de Investigaciones y Estudios Superiores en Antropología Social (CIESAS) - Universidad Intercultural de Chiapas (UNICH), Quito, Ecuador, 259–288.

Tuaza C., L. A. (2010). Concepciones del Estado y demandas de las organizaciones campesinas e indígenas (1940-1960): In In Burbano de Lara, F. (ed.), Transiciones y rupturas. El Ecuador en la segunda mitad del siglo XX, Flacso Ecuador - Ministerio de Cultura, Quito, Ecuador, 465–513.

Untermaier, J. (1996). Représentation et pesée globale des intérêts en droit français de l'aménagement du territoire et de la protection de l'environnement: In Morand, C.-A. (ed.), La pesée globale des intérêts. Droit de l'environnement et de l'aménagement du territoire, Helbing & Lichtenhahn, Basel-Frankfurt am Main, Switzerland-Germany, 129–150.

Velasco J. C. (2000). El Multiculturalismo, ¿una nueva ideología? Alcance y límites de la lucha por las identidades culturales: In Alcina Franch, J., Calés Bourdet, M. (eds.) Hacia una ideología para el siglo XX — Ante la crisis civilizatoria de nuestro tiempo, Akal, Tres Cantos, Spain, 146–163.

Von Bogdandy, Armin (2006). Constitutional Principles for Europe: In Riedel, E., Wolfrum, R. (eds.), Recent Trends in German and European Constitutional Law, Springer, Berlín-Heidelberg-New York, Germany-US, 1–35.

Wallerstein, I. (2007). Geopolítica y geocultura. Ensayos sobre el moderno sistema mundial, Kairós, Barcelona, Spain

White, L. (1967). The Historical Roots of Our Ecological Crisis, Science, 155: 1203–1207.

# The Indigenous Question and the Territorial Organisation of the State in Latin American Refounding Constitutionalism

Andoni Perez Ayala

## Constitutional Changes: Refounding Constitutionalism and the Indigenous Question in Latin American

The turn of the twentieth century was marked in Latin America by intense constitutional activity that extended to practically all the countries of the Central and South American subcontinent. In the last decade of the twentieth century and the first of the present one, important constitutional changes took place in this field, not only in quantitative terms as a consequence of the number of new texts and constitutional reforms carried out but also because of the innovations that some of these changes have introduced in contemporary constitutionalism, particularly in the case of Latin America, in the early years of the present century.[1]

After the gradual disappearance of the dictatorial regimes, which in some countries lasted well into the 1980s, a new period of constitutional recomposition commenced in Latin American countries,[2] in some cases by, on occasions, substantially revising already existing constitutional texts as in Argentina, 1994, and to a certain extent Chile, 1989, although the latter is a special case as it entailed a Pinochet-inspired "constitutional" text. In other instances, entirely new constitutional texts were adopted (Brazil, 1988[3]; Colombia, 1991), and finally, in some

---

[1] An overview of Latin American constitutionalism up to the last decade of the twentieth century can be seen in the extensive: "Estudio introductorio" by Quiroga Lavie (1994), pp. 7–117. Likewise, see the wide ranging: "Estudio preliminar" by Hector Fix Zamudio in the classic work by Biscaretti (1996), pp. 28–69.

[2] See Reinaldo Vanossi (2007), pp. 407–424.

[3] Regarding the Brazilian constitutional experience, in particular, see Figueiredo (2010), pp. 1509–1535. Likewise, the monographic section to mark the first two decades of the Brazilian constitutional experience: AA.VV. (2008), pp. 1340–1450.

A. Perez Ayala (✉)
Department of Constitutional Law and History of the Political Thought, University of the Basque Country, Campus of Sarriena, Post Box 644, Bilbao 48080, Spain
e-mail: andoni.perez@ehu.es

A. López-Basaguren and L. Escajedo San Epifanio (eds.), *The Ways of Federalism in Western Countries and the Horizons of Territorial Autonomy in Spain*, Vol. 2, DOI 10.1007/978-3-642-27717-7_35, © Springer-Verlag Berlin Heidelberg 2013

cases, a constitutional order was established that was not only different but also *refounding* in nature, in accordance with the term that the constituent assemblies themselves used to describe their work: Venezuela, 1999; Ecuador, 2008; and Bolivia 2009. This entailed a process of constitutional changes that, both in terms of their scope (it includes, generally speaking, all the countries of Latin America) and the changes it introduced, is of undoubted interest for a better understanding of the current evolution of contemporary constitutionalism.

Such is the framework of generalised constitutional changes in Latin America during the final years of the last century in which the new phenomenon of *refounding constitutionalism* emerged, a term by which the constituent assemblies of certain Latin American countries (Venezuela, Bolivia, and Ecuador) referred to their desire to "refound" (and not only reform) the existing political order: a refoundation undertaken in the terms envisaged in the Constitution, and which became one of the most valuable mechanisms (the most important at the legal level) for carrying out the refounding project. This conception of the Constitution, which did not coincide with that which, lacking refounding pretensions, was in existence until that time, meant that the structure and content of the Constitution revolved around the refounding objective, and it is precisely that aim that helps to explain the particular characteristics these new constitutional texts were to have.[4]

It was Venezuela that, coinciding with the end of last decade of the twentieth century, inaugurated the refounding constitutional experience in Latin America after the intense constituent process that was undertaken in this country in 1999 and that culminated in the establishment in the Bolivarian Republic of Venezuela, bringing to an end almost four decades, during which the constitutional regime established at the beginning of the 1960s had remained in force. The election of Evo Morales as President of Bolivia in December, 1995, heralded a prolonged and bitter constituent process in the country (2006–2009) through which Bolivia was to set in motion its own refounding experience, which in this case displayed its own distinctive features due to the considerable influence of the indigenous population. Finally, and almost simultaneously (2007–2008), Ecuador was to carry out its own refounding constitutional experience in which the indigenous factor was also to play an important role in the development of the refounding political process.[5]

The new Constitutions (Venezuela, 1999; Ecuador, 2008; and Bolivia, 2009), which arose from these refounding constituent processes, introduced a series of new elements that, to a large extent, modified the classical Latin American constitutional blueprints, such as a different approach to regulating economic and social relations and the role of the State therein, a question to which the refounding constituent assembly devoted priority attention. The newly refounded constitutional texts also reformulated regulation of classical constitutional content, such as in the matter of rights and freedoms, which were considerably extended by embracing a new generation of rights. While still retaining the Presidential format

---

[4] See Clavero (2005), pp. 195–211.

[5] Regarding these latter countries, see Cruz and Guerra (2010), pp. 97–124.

characteristic of Latin American political regimes, new mechanisms were introduced aimed at promoting popular participation (the extension of referenda and revocation processes for elected authorities, including the Head of State) in an effort to address another classical constitutional concern: the structure of state powers.

One of the new topics that was to be the subject of special attention in the refounding constitutional texts was the *indigenous question*. This has special relevance from the constitutional standpoint, given that the subject has barely been dealt with by constitutionalism as a whole and by Latin American constitutionalism in particular,[6] despite the fact that in some countries, particularly those of the Andean region, the indigenous population has a considerable influence, at least in quantitative terms, in their respective countries (as is the case of Bolivia and Ecuador, which we deal with in this paper). Moreover, it is important to note that the indigenous question is not just another subject that received only passing treatment on the part of the constituent assembly but indeed occupied a central role in the refounding political project, at least in those countries where the indigenous population is demographically significant. A further point is that the treatment of this subject in the refounding constitutional texts was to fill a vacuum that had existed up until that time in Latin American constitutionalism.

The treatment of the subject that concerns us in this section (the effect of the indigenous factor in Latin American refounding constitutionalism and in the territorial (re)organisation of the State) will be dealt with along three lines. First, the constitutional redefinition of the State will be examined in accordance with recognition of the plural composition of its population, in particular of the indigenous population, a point ignored in constitutional terms until now. Second, within the framework of the new and more extensive regulation of constitutional rights and freedoms, the specific rights of the indigenous population will be examined, an issue to which the refounding constitutional texts, for the first time, devoted particular attention. Finally, the specific forms of territorial organisation and of exercising self-rule in indigenous communities will be examined, which, for the first time, were to be set out and reflected in the constitutions. The development of the three lines described will be carried out on the basis of the three refounding experiences (Venezuela, Ecuador, and Bolivia), which have taken place up till now and of the constitutional texts in which these have, up to the present, been given effective legal-political expression.[7]

---

[6] On this subject, see Bidart Campos (2003), pp. 267–288.

[7] Regarding the processes of constitutional change in these countries, see the introductory study by Luis Aguiar de Luque and Reviriego (2006), pp. 227–243. Likewise: Shifter and Joyce (2008), pp. 55–66.

# Bolivarian Constitutional Refoundation in Venezuela: Aspects Relating to the Indigenous Question and the Territorial Organisation of the State

## *Constitutional Recognition of the Multi-ethnic and Multicultural Nature of Venezuela*

As is known, Venezuela was the first Lain American country in which the refounding theses were to be effectively implemented after the collapse, at the end of the last century, of the constitutional regime (more apparent than real) that had ruled the country for over four decades.[8] It should be said, nevertheless, that neither in the collapse of the previous regime nor in the refoundation of the new one did the indigenous question or territorial reorganisation of the State have any real impact. The questions (basically those of corruption and related affairs) that polarised Venezuelan political life in the 1990s and that finally gave rise to the exhaustion and final collapse of the previous political regime were different.

Unlike other Latin American countries such as Ecuador and Bolivia (with which we deal below), which also share with Venezuela the refounding constitutional experience, the indigenous population in Venezuela is small. This logically also means, in comparative terms, that the indigenous factor has less of an impact at the constitutional level in the Caribbean country than in the Andean countries previously referred to and does not play the same role in the different cases, as we will later see, in the constitutional formulation of the State. This distinct situation should be borne in mind as a starting point, given that it is thus easier to understand how this issue has been treated differently in the Venezuelan constitutional text in relation to its Ecuadorian and Bolivian counterparts.

Yet, the Venezuelan refounding constituent assembly of 1999 did not forget this matter, and although to a lesser extent than in Ecuador and Bolivia, it was also dealt with constitutionally in the terms that will be examined below. It is interesting to draw attention to this fact, given that, unlike some other Latin American countries (in particular, the Andean and Central American ones),[9] in Venezuela the indigenous question had barely been reflected in the preceding constitutional texts. It is within the framework of refounding constitutionalism, which was given expression in the 1999 Venezuelan constitutional text, in which the indigenous question was to be specifically and explicitly addressed for the first time in Venezuelan constitutionalism.

Prior to the present constitutional text, in force for the last decade, the indigenous question had, at best, enjoyed a marginal presence (as occurred in the majority

---

[8] See Rachadell (2003), pp. 95–148.

[9] The cases of Guatemala (Constitution of 1985) and of Colombia (Constitution of 1991) should be mentioned. Regarding these, see: Garcia Laguardia (1985), pp. 211–232; Osuna et al. (1991); both in pp. 211–232 and 261–278, respectively.

of Latin American constitutional texts). The previous Venezuelan Constitution of 1961,[10] whose formal validity extended over the last four decades of the twentieth century, contained a fleeting reference to it, within the framework of a regulation devoted to improving the living conditions of the rural population (Article 77) and, in the best paternalistic tone, to *the indigenous communities*, which the State promised to "protect"[11] in order to facilitate their gradual incorporation into the life of the nation. As can be observed, it entailed a passing reference that did not go beyond the typical rhetorical clause in which constitutional texts are usually dressed up.

The Bolivarian Constitution of 1999 was to treat this subject in a completely different manner, beginning with the constitutional recognition of the indigenous reality. Reference is made to the "indigenous ancestors", precursors of the present indigenous communities, in the Preamble and in the preliminary paragraphs.[12] Together with the refounding statement of the Bolivarian Republic, a specific reference is also made for the first time to the *multi-ethnic and multicultural* component of Venezuelan society. This constitutes something new in Venezuelan constitutionalism as is also the reference that is made, among the *Fundamental Principles* (Title I: Articles 1–9), to the principle of joint official use of the *indigenous languages*, "of official use in the indigenous villages", compatible with the official language, Spanish, throughout the country (Article 9).

Also among the *Fundamental Principles* (included in Title I) of the refounded Bolivarian Republic of Venezuela, we find the description of this as a *Decentralised Federal State* in the terms envisaged by the Constitution (Article 4). In this case, the Bolivarian constituent assembly did not introduce any change since Venezuela is one of the Latin American countries (together with Mexico, Brazil, and Argentina) that has traditionally adopted a federal model of territorial organisation,[13] although it is necessary to note that Latin American federalism, in general, and the Venezuelan one, in particular, are difficult to classify within the authentic federal model, resembling more a specific type of political decentralisation.[14] In this respect, the terms that the Venezuelan constitutional text itself uses are highly illustrative (Article 4) as it defines the State as *decentralised federal*, which reveals a conception of federalism closer to political decentralisation than to the federal model, strictly speaking.

---

[10] See: Brewer-Carias (1992), pp. 773–815

[11] Article 77 of the Venezuelan Constitution of 1961 is drafted in the following terms: "The State will propose to improve the living conditions of the rural population. The Law will establish a special regime which requires the protection of the indigenous communities and their progressive incorporation into the life of the Nation".

[12] Regarding the Venezuelan Constitutional Preamble, see Canova Gonzalez (2001), pp. 409–446.

[13] With respect to Latin American federalism, see Fernandez Segado (2003), 169 pp. Likewise, a shorter version regarding the subject by the same author: Fernandez Segado (2003), pp. 699–734.

[14] Regarding Venezuelan federalism, in particular, see Brewer-Carias (1992); *Informe sobre la descentralización en Venezuela (1993–1994)*, Arte, Caracas, 1994.

With regard to the multi-ethnic composition and decentralised federal territorial organisation of the Venezuelan State, it should be remembered that the two have no mutually corresponding relationship: that is to say, the federal organisation of the State is not structured on the basis of the multi-ethnic or multicultural composition of the population but is, rather, independent of it. We are not, therefore, dealing with a federalism that has an ethnic-cultural origin in which each indigenous community has its own federated State, nor is this reorganised in accordance with the ethnic-cultural composition of the population. Rather, the pre-existing federal territorial delimitation is reproduced (which undergoes no change)[15]; within whose framework, the indigenous population was to see a series of linguistic and cultural rights recognised to which, up to that point, no reference had been made (in this field there *were* substantial changes).

## Constitutionalisation of Indigenous Peoples' Rights

The most notable innovation in the Venezuelan Constitution, with regard to the indigenous population and (in accordance with the constitutional preamble) the previously mentioned multi-ethnic and multicultural composition of the Republic, was the introduction of a series of constitutional regulations specifically devoted to *the rights of the indigenous peoples* (Articles 119–126, Chapter VIII of Title III). Contained in the extensive Title III of the Constitution (more than one hundred Articles), related to "the human rights, safeguards and duties" (Articles 19–135), the constitutional text of 1999 deals for the first time with a series of rights (of the indigenous peoples) on which it confers its own, differentiated entity in relation to the rest of the rights and that, in consequence, are grouped in a specific Chapter (VIII). The Venezuelan constituent assembly thus incorporated into its legal code at the highest level what, until that time, had been no more than declarations and heterogeneous agreements concerning matters related to the indigenous question.[16]

This is based on constitutional recognition of the existence of the *indigenous peoples and communities*, invested with their own "social, political and economic organisation, their cultures, uses and customs, languages and religion" (Article 119). The right is likewise recognised that helps the indigenous peoples "to maintain and develop their ethnic and cultural identity, view of the world, values, spirituality and their sacred sites and places of worship" (Article 121). It is necessary to add that the Venezuelan Constitution not merely is limited to recognising the indigenous reality and the generic right to preserve their indigenous identity or identities but also

---

[15] See Crazut (2000), p. 40 onwards.

[16] An account of the different declarations, agreements, accords, etc. regarding indigenous rights up to approval of the Venezuelan Constitution can be found in AA.VV. (1998), 710 pp.

assigns to the State an active role in promoting the valuation and diffusion of the cultural expressions of the indigenous peoples.

In line with this recognition of a cultural specificity, constitutional cover is provided for a specific educational model "of an intercultural and bilingual nature, bearing in mind the socio-cultural peculiarities, values and traditions (of the indigenous peoples)" (Article 121). Constitutional cover is also provided, within recognition of the specificities unique to the indigenous peoples, for more debatable practices such as the provision that "the State will recognise their traditional medicine and complementary therapies" (Article 122), a formulation that is more than dubious, in particular in constitutional terms,[17] even though it is accompanied by the specification that such a recognition will be made subject to bioethical principles.

One striking peculiarity is the constitutional safeguard and protection accorded to "the collective intellectual property of the knowledge, technologies and innovations of the indigenous peoples", with a specific constitutional prohibition of "the register of patents regarding these ancestral resources and knowledge" (Article 124). The problem that this type of constitutional formulations poses, even while recognising that the intention that undoubtedly inspired the constituent assembly to protect the specific cultural heritage of the indigenous peoples is praiseworthy, is that it is somewhat difficult to determine what the knowledge or innovations of the indigenous peoples are exactly or, at least with a minimum of accuracy, which should be subject to special attention and cannot be registered as patents.

The provisions relating to the "habitat and native rights to the lands which ancestrally and traditionally they (the indigenous communities and peoples) occupy and which are necessary to develop and safeguard their life styles" (Article 119) are especially interesting. In this respect, the national executive is assigned, specifying that it must do so with the participation of the indigenous peoples, the demarcation and guarantee of the right to collective ownership of their lands, on the basis of the principles of "inalienability, imprescriptibility, unseizability and untransferability", in accordance with that established in the Constitution and in law. Likewise, the constitutional text expressly establishes that "the exploitation of the natural resources in the indigenous habitats on the part of the State will be conducted without infringing on the cultural, social and economic integrity of the former", establishing "prior information and consultation for the respective indigenous communities" as a condition (Article 120).[18]

The right to *political participation* is the subject of specific constitutional treatment in view of the particular characteristics that the indigenous population

---

[17] Despite this, it is necessary to point out that we will also find it in similar terms in the constitutions of Ecuador and Bolivia.

[18] Regarding the specific problem posed by this group of rights and social rights, in general, in Latin American and refounding constitutionalism, in particular, see Noguera (2010), especially Chapter VI, which deals with the group of countries immersed in refounding processes, pp. 159–233.

display, both with reference to its quantitative size and as regards their territorial distribution. In this respect, the constitutional text envisages specific ways of participation in order to guarantee indigenous representation in the National Parliament, as well as in the deliberating bodies of those federal and local entities with an indigenous population (Article 125). With respect to the National Parliament, "the indigenous peoples of the Bolivarian Republic of Venezuela are reserved three members of parliament in accordance with the stipulations set out in electoral law and respecting their traditions and customs" (Article 186).[19] In this way, representation of the indigenous peoples is guaranteed in the National Parliament.

One final observation should be made regarding the provision (Article 126) that closes the Chapter devoted to the rights of the indigenous peoples: In accordance with this provision, the constitutional recognition of these peoples is made by explicitly stating that "they form part of the Nation, of the State and of the Venezuelan peoples as unique, sovereign and indivisible", specifying immediately afterwards, such that there is no room for any doubt, that "the term people cannot be interpreted in this Constitution in the sense which it is given in international law" (Article 126). In accordance with the constitutional clauses we have mentioned, it is not therefore possible to invoke the right to self-determination for its application to the indigenous peoples in order to accede to a political status that implies any form of disassociation from the Republic of Venezuela.

## *"Federal" Continuism of the Territorial Organisation of the State*

Unlike the Chapter previously commented upon regarding constitutional recognition of the rights of the indigenous peoples in the terms described, which represents an important innovation in Venezuelan constitutionalism, the Chapter related to the federal structure of the State (Chapter III of Tile IV: Articles 159–167) barely offers anything new with regard to the framework of territorial organisation existing up to that moment. In this respect, it can be said that this issue is one of the few that did not undergo any significant change in the new Bolivarian constitutional text, which in this area was to maintain a position that could be described as federal continuism, in line with what had been traditional in Venezuelan constitutionalism (and, in particular, in the previous constitutional text of 1961).

The explanation for this continuism (which contrasts with the major changes introduced by refounding constitutionalism in almost all other fields) is to be found in the fact that the federal question was far from being one of the main concerns for

---

[19] As a comparative reference, it should be said that the same constitutional provision (Article 186) also sets as three the number of representatives of each State in the National Parliament, to which we have to add a variable additional number according to the population. There is no Senate that, in principle, is the ideal Chamber for territorial representation.

the Bolivarian constituent assembly of 1999.[20] The same could be said for the opposition, which did not raise any important objections regarding this question either, unlike others, especially in the economic and social fields, which were the focus of confrontation with the new Bolivarian power. Consequently, the model of federal territorial organisation in the version that this had up till then in Venezuelan constitutionalism was adopted, without this question being the subject of special controversy.

The abolition of the Senate, which is the ideal Chamber for organising the federal structure of the State, should be noted as an innovation: at least, it has thus been historically in all federal states since the Philadelphia Convention (1787) gave rise to the first of them. In fact, it is merely one further instance of the scant attention that, for the Bolivarian constituent assembly of 1999, the federal institutionalisation of the State was given, in which the Senate or Chamber for territorial representation is always a fundamental element. The new institutional framework established by the constituent assembly of 1999 abolished the bicameral model, which had been the traditional one in Venezuela, and replaced it with a single-chamber system whose institutional expression was to be the National Parliament (Article 186 onwards).[21]

The Bolivarian Constitution of 1999 devotes a brief Chapter (Ch. III of the State Public Power: Articles 159–167) within Title IV (of Public Power: Articles 136–185) to the regulation of federal entities (which, unlike the previous Constitution of 1961, it does not mention). In accordance with the design that the current constitutional model establishes, *state* public power (of the federal States that make up the Venezuelan Republic) integrates, together with *national* public power and *municipal* public power (the subject also of constitutional regulation in Title IV relating to *public power*), the basic structure of the territorial distribution of power, which in this respect evidences no substantial differences to the previous Constitutions.

The States that form the Republic are configured as "autonomous and equal political entities" (Article 159), endowed with an institutional organisation headed by a *Governor* or *Governess*,[22] who holds office for a period of 4 years, with the possibility of re-election [Amendment Number 1 of 15/02/09] (Article 160). It is expressly envisaged (Article 161) that they must give an account of their governance before the *State Board of Control* and present an annual report of the latter before the *Legislative Council* and the *Planning and Coordination Council* for Public Policy.

---

[20] Regarding the Bolivarian constituent assembly in Venezuela, see Viciano and Martinez Dalmau (2001), p. 169 onwards.

[21] Regarding the new institutional organisation of the Republic, see Viciano and Martinez Dalmau (2001), op. cit., in particular, the section devoted to "the configuration of powers", p. 229 onwards.

[22] It is interesting to note the linguistic gender used by the Venezuelan Constituent Assembly throughout the constitutional text. This is a characteristic feature of refounding constitutionalism that we also find in the Ecuadorian and Bolivian constitutional texts.

The *Legislative Council* is the organisation that exercises legislative power in each state, approving the corresponding norms with the status of law in the subject matters of state competence, as well as approving the Budgets in each state and exercising the competences established in the Constitution and by law. It comprises a small number of Councillors (between 15 and 7), which makes it more similar to a smaller body with the nature of a Council than a parliamentary-type body (as occurs in Spain with the Autonomous Parliaments). Its members are elected for a period of 4 years, as happened with the Governor/Governess, and they can be re-elected (Article 162).[23]

As well as the executive bodies referred to (Governor/ness and Legislative Council), the institutional organisation of the States is completed by the *Board of Control*, formed as a body endowed with organic and functional autonomy charged with the task of exercising "the control, monitoring and auditing of the revenue, expenditure and state assets" (Article 163). Lastly, the Constitution envisages the existence of a *Council for Planning and Coordination of Public Policy* (Article 166), which under the Presidency of the Governor/Governess and with the participation of the Mayor/Mayoress and elected officers in the National Parliament and the Legislative Assembly, as well as representatives of "the organising communities, including any indigenous ones", have the task of promoting and developing public policies in their respective areas.

As regards the area of State competences, the Constitution distinguishes between *exclusive* competences, grouped into a list of eleven subject matters specified in the Constitution (Article 164), also envisaging that the residual power clause operates in favour of the States, and *concurrent* competences, which "will be regulated through basic laws passed by the National Government and development laws approved by the States" (Article 165). Without examining the list of competences in detail (which is not the object of this work and which would also be impossible), it can be said that it is an area of competences of a predominantly administrative nature and content which, as has already been indicated, characterises Venezuelan federalism.

Finally, the Constitution envisages limited financial autonomy for the federated States (Article 167). As well as revenue from their assets and the administration of their properties and the taxes for the use of their services, the previously mentioned provision envisages a source of financing (the "constitutional revenue" according to its own denomination) comprising the assignment to the States of a budgetary allocation equivalent to 20 % of the total revenue estimated annually by the national Treasury. This amount is distributed between the States in accordance with certain criteria established by the constitutional provision. Likewise, it is foreseen that the federated States can have at their disposal "the taxes, rates and special contributions which they are assigned by national law", reflecting the limited nature of financial

---

[23] This possibility of re-election was introduced by constitutional amendment number 1 of 15/02/09, the only constitutional reform carried out up till now.

independence. Lastly, an Inter-territorial Compensation Fund was established,[24] which is entrusted with correcting any inter-territorial imbalances.

To conclude this brief study of the Venezuelan refounding constitutional experience (the first of this nature and one that was later to spread to other Latin American countries), we should note the innovation that the constitutional recognition of the multi-ethnic and multicultural nature of Venezuela entails, which is unprecedented in Venezuelan constitutionalism. Likewise, we should also note, the no less important innovation of the constitutionalisation of the specific rights of the indigenous population, which had at no time previously occurred. Yet, at the same time, it is also necessary to state that the territorial organisation of the State did not undergo substantial changes, the "federal" system, with small variations, (although more nominal than real) which was in existence prior to the Bolivarian refounding experience being maintained.

# Ecuadorian Constitutional Refoundation: Its Repercussion on the Indigenous Population and the Territorial Organisation of the State

## *Constitutional Recognition of the Multinationality and Interculturality of the Ecuadorian State*

In Ecuador, as in the rest of the countries of the Andean area (Bolivia, Peru, and Colombia), the indigenous population is large, which means the indigenous question is a factor that has to be taken into account in any political project concerning the country. Nevertheless, it is a fact that Ecuadorian constitutionalism, as in Latin America constitutionalism in general, has barely attended to the subject over its long, turbulent history.[25] This constitutional indifference towards the indigenous situation, which is undoubtedly a basic structural component in Latin American countries, especially in the Andean ones, has been corrected to a large extent in the recently refounded constitutional texts, which award the indigenous question a treatment that it had not had until then.

The recent Ecuadorian Constitution of 2008 (like the Bolivian one of 2009, which we will deal with below) pays special attention to this subject, making it one of the fundamental elements of its refounding project. It is necessary to state,

---

[24] The similarity is noteworthy in the denomination of this body with the Spanish ICF, which reveals the influence of the Spanish Constitution on the Venezuelan one. Regarding this subject, see Brewer-Carias (2003), pp. 765–786.

[25] The numerous constitutional texts that appeared in Ecuador between 1822 and 1978 reveal the scant interest that this subject has aroused. Regarding the previous Ecuadorian Constitution of 1978 (prior to that of 1998, which we deal with in this paper, and the current one of 2008), see Salgado (1992), pp. 325–350.

nevertheless, that in the Ecuadorian case, incorporating the indigenous factor into the Constitution has a close precedent: the previous constitutional text of 1998,[26] which had already embraced a series of constitutional provisions related to indigenous rights and the territorial organisation of the State, which were innovative in the refounding scenario of the late 1990s and which, to a large extent, served to elaborate the current constitutional regulation of 2008 (which also forces us to refer back to the previous constitutional provisions of 1998).

As early as the introductory paragraphs, the Ecuadorian constituent assembly of 2008 referred to *the different peoples* who make up *the sovereign nation* of Ecuador, as well as *the cultures* (in plural) that enrich Ecuadorian society. This entails a new conception, different from that which had existed until then, of the plurality of Ecuador and its cultural diversity.[27] In accordance with these preliminary premises, Article 1 of the Constitution defines the Ecuadorian State as *multinational and intercultural* (as well as the features already known and included in the previous constitutional texts: social, democratic, sovereign, independent, secular, and unitary). It has to be said, nevertheless, that the previous constitutional text of 1998 had already opened the way in this direction, recognising in its preamble the diversity of the regions, peoples, ethnic groups, and cultures that make up the Ecuadorian nation and the multicultural and multi-ethnic nature of the State (Article 1). In this regard, a line of continuity can be discerned between both texts (which as we shall see below will again be evident in other questions, although perhaps stated with greater emphasis and forcefulness in the text currently in force since 2008).

Likewise, together with the official language of Ecuador (Spanish), the joint validity of the indigenous languages (Kichwa, Shuar, and "the other ancient languages") is recognised in the corresponding regions and in the terms established by law, with the State promising to respect and encourage their preservation and use (Article 2). Equally, the State assumes as a *fundamental duty* "the strengthening of the process of autonomies and decentralisation" (Article 3.6). These statements regarding autonomy and plurality should be combined with the unitary aspect: the State is expressly defined as *unitary* (Article 1). It also assumes, as a *fundamental duty*, the strengthening of "national unity in diversity" (Article 3.3) and, so that there is no room for doubt, specifically establishes that "nobody shall place territorial unity in jeopardy nor promote secession" (Article 4).

## Constitutionalisation of the Rights of the Communities, Peoples, and Nationalities

The Ecuadorian Constitution of 2008 devotes a specific Chapter to the *rights of the communities, peoples and nationalities* (Articles 56–60), within the extensive

---

[26] Regarding this Constitution, see AA.VV. (2005).

[27] There is a marked contrast between the current preliminary text and the previous one of 1998, although the latter already contained a reference to the diversity of peoples, ethnic groups, and cultures. Regarding this, see Verdesoto (2001), pp. 183–192.

Title II (Articles 10–83) addressing *rights*. The inclusion of the specific rights of indigenous peoples in the constitutional texts as such is one of the distinctive features of refounding constitutionalism (both in Ecuador and, although in different ways, in Venezuela and Bolivia), in contrast to the silence that Latin American constitutionalism had traditionally maintained in this regard. It is necessary to specify, nevertheless, that in the case of Ecuador the previous Constitution of 1998 had already taken the first steps in this direction, devoting a specific section (Section 1 of Chapter V of Title III) to the rights of the *indigenous, black and Afro-Ecuadorian peoples* (Articles 83–85).[28]

The 2008 Constitution currently in force almost totally reproduces (Article 57) the extensive list of specific rights of the indigenous peoples already recognised in the constitutional text of 1998 (Article 84), adding in turn certain new clauses in order to extend or strengthen the protection of rights.[29] Thus, the right to maintain, develop, and strengthen their own collective *identity* is recognised (both in the 1998 text and in the text of 2008). The latter text adds, however, two new clauses to strengthen the protection of this right, making specific mention to racism and whatever form of "discrimination founded on origin and ethnic or cultural identity" (Article 57.2) and to the due "reparation and compensation for those groups subject to racism, xenophobia and other related forms of intolerance and discrimination" (Article 57.3). Likewise, the right "not to be evicted from their ancient lands" (Article 57.11) is also recognised (previously contained in the 1998 Constitution: Article 84.8).

With regard to the *property* of the indigenous communities, a specific regime is constitutionalised for this, based on recognition of the right to "preserve the imprescriptible property of their community lands, which will be inalienable, unseizable and indivisible", to "maintain possession of the ancestral lands and territories and to obtain their free adjudication", as well as to "participate in the use, usufruct and administration of the renewable resources which are found on their lands" (Article 57.4, 5 and 6). Likewise, and in relation to the protection of the properties owned by the indigenous communities, a prior consultation procedure is envisaged regarding "the plans and programmes for prospecting, exploitation and marketing of non-renewable resources which are found on their lands and which may affect them environmentally and culturally". Consultation is obligatory, but "should the consent of the community consulted not be obtained, things will proceed in accordance with the Constitution and the law" (Article 57.7); the latter clause introduced in the constitutional text of 2008 that was not present in that of 1998, which in all other respects regulated this matter in the same way.

In the organisational sphere, recognition is reiterated (it was already envisaged in the 1998 text, Article 84.7) of the right to "preserve and develop their own ways of coexistence and social organisation and of generating and exercising authority" (Article 57.9), although the 2008 constitutional text specifies that such a right

---

[28] See Pacari (2005), pp. 143–172.
[29] See Baltazar (2009), pp. 211–234.

remains confined to the territory of the indigenous community. A new clause was also introduced that envisaged that the creation and maintenance of the representative organisations of these communities should be carried out "within the framework of respect for pluralism and cultural, political and organisational diversity" (Article 57.15). The new clause offers special interest that, recognising the right of the indigenous communities to "create, develop, apply, and practise their own or common law", expressly introduces the constitutional provision that this "cannot violate constitutional rights, especially those of women, girls, boys and adolescents" (Article 57.10). This clause is especially suitable for preventing those practices that may involve violations of the fundamental rights of the most vulnerable social groups, invoking the traditional indigenous customs.[30]

In the area of participation, specific ways of participating for the indigenous communities in official organisations are foreseen, by means of their own representatives, "in the definition of those state policies which concern them, as well as the design and decision of the priorities in the plans and projects of the State" (Article 57.16), determining the specific field of the indigenous communities' right to participation with greater precision that, although it was recognised in the previous text of 1998 (Article 84.14), was limited to expressing the general principle of participation.

The extensive constitutional provision commented upon (Article 57), regarding the rights of the indigenous communities, also contains a series of new clauses not set out in the previous text of 1998, which should be emphasised. These include restricting military activities in the territory of the indigenous communities (Article 57.20), although it should be pointed out that this limitation is made "in accordance with the law" that obliges it to be referred to in order to determine the scope of this constitutional provision. Mandatory consultation is also envisaged (it is understood of which representative organisations of the indigenous communities) "before adopting a legislative measure which might affect any of their collective rights" (Article 57.17), and likewise, there is the commitment that "the dignity and diversity of their cultures, traditions, histories and aspirations be reflected in state education and the media" (Article 57.21).[31] Finally, maintaining and developing cooperative relations with other peoples is envisaged, "in particular those which are divided by international borders" (Article 57.18). This allusion to peoples divided by international borders, exceptional in comparative constitutionalism, takes on special significance in the case of Ecuador, given that in accordance with the Constitution (Article 7) Ecuadorian citizenship is awarded to "those persons belonging to communities, peoples and nationalities recognised by Ecuador who are present in border areas", which also constitutes an exceptional constitutional clause not devoid, however, of possible conflicting consequences with the bordering countries where indigenous communities also dwell.

---

[30] Regarding the specific problem that the coexistence of indigenous rights with the constitutional ones poses, see Vitale (2008), pp. 3–16.

[31] Regarding the new rights incorporated into current Latin American constitutionalism in general, see Noguera 2010, op. cit.

In the same provision (Article 57), the 2008 Ecuadorian Constitution introduces a specific reference to *the peoples in voluntary isolation*, an allusion to the aboriginal peoples of the Amazon region. The reference to this group of the population, who should not be confused with the *indigenous* population given that they do not live in isolation from the rest of the population, constitutes a new element in the constitutional text, both in relation to the previous one of 1998 and as regards current comparative constitutionalism in which specific provisions related to this question are not found. The current Ecuadorian Constitution deals with this subject by establishing the principle of the intangibility of the ancient possession of these peoples' territories, vetoing any type of mining activity there.[32] Likewise, the State promises to adopt the necessary measures "to make their self-determination and desire to remain in isolation respected and to ensure observance of their rights", whose violation will constitute a crime of ethnocide in the terms defined by the law.

As well as the extensive general provision commented upon in the preceding sections relating to the collective rights of the indigenous peoples, the 2008 constitutional text devotes two brief specific constitutional provisions to these, the first to the *Afro-Ecuadorian peoples* (Article 58), whose differentiated identity with regard to the indigenous populations is thus constitutionally reflected and to which "the collective rights established in the Constitution" are recognised, and the second devoted to the *Montubio peoples*[33] (Article 59), also with a differentiated identity, to which it constitutionally recognises "their ways of associative administration . . . . . . and respect for their own culture, identity and vision, in accordance with the law".

Finally, Chapter (IV), which we have commented upon, devoted to the *collective rights of the communities, peoples and nationalities* of the Ecuadorian Republic, concludes with a provision (Article 60) common to "the ancient, indigenous, Afro-Ecuadorian and Montubio peoples",[34] whose right to constitute *territorial districts* for the preservation of their culture is recognised. This is a constitutional provision that, in principle, offers undoubted interest from the perspective of the effect of the indigenous factor on the territorial organisation of the State. However, this obliges the subject to be treated within the framework of the constitutional provisions relating to the territorial organisation of the State that we will deal with below.

---

[32] This is a subject of maximum topicality that also affects the indigenous population and the cause of frequent conflicts between these population groups and the (normally foreign) mining companies. The media at times report these disturbances regarding this question, which are on occasions very serious (at the time of writing this paper, October–November 2011, there were incidents in Bolivia caused by the construction of the inter-oceanic road).

[33] A minority ethnic group, located on the Ecuadorian coast, the result of Indo-Afro-Hispanic cross-breeding.

[34] The statistics regarding the ethnic composition of the population, including the official ones, vary according to the classificatory criteria, in particular with respect to the mixed race population. One of those drawn up by the Official Institute (INEC) distributes the population in the following way: mixed race (55 %), Amerindians (22 %), whites (17 %), African descendants (3 %), and others (3 %). For more precise data, see Instituto Nacional de Estadística y Censo (INEC) (http://www.inec.gob.ec).

## A Limited Autonomous Territorial Reorganisation of the State

The 2008 Ecuadorian Constitution does not introduce important changes in the territorial organisation of the State, maintaining, in its basic aspects, the model already designed in the previous constitutional text of 1998.[35] We would merely point to the incorporation of the *regional* entities (dealt with below), together with the already existing municipal and provincial ones, into the territorial institutional structure of the State. It can be stated that the Ecuadorian refounding constitutionalism (as we have already seen in the case of Venezuela) has not entailed any important changes in this area, unlike in others (in particular, in the socio-economic field) where its impact has been greater.

The 2008 Ecuadorian constituent assembly devoted an extensive Title to the territorial organisation of the State (V: Articles 238–274), subdivided into five chapters in which, as well as establishing the general principles of the model, those aspects related to institutional organisation, area of competences, and economic resources are laid out. Although the 2008 refounding constituent assembly dealt with this subject more extensively (36 constitutional provisions in the 2008 text against 17 (less than half) in that of 1998 and even fewer in the previous ones that, at the very least, is indicative of the growing attention devoted to this subject), all it reveals is that the questions relating to the remodelled autonomous constitutional regime of 2008 are regulated in greater detail without it involving the adoption of a new model of territorial organisation different to that existing up till then.[36]

The Ecuadorian Constitution of 2008 establishes a model of political, administrative, and financial *autonomous decentralisation*, which is governed by principles of solidarity, subsidiarity, and inter-territorial equality, expressly specifying subsequently that "in no case will the exercise of autonomy allow secession from the national territory" (Article 238). The same constitutional provision then establishes the *decentralised autonomous* government bodies that exercise this autonomy: rural parochial boards, municipal councils, metropolitan councils, provincial councils (all of which previously existed), and *regional councils*, inexistent up till that moment and constitute the territorial-autonomous innovation of this Constitution (with which we will deal below). The silence regarding the *indigenous territorial districts* is striking (which we will also specifically look at further on and to which we have already referred in previous sections when dealing with the rights of the indigenous communities), although it has to be said that there is a passing reference

---

[35] Regarding the territorial organisation of the State in the previous Constitution of 1988, see Perez Loose (2005), pp.173–192.

[36] Regarding the model of territorial organisation in the 2008 Constitution, see Viciano (2009), pp. 105–118.

to them (in my opinion unsystematically, given that they are also autonomous bodies) in another provision (Article 242) devoted generically to the organisation of the territory.

With regard to the distribution of competences between the different *decentralised autonomous* entities, the 2008 Constitution substantially corrects the model established a decade earlier by the previous Constitution (1998),[37] based on the *dispositive* principle, by virtue of which the decentralised autonomous entities freely assumed (within the constitutional framework) the competences they deemed convenient, which at times gave rise to excessive dispersion of competences. The 2008 constitutional text, on the other hand, envisages establishing "a national system of obligatory competences" (Article 239) by which all the *decentralised autonomous governments* have to be ruled. In contrast to that previously available in the system of competences, this obligation is further reinforced by the express constitutional provision of "obligatory *planning* for all the decentralised autonomous governments" (Article 241). Likewise, a technical organisation is set up, comprising a representative of each level of government, to make the national system of competences effective (Article 269).

It is necessary to make two critical observations regarding the inadequate way in which distribution of competences is regulated[38] between the different *decentralised autonomous* entities (according to the repeatedly used terms in the Ecuadorian constitutional text). The first refers to the lack of rigour, which means the indiscriminate assignment of *legislative* powers to all "the decentralised autonomous governments of the regions, the metropolitan districts, the provinces and cantons" (Article 240), inevitably leading to confusion in the nature of the competences attributed to each level of government. The second is describing every competence of all the decentralised autonomous entities (Articles 261 onwards) as *exclusive,* which in practice is neither reasonable nor viable. It is not surprising, therefore, that the Constitution itself corrects this deficiency by attempting to reconcile the exclusive nature with that concurrent in the competences: "exercising exclusive competences will not exclude concurrent exercise of management in the provision of public services" (Article 260), thus creating a new, hybrid type of competence of an exclusive and concurrent nature, at the same time as merely increasing the confusion over the nature of the competences.

We will not attempt in this paper to examine the autonomous structures in the municipal and provincial entities, given that it is not the aim of the present work and, further, they do not display any significant innovations (except those already mentioned in the previous sections) with regard to the previous autonomous constitutional system. However, it is necessary to give a brief, critical consideration regarding the advisability of continuing to maintain the autonomous provincial entities when the Constitution of 2008 introduced the new regional autonomous

---

[37] See Perez Loose (2005), op. cit.
[38] See Viciano 2009, p. 108, op. cit.

entities into the territorial structure. This is precisely one of the principal constitutional changes with respect to the territorial organisation of the State, which we will now analyse.

The configuration of the *autonomous regions* in Ecuador, as envisaged in the constitutional text of 2008, poses an initial problem: namely, the lack of tradition and regional feeling in this country in which, up to that moment, only the municipalities and provinces existed as territorial organisations. From the territorial point of view, three major natural areas or "regions" can be distinguished in Ecuador: the coast, the mountain chain, and the Amazon region, although they have never had any common entity, at least in legal-political terms. To this we have to add the historical rivalry between the two major urban and economic centres of the country: Guayaquil and the capital, Quito, which more than regional entities, strictly speaking, are built-up urban areas. It is not surprising, therefore, that the Ecuadorian constituent assembly, in spite of setting up the *autonomous regions* as a central element of the territorial organisation of the country, was not able to determine or delimit territorially the regional bodies.

In the absence of this constitutional realisation, the Ecuadorian constituent assembly was limited to indicating how the regional organisations could be set up, something that the Constitution envisaged but did not determine. In this respect, the dispositive principle was established, by virtue of which two or more provinces with territorial continuity, on condition that they jointly cover over 20,000 square kilometres and more than 5 % of the national population, would be able to form an *autonomous region*.[39] In accordance with the constitutional statement, with the conformation of the new regional bodies, "interregional balance, historical and cultural affinity, ecological complementarity and the integrated management of the basin will be secured" (Article 244). This same provision expressly envisages "economic and other types of incentives so that the provinces are integrated into regions", reflecting the interest of the constituent assembly in making the new regional bodies the focal point of the territorial organisation of the State.

The autonomous regions thus set up have a Statute whose project is drawn up jointly by the representatives of the provinces that comprise the new autonomous region (given that this is based on the provinces). It is finally approved by the National Parliament (which can only reject it by a majority of 2/3 of its members) and is then sent to the Constitutional Court to ensure that it conforms to the Constitution. Ultimately, it is voted on in a referendum by the population of the new region (Article 245). Once this procedure is complied with, "the approved Statute will be the basic institutional norm of the region and will establish its name, symbols, principles and institutions of the regional government".[40]

---

[39] The 24 provinces, already in existence prior to the current Constitution, are grouped into seven regions (newly created bodies) and two metropolitan districts: Quito and Guayaquil.

[40] The similarity between the Spanish Constitution in the definition of the Statutes as a "basic institutional norm" is striking, which denotes the influence that this exercised on the Ecuadorian constituent assembly. Regarding this question, see Salgado (2003), pp. 445–458.

Although the Constitution does not determine, as we have already indicated, the regional political map of the country, it *does* directly delimit, however, the area of competences of the new regional bodies (observe the similarity also in this respect with the Spanish autonomous constitutional model). In accordance with the terms in which the constitutional text regulates this matter (Article 262), it can be stated that it is a very limited regional autonomy, formulated on the basis of the pre-existing provincial structure and focused, above all, on the planning of economic develop-ment and territorial organisation,[41] with a specific mention of the water basins and the regional road and transport system. Likewise, the list of *exclusive* competences assigned to the newly created regional bodies also envisages promoting regional productive activities and food safety and finally extends to registering and controlling regional social organisations and international cooperation for the fulfilment of their competences.

Given the reduced scope of competences of the autonomous regions thus delimited, it is yet to be seen how this will evolve in the future: whether the provincial structure is to be reproduced on a larger scale, given the shallow roots of regional awareness in Ecuador, or whether an expansive dynamic is opened up, as has already occurred in other similar autonomous processes, in which the regional bodies widen their sphere of competences to reach the level of exclusive State competences. Lastly, and to round off the regional autonomous field of competences, special attention should be drawn to the fact that no constitutional reference exists regarding the indigenous question, once again evidencing in the Ecuadorian refounding consti-tutional structure (as we saw previously in Venezuela) the lack of connection between this question and the territorial reorganisation of the State.

## Bolivian Constitutional Refoundation: Its Impact on the Status of the Indigenous Population and on the Territorial Reorganisation of the State

### Constitutional Redefinition of Bolivia

Bolivia is, without doubt, one of the countries in which the importance of the indigenous population is greatest.[42] From the outset, this determines the effect (much greater than in other countries) that the indigenous factor has on all aspects

---

[41] Regarding this subject, see Suing Nagua (2009), op. cit., pp. 383–401.

[42] 68 % of the Bolivian people identify themselves as cross-bred, 18 % as indigenous-native, and 37 % as white (descendents of Hispano-Europeans), according to data from the National Survey carried out by the Fundación Boliviana para la Democracia Multipartidaria (FBDM) and the Fondo para la Democracia de las Naciones Unidas (UNDEF). To determine the ethnic composition of the Bolivian population more accurately, see the Reports of the Bolivian National Statistics Institute (INE) at: http://www.ine.gob.bo

of Bolivian social and political life and also on the constitutional sphere. Moreover, the constitutional refoundation movement, which burst upon the scene in the first decade of the twenty-first century in some Latin American countries and which was to have one of its clearest manifestations in Bolivia, focuses particular attention on the indigenous question and makes it one of the core elements of its refounding project. The Bolivian refounding constituent assembly's interest (2007–2009) in the indigenous question, to which it was to give a highly original treatment, is not therefore surprising.

As previously indicated, apart from specific exceptions (Guatemala, 1985, and Colombia, 1991), Latin American constitutionalism has barely concerned itself with the indigenous question until very recently. This general rule is also applicable to Bolivia, despite the great importance that the indigenous population has in this country, something that aggravates the imbalance between the norms and institutions derived from the constitutional texts, on the one hand, and the social medium in which they operate, on the other. Even before the appearance of refounding constitutionalism, it is this fact that gave rise to the inclusion in the constitutional texts of certain references related to what might generically be termed the *indigenous factor*. As in the case of Ecuador, which we have just examined (whose 1998 constitutional text had already dealt with the indigenous question), Bolivian constitutional reforms of 1994 and 2004[43] also dealt with this question prior to the approval (2009) of the constitutional text currently in force.

Thus, after the constitutional reform of 1994, the Bolivian Republic, as well as being free, independent, and unitary, as defined in previous texts, was to add the defining characteristics of *multi-ethnic and multicultural* (Article 1), in reference to the indigenous components of the Bolivian population: a reference that was strengthened with the specific constitutional recognition (Article 171) of "the social, economic and cultural rights of the indigenous peoples...especially those related to their original community lands....and to their identity, values, languages and customs or institutions", accompanied by the provision of a recognition on the part of the State of "legal status for the indigenous communities". Finally, it was envisaged that "the natural authorities of the indigenous communities and rural dwellers will be able to exercise administrative functions and apply their own norms...in accordance with their customs...provided they do not conflict with the Constitution and the laws" (Article 171).

In the long and bitter process that the Bolivian refounding constituent assembly undertook in the second half of the last decade,[44] the indigenous question was to

---

[43] The modifications introduced by these constitutional reforms can be consulted in the compilation of the Bolivian Constitutions (and Hispano-American ones, in general), which the Cervantes virtual library offers, at http://bib.cervantesvirtual.com/portal/constituciones. A commentary on the previous Constitution of 1967, of which these reforms are made, can be seen in Harb (1992), pp. 99–125.

[44] The Bolivian constituent process was particularly conflictive and prolonged. It began with the victory of Evo Morales in the Presidential elections of December, 2005, and continued until January, 2009, when the referendum was held to approve the new Constitutional text currently in force. See Storini and Noguera (2008), pp. 1285–1304.

have a relevance it had never before had in Bolivia and that was much greater than it had enjoyed in any other Latin American country. That was to be reflected, logically, throughout the unusually long Bolivian constitutional text (more than 400 Articles) and, in particular, in the constitutional passages devoted to the description of the State, the rights (especially of the indigenous population), and the territorial organisation of the State, subject matters that we will now look at.

Already in the Preamble, when expressing the constituent assembly's desire *to build a new State,* the *plural composition* of the Bolivian people is alluded to and specific mention is made of the indigenous factor as a constitutive element: specifically, the *indigenous anti-colonial uprisings* and the more recent *indigenous marches* by land and water (second paragraph). In accordance with these premises, the new refounding State added to the descriptive notes that it already had in previous texts (unitary, democratic, social justice) the new description of *multi-national community* (fourth paragraph), in clear reference to the indigenous communities that make up the State. Finally (sixth paragraph), the "mandate of our peoples" is alluded to (in plural, although the reference to "the original power of the people" is also employed in singular, a titular subject of the constituent power) as an authorising title for adopting the constituent assembly decision to *refound* Bolivia in the terms specified throughout the extensive Bolivian constitutional text (411 Articles).[45]

In this aspect, the first provisions of the constitutional text relating to the *State model* concern the definition of this, together with the traditionally mentioned traits (free, independent, sovereign, democratic, etc.), as *decentralised and with autonomous regions*, embracing the principle of *cultural and linguistic* (as well as political, economic, and legal) *pluralism* "within the integrating process of the country" (Article 1). Of particular interest, from the standpoint of the communal composition of the population, is the following constitutional provision (Article 2) since it introduces the notion of indigenous multinationality (*rural native indigenous peoples and nations*), which should not go unnoticed in the Bolivian refounding constitutional structure[46] and which was to be constantly reiterated, as we will have occasion to see below, throughout the constitutional text. The Constitution "guarantees free self-determination" for these bodies although the same constitutional text is quick to clarify that this has to be considered "within the framework of State unity" and that the content of self-determination for these entities "consists of their right to autonomy, self-government, their culture, recognition of their institutions and consolidation of their territorial bodies, in accordance with the Constitution and the law" (Article 2).

---

[45] The extensive preamble to the present Constitution contrasts with the absence of a preamble in the previous constitutional texts, which has led Bolivian constitutionalists to consider the Act of Independence and the Declaration of 1825 as the foundational text. In this regard, see Harb (2001), p. 61 onwards.

[46] See del Real Alcala (2011), p. 115.

One characteristic and distinctive feature of Bolivian constitutional refoundation is that it is not limited to the state institutional system but rather extends to the Bolivian nation itself,[47] "made up of all Bolivians, the rural native indigenous nations and peoples, and the intercultural Afro-Bolivian communities, which together constitute the Bolivian people" (Article 3). The common language of Bolivia, which is Spanish, is directly constitutionalised, moreover, as the joint official language along with "all the languages of the rural native indigenous nations and peoples", which the Constitution (Article 5) lists (36 languages as well as Spanish). To guarantee linguistic plurality, it was envisaged, likewise, that both the multinational government (Bolivian) and the departmental governments (we will later deal with these departments) must use at least two official languages, Spanish being one of them (Article 5.II).

Although we will return to this theme, as we are dealing with the recognised constitutional rights of the indigenous population, it is necessary to make a brief critical comment regarding the notion, to which the constitutional text repeatedly refers, of *rural native indigenous nations and peoples*. In this regard, and concerning only their relationship with the subject under discussion regarding the description of the State, the suitability of this name to refer to the whole of the indigenous population is debatable since not all the indigenous population(s) are of a rural nature, as is shown by the important presence of the non-rural indigenous population in mining and craftworks in the urban centres. Even more debatable is the description of each and every one of the existing indigenous communities as *nations*, merely because they make up distinct linguistic groups (no less than 36, according to the report on official languages of the previously mentioned Article 5 of the Constitution), thus identifying the nation with the distinct ethno-linguistic group,[48] although it *is* true that all of this is accompanied by the simultaneous and prevalent affirmation of the Bolivian nation and people, titleholders to constituent power and sovereignty (Article 7).

The fact that the State assumes and promotes (Article 8) the *ethical-moral principles* typical of the indigenous communities, which remain expressly constitutionalised as such (Article 8.I), strengthens the indigenous component of Bolivian constitutional refoundation. Nor is there any shortage of references to national, cultural, and linguistic plurality derived from the indigenous factor when pointing to the *essential aims and functions* of the State (Article 9). Leaving aside the debatable mixture of aims and functions (which are different concepts) in the same constitutional provision, we should note the references to the consolidation of multinational identities (Article 9.1), the promotion of intra-cultural, intercultural, and multicultural dialogues (Article 9.2), and the preservation of

---

[47] See Nuñez Rivero (2009), p. 566.

[48] Regarding the question of multinationality in Bolivia, see the debate on the subject between Noguera 2008, no. 84, pp. 147–167, and Noguera 2009, no. 87, pp. 241–269; Arevalo, no. 85, pp. 187–199 and Arevalo, no. 89, pp. 195–217.

multinational diversity, although these are compatible with the reaffirmation of the unity of the nation (Article 9.3).

Lastly, regarding the principles that inspire the system of government and the kinds of democracy, as well as the well-known classical forms of direct and representative democracy, we should mention the specific reference to *communal democracy*. This is, in accordance with the Constitution, one further kind of democratic exercise in the specific field of indigenous populations that envisages "the election, appointment or nomination of authorities and representatives by norms and procedures typical of the rural native indigenous nations and peoples", specifying that all of this should be performed "in accordance with the law" (Article 11.II.3).

## Constitutionalisation of the Rights of the Rural Native Indigenous Nations and Peoples

As we have already seen in the previous cases of Venezuela and Ecuador, the refounding constitutional texts devote a specific section to the rights of the indigenous communities, this being, further, one of the distinctive features of the recent constitutional trends that draw upon this orientation.[49] Bolivia, where the effect of the indigenous factor is stronger than in any other Latin American country, is no exception, and its recent Constitution also addresses this question, devoting a specific Chapter to it, as part of Title II, related to *fundamental rights*, expressively entitled "Rights of the rural native indigenous nations and peoples".

Before examining these specific rights, it is necessary to identify who they refer to, which leads us once again to the notion of *rural native indigenous nations and peoples*. In this regard, the constitutional text provides us with a definition of these, considering as such "all human groups which share a cultural identity, language, historical tradition, institutions, territoriality and view of the world, whose existence is prior to the Spanish colonial invasion" (Article 30.1). We should reiterate the critical observations expressed previously regarding the questionable suitability of the name and definition employed in the constitutional text to refer to the indigenous communities, given that it is more than debatable, in our opinion, that the term *nation* can be attributed to all the distinct indigenous groups (many, indeed the majority, of whom are very small and show no awareness of, or interest in, becoming a nation). Another entirely different matter is recognising and protecting a series of specific rights for those people as members of these indigenous communities, which the constitutional text also deals with in the terms that we describe below.

---

[49] Regarding recognition of the rights of the indigenous peoples in general, see AA.VV. (2007), especially the second part specifically devoted to "exercising the rights of the indigenous peoples", pp. 161–333.

In the extensive list of rights constitutionally recognised for the indigenous population (Article 30.II. Numbers 1–18), some of which are of a very diverse nature, of special interest to us are those that have a greater effect on the institutional structure of the State and on the most relevant economic and political aspects of the life of the indigenous communities.[50] In this respect, together with the obvious right "to exist freely" (Num. 1) and to their own "cultural identity" (Num. 2), which is specified in greater detail in the different sections of the list, we should make an initial observation regarding the field in which the rights are recognised, which the provision itself expressly establishes, delimiting it within "the framework of State unity and in accordance with this Constitution" (Article 30.II).

Thus, it is necessary to embrace the right to *free determination and territoriality* (Num. 4) within this framework, as well as the right to "exercise their political, legal and economic systems in accordance with their view of the world" (Num. 14), which perforce must be framed within the principles of state unity and in accordance with constitutional norms. They should equally have the right to enjoy their own institutions and to form part of the general structure of the State (Num. 5) and, in the institutional field, have the right to *participate* in the bodies and institutions of the State (Num. 18). Finally, the right to *consultation* is established through the indigenous communities' own institutions "whenever legislative or administrative measures are envisaged which might affect them" (Num. 15).[51]

In the sphere of economic and social rights, we should mention the right "to the collective ownership of the lands and territories" (Num. 6), which is thus constitutionally formulated explicitly as a collective right of the indigenous community and of the members that comprise it regarding the land that belongs to them and the territory they inhabit.[52] In relation to this collective territorial right, we should also mention the right "to participate in the profits from exploiting the natural resources of the territories" (Num. 16), from which the whole of the indigenous community collectively benefits. In this same group of rights, we should also include the right related to "the autonomous indigenous territorial management and exclusive use and exploitation of the renewable natural resources existing in their territory" (Num. 17), compatible with the rights legitimately acquired by third parties in accordance with the constitutional provisions.

The catalogue of specific rights unique to the indigenous population is completed by a series of miscellaneous rights, although linked in different ways

---

[50] Regarding the problem that this subject raises, see Noguera (2010), pp. 87–116.

[51] It would be more appropriate to talk of a *right to consultation* on the part of the institutions when these adopt a decision that affects the indigenous population. It is a highly topical question that often causes organised protests of the indigenous population (such as that which was taking place at the time the present paper was written (October–November 2011) in Bolivia as a result of construction work on the inter-oceanic road running through the Bolivian indigenous territories).

[52] Regarding this question, set in the more general context of globalisation, see Assies (2007), op. cit., pp. 227–246.

to the cultural identity/identities of the indigenous population.[53] Among these should be mentioned, firstly, that related to the public expression of the cultural identity of the people, who can make their personality expressly known, if they so wish, in their identity card, passport, or any other identification document (Num. 3). It is interesting to underline that public manifestation of the cultural identity of the people is not posed as an alternative to common Bolivian citizenship but complementary and compatible with it.

Other rights also related to the different manifestations of cultural identity are those concerning respect for their own religious beliefs and spirituality (Num. 2) and to the protection of their sacred places (Num. 7). In educational matters, the right is recognised to "an intra-cultural, intercultural and multilingual education throughout the educational system" (Num. 12). Over and above the literalness of the statement, this has to be understood not so much as a right in the strict sense but as a programmatic principle in favour of multilingualism and interculturalism since it is highly problematical to effectively guarantee education in any educational system in the 36 languages constitutionally recognised.[54]

Lastly, within the sphere of cultural identity, there are allusions to respect, that is, allusions to promoting and developing "traditional learning and knowledge" (Num. 9), as well as (a question that poses greater legal problems vis-à-vis their delimitation) to the right "to the collective intellectual property (of the indigenous communities) of their learning, sciences and knowledge" (Num. 11). It would be necessary to examine, in any case, what learning, sciences, and knowledge we are dealing with, given that these do not necessarily always have to be subject to promotion and development. We should make similar considerations regarding the allusion to the valuation, respect, and promotion of "traditional medicine" and to the idea that the health system should "respect the view of the world and traditional practices" (of the indigenous population) (Num. 13). In this regard, we should say that the constitutionalisation of notions such as that of *traditional medicine* (above all, if it has to be the subject of valuation and promotion) is more than doubtful (Num. 9) or the provision that the health system has to respect their view of the world and traditional practices (Num. 13). Finally, there is an allusion to a special category of indigenous nations and peoples: those that are "in a situation of voluntary isolation and out of contact" (Article 31), to which the Constitution affords protection and respect for their individual and collective ways of life, something that also seems somewhat dubious from the constitutional perspective and poses serious problems as regards effective compliance.

---

[53] Rights that are closely linked to the formulation of indigenous autonomy. Regarding this, see Aparicio Wilhelmi (2007), op. cit., pp. 247–28.

[54] Article 5 of the present Bolivian Constitution lists no less than 36 official languages, the majority of them spoken by very small groups, which means that their official status is more formal than real and effective.

## Territorial Reorganisation of the State Within the New Constitutional Framework

In Bolivia, as in the other two countries previously examined (Ecuador and Venezuela) with which it shares the refounding constitutional experience, territorial organisation of the State has not been one of the topics that has historically merited special attention, either in Bolivian political discourse in general or in the specifically constitutional sphere.[55] From the beginning, the territorial organisation of the Bolivian State has corresponded to a unitary model, in particular in its Spanish version, which is logical given the close political relationships between both countries. However, it is also necessary to highlight the French influence,[56] which has historically constituted the reference model for this type of territorial organisation. Whatever the case, what is certain is that adopting the centralised unitary model was commonly and generally accepted and posed no constitutional problem.

The recent appearance, especially in Bolivia over the last two decades, of the movements and demands of the indigenous peoples introduced a new factor that was to decisively affect the development of political processes and, likewise, the constitutional sphere in particular. One direct consequence of this was the constitutional changes that took place in the countries in which the indigenous question had the greatest impact, in particular, in the Andean countries[57] and, specially, Bolivia. The refounding constituent process that recently took place in this country (2006–2009) was to provide the perfect framework for the indigenous question to have a wide constitutional expression linked to the territorial reorganisation of the State.

Together with the appearance of the movements and demands of the indigenous peoples,[58] whose effect on the development of the constituent process was to prove notable, a further factor was present on the Bolivian political scene during the constituent assembly period: namely, the demands for greater departmental autonomy to manage economic affairs on the part of the dominant social groups in their respective departmental territorial spheres. These were two movements of a different and even opposing nature in certain cases but that converged in demanding a change to the model of territorial organisation of the State, although this temporary consensus in the common objective of territorial reorganisation should not hide the disparity of the aims that were pursued: the constitutional recognition of the

---

[55] A brief overview regarding the Bolivian historical constitutional evolution and, in particular, the previous Constitution of 1967 to the present one can be seen in Harb (1992), pp. 99–125.

[56] The terms used in the constitutional text (and in the laws) to refer to the territorial units—*Departments*—and to the authorities that head them—*Prefect*—are very illustrative, in this respect.

[57] As well as the Ecuadorian and Bolivian Constitutions which we examine in this paper, we should also mention the 1991 Colombian and 1993 Peruvian Constitutions. Regarding the latter, see Eastman (1991), pp. 233–253 and Palomino (2000), pp. 279–290.

[58] See Marti i Puig (2007), op. cit., pp. 127–148.

indigenous identity, in the one case, and that of departmental autonomy for managing economic affairs, in the other.

It is precisely this duality, by which we refer to the components that gave rise to and that operated on the process of territorial reorganisation of the State in Bolivia, which enables us to explain the peculiar characteristics that, as we shall see below, the Bolivian autonomous model displays. Understandably, this reflects the tensions and contradictions typical of Bolivian society and, more specifically, the response that the refounding constituent assembly gave to these by structuring a complex and diversified autonomous system that can only be correctly understood by starting from the plurality of autonomous peoples, each with their own mutually different aims and demands.


## A Diversified and Plural Autonomous System

The current Bolivian Constitution, the product of an eventful constituent process lasting over 3 years (2006–2009),[59] established a diversified system of territorial organisation. According to the constitutional provision that opens Title (I of the Third Part) regarding the *Territorial Organisation of the State*, "Bolivia is organised territorially in departments, provinces, municipalities and rural native indigenous territories" (Article 269.I), to which have to be added "the regions (which) will form part of the territorial organisation, in the terms and conditions determined by the law"[60] (Article 269. III). Therefore, already existing territorial bodies—municipalities, provinces, and departments—are now joined by newly created ones: rural native indigenous regions and territories, the departments undergoing a reconfiguration as autonomies in the terms we will examine later.

Although the Constitution makes express reference to the principle of equality between all the entities referred to—"the autonomous territorial entities will not be subordinated among themselves and will have equal constitutional rank" (Article 276)—what is true is that we have entities of a distinct nature from the autonomous point of view.[61] In this regard, the new rural native indigenous autonomies (according to their constitutional name) and the reconfigured departmental autonomies constitute the basic elements around which the territorial organisation of the Bolivian State revolves. Regarding regional autonomy, introduced by this constitutional change, it is still difficult to express an opinion given the imprecision with which this new figure is envisaged in the constitutional text (unlike the

---

[59] Regarding the drawn-out and conflictive Bolivian constituent process, see Storini and Noguera (2008), pp. 1285–1304.

[60] Framework Law for Autonomy and Decentralisation (LMAD, in Spanish). The unabridged text of this important constitutional developmental law regarding the territorial organisation of the State can be seen at http://file.minedu.gob.bo/ves/ves_11.pdf.

[61] Regarding the distinct nature of the different autonomous bodies—departmental, indigenous, and regional—see Clavero and Noguera 2005, in the debate about multinationality and autonomy in nos. 84, 85, 87, 89, op. cit.

remaining autonomies, except the provincial ones, they do not have their own defined area of competencies). For its part, municipal autonomy poses another different problem that has no direct relationship with the autonomous reorganisation of the State.

The Constitution delimits the autonomous field in general, which covers, "the exercise of the legislative, regulatory, executive and taxation powers by the autonomous government bodies in the area of their jurisdiction, competences and powers" (Article 272), as well as the administration of their own economic resources. This same constitutional provision links autonomy with "the direct election of their authorities by the citizens", which excludes the external designation (of the central state powers) of the autonomous authorities. The Constitution also envisages drawing up a "Statute or Organic Charter" of the autonomous territorial bodies "which will have to be approved by two thirds of the total of its members (representative body) and, with prior constitutional control, will come into force as a basic institutional norm of the territorial entity through a favourable referendum in its jurisdiction" (Article 275).[62] The express constitutional demand for democratic conformation of the autonomous entities should be underlined both as regards the election of their authorities and as to the establishment of their institutional framework.

Finally, the Bolivian constituent assembly remits to the constituted powers, in particular to the Multinational Legislative Assembly, the task of approving a specific law regarding the subject matter (the Framework Law for Autonomies and Decentralisation),[63] specifying that a qualified majority of two-thirds of the members of the said Assembly present will be required for this (Article 271). The large majority required for its approval is striking, the same that is required for reform of the Constitution (Article 411), which explains the importance the constituent assembly attached to this law. The twin reference in its title to the *autonomies* and to *decentralisation* should also be highlighted and is indicative of the duality of the entities (strictly speaking, autonomic or merely decentralised), which the Bolivian constituent assembly contemplated when reorganising the State.

## Departmental Autonomy

The Bolivian Constitution currently in force (since 2009) maintains the *Departments*, already existing under the previous constitutional regime (Constitution of 1967, modified in 1994, 1995, and 2004), as a basic structural element of the territorial organisation of the State, although these underwent a major restructuring

---

[62] As already pointed out on previous occasions in relation to Venezuela and Ecuador, the lexis used in the Bolivian constitutional text, and in particular in its provisions relating to territorial organisation (Statute of Autonomy, a basic institutional norm), also reflects the influence of the Spanish constitution. In this regard, see Rivera (2003), pp. 177–195.

[63] Regarding the role of this law (LMAD) of constitutional application in the Bolivian autonomous process, see Barrios 2011, p. 84 onwards.

as entities endowed with political autonomy (which they previously lacked). In the previous Constitution, the Departments were configured as territorial districts for exercising central political power. This is reflected by their inclusion in the previous constitutional text in the Chapter relating to executive power, together with the provinces and other local entities (Article 108). Heading the Department was a Prefect, directly appointed by the President of the Republic, titleholder of executive power (Article 109), and as specified by the Constitution itself, power was exercised in this territorial sphere in accordance with the principle of administrative decentralisation (Article 110).[64]

Within the Title relating to the "Territorial Organisation of the State" (Title I of the Third Part), the present Constitution devotes a specific Chapter to *departmental autonomy*, a term that is indicative of the (previously lacking) autonomous nature of the new departmental entities. In accordance with the new Constitution, it is understood that a territorial body (in this case, the Departments) is autonomous when its authorities are directly elected by the population living there (and are not externally appointed by the central power, as previously occurred), when it administers its own economic powers and, through its own bodies of autonomous government, exercises legislative, regulatory, executive, and controlling powers in its own area of competences (Article 272).

The institutional organisation of the departmental autonomies that the Constitution envisages is based on an executive body, "directed by the Governor in his/her capacity as the supreme executive authority" (Article 279). Although the Constitution says nothing specifically about how they are elected, in accordance with the Presidential-style institutional system typical of the Bolivian political regime (as well as Latin American countries in general), it is understood that the Governors have to be elected directly by the whole of the population, as occurs with the election of the President of the Republic. Likewise, it should be understood that, once the head of the departmental executive has been elected, he/she freely names the members of the team who comprise it.

The Departmental Assembly is the other body that, together with the previous one, completes the institutional system of the departmental autonomy. The Constitution specifically assigns to this the "deliberative, fiscal and legislative power. . ..in the area of their competences" (Article 277),[65] likewise envisaging its election by "universal, direct, free, secret and obligatory ballot" (Article 278). In this case, however, it is necessary to draw attention to the constitutional prevention that this provision establishes over representation in the Departmental Assembly, reserving a quota (which is not determined in the Constitution) to the "departmental assembly

---

[64] Regarding territorial organisation prior to that established by the current Constitution, see Barrios (2011), op. cit., in particular, the section devoted to "the Bolivian territorial organisation prior to Constitution reform", p. 66 onwards. Likewise, regarding the origin of the new departmental autonomies, see Urenda (2005).

[65] Including the departmental legislatures in the institutional system affects the reconfiguration of state legislature, a question already posed during the course of the constituent debate. See, in this regard, Asbun (2007).

members elected by the rural native indigenous nations and peoples, in accordance with their own norms and procedures". In this same line, it is also envisaged that the law that regulates the departmental assembly members takes into account, among others, the factor of "cultural and linguistic identity when the rural native indigenous peoples are in a minority" (Article 278. II). Specific constitutional cover is also given to the indigenous and linguistic-cultural factor in the composition of the representative bodies of the Departments, which up till then had been formulated disregarding any consideration concerning these factors.

The Constitution also directly delimits the constitutional field of departmental autonomy (Article 300) through a long list of *exclusive* competences (36). Without examining all 36 of the exclusive departmental competences (which is impossible in this study), it is interesting to point out that on many occasions such exclusivity does not exist, given that the "exclusive" competences in many cases are exercised (employing a language already familiar to us and that has possibly influenced the Bolivian one) "within the framework of"... "in coordination with", etc. In other cases, a confused situation occurs given that on occasions the "exclusive" departmental competences overlap or are duplicated in relation to the, almost "exclusive", competences either of the State or of the municipalities. A period of running in of the new system of territorial distribution of power will also be necessary in order to duly correct the imbalances with respect to the competences, a likely result of the novel autonomous experience that has only just commenced.

Among the competences assigned to the Departments by the Constitution and the development legislation, it is necessary to make a specific reference to those of a fiscal or budgetary nature.[66] In this regard, the Departments are recognised as having the power to "create and administer departmental taxes" (Article 300. I. 22), although it is specified that the taxable items cannot be analogous to those of the national or municipal sphere. Likewise, the Departments are recognised as having the power to draw up, approve, and execute their own budgets (Article 300. I.26). These competences in the tax and budgetary area are completed by a large block of economic matters, which range from the defence of competition (Num. 24) and promotion of private investment (Num. 34) to the creation of public enterprises or economic planning in the departmental sphere. It is worth noting this specific mention to tax, budgetary, and economic matters in general, given that these were at the heart of the "autonomous" demands of the economic groups that made up the departmental establishment,[67] which finally, as can be observed by reading the constitutional text, were included in it.

---

[66] See Barrios (2010).

[67] Especially the eastern Departments (Santa Cruz, Beni, Pando, Tarija), where the demands for departmental autonomy were stronger and, in particular, the Department of Santa Cruz, which has the greatest economic and demographic importance in Bolivia. See, in this respect, Barrios (2005).

## Rural Native Indigenous Autonomy

Constitutional recognition of *rural native indigenous autonomy* is one of the most outstanding innovations of the complex system of territorial organisation of the State established by recent Bolivian fundamental law. A specific Chapter is devoted to this (Chapter VII, Articles 289–296), in which the nature of this new autonomous concept is delimited. This does not prove at all easy at times, given its peculiarity and lack of correspondence with equivalent concepts in comparative constitutional experience. It should be pointed out, moreover, that this new autonomous entity, conceived by the Bolivian refounding constituent assembly for the *indigenous* population to be included in it,[68] was to coexist in the complex Bolivian autonomous system, with other autonomous entities such as the *Departments*, already referred to, and the *Regions*, with which we will deal below.

In accordance with the constitutional provisions that deal with the question, "rural native indigenous autonomy consists of self-government as the exercise of the free determination of the rural native nations and peoples, whose population share their own territory, culture, history, languages as well as legal, political, social and economic organisation or institutions" (Article 289). In view of this constitutional definition of the *indigenous autonomy*, we should carry out similar critical considerations to those already made when commenting on the provision relating to the constitutional definition of the *rural native indigenous nations and peoples* (Article 30), with which it is closely related. In this case, as well as reiterating the critical considerations regarding the description of all the different ethno-linguistic groups as a *nation* (some consisting of several or a few thousand individuals), critical objections to the comparison made of the notion of indigenous self-government and that of free national self-determination have to be understood.

It is certainly true that, immediately following, it is specifically and repeatedly emphasised that exercising indigenous self-government is framed within what is established in the Constitution and the law (Article 290 I and II, Articles 291 and 292), which delimits its scope in legal terms irrespective of allusions to the free national determination referred to. The Constitution envisages, likewise, that rural native indigenous autonomy has to be expressed in legal terms through a *Statute* that, although drawn up in accordance with the norms and procedures typical of the indigenous community that accedes to self-government, should be done so, it is again stressed, in accordance with the Constitution and the law (Article 292). In any case, the very recent creation of the indigenous autonomies makes it impossible, at the moment, to make any well-founded evaluation of the role they play (or that they might play in the future) in the Bolivian institutional system and political process.[69]

Given that the indigenous autonomies are newly created entities, unlike the municipalities and Departments that had already existed (although the latter underwent major reconfiguration), the Constitution envisages the possible channels

---

[68] See Albó and Romero (2009).
[69] See Mendoza (2009).

for the composition of these new autonomous entities. In this regard, it is based on the principle that the creation of an indigenous autonomy has to be the result of "the will expressed by its population in accordance with its own norms and procedures" (Article 293.I). Establishing minimum population requirements is accepted (Article 293. III) in order to avoid the risk of excessive autonomic fragmentation, and finally, specific reference is made to coordination and cooperation in the exercise of self-government, remitting to the law[70] to establish the mechanisms that formulate them (Article 293. IV).

The municipalities can adopt the decision to form themselves into a rural native indigenous autonomy, although this decision has to be taken with the direct participation of the peoples concerned through a referendum and in accordance with the conditions and requirements established by law (Article 294. II). Likewise, in the municipalities where indigenous communities exist and that have "their own organisational structures which coordinate them", these can form a new municipality. In this case, however, for its definitive approval it is necessary to follow the procedure established by the Multinational Legislative Assembly (Article 294. III). With regard to self-government of the rural native indigenous autonomies, as well as envisaging that it be exercised "by means of their own norms and types of organisation", it is reiterated that it must be done in accordance with the Constitution and the law (Article 296).

As we have already seen with departmental autonomy, the Constitution directly delimits the area of competences pertaining to the rural native indigenous autonomy via a very extensive, triple list of competences: exclusive, shared, and concurrent (Article 304), to which would have to be added the remaining ones of the constitutional clause (Article 303) that assigns the municipal competences to the indigenous autonomies in those cases contemplated in the Framework Law for Autonomies and Decentralisation. Without attempting an individual examination here of the subject matters that comprise the area of competences of the indigenous autonomy (which is impossible in a study such as this), critical observations can be carried out similar to those already made when dealing with departmental autonomy regarding the dubious exclusivity of many of them, as well as the duplications (or triplications at times) that can be seen in the different, and numerous, lists of competences.

Among other issues, competence should be mentioned with regard to cultural, tangible, and intangible heritage (Num. 10) or the development and execution of the mechanisms of previous consultation with respect to the application of legislative, executive, and administrative measures that affect the indigenous population (Num. 21). Due to the implications it has in the legal sphere, special mention should be reserved for the competence regarding the "exercise of rural native indigenous jurisdiction for the application of justice and the resolution of conflicts through their own norms and procedures" (Num. 8), which may pose problems, given that such norms and procedures are not always compatible with constitutional

---

[70] The Framework Law for Autonomies and Decentralisation (LMAD), cit.

norms.[71] As already highlighted on so many other occasions, this possible contradiction is once again overcome through the express provision that exercising indigenous jurisdiction should be carried out "in accordance with the Constitution and the law", which excludes the possibility of indigenous justice being outside or contrary to the constitutional norms.

## Regional Autonomy

The current Bolivian Constitution introduces a new entity into the territorial organisation of the State: the *Regions*, which previous Constitutions did not contemplate and which in this one are added to the departmental and indigenous autonomous entities already examined. The scant constitutional regulation of the new *regional autonomy* (Articles 280–282) does not allow any defined profile for this new autonomous entity, although it can be said, in accordance with the constitutional provisions that deal with this subject, that they are constituted as "a sphere of planning and management" based on the municipalities or provinces that have geographical continuity and that "share a culture, languages, history, economy and ecosystems in each Department" (Article 280. I). This same constitutional provision remits to the Framework Law for Autonomies and Decentralisation (LMAD, in Spanish) for specifying its organisation and functioning as a new autonomous entity.[72]

What the constitutional text *does* directly determine is that in order "to be constituted as a regional autonomy", the regions should do so "at the initiative of the municipalities which comprise it via referendum in their jurisdictions" (Article 280. III) and should have a Statute of Autonomy (Article 280. II) that details all aspects concerning regional autonomy. The existence of a regional executive body is likewise envisaged, without further clarification, and of a Regional Assembly, whose members will be elected in each municipality, together with the lists of candidates for municipal councillors, which will have deliberative, normative-administrative, and tax-raising powers in the area of their competences (Article 281).

Unlike departmental and indigenous autonomy, whose respective areas of competences (as well as the municipality) remain directly delimited by the Constitution through an extensive list of subject matters (Article 300: the Departments,

---

[71] Although it is not possible to develop the subject in this study, it has to be said that it is one of the topics to have given rise to the most doctrinal commentaries (and political controversies). Regarding this problem, see AA.VV. (Laura Giraudo, ed.) (2008), in particular, Ahumada Ruiz (2008), pp. 233–241; Sanchez Botero (2008), pp. 215–232; Borja Jimenez (2008), pp. 185–213; Molina Rivero (2008), pp. 95–125.

[72] Although the constitutionalisation of the regions as autonomous entities is very recent (2009), regionalist approaches already existed prior to the present constitutional text. Regarding this, see Roca (1999).

Article 304: the rural native indigenous autonomies), the matters that comprise the area of competences of the regional autonomy are not expressly determined by the Constitution. In their absence, two brief constitutional provisions refer to the subject, one envisaging that the "Region, once constituted, as a regional autonomy, will receive the competences which are transferred or delegated to it" (Article 301) and the other, complementary to the previous one, envisaging that such regional competences should be approved by the Departmental Assembly in which the autonomous region is located by a qualified majority of two-thirds of the total number of its members (Article 280. III). These constitutional provisions place the regions and the regional autonomy in a position of subordination and dependence in relation to the Departments.

This lack of constitutional specification of the area of competences of the new regional entities contributes towards making the nature of the recently inaugurated regional autonomy less precise. Only the institutional running in of these new autonomous entities, which in the complex Bolivian constitutional structure coexist with the departmental and rural native indigenous autonomies, will allow the real nature of the regional autonomy established by the current Constitution to be defined. In any case, it is not out of the question that the present autonomous triplication (Departments, Regions and Indigenous Autonomies) will give rise, after the adjustments that the practical working of this overloaded autonomous system will bring, to a more simplified and integrated autonomous model than that designed by the Bolivian refounding constituent assembly.

# Conclusions

1. Until recently, Latin American constitutionalism has paid little attention to the indigenous situation that, however, constitutes one of the basic structural elements of Latin American political and social reality, especially in some countries in which the importance of the indigenous population cannot be ignored. Recently, in the last two decades, new trends have been appearing in different Latin American countries that, as well as advocating overall constitutional changes, champion, in particular, constitutional recognition of the indigenous situation. It is within this constitutional framework in Latin America in which the constitutional experiences described by the key players themselves as *refounding* have to be situated, in which the *indigenous question* will be the subject of special attention as an integrating element of the refounding project.
2. Given the variety of situations in the different countries regarding the importance of the indigenous population in each, the effect of the indigenous factor on the territorial reorganisation of the State is very distinct, as can clearly be seen in the experiences analysed in this study (Venezuela, Ecuador, and Bolivia and is also likely to be so in other countries that will soon introduce constitutional changes along these lines). Nevertheless, introducing the indigenous factor into the Constitution gives rise, in all the cases, to a redefinition of the State on the

basis of the recognition of the plural composition of their population, to a constitutionalisation of a group of specific rights of the indigenous population, and to a territorial reorganisation of the State in accordance with the plural composition, in particular as regards their indigenous component, of the population.

3. Constitutional redefinition of the State, bearing in mind the multi-ethnic and multicultural nature of the population, in comparison with the absence of any reference to this plural composition in previous constitutional texts, is one of the distinctive features of the new Latin American refounding constitutionalism. This clearly shows that the *indigenous question* is not merely a decorative element to which rhetorical clauses are dedicated, as had previously occurred in historical Latin American constitutionalism, but rather a determinant factor in the conformation of the new constitutional order arising from the refounding process. It also has to be said that the conception of multinationality that the constitutional texts reflect is, in our opinion, somewhat debatable (in particular, in Ecuador and, above all, in Bolivia), which describes any differentiated ethnic group as a nation. In any case, it is the constitutional redefinition of the State that will make possible, and even obligatory, the constitutionalisation of the specific rights of the indigenous population, as well as the commencement of diverse processes, according to the conditions of each country, of territorial reorganisation of the State.

4. One common and distinctive feature of the refounding experiences is the express constitutionalisation of a series of rights referring specifically to the indigenous population. It is necessary to highlight the important innovation that this signifies when endowing the highest legal authority, the Constitution, with a set of rights that until recently had only been included in disperse declaratory texts that lacked any legal value. However, we have to be aware of the difficulties and problems that incorporating this set of rights into the constitutional code poses, be it only as a result of their novelty and lack of precedents, in particular with regard to the distinction that must be made between what are the rights of the members of the indigenous population, strictly speaking, and which are merely indigenous practices and customs that would be dubious to enshrine in the Constitution as rights (as, at times, is done in the refounding constitutional texts).

5. In accordance with the constitutional redefinition of the State and the constitutional recognition of indigenous rights, refounding constitutionalism deals with territorial reorganisation of the State. This, however, is one of the most undefined and least innovative aspects of the refounding project, given that, rather than designing a new model of territorial reorganisation, the continuity of the previous one is maintained, adding, where necessary, new elements to it whose harmonisation with those that remain of the previous one is very debatable. The influence of Spain's autonomous model should also be highlighted on the conformation of the new autonomous entities by means of which the territorial reorganisation of the State is structured. Nevertheless, a period of running in will be necessary for the new autonomous institutions so as to be able to evaluate

with any certainty the viability of the territorial reorganisation embarked upon, without ruling out its restructuring in the short term, in the light of the evolution of the process of territorial reorganisation of the State.

# References

AA.VV.: *Derechos de los pueblos indígenas*, Servicio de Publicaciones del Gobierno Vasco/ Eusko Jaurlaritza, Vitoria-Gasteiz, 1998, 710 pages.

AA.VV. (Laura Giraudo, ed.): *Derechos, costumbres y jurisdicciones indígenas en la América Latina contemporánea*, Centro de Estudios Políticos y Constitucionales (CEPC), Madrid, 2008.

AA.VV.: "Brasile: venti anni di Costituzione democratica", in *Diritto Pubblico Comparato ed Europeo*, no. III-2008, pages 1340–1450.

AA.VV. (F. Fernández Segado, coordinator.), *La Constitución de 1978 y el constitucionalismo iberoamericano*, Centro de Estudios Políticos y Constitucionales, Madrid, 2003, pages 445–458.

AA.VV. (Salvador Martí i Puig, ed.): *Pueblos indígenas y política en América Latina. El reconocimiento de sus derechos y el impacto de sus demandas*, CIDOB, Barcelona, 2007 pages 161–333.

AA.VV. (R. VICIANO, J. C. TRUJILLO y S. ANDRADE, Editors): *Estudios sobre la Constitución ecuatoriana de 1998*, Tirant lo blanch, Valencia 2005.

Adolfo MENDOZA: *Tendencias y viabilidad de las autonomías indígenas originarias campesinas en Bolivia,* Ministerio de la Presidencia, La Paz, 2009.

Albert NOGUERA: *Los derechos sociales en las nuevas Constituciones latinoamericanas*, Tirant lo blanch, Valencia, 2010.

Albert NOGUERA: "¿De qué hablamos cuando hablamos de constitucionalismo multicultural?", *Anuario de la Facultad de Derecho de la Universidad de Extremadura*, no. 28, 2010, pages 87–116.

Albert NOGUERA: "Plurinacionalidad y autonomías...", *Revista Española de Derecho Constitucional*, no. 84, 2008, pages 147–167.

Albert NOGUERA: "Diálogos sobre la plurinacionalidad y la organización territorial del Estado en Bolivia", *Revista Española de Derecho Constitucional*, no. 87, 2009, pages 241–269.

J. Alberto DEL REAL ALCALA: "Constitución de 2009 y nuevo modelo de Estado de Derecho en Bolivia: el Estado de Derecho Plurinacional", *Cuadernos Manuel Giménez Abad*, no. 1, June 2011, page 115.

Allan R. BREWER-CARIAS: "Los problemas de la federación centralizada", *IV Congreso Iberoamericano de Derecho Constitucional*, UNAM, México, 1992.

Allan R. BREWER-CARIAS: "El sistema constitucional venezolano", *Los sistemas constitucionales iberoamericanos*, Dykinson, 1992, pages 773–815.

Allan BREWER-CARIAS: "La Constitución española de 1978 y la Constitución de la República bolivariana de Venezuela de 1999: algunas influencias y otras coincidencias", in AA.VV (Director: F. Fernández Segado): *La Constitución de 1978 y el constitucionalismo iberoamericano*, Centro de Estudios Políticos y Constitucionales (CEPC), Madrid, 2003, pages 765–786.

Antonio CANOVA GONZALEZ: "Venezuela" (preámbulo constitucional), AA.VV. (Antonio Torres del Moral and Javier Tajadura dirs.), *Los preámbulos constitucionales en Iberoamé rica*, Centro de Estudios Políticos y Constitucionales (CEPC), Madrid, 2001, pages 409–446.

J. Antonio RIVERA: "La Constitución española de 1978 y su incidencia en el sistema constitucional boliviano", AA.VV. (F. Fernández Segado, coord.): *La Constitución de 1978 y el constitucionalismo iberoamericano*, Centro de Estudios Políticos y Constitucionales (CEPC), Madrid, 2003, pages 177–195.

Bartolomé CLAVERO: "Novedades constitucionales y continuidades constituyentes: Ecuador, Venezuela, México, Bolivia (1998–2004)", *Revista Española de Derecho Constitucional*, no. 74, 2005, pages 195–211.

Bartolomé CLAVERO and Albert NOGUERA (2005), in the debate about multi-nationality and autonomy in the Revista *Española de Derecho Constituional*, no. 84, 85, 87, 89, ops. cit.

Benjamín Miguel HARB: "El sistema constitucional boliviano", *Los sistemas constitucionales iberoamericanos*, Dykinson, Madrid, 1992, pages 99–125.

Benjamín Miguel HARB: "Comentario al preámbulo de la Constitución política del Estado", *Los preámbulos constitucionales en Iberoamérica* (Antonio Torres del Moral and Javier Tajadura, directors), 2001, page 61 onwards.

G. J. BIDART CAMPOS: "La diversidad cultural en el constitucionalismo democrático: los pueblos indígenas", AA.VV.: *Visión iberoamericana del tema constitucional*, Fundación Manuel García-Pelayo, Caracas, 2003, pages 267–288.

P. BISCARETTI: *Introducción al Derecho Constitucional Comparado*, Fondo de Cultura Económica (FCE), Mexico, 1996, pages 28–69.

Cayetano NUÑEZ RIVERO: "El principio autonómico en el texto constitucional boliviano", *Teoría y Realidad Constitucional*, no. 24, 2009, page 566.

Claudia STORINI and Albert NOGUERA: "Processo costituente e Costituzione in Bolivia. Il difficile cammino verso la rifondazione dello Stato", *Diritto Pubblico Comparato ed Europeo*, 2008-III, pages 1285–1304.

Clavero AREVALO: "Nota sobre el sistema de autonomías en la Constitución de Bolivia" in *Revista Española de Derecho Constitucional*, no. 85, pages 187–199.

Clavero AREVALO: "Apunte para la ubicación de la Constitución de Bolivia" in *Revista Española de Derecho Constitucional*, no. 89, pages 195–217.

Edwin CRUZ and Hugo GUERRA: "El tránsito hacia el Estado plurinacional en Bolivia y Ecuador (1990–2008)", *Historia Contemporánea*, no. 28, 2010, pages 97–124.

Emiliano BORJA JIMENEZ (2008): "Derecho indígena sancionador y derechos humanos", pages 185–213.

Ermanno VITALE: "Derechos (de los) indígenas y derechos fundamentales. Una reflexión crítica", en AA.VV. (Laura Giraudo ed.) *Derechos, costumbres y jurisdicciones indígenas en la América Latina contemporánea*, Centro de Estudios Políticos y Constitucionales (CEPC), Madrid, 2008, pages 3–16.

Esther SANCHEZ BOTERO (2008): "La jurisdicción especial indígena", pages 215–232.

M. FIGUEIREDO: "Evolutions récentes du constitutionnalisme brésilien", *Revue de Droit Public*, no. 5, 2010, pages 1509–1535.

Francisco FERNANDEZ SEGADO: *El federalismo en América Latina*, Cuadernos constitucionales México-Centroamérica, no. 41, UNAM, Mexico, 2003, 169 pages.

Francisco FERNANDEZ SEGADO "El federalismo en América Latina", AA.VV., *Visión iberoamericana del tema constitucional*, Fundación M. García-Pelayo, Caracas, 2003, pages 699–734.

Hernán PEREZ LOOSE: "La organización territorial en la nueva Constitución", AA.VV. (R. Viciano, J. C. Trujillo and S. Andrade, editors), *Estudios sobre la Constitución ecuatoriana de 1998*, Tirant lo blanch, Valencia, 2005, pages 173–192.

Hernán SALGADO: "Influencia De la Constitución española en el Ecuador", AA.VV. (F. Fernández Segado, coordinator.), (2003), pages 445–458.

Hernán SALGADO: "El sistema constitucional ecuatoriano", *Los sistemas constitucionales iberoamericanos*, Dykinson, Madrid, 1992, pages 325–350.

Jorge ASBUN: "Composición del Legislativo en un Estado con autonomías departamentales", *Contrapuntos al debate constituyente*, Prisma/Plural, La Paz, 2007.

Jorge Mario EASTMAN: "La nueva Constitución colombiana", *Constituciones políticas comparadas de América del Sur*, Parlamento Andino, Bogotá, 1991, pages 233–253.

José F. PALOMINO: "Problemas escogidos de la Constitución peruana de 1993", AA.VV., *Constitucionalismo iberoamericano del siglo XXI.*, UNAM, Mexico, 2000, pages 279–290.

Jose Luis ROCA: *Fisonomía del regionalismo boliviano*, Plural, La Paz, 1999.

José SUING NAGUA: "El sistema nacional descentralizado de planificación participativa", *La nueva Constitución del Ecuador*, 2009, pages 383–401.

Juan Carlos URENDA: *Bases para construir las autonomías departamentales*, Ildis/Comité pro Santa Cruz, 2005.

Luis AGUIAR DE LUQUE and Fernando REVIRIEGO: "Implicaciones constitucionales del giro político en algunos países iberoamericanos", *Cuadernos de Derecho Público*, no. 27, 2006, pages 227–243.

Luis VERDESOTO: "Ecuador" (Preamble), AA.VV. (Antonio Torres del Moral and Javier Tajadura, directors), *Los Preámbulos constitucionales en Iberoamérica*, CEPC, Madrid, 2001, pages. 183–192.

Manuel RACHADELL: "El proceso político en la formación y vigencia de la Constitución de 1961", AA.VV.: *Visión iberoamericana del tema constitucional*, Fundación Manuel García-Pelayo, Caracas, 2003, pages 95–148.

Marco APARICIO WILHELMI (2007): "La construcción de la autonomía indígena: Hacia el Estado intercultural como nueva forma de Estado", AA.VV. (S. Martí y Puig, ed.): *Pueblos indígenas y política en América Latina. El reconocimiento de sus derechos . . .*, pages 247–280.

Marian AHUMADA RUIZ (2008): "Derecho indígena y constitucionalismo democrático: una mirada crítica", pages 233–241.

J. Mario GARCIA LAGUARDIA (1985): "Transición democrática y nuevo orden constitucional. La Constitución guatemalteca de 1985" in AA.VV.: *Constitucionalismo Iberoamericano del siglo XXI*, Universidad Autónoma de México (UNAM), pages 211–232.

Michael SHIFTER and Daniel JOYCE: "Bolivia, Ecuador y Venezuela, refundación andina. Las reformas constitucionales de Morales, Correa y Chavez . . .", *Política Exterior*, no. 123, 2008, pages 55–66.

Nina PACARI: "Derechos colectivos y de indígenas en la nueva Constitución Política", AA.VV.: *Estudios sobre la Constitución ecuatoriana de 1998*, op. cit., Tirant lo blanch, Valencia 2005, pages 143–172.

N. OSUNA, H. SIERRA and A.J. ESTRADA (1991): "La Constitución colombiana de 1991" in AA.VV.: *Constitucionalismo Iberoamericano del siglo XXI*, Universidad Autónoma de México (UNAM), pages 261–278.

H. QUIROGA LAVIE to: *Las Constituciones Latinoamericanas. El constitucionalismo en las postrimerías del siglo XX*, Tomo I, Universidad Nacional Autónoma de México (UNAM), Mexico, 1994, pages 7–117.

Ramiro MOLINA RIVERO (2008): "La justicia comunitaria en Bolivia:cambios y continuidades", pages 95–125.

Ramón CRAZUT: "Comentarios al Título II de la constitución de 1999 sobre el espacio geográfico y la división política", *Revista de Derecho Público*, no. 81, Caracas, 2000, page 40 onwards.

J. REINALDO VANOSSI: "Los rifirrafes constitucionales de la década pasada", *Anuario Iberoamericano de Justicia Constitucional*, no. 11, 2007, pages 407–424.

Roberto VICIANO and Rubén MARTINEZ DALMAU: *Cambio político y proceso constituyente en Venezuela (1998-2000)*, Tirant lo blanch, Valencia, 2001, pages 169.

Roberto VICIANO: "Algunas consideraciones sobre la organización territorial del Estado en la Constitución ecuatoriana de 2008", AA.VV. (S. Andrade, A. Grijalva and C. Storini, editors), *La nueva Constitución del Ecuador*, Universidad Andina Simón Bolivar (Ecuador, Quito), 2009, pages 105–118.

Rosa BALTAZAR: "Derechos de las comunidades, pueblos y nacionalidades", AA.VV. (S. Andrade, A. Gijalba, C. Storini, Editors), *La nueva Constitución del Ecuador* (2008), University of Andina Simón Bolivar (in Ecuador), Quito 2009, pages 211–234.

Salvador MARTI I PUIG (2007): "Emergencia de lo indígena en la arena política: ¿un efecto no deseado de la gobernanza?, AA.VV., *Pueblos indígenas y política en América Latina*, pages 127–148.

STORINI and Albert NOGUERA: "Pocesso costituente in Bolivia. Il difficile cammino verso la rifondazione dello Stato", *Diritto pubblico Comparato ed Europeo*, III-2008, pages 1285–1304.

Willem ASSIES: "Los pueblos indígenas, la tierra, el territorio y la autonomía en tiempos de globalización", AA.VV. (S. Martí i Puig, ed.), *Pueblos indígenas y política en América Latina. El reconocimiento de sus derechos* pages 227–246.

Xavier ALBÓ and Carlos ROMERO: *Autonomías indígenas en la realidad boliviana y su nueva Constitución*, Vicepresidencia de la República, La Paz, 2009.

F. Xavier BARRIOS: *Propuesta autonómica de Santa Cruz*, Ildis/Plural, La Paz, 2005.

F. Xavier BARRIOS: "La ley marco de autonomías y un nuevo régimen financiero territorial", *Nueva Crónica y Buen Gobierno*, no. 62, 2010.

F. Xavier BARRIOS: "Ni unitario, ni federal, ni autonómico: ¿contiene la nueva Constitución boliviana un intento de estructura territorial estatal?", *Revista d'Estudis Autonòmics i Federals*, no. 13, 2011.

# The Qualitative Development of the Spanish System of Autonomous Communities: Changes to the Statutes of Autonomy

Esteban Arlucea Ruíz

At this stage in the history of autonomy in Spain, it may seem a little out of context to reflect on what meaning the Autonomous Communities, these new territorial public administrations referred to as early as Article 2 and delimited in Title VIII, have for the Constitution, their creator. Yet, we do not feel such a reflection to be out of place when said territorial distribution of political power has proved to be one of the Constitution's most important and innovative contributions and since the current system now differs so much from the early 1980s, when it was created, and from the 1990s, when the first changes were made. As Professor Cruz Villalon has pointed out, it seems to have taken on another variation of itself.[1] The expansion of certain Statutes of Autonomy (250 Articles in the Andalusian Statute, 223 in the Catalonian, 139 in the Balearic Islands, 115 in Aragon, 93 in Valencia, and 91 in Castilla y León and Extremadura) and the controversy surrounding the revised content thereof bear testimony to the fact that something is changing in the Statutes.

A considerable qualitative gap has emerged between the time of the initial debates concerning the political and administrative content of autonomy and whether or not a general right to autonomy should be granted (both issues resolved by the autonomous agreement of 1981): in other words, regarding the creation of an organic-institutional structure that led the Constitutional Court to describe these statutory norms as "paradigms of the legal instruments of self-organization" (Constitutional Court Ruling 56/90, dated 29 March) and "competences" (Constitutional Court Ruling 247/2007) and the debates that have arisen since the latest reforms. This, I think it is safe to say, was never in the minds of those who laid the foundations for the model since, in all the cases that have emerged to date, there

---

[1] Cruz Villalon (2006), p. 79.

E. Arlucea Ruíz (✉)
Department of Constitutional Law and History of the Political Thought, University of the Basque Country – Campus of Sarriena, Post box 644, Bilbao 48080, Spain
e-mail: juanesteban.arlucea@ehu.es

A. López-Basaguren and L. Escajedo San Epifanio (eds.), *The Ways of Federalism in Western Countries and the Horizons of Territorial Autonomy in Spain*, Vol. 2, DOI 10.1007/978-3-642-27717-7_36, © Springer-Verlag Berlin Heidelberg 2013

has been total reform that has led to one statute being replaced by another.[2] This has been taken even further in the failed attempt at a political Statute for the Basque Country (25 October, 2003, and approved by the Basque Parliament in December 2004), which the Basque Nationalist Party (PNV) now seems to want to revive as a fresh political framework between the Basque Country and Spain for 2015.[3]

Although in constitutional terms some of these Autonomous Communities were conceived applying a dispositive interpretation ("right to autonomy", "Autonomous Communities which are constituted", being some of the expressions that have provided scholars and jurisprudence with support to justify the principle), said criterion soon became blurred in political terms after the first autonomic agreement of 1981[4] and because of certain scholars who drew from Article 137 "a constitutional option to form the basis of the State/System of Rules grounded on a network of autonomous communities",[5] such that these new administrations have proved the key to the internal distribution of political power. Said dispositive principle has been hotly contested, if not indeed cast aside, by the autonomous pacts drawn up to date[6] but has been reconsidered in Constitutional Court Rulings such as 247/07, 249/07, and 31/2010 as a crucial element in constitutional analysis of possible statutory content.

Such a generalization of the autonomous system bears witness to the shift in the perspective from which we visualize the meaning of these new administrations. This is reflected in the transition over the last 30 years from the original dispositive principle to the *de facto* imperative. Strangely enough, both previously and at present, what has remained constant has been the lack of any reflection concerning what, in sum, many suspected might come about: the appearance of a territorial model that in its everyday application has been subject to improvization and the private interests of politicians with a parliamentary majority that is often the result

---

[2] All of them, except Organic Law 1/2007, which amends the Statute of the Balearic Islands, contain a single derogatory provision repealing the previous statute. Organic Law 1/2007 is applicable, although with similar effects, to an almost total amendment of the previous Organic Law LO 2/83, as may be interpreted from its single article.

[3] See El País newspaper, 1 November 2011.

[4] The map of the Autonomous Communities set out by said agreements establishes that the State will be organized into territories in the Autonomous Communities cited: all the Statutes of Autonomy having to come into force before 1 February 1983. Nevertheless, these agreements merely followed the path of Organic Law 12/80, dated 16 December, which rendered provincial ratification of Article 151.1 null and void in the interests of a ratification over "all territories aspiring to self-government".

[5] Ibarra Robles (1982), p. 128.
This is an example of what was highlighted by Professor Lojendio e Irure shortly after the proclamation of the Constitution: "Between what a Constitution initially is and what it means in its historical context and the subsequent process of developing its normative content, it is common for contrasts to appear which call into question (...) the appropriateness of the rigid mechanisms which sought to ensure it a long life" (1982).

[6] Not forgetting the 2006 report issued by the Council of State on constitutional reform, published in the Council of State joint edition/CEPC, Madrid, 2006, particularly page 127.

of pacts that are hard to comprehend. As Lasagabaster reminds us, this is no doubt a consequence of the unclear ideas concerning the direction to be taken when regulating Title VIII of the Constitution.[7]

Going about things in such a manner led to two well-known and far from desirable consequences that, however, seem to be reemerging in recent years. We will make a general reference to these before moving on to focus on a particularly meaningful example of the second.

## The Relative Unimportance of Constitutional Dictates

During both the period subsequent to the early autonomic pacts and during these early years of the twenty-first century, the State has been structured in a manner that lacks any legal-political roadmap resulting from consensus amongst stakeholders. However, one clarification that should immediately be made is that the early autonomic pacts were the fruit of the work carried out by a broad committee of expert jurists whose reputation is unquestionable. Yet, where their work has been undone is in the subsequent application of the measures set out in said committee's report[8] and in the emerging political pact.

Both after 1981 and at the present time, the issue of the Autonomous Communities has been turned into a kind of legally "constituent" process, by which I mean that on both occasions we have started from a minimum conception of what a constitutional text represents, only focusing on the idea of the institution that is to be regulated whilst neglecting, above all, the limits surrounding it. It is not that we are undoing the Constitution's approach as an open system[9] but rather that we are seeking to empower such a description by using it as a basis, as Professor Diaz Revorio has quite rightly pointed out, by drawing on it as a foundation and by adhering to it, intervening therein by applying constitutionally hermeneutic criteria.[10] At both points in our history, an abstract idea of the autonomous state has been drawn from the indecisions inherent in the constitutional text itself. Said indecisions have then been developed depending on the available legal (but not necessarily legal-constitutional) and political possibilities. The consensus that was reached in 1981 in political terms today seems to have been replaced (in the face of dissension) by the constitutional legitimacy afforded by the rulings of the Constitutional Court, a court which, if I may say so, has changed from being a negative legislator to a derived constituent power.

On both occasions, failure to pay close attention to the provisions set out in the Constitution, coupled with political opportunism, has given rise to a second

---

[7] Lasagabaster Herrarte (2005), p. 21.

[8] Nor should we forget the report drafted on funding.

[9] Aparicio (2005), p. 2.

[10] Diaz Revorio (1997), pp. 209–210.

"Constitution", running parallel to the one approved in 1978 by the Spanish people. We feel that ignorance of the dispositive principle, reflected in the early autonomic agreement, as well as our Constitutional Court's present-day interpretation of Article 139, conveyed through Constitutional Court Rulings 247 and 249 of 2007 and 31/10, dated 28 June, are two examples of a single criterion, namely that all written texts are open to interpretation depending on contemporary political criteria.

## The Change in the Statute's Legal Nature

On 12 December 2007, judgment no. 247 was issued in which the Constitutional Court ruled on the challenge of unconstitutionality (7288-2006) filed by the regional government of Aragon against reform of the Statute of Autonomy of Valencia approved under Organic Law 1/2006, dated 10 April.[11] The following day, Constitutional Court Ruling 249/07 was issued, which resolved the challenge of unconstitutionality 7289-2006 filed by the regional government of Castilla-La Mancha against the above-mentioned Organic Law. As Constitutional Court 249 ruling set outs in its second legal basis, the judgments essentially concur as they evidence similar rationale with regard to the issue under debate.[12] These were the first Constitutional Court rulings on the new statutory reforms. The long awaited ruling 31/2010 on the Statute of Catalonia was to appear in 2010.

This third autonomous phase, following on from the first group that was shaped by the early autonomic agreements of 1981 and the second, subsequent to the 1992 agreements, represents the most important of the three key moments in the Autonomous Communities to date in qualitative terms: the beginning, covering the early Basque and Catalonian statutes of 1979 up to 1983, when the autonomization of Spain concluded, with the exception of Ceuta and Melilla, which was put back until 1995;[13] the first phase of reforms applied the provisions of Article 148.2 of the Spanish Constitution and commenced in 1992 after the second round of autonomic agreements, formally set forth in Organic Law 9/92, concluding in the late 1990s; and the third phase, which commenced in the early twenty-first century, subsequent to the doomed Ibarretxe Plan[14] and which for the time being includes statutory

---

[11] BOE no. 13, dated 15 January 2008.

[12] Appeal 7288/06 was filed against the whole of Article 17.1; appeal 7289/06 was filed against the second subsection of the first paragraph of 17.1.

[13] It should be remembered that despite having statutes of autonomy, these are not Autonomous Communities like the rest, as highlighted by the Constitutional Court in rulings 201 and 202 of 25 July 2000. The political agreements between UCD-PSOE in 1981 with regard to these two cities pointed out, however, that the only two possibilities open to them were to continue as local bodies or to become an Autonomous Community.

[14] On 1 February 2005, Congress refused to consider it.

reform of Valencia, Catalonia, the Balearic Islands, Andalusia, Aragon, Castilla y León, Navarre, and Extremadura.

Nevertheless, in qualitative and quantitative terms, reform of the Statute of Catalonia (Organic Law 6/06, dated 19 July) may be said to have eclipsed previous (Valencia)[15] and subsequent reforms (Balearic Islands: Organic Law 1/07, dated 28 February; Andalusia: Organic Law 2/07, dated 19 March; Aragon: Organic Law 5/07, dated 20 April; Castilla y León: Organic Law 14/07, dated 30 November; Navarre: Organic Law 7/2010, dated 27 October and Extremadura: Organic Law 1/2011, dated 28 January), which, taking advantage of the breach opened up by the Statute of Catalonia, have repeated certain issues that are at the very least controversial when indeed not openly unconstitutional.[16] The judgment on the appeals lodged against some of these amended organic laws should examine these thorny issues, despite the fact that there are others of at least equal importance that, as a result of not being challenged with regard to their unconstitutionality, will remain excluded from Constitutional Court pronouncements (e.g., the innovative second additional provision of the reform of the Statute of Valencia, better known as the *Camps clause*). There is also a need to address in clear terms thus far peaceful constitutional matters that since 2006 have been in need of clarification from the "only body competent to give true and unquestionable definitions of constitutional categories and principles", as our Constitutional Court defined itself in ruling 31/2010 (legal basis 7). Constitutional Court Ruling 247/2007, dated 12 December, the first issued on these reforms, takes up several of these controversial issues, in turn evidencing the numerous interpretations of what are apparently unequivocal constitutional principles, the many personal votes (five) being a clear indication of this.[17]

These laws contain issues that are indeed controversial since they affect the very structure of the Autonomous State: in other words, the balance between the State and Autonomous Communities. However, these matters did not receive the attention of the founding fathers of the statutes either in the 1980s or in the subsequent reform processes, which focused far more on the question of competences than on matters that might be termed dogmatic, perhaps because the concept of statute of autonomy was still very much present in Article 147 of the Spanish Constitution, in the sense that it was primarily a basic institutional rule of the Autonomous Community. Yet, without exhausting the possibilities thereof in terms of competences, either because there were still competences under the control of the state that might be transferred or because some that had already been transferred were awaiting Royal Decrees on the transfer of services, we witnessed a "constitutional turnaround" (after the doomed Ibarretxe project, in certain matters, diametrically opposed to the text of 1978), which far outstripped what may have been interpreted

---

[15] Despite the innovative second additional provision known as the *Camps clause*.

[16] Excluding reform in Navarre, which has only effected institutional changes.

[17] These were cast by judges: Conde Martín de Hijas, Delgado Barrio, García-Calvo y Montiel, Rodríguez-Zapata Pérez, and Rodríguez Arribas.

in Article 2 and Title VIII of the Spanish Constitution with regard to political decentralization of the State.

Much of this is due to what has been provoked in certain sectors, which are not just nationalist but also regionalist, as well as by a lack of clarity concerning ideas over sovereignty and autonomy and the transformation that *de facto* said sectors are seeking to impose on autonomy in order to make it fit in with sovereignty. At the time, the so-called Ibarretxe Plan was a blatant conceptual innovation (co-sovereignty), which failed in the national parliament,[18] a parliament that, it has gradually emerged, lacks sufficiently sound legal-political *acquis* to know how Autonomous Communities can respond when attacked, not head on but from the rear.

The autonomous constitutional state is the creation of a single nation in a single State which may be internally divided (dispositive principle, as highlighted by Portero Molina,[19] although amended—repealed—in the early autonomic pacts) into new territorial administrations endowed with autonomy to manage their respective interests. Thus, as a part that is (Article 2 of the Spanish Constitution) an integral component of a single nation, the institutional rules of the autonomous constitutional state must reflect those aspects that merely constitute its legal reality, at the risk of being unconstitutional, either by defect or excess. Drawing on the words of Aguiar de Luque, we are dealing with rules that create and make up the basic elements of a specific organizational structure endowed with numerous levels of self-government,[20] which are not the reflection of sovereign power (Constitutional Court Ruling 4/81, dated 2 February, legal basis 3). Anything else would go beyond the bounds of the task that is constitutionally assigned to them, either in terms of the organic law (formally) or in terms of the *sui generis* organic law (materially), which, as is well known, merges two distinct wills (Constitutional Court Ruling 99/86, dated 11 July).

Thus far, we have seen that all the claims put forward by the autonomies have been preceded by short, insufficient periods of reflection concerning the substance of the issue under debate, constituent debates giving rise to a Title VIII, which can at best be described as complicated.[21] The report issued by the commission of experts on territorial autonomies provided the basis for the first autonomic pacts back in 1981, pacts that, after the recently approved Constitution, redesigned some of the basic aspects thereof[22] (e.g., the dispositive principle referred to earlier). Years later, the second round of autonomic pacts in 1992 addressed extensions and

---

[18] As Corcuera Atienza has rightly highlighted (2005, p. 65), "the only theoretical justification for anybody used to justify statutory reform which is clearly contrary to the Constitution stems from the latter's subordination to a well-grounded Constitution, creation of which allows the formal Constitution to be overlooked or devalued".

[19] Portero Molina (2005) cited, p. 40.

[20] The author's reflections cited in *Teoría y Realidad Constitucional*, no. 20/2007, p. 33.

[21] "Unfinished and ambiguous, open to uncertain and conflictive developments." This perfectly sums up a widely held view concerning the content thereof (Balaguer Callejon 2007, p. 302).

[22] A rewriting that, as Aragon reminds us, was soon described as constitutional convention by Vandelli (Aragon Reyes 2007, p. 16).

reorganization of competences. Yet, this formula of political consensus has, for the moment, been set aside and replaced by bilateral negotiations in exchange for contrived support. In this instance, it is not that Rousseau's maxim expressed in his Social Contract ("...the more grave and important the questions discussed, the nearer should the opinion that is to prevail approach unanimity...") has been abandoned but simply that such an approach has been ignored. It is not therefore surprising that some of the new statutes drafted at the start of the twenty-first century reflect the lack of a previously agreed upon model, such that some might be said to bear a striking resemblance to constitutional texts[23] (particularly the new statutes of Catalonia and Andalusia), any prior debate having been postponed until later and transferred to the "negative legislator" that is the Constitutional Court.

We have reached this situation due to central authority failure to impose limits, which has virtually allowed and indeed generated confusion between the Constitution and the statute of autonomy, contradicting the constitutive definition of Article 147 of the Spanish Constitution, which sets out that statutes should provide the basic institutional rules for any Autonomous Community. This is precisely one problem that, after 30 years of the Constitution, still persists. It is by no means a trivial matter, if we take account of the kind of state that such a norm permits. Put directly, the option of a decentralized territorial formula should be founded on a fine balance between what Rousseau referred to as justice and usefulness,[24] a model that seems to have been applied to good effect in modern times to consolidate decentralization in countries neighboring Spain.[25]

Despite the complexity of the task, the present Constitution quickly gave rise to Autonomous Communities that, unlike other countries such as Portugal or Italy, were institutionalized through certain *ad hoc* rules that have concluded the structuring of what some have termed the deconstitutionalization of the State.[26] Although on balance the experience in our view has proved to be positive, we should not overlook the fact that in Spain progress in the issue of autonomy is leading to a phenomenon where a love of regionalism is turning into nationalism[27]

---

[23] Ruggiu (2007), p. 291.

[24] Rousseau (1990), p. 37.

[25] I am referring to the case of Italy, particularly to its constitutional law 3/2001, dated 18 October, as has been well pointed out by Prada Fernandez De Sanmamed in "Continuación de las reformas institucionales italianas (enero 2000-mayo 2002)" (*REP* no. 126/04, p. 338 et seq.), although significant differences may also be found such as the residual clause in favor of the regions (Art. 117.4 of the Italian Constitutional) or its original name given by the government of D'Alema, the driving force behind the "Federal Organization of the Republic", which was ultimately amended by "Title V of Part II of the Constitution".

[26] "It does not contain all the extremes which might be desirable to derive from within it a territorial model of the State", Professor Aparicio points out in 2005 already cited, p. 6.

[27] A. Rojo Salgado states clearly: "...communities which proclaimed themselves regions and only regions and which fully accepted the autonomous model, now, in clear imitation of nationalisms, profess to be nationalists... at the same time demanding full and identical treatment, both institutionally and in terms of competences, as has been given to historical communities" (2005, p. 237).

and in which the foundational rules are thus seeking to acquire a constitutional *paruenza* that equates their structure and content to those typical of constitutions.[28] This is a key constitutive issue in the organization of the state that, rather than reappearing, seems to be emerging for the first time in the twenty-first century in the light of the new statutory reforms approved.

Exceeding constitutional limits has mainly been caused by including reforms that do not reflect greater or fewer competences but that extend to the area of dogma through a list of rights and institutions disguised, to a greater or lesser extent, as their own and that, in fact, mirror mechanisms that belong exclusively to the state.

It is not surprising that doctrine is divided over the matter. The numerous opinions expressed have given rise to discussion concerning aspects that had remained buried and dealt with only superficially. Controversies that, for many years, seemed to have given way to other issues now emerge as part of the ongoing polemic, yet must, nevertheless, be addressed if the debate is to be brought to a satisfactory conclusion: whether it is an Autonomous Community, whether it is a Statute, what constitutional content is, what the nature of said content is, and what Article 139.1 of the Spanish Constitution means are just some of the questions that had ceased to be topical but that have reemerged as issues, clarification of which is key to finding a reasoned answer to this fresh controversy.

The original debate that sprang up in the 1980s concerning what autonomy meant compared to the conventional concept of sovereignty concluded with a series of rulings highlighting the conceptual differences and the former's subservience to the latter. Autonomy was to refer to a limited power within the already delimited power of sovereignty, the task of the Constitution being to mark the boundaries within which these new politically oriented territorial administrations could legitimately move. Within such a dynamic, it was the constitutional norm that became the necessary area in which to establish what action could be carried out in a decentralized state.

In early February 2005, Congress took the decision not to consider the reform proposal put forward under the Basque Statute of 1979 mainly because it was framed outside the Constitution and assumed the same sovereign powers reserved exclusively for the Spanish state. A particular and partisan reinterpretation of the First Additional Provision of the Spanish Constitution, in the view of those proposing reform, allowed for the creation of "self-government through a particular political relation with the Spanish state, based on free association" (Articles 1 and 12). These provisions were framed more within the sphere of national functions than merely, with all due respect, autonomous functions and closely resembled the second paragraph of amendment 689 of the constitutional bill that sought the return to the three Basque provinces and Navarre of unspecified political institutions and powers of uncertain origin, which "virtually removed all limits from the Constitution and which indeed meant an added constitution to the one

---

[28] Anguita Susi (2007), p. 199.

already being drafted".[29] In other words, it was no more than a clash between Constitution and historical rights, between constitutional legitimacy and historical legitimacy.

Put differently, Congress had a very clear idea of where the line was to be drawn with regard to constitutional power and that said line could not be overstepped even under the supposed guise of historical rights that were embraced and respected by fundamental law. Ultimately, these historical rights should be *secundum constitutione*.[30]

Furthermore, the right to autonomy in constitutional terms belongs to nationalities and regions that, in sum, are merely a constitutional expression of a desire to prevent over-fragmentation at a territorial level whilst, regarding the former, adding recognition to the autonomy they enjoyed during the Republican period. Within both categories, provincial government bodies are privileged actors in the autonomic process that may be replaced by official higher ranking bodies should there be a provisional autonomous regime (first transitional provision of the Spanish Constitution). In sum, it is exclusively administrative bodies (provincial councils, preautonomous governments) that promote the creation of new territorial administrations under Title VIII, which in the framework of constitutional procedure will evolve until they are able to form part of the political arena. This is what is known as the statutory process or the specific legislative path (Articles 146 and 151.2) towards drafting basic institutional rules (Article 147.1), which take on the legal form of an Organic Law (Article 81.1) and which, when constitutional provisions are enacted (essentially Title VIII), create an Autonomous Community.[31]

Within this process, certain political stakeholders play an increasingly important role (assemblies made up of elected representatives chosen in the various provinces or only chosen by said representatives in the case of Article 151.2) until the process is finally debated and discussed in the political arena *par excellence*, the national parliament, which will endow the rules that create said bodies with the aura *par excellence* of all the constituted power or importance of the law: in this instance, in the legal form of an Organic Law. This somewhat peculiar means of creation is

---

[29] Lojendio (1988), p. 33.

[30] A thorough analysis of the various positions may be found in Larrazabal Basañez (1997), p. 431 et seq.

[31] Although aside from the somewhat sketchily drawn out system, the national parliament has the power to authorize the creation of an autonomous community, authorize or agree to a statute of autonomy, and replace the initiative of local corporations in Article 143.2. All of this is possible if the previously mentioned conditions set forth in Article 144 are met. Some of these are objective (a smaller territorial block than the provincial, nonintegration in the provincial organization), others undetermined (national interest, certain conditions of 143.1) and with the possible paradox, already denounced in constituent instances themselves by senators Zarazaga and Sánchez Agesta, of the imposition of autonomous community initiative, contrary to the will of local corporations (parliamentary records of 12 September 1978).

what has enabled statutes to become known as *sui generis* rules, merging two wills whilst remaining, however, national rules (Constitutional Court Ruling 99/86).

This evidences the fact that the institutions created come under the provisions of the fundamental rules that structure the coexistence of central bodies belonging to the single state of the Spanish nation with the politically based administrations into which it is internally divided, in application of the rules, limits, and possibilities marked out.

The situation to emerge vis-à-vis the autonomies subsequent to their evolution has depended on four fundamental factors: the imprecision of the constitutional text, the jurisprudence established by our Constitutional Court, the temporary arrangements of governments with centrifugal political formations, and the Statutes of Autonomy conceived as necessary norms that contribute to defining the model. Yet, of the four factors mentioned, the latter as a final summary of the situation is where all the rest converge, emerging as the final binding element resulting from an interpretation of the Autonomous State that has undergone numerous changes compared to the undefined but nevertheless definable model outlined in the basic text. One simple point will, I feel, suffice to illustrate clearly this shift in criterion: the mere extension already referred to concerning the basic institutional rules that were reformed. All of them, with the exception of reform in Navarre in 2010, are at least twice the size of the original, the texts in some instances stretching to over 200 articles (in the case of Catalonia and Andalusia), their corpus evidencing an internal distribution similar to that of the constitutional text. Yet, despite the impreciseness and ambiguity found in the Constitution, the clearly defined limit for the Autonomous State is that Autonomous Communities are not sovereign and that their statutes cannot be constitutions or imitations thereof. This is the line that the confluence of the factors referred to is attempting to cross.

In addition to the above-mentioned extensions that are beyond all logic when compared to the previous texts, they also contain a series of matters that have sparked a lively, controversial, and, to date, inconclusive debate, resulting from the opening out that is so evident in Article 147.1 and 2 of the Spanish Constitution. Said precept, structured in its three paragraphs, sets out an ethos in the first, describing its nature. The Statutes of Autonomy are to be the basic institutional rule for each Autonomous Community, which is to reproduce, with no variation, the definition that the constituent assembly already set out in Article 132.1 of the draft Constitution on 5 January, 1978. Such was the consensus at the time concerning the definition that no amendments were put forward. All statutes are, constitutionally speaking, the basic rules of the respective Autonomous Communities, a rather unfortunate definition since, if we are to understand such a rule drafted by the respective Autonomous Community, the latter is yet to be created (the statute is precisely the foundational rule of the Autonomous Community—for all cases, see Constitutional Court Ruling 76/88 dated 26 April). If it is perceived as a nonautonomous rule in the sense that it is drafted by nonautonomous bodies (national parliament), it would be one of the basic institutional rules, together with the Constitution itself, highlighted by certain bodies in Article 152.1. Bearing all of this in mind and leaving aside the debate, what is characteristic of such provisions is that they are basic, in the sense that they are the main basis of the constitutional autonomy that they implement, as has been understood since 1947 in the Italian Constitution regarding the matter of the regions in Article 123,[32] this being the Constitution that "most resembles the one we wish to create", in the words of Member of Parliament Fraga Iribarne in his address to Parliament on 14 June, 1978.

In addition to proving essential, nonautonomous bodies are described further in the following paragraphs through content that is necessary and indispensable: denomination, territory, reform procedure, their own institutions, assumed powers, and bases for transfer of services so as, in the words of Member of Parliament Martin Toval, to avoid repeating previous historical errors such as those experienced under the Catalonian Statute of 1932 of failing to take account of all the services required.[33] Nothing more is referred to in Title VIII of our foremost rule with regard to content (the legal nature of the statute and the required content).

For its part, the Constitutional Court has addressed the matter in a number of judgments, analyzing this much debated Article 147 of the Spanish Constitution from a more constitutional perspective, basing its view on the discourse concerning the possible statutory content allowed by the dispositive principle that hangs over Title VIII of the Spanish Constitution. Even so, the issue is far from being an amicable one.

Within the terms of the Constitution, the Constitutional Court has identified three kinds of content in these basic rules: the minimum or necessary content corresponding to sections of Article 147, additional content, the other constitutional possibilities that may be embraced by the statute, and complementary content or that which is not reflected constitutionally. This is defined in Constitutional Court Ruling 247/07 and rectified in subsequent rulings, such as that which, not being expressly set out in the Constitution, proves a suitable addition due to its link to constitutional provisions, a suitability that refers to the function that the Constitution entrusts to the Statutes of Autonomy.[34]

This paradox between the shortcomings in the content of the statutes and the definition as a basic institutional rule is striking. This has led to extensions of the organic laws such as those referred to previously, which go far beyond the early Statutes of the 1980s. Comparing them clearly involves taking account of the quantitative and qualitative differences, the latter being those that allow discussion concerning how the Statutes have evolved. By way of an example, we may take the case of Catalonia. The 57 Articles contained in its Organic Law 4/79 increased to 223 in Organic Law 6/06, additional and transitional provisions being excluded in both. The first contained four Titles and the second seven, the latter including Titles devoted to judicial power in Catalonia (III), embracing the innovative Board of Justice; another addressing rights, obligations, and governing principles (I); and a further final one dealing with institutional relations (V).

---

[32] "Each region shall have a statute which, in accordance with the Constitution, determines its form of government and its fundamental principles of organization and self-government...".

[33] Toval (1980).

[34] One illustrative example in this regard is the article by Professor Espierrez (2008). See also Aparicio Perez (2011).

What is beyond question is that there has been a step forward regarding how the nature of the Statutes of Autonomy may be understood and without any changes to what is set out in Article 147 of the Spanish Constitution. From being a basic institutional rule that creates a nonsovereign public authority, it seems to have become a rule that has created a territorial authority that rivals any national formation in terms of institutional structure and powers that, obvious differences aside, often proves merely linguistic, very possibly aware that it may be challenged by a Constitutional Court and conscious of the latter's determination and clear doctrine regarding the qualitative differences between autonomy and sovereignty. Strangely enough, or perhaps not so strangely, this is a trend that seems to have become part of our constitutional state.

# References

Anguita Susi, A. (2007): "Naturaleza y alcance de las declaraciones estatutarias de derechos en España e Italia", in *REDC* no. 80/07, page 199

Aparicio, M.A. (2005): "La adecuación de la estructura del Estado a la Constitución (reforma constitucional vs. reforma estatutaria), in *RCDP* no. 31/05, page 2

Aparicio Perez, M.A. (2011): "Posición y funcionamiento de los estatutos de autonomía en la STC 31/2010", in *REAF* no. 12/2011

Aragon Reyes, M. (2007): "La organización institucional de las comunidades autónomas", in *REDC* no. 79/07, page 16

Corcuera Atienza: Derechos históricos, democracia y ley de la claridad (más sobre el "plan Ibarretxe"), in AAVV.: El estado autonómico: integración, solidaridad y diversidad, vol. II, joint edition Colex/INAP, Madrid, 2005, page 65

Balaguer Callejon, F. (coord.): *Manual de derecho constitucional*, vol. I, ed. Tecnos, Madrid, 2007, page 302

Cruz Villalon, P. (2006): "La reforma del estado de las autonomías", in *REAF* no. 2/06, page 79

Diaz Revorio, F.J.: *La Constitución como orden abierto*, ed. McGraw Hill, Madrid, 1997, pages 209–210

Cabellos Espierrez (2008) "La relación derechos-estado autonómico en la sentencia sobre el estatuto de Valencia", *REAF* no. 7/2008

Ibarra Robles, J.L. (1982): "La autonomía en su dimensión de principio general de la organización del Estado/Ordenamiento. Artículo 137 in fine de la Constitución", in *RVAP* no. 2/1982, page 128

Lojendio e Irure: "Normativa constitucional y política autonómica", in *RVAP* no. 4/82, p. 23

Larrazabal Basañez, S.: *Contribución a una teoría de los derechos históricos vascos*, ed. IVAP, Oñati, 1997, pages 431

Lasagabaster Herrarte, I. (2005): "La reforma de los estatutos de autonomía: una reflexión sobre su teoría y práctica", in *Revista Catalana de Dret Public*, no. 31/05, page 21

Lojendio, I. Mª.: *La disposición adicional primera de la constitución española*, ed. IVAP, Oñate, 1988, page 33

A. Rojo: "La experiencia del estado regional en Europa: un referente para el caso español", in *REP* no. 127/05, page 237

Rousseau, J.J.: *Contrato Social*, ed. Espasa Calpé, Madrid, 1990, page 37

Ruggiu, I.: "Il nuovo Statuto Catalano", in *Le Regioni*, no. 2/2007, page 291

Martin Toval: *Constitución española. Trabajos parlamentarios*, vol. II, ed. CCGG, Madrid, 1980, page 1560

# Statutory Rights and the Federal System

M. Agudo Zamora and C. Milione

**Abstract** The protection of rights and liberties demands an element inseparable from the constitutional model of the Rule of Law. Together with the dominion of laws and the separation of powers, the axiological requisite is formed, underpinning this model of state.

In decentralized States, it is essential to establish the model of the distribution of powers in relation to the protection of rights. In the federal model, together with the necessary role of the federal state, the States stipulate a scope of power superior to that of States with a regional or autonomous model, as is the case in Spain.

In its Sentence of 31/2010, the Constitutional Court validated the existence of a recognition of rights and liberties through the Statutes of Autonomy, be it with a limited character, since the Tribunal finds that these statutory rights are not subjective rights but rather mandates for lawmakers, to differentiate them from basic rights recognized by the Constitution and, therefore, statutory rights of lawmakers in the autonomous communities. According to the Constitutional Court, this means that these rights will only be fulfilled before judicial organs when legislators from autonomous communities have passed them into law. Likewise, statutory rights are materially bound to the scope of powers within that autonomous community; that is to say, the powers recognized by the Statute are the ones that delimit the scope in which statutory rights can operate.

In this paper, we would like to make the case, firstly, for the importance of the model of the Rule of Law in the recognition of rights and liberties; secondly, for the possibility and necessity that, in Spain, the Statutes of Autonomy integrate a list of rights regulating their essential content; and, thirdly, to offer an analysis of the range of constitutionality of the inclusion of statutory rights, following the Sentence of the Constitutional Court 31/2010, which resolved the appeal to unconstitutionality filed against certain aspects of the 2006 Statute of Autonomy of Catalonia.

M. Agudo Zamora (✉) • C. Milione
Area de Derecho Constitucional, Facultad de Derecho de Córdoba, Universidad de Córdoba
(España), C/ Puerta Nueva s/n – 14071, Córdoba, España
e-mail: miguelagudo@uco.es; ciromilione@uco.es

A. López-Basaguren and L. Escajedo San Epifanio (eds.), *The Ways of Federalism*     587
*in Western Countries and the Horizons of Territorial Autonomy in Spain*, Vol. 2,
DOI 10.1007/978-3-642-27717-7_37, © Springer-Verlag Berlin Heidelberg 2013

# The Recognition of Rights as an Indispensable Element and Guarantee of the Rule of Law

The Rule of Law, that is, the State "subjected to Law," the State whose activity is subjected to judicial control, is borne bound to the liberal State and constructed under the doctrine of the "dominion of law." The establishment of liberal regimes brings with it then the generalization of the formula "Rule of Law," whose first important expression was articulated in the 1789 Declaration of the Rights of Man and of the Citizen. In this text, we find the proclamation of the absolute primacy of law in terms of the expression of the general will (articles 3 and 6), as well as the requirement of the separation of powers and the guarantee of rights (article 16).

The "Rule of Law," a term coined definitively by Robert von Mohl in 1832, is characterized by three elements:

a) Dominion of law. This, without a doubt, is the key defining element of this formula. Laws must be created by a representative organ that expresses popular will. Laws then must be drawn up by the Spanish Parliament, which in turn must be elected under universal, free, and periodic suffrage, with voter anonymity. These laws must regulate all state activity, including the administrative sphere—the principle of legality of the Administration is guaranteed by a system of appeals that permits those potentially affected to react—as well as the judicial sphere, without forgetting that all citizens are subjected to the same rule. In any case, laws will be subject to the Constitution and subsequent constitutional controls.

   The subordination of power to Law finds its most forceful expression in article 9 of the Spanish Constitution (SC), which establishes in its first section that "citizens as well as authorities are subjected to the Constitution and the rest of the legal system", specifying in the third section the principles that put into effect this subordination, which is to say, the principles of legality, normative hierarchies, publicity regarding the norms, the non-retroactive nature of provisions penalizing laws unfavorable or restrictive toward individual rights, legal certainty, and the responsibility and interdiction of the arbitrariness of authorities.

b) Division of powers. The primacy of law should be accompanied by a system of separation of powers as a guarantee and check against themselves. This separation need not be understood in an absolute sense but rather as a system of distribution of functions within a network of relations and mutual controls. The point of this separation is none other than to avoid the concentration of power, establishing a balance that should be to the benefit of the citizen, an essential piece of which balance is the existence of a completely independent Court System, as well as a process that guarantees the most essential freedoms. The classic diagram of the division of powers thus sees an adaptation to the new exigencies of the social State, said adaptation being supported by the expansion of the areas of state action, as well as in the modification of relations between the Parliament and the Government, above all, after the advent of universal suffrage and the conversion of political parties into authentic protagonists within the political system.

c) Recognition of Rights and fundamental freedoms. If the dominion of the law is the key defining element of the Rule of Law, the fundamental element from a more judicial, axiological, and even ethical standpoint is the recognition and guarantee of a series of rights and liberties that belong to every citizen. Human dignity is the motive for declaring a series of personal rights, and this is precisely the point of the catalogue of rights and freedoms that our constitutional text contains, proclaiming in article 10 that "human dignity, inviolable and inherent rights, free development of the personality, respect for the law and for the rights of others are the foundation of political order and social peace". This stipulation, as well as the comprehensive catalogue of rights and liberties, takes responsibility for the principles of immediate efficacy and favorable interpretation, while all laws must respect its essential content. Together with this proclamation, and with the objective of giving it full effectiveness, the constitutional text guarantees a series of instruments protecting the rights— reinforcing especially those considered the most basic—which constitute the most essential guarantee of the State of Law in each and every one of its dimensions.

## Autonomous State and Statutory Rights

Just as the federal State stipulates the recognition of various constituent, legislative canters within the State that result in a plurality of constitutional regulations—these constitutional regulations falling under another superior set of regulations in which they also participate—in the Autonomous State there are entities that stipulate a certain level of autonomy while maintaining the principle of state unity. These entities have determined capacities for self-government, on the executive level as much as, on occasions, the legislative. On the one hand, there exists national constituent political power, whose legislative reach is logically established by the Constitution, and, on the other, there exist territorial communities, be they referred to as regions or nationalities—other canters of political decision—with exclusively legislative power granted by the same Constitution. These territorial communities are bodies endowed with legislative autonomy and have a judicial personality distinct from that of the central political Power.

There are authors who argue that only two types of States exist, the unitary and the federal, the regional or autonomous being subspecies of the federal model. There are even those who frame the concept of the federal State in its highest degree of constitutional protection in terms of the autonomy its members encounter, a protection that takes form in constitutional rigidity and in a system of constitutional justice in charge of conflicts between different political bodies.

In the case of Spain, as we have shown, respecting rights constitutes the foundation of political order and social peace, a narrow nexus of genetic and functional interdependence establishing itself between the Rule of Law and rights, since the Rule of Law demands it be so in order to guarantee these rights, which in turn demand their realization from the Rule of Law. The greatest or smallest expansion of the constitutional recognition of rights, as well as the level of protection or guarantees for those who enjoy them, will be a parameter sufficiently indicative of the democratic legitimacy of political order, while there exists a profound relation between the role assigned to rights and liberties and the system of organization and the exercise of state functions. In constitutional guidelines of democratic countries, basic rights enjoy then a double character, presenting themselves as a set of basic objective values and as the framework for the protection of subjective judicial situations. Currently, therefore, these rights have a double function: On the subjective plane, they act as guarantees of individual freedoms, as well as social and collective aspects of subjectivity, while on the objective plane, they assume an institutional component, functioning as a means to achieving constitutional aims and values.

Building on the role rights have in the foundation of political order, the Spanish Constitutional Court has formulated the doctrine regarding the double nature—subjective and objective—of basic rights. In the Sentence 25/81 of July 14, the Court declared that "firstly, basic rights are subjective rights, rights of individuals not only in relation to the rights of citizens in a strict sense, but also in relation to how they guarantee judicial status or freedom within the scope of existence. But at the same time, they are essential elements of an objective system of the national community which forms a frame for a just, human, and peaceful communal fellowship, expressed historically through the Rule of Law, and later in the social Rule of Law or the social, democratic Rule of Law, in accordance with our constitution".

The first article of our Constitution, after defining the form of State, proclaims as the paramount values of our legal system the following: liberty, justice, equality, and political pluralism. This precept is narrowly connected with another, that which marks the beginning of Title I, which, among the basic principles of political order and social peace, includes the dignity of the human person; it is evident then that these said paramount values of the system need as a basic assumption for their full existence the honorable ethical participation of the members of the society, which is itself governed by them. Therefore, the recognition of rights is none other than the manifest obligation of the primacy of ultimate constitutional value: the dignity of the human person to which is intimately linked the free development of the personality. In this way, the older, strictly subjectivist conception of basic rights is broken away from, allowing them to be considered elements of the judicial system, that is, as objective judicial standards that are the apogee of the axiological system that informs all sectors of the Law.

The natural next question to ask is if the Autonomous Communities—politically decentralized bodies in Spain—can or cannot regulate rights.

It could be understood then, *prima facie*, that if a reductionist reading of the Constitution is applied, the resulting margin—the margin, that is, to include regulatory clauses regarding rights and duties that in their legal application have constitutional links—left at the disposal of the Autonomous Communities would be extremely small and, hence, that of the Statutes of Autonomy as well.

In this sense, Diez-Picazo (2006) holds that there are substantive formal arguments that show that the inclusion of declarations of rights in the Statutes of Autonomy is not in accordance with the Spanish Constitution. This theory is answered by Caamaño (2007), who believes that the content of the Statutes of Autonomy that the SC establishes as necessary in article 147.2 does not have an exclusive or excluding character, which makes the inclusion of other matters in statutory texts possible, such as a list of rights and duties, which furthermore, in the opinion of this author, is logical since "in a system of multilevel distribution of political power the simultaneity of lawmakers working in relation to basic rights is inevitable".

The principle of autonomy of nationalities and regions, which shape the Spanish State, made real *ex constitutione*, and the evolution territorial bodies have fostered, for the sake of achieving increased protagonism in political life, has resulted in a plurality of differentiated political systems that coexist harmoniously by their bond to a common order, one that emanates from the application and efficiency of the constitutional system.

From this it can be inferred, as a structural consequence of the principle of autonomy recognized by our Constitution, that in the Spanish State a uniformity of rights and obligations for all citizens cannot exist, and to this extent, in spite of their being connected by a common system inside of whose vertices the Constitution is found, they are also subjected to differentiated judicial systems.

Aguado (1996) sustains, with a differing opinion, that the recognition of a catalogue of rights in a Statute is hardly compatible with our Constitution, a reading not shared by various autonomous Advisory Boards that have deliberated on this matter, leaning favorably toward the inclusion of a catalogue of rights and duties in new statutory texts.

Therefore, as Porras Nadales (2007) points out, "the rigorous vision of things seems like it should be predicated, strictly speaking, on 'authentic' basic rights, which is to say, on those which in theory are integrated in Section One of Chapter II of Title I of the 1978 Spanish Constitution: but at the same time the existence of an autonomous State implies the subsistence of a plurality of systems that would be incompatible with absolute uniformity in terms of the rights and duties of Spanish citizens, as recognized by our Constitutional Court". Hence, if the fundamental nucleus of said rights was then resistant to any incursion of inequality derived from the process of territorial decentralization. On the other hand, the package of social rights and governing principles of social and economic policy, which normally adjusts to the profile of powers belonging to the Autonomous Communities, would be able to elude the possibility of complete and exhaustive state regulation, permitting the Autonomous Communities to prioritize, or not prioritize, certain values inherent to the Welfare State.

It is true that the Spanish Constitution does not contain any provision by which to expressly empower the Autonomous Community to create its own catalogue of rights and duties. Moreover, previous Statutes of Autonomy tended to include clauses of pardon in which it was indicated that the rights and duties of citizens of Autonomous Communities were established by the Constitution.

At this point, one question is whether all Spaniards hold the rights and duties recognized by the Constitution and another is if Autonomous Communities cannot implement aspects related to the content or exercised conditions of the rights and duties or recognized new rights and duties—that is, beyond those constitutionally recognized.

Naturally then it stands to ask: Are there constitutional limits to including a set of rights in a Statute of Autonomy? To this question, one should respond with three substantial pieces of information: First, the Constitution does not impede this; second, the content provided by article 142.7 of the Constitution as the necessary content of the Statutes of Autonomy is the bare minimum, hence it can regulate other issues; and, third, it is recommended to include the abovementioned set as an expression of political pluralism that, as a paramount value of the legal system, strengthens and preserves democratic principles, the vertebrae of our State.

Now, what rights could be included in the Statutes?

Basic rights and public freedoms cannot be regulated. By virtue of the combination of articles 53 and 81 of the Constitution, this matter remains reserved for "organic" lawmakers, in other words, for the state. Because of this, the essential content of these rights and freedoms are impossible to modify in the Statutes of Autonomy. This does not mean that aspects beyond the most basic cannot be regulated by the Autonomous Communities, as long as the implementation is carried out competently in the context in which the right in question is raised.

The rights contained in the Second Section of Chapter II of Title I and those in Chapter II of the same Title fall under exclusive federal jurisdiction or the reserve powers of the autonomies, depending on the corresponding title of responsibility. Perhaps it would be convenient, with respect to rights containing particular social import, to provide increased capacity to the Autonomous Communities, with which a more stable and efficient space of power would be institutionalized.

Before continuing, we should succinctly point out two constitutional clauses that could affect the exercise of autonomous latitude in this context. This concerns two provisions found in articles 139.1 and 149.1.1º of the Constitution. The literal text of article 139.1 ("All Spaniards have the same rights and obligations in every State territory") does not impede different regulations by Autonomous Communities but rather protects Spaniards from discrimination.

As such, that the State has the exclusive ability to regulate the basic conditions that guarantee equality for all Spaniards in the exercise of rights and in the fulfillment of constitutional duties impedes Autonomous Communities from regulating the essential content of these rights, but it does not exclude the possibility of regulating certain aspects of them by virtue of the delegated titles of responsibility.

Therefore, we can say that Autonomous Communities have a recognized capacity for action with regard to rights and duties in three areas:

- To regulate, to the extent that they are competent (regulation of the content of the rights of the conditions in which they are exercised), the rights and duties found in the Constitution.
- To transform into subjective rights the "governing principles" of Chapter III, Title I.
- To recognize new rights not contemplated by the Constitution, whose establishment could be derived from a certain autonomous title of responsibility.

As such, to the extent that the Statutes register new rights and broaden those already existing, they will undertake the realization of the ultimate goal of States, rights known as Welfare: to advocate the quality of life of citizens, and ultimately, the realization of their dignity. More specifically, the Spanish Constitution lays out a series of paramount values in its system—liberty, justice, equality, and political pluralism—which holds the Autonomous Communities responsible as authorities, especially when the Constitution has entrusted them with the task of "promot[ing] (inside its scope of power) the conditions in which freedom and equality of the individual and groups is real and effective; to remove obstacles that impede or obstruct its plenitude..." (article 9.2., SC), these values that necessarily illuminate a statutory catalogue of rights and duties. Therefore, the regulation of this catalogue is an issue reserved for the Statute, firstly, to the extent that it expresses the framework of judicial conditions and power between the Autonomous Community and its own citizens, derived from the powers assumed by the Community, and secondly, because the institution in the Statute of this fundamental frame of judicial relations between citizens and authorities links directly to these powers in the moment that they exercise their normative powers to act.

# Range of Constitutionality of the Inclusion of Statutory Rights, after Sentence 31/2010

The 31/2010 Sentence of the Constitutional Court (SCC), which decided the appeal to unconstitutionality lodged against various precepts of the 2006 Statute of Autonomy of Catalonia, is not the first sentence in which the Constitutional Court has made a judgment regarding constitutional legitimacy based on a declaration of rights and governing principles included in the Statutes of Autonomy. SCC 247/2007, which decided the appeal against the reform of the Statute of Autonomy of Valencia, established that the content of the Statute can go beyond that already established, such as the necessary fulfillment of article 147.2 SC, for which no impediment exists preventing the Statute, as a basic institutional standard for the Autonomous Community, from including rights in its text. At the same time, as Carrillo (2010) explains, "after introducing a singular distinction between 'institutional rights' and 'rights of jurisdiction,' the Court determined that, no matter the denomination used by the Statutes, the said statutory rights are not in reality subjective rights but rather simple mandates to the autonomous authorities. Now, in consideration of SCC 31/2010 (legal basis (l.b.) 16), the Court maintains that statutory rights—those referred to with this denomination—are not subjective rights but rather mandates to authorities, but this seems to abandon the controversial distinction because it makes no distinction—established in SCC 247/2007— between those rights which remain bound to the function of institutions and the specific exercise of power".

Thusly, Carrillo points out that "in the very Constitution under the term 'right' there are understood to be true subjective rights, like clauses of legitimization for the drawing up of certain legislative options, be they always in the end mandates (in both cases) addressed to lawmakers, imposing on them a job or omission which is built on a subjective aim accountable before the Courts of Justice; obligating them to pursue a result without prescribing specifically how to achieve it and without using this obligation as a basis for a subjective right, which in this case will only be born from regulations dictated in the fulfillment of the given pursuit. Regulations which ultimately prescribe ends without imposing means or, to be more precise, which provide the legitimization of the political administration of public means in the service of a certain end".

The Court holds then that these statutory rights are not subjective rights but are instead mandates for the lawmaker to differentiate them from basic rights recognized by the Constitution and that, therefore, statutory rights only are bound to the autonomous lawmaker. According to the Constitutional Court, this means that they will only be accountable before judicial organs when autonomous lawmakers have passed them into law. Likewise, statutory rights are materially bound to the scope of powers within that autonomous community; this is to say, the powers recognized by the Statute are the ones that delimit the scope in which statutory rights can operate.

At this point one must recall that magistrates Conde Martín de Hijas and Delgado Barrio, in their respective opinions on SCC 31/2010, took dissenting positions on the issue. Conde Martín de Hijas finds that statutory rights are not only mandates to authorities but *are* the authority, which is regulated by a set of guarantees given by the very same statutes, to the point of taking on a jurisdictional character. As the magistrate reasons, the inclusion of rights does not belong in the statutory text and finds the contested articles related to rights unconstitutional. Delgado Barrio argues, given that the Statutes of Autonomy are a source of differentiation among the Autonomous Communities, that the Statues are hence not the adequate normative context in which to establish rights that should entail differences, which by their inclusion in the Statute should be inspired by profoundly restrictive criteria. He concludes, therefore, that, save for exceptions, the general rule should be that the inclusion of rights in the Statutes is not viable.

As such, the Court, in l.b. 16 of SCC 31/2010, reminds that "basic rights are strictly those which, in the guarantee of liberty and equality, bind all lawmakers, that is, the Parliament and legislature of the Autonomous Communities, without exception". This limiting function can only be realized through a common standard superior to lawmakers, which is to say, through the Constitution, the supreme standard that gives to the rights recognized in it a limit unsurpassable by all powers constituted and endowed by contents that are equally opposed, and with the same substantive reach by virtue of the unity of the jurisdictions of power (ordinary and judicial) for its definition and guarantee. Rights, hence, that are not recognized as basic by the constitution, but are rights precisely for having come from an expression of constituent will. Because of this, statutory rights "should be, ergo, something else."

The issue at hand then is rights that are bound solely to the autonomous lawmaker and, furthermore, fall under the scope of power of Autonomous Communities. Meanwhile, according to SCC 31/2010, "under the same category of 'right' distinct normative realties can be understood, and it is these which must be addressed, beyond the pure *nomen*, to conclude whether their inclusion in a Statute is or is not constitutionally possible".

These types of statutory rights, as established in SCC 247/2007, are not subjective rights but rather mandates to authorities, acting as technical guides, prescriptive or directive, depending on the case, for the exercise of autonomous powers. This, therefore, presupposes a principle of differentiation that cannot be confused with inequality or privilege, prohibited by articles 138.2 and 139.1 of the SC, since this principle "only abounds in the inherent diversity of the autonomous State", as was declared in the decision SCC 76/1983.

On the other hand, the Court argues that the function of the oversight of basic rights does not correspond to the Statutes of Autonomy but rather to the autonomous legislator, pertaining to the ordinary legislator, and according to the constitutional distribution of power, but not to the organic statutory legislator. In this sense, according to the criteria of the Court, and as Carrillo critically points out, there is no contradiction with which an ordinary legislator can impede a statutory legislator because, as he affirms, "in reality, it is not that it can be done more through autonomous law; it is that something distinct happens, which corresponds in the set of established standards to the criteria of power". Carrillo argues that this interpretation of the constitutional legitimacy of the statutory provision over rights, duties, and principles suffers from weaknesses. Firstly, statutory rights are not always different from the basic rights recognized by the Constitution. Secondly, it is not clear to the statutory legislator—always within his or her scope of power—if he or she can mould the content of the rights he or she receives with greater or lesser exactitude.

In conclusion, SCC 31/2010 is not the first sentence decided by the Constitutional Court regarding the constitutional legitimacy of a declaration of rights and governing principles included in the Statutes of Autonomy. Sentence 247/2007, which decided the appeal against the reform of the Statute of Autonomy of Valencia, established that the content of the Statute can go beyond that already established, as necessary fulfillment of article 147.2 of the Spanish Constitution, for which no impediment exists to block the Statute, as a basic institutional standard, from including rights in its text. However, the Court specified that statutory rights are not in reality subjective rights but rather simple mandates for autonomous authorities. Now, in consideration of SCC 31/2010, this doctrine reiterates and maintains that statutory rights are not subjective ones but instead mandates for authorities, abandoning the established distinction in SCC 247/2007 between those rights that remain linked to the function of institutions and those whose exercise falls under the scope of specific powers.

The court reasons that these statutory rights are not subjective rights but mandates for lawmakers to differentiate them from basic rights recognized by the Constitution, and therefore statutory rights are bound only to autonomous lawmakers. This, according to the Constitutional Court, means that these rights are only accountable before judicial organs when autonomous lawmakers have passed them into law. Likewise, statutory rights are materially bound to the scope of powers within the autonomous communities; that is, the powers recognized by the Statute are the ones that delimit the scope in which statutory rights can operate.

In any case, and in spite of the judicial reservations expressed, which are fundamentally related to the limited nature of their reach, the constitutional "validation" of the inclusion of the catalogue of rights in the Statutes of Autonomy does not cease to be an important contribution of Constitutional Court Sentence 31/2010.

# References

Aguado Renedo, C. (1996). *El Estatuto de Autonomía y su posición en el ordenamiento jurídico.*
Caamaño, F. (2007). "Sí, pueden (Declaraciones de derechos y Estatutos de Autonomía)". *Revista Española de Derecho Constitucional REDC* 79; 33–46.
Carrillo, M. (2010) "Derechos y garantías jurisdiccionales". Revista Catalana de Derecho Público. Número especial sobre la STC 31/2010.
Dictamen 268/05 del Consejo Consultivo de la Generalitat de Cataluña.
Dictamen 782/05 del Consejo Consultivo de Galicia.
Dictamen 72/06 del Consejo Consultivo de Andalucía.
Dictamen 68/06 del Consejo Consultivo del Principado de Asturias.
Dictamen 713/06 del Consejo Consultivo de Castilla y León.
"Dictámenes sobre las reformas estatutarias" en *Revista Española de la Función Consultiva, nº extraordinario de 2007.*
Diez-Picazo, L.M. (2006). "¿Pueden los Estatutos de Autonomía declarar derechos, deberes y principios?". *Revista Española de Derecho Constitucional,* 78; 63–75.
Porras Nadales , A. (2007). "Derechos sociales y políticas públicas". *El* Estatuto *de Autonomía de Andalucía de 2007* (Coord. Agudo Zamora, M), Centro de Estudios Andaluces; 62 y sgs.

# Multilevel Rights Protection in Canada

Cecilia Rosado Villaverde

**Abstract** As a federal State, Canada has a multilevel protection of rights and freedoms. The Constitutional Act of 1982, the anti-discrimination laws, and the bills of rights of the provinces and territories are the legal rules that protect the rights of citizens. The system of rights guarantees needs to be mentioned too because the instruments of protection are, in many cases, a combination of judicial and administrative institutions.

## Introduction

Canada was founded in 1867, when three British colonies of North America decided to join in a federation. One colony was divided into two, forming Quebec and Ontario. This division responds to the earlier history of these territories and to their colonization by Britain, in the case of Ontario, and by France, in the case of Quebec. Canada is currently composed of ten provinces and three territories.

Canada is a federal state. Although it was a British colony, the Canadians decided to create a federation and not a unitary state, on the one hand, because of the existence of indigenous peoples and, on the other hand, because English settlers and French settlers lived in the same territory (Mitjans Perellò and Chacón Piqueras 1999). Therefore, given these differences, it would have been very difficult to create a unitary state; moreover, in the future, it could have been a source of future nationalistic problems in the future, as it has happened in other States.

It is at this historical moment, when Canada was created, that the English Parliament approved the Constitutional Act of 1867. Focusing on our matter of interest, the Constitution Act of 1867 includes a tool that had no rights protection.

C. Rosado Villaverde (✉)
Facultad de Ciencias Jurídicas y Sociales, Rey Juan Carlos University, Paseo de los artilleros s/n, 28032 Madrid, Spain
e-mail: cecilia.rosado@urjc.es

A. López-Basaguren and L. Escajedo San Epifanio (eds.), *The Ways of Federalism in Western Countries and the Horizons of Territorial Autonomy in Spain*, Vol. 2, DOI 10.1007/978-3-642-27717-7_38, © Springer-Verlag Berlin Heidelberg 2013

The absence of a bill of rights is due to two reasons: firstly, the principle of parliamentary sovereignty, which means that it is not possible to limit the powers of this institution (such would be the consequence of the introduction of an instrument of rights protection in a constitution), and secondly, the rule of law, which means that the protection of rights is done through ordinary laws and judges (Castellà 2005).

However, it is true that Canada's own situation did not permit the total lack of recognition and protection of rights, and for this reason the Constitution Act of 1867 included some rights (Articles 93 and 133), such as linguistic and religious freedom. However, the scope of those rights was limited (Relaño 2005; Ruiz Robledo 2005).

This situation continued until 1960, when the Canadian Parliament passed the Bill of Rights. This norm recognizes and guarantees civil and political rights in relation to the performance of federal agencies. It should also be noted that the Bill of Rights applies only to federal Parliament. In addition, this norm is an ordinary legislative text; it can be changed through a simple majority in parliament, that is, it is not a superior text and difficult to modify. This norm had little impact on Canadian society (Hiebert 2001).

Another legal instrument adopted to protect the rights and freedoms was the law against discrimination in 1977, although its impact on Canadian political culture was minimal. Finally, in 1982 the new Constitution Act was adopted, containing the Charter of Rights and Freedoms. With the adoption of the Constitution Act, the Canadian Human Rights Declaration was weakened and is now almost out of use. However, there are some rights that are not included in the Constitution of 1982; however, the Declaration recognizes rights and freedoms, such as the right to property.

## Sources of Law in Canada with Respect to the Regulation of Rights

In Canada, rights and freedoms are regulated at two levels, the federal level and the provincial or territorial level. How can one define who is competent in this area at all times? Well, in Canada, it is "generally considered that the rights and freedoms is an area of competition as such, which could be attributed to a government order or another, it is rather a matter whereby the federal government and provinces may exercise its powers, either to protect the rights and freedoms in order to change or to limit them" (Woerhling 2005).

That is, the competence on rights will depend on substantive matters; so, for example, if the provinces are responsible for education, they will also be responsible to legislate on the right to education. Also, if criminal jurisdiction is federal, the federal level will be responsible for regulating the rights of prisoners and detainees. Therefore, both levels are competent on rights and freedoms.

It should also be noted that the provinces began to enact laws guaranteeing rights 35 years before the federal level did. The first province to adopt a law on this matter was Saskatchewan in 1947. That is, the provinces (and territories), in view of the constitutional vacuum that existed at the federal level, decided to provide Declarations of Rights and Freedoms to limit power while protecting its citizens from potential rights violations. However, the rules that protect rights and freedoms in the provincial and territorial levels are usually anti-discrimination clauses, that is, it is not very common these days to find a Bill of Rights in the Canadian subunits (Brun 2003).

In addition, the Declarations of provincial rights and anti-discrimination laws are constantly reviewed in order to modify them to fit social reality. This is also because the laws governing rights in the provinces are ordinary laws, and therefore their modification is much simpler than the reform of the Constitution Act of 1982 (Brun and Tremblay 2002).

Finally, it is necessary to mention at this point that there are two instruments to guarantee rights and freedoms, both at the federal and provincial levels. These two instruments are, on the one hand, the aforementioned anti-discrimination laws and, on the other hand, laws that recognize the rights of the individual (in 1960, Canada passed at the federal level the Canadian Human Rights Declaration, and in 1977, it entered into force the law against discrimination).

## The Canadian Charter of Rights and Freedoms (1982)

The adoption of a new constitutional law began to take shape in the second half of the twentieth century, when more and more voices were calling for a complete overhaul of the Canadian constitutional Law. However, the differences among experts were great, especially on the question of the model to be adopted, that is, in accordance with the British model itself or supplemented with a more American model (especially in relation to the power of judges to the detriment of the power of Parliament, sovereign in British political model).

In addition, we have to mention the total reform of the Constitution Act (1867) that would have to be approved by the English Parliament, which entailed more difficulties for the Canadian situation. Finally, after years of debate, in 1982 the Canadian government got the British Parliament to adopt a new Constitutional Act for Canada with a process of constitutional reform where only Canadian authorities may intervene and the inclusion of the aforementioned Canadian Charter of Rights and Freedoms. This agreement received the affirmative vote of nine Canadian provinces, with one voting against it (Quebec), which, as we will show, will be important for the development of federal rights in this province. So far, we mentioned the multiple complications in the external front; however, it really was difficult to reach an internal agreement, that is, an agreement among all provinces and territories and between Canadian political voices.

The Canadian Charter of Rights and Freedoms represents, according to Janet L. Hiebert, "the most radical change ever conducted in the Canadian Constitution" (Hiebert 2001). Before the adoption of the Charter, the prevailing principle is parliamentary supremacy, that is, while the parliament did not exceed its scope, the judges did not examine the legislative texts. However, the Charter of 1982 requires the courts to interpret the rights recognized therein, and they are also responsible for protecting and repairing the damage when they are violated.

The Charter not only recognizes individual rights or freedom as freedom of association, equality, or freedom of expression but also recognizes another series of rights that are proper to the history of Canadian society. These are collective rights that have arisen as a result of the different languages, races, and cultures that live throughout Canada. The French Canadians not only have a different language but also are governed by different rules in specific cases (for example, by the civil law heritage of France); other ethnic groups with large settlements in Canada, such as the Inuit, have their own language (not recognized as an official language) and ancestral customs. In addition, we cannot forget the claims that, for years, have maintained cultural groups as a result of immigration. It should not be forgotten that 14.03 % of the population is of Scottish origin, 12.90 % of Irish origin, or 9.25 % is of German origin and that there are more than 15 different origins among the Canadian population.

Some of these rights are freedom of movement, respect for treaties signed with Aboriginal peoples, or the rights of linguistic minorities in education. Paradoxically, the Charter does not recognize any economic, social, or cultural rights; that is, it practically focuses on the rights of individual character, in the first generation rights (Brun 2003).

Another important highlight of this Charter is that the rights contained therein are not applicable to relations between individuals; that is, they only apply to relationships between an individual and a public body, be it federal, provincial, or territorial. The Canadian Supreme Court has sought to remedy this situation and therefore has made a broader interpretation of this provision of the Charter. For the Supreme Court, the rights under this federal instrument can also be invoked in relations between an individual and non-governmental entity such as a hospital or university, provided that they perform a "governmental function" (Woerhling 2005). However, relations between individuals are completely outside the federal protection, and thus if a private company (for example) violates the right of a citizen, that citizen cannot go to the mechanisms of protecting federal rights and this possibility is beyond the scope of the Canadian Charter of Rights and Freedoms of 1982.

Finally, we turn our attention to two articles of this Charter, two peculiar possibilities of the Canadian system in terms of rights. We're talking about Article 1 and Article 33 of the Constitution Act 1982. The first precept we are going to analyze, art. 33 of the Canadian Charter of Rights and Freedoms, states that "(1) Parliament or the legislature of a province may adopt a law (or regulation having the force of law) expressly declares that it or one of its provisions, shall have effect notwithstanding the provisions of Article 2 or sections 7 to 15 of this Charter". That is, the federal

Parliament and provincial legislatures can set limits to the exercise of most of the rights recognized and guaranteed in the Canadian Charter through ordinary laws. The limitation on the exercise of rights has a maximum of 5 years, after which a new vote is necessary to see whether or not the limitation is maintained (Mitjans and Castellà 2001).

There are three categories of rights that cannot be limited in their exercise: democratic rights (political rights, the right to effective judicial protection, and gender equality), freedom of movement and settlement, and finally, the linguistic rights of the Anglophone minority in Quebec and of French-speaking minorities in the rest of the Canadian territory. These are rights that can never be limited by a federal or territorial ordinary law. To proceed to its elimination is necessary to start the procedure to amend the Constitution Act.

The reason for a provision of this nature is the disjunction between political and legal models in Canada. That is, the Canadian constitutional court tried to reach a balance between, on one hand, the primacy of the rule of law, which is the Constitution, and the judicial review to be carried out on all the state laws that are capable of contradicting the Constitution and, on the other hand, the democratic principle that upholds the importance of the decision of the representatives who are elected by citizens (Fremont 2008). Likewise, the existence of this article is also due to a concession from the federal government to the provinces so that they do not oppose the Constitution, which limited the powers through their legislatures. All provinces accept this text, except Quebec, although it has been the province that has used the article 33 precept more often, while others have not used it or have only exceptionally done so.

Article 1 says that "The Canadian Charter of Rights and Freedoms guarantees the rights and freedoms here under. They can only be restricted by a rule of law, with limits that are reasonable and which can be demonstrably justified in the context of a free and democratic society". That is, there is a limitation clause that allows, in general, the limitation of rights (Woehrling 1993; Hiebert 1996). That provision guarantees, at first, the rights enshrined in the Charter; however, it is later acknowledged that they are not absolute and may be limited to the extent of the reasonable limits prescribed by law, which would also be justified in a free and democratic society.

Therefore, the Canadian bill of rights may be limited by non-constitutional laws, but it is necessary that all the guarantees imposed by the Constitution for this process are satisfied (Russel 1983). Nonetheless, how can we know if a law protected by Article I of the Charter of Rights is constitutional? The Supreme Court has set a two-phase control of laws limiting rights. In the first phase, it decides whether or not the law restricts some of the rights recognized in the Charter. If it does not restrict any rights, it is declared constitutional. However, if the Court finds that there are restrictions on rights, it opens a second phase in which it is decided whether the restriction is constitutional or not, following the guidelines issued by the first article of the Charter. Therefore, these laws are subject to proper control of the system of democratic modern states, namely the control of constitutionality of laws.

Finally, we should add that this constitutional provision has been used frequently by the Canadian Provinces, through their parliaments, in part because provision 33 of the Charter has been impractical in the Canadian reality.

## Provincial and Territorial Instruments of Protection of Rights and Freedoms

As we already said in the introduction to this section, the instruments used to recognize rights are of two types: anti-discrimination laws and laws that recognize the rights of the individual. This is because there is no "formal or codified concept" of the provincial constitutions (Castellà 2006); therefore, there are two standards that recognize and protect rights in the provinces and territories of Canada, and neither is a constitution in the formal sense.

Anti-discrimination laws are the most common standards in the provinces and territories in terms of rights. Though in general they often look to each after, there are variants that need to be highlighted. In most cases, they're going relate these variants or difference to the anti-discrimination law in the province of Quebec.

The content of these laws focuses on prohibiting forms of discrimination that are based on certain grounds, which are exhaustively listed. These reasons may be race, handicap, or sex, which appear on all anti-discrimination laws. Others, which are foreseen only in certain laws, are language, color, sex or condition, among others. Quebec anti-discrimination law includes 14 prohibited grounds: race, color, sex, pregnancy, sexual orientation, marital status, age, religion, political belief, language, ethnicity, and handicap or means to overcome this handicap.

Moreover, these anti-discrimination laws prohibit discrimination only in some areas of activity, such as access to transportation, services available to the public, or employment and pay, for example. Thus, discrimination is forbidden not in general but only in some areas. This regulation is specific to the historical tradition of common law, which has a decisive influence on various aspects of protection of rights and freedoms in Canada. On the other hand, it is necessary to emphasize that discrimination is prohibited whether conducted by private individuals or public bodies at provincial level.

With regard to exceptions that may exist to discrimination, anti-discrimination laws, both provincial and territorial, allow for a few. Among the most remarkable we find social promotion programs that seek to improve the position of those groups of individuals who are disadvantaged in society due to a prohibited ground of discrimination. However, we must not forget that although this is the general tone of anti-discrimination codes, there are some that allow all those discriminations that are reasonable.

Only three provinces (Saskatchewan, Alberta, and Quebec) and a territory (Yukon) recognize rights and freedoms in a provincial and territorial bill of rights. Except Alberta, other provinces, and the territory mentioned, the rights and liberties and anti-discrimination provisions found in one document, i.e., anti-discrimination laws and bills of rights are brought together in a single piece of legislation. However, within this same document, anti-discrimination content is more important than the General Declaration of Rights and Freedoms.

In general, these four bills of rights contained only individual rights and freedoms. Therefore, they focus on first generation rights—some of them are freedom of religion, freedom of expression, freedom of peaceful assembly and association, freedom of conscience, and the right to freedom from arbitrary detention, etc. In addition, Saskatchewan and Alberta collect political rights (Castellà 2005). However, the province of Quebec shows a difference in this regard because it is the only bill of rights that recognizes and guarantees not only individual rights but also political rights and liberties, judicial rights, and economic and social rights. However, these economic and social rights lack the protection afforded to other rights. For instance, the supremacy clause contained in art. 52 of the Charter of Rights and Freedoms of the individual in Québec only applies to articles 1–38. This means that the rights enshrined in arts. 39–48 may not be used to challenge a statute.

Finally, it should be mentioned that in all charters of rights in Alberta, the provisions apply to both provincial and territorial authorities and to relations between individuals. In Alberta, the charters of rights only apply to the provincial government, but anti-discrimination law in this province does apply to relations between individuals (it should be kept in mind that in Alberta anti-discrimination law and the Bill of Rights are separated; they appear in two separate documents, as opposed to Saskatchewan, Quebec, and Yukon).

## The Position of Canadian Law Concerning Rights and Freedoms in the Source System

Almost all of the laws that recognize rights at the provincial and territorial levels have a mechanism that provides for their supremacy over other laws, whether they are enacted before or after these laws on rights.

The mechanism that gives them such a position is called "supremacy clause"— for example, article 52 of the Charter of Rights and Freedoms of the individual in Quebec or art. 1.1 of the Human Rights, Citizenship and multiculturalism Act of Alberta. That is, an article in the Bill of Rights, provincial or territorial, provides that no law may "repeal" a law that recognizes rights unless it expressly declares the will to repeal or abolish any of its provisions. Therefore, the primacy of the laws that contain statements of rights is linked to a "requirement of express repeal" (Woerhling 2005). That is, the provincial or territorial bills of rights are different from other laws, and this means that none of these other laws may be contrary to the rule that recognizes rights, and if it were the case, then the contrary law would not apply. Therefore, rules governing rights of individuals are used in the control of the constitutionality of laws.

Now, if an ordinary law clearly states its willingness to repeal the law that recognizes rights or any of its provisions, then such rights shall not apply in the course of 5 years at the end of which a legislative vote to confirm or not the abrogation of the rights in question shall be re-executed. Therefore, strictly speaking we would not be before a law that works as a constitutionality parameter but rather before a quasi-constitutional parameter. The reason for this mechanism is based on the democratic principle.

Finally, note that some provinces or territories do not include in their Declaration of rights a "supremacy clause". However, the Supreme Court has intervened in this matter, and since the 1980s it grants these declarations of rights without "supremacy clause" the same status as those that contain such a mechanism.

Consequently, even if a provincial bill of rights did not want to give a position of primacy to its provisions and did not include the requirement of an explicit declaration of the legislature to repeal, even in these cases, the Supreme Court's interpretation is compelling to somehow discredit the will of the legislature of that province or territory.

## The System of Rights Guarantees in the Canadian State

The provincial rights guarantees are relatively original in comparison with other states where judges and courts, or a specific court, are responsible for the protection of these rights. Additionally, in Canada there are highly effective mechanisms that are not part of the judiciary, which are also responsible for protecting the rights and freedoms of citizens. However, the judiciary holds its leading position in the system of guarantees of rights and freedoms (David 1968; Dickinson 1995).

First of all, we will deal with the protection afforded to anti-discrimination laws and the declarations of rights of the provinces and territories. Provincial Judges and courts do not apply the laws governing the rights directly (Woerhling 2005); it is for this reason that these laws have created an administrative body, generally called "Commission for the rights of the person", which not only has preventive functions but also a deeper adjudicative function (Howe and Johnson 1990).

The Commission's preventive function means that it is responsible to prevent those acts contrary to the rights enshrined in the law through information and the education of citizens. With the adjudicative function, the Commission is tasked to study the demands filed by those stating the existence of these acts. Any person or group can file a complaint with the Commission. Once it has been examined, if it is accepted it would open an investigation in order to get appropriate evidence and testimony. After the investigation, the report shall be presented to the Commission, who rejects the application or declares it founded.

If the claim is accepted, then the Commission must appoint a conciliator to attempt to reach a negotiated agreement between the parties. If no agreement is reached, the Commission will request the establishment of the so-called Court of the rights of the person, which is an administrative body composed of people of great experience and sensitivity to the problems posed by rights who may not be members of the judiciary. The Tribunal will consider the demand and the reports made during the research process, and if said demand is accepted, the Tribunal must decide on a way to correct or repair the situation.

The decision of the Court of the rights of the person may be appealed by the Commission or the parties before a specialist, in some cases a judicial body. The decisions of these courts can be reviewed by the courts, more specifically the Provincial High Courts (Howe and Johnson 1990). Therefore, to resolve conflicts of rights we are facing an administrative process, free and relatively uncomplicated, which in most cases avoids litigation before judges and courts, at least in what might be called the first instance. Professor Richard W. Bauman does not entirely agree with this statement because he suggests that major problems in the system of guarantees could be improved. In this context, the court is not trying to determine the reasonable limits of government action.

Of course, there are different and special cases that do not follow the process just described. This is the case of the Charter of Rights and Freedoms of the person of Quebec; it establishes the "court of the rights of the person of Quebec", which must be composed of judges of the judiciary, that is, judges of the Court Quebec. This Charter provides for a special case, in which all elderly or disabled people who consider themselves victims of discrimination, harassment, or exploitation may choose to go to the courts or the "Commission on the rights of the individual and the rights of youth" of Quebec.

Also, Alberta has a different process for matters regarding its Bill of Rights (for anti-discrimination law, it has the same administrative process set out above). Any violation of a right recognized in the Declaration shall be reported to the ordinary courts, i.e., there is no Commission or a specialized court for the rights contained in the articles of the Alberta Bill of Rights.

As for the federal protection system, there is a Commission of an administrative nature that follows the same process as other provincial commissions. The appeal of the decisions of the Federal or specialized federal courts (consisting of members from outside the judiciary and, therefore, administrative bodies) shall be made before the Federal Court of Canada. As a final court within the jurisdictional guarantees, one may go to the Supreme Court.

# References

H. Brun and G. Tremblay (2002). Droit constitutionnel. Éditions Yvon Blais. Cowansville.
H. Brun (2003). Chartes des droits de la personne – législation, jurisprudence, doctrine. Wilson & Lafleur. Montreal.
J. Mª. Castellà Andreu (2005). El doble nivel de protección de los derechos en Canadá: la Carta de derechos y libertades de 1982 y las Cartas de Derechos provinciales, en especial, la de Quebec. In E. MITJANS (ed.) and J. Mª. CASTELLÀ ANDREU (coord.), Derechos y libertades en Canadá, Atelier, Barcelona, 123–144 pp.

J. Mᵃ. Castellà Andreu (2006). Constitucions de les províncies del Canadâ. El cas de la Constitució del Quebec. In V. V. A. A. L'abast de l'autonomia política del Quebec. Parlament de Catalunya. Barcelona.

R. David (1968), Los grandes sistemas jurídicos contemporáneos (derecho comparado), Aguilar, Madrid.

B. Dickinson (1995). Federalism, Civil Law and the Canadian Judiciary: an Integrated Vision", Revue Juridique Themis, n. 28, 1995, 459 – 480 pp.

J. Fremont (2008). Derechos fundamentales en el sistema constitucional canadiense: entre la carta Constitucional y los Códigos provinciales. Revista Vasca de Administración Pública, n. 82, 2008, 181 – 195 pp.

J. Hiebert (1996). Limiting Rights. The dilema of judicial review. Montreal &Kingston, Mc-Gill-Queen's University Press.

J. L. Hiebert (2001).Los efectos de la carta de derechos y libertades en la política canadiense. In E. Mitjans and J. M. Castellà (coord.). Canadá. Introducción al sistema político y jurídico. Universidad de Barcelona. Barcelona. 196 pp.

R. B. Howe and D. Johnson (1990). Restraining Equality – Human Rights Commissions in Canad., Carleton University Press. Ottawa.

E. Mitjans Perellò and C. Chacón Piqueras (1999). Canada, Diversity and federalism in Canada. In Miguel Angel Aparicio Pérez (ed.). Decentralization and federalism: new models of political autonomy (Spain, Belgium, Canada, Italy and UK). Cedecs. 99-114 pp.

E. Mitjans and J. M. Castellà (2001) (coords.). Canada. Introducción al sistema político y jurídico. Barcelona University. Barcelona. 214 pp.

E. Relaño Pastor (2005). La libertad religiosa y el pluralismo religioso en la Constitución canadiense. In E. Mitjans (ed.) and J. Mᵃ. Castellà Andreu (coord.). Derechos y libertades en Canadá. Atelier. Barcelona. 145 – 194pp.

A. Ruiz Robledo. Los derechos lingüísticos. In E. Mitjans (ed.) and J. Mᵃ. Castellà Andreu (coord.). Derechos y libertades en Canadá. Atelier. Barcelona. 209 – 226 pp.pág.

P. Russel (1983). The Political Purposes of the Canadian Charter of Rights and Freedoms. Revue du Barreau Canadien. n. 31.

J. Woehrling (1993). La Cour Suprême du Canada et la problématique de la limitation des droits et libertés. Revue trimestrielle des droits de l'homme. n. 4.

J. Woehrling (2005). Superposición y complementariedad de los instrumentos provinciales de protección de los derechos del hombre en Canadá. In M. A. Aparicio (ed.). Derechos y libertades en los Estados compuestos. Atelier. Barcelona. 71 pp.

# Difference, Dissent, and Community Identity: Striking the Balance in Rights Theory and Jurisprudence

Ian Peach

**Abstract** Striking an effective, principled balance between the right of communities to protect their distinctiveness as communities within federal states and the right of individuals to protect their distinctiveness as individuals within the community, including their right to dissent from community-imposed norms is a challenge for all liberal democratic, multinational states. Where to strike this balance is more than merely a theoretical question for law, political science and philosophy scholars, it is the stuff of democratic politics and law in a multinational state. At heart, the task is to respect individual rights and, in particular, the right to individual self-determination, without eliminating the distinctiveness of minority communities, and the right to collective self-determination in the case of national minorities, in the face of the force of liberal individualism.

While this is an important issue for all minorities, where national minorities are involved, the conflict between collective rights and individual rights runs deep. In these cases, the conflict engages the hard question of the extent of the right to self-government for national minorities within a federal constitutional system that is committed to the reconciliation of competing sovereignties. This paper reviews both the theoretical underpinnings of this debate and how, and how well, Canada has addressed the debate in balancing collective and individual rights in rights jurisprudence, in the hope of drawing out of the Canadian experience, thoughts and lessons for other multinational federations.

I. Peach (✉)
University of New Brunswick, Box 4400, Fredericton, NB, Canada E3B 5A3
e-mail: ipeach@unb.ca

A. López-Basaguren and L. Escajedo San Epifanio (eds.), *The Ways of Federalism in Western Countries and the Horizons of Territorial Autonomy in Spain*, Vol. 2, DOI 10.1007/978-3-642-27717-7_39, © Springer-Verlag Berlin Heidelberg 2013

# Introduction

Everyone carries with him multiple identities, such as his gender, ethnicity, place of residence, and profession, each of which is more or less relevant to the individual in different circumstances. As one thinks about the multiplicity of ways in which individuals define themselves, the challenge of respecting the diversity that exists not only among communities but also among the individuals within those communities becomes apparent. Striking an effective, principled balance between the right of communities to protect their distinctiveness as communities and the right of individuals to protect their distinctiveness as individuals within the community, including their right to dissent from community-imposed norms that are in conflict with their values, is a challenge to which a perfect resolution within multicultural or multinational democratic societies does not exist.

Where to strike this balance is more than merely a theoretical question for scholars; it is an issue with significant, practical implications within society, being part of political and legal discourse on such issues as polygamy, coerced participation in the traditional cultural ceremonies of a community, access to education in one's language, funding of faith-based schools and other services, accommodation of the traditional dress of religious and cultural minorities in the public sphere, and even the right to membership in the community itself. At heart, the task is to respect individual rights and, in particular, the right to individual self-determination, without eliminating the right of minority communities to retain their distinctiveness, and the right to collective self-determination in the case of national minorities, through a single-minded commitment to liberal individualism. How, and how carefully, the political and legal institutions of a society secure this difficult balance between the individual and the community will have a significant effect on the legitimacy of those institutions in the eyes of both minority communities and the members of the majority.

A commitment to liberal individualism promotes a view that individual rights should supersede collective rights when the collective rights have the potential to harm personal security, equality, or freedom from overt coercion by the community in making personal choices about how to live one's life. On the other hand, protection of the right to be distinctive, and to express that distinctiveness within a distinct community that has meaning for its individual members, can make an important contribution to an individual's capacity for self-determination as an equal person within the broader society. Thus, respecting minority rights can enlarge the freedom of individuals, as freedom is intimately linked with and dependent on culture and respect for the cultural context within which one sees oneself (Kymlicka 1995, 75). As such, the justification for the existence of group rights can be found in the need to protect the well-being of individual members of the minority group. If, however, collective rights are exercised in a manner that does not protect and promote the well-being of individual members, the justification for group rights itself becomes questionable (Isaac 1991, 627).

For immigrant or ethno-cultural minorities, such an approach requires a genuine sensitivity to and respect for cultural difference in approaching individual rights claims on the part of the state. Indeed, respect for cultural difference has the status of a constitutional commitment in Canada, as section 27 of the *Canadian Charter of Rights and Freedoms* declares that "This Charter shall be interpreted in a manner consistent with the preservation and enhancement of the multicultural heritage of Canadians" (*Constitution Act* 1982, s. 27). The question remains, however, how to apply this commitment to balancing respect for individual rights and cultural distinctiveness when community norms and dissent come into conflict. As Timothy Dickson notes, while the multicultural dilemma will always elude a perfect solution, the importance of the interests involved demands that we formulate sophisticated approaches that encourage, as much as possible, the co-existence of both individual and group rights (Dickson 2003, 157).

## Liberal Theory and Minority Rights

Probably the most prominent Canadian liberal theorist to tackle this question is Will Kymlicka. In attempting to establish a principled basis for approaching this question, he has identified two classes of what one might call "minority exemptions" to liberal individualism. The first, which he labels "external protections", are those group rights that are designed to protect the group against the external pressures on their distinctiveness that majoritarianism would impose (Kymlicka 1995, 152). Because decision-making in liberal democratic states is naturally dominated by the interests of the numerical majority, external protections recognize that it is a fiction to suggest that these states are ethnoculturally neutral and do not privilege a conception of society that reflects the majority's cultural touchstones and interests. Some minority rights therefore eliminate, rather than create, structural inequalities, as some groups are unfairly disadvantaged in the cultural "marketplace" created by liberal individualism; political recognition and support for minority rights rectify this disadvantage (Kymlicka 1995, 109).

The second, illegitimate, exercise of collective rights is what Kymlicka refers to as "internal restrictions" (Kymlicka 1995, 152). These are collective rights claims against a minority's own members that are designed to reduce or eliminate the destabilizing impact of internal dissent. For Kymlicka, these must be of concern to liberal theorists because of the strength of liberalism's commitment to individual autonomy; they should reject the idea that groups can restrict the basic civil and political rights of their own members in the name of preserving the purity and authenticity of the group's culture and traditions, as stifling the individual's capacity for choice about which attributes of a culture to value and respect is inherently illiberal (Kymlicka 1995, 152). One particular understanding of a community's tradition may be dominant at any given time, but this cannot justify the assertion that the traditions are uncontestable or that dissenters from the dominant understanding are heretical (Leclair 2006, 525). Individuals should have the freedom and capacity to question and possibly revise the traditional practices of their community, should they come to see them as no longer worthy of allegiance (Kymlicka 1995, 152).

Kymlicka's distinction, however, has been subject to some criticism, generally focusing on the difficulty of distinguishing between the two categories. The critics argue that Kymlicka's conceptual framework has not progressed very far in providing guidance on when the commitment to individual equality that underlies the opposition to internal restrictions might justify a limit on self-determination claims characterized as external protections in the world of specific conflicts between collective and individual rights (Spaulding 1997, 72). The root of the problem is one of characterization and competing perspectives. Inevitably, when a challenge arises, the minority community will characterize its actions as external protections necessary to protect its cultural distinctiveness from being undermined by the dominance of the cultural majority's practices. Meanwhile, the individual claimant of individual rights will argue with equal force that the community's action is an illegitimate internal restriction, designed to limit their personal autonomy, equality, and right to self-determination in the name of cultural preservation. How, then, do Canadian courts, which are most frequently tasked with defining this balance, approach their task when minority group interests conflict with majoritarian interests? Even more challenging, how do the courts find a legitimate balance when one *Charter* right (such as freedom of religion) conflicts with another (such as equality)?

## Minority Rights Jurisprudence in Canada

In such cases, the courts have generally trod carefully. There are several cases that provide examples of the courts' treatment of these issues. In the case of conflicts between the claims of individual members of minority groups of a right to express their cultural difference and majoritarian interests, the courts generally come down on the side of minority rights. One of the earliest *Charter* cases was a religious freedom case, in which non-Christian store owners defended themselves against charges of violating a legal requirement that all stores close on Sundays by claiming that the law violated the *Charter* protection of freedom of religion. In this case, *R. v. Big M Drug Mart*, the Supreme Court of Canada decided that the law did violate freedom of religion, as its avowed purpose was to enforce Sunday religious observance (*Big M* 1985, paras. 78–81, 150). In the course of his decision, Dickson J. also noted that the power to compel the universal observance of one religion's preferred day of rest was inconsistent with the preservation of the multicultural heritage of Canada protected by s. 27 of the *Charter* (*Big M* 1985, para 99).

The Supreme Court of Canada later decided, in *Syndicat Northcrest* v. *Amselem*, that condominium by-laws that prevented orthodox Jews from setting up succahs on their balconies violated the guarantee of freedom of religion under s. 3 of Quebec's *Charter of Human Rights and Freedoms* (which is similar to s. 2(d) of the *Canadian*

*Charter of Rights and Freedoms*) (*Amselem* 2004, para. 103). Iacobucci, J., for the majority, also concluded that the alleged negative effects on the interests of the other occupants of the condominium by having succahs on some balconies for the 9-day Succat holiday were, at best, minimal and could not validly limit the exercise of the appellants' religious freedom (*Amselem* 2004, para. 84). In this context, he commented that

> In a multiethnic and multicultural country such as ours, which accentuates and advertises its modern record of respecting cultural diversity and human rights and of promoting tolerance of religious and ethnic minorities — and is in many ways an example thereof for other societies —, the argument of the respondent that nominal, minimally intruded-upon aesthetic interests should outweigh the exercise of the appellants' religious freedom is unacceptable. Indeed, mutual tolerance is one of the cornerstones of all democratic societies. (*Amselem* 2004, para. 87)

The Supreme Court of Canada has also ruled, in *Multani* v. *Commission scolaire Marguerite-Bourgeoys*, that the banning of the Sikh kirpan (a ceremonial dagger that all Sikhs are required to wear on their person) in public schools violated the freedom of religion of Sikh students (*Multani* 2006, para. 41). In discussing the question of whether the ban was justifiable as a reasonable limit "demonstrably justified in a free and democratic society" (*Constitution Act* 1982, s. 1), the Court also concluded that there were alternative ways to ensure the safety of students and staff in schools that would have impaired the Sikh students' religious freedom less than a complete ban on the wearing of kirpans (*Multani* 2006, paras. 58, 77). Charron, J., for the majority, also commented that

> Religious tolerance is a very important value of Canadian society. If some students consider it unfair that Gurbaj Singh may wear his kirpan to school while they are not allowed to have knives in their possession, it is incumbent on the schools to discharge their obligation to instill in their students this value that is ... at the very foundation of our democracy. (*Multani* 2006, para. 76)

On the other hand, the courts are much more circumspect about protecting freedom of religion when vulnerable persons, such as children, are involved. Thus, in the case of *B(R)* v. *Children's Aid Society of Metropolitan Toronto*, which involved questions of freedom of religion and parental rights to make decisions about their children's medical treatment, the Supreme Court recognized that state intervention violates the freedom of religion of parents but justified such interventions in order to protect the child (*B(R)* 1995).

When different rights come into conflict, the balancing that the courts must undertake is a more difficult task. For example, in *Trinity Western University* v. *British Columbia College of Teachers*, the majority of the Supreme Court of Canada held that neither freedom of religion nor equality is an absolute and that they must, instead, be balanced against one another (*Trinity Western University* 2001, paras. 29–31).[1] For the majority, this balancing allowed members of a

---

[1] This was a case in which the British Columbia College of Teachers denied the appellant university full responsibility for the conduct of its teacher education program because of concerns that teachers trained at the university would discriminate against homosexuals.

religious group to hold whatever beliefs they chose, though they could not act on the basis of those beliefs in a way that undermined equality (*Trinity Western University* 2001, paras. 36–7). As there was no evidence in this case that the university's teacher education program fostered discrimination in British Columbia schools, however, the Supreme Court of Canada decided against the College of Teachers, concluding that the freedom of College members educated at the university to hold their religious beliefs should be respected (*Trinity Western University* 2001, para. 36). The Supreme Court has also concluded that, while same-sex marriage itself does not violate freedom of religion, compelling religious officials to perform such marriages against their religious beliefs would (*Reference re. Same-Sex Marriage* 2004). There is thus still room for freedom of religion, even in the face of a challenge based on equality.

## Individual Rights, Collective Self-Determination, and the Multinational State

Where national minorities are involved, the challenge is even more significant than simply applying the liberal rights paradigm of the *Charter* sensitively and in a way that respects section 27. For Canada's two generally recognized national minorities, Quebec and Aboriginal peoples, the conflict between collective rights, or collective self-determination, and individual rights runs deeper, as the interpretation and, indeed, the very legitimacy of the application of the *Charter* to their communities becomes a live question.

Within Quebec, this debate has centered around language policy, particularly limitations on the use of the English language in the public sphere and access to English-language education. In *Ford* v. *Quebec (Attorney General)*, a key freedom of expression case about Quebec's ban on the use of English on outdoor commercial signs, the Supreme Court of Canada decided that the French-only rule for outdoor signs interfered with the freedom of expression guaranteed by s. 3 of Quebec's *Charter of Human Rights and Freedoms* and s. 2(b) of the *Canadian Charter of Rights and Freedoms* and could not be justified as a reasonable limit on that freedom (*Ford* 1988, para. 83). In coming to this conclusion on the justification analysis under s. 1 of the *Charter*, however, the Supreme Court stated that

> The aim of such provisions as ss. 58 and 69 of the *Charter of the French Language* was, in the words of its preamble, "to see the quality and influence of the French language assured." The threat to the French language demonstrated to the government that it should, in particular, take steps to assure that the "*visage linguistique*" of Quebec would reflect the predominance of the French language.
>
> The section 1 [of the Canadian *Charter*] and s. 9.1 [of the Quebec *Charter*] materials establish that the aim of the language policy underlying the *Charter of the French Language* was a serious and legitimate one. They indicate the concern about the survival of the French language and the perceived need for an adequate legislative response to the problem. Moreover, they indicate a rational connection between protecting the French

language and assuring that the reality of Quebec society is communicated through the "*visage linguistique.*" (*Ford* 1988, paras. 72–3)

These comments suggest a sensitivity on the part of the Supreme Court of Canada to the concerns of national minorities about protecting their collective identity.

When it came to questions of access to English-language education in Quebec, in *Gosselin (Tutor of)* v. *Quebec (Attorney General)*, the Supreme Court of Canada upheld Quebec's laws limiting access to English-language education to those whose parents were educated in English in Canada against an equality rights challenge, on the basis that s. 23 of the *Charter*, which provides constitutional rules for access to minority-language education in Canada, cannot be invalidated by an equality claim (*Gosselin* 2005, para. 34). Here, showing a sensitivity to Quebec's cultural context similar to that shown in *Ford*, the Court stated that

> In rejecting "free access" as the governing principle in s. 23, the framers of the Canadian *Charter* were concerned about the consequences of permitting members of the majority language community to send their children to minority language schools. The concern at the time (which the intervener, the Commissioner of Official Languages for Canada, submitted is a continuing concern today) was that at least outside Quebec minority language schools would themselves become centres of assimilation if members of the majority language community swamped students from the minority language community. Within Quebec, the problem has the added dimension that what are intended as schools for the minority language community should not operate to undermine the desire of the majority to protect and enhance French as the majority language in Quebec, knowing that it will remain the minority language in the broader context of Canada as a whole. [emphasis in original] (*Gosselin* 2005, para. 31)

Even in the accompanying case of *Solski (Tutor of)* v. *Quebec (Attorney General)*, in which the Supreme Court ruled that the claimants have a right to an English-language education in Quebec, the Court nonetheless upheld the minority language education rules of the *Charter of the French Language*, deciding that the law was being interpreted too narrowly in its application and that it could be interpreted in a way that would be consistent with s. 23 of the *Charter* (*Solski* 2005, paras. 27–8, 46). The Court commented, in the course of its decision, that

> The application of s. 23 is contextual. It must take into account the very real differences between the situations of the minority language community in Quebec and the minority language communities of the territories and the other provinces. The latitude given to the provincial government in drafting legislation regarding education must be broad enough to ensure the protection of the French language while satisfying the purposes of s. 23. (*Solski* 2005, para. 34)

This decision, too, suggests that the Supreme Court of Canada exercises care when deciding cases that involve the balancing of individual rights and the protection of core elements of the identity of national minorities, especially in the case where the national minority has an element of sovereignty, through the federal system, and has a recognized place in the constitutional system.

The courts have also dealt with these conflicts between individual rights and right of national minorities to autonomy in cases involving Aboriginal communities, although with somewhat different results, possibly as a consequence of their different status within the federation. In *Thomas* v. *Norris*, for example, the Supreme Court of British Columbia concluded that the Aboriginal rights of Coast Salish First Nations did not extend to a right to seize an individual and force him to participate in a "spirit dance" (*Thomas* 1992). There have also been several cases involving the right of First Nations to control who votes and runs for positions on First Nation band councils under First Nation election laws and the right of First Nations to determine who is a member, or citizen, of the First Nation under First Nation membership rules. For example, *Francis* v. *Mohawk Council of Kanesatake* and *Clifton* v. *Hartley Bay (Electoral Officer)* were both voting rights cases heard by the Federal Court of Canada. In *Clifton*, the Federal Court quickly found that there was a discriminatory distinction in the election code and that the complete exclusion of off-reserve status of Indians from voting is a violation of section 15 of the *Charter* and cannot be justified (*Clifton* 2005, para. 58).

In *Scrimbitt* v. *Sakimay Indian Band Council*, Scrimbitt, a member of the Sakimay First Nation who regained her status under the 1985 amendments to the *Indian Act*, was struck from the Band list due to the operation of the Band's membership code, which was designed to disenfranchise potential band members who had received status by the operation of the 1985 amendments. She challenged this exclusion as incompatible with section 15 of the *Charter* and won. The Federal Court, Trial Division, decided that the refusal of the right to vote discriminated against her and was an affront to her dignity, resulting in a violation of her equality rights.

A similar challenge was brought in the case of *Grismer* v. *Squamish First Nation*. In this case, the adult adopted children of a Squamish First Nation member were denied membership because of the rules of the First Nation's membership code. In deciding this case, the Federal Court, Trial Division, decided that, while the Squamish First Nation had the right to develop its own membership code, its provisions discriminated between adopted and biological children, as well as among adopted children themselves (*Grismer* 2006, para. 57). Thus, the Court found the membership code was contrary to section 15 of the *Charter*. The Court, however, went on to find the code to be justified under section 1 of the *Charter*, concluding that,

> Considerable deference should be accorded to the Squamish in making this policy decision, particularly since it concerns questions of citizenship, Band custom and lineage... (*Grismer* 2006, para. 73)

The Court did, however, note that, "in another case, based on a differently constituted evidentiary record, another judge may have come to a different conclusion" on the issue of whether an infringement is justified (*Grismer* 2006, para. 83).[2]

---

[2] It is also worth noting the case of *Sawridge Band* v. *Canada*, an Aboriginal rights case in which the requirement of the *Indian Act* that band membership codes provide membership to individuals who gained their status by virtue of the 1985 amendments to the *Indian Act* was challenged as a violation of the Aboriginal rights of bands that wished to exclude these individuals. The courts, however, never had a chance to provide a definitive decision on the substance, despite more than 20 years of litigation, as the case collapsed on procedural grounds and the claimants sought the dismissal of their case. See *Sawridge Band* 1997; *Sawridge First Nation* 2008, 2009.

While the courts have taken some care with the rights analysis in these cases, one can see in them a reflection of Kymlicka's concern about internal restrictions; the courts seem to have established security of the person and equality as higher order values than freedom of religion or Aboriginal rights when these rights come into conflict, though these latter two are worthy of protection in the face of general majoritian interests. Yet in its recent decision in *Alberta (Aboriginal Affairs and Northern Development)* v. *Cunningham*, the Supreme Court of Canada upheld the provision of the *Métis Settlements Act* that automatically excluded individuals who sought registration as an "Indian" from membership in the Métis settlements in Alberta in the face of an equality rights challenge (*Cunningham* 2011, para. 96). The Supreme Court decided that the *Métis Settlements Act* was designed to ameliorate the disadvantage of Métis, a disadvantaged group and, as such, was protected from equality rights challenges by subs. 15(2) of the *Charter* (*Cunningham* 2011, paras. 83–88). This suggests that equality will not always trump the right of Aboriginal peoples to some forms of self-determination, especially if the Aboriginal community can claim the protection of subs. 15(2).

As noted above, the balancing of respect for the collective rights of national minorities to self-determination and individual freedoms and equality has led to debates about the very legitimacy of the application of the *Canadian Charter of Rights and Freedoms* to national minorities, a debate that has, periodically, had a prominent place on Canada's political agenda. While Canadians, even those who are members of national minorities, demonstrate a strong attachment to the *Charter*, the question nonetheless remains whether the full application of the *Canadian Charter of Rights and Freedoms* is really the best approach to balancing the collective rights of national minorities, particularly Aboriginal peoples, with individual rights. The language of the *Charter* is not the only way to articulate a commitment to the constitutional protection of individual rights. As Webber notes, even given a shared commitment to individual rights, the specific expression of those rights in a concrete legal order is always marked by cultural features that have little or nothing to do with respect for the individual (Webber 1994, 237). This is likely to remain a matter of debate in Canada, as well as in other multinational states.

## Conclusion

The lesson in this for democratic politics is that the political and legal debate over balancing the right to preserve a collective identity as a minority community against the right of individuals to exercise their individual self-determination, even to the point of dissenting from community norms, is a complex, difficult, and multifaceted one. For immigrant or ethno-cultural minorities, it raises difficult issues about the right balance between respect for cultural distinctiveness and respect for individual autonomy within a liberal society. For national minorities, however, even bigger questions, ones that go to the heart of our constitutional order, arise. The application of an individual rights regime that arises out of the cultural context of the majority and is interpreted and applied by the institutions of the majority society to national minorities of necessity raises questions about the commitment of the state to respecting the role of those national minorities within what is meant to be a shared constitutional order.

While certainly not perfect, we have done relatively well in Canada to strike a balance between the individual and the collective in a way that preserves the legitimacy of our political and legal institutions in the eyes of both the majority culture and minority communities. Yet we still have much to learn, including from political philosophy, law, and history, to create a just society that fully includes Quebec and Aboriginal peoples. Our commitment to liberalism must not prevent us from thinking hard thoughts about cultural, political, and legal pluralism so that we can effectively use what we have learned to date about respect for minorities, and particularly national minorities, to continue to build a genuinely multicultural and multinational state on a foundation of mutual concern, respect, and reconciliation.

# References

*Alberta (Aboriginal Affairs and Northern Development)* v. *Cunningham*, 2011 SCC 37.
*B(R)* v. *Children's Aid Society of Metropolitan Toronto*, [1995] 1 S.C.R. 315.
*Clifton* v. *Hartley Bay (Electoral Officer)*, 2005 FC 1030, [2006] 2 F.C.R. 24, [2005] 4 C.N.L.R. 161 (F.C.T.D.).
*Constitution Act, 1982*.
Dickson, Timothy (2003). Section 25 and Intercultural Judgment. University of Toronto Faculty of Law Review 61: 141–174.
*Ford* v. *Quebec (Attorney General)*, [1988] 2 S.C.R. 712.
*Francis* v. *Mohawk Council of Kanesatake*, 2003 FCT 115, [2003] 4 F.C. 1133 (F.C.T.D.).
*Gosselin (Tutor of)* v. *Quebec (Attorney General)*, 2005 SCC 15, [2005] 1 S.C.R. 238.
*Grismer* v. *Squamish First Nation*, 2006 FC 1088, [2007] 1 C.N.L.R. 146 (F.C.T.D.).
Isaac, Thomas (1991). Individual Versus Collective Rights: Aboriginal People and the Significance of *Thomas* v. *Norris*. Manitoba Law Journal 21: 618–630.
Kymlicka, Will (1995). Multicultural Citizenship. Oxford University Press, Oxford, United Kingdom, 280 pp.
Leclair, Jean (2006). Federal Constitutionalism and Aboriginal Difference. Queen's Law Journal 31: 521–535.
*Multani* v. *Commission scolaire Marguerite-Bourgeoys*, 2006 SCC 6, [2006] 1 S.C.R. 256.
*R.* v. *Big M Drug Mart*, [1985] 1 S.C.R. 295.
*Reference re. Same-Sex Marriage*, 2004 SCC 79, [2004] 3 S.C.R. 698.
*Sawridge Band* v. *Canada*, [1997] 3 F.C. 580.
*Sawridge First Nation* v. *Canada*, 2008 FC 322.
*Sawridge First Nation* v. *Canada*, 2009 FCA 123.
*Scrimbitt* v. *Sakimay Indian Band Council*, [2000] 1 F.C. 513, [2000] 1 C.N.L.R. 205 (F.C.T.D.).
*Solski (Tutor of)* v. *Quebec (Attorney General)*, 2005 SCC 14, [2005] 1 S.C.R. 201.
Spaulding, Richard (1997). Peoples as National Minorities: A Review of Will Kymlicka's Arguments for Aboriginal Rights from a Self-Determination Perspective. University of Toronto Law Journal 47: 35–113.
*Syndicat Northcrest* v. *Amselem*, 2004 SCC 47, [2004] 2 S.C.R. 551.

*Thomas* v. *Norris*, [1992] 2 C.N.L.R. 139 (B.C.S.C.).

*Trinity Western University* v. *British Columbia College of Teachers*, 2001 SCC 31, [2001] 1 S.C. R. 772.

Webber, Jeremy (1994). Reimagining Canada: Language, Culture, Community, and the Canadian Constitution. McGill-Queen's University Press, Montreal and Kingston, Canada, 373 pp.

# Exploring the Social Origins of Elite Accommodation: Recognition and Civil Society Integration in Divided Societies

Alexandre Pelletier and Michael Morden

**Abstract**  This chapter identifies a lacuna in the literature on consociational accommodation in multinational societies. We argue that civil society is discussed in "bottom-up" theories of peace-building, but often overlooked in classical approaches to political accommodation. We seek to address this gap by looking at the dynamics of accommodation from a civil society perspective, stressing the importance of relational structures across social actors and segments in explaining accommodative outcomes at the political level. The chapter is organized into two parts. First, we look at civil society in the context of divided societies, and develop a framework that connects relational topography with elite-level dynamics. Second, we consider recent Canadian political history and the role of civil society in two efforts at recognition and accommodation with divergent outcomes: the Meech Lake Accord and the official apology to Indigenous survivors of residential schools. These cases illustrate the impact of civil society segmentation, the nature of horizontal linkages, and the oppositional potential of civil society groups. By addressing the structural conditions that promote or constrain cooperative behavior, this chapter intends to contribute to our theoretical understanding of accommodative outcomes in divided societies.

A. Pelletier (✉) • M. Morden
Department of Political Science, University of Toronto, Sidney Smith Hall, , Room 3018100 St. George Street Toronto, Ontario M5S 3G3, Canada
e-mail: alex.paquin.pelletier@utoronto.ca; michael.modern@utoronto.ca

A. López-Basaguren and L. Escajedo San Epifanio (eds.), *The Ways of Federalism in Western Countries and the Horizons of Territorial Autonomy in Spain*, Vol. 2, DOI 10.1007/978-3-642-27717-7_40, © Springer-Verlag Berlin Heidelberg 2013

# Accommodation, Divided Societies, and Civil Society: Uncharted Links?

## Understanding Accommodation: From Top-Down to Bottom-Up Approaches

This project flows from a discrepancy between two literatures on divided societies, which have yet to engage each other in a potentially fruitful dialogue (see Morden and Pelletier 2011).

The first is a *top-down* approach (Lijphart 1977). It argues that elites are better able to mitigate conflict, as long as they enjoy predominance over stable communal cultures (McGarry and O'Leary 1995). Dense *intra*-communal political ties, instead of *inter*-communal ones, are seen as beneficial for accommodative behavior. Lijphart argues that keeping transactions among antagonistic subcultures to a minimum helps ensure elite deference (1969: pp. 220–221). By increasing the organizational strength of the segments, restraining intercommunity contact allows elites more autonomy, which in turn helps to downplay the destructive logic of intergroup conflict (Dixon 1997: p. 6). Social dynamics are often taken as constant, based on the assumption of a deeply segmented pluralism.

Failing to account for the social condition of unity, the study of power-sharing has generally focused on top-level leadership and formal institutions in explaining accommodative outcomes. Institutionalists have looked at the effect of institutions on national minorities, as well as their capacity to accommodate or exacerbate ethnic conflict (Amoretti and Bermeo 2004). Some work has sought to clarify the types of institutions and constitutions, as well as normative conceptions that are more likely to lead to accommodation (see Stepan 2001; Hueglin 2003). However, when it comes to accommodation *per se*, authors generally adopt a *voluntarist* conception. Building on Taylor (1994), recognition is seen as the source of accommodative behavior, which ought to be accompanied by other positive behavior such as mutual consent, mutual understanding, and self-criticism (Tully 1996). However, few studies have questioned the empirical conditions leading to this ethic of intergroup relations (James 2003; Deveaux 2003). Recently, scholars have started to address the dynamics of majority/minority relations (Gagnon et al. 2007) and the causal importance of trust in divided societies (Weinstock 1999; Rocher and Karmis 2012). Building on the idea of "nested games", some authors have tried to link political actors' accommodation calculations with intrasegmental (Tsebelis 1990) and intersegmental dynamics (Zuber 2010). In general however, theories of federal accommodation largely focus on political actors and formal institutional dynamics, assuming the stability of the cleavages on which those systems are based.

A second approach has slowly emerged as a challenge to the traditional top-down approach in the peace building literature, although its theoretical contribution remains limited. The *bottom-up* approach (Dixon 1997: p. 8) draws on a well-established but still contested social psychological tradition (Forbes 1997; Olzak 1992), which argues that intergroup contacts are beneficial and that they contribute to the attenuation of cross-group hostility and prejudice (Allport 1954; Petitgrew 1998). Also, borrowing insights from the idea of "track II" diplomacy, which consists of informal diplomacy by non-state actors, this literature argues that peace settlements should take place through mechanisms that bridge social segments at different levels of society. The model developed by Lederach, for instance, involves peace processes at top-level leadership, undertaking high-level negotiations, and also at middle-range (e.g., NGOs, academics, ethnic leaders, social leaders) and grassroots leadership (e.g., local leaders, community actors) (1998: pp. 38–55; see Dugan 1996; Nan 2008).

The bottom-up approach argues that civil society is often less affected by the positional logics of high and symbolic politics, and so it aids actors to circumvent strategic logics of conflict that are detrimental to accommodation processes (James 2003). For example, Cochrane and Dunn show that in the case of Northern Ireland, the logic of civil society was *process* driven rather than *outcome* driven, with the majority of peace and conflict resolution organizations immersed in consensus-building exercise rather than zero-sum political deals (2002: p. 5). They argue that this process eventually "filtered up into track-one level negotiations and made a positive contribution to the political process" (idem). Hence, the bottom-up litera-ture establishes a causal connection between social dynamics and political dynam-ics, whereas the top-down approach tends to isolate the political arena on the assumption of elite deference and segmental stability.

If the top-down approach has ignored civil society dynamics, it is less the result of an absence of explanatory power than because of theoretical inclinations. Questions such as what makes a divided society stable have been on the agenda now for decades. However, if we know more about the institutions and behavior that bring stability, few answers have been given about the favorable conditions that facilitate or induce accommodative behavior. Rather, we observe a tendency in the last decade or so to limit those explanatory conditions to *voluntarist* explanations, such as *deliberate* cooperation and *personal commitment* to the maintenance of the system by elites (Andeweg 2000; Bogaards 1998). If this optimism is welcomed in post-conflict societies seeking stability, it does not inform comparative theories of state dynamics, especially those dealing with federal or consociational states. As a result, its predictive power is greatly limited (Pappalardo 1981).

In conclusion, when it comes to the conditions fostering accommodation, theories have mainly adopted *top-down* and *voluntarist* approaches. Conse-quently, they have focused on elite behavior, whether it is framed as a problem of moral, rational, or strategic behavior. In contrast, when they adopt an institutionalist perspective, they have inscribed the evolution of accommodative behavior in the idea of legacies, making it hard to account for punctual shifts from, for instance, cooperative, competitive, and collaborative behavior (see Simeon and Robinson 2004).

## Civil Society in Divided Contexts: Temporal and Sectoral Variations

The voluntarist top-down approach does not make enough space for the shifting dynamics that take place *within* and *across* social segments. While the literature takes social blocs as constant, they are in fact in a state of continuous change, evolving in part independently from the interference of the state. If the state has a structuring role on civil society (Pal 1993), it also responds to logics of its own: citizens not only build, transform, or deconstruct coalitions *in* and *between* social segments but also face conflict and eventually even accommodate themselves.

In trying to overcome the *voluntarist* and rather *static* conditions of the top-down approach, Adriano Pappalardo draws our attention to societal factors like the patterns of intrasegmental stability and intersegmental social and organizational ties and alignments (1981: p. 369). He argues that the emergence of floating voters is detrimental to power-sharing schemes since it renders catchall strategies profitable and compromise unnecessary (Pappalardo 1981: p. 375). In contrast, Ronald A. Kieve argues that the acceptance of accommodationist procedures is the outcome of social and political conflict that reflects significant changes in the balance of social and class forces (1981: p. 322). Since the creation of cross-segmental coalitions threatens the position of some political and social elites who benefit from ethnic politics, they maintain positive attitudes toward accommodation as a means to ensure the continuance of their structural position (*idem*). Despite the functionalist tone of the second argument, both authors highlight the potential effect of a change in the patterns of segmentation through coalition building on the stability of accommodationist systems.

In his study of ethnic conflict, Ashutosh Varshney found that the critical variable distinguishing conflict-prone and conflict-proof communities is the vitality of interethnic associational life. He argues that integrated civil societies promote communication that, in times of intense exogenous tensions, act as a buffer to community conflict (2001: p. 375). They, for example, kill rumors, remove misunderstandings, and often police neighborhoods. In turn, social actors pressure political actors towards settlement and offer very practical reasons for it: they would, for instance, lose from a split fight for their turf (ibid: 378). Varshney's model allows for a refined understanding of ethnic conflict by making room for intracase and cross-temporal variations, as well as by stressing concrete mechanisms linking civil society and political actors. In a potential complement to Varshney, Val R. Lorwin shows the extent to which segmentation is sector-specific rather than system-wide as it is often argued. He shows that in small European countries, workers and farmers have been much more inclined than employers and members of the liberal professions to act through segmented organizations (1971: p. 153). Similarly, an edited survey of civil society in multi-national federal contexts shows that there is more convergence and contacts between segments than one would normally expect (Kramer and Schneider 1999). It highlights how organization's leaders, and sometimes even members, are sometimes deeply involved in cross-group networks, thus opening space for the negotiation of similar policy positions.

In general, these social-structural perspectives on divided societies show that segmentation varies across sectors and through time. Dynamics of civil society are not reducible to a unidirectional movement toward greater segmentation (Geertz 1973) or toward greater integration, as classic modernist theories would predict. If temporal and sectoral patterns were observed, they have yet to be integrated in a theory of accommodation. The *bottom-up* literature is useful in pointing in that direction yet remains limited. It is more often concerned with peace-building contexts and looks at temporary organizations created as a means to resolve conflict. In other words, it is more often concerned with the *genesis* of power-sharing rather than the *functioning* of already established (more or less) accommodative systems (see Rustow 1970).

While accommodative models have been voluntarist, top-down, and institutionalist, there is reason to believe that the study of changing patterns of intersegmental relations may help to bring more dynamism to these models. The next section aims at proposing a tentative framework stressing the function of civil society and its impact on political dynamics.

## Relational Topography and Political Society: Functions and Role

A concern for relational structures begins with the idea that political actors are interdependent rather than independent and that their behavior flows in part from their relational position rather than simply their individual characteristics (Cinalli 2005: p. 173, 176). According to one classic definition, associational life helps foster norms of reciprocity and encourages the emergence of social trust (Putnam 1994: p. 67). These norms and values, in turn, help to resolve dilemmas of collective action and smooth political negotiations by broadening participants' sense of self and turning their "I" into a "We" (idem). Many of Putnam's followers have been concerned with the nature of social capital and have distinguished between "bonding" and "bridging" social capital. The latter, it is argued, is more beneficial in multicultural contexts.

One problem with Putnam's notion of social capital is that it conveys a moral and ethical tone, while it used to be a neutral concept (see Bourdieu 1990; Coleman 1990). It is now commonly seen as inherently positive, as bringing and sustaining democratization for instance. Social capital is a relational-structural concept, which either facilitates or constrains actions, rather than a psycho-sociological attribute (namely trust). Therefore, under certain circumstances a robust civil society may not produce beneficial effects but rather signal a democratic regime's degeneration (Berman 1997) or fuel its fragmentation into "ferociously jealous small republics" (Foley and Edwards 1997: p. 39). In other words, civil society and social capital are ethically neutral; they may enhance inclusion and accommodation as much as they can foster exclusion and violence.

Social networks display many horizontal functions, of which three are our particular concern. First, social networks are the site of "on-going conversations" among network agents, between agents and challengers, and between activists and their publics (Tilly 1998). Conversation "shapes social life by altering individual and collective understandings, by creating and transforming social ties, by generating cultural materials that are then available for subsequent social interchange, and by establishing, obliterating, or shifting commitments [...] of participants" (Tilly 1998: p. 507, cited in Mische 2003). For Eliasoph (1996) and Lichterman (1999), the expression of identity, commitment, and public concern varies systematically according to the particular group settings in which conversation takes place (Mische 2003). In other words, interest and identity are linked, and associational life offers the arena to renegotiate them. The topography of relational structures, and particularly those that cut across or exclude social segments, thus weigh on groups' potential experience, appreciation, and acceptation of accommodation.

Second, the topography of social networks influences the extent to which they may support inclusive agendas. Mische (2003) argues that activists at the intersection of many overlapping organizational networks may develop greater adeptness at using bridge-building strategies in order to manage their multiple relationships. In contrast, less embedded or more marginalized actors may result in more univocal narratives. Political elites are not divorced from these dynamics; they actively build on existing narratives, yet sometimes try to shape them (Deegan-Krause 2006), which act as one of their central resource in negotiation settings.

Third, not only does the relational topography matters, but also the very nature of civil society *linkages* influences both the nature of the conversation and also its susceptibility to endogenous shocks. For instance, Stolle and Rochon (2001) demonstrate that all associations are not alike and that they do not all contribute to social capital to the same degree. Pelletier and Simeon (2012) suggest that substantial linkages across voluntary organizations tend to foster accommodation and resistance to conflict, while instrumental linkages tend to be somewhat depoliticized, circumscribed, and conditional.

Since political actors are connected to social actors (Knoke 1993), civil society dynamics in turn influence broader political dynamics.

First, and most obviously, civil society may either reject or push for institutional or even regime change. Berman (1997) argues that where the political system is perceived as illegitimate, civil society may become an alternative to politics and actually deepen political cleavages. It may also support political accommodation in order to keep cross-communal associations alive. Alternatively, exclusion in civil society networks may fuel demands for inclusion at the political level (see Lemieux 1973).

Second, since cleavages are not simply the outgrowths of social stratification (Lipset and Rokkan 1967), they are a form of dynamic closure of social relationships. Chibber argues that weak associational life gives greater capacity to elites to exert influence on social cleavages (2001: p. 12). In other words, in the absence of a civil society that structures relevant cleavages, pockets of "exploitable cleavages" are formed (Netto and Cox 1997). In this case, political actors may benefit from divisive policy since civil society actors also benefit from it. In other words, civil society fractionalization can foster elites' fracture, thus encouraging competitive strategies at the top (Castañeda 2011).

## Lessons from Canada (1): Civil Society and Meech Lake

In 1982, the Canadian constitution was altered to include a charter and an amending formula. It was adopted after a lengthy period of wrangling between the federal and provincial governments, which left Québec isolated as it refused to consent to the new constitution. A new government came to power in 1984 and vowed to rectify this problem by achieving a new constitutional settlement that would satisfy Quebec's traditional demands. From 1986 to 1987, these proposals were discussed in a series of closed-door bilateral and multilateral meetings between the premiers and the prime minister. An agreement was reached in the spring of 1987, after the prime minister had generalized Quebec's demands out to all of the provinces in a manner that won the support of the English Canadian premiers. The final product—the Meech Lake Accord—offered a series of reforms that would substantively decentralize the federation and institute a form of consociational power-sharing by way of the "distinct society" clause, an asymmetrical component referring only to Quebec. Having won the endorsement of all the first ministers, the Accord automatically entered into a 3-year ratification period. The Accord attracted fierce and unanticipated opposition in English Canadian civil society despite the unanimity of the political class. It failed to achieve ratification in every provincial legislature and officially expired in 1990.

The Meech Lake Accord was the most recent attempt in Canada at consociational accommodation within a framework of binational federalism. Its negotiation process is often thought of as a textbook example of elite accommodation. There was no process of public dialogue or consultation. Instead, intergovernmental elites worked closely with each other over a lengthy time period in isolation from public scrutiny. The prevailing view was that the stakes were so high that nothing should be public or formal until success was assured.

This paper locates the failure of Meech Lake in an historical understanding of the evolution of civil society in Canada. It highlights three important findings regarding the theoretical and empirical significance of civil society on political accommodation.

First, ethnolinguistic divisions in civil society precluded the possibility that it could host bridge-building dialogue. The engagement of English- and French-Canadian civil society actors was vertical, with the state, rather than horizontal, with each other. *This points to the importance of examining the condition of integration/segmentation of civil society in divided societies, which vary temporally and sectorally.*

Second, *the nature as well as degree of integration in civil society has theoretical significance for successful political accommodation.* Where horizontal trust ties exist in associational life, they may be instrumental or substantial, and this impacts their ability to facilitate accommodative dialogue and resist broader political changes or shocks.

Third, given the relative unanimity of the political class and because of the incapacity of civil society to host integrative dialogue, civil society instead became the primary site of opposition to the accord, attenuating the force of elite compromise and negotiation. *Here, the oppositional potential of a divided civil society altered the calculus of consociational game playing, demonstrating its theoretical importance for understanding why elite pacts break down.*

## The Degree of Civil Society Segmentation

An already divided civil society was unable to provide space for interethnic associational engagement throughout the ratification period. Beginning in the mid-nineteenth century, when a meaningful civil society began to develop in Canada, there has been a tendency towards an associational life divided along ethnic, religious, and linguistic lines. Sectoral organizations and business associations, which de facto became sites for discussion of public affairs, were typically wholly or largely Anglophone. Francophones formed parallel organizations in an effort to organize francophone communities scattered across the country to preserve language and religion (Prang 1986). The Catholic Church actively created and sustained dense social networks that cut across provincial boundaries. Initially then, two pan-Canadian civil societies, segmented along religious and linguistic lines, developed in relative isolation from each other.

After WWII, it is possible to observe a dynamic of convergence, leading to a renegotiation of English- and French-Canadian relations. Associations that sought to be truly pan-Canadian underwent structural reforms aimed at entrenching bilingualism and some measures of power-sharing (see Meisel and Lemieux 1972). This moment was short-lived, however, as many of these rapprochements led to bitter conflict within the associations. Unable to resolve the linguistic issue, and even less the question of mutual representation, many pan-Canadian associations broke apart.

Similarly, in French-Canadian associations, members from Quebec became more activist and started to look for new policy arenas to occupy. Turgeon (1999) explains that on the eve of the Quiet Revolution, during which Québec's government actively nation-built, Québec's civil society strengthened and became denser. This occurred partly as a result of the break-up of pan-Canadian francophone organizations into both Québec and French-Canadian organizations. Therefore, the passage from a religious to a linguistic non-confessional basis of organization contributed to the disintegration of the cross-provincial linkages that united French Canadians across the country. The existence of two linguistic pan-Canadian civil societies gave way to a pan-Canadian Anglophone and a provincialized Francophone civil society.

By the 1980s, there were few functional pan-Canadian associations with strong representation from both linguistic groups, and the ones that existed allowed for only essentially perfunctory contacts between the groups. As a result, there was little opportunity for direct horizontal exchange between English and French Canadians during the Meech debate. Feminist activism during the ratification period constitutes a classic example. English Canadian feminists opposed the Accord out of fear that the distinct society clause would water down the rights protection of the Charter for women in Quebec, while French Canadian activists were largely in favor of Meech (Monahan 1991:p. 141). Dobrowlosky argues that few contacts between French and English-Canadian organizations and the relatively homogenous composition of pan-Canadian feminist activist networks explain why Anglophone organizations found themselves at odds with Francophone feminists during the Meech period (1998: p. 723). The Ad Hoc Committee of Canadian Women on the Constitution and other feminist organizations based in English Canada testified against the Accord at parliamentary hearings. Quebec-based women's organization, such as the Quebec Council on the Status of Women, testified in favor. They also charged English-Canadian feminists with being "maternalistic" and harboring an anti-Quebec bias (Monahan 1991: p. 142). In turn, there was genuine confusion on the part of English-Canadian feminists about this response (Dobrowlosky 1998: p. 729).

The important point is less that French- and English-Canadian feminists drew different conclusions about the Accord but that there was no associational framework in which they could engage each other directly in the interest of finding common ground, as well as in rethinking their interests (see Dobrowolsky 1998). Instead, their opposition or support was funneled upward toward the state, effectively as dueling lobbies. Those crosscutting cleavages that might otherwise have acted as a safety valve for rising interethnic tensions were unable to do so because they were organized in civil society around the prevailing linguistic cleavage.

## The Nature of Civil Society Integration

The degree of civil society integration or segmentation is important. However, the *kind* of integration is also significant, and this also is illustrated by the Meech experience. In other words, mere cooperation between Anglophone and Francophone associations on a range of issues tells an incomplete story. Our findings suggest that while this does indicate a certain level of trust, the nature of these relations proved unable to sustain dialogue during the Meech Lake period.

English and French civil society groups have indeed been able to cooperate moderately with each other and accommodate the linguistic difference under certain circumstances (Cameron and Simeon 2008). The Meech experience demonstrates, however, that some kinds of relationships can break down quickly. English and French Canadian Women's Groups were able to work together on issues of mutual concern that left the identity question aside but less able to sustain a conversation during the accommodative moment. Linguistic segmentation and integration is fluid and depends on not only the context but also the nature of cross-linguistic associational ties. During Meech, intramovement linkages across groups were replaced by new intragroup cross-movement alliances. In other words, identity and interests converged, with sectoral organizations becoming segmented and seeking allies in other sectors within the segment. For instance, English Canadian feminists sought active cooperation with English Canadian anti-globalization actors (Dobrowlosky 1998: p. 728)—another associational sector that has demonstrated a tendency to alternate between linguistic segmentation and integration depending on which issues are contested (Dufour 2006). These dynamics suggest that in the Canadian case, civil society integration often occurs on the basis of *instrumental* rather than *substantial* trust (Pelletier and Simeon 2012). In other words, they rest upon interdependency and convergent interests and are sustained by the shelving of divisive issues. This explains why they proved unhelpful during attempts at resolving issues that were excluded from conversation in daily exchange (Simeon and Cameron 2008: p. 178).

## The Oppositional Potential of a Divided Civil Society

In the structural context of segmentation and instrumental cooperation, civil society can galvanize opposition and undermine political accommodation. When it is unable to sustain a parallel process of dialogue and compromise, its oppositional potential creates new players in the accommodative game, not well accounted for in the classical consociational imagination.

This dynamic was made clear in two ways. First, civil society actors encountered deadlocks on issues of bilingualism and representation in their association in the mid-twentieth century. As a result, the question was punted into the political arena. Pan-Canadian civil society organizations effectively participated in the same debate that would take place in the political and constitutional arena 20 years later, involving language rights, group representation, asymmetry, etc. The exclusion of those issues from civil society organizations clearly had an impact on subsequent political dynamics, as well as the nature of the conflict.

Second, this dynamic was made even clearer by specifically anti-Meech organizing during the ratification period. Within weeks of the Accord's public announcement, formal and semi-formal anti-Meech committees had been founded. Some accounts of the Accord attribute inclement public opinion primarily to the anti-Meech interventions of former Prime Minister Pierre Trudeau, who testified in opposition and published a series of open editorials. In fact, prior to Trudeau's taking any stand publicly, English Canadian mobilization at the level of civil society had already signaled strongly that the ratification process was going to be more fractious and difficult than political leaders had imagined.

The most prominent oppositionist civil society organization was the Canadian Coalition on the Constitution (CCC). Its organizers recruited spokespeople in each province to ensure a sustained anti-Meech presence in the media. The *de facto* head of the organization, Deborah Coyne, explained: "I regarded our role as simply building up... an ability to demonstrate—giving the total absence of political leadership—a critical mass of people opposed" (Coyne 2011). Because political elites had closed ranks (initially) around the Accord, CCC focused much of its efforts at the level of civil society. It provided myriad other groups—professional, interest based, even charitable—with research and analysis and encouraged them to take positions publicly (*ibid.*). The group was based predominantly in English Canada and struggled to maintain representation in Quebec (*ibid.*). More importantly, it built on existing networks, particularly feminist networks, which given the absence of integration were not a site for engaging in dialogue with Québec-based organizations.

Eventually, this citizen-driven opposition broke through into formal politics. It immediately caused disquiet in the ranks of the federal parties that had originally endorsed the Accord (Cohen 1990: p. 135; see also Jeffrey 2010). In the three provinces that held elections during the ratification period, anti-Meech political parties (of both strong and ambivalent varieties) did uniformly well. In Newfoundland and Labrador, Clyde Wells was elected with a large majority on the promise to demand dramatic changes to the Accord or rescind the signature of his predecessor. He became the figurehead of the anti-Meech movement and one of the most popular politicians in the country (Fournier 1991: p. 65). He hired leading anti-Meech civil society activists to advise him and had them work constantly to build and nourish networks of opposition across the country (Coyne). Division among civil society actors thus built and activated anti-Meech resources, which political elites were able to mobilize.

Here, the important lesson is simply that voices that were excluded from and disenchanted with the elite-level dialogue found alternative means to oppose the act of accommodation in a divided civil society. The consociational theory argues that behind closed doors, elites have the flexibility to find compromise by horse-trading instrumental incentives. In the case of Meech Lake, however, the "winning" of the political class was wholly insufficient for earning the acquiescence of the citizenry. Opposition simply moved to civil society. In the absence of a cohesive pan-Canadian civil society, this meant that there was little opportunity for dialogue. Furthermore, citizen-driven opposition inevitably weakened the commitment of the political class and encouraged non-compromising strategies. Broad public opposition altered the incentive structure for the politicians who initially supported the Accord and ultimately provoked a cracking of the political consensus in the election and leadership of Clyde Wells. The theoretical top-down and voluntarist perspective exaggerates the degree of autonomy that elites enjoy by largely ignoring the role of non-state actors, both as political agents themselves, and altering the political calculus of elites (Table 1).

**Table 1** Summary of findings: horizontal and vertical dynamics in two Canadian cases

|  | Meech lake | Official apology |
|---|---|---|
| Political elite behavior | Initially cooperative | Initially uncooperative |
| **Horizontal dynamics** | | |
| *Integration/segmentation* Networks as site of "on-going conversations" and identity formation | Mostly segmented French- and English-Canadian networks Few supporting structure for dialogue either before or during the ratification | Cross-community nonsegmental sectorial networks Supporting structure before and during recognition |
| *Nature of linkages* Networks as site of exchange, either substantial or instrumental | Instrumental, depoliticized | Substantive, identity oriented |
| **Vertical dynamics** | | |
| *Mobilization* Networks as site of support, opposition, or initiation of accommodation | Mobilization against elite recognition and accommodation | Mobilization in favor of elite recognition and accommodation |
| *Discursive* Networks as resources and constraints on discursive politics | Segmented networks allowed for discursive work of presenting the accommodation as a rights infringement Gave support to anti-Meech politicians | Cross-community networks allowed for reframing the issue as a moral one Constrained elites to recognize and apologize |
| Outcome | Weakening of political support, no accommodation | Weakening of political opposition, accommodation |

# Lessons from Canada (2): Civil Society and the Indian Residential Schools Official Apology

We have argued that the divided nature of Canadian civil society is a structural factor mitigating political efforts at accommodation. It is, therefore, a relatively constant independent variable in recent political history. Nevertheless, there are some *sui generis* instances where, for issue-specific reasons, horizontal linkages at the level of civil society have facilitated accommodation. We take, tentatively, the 2008 apology to Indigenous survivors of the Indian Residential Schools as an example of this. Direct intergroup relationships existed in civil society because of the churches' involvement in the administration of residential schools and Indigenous civil society leaders' decisions to engage them directly. This may help to explain why, at what was arguably a politically inauspicious moment, an act of accommodation resulted.[1]

We draw two elements from the political process leading to the apology, which suggest its relevance to this discussion:

*First*, the political calculus of the moment appeared unfriendly to the possibility of an accommodative outcome. Here again, we test the theoretical voluntarism of classical work on consociational power-sharing. In this case, there was little incentive or seeming inclination on the part of political elites to accommodate this demand of the numerous Indigenous nations that constituted only a tiny minority of Canadians. The Truth and Reconciliation Commission emerged as a condition of the Indian Residential Schools Settlement Agreement, the largest class-action settlement in Canadian history (Stanton 2010: p. 4). The promise of an apology itself was only ambiguously present in the settlement agreement. As a result, even after the settlement had been reached, the Conservative government of the day resisted issuing an apology. Initially, in early 2007, the Minister of Indian Affairs resolutely denied that an apology was appropriate or necessary. Later, he argued that it should only come after the commission completed its 5 years of hearings. To some Indigenous leaders, this was viewed as evidence that the government "[didn't] see us as a big voting bloc" (Curry 2007) and felt no pressure to participate in a symbolic act of recognition.

The prime minister was notably disinterested in Indigenous issues. In fact, one of his very few interventions on the subject prior to becoming the leader of his party had been to publicly oppose an official posthumous apology to the executed Indigenous leader, Louis Riel (Curry 2009). The non-Indigenous public was only dimly engaged on the issue, with parts of it moderately antagonistic to Indigenous demands generally, given recent highly controversial acts of contentious collective action by Indigenous groups. With a divided House of Commons and minority parliament, non-Indigenous political elites did not enjoy a substantial degree of societal segmental stability. Given all this, reading only the political dynamics of the moment the accommodative outcome seems anomalous.

*Second*, the residential schools issue is distinct in that there was direct, horizontal engagement at the level of civil society prior to the political act of recognition. We hasten to qualify this: It was only true of the residential schools issue specifically and not more broadly of Indigenous-non-Indigenous social segments, which are typically deeply divided. It also only involved a limited range of civil society actors. Specifically, a number of Christian churches became involved in the pursuit

---

[1] It is necessary to justify the discussion of an official apology in a paper about power sharing. The relationship between public reconciliation—which might be categorized as belonging to "the politics of recognition" broadly—and power sharing is ambiguous and under-explored (Loizides 2010). Reconciliation policy typically occurs alongside power sharing innovation in post-conflict contexts. It is intended to reconstitute the political community, and entails a sharing of symbolic resources, but clearly falls short of power sharing *per se*. Instead, we have opted to treat it as a form of accommodation within an ethnically-divided society and therefore, procedurally similar in some meaningful ways to the politics of power sharing.

by survivors for recognition. The reason for this was the obvious culpability of the churches themselves, which were empowered by the Canadian state to administer the residential schools and were therefore intimately involved in the pervasive abuse of Indigenous children. Nevertheless, after the majority of schools were closed, the churches played an independent role in reconciliation processes with Indigenous victims.

Beginning in the late 1980s, allegations of systemic sexual, physical, and emotional abuse were leveled against the churches. Phil Fontaine, then leader of the Manitoba Chiefs, was amongst the first public figures to make these accusations publicly and pursue redress from the churches directly. After a period of lobbying, the churches began to issue their own apologies. The United Church of Canada apologized in 1986 and again in 1998. The Anglican Church apologized in 1993. The Presbyterian Church issued a "Confession" in 1994. Some acknowledgement short of an apology on behalf of the entire Canadian Conference of Catholic Bishops was made to the Royal Commission on Aboriginal Peoples in 1993 and, again, by various Catholic authorities in other settings. Subsequently, some of the churches participated in fundraising and awareness campaigns on behalf of survivors and even conducted some soft lobbying of the government in the run-up to the official apology (United Church of Canada (2) 2007a, b).

What is unique about this issue then is that the act of recognition began at the level of society and subsequently filtered upwards. This lends some credence to the notion that the "strategic logics" of conflict (James 2003) can be circumvented in bottom-up reconciliatory processes. Political elites had a clear incentive, driven by political and resource logics, to resist the act of accommodation. Recognition of past abuses committed them to future accommodation, as well as redistribution of resources. The latter was true of church leaders too, given their own legal liability and participation in the settlement to come, but they did not face the same open-ended implications of recognition. Individual citizens lacked the information and organization requisite for meaningful participation in dialogue. As a result, church leaders, the "middle level actors" often identified in the peacebuilding literature, were best positioned to engage in recognition (James 2003: p. 175).

Moreover, we are able to recognize the causal importance of the structure of civil society. The residential schools issue, and the relationship between churches and Indigenous advocates, represents a distinct micro-structure. The horizontal linkages that existed were sector-specific—not replicated between Indigenous and non-Indigenous civil society on other issues. The nature of the linkage was significant too. It was substantial rather than instrumental—structured explicitly around the accommodative issue and a stated desire to improve intergroup relations. The churches, originally adversarial, became after dialogue and acknowledgement cooperative or at least sheepishly compliant in pursuit of accommodation.

This is quite distinctive from other Indigenous-non-Indigenous civil society linkages. For example, much has been made of recent "alliances" between Indigenous groups and environmentalists (Davis 2007; Larsen 2003). However, these linkages have often proven sustainable only where Indigenous claims to recognition and accommodation have engaged environmental themes. Some Indigenous actors have expressed disappointment by a lack of support on issues that refer only to the recognition of Indigenous peoples, and not simultaneously to environmental issues, suggesting instrumental rather than substantial ties. The nature of linkages in the case of residential school survivors and the churches was unique, and largely absent during Meech Lake.

We recognize the difficulty in offering a definitive causal explanation for why the government of Canada finally offered a public apology to Indigenous peoples in 2008. Nevertheless, the unique role played by civil society, as well as the lack of elite political cooperation, suggests a theoretically interesting case that should be pursued through more substantial process-tracing analysis.

# Conclusion

In the case of Meech, when Canadian elites attempted to engineer an act of accommodation using the processes of executive federalism, they were undermined by a divided and highly mobilized civil society. The structure of civil society did not allow for horizontal engagement between peoples that did not share a vision for the country. Instead, heavy mutual incomprehension prevailed. In the case of the official apology to residential school survivors, uncooperative political elites were supplanted in the accommodative process by engaged civil society actors. Both events highlight the important—and neglected—role that the structure of civil society plays in determining the outcome of political accommodation. It is the site of the ongoing dialogue that shapes collective understandings of societal goals. When it is highly segmented, competing visions of the country are likely to exist in parallel without regular meaningful engagement with each other. The nature of civil society linkages between groups also shapes the capacity of a multinational state to host bridge-building dialogue. All trust ties are not made equally, and they will respond differently under different circumstances and subjected to different stresses and shocks. Furthermore, these structural conditions of civil society feed back upon political dynamics, constraining and altering elite behavior, as well as introducing new actors into negotiation and accommodation. In short, our understanding of the "multinational game" (Zuber 2010) in any given federation is enhanced by paying systematic attention to the condition of civil society.

# References

Allport, G. (1954). The Nature of Prejudice. Reading MA: Addison-Wesley.

Amoretti, U. and N. Bermeo (eds) (2004) Federalism and Territorial Cleavages. Baltimore: John Hopkins University Press.

Andeweg, R. B. (2000). Consociational Democracy. Annual Review of Political Science, 3(1), p. 509–536.

Berman, S. (1997). Civil Society and Political Institutionalization. American Behavioral Scientist, 40(5), 562–574.

Bogaards, M. (1998). The favourable factors for consociational democracy: a review. European Journal of Political Research, 33(4), p. 475–496.

Bourdieu, P. (1990) The Logic of Practice. Stanford: Stanford University Press.

Cameron, D. and R. Simeon (2008). Language Matters: How Canadian Voluntary Associations Manage English and French. Vancouver: UBC Press.

Castañeda, G. (2011). Alternative Routes of Political Change: Elites Fracture or Social Mobilization, Economic Incentives or Cultural Thresholds. The Journal of Socio-Economic. 40. p. 178–91.

Chhibber, P. (2001). Democracy without Associations: Transformation of the Party System and Social Cleavages in India. Ann Arbor: University of Michigan Press.

Cinalli, M. (2005) "Below and Beyond Power Sharing: Relational Structures across Institutions and Civil Society." In O'Flynn, Ian and Russel, David (eds.) Power Sharing New Challenges for Divided Societies. London : Pluto Press, 2005, p. 172–187.

Cochrane, F. and S. Dunn. (2002). People Power? The Role of the Voluntary and Community Sector in the Northern Ireland Conflict, Cornwall: Cork University Press.

Cohen, A. (1990). A Deal Undone. Douglas and McIntyre Ltd.

Coleman, J. S. (1990). Foundations of Social Theory. Boston: Harvard University Press.

Coyne, D. (2011). Interview by Michael Morden. Tape Recording. Toronto ON., July 9.

Curry, Bill. (2007) "No residential schools apology, Tories say." Globe and Mail, March 3.

Curry, Bill. (2009) "Residential Schools Apology Deeply Moved Harper, Changed His Views." Globe and Mail, January 6.

Davis, Lynne (ed.). (2007) Alliances: Re/Envisioning Indigenous-non-Indigenous Relations. Toronto: University of Toronto Press.

Deegan-Krause, K. 2006. New Dimensions of Political Cleavage. Oxford Handbook of Political Science, eds. R. Dalton and H.-D. Klingemann. Oxford: Oxford University Press.

Deveaux, M. (2003) "A Deliberative Approach to Conflicts of Culture," Political Theory, 31:6, p. 780–807.

Dixon, P. (1997). "Paths to Peace in Northern Ireland (I): Civil Society and Consociational Approaches, Democratization, 4:2, p. 1–27.

Dobrowolsky, A. (1998). "Of 'Special Interests': Interests, Identity and Feminist Constitutional Activism in Canada." Canadian Journal of Political Science 31:4, p.707-742.

Dufour, P. (2006) « Projet national et espace de protestation mondiale : des articulations distinctes au Québec et au Canada. » Canadian Journal of Political Science 39 :2, p. 315–342.

Dugan, M. (1996) "A Nested Theory of Conflict" Women in Leadership, 1:1, p. 9–20.

Eliasoph, N. (1996) Making a Fragile Public: A Talk-Centered Study of Citizenship and Power. Sociological Theory. 14. p. 262–89.

Foley, M. W., & Edwards, B. (1997). Editors' Introduction: Escape From Politics? Social Theory and the Social Capital Debate. American Behavioral Scientist, 40(5), p. 550–561.

Forbes, D. (1997) Ethnic Conflict, New Haven: Yale University Press.

Fournier, P. (1991). A Meech Lake Post-Mortem: Is Quebec Sovereignty Inevitable? Montreal: McGill-Queens University Press.

Gagnon, A.-G., A. Lecours, and G. Nootens. (eds) (2007) Les nationalisms majoritaire contemporains: identité, mémoire, pouvoir. Québec: Québec Amérique.

Geertz, C. (1973). "The Integrative Revolution: Primordial Sentiments and Civil Politics in the New States." In Clifford Geertz (ed.), The Interpretation of Cultures. New York: Basic Books.

Hueglin, T. (2003) "Federalism at the Crossroads: Old Meanings, New Significance," Canadian Journal of Political Science, 36: 2, p. 275–294.

James, M.R. (2003) "Communicative Action, Strategic Action, and Inter-Group Dialogue," European Journal of Political Theory, 2:2, p. 157–81.

Jeffrey, B. (2010). Divided Loyalties: The Liberal Party of Canada, 1984–2008. Toronto: University of Toronto Press.

Kieve, R. (1981). "Pillars of Sand: A Marxist Critique of Consociational Democracy in the Netherlands" Comparative Politics, 13(3), 313–337.

Knoke, D. (1993) Networks of Elite Structure and Decision Making, Sociological Methods and Research. 22:1. p. 23–45.

Kramer, J. and H.-P. Schneider (1999) Federalism and Civil Societies: An International Symposium, Baden-Baden: Nomos, 384 p.

Larsen, S. C. (2003) Promoting Aboriginal Territoriality Through Interethnic Alliances: The Case of the Cheslatta T'en in Northern British Columbia. Human Organization, 62:1, p. 74–84.

Lederach, J.P. (1998) Building Peace: Sustainable Reconciliation in Divided Societies, Washington: United States Institution of Peace.

Lemieux, V. (1973) "Le conflit dans les organisations biculturelles" In Recherches sociographiques, 14:1, p. 41–57.

Lichterman, P. (1999) Talking Identity in the Public Sphere: Broad Visions and Small Spaces in Sexual Identity Politics. Theory and Society.

Lijphart, A. (1969) Consociational Democracy. World Politics. 21:2 p. 207–25.

Lijphart, Arendt (1977) Democracy in Plural Societies: a Comparative Exploration, New Haven: Yale University Press

Lipset, S. M. and S. Rokkan. 1967. "Cleavage Structures, Party Systems, and Voter Alignments." In Seymour Lipset and Stein Rokkan (eds.), Party Systems and Voter Alignments: Cross-National Perspectives. New York: Free Press.Lorwin 1971, 1–64.

Loizides (2010). "Introduction: Federalism, Reconciliation and Power Sharing in Post-Conflict Societies." Federal Governance 8:2, p. 1–14.

Lorwin, Val R. (1971) Segmented Pluralism: Ideological Cleavages and Political Cohesion in the Smaller European Democracies, Comparative Politics, Vol. 3, No. 2 (Jan., 1971), p. 141–175

McGarry, J. and B. O'Leary (1995) Explaining Northern Ireland. Oxford: Blackwell

Meisel, J. and V. Lemieux (1972). Ethnic Relations in Canadian Voluntary Associations, Documents of the Royal Commission on Bilingualism and Biculturalism, no. 13.

Mische, A. (2003). Cross-talk in movements: Reconceiving the culture-network link. Social Movements and Networks - Relational Approaches to Collective Action (pp. 258–80). Oxford University Press Oxford.

Monahan, P. (1991). Meech Lake: The Inside Story. Toronto: University of Toronto Press.

Morden, Michael et Alexandre P.Pelletier (2011) Multinational Studies and the Problem of Unity: Bringing the Citizen In. Unpublished manuscript, Canadian Political Association Conference, Waterloo.

Nan, S. A. (2008) "Conflict Resolution in a Network Society" International Negotiation, 12, p. 111–131.

Netto, O. and G. Cox (1997) Electoral Institutions, Cleavage Structures, and the Number of Parties. American Journal of Political Science. 41, p. 149–74.

Olzak, S. (1992) The Dynamics of Ethnic Competition and Conflict, Stanford: Stanford University Press.

Pal, L. (1993) Interests of State: The Politics of Language, Multiculturalism, and Feminism in Canada, Montréal: McGill-Queen's University Press.

Pappalardo, A. (1981). The Conditions for Consociational Democracy: a Logical and Empirical Critique. European Journal of Political Research, 9(4), 365–390.

Pelletier, A. and R. Simeon (2012) Groupes linguistiques et société civile: confiance, cooperation et accommodements au sein des associations volontaires au Canada. F. Rocher and D. Karmis. La Dynamique confiance méfiance dans les démocraties plurinationales: Le Canada en perspectives comparées, Québec: Presses de l'Université Laval, p. 245–268.

Petitgrew, T. (1998). Intergroup Contact Theory. Annual Review of Psychology, 49, 65–85.

Prang, M. (1986). "Networks and Associations and the Nationalizing of Sentiment in English Canada" in Carty and Ward (eds) National Politics and Community in Canada, Vancouver: University of British Columbia Press, p. 48–63

Putnam. 1994. "Bowling Alone: America's Declining Social Capital", Journal of Democracy, 6, p. 65–78.

Rocher François and Karmis, Dimitrios. (2012). La Dynamique confiance/méfiance dans les démocraties multinationales: Le Canada sous l'angle comparatif, Ste-Foy: Presses de l'Université Laval.

Rustow, D. 1970. "Transitions to Democracy: Toward a Dynamic Model." Comparative Politics, vol.2, no.3: 337–364.

Simeon, R. and I. Robinson (2004) "The Dynamics of Canadian Federalism" in J. Bickerton and A.-G. Gagnon (2004) Canadian Politics, Peterborough: Broadview Press.

Simeon, R. et D. Cameron (2008). "Accommodation at the Pinnacle: The Special Role of Civil Society's Leaders" In Cameron et Simeon (dir), Language Matters: How Canadian Voluntary Associations Manage French and English, Vancouver: University of British Columbia Press

Stanton, Kim. "Canada's Truth and Reconciliation Commission: Settling the Past." International Indigenous Policy Journal 2, 3: August 2010, p. 1–18.

Stepan, A. (2001) "Toward a New Comparative Politics of Federalism, (Multi)Nationalism, and Democracy: Beyond Rikerian Federalism" in Arguing Comparative Politics, Oxford: Oxford University Press.

Stolle, D. and T.R. Rochon (2001) "Are All Associations Alike? Member Diversity, Associational Type, and the Creation of Social Capital" in B. Edwards, W. Foley and M. Diani, Beyond Tocqueville: Civil Society and the Social Capital Debate in Comparative Perspective, Hanover: University Press of New England.

Taylor, C. (1994) Multiculturalisme: différence et démocratie, Paris: Champs.

Tilly, C. (1984) Social Movements and National Politics. C. Bright and S. Harding. Statemaking and Social Movements: Essays in History and Theory. Ann Arbor: University of Michigan Press.

Tilly, Charles. (1998) "Contentious Conversation" Social Research, Vol. 65, No. 3, p. 491–510

Tsebelis, G. (1990) Elite Interaction and Constitution Building in Consociational Democracies. Journal of Theoretical Politics, 2:5, p. 5–29.

Tully, J. (1996). Strange Multiplicity: Constitutionalism in an age of diversity, Cambridge: Cambridge University Press.

Turgeon, Luc. (1999). La grande absente. La société civile au coeur des changements de la Révolution tranquille. Globe: revue internationale d'études québécoises, Vol. 2, No. 1, p. 35–56

United Church of Canada (2007a). "The Healing Fund." Official Website of the United Church of Canada. Retrieved from: http://www.united-church.ca/funding/healing/about on November 3/ 2011. N.D.

United Church of Canada (2007b). "United Church Encouraged by Government Commitment to Search Residential Schools Records." April 25, 2007. Retrieved from: http://www.united-church.ca/communications/news/releases/070425.

Varshney, A. (2001) "Ethnic Conflict and Civil Society" in World Politics, 53, p. 362–398.

Weinstock, Daniel. "Building Trust in Divided Societies." Journal of Political Philosophy 7, no. 3 (September 1, 1999): 287.

Zuber, I.C. (2010) "Understanding the Multinational Game: Toward a Theory of Asymmetrical Federalism" Comparative Political Studies, 44:5, p. 546–571.

# Part III
# Territorial Autonomy in Spain: Other Issues

# Openness, Complexity, and Asymmetry: A Comparative Perspective on the Challenges of the "Autonomic State"

María Salvador Martínez

**Abstract** The purpose of this paper is to analyse the three most characteristic and problematic features of the so-called "state of autonomies": its openness (or open-endedness), its complexity, and its asymmetry. Clearly, we shall make our analysis from a constitutional perspective. However, we shall pay particular attention on the politico-constitutional circumstances that determine the form of territorial organisation and particularly its dynamics. We shall also examine the situation from a comparative perspective to determine whether these characteristics are common to all states with a federal structure and to what extent Spain has distinct features and issues.

## Some Initial Questions

The way in which a state organises itself territorially is determined by basic decisions as to how the exercise of power is to be distributed within that territory. The resulting organisation may be more or less centralised, given that any state combines a certain level of centralisation with a certain level of decentralisation. It is important to remember that the state, as a form of political organisation capable of ensuring unity, exists precisely by virtue of an essential minimal amount of centralisation. Absolute centralisation may be politically and functionally impossible today, but it is equally true that absolute decentralisation makes the state as an organisation inoperative.

This contribution has been developed under the Research Project DER 2009-10375/JURI "Constitución y Globalización: Transformaciones del Estado constitucional y constitucionalización de espacios supranacionales".

M. Salvador Martínez (✉)
Facultad de Derecho, Departamento Derecho Politico, UNED, C/ Obispo Trejo, 2, 28040 Madrid, Spain
e-mail: msalvador@der.uned.es

A. López-Basaguren and L. Escajedo San Epifanio (eds.), *The Ways of Federalism in Western Countries and the Horizons of Territorial Autonomy in Spain*, Vol. 2, DOI 10.1007/978-3-642-27717-7_41, © Springer-Verlag Berlin Heidelberg 2013

What, then, determines the degree of centralisation or decentralisation to be found in any given state? In a democratic state, the answer lies in sociopolitical elements: in the features of the political community that organises itself into a state and, very specifically, in that community's degree of political integration. This is particularly obvious in politically more decentralised (federal) states. Such states are organised not to some prior design or model; rather they are the result of a range of specific historical and political/social circumstances, which tend to vary greatly from case to case. During the constituent process in which a political community organises itself into a federal state (whether it uses this term or another, such as "regional state", "autonomic state"[1], etc.), the various political forces set out the different positions on the issue. They then seek a means of articulating centralisation and decentralisation in such a way that the resulting territorial organisation matches the characteristics and satisfies the needs of that political community. As a result, there is no unique model and it would be difficult to list concepts that can be applied to all. Any analysis of the way a given federal state is organised requires an empirical study of that specific case and an understanding of the sociopolitical context in which it was developed.

However, even if we are unable to come up with a single all-encompassing concept of federal state that can be applied to all such organisational structures, we can nonetheless identify a series of structural elements that are common to all the federal states in the western world. These include (1) the existence of territorial institutions with legislative and political powers, as well as administrative ones; (2) distribution of powers with the corresponding financial resources; (3) participation by the territorial institutions in the central organisation, normally by way of a second chamber; (4) a guarantee that the aforementioned characteristics cannot be altered by an act of the central parliament; and (5) a mechanism for solving disputes essentially by the judicial way.[2]

With these minimum features as a starting point, each specific federal state may have other very diverse features since the constitutional balance struck between centrifugal and centripetal forces may vary greatly from case to case.

In Spain, the "autonomic state" was developed out of the provisions of the 1978 Constitution. This arrangement was considered original in terms of its territorial organisation of power, but it nonetheless contains the minimum characteristics common to all federal states we have seen above. We shall leave to one side the debate as to whether Spain is a federal or federalising state; given that it has the

---

[1] Translator's Note: in order to avoid confusion of terminology, throughout the text, *autonómico* has been translated as "autonomic" (rather than regional) when it refers to the framework of devolution but as "regional" when it refers to the specific administrations of the various autonomous communities, hence "autonomic state" (*estado autonómico*) but regional parliament (*parlamento autonómico*).

[2] For the Spanish case, see for example J. Juan González Encinar (1985), pp. 88–89; foreign studies include Anderson (2008), pp. 21–22.

minimum features common to any federal structure, we can make a comparative analysis of our "autonomic state" and other federal states.

Any federal structure, by its nature, is subject to continuous tensions and challenges, insofar as it is a compromise between unity and plurality, between centrifugal and centripetal forces. In addition, however, the Spanish "autonomic state" has to deal with important problems related—as we shall now see—to the openness, complexity, and asymmetry of its territorial organisation.

## The Openness of the Spanish "Autonomic State"

To explain the "openness" (or open-endedness) of the Spanish "autonomic state", we need to refer back to two separate, though closely associated phenomena: the first is the "de-constitutionalisation" of the model (i.e., the failure to enshrine it in the constitution), in that the constitution only contains the fundaments of territorial organisation and not its specific design; the second is the "openness" of the model in the strictest sense, given that the way it is determined has depended (and continues to depend to a large extent) on the will of the political and legal actors involved.

### *"Deconstitutionalisation"*

The Spanish Constitution did not confer any politically decentralised shape on the state; rather, it established the rules for a voluntary and gradual process of decentralisation. A foreign jurist wanting to find out how the Spanish state has been territorially organised would not find the answer in the constitution.[3] So what does the constitution actually contain? It holds the pieces for developing a politically decentralised state. More specifically, it establishes which territories can decide to constitute themselves into "autonomous communities" (referred to hereinafter as ACs)—the politically decentralised entities making up the "autonomic state"—the procedure by which they should go about this, a list of powers from which they may decide to assume some or all, and an entirely minimal definition of how they should be organised (which does not apply to all the potential ACs). In other words, the constitution did not design the "autonomic state" we know today; it only made it possible. The constitution established the entitlement to self-government and set out the procedural rules whereby, freely exercising that right, the nationalities and regions could shape the territorial organisation of the state.

Spain's form of territorial organisation is defined, therefore, not in the constitution, but in lower tiers of legislation and in the jurisprudence of the Constitutional

---

[3] An idea developed by P. Cruz in the well-known Cruz (1982).

Court. All territories that have opted for self-government have approved a "statute of autonomy" (SA). This is their basic institutional legislation. It regulates the way the autonomous community is organised and adopts certain powers from amongst those permitted under the constitution. In addition to the SAs, there are also other regulations of very diverse categories appertaining both to the central state and the ACs, which regulate some of the defining elements of the "autonomic state". They relate to the distribution of powers, financing, mechanisms of cooperation, and the participation of the ACs in certain central powers of the state. Finally, the Constitutional Court has played an extremely important role in resolving all the conflicts that arose while the "autonomic state" was being developed, since the constitutional provisions in this regard are minimal and the constitutionality of their developing rules is open to question. So for example, Constitutional Court jurisprudence includes some defining elements of the system. These relate especially to the distribution of powers and also impact the extent of the SAs' powers of reform, the scope of the central state's entitlement to "harmonise" autonomic legislation, the principle of solidarity and the contents thereof, and relations of cooperation and collaboration, among other central issues.[4]

The reasons the 1978 Constitution left design of the form of territorial organisation open-ended are essentially historical and political in nature.

The first attempt at a federal arrangement in Spain came in 1873 with the "Draft Federal Constitution" of the First Republic. However, it was never passed into law because, before it could be, there was an anarchic pro-independence outbreak. As a result, a conscious or unconscious association remains in the historical memory of many Spaniards between federalism and anarchy. This explains why for so long, any use of the term "federal" has been avoided. The constitution of the Second Republic (1931) established the first federal regime in Spain. It was very similar to that inaugurated under the current constitution, and allowed access to self-government for any regions so deciding. Under the constitution, statutes were drawn up for Catalonia, the Basque Country, and Galicia (the latter, although passed in a referendum, was never enacted). After the 1936–1939 civil war, the victorious Franco regime brought centralisation of the apparatus of the state that was to last for nearly 40 years.

After Franco's death and at the start of the "political transition", a number of territories with a particular drive for political self-government called for the constitutional state to establish a politically devolved arrangement. While there was a general desire to satisfy this demand, it was feared that negotiations on the issue might exceed the scope of the process of political transition. Consequently, a parallel process was set up between 1977 and 1978, initiating a regime of "pre-autonomies" throughout the territory of the state.[5]

---

[4] Inter alia, see Fernández Farreres (2005).

[5] With all the resulting "theft of the activity of the constitution-framing power and of the very design of the constitution [*hurto a la actividad del poder constituyente y al propio diseño constitucional*]" (García Roca 1988, p. 123).

Throughout the process of drafting the constitution, negotiations were influenced by the fact that the nationalist parties of Catalonia and the Basque Country, which enjoyed majority support in their respective regions, held a position of strength and were capable of altering the general design of the state's form of territorial organisation. The other political parties felt they were in no position to deny the Basque and Catalan nationalists the level of self-government they demanded, as without the consensus of Basques and Catalans the constitution would lack legitimacy from the outset. At the same time, however, they did not believe that the large degree of political devolution claimed by the Basques and Catalans could be extended to other parts of Spain that lacked the necessary resources and experience. As a result, the framers of the 1978 Constitution, having inherited a strongly centralised state and needing to forge a difficult consensus, retained a certain formal ambiguity as to the issue of political decentralisation, leaving the model open-ended and allowing its precise design to be determined in a subsequent legal-political debate.[6]

## *The Openness of the Model*

Spain's system of territorial power distribution is "open" because it has been constructed and continues to be constructed on the initiative of the territorial institutions—i.e., on the basis of what is called *principium dispositivium*, the principle of determination [*principio dispositivo*]. It also contains other additional elements of openness.

a) The *principium dispositivium* is derived from the right to self-government of nationalities and regions set out in the constitution.[7] In consonance with the aims of the framers of the constitution, it has become a central feature of the system; applying this principle, it is the legitimised territories that decide voluntarily (dispositively) whether to become ACs, what powers to assume, and how they are to organise themselves.[8]

   In this conception, the *principium dispositivium* operates at two points in time: initially, immediately upon approval of the constitution, when the different territories decide whether they choose to constitute themselves into autonomous communities and the degree of self-government they wish to exercise (initial openness) and, at a later point in time, after they have already organised themselves into autonomous communities, when they decide whether to initiate

---

[6] On the action of the political parties in the process of framing the constitution and subsequent development, see Alzaga (2011).

[7] Essential reading on the difference between nationalities and regions include Corcuera (1992–1993).

[8] Aguado (1997) and Fossas (2007), among many other studies.

a procedure of reform of their Statute of Autonomy to modify their legal system and redefine their area of self-government (openness via reform).

Given that the decision as to whether or not to form an AC lies with the territories, there could have been just three ACs—or five or seven—with the rest of the country remaining outside this arrangement. However, this was not what happened. Between 1978 and 1983, SAs were approved throughout the country, with the regime of the autonomous cities of Ceuta and Melilla being enacted in 1995. Now that all of Spain is organised into ACs, that initial openness has ceased to exist; although the "regional map" is open to changes at any time, a "map" of the ACs comprising the Spanish state now exists.[9]

However, the initial openness did affect not only the number of ACs that were to be created but also the contents of each one's self-government. The constitution, it should be remembered, limits itself to listing the powers that can be assumed by the ACs; sketching out the minimum features of their organisation (and not even in all cases); setting out the bases of the financing system; and little else. Starting from this point, each AC has determined the scope of its own self-government and how it organises itself and relates to other ACs and to the central state.

With the initial period of openness now, as we have seen, completed (i.e., a "map of autonomies" now exists), the *principium dispositivium* leaves the model open, insofar as it allows it to be reformed through modification of the SA. This openness is by no means insignificant: as we know, the specific design of the form of territorial organisation is contained not in the constitution but in the SAs. The powers, internal organisation, and other matters regulated in the SAs can all be modified. Indeed, in 2006 and 2007, some of those statutes were importantly and controversially reformed, redefining the powers of the ACs, creating new bodies, introducing new measures on financing, and establishing new paths for the (bilateral) relationship with the central state.[10]

As a result of the issues they raised, the constitutionality of some of these reforms was challenged in the Constitutional Court, evidencing the importance of the Court's role in the "de-constitutionalisation" and "openness" of the model.

The 1978 Constitution remains unchanged, yet the form of territorial organisation is not as "de-constitutionalised" as it was when it was first passed. Over the last thirty-odd years, the Constitutional Court has interpreted the text of the constitution, settling its precise sense and meaning. The result is that there is now a body of constitutional jurisprudence on the "autonomic state", fleshing out the constitution itself. Thus, the openness of the system through reform of the statutes is restricted both by the boundaries placed in the constitution, i.e., the

---

[9] To confirm that the initial period of openness was now over, in 2005 the government asked the Council of State to issue a report on possible reform of the constitution which was to include the 17 existing ACs. However, after the council issued its report, the reform procedure was never initiated.

[10] *Inter alia*, Ruiz-Rico Ruiz (2006).

constitutional text—with all its limitations and deficiencies—and by the Court's interpretation of it.

In this task, however, the Court is fatally hobbled by the fact that the constitution does not enshrine any given model therein. The model remains open because no basic decision was taken to organise a homogenous federal state, an asymmetric federal state, a quasi-federal state, or any other kind of federal state. The reason that did not happen was that different conceptions existed that prevented any such decision from happening. The result is that, while there will be conflicts that the Court can resolve relatively easily, there will be others that affect the essence of the model and place the court in a position that does not correspond to it. The Court can, with its jurisprudence, flesh out the constitution, but it cannot take the place of the framers of the constitution by making decisions that they did not.[11]

b) As well as the openness introduced by the *principium dispositivium*, there are also, as we have already noted, other additional elements of openness.

Specifically, in the matter of powers, the limits on openness are set by the powers held exclusively by the state, as listed in Art. 149 of the constitution. The ACs can assume any powers they wish to except for those exclusively attributed to the state under the constitution. Nonetheless, the constitution itself provides the state with the possibility of going further by enacting different types of law: first, framework laws (Art. 150.1 CE) allow the central state, in matters of its competence, to confer upon all or any of the ACs the power to enact legislation within the framework of the principles, bases, and guidelines established by state law, and, second, the organic laws of transfer or delegation (Art. 150.2 CE) allow it to transfer or delegate to all or any of the ACs powers appertaining to it (the powers of various ACs have been extended by way of the technique of the organic laws of transfer).

The laws that have sparked the greatest debate have been the so-called transfer or delegation acts. These keep the system open-ended because even if the ACs have reached the ceiling of their competences, the central state can transfer further powers that the constitution attributes exclusively to the state. These laws were introduced into the constitutional text as an element of flexibility or openness, with a view to helping adapt the system of distribution of powers to new circumstances; in effect, they are in keeping with the idea of "openness" that infuses the entire model. Nonetheless, some commentators have recommended that limits be placed on jurisdictional openness. This could be achieved, for example, by earmarking certain powers as appertaining "exclusively" to the central state, meaning that they cannot be transferred or delegated to the ACs under such an act. These powers would define the irreducible power

---

[11] In this regard, the results of a survey on Constitutional Court Ruling STC 31/2010 on the Statute of Catalonia answered by various lecturers (published in *TRC*, No. 27, 2011) are particularly interesting.

core of the central organs of government and would also constitute the only absolute limit to jurisdictional openness.[12]

## The Complexity of the "Autonomic State"

The organisation of any federal structure is imbued with a certain complexity, comprising as it does at least two levels of government that need to be regulated and coordinated. However, in the Spanish case, the complexity is increased by legal and political circumstances.

a) In legal terms, the complexity of the model derives both from the constitutional provisions on the form of territorial organisation and from the subsequent development of these provisions.

  i) The constitution created a significant initial degree of complexity. Leaving the model open, it sought to establish different requirements and procedures for different situations, thus enabling each territory to accede to self-government at the pace and to the extent that it chose (in particular, it was intended to enable faster and broader recognition of powers for territories that had most clearly demanded self-government). This initial complexity can be seen, for example, in the constitutional regulation of the following issues:

  – Procedures for acceding to self-government and enacting the Statute of Autonomy. The constitution leaves it up to each territory to decide whether to opt for self-government by passing a statute of autonomy but provides five different procedures for the purpose. The first is a special procedure for Catalonia, the Basque Country, and Galicia, i.e., the three territories that had passed a statute of autonomy during the Second Republic (Art. 151 and transitory provision 2). The second is a speeded-up procedure for "first tier" or fast-track communities—i.e., Andalusia (Art. 151); The third, "ordinary" procedure, is for second-tier or slow-track ACs—all those not included in the other cases (Art. 143 and Additional Provision 1). There is also a specific procedure for Navarra (Transitory Provision 4) and, finally, a special procedure for the cities of Ceuta and Melilla (Transitory Provision 5).

  – The form of distribution of power. The constitution establishes a "twin list" system—powers held exclusively by the state (Art. 149) and powers that may be assumed by the ACs (Art. 148)—the interpretation of which has proved anything but simple. Article 149, with its especially elaborate wording, includes not only powers of the central state but, in many cases, shared powers as well. In some cases, it allocates "legislation" to the state

---

[12] "Informe sobre modificaciones de la Constitución Española", in *El informe del Consejo de Estado sobre la reforma constitucional*, CEPC, Madrid, 2006, pp. 175–177.

in a certain matter, whose "execution" may appertain to the ACs. In others, it attributes the establishment of the "bases" in an area to the state, while the "development" corresponds to the ACs. At the same time, the list provided in Article 148 is neither general nor definitive; by a variety of means provided for in the constitution, the ACs have—sooner or later—managed to break through this "jurisdictional ceiling". As well as these two lists, there are other matters that are reserved to the state by other articles of the constitution not specifically dealing with the division of powers. This is the case of matters that can only be regulated by an organic law (passed by the central parliament). Also, there is a double clause of distribution of powers (matters not attributed to the state may be assumed by the ACs, and matters not assumed by the ACs shall appertain to the state), a prevalence clause—which has proved utterly inoperative since it applies only to concurrent powers (which, in practical terms, do not exist)—and a subsidiarity clause, the interpretation of which has proved particularly contentious and problematical. Finally, one should not forget that under the principium dispositivium, it is the SAs that define the scope of the powers of the corresponding ACs and—inversely—those of the central state.

ii) In some cases, the subsequent development of legislation and jurisprudence has added greater complexity.

– In terms of legislation, it is worth mentioning the deficient and fragmentary regulation of the procedures for amending the SAs, a central feature of the system. The constitution establishes only that the amendment must be approved by an organic law of the central parliament and that in certain ACs a referendum must be held. Starting from this basis, the procedure is regulated by the SAs and by parliamentary acts of the central and regional parliaments. These establish five different procedures, depending on the ACs in question, with important differences between them.

– As for the development of jurisprudence, the clearest example can be seen in the jurisprudence on the determination of powers. This is a complex issue in any federal state, but it is all the more so if the rules of jurisdictional distribution are not sufficiently clear. The Constitutional Court has had to rule on the interpretation of these provisions, on many occasions making them more, rather than less, complex. For example, jurisprudence on the technique used for distributing power over "bases" and "development"—which is central to the Spanish system—has been changeable and has failed to provide a sufficiently clear and operative concept of "bases". The result is that disputes over powers, rather than being reduced, have actually increased.[13] Another example is the ruling that even in areas exclusively allocated to the state under the constitution

---

[13] Fernández Riveira (2009).

(international relations and administration of justice), some powers may be conferred upon the ACs. One might cite further examples.

b) Finally, the political factors contributing to the complexity of the system relate to features of the party system in Spain.

There are a number of nationalist parties, but only in certain ACs, where they enjoy strong support. As well as acting within the ambit of their autonomous community, they also operate nationally, where they hold a strong position, for two reasons: firstly, the characteristics of the electoral system give them a large number of seats in the central parliament, and secondly, they act as kingmakers, giving the majority party the backing it needs to take certain decisions in the absence of an absolute majority. When this occurs, the nationalist parties can have a decisive influence on the decisions of the central organs of the state.

At the same time, by the very fact that they are nationalist parties, they necessarily have to maintain a constant struggle with the central power, claiming for their communities greater and greater quantities of powers and resources. Combined with the fact that the constitution recognised self-government as a right, but left the process of territorial organisation open, this has meant that in the ACs in which these parties operate, political debate has always centred on making greater demands on the state, exercising a right that was not sated by the formation of the ACs.[14]

The nature of the nationalist parties and their strong bargaining position left its mark on constitutional provisions on territorial matters, and it has subsequently conditioned the political and legal debate on the openness of the model. It has increased its complexity and, in particular, its heterogeneity and asymmetry, as we shall now see.

## The Heterogeneity and Asymmetry of the "Autonomic State"

Finally, the Spanish form of territorial organisation must be considered diverse and asymmetric since legally not all ACs have the same degree of autonomy or the same position within the "autonomic state". In analysing this aspect, it will help if we identify two of the reasons for this heterogeneity:

a) Firstly, the lack of homogeneity derives from the principium dispositivium, which, as we have seen, was adopted with a view to giving each territory access to self-government in accordance with its demands.

   i) The constitution reflects an initial situation in which the various parts of the country did not all feel the same need to form an autonomous community. Indeed, it was initially thought that the exercise of the right to self-government

---

[14] As pointed out, for example, by Balaguer Callejón (2006), p. 567.

might lead to a structure with two asymmetric tiers of devolution: real political decentralisation in Catalonia, the Basque Country, and Galicia, where there was a clear call for self-government, and a more or less administrative decentralisation for the other ACs, which had not expressed that same "vocation for self-government". As we know, however, this did not turn out to be the case.

From this initial starting point, the constitution established the following differences:

- Procedural differences. These are the different types of procedure for approving the SAs, allowing faster or slower access to self-government, depending on individual cases.
- Jurisdictional differences. The constitution distinguished between two types of AC, depending on the degree of self-government they could initially assume. Some could adopt all the powers allowed under the constitution immediately. Others, however, were limited during the first 5 years to those provided for under Art. 148. After that initial 5-year period, the maximum ceiling of self-government became the same for all the ACs.
- Organisational differences. Similarly, the only requirement the constitution places on ACs eligible to accede to the maximum level of self-government from the outset is that they have an internal organisation comprising a legislative assembly, a council of government, and a president [first minister].

The issue here is to determine whether the differences established in the constitution as to the speed and scope of access to self-government were merely transitory or whether, conversely, they should be retained in some form. Most commentators believe that those initial differences only sought to order access to self-government by territories with initially varying needs; now that that first period has passed, therefore there is constitutionally no difference between the various ACs. However, a minority, operating from the perspective of the "fast-track" ACs, argues that the differences should be maintained.

ii) Tt the same time, under the principium dispositivium, each AC freely decides which powers it assumes, and the result is therefore necessarily diverse. There could have been up to seventeen different levels of self-government; fortunately this was not the case, but nonetheless there are important differences between some ACs and others.

All ACs that were eligible to do so assumed all the powers the constitution allowed them from the outset. Since then, these communities have formed a select group that has always stood out from other ACs for this reason. When it came to the other ACs, the majority political parties signed "Acuerdos Autonómicos" to avoid excessive disparity in 1981 (on the eve of the enactment of the statutes of autonomy, to ensure that the communities assumed similar areas of power) and in 1992 (with a view to ensuring a uniform extension of powers).[15]

Thus, between 1992 and 2005, two elements contributed to maintaining uniformity and keeping the differentiating effect of the principium dispositivium in check: firstly, the central state's need for a certain degree of uniformity to order its responsibilities and resources—the reason the majority political parties signed the accord of 1981 and 1992 (an objective element)—and, secondly, a spirit of emulation that has developed between ACs (subjective element) under which any extension of powers or differentiating feature secured by one AC is immediately claimed by the others.[16] By the middle of the last decade, therefore, while there were differences between "fast-track" and "slow-track" ACs, they were not as great as they might have been.

Between 2006 and 2007, however, a number of SAs were reformed, and the balance was broken. As a result, there are now very significant differences between some ACs and others. Moreover, these reforms have revealed profound deviations as to the conception of the model of state. They have also exposed the incapacity of the majority parties to act with a vision of statehood on this occasion and see beyond the most immediate partisan interests to reach a consensus on the basic elements of the reforms. These most recent reforms have shown that, from the perspective of the principium dispositivium, the path of reform of the SAs remains ever open. Constitutionally, the heterogeneity arising out of the principle is unlimited, and the result will depend on the agreements the political parties are capable of reaching.[17]

b) Secondly, for only a limited number of ACs, the constitution itself recognises certain distinguishing peculiarities, known as "differentiating features" [hechos diferenciales]. These are particular characteristics linked either to some given historical legal situation (the "historical rights" of the "territorios forales" [the Basque provinces and Navarra, which enjoyed certain historical jurisdictional privileges or "fueros"] or local civil law), geographical peculiarity (islands and their distance from the mainland), or cultural difference (language). Geographical and cultural differentiating features are objective and have sparked little debate, but the same cannot be said of the civil law of the "fueros" and, in particular, the historical rights of the "territorios forales". Above all, however,

---

[15] Most of the time, there has been an identifiable distinction between two groups of communities: on the one hand, the ACs with a greater degree of self-government (Catalonia, the Basque Country, Galicia, Navarra, Andalusia, Valencia, and the Canary Islands) and, on the other, the ten remaining communities (Asturias, Cantabria, La Rioja, Murcia, Aragon, Castile-La Mancha, Extremadura, the Balearic Islands, Madrid, and Castile and Leon).

[16] "Informe sobre modificaciones de la Constitución Española", in *El informe del Consejo de Estado sobre la reforma constitucional*, CEPC, Madrid, 2006, pp. 130–131.

[17] Tudela (2010), pp. 111–151.

there has been much discussion as to the consequences that have arisen out of these "differentiating" features, specifically the special fiscal powers of the Basque Country and Navarra.

With regard to these "differentiating features", the debate relates to both the number (with some commentators defending the existence of other additional features) and their consequences. In principle, it would be logical to assume that a "different feature" justifies a different treatment directly related to that feature: in the case of language, for example, specific powers and faculties for the promotion, protection and regulation of its use. However, others uphold a broader interpretation, maintaining that a recognition of differences should imply a separate status, a distinct area of political power, and a different relationship with the state.[18]

c) All of these debates highlight the ongoing tension that exists in the Spanish state, essentially between two models: one conceiving of the "autonomic state" as a means of organising territorial institutions of equal status and, therefore, with a system of multilateral relations amongst equals and another, which considers that the territorial institutions of the state are different to one another—given that some have elements of differentiation not possessed by the others—and that their status cannot therefore be the same; for this reason, it is argued, the basic type of relationship with the central state should be bilateral.[19] As a result, the tension between homogeneity and difference amongst the different communities has not abated and the debate on the "symmetric" or "asymmetric" nature of the Spanish autonomic model centres not so much on existing differences but on demands for establishing new ones.

The problem of the "asymmetry" of Spain's "autonomic state" is therefore that it is unclear where the limit of the heterogeneity lies. It is clear that the heterogeneity between the different communities cannot grow unchecked; it is also clear that a minimum degree of homogeneity is essential in order to keep them united within a single state. The problem lies in setting the boundaries to heterogeneity.

In principle, it seems clear that heterogeneity is delimited by the principle of equality. However, neither the literature nor the jurisprudence of the Constitutional Court offers a solid enough construction to allow this principle to be fully deployed. The Court, for example, has clearly stated that there is no constitutional grounds for the calls for equality between the ACs (STC 76/1983), while some legal authorities argue that the process of differentiation—not the differences themselves—could and should be maintained indefinitely provided it is balanced by the principle of solidarity.[20]

---

[18] Among other studies on this issue, see Aja (1999) and López Aguilar (1998); see also Blanco Valdés (2005).

[19] This view is expressed by Balaguer Callejón (1997), pp. 129–160.

[20] On the role of the principle of equality, asymmetry, and openness, see Solozábal Echevarría (2001), pp. 231–251.

## Openness, Complexity, and Asymmetry in a Comparative Perspective

As we noted at the beginning of this piece, each federal state has its own character and there is no single model of federalism; however, a comparative view of other experiences can provide a wider and more enriching perspective with which to assess the problems we are considering here.

From this perspective, we can see that any federal structure has flexibility clauses that give the system a certain openness.[21] Indeed, the territorial distribution of power has a dynamism that it is not found in vertical divisions of power. The result is that all federal states evolve and are transformed by the particular balance struck between centripetal and centrifugal forces. At a constitutional level, these changes may be accompanied by reforms to the constitution (examples are to be found in a number of federal states such as Italy, Mexico, and most particularly, Germany, which have undertaken major reforms in territorial matters). On other occasions, they take place without being reflected in the constitution (the clearest example is the USA, where federalism has evolved in different ways with no change to the constitution at any point).

Nonetheless, the degree of openness—and the de-constitutionalisation—of the Spanish model is unmatched in any other federal state.

A federal state must be backed by a written constitution that sets out the model of territorial organisation and reflects the fundamental decisions in this area. The constitution is the supreme legal standard. It acts as the framework within which the two orders of government of the federal structure will operate. Moreover, it has a symbolic value that is decisive in fostering the unity of the state. The constitutions of federal states may vary greatly in terms of the extent and detail of their regulation of territorial organisation, but they all define the form of state. After defining the model, different constitutions go on to regulate it in greater or lesser detail. In this regard, when it comes to deciding which matters are to be regulated in the constitution and which are to be left to ordinary laws, it is essential to determine which elements in that political community require symbolic recognition or the copper-fastened protection of the constitution.[22]

In a federal state, the role of the interpreter of the constitution is an essential one. However, when the constitutional design is deficient, it plays a superlative role; its interpretation can significantly change the form of territorial distribution of power, making the federation more or less centralised than was originally intended. This is especially true of the oldest and least detailed of constitutions, as is the case with the United States. The American Constitution defines the model of state, but its regulation is very short and does not provide for situations that would have been unimaginable over two centuries ago; as a result, the Supreme Court has at different

---

[21] Watts (2006), pp. 166–168.
[22] Anderson (2008), pp. 77–78.

times, lent its support to more or less centralising interpretations, and likewise, American legal authorities have constructed different theories and models of US federalism. Those same authorities have warned of the dangers arising out of the deficient constitutionalisation of the federal state: excessive room for manoeuvre, with the Supreme Court interpreting the constitution on the basis of varying models of federalism; a lack of transparency and certainty; and resulting problems of accountability, among others.

As for the *principium dispositivium*, examples can be found in which it is applied to specific questions; for example, the Canadian constitution entitles the provinces to choose whether to assume powers in developing and assuring certain rights, with the result that Quebec has assumed the corresponding powers while other provinces have not. Nonetheless, in no other federal state has the model been driven entirely by this principle, as it has in Spain.

Nor is the complexity derived from the "de-constitutionalisation" and the openness of the Spanish model reflected in other federal states. That said, a certain degree of complexity with regard to the distribution of powers is common. The constitution of any federal state contains provisions relating to the territorial distribution of power and the specific distribution of competences, although there are major differences as to the degree of precision, the system of allocation of powers, and the type of powers allocated at each territorial level. All states have their own debates on this issue and there is no simple formula to determine the most suitable way of distributing power between the different tiers of government.

As for the issue of heterogeneity and asymmetry, all federal states contain a certain degree of historical, social, economic, or cultural diversity. Indeed, the federal state is precisely the form of organisation designed to integrate communities with different features. In juridical terms, however, the general rule has been to assign the same powers to all territorial institutions making up the state, as we see in all the classical federations (the United States, Australia, Germany, Switzerland, etc.). The concept of "asymmetric federalism" has been forged over the last 50 years to refer to federal states in which the territorial institutions do not have the same position of self-government, as is the case in Canada, Spain, Belgium, Italy, Russia, and India. Canada has had an asymmetrical arrangement from its origins due to the linguistic, legal, and religious differences between Quebec and the rest of the country. Belgium has been organised asymmetrically into regions and linguistic communities. In Italy there are two types of region, those with an "ordinary statute" and those with a "special statute". Nevertheless, it is important to remember that asymmetric federations are a minority and that there are also significant differences between them, with Spain being one of the examples of greatest heterogeneity and asymmetry.

As to the reasons, asymmetries are classed as "transitory" if—as in the Spanish case—the constitution provides for different paces of access to self-government. Another issue is the "differentiating features" (language, ethnicity, religion, etc.) that require different powers to be assumed in this regard. This is the case in Switzerland, Belgium, Canada, and Spain in terms of language and in Canada and Spain with regard to differences in legal systems.[23] In all these cases, the asymmetry must be limited,[24] and in this regard, what marks Spain out from other federal states is the non-existence of limits to the heterogeneity arising out of the *principium dispositivium*.

All comparative studies of federalism recognise asymmetry as being the solution for integrating territories with significant differences between them, but it introduces a greater degree of complexity and a specific set of problems. Any state, including a federal one, is founded on a vocation to integrate and create unity; that objective is all the more challenging in federations in which there exists a greater diversity (of language, ethnicity, religion, etc.) and in which there are groups with different identities. The problem lies not in the diversity—which is in itself enriching—but in the way in which it is addressed, the way in which channels are sought to ensure that the model does not destroy itself. Here, comparative studies show that asymmetric federal states tend to host two different and more or less opposing positions: a majority position that considers that the state must be integrating and a minority position that demands more powers and more self-government. The best strategy for preventing the break-up of the state is to strike a balance between the two positions, to reconcile the maintenance of unity with accession to the main aspects of the territorial institutions' demands.

Here it is clear that the political and legal players, especially the political parties, have a decisive role to play in the design and operation and in the success or failure of a federation since they determine whether a federal structure develops in an integrating or disintegrating direction.[25] Because of this, the most recent comparative studies of federalism also warn of the ailments to which federal states are susceptible and the factors that contribute to creating tension and that can, in certain cases, lead to the break-up of the federation.[26] They include differences in language, cultural tradition, social structuring, and economic development, which can exacerbate division and resentment between territorial institutions and, at the same time, the action of the political players, who can contribute to moderating or accentuating the political conflict.

In the light of this analysis, and as the literature broadly accepts, we would be well advised to consider certain reforms of the Spanish "autonomic state". Without abandoning its openness and asymmetry, which are in effect essential characteristics of the model, it is high time we undertook a reform of the constitution: constitutionally defining our federal *state of autonomies*, enshrining the model we have already developed; removing all provisions regulating access to self-government that will not apply again in the future, polishing up any provisions that have proved ineffective, and adding some new and necessary ones; and setting the limits to openness and asymmetry, so that these aspects can be fully effective within a stable framework.

---

[23] Watts (2006), p. 179.

[24] Anderson (2008), pp. 77–78.

[25] Watts (2006), pp. 175–179, Burgess (2006), pp. 209–222.

[26] Watts (2006), pp. 234–244, Burgess (2006), pp. 269–281.

# References

C. Aguado, "El principio dispositivo y su virtualidad actual en relación con la estructura territorial del Estado", *REP*, *No*. 98, 1997.

E. Aja, *El Estado autonómico (Federalismo y hechos diferenciales)*, Madrid, 1999.

O. Alzaga, *Del consenso constituyente al conflicto permanente*, Madrid, 2011.

G. Anderson, *Una introducción al federalismo*, Madrid [Federalism, An Introduction. Oxford University Press, 2008].

F. Balaguer Callejón: "La constitucionalización del Estado autonómico", *Anuario de Derecho Constitucional y Parlamentario*, *No*. 9, 1997, pp. 129 to 160.

F. Balaguer Callejón: "Reformas constitucionales relativas al Título VIII" in *El informe del Consejo de Estado sobre la reforma constitucional*, CEPC, Madrid, 2006, p. 567.

R. L. Blanco Valdés, *Nacionalidades históricas y regiones sin historia*, 2005.

M. Burgess, *Comparative Federalism in Theory and Practice*, London, 2006, pp. 209 to 222.

J. Corcuera, "La distinción constitucional entre nacionalidades y regiones en el 15 aniversario de la Constitución", *Documentación administrativa*, *No*. 232–233, 1992–1993.

P. Cruz "La estructura del Estado o la curiosidad del jurista persa", *Revista de la Facultad de Derecho de la UCM, No. 4, 1982.*

G. Fernández Farreres, *La contribución del Tribunal Constitucional al Estado autonómico*, Madrid, 2005.

R. Fernández Riveira, *Una nueva etapa en la identificación de las bases*, Madrid, 2009.

E. Fossas, *El principio dispositivo en el Estado autonómico*, Madrid, 2007.

J. García Roca, "El principio de voluntariedad autonómica: teoría y realidad constitucionales", *REDC*, *No*. 23, 1988, p. 123.

J. Juan González Encinar, *El Estado unitario-federal*, Madrid, 1985, p. 88–89.

J. F. López Aguilar, *Estado autonómico y hechos diferenciales*, Madrid, 1998.

G. Ruiz-Rico Ruiz (Coord.), *La reforma de los Estatutos de Autonomía*, Jaen-Valencia, 2006.

J. J. Solozábal Echevarría, "Estado autonómico", in M. Aragón (Coord.), *Temas básicos de Derecho Constitucional II*, Madrid, 2001, pp. 231 to 251.

J. Tudela, "Heterogeneidad y asimetría en un Estado indefinido", in Tudela/Knüpling (eds.), *España y modelos de federalismo*, Madrid, 2010, pp. 111 to 151.

R. L. Watts, *Sistemas federales comparados*, Madrid, 2006 [Comparing Federal Systems. Institute of Intergovernmental Relations. 1999], pp. 166 to 168.

# Prevalence and Primacy: An Essay on Their Scope

Francisco J. Matia Portilla

## The Prevalence of the State

### Prevalence and the Spanish Autonomous Regions (Introduction)

One of the many paradoxes of the Spanish Constitution is that while it scarcely defines the Regional framework, it goes into detail regarding the limits of the sources of law. Following the widely known work by Professor Cruz Villalón (1981), it is interesting to note that in December 1978 there were few certainties about what territorial structure the Spanish State would finally adopt, both regarding the scope of the decentralisation and the degree of self-governance. These questions would only be answered 3 years later in the regional agreements.

Against this vagueness, the system of sources provided for in the Spanish Constitution established more sound foundations. Schematically, the Constitution is the supreme law within the Spanish legal system, as proved by its special rigidity and its supra-legal status. It is established by the Constitution and the Central State Law that the Autonomous Regions may assume those competences conferred on them by virtue of their Statutes of Regional Autonomy. It is therefore logical that the relationship between the State Law and territorial standards are ruled by the competence criterion since the first requirement for a standard to be valid is to have been issued under an own title.

Normative conflicts may, however, arise between a State standard and a regional one, both issued under sectoral agreements, if two of them regulate the same matter or legal relationship, regulate the same territory, and contain rule discrepancies (Santamaría 2009, p. 141). In order to solve those normative contradictions, the principle of prevalence establishes that State law takes preference over all others.

F.J. Matia Portilla (✉)
Facultad de Ciencias Sociales, Jurídicas y de la Comunicación, University of Valladolid, Palacio de Mansilla, c/ Trinidad 3, Campus of Segovia 40001 Segovia, Spain
e-mail: javierfacultad@gmail.com; javier@der.uva.es

A. López-Basaguren and L. Escajedo San Epifanio (eds.), *The Ways of Federalism in Western Countries and the Horizons of Territorial Autonomy in Spain*, Vol. 2, DOI 10.1007/978-3-642-27717-7_42, © Springer-Verlag Berlin Heidelberg 2013

This principle ensures, from a purely normative perspective, the supremacy of the State legal system over the regional one (García de Enterría and Fernández 1989, p. 355), linked to the general interest (Parejo 1981, p. 110). Regarding prevalence, it is especially interesting to look at its relationship with the principle of primacy of the Community Law over national law, an interrelation initially marked by the widely known Declaration of the Constitutional Court (DTC) 1/2004, which has been recently brought up again in the very interesting and questionable Constitutional Court Order of 9 June 2011, with the separate opinion of Senior Judge Pérez Tremps.

## Some Background on Prevalence with Special Reference to Federal States

The first references to the principle of prevalence, before the rise of the federal States model, dates back to the plurality of personal and territorial systems existing after the collapse of the Roman Empire. Then it adopted the opposite position (i.e., the local law took preference over the laws of the Reich; Otto 1981, p. 60), apart from the then unknown principle of competence (Lasagabaster 1991, p. 109).

It is, however, in the context of the rise of the Federal Republic of the United States of America that the principle of prevalence is developed. It was specifically provided for in Art. 6.2 of the 1787 Constitution and in other federal rules (particularly, in Art. 31 of the German Basic Law—and before, in Art. 2.1 and Art. 13 of the Constitution of the German Empire of 1871 and the Weimar Constitution) and implicitly in the Swiss legal system. This approach has not been included in the Austrian Constitution (Otto 1981, pp. 59–60). It was introduced in the Spanish Constitution of 1931, embracing the idea of the integral State.

## Doctrinal Debate

The nature, content, and scope of the prevalence clause has been the subject of a lively debate in the doctrine, where doubts regarding its appropriateness in our model of Autonomous Regions have been raised. It is worth noting, among other things, the contributions made with regard to this matter by Luciano Parejo, Ignacio de Otto, and Iñaki Lasagabaster.

Almost all these doctrinal orientations encapsulate an understanding of the Spanish territorial decentralisation model. While for some authors, it is similar to the federal approach (highlighting the competence transfer of Germany or the limited powers of the federal power in the United States); for others, it reminds them that the regional model is actually characterised by the contrary, i.e., by the introduction of general and full power for the regions. It is fair to note that the constitutional clause has been widely contested, among others, at federal state level. While some classic authors argue that it belongs (Schwartz or Maunz; Otto 1981, p. 60–); others advocate for its exclusion (Imboden; Von Mangoldt and Klein and, particularly, Schmitt and Kelsen) (*cfr*. Lasagabaster 1991, pp. 96 & ff.). Ignacio de Otto is especially belligerent in this regard and defends in a classic paper the point that the central power is of a general and complete nature while that of the regional administrations is competence-limited in character. He considers that the principle of prevalence "is designed to avoid the effect of combining the principle of specialty [of the regional law] and the principle of concentration of the constitutional jurisdiction" (p. 87). For this reason, "if the competent body considers that Regional legislation is null and void, there will be no obligation to apply it under the aforementioned principles. The State Law, i.e., the general law shall be applied instead, without prejudice that subsequently it may be proved that this conclusion was erroneous and that, therefore, the specialty rule should have been used and that the regional law should have been applied. Far from being forced to make an assumption, the prevalence rule states that if there is a doubt regarding the regional law it shall not be applied and that the general State law should apply instead" (Otto 1981, p. 87). In turn, Luciano Parejo defends the prevalence of the State law pursuant to Art. 149.1 of the Spanish Constitution (pp. 103–104), since he considers that it also works as a "competence rule" (ibidem, p. 110) and Gómez Ferrer (1987) links it with a theoretical *constitutional function* (pp. 33–36). Rubio Llorente (1993, p. 123) also calls for the non-application of the regional law. A totally opposite position is held by those who, according to Kelsen, argue that the principle of prevalence is pointless in a model based on the territorial distribution of powers. These professors highlight that "prevalence proves that the constitutional or contractual transfer of powers is useless, since in order to be meaningful it shall not be available at least against the will of one of the parties"(Arroyo 2007, p. 418).

Without going into the details of all those doctrinal approaches on prevalence, it is worth highlighting that due to the development of the Autonomous Regions, the principle of prevalence has been bypassed by the Spanish Constitutional Court and its eventual application, if any, has been unnoticed.

Regarding the first of the aforementioned questions, it should be noted that among us the feeling has grown that the Spanish Regional Framework sets the central and regional governments at the same level. Although the rationale argued by Ignacio de Otto is reasonable, it does not consider some of the facts that are worth bearing in mind. For instance, the fact that the Legislative Assembly of an Autonomous Region may withdraw a proposal to amend its Statute of Autonomy at any stage of the procedure encourages this pactism idea. The Spanish Constitutional Court has also provided greater support to this approach with some of the decisions adopted over the years. For instance, it has expressed that the national regulator is no longer permitted to regulate competences that have be transferred to all the Autonomous Regions; it has also stated that any conflict between State and Regional rules shall be solved through the exclusive application of the competence principle.

The prevalence clause can be useful where the State and Regional regulations are issued pursuant to their own and different competence agreements (Santamaría 2009, pp. 141–142). At this point, the Constitutional Case Law is particularly interesting regarding the relationship of the State legal foundations and the regional rules developing them. While for some authors these are concurrent jurisdictions and therefore the prevalence principle is applicable (García de Enterría and Tomás Ramón Fernández 1989, p. 356; Borrajo 2009, p. 2497; Alonso Más 2003, p. 345), some others argue that there is a functional delimitation (legal foundations on one hand and developing rules on the other hand), which involves an accountable constitutional division of competences making it unviable to apply the prevalence criterion (Otto 1987, p. 282).

The Spanish Constitutional Court has understood that regional rules contrary to the State foundation are unconstitutional [Constitutional Court Judgments (CCJ) 27/ 1987 and 151/1992] directly or indirectly in connection with the foundations (CCJ 60/1993, 166/2002 and 109/2003, among many others). Such unconstitutionality may also occur where regional legislation, although valid in its origin, is contrary due to amendments to the state foundation (CCJ 1/2003). Lasagabaster considers that, in that event, common courts could apply the fundamental provision (always provided that it has been defined as such by the national legislator or, in the case of regulations, when the national Law establishes its fundamental character) in detriment to the former regional standard but not if it was passed subsequently. To propose the correspondent unconstitutionality, appeal would be possible in the latter case (pp. 148–156). Santamaría Pastor goes further and considers that the Regional standard affected by new State foundations shall be considered derogated (p. 143).

It is, however, true that this understanding of the matter may be called into question. For instance, Constitutional Court Judgment 1/2003 was accompanied by a separate opinion where three Senior Judges considered that the prevalence clause was applicable (see also, from the doctrinal perspective, Borrajo 2009, p. 2497).

Regarding the second issue, and closely related to the relegation of the prevalence in the Constitutional case law as regards the competence principle (CCJ 69/ 1982, of 23 November, FJ 2.c), it has been taken into consideration by common courts resulting in a discretionary application that makes its analysis difficult. For this reason, it has been argued that its practical application is invisible (Borrajo 2009, p. 2496).

To this it must be added, obviously, that the powers of legal participants are very limited because, on the one hand, all of them (and, particularly, Courts and Tribunals) are subject to the rule of law and, on the other hand, because the Constitutional Court itself has stated that common courts cannot disregard regional standards with the force of law without proposing the corresponding unconstitutionality appeal before the Constitutional Court (CCJ 163/1195, of 8 November, which was noted before by Lasagabaster pp. 124 or 127, vid. Borrajo 2009, pp. 2498–2499). This places the competence principle again at the heart of the discussions, leaving out the efficiency of the prevalence principle.

## *Characteristics of Prevalence*

a) Regardless of what the word "principle" may suggest, prevalence is a legal rule establishing that State law takes precedence over regional laws. This idea on the Supplitary feature, expressed by Professor Biglino, is equally applicable to prevalence (Biglino 1997, p. 56).

b) In any case, this rule is applicable to a conflict between two valid standards, i.e., one that cannot be solved by applying the competence criterion because if the latter is used, "there is no room for prevalence, since the conflict is solved at a previous stage, that of the competence" (Arroyo 2007, p. 416; vid. Santamaría 2009, pp. 140–141). For this reason, prevalence only begins to be meaningful when it refers to competences, at least to shared competences, and being only as sufficient as this due to the lack of a material regulation in our constitutional model.

c) Prevalence is not hierarchy; instead, it operates among rules that may be at the same hierarchical level of different legal subsystems. Since "the non-existence of a hierarchical rule is explained by the political foundation of the system itself: no source of Law (except the Constitution itself) has the immanent competence vested by Law as the expression of the national will in a state of law" (Balaguer 2003, p. 201).

d) As a consequence of the above, the prevalence does not involve the nullification of any standard, nor does it involve the derogation of one of the standards by the other (Borrajo 2009, pp. 2495–2496). "The standard remains valid and in force, but only regulating instances different from those under the mandate of the prevalent standard" (Borrajo 2009, p. 2496). It is just a non-application of the rule to the specific situation.

e) Finally, prevalence is not exercised by neither the Spanish Constitutional Court (Alonso Más is in favour of establishing a procedure for a better understanding of these matters, esp. pp. 346–347) nor the legislator (be it the State or a Regional legislator—cf. CCJJ 76/1983, on the one hand, and 132/1989 and 331/2005, on the other).

## The Primacy of the European Union Law and Its Remoteness from the Constitutional Clause of Prevalence

It is common to refer to the primacy of the European Union Law (to the well-known CJEU Costa-Enel) in the academic studies on prevalence (Lasagabaster 1991, pp. 39–40, uses them as synonyms). In turn, Borrajo considers that both principles are similar, but he introduces two points: (a) the primacy of EU law is not expressly laid down by the Treaties; (b) the Spanish prevalence is limited (since it is not applicable to the exclusive competences of the Regions, as set forth in Art. 149.3 of the Spanish Constitution) (p. 2496).

Without questioning these assumptions, it is worth taking into consideration two additional pieces of data. The first one is that while the European Union (whose law is superior to the national laws of the Member States) is an international body with granted powers (and thus limited to these powers), it is not the same for the Spanish central State vis-à-vis the Regions. In our country, Autonomous Regions are the only territorial organisations with granted legislative competence. Another question is that, once competences have been granted, the central State is not entitled to regulate them anymore. It is nonetheless significant that both UE and the Regions were established with an enumeration of powers and that the power of the State to amend the Constitution is still exclusively linked to the Central Administration of the State.

The second idea to be added to the arguments by Professor Borrajo is that the primacy of the EU law over the national legislations is not absolute. All Constitutional Courts have retained jurisdiction, in more or less accurate but evident terms. Thus, for instance, Declaration of Constitutional Court (DCC 1/2004, of 13 December), goes as far as to state that "in a final instance, the conservation of the sovereignty of the Spanish people and the given supremacy of the Constitution could lead this Court to approach the problems which, in such a case, would arise"(FJ 4). Primacy yes, *ma non troppo*.

It is, however, true that that Declaration states a basis in favour of the primacy principle, admitting also that the constitutional text (namely, Art. 93 of the Spanish Constitution) may set forth "its own displacement or non-application" (FJ4). This statement is not noted here in order to reiterate the discrepancies brought to light in the past in this regard (Matia 2005, esp. pp. 345 & ff.) but because the Constitutional Court Order regarding the appeal for protection of fundamental rights 6922-2008, where three preliminary rulings were requested from the Luxembourg Court, examines this question in greater detail. For the purpose of this essay, this recent decision will be analysed only from the primacy perspective notwithstanding that, in a more general context, other complementary questions may be discussed (for instance, if it is possible to lodge a preliminary ruling on the specific wording of a standard that is not in force at the moment, its application is required).

From this perspective, we aim to analyse the relevant and worrying issue that a question is lodged before the European Union Court of Justice about whether a provision of secondary EU law should be interpreted such that it prevents authorities from submitting a European arrest warrant according to standards that the Spanish Constitutional Court has recognised as essential to guarantee the fundamental right of defence (Art. 24.2 CE). The Luxembourg Court is also requested to explain whether such a provision is compatible with the Charter of Fundamental Rights of the European Union. Finally, the third question refers to whether, if the EU law at issue is compatible with the Charter of Fundamental Rights of the European Union and pursuant to Art. 53 of the Charter, a Member State could limit the scope of a European arrest warrant to make it compatible with respect to the constitutional rights of the individual.

The conflict in question does refer not only to the legality of the secondary Community law (in a broader sense) concerning the primary law (particularly, the above-mentioned Charter, which has the same force as Treaties), but also to the binding influence that such a provision passed by the Council of the European Union may have on the fundamental rights originating from the constituent powers. From this narrow point of view summarising the Gordian knot of the Constitutional Court Order, the Order may be called into doubt for different reasons.

We shall start with the most obvious issues. Even in the event that it was admitted that the national Constitution could be partially displaced by an international treaty (and even more, admitting that such displacement is made by a secondary community law, although obviously international treaties are subject to the compliance with the Constitution), it is clear that fundamental rights could never be affected by such an effect. It is because the purpose of the Constitution (as the most complete form of constitutionalism) is to guarantee the freedom that it is inadmissible to assume that Community law (primary and secondary) consents to the violation of (or the suspension of the binding force) fundamental rights. This is precisely the message contained in the Judgments with regard to this matter of the main European Constitutional Courts (also of the Spanish Constitutional Court, CCJ 64/1991). Apart from diverging from those who argue the case for the Constitutional Court requesting preliminary rulings before the European Union Court of Justice (Alonso 2003) since—strictly speaking—they are neither judges nor applicants of secondary Community Law, it seems therefore that, in any case, that direction should not be followed when fundamental rights are at stake.

If the supreme Community jurisdiction were to understand, as the higher Community law interprets, that the provision under discussion respects the Nice Charter, it would put the Spanish Constitutional Court in a delicate position. It is unlikely that special regimes based on the equality and on the good faith of the State can be consented to in a system such as the European arrest warrant. That would force the Constitutional Court to either abandon the case law of previous decisions (JCC 91/ 2000, 134/2000, 162/2000, 156/2002, and 183/2004) where constitutional law is interpreted and instead accept an intergovernmental decision that was adopted within the European Union, which would be a surprising action to undertake, or to rebel against EU jurisdiction (if the Luxembourg Court were to dismiss State requests on fundamental rights). It is worrying to consider any of these possibilities. From the strictly strategic perspective, the preliminary ruling is risky, apart from being dogmatically unfortunate. If it is the Court's will to be coherent with its previous case law, it would be closer to rebellion than to understanding since in the above-mentioned 2004 Declaration it is stated expressly that "it is clear that the Charter is conceived, in whatsoever case, as a guarantee of minimums on which the content of each right and freedom may be developed up to the density of content assured in each case by internal legislation", and if the option chosen was to forget this assumption and to be submitted to community jurisdiction, it would not be impossible that the European Court of Human Rights inform our Constitutional Court, which would not be positive either.

Those who agree with the arguments made so far are also likely to endorse the view that perhaps the Constitutional Court should have explored other approaches. One of them, suggested by Senior Judge Pérez Tremps, is to give serious consideration if constitutionally relevant defencelessness may occur by virtue of a judgment by default when there is evidence that the defendant was duly summoned and he freely decided not to show and that he also had the opportunity to be represented by an attorney for the protection of his interests (section 6 of the separate opinion attached to the Order). This line of argument (incidentally linked to the Strasbourg Court's case law and not to the European Union Charter) makes it unnecessary, in accordance with the opinion of the dissenting Senior Judge, to resort to the preliminary ruling in this case. Moreover, the Court could have questioned if the publication of a new European catalogue of human rights, undoubtedly relevant for establishing the constitutional content of the fundamental rights, requires (or consents) reading in an innovative way the fundamental rights that have also been enshrined in the Charter.

Back to the aim of the present essay and to conclude, it must be made clear that the primacy of the Community law and the constitutional prevalence clause can hardly be compared. While the subsystems of the Central State and of the Regions are linked to a Constitution that is superior, European Treaties establish international bodies, the masters of which are still the sovereign Member States and, this is what is relevant to this article, the founding of rules that should be adopted in accordance, both procedural and substantive, with the different national Constitutions.

## Some Points by Way of Conclusion

It has been highlighted above that there are some major differences between the principle of prevalence of the State law over the regional law and the principle of primacy of the Community Law over national laws of Member States. Due to these differences, it is recommended that a thorough and separate analysis of them is carried out. This first conclusion is not surprising since the best doctrine has repeatedly pointed out that the principle of prevalence has specific connotations in each of the legal systems where it is present (Lasagabaster 1991, p. 100). It has also been highlighted that the Spanish Constitution remains important in our legal order, as a consequence of its constituent powers and as a supra-legal law and guaranteed through the nomophylactic control of the legislation enacted by any constituent power.

It would be unfair to conclude without mentioning that both the European and Regional integration processes share another common feature. Both are open processes and, for this reason, unstable.

At a national level, this instability was recently proved when the Constitutional Court (CCJ 31/2010) did not authorise the amended Statute of Autonomy of Catalonia, provoking political and doctrinal reactions. The European Union has not been immune to tensions due to the lack of definition of the chosen international model (which over the years, it is fair to note, has been allowed to reach a profound level of social integration, as well as political and strategic interdependence).

Some of the decisions from the national Constitutional Courts illustrate this (being the most recent the German declaration on the Lisbon Treaty), which, far from holding a debate with the Luxembourg Court, establish the constitutional limits that condition the development of the European Union.

It is clear that the future of both processes for the territorial integration of powers would depend on the political decisions to be adopted. It is also clear that the option adopted in relation to any of these integration processes will have an impact in the other one. Thus, for example, if the European Member States would follow today the path of the United States of America, forming a European State, the role of the Autonomous Regions in our country or the Länder in Germany would lose importance.

It would be risky to speak about the future of the European Union, but it would not be so risky to talk about the possible development of our present Autonomous Regions since their creation was very different from that of federal states in other countries. It is widely known, for example, that the American federalism has traditionally been considered as a second degree or territorial separation of powers, which overlaps with the horizontal or functional one (Ballbé and Martínez 2003, p. 26). However, as it is commonly understood that, from such horizontal perspective, the political system should be based on the Parliament because it represents the minority (its existence and respect is the essence of democracy, cfr. Kelsen 2006, pp. 154–155), it is commonly argued that the central State shall retain some political supremacy over the institutions with territorial decentralisation.

This fact that in no way questions the independency between central and regional institutions, and the fact that they are at the same hierarchical level is also applicable to our constitutional system. Some examples are the principles of indissoluble unity and solidarity (Art. 2 Spanish Constitution), being the latter ontologically weighted and required by the central State, and the subordination of the entire wealth of the country to the general interest (Art. 128.1 Spanish Constitution), to the states of emergency (Art. 116 Spanish Constitution), and particularly, in the context of the present essay, in the eventual substitution of the regional powers by central state authorities (Art. 155 Spanish Constitution).

It could be argued that the supremacy is not recognised in the law, pursuing the idea that the Statutes of Autonomy are pursuant to the agreement between the State and the Regions, a theory that has been given further impetus after the Resolution by the Presidency of the Spanish Parliament (Congreso de los Diputados), 16 March 1993, on the procedure to be followed when reforming the Statutes of Autonomy which allows the proposing Legislative Assembly to withdraw its proposal at any stage of the procedure. Indeed, the consensus between the central State and the Autonomous Region will be necessary. It should be noted, at least from a de facto perspective, that this is an agreement between territories.

Since this is certainly true, it should be pointed out that the constitutional review that can (and must) close the door on the Spanish regional model, whatever the adopted political direction is, does not require the involvement of the Autonomous Regions (Groppi 2002, p. 10). By reviewing the Constitution, any decision in this regard could be adopted (ranging from a centralized State model to a Federal State).

It could be argued, however, that Autonomous Regions would also take part in that process through the Spanish Senate since it is the House of territorial representation (Art. 69.1 Spanish Constitution), but this is nothing but an unrealizable notion at the time of writing this article.

The supremacy of the central State is not only a provision of a theoretical model but a consequence of the way we have achieved the territorial decentralisation moving away from a centralised State. Although there is no doubt that the experiment launched by the Constitution has been very positive, this may be a good time to reconsider the model, in whatever manner, and end the process providing it with a stability that is both appropriate and necessary.

# References

Alonso García, Ricardo: *El juez español y el derecho comunitario: jurisdicciones constitucional y ordinaria frente a su primacía y eficacia.* Consejo General del Poder Judicial. Madrid, 2003.

Alonso Más, Mª José: "La prevalencia del Derecho del Estado y la inaplicación judicial de las leyes autonómicas: el caso de las cesiones de aprovechamiento en suelo urbano". *Revista de Administración Pública* 161 (2003).

Arroyo Gil, Antonio: "Los principios de competencia y prevalencia en la resolución de los conflictos competenciales: una relación imposible". *Revista Española de Derecho Constitucional* 80 (2007).

Balaguer Callejón, Francisco: "Fuentes del Derecho, espacios constitucionales y ordenamientos jurídicos". *Revista Española de Derecho Constitucional* 69 (2003).

Ballbé, Manuel y Martínez, Roser: *Soberanía dual y Constitución integradora.* Ariel. Barcelona, 2003.

Biglino Campos, Paloma: "La cláusula de supletoriedad: una cuestión de perspectiva". *Revista Española de Derecho Constitucional* 50 (1997).

Borrajo Iniesta, Ignacio: "El orden constitucional de competencias y ordenamientos (art. 149.3 CE)". En Casas Baamonde, María Emilia y Rodríguez-Piñero Bravo-Ferrer, Miguel (dirs.); Borrajo Iniesta, Ignacio y Pérez Manzano, Mercedes (coords.): *Comentarios a la Constitución española (XXX aniversario).* Fundación Wolters Kluwer. Toledo, 2009.

Cruz Villalón, Pedro: "La estructura del Estado o la curiosidad del jurista persa" (1981). Incluido en *La curiosidad del jurista persa y otros estudios sobre la Constitución.* 2ª ed. Centro de Estudios Políticos y Constitucionales. Madrid, 2006.

García de Enterría, Eduardo y Fernández, Tomás-Ramón: *Curso de Derecho Administrativo I.* 5ªed. Civitas. Madrid, 1989.

Gómez-Ferrer Morant, Rafael: "Relaciones entre leyes: competencia, jerarquía y función constitucional". *Revista de Administración Pública* 113 (1987).

Groppi, Tania: "La reforma constitucional en los Estados federales: entre pluralismo territorial y no territorial". Ponencia presentada en el VII Congreso iberoamericano de derecho constitucional, México, 12–15 de febrero de 2002. Consultado el 23 de julio de 2011 en *http://www.unisi.it/ricerca/dip/dir_eco/COMPARATO/pub.html.*

Kelsen, Hans: *Esencia y valor de la democracia.* KRK. Oviedo, 2006.

Lasagabaster Herrarte, Iñaki: *Los principios de supletoriedad y prevalencia del Derecho estatal respecto al Derecho autonómico.* Civitas. Madrid, 1991.

Matia Portilla, Francisco Javier: "Dos constituciones y un solo control: El lugar constitucional del Estado español en la Unión Europea". *Revista Española de Derecho Constitucional* 74 (2005).

Otto y Pardo, Ignacio de: "La prevalencia del Derecho estatal sobre el Derecho regional". *Revista Española de Derecho Constitucional* 2 (1981).

Otto y Pardo, Ignacio de: *Derecho constitucional. Sistema de fuentes.* Ariel. Barcelona, 1987.

Parejo, Luciano: *La prevalencia del Derecho estatal sobre el regional.* Centro de Estudios Constitucionales. Madrid, 1981.

Rubio Llorente, Francisco: "El bloque de la constitucionalidad", incluido ahora en *La forma del poder (estudios sobre la Constitución).* Centro de Estudios Constitucionales. Madrid, 1993.

Santamaría Pastor, Juan Alfonso: *Principios de Derecho administrativo general I.* 2ª ed. Iustel. Madrid, 2009.

# The Primacy Clause in the Spanish Constitution: A Contribution to the Debate

Josu de Miguel Bárcena

## Introduction

Article 149.3 of the Spanish Constitution contains a clause establishing the primacy of State law over regional law. Over the past 30 years, both in theory and in the case law of the Constitutional Court (hereinafter: CC), the validity of this clause has been discussed, basically because the application of this principle is better suited to a composite federal State than to a decentralized regional State such as Spain.

Professor Ignacio de Otto was the first to grasp the problematic character of the primacy clause within the Spanish constitutional order.[1] In truly federal systems, that is, where the State is the aggregate sum of its parts, the general competences of the Federation are limited to specific matters. As a result, any rules created outside this general competential framework are void. The way to allow the general legal order to coexist with the particular legal orders is by materially limiting the former to the areas established in the competential system. The Federation's legislative power is thus materially limited, which allows for all excluded matters to be regulated by the particular legal systems of the States.

However, constructing a general legal order out of particular ones, as is the case of, for instance, the United States, Germany, or the European Union, implies the existence of concurring or parallel competences, which are applied to the same subject matter on two different territorial levels. In this context, the primacy clause acquires its full meaning, for faced with a conflict between rules, the Constitution (e.g. art. 72 of the German Basic Law) chooses to attribute a higher value to federal law.

---

[1] Otto y Pardo (1981).

J. de Miguel Bárcena (✉)
Facultad de Derecho, Universidad Autónoma de Barcelona, Edifici B. Campus de la UAB, 08193 Bellaterra (Cerdanyola del Vallès), Spain
e-mail: jesusmaria.demiguel@uab.cat

A. López-Basaguren and L. Escajedo San Epifanio (eds.), *The Ways of Federalism in Western Countries and the Horizons of Territorial Autonomy in Spain*, Vol. 2, DOI 10.1007/978-3-642-27717-7_43, © Springer-Verlag Berlin Heidelberg 2013

The Spanish case is different. Not only because formally there exist few concurring competence[2] but also because, as a regional (autonomic) State, the overlap of competential systems is resolved using a different technique. Theoretically, the legislative competence of the State has no limits; it has a general competence. The only existing limits appear during the application of these rules: in those cases where the Autonomous Community is competent, the valid State rule retains a residual force. This follows from art. 149.3 of the Spanish Constitution, which establishes that State law shall, in any case, act as suppletory law to the law of the Autonomous Communities. The rule of suppletion therefore means that, when State law addresses matters that are competence of an Autonomous Community, it will not be void as in federal law, but its application will be suppletory, i.e., valid but of reduced force in cases where valid autonomic law exists. Even though this is a case of inverse concurrence,[3] the primacy clause proves difficult to apply because the State should not be colonizing legal areas pertaining to its own competence and because the Spanish legal order is a system in which shared competences predominate.

The Spanish autonomic State, however, has gradually advanced towards a federal system due to the work of the Constitutional Court. The Court has constructed a decentralized legal system by using almost exclusively the principle of competence.[4] Since the 1990s, the CC progressively changed the relations between the State and the Autonomous Communities, rendering inoperative the suppletory clause provided in the Constitution. To some authors, this meant that the Regions were faced with the responsibility of choosing to regulate the matters attributed to them by the Constitution or abstain from doing so, according to their political criteria and the shared or exclusive nature of the competences in question.[5] To others, the disappearance of the general character of the state legal order led to the creation of normative gaps conducive to a minimal intervention by the State, leaving in a precarious state the shared competences that required the Communities to complement the State's framework laws.[6]

The debate on the primacy clause was concluded by judgments 76/1983 and 77/1984 of the Constitutional Court. Until then, theory had considered the primacy rule as a clause attributing competences.[7] However, as a result of the

---

[2] Fernández Farreres (2005), p. 433.

[3] Ignacio de Otto states that "it is obvious that, strictly speaking, all competences are concurring or, put differently, that when a competence is attributed to an Autonomous Community, it is attributed in concurrence with the subsisting competence of the State, which is the reason why in our legal system the rules of collision are not rules to applied in exceptional cases only, but generally applicable rules, as each and every rule of the Autonomous Community, even those that are adopted within its strictest competence, enters into conflict with a state rule", Otto y Pardo (1981), p. 80, *op. cit.*

[4] Biglino Campos (2007).

[5] Balaguer Callejón (1998), p. 305.

[6] Tajadura Tejada (2000a).

[7] Parejo Alfonso (1981), p. 113 ff.

new interpretation of the suppletory clause and the increasingly broad use of the principle of political autonomy by the Regions, proposals are made to reconsider the possibility of finding mechanisms to avoid the fragmentation of the legal order, a fragmentation that has only continued to increase due to the successive reforms of the Autonomic Statutes over the past decade.[8] This has lead to a renewed debate on the primacy clause of art. 149.3 of the Spanish Constitution.

## The Spanish Territorial Organization: Competence and Primacy

In Spain, both theory and the case law of the Constitutional Court have maintained that the relations between the state legal order and the regional ones are essentially based on the principle of competence. Consequently, there is no possibility of applying the rule of art. 149.3 CE establishing the primacy of state law. In this respect, the most radical thesis is upheld by Arroyo Gil, who in various works has asserted that the logic of the federal constitution (among which he includes the Spanish Constitution) suggests that all competences are, by definition, exclusive: Competences are considered concurring or shared by virtue of the subject matter they regulate; the scope of the legislative or executive power is, however, always exclusive. In this situation of perfect competential distribution, the primacy clause proves ineffectual since the State, whenever it wants to impose its law, will have to show the higher value of its law as defined by the general interest it represents.[9] As Kelsen showed, the primacy clause goes completely against the idea of the federal constitution, which guarantees the principle of political autonomy and should therefore be rejected as an instrument to integrate a decentralized legal order.[10]

In essence, we agree with Arroyo Gil's theory. Nonetheless, as he himself recognizes, competential distribution criteria are necessarily heterogeneous, so that they do not always coincide. Of course when competences concur due to new framework laws adopted by the State based on art. 149.1 of the Spanish Constitution, state law has precedence without the need to render null the regional rules of implementation. A different case is the collision of rules that might result from the concrete application of state framework laws. The rule on the primacy of state law could also be effectively applied in cases where the State is required to harmonize the legal order within the framework of principles established by the State (art. 150.1 CE).[11] Finally, it is commonly accepted that the competence regarding culture, as recognized explicitly in art. 149.2 CE, and the derived competence to guarantee the use of the Castilian language in the entire Spanish

---

[8] Sosa Wagner (2011).

[9] Arroyo Gil (2007, 2009).

[10] As recalled by Otto y Pardo (1981), p. 60, op. cit.

[11] Cantero Rodríguez (1996), p. 132 ff.

territory, are matters regarded as concurring competences. As a result, the rule on the primacy of state law should be applied to these competences.[12]

Are there more situations to be found where the principle of competence does not offer a solution to normative conflicts and the primacy clause must be used? The Spanish Constitution does not contain any explicit competential titles that attribute the regulation of a specific matter on equal terms to the State and the Regions (concurring competences). Only if we were to consider the Constitution as a normative body integrated into the multilevel European Constitution and its distribution of powers,[13] this possibility might be accepted: After all, art. 2.2 of the Treaty on the Functioning of the European Union provides that "When the Treaties confer on the Union a competence shared with the Member States in a specific area, the Union and the Member States may legislate and adopt legally binding acts in that area. The Member States shall exercise their competence to the extent that the Union has not exercised its competence." Consequently, an analysis is required of the different interactions that occur between state law and regional law on a national level, based on the competential typologies that can be found in the Spanish Constitution.

# The Scope of Application of the Primacy Clause in the Spanish Legal Order

As we just pointed out, the rules on exclusive competence do not exclude the possible concurrence of rules emanating from different territorial levels.

## *Collisions Produced by the State and Regions Exercising Different Material Competences on the Same Territorial Level*

The Spanish Constitution foresees the coexistence of competential titles exercised within the same geographical area. It is exactly this possible concurrence of competential titles with regard to the same space that requires methods of cooperation to be found, which allow for their effective application in each concrete case.[14] In principle, these methods should allow for the optimal exercise of state and regional competences, bearing in mind, though, that conflicts still may arise, which cannot be resolved through cooperation and which therefore need to be

---

[12] López Castillo and Tajadura Tejada (2011), pp. 9–24.

[13] Pernice (1999).

[14] On cooperation within the autonomic State, see Tajadura Tejada (2000b).

resolved using the principle of primacy.[15] As none of the territorial bodies exceeds its competences, the collision becomes a matter of interests, requiring a decision on which interest should come first, the general interest or the broadest interest, in order to declare it prevalent or preferential. Without doubt, in an autonomic State the principle of unity acts as a force that can be used in favor of the prevalence of the general interest (which is guaranteed by the State) every time territorial interests exceed their material or functional limits.

Theory has shown that, however complex reality may be, from a strictly legal point of view there cannot be two territorial bodies having the same competence over the same subject matter. For this reason, a competential delimitation is required by the Constitutional Court without resorting to the primacy clause since these situations do not represent a collision between rules but the excessive use by a body of its competences on one of the territorial levels.[16]

Nevertheless, the Constitutional Court has declared that the State cannot be impeded from exercising its exclusive competences by the existence of an auto- nomic competence, even though exclusive. The reason for this is that there exists a general interest that prevails over the fragmented interests that other affected territorial bodies might have (CC Judgment 40/1998, ground nº 3). In this way, the primacy clause can help to establish which rule is applicable when several political levels have validly exercised their competences. Establishing the applicable rule in this way can, in our opinion, be done by any judge or court, even though the Constitutional Court has observed that the State must use this method in a legiti- mate way (CC Judgment 65/1998). This solution means accepting that the exercise of competences by the Regions may be affected by the exercise of its material competences by the State.[17] This method can therefore be applied, although the Constitutional Court normally resorts to the principle of competence to resolve normative conflicts, establishing wherever possible whether at one of the levels competences have been exceeded.

## Shared Competences and the Principle of Primacy

As indicated, the primacy rule laid down in art. 149.3 CE is only applicable in case of collision between valid rules. However, when the State, pursuant to art. 149.1 CE, modifies the basic legislation, this may retroactively render regional rules invalid, as these find the origin of their validity in the basic state legislation. This, though, from a practical point of view constitutes a fundamental problem for institutional actors who have to apply the law: They either have to wait for the

---

[15] For instance, in the case of the Natural Reserves Protection Act, the Highway Act, as well as the Water Act and the Coastal Act; in this respect, see Peñarrubia Iza (1999).

[16] Fernández Farreres (1991), p. 545; and Biglino (2005), pp. 194 and 195.

[17] García De Enterría and Fernández (1999), p. 351 ff.

Autonomous Communities to adopt new rules implementing the basic state legislation or, where possible, submit a question to the Constitutional Court regarding the possibly conflicting rules (or competences).

In order to avoid this, an important part of theory has proposed to apply the clause on the primacy of state law to resolve potential conflicts between basic state rules and autonomic rules of implementation.[18] Moreover, Judges Jiménez de Parga, Delgado Barrio, and Rodríguez-Zapata have defended, in a dissenting opinion to CC Judgment 1/2003, that "collisions between autonomic laws and basic state laws modified after the first were approved, can and must be resolved immediately [...] through implementation of the basic state rule". It is necessary to understand that the basic legislation of the State is not static but dynamic and is constantly modified depending on the different policies that the state legislator may legitimately choose to adopt at various points in time.[19] Therefore it can be maintained that subsequent modifications of basic state legislation can displace incompatible autonomic rules without declaring them unconstitutional or void, which would allow for a rational and prompt application of an increasingly complex legal system.

Thus, considering that the determination of the scope of each regional competence depends, to a large extent, on the ordinary state legislation,[20] nothing would prevent ordinary judges and courts from assuming the power to directly resolve the collisions that occur between autonomic rules, at one time validly adopted, and subsequent state laws modifying the basic legislation in a specific area. This approach, however, presents serious problems.

The most important problem, of which the Constitutional Court itself reminds us in Judgment 1/2003, is that the principle of primacy can only be applied in case of collision between valid rules; however, when the State modifies the basic legislation, this invalidates the autonomic rule as a result of the competential delimitation produced by the new basic rule. We are therefore not faced with a conflict between applicable rules but of competences, which necessarily must be resolved by the Constitutional Court, which is the indicated organ to decide whether the State has exceeded itself in the exercise of its competences or whether regional law has become unconstitutional due to the revision of framework legislation by the State.[21] This obviously does not exclude the possibility of seeking provisional formulas of correctly applying the law at stake, as well as the Constitution itself.[22]

---

[18] Solozábal Echevarría (1998), p. 167; Jiménez Campo (1989); and Borrajo Iniesta (2009), p. 2498 ff.

[19] García Morillo (1996).

[20] Quadra-Salcedo Janini (2006).

[21] Constitutional Court Judgment 163/1995. Albertí Rovira (1991), pp. 311–344.

[22] Tornos Mas (1991), where he vindicates that the primacy clause should be applied provisionally to state law until the Constitutional Court decides which law is to be applied by virtue of the principle of competence.

## *The Primacy Clause and the Horizontal Competences of the State*

The latest contribution to the debate about the primacy clause in the Spanish constitutional system was made by De la Quadra-Salcedo Janini.[23] This author points out that the Spanish Constitution of 1978, just like other federal constitutional systems, contains competential titles that are based on objectives rather than on subject matters.[24] Art. 149.1.1 CE, for instance, reserves to the State the regulation of the basic conditions guaranteeing the equality of Spanish citizens in the exercise of their rights; art. 149.1.13 CE reserves to the State the basic legislation and general coordination of economic activity. These competences are expressed by the adoption of state measures, which might condition the various areas or matters regulated by the Regions by virtue of their own material competences.

In other words, we are faced with a kind of "concurring competences". After all, in this last model, collisions may occur between rules adopted pursuant to different competences derived from objectives (State) and others based on subject matter (Autonomous Communities). In this case, the conflict between two rules adopted through the exercise of different, non-material, competences cannot be resolved exclusively by applying the principle of attribution, considering that the Autonomous Community may in the exercise of its competence adopt a certain rule, while the State may, in the exercise of its own competence, adopt a rule that might enter into conflict with the autonomic rule. As this normative conflict, in terms of competence, occurs between legitimate rules, it may be resolved using the same conflict resolution principle that is used in the case of concurring competences: the clause on the primacy of state law over regional law.[25]

Until now, however, constitutional practice does not follow this interpretation. According to the Constitutional Court (Judgments 54/2002 and 135/2006), collisions that are produced by the State exercising the horizontal competences of articles 149.1.1 and 149.1.13 CE constitute a competential issue to be resolved, just as in the case of shared competences, by declaring the autonomic rule void, thus not allowing for ordinary judges and courts to apply the primacy principle by declaring ineffective the autonomic law. We concur with De la Quadra-Salcedo Janini in that it would have been more correct if the Constitutional Court had defined the problem in terms of the concurrence of rules, which might be resolved through the application of art. 149.3 CE. This can rightly be argued because, as the author indicates,[26] when the State regulates the basic conditions that guarantee the equal exercise of rights or the general coordination of economic activity, the truth is it does not limit

---

[23] Quadra-Salcedo Janini (2009).

[24] As examples of horizontal competences, he mentions the United States' commerce clause and the power of the EU to achieve the establishment of the internal market as recognized by Art. 114 TFEU.

[25] Quadra-Salcedo Janini (2009), p. 232, op. cit.

[26] Quadra-Salcedo Janini (2009), p. 236, op. cit.

itself to delimiting the scope of material regional competences. On the contrary, an overlap occurs between regulations derived from competences that pertain, in a way exclusively, to each level.[27]

Based on the preceding arguments, ordinary judges and courts, who are responsible for establishing the law applicable to each case, could apply the primacy principle to resolve conflicts between state and regional rules. Nonetheless, in our view, this option has its limitations: Art. 149.3 CE states clearly that state law will prevail in all matters that are not the *exclusive* competence of the Regions.[28] In these cases, two interpretations are possible: on the one hand, to apply the text of art. 149.3 CE literally and therefore let autonomic rules prevail when they have been adopted pursuant to an exclusive regional competence. This interpretation has the drawback that the State may have adopted the law based on a legitimate title. Furthermore, due to an ever more complex social reality, it is difficult to clearly define "exclusive competences", even more so when horizontal titles enter into play. On the other hand, the second interpretation would allow ordinary judges and courts to submit questions to the Constitutional Court, an option for which probably a new constitutional procedure would have to be created based on art. 161.1 d) CE. After all, the constitutional jurisdiction's purpose fundamentally is to establish the validity of rules, and in this case, when referring to primacy, the question to be decided is the applicability of rules, which corresponds to the ordinary jurisdiction, just as in EU law.

## Conclusions

The aim of this article has been to provide a brief analysis of the theoretical debate on the primacy clause in Spanish constitutional law, to which we have tried to make a small contribution. The analysis shows that there is no consensus in theory or in case law regarding the competential cases in which the principle of the primacy of state law over regional law can be applied. An additional effort is therefore required to identify these cases, especially since the Constitutional Court deprived the suppletion of autonomic law by state law of its constitutional value. The Spanish territorial legal system has become particularly complex due to the increasing normative weight of regional law and the frequent use by the State of horizontal competential titles in order to solve problems related to the implementation of EU law and what has come to be called "crisis law".[29] From this point of view, the present article calls for a greater use of the primacy clause by ordinary legal actors responsible for the application of the law.

---

[27] Thus, the autonomous decision-making scope of the Regions would only be affected in case the State was to effectively exercise horizontal competences (practical concurrence). See Quadra-Salcedo Janini (2009), p. 232, op. cit.

[28] As shown by Alonso Mas (2003), p. 344.

[29] Embid Irujo (2009).

# References

ALBERTÍ ROVIRA, E.: "La noción de "bases" y el derecho estatutario", VV.AA.: Estudios sobre el Estatuto de Autonomía del País Vasco, Vol. II, IVAP, Oñate, 1991, pp. 311–344.

ALONSO MAS, M.J.: "La prevalencia del derecho del Estado y la inaplicación judicial de las leyes autonómicas: el caso de las cesiones de aprovechamiento en suelo urbano", Revista de Administración Pública, n° 161, 2003, p. 344.

ARROYO GIL, A.: "Los principios de competencia y prevalencia en la resolución de los conflictos competenciales. Una relación imposible", Revista Española de Derecho Constitucional, n° 80, 2007.

ARROYO GIL, A.: "Competencia versus prevalencia en los Estados territorialmente descentralizados, con especial referencia al Estado autonómico español", Revista Jurídica de la Universidad Autónoma de Madrid, n° 20, 2009.

BALAGUER CALLEJÓN, F.: "Las relaciones entre el ordenamiento estatal y los ordenamientos autonómicos. Una reflexión a la luz de la regla de supletoriedad", Revista de Derecho Político, n° 44, 1998, p. 305.

BIGLINO, P.: "El poder de la Unión y el poder de los Estados miembros en el Proyecto de Constitución: una forma distinta de entender la competencia", VV.AA.: Coloquio Ibérico: Constituçào Europeia. Homenagem ao Doutor Francisco Lucas Pires, Coimbra editora, Coimbra, 2005, pp. 194 and 195.

BIGLINO CAMPOS, P.: Federalismo de integración y de devolución: el debate sobre la competencia, CEPC, Madrid, 2007.

BORRAJO INIESTA, I. "Artículo 149.3 CE. El orden constitucional de competencias i ordenamientos", in: CASAS BAAMONDE, M.E. and RODRÍGUEZ-PIÑERO and BRAVO-FERRER, M. (ed.): Comentarios a la Constitución española, Wolters Kluwer, Madrid, 2009, p. 2498 ff.

CANTERO RODRÍGUEZ, J.: "Nuevas reflexiones sobre la cláusula de prevalencia", Revista de Estudios de la Administración Local y Autonómica, n° 269, 1996, p. 132 ff.

EMBID IRUJO, A.: El Derecho de la crisis económica, Zaragoza University, Zaragoza, 2009.

FERNÁNDEZ FARRERES, G.: "Colisiones normativas y primacía del derecho estatal", VV.AA.: Estudios sobre la Constitución española. Homenaje al Profesor García de Enterría, Vol. I, Civitas, Madrid, 1991, p. 545.

FERNÁNDEZ FARRERES, G.: La contribución del Tribunal Constitucional al Estado Autonómico, Iustel, Madrid, 2005, p. 433.

GARCÍA DE ENTERRÍA, E. and FERNÁNDEZ, T.R.: Curso de Derecho Administrativo, Civitas, Madrid, 1999, p. 351 ff.

GARCÍA MORILLO, J.: "La versatilidad de lo básico", Revista de Administración Pública, n° 139, 1996.

JIMÉNEZ CAMPO, J.: "Qué es lo básico? Legislación compartida en el Estado autonómico", Revista Española de Derecho Constitucional, n° 27, 1989.

LÓPEZ CASTILLO, A. y TAJADURA TEJADA, J.: "El Estado Autonómico en la encrucijada", Revista de Estudios Políticos, n° 151, 2011, pp. 9–24.

OTTO y PARDO, I.: "La prevalencia del derecho estatal sobre el regional", Revista Española de Derecho Constitucional, n° 2, 1981.

PAREJO ALFONSO, L.: La prevalencia del Derecho del Estado, Centro de Estudios Constitucionales, Madrid, 1981, p. 113 ff.

PEÑARRUBIA IZA, J.Mª.: "Preferencia, coordinación y prevalencia en el ejercicio de competencias concurrentes", Revista de Administración Públicas, n° 149, 1999.

PERNICE, I.: "Multilevel constitutionalism and the Treaty of Amsterdam: European constitution-making revisited?", Common Market Law Review, Vol. 36, n° 4, 1999.

QUADRA-SALCEDO JANINI, T. de la: "La reforma de los Estatutos de Autonomía y sus límites constitucionales. La imposibilidad de "blindar" las competencias autonómicas a través de una mera reforma estatutaria", Cuadernos de Derecho Público, n° 24, 2006.

QUADRA-SALCEDO JANINI, T. de la: "Los principios de competencia y prevalencia como reglas de resolución de conflictos en el Estado autonómico", Revista Jurídica de la Universidad Autónoma de Madrid, n° 20, 2009.

SOLOZÁBAL ECHEVARRÍA, J.L.: Bases constitucionales del Estado autonómico, McGraw Hill, Madrid, 1998, p. 167.

SOSA WAGNER, F. and FUERTES, M.: El Estado sin territorio. Cuatro relatos de la España autonómica, Civitas, Madrid, 2011.

TAJADURA TEJADA, J.: La cláusula de supletoriedad del derecho estatal respecto del derecho autonómico, Biblioteca Nueva, Madrid, 2000.

TAJADURA TEJADA, J.: El principio de cooperación en el Estado autonómico, Comares, Granada, 2000.

TORNOS MAS, J.: "Ley de bases y legislación de desarrollo. El problema de su articulación por modificación de la ley de bases. la cláusula de prevalencia", Revista Española de Derecho Constitucional, n° 33, 1991.

# Asymmetry as an Element of Federalism: A Theoretical Speculation Fifty Years Later—Readdress the Spanish Case

Esther Seijas Villadangos

**Abstract** Two essential and complementary parts are integrated in this article: a theoretical reflection about asymmetrical federalism and a pragmatic approach to the situation in Spain.

The former has sought to consolidate the key defining elements of asymmetry. Asymmetry for Constitutional Law is a form of state organization where territorial units with political autonomy enjoy a differentiated constitutional treatment, legitimized for the positive recognition of having different types of singularities (linguistic, juridical, fiscal) with respect to the other units of the State. Linked to asymmetry, we had proposed a neologism, *dissymmetry*, in an attempt to refine the concept. Dissymmetry will be applied to those situations where a proportional or symmetrical situation was broken in an anomalous or faulty way.

The latter has tried to cast some light on the Spanish situation through a series of dilemmas: We have paid attention to the transition from autonomism to federalism and the cohabitation between two types of federalism, a functional federalism and a nationalist federalism, that would result in an asymmetric federalism.

The tension between equality and asymmetry has put on the table the main problem of asymmetric federalism: not considering the differences as grievances. For that, our policies must distinguish what is really essential for citizens.

The last dilemma refers to the risk of emulating asymmetries by other territories, which united with a warning of avoiding a form of autistic federalism could illuminate our future—a future necessarily based on unity and solidarity.

This short essay is mainly speculative. It attempts to highlight a principal weakness in theoretical treatments of the concept of federalism, and to offer modifications of the federal concept. It is not in any sense a complete theoretical statement of federalism. Nor is it meant to survey writings on federalism, although it is generally based on a wide sampling from those writings (Tarlton 1965: 861).

E.S. Villadangos (✉)
Facultad de Derecho, Departamento de Derecho Público, Universidad de León, Campus de Vegazana, 24071 León, Spain
e-mail: meseiv@unileon.es

A. López-Basaguren and L. Escajedo San Epifanio (eds.), *The Ways of Federalism in Western Countries and the Horizons of Territorial Autonomy in Spain*, Vol. 2, DOI 10.1007/978-3-642-27717-7_44, © Springer-Verlag Berlin Heidelberg 2013

Approximately 50 years after Tarlton's essay about symmetry and asymmetry, really focused on symmetry, we would try to make a reflection about asymmetry, which for Spain appears as more interesting one for the reasons than we will explain in the following pages.

# Introduction

Asymmetry has been introduced in the federal theory since the beginning of its existence, but it was in 1965 when Charles D. Tarlton rediscovered the importance of linking federalism to symmetry and asymmetry. The pragmatic implementation of federalism has required the creation of different ways of adapting flexible federal principles to the complex reality of several states.

This work has two targets: first, to develop a theory about the meaning of introducing asymmetrical elements into a federal system; second, to resolve the main problems that it could create, especially connected to the acceptance of the formula for a State, with special attention to the case of Spain.

The format of what follows can be outlined briefly at the outset. The first section is a general assessment of approaches to asymmetry through the answers to different capital questions: Why, what, how, and how many asymmetries? The second half is a brief discussion about the main issues of the Spanish decentralization, using the concept of asymmetry and the useful methodology of dilemmas or antithesis. A final reflection will conclude this study.

# Can a Federal System Be Asymmetrical? A Brief Theory About Asymmetry in a Federal Context

Symmetry in federalism refers to sharing by component units, whereas asymmetry expresses the extent to which component units do not share in these common features. "Weakness" is the key concept, the reference for analyzing asymmetry, according to Tarlton's speculation. This pathology should be treated or should be integrated in the State, in a way of cohabitation. Apart from studying the different types of asymmetries and their consequences, the main discussion must show how important it could be to design a compatible way of federalism that could include several degrees of asymmetry and their limits. Now, we will speculate.

## *Justification: Why Asymmetry?*

The main reason for an asymmetrical performance of a decentralized State is to search for an instrument in order to accommodate the differences for achieving a stable State. States with a variety of cultures, languages and religions could find in asymmetry a *modus operandi* for managing them. Nonetheless, asymmetry can neither be regarded a priori as useless nor a panacea. With that considered, we will try to justify the asymmetrical resource in these first paragraphs: Why develop a theory about asymmetry? Why asymmetry?

Why make a dissertation about asymmetry? In 1965, Charles Dudley Tarlton wrote a brief essay about symmetry and asymmetry, which is the core of our article. Tarlton wrote three interesting studies about federalism and asymmetry: "Symmetry and asymmetry as elements of federalism: a theoretical speculation" (1965); "Federalism, political energy and entropy: implications of an analogy" (1967) and "The study of federalism: a skeptical note" (1971). The Voting Rights Act, a law that consolidated an only-citizenship-in-North-America provision, was his main reference. From this academic point of view, we could differentiate three main stages in the study of asymmetry: the first one, the beginning of the concept, in Tarlton's works; the second one, the consolidation of asymmetry in the theory about federalism, Agranoff's (1999) volume; and the last one, with two capital references for any comparative study about asymmetrical federalism, with Watts and Burgess's works.

Why asymmetry? We will try to solve the beginning and the end of asymmetry, legitimacy and challenges of asymmetry. Looking back to history, we could find special differences in political organizations, maybe the ancestors of asymmetry: *foedera aequa–foedera iniqua*, German hegemony federalism (Seijas 2003: 222–251). These types of differences were justified by the Latin expression *exceptio firmat regulam*, which we adapt to a theory about asymmetry in exceptions to help fulfill rules. We link the legitimacy of asymmetry with the need of searching for an instrument to link the different parts of a State. A pragmatic approach in order to join the different units in a State legitimizes asymmetry. This is very close to the main challenge of asymmetry. The aim of asymmetry is to integrate the different units in search of stability.

## *Definition: What Is Asymmetry?*

The notion of asymmetry refers to the situation where some territorial units should be allowed some scope for reflecting on their specific characteristics and needs.

In an etymological approach to asymmetry, we must refer to the Greek word ασυμμετρια, which means disproportion. In other words, asymmetry is a lack of symmetry that implies another element for making a comparison. This is an aseptic meaning. A situation where a heterogeneous element is introduced, breaking the proportionality of the parts, between them and in relation to the whole. A second meaning, in a pejorative sense, what we call dissymmetry—the prefix dis-expresses negation or completeness or intensification of an unpleasant or unattractive action—will be applied to those situations where a proportional or symmetrical situation was broken in an anomalous or faulty way (i.e., for political pressures, the threat of secession or self-determination, the confusion between powers—if you have differences in culture, religion, language ... you could reach more powers in economy, social services, or foreign policy or more representatives in state institutions). When a territorial organization is based on *dysymmetries*, we have to speak about the pathology of federations, meaning the failure of them (Watts 1999: 109–115).

Asymmetry for Constitutional Law is a form of state organization where territorial units with political autonomy enjoy a differentiated constitutional treatment, legitimized for the positive recognition of having different types of singularities (linguistic, juridical, fiscal) with respect to the other units of the State.

The main aftermath of asymmetry is the qualitative intensification of powers of one unit without reducing the powers of the others, *ad intra*, and the reflection of these singularities in the state institutions and intergovernmental relations, *ad extra*. A proper asymmetrical Constitution must include limits to the positive asymmetries regulated by it. Because asymmetry is not less essential to federalism than symmetry, it is basic to strengthen the stability of the system from the periphery. The main limits of asymmetries are equality and solidarity.

## Description: How Is Asymmetry?

We wish to emphasize four features of asymmetry: first, *singularity*. The root of any asymmetry has to be a differential fact that must not be shared with the rest of the territorial units. Second, *identity*, a difference is not enough to speak about asymmetry. It is considered that an asymmetrical element is the channel to express the demands of citizens and its bond of union; Third is *gradual implementation and flexibility*. We could use asymmetrical arrangements according to the variety of situations that we could face. In other words, it could simply create more problems than solutions, and it could be disastrous. In the development of policies or legislation according to an asymmetrical pattern, it is important to have some degree of flexibility within the constitutional system. Last feature is the *instrumental nature reflected in the Constitution*. Linked to the essence of asymmetry, we stress its subsidiary feature, subordinated to fill other values and principles regulated in the Constitution and the reasons it was adopted basically—unity and stability.

The implementation of asymmetrical arrangements implies different measures concerning legislative powers, functions, distinct administrative status, Civil Law, Fiscal powers, representation in national parliament, reservations of posts in the national executive, language, distinct party system, religion, or symbolism (Keating 1998: 196).

## Typology: How Many Asymmetries?

"Among the several states in a federal union, cultural, economic, social, and political factors combine to produce variations in the symbiotic connection between those states and the system" (Tarlton 1965: 861). Those types of factors would be described as preconditions to asymmetry. We could simplify those types of preconditions of asymmetry in socio-economic and cultural-ideological aspects. If we consider them separately, they only constitute a test of the differences that exist in a plural political organization, especially "federal systems". We need to add the features that characterize asymmetry (*singularity, identity, gradual implementation, flexibility* and *instrumental nature reflected in the Constitution*) in order to consider them as asymmetrical.

Focusing only on asymmetries, we could distinguish different types from a conceptual distinction that could be useful for a practical analysis:

The first type is *de iure* and *de facto* asymmetries. The former refers to those asymmetries formally entrenched in constitutional level and in other types of laws, i.e., in the Spanish case, Statutes of Autonomy, so that territorial units are treated differently by the lawmaker. *De facto asymmetries* refer mainly to political practice or intergovernmental relations where asymmetrical preconditions are reflected. One of the most important *de facto asymmetry* is the existence of different territorial units, according to the size or the population of each unit. Those preconditions produce a diversity of factors of power in every State and reflect, in the perception that everyone has of the others, supremacy and, on the other side, fear and distrust of the less powerful units.

Very close to the former category, Watts has distinguished political and constitutional asymmetries. Political symmetry, which is a common feature in all federal systems, refers to relative influence of the various constituent units within a federation that arises from the impact of cultural, economic, social, and political conditions. Constitutional asymmetry implies the constitutional assignment of different powers to different constitutional units, which is not such a common feature in many federal systems (Watts 1999: 63).

Structural and relational asymmetries are the result of considering the scope where they are implemented. Structural asymmetries are the result of a static analysis of a plural State and refer to the differentiated position of the territorial units due to different factors like population, race, culture, religion ... From those conditions it has determined a singular position of those territorial units in the State that affects decisively the general policy, i.e., elections, fiscal policy ... Relational asymmetries are the consequence of projecting those structural asymmetries *ad extra*. They determine the special status of a territorial unit, i.e., the bilateralism in the relations between the center and those States or Regions.

The different degree of asymmetrical outcomes has generated quantitative types of asymmetry. For instance, a Constitution could provide an asymmetric assignment of powers to the various territorial units to increase provincial or regional autonomy. On the other hand, a Constitution, a subconstitutional law, or a political decision could establish an increase in national or federal powers over specific territorial units for some specific functions, i.e., very expensive powers like health care or education. This was a claim of several Spanish Autonomous Communities (i.e., Valencia, Madrid, and Murcia), sustained from summer of 2011. The consideration of Autonomous Communities as responsible for the crisis, and not as victims, has forced that situation. Nonetheless, this is not new because in 2009, Canary Island proposed to give back to the State the autonomous power over immigrant children. Times of crisis and economic difficulties are times for rolling back to the State.

Finally, the existence of asymmetries, which could be described as transitory or permanent, is explained according to the circumstances of acceptance or refusal that generate the integration of differentiated elements inside the State. Time is the key question in these types of asymmetries. The different ways of reaching autonomy in Spain is an excellent example.

The permanent asymmetries are entrenched in the Constitution or at a subconstitutional level, and its aftermath is to define the system qualitatively.

## Asymmetric Federalization in Spain: Main Challenges

According to the brief theory assessments about asymmetry that we have done in the first chapter of this article with a dogmatic presentation, we will try to change the perspective, adopting a practical point of view and paying attention to the situation of Spanish decentralization. To complete that objective, we have chosen a dynamic method consisting of expressing the main issues through a series of dilemmas, according to a dialectic way of thinking. The result of this proposal is reflected in the last chapter.

### *Autonomism* Versus *Federalism: Spanish Virtual Federalism*

The first dilemma that we propose reflects the tension between *status quo* and the future: preserve the success of the existing autonomous system (more or less workability) *versus* the desire to adopt a federal system.

The long shadow of federalism has been projected over our State with different degrees of intensity from the same moment of the creation of the Spanish Autonomous System. However, we must recognize that the unique substantive reference to federation in the Spanish Constitution of 1978 is negative—sec. 145.1: "Under no circumstances shall a federation of Autonomous Communities be allowed". Nevertheless, it is very common that Spain, especially for foreign academics, was considered federal (Elazar 1994, Watts 1999, Gagnon 2009). According to Elazar's description of federalism, "self-rule and shared rule", Spain could be considered a federation or a "federation-in-the making" (Palermo et al. 2010: 12) or a protagonist of an "unfulfilled federalism" (Beramendi and Máiz 2004).

Different substantive features of our system sustain that consideration: (1) We have a system of shared powers (secs. 148 and 149). (2) The process of preparing Statutes of Autonomy followed a covenant pattern with a keenly felt federal nature, especially according to section 151.2. (3) This federal nature is strengthened when we pay attention to LORAFNA, a Statute of Autonomy especially endorsed for Navarra Foral Autonomous Community. (4) The first final clause for closing the system of shared powers is very close to a federal proposal (sec. 149.3): "Matters not expressly assigned to the State by this Constitution may fall under the jurisdiction of the Autonomous Communities by virtue their Statues of Autonomy". (5) The prevalence clause (sec. 149.3) "State, whose laws shall prevail". (6) The system for controlling Autonomous Communities established by the Constitution is based on legal principles of jurisdiction, sec. 153—"Control over the bodies of Autonomous Communities shall be exercised by: (a) The Constitutional Court, in matters pertaining to the constitutionality of their regulatory provisions having the force of law. (b) The Government, after the handing down by the Council of State of its opinion, regarding the exercise of delegated functions referred to in section 150, subsection 2. (c) Jurisdictional bodies of administrative litigation with regard to autonomic administration and its regulations. (d) The Auditing Court, with regard to financial and budgetary matters". (7) Final substantive feature is the Autonomous Communities' participation in State decisions through the Senate (sec. 69) and through legislative process (secs. 87.2 and 109) or in the planning of general economic activity (sec. 131.2).

Readdressing these characteristics, we can sustain that Spain is a "virtual federal State", according to the meaning of virtual, "almost or nearly as described, but not completely or according to strict definition". So we could dissert about "the federal appearance of the Spanish Autonomous system". The hitherto backward-looking review of Spanish decentralization leads us to the next step. We will try to draw the main steps to become a fulfilled federation, the federal transition in Spain.

From a formal point of view, we have two options: a constitutional reform or a constitutional implementation in a federal sense, federal reform *versus* federal mutation (according Constitutional Law classic term). The former option will lead us to follow the ruled process fixed in Title X of Spanish Constitution, "too easy" if we pay attention to the last reform of sec. 135 against what scholars have sustained for a long time. It is important to introduce the reform of this title, including the Autonomous Communities participation in future constitutional changes. The latter option would consist of interpreting the Constitution and the States of Autonomy in a federal way (deconstitutionalization). This option has been reinforced in the VIII and IX Legislatures (2004-2008/2008-2011) with the reforms of seven Statutes of Autonomy (Valencia, Aragon, Illes Balears, Catalonia, Andalucia, Castilla and León, and finally, Extremadura) and by the absence of a consensus between the major political forces in Spain.

In a material perspective, the first proposal is to achieve a global consensus, with the same degree of support that the Constitution of 1978 has got. That substantial change would have to include, at least, the following topics: identifying the federal States and reforming the Senate in a symmetrical (USA pattern) or an asymmetrical way but never dissymmetrically. This means to give a qualitative reception of differential facts, but never in a quantitative way. The essence of democracy is to change quantitative items, number of votes into qualitative decisions or policies.

A transparent and stable system of intergovernmental relations and the inclusion of plural symbols in the State (plurinationalism) should be key elements in this reform.

Three basics steps in that transition would be:

First, *to create a federal culture*. The main target is to prepare civil society to assume the values of federalism connected to stability and unity. Political forces must communicate these ideas to the citizens in order to build a leadership culture linked to federal ideas. It would be basic that federal proposal, federal culture would be able to gain the same support that, currently, nationalist culture enjoys;

Second, *to specify the main characters and the main sceneries of the federal evolution in Spain*. An advanced Spanish federal map would be focused on asymmetry, the union of a functional federalism, and a nationalist federalism, in a redefinition of the current autonomous system where the differences would be minimized and linked only to real differential facts. With the slogan of "rolling back the States", we would try to underline the advantages of recovering the common features of the central autonomous communities with a protagonist of national territories. We are at the moment when welfare of citizens must prevail. It would have to fight with the strong desires of self-determination that we find in some autonomous communities and the lack of confidence in federalism from the central autonomous communities. The main challenge is making asymmetry workable and fair, so we have to know the limits of asymmetry;

Third, *to translate that proposal to a legal challenge, especially at the constitutional level*. The last point in this journey towards a Federal Spain is to consolidate it at constitutional level and, from the point of view of its legitimacy, with the same high degree of support that the present Constitution has enjoyed since its approval in 1978.

To federalize Spain does not mean to weaken it, neither does it mean to open the door to disintegration or secession. Federalism means to stress union in a noncentralized way. The resource of asymmetry is a tool for achieving harmonization, for managing the conflict; asymmetry is not an end in itself.

The following dilemmas should illustrate more details of our proposal. First, the map of federal implementation could be a mixture of two types of federalism (functional federalism and nationalist federalism); the result would be an asymmetrical federalism. Second, the major problem in Spanish decentralization is the combination between equality and asymmetry. Third, here is a warning about the main risk of the process: the proliferation of elements of divergence.

## *National Federalism* Versus *Functional Federalism*

In an attempt of sketching the map of a future scene of a federal Spain, with the only purpose of stimulating a debate on this issue, we will not advocate a particular model. Our line of reasoning is to propose a global idea that reflects our aim of searching for a workable proposal. The limit is not to perpetuate and exacerbate old problems and, at the same time, not create new ones.

The fundamental issue is to link those parts of Spain with a strong nationalist feeling with the rest of Spain (ROS) that lacks this feeling, but at the same time they do not want to lose the advantages of living in a decentralized system in terms of democracy and social rights.

With the aim of accommodating linguistic, civil law, and fiscal powers, we could demand a federal pattern for the peripheries that support demands for autonomy, a nationalist federalism.

The rest of Spain could enjoy a functional federalism whose core elements were an efficient policymaking. They look for a basic equal status for citizens. These introduce the topic of equality and asymmetry. A functional federalism, especially in times of crisis, means a reduction of bureaucracy and institutions. At the same time, the cooperation between territories must increase in order to avoid superfluous duplication. Of course, intermediate administrative levels between citizens and states must be reduced or disappear.

## *Asymmetry* Versus *Equality*

Diversity is inherent to each process of decentralization, and it is not necessarily negative, but it can cause the risk of unequal treatments among Spanish citizens. The risk of inequality can be easily understood by testing different policies, i.e., health policy, education, or civil servants' salaries.

One of the most important issues in a federal State is to clarify what equality means. Can we talk about the same equality in a unitary State or in a federal State? What happens with equality in asymmetric federations?

There are two references for comparing, constituent units and citizens, and two conceptualizations of equality, arithmetic equality and geometric equality.

On the one hand, arithmetic equality postulates absolutely equal treatment under the law. On the other hand, geometric equality requires differentiation of treatment according to real differences. This was Plato's main theory. If we apply this theory to constituent units, under an arithmetic equality all these units would be considered absolutely equal under the law. If we differentiate the legal status between them according to real differences, such as territorial size, population, tradition, language, religion, we should apply a geometric concept of equality. The justice of this application depends on the reality of these differences and on the limits to the consequences of the assignment of that singular status.

In the case of individuals, we have to reinforce the jurisprudential concept of "fundamental juridical positions" (STC 37/1987, FJ.10). That cryptic expression refers to the heart of equality, its essence. This is the only way for making that concept compatible with asymmetry. In that case, there is enough room for differences but not for discriminations among citizens.

Connected to the study of equality, we have to take a look at the interesting question of its perception. First of all, asymmetry can cause grievances among citizens. A demand for symmetry would be necessary for counterbalancing the situation. It is quite common that a phenomenon of policy contagion happens. It means that policy choices made in one territorial unit may be copied in the rest. This could lead to a surrealistic situation, like we will see in the next paragraph, when the goal of copying other Autonomous Communities is only *per se* an asymmetric element (if you have a proper language, me too).

Another very important issue linked to equality and asymmetry is that there is a dilemma with respect to the distribution of resources and the way the territorial units are financed. The richest units perceive that they subsidized decentralization. This is the case of Catalonia that has been clearly reflected in the amendments to section 135 of the Constitution in its recent reform. Amendment 12 signed by the Catalan Group: "The State will ensure that under no circumstances will alter previous positions per capita contribution to gross domestic product by each Autonomous Community over the final positions in disposable income per capita adjusted for prices" (Official Bulletin of the Congress of Deputies, 05/09/2011).

Catalonia, Western Australia, and a long list of federal States feel exploited as a cash cow. Their usual answer is to propose to secede from Spain, Australia … because of the high burden they had carried in financing poorer units. In Spain, we have on the table for the new Legislature the proposal of "Catalan Fiscal Covenant", similar to "Basque Country Concierto" and "Navarra Convenio". This is a proposal that can be included in a type of federalism that Watts called "fend-for-yourself" (Watts 1999: 45); this is a clear root of a pathology of federalism. We have to remember again the two clear limits to asymmetric federalism: unity and solidarity.


## *Asymmetry for Every One* Versus *Designed Asymmetries*

The formula of "Coffee for everyone" has been one of the most democratic elements of Spanish decentralization, also one of the most criticized. Current preoccupation is the adaptation of this famous slogan to an asymmetrical context, "asymmetries for everyone."

If someone checks one of the recent reformed Statues of Autonomy, i.e., Castilla and León, LO 14/2007, 30th November, it will be evident that there are plenty of asymmetrical references, even in the traditional center of Spain. So we could find singular historical reasons of the Autonomous Community; different proper languages, "leonés", "gallego" (sec. 5); a Charter of Rights for the Castilian and León citizens (Title I); new territorial organizations inside the Autonomous Community, with a differential fact (El Bierzo sec. 46.3); and the legal recognition of internal plurality that determines the need for phasing out economic and demographic imbalances between the provinces and territories of the Autonomous Community (D.A. 2.°).

This is not the proper way to get to federalism but an option for a failed formula. A federation is not a mechanism for manufacturing asymmetries; this path will lead to a disaster; it will start to crumble.

Nevertheless, what can we do when political forces, especially those from periphery, are tightening rope and when the rest of Spain (ROS), in an effort not to be outdone, triggers further demands (i.e., Camps clause)? The strengthening of the integrative function of the state and horizontal cooperation are the main solutions.

We have to add another challenge, the dilemma between an executive federalism and a participatory federalism. The recent Statutory reform process and the constitutional reform have shown the absence of popular participation, e.g., referendum on the Catalan Statute of Autonomy held on 18th June 2006, with a 49 % participation. Federalism without the counterbalance of the people would be an autistic federalism.

## Proposals and Final Reflection

Following this reasoning and applying it to a brief discussion of the quality of asymmetrical federalism in Spain, certain interesting conclusions are reached:

Firstly, we could develop the asymmetrical federalism theory, adding the category of *dissymmetry*. *Dissymmetry* will be applied to those situations where a proportional or symmetrical situation was broken in an anomalous or faulty way (i.e., for political pressures, the threat of secession or self-determination, the confusion between powers—because you have different culture, religion, language ... you could reach more powers in economy, social services, or foreign policy or more representatives in State institutions). The risk of falling into a pathological federalism, founded in *dissymmetries*, is too high. All deceived federations could corroborate this premise.

Secondly, we could suggest a list of stages for what we have called "the Spanish transition to federalism": First is *to create a federal culture*. The main target is to prepare civil society to assume the values of federalism connected to stability and unity. Political forces must communicate these ideas to the citizen in order to build a leadership culture linked to federal ideas. It would be basic for that federal proposal that a federal culture would be able to gain the same support that, currently, nationalist culture enjoys. It is crucial to emphasize the importance of limits. The essence of federalism—unity and self-government—is not compatible with secession.

Second is *to specify the main characteristics and the main sceneries of the federal evolution in Spain*. An advanced Spanish federal map would be focused on asymmetry, union of a functional federalism, and nationalist federalism, in a redefinition of the current autonomous system where the differences would be minimized and linked only to real differential facts. With a slogan of "rolling back the States", we would try to underline the advantages of recovering the common features of the central autonomous communities without forgetting the importance of national territories. We are in the moment when welfare of citizens must prevail. It would have to fight with the strong desires of self-determination that we find in some autonomous communities and the lack of confidence in federalism from the central autonomous communities. The main challenge is making asymmetry workable and fair, so we have to know the limits of asymmetry.

Third is *to translate that proposal in a legal challenge, especially at the constitutional level*. The last point in this journey towards a Federal Spain is to consolidate it at a constitutional level. It must have the same high degree of support that our present Constitution has enjoyed since its approval in 1978.

Our last reflection refers to how difficult it is to find comprehensive answers to the questions raised by asymmetrical federalism. We cannot stop trying to get them. Our dilemmas have tried to contribute to this effort.

"The concept of federalism has been a major panacea in Western political thought for an incredible range of problems ... Whenever events have seemed to demand cooperation and coordination, while interests and anxieties have held out for the preservation of difference and diversity, the answer has almost unfailingly been some form of federalism" (Tarlton 1965: 874). In the future, it is possible for Spain to become federal, and this federalism could be an asymmetrical federalism.

# References

Agranoff, R. (ed) (1999). Accommodating diversity. Asymmetry in Federal States. Nomos. Baden-Baden.

Beramendi, P., Máiz, R. (2004). Spain. Unfulfilled federalism (1978–1996). In: Amoretti, U., Bermeo, N. (eds.) Federalism and territorial cleavages. John Hokins University Press. Baltimore and London.

Elazar, D. (1994). Federal Systems of the world. A handbook of Federal, Confederal and Autonomy Arrangements, Longman, London.

Gagnon, A. (2009). The case for Multinational Federalism: beyond the all encompassing Nation, Routledge, London.

Keating, M. (1998). What´s wrong with asymmetrical government? Regional & Federal Studies 8: 195–218.

Palermo, F., Zwilling, C., Kössler, K. (2010). Asymmetries in Constitutional Law. Recent developments in Federal and Regional systems. Eurac. Bolzano.

Seijas Villadangos, E. (2003). Configuración asimétrica del sistema de Comunidades Autónomas. Universidad de León, León.

Tarlton, Ch. D. (1965). Symmetry and asymmetry as elements of federalism: a theoretical speculation. The Journal of Politics 27.4: 861–874.

Tarlton, Ch. D. (1967). Federalism, political energy and entropy: implications of an analogy. *W.P.Q.* vol. XX, n.° 4: 866–874.

Tarlton, Ch. D. (1971). The study of federalism: a skeptical note. In RIEDEL, A., (Ed.), New Perspectives in State and local government. Xerox College Publishing, Waltham: 97–100.

Watts, R. (1999). Comparing Federal Systems. McGill-Queen´s University Press, 1999.

# The Principle of Federal Loyalty and Trust in the Estado De Las Autonomías

Sebastian D. Baglioni

**Abstract** Federalism is often presented as a workable solution for the accommodation of multinationality. Combining self-rule with shared rule, a federal polity
opens up the space to recognise and accommodate the diverging demands coming
from different actors and/or governments. The unity of a federal polity is
guaranteed by the existence of a central government, whereas its diversity is
guaranteed by the second level of political authorities who enjoy political autonomy
and the proper constitutional protections. However, federalism is neither an automatic process nor a magical solution for political conflicts.

The present paper discusses the principle of federal loyalty and trust as important
elements conducive to the legitimacy and efficacy of federal systems. This is
especially relevant for the Spanish case for a number of reasons. First, the existence
of national minorities demanding the political recognition of certain rights presents
a significant challenge to the system. Second, Spain has adopted a 'federalising'
direction whereby institutions and practices display the classic characteristics of
federal systems with varying degrees of success. Third, taking together the last two
points, the *Estado de las Autonomías* displays interesting characteristics to analyse
the ways in which federalism is a proper normative and institutional option for the
accommodation of multinational demands and to assess the conditions under which
a federal system gains legitimacy and realises the principles of democratic rule and
political inclusion.

S.D. Baglioni (✉)
University of Toronto, 100 St. George Street, Toronto, ON, Canada M5S 3G3
e-mail: sebastian.baglioni@utoronto.ca

A. López-Basaguren and L. Escajedo San Epifanio (eds.), *The Ways of Federalism*
*in Western Countries and the Horizons of Territorial Autonomy in Spain*, Vol. 2,
DOI 10.1007/978-3-642-27717-7_45, © Springer-Verlag Berlin Heidelberg 2013

# Introduction

The present paper examines the evolution of the *Estado de las Autonomías* since its establishment in 1978, highlighting the progressive adoption of federal institutions and practices and the ways in which these have been incorporated into the normal functioning of the system. Intergovernmental relations and the inclusion and participation of regional governments in Spanish state institutions are emphasised so as to show the extent to which there exist federal loyalty and trust as sustaining factors of a legitimate and democratic federal system in a multinational context like the Spanish one.

The first section briefly presents the background conditions under which the current Spanish political system was adopted, emphasising the tension between the unity of the polity, on the one hand, and the process of decentralisation and political autonomy, on the other. The second section discusses the principle of federal loyalty and the constitutional reading and interpretation of it made by the Spanish Constitutional Court (SCC). The third section stresses the potential conflict between the role of the Court as a guarantor of the principle of federal loyalty and the ongoing patterns of relations between the different tiers of political authorities in the country. Finally, the conclusion emphasises the possibilities and limits that a federal political system, in general, and the principle of federal loyalty, in particular, display when accommodating multinational demands.

# The Indissoluble Unity of Spain and the 1978 Constitution

In 1978, Spain adopted a new constitution, inaugurating a period of democratic rule after decades of dictatorship under Franco. However, the constitutional framers were faced with deep historical problems stemming from the previous political evolution of the country. Put it succinctly, the conflict involved multiple layers of political belonging and identification that, at the same time, fostered a diversity of national conceptions and projects that called into question the unity of the polity. This last element either challenged directly the unity of Spain or, at least, required a redefinition of the terms that make up that unity.

As it is well known, the drafters of the 1978 Constitution chose a middle course between two opposing options: either prolonging the centralising features of the Francoist regime or adopting a fully fledged federal system. Their solution was to combine the 'indissoluble unity of the Spanish Nation' with 'the right to self-government of the nationalities and regions of which it is composed' (Section 2, Spanish Constitution (Congreso Español 1978). This meant that the principle of sovereignty was established as an exclusive right of the Spanish people, whereas the principle of political autonomy and self-government was recognised for the units composing the polity.

Thus, the constitution tries to strike an uneasy balance between unity and diversity, between the encompassing idea of Spain as the overarching political unit and the more particular attachments based on regional units (notably, though not exclusively, the three historical communities: Galicia, the Basque Country, and Catalonia). Several analysts have agreed that the wording of the constitution and its degree of generality and ambiguity are both the product of the historical circumstances and a conscious balancing act between seemingly mutually exclusive demands (Blanco Valdés 2005; Moreno 2008; Solozábal 1998).

The general mechanism adopted was the establishment of a system of autonomous regions, known as Estado de las Autonomías. The system divided the country into seventeen different regions, with different degrees of competences and powers. Among these regions, Galicia, the Basque Country, and Catalonia stood out, given their defined identity, cultural characteristics (including their own languages), and distinct political institutions. Moreover, in the case of Catalonia and the Basque Country, they had already enjoyed a considerable degree of autonomy at the beginning of the twentieth century, and later was a staunch focus of resistance against the Francoist dictatorship. As a consequence, it was felt that at least these regions had a strong claim to organise themselves politically, although both the specific right to self-determination and the idea of shared sovereignty were explicitly rejected.

The Estado de las Autonomias has evolved dramatically during the last three decades, making Spain one of the most decentralised countries in Europe. This is most remarkable, given the political history of the country and the ever-present demands from regions with a strong national sentiment. Equally, the interactions among political elites and authorities in Spain have also undergone a complex and long process during these years. Periods of high levels of conflicts have been followed by others characterised by some level of cooperation. This is a natural consequence from the creation of a completely new level of government to the progressive adoption of powers and competences by those governments and the realisation of the necessity to interact with one another. Concrete decisions like the Autonomous Pacts of 1981 and 1992 have created new sources of conflict and reignite old controversies; however, it is also true that cooperation has equally been an ongoing feature of the Spanish system. Intergovernmental relations and the degree of participation and representation of regional governments at central government decision-making mechanisms are still relatively weak and could be improved in many ways (García Morales 2006). However, the number of meetings and collaborative initiatives between both levels of government has been increasing in recent years, indicating that the Spanish political system is slowly moving towards a more clearly defined model of cooperative federalism.

# Federal Loyalty and the Spanish Constitutional Court

The modern concept of federal loyalty (*Bundestreue*) was developed by the Federal Constitutional Court of Germany as a non-written principle that stems directly from the constitution. Federal loyalty and trust basically mean that the different levels of government have the constitutional duty to cooperate in order to sustain the constitutional regime and advance the legitimate interests of the polity. More precisely, the Court has affirmed that "both the federation and the Lander are obliged to cooperate pursuant to the nature of the constitutional 'pact' between them and have to contribute to its consolidation as well as to the maintenance of the well-understood interests of the federation and the constituent states" (quoted in Gamper 2010: 160).

The SCC has adopted a similar principle, inspired by the doctrine of its German counterpart. This means that all levels of government in Spain have the duty to obey and respect the principle of solidarity as enshrined in Section 2 of the Spanish Constitution (Constitutional Court Sentence 25/1981, CCS 64/1990), the duty of reciprocal help among them (CCS 18/1982, 96/1986), and the principle of loyalty to the constitution (CCS 11/1986) (Tribunal Constitucional Español 2011).

More specifically, the doctrine of the SCC determines that both the central government and the regional ones must collaborate positively and negatively. In the former case, the Spanish State and the Autonomous Communities must respect (i.e., do not encroach upon) both their respective prerogatives and the shared interests of the polity as a whole; in the later case, both levels of government must help and support each other in order to effectively exercise their respective powers (Aja 1999: 143, Albertí 1996; Álvarez 2009).

Clearly, federal loyalty and trust cannot be dictated by a court but, rather, should be the logical outcome of a structure of relations in which political authorities engage, ensuring at the same time a certain degree of collaboration and mutual respect, beyond the obligation to obey the law. Moreover, the values and practices that the idea of federal loyalty entails are certainly elusive qualities. It presupposes that the actors involved trust one another and establish relations of good faith with one another. This may very well not be the case in multinational polities. If political processes and overall agreements about the nature of the polity are not solid enough to sustain the future of a multinational polity, then the assertiveness of certain demands and right claims will become a divisive political factor. Such conflictive scenarios can involve the distribution of competences between levels of government or the political recognition of symbols and identities. However, they can also include the territorial distribution of power (or the territorial division of the polity itself) or the very definition of what democracy means.

The Spanish case illustrates both the possibilities that a federal institutional framework presents and its limitations. It provides reasons for hope in relation to the capacity of federal arrangements to accommodate multinationality. Nevertheless, it also shows the tensions and eventual conflicts that such a system may face. Federal loyalty is at the heart of these tensions; moreover, it can constitute a key element for the progressive institutionalisation of constructive practices and patterns of relations among the different levels of government in a federal system characterised by multinationality.

# From Court Rulings to Political Relations

The 1978 Spanish Constitution and the subsequent political evolution of the country since then constitute a serious attempt at addressing the issue of accommodating the nationalist claims of Catalonia, the Basque Country, and Galicia. Not surprisingly, this issue has proved to be highly controversial, and the overall assessment of Spain as a multinational democracy with adequate level of political recognition displays a mixed record of success and failures. The principle of political recognition implies a series of specific characteristics that the political order of a country should reflect. First, at the constitutional level, there should be a number of basic rights and guarantees conducive to the expression and protection of nationalist claims explicitly enshrined in the constitution. Second, at the institutional level, there should be a series of rules and decision-making mechanisms that make possible an adequate inclusion and participation of all constituent units in collective binding decisions of the polity. Third, at the political level, there should be general patterns of interaction and cooperation that create enough room for publicly sustained democratic practices (i.e., deliberation, negotiation) among all relevant actors.

At the constitutional level, in 1978, Spain recognised for the first time in its history that it is composed by 'regions and nationalities' and that they enjoy a right to political autonomy or self-government (Section 2, Spanish Constitution). This went against the long-standing Spanish tradition of homogeneity and unity of the polity. It also broke away from the past legacy of centralisation and cultural assimilation of the Francoist years (1939–1975). However, the constitution did not establish the precise ways in which that right to self-government would be exercised; moreover, the exact contents and limits to political autonomy were left indeterminate. This is what the Spanish constitutional doctrine has called *principio dispositivo*: the constitution established only general principles around Spanish unity and sovereignty, coupled with the political autonomy of the regions and nationalities. As a result, the Estado de las Autonomias could evolve in different directions, depending on particular interpretations and understandings. The wording of the constitution, its ambiguity and indeterminacy, and the *principio dispositivo* all have made constitutional (and political) disputes in Spain struggles to define the overall system along symmetrical or asymmetrical lines. In the former case, certain homogeneity among all the constituent units is secured, blurring the distinction between regions and nationalities. In the latter case, nationalities are favoured on the understanding that they constitute national minorities with a right to enjoy certain powers and competences that regions do not.

The SCC has been a fundamental actor in defining the terms of these disputes by advancing a jurisprudence and case law record conducive to the clarification and realisation of the principles contained in the constitutional text. This has paved the way to the recognition and accommodation of certain rights claimed by Catalonia, the Basque Country, and Galicia. However, Spain has rejected any confederal arrangement whereby these nationalities would enjoy a right to shared sovereignty. Federal loyalty and trust, as understood and upheld by the SCC, may play an important role in guaranteeing a minimum level of cooperation among the competing actors and authorities. However, the Court itself does not have the power to impose such an outcome. Rather, it should be the natural outcome of a slow, progressive learning process whereby all parties involved adopt values and practices conducive to a legitimate and stable federal system, even in the face of multinational demands and claims.

At the institutional level, Spain has embarked itself in a general and deep process of decentralisation, in parallel with the just mentioned process of political devolution. All constituent units created their own institutions and bureaucracy in order to fulfil the newly acquired powers and competences at the level of regional governments. This represented an improvement in terms of subsidiarity and better representation of regional interests throughout the country. However, the formal and genuine inclusion of regions and nationalities in decision-making mechanisms and institutions of the central government has proved to be more difficult. It is widely accepted, for example, that the Senate has not adopted the expected role of a chamber of territorial representation, and other mechanisms conducive to the direct involvement and participation of regions and nationalities in collective binding decisions turned out to be less than satisfactory. There are a series of instruments and meetings whereby the different levels of government share information and coordinate their efforts in a whole array of policy areas. However, these do not yet inform the normal government machinery, and much more progress could be achieved in terms of better representation and articulation of interests of regions and nationalities when adopting policy decisions and objectives at the level of the central government (García Morales 2006; Cámara 2011). On the other hand, Colino (2008) and Arbós et al. (2009) emphasise the fact that there have been, in recent years, promising developments in the area of intergovernmental relations. Both the nature of the instruments and the number of exchanges have increased significantly in the past few years. This could affirm a tendency towards a type of institutional relations more clearly defined along the lines of a system of cooperation.

At the political level, the interactions between the different political elites have also been characterised by conflict and cooperation. During the first years of evolution of the Estado de las Autonomias, the relations between all three historical communities and the central Spanish government have been characterised by a high level of conflict. This was, to a large extent, expected due to the fact that the constitutional text only provided principles and general guidelines for the system but did not specify enough fundamental issues like the distribution of power and the territorial organisation of the country. In this context, the SCC, as arbiter of disputes between levels of government and final interpreter of the constitution, became the central actor in all these conflicts. The activity of the SCC has been crucial in order to imprint a specific direction in the overall evolution of the system and affirm specific features of it among several possible ones. It is worth mentioning, among others, its landmark rulings regarding the contents of state basic laws, the block of constitutionality, and the principle of institutional loyalty and cooperation. However, the SCC cannot replace the necessary interaction and mutual cooperation between Galician, Basque, and Catalonian elites, on the one hand, and the Spanish elite, on the other. There were periods during which neither the socialists (PSOE) nor the conservatives (PP) achieved a clear majority to form government and thus were forced to accept the electoral-political support of nationalist political parties (Catalans and Basques). As a result, elites' relations displayed a relatively stable mode of cooperation based on mutual gains: Catalans and Basques demanded and acquired specific powers and competences in return for their participation in a Spanish coalition government. However, this is not necessarily a good thing insofar as cooperation can be seen as the result of political necessity or bargain and not based on the intrinsic merits or legitimacy of the claims advanced (Fossas 1999). It is important to note here that the limited cooperation among nationalist-Spanish political parties and leaders can be the result of either an intransigent dogmatic position defended by the former or a principled non-negotiable attitude displayed by the latter.

## Conclusion

Taking all these three levels of analysis (constitutional, institutional, and political), the display of federal loyalty and trust among Spanish political authorities has adopted different patterns depending on the specific features of each of the three historical communities.

In the Basque case, political violence and the presence of the terrorist organisation ETA have certainly influenced the level of conflict with the Spanish state. This, coupled with an aggressive nationalist discourse and programmes endorsed by the successive PNV's regional governments, has made the relations between that region and the rest of the country highly conflictive and dominated by ideological disputes where negotiation and compromise are rarely invoked, let alone secured. The ways in which the failed proposal to amend the Basque Statute (i.e., the Ibarretxe Plan) nicely illustrates this point: dogmatic positions and maximalist demands clashed against accusations of manipulation and disloyalty. The end result, unsurprisingly, has been an overt unconstitutional proposal sent by the Basque Parliament to the Spanish Parliament and the outright refusal of the latter to even consider the proposal (Muro 2009; Fernández Farreres 2009). The current socialist-led Basque government seems to be opening up new possibilities in this regard, though it is too soon to tell how far this development can go. In terms of federal loyalty, the Basque Country has remained, ever since the establishment of the Estado de las Autonomias, suspicious about the adequacy or even legitimacy of the current political system. However, this position varies depending on the ideological bent of different forces in the Basque nationalist camp. Moreover, periods of high levels of conflict have been followed by others where cooperation is accepted, and the participation of the Basque Country in regular meetings for policy coordination with other regions and/or the Spanish State is not significantly lower than the national average (Arbós et al. 2009).

In the Catalan case, the relations with the rest of Spain have been dominated by 'Catalanism' as presented and defined by the centrist Catalan political party Convergence and Union (CiU), in office from 1980 to 2000. As a result, the overall pattern of claims and demands coming from this region has been characterised by a clever combination of principled positions and a pragmatic sense of opportunity. Ideological compromises and aggressive positions are certainly present, but they do not dictate the nature and content of relations with the Spanish government (Muro 2009). Therefore, Catalan elites have been able to defend and advance their interests without resorting, for the most part, to zero-sum situations and political deadlocks, as has often been the case with Basque demands. In recent years, this tendency has been reinforced by regional coalition governments led by the socialists, which guarantees a minimum level of understanding and mutual interest with the socialist Spanish government of Zapatero. However, the proposed and ratified new Catalan Statute of Autonomy (2006) has proved to be a divisive issue and an important source of conflict. The strong reaction of the conservatives and the subsequent ruling of the SCC cutting down some provisions of the proposal seem to indicate specific limits of acceptable demands. More broadly, this could also reduce the level of understanding and cooperation that Catalan elites have traditionally displayed towards their Spanish counterparts.

In the Galician case, the demands and overall relations with the rest of Spain have been characterised by a low level of conflict. This is due to a number of reasons: first, the lack of a strong nationalist political party in control of the regional government, as it has been the case of the Basque Country and Catalonia. Second, the ability of the conservatives (PPG) to appropriate Galician demands and claims and convert them into a moderate programme favouring 'autonomism' and not nationalism. Third, and related to the previous points, there has been a marked inability of Galician nationalist forces to articulate an attractive programme with which to gain electoral support and form government (Máiz 2001). Certainly, this region advances specific claims and demands (notably, the protection and promotion of Galego as co-official language of that Autonomous Community), but the intensity of these and the overall level of conflict with the Spanish state has been much less pronounced when compared to the Basque Country and Catalonia. The experience of a failed initiative to amend the Galician Statute of Autonomy clearly shows the limited scope of nationalist sentiments or, at least, the inability to translate that sentiment into concrete political plans. However, Galicia has been historically well integrated in the Estado de las Autonomias, both at the institutional and political levels, exhibiting a reasonable degree of cooperation and collaboration with Spanish State authorities.

Spain has gone a long way from the legacy of Francoist dictatorship and the traditional model of a centralist homogenising state. However, this does not mean that the Estado de las Autonomias has solved once and for all the nationalist demands of the Basque Country, Catalonia, and Galicia. Further, to expect a final resolution of these conflicts is to misunderstand the nature of politics in a multinational polity. Conflict and disagreements about the proper way to recognise claims put forward by national minorities are part of the dynamic of a country characterised by multinationality. It is not so much finding a way to avoid these conflicts but, rather, exploring the possible alternatives to accommodate seemingly mutually exclusive claims. The Spanish political system is prone to regular challenges from these three regions in order to make the political order more responsive to their identities and interests. More precisely, the issue includes a triple relation: first, the historical communities and their claims; second, the reaction of the Spanish government towards those claims; third, the predictable feeling of comparative grievance that all other component units may express.

The overall assessment of the political evolution of the Spanish Estado de las Autonomias and the ways in which it has responded to multinationality should be seen as an ongoing struggle whereby different political actors advance a series of claims and engage in public debates and reasoning as to what extent those claims are legitimate and how to accommodate them. The degree of federal loyalty and trust exhibited by the different political elites at different moments in time is crucial to assess the success or failure of the system as a whole when it comes to the accommodation of the multinational character of the polity.

Related to this last point, there is a difference between decentralisation and devolution (Requejo 2005). The Spanish political system displays a high level of decentralisation whereby all the constituent units enjoy a wide array of powers and competences. This in itself can be seen as a good thing, insofar as that process is conducive to political authorities being closer to the people and more responsive to their needs. However, devolution (i.e., self-government) and the ways in which nationalist claims are being recognised do not necessarily go hand in hand with decentralisation. The constitutional enshrinement of Basque, Catalan, and Galician demands, together with a symbolic and institutional recognition of their identities and interests, becomes the heart of political debates in Spain.

Federal loyalty and trust constitute a basic value to make a multinational federal system work, even in the face of unresolved and divisive disputes among the constituent units of the polity. By learning to cooperate and embrace shared interests, the different levels of government of such a system strengthen their mutual belonging. This, obviously, does not deny their differences and sources of conflict. However, it does point to a fruitful direction whereby those differences can be accommodated in a democratic manner. Spain is far from having found 'the' solution to these issues (assuming that that is a possible and desirable condition), but the country has indeed come a long way in terms of incorporating basic values and attitudes conducive to mutual respect and recognition of each other's identities.

700                                                                 S.D. Baglioni

# References

Aja, E. (1999). El Estado Autonómico. Federalismo y hechos diferenciales. Alianza Editorial, Madrid, 357 pp.

Albertí Rovira, E. (1996). El federalismo actual como federalismo cooperativo. Revista Mexicana de Sociología, Vol. 58, No 4: 51–68.

Álvarez, L. (2009). La función de la lealtad en el Estado Autonómico. Eikasia. Revista de Filosofía, Año IV, No 5: 135–168.

Arbós, X., Colino, C., García Morales, M. and Parrado, S. (2009). Las relaciones intergubernamentales en el Estado autonómico. La posición de los actores. Institut d'Estudis Autonomics, Barcelona, 312 pp.

Blanco Valdés, R. (2005). Nacionalidades históricas y regiones sin historia. Alianza Editorial, Madrid, 231 pp.

Cámara, G. (2011). El principio de colaboración entre el Estado y las Comunidades Autónomas. Available at: www.unisi.it/ricerca/dip/dir_eco/COMPARATO/camara.doc

Colino, C. (2008). The Spanish model of devolution and regional governance: evolution, motivations and effects on policy making. Policy and Politics. Vol. 36, No 4: 573–586.

Congreso Español (1978). Constitución Española. Available at: http://www.congreso.es/docu/constituciones/1978/1978_cd.pdf

Fernández Farreres, G. (2009). El Tribunal Constitucional ante las reformas estatutarias. Fundación Manuel Giménez Abad, Navarra, 24 pp.

Fossas, E. (1999). Asymmetry and Plurinationality in Spain. Working Paper 167. Institut de Ciencies Politiques i Socials, Barcelona, 20 pp.

Gamper, A. (2010). On loyalty and the (federal) constitution. International Constitutional Law Journal. Vol. 2, No 2: 157–170.

García Morales, M. (2006). Las relaciones intergubernamentales en el Estado Autonómico: estado de la cuestión y problemas pendientes. Fundación Manuel Giménez Abad, Zaragoza, 32 pp.

Maíz, R. (2001). El nacionalismo gallego en el siglo XXI. In: Morales, M. (Coord.). Ideologías y movimientos políticos. España Nuevo Milenio Editores, Madrid, 368 pp.

Moreno, L. (2008). La federalización de España: poder político y territorio. Madrid: Siglo XXI España Editores, Madrid, 224 pp.

Muro, D. (2009). Territorial Accommodation, Party Politics, and Statute Reform in Spain. South European Society & Politics. Vol. 14, No 4: 453–468.

Requejo, F. (2005). Multinational Federalism and Value Pluralism. Routledge, London, 168 pp.

Solozábal, J. (1998). Las bases constitucionales del Estado Autonómico. McGraw-Hill Publishers, Madrid, 367 pp.

Tribunal Constitucional Español (2011). Sentencias del Tribunal Constitucional. Available at: http://www.boe.es/aeboe/consultas/bases_datos/jurisprudencia_constitucional.php

# Brief Considerations Regarding the Structure of the Spanish Senate and the Boundary Between Federal Covenant and Autonomous State

Elena García-Cuevas Roque

**Abstract** Over 30 years after the Spanish Constitution was approved in 1978, the *Estado autonómico* or "autonomic State" for which it provides has evolved in a series of phases coinciding with different legislatures of the Spanish parliament, culminating in the configuration of a new model of the State. The key players in this process have been the political parties and the Spanish Constitutional Court. However, this new model as outlined in the proposals of the Catalan, Basque, and Galician nationalists and, in particular, as framed in recent reforms of certain statutes of autonomy, is wholly incompatible with the Constitution, which has led to calls for a definitive solution in the form of a pact to proceed openly with constitutional reform or to return powers to Spain's central government.

**Keywords** Nationalism • federation • autonomy

## The Problem

The ongoing autonomic process is undeniably one of the most important current issues in Spanish politics. In view of the progressive achievements and conquests made in this field, it has become necessary to bring Title VIII of the Spanish Constitution into line with the new circumstances of Spain's nationalities or, more accurately, the Autonomous Communities (*Comunidades Autónomas*—CCAA—in Spanish), as the regions are known. Title VIII establishes a decentralised model for the State, but it is ambiguous and vague in a number of respects.

E. García-Cuevas Roque (✉)
School of Business and Economics, San Pablo CEU University, Julián Romea 23, 28003 Madrid, Spain
e-mail: garcue@ceu.es

A. López-Basaguren and L. Escajedo San Epifanio (eds.), *The Ways of Federalism in Western Countries and the Horizons of Territorial Autonomy in Spain*, Vol. 2, DOI 10.1007/978-3-642-27717-7_46, © Springer-Verlag Berlin Heidelberg 2013

# Evolution of Spain's Territorial Structure

The Constitution sets no limits on the number of the CCAA or deadline for their creation. Moreover, it does not impose the autonomic structure nationwide (art. 137); again, two different procedures exist for the formation of Autonomous Communities. The first, applied in Catalonia, the Basque Country, Galicia, and Andalusia, requires a referendum on the autonomic initiative under art. 151.1 of the Constitution. The second procedure applied by the remaining Autonomous Communities is regulated in art. 143 and does not require a referendum. Finally, the Constitution does not expressly create or recognise the Autonomous Communities, which are formed via their Statutes as the basic law governing the organisation of the region concerned. The key point here is that the Constitution established variable requirements for the drafting and approval of the regional Statutes, which constitute the legislation that actually determines the extent of regional autonomy. Furthermore, two procedures exist for reform of the Statutes enacted under art. 151. The Constitution links the principle of autonomy to the "prerogative" of access to political autonomy (Judgment 247/2007, of 12 December, the Constitutional Court, hence forward STC).

The CCAA are, then, far from uniform, although their differences may not on any account imply economic or social privileges (art. 138.2), and the contents of their Statutes vary widely within the framework provided by art. 148 and 149 of the Constitution. In the initial phase, considerable differences existed between the so-called "historic" Communities (Catalonia, the Basque Country, Galicia and Andalusia), the regions equated with them (Valencia and the Canary Islands) and the rest (see STC 1/1982, of 28 January). Eventually, the devolution of powers was evened out by the *Pactos Autonómicos* (Autonomous Pacts) of 1992. These agreements were enshrined mainly in Basic Law 9/1992, of 23 December, by which additional powers were assigned to the regions that had gained their autonomy under art. 143 of the Constitution, and in subsequent Acts of the Spanish Parliament amending their Statutes. The twins aims of these measures were to expand the powers devolved to the "second division" CCAA (formed under art. 143) in order to align them with the art. 151.1 regions, and to enhance cooperation between the State and the CCAA.

The reforms of the Statutes of Autonomy undertaken between 1996 and 2004 practically levelled out the powers devolved to the CCAA, with some notable exceptions such as policing, which has not been devolved even to all of the historic (art. 151) Communities. Finally, the 2004–2008 legislature saw the reform of the Statutes of Valencia and Catalonia in 2006 and the Balearic Islands, Andalusia, Aragon and Castile and León in 2007, as well as the creation of new cooperation mechanisms institutional, rather than of subordination, in order to expand the concept of solidarity (see STC 237/1992, of 15 December, 109/2004, of 30 June and 247/2007, of 12 December, concerning the principle of territorial solidarity and balance). The reform proposed by the Basque Regional Parliament was rejected in 2005, however. The *Estatuto Político de la Comunidad de Euskadi*, known as the

"Plan Ibarretxe" after the Basque regional premier, was considered to enshrine a model that would not fit within the framework of the Spanish Constitution (see Castells and Cajal 2009 for a fascinating discussion of Basque nationalism and its origins). Finally, the new Catalan Statute of 2006 aroused heated debate, as will be explained in the last section of this paper. The Catalan model was copied by the new Andalusian Statute after the elision of certain aspects found to be incompatible with the model of the autonomic State.

# The Clash Between the Autonomic State and the Federal State

The very formulation "boundaries of the Federal Pact and the Autonomic State" provides some idea of the direction of this paper. This is certainly a controversial question, beginning with the matter of "sovereignty". In principle, the CCAA have only limited political autonomy but lack sovereignty, as the Spanish Constitutional Court has found in various judgments. Consequently, they do not enjoy the original, constituent power that is proper to the members of a federal State. The autonomic State, then, emerges from the polarisation or segregation of the original whole, and there is therefore no pact between pre-existing sovereign entities. In contrast, the members of a Federation have, or once had, "sovereignty" because they were joined together in a "federal pact" resulting in a concentration of power.

What is the principle of autonomy? In the first place, it is a general organisational or structural principle of the State (STC 32/1981, of 28 July and 4/1981, of 2 February) that entails a distribution of power between different entities. These are the State itself, in which sovereignty resides, the CCAA as politically autonomous entities, and the provinces and municipalities (local corporations) as administratively autonomous entities (art. 137). The existence of a unified, sovereign nation-state was at all times latent in the debates preceding the drafting of the Constitution (i.e. there was no federal pact), insofar as the Spanish State "is founded on the indissoluble unity of the nation" (art. 2), in which national sovereignty uniquely resides. Hence, constituent power lies with the State and is common to all of the regions and peoples of Spain, and there is in principle no place in the Constitution for a "Catalan State" or a "Basque State" as such, but there is room for regional governments.

In the general parliamentary debate of July 1978, the PSOE, among others, proposed defining the new Spain as a federal State or at least as a State based on the federal principle. However, other parties, including the governing UCD, stressed the incompatibility of the federal concept with a State based on Statutes of (regional) Autonomy. As González argued, "Only when the optimum powers available to all of the territorial entities had been devolved to them would we arrive at a federal State". Thus, the Socialists' proposal over the constituent period was based on an "underlying model of the State that is tendentially federal" (Fajardo 2009, pp. 52–53).

Given the diversity of the 17 CCAA (and the two autonomous cities), however, a "federal pact" between them similar to that existing in Germany, for example, appears unlikely unless the actual make-up of the Spanish Senate is "redesigned". Meanwhile, the lack of uniformity between the regions has led to the constant use of the term "asymmetry" (in phrases like "asymmetric model", "asymmetric federalism" see Requejo and Nagel (2011), "asymmetric Catalan nationalism") to refer to the so-called *hechos diferenciales* (the exceptions differentiating the historic regions, in particular Catalonia). It has even been argued (Elorriaga 2011, p. 16) that this asymmetric model was enshrined in the Constitution from the moment of its approval, because, among other grounds, it differentiates the channels of regional autonomy and avoids closing the list of powers that can be devolved to the CCAA. Let us now clarify the concepts of "nationality", "nationalism" and "federalism". A "nationality" is the specific condition and nature of a nation's members, who should form a politically independent State. The term may also sometimes be used to refer to the common language, law and art that form a nationality, and so a nationality would be a cultural unity or civilisation. Thus, art, science, customs, laws and so forth are all rooted in nationality (Prat 1917, pp. 52, 71).

In this context, the term "nationalism" suggests a federal structure (Smith 2004 provide illuminating discussions of the theory of nationalism). Nationalism entails a close attachment to local traditions and the distinguishing features of the nation concerned, and nationalist doctrines are therefore based on feelings of belonging that are designed to stress all aspects of the national identity and, above, all to seek and defend sovereignty. Catalonia and the Basque Country provide the paradigms for the concept of "nationality" given their desire to achieve sovereignty, although the term may sometimes be used ambiguously. In this context, we may recall that the regions with a higher political consciousness and separatist outlook in 1930 were precisely Galicia, the Basque Country and Catalonia. The latter obtained its own Statute early on in the period of the Second Spanish Republic. When the Constitution of 1978 came into force, it was the Basque Country that was the first to present a bill for a Statute of Autonomy to the Spanish Parliament, just a few hours before the Catalan bill was filed, and the Basque Statute was also the first to be approved. The Constitution largely frustrated the expectations of the two longest standing nationalist movements (Catalonia and the Basque Country), however, because they believed its structure and dynamics curtailed the devolution of powers.

It has become common in Spain to speak of "peripheral nationalism" to distinguish these nationalist movements from "Spanish nationalism" or, to put this another way, to differentiate between the stateless nationalities and the Spanish nation (Béjar 2008, p. 13). However, we may still consider this matter in an optimistic light, following authors like Sevilla et al. (2009, p. 11), who argue that "Our system enjoys high levels of political and social legitimacy via the feeling of dual belonging that is both regional and national", as the constitutional edifice is the shared work of the whole Spanish people and in it they have found their place in the European process.

To complete this series of definitions, "federalism" is the system by which various states, each of which is governed by its own laws (and therefore conserves its own autonomy), submit in certain cases and under certain circumstances to the decisions of a central government or power. A "federation" always emerges from an internal pact, in contrast to a "confederation" that arises from an international union or league that may sometimes be externally imposed, even by force. Hence, the member states of a federation share power with a central (federal) government with its seat in the federal capital. The member states "form a league and subordinate themselves to the union of their peers for all common purposes without losing their autonomy in matters that are peculiar and proper to themselves", or, as Pi y Margall (2002, p. 115) puts it, they "establish unity without destroying variety or changing their nature as nations". (For a discussion of federalism as a form of government and political integration, see Boogman and Van der Plaat 1980.)

## The Long-Awaited Reform of the Senate and Other Outstanding Reforms

Leaving aside the controversy outlined in the preceding section, the Spanish Constitution is not formally federal, if only because the text itself declares that "Federation of the CCAA shall not be permitted under any circumstances" (art. 145.1). Meanwhile, one need only compare the composition of the German *Bundesrat* (articles 50 to 53 of the *Grundgesetz*) with that of the Spanish Senate.

Constitutional regulation has failed to tame the complexities of the regional reality. Thus, it has for some time been recognised that reform of the Senate is "indispensable" in order to correct flaws in article 69 of the Constitution and the major shortcomings in the functioning of the Senate as a territorial Chamber. The necessary reform would ensure that it was the CCAA (and not the provinces) that were represented. At the time of the agreements made between the Socialist Party and the conservative *Partido Popular* to amend the Statutes approved under art. 143 of the Constitution in the mid-1990s, various working groups and commissions were set up to examine reform of the Senate, which had retained the structure it had when the Constitution was approved, even though the autonomic State was by then a reality and despite the frequently invoked need for "federalising progress" (cf. Fajardo 2009, pp. 154–155). The PSOE launched various political initiatives to seek agreement in this regard, but the matter was dropped during the first PP government of 1996–2000. Nevertheless, it resurfaced in 2001 and has been aired by the present Socialist government, although without results.

Not in vain, the reform of the Senate was one of the four issues addressed in the Council of State's 2006 "Report on amendments to the Spanish Constitution", following the consultations raised and proposals made by the Government. Among other matters, the Council of State proposed various reforms related to the functions of the Senate as the territorial Chamber and to its composition, among other matters. To begin with, the Council of State recommended strengthening the Senate's position in relation to "autonomic legislation" (legislative matters). It also proposed to enhance the Senate's role as a forum for agreements and cooperation between the CCAA and the State by assigning it a harmonising function. With regard to the composition of the Senate, meanwhile, a new wording was proposed for certain paragraphs of art. 69. Thus, each Autonomous Community would elect six senators, as opposed to the four currently elected by each province, which would of course reduce the total number of senators (see Rubio and Álarvez 2006).

As mentioned above, these debates reflect both nationalist or separatist views and unionist positions, depending on the political ideology of their authors. It was this situation that gave rise to the wording of art. 2 of the Constitution, which enshrines the unity of the Spanish nation, on one hand, while recognising the plurality of the nationalities, on the other, though these are not mentioned in Title VIII, and it was in fact the Statutes of Autonomy that christened them as such. This lacuna has multiplied the activity of the Constitutional Court, which is never beneficial in a democratic society. However, this is nothing new. It is well known that the actual structure of the autonomic State has been developed fundamentally by the Court's jurisprudential contributions, along with other constitutional factors.

For all of these reasons, the inclusion of the names of the CCAA and Cities in the Constitution was also addressed in point IV of the above-mentioned Council of State's Report, where it was proposed to make a material change to Title VIII in order to expressly mention the Autonomous Communities in arts 2, 137, and, 143 and to list them. This proposal is based, in the main, on the advisability of removing the autonomic prerogative, which the Council of State considers to have had scant effect, and on the need to close the process of political decentralisation without entirely shutting the door on the possibility that new Autonomous Communities might be created or that further reforms might be made to the Statutes of those already in existence.

A new regime is also needed for local government, and this will obviously mean establishing the formal channels by which such a reform could be carried out. "Autonomy" requires that the actions of regional government will not be controlled by central government, and this excludes any kind of hierarchical dependence proper to a centralised organisation with respect to the Administration of the State. Meanwhile, powers over Health have already been devolved (Royal Decree 1207/2006, of 20 October, concerning management of the Health Cohesion Fund), but other services such as the Administration of Justice and Prisons are still centralised. Further devolution would enhance the efficiency with which public services are delivered. After the Local Government Modernisation Act (Law 57/2003, of 16 December), an attempt was made to implement the *Proyecto Sevilla* (a reform plan named after the former PSOE Minister of Public Administration, Jordi Sevilla) and the "White Paper on the reform of local Government in Spain". The Project was abandoned when J. Sevilla was sacked in 2007, however.

So, progress has been made towards political decentralisation, recalling the Canadian model. Meanwhile, every effort has been made to establish a funding model that can be applied generally to all of the Autonomous Communities in order to avoid inter-regional imbalances (Law 50/1985, of 27 December and Law 22/2001, of 27 December). Finally, the CCAA have been allowed the maximum possible autonomy in the management of their finances. Despite all of these good intentions, however, numerous failings have been found in the application of the funding model, caused among other factors by the differing revenue structures of the CCAA.

We may affirm that it is only through a full-blown constitutional reform that some of these measures could be implemented, including, for example, the recurring proposal to reduce the powers enumerated in the Statutes of Autonomy to the simple rule that all and any powers not exclusively reserved to the State by art. 149.1 shall be exercised by the Autonomous Communities. This would require amendment of art. 149.3. Arguments are now beginning to be openly voiced in favour of constitutional reform to establish a confederate or quasi-confederate model for the State, instead of changing its territorial structure without a general design via the reform of the Statutes of Autonomy. However, it is not likely that this step will be taken, given the scant enthusiasm shown by citizens in the CCAA where reforms of this kind have been mooted.

This raises serious issues. Let us not forget that Title VIII, Chapter III of the Constitution, "The Autonomous Communities", is very rigid, and it enjoys special constitutional protection as it is referred to in the Preliminary Title (art. 2). Moreover, great care would be required with any reform. It is because of this that the Socialist Party has shied away from "opening the can of worms of constitutional reform" as it has been put, despite recognising the need and launching the political initiatives described above in order to seek agreement.

Given the developments described and the direction now being taken by the autonomic process, there can be no doubt that change is urgently needed unless powers are to be returned to the central government of Spain, but such retro-devolution by the CCAA also has its detractors, who argue that the scope of powers can sometimes be revised in federal States (as recently occurred in Germany), but it would be neither possible nor effective in Spain as the problem is for each part of the State (i.e., central government and the governments of the Autonomous Communities) "to exercise its constitutional powers" (Sevilla 2009, p. 18).

## Towards a Federal State?

Despite the appeals to the federal model in Spain, realism is needed, and we may conclude with Fajardo (2009, pp. 143, 145) that it is unlikely such a model would allow the changes to the texture of regionalisation witnessed in Spain because it is essentially based on integration. Thus, the *Länder* in Germany's federal system, for example, may occasionally act in a self-interested manner, but they are all aware of the maxim that "the parts believe in the whole and fit into it", especially since the federal reforms of 2006. Unfortunately, this is not the case in Spain. Furthermore, not all federal States are the same. In fact, Spain has already surpassed the levels of decentralisation found in other supposedly federal countries.

While it is true that the mooted Statute reforms suggest an effort to treat Spain as an integrated and harmonious country in which the parts believe in the unity of the whole, the reality is quite different, as the regions of Spain in fact display distinct separatist tendencies. The process of change that has affected Spain's territorial organisation over the last decade or so is a clear sign of a "country divided in its feelings of belonging" (Béjar 2008, p. 23), which has led some to argue that the State is incomplete and its structure is an unfinished edifice. The situation is grave because the dysfunctions between the agents making up the Spanish State are far from trivial. Quite the reverse, they affect key issues such as education, health care, and the funding of scientific research.

In this context, we may recall that the most far-reaching reforms of the Statutes of Autonomy were made after the approval of a Devolution Act pursuant to art. 150.2 of the Constitution and the incorporation of the powers concerned into the Statutes of the Autonomous Communities (see STC 56/1990, of 29 March). Certain contents of the Statutes were also amended between 1997 and 1999, culminating in the reform of the funding system in 1997 and 2001. While certain Communities have provided for the existence of a mixed Commission of the legislative powers of the State and the Autonomous Community in certain circumstances, if any of them were to undertake the changes to their Statutes that their governments desire without previous agreement on fundamental issues such as powers or funding, the outcome would be more of a confederate cast than a federal model (cf. Sosa 2007, pp. 142 ff.).

## Catalan Nationalism: The Confederate Model

Catalonia has spent over a century seeking to construct a federal State based on the effective popular sovereignty and political autonomy of [Spain's] peoples. The region has a long history, its own distinctive language, certain marked local characteristics, and its own civil law. In short, it is possible to talk of a true "Catalan nationalism", "national reality", and "national movement", which was believed to produce the right to the creation of Catalan State. An interesting discussion of Catalan nationalism will be found in Torres (2008).

It is for this reason that the current situation of Catalonia as an Autonomous Community merits special attention here, given its federalist or confederate tendencies (as opposed to the "associated State" model proposed by the former Basque premier Ibarretxe for Euskadi) since the *Pacto de Tinell* on 14 December 2003, following the ideas of the then leader of the Catalan Socialists, Pasqual Maragall. Let us not forget that Maragall's intention in 1999 was for "Catalonia to lead the transformation of Spain", and 2 years later he began using the term "plural Spain", which was adopted by the Pacto de Tinell. At a meeting of all the main peripheral nationalist parties held in Cantabria, the Catalan parties rejected the federal formula and supported the idea of confederation. A commitment was made to include far-reaching initiatives in the new Catalan Statute of 2006. However, the window opened by Maragall was closed in 2006 by the Mixed Commission of the Spanish National Parliament and the Catalan Assembly, which significantly modified the proposed Statute.

The controversial new Catalan Statute of 2006 aroused heated debate in the context of the reform of the Statutes of Autonomy in Spain (art. 147.3 of the Constitution), as it was viewed by some as legal and political madness that threatened the disappearance of the State as it was conceived during the transition to democracy (Leguina, Prologue to Sosa 2007, p. 11). Without going quite so far, there can be no doubt that the proposed Statute would have incorporated a different model into the Constitution had it not been modified by the Spanish Parliament. Moreover, the reformed Catalan Statute has exacerbated regional tensions, especially since STC 31/2010, of 28 June, on an issue that was indisputably political and financial.

## Concluding Remarks

Unfortunately, the judgment of the Constitutional Court, which firmly declared that "the Constitution does not recognise any nation other than Spanish nation", has not closed the debate surrounding the model of the State, and in general terms the situation remains the same as it was before the approval of the Catalan Statute. Once again, it will be "a political decision that will restore the lost legal and constitutional stability [*of the State*]" (Vallés 2011, p. 31). Since the Statute reforms of 2006 and 2007, some now consider that the Socialists' "can of worms" has been opened by the latest nationalist proposals, which outline a new model for the State. There can be no doubt that change is urgently needed unless powers are to be returned to the central Government of Spain, which today seems unlikely.

However, I wish to offer a positive view of these problems. If endeavours are focused on "achieving an efficient and rational territorial organisation of government, which acts from a position of openness, integration of different political goals, Europeanism, increasing attainment of democratic participation, mutual respect and good faith between institutions, and the assurance and extension of individual rights as the fulcrum on which the action of government turns, without ignoring cultural peculiarities as a basic principle", it may be possible to find support for this contentious federalising drive. Contentions arise because both peripheral nationalists and centralists do not always see eye to eye with the federalists. It will therefore be necessary to seek a balance to ensure that the national peculiarities of the parts are not relegated to a subordinate position, and that these singularities do not fragment the unity of the whole. Each must rather enrich the other. Otherwise, a State containing different nationalities that is organised around the national principle will run the risk of allowing a key role for one or more of its component parts, to the detriment of others. This is the view of the Spanish State taken by Arroyo (2011, pp. 12 ff.).

Obviously, the political parties have key role to play in this difficult task, but no less so the citizens of Spain themselves. The current economic crisis has raised awareness of and concern about the excesses of Government in Spain, and this will do little to help consensus and compromise. Opinions with regard to the territorial structure of the Spanish State remain sharply divided, but whether the preferred option is an autonomic State, a federal State, or a confederate State, only a generous, high-minded, and trusting attitude to dialogue will bring us any closer to a reasonable, unambiguous agreement on shared objectives.

**Acknowledgements** This contribution has been developed under the research project DER 2009-10375/JURI "Constitución y globalización: transformaciones del Estado constitucional y constitucionalización de espacios supranacionales".

# References

Arroyo, A. (2011). El Estado (federal) español. El Notario del Siglo XXI. Revista de Colegio Notarial de Madrid n° 37, mayo-junio, 11–15 pp.

Béjar, H., (2008) La dejación de España. Nacionalismo, desencanto y pertenencia. Katz, Buenos Aires, 290 pp.

Boogman, J.C. and Van der Plaat, G.N. (eds.) (1980). Federalism. History and current significance of a form of Government. The Hague, Martinus, Nijhoff, 307 pp.

Castells, L. and Cajal, A. (eds.) (2009). La autonomía vasca en la España contemporánea (1808–2008). Marcial Pons Historia, Madrid, 396 pp.

Elorriaga, G., (2011) La gran reforma pendiente. El Notario del Siglo XXI. Revista de Colegio Notarial de Madrid n° 37, mayo-junio, 16–21 pp.

Fajardo, L. (2009). ¿Hacia otro modelo de Estado?. Los Socialistas y el Estado autonómico. Aranzadi, Pamplona, 236 pp.

Pi y Margall, F. (2002). Las nacionalidades. Biblioteca Nueva, Madrid, 364 pp.

Prat, E. (1917) La nacionalidad catalana. Imprenta castellana, Valladolid, 143 pp.

Requejo, F. and Nagel, K.J. (eds.) (2011). Federalism beyond federations. Farnham, Surrey, Burlington, VT, 279 pp.

Rubio, F., Álvarez Junco, J. (2006). El Informe del Consejo de Estado sobre la reforma constitucional. CEPC, Madrid, 932 pp.

Sevilla, J. *et al.* (2009).Vertebrando España. El Estado Autonómico. Biblioteca Nueva, Madrid, 281 pp.

Smith, A. D. (2004). Nacionalismo. Teoría, ideología, historia. Alianza, Madrid, 208 pp.

Sosa, F. and Sosa, I. (2007). El Estado fragmentado. Modelo austro-húngaro y brote de naciones en España. Trotta, Madrid, 2007, 220 pp.

Torres, X. (2008). Naciones sin nacionalismo: Cataluña en la monarquía hispánica (siglos XVI-XVII). Servicio de Publicaciones, Universidad de Valencia, 392 pp.

Vallés, J. M. (2011). El Estatuto catalán de 2006 y la sentencia de 2010. El Notario del Siglo XXI. Revista de Colegio Notarial de Madrid n° 37, mayo-junio, 26–31 pp.

# The Adhesion of the Spanish Autonomic State to the Disaggregative Model of Federalism: A Possible Way

Anna Mastromarino

1.—The multinational tensions that have been gaining momentum in Spain for some time seem to have escalated to such an intensity as to threaten the social unity of the Country, if not the territorial one as well.

The Spanish national system is regarded as a multinational organization, a fact that was recognized by the Constitutional authorities as early as 1978. Over time, seeds of differentiation have taken root to distinguish—at least on a theoretical plan—the various communities, be they of a sociological or institutional nature. Article 2 of the Constitution, for example, and terms like *nacionalidad* or *comunidad historica*, find their validation in a willingness to give juridical form to a difference—be it real or alleged—that is perceived at social and political level.

The definition of such claims as "real or alleged" refers to the fact that at the time of the drafting of the Constitution the historical and institutional context held no certainty for the future.

The Spanish Constitution of 1978 is, in many ways, a multifunctional text: the fact that the question of the form of the State was in itself an acknowledgement of the impossibility to predict future events, particularly with reference to the direction that local nationalistic sentiments would take. It could have either consolidated or progressively dissolved, the latter being by far the preferable option but not the only viable one or the sole to be encouraged.

Neither was it the only option available in absolute terms. Comparative law provides clear examples of the limits that characterize policies aimed to disavow the existence of minority groups: distances grow wider, borders turn into

A. Mastromarino (✉)
Facoltà di Scienze Politiche, Centro Studi sul Federalismo, University of Turin, Via Vicolo Benevello 3/A, 10124 Torino, Italy
e-mail: anna.mastromarino@unito.it

A. López-Basaguren and L. Escajedo San Epifanio (eds.), *The Ways of Federalism*
*in Western Countries and the Horizons of Territorial Autonomy in Spain*, Vol. 2,
DOI 10.1007/978-3-642-27717-7_47, © Springer-Verlag Berlin Heidelberg 2013

insurmountable frontiers, "*exit* and *voice*"[1] practices grow stricter. Political claims take more radical stances, and self-determination becomes the ultimate goal.

However, irrespective of the processes of self-representation and collective, spontaneous mythopoeia that often characterize nationalist movements, there persist recurring questions that arise in Spanish legal theory on the legitimacy of the political claims made by some nationalist movements, starting from a purely historical standpoint, for the purpose of gathering data that would objectively support—or dismiss—a social and institutional differentiation policy.

With what results? It is difficult to identify universally accepted elements on which to base the definition of "ethnic group" or "nation." Should a minority be denied the status of national group, it would nevertheless remain an active interlocutor in public policy-making in the Spanish context, one that could not be ignored, a standard-bearer of specific claims and demands of recognition. The latter can be met either through a sectoral and occasional approach, with one-off policies that reflect the coalitions and political balance of a specific point in time, or through a radical transformation of the country so that the resulting form of the State is truly representative of the multinational nature of Spain.

Much has been said about the transition towards a federal State, at times going as far as to conclude that an explicit definition of the federal nature of the Spanish system is now entirely unnecessary since it has become evident in practice.[2]

In fact, none of the institutional actors appears to be willing to take the route to federalism: some for fear of undermining the Country's unity, others for fear of losing the flexibility and bilateral dimension that the current autonomic State seems to ensure.

---

[1] Group dynamics with reference to subjects in constant transformation from a quantitative and qualitative perspective can also be viewed with reference to the paradigm of Hirschman (1967), who starts from a Parsonian social scheme and identifies three elements at the foundation of social change. According to Hirschman, every community lives in a state of constant tension between an effort to defend and preserve its borders and prevent their downscaling. The elements that fuel this tension consist, first, in mechanisms of loyalty—maintenance structures that force social components to remain within set contexts; voice—processes that ensure communication between individual social components and between one system and the other, also in terms of opposition and not merely adherence, in order to ensure the regular supply of information from the outside in and vice-versa; and lastly, exit—referring to sources of change, in terms of collapse, transformation, and transcendence of the group, that represent a crucial event that can determine the crossing of a consolidated social boundary. The "*voice/exit*" dialectic presents an inexorable process of construction of borders and their overcoming that applies to all levels of human life. In this sense Rokkan (2002), 138 ss., attempts to articulate the "exit-voice" paradigm for a comparative study of territorial social systems: systems with limited *membership* and codes of interaction within borders that are identified in space. See also Hirschman (1978), 90 ss.

[2] For a federal view of the Spanish system, see, among others, Vilanova (2008), 5 ss.; Subra De Bieusses (2008), 19 ss.; Viver Pi-Sunyer (2004), 133; Aja (2003); Blanco Valdés (2003); Milano Giuffre (2003), cit., 103 ss., and also, more recently, in Italian, by the same author, Blanco Valdés (2006), 321 ss., as well as Blanco Valdés (2008), in particular 10. Non-Italian references include Agranoff (1996), 386 ss.

It is also a fact that the constitutional framework is often expanded to adjust to extensive exercises in interpretation, and it is no more suitable to perform a descriptive or a prescriptive function with reference to the form of the State.[3] The Constitutional Court decision no. 31/2010—which will likely become a milestone in public Spanish law—on the constitutionality of the Catalan Statute seems to acknowledge this scenario with this controversial and ambiguous decision, which promotes greater adherence to the Constitution itself.

Spain appears suspended, therefore, in a balancing act between fear of change and the struggle to guarantee answers and policies that are generally accepted by a social body that, in turn, is more and more divided.

In spite of all the fears, it would seem that the time has come to engage in a responsible reflection on which type of State would best suit Spain, a reflection that would allow Spain to maintain its unity while taking an active role in the management of diversity and change.

The adherence of Spain to the federal model through a disaggregative process of the autonomic State appears to offer good prospects to ensure the stability and cohesion of a country that is undergoing a serious identity crisis. This point is illustrated in greater detail in the following considerations on the characters of the paradigm of the dissociative federal State.

2.—An analysis of contemporary federalism cannot overlook the fact that while interest towards the aggregative federal State may be decreasing, it is not so for its appeal in its disaggregative form.[4]

The latter appears particularly suitable to respond—in both political and legal terms—to the progressive resurgence of ethnic-nationalist feelings that, contrary to the assumptions of liberal theory and far from imploding onto themselves, have made a significant comeback in public debate and social practice in several countries, also in Europe.

Today's societies are called to deal with a growing number of minority-related issues whereby claims are made for the recognition of a minority group's identity and the acceptance of their cultural differences. Such demands often lead to violent clashes between different cultures sharing the same institutional milieu.[5] In this scenario a merely formal description of the principle of equality appears to be inexorably inadequate. Consequently, while the liberal project still functions as the

---

[3] According to Balaguer Callejón (1997), 158 et seq., "el Estado autonómico, en cuanto formulación constitucional superadora del estado regional clásico y cercana a la filosofía del estado federal, ha culminado su desarrollo posible dentro del marco constitucional. Esta culminación significa tambien un agotamiento de su consideración como "proceso" inspirada en el principio dispositivo. La madurez del Estado autonómico implica, por tanto, la imposibilidad de estirar más el marco constitucional aportando soluciones a problemas estructurales que difícilmente se podrán resolver sin una actuación a nivel constitucional que permita consolidar y cerrar el modelo. La consolidación del Estado autonómico exige, ante todo, la superación definitiva del principio dispositivo, pero, no sólo de este principio".

[4] For a more in-depth analysis, see Mastromarino (2010).

[5] On this point, see Kymlicka (1995), 21; Holzner (1983), 119 et seq.

backdrop against which contemporary democracies move about today, it could be argued that this approach is no longer effective, at least in its purest form, to meet the challenges of pluralist societies[6] that are characterized by a growing complexity and that are, therefore, reluctant to classify differences as a mere "representation" or "superstructure" of any individual. It is actually a stance that institutions should reject and that the population, as far as it is ontologically possible, will also have to leave behind as living conditions improve on a vast scale and mature democratic systems consolidate.

Hence, there is the need to investigate the reasons that, from a practical point of view, have led over the past few years to the rise of the federal model as a means to fulfilling the needs of a multinational State, thus, in turn, the need to investigate the characteristics of the federal State in its disaggregative form, as well as the nature of what has been rapidly defined as *ethnic revival*. It is an exercise that serves to evaluate how suitable the "treatment" is to the "clinical picture" in order to overcome a long-standing prejudice that sees federalism and nationalism as incompatible and to view the relation between the two as a result of the very nature of federalism itself, as a tool to organize the community while preserving both unity and diversity, thanks to the autonomy and mutual independence that are guaranteed to the central government and to the governments of federated units,[7] respectively, in their actions.

3.—This is not the place to engage in a comprehensive examination of the common traits that seem to be shared by nationalist movements over the past decades, across all differences.

However, it is essential to provide an overview of the nature of the claims that are put forth and to identify the stances that animate the various groups, in that this

---

[6] See Trujillo (2007); Kymlicka (1995), 313, cit; Hooghe (1997), 270 ss. Cf. also Domenichelli (2002), 12, where it is stated that "concezione liberale della cittadinanza non tiene però conto del fatto che i fattori di discriminazione che impediscono attualmente la piena partecipazione alla vita della comunità politica da parte di alcuni suoi membri, almeno nelle società occidentali, sono sempre meno legati al riconoscimento dei diritti individuali. Le ragioni dell'esclusione, alla fine del XX e all'inizio e del XXI secolo, vanno spesso ricercate nel mancato riconoscimento della differenza culturale, per cui, pur possedendo i comuni diritti di cittadinanza, a molte persone è precluso un pieno godimento di diritti in teoria riconosciuti a tutti, proprio a causa della loro appartenenza a gruppi culturalmente discriminati".

[7] This could be done through a reevaluation of the intuitions that can be found in classic treatises on federalism like Wheare (1963), Elazar (1987), Lijphart (1984). Cf. also Requejo (2005); Ventura (2004), 407; Linz (2006), 558 ss.; Langer (1994), 89 ss.; Gagnon (2008), 18. On this point, Elazar (1987), 7, describes federalism as an important attempt to reconcile the widespread desire of peoples to preserve and reinstate the advantages of smaller societies with the growing need to combine into larger systems, in order to use common resources or to maintain or reinforce one's cultural peculiarities in wider communities. While searching for the reasons of the federalist revival, corresponding to the rise of ethnic-national claims, Ronald Watts wrote in his publication *The Contemporary Relevance of the Federal Idea*, in 1994, that federalism provides a technique for political organization that provides not only for the initiative of a central government to achieve shared objectives but also for the autonomous initiative of regional government units for objectives related to the safeguard of regional peculiarities. See also Ryker (1964), in particular 2.

point becomes relevant to the legislator when such claims threaten to undermine the foundations of the State.

Defending the pluralist nature of the liberal-democratic State entails the recognition and the support of the various social formations that—in a natural or associative form—ensure the expression of the individual and his/her development.

As social pluralism becomes more and more manifest, it should be noted that not all social groups take stances that break away from the State community.

The recognition of the rights of minorities—notwithstanding the primary and vital question of identifying a common meaning to be attributed to the concept of minority group—is an issue only with respect to the formations in which individuals do not simply pass through and preserve their individuality but with which they identify as a collective body. This does not refer to a spontaneous adherence to the activities of the community but requires a determination to participate in the destiny of the community to which the individual feels he/she belongs and that is a fundamental component of the individual's own *self*.

In such cases, individuals not only demand the commitment of the State to protect their right directly; they also request a mediated action that gives voice to the group to which they belong. They are not satisfied by a sector-based approach focusing on one specific characterizing element, e.g., language: They are requesting a comprehensive acknowledgement of their otherness and their identity.

The emphasis that is placed on the peculiarities of each community, that certainly deserve recognition, should be accompanied by a search for other factors that better represent the instances of the minority and that bring together—rather than tell apart—the experiences and scenarios of the various minority groups.

Therefore, regardless of other forms of differentiation, the communities that make up the social body could be classified starting from the very nature of their instances. Alongside groups that put forwards claims of an eminently cultural nature, it can be recognized that other social groups exist whose requests are of a political nature and whose behavior reflects clearly and inevitably into public life.

The fulfillment of the claims that are put forth by groups of the first type requires State action on the normative plan but does not entail any change at the institutional level. In this case, it could be argued that the recognition of the principle of the protection of cultural pluralism at constitutional level, supported by adequate legislation—sanctioning freedom of expression and the manifestation of one's culture—could in and by itself be regarded by minorities as an effective tool to meet their requests.

However, if the group's collective action is not aimed to the obtainment of the mere recognition of one's language, religion, or ethnic group in an abstract sense but to the granting of rights that ensure the participation of the minority in the political life of the State, the claims put forward will inevitably bring about institutional consequences. For groups with a "political vocation", language, religion, and ethnic group are not the point of their claims, which are regarded as instruments to gain access to the State's public life for the recognition of an identity and a diversity that finds in language, religion, and ethnic group only its most tangible expressions.

Instead of a "static" recognition, more "dynamic" policies are now preferred that entail the interaction of different social groups. This applies in particular to modern multinational States in which the territorial dimension is such a powerful binder as to lead autochthonous communities to develop a deep-set conviction that they are legitimately entitled to self-government, and it fuels the political aspirations of certain communities that wish to express their identity in a dimension that is not merely cultural but also political. It is an ambition to participate in the institutional life of the country, where the group lives together with other social entities, consolidating stable relations that are defined by the prevailing of one social component over another depending on existing relationships.

This is the starting point for an analysis of the current ethnic-national sentiments that will inevitably debunk the concept of a minority *deserving* recognition, as we know it. It is not always the case that the communities that come knocking on the door of the State possess the historical, ethnic, and social characteristics that have granted the dignity of a *people* to a collective body for the past few decades.

This does mean that such an approach would not give rise to issues of compatibility in a majority system: Denying the existence of a minority that lacks traditional standards does not shelter society from conflict. Minority communities result from a process of self-reflection and hetero-representation and mark a boundary that separates them from the majority group, in spite of the past and in view of the future.[8]

Empirical experience shows a certain inclination on the part of autochthonous minorities in multinational States to recognize themselves not in one tangible historical trait but in a wider framework to which that trait refers, a certain way of *feeling*, which may not coincide with their *being*, in the adoption of a *habitus* that leads to their juxtaposition to the majority. It is a distinction between *us* and *them*, a certain idea of the world and oneself that results from a mix of both voluntary and involuntary traits of the individual, that do not coincide with language or religion as such, an ethnic group, or a nation. It is closer, indeed, to the concept of *identity*, which better reflects a comprehensive reification of their collective entity and provides references for the consequent legal adjustments required. At least three characteristics make this option preferable over other, more traditional categories that are not necessarily more precise.

Identity is, at the same time, inevitable, ideal, and dynamic.

---

[8] The interpretation of ethnic-cultural identity as a fact and not as a process can be ascribed to romantic theory, critics of the Enlightenment, and the industrial society. Over time, this position was replaced by the idea that ethnic groups are rooted in a system of reciprocal actions that are put in place by the members and by the groups themselves. The construction of a community would go through a process of selection, within the community itself, of cultural factors regarded as essential. Emblematic in this sense is the theory of groups and boundaries by Barth (1969), whereby a inexhaustible process of transformation of identity-based communities is always afoot, and they represent the instrument, as well as the result of a constant effort to define and classify boundaries that require a continuous redefinition of the group's distinctive traits. On this point, see in particular, Scarduelli (2004), in particular, 35 ss.

It is *inevitable* because the human being is subject to an inevitable urge to ask questions concerning one's own nature. Hence, the need and the consequent development of the ability to "di tracciare dei confini e di 'collocarsi', di integrare le esperienze passate, presenti e future in una biografia più o meno coerente, di dare cioè continuità e stabilità al proprio sé", which requires "una *continuità* di relazioni sociali nella vita di un individuo, una memoria collettiva e un *mondo comune* che l'individuo condivide non solo più con l'altro dei mutevoli rapporti faccia a faccia, ma con tutti gli altri, anche quelli più lontani e anonimi".[9]

It is *ideal*, in that it can only be described "attraverso un racconto, attraverso un 'movimento mimetico', come il 'prodotto di una finzione', di una 'costruzione mitica'".[10] In this sense, identity would be nothing other than the result of a process of self-assumption based on the recognition of *us* as distinct from *them*.[11] It is the result of a process that is both *self* and *hetero* identification: "non è una proprietà intrinseca al soggetto, ma ha un carattere intersoggettivo e relazionale. Ciò significa che l'identità è il risultato di un processo sociale nel senso che sorge e si sviluppa nell'interazione quotidiana con gli altri".[12]

Lastly, by virtue of its being inevitable and ideal, it is also *dynamic* or subject to transformations that, in the medium to long term, alter its structure and its contents so that it becomes suitable to answer the ancestral question of all human beings—"Who am I?"—and to fulfill human relational needs. It is a result of a social process, and as such it feeds on symbols and meanings, and for this reason it

---

[9] L. Sciolla, *Teorie dell'identità*, in Id. (a cura di), *Identità*, cit., 23 et seq. According to Sen (1999), 14, identity takes precedence over reasoning, so much so as to represent for the individual "qualcosa di intrinseco più che qualcosa che egli può determinare".

[10] See Tucci (2004), 111 and bibliography thereof. A.D. Smith mentions *mythopoeic* processes when discussing the ethnic origins of nations, while Mosse (1974), 26 ss., with reference in particular to the totalitarian experience in Germany and Italy in the aftermath of the First World War, acknowledges that myth was the engine that transformed shapeless masses into an active subject, deceptively corresponding to the expression of the general will. Lombardi (1979), 20, notes that with the affirmation of the idea of nation, "al tempo stesso, si evidenziano, da un lato la vocazione (o per meglio dire l'autoinvestitura) rappresentativa della borghesia; e dall'altro canto la sottile mimesi attraverso la quale sotto il nuovo concetto politico-costituzionale si consuma la sostanziale spogliazione ed estromissione dal potere (a ben vedere più che di una estromissione si tratta di una esclusione preventiva) dei ceti subalterni sotto la forza legittimante (e mistificante) di una ideologia, quella nazionale che, se pure li fa sentire partecipi a livello di identificazione emotiva, li esclude nella forma e nella sostanza dall'esercizio del potere".

[11] In this sense, the words used by the anthropologist Benedict Anderson could be useful to define the concept of nation as an *imagined political community* in which individual members will never know, or meet, most of their fellowmen or hear their voice, but in the mind of each one of them they nurture the image of themselves as a community. Cf. Anderson (1991). As noted by Linz and Stepan (2000), 35, a nation requires some measure of internal identification since as such it does not possess organizational traits that can be compared to those of a State. It lacks autonomy, representatives, and rules, and it only possesses the resources that derive from the psychological identification with the persons that make it up.

[12] See L. Sciolla, *Teorie dell'identità*, cit., 21.

appears to be less *physiologically* determined than other terms like race, ethnic group, and nation appear to be.

It could not be otherwise since it functions as a catalyst of human needs and fears that change over the years, in line with the human inclination to belong to kin groups and units and to share a certain cultural symbolism that ensures communication and signification.[13]

Identity is therefore a multifaceted concept, which is versatile and referable to different situations and therefore is ill-fit to adjust to sector-based protection and development policies. It requires actions of a wider scope that reach beyond the individual dimension to focus on the collective subject that embodies that identity. Notwithstanding the willingness of the State to recognize certain minority groups characterized by a strong sense of identity, the latter will likely pose a question of *public recognition*[14] that translates into political claims that may find an answer in the constitutional instruments available to create political integration tools that are in line with the nature of a multinational State.

The ensuing public dialogue on the integration of minorities is therefore not only useful; it is also inescapable. The fact that contemporary multinational democracies are not tackling the issue in institutional terms appears to be a false option.

Differences are perceived and are taken on by the group as an ineludible boundary in meaning. They cannot be taken out, but they can be mitigated by virtue of the dynamic and ideal nature of identity and subject to changes imposed by the group through a convergence of the traits that characterize the group.

Breaking away from a static view of culture-based affiliation, the postmodern approach to "ethnic revival",[15] along with the ambition of groups to hand down their historical and cultural heritage, allows a discussion of the differences between social groups as factors that are the result of a construction (instrumental to the modern industrial society or traced back to ancient and premodern society). This allows for a full grasp of the *mythical* aspect of the group as the repository of the ancestral character of the community that is hidden behind its ever-changing nature.

Based on the assumption that human groups—also those that are defined on an ethnic or national basis—are constantly evolving, this perspective contributes to

---

[13] Smith (1987), 48.

[14] As a *process of recognition*, the construction of an identity represents a modern phenomenon because "è solo a partire dalla modernità che il riconoscimento non è più un elemento scontato, agevolmente reperibile all'interno di una società organizzata gerarchicamente, in cui ogni individuo occupa il suo posto per nascita" (cf. Loretoni 1996, 106). Berlin (1958), highlighted the role played by public recognition on the perception of personal freedom and clams that one may feel he or she is not free in the sense that he or she is not recognized as an individual self-governing human being, but one can feel free as a member of a group that is not recognized or not adequately respected, hence the desire for emancipation of a whole class or community, nation, race of profession to which one belongs (*ibid.*, 58). On *the fight for recognition* and recognition as a driver for nationalist movements and on the connection with the idea of identity, see Habermas and Taylor (2002), which contains two classic treatises by the authors; also, Taylor (1992).

[15] Based on the definition by Smith (1981).

highlighting the key role that public law has to play in the process of creation of the identity of a minority and in the solution of conflicts and social tensions.

If changes to which human identity is subject are driven by the environment, then it is indisputable that the public *habitat* will also influence its definition. Over time, participation in public life to State institutions can give rise to processes of *comunizazione* that generate stronger consensus and a desire to live together, thus altering the boundaries of the identity described above as "*us.*" The interaction of such different cultures can give rise to a new cultural model based on the sharing of public space.

The impact of this vision, whereby identity characters are endlessly evolving, on public law is immediately self-evident. A relative approach to minorities prevents an entrenchment behind a rigid and absolute concept of identity as an immutable condition, and it makes it possible to contrast attempts to falsify reality and influence human beings in their search for a "community" to belong to, in order to fuel a permanent ethnic-cultural conflict.

Most significantly, it allows State institutions to interfere in the processes leading to the self-shaping of an identity, which as a result lose their self-referential dimension in favor of participation in a process of social integration and reconciliation.

While fundamental identity traits are nonnegotiable in the short term, in the medium-to-long term, like all aspects of human nature, they are subject to change induced by the social interaction of individuals. Consequently, a progressive distancing from the Nation-State model—in favor of more inclusive forms of political organization—paves the way to the construction of collective mythopoeic platforms that reach out to the largest possible target population. The definition of a widely shared culture in society thus becomes a feasible achievement.

In this sense the legal instrument on which integration projects can be based is found not in the theoretical adherence to the principles of democracy but in a common feeling of being subject to a Constitution that regulates decision-making processes. These projects can successfully replace the outdated concept of the Nation-State with the one of *civic nation* that stems from the classic dichotomy *ethnos-demos* and that refers to a voluntary interpretation of the idea of nation whereby the institutions and the Constitution[16] are entrusted with the setting of common rules of civil and democratic life as the expression of the passion that lies

---

[16] In this perspective "gli individui acconsentono alla forma associativa delineata dalla costituzione in virtù del riconoscimento costituzionale della loro *sostanziale diversità culturale*. In altri termini: la costituzione deve essere la "forma di compromesso" della diversità culturale" (cf. Gozzi 2009, 193), hence the idea whereby the Constitution "non è soltanto un ordinamento giuridico per i giuristi, da interpretarsi da questi in base a regole d'arte vecchie e nuove—essa funge anche da linea-guida per i non giuristi: per i cittadini. La costituzione non è solo un testo giuridico o un armamentario di regole normative, ma anche l'espressione di uno stadio evolutivo culturale, un mezzo di auto rappresentazione culturale del popolo, lo specchio di un patrimonio culturale e fondamento delle sue speranze". See Häberle (2006), 11. See also Tully (1997), in particular 30; Belvisi (2000), in particular 112 ss.

at the heart of an ethnic-national sense of belonging, in the quest for a spiritual unity. No society can exist without a sense of common belonging: It is this sentiment that turns the interests and the needs of others into one's own; that leads to the recognition of the authority in charge of making decisions and laws that must be respected, even when they are not in the immediate interest of the individual; and that provides a criterion to tell apart those who are entitled to the sacrifices deriving from this belonging from outsiders. If experience is detached from the concept of belonging, the social contract is doomed to dissolve: social obligations become temporary, negotiable, ephemeral, and the idea that someone may be called to sacrifice his or her life for a group of strangers becomes plainly absurd.[17]

Thus, democracy stops being an end in itself; it becomes a means to an end for the achievement of the primary objective of complex contemporary societies: the cohesion of a social body as opposed to the original fragmented state with its plurality of interests.

It is not democracy itself but the instruments and the institutions of democracy that become a seat of cohesion and catharsis, a place where the collective and otherwise fragmented identity of a society is formed and where individual social components shed their most extreme particularisms.

In order for this to happen, form has to become substance, by placing emphasis not only on procedures but also on contents.

In a plural society, it is not enough that decisions are made after public debate. Decisions are required to embody the very outcome of that debate, which must represent an act of summing up, the overcoming of a boundary, the subsumption of the particular into the general, to draw a new border that is wider and more inclusive.

The binding nature of decisions taken by the institutions will be legitimate as far as the decisions take into account the interests of all.

The choice of which type of democracy will guide the public hand appears inevitably central. It will be regarded as a model for the organization of the collective and public exercise of power in the fundamental institutions of society. This, in turn, will be based on the principles whereby decisions on the well-being of the community are the result of a free and reasoned deliberation of individuals that are regarded as morally and politically equal.[18]

It is through this model of participatory and deliberative democracy that a civic nation can issue not as the representation of an assumption, an original element, but as an objective that is achieved after a long transformation that involves first and foremost the State—both in terms of territorial organization and respect for the central political organization.

---

[17] See Scruton (2004), 9. On this point, see also Reale (2003).

[18] Cf. Benhabib (2002), 145. On the deliberative democratic approach, see, in general terms, Benhabib (1996), 67 ss.; Gutmann (1996); Habermas (1992); Frishkin (1991); Dryzek (1990); Cohen (1989), 17 ss.

When put into practice, the paradigms of democracy will require participation in decision-making so that they truly come to embody the normative foundation of community life. Thus the venue where public debate takes place, the subjects eligible to participate, the outcome of the debate itself become essential to ensure that the decision is perceived as a widely accepted outcome, in which one can reflect as an individual and as a group.

4.—In multinational contexts, it is the nature of the social body that influences the choice of a State's government organization over another. Irrespective of any sociological, historical, or ethnographic consideration on the origin and the foundation of nationalist movements, it is the responsibility of the legislator to give shape to pluralities on the institutional plan, to reconcile and manage conflicts that could become irretrievable.

Federal principles and their practical application in a Federal State seem fit to serve this purpose, according to a trend that breaks away from traditional federalism characterized by a centrifugal force.

Consequently, at least from a legal point of view, the time has come to make a clear distinction between a so-called aggregative form of federalism (ascribable to the US model) and more recent dissociative patterns (e.g., Belgium) that result from a disarticulation of the unitary State.

Until recently, studies on federalism have largely neglected to investigate the differences that issue from the different process leading to the creation of a federal system, perhaps because it was only recently that disaggregative systems have gained momentum and they remain limited in number.

Undoubtedly, from an ideological point of view and in terms of theory of the State, the federalization of a unitary State appears similar to the experiences of major federal States, like the U.S.A. The term "federalism" can be used to define not only a type of State—namely the Federal State[19]—but also a current of thought, an ideology, a political and social project that is regarded as desirable in order to ensure good government and peace among peoples.[20] In this sense, the federal idea, which necessarily entails a structural analysis, is rooted in its symbolic aspects, which should not be confused with other forms of decentralization that stem from an asymmetrical form of regionalism, which take inspiration from federal principles.

From a strictly legal perspective, it is not possible to carry out an analysis leading to observations that can apply to both forms of federalism: The disaggregative one is much closer to other types of State organization than to aggregative federalism, like the Regional State that represents the greatest level of decentralization while preserving the State's territorial unity.

---

[19] Hence the distinction between "federation" and "federalism" that is often found in theoretical arguments on the issue. In particular, King (1982). Cf. Croisat (1992), 15 ss.; Albertoni (1995), 23 et seq.

[20] As noted by Mario Albertini in the introduction to his anthology Mario Albertini (1963). See also Bognetti (2005), 82 ss.; Malandrino (1998); Luciani (1997), 215 ss.; Pasquino (1996), 13 ss.

These are the premises that have led to an *impasse* that is ill-suited to offer a comprehensive analysis of federalism that would include its philosophical, political, as well as structural dimensions.

The two options—the federal disaggregative versus the regional system—are inextricably connected in their very essence, like two faces of the same coin, and a different perspective would diminish the traits of each version. Regarding as minimal the "ideological" distance between the federal experience—even in its disaggregative form—and the regional one would mean rejecting federalism as a political thought in favor of a one-way interpretation of decentralization in merely legal terms. However, choosing an approach to federalism as a principle rather than as the application of a "Federal State" would not take into account the technical and organizational aspects that are of primary importance to the legislator.

Could it be that *tertium non datur*? The solution may lie in the complex nature of federalism itself, on the condition that disaggregative federalism is regarded as a type of hybrid State that is other than an aggregative form of federalism, but just as distant in terms of institutional dynamics from the regional paradigm.

A careful analysis of the recent federalization process, while placing emphasis on the legislator's priorities, may come to regard disaggregative federalism as independent from either aggregative federalism—with which it shares its ideological framework—or other forms of decentralized State government—of which it is an expression and with which it shares some of its structural features.

The immediate consequences of such considerations should not be underestimated. If an exercise in classification serves to fulfill a descriptive as well as a prescriptive necessity, disaggregative federalism as a form of State government serves to bring the theory of State forms closer to reality. At the same time, it also clarifies the premises and the traits that characterize the regional State and the federal State, which appear to be inexorably converging as the associative federal option gains momentum.

It should also be noted that from a pragmatic point of view, the question of defining the regional versus the federal state seems to have led to the definition of the category of the Composite (or decentralized) State, while from a juridical, speculative standpoint it would appear preferable to maintain some distinction that would highlight the distance between the possible expressions of decentralization.

The historical-ideological element that characterizes federalism as a current of thought and as a category of State organization represents an essential element that is not suitable to a merely empirical approach.

It can be recognized that both the regional option and the federal one—the latter intended as a disaggregation from a unitary whole—possess decentralized and composite traits and that there may be similarities of these parallel experiences on the two models. However, it is not possible for this reasoning to go any further, for ontological as well as aethiological reasons: it would not be possible, in particular, to trace the two experiences back to the same type of State without stripping both systems of their political essence.

On the other hand, viewing disaggregative federalism as a type of State that is distinct from aggregative federalism would entail advantages also in terms of a revival of the descriptive and prescriptive functions of federalism. This is because it would contribute to a systematic classification of the federal State model that recent experiences seem to have made unclassifiable because most recent federal States appear not to reflect the characters that identify a federal State type according to a traditional theoretical approach.

The systematic differentiation between disaggregative and aggregative forms of federalism and the identification of the factors leading to the creation of a Federal State—and therefore the nature of the federal process afoot—can contribute to restoring a more accurate overall view.

Clearly, the two processes are triggered by different needs and reasons, and their structural, institutional, and organizational outcomes also differ.

In the current scenario, the aggregative formation of major Federal States appears to be losing steam, at least in its classic form. Eighteenth and nineteenth century federalism rested on the need on the part of the State to consolidate its borders and its offensive power. It was intended to ensure an adequate defense against external threats, and it led individual States to relinquish part of their sovereign prerogatives in favor of a wider institutional association.[21]

Federalism by disaggregation, on the other hand, has a more recent inception and responds to completely different needs.

It appears better suited to States characterized by a more composite social body subject to stronger separatist tensions. In these cases, the process of federal disarticulation of State institutions starts at Constitutional level, in order to meet the system's internal needs,[22] to answer demands for self-government that come from the social body and that could lead eventually to the dissolution of the State itself, were they to remain unheeded.[23] In this sense, dissociative Federalism strikes a balance between the conservation of the State's territorial unity and the fulfillment of the interests of the social body itself.[24]

---

[21] In this sense see Wheare (1963), 91 ss. In the same years, Riker (1964, 1975), 93 ss.

[22] On this point Russell (1994).

[23] According to the study by S. Ventura (a cura di), *Da stato unitario a stato federale*, cit., 195, "i processi di riorganizzazione del governo del territorio mostrano chiaramente ... che la mobilitazione delle periferie contro il centro, promotore del processo di costruzione della nazione, è da ricollegare a processi di *nation-building* "incompleti"".

[24] In this sense, the American politologist Stepan (2001), 181 ss., insists on the distinction between *coming together* federative processes (of the associative type) and *holding together* ones, where the federal option is the only option available to prevent the dissolution of the State. In this sense, "una forte mobilitazione etnica *non* sfocia nella disintegrazione dello stato ma in effetti lo sostiene": L. Hooghe, *Il Belgio: una missione per eccellere in Europa*, cit., 273. Vedi anche Linz (2006), cit., 549 ss.; Paddison (1995), 27, which identifies the essence of federalism in "nel facilitare l'espressione di interessi regionali distinti all'interno di un'unione politica complessiva". Specifically, federalism would be "potenzialmente utile a risolvere i problemi della diversità etnica, laddove i vari gruppi etnici sono territorialmente segregati: laddove, in altre parole, essi possono avere un'autonomia regionale" (*ivi*, 28); Dikshit (1975).

The two systems also differ in substance. In particular, their ontological difference reflects in the allocation of sovereignty, a point that has been at the heart of the federalist debate for centuries.

Aggregative federalism begs the question of the distribution of sovereign power between the Federal State and the Member States, which possess an original nature and which, in the exercise of their sovereignty, adhere to a supranational process, whereas in disaggregative federalism the question must be posed from a different perspective.

It can be argued that in a process of federalization of a national territory, it is the State that creates federated entities. From a strictly juridical and institutional viewpoint before being sanctioned by a Constitution, the latter simply do not exist[25]: Consequently, the question of the attribution of power to the federated entities rather than to the Central State is made irrelevant by virtue of the derived nature of the members of this type of federation.

The dissociation of a State into derived federal entities does not jeopardize the sovereignty of the central federation that will continue to benefit from all the prerogatives of the original entity. The federal entities that derive from the disaggregation of a unitary State are autonomous but not sovereign ones, in that they result from a decision of the Central State to seek new forms of political integration through the disarticulation of its power and its territory.[26]

A number of consequences contribute to further distinguishing the aggregative from the disaggregative federal model.

In terms of State theory, the differences that characterize aggregative experiences from the disaggregative ones also reflect on the institutional level so that, as previously noted, most States based on a disaggregative federal model, do not possess the traits that are traditionally regarded as distinctive of a Federal State if compared to a unitary or regional one.

The autonomous and nonsovereign nature of the members of the federation, from a strictly juridical point of view, makes it impossible to attribute to them the same powers that are recognized to States that engage in aggregative federalist processes, and it also influences their constitutional framework.

The consequences are twofold: on the one hand, federated entities in disaggregative processes do not have the prerogative to adopt a local Constitution. They possess, however, a statutory power, the expression of their autonomic faculties that reflect their derived and nonoriginal nature.

---

[25] The same expression that was used in the past by A. Ambrosini to describe that regions could be applied, *mutatis mutandis*, to these entities as well: They are described as "frammenti di Stato" (*Un tipo intermedio di Stato fra l'unitario e il federale caratterizzato dall'autonomia regionale*, in *Rivista di Diritto pubblico*, 1932, 95 ss.), with an explicit reference to the theory of G. Jellinek on the nature of regional entities.

[26] Nor would it appear to be enough to disprove the aforesaid through the extensive use of the terms "autonomy" and "sovereignty", which are made by some Federal Constitutions like the one of Austria. Cf. Pernthaler (1992), 30 ss.

Furthermore, since they did not participate in the act that laid down the State organization, they are not always entitled to direct participation in the process of constitutional revision,[27] while their participation is not precluded in an absolute sense. They are actively involved in the construction and safeguard of their self-government as sanctioned by the Constitution, not as protagonists or coprotagonists along with the State in the Constitutional revision process (which sees federal entities in a subordinate position with respect to the central power) but as active forces in "Constitutional policy-making", in the application of the Constitution, the content of which "non coincide con i principi politici fondamentali di cui sono (e sono state nel momento costituente) portatrici le forze politiche dominanti, ma è quello che consegue all'insieme delle attività diffuse". Constitutional policy making "non è dunque affatto sinonimo di attuazione della Costituzione, ma è invece, innanzi tutto, causa della sua validità (in una prospettiva istituzionalistica), o sintomo essenziale della sua validità (in una prospettiva normativistica)".[28]

As regards the forces that fuel the disaggregative federal process of a State, notwithstanding the form and the degree of participation to the constitutional reform on the part of local entities, other considerations come into play on the validity of the Constitution, in that it "è valida non perché voluta (o riconosciuta come punto di equilibrio) dalle forze politiche dominanti, ma perché riconosciuta come punto di riferimento pratico, e cioè come oggetto di interpretazione (e simultaneamente come parametro per le questioni successive), dai diversi soggetti cui essa stessa affida la propria applicazione. Fondazione della validità e determinazione del contenuto (del significato complessivo, unitario) della Costituzione, in questa prospettiva, dunque, si fondono".[29] Therefore also in disaggregative federal systems, regardless of established procedure, local forces participate in the definition of a new constitutional balance for the purpose of ensuring its endurance.

Moreover, the disaggregative origin of the federal system, unlike the aggregative one, also reflects in the judiciary and fiscal organization of the new framework: Federated subjects do not possess jurisdictional or tax-levying powers. The power to render justice, like the power to levy taxes, rests with the "sovereign" entity and not with ones that are simply autonomous.

The different process that leads to the formation of the two models also has evident consequences not only on the institutional and political aspects of disaggregative federal systems but also on the pre- e *praeter*-constitutional bond between the federal State and the federated entities.

Traditionally, the Federal State—which results from the aggregation of several sovereign entities—represents a virgin territory, entirely to be formed, that stems

---

[27] The disaggregation process of the unitary State evolves through a constitutional transformation that stems from the demands put forward by social forces, which may not have been part of the constitutional pact in origin but operates through the instruments of established power.

[28] Cf. Dogliani (1996), 293 ss., in particular 295.

[29] *Ibidem*, 295.

from a common willingness expressed by the original subjects involved. Vice versa, in disaggregative federal systems, the federated entities operate within a system that is characterized by consolidated power relations, contrapositions. or solid alliances between different parts of the social body and the national territory that, while often in a nonofficial capacity, predate the federation itself and inevitably influence its institutional and constitutional developments.[30] In federal States that result from a disaggregative process, factual and prejuridical elements become central and are the foundations of new federal relations, which are destined to replace the unitary structure of central power and which often acquire relevance also with reference to other structural aspects of the Federal State organization.

In this perspective, the role of a party-based system becomes pivotal in determining institutional directions. However, while political parties represent a specific topic in the study of federal systems,[31] in the case of disaggregative processes the presence of regional forces that have strong territorial roots leads to a reflection on the differences that appear evident if compared to the aggregative process. These consist in the fact that "local" parties predate federalism itself, or rather their claims and their activity on the local scale make them in fact the promoters and the inspirators of federalism, since it could be argued that they are the subjects that will actually "negotiate" its creation with the central power. In an aggregative process, on the other hand, parties stem from a unitary structure and tend to regionalize only in order to take advantage of all the opportunities offered by the various political arenas.

In a dissociative federal State, negotiation would therefore be identified as the prevailing element, both on the political and the institutional levels. Unlike the pact among equals that anticipates the creation of aggregative federal States, the relationship between autonomous federated entities and the Central State would be founded on federative bonds that are, by far, much more complex in their stipulation because they are the result of bilateral negotiations between the State and each *federating* entity.[32]

As a result disaggregative federalism, experiences are characterized by an innate asymmetry, both vertically and horizontally.

Unlike more traditional federal experiences, disaggregative processes never result in a perfectly equal status of the various levels of government since the central authority maintains a certain supremacy over the others, thanks to persisting rules that attach a certain preeminence to the federal organization and that therefore lead to a vertical asymmetry that is atypical of traditional federalism categories.

---

[30] Cf. Bauböck (2001), 6 ss.

[31] Starting with Truman (1955), 115 ss., and also Elazar (1987), cit. See also Weaver (2004), 228; Chandler (1987), 149 ss.

[32] In a dissociative form of federalism, new meaning is attached to the warning that was formulated in the past by William Riker (1964, cit., 16) as an invitation not to fall into what he defined as *reductionist fallacy.*

The federal State that is based on a process of power and territorial disaggregation is, by its very nature, a horizontally differentiated system that may translate only in a partial federation of the territory.[33] Dissociation will be promoted by one or more groups that are part of the country's social body but that take a different stance with regard to the national sociocultural model. Clearly, they have developed a pluralist view of the political and physical space in which they live, as required by a plural reality: They accept to keep the State to which they adhere alive on the condition that it evolves from a unitary and possibly decentralized one into a federal State that is willing to grant room for political autonomy to reflect the characters of each federated community, thus responding to the demand for self-government.

5.—Also in light of the foregoing considerations, which future can be expected for the Spanish Autonomic State? Is federalism a viable option for the Spanish State organization?

It can certainly be argued that the "liquid form" of the Spanish State organization represents a winning option also for the future because it can adapt over and over again to the needs and the demands of the various components of society.[34] Nevertheless, in the long term, the social system will be called to pay a price in terms of cohesion.

The "liquid" system requires that the structure does not remain crystallized, and therefore, in this particular case, it may give rise to new claims and additional demands. It presupposes the definition of more and more virtual borders—in that they are rooted in less tangible traits—and therefore it also advocates the persistence of a more or less latent state of conflict. The distance between *us* and the *others* becomes less objective and more rooted in a subjective *self* and for this reason all the more difficult to eradicate, particularly in a State that is perceived as delegitimized by part of the social body.[35]

Could it be that the time has come for Spain to constitutionalize its State organization? The Constitutional definition of a federal organization based on the disaggregative model described above, at least in the short term, would certainly entail a redefinition—most likely in favor of asymmetry—of the autonomy of individual communities and therefore a downscaling of the liquid nature of political relations between the center and the periphery.

However, based on the considerations on multinationalism and dissociative federalism, it is possible that the explicit adoption at Constitutional level of a federal State model—not simply an abstract adherence to the principles that lie at the heart of federal theory—would unquestionably bring about benefits in terms of

---

[33] According to Linz, (2006), cit., 544, there exist some institutional forms that Federalist scholars like Daniel J. Elazar call *federacies*, in which the smaller units—generally one or more islands—are granted a special constitutional status, while the remaining portion of the State is governed as a unitary State. Cf. Elazar (1995), 474 ss. and Elazar (1991).

[34] In this sense, cf. Rodríguez-Arana Muñoz (2002), 111.

[35] Consider the concept of *hecho diferencial*, which is perpetually losing its juridical traits to adopt a nature that appears to be increasingly political, sociological, a more "extremist" character that it lacked almost entirely in origin.

social harmony and the construction of a public space. This, in turn, would contribute to building a consensus around the State project, enhancing a civic sense of nation, completing the unfinished process of construction of the national unity, and promoting a sense of togetherness as noted earlier.

This is the option that lies ahead if Spain intends to turn a new leaf in its institutional history: a complete rethinking of the form of government and of State to opt for. The acceptation of the country's multinational nature (to what good all the soul-searching on the existence of a national tradition of communities that do not aspire but actually demand to have a future?), a proactive approach towards differences, also in view of the construction of a civic identity at State level, that looks beyond ethnic or linguistic differences and aims at recognizing the Constitution as a common heritage, an opening to the disaggregative federal system as the option that can both preserve the unity of the State while providing recognition for the political and institutional role of the various social components: it is from these premises that the journey can finally begin.

# References

R. Agranoff, *Federal Evolution in Spain*, in *International Political Science Review*, vol. 17, n. 4, 1996

E. Aja, *El Estado autonómico. Federalismo y hechos diferenciales*, Madrid, Alianza, 2003

A. Albertoni (a cura di), *Il Federalismo nel pensiero politico e nelle istituzioni*, Milano, Eured, 1995, 23

Amartya. K. Sen, (*La ricchezza della ragione*, (1999), trad. it., Bologna, il Mulino, 2000, 14

B. Anderson, *Comunità immaginate*, (1991), trad. it., Roma, Manifesto libri, 1996, 27

F. Balaguer Callejón, *Constitucionalización del Estado autonómico*, in *Anuario de derecho constitucional y parlamentario*, n. 9, 1997, 158

F. Barth, *I gruppi etnici e i loro confini*, (1969), trad. it., in V. Maher (a cura di), *Questioni di etnicità*, Torino, Rosenberg & Sellier, 1994

R. Bauböck, *United in Misunderstanding? Asymmetry in Multinational Federations*, Vienna, Austrian Academy of Sciences, Research Unit for Institutional Change and European Integration, Working Paper n. 26, 2001

F. Belvisi, *Società multiculturale, diritti, costituzione*, Bologna, Clueb, 2000

S. Benhabib, *Deliberative Rationality and Models of Democratic Legitimacy*, in Benhabib (ed.), *Democracy and Difference: Contesting the Boundaries of the Political*, Princeton, Princeton University Press, 1996

S. Benhabib, *La rivendicazione dell'identità culturale*, (2002), trad. it, Bologna, il Mulino, 2005, 145

J. Berlin, in *Due concetti di libertà*, (1958), trad. it., Feltrinelli, Milano, 2000

Blanco Valdés, *Constitución, descentralización, federalismo: que se puede aprender de la experiencia española*, in M.P. Viviani Schlein, E. Bulzi, L. Panzeri (a cura di), *L'Europa tra federalismo e regionalismo*

R.L. Blanco Valdés, *La Constitución de 1978*, Madrid, Alianza, 2003

Blanco Valdés *La Spagna, il federalismo e Godot*, in *Politica del diritto*, 2006

Blanco Valdés *La seconda decentralizzazione spagnola: tra riforma confederale e Stato possibile*, in *Federalismi.it*, n. 17, 2008

G. Bognetti, *Federalismo*, Torino, Utet, 2005

W.M. Chandler, *Federalism and Political Parties*, in H. Bakvis, W.M. Chandler (ed.), *Federalism and the Role of the State*, Toronto, University of Toronto Press, 1987

J. Cohen, *Deliberation and Democratic Legitimacy*, in A. Hamlin, P. Petit (eds.), *The Good Polity: Normative Analysis of the State*, London, Blackwell, 1989

M. Croisat, *Le fédéralisme dans le démocraties contemporaines*, Paris, Montchrestien, 1992

R. Dikshit, *The political geography of Federalism*, London, Macmillan, 1975

M. Dogliani, *La lotta per la Costituzione*, in *Diritto Pubblico*, 1996

L. Domenichelli, *Asimmetria territoriale e cittadinanza differenziata come strumenti di protezione dell'identità*, in *Diritto pubblico comparato ed europeo*, 2002, 12

J.S. Dryzek, *Discursive Democracy*, Cambridge, Cambridge University Press, 1990

D.J. Elazar, *Idee e forme del federalismo,* (1987), trad. it., Milano, Mondadori, 1998, 7

D.J. Elazar, *Federalism*, in S.M. Lipset (ed.), *The Encyclopedia of Democracy*, vol. II, Washington, Congressional Quarterly, 1995

Elazar *Federal Systems of the World. A Handbook of Federal, Confederal and Autonomy Arrangements*, Harlow, Longman, 1991.

J.S. Frishkin, *Democracy and Deliberation: New Directions for Democratic Reform*, New Haven, Yale University Press, 1991

A.-G. Gagnon, *Oltre la "nazione unificatrice" (in difesa del federalismo multinazionale)*, Bologna, Bononia University Press, 2008, 18

G. Gozzi, *In difesa del relativismo*, in *Il Mulino*, 2009, 193

A. Gutmann, D. Thomson, *Democracy and* Disagreement, Cambridge, Harvard University Press, 1996

P. Häberle, *Costituzione e identità culturale*, Milano, Giuffrè, 2006, 11

J. Habermas, *Fatti e norme: contributi a una teoria discorsiva del diritto e della democrazia*, (1992), trad. it., Milano, Guerini, 1996

J. Habermas, Ch. Taylor, *Multiculturalismo. Lotte per il riconoscimento*, Milano, Feltrinelli, 2002

A.O. Hirschman, *Exit, Voice and Loyalty. Reponses to Decline in Firms Organization, and States*, Cambridge, Harvard University Press, 1967

A.O. Hirschman, *Exit, Voice and State*, in *World Politics*, vol. 31, n.1, 1978

B. Holzner, *La costruzione di attori sociali. Saggio sulle identità sociali*, in L. Sciolla (a cura di), *Identità. Percorsi di analisi in sociologia*, Torino, Rosemberg & Sellier, 1983, 119

P. King, *Federalism and Federation*, London and Canberra, Croom Helm, 1982

W. Kymlicka, *La cittadinanza multiculturale*, (1995), trad. it., Bologna, il Mulino, 1999

L. Hooghe, *Il Belgio: missione per eccellere in Europa. Federalizzazione e integrazione europea*, in Aa.Vv., *Governare con il federalismo*, Torino, Fondazione Agnelli, 1997

A. Langer, *Nazionalismo e federalismo nell'Europa attuale*, in G. Zagrebelsky (a cura di), *Il federalismo e la democrazia in Europa*, Roma, La Nuova Italia Scientifica, 1994

J.J. Linz, *Democrazia e autoritarismo. Problemi e sfide tra XX e XXI secolo*, Bologna, il Mulino, 2006

J.J. Linz, A. Stepan, *Transizione e consolidamento democratico*,(trad. it.), Bologna, il Mulino, 2000, 35

A. Lijphart, *Democracy. Patterns of Majoritarian and Consensus Government in Twenty-one Countries*, Yale University Press, 1984

G. Lombardi, *Principio di nazionalità e fondamento della legittimità dello Stato*, Torino, Giappichelli, 1979, 20

A. Loretoni, *Identità e riconoscimento*, in F. Cerutti (a cura di), *Identità e politica*, Roma-Bari, Laterza, 1996, 106

M. Luciani, *A mo' di conclusione: le prospettive del federalismo in Italia*, in A. Pace (a cura di), *Quale, dei tanti federalismi?*, Padova, Cedam, 1997

C. Malandrino, *Federalismo*, Roma, Carocci, 1998

Mario Albertini *Il federalismo e lo Stato federale. Antologia e definizione*, Milano, Giuffré, 1963

A. Mastromarino, *Il federalismo disaggregativo. Un percorso costituzionale negli Stati multinazionali*, Milano, Giuffrè, 2010

G.L. Mosse, *La nazionalizzazione delle masse*, (1974), trad. it., Bologna, il Mulino, 1975

R. Paddison, *Il federalismo: diversità regionale nell'unione nazionale*, in G. Brosio (a cura di), *Governo decentralizzato e federalismo. Problemi ed esperienze internazionali*, Bologna, il Mulino, 1995

G. Pasquino, *Lo stato federale*, Milano, Saggiatore, 1996

P. Pernthaler, *Lo Stato federale differenziato* (1992), trad. it., Bologna, il Mulino, 1998

G. Reale, *Radici culturali e spirituali dell'Europa*, Milano, Cortina, 2003.

F. Requejo, *Multinational Federalism and Value pluralism*, London & New York, Routledge, 2005

W.H. Riker, *Federalism: Origin, Operation, Significance*, Little Brown and company, Boston, 1964

W.H. Riker., *Federalism*, in F.I. Greenstein, N.W. Polsby (eds.), *Handbook of Political Science*, Reading, Addison-Wesley, 1975, vol. 5

J. Rodríguez-Arana Muñoz, *Estudios sobre la Constitución*, Madrid, La Ley, 2002, 111

S. Rokkan, *Stato, nazione e democrazia in Europa*, (1999), trad. it., Bologna, il Mulino, 2002

P.H. Russell, *Canada's Mega Constitutional politics in Comparative Perspective*, essay presented at the conference of the International Political Science Association, 21–25 August 1994.

W.H. Ryker, *Federalism,* Boston, Little Brown, 1964

P. Scarduelli, *La costruzione dell'etnicità*, Torino, L'Harmattan Italia, 2004

R. Scruton, *The Need for Nations*, London, Civitas: Institute for the Study of Civil Society, 2004, 9

A.D. Smith, *Il revival etnico*, (1981), trad. it., il Mulino, Bologna, 1984

A.D. Smith, *Le origini etniche delle nazioni,*(19879, trad. it., Bologna, il Mulino, 1992, 48

A. Stepan, *Toward a New Comparative Politics of Federalism, (Multi) Nationalism, and Democracy: Beyond Riker Federalism*, in A. Stepan, *Arguing Comparative Politics*, Oxford, Oxford University Press, 2001

P. Subra De Bieusses, *Un Etat unitaire ultra-fédéral, Pouvoirs,* n. 124, 2008

Ch. Taylor, *Multiculturalismo. La politica del riconoscimento*, (1992), trad. it., Milano, Anabasi, 1993

J. Tully, *Strange Multiplicity. Constitutionalism in an Age of Diversity*, Cambridge, Cambridge University Press, 1997

I. Trujillo, *Giustizia globale. Le frontiere dell'eguaglianza*, Bologna, il Mulino, 2007

D. Truman, *Federalism and Party System*, in A.W. MacMahon (ed.), *Mature and Emergent*, New York, Russel and Russel, 1955

A. Tucci, *Ripensare l'identità nell'epoca della globalizzazione. Il contributo delle discipline sociali e antropologiche*, in *Sociologia del diritto*, n. 1, 2004, 111

S. Ventura, *Federalismo e nazionalismo: il federalismo asimmetrico*, in *Rivista italiana di Scienza Politica*, 2004, 407

P. Vilanova, *Espagne, trente ans de démocratie: notes pour un bilan, Pouvoirs*, n. 124, 2008

C. Viver Pi-Sunyer in the survey coordinated by E. Argullol Murgadas, *Federalismo y autonomía,* Barcelona, Ariel, 2004, 133

R.K. Weaver, *Electoral Rules and Party System in Federations*, in U.M. Amoretti, N. Bermeo (ed.), *Federalism and Territorial Cleavages*, Baltimore & London, The Johns Hopkins University Press, 2004

K.C. Wheare, *Del governo federale*, (1963), trad. it., Bologna, il Mulino, 1997

# Democratic Citizenship and Spanish Multinational (*Dis*)Order: Procedural Democracy *Versus* Secession Clause

José A. Sanz Moreno

## National Identities, Federalism, and the Spanish Order

The link between collective sovereignty and the individualistic safeguard of rights marks the beginning of the modern state and the mutation of its legitimacy. Ideals of universal neutralism and equal human nature are eclipsed by artificial nation-building and their monopolistic identities. Political will, law creation, and social order are defined by the new state's configuration, and its *rising nation* is seen as the legitimate sovereign.

The nationalistic theory divides the world into different peoples with national consciousnesses. In this sense, the ontological nation and its presupposition of substantial equality among citizens were enough to transcend single human beings or even the essential value of democracy: the idea of freedom as a form of citizen self-determination and participation in the creation of legal order. With the metamorphosis of legitimacy—from divine to popular sovereignty—the transcendental volition of God did not transform into the immanent decision of all the citizens but the monolithic and omnipresent will of the nation. However, the old models of homogeneous nation-states are not the present answers for "the concept of the political" (Schmitt 2007: p. 19).

The Westphalian system of sovereign states and its policies of *assimilation*, *exclusion*, *segregation*, *expulsion*, or worse, *genocide*, cannot be imposed in the name of the Holy Nation. The fiction of national homogeneity was constructed by the state and strengthened through public policies. With regard to this *imaginary* nation-state, heterogeneous countries and plural nationalities were seen as regrettable mistakes that needed to be rectified. Carl Schmitt was categorical in the *Weimar-era*, 1928: "A state lacking this homogeneity has an abnormal quality

J.A. Sanz Moreno (✉)
Derecho Constitucional, Universidad Complutense de Madrid, c/ Sánchez Pacheco 64, 2° 4, 28002 Madrid, Spain
e-mail: sanzmorenoja@cps.ucm.es

A. López-Basaguren and L. Escajedo San Epifanio (eds.), *The Ways of Federalism in Western Countries and the Horizons of Territorial Autonomy in Spain*, Vol. 2, DOI 10.1007/978-3-642-27717-7_48, © Springer-Verlag Berlin Heidelberg 2013

that is a threat to peace" (2008: p. 262). However we cannot think about state, nation, and sovereignty using obsolete categories and destructive theories: democracy is not a substantial identity, a concentration of powers, or one volitional decision. As Yael Tamir said, "the era of homogeneous and viable nation-states is over". When it is not possible to maintain the nationalistic ideology that proclaimed "a State to Each Nation", you must see it as "an Unattainable Ideal". Thus we need to leave the chimera of a uniform world of nation-states and redefine the most important political concepts (1993: pp. 3, 142–145 and 150). Nevertheless, this does not mean, as some authors suggest, that we can think about a state without national ideology or as being culturally neutral.

The state can be—and even should be—more plural in recognizing the rights of its national minorities, historic nationalities, and recent immigrants. However, it cannot ignore its own main culture and national projection. The ethical potential for rejecting a single national identity as an indissoluble element to state formation is not enough to forget the basics of a *distinct identity*; the communities must be less coercive and more inclusive with other cultural shapes in a reciprocal movement, but their public institutions will always need to work with some specific identities that are incompatible with aseptic neutrality. Even a sophisticated multination-state cannot include every language, custom, or national culture in its own background as intrinsic elements of public action. The states usually present "nested national identities" and plural societies, but the public entities carry on with their bases and developments over communal forms and, in many cases, through rival national projects. Thus, whether the *homogeneous nation-state* is an *anachronistic idea*, the *national neutrality*—the private sphere, as well as religious, separated from the state—is its *utopian reverse*.

Shared civic principles are essential to improve the democratic system. However, the Renan's "voluntary desire" is not enough reason to belong to one concrete nation; no one loses his or her birth-nationality because he or she refuses constitutional values. Hence, the question is not the *naive choice* between *ethnic* or *civil* nations. The real problem is when nationalism is based on an exclusive identity and sees the state, or its historic homeland, as its sole expression. Here, from a democratic point of view, the answer is divided between *two unequal options*: (1) *a solution from the past*, to build an exclusive nation, with the fiction of its homogeneity and the illness of national plurality, or (2) a *balance of the present and beyond*, in order to recognize the reality of multinational states and guarantee the collective rights of every nationality with territorial presence and the individual human rights of the whole population. A true democratic system consists of not only following formal rules but also protecting human rights, safeguarding political freedoms, and maintaining accountability of all citizens.

The problem of sovereignty cannot be solved with one ontological presupposition about nation and concurrent spheres between citizenship and nationality. So we need to reject not only the more ethnocentric and xenophobic features of nationalism but also its basic existential volition: the idea of a nation as absolute actor with univocal will and monolithic identity of its members. The plural existence of national identities and its confrontation with antagonistic national projects are going to be present for an indefinite time, and the existing social order has to deal with that reality.

The inherent pluralism of the real world denies the simplicity of the homogeneous state and its permanent goal to impose a common language, culture, and historical vision. The shift has been so deep that many Western democracies have accepted the existence of national minorities as an intrinsic part of their own plural identities and not as anomalies to overcome. The multinational state answers the question about national minority demands with the consolidation of territorial sub-units in which the minority group could be the majority and, thus, exercise its right to self-government. We cannot divide the states between one legitimate nation-construction (a dominant majority) and many spurious national discourses (inferior or necessarily assimilated minorities). If we are sharing the same constitutional order and plural identities, we must break the zero-sum relationship between different models of national legitimacy and the goals of democracy. When every group is protecting liberal-democratic values, the consensus over accommodating diversity is not an ontological fight between winners and losers about its own existence. The *friend-enemy* dichotomy (Schmitt 2007: pp. 27–37) had its political wars and extermination camps, but this should be over by now. We need to forget not only the volitional conception of the majority nation and its cultural determinism but also the ethnic peripheral nationalists, their belief in an exclusive identity, and with this unreasonable logic, their continuous search for independence. It is evident that national belonging is not a question of choice for most members of national group but rather a matter of birth. Nationalism, with or without the state, from the oldest to the newest, is a hybrid of civic and ethnic origins, political and cultural roots, subjective and objective elements, rational and irrational actions, etc., and it cannot be reduced to a struggle between *good*-civic and democratic- and *bad*-ethnic or biological *nations*. When the national identity played with the absolute ethos of ethnicity and race, we suffered its consequences, but it does not mean we should accept Manichean oppositions between good and bad nation projects, much less between *true nations* (natural and with state majority) and *false nations* (invented or without its "own" state). Likewise, we are not predestined to belong to one single identity but to create ourselves by choosing private relationships and public loyalties. The path needs to follow the freedom of choice in a substantial democracy with multiple identities. In this regard, the *right to self-determination*, with its distinction between *internal* and *external perspectives*, always means a certain type of self-rule but not necessarily the *total sovereignty*, for this concept is a vain *fiction*.

The theory of self-determination must include the not only right to secede "but also ... one that does not assume that independent statehood is the natural goal or inevitable culmination of aspirations for self-determination" (Buchanan 2004: p. 332). In order to gain more freedom to pursue the project of nation building, the quest for political self-determination cannot always be confused with the right for a group to break away from its previous state and to create a new independent one. What's more, Norman says that the premise in Buchanan's argument—the independent statehood in many cases as the least suitable exercise of self-determination—is a spectacular understatement. "There are about four times as many "nations". . . as there are states in the world today" (2006: p. 74). Thus, in the majority of cases, national minorities have their specific form of exercising the right to self-government. It is not external but within the multinational state as internal self-determination in matters related to their own affairs, with the observance of both the constitutional state order and the internationally recognized human rights. We can say, like Tamir, that *liberal nationalism* does not necessarily link the right to self-determination with political independence but with "the right to preserve the existence of a nation as a distinct cultural entity" (1993: p. 57).

Nevertheless, it could create the grave confusion of a false identification between "nation" and "differentiated culture" and the inclusion of all persons into a solely national identity, as Will Kymlicka seems to maintain. Moreover, his description of history is too anachronistic, like many theories of multiculturalism, particularly when they speak about the Spanish case. In many Western countries, state unification was prior to nation building, with another type of legitimacy and more plural identities. Kymlicka should not transfer to national minorities what he denies to the dominant nation. To immerse individuals in an exclusive culture and national context is as naive as to say that classical nationalism demands the Gellnerian congruence between national and political unity. When the protection of the basic civil and political rights are guaranteed to everybody, regardless of their nationality, and the democratic state has more than one national identity, we need to think of what could be the level of recognition and achievement for the different minority groups and their relationships with the majority rule. However, we would also have to abjure collective identities that see themselves as the absolute political form. In contrast to the lineal idea between "Us" and "them", citizens and community groups are now better defined with multiple and overlapping identities.

Thus, we can distinguish two forms of *state federalism*: *multinational federation* and *territorial autonomy*. The first seeks to satisfy the longing for self-rule of historic minorities with differentiated national identity (Canada). The second, while not questioning the existence of a purely national community, seeks more public efficiency from a vertically organized territory (USA). Now the question is, of these two models of federalism, *which is the Spanish type?* The problem is the hybrid movement between both systems that makes it difficult to define. The *state of autonomies* was born to solve the national minorities' desire for self-government, but it was implemented in every territory so as to work out mere administrative decentralization.

The open "dispositive principle" joins the national minority demands with simple democratic proximity as a way of neutralizing the wish for shared sovereignty. "The right to autonomy of nationalities" from article 2 of the *Spanish constitution* (*SC*) is undermined by article 137 and the development of the autonomic-state model for all provinces and regions, with or without singular national identity. A federal asymmetrical solution for a *multinational state* is combined with a *territorial autonomy* and systemic homogeneity, the *explicit asymmetry* between national majority and peripheral nations, with the *implicit equality* to citizens and "autonomous communities". This evil formula—*coffee for everyone*—was the beginning of many unsolvable problems. The right distinction between nationalities and the rest of territories of article 2 was dissolved by *Title VIII* on *Territorial Order* and, further more, with the post-constitutional development and its successive stages. With this "pioneer method", the transition to democracy was able to close the territorial map, but it did not end the constant claims for recognition by national minorities. The race towards more symbolic and nationalistic denomination, higher level of self-government, and more parochial education and feelings of local patriotism poisons the relationships between central powers, autonomous communities, and neighbouring territories or, worse still, between nested social identities with antagonistic political viewpoints. Thus, the struggles between majority nation building and the national projects of minorities are transformed into the chaotic territorial (*dis*)order, without a plain conception about symmetrical or asymmetrical results.

Against the equal uniformity of territories, we can consider *asymmetrical federalism* as the model in which minority nationalities "marry" the state. This exceptional interaction and its specificity on powers and privileges can be seen as a threat to basic state definitions: collapse of equality citizenship and loyal patriotism, national majority weakness and federal incapacity, unfairness and disunity among regions, disaffection with juxtaposed identities, etc. Nevertheless, without asymmetry, it is not possible to accommodate the political construction of the different nationalities. The matter is not between legal symmetry or asymmetric dynamics but "the type and degree of asymmetry which would be tolerable" (Keating 2001: p. 274). In this regard, Requejo has pointed out some kinds of asymmetries: de facto (social, economic, cultural, linguistic diversities, etc.), de jure (constitutional varieties among federated entities about the degree or nature—quantitative or qualitative—of their self-government), and those produced through the differentiated exercise of the right to self-determination (2010: p. 286). With these three types—*factual differences* (real plurality), *constitutional distinction* (possible legal acknowledgment), and *self-government ways* (changeable direction)—we make out the complexity and heterogeneity among territories. From there, we can present, with Norman, the most important principles of recognition to national minorities: *collective assent, commitment and loyalty, anti-assimilation rules, territorial autonomy as national self-determination, equal right of nation building*, and *multiple and nested national identities* (2006: pp. 165–168). However, the practice of multinational federalism is not only a sort of recognition but also a way to redistribute political power between self-governing territories. This has been presented as an effective instrument for decreasing the hierarchal relationship between a state's national majority and substate minorities (Kymlicka 2007: pp. 141–143). For this reason, the antagonism between formal democracy and substantial constitutional values cannot be hidden.

## Procedural Democracy and Constitutional Interpretation

Identity claims should not be any alibi to cut back democratic dialogue. Every nation-building project must be seen as legitimate as any majority nation-making process. Nevertheless, the right to develop common cultural traditions and collective identities cannot be invoked to deny the protection of universal human rights (*Universal Declaration on Cultural Diversity*, 2001, article 4). The *basic crimson line* has been drawn and nobody can step over it. Here, the antagonism between *universal liberalism*, *multiculturalism*, and *cosmopolitanism* ought to be controlled. The protection of human rights and fundamental freedoms is not only the constitutional commitment to interpret the norms related to basic rights and liberties, which are recognized by the *Spanish constitution* (article 10.2 *SC*). First of all, human dignity and inviolable rights constitute a material limit impossible to break, neither through a super-aggravated amendment nor through a total revision, even when, literally, *Title X* only demands formal requirements. If the right to self-determination is an essential condition to guarantee not only individual rights but also collective ones, the Constitutional order is not a mere juridical procedure but a system to protect universal and democratic values. In the balance between the safeguard of human rights and the right to cultural preservation, the first always has priority; human rights should never be sacrificed in order to integrate practices that violate those rules.

For this premise, the *Spanish constitutional court* (*Scc*) cannot declare that the citizens do not have any material restriction over the Constitutional changes ("only the citizens, undertaking necessarily at the end of the process of reform, can have the supreme power, this is, the power to modify without limits their own Constitution", *103/2008 Judgment of Scc*, 2°JF, September-11, which declared unconstitutional *Law 9/2008 of Basque parliament* on popular consultation). Through amendments and revisions of the Constitution, citizens cannot override the democratic system.

The connection between human rights and democratic constitutionalism prevents an absolute voluntarism on the sovereign power's part. The particularity of a nation ought to be completed with the universality of human rights, and these cannot be at the expense of a contingent *national will*, which is always artificially created, and it is never a unanimous decision. The state carries out its roles of law creation and coercion control, but it is not a sovereign entity that stands outside of the international order. Thus, the Court's claims that the citizens could change the constitutional order without any restrictions are as unreal as they are "unlawful". The states operate within an international world with its own juridical order and rights, and so it is very ingenuous to think about one separate state system *for* and *by* itself. The constitutional interpretation cannot forget that the state and its sovereign power—the people transformed into citizens with political rights within the national legal order—do not stand alone and can do what they want. For that precondition, it would be self-contradictory for a country like Spain to base its "political order and social peace" on "human dignity and inviolable rights" (article 10.1) and assert, at the same time, that their citizens can alter without limits every constitutional obligation.

Moreover the *Scc*, with its conception of "nation", keeps the conventional notion of sovereignty when it is absurd to believe in the holder of the power *as if* it could create law and order from the void. The sovereign nation is not an omnipotent power without any restrictions, and its expression, the citizens—with political rights and through their practices—cannot destroy the constitutional order *ad infinitum* (article 1.2, 23 and Title X). Of course, the Constitutional amendment is in many ways so unwieldy that it could be seen as an *undercover intangible clause*, but we can never confuse the substantial definition of Constitution with its change process. The *procedural positivism* or, even worse, the implicit *decisional thought* by this judgment does not defend democracy, but it can be its unexpected enemy. In the clash between democratic universal values and national ideology, the *Scc* seems to forget the firsts with the sublimation of the national concept and its tendency towards procedural and majority rule. However, the role of a Constitution is not only to produce a way but also to define, *on the one hand*, the juridical order, the sovereign power, and its exercise forms and, *on the other hand*, the values and aims to guarantee and improve. The *formal super-legality* is completed with the *material super-legality* and by linking both brought into being the constitutional defence mechanism in continental Europe. The *Constitutional court*, as the *guardian* with monopoly over judicial review of constitutionality, and the *Constitutional amendment*, as *normal procedure* to protect the Constitution and not a form to destroy, eliminate or create a totally new one. Yet, this could be the final result of a juridical doctrine that allows an unlimited material transformation of the constitutional order.

Even when a dominant national group could have control over the procedures, we must not fall down under the despotism of an arithmetic process. Majority rule should not be seen as an absolute and isolated principle. We need to choose between Kelsen and Schmitt, and here it is not possible to have *checks and balances*, as the SC desired. Self-determination and sovereignty are defined: (a) *over* individual freedom, political pluralism, and citizens' right to participate in public affairs (articles 1.1, 6, 9.2, 10.1, 23; *the democratic values*) or (b) *under* the "democracy of identity" and its total immersion of equal Spaniards within one overarching will and national unity, indissoluble and indivisible (Preamble, articles 2, 8.2, 13.2, and 14; *the irrational and unlimited volition of a sovereign nation*).

The rhetorical supposition of an ontological and collective entity, called the Spanish nation, cannot be transformed into a numeric citizenship with a limitless capacity for political action. The principle of protecting against the tyranny of the majority is not a useless declaration about democracy but its own essential core. Without it, the democracy would lose all possibility to build a substantial definition in favor of procedural relativism, and in this case it would leave the constitution-making power in the hands of one despotic majority. Of course, as Will Kymlicka affirms, "this is what democracy is all about: multiple and shifting points of access to power" (2007: p. 111), but it is not *only* that. The real value of democracy is not merely numbers, procedural rules, and fights for power, as was Schumpeter's view.

Even as "only a *form*, only a *method* of creating a social order" "there is no absolute rule of the majority over the minority" (Kelsen 2000: p. 106; 2007: p. 287).

In Spain, the basic foundations of liberal democracy are well consolidated, but *could we forget its parameters and present the constitutional system over merely one basic procedure without any material constraints*? I fear that this was the answer that the *Scc* did not think enough about. In order to prevent future (external) self-determination rights from the territorial parts against the national will, the *Scc*'s voluntarism must have misunderstood the axiological root of the Spanish system.

Our dilemma is between procedural (descriptive) and substantial (prescriptive) concepts of democracy. So the *SC* or, rather, its "Supreme interpreter", should abandon a radical nationalistic language that recognizes only one nation: the majority group. To define the concept of nation as *extraordinarily protean* and *polysemous* is as obvious as it is dangerous to shake national consciousness (*31/2010, Judgment of Scc*, 12th JF, June-28, on *Catalonia statute*). It is one thing to say that the people are sovereign, and it is quite another to declare that the Constitution would only permit the use of one national definition in a juridical-constitutional sense. The problem of sovereignty cannot be solved with such a monolithic conception of the nation. The *Scc*'s return to dead definitions is not the path to answer living problems; its duty is to adapt legal definitions to their context and social reality (article 3.1 *Civil code*). Wherefore a dynamic constitutional interpretation rejects the fiction of the Spanish nation as an ontological condition of political unity with total decision over state form, it could be better to recognize the commitment not only in a plural political sphere but also between territorial communities and the state, so as to build a union within the same democracy.

The *SC* does not rest on the foundation of one transcendent national unity but on the democratic referendum that took place in 1978. It was the beginning of the new source of legitimacy for the constitutional system. However, more than 33 years later, we need to rethink the sense of such a plebiscite. The living citizens would need to rule themselves, but when the model is a multinational federation with different and nested spheres of membership, we have to consider the interplay between distinct majorities and their agreements as well.

The explicit constitutional recognition of national minorities could always have a different meaning to them than to the majority group. However, the constitutional order resolved this discussion: In times of political normality, the sitting judges on the Constitutional court have the last word. For that, as Rodriguez-Zapata criticized with his particular vote on the *247/2007 Judgment* (*Valencia statute*), "the SC says what the Scc says it is", in other words, a qualified interpretation as a negative and even a positive legislator. However, the long arm of constitutional jurisprudence cannot change our system or fulfill the role of constituent power in one *exceptional situation*. The *justices* can write new laws with their supreme hermeneutics, but they never ought to rewrite their own Constitution.

Therefore, we need to guarantee the most essential values of constitutional order in democratic defence, even when the *Scc* declared our model as *un-militant democracy* (*126/09*, 9thJF, May-21). Procedural democracy and unlimited constitutional revision are being combined with the most out-of-date form to define the concepts of nation and nationalism. Yet the simple objective of education—article 27.2—tells us what the essential value of democratic citizenship is. The existence of an indestructible constitutional content and the defence of democracy against its enemies are the capital instruments for establishing "an advanced democratic society", and an erratic jurisprudence cannot invalidate the basics of our shared system. If the constitutional interpretation can sometimes fail, the juridical order has its own extraordinary instrument of modification: the constitutional amendment. Thus, in a multinational state, it would be better to define clearly what the right to self-determination is and even to debate the necessity of introducing a secession clause as constitutional procedure to resolve the eternal challenge of pro-independence groups within national minorities and the host state.

## The Secession Clause

"A multinational democracy is free and legitimate, therefore, when its constitution treats the constituent nations as peoples with the right of self-determination in some appropriate constitutional form, such as the right to initiate constitutional change" (Tully 2008: p. 219).

In the Spanish case, the national minorities are not *constituent nations*. Nonetheless, at the same time, some of their members—notwithstanding formal nationality—might feel alienated by the nation-state, so the constitutional order should determine when a territorially concentrated disaffection is overwhelming. The ontological foundation of the *SC* and its unique sovereign power cannot forget the axiological root of human dignity and political pluralism. However, the defence mechanisms of minority groups, as isolated individuals, do not protect their life-forms as communal entities. In order to guarantee a democratic relationship, citizens of a multinational state must protect the same constitutional values when the ownership of the constituent power is on the table. From the outset, the rules of the game should be defined and accepted by every political actor. We need to recognize that individual citizens are not the only players, as the Constitutional court said in its transmutation from the collective sovereignty of the people into citizens with political rights. There is also the question of the *nested communities*: the *Spanish nation* (the isolated "juridical-constitutional nation"—for an obsolete and very moot interpretation—and its metamorphosis into the whole citizenship) and the *nationalities* and *regions* (with or without national identity, as differentiated peoples and their conversion on the Spaniards with administrative residence in a concrete "community").

The federal agreement must not be seen as a single level of territorial autonomy; it is also a form of singular recognition with a sense of divided and shared sovereignty. Federalism, for some authors, is the solution to territorial conflicts and, for others, a previous step to total statehood. Here, we can see the *federalist paradox*, which could be used either to induce or to calm external wishes of self-determination.

Never a world panacea, the first and most romantic interpretation of national self-determination as the right of all peoples (or better, their formation as a homogeneous nation) to choose their political status was as naive as it was dangerous. Against the openness of Wilson's doctrine, the principle of self-determination was combined with the right of territorial integrity, and its range had been rigorously reduced in international law (*Charter of the United Nations* and *Covenant on Civil and Political Rights*). Moreover, the 1960 *Declaration on the Granting of Independence to Colonial Countries* said that all people have the right to self-determination, yet it banned the disruption of national unity and territorial integrity. The later 1970 *Declaration concerning Friendly Relations among States* recalled the codification of these principles and their contradictory answer: "the territorial integrity and political independence of the State are inviolable". The classical sovereignty prohibits secession, but only when the State in question submits itself to the principle of self-determination. The right to secession is the last resort against unfair violations of individual rights: in particular, political rights associated with the improvement of democracy. It is a complex solution that combines *ethnos* with *demos*, that is, individual rights and linguistic, cultural, and collective rights, with the real use of self-government. However, one conclusion is certain: International law does not recognize a unilateral right to secede. The majority vote of citizens from substate nations is not enough reason, or even fair cause, to break the integrity of the state. To sum up, self-determination means the right to participate in the political system within a state, but secession is only allowed by mutual negotiation between central rulers and territorial minorities.

In this regard, it is crucial to come back to constitutional law or, more precisely, to the very legitimacy of multinational constitutionalism. When the fact and its range are mainly internal actions, when the search of secession is from inside, we cannot only glance at the basic principles of international law and its ethics. The international community could play a more active role in protecting the right to self-government of national minorities within a state. Nonetheless, the key role must be played by the constitutional order, and then the possibility of picking up a secession clause should not be overlooked. To block the existence of secessionist movements might strengthen their popular support more than undermine it.

Thus, we can roughly describe three conflicting *theories of a unilateral right to secede*: *national decision* (every nation, territorially concentrated, as a political mature people, could secede if the majority of its members want to do it), *territorial choices* (every geographic group, with or without nationalistic "pedigree", may secede if the majority of the people choose through a plebiscite to create their own state), and *remedial right* or *just-cause* (the fair and unilateral answer for persistent and severe violations of individual human rights, unjust annexation, or even grave and continuous limitation of self-government rights). Although our first option could be the *remedial right only theories* (Buchanan 2004: pp. 369–371), it is difficult to achieve a deal between antagonist nationalities in knowing when a continuous and grave violation of rights over a singular community is being committed. The *remedial right theories* would be an important ethics law on the international field. However, from a constitutional viewpoint, we need also to consider the values of democracy.

On that account, one congruent position with democratic logic is Kymlicka's standpoint: "if a national minority gets a clear majority in favor of secession in a free and fair democratic referendum, then there is little that the state can do to prevent secession", and it must be allowed, though explicitly the constitutional order can forbid it. The evolution of political systems does not depend on the presence or absence of the right to secession "but rather deeper liberal values of democracy, individual liberty, peace and mutual respect" (2005: pp. 115–116). When it is undeniable that there are many pro-independence campaigners with large popular support, a true democratic reasoning would validate the constitutional amendment to clarify the method of juridical secession because its gap could be an incentive—or excuse—to achieve the separation without legal procedure or through more violent actions.

In the Western world, the question of minority nationalism is only seen as a security issue when it involves totalitarian secessionism or terrorism. However, as Kymlicka stresses, so long as a substate nationalism is peaceful and democratic, it stops being a security problem, even when it is working explicitly to achieve its independence (2007: p. 194). Thus, we must be aware of the necessity to adopt a secession clause as a qualified procedure to resolve the tension between democratic rules and the separatist desires of a national minority. From a democratic position, when the majority of a national and territorial community does not want to maintain the *status quo* in its union with the host state, it is unreasonable to say that all citizens of the state hold the only key to solve the impasse. The wishes of the inhabitants cannot be overlooked when they are freely expressed by means of a fair plebiscite, yet the constitutional orders generally do not have a self-determination clause.

We discovered a paradigmatic resolution about an implicit possibility to interpret the Constitution in agreement with secession, the *Canadian Supreme Court* and its *Opinion* over the Quebec case. Even though the Court rejected the validity of a unilateral attempt to secede, the constitutional principles and the democratic legitimacy were enough to show the lawful procedure: *clear question, clear majority* in favor of secession, and *mutual negotiations* between central and territorial powers. What would be a "clear question" and a "clear majority" were odd categories *without a clear answer* from the judges. Precisely, this one is the explicit role of a constitutional clause, and indeed the Quebec affair is the best lesson to check the costs and risks to preserve a constitutional system without a legal secession procedure (Norman 2006: pp. 192–203).

It is evident that the very idea of secession procedure can be seen as schizophrenic and against the own right of self-preservation, especially when the nation is considered the constitutional base and is declared indissoluble. However, these last precepts do not have any fundamental relation with the values of democratic constitutionalism but rather with an *existential collective notion* and its identification with a *dominant nation and exclusive national identity*. Therefore, when the presence of pro-independence movements has an important support—between 20 % and 60 % of the population (Norman 2006: p. 202)—the climate for discussion about secession should be analogous to any other matter, even if these arguments could be more distressing to our political identities.

The suitability of including a rigid and qualified secession clause must not be understood as believing in its own legitimacy to the secession process but as the best answer to assure the good health of the constitutional democracy. When a distinct community begins to escalate its demands from internal autonomy to external self-determination, we need to know what the steps are.

In short, a clear secession clause and its qualified prerequisites could correct the *original sin* of sovereign power, and thus the theological description of uniform nations would be transformed into an *advanced democratic citizenship*.

# References

Buchanan, A., Justice, Legitimacy, and Self-Determination. Moral Foundations for International Law, Oxford Univ. Press, Oxford-New York, UK-USA, 2004, 506 pp.

Keating, M., Nations against the State. The New Politics of Nationalism in Quebec, Catalonia and Scotland, Palgrave, New York, USA, 2001, 320 pp.

Kelsen, H., On the essence and value of democracy, 1929, in Weimar: a jurisprudence of crisis, Univ. of California Press, Berkeley, USA, 2000, pp. 84–109.

Kelsen, H., General Theory of Law & State, 1945–49, Transaction Publishers, New Brunswick-London, USA-UK, 2007, 516 pp.

Kymlicka, W., Federalism and secession: East and West", in Democracy, nationalism and multiculturalism, Frank Cass, London-New York, UK-USA, 2005, pp. 108–206.

Kymlicka, W., Multicultural Odysseys. Navigating the New International Politics of Diversity, Oxford Univ. Press, New York, USA, 2007, 374 pp.

Norman, W., Negotiating Nationalism. Nation-building, Federalism, and Secession in the Multi-national State, Oxford Univ. Press, Oxford-New York, UK-USA, 2006, 250 pp.

Requejo, F., Federalism and democracy. The case of minority nations – a federalist deficit, in Federal Democracies, Routledge, New York, USA, 2010, pp. 275–298.

Schmitt, C., The Concept of the Political, 1932, Univ. of Chicago Press, Chicago, USA, 2007, 126 pp.

Schmitt, C., Constitutional Theory, 1928, Duke Univ., Durham, USA, 2008, 468 pp.

Tamir, Y., Liberal Nationalism, Princeton Univ. Press, Princeton, New Jersey, USA, 1993, 194 pp.

Tully, J., Public Philosophy in a New Key, Cambridge Univ. Press, Cambridge, UK, 2008, 360 pp.

# The Decentralisation of the Advisory Function in the Autonomous State: The Position of the Council for Statutory Guarantees of Catalonia Following CCS 31/2010, of June 28

L. Delgado del Rincón

## The Decentralisation of the Advisory Function in Spain: From the Advisory Council to the Council for Statutory Guarantees of Catalonia

In Spain, the introduction of the concept of regional State has involved a process of decentralisation of the different functions of the State, not only those of a political nature but also others such as the classical advisory function, which since the very origins of our constitutional history has been exercised by the Council of State.

The Spanish Constitution of 1978 (SC) contains no provision specifically acknowledging the power of the Autonomous Communities to create autonomous advisory bodies. However, some Autonomous Communities like Catalonia, the Canary Islands, and Extremadura soon added an article to their Statutes of Autonomy of 1979, 1982, and 1983, respectively, in which they anticipated the creation of an Autonomous Advisory Council via the publication of the corresponding autonomous law. The creation of this body is based upon art. 148.1.1 SC, which confers upon Autonomous Communities competence with regard to the organisation of their institutions of self-government. Thus, Catalonia, which is the Autonomous Community where the process of decentralisation of the advisory function in Spain began, provided for, in art. 41 of its Statute of Autonomy (SAC) of 1979, the creation of the Advisory Council of the *Generalitat*, referring to a law passed by the Catalan Parliament for its development: Law 1/1981, of February 25 (Cano Bueso 2009, pp. 58–66).

The Catalan and Canarian Statutes of Autonomy granted the Advisory Councils competence in deciding upon the conformity to the Statute and the Constitution of projects and legislative proposals. However, with legislative development, a difference emerged between the Catalan and Canarian bodies. Whilst the former, the

L. Delgado del Rincón (✉)
Universidad de Burgos, Hospital del Rey s/n, 09001 Burgos, Spain
e-mail: ldelgado@ubu.es

A. López-Basaguren and L. Escajedo San Epifanio (eds.), *The Ways of Federalism in Western Countries and the Horizons of Territorial Autonomy in Spain*, Vol. 2, DOI 10.1007/978-3-642-27717-7_49, © Springer-Verlag Berlin Heidelberg 2013

Catalan Advisory Council, is fundamentally an institution the purpose of which is preventative examination of the constitutionality and the "estatutoriedad" of the laws passed by the autonomous Parliament, the latter, the Canarian Advisory Council, assumes in addition the classical advisory function of supervising the legality of general regulatory and administrative activity. This difference is due to the fact that in Catalonia the traditional advisory function had been assigned to another body, the Advisory Legal Commission, established by the Decree of October 17, 1978 and currently regulated by Law 5/2005, of May 2. Thus Catalonia adopted a unique model of advisory function that has no equivalent in the autonomous sphere, given the assignment of the function to two different bodies.

Also present in the origins of the autonomous Advisory Councils was the need to fill a gap that existed in the design of constitutional jurisdiction, which prevented the Governments of the Autonomous Communities or sections of their legislative Assemblies from applying to the Constitutional Court to appeal against the possible unconstitutionality of a law passed in the respective autonomous Parliaments (Biglino Campos 2003, pp. 176–177; Albertí Rovira 2008, pp. 20–21).

The Constitutional Court, in sentence (CCS) 204/1992, of November 26, confirms the constitutionality of the competence of the Autonomous Communities to create, by virtue of their powers of self-organisation, their own advisory bodies. Following this decision by the Constitutional Court, most Autonomous Communities opted for the creation of their own advisory bodies, the main competence of which would be the supervision of the legality of regulatory and administrative activity, without prejudice to some of them also assuming the function of examining the constitutionality and "estatutoriedad" of legislative proposals in the process of parliamentary consideration. A function implicit within which would be a relationship between the legislative Assembly and the autonomous advisory body (Jover Presa 2007, pp. 77–93).

The autonomous Advisory Councils share some common functional and organic characteristics, though there are also numerous differences between them that affect both their organic and functional dimensions, as well as their definition in regulatory Statutes and laws, the criteria employed in designating their members, their organisation, and the system of internal functioning or the attribution of diverse functions (Delgado del Rincón 2011, pp. 232–233).

With the reform of the Statute of Autonomy of Catalonia by the Organic Law 6/2006, of July 19, arts. 76 and 77 established the creation of a new body, the Council for Statutory Guarantees. These provisions include the regulation of certain aspects related to their definition, functions, composition, and functioning, referring to a Parliamentary law for their development. This was Law 2/2009, of February 12, of the Council for Statutory Guarantees (LCSG). The Catalan Statute also mentions the Council for Statutory Guarantees in another provision, art. 38.1, within "the guarantees of statutory rights", to confer upon it the protection of the rights recognised in chapters I, II, and III of Title I SAC and of the Charter of the rights and duties of the citizens of Catalonia.

For a sector of the scientific literature, the substitution in 2009 of the Catalan Advisory Council by the Council for Statutory Guarantees was accompanied by a new phase in the evolution of the autonomous advisory bodies, as the Catalan institution considerably extended the number of functions previously assumed by the body that preceded it, the Advisory Council (Vintró 2008, pp. 357–359). This is also acknowledged in the Preamble to Law 2/2009, of February 12, governing the Council for Statutory Guarantees, when it states its objective of designing a new institution in accordance with the superior levels of self-government implicit within the reform of the Catalan Statute. In this sense, and in accordance with the functions acquired, the Council for Guarantees is configured as an advisory body and as an organ of legal control that assumes the functions of guaranteeing the statutory and constitutional correctness of certain regulatory provisions and protection of the legislative activity of the Parliament in the development of statutory rights.

In Italy, with the process of statutory reform undertaken during the first decade of the twenty-first century, after the modification in 1999 of art. 123 of the Italian Constitution (which affects the nature, elaboration, and control of the Statute as a source of Law), almost all the regions, with the exception of Las Marcas, have anticipated in their new statutes, with different denominations, the creation of an organ of statutory guarantee, referring to a regional law that regulates its organisation, functioning, and competences. Most of these regions have proceeded to pass the corresponding regional law and the constitution of the Council for Statutory Guarantees (Poggi 2009, pp. 88–90; Romboli 2009, pp. 38–39; Catelani 2011, p. 356). Nevertheless, one also notes that recently, in the region of Calabria, a new statutory reform through regional Law n° 3, of January 19, 2010, resulted in the repeal of art. 57 of the Statute of October 19, 2004, which established, as an advisory and assessment body in the region, the Statutory Consultation, an institution that had also been developed by regional Law n° 2, of January 5, 200 (Spadaro 2010, pp. 8 and 9).

The Italian Councils of Guarantee are collegiate bodies whose composition varies between three and seven members. They are elected by the Regional Council via absolute majority, which obliges the political forces with parliamentary representation to agree with regard to their designation. The council members have to be magistrates, lawyers, university professors, or civil servants, with several years' experience in their profession. This legal qualification of the councillors reflects the markedly technical activity to be undertaken by the organ of statutory guarantee. The members of the Councils of Statutory Guarantee are nominated, as a rule, for a period of 6 years, 1 year more than a parliamentary term (Romboli 2009, pp. 40–43; Baldazzi 2005, pp. 857–860).

The main function of the Italian Councils of Statutory Guarantee is that of preventative control of the "estatutoriedad" of draft bills or regional regulations, in other words, issuing a judgement regarding the appropriateness or otherwise of these bills vis-à-vis the Statute, which also involves their interpretation and compliance with the Constitution. Other functions that the Statutes attribute to the Councils for Statutory Guarantee are emitting a verdict of admissibility with respect to proposals of referendum and popular initiative and resolving contributions of attribution between regional bodies or between regional bodies and local bodies (Conte 2009, pp. 12–19; Romboli 2009, pp. 44–52; Baldazzi 2005, pp. 860–863).

# The Broadening of Competences of the Catalan Council for Statutory Guarantees: The Protection of Statutory Rights with Regard to Draft Legislation or Bills That Develop or Affect them

Article 76.1 SAC defines the Council for Statutory Guarantees as that institution in the *Generalitat* whose function is to ensure the suitability for the present Statute and the Constitution of the provisions of the *Generalitat* in the terms established by this rule in its second section, a definition that is reiterated in art. 2.1 LCSG.

The function developed by the Council for Statutory Guarantees, as a body that supervises the constitutionality and "estatutoriedad" of legislative proposal with the force of law, fulfils a dual role: that of controlling its suitability for hierarchically superior provisions and that of guaranteeing the laws finally passed by Parliament (Rubio Llorente 2004, p. 105).

According to art. 76 SAC and arts. 16 and 17 LCSG, the advisory function of the Council for Statutory Guarantees may be divided into three types of competences:

1) One competence assigned to the Council of Statutory Guarantees is prior scrutiny of the constitutionality and "estatutoriedad" of legislative proposals with force of law and proposals and projects for statutory reform, draft bills and legislative proposals, draft legislative decrees or decree-laws subject to Parliamentary approval (arts. 76.1 and 2 a)–e) SAC, as well as art. 16.1 a)–e) LCSG).

   The judgement issued by the Council for Statutory Guarantees in the exercise of this competence is optional and non-binding. The following are entitled, depending on the case, to consult the decision: two parliamentary groups, one-tenth of the members of Parliament, the Government and the municipalities or "veguerías" (arts. 26 a 29 LCSG);

2) Another competence assigned to the Council of Guarantees is that of making a decision, in advance, with regard to the presentation before the Constitutional Court of a claim of unconstitutionality, of a conflict of competences, or of a conflict in defence of local autonomy by the bodies thereby legitimised (arts. 76.3 SAC and 16.2 LCSG).

   The ruling issued by the Council for Statutory Guarantees in the exercise of this competence is mandatory in that it must be requested by the authorised bodies, which are, as the case may be, two parliamentary groups, one-tenth of the Members of Parliament, the Government or certain local institutions, in accordance with art. 23 LCSG in relation to the Law Organic of the Constitutional Court. The decision is non-binding for the requesting bodies, so they are not obliged to act upon the conclusions included therein.

   The competences referred to in arts 76.2 and 3 SAC are ordinary competences, characteristic of all advisory bodies and, in practice, already possessed by the previous Advisory Council of the *Generalitat*. In assigning the first competence to the Council for Statutory Guarantees, the Catalan Statute of Autonomy opts to establish a prior control of the "estatutoriedad" and constitutionality of certain legislative proposals with the power of law, a control included within the phases of legislative procedure and, in any event, previous to its final approval by Parliament. This is also an external control exercised by a technical-legal body within Autonomous Community, hence the interpretation of the Council for Statutory Guarantees as "an organ of collaborative legislation" (Aparicio Pérez 2009a, p. 4).

The fact that the Council for Statutory Guarantees assumes the competence of prior control of the "estatutoriedad" and constitutionality of draft legislation does not lead, in principle, to a clash with the Constitutional Court in the exercise of the function of control of the constitutionality of laws, since the parameter of control—the Constitution and the Statute—is similar, but the objective of control is different: a draft bill or draft legislation in the preparation stage, in the case of the supervision of the Council for Statutory Guarantees, or a fully approved law, in the case of the exclusive control exercised by the Constitutional Court (Aparicio Pérez 2009a, p. 22).

Neither are Italy's Councils for Statutory Guarantees regarded as "small constitutional courts" due, amongst other reasons, to the principle of unity of constitutional jurisdiction and the regions' lack of competence to create institutions with jurisdictional functions. They are more regional bodies of an administrative nature, possessed of the competence to guarantee statutory supremacy and rigidity (Romboli 2009, pp. 63–65). They are not constitutionally necessary bodies, although they may be necessary in order to maintain a balanced form of regional government (Spadaro 2010, pp. 2 and 4). The Italian Constitutional Court also interpreted them, thus, in sentence 200/2008, of June 13, in which it states that the institutions of statutory control are of an "administrative character" and their decisions are "administrative decisions", the object of which is to "eliminate doubt and controversy regarding the interpretation of statutory provisions and of regional laws referring to the relationship between the region and other institutions operating within their territorial context" (FJ 5.1). In this sentence, the Constitutional Court also recognises that the intervention of the Council for Statutory Guarantees must be of a "preventative nature, and must be developed during the procedure of formation of legislative acts", without possible recourse to this body "following the enactment of the laws or the issue of the regulations", as "any assessment with regard to their legitimacy is exclusively the competence of the Constitutional Court and of the judges, ordinary and administrative" (FJ 5.2).

3) Another of the competences assigned to the Council for Statutory Guarantees is the protection of statutory rights in relation to the draft laws and legislative proposals that develop or affect them (arts. 38.1 y 76.4 SAC y 17.3 LCSG).

The ruling emitted by the Council in the exercise of this competence is optional, not obligatory, so that it is at the discretion of the legitimate bodies whether or not to request it from the Council of Guarantees. In the event of it being requested, the ruling emitted is binding for Parliament if its opinion is negative or unfavourable. The following are authorised to request the ruling: two parliamentary groups, one-tenth of the Members of Parliament, the Government, and the *Síndic de Greuges* (art. 23 LCSG). The assignment of this power to the *Síndic de Greuges*, whose main activity is the defence of citizens' rights with regard to the Administration's actions, is not particularly fortunate, as it gives rise to the suspension of parliamentary procedure, even in "scenarios in which the legislation is supported by all the political forces represented in the Catalan Parliament" (Santolaya Machetti 2009, p. 85).

The binding nature of the Council of Guarantee's ruling is "one-way", as it operates only when the judgement is negative or unfavourable, in other words, when it declares the "antiestatutoriedad" or unconstitutionality of the draft bill or legislative proposal but not when this is positive or favourable, that is, when the draft bill or legislative proposal is in accordance with the Statute or the Constitution (Aparicio Pérez 2009a, p. 7). In the first case, if in the conclusions of the Council of Guarantee's rulings it is specifically stated that one or more provisions, or a part of these, are contrary to the Constitution or the Statute, the parliamentary drafting of the text cannot proceed without the elimination or modification of these provisions or parts thereof (Art. 18.2 and 3 LCSG).

For a sector of the scientific literature, this new competence of the Catalan statute, in direct response to the creation of the category of "statutory rights", conferred upon the Council for Statutory Guarantees the nature of organ of protection or institutional guarantee of the statutory rights of the Catalans (Tornos Mas 2010, p. 1; Albertí Rovira 2008, p. 19), as it could exercise preventative control of Parliament's legislative activity in defence of their rights (Aparicio Pérez 2009b p. 177; Balaguer Callejón 2010, p. 69).

In fact, the competence anticipated in art. 76.4 SAC is the same as that regulated by art. 76.2 b) SAC but with reference to the question of statutory rights. What changes is the effect of the ruling, which will be binding in nature when declaring the existence of a contradiction between a particular provision of the draft bill or legislative proposal consulted and the statutory regulation with regard to this matter. This binding aspect of the ruling modifies the nature of the institution, transforming it into an organ of legal control and "objective guarantee of the Statute and the Constitution" (Jover Presa 2007, p. 84; Vintró 2008, p. 358; Fossas Espadaler 2011).

The assignment to the Council for Statutory Guarantees via art. 76.4 SAC, in relation to art. 38.1 SAC, of this new competence of protection of statutory rights with regard to draft bills and legislative proposals that develop or affect them, issuing binding rulings for Parliament, has given rise to an interesting debate within the literature about the nature of the organ, the latter's exercise of a function that is jurisdictional in character, similar to that of the Constitutional Court, and how the Council's binding ruling limits the freedom of action of Parliament. Furthermore, the assignment of this competence to the Council for Statutory Guarantees in the provisions quoted from the Catalan Statute of Autonomy, along with other aspects contained in art. 76.1 and 2, was contested in the Constitutional Court in the claim of unconstitutionality lodged by 99 members of the Popular Parliamentary Group of the Lower House.

In Italy, the effectiveness of the decisions of the Councils for Statutory Guarantees in exercising the function of controlling the "estatutoriedad" of regional legislative proposals or regulations, if their decisions are negative, in accordance with principles stated in the Constitution, cannot be binding in nature for the competent political bodies (in particular, for the regional Council) when they pass the corresponding laws, although some Statutes require that the draft bill be examined again or passed by a qualified majority or by reasoned decision (Romboli 2009, pp. 55–59, bearing in mind the decisions of the Constitutional Court in sentences 378/2004, of November 29 and 12/2006, of January 11; Baldazzi 2005, pp. 864–871; Spadaro 2010, p. 16 and 17).

## CCS 31/2010, of June 28, Regarding the Catalan Statute of Autonomy and Its Impact upon the Council for Statutory Guarantees

In the aforementioned appeal on the grounds of unconstitutionality against certain provisions of the SAC, with reference to art. 76.1, 2, and 4, the appellants claim that the functions attributed to the Council for Statutory Guarantees in this provision infringe upon the function of control of constitutionality of legislation with force of law attributed to the Constitutional Court by art. 161 SC. Moreover, they believe that the binding effectiveness that art. 76.4 SAC confers upon the Council's rulings may give rise to conflicts of legitimacy with the decisions of the Constitutional Court, in addition to the problems arising from the guarantee scheme established in art. 38 SAC.

It is section 4° of art. 76 SAC, which assigns to the Council for Statutory Guarantees the competence to issue a binding ruling with regard to draft bills and legislative proposals in Parliament that develop or affect statutory rights, that would be declared unconstitutional by the Constitutional Court. The Tribunal employs two arguments in declaring the unconstitutionality and nullity of art. 76.4 SAC, depending on precisely when the Council exercises control:

1) If the Council's control is exercised at the time of presenting the legislative proposals before the Chamber or whilst they are debated, a negative ruling by the Council will prevent "parliamentary approval of the proposal or, alternatively, continuation of the debate". For the Tribunal, this consequence of the binding nature of the unfavourable ruling would represent "an inadmissible limitation of parliamentary authority and competence, to the severe detriment of the rights of political participation recognised by art. 23 SC, to guarantee the parliamentary freedom fundamental to democratic systems" (CCS 31/2010, of June 28, FJ 32°).
2) If the Council's control is verified subsequent to the legislative procedure but prior to the publication of the law, a negative ruling by the Council will prevent "the publication of the law and its entry into force". For the Tribunal, this

consequence of the binding nature of the unfavourable ruling "would configure the control exercised by the Council in terms excessively close (essentially equivalent, certainly) to a jurisdictional control over laws that are thoroughly perfected in terms of content, to the detriment of the monopoly on rejecting laws with the force of law reserved by art. 161 SC for this Court" (CCS 31/2010, of June 28, FJ 32°).

A broad sector of the public legal literature, especially in Catalonia, has interpreted the CCS 31/2010 as a backwards step in the evolution of the Catalan institution, preventing it from becoming an autonomous organ of preventative control of the constitutionality and "estatutoriedad" of specific autonomous provisions. Some of the arguments employed by this sector of the literature are the following:

1) The function of control regarding the "antiestatutoriedad" or not of draft legislation related to the statutory rights exercised by the Council for Statutory Guarantees is conceived as a form of self-control based upon the institutional autonomy and the political autonomy of art. 2 SC (Carrillo 2010, pp. 35–36).
2) The binding decision of the Council for Guarantees is valid only at the initial moment of the legislative procedure and applicable to draft legislation and proposals, to "a mere intention of a law", not to existing laws that already result in subjective rights. Hence, in the event of an unfavourable ruling, there is no elimination of any law because no such law yet exists (Aparicio Pérez 2009b, p. 176).
3) The Council for Statutory Guarantees is not an autonomous Constitutional Court, nor is it a body that encroaches upon the function that the Constitution reserves exclusively for the Constitutional Court concerning the control of the constitutionality of laws (Aparicio Pérez 2009a, p. 4).
4) The assignment of binding nature to the Council for Statutory Guarantees' ruling configures the latter as an organ of legal control of the constitutionality and "estatutoriedad" of draft legislation (on a preventative or cautionary basis), similar to the control currently exercised by the French Constitutional Council (Carrillo 2010, p. 36; Balaguer Callejón 2010, p. 66).

In our opinion, we coincide with the view taken by the Constitutional Court with regard to the declaration of unconstitutionality of art. 76.4 SAC, with respect to the binding ruling of the Council for Statutory Guarantees, although we believe that, given the significance of the judgement, the Court should have further developed the reasoning employed to justify its decision (Delgado del Rincón 2011, p. 252).

We consider that the attribution of binding nature to the ruling by the Council for Guarantees with regard to the constitutionality or "estatutoriedad" of draft bills with status of law in the area of statutory rights would represent an attack on the democratic principle, the principle of the separation of powers, and the autonomous parliamentary form of government.

This would be an attack on the democratic principle because it would constitute interference with the process of formation of the political will of the Chamber and limitation of the full autonomy of the Parliament, as representative of the Catalan people, to exercise their legislative power and to express themselves freely with regard to the contents of legal drafts or proposals concerning statutory rights being considered in the Chamber. The consequence of this type of binding ruling would be the introduction of obstacles to the free development of the public debate between the different Catalan political forces with parliamentary representation.

The binding ruling by the Council for Guarantees would also be contrary to the principle of separation of powers, as the political will of the Catalan Parliament would be dependent upon the will of an external organ of statutory control, in such a way that Parliament could not continue processing a draft bill in the area of statutory rights without the suppression of those provisions declared anti-statutory or unconstitutional by the Council for Guarantees (art. 18.2 and 3 LCSG) (Santolaya Machetti 2009, p. 81).

This would also affect the autonomous parliamentary form of government, to which art. 152.1 SC refers, due to the fact that the Council for Statutory Guarantees, to which the Catalan statute assigns the authority to issue binding decisions, would become a statutory organ of control that would influence the functioning of one of the institutions of Catalan political autonomy, the Parliament, involving itself in the process of elaborating norms with force of law that develop or affect statutory rights.

In other words, the binding effect upon Parliament of the negative ruling by the Council for Guarantees would mean the introduction into the originally intangible sphere of the Chamber (or into the very heart of the legislative process) of an external organ of legal control that would exercise (as a consequence of its decisions) a function of a jurisdictional or quasi-jurisdictional character. Until now and because of its inclusion in the basic rule, the only constitutional body that is assigned this function and also has the capacity to limit the Parliament's legislative activity is the Constitutional Court. The creation of other autonomous bodies with this type of function would require reform of the Constitution.

Moreover, as the Constitutional Court has acknowledged on numerous occasions that not even the Board of the Chamber is authorised to issue a judgement of constitutionality of a legislative proposal introduced by a parliamentary group on the ground that it transcends the field of competence of the Autonomous Communities. Otherwise, the Board "would not only be assuming under a supposedly technical pretext a political decision corresponding solely to the Plenary, but, in addition, and from the perspective of democratic representation, would be hampering the possibility of celebrating a public debate between the different political forces with parliamentary representation, the representative effect of which before the electorate is guaranteed by its mere existence, regardless, needless to say, of whether the initiative, where applicable, prospers". It corresponds to the Plenary of the Chamber to reject a legislative proposal or opt to "take it into consideration and rid it of possible unconstitutional flaws during the different phases which form a part of the legislative process. Furthermore: in the event of the potentially unconstitutional legislative proposal achieving the status of definitive law and those possible unconstitutional flaws enduring, this Constitutional

Court alone, when legally legitimated subjects demanded that it do so, would be authorised to pronounce upon la constitutionality or not of that future law" (By all, the CCS 95/1994, of July 18, FFJJ 2° y 4° y 78/2006, of March 13, FFJJ 3° y 4°).

Furthermore, as Santolaya Machetti correctly observes (2009, pp. 82–83), the attempt to restore the instrument of prior control of the constitutionality or "estatutoriedad" of the draft legislation via the binding rulings of the Council for Guarantees—with the object of achieving a greater degree of autonomy in Catalonia—could create serious problems for the government of Catalonia. More-over, the fact is that the mechanism of prior control of the constitutionality of organic laws and of the Statutes of Autonomy constituted a negative experience in the Spanish legal system during the period in which it was in effect since, amongst other of its drawbacks, it provided the opposition with opportunity systematically to block and obstruct the legislative proposals of the parliamentary majority.

In short, following CCS 31/2010, of June 18, which declared the unconstitution-ality of the competence of the Council for Statutory Guarantees to issue binding rulings to Parliament regarding legislative proposals in the area of statutory rights, the Council for Statutory Guarantees is conceived as an advisory body of the *Generalitat* (similar to the previous advisory council although with extended competences) that exercises the function of monitoring the constitutionality and the "estatutoriedad" of the legislative proposals referred to in art. 76.2 SAC, including those relating to statutory rights. In this sense, the Council may also be configured as an organ of guarantee and institutional protection of these rights, although the rulings emitted with regard to legislative proposals concerning this matter, as a result of the declaration of unconstitutionality of art. 76.4 SAC, will not be binding in character for the Parliament of the *Generalitat*.

Finally, it is worth noting that in the wake of CCS of 31/2010, of June 28, the Catalan Parliament has modified the Law of the Council for Statutory Guarantees via Law 27/2010, of August 3, with regard to the processing rulings concerning legislative proposals and draft legislations passed on first reading. However, Parlia-ment has not taken advantage of the opportunity to abolish arts. 17.3 and 18 LCSG, relating to binding rulings, developed by art. 76.4 SAC, declared unconstitutional by the CCS 31/2010. In any case, this situation would give rise to another problem, the question on whether or not it is possible to extend the annulling effects of a sentence emitted by the Constitutional Court declaring the unconstitutionality of one or more provisions of the Catalan Statute of Autonomy to identical or similar provisions contained in a Law passed by the Catalan Parliament.

# References

Albertí Rovira, Enoch, (2008). "El nuevo Consejo de Garantías Estatutarias del Estatuto de Autonomía de Cataluña como instrumento de garantía de los derechos". Revista Vasca de Administración Pública, n° 82.

Aparicio Pérez, Miguel, (2009), a). "Protección del autogobierno y control de estatutoriedad. El Consejo de Garantías Estatutarias". Revista catalana de dret públic, n° 39.

Aparicio Pérez, Miguel, (2009), b). "Órganos de garantía estatutaria y tutela de derechos". In: Aparicio Pérez, M. and Barceló i Serramalera M. (coords.) Los órganos garantes de la autonomy política. Barcelona.

Balaguer Callejón, Francisco, (2010). "Las cuestiones institucionales en la STC 31/2010, de 28 de junio". Monográfico El Tribunal Constitucional y el Estatut. El Cronista, Iustel, n° 15, (octubre).

Baldazzi, Davide, (2005). "Gli organi di garanzia statutaria: arbitri o vittime della politica regionale?". Istituzioni del federalismo: Rivista di studi giuridici e politici, n° 5. http://www.regione.emilia-romagna.it/affari_ist/rivista_5_2005/855-873

Biglino Campos, Paloma, (2003). "Algunas reflexiones finales". In: Biglino Campos, P. (coord.) Consejos Consultivos y Comunidades Autónomas: la institución en Castilla y León. Cortes de Castilla y León and Universidad de Valladolid. Valladolid.

Cano Bueso, Juan (2009). "Consolidación de los Consejos Consultivos en Spain y su papel como garantes de la autonomía". Revista catalana de dret públic, n° 39.

Carrillo, Marc, (2010). "Después de la sentencia un Estatuto desactivado". Monográfico El Constitutional Court y el Estatut. El Cronista, Iustel, n° 15 (octubre).

Catelani, Elisabetta (2011). "La reforma de los Estatutos en las regiones italianas". Revista de Estudios Políticos, n°. 151.

Conte, Giovanna (2009). "El control de estatutariedad de las leyes regionales y los órganos de garantía: ¿hacia un pseudomodelo de justicia constitucional?". Revista catalana de dret públic, n° 39.

Delgado del Rincón, Luis, (2011). "El Consejo de Garantías Estatutarias de Catalonia: de órgano consultivo de la Generalidad a órgano de control jurídico y de tutela institucional de los derechos estatutarios". In: Matia Portilla, F. (dir.). Pluralidad de ciudadanías, nuevos derechos y participación democrática. Centro de Estudios Políticos y Constitucionales, Madrid.

Fossas Espadaler, Enric, (2011). "El control jurídico y la posición de los Tribunales Constitucionales y de los Consejos de Garantías Estatutarias". In: P. Biglino Campos and C. Mapelli Marchena (dirs.) Garantías del Pluralismo territorial, Centro de Estudios Políticos y Constitucionales, Madrid.

Jover Presa, Pere, (2007). "función consultiva y función de control: la posición institucional del Consejo de Garantías Estatutarias de la Generalitat de Catalunya". Revista Española de la Función Consultiva, n° 7 (enero-junio).

Poggi, Ana, (2009). "Órganos de Garantía Estatutaria y "forma de gobierno" de las regiones". In: Aparicio Pérez, M. and Barceló i Serramalera M. (coords.) Los órganos garantes de la autonomía política. Barcelona.

Romboli, Roberto (2009). "Los Consejos de Garantía Estatutaria en la experiencia italiana". In: R. Romboli and M. Carrillo (coords.). Los Consejos de Garantía Estatutaria, Fundación Coloquio Jurídico Europeo, Madrid.

Rubio Llorente, Francisco (2004). "La función consultiva en el Estado de las Autonomías", *Revista Española de la Función Consultiva*, n° 2 (julio-diciembre).

Santolaya Machetti, Pablo (2009). "Posición del Consejo de Garantías Estatutarias de la Generalidad de Catalonia en el sistema institucional". In: Aparicio Pérez, M. and Barceló i Serramalera M. (coords.) Los órganos garantes de la autonomía política. Barcelona.

Spadaro, Antonino (2010). "Ancora sugli organi regionali di garanzia statutaria, fra tante luci e qualche ombra", n° 3. http://www.forumcostituzionale.it/site/images/stories/pdf/documenti_forum/paper/. Also in Le Región. Bimestrale di analisi giuridica e istituzionale.

Tornos Mas, Joaquín (2010). "El Consell de Garanties Estatutàries". Revista catalana de dret Públic. Especial Sentència sobre l'Estatut.

Vintró, Joan, (2008). "Les institucions de la Generalitat (III): El Consell de Garanties Estatutàries, el Sindic de Greuges, la Sindicatura de Comptes i el Consell de l'Audiovisual de Catalunya". In: M. Barceló and J. Vintró (coords.). Dret Públic de Catalunya, Barcelona.

# The Senate Territorial Groups

Ignacio Durbán Martin

## Territorial Groups and Their Rules

### *Origin and Normative Sources*

The Senate Rules draft submitted to the House in July 1980 already contained the main elements of the current territorial Groups Rules. However, that version offered nuances of interest that are worth underlining. First, the Senators composing a territorial Group initially should come from at least three different Autonomous Communities. Then, it wasn't required that the notification of establishment of the Group submitted to the House Presidency should contain an express reference to the territory and the party (or federation, coalition, or association) to which its members belong, as planned in the current Rules. Finally, the Group's representative had the specific title of Speaker. Regarding the first of these differences, we know that the amendments that achieved to reduce the minimum number of Autonomous Communities represented in the parliamentary Group to "two or more" in the Rules Commission's report were the 38th amendment by Senator Casademont Perafita and the 166th amendment by the Senators of the Basque parliamentary Group. The justification for these amendments was based on the House's structure. As it is the House of territorial representation, all the opportunities couldn't be met if there was a minimum of three represented Communities.

The substitution of the figure of the Speaker for a mere representative and the required reference to the territory and the party (federation, coalition, or association) to which the members of the territorial Groups belong are changes that ended up being part of the proposal (amendments 268 and 269, among others) of the then majority party in the House: U.C.D. Obviously, such a restrictive rule regarding the autonomy of the territorial Groups was aiming at increasing their connection and

I. Durbán Martin (✉)
University of Valencia, Spain
e-mail: Igdurmar@alumni.uv.es

A. López-Basaguren and L. Escajedo San Epifanio (eds.), *The Ways of Federalism in Western Countries and the Horizons of Territorial Autonomy in Spain*, Vol. 2, DOI 10.1007/978-3-642-27717-7_50, © Springer-Verlag Berlin Heidelberg 2013

subordination to the parliamentary Groups to such an extent that it wouldn't be possible for the former to communicate *ad extra* without the mediation of the latter.

However, after the approval of the Senate Rules in 1982, the first territorial Group to be set up was the Castilian-Leonese Popular Group, formed by 13 Senators, whose constitution was notified to the Speaker of the House on March 8, 1983. The creation of territorial groups would then become gradually generalized. During the second term of office (1982–1986), 17 territorial Groups were formed, the maximum allowed (one for each Autonomous Community) within the socialist parliamentary Group, 10 within the Popular parliamentary Group and 2 within the mixed Group. Through this tepid and limited representation of the Autonomous Communities, a new step began, which seemed to be able to lead to the rectification of the House's dynamics that were not at all territorial up to this date (Fernández Segado 1982).

Beyond the Senate Rules it's worth mentioning that, in relation to territorial Groups, the following rules also constitute normative sources in current law: the internal parliamentary Group rules, the Party status, and the specific internal rules that the territorial Group can draw for itself. It is unclear though whether we could take all the legal-private rules as normative sources for territorial Groups.

According to Javier García Fernández, we are faced with flawed private Law entities, as long as "their patrimonial, contractual and legal capacity isn't submitted to administrative Law (. . .) and the civil capacity of these Groups isn't regulated at all (. . .) by the House Rules but by their status that do not have a public legal nature either". He adds that it is so without affecting the fact that this private Law entity is of public interest, "as being of interest does not have as a reference the legal regime that frames its existence, but the gain or profit pursued in its goals" (García Fernández 1985). Be as it is, parliamentary uses, conventions, and customs should be added to those basic sources. As we will see further on, this customary source has had a particular relevance in regard to the functionality of territorial Groups.

## *Formation*

The Senate Rules regulate parliamentary and territorial Groups in its Title I chapter II. The 32nd article, in its first two sections, sets up the possibility of forming the last ones, as long as the following requirements are met:

1. They have to be formed within a parliamentary Group.
2. This parliamentary Group has to be composed of Senators belonging to two or more Autonomous Communities.
3. The minimum number of members has to be three Senators, elected by the territory electorate or appointed by the legislative Parliament of the respective Autonomous Community.
4. Each Senator can only be part of one territorial Group.

So we see that inside parliamentary Groups incorporated by Senators appointed *in more than one Autonomous Community*, it is possible to form territorial Groups. This leads us to think that the territorial Group is a parliamentary subgroup or a "deconcentration of the parliamentary Group" (Sánchez García 1985). Submission to political parties (parliamentary Groups being its expression within the House) and the awareness of the necessity of looking for a type of territorial representation would be, in the end, the defining elements of territorial Groups.

It is also worth mentioning that the same 32nd article does not make any difference between Senators elected by the electorate or appointed by the legislative Parliaments, thereby adding the possibility for territorial Groups that could not be formed at first to be formed afterwards whenever a member coming from the autonomous institutions joins a parliamentary Group.

Moreover, no Senator can participate in more than one of this kind of Groups since the elements determining which territorial Group one can be part of are, first, membership in a determined parliamentary Group and, second, place of origin. For example, an Aragonese Senator (at a provincial or community level), registered to the socialist parliamentary Group, could only be a member of the territorial Group of the Autonomous Community of Aragon if it is made up (as we know it has to have at least three Senators) within its parliamentary Group. That is to say that he will neither be able to join territorial Groups with a different name that have been made up within his parliamentary Group (it would make no sense for him, following up with our example, to join the socialist territorial Group of Madrid made, as it is natural, of Senators elected or appointed only in that Autonomous Community) nor be able to join territorial Groups of the same name but made up outside of the parliamentary Group (the Popular territorial Group of the Autonomous community of Aragon could not count in its ranks Senators that, as the one in our example, are registered to a parliamentary Group that is not the Popular one in the Senate).

The 33rd article of the Rules sets up the following steps that have to be followed in order to make up territorial Groups:

1. Hand in to the Speaker of the House the list of its members' names through the corresponding parliamentary Group.
2. This list will have to be endorsed by all its members and by the speaker of the parliamentary Group they belong to.
3. It will have to specify the territorial Group denomination too, stating the territory, party, federation, coalition, or association to which its members belong.
4. Finally, it is mandatory to indicate the name of the representative and of its substitutes.

There is a clear parallel between the requirements for the formation of parliamentary Groups and of territorial Groups (requiring a name for the group, the designation of a representative and substitutes, etc.). There is an important difference however: There is nothing in the Rules about the dates of constitution and dissolution of the territorial Groups. From this silence, it was interpreted that they can be freely formed at any time during the term of office and that, similarly, their dissolution will depend on their members' will or, of course, on when the required minimum number of members is not met (Sánchez García 1985).

In any case, it is really interesting to note that the steps required for forming territorial Groups impose on them a strong level of submission towards parliamentary Groups. First, the constitution of a territorial Group has to be posterior to the one of the parliamentary Group from which its members come. Furthermore, when the time comes, not only is the concurrence of will of those Senators wanting to make up the Group needed, but it is also imperative to have the external intervention of the Speaker of the parliamentary Group they have previously joined. Therefore, there is no act expressing the autonomy of the Senators' will but only an authorization granted by the parliamentary Group that the Senator has previously joined and with which discipline he complies.

This political or ideological connection also affects the territorial Group internal discipline. It is so much so that, according to Javier García Fernández, "the Speaker's participation and the specific reference to the party of origin in the constitutive procedure make it possible to think that the general regime of discipline of the parliamentary Group extends to the territorial Group" (García Fernández 1985).

Nevertheless, the attention territorial Groups have encountered in the rules of the parliamentary Groups has been limited. The rules of the socialist Group (article 11) only recognize them internally, without any requirement of a minimum number, in order to use them as channels for electoral circumscriptions problems. The ones of the Popular Group (article 3), after recognizing them, require them to keep a tight and permanent institutional contact with Popular Party members of Parliament in the assemblies of the Autonomous Communities (García Guerrero 1996).

## *Functioning*

The intervention of the territorial Groups in the work of the House is made through the following ways:

1. Through the attendance of its representatives to the Speakers' Board (arts. 32.3 and 43.2);
2. Through the participation of its representatives in plenary sessions affecting, in a special way, the Autonomous Communities from which the name of the Group comes (arts. 32.3 and 85.1);
3. Originally[1] under article 137, which establishes that, in addition, the representatives of the territorial Groups whose Communities would have signed an agreement for the management and assistance of their own services could

---

[1] This function has been removed after the reform of the article 137.3, passed during the plenary session of the Senate on January 11, 1994 (BOCG, Senate, Term of office V, issue III A, num. 5 (h), January 17, 1994).

participate, with voice but without vote, to the commission which would decide whether the agreement would have to receive the General Court's authorization, even though they would not be members of the commission.

From the redaction of article 43.2 we can infer that it is possible for up to two representatives of the territorial Groups existing within one parliamentary Group to attend the Speakers' Board meetings. It is, however, a power granted to the Speaker, who may or may not make use of it, and if he does, he is free to choose one or two representatives. The assumption is different if the Board is holding a discussion on a matter affecting particularly one Autonomous Community, in which case there is not an option but an obligation for the Speaker of the Senate to communicate about it and a right for the representatives of the concerned territorial Groups to attend. For Álvarez Conde, however, the territorial Groups do not attend the Board's meetings as members (Álvarez Conde 1987). In any case, this may be the only time when the activity of the territorial Groups does not seem to be directly depending on the parliamentary Groups (although the Speaker of the House's announcement is processed through those Groups).

The second function, as planned in article 85.1 of the Rules, finds its raison d'être precisely in the very existence of the territorial Groups, which justification is no other than the defence of the entity and of the interests of the different Autonomous Communities in the Senate. Therefore, it seems reasonable that, as stipulated in the article, it is possible to increase at any time the number of interventions during the plenary sessions of the Upper House in order to allow the representatives of the affected territorial Groups to participate. This article gives them great opportunities as it allows them to take part in plenary sessions. However, this is a rule full of reservations and uncertainties. On the one hand, it is the Speaker of the House who determines which issues under discussion will affect "in a particular way" one or various Autonomous Communities (so that a restrictive interpretation of the Rules would prejudice the territorial Groups that could do little about it). On the other hand, there has to be an agreement between the Speaker of the parliamentary Group and the Speaker of the House in order to increase the number of interventions, thereby demonstrating again the deliberated intention to make Speakers act as mediators and liaisons before any possible intervention of the territorial Groups.

Yet, if one considers that in articles 43 and 85 of the Rules are regulated, respectively, the Speaker's Board and the procedure planned for plenary sessions of the House (regarding discussions on issues affecting in a special way one or various Autonomous Communities), one can assess the true scope of the territorial Groups, which, according to Nicolás Pérez-Serrano Jáuregui, consists in "letting its local voice be heard in the organ of fixation of the orders of the day and on specifically autonomous matters" (Pérez-Serrano Jáuregui 1989).

## Territorial Groups Formed in Accordance with the House Current Composition

In the IX Term of office, the number of territorial Groups within each parliamentary Groups was as follow:

| Parliamentary Groups | Territorial Groups |
|---|---|
| *Populars in the Senate* | 12 |
| *Socialist* | 10 |
| *Entesa Catalana de Progrés* | 0 |
| *Catalán en el Senado de Convergència i Unió* | 0 |
| *Nationalist Senators* | 0 |
| *Mixed* | 0 |
| Total | 22 |

The Entesa Catalana de Progrés and Catalán en el Senado de Convergència I Unió parliamentary Groups are entirely composed of Senators coming from only one Autonomous Community (Catalonia), therefore making it impossible to constitute territorial Groups within them, in accordance with article 32.1 of the Rules. It is interesting to note that the Senators belonging to the Socialist Party of Catalonia have joined the Entesa Catalana de Progrés parliamentary Group and not the socialist parliamentary Group within which they could have formed a territorial Group. However it seems clear that forming a parliamentary Group helps developing a better capacity of defence of the entity and of the interests of the Autonomous Communities. However, the Nationalist Senators parliamentary Group would be able to form at least one territorial Group (of the Basque Country) as is has in its ranks three Basque Senators and one Galician (José Manuel Pérez Bouza).

Regarding the mixed Group there is no obstacle, according to the Rules, for it to form territorial Groups. However, due to its current composition (nine members from five different communities), there is no margin to constitute one.

| Territorial Groups made up within the Popular parliamentary Group in the Senate | | | |
|---|---|---|---|
| | Number of Senators | | |
| Name | Elected | Appointed | Total |
| *P.t.G. of Andalusia* | 10 | 4 | 14 |
| *P.t.G. of Aragon* | 3 | 1 | 4 |
| *P.t.G. of the Canary Islands* | 2 | 1 | 3 |
| *P.t.G. of Cantabria* | 3 | 0 | 3 |
| *P.t.G. of Castile and León* | 24 | 2 | 26 |
| *P.t.G. of Castile-La Mancha* | 14 | 1 | 15 |
| *P.t.G. of Extremadura* | 2 | 1 | 3 |
| *P.t.G. of Galicia* | 11 | 1 | 12 |
| *P.t.G. of Murcia* | 3 | 1 | 4 |
| *P.t.G. of La Rioja* | 3 | 1 | 4 |
| *P.t.G. of the Balearic Islands* | 2 | 1 | 3 |
| *P.t.G. of the Valencian Community* | 10 | 2 | 12 |

Territorial Groups made up within the Socialist parliamentary Group in the Senate

| Name | Number of Senators | | |
|---|---|---|---|
| | Elected | Appointed | Total |
| *Aragonese Socialists* | 9 | 0 | 9 |
| *Asturian Socialists* | 3 | 1 | 4 |
| *Socialists of the Canary Island* | 7 | 1 | 8 |
| *Socialists of Andalusia* | 22 | 5 | 27 |
| *Socialists de Castile and León* | 11 | 1 | 12 |
| *Socialists de Castile-La Mancha* | 6 | 1 | 7 |
| *Socialists of Extremadura* | 6 | 1 | 7 |
| *Socialists of Galicia* | 4 | 1 | 5 |
| *Socialists of Madrid* | 1 | 3 | 4 |
| *Basque Socialists* | 8 | 1 | 9 |

We can see that almost all Senators from both parliamentary Groups are included in their own territorial Groups (91 out of 105 for the Socialists and 103 out of 123 for the Popular Party). It should also be noted that nearly all the territorial Groups that could be formed in each parliamentary Group have been formed, and that nearly all the Senators that could be part of them[2] have joined in, which shows the great success that keeps having the 32nd article of the Rules, after 30 years of existence. However during the current Term of office none of the two parliamentary Groups managed to reach the maximum number of territorial Groups authorized by the Rules, 17, one for each Autonomous Community.

The Autonomous Communities of Andalusia, Aragon, the Canary Islands, Castile and León, Castile-La Mancha, Extremadura, and Galicia are the only ones having two territorial Groups in the Senate, the other ones having only one (except for Catalonia and Navarre,[3] which have none).

The territorial Groups of the Balearic Islands, the Canary Islands, and Cantabria are made up with the minimum number of members required. In addition, only the latter and the socialist territorial Group of Aragon do not have appointed Senators. On the contrary, the socialist Group of Madrid is the only one to have more appointed Senators (3) than elected ones (1). In addition, it is important to note

---

[2] The only ones that could have been formed but were not are the territorial Group of the Valencian Community within the socialist parliamentary Group (which has five Senators coming from this community) and the territorial Group of the Madrid Community within the Popular parliamentary Group (which has seven Senators from Madrid). On another level, the only Senators not joining a territorial Group of which they could have been members according to their origin are, within the socialist parliamentary Group, five Andalusian Senators and the Basque Senator and Speaker of the House Francisco Javier Rojo García and, within the Popular parliamentary Group, Ildefonso Rafael Pastor González (Castilian-Leonese) and Almudena Monserrat de León (from the Canary Islands).

[3] At the beginning of the IXth Term of office, the People's territorial Group of Navarre was formed, but as a result of the breaking off (announced on October, 2008) of the pact uniting the PP and the UPN since 1991; Senator María Caballero Martínez left the Popular parliamentary Group and, subsequently, the territorial Group of Navarre, which then had to be dissolved, not having the required minimum number of three members anymore.

that the Popular territorial Groups of the Canary Island, Extremadura, and the Balearic Islands could not have been formed if there had not been appointed Senators in their ranks.


# Conclusions

As a conclusion or a general result, it should be noted first that the existence of the territorial Groups opens the possibility of a limited territorialization, not yet of the House but of the parliamentary Groups. It is indeed established that, within the latter, a number of Senators elected by a territory, either a province or a community, being at least three, can come together, having to communicate it in writing to the House's Presidency, which writing has to be endorsed by all the members of the future Group and, in any case, by the Speaker of the parliamentary Group that the Senators are part of (which subordinates totally the territorial Groups to the parliamentary Group they belong to). In this way, the words of Manuel Martínez Sospedra are significant when he points out that "the role of the territorial Groups is rather limited" (Martínez Sospedra 1990).

Following this position, Piedad García-Escudero has come to declare that "the statutory prevision of the territorial Groups existence has showed itself as being totally inoperable and ineffective as they have to be formed within the parliamentary Groups, thereby giving precedence to political affiliation and party discipline over territorial nature" (García-Escudero 1995). It does not appear as if any of the requirements for these territorial Groups, being of a quantitative or ideological nature, allows these Groups to have a prominent role in the Senate configuration. Only the possibility for these Groups to be formed at any moment during term of office, allowing the incorporation of Senators appointed all along the term, can favor these Groups' existence, as their worthless operating capacity has been their main characteristic up until now. Despite this limited functional range, Javier García Fernández maintains that "a wider autonomous interpretation of the Rules in force which would be based on the gradual use and consolidation of parliamentary practices and conventions would give a more prominent role to the territorial Groups while territorially energizing the House" (García Fernández 1985).

Finally, we can say that the practical role of these territorial Groups has been rather limited and the parliamentary Rules that apparently activate its participation have not succeeded in their objective, so that it seems that we can agree with Álvarez Conde when he says that "the territorial Groups are lacking the necessary organizational and functional autonomy, their dependence towards the parliamentary Group to which they are attached is total, that way becoming a real parliamentary fiction, as showed by their role and presence during the House debates" (Álvarez Conde 1987).

# References

Álvarez Conde, E. (1987). El régimen político español. Tecnos, Madrid, 715 pp.

Fernández Segado, F. (1982). El bicameralismo y la naturaleza del Senado. Revista Española de Derecho Constitucional 6: 61–114.

García Fernández, J. (1985). Los Grupos territoriales del Senado. I Jornadas de Derecho Parlamentario. 21–23 de Marzo de 1984. Vol. 2. Madrid, pp. 1105–1136.

García-Escudero Márquez, P. (1995). Los Senadores designados por las Comunidades Autónomas. Centro de Estudios Políticos y Constitucionales, Madrid, 583 pp.

García Guerrero, J. L. (1996). Democracia representativa de partidos y grupos parlamentarios. Congreso de los diputados, Madrid, 554 pp.

Martínez Sospedra, M. (1990). La reforma del Senado. Fundación Universitaria San Pablo CEU, Valencia, 270 pp.

Pérez-Serrano Jáuregui, N. (1989). Los Grupos parlamentarios. Tecnos, Madrid, 260 pp.

Sánchez García, J. (1985). Los Grupos territoriales del Senado. I Jornadas de Derecho Parlamentario. 21–23 de Marzo de 1984. Vol. 2. Madrid, pp. 1175–1196.

# Reinforcement for the Position of Local Government in the New Statutes of Autonomy

José M. Porras Ramírez

## The Effective Assumption of Local Governments into the Autonomic System

It seems to be increasingly widely accepted that the best means of guaranteeing the position of local governments is to integrate them effectively into the autonomic system, along the same lines as certain European federal systems.[1] This means that the statutes of autonomy of the different regions need to have the power to designate the jurisdictional powers of local government *vis-à-vis* those held by the autonomous communities.[2] Given that the statutes form an integral part of the "bloque de la constitucionalidad"—the body of constitutional law—assigning this important task to them will help make them the undisputed parameters of the validity of any laws that might affect the delimitation of local self-government related to the jurisdictional area of the autonomous region. At the same time, it will avoid the error of a rigid uniform treatment that does not reflect the real situation of the local government systems of Spain, whose diversity and heterogeneity are becoming increasingly evident and elude the excessive homogenising zeal commonly encountered in the fundamental provisions of state laws.[3]

While this is no panacea and needs be implemented in parallel with a reform of the law regulating the bases of the local government system (to include, at least, the common uniform regulation for the entire state, pursuant to the strict provisions of

---

[1] For a general overview, see Watts (2008), p. 132 et seq.

[2] Font i Llovet (2006), p. 20 et seq. Also, by the same author, Font i Llovet (2006), p. 19 et seq.

[3] On this issue, see Caamaño Domínguez (2000–2001), pp. 87–110. Also, Porras Ramírez (2005), pp. 211–237; particularly, p. 233 et seq., Requejo Pagés (2007), pp. 53–58; particularly, p. 57; and Zafra Víctor (2009), pp. 35–66.

J.M.P. Ramírez (✉)
Facultad de Derecho, Universidad de Granada, Plaza de la Universidad 1, 18071 Granada, Spain
e-mail: jmporras@ugr.es

A. López-Basaguren and L. Escajedo San Epifanio (eds.), *The Ways of Federalism in Western Countries and the Horizons of Territorial Autonomy in Spain*, Vol. 2, DOI 10.1007/978-3-642-27717-7_51, © Springer-Verlag Berlin Heidelberg 2013

Article 149.1.18 of the Constitution, thus making it a proper "set of legal principles"), it would certainly mark a great step forward. It would enable regulations to be drawn up that were less abstract and therefore more in touch with reality, in other words, with the political and territorial pluralism that, according to the Spanish constitution, should inform the decentralised structure of the state. This would be a major advance towards configuring a diversified system that would, at the same time, reflect the importance of reallocating powers and responsibilities to these local governments, in keeping with the principle of subsidiarity.[4] Because these tiers of government are a more developed expression of an advanced grassroots democracy, strengthening them would necessarily lead to the construction of a political system of greater quality, favouring citizen participation, transparency, and greater control over the actions of the public authorities.

Given the dissatisfaction generated by successive legislative reforms—whose repeated lack of success can be put down to their distorted approach—with the implementation of different proposals for statute reform, the time has at last come for local governments to be accommodated, once and for all, within the autonomic system. Indeed, this is precisely what Article 148.1.2 of the constitution appears to call for. We need to do away with the disproportionate and frequently inappropriate use of Article 149.1.18 of the constitution which to date has been used solely to enable the state to supplant the role that rightfully belongs to the autonomous communities, by forcibly linking the constitutional guarantee of local autonomy (Arts. 137, 141 and 142) with the "basic rules of the legal system of public administrations".

Given the extensive margin of action available to the statutes of autonomy, they can perform this qualified function while respecting the minimum common regulation that the state is responsible for establishing, by reinforcing the jurisdictional status of the local governments while at the same time catering for their singular nature in the various different autonomous communities. On the one hand, their very position within the system of sources, which is a result of their peculiar dual nature and the qualified constitutional guarantee applying to them and explains their rigidity, is manifested both in their passive strength, which allows them to resist, where necessary, the state parliament, and in their capacity to actively condition any legislative developments that may be made by the regional parliaments, depending on the powers assumed.[5] On the other hand, the basic institutional rules of the autonomous communities can be seen to be the ideal vehicle for properly projecting the very significance of the principle of subsidiarity, in terms of the distribution of powers between the different territorial authorities or tiers of government, regional and local.[6]

It is not surprising that Council of Europe Recommendation 121 (2002) on local and regional democracy in Spain called for this guiding principle to be included in

---

[4] Font i Llovet (2004), pp. 13–36; particularly, p. 24 et seq.

[5] Inter alia, Porras Ramírez (2007), p. 14 et seq.

[6] See also Velasco Caballero (2004), pp. 117–159.

all statutes, in order to favour the attribution to local collectives of a certain number of powers pertaining to them, which are currently still centralised. This resource will make it possible to assess the impact of the decentralisation process begun in recent years by taking it out of the arena of mere political rhetoric. This "radical improvement", as the Council of Europe calls it, therefore requires open territorialisation of the legal and financial procedure attending local governments, in other words, a clear assumption of the local space into the sphere in which it undisputedly belongs: the autonomic area. The European Charter of Local Self-government backs this desire: Article 4.3 expresses a general preference for public responsibilities to be exercised by those authorities that are closest to the citizen. These powers must therefore be allocated, with the subsequent provision of services to the community, to those who can exercise them most effectively and immediately, and the upper echelons of government should not be called in except when the lower tier proves incapable of fulfilling these responsibilities. Political organisation must therefore be built from the bottom up, resulting in an intensification of the processes of decentralisation of power and a consequent redistribution of powers and responsibilities.

In this respect, the round of statutory reforms undertaken during the period from 2004 to 2011, taking strictly into account the restrictions imposed by the Constitution, have been used, with different degrees of success and intensity, to reinforce the position of local government. Some statutes include a list of the decentralised autonomic powers that are allocated to local government, taking their interests into account. As well as detailing these powers, this has meant forgoing the common—and problematical—resort to non-specific general clauses and the introduction of a detailed guarantee *vis-à-vis* the regional parliament, which is commonly tempted to evade or diminish the impact of such clauses.[7]

## Local Government in the New Statutes of Autonomy

In this sphere of demands and proposals, the new statutes of Valencia, Catalonia, Andalusia, the Balearic Islands, Aragon, Castile-Leon, and Extremadura have introduced amendments of varying significance. Given the expectations that had been raised, some, as we shall see, have proved quite disappointing. Others, however, mark an important sea change, notably reinforcing the position of local government institutions within the framework of their respective autonomous communities. All of the new statutes seek to establish a more detailed regulation of the territorial organisation, involving greater diversification and heterogeneity in the way the issue of local government is dealt with. The most significant development is a shared belief that the statute must act as the guarantor of local self-government.

---

[7] Porras Ramírez (2007), pp. 219–236; particularly, pp. 230–231.

For example, although the *Statute of Autonomy of the Community of Valencia*, extensively amended in 2006, included an entire new Heading (Heading VIII) devoted to "Local Administration", it contains few new features, somewhat limiting its scope in practice. This statute first asserts the benefit of establishing organs of cooperation between regional and local administrations on matters in which they share powers (Art. 63.3). Article 64 entrusts to the parliament the task of promoting local self-government and provides for delegation of the execution of functions and powers to municipal authorities and other local supra-municipal organs, in accordance with their capacity for management and the nature of the representative authority in question. It also appeals to the principles of subsidiarity and differentiation but ends up leaving it up to the regional parliament to decide what powers are to be decentralised and what economic resources are required for this purposes. It goes on to establish the creation of a municipal cooperation fund and a joint committee of the government of Valencia (the Generalitat) and the Valencian Federation of Municipalities and Provinces, which shall be entitled to be consulted in all legislative initiatives by the parliament of Valencia that affect local entities or that refer to the adoption of plans and regulations of this nature (Art. 64.4). Article 65 of the Statute provides for the creation of *comarcas* (sub-regions), metropolitan areas and groupings of *comarcas*, by an act of the regional parliament approved by a two-thirds majority.

Finally, the controversial Article 66, dealing with the provincial councils (*Diputaciones Provinciales*), echoes a particular concern with overseeing the activities of these bodies—an attitude that tends to impinge on their constitutionally guaranteed field of self-government. Initially, the statute provides for the transfer or legislative delegation of the Generalitat's powers. At the same, it reiterates the Generalitat's right to coordinate functions pertaining to the provincial governments that are of general interest for the autonomous community, on the basis of formulae established in an act approved by an absolute majority of the regional parliament. However, having emphasised that their budgets must be united to those of the regional government, it further states that in executing these delegated powers, the provincial councils act as institutions of the Generalitat, fully submitting to its legislation, regulation, and inspection. Hence, it establishes that if a provincial council fails to comply with the orders of the Statute or those imposed by regional laws, the government of the Generalitat may take any measures necessary to enforce its compliance, although the provincial authorities may appeal any such decision to the Higher Court of Justice of the Community of Valencia.

Finally, Article 70, apart from some general references, avoids establishing or providing effective guarantees of the financial capacity of the local entities.

The result, as we have said, is something of a disappointment: the statute adopts no measures to ensure a significant reinforcement of the status of local governments in the region. It only introduces certain enabling articles that empower the regional parliament, with a very wide margin or freedom of formation, to act on grounds of mere convenience or political expediency, a provision that may, as is often the case, result in an infringement on the existing material sphere of local self-government. Thus, in practice and taken as a whole, these measures, far from assuring a statutory improvement in local government, to a great extent frustrate the very reasonable expectations raised; indeed, they might even be viewed as a retrograde step, in their disproportionate desire to supervise the activities of the provincial councils.

The new *Statute of Catalonia* offers a genuinely novel and intense approach to the issue,[8] with Heading II, Chapter VI given over to regulating the basic profiles of local government in the region. Nonetheless, the intensive reinterpretation of the scope of this chapter made by the constitutional court's controversial ruling, STC 31/2010 of 28 June 2010, has to a great extent limited the significance of its primary contributions. In broad terms, the ruling states that any such statutory arrangement shall be made "...without prejudice to the relations that the state may, in turn, legitimately establish, under Article 149.1.18 of the Spanish Constitution with all local bodies" (FJ 37).[9]

Initially, Section I of this Chapter establishes the local territorial organisation of Catalonia on regional criteria, i.e., based on the particular features of regional divisions in this autonomous community. Thus, it is essentially divided into municipalities and *veguerías*, and the supra-municipal area is deemed to be made up, in all cases, of *comarcas*, as regulated by an act of the regional parliament. This express reference to these bodies does not signify any exclusion either of other supra-municipal bodies that the regional government (Generalitat) may choose to designate, grounded on a desire for collaboration and association between municipalities (Art. 83) or, naturally, of the provinces, given the non-transferability of ownership [*indisponibilidad*] of their powers under the constitution.

Article 84 Paragraph 2 of the Statute establishes an extensive and very thorough list of fourteen matters subject to autonomic jurisdiction, over which "a core set of powers" shall be reserved to the municipalities "which shall be exercised by them with full autonomy" (Paragraph 1), "in the terms established by [regional] laws", in accordance with basic state legislation under Art. 149.1.18 of the Constitution (Ruling STC 31/2010, FJ 38). These competences must take into account criteria such as the "management capacities" of the local entities in question and the principles of subsidiarity, differentiation, and financial capacity (Art. 84.3). To this end, the Generalitat must establish the mechanisms for financing the new services resulting from the expansion of local government powers (Art. 84.4).

Interestingly too, Article 85 of the Statute provides for the creation of a council of local governments to be developed by means of an act of the regional parliament. As the representative body for municipalities and *veguerías* in the institutions of the Generalitat, the council has the right to be taken into account in parliamentary procedures for legislative initiatives that affect local administrations and in any matters referring to the preparation of plans and regulatory rules.[10]

---

[8] Inter alia, see Argullol Murgades (2008), p. 67 et seq., and also Tornos Más and Gracia Retortillo (2008), p. 75 et seq.

[9] For an initial assessment of the sentence, see the contributions by Bayona Rocamora et al. (2010), pp. 213–248; and also Galán Galán and Gracia Retortillo (2011), p. 237 et seq.

[10] Act 12/2010, of 19 May 2010 (Ley del Consejo de Gobiernos Locales).

Heading II, Chapter VI, Section II of the statute is given over to the municipalities. It starts by reiterating the guarantee of the necessary autonomy for the exercise of their powers and the defence of the interests of the communities they represent (Art. 86.3), from which derives their full authority for self-organisation (Art. 87.1) and the exercise of the corresponding regulatory power (Art. 87.3). It then goes on to establish their right to enter into association with others and to co-operate amongst themselves and with other public bodies, to exercise their powers and tasks of common interest. To this end, it recognises their capacity to enter into agreements and create and participate in *mancomunidades*, consortia, and associations, with no legal restriction whatsoever other than to guarantee the recognised autonomy of other entities (Art. 87.2). In any case, "the Generalitat has the authority to check that any act or decision adopted by municipalities complies with the legal system and, if appropriate, take the necessary action to bring the issue before the contentious-administrative courts, without prejudice to any actions which the State may take in defence of its powers" (as recalled by constitutional court decision FJ 38, STC 31/2010)".

Another very important feature of the statute is its consecration of the principle of differentiation. Article 88 states that the laws affecting the legal, organic, functional, jurisdictional, and financial systems of the municipalities shall take into account their different demographic, geographic, functional, and organisational characteristics and also their size and capacity for management. Article 89 very specifically alludes to the special system established for the municipality of Barcelona in an act of the Catalan parliament. This must recognise the initiative, both to propose a modification in this special system and to participate in preparing government bills affecting this special system, for which reason the municipality shall be consulted during the parliamentary proceedings of any legislative initiatives affecting the special system.

Also in accordance with the principle of differentiation and with a view to recovering a local form of territorial division, deemed to be an inseparable feature of Catalonia, Heading II, Chapter VI, Section III of the statute determines that the *veguería* is a specific territorial area for the exercise of inter-municipal government for local cooperation. It has legal personality and autonomy in the management of its interests. The *veguería* is therefore "the territorial division adopted by the Generalitat for the territorial organisation of its services" (Art. 90.1). It is therefore provided with an organ of government and autonomous administration, the *Veguería* Council, whose legal system shall be determined by an act of the regional parliament, which can functionally replace the provincial council, without, for this reason, affecting the provincial boundaries, which would, under Article 141.1 *in fine* of the Spanish Constitution, require approval of the Cortes Generales by way of an organic law (Art. 91).

In any case, as the Constitutional Court ruled in STC 31/2010, FJ 40, the creation of the *veguerías* does not prevent the province from continuing to be the territorial area taken as a reference by the Central Administration of the State for carrying out the tasks within its power (Art. 141.2 of the Spanish Constitution) and, at the same time, the area of the electoral constituencies regulated by the State under Articles

68.2 and 69.2 of the Constitution. Neither, of course, does the creation of the *veguerías* exclude the existence of other bodies of supra-municipal government. Against the claims of those contesting the section of the statute referring to the *veguería*, one might therefore argue that neither of the two dimensions of the *veguería* set out in the statute—as a division of the territory for intra-regional purposes and as a local government intended for inter-municipal cooperation that enjoys self-government for the management of its interests—infringes on the constitutional concept of the province as a territorial division of the state and as a local entity or on the constitutional functions pertaining to the province, essentially in its condition as an electoral constituency. As the Constitutional Court has established, therefore, "the statutory provisions of the existence of the *veguerías*, whatever their geographical boundaries, cannot entail the abolition of the provinces in Catalonia, nor of their constitutional functions" (STC 31/2010, FJ 40).

In any event, the references to the *veguerías* whose constitutionality have been called most into question are those concerning their creation, modification, and abolition and their organ of government, as set out in Art. 91, given the limitations imposed by the constitution with regard to the legal system of the provinces (Art. 141). Given the potential conflict between constitutional and statutory regulation, the Constitutional Court (FJ 41 STC 31/201) argued that any ratification of the validity of the contested statutory precepts would have to be grounded either on the assumption that *veguería* is merely the name given to a province in Catalonia, for strictly regional purposes, since it fulfils the typical features of the province in the statute; or an assumption that this is a different local entity, with all the associated consequences of each of these very different premises. If the first of these interpretations is accepted, it would be legitimate to consider that the "*Veguería* Councils", as the organ of "government and autonomous administration of the *veguería*" (Arts. 91.1 and 91.2), effectively "replace the provincial councils" (Art. 91.3), without affecting the fact that it is still state legislation that regulates their composition and the means whereby their members are chosen. However, if one takes the second option, any interpretation of the statute in accordance with the Constitution would have to accept that the *Veguería* Councils only replace the provincial councils in situations in which the geographical limits of the *veguería* coincide with those of the province and not in others.[11]

At the same time, in keeping with the trend towards promoting the principle of differentiation that we have already discussed, Heading II, Chapter VI Section IV, of the Statute seeks to counter the divisive situation of both infra-municipalism and multi-municipalism suffered in Catalonia,[12] with the *comarca*, as a grouping of municipalities, being seen as a local entity with its own legal personality, oriented towards management of local powers and services. It further provides that the creation, modification, and abolition of the *comarca*, as well as the establishment

---

[11] See, for example, Mir i Bagó (2006), pp. 79–103; particularly, p. 97 et seq.

[12] Cf., Pereira i Solé (2004), pp. 199–207; particularly, pp. 201–202.

of its legal procedure, shall be regulated by an Act of the regional parliament (Art. 92).

Along similar lines, Article 93 of the Statute also refers to the possibility of creating, modifying, and abolishing other systems of local entities of a supra-municipal nature—among which it mentions the metropolitan areas—by way of an act of Parliament regulating their legal system. The stated purpose is to facilitate and recognise the municipalities' wish to collaborate and enter into association.

Article 160.1 of the statute (Local Government System) is closely related to this local territorial organisation. Coming within the framework of the highly important Heading IV (Powers), it states that the Generalitat has exclusive power over the local government system, respecting the principle of local autonomy, in order to foster the effective assumption of Catalonia's local government system. Not surprisingly, it is in this clause, necessarily linked to those discussed above, that this goal is most precisely expressed. It lists all the areas in which the Generalitat aspires to exercise its exclusive capacity of regulation, painstakingly listing each sub-matter. Inter alia, it states that it is the exclusive power of the Generalitat to determine the relations between the institutions of the Generalitat and local government entities and also the methods for organisation and liaison in regard to cooperation and collaboration between local government entities and between these and the administration of the Generalitat, and including the various forms: associations, *mancomunidades*, conventional associations, and consortia. The Generalitat shall determine the powers and jurisdiction of municipalities and other local government entities, in the areas specified in Article 84. It shall also regulate the system of publicly owned communal and patrimonial property and the modalities of public service provision. Furthermore, it shall determine the governing bodies for local government entities created by the Generalitat, i.e., *comarcas* and *veguerías*, and the functioning and decision-making system of these bodies. The Generalitat shall also hold power over the system governing complementary bodies in the organisation of local government entities.

However, after an appeal was lodged on the grounds of unconstitutionality, the Constitutional Court issued its very debatable ruling in STC 31/2010, restricting the scope of this section of Article 160. In FJ 100 it rules that the determination of the exclusive nature of the powers in this article "was made improperly" and that therefore "there is no impediment to full application of the state bases, namely those contained in Art. 149.1.18 of the constitution to these regional powers...". Art 160.3 of the statute additionally gives the Generalitat power to regulate the electoral system for the local entities it creates, i.e., the *comarcas* and the *veguerías*; however, in the case of local governments that are constitutionally guaranteed, this power is deemed to belong to the state and not the Generalitat. The Constitutional Court recognises that this clause does not, in any way, infringe upon the power of the state, given that it is unnecessary for the statute to confirm the state's power to establish the general electoral system (Art. 149.1.1, in relation to Art. 81.1 of the Constitution) (STC 31/2010, FJ 100). For all other matters, the statute considers that the Generalitat has shared powers with the state (Art. 160.2), in accordance with Article 149.1.18 of the Constitution.

In any case, it links these exclusive powers to the—also exclusive—power assigned to the Generalitat, under Art. 151 of the Statute, on territorial organisation, to determine the creation, modification, and abolition of local government entities; to create, abolish and alter boundaries both of municipalities and local government entities of lesser territorial scope; to denominate their capital and establish their symbols and special systems; and to establish the procedures for relations between local government entities and the population.

As a corollary, the Statute establishes that in Catalonia the Council for Statutory Guarantees shall rule on compliance of government bills and members' bills and draft legislative decrees approved by the government with local autonomy (Art. 76.2 d). This shall be independent of the prior lodging of claims of conflict over the defence of local autonomy before the Constitutional Court (Art. 76.3).

To sum up, the original version of the new Statute of Catalonia can be seen to have advanced a truly radical development in its approach to the local government system; it arranged matters in such a way that, while fully respecting the constitutional framework established, it significantly reinforced the position of the local governments. It did so by recognising and guaranteeing their reserved areas of action, associated with the sphere of influence of the Autonomous Community, and in this regard the regional parliament was ordered to determine their own powers, based on expressly stated orders and restrictions. The Statute also openly broke ranks by introducing the principle of differentiation, in recognition of the real political and territorial situation at local level. In short, it marked a change in orientation, inclining towards creating a "model of local government model of its own".[13] However these ambitions were, to a considerable extent, thwarted by STC 31/2010 of 28 June 2010, which introduced major restrictions to the scope of these plans. The ruling, which restated the oldest, most regressive and most widely criticised doctrine in the matters of the Court, insisted that the two-front nature of the regulation must be retained, and it stressed, beyond reasonable bounds, the role that the state, through its basic legislation, as set out in Art. 149.1.18 of the constitution, must continue to play. Despite the undisputed advances made, therefore, full inclusion of the local government system in Catalonia—as promoted in the statute's rigorously federal logic—has largely been neutralised.

Following the trend initiated in Catalonia, the new *Statute of Autonomy of Andalusia* also regulated this area in considerable detail. Heading II, Article 60.1, states that, in accordance with the distribution of powers inferred from the Constitution, the Autonomous Community of Andalusia possesses "exclusive powers" while respecting both the principle of local self-government and "Article 149.1.18 of the Constitution". This reference is made to forestall any objections and in the full knowledge that the article's reference to state powers is intended solely to establish the exact bases of the legal system governing public authorities. In law, therefore, these powers affect only the regulation of relations between the government of Andalusia and the local government entities. They determine the methods

---

[13] See Font i Llovet (2006), pp. 13–34; particularly, p. 29.

of organisation and relationship for co-operation and collaboration between the local government entities and between them and the regional government and set out the various forms they can take: associations, *mancomunidades*, conventional associations, and consortia; they determine the powers of the municipalities and other local government entities; they establish the system of property and the systems for provision of public services; they determine the organs of government, the system for operating and for adopting agreements of the local government entities created by the regional government (the Junta) itself; they establish the system attending the complementary organs of the local government bodies; and they indicate the electoral system for bodies created by the government of Andalusia, which therefore do not come under the aegis of the constitution. Within the framework of state legislation, the autonomous community has shared powers in all matters not previously set out (Art. 60.2), in particular, with regard to local revenue departments and the financial protection of local government entities, without prejudice to their self-government (Art. 60.3).

Heading III of the Statute (Territorial Organisation of the Autonomous Community) details many of these provisions. The introductory text of the Heading states that "Andalusia is organised territorially in municipalities, provinces and any other territorial entities that may be created by law" (Art. 89). This territorial organisation shall be governed by the "principles of autonomy, responsibility, cooperation, deconcentration, decentralisation, subsidiarity, coordination, financial capacity and institutional fealty" (Art. 90).

Article 91 recognises the municipality as the basic territorial entity of the Autonomous Community, attributing to it the organisational features assigned by the Constitution, with which we are now familiar. It establishes that "any modification to municipal boundaries and the merger of adjoining municipalities within the same province shall be performed in accordance with the legislation ordered by the autonomous community within the framework of the basic legislation of the state". The statute's most significant contribution is a list of fourteen matters (it allows for the possible inclusion of others at the behest of the parliament) in regard to which, and in accordance with developments made by the laws of the Autonomous Community, the municipal authorities may exercise powers of their own, "with full autonomy" and "subject only to confirmation of their constitutionality and legality" (Art. 92). The statute further provides for the transferral and delegation of powers from the Junta to the municipal authorities, which shall "at all times have the necessary financial capacity to develop same". The transferral must be approved by an act of the regional parliament approved by an absolute majority. In all cases, the Junta retains its powers of planning and control (Art. 93). Likewise, an act shall regulate the functions of the metropolitan areas, *mancomunidades*, consortia, and other groupings of municipalities that may be established, based on criteria of demography, geography, functions, organisation, dimension, and management capacity (Art. 94). The Andalusian statute, like those of other regions, provides for the creation of a mixed body, with representation of the Junta and municipal authorities, to act as a permanent forum for institutional dialogue and collaboration.

This body must be consulted in parliamentary proceedings on bills that affect the local corporations (Art. 95).

Article 96 of the Statute reiterates the constitutional references to the province, setting out its most characteristic powers and referring back to the basic legislation of the state and the developing legislation of the autonomous community. The Junta nonetheless reserves the power to coordinate the action of the provincial councils in relation to the powers attributed thereto in the statute itself in matters that are of general interest for Andalusia. The designation of a matter as being of general interest and the formulae for such coordination is to be established by an act approved by an absolute majority of the Parliament of Andalusia.

Article 97, taking as its basis the principle of differentiation, provides for the existence of *comarcas*, the creation and powers of which would be regulated by law. In all cases, creation of these *comarcas* requires the agreement of the municipal authorities affected and approval from the government.

Finally, Article 98 of the Statute refers to an act governing the local government system that must be passed by the parliament, within the framework of the basic legislation of the state, in order to regulate relations between the government of Andalusia and local government entities; the methods for organisation and relations for co-operation and collaboration between the local government entities and between these and the regional administration, including the different forms: associations, *mancomunidades*, conventional associations, and consortia. This law will also regulate the matters set out in Article 60 of the Statute, which are the exclusive power of the autonomous community.

This regulation has already resulted in essential specification by way of an important act of basic statutory development,[14] and it has also merited an equally important financial law, part of a new trend seen amongst the most ambitious reforms promoted to date. This law promotes an effective reinforcement of the position occupied by local governments in the territorial organisation of the autonomous community. Nonetheless, despite the evident caution taken, it is affected by the doctrine established in STC 31/2010 in relation to the Statute of Autonomy of Catalonia, given that the ruling empowers the state to intervene in the regulation of areas of power that the Andalusian statute seeks to reserve to the autonomous community. This circumstance potentially limits the area of powers it seeks to attribute to the community.

The reformed *Statute of Autonomy of the Balearic Islands* introduces a considerable legal change that significantly improves the status of intermediary local governments in the autonomic area. In particular, it elaborates on the recognition that the fact that the autonomous community is made up of islands comprises a "differentiating feature", deserving "special protection" (Art. 3). Having established that the autonomous community possesses powers of legislative

---

[14] The Andalusia Local Self-Government Act of 11 June 2010 (Act 5/2010) and Act 6/2010, of 11 June 2010, regulating participation of local entities in the taxes of the Autonomous Community of Andalusia, ordered in development of Article 192.1 of the Statute.

development and execution in the matter of the "local government system", Article 31.13, of the Statute devotes its primary attention, within the framework of a regional territorial structure formed by islands and municipalities (Art. 8), to regulating the singular institutions of government and, in particular, the Island Councils or *Consejos Insulares* (Chap. IV of Heading IV), setting out their organisation, composition, structure, and system of operation, although it leaves development up to an act to be passed by two-thirds of the members of the parliament the Balearic Islands (Arts. 61–68). The most significant feature is a comprehensive list of matters in which these Islands Councils shall exercise their powers and which the autonomous community undertakes to transfer by means of the corresponding decree of transferral. In addition, a number of additional powers are attributed to them under Spanish state legislation (Art. 70). As already established in the preceding statute, within their territorial area these Island Councils have executive and managerial functions over a long list of matters that are the power of the regional executive. Other areas affecting their respective interests and not expressly set out in the statute, may be added in accordance with transfers or delegations that may be established, following the procedure determined by an act of the parliament of the Balearic Islands (Art. 71).[15]

On the other hand, the municipalities are subject to a less innovative statutory regulation; although the exercise of their own powers is safeguarded, no list of matters affected by these powers is given. Instead, the statute choses to recognise their initiative in any matters not excluded from their powers or attributed exclusively to another administration or authority (Art. 75.4). In short, the statute recognises their capacity to be delegated powers by the State, the Autonomous Community, the Island Councils, and other administrations (Art. 75.5). In any case, the municipalities of the Balearic Islands may assume the executive and management powers pertaining to the Island Councils or those that have been transferred to them (Art. 75.6). The statute recognises their right to association and inter-municipal cooperation, and in this respect it is receptive to the establishment of *mancomunidades*, consortia, and associations of municipalities, at the behest of the municipalities (Art. 75.7). Based on the principle of differentiation, the upcoming act governing the local government system of the Balearic Islands will therefore treat the different local governments as befits their particular features (Art. 75.8). Moreover, the Statute guarantees the financial capacity of the municipalities and any other local government entities that may be created; to this end, it orders the creation of an unconditional local cooperation fund, to distribute resources in accordance with the socio-economic and territorial characteristics of the municipalities (Art. 75.9). Finally, it establishes that an act of parliament shall

---

[15] See the references in the very interesting Green Paper "Los Gobiernos Locales en España. Diagnóstico y propuestas para reforzar el valor institucional de las Diputaciones y de los demás Gobiernos locales intermedios en el Estado autonómico", Madrid, Fundación Democracia y Gobierno Local, 2011, p. 159 et seq.

stipulate the special system for the city of Palma, as the capital of the Autonomous Community, for which its participation shall be required (Art. 75.10).

The first *Statute of Autonomy of Aragon*, enacted in 1982, contained practically no references to the system of local government. The new statute introduces some more significant references, although in terms of its scope and significance, it is a far cry from the other statutory reforms discussed here. Art. 71.1.5 of the new statute, for example, deems it to be the exclusive power of the autonomous community, "in matters of local government", to determine the attributes of the municipalities and other local government entities, in matters lying within the power of the autonomous community of Aragon, the local property system, the systems for the provision of local services, relations for co-operation and collaboration among local government entities and between these and the administration of the autonomous community and to determine the organs of government of the local government entities created by the autonomous community and their electoral system. It views development of the bases provided for in Article 148.1.18 of the constitution, insofar as they refer to local administration, to be a shared power (Art. 75.11).

The newly added Heading VI, entitled "territorial organisation and local government", regulates the matter in question in summary and general terms. The regulation is notable only for its insistence that the agents in the matter shall be the municipalities, *comarcas*, and provinces; it leaves the creation, organisation, and provision of powers of the metropolitan areas and local government entities of lesser territorial scope up to a regional act (Art. 81). Otherwise, the references to the municipality (Art. 82) and the province (Art. 84) contain no new features, reiterating the terms already set out in the Constitution and in the act governing the bases of the local government system. The references to the *comarca* (Art. 83) are more interesting, demonstrating as they do the Statute's intention to turn this territorial entity, composed of adjoining municipalities, into a structural feature of the autonomous community. The purpose is to alleviate the problems of the region's sparse and scattered population—in other words, the acute prevalence of multi and infra-municipalism, a phenomenon that has been widely censured.

Article 85 of the Statute establishes that the activities of the territorial entities of Aragon should be guided by principles of subsidiarity, proportionality, and differentiation, together with the criteria of mutual information, collaboration, coordination, and respect for the respective areas of power that should govern the relations between the government of the Autonomous Community and the local entities. It also establishes—albeit without being specific—that the administrative responsibilities of the different tiers of territorial organisation shall be distributed by an act of the parliament of Aragon (the Cortes), which shall provide sufficient financial resources.

Art. 86 of the Statute provides that the Local Council of Aragon [*Consejo Local de Aragón*], as the organ of collaboration and coordination between the regional government and local governments, must rule on any legislative, regulatory, or planning initiatives undertaken that specifically affect the local governments.

Finally, Article 114 again stresses the principle of the financial capacity of the local entities of Aragon, expressly calling on the Aragonese parliament to distribute any unconditional allocations it considers necessary in accordance with the criteria established in law, taking into account the spending requirements and the fiscal capacity of the local government entities.

By any measure, this regulation has to be seen as insufficient and underambitious; the constant referral back to the law avoids projecting the rigidity of the statute on a more comprehensive and original regulation of the local government system of Aragon, involving its effective assumption into the autonomic sphere.

Unlike its predecessor, which contained few references to the matter, the *new Statute of Castile and Leon*, passed into law in 2007, devotes an entire chapter (Chapter III) to the territorial organisation of the autonomous community. Nonetheless, this regulation cannot be considered particularly innovative, given its constant and indeterminate remissions to the parliament, which is thus provided with a very wide margin of free disposition in this regard. This is the case, for example, with the determination of the municipalities' powers, an area in which the statute avoids listing the matters affected by these powers (Art. 45.2). Nonetheless, it recognises their intervention in all matters of local interest, unless excluded as being the power of the state or the regional government (Art. 45.3). The organisation and legal system of the *comarcas* created is also left up to the law (Art. 46.4). The statute says nothing significant about the province, beyond repeating the constitution and state legislation (Art. 47). It allows for the delegation and transfer of powers from the autonomous community to the local entities, under an act of the regional parliament approved by absolute majority (Art. 50) and the creation of a Local Cooperation Council (Art. 51)

In short, as we can see, the regulation is little more than descriptive. It is clearly reluctant to make serious decisions that might involve the effective bolstering of local self-government with a statutory guarantee.

Finally, it is worth referring to the new *Statute of Autonomy of Extremadura*. Heading IV, devoted to the territorial organisation of the autonomous community, fails to introduce any original regulation of the area, missing out on the opportunity presented by the drafting of a new statute. As a result, the passing references made, for the purposes of definition, to municipalities (Art. 54), provinces (Art. 56), *comarcas* (Art. 57), and other minor local government entities (Art. 58) go no further than to reiterate the terms of the basic legislation of the state. The statute entrusts any subsequent development to regional law, upon which it imposes no contents. Significantly, therefore, it is left to an act of the Assembly of Extremadura to determine how "powers in matters that come under the jurisdiction of the Autonomous Community" shall be transferred or delegated to the local entities of Extremadura, with the corresponding provision of financial, personnel, and material resources (Art. 59.3). It is also left to an act of the assembly to establish, where necessary, an unconditional fund, funded by the tax revenue of the Community, to be distributed among the Municipalities, in accordance with their populations, spending requirements, and fiscal capacity (Art. 60.2).

In conclusion, we can see that the various statutory reforms introduced with regard to the organisation of the "local government system" are inspired by very different ambitions. The statutes of Catalonia and Andalusia clearly stand out from the rest for their rigour and their attempt to reinforce the position of local governments, encouraging their effective integration into the framework of the autonomous community. However, one must fear that the legal effects of STC 31/2010 will considerably limit their scope. It is also worth noting the terms of the Statute of the Balearic Islands. Although more limited in their aims, they show a clear interest in raising the position of intermediary local governments in the institutional and jurisdictional organisation of the autonomous community. The contributions of the statutes of the Community of Valencia, Aragon, Castile and Leon, and Extremadura, on the other hand, are considerably less significant; apart from setting out some general principles, they involve no more than a call to action by the regional parliament, leaving it up to the parliament to develop, with considerable self-determination, those areas that the statutes merely set out in programmatical form.

# References

E. ARGULLOL MURGADES, "El desarrollo estatutario de los gobiernos locales en Cataluña", in Anuario del Gobierno Local 2008, pp. 67 et seq.

A. BAYONA ROCAMORA, J. R. FUENTES i GASÓ, A. GALÁN GALÁN and R. GRACIA RETORTILLO, and J. MIR BAGÓ in Revista Catalana de Dret Públic. Especial Sentencia 31/2010 del Tribunal Constitucional sobre el Estatuto de Autonomía de Cataluña de 2006, 2010 pp. 213–248

F. CAAMAÑO DOMÍNGUEZ, "El abandono de "lo básico": Estado autonómico y mitos fundacionales", in Anuario de Derecho constitucional y parlamentario, numbers 12–13, 2000–2001, pp. 87–110

T. FONT i LLOVET, "Autonomía local y Estatutos: crónica de un compromiso", in Various Authors, Anuario del Gobierno Local 2006, pp. 13–34

T. FONT i LLOVET, "El gobierno local en la reforma del Estado de las autonomías", in "Anuario del Gobierno Local 2004", pp. 13–36

T. FONT i LLOVET "El régimen local en la reforma de los Estatutos de Autonomía", in Various Authors, "El régimen local en la reforma de los Estatutos", Madrid, Centro de Estudios Políticos y Constitucionales, 2006, pp. 19 et seq.

T. FONT i LLOVET, "Estado autonómico y gobierno local: el inicio de un nuevo ciclo", in Anuario del Gobierno Local 2005, Barcelona, Fundación Democracia y Gobierno Local-Institut de Dret Public, 2006, pp. 20 et seq.

A. GALÁN GALÁN and R. GRACIA RETORTILLO, "Estatuto de Autonomía de Cataluña, Gobiernos locales of Tribunal Constitucional", in Revista d'Estudis Autonòmics i Federals, No. 12, 2011, pp. 237 et seq.

J. MIR i BAGÓ, La regulación de las veguerías en el nuevo Estatuto de Cataluña", en, Anuario del Gobierno Local 2006, pp. 79–103

A. PEREIRA i SOLÉ, "El régimen local en la reforma del Estatuto de autonomía de Cataluña", en Anuario del Gobierno Local 2004, pp. 199–207

J. M. PORRAS RAMÍREZ, "El autogobierno local en el Estado autonómico. Premisas para una reforma necesaria", in Revista Española de Derecho Constitucional, No. 75, 2005, pp. 211–237

J. M. PORRAS RAMÍREZ, "Las reformas estatutarias y el nuevo sistema autonómico de fuentes del Derecho", Madrid, Civitas, 2007

J. M. PORRAS RAMÍREZ, "Régimen local", in F. BALAGUER CALLEJÓN (dir.), "Reformas estatutarias y distribución de competencias", Sevilla, Instituto Andaluz de Administración Pública, 2007, pp. 219–236

J. L. REQUEJO PAGÉS, "Garantía de la autonomía local y Estatutos de Autonomía", in Anuario del Gobierno Local 2006: la reforma de los Estatutos y la legislación local, Barcelona, Fundación Democracia y Gobierno Local-Institut de Dret Public, 2007, pp. 53–58

J. TORNOS MÁS and R. GRACIA RETORTILLO, "La organización territorial en los nuevos Estatutos de Autonomía. En especial, el nivel local supramunicipal en Cataluña", in Anuario del Gobierno Local 2008, pp. 75 et seq.

F. VELASCO CABALLERO, "Autonomía local y subsidiariedad en la reforma de los Estatutos de Autonomía", en Anuario del Gobierno Local 2004, pp. 117–159

R. L. WATTS, "Comparing Federal Systems" Montreal, McGill-Queen's University Press, 2008

M. ZAFRA VÍCTOR, "Garantía estatutaria de la autonomía local", in Anuario del Gobierno Local 2008, Barcelona, 2009, pp. 35–66

# A Basque (and Catalan) Republic Within a Federal Context: Reflections on New Scenarios in the Crisis of the Autonomous State

Iñigo Bullain

## Introduction

This article reflects on the crisis facing the Autonomous State and, with the end of ETA's armed struggle,[1] speculates on the prospects of a federalist political alternative. Although it is normal for academic reflection to obviate the existence of different national identities when analysing the constitutional framework and autonomic problem, the existence of disparate political behaviour in Spain and the Basque Country and also, to a lesser extent, in Catalonia is evident and is expressed in antithetical and contradictory electoral majorities. Over the years, Basque nationalist majorities have often approached the criterion by which a clear qualified majority can be identified: 60 %. While in Spain the two dominant parties, the PP and PSOE, obtain around 90 % of the vote, in the Basque Country these two political groups are usually in a minority.[2] Specifically, in 2011, on the occasion of the last municipal and autonomous elections, they barely received the support of a third of the electorate. On the other hand, the Basque pro-independence parties,

---

[1] A reflection regarding a new political scenario in the Basque Country in Bullain (2011).

[2] Except in the last legislatures in which, as a consequence of the effects of the Law on Political Parties, the results have been different. The present composition of the autonomous Parliament and the political majority that has sustained the Basque Government since 2009 is directly related to the ban by the courts imposed on the so-called Basque National Liberation Movement (MLNV in Spanish) to stand in the elections, given their connection to ETA violence. Their absence left Basque nationalism in a minority for the first time since 1980. In 2011, after breaking with the strategy of violence, the State allowed the left-wing Basque nationalists to run for local election as part of an electoral coalition called Bildu. See archive of electoral results of the Basque Government Home Office where the results of all the elections that have taken place in the Autonomous Community since 1977 can be consulted. The elections that took place during the period of the Second Republic can also be consulted: www.euskadi.net/elecciones.

I. Bullain (✉)
Department of Constitutional Law and History of the Political Thought, University of the Basque Country, Campus of Sarriena, Post Box 644, Bilbao 48080, Spain
e-mail: inigo.bullain@ehu.es

A. López-Basaguren and L. Escajedo San Epifanio (eds.), *The Ways of Federalism in Western Countries and the Horizons of Territorial Autonomy in Spain*, Vol. 2, DOI 10.1007/978-3-642-27717-7_52, © Springer-Verlag Berlin Heidelberg 2013

PNV and Bildu, obtained majorities bordering on two-thirds in the Basque Auton-omous Community. After a complicated journey of 30 years, the "drinks all round" formula employed to diffuse and stifle the desire for autonomy in the Basque Country, and Catalonia has led the Autonomous State to a critical situation. This article will seek to present the reasons that have sparked such a crisis and to propose some alternatives: in particular, from the perspective of the Basque political context, although I also consider that the Catalan political reality requires a specific solution. Implementing an asymmetrical federal model to accommodate both Basque and Catalan republics might constitute a provisional alternative to the growing deterioration of the autonomous system and uncertain future it faces. The majority desire for sovereignty in the Basque Country, which is also growing in Catalonia, could find a compromise solution within the framework of an asym-metrical federation.

Throughout these decades of democracy, Spanish political reality has quite clearly evidenced the existence of at least two complex national realities: one common to a majority of Spaniards and another specific to Basques and Catalans. Although other Autonomous Communities are also recognised as nationalities, the national identities of Galicia, Andalusia, the Canary Islands, and Aragon are not as overwhelmingly asserted as in the Basque Country and Catalonia, and in any case, their nationalisms approach a paradigm of dual identity that they share with the Spanish identity.

While in Spain we can talk of a Basque and Catalan national minority, in the Basque Country or in Catalonia it can be said that a Spanish national minority exists.[3] The coexistence of these two majorities and minorities seems to posit the need for reflection that, assuming such a paradox (that those who form part of a majority in one political sphere are also a minority in another), also seeks to offer solutions aimed at securing democratic coexistence. From my point of view, asymmetrical federalism offers an appropriate conceptual framework for develop-ing an imaginative constitutional structure that might offer the various nationalist programmes a framework, at least temporarily, for peaceful and democratic coex-istence. At the moment, however, it is the pro-independence perspective that is gaining ground, given the level of discredit that the autonomic model has progres-sively accumulated in the Basque Country and Catalonia.

After decades of reformist delay, during which time constitutional modification was systematically rejected in Spain by the two majority parties, a dilemma looms on the political horizon: either Spanish nationalism finally commits itself to ensur-ing that the Basque Country and Catalonia have an opportunity to fulfil their desire for self-government without the present constitutional strictures or it will face the alternative of governing in the Basque Country and Catalonia as if they were a kind

---

[3] In Catalonia, a feeling exists of considering "Catalanness" (to coin a word) as a way of being Spanish, while in the Basque Country the link between Basqueness and Spanishness is less deeply rooted. In the Basque Country, the dominant perspective is, rather, a dilemma: either Basque or Spanish. The Basque–Iberian historical tradition, on the other hand, made the Basques representatives of the original Spanish.

of Spanish Protectorate. That is to say: to subject the Basque and Catalan parliamentary majorities that demand more self-government to what a majority in the National Parliament lays down. The frustration associated with this scenario will probably feed the prospect of secession even more.

After the announcement by ETA of a final ceasefire[4] and the end of the political-military strategy that has conditioned political life for half a century, the legitimacy of the Basque Parliament's decisions regarding self-government will, in future, carry certain democratic credentials different to those that accompanied the so-called Ibarretxe Plan. Then, the parliamentary majority favourable to the Project for a New Basque Political Statute was reached with support of some representatives of the MLNV (Basque National Liberation Movement), at the time a political-military organisation.[5] On the other hand, after the end to the violence, the decisions concerning the democratic reformulation of Basque self-government will probably have the broadest and most legitimate parliamentary majorities. The Spanish national minority in the Basque Country will find it difficult to prevent political debate, to deny the Basque national majority their democratic right to take decisions concerning self-government or limit it "sine die" to the present autonomic framework. Although constitutionally necessary, a parliamentary majority in Madrid is not equivalent to a politically sufficient legitimacy "ad aeternum" if it is confronted by a local majority will in the Basque Country. Moreover, the Basque majority in favour of sovereignty cannot obviate the Basque–Spanish minority present in the Basque Parliament, nor can it ignore the majority politically represented in the Spanish Parliament, dominated by the PP after the elections of 20th November 2011. In consequence, the political scenario for the next few years looks quite complicated.

Except for those who are determined to make the 1978 Constitution an insurmountable hurdle, the present framework of the Autonomous State does not appear even remotely to be the most adequate system for accommodating the political future of the Basque Country (or that of Catalonia). However, the road to statutory reform seems to be closed after the recent Ruling regarding the New Catalan Statute. In a highly criticised decision, the Constitutional Court rejected the possibility of autonomous development, which the Catalan Parliament proposed, supported by 90 % of its MPs, and subsequently ratified in a referendum by the Catalan people. If, within reform of the Autonomous Statute, it is impossible to extend autonomic self-government by ring-fencing autonomous competences, then what can we do?

---

[4] During the days of the International Congress: "The roads to federalism and the prospect of the Autonomous State" held in Bilbao between 19 and 21 October, 2011, ETA announced "the definitive cessation of armed activity" after more than 50 years of violence. This communiqué, awaited for so long by Basque and Spanish society, represents the beginning of a new political cycle of which we can presumably expect a new political status for the Basque Country. See content of the ETA communiqué in the Deia newspaper of 20 October, 2011.

[5] Regarding the political violence in the Basque Country, see Bullain (2011).

From my point of view, it is a democratic right that assists a political community to demand a political agreement modifying the present constitutional framework. If that is what a broad majority in an Autonomous Community wishes (a political reality limited to the Basque Country and Catalonia), making Basque and Catalan autonomous self-government possible without it being subject to the strict constitutional limits marked out thus far by the decisions of the Constitutional Court, it will lead to a new constitutional agreement for the Basque Country and Catalonia. For ample Basque and Catalan majorities, the present constitutional limits are interpreted very narrowly. Although at the moment the majority in the Spanish Parliament has preferred to avoid giving a political response and making it a jurisdictional matter, the relations of these two Communities with the Spanish State demand to be the object of a specific bilateral agreement with the State. Instead of trying to subject Basque and Catalan autonomies to the discipline of a multilateral system of "drinks all round", sustained in a model of homogenous cooperative regionalism whose reference is Germany, promoting an asymmetrical solution is, in my opinion, better adapted to political reality. This would be a question of promoting a two-speed model closer to the Canadian model sustained in both autonomous political frameworks acknowledged for Catalonia and the Basque Country and a general framework for the rest of the Communities. A Federal Agreement with the republics of the Basque Country and Catalonia could incorporate, in said event, an agreement between the Basque Provinces and Navarre.[6] Likewise, bilateral relations between the Basque Country and Catalonia and the projection of those autonomous republics abroad would be guaranteed by a political agreement with the State.

This alternative panorama, with particular attention to the European framework and the prospect of asymmetrical federalisation, will be the focus of this work concerning the crisis and future of the Autonomous State.

## The Autonomous State in Crisis

Almost without exception, federal states and federative systems are advanced democratic and politically cooperative models. Although it has certain features that make it more similar to a federation, the Autonomous State, partially enshrined in the 1978 Constitution and implemented over more than 30 years, cannot, either theoretically or practically, be compared to a federal model. However, while some characteristics of federations are present in the Autonomous Communities of Spain, and despite the hopes of a sector of the doctrine to compare the reality to

---

[6] With the support of a majority of people from Navarre, a common political ground could be formulated in a kind of Basque-Navarre Confederation. It is significant that the only two Autonomous Communities where there is a political agreement between PP and PSOE are the Basque Country and the Community of Navarre.

a federation, the Autonomous State is more accurately a regionalised unitary State. This is evidenced by the scant Autonomous Community participation in central state power. The combination between *self-rule* and *shared rule*, characteristic of federalism, is very weakly developed in Spain. The Autonomous State undoubtedly heralds a major step forward compared to the Centralist State of the Franco dictatorship and other previous formulae of nineteenth century liberalism. Despite the serious flaws that afflict its democratic model, an autonomous Spain also represents great progress *vis-à-vis* the brief and convulsive period of the Second Spanish Republic. However, these achievements do not mean that the present autonomic model is an unqualified success. Indeed, wide political majorities reject it in the Basque Country and Catalonia. Hence, we can only speculate about other models that might be better adapted to the diverse political wishes present in the complex reality that is Spain.

The autonomic model implemented in Italy and Spain has its origin in the Kelsen-inspired Austrian Constitution. Nevertheless, while in the United States and Switzerland the federal desire was to acknowledge the powers of the political centre, in Spain and Italy regionalisation sought to endow sub-states with autonomous power. In federal or regional practice, especially within the framework of the European Union, hardly any watertight competence areas exist, but rather what is usual is the combination of different levels of power over the same material areas. The problems that the multiple accusations pose are complex, and a lack of political agreements has ensured that the Constitutional Court takes on tasks that do not correspond to it, such as the demarcation of the rules, functions, or objectives of the competences. Given that there is no directly recognised participation of the Autonomous Communities in the composition of the Senate, the interests of central power represented by the PP and PSOE are mainly reflected in the jurisprudential work of the Constitutional Court in whose composition only representatives of the central power participate. It is clear that not only jurisdictional safeguards but also the political guarantees through the Senate or intergovernmental relations between parties have not been developed sufficiently and merge to the detriment of the Autonomous Communities. One consequence of this combination of factors is that the prestige of the Constitutional Court has been seriously undermined.

Spain has been a Member State of the European Union since 1986. Adaptation to a supra-state framework has entailed profound changes as it has with regard to the Autonomous State. However, these changes have taken place without resorting to constitutional reforms. As a result, there is a serious disparity between what the text of the 1978 Constitution says and what the constitutional reality is. After the impact of the European Treaties and their reforms, we can speak of true constitutional change. Although partially attenuated after the reforms of certain autonomous statutes, something similar can be said in relation to the autonomic frameworks that have also undergone profound changes since many autonomous subject matters have come under the control of the European Union with the European treaties and their reforms, without these alterations having given rise to formal changes in the texts. We have to add the level of power of the European political centre to the distribution of power of the Autonomous State between the central power and the Autonomous Communities. In consequence, the design of territorial distribution of power characteristic of federal models and also of the Autonomous State has no option but to adapt to this multilevel reality. However, the system developed around the Sectorial Conferences is highly inadequate and de-autonomisation has taken place in favour of Central Power, which, through its dominant position in the European decision-making process, has gained control of many autonomous functions and competences.

A federal reform that transformed the Senate into a representative chamber for the Autonomous Communities and that was also endowed with certain functions and competences that at present it lacks, could serve not only to improve the position of the Autonomous Communities in the management of the State but also to promote the position of the Communities in the European framework. The German Bundesrat model of executive federalism of cooperation would, without doubt, herald a step forward from the present situation of autonomic exclusion from the management of the State and participation in European affairs. However, to my mind, that alternative must be pursued without detriment to a paradigm shift to accommodate Catalan and Basque self-government within the State and the EU. The model of multilateral federalism between central power and Autonomous Communities within the framework of the European Union is of no use to Catalonia and the Basque Country, whose national political realities are different and cannot be likened to the rest of the Autonomous Communities. Federal reform would be the consequence of prior recognition of the specific national realities of the Basque Country and Catalonia and would entail the State maintaining three federative orders: one common to the majority of the Autonomous Communities, another with Catalonia, and a further one with the Basque Country.

Ortega y Gasset's belief that the circumstances are inseparable from the analytical moment cannot be obviated. The crisis that is affecting Europe, and especially Spain, is a serious threat to the Autonomous State. The budgetary situation and the socio-economic future of certain Autonomous Communities are dramatic. The responsibility of the parties and institutions for this deterioration cannot be denied. Irresponsible management of many of the Savings Banks under autonomic control is evidence of political recklessness in the Autonomous State, as is the lack of accountability of the institutions for controlling the State, which have obviated their tutelary functions and allowed speculation and fraud to plunder the assets of generations of savers. Only from the perspective of the paradigm of systematic recklessness and corruption that has dominated the Autonomous State in the name of the Market can the excesses and absence of political and media criticism be made intelligible. A kind of narcissistic delirium of self-satisfaction has dominated political life over the years to which, to a large extent, the academic world has given shelter. The devastating effects of the crisis on public power will have serious consequences for the Autonomous State, and its reconfiguration in the coming years will come under the leadership of the majorities that the Partido Popular (PP) controls in almost all the Autonomous Communities and, after the November 2011 elections, in the central power.[7] It seems likely that recentralisation of competences and privatisation of public services will be some of the central themes of future autonomic policy.

Indeed, the financial deficit that accompanies regional autonomy is converted into possibilities that the central power often uses to cut back normative autonomy. Loss of autonomy in favour of the central powers has been a constant feature of decentralised systems, especially since the Second World War. Within the framework of the European Union, regional autonomy tends to project an image of itself as an autonomy with functions for implementing norms and programmes of a higher level: i.e., of the State or EU. Not only has de-autonomisation taken place coterminously with the European process of integration, but a very marked deterioration has also taken place within the constitutional framework. The 31/2010 Ruling of the Constitutional Court regarding the New Catalan Statute constitutes a milestone that marks the limits of autonomous self-government.[8] Attempts through statutory reform to prevent assignment of competences from remaining discretionally in the hands of the central legislator, and to allow competences to be specifically set out in the autonomic text and to be ring-fenced, have been rejected by the Constitutional Court, which has further declared itself to be the only interpreter of the distribution of competences.[9] Thus, the aim of improving the quality of the competences, that is to say, of autonomous policy, has been roundly rejected. The Ruling on the New Catalan Statute consequently favours a symmetrical model of the Autonomous State since it prevents, by means of statutory reforms, the autonomic texts from improving and modulating the quality of self-government. On the other hand, the economic crisis and the majority of the PP in the National

---

[7] On the eve of the general elections of 20 November, 2011, opinion polls gave an absolute majority to the PP in the Spanish Parliament, which they duly attained. See the newspaper El País of 16/10/2011.

[8] Unlike the jurisprudence found in previous rulings such as that of 247/2007 on reform of the Valencian Statute, the Constitutional Court, in accordance with the provisions of Ruling 31/2010, rejects the possibility that the Statutes can specify autonomic competences and, thereby, State competences, too. According to the Ruling regarding the supra-territoriality of the River Guadalquivir envisaged in the reform of the Andalusian Statute, the State can have at its disposal all the subject matters, even those pertaining to the Autonomous Community. Further, the autonomous laws will have to be adapted to that envisaged by the civil legislator. In the opinion of the majority of Catalan jurists, this is an unfortunate decision that heralds the closure of the autonomic model to the hopes of statutory reforms. See The Catalan Journal of Public Law, 2010. Special Ruling 31/2010 of the Constitutional Court on the 2006 Catalan Statute of Autonomy.

[9] The important jurisprudential work on the configuration of the Autonomous State has to do with the lack of precedents in the brief constitutional history of Spain. To the existence of overlapping central and autonomous powers has been added the more recent appearance of a European power. Although various centres of sovereignty are not recognised, the definition and configuration of the State, Autonomous and European competences do not correspond exclusively to the civil legislator or to the Constitutional Court. However, in repeatedly cited Ruling 31/2010, the Constitutional Court issues statements such as "the Statute of Autonomy cannot delimit competences", "it is merely another law", "the civil legislator is not negatively limited by the Statutes" or that "the constituent assembly performed a perfectly finished job".

Parliament, together with the majority of regional parliaments, seem to favour recentralisation of the autonomous model.

Central power has been the major beneficiary of civil legislative intervention. Lack of Autonomous Community involvement in the management of the central power of the State has meant that the civil legislator represented by the PP and PSOE has gradually reduced autonomous political power. In the patient task of recentralisation, the civil legislator has employed several mechanisms. On the one hand, it has made abusive use of Royal Decrees to extend the competence rules of the subject matters and functions of the central power. Further, it has used certain horizontal Titles such as that laid out in Article 149.1.13: "rules and coordination of the general planning for economic activity" to recentralise the competences pertaining to the Autonomous Communities. The Autonomous Communities' own lack of financial resources has also been taken advantage of by the central authorities that have used their financial muscle to shape regional policy. Likewise, central power has resorted to the criterion of supra-territoriality to expand its competences or to specify in detail the normative framework of the European directives by eliminating the Autonomous Communities' role of normative development, in accordance with their way of understanding the transfer of competences. It has also used the reserve set aside in organic law to eliminate the Charters of autonomous rights by claiming exclusivity over fundamental rights.[10]

Although the Autonomous Communities control almost a third of public expenditure and, together with local authorities, account for nearly half of the total national public expenditure budget, intergovernmental relations are not on a par with the autonomic framework.[11] The Sectorial Conferences that have arisen since the 1980s, and that have blossomed over the last decades, are dependent on the wishes of the Central Power both as regards their convening and the agenda.[12]

---

[10] Some questions, such as the Declarations or Charters of Rights contained in the reformed Autonomous Statutes, have been interpreted as anti-constitutional by the Constitutional Court for whom they do not fit into the statutory framework but rather in that of the civil legislator, except if they are limited to copying or plagiarising that already specified. The Declarations of Rights are interpreted as statements of a statutory constituent power that they assign. The question of autonomous citizens also poses difficulties, given that they are required to be Spanish and administratively resident in the Autonomous Community. Indeed, the conditions of said residence are regulated in a new State law (Organic Law of Local Administration), whose time periods are established by the Central Power. It is thus made possible for the will of those outside the Autonomous Community to modify the criteria of autonomous citizenry.

[11] See Arbós et al. (2009).

[12] The agriculture and fisheries sector within the framework of European issues is that which most frequently calls for meetings to be held. The Conference on Issues Related to the European Union established in 1989 and denominated (CARUE), with its head offices in the Senate, since April 2010, is the most important. The Autonomous Communities have obtained certain rights to information, participation, and representation in EU matters that have led to the adoption of certain common positions, such as the presence of some autonomous representatives in the Spanish delegations before the EU Council of Ministers. A 6-month rotation system is used with coordination through the Offices that the Autonomous Communities have in Brussels and the intervention of the Minister for autonomous issues attached to Spain's permanent representation before the EU. See Tajadura Tejada (2010).

This dominant role has been confirmed by the Constitutional Court. In consequence, Central Power has promoted this type of multilateral forum whose principal function is to share money among the Autonomous Communities to the detriment of the development of Bilateral Commissions and the Central Power/Autonomous Community. Indeed, this occurred, after the statutory reforms of the 2000s (in particular the Statutes of Catalonia and Andalusia), when bilateralism has been envisaged for relations with the Central Authority.[13] Specifically, the New Catalan Statute envisages bilateralism as a general and permanent framework with statutory status. As often occurs, Autonomous Communities emulating the steps of Catalonia and, previously, the Basque Country and Navarre, *vis-à-vis* the granting of special "historical" rights, has consequently meant that bilateralism has become generalised and, thus, has ceased to be so.

As regards horizontal cooperation between Autonomous Communities, it can be said to have proved extremely inadequate, among other reasons, due to the lack of means and infrastructures to sustain it, in particular, due to lack of resources in certain Autonomous Communities. Only intergovernmental relations at the maximum level—Presidential Conferences—have, since they were introduced in 2004, enjoyed the support of having the Senate as their headquarters. Insofar as the role of the political parties is fundamental in intergovernmental relations, within the framework of the Autonomous State, the model of multilateralism through PP and PSOE control predominates over State/Autonomous Community institutional bilateralism.

## De-autonomisation Within the Framework of the European Union

At the end of the 1970s, Spain undertook the transformation of a national-catholic dictatorship: the transition from a regime with corporative features to a parliamentary democracy. The isolation that accompanied the 40 years of Franco's regime led to a remoteness compared to the State model that was being implemented in Europe and, in consequence, also in relation to the supra-state process of integration.

---

[13] Specifically, the New Statute recognises bilateralism as one of the main regulators of relations between the Generalitat (Catalan Parliament) and the State, establishing in Article 183 the Generalitat Bilateral Commission/State as a "general and permanent framework for relations between the Governments of the Generalitat and the State". In the framework of said Bilateral Commission, a Sub-commission has been set up for European Affairs and Foreign Action comprised of two Working Groups: EU and Foreign Action. Since 2007, the Bilateral Commission has met approximately every 2 months. In Article 220, the Statute of Andalusia regulates the Government of Andalusia Bilateral Commission/State. In Article 220 (2.g), its functions include monitoring European policy to ensure effective involvement of the Autonomous Community of Andalusia in European Union affairs. As an exception, the New Statute envisages the presentation of an annual report to the Catalan Parliament regarding the activity of the Bilateral Commission.

In fact, as is perfectly reflected in the 1978 Spanish Constitutional text, the European perspective is conspicuous by its absence. The incorporation of Spain in the EEC (European Economic Community), barely 8 years later (1986), was not accompanied by any constitutional reform or with the successive reforms of the European Treaties (Single Act, European Union Treaty, Amsterdam, or Nice). More recently, the Treaty of Lisbon did not involve any constitutional reform. Even when Spain became a member of the European Union, it did not lead to any statutory reform, despite the marked effects that implementing the process of European integration was to have on the competences of the State and Autonomous Communities.

Thus, the 1978 Spanish Constitution does not contain any specific reference to the European Union except the recent mention of the EU found in the reform of Article 135.[14] With regard to the distribution of subject matters between the competence of the State and the European Union, only in Article 93 of the Spanish Constitution is it mentioned that "by means of an organic law the signing of treaties may be authorised by which an international organisation or institution is assigned to exercise the competences derived from the Constitution". In the same Article, reference is made to the fact that "ensuring fulfilment of these Treaties and of the resolutions derived from the international or supranational organisations to which transfer pertains corresponds to the National Parliament or Government". In fact, except for the previously mentioned reform of Article 135 of the Spanish Constitution, reference to "supranational organisations" in Article 93 is the only indirect reference to the process of European integration contained in the constitutional text. The majority of the Statutes of Autonomy of the Autonomous Communities previously drafted between 1979 and 1982 do not contain references to the former European Economic Community either. A significant *European blindness* is evident in both the constituent assembly and the regional political elites responsible for drawing up the Statutes that, except for certain exceptions such as the New Catalan Statute and the subsequent Andalusian Statute, are still present almost 30 years later.

However, successive and continued assignment of new subject matters in favour of the competence of the Autonomous Community and the European Union has been carried out at the expense of the competences attributed to the Member States. In those with a regional structure, such as Spain, competences of the State that become competences of the EU are assigned at the national level to both the central power and the Autonomous Communities. However, whereas the central power compensates for the European assignment of its competences by means of its position in the EU decision-making structure, where it shares the decisions concerning the subject matters distributed at the European level with representatives of other Member States, the Autonomous Communities, on the other hand, are subject to a "zero-sum game". Thus, although Europeanised subject matters coincide with subjects of regional competence to a large extent, given the

---

[14] BOE 27/09/2011.

lack of appropriate mechanisms for participation and representation in the EU (monopolised by central power), the regional position tends to grow weaker as the process of integration advances. Not only do the heads of the Autonomous Communities lose decision-making capacity over the subject matters assigned to their competence by the Constitution and the respective Statutes of Autonomy, but also the loss of autonomic power is particularly severe in relation to the Autonomous Parliaments which that are stripped of their norms in favour of European institutions and the organs of central power. The latter take advantage of the transfer or assignment of regional subject matters in favour of EU Institutions in order to take decisions regarding them in the name of the State in clear detriment to the decision-making capacity internally attributed to the Autonomous Communities.

Although it affects all the Autonomous Communities, this process of de-autonomisation as a consequence of European integration is clearly not experienced in the same way by all of them. Some, especially the Basque Country and Catalonia, suffer especially from their European marginalisation and pose a unique problem. An Autonomous Community where its citizens mainly identify with what the State represents does not pose the same problem as those where there is a national conflict of identity and whose autonomous governments and authorities are usually in the hands of political forces different from those dominant in Central Power. Neither is the European appraisal shared in the same way when, for example, one of the regional languages (i.e., Catalan or Basque) does not have European recognition (and neither by the central State). Furthermore, another element of divergence is that the government parties are not one of the two majority Spanish parties.[15] Likewise, in the Basque case, as well as the national political conflict, a revolutionary movement has been operating whose socio-communist ideology conflicts with the liberal parliamentary model characteristic of the European integrative process.[16]

As well as the previously mentioned *European blindness*, other factors that have a powerful influence on the position of the Autonomous Communities regarding European integration should also be identified. Thus, an important factor for explaining the position of the Autonomous Communities in relation to the European Union derives from the weight of the political parties on the regional structure. In regionalised States such as Italy or Spain, party logic imposes itself over institutional logic. The dominant parties (in Spain, the PP and PSOE) eclipse the central power dialectic: the Autonomous Communities imposing their criteria on the regional representatives subject to party discipline. Only occasionally have regional representatives refused to comply with party leadership mandates.

---

[15] Convergencia i Unió governed for more than 20 years in Catalonia. After a period of 8 years in which a coalition of three Catalan parties led by the PSC, an autonomous party federated to the PSOE, governed, CiU recovered both its parliamentary majority and government of the Catalan Parliament in 2010.

[16] It is still too soon to know if the renouncement of the political-military strategy will involve a review of their revolutionary ideology. See Bullain (2011), op. cit.

In consequence, the party system dominates the political-institutional game. In federations such as Germany, institutional logic coexists with that of the party. The implementation of cooperative federalism in Germany and the degree of institutionalisation it has attained within the framework of the Fundamental Law of Bonn is very high. Given the existence of the CDU in Bavaria and the CDU/CSU agreement not to compete in Bavaria and Germany, the position of Bavaria within the federation is very unusual. In Belgium, the non-existence of Belgian parties confers on Belgium federalism a characteristic feature. In Spain, the electoral majorities that the Basque, Catalan, and Navarre parties locally attain confer on these Autonomous Communities a special position.[17]

The position of the Italian Autonomous Regions or that of the Spanish Communities in the running of the State is not comparable to that enjoyed by the federated powers in Germany or Belgium, either through the Bundesrat or other mechanisms of participation. In consequence, their position within the framework of the European Union is very different. While the German Länders and the Belgian cultural Regions or Communities have recognised informative rights of participation and representation that prevent their marginalisation in the decision-taking process, those rights are, however, much weaker for regions and autonomous communities whose position in Europe is clearly peripheral. That is why European integration has had certain devastating effects for both self-rule and in relation to shared regional rule with regard to the EU.[18]

There is no doubt that the political dynamic maintained by the parties is stronger than that derived from regional institutions. This is due to several factors. First, because the regional structures inherent in Autonomous Communities are new: only Catalonia and the Basque Country had prior experience of autonomous self-government until Franco's dictatorship brought them to an end. Second factor is because the autonomic structure is not accompanied by representation and participation of the Autonomous Communities in the management of the central power of the State. Unlike in other federalised states such as Germany or Austria, where the Länders have a political body (the Bundesrat) that represents them and through which they participate in the management of the State, as well as in decision-taking at the European level, in Spain the position of the Autonomous Communities is very different, their internal marginalisation being maintained. Their participation continues to depend on the workings of various Sectorial Conferences, characteristic of an administrative relationship between executive bodies that work (when they do work) fitfully. In said functioning, the key is the will of the political parties, above and beyond the institutional role corresponding to the Autonomous Communities. With a few exceptions, the Autonomous Communities dominated by the Partido Popular work *en bloc*, and the same occurs with those governed by the Socialist Party. Given that both parties are in a majority and dominate the government of

---

[17] Hrbek (2004).

[18] A comparative study of the position of the sub-state entities in the EU, in Bullain (2005), pp. 11–47.

almost all the Communities, the positions that the Autonomous Communities adopt in regard to the majority of issues are decided in extra-community headquarters and are imposed on the autonomic representatives. Further, the game played by the parties imposes its electoral logic and usually favours the transfer of inter-party conflict to inter-regional relations.

## Participative Deficit of the Autonomous Communities in EU Matters Within the State

With regard to the participative marginalisation of the Autonomous Communities in European matters, two phases can be distinguished. The first covers the period from when Spain joined the European Economic Community in 1986 to the 2004 Agreements, and the second, from said Agreements onwards.[19]

### 1986–2004

For a long time[20] the Autonomous Communities were almost entirely marginalised from European issues. Even today, 26 years after Spain joined the EEC, they have no constitutional recognition regarding information, participation, or representational rights. It can be said that, through Europe, a majority of the autonomous competences have fallen into the hands of the central Government, to a large extent, due to the indifference of the Autonomous Communities themselves. The method employed to link the Communities to the EU has been the so-called Sectorial Conferences, more specifically, the Conference on Issues Related to the European Communities (CARCE, in Spanish), renamed CARUE in 2011 (Conference for Issues Related to the European Union).[21] However, as the Central Administration itself has recognised, it has not served to effectively incorporate the Autonomous Communities into the decision-making process.[22] This shortcoming has also been shown annually in the well-known Autonomous Community Report.[23]

---

[19] See Bullain (2008), pp. 19–41.

[20] In accordance with the Agreements of December, 2004, endorsed by the central Government and the Autonomous Communities, representatives of the Communities could participate in some EU Councils of Ministers, always within the Spanish delegation. Likewise, two representatives of the Autonomous Communities will join the Permanent Representation of Spain.

[21] The institutionalisation agreement of CARCE is from 29 October, 1992 (BOE 241 of 8-10-9393). The internal regulation is found in BOE 269, 10-11-1994, currently in force in accordance with BOE 189 of 8-8-1997. Since its institutionalisation, it has met on more than 50 occasions: that is to say, approximately once every 6 months.

[22] The Minister for Public Administration has acknowledged in several documents that the system via Sectorial Conferences has not served to ensure the participation of the Autonomous Communities in European issues. See, Bullain (1998).

[23] For example, in the report published in October, 2004, corresponding to the year 2000, the Secretary of CARCE highlights how inadequate the working of the Conference is. See Vid. Roig

During this first phase, the Autonomous Communities received European information very asymmetrically and could barely adopt decisions jointly.[24] Furthermore, Autonomous Community participation in the European Union was limited to certain committees of the European Commission.[25] In these, the situation of the Autonomous Communities lacked any formalisation in relation to the criteria by which they could shape the position of the Communities. Furthermore, some of those committees frequently had no work or simply disappeared. Moreover, due either to their functions or to their appointment, the autonomous Ministers within the Spanish Permanent Representation could hardly be called an autonomic representative. They are, rather, diplomatic ministers designated by the central authorities to work as an intermediary with the autonomous authorities.

## The Agreements of 9th December 2004[26]

The content of the Agreements[27] enabled the Autonomous Communities to participate in four of the nine different compositions of the EU Council of Ministers: (1) agriculture and fisheries; (2) environment; (3) employment; social policy, health, and consumer affairs; and (4) education, youth and culture, which in 2009 was enlarged to create another formation with Competition/Consumption. Likewise, autonomic participation was transferred to the working groups of the Council and COREPER. Therefore, representatives of the Autonomous Communities have been able to participate as members of the Spanish delegation in meetings of the EUMC in accordance with a system of 6 monthly turns. Furthermore, two functionaries as representatives of the Autonomous Communities have become members of the Permanent Representation (REPRE), their mission being to serve as liaison between the Offices of Representation of the Autonomous Communities in Brussels and the rest of the members of REPRE in order to provide the Communities with European information, monitor autonomic participation in the Sectorial Conferences, and report on the negotiations in Brussels. The agreements, however, are not incompatible with those bilateral channels that the central

---

(2000), p. 508. At the end of the decade, the report corresponding to the year 2009 states that, for example, in the years 2007 and 2008 the two annual meetings legally envisaged were not even held due to a lack of quorum. See Donaire Villa (2009), p. 691.

[24] According to this system, the central Government requires the unanimity of the Autonomous Communities: failing that, it does not have to respond to the majority positions attained by them. Regarding the failure of the 1994 system, see Alberti Rovira (2003), especially, p. 187.

[25] This concerns between 50 and 100 of approximately 350 committees of the European Commission with normative functions for the application of community policies in which functionaries of the Autonomous Communities participate.

[26] See Roig Molés (2004), pp. 602–623.

[27] This deals with the following agreements: Agreement on autonomic participation in the Spanish delegations; Agreement on the Department for Autonomic Affairs in the Permanent Representation of Spain before the European Union and on the participation of the Autonomous Communities in the Working Groups of the European Union Council.

Government might endorse with certain Autonomous Communities, maintaining the special status of the Canary Islands, Ceuta, and Melilla intact.[28] The 2004 agreements should be seen in the context of the failed attempt to design a new autonomic framework: i.e., a project linked to establishing the Conference of Autonomic Presidents,[29] to reforming the Senate, and to proposing a reform process for certain Autonomous Statutes.[30]

However, the new Autonomous Statutes of Andalusia and Catalonia include rights to information, to participation in the formation of the will of the State, and to decisions and representation in the EU (Articles 230–239 of the Andalusian Statute of Autonomy and Articles 184–192 of the New Statute of Catalonia), as well as a reserve of competence for the development, application, and execution of the EU norm when it affects the area of their competences. In any case, it should be highlighted that, for the autonomic Parliaments, de-autonomisation as a consequence of European dynamics is overwhelming. They barely implement European norms in subject matters that previously corresponded to them. It is the Spanish Parliament that has basically, through the normative function of the executive power, dealt with legislative implementation. Moreover, it should be borne in mind that, frequently, both the regulations and the EU directives are quite detailed and, thus, the function of implementing the norms of the Member States is greatly reduced as regards their legislative capacity and that the use that the Spanish Parliament makes of Article 149.1.13 of the Spanish Constitution, which authorises it to establish the general codes of economic regulation, also allows it to limit considerably the function of the autonomic parliaments. Further, the scant interest shown by these parliaments in European issues should be highlighted, even though their legislative function has been severely restricted.[31]

It is still too soon to gauge the effects that the provisions envisaged in the Treaty of Lisbon, in particular Protocol 1 on the mission of the national parliaments in the EU,

---

[28] As contained in the Agreements: "that established in the present Agreement will be applied without detriment to the singularities derived from the specific system of integration of the Canary Islands, as well as the special community system of Ceuta and Melilla".

[29] Four Conferences of Autonomic Presidents have been held: in 2004/05/07 and 2009.

[30] Specifically, the 2007 New Andalusian Statute of Autonomy contains in Chapter III of Title IX, Articles 230–239, the relations with the EU institutions. In Article 1.4, it expressly states that the European Union is the area of reference of the Autonomous Community, which assumes its values and ensures the fulfilment of its objectives and respect for the rights of European citizens.

[31] The autonomic parliaments usually approve an average of 12 laws per year. Thus, in the previously cited Autonomous Community Report of 2000, it is stated that, while Catalonia (first in the ranking) approved 23 laws, the Basque Country only passed 4, Galicia 5, Andalusia 1, Navarre 20, and the Canary Islands, Cantabria, or La Rioja 7. For its part, in the same year, the Spanish Senate approved 14 laws and 50 International treaties. At the end of the decade, in 2009, except for the Autonomous Communities with new statutes such as Catalonia, which approved 26, others such as the Basque Country, with an old statute and which had held autonomic elections, only passed 3, while Madrid with 10 came close to the overall average of legislation. The State, for its part, approved 46 norms with the status of law in 2009.

might have on regional parliaments.[32] Specifically, by virtue of its constitutional law, Belgium has established the need for both the House of Representatives and the Senate of the Federal Parliament, as well as the Parliamentary Assemblies of the Communities and Regions to act, in accordance with the competences exercised by the Union, as components of the national parliamentary system or Houses of the National Parliament. At present, in Spain, in accordance with a new law, as soon as the Congress and the Senate receive a legislative initiative from the EU, they will remit it to the parliaments of the Autonomous Communities, which will have a period of 4 weeks to issue a detailed report.[33] In this vein, and in relation to the principles of subsidiarity and proportionality, the New Andalusian Statue expressly states in Article 237 that: "The Parliament of Andalusia will be consulted prior to the National Parliament issuing the report concerning European legislative proposals within the framework of the control procedure of the principles of subsidiarity and proportionality which EU law establishes", which is similar to that established in Article 188 of the New Catalan Statute, which also specifies the participation of the Catalan Parliament in the control procedures of subsidiarity and proportionality. However, as seems to be deduced from the Subsidiarity Monitoring Network, the reports, which in accordance with the parliamentary warning procedures some regional legislative assemblies, such as the Catalan Parliament, send to the Congress-Senate Cross-Party Commission regarding EU matters that affect autonomic competences, point out that regional participation is not working effectively.[34]

## The Autonomous Communities in European Institutions

We will now attempt to offer a brief outline regarding the presence of the Autonomous Communities in European Union institutions. Let us bear in mind that according to what is established in Article 4.2 of the Treaty of Lisbon: "The Union will respect the equality of the Member States *vis-à-vis* the Treaties, as well as their national identity inherent in the fundamental political and constitutional structures and also with regard to local and regional autonomy". We will begin our analysis with that body where they have a consolidated representation (the Committee of the Regions) and continue with its presence in other institutions such as Parliament, Council of Ministers, and European Commission.

---

[32] Rights to information and participation in the national parliaments are contained within the framework of the community decision-taking process in said Protocol.

[33] Law 24/2009, BOE of 23/12/2009, where Law 8/1994 of 19 May is adapted, in which the EU Cross-party Commission is regulated and adapted to the Treaty of Lisbon. For its part, Article 4 of the Protocol regarding the mission of the national parliaments in the EU establishes a period of 8 weeks between the date on which a project for a legislative act is processed and the date on which it is included in the provisional agenda of the EU Council of Ministers.

[34] Palomares Amat (2011). The author suggests active participation of the Conference of European Regional Legislative Assemblies (CALRE, in Spanish) and certain corrective measures to prevent the risk of trivialising the procedure.

## The Committee of the Regions

This is a body that does not attain the status of EU Institution and occupies a peripheral position in the decision-making structure. It acts as a consultative body for certain areas and was created at the time of the Maastricht Treaty in 1992. Despite its name, the majority of its members do not represent regions but rather a varied typology of local entities. The Treaty on the Functioning of the European Union regulates the composition and functions of the Committee of the Regions in Articles 305–307. For its part, Article 13.4 of the European Union Treaty awards the Committee of the Regions a consultative function and aid to Parliament, the Commission, and the Council. Since its origin in Maastricht, a share of representatives was established for the CoR between the Member States, coinciding with that established for the composition of the Economic and Social Committee.[35] This coincidence in the assignment of representation, without taking into account whether in the Member States a regional institutionalisation exists or not, poses serious doubts about the nature of the Committee of the Regions. The impression is given that, more than a body for institutionalising regional participation (a desire that motivated the German Länders who promoted the initiative[36]), the European Community wished to create a forum for incorporating the different sub-state entities into the management of the Internal Market. In fact, only a minority of the representatives of the CoR represent regions, and of those only a few are representatives of autonomous regions: around 75 of the almost 350 members of the Committee. These are the representatives of the German and Austrian Länders, together with the regions and cultural communities of Belgium: the three Federal States of the EU. The Italian autonomous regions are also represented, together with the Spanish Autonomous Communities, as well as the autonomous archipelagos of Portugal (the Azores and Madeira), Scotland and Northern Ireland, and the Aland Islands, which have Autonomous Parliaments unlike Wales or the French regions whose legislative Assemblies do not have the capacity to draw up norms with the status of law and can only complete state norms.

The heterogeneity in the composition of the Committee poses important difficulties since not all its members have competence over the areas assigned to it: education, culture, public health, trans-European networks, economic and social cohesion, as well as others assigned at the time of the successive reforms of the

---

[35] See, previous Article 258 of the EUT.

[36] In fact, it was the pressure of the German Länders on the Federal Government, given the position that these occupy in the Senate, which encouraged the European Community to create the Committee of the Regions. The German Government relied on the support of Belgium, which had just culminated the federalisation of the State in which regions and cultural communities have important powers.

European Union Treaty: transport, employment, vocational training, European social fund, environment, and cross-border cooperation. These are subject matters regarding which, in certain aspects, consultation with the CoR is envisaged. The list of subjects is small if compared to the competence areas of the autonomic regions, whose sphere of competence is much wider. However, on the other hand, it is also a question of subject matters concerning which many of the representatives of the CoR do not have competence: municipal representatives of different Member States, non-autonomous regions with representation in the CoR, or representatives of other types of sub-state entities that, within the State, do not have competence over such matters. Such heterogeneity makes decision-taking difficult, as does the fact that numerous members of the CoR combine their representation with that of other institutions, since it promotes absenteeism or lack of rigorous attention to the tasks of the CoR.[37] Further, including an important number of new members of the Committee after the last incorporation of countries from Central and Eastern Europe has meant that a substantial number of members come from non-regional States, given that the centralised communist structures via a single party were contrary to territorialisation of power. It might be speculated that the CoR, given its composition, is a body that in future will encourage regionalisation in those Member States (the majority), which still do not have regional structures. However, for the present autonomous regions, it is a body that remains at a much lower level than in the autonomous communities. Obviously, its existence favours the relationship between regional representatives and constitutes an opening for developing new initiatives.

With respect to the working of the CoR, it should be pointed out that a latent unease exists due to the lack of attention that institutions, which in accordance with the Treaty must request the opinion of the Committee, receive from the Council of Ministers or the Commission[38] and which with relative frequency in the past they had not done. Finally, and addressing an old demand of the CoR, the Treaty of Lisbon in Article 263 (Treaty on the Functioning of the European Union) has recognised the legitimacy of the CoR to lodge an appeal in order to safeguard its prerogatives before the Court of Justice in Luxembourg,[39] thus improving its institutional position.[40] However, it is criticisable that, unlike the consultative recognition in favour of the Economic and Social Committee concerning areas such as industry, technological research, and development, a similar consultation is

---

[37] In accordance with the Nice Reform, representatives in the CoR have to be locally or regionally elected posts or politically responsible in an elected assembly.

[38] Complaints about this attitude have even been publicly lodged from the Presidency of the Committee. See Pellisé (1999), pp. 522–533.

[39] On the occasion of the Intergovernmental Conference from which reform of the Treaty signed in Nice arose, the Committee of the Regions requested recognition of its active legitimacy before the Court. This initiative had the support of Belgium. See, DOC Conference, 12 May 2000.

[40] Unlike that stipulated in favour of the Economic and Social Committee, whose consultation proved preceptive according to that established in the previous Article 262 of the EUT, a similar preceptivity of the consultation was not expressly included in favour of the CoR.

not established for the CoR, although they are matters over which the autonomous regions usually have competence.

Whatever the case, it should be remembered that the opinions of the Committee are not binding and that it is frankly difficult to evaluate to what extent the opinions of the Committee are addressed by the Council of Ministers or the Commission. EUT reforms have also enabled the European Parliament to request the opinion of the CoR and to allow it, on its own initiative, to draw up its own opinion regarding any issue deemed relevant.[41] The CoR has eight permanent commissions: territorial cohesion policy; economic and social policy; sustainable development, culture, education and research; constitutional affairs, European governance and freedom, security and justice; external relations and decentralised cooperation; administrative and financial affairs and a temporary *ad hoc* commission for review of the EU financial framework.

These reflections regarding the CoR may be concluded with the observation that, in accordance with Article 300.3 of the TFEU, its members must be representatives of regional or local entities, but since no category of European region exists, it corresponds to each Member State to determine who is recognised under this category. Neither has it been decided in what proportion representation of regions and local entities should be established in the Committee of the Regions, nor has it been decided in what proportion, between both categories, their representation should be appointed by the Member States.


**European Parliament**

Although envisaged by the founding Treaties, the European Parliament has been unable to provide itself with a uniform electoral procedure. Consequently, each Member State decides on the procedure to appoint the representation that the EUT assigns to it in the European Parliament. Thus, it is possible that, while some regions have elected representatives in the European Parliament, others, as is the case of the Spanish Autonomous Communities, have no representation, given that the entire Spanish State constitutes a single electoral district, unlike the Belgium regions or the electoral districts that in the United Kingdom are recognised for Northern Ireland, Scotland, or Wales whose EMPs can be assigned said representation. For elections to the European Parliament in Italy and France, super-regional districts exist, which group together different regions. The mixed system of Germany enables the election of EMPs in the Länders.

Given that in Spain the National Parliament has imposed a single electoral district for European elections, a majority of regional political parties need to

---

[41] The possibility that the European Parliament requests its opinion is due to the Amsterdam reform that currently figures in Article 307 of the TFEU and that further stipulates that the own initiative opinion also be sent to the Council and Commission, together with the minutes of the deliberations.

participate in those elections in coalitions, which bring together various forces from different Autonomous Communities. These are *ad hoc* electoral mechanisms that are used to win votes and obtain parliamentary representation. Diverse regional political parties are normally represented in the European Parliament: for example, the Catalan nationalists of CiU and the Basque Nationalist Party. At other times, the following parties have been represented: Esquerra Republicana de Catalunya; the Basque parties, Eusko Alkartasuna, and Herri Batasuna; O Bloque Nacional Galego or the Partido Andalucista. Be that as it may, representation of the regional parties in the European Parliament is scarce: around 20 seats out of a total of 754.

## European Commission

Representation of the Autonomous Communities in the European Commission takes place through the committees for applying those norms assigned to the European Commission. These committees are distinct from those advising the Commission on the drawing up of budgets (consultative committees) during the ascendant phase. Committee representation deals with technical matters of scant political relevance. For participation in these committees, the Autonomous Communities have established shared turns between two communities for periods of 4 years.[42]

## Council of Ministers

According to Article 16.2 of the European Union Treaty, representation in the Council of Ministers is permitted for members of institutions other than the central governments: "one representative from each Member State, of ministerial rank, authorised to commit the Government of the Member State which they represent and to exercise the right to vote". Before Maastricht, however, only central government representation was accepted (previous Article 145, EECT). Representation of the Autonomous Communities takes place in the name of the Kingdom of Spain since direct representation of the Autonomous Communities is not possible. Be that as it may, within the Spanish representation, the agreements of December, 2004 envisage Autonomous Community access to the meetings of four different compositions of the Council of Ministers of the European Union, to which a fifth formation has subsequently been added in accordance with a system of six monthly

---

[42] See Astola (2004), pp. 45–75 regarding foreign activities of the Basque Country, Castro Ruano (2004). Between 1997 and 2003, 13 corresponded to the Basque Country and between 2003 and 2006, another 14. Matters such as gas apparatus, incineration of dangerous materials, air quality, or ecological labelling. On the other hand, the so-called Bilateral Commission of the Central and Basque Authority for European Community Affairs has met barely 12 times since its creation in 1995. The Committees of the Commission are envisaged in Decision 2006/512 EC of the Council, 17 July, 2006.

turns. These are the previously cited: agriculture and fisheries; environment; employment, social policy, health and consumer affairs; education, youth and culture, and competition/consumption, although said participation has been more symbolic than effective.

Said conditions of participation clash with the EU system of negotiation, in accordance with which around 100 annual meetings of the Council of Ministers are held, distributed formally in nine formations different from the Council. In fact, the Member States negotiate amongst themselves regarding all the fields of EU competences without the negotiation being divided into watertight areas. Indeed, the decisions of the Council of Ministers are on the whole formal since in practice the decisions have been adopted within the working groups or the Committee of Permanent Representatives (COREPER). The negotiating formula means that the affairs to be dealt with are linked to previous or future negotiations in the form of "package deals", in such a way that, for the decision regarding a certain issue, the stances regarding other past and future matters that the whole of the state delegations have maintained or might maintain are usually taken into account. Hence, going to Brussels twice a year to deal with a specific matter is not relevant for negotiating. The interest of the Autonomous Communities in being present at the meetings of the Council of Ministers of the European Union (CMEU) corresponds more to questions of publicity—to associating the image of the Autonomous Community to a political forum as important as the Council. In practice, the autonomic representatives have formed part of the Spanish delegations in around one-fifth of the meetings of the Council, taking part orally on 3 % of the occasions.[43]

It can therefore be concluded that the Treaty of Lisbon has not substantially modified the presence of the Autonomous Communities in the European institutions, which continues to be a token gesture except in relation to the Committee of the Regions, while the position of the Committee in the decision-making structure is peripheral.[44] This EU marginalisation is not perceived by the Autonomous Communities as an important political issue. European questions play (when they do so) a very secondary role in the political agenda, and the majority of regional parliaments scarcely devote any time to these matters. The regional political class, with the possible exception of Catalonia (reflected in the important number of provisions of the project for a new Statute devoted to the EU, many of which have also been incorporated into the new Andalusian Statute), lacks a European perspective. A good example of this short-sightedness is that the project for the new Basque Statute, known as the "Ibarretxe Plan", devoted only one article to the EU.[45]

---

[43] See data corresponding to 2009 in Donaire Villa (2010), pp. 691–700, which states that the Autonomous Communities attended 21 meetings and spoke on 3 occasions, p. 697.

[44] See Olesti Rayo (2009), pp. 68–88.

[45] Specifically, Article 65 of a total of 69 Articles. The project was approved by the Basque Parliament in December 2004, and was rejected for consideration in plenary session by the Spanish Parliament in February 2005. Regarding possible improvements in relations between the Basque Country and the EU, see Bullain (2011), pp. 57–61.

# Basque and Catalan Asymmetry in a Federal Perspective

The crisis of the autonomic model offers the opportunity to rethink a new constitutional framework. It is also an opportunity to reformulate relations with Catalonia and the Basque Country by truly integrating regional self-government within the European framework. The economic crisis and failure of Catalan statutory reform also poses additional challenges. Modification of the realities of identity, such as the Basque and Catalan, is not best fitted to a homogenising framework that, like the German one, does not seek to respond to the problem of distinct nationalities. Although a system of executive and cooperative federalism may serve to articulate a common framework, the national specificities of Catalonia and the Basque Country require a different formula. The "drinks all round" philosophy is not suitable, especially when there are not enough drinks for everyone. A further point to remember is that the autonomous structure, linked to a specific system of assigning competences, resulting in the absence of sufficient safeguards to ensure autonomic demands, is not contemplated in the same way from the common autonomic perspective, as it is from the wish for self-government of the Basque Country and Catalonia.

A Basque and Catalan Republic federated to the Spanish State within the framework of the European Union could constitute an alternative to the autonomic model and be interpreted as a formula that shows greater respect for the recognition of and respect for the distinct political will existing in Spain. It would also be a comprise solution between unionism and separatism, between independent sovereignty and Spanish nationalism of indissoluble and indivisible nations. Rather than opting to minorate and ignore any political majorities other than that dominant one in Spain, reflected in the PP/PSOE binominal, recognising Basque and Catalan republics federated to the Kingdom of Spain might constitute an ideal framework for developing Basque and Catalan self-government, as well as for a more effective management of the State. Until now, however, the emulation and contagious effect in other Autonomous Communities to proposals favourable to Basque and Catalan self-rule have led, on the one hand, not only to autonomic excesses that have affected the governance of the State but also to a reduction and limitation of the autonomic demands of Catalonia and the Basque Country. While a majority of the Autonomous Communities have taken advantage of the wish for Basque and Catalan self-government, the latter have been the ones to lose out as a result of the tutelary eagerness, which the State has displayed in its desire to control the autonomic structure.

The right of political communities to freely decide their future should be consummated by the right of individuals to freely decide their own destiny. The history of Spain is an example of the opposite. The unity of Spain, like that of so many other political units, was not the consequence of the free self-determination of its component nations and citizens but rather the result of wars (conquests of the Kingdoms of Granada and Navarre) and family bonds between dynasties and their hereditary effects (Castile and Leon, Aragon and Castile). In Spain, especially, the inquisitorial inheritance is culturally and politically highly relevant. The desire for power in order to impose an orthodoxy (a canonical model) is a basic feature. In this sense, it can be said that nationality has replaced religion. The absence of respect for the free choice of nationality is a reminder of the persecution of religious dissidence. The desire for assimilation—to the benefit of the Spanish—seems to reflect a continuing desire to maintain a single religious faith. In this sense, rejecting asymmetrical formulae may be interpreted as a reflection of the hostility that the spirit of orthodoxy maintains in order to coexist with heterodoxy.

In this vein, the uneasy coexistence between liberalism and the nation-state is highly relevant. The relationship between individual rights and the cultural project of a majority poses questions of undoubted theoretical and practical difficulty. The mono-linguistic commitment of many nation-states and their persecution or formal ignorance of bilingualism or multilingualism should lead to a reflection on the history of liberalism in the West. Given that, within the European Union framework, multinationality is a common feature, it would seem that recognising such a characteristic within EU Member States should not constitute an insurmountable conceptual hurdle. However, in a system of multilevel governance, opening the door to the privatisation of nationality has still not been posited.[46] Nor has speaking in a language other than Spanish in the Upper House of Parliament been authorised.[47]

The federal model of democracy, that is to say the combination of federalism and liberal democracy, is the generalised system in the main political units of the world, with the notable exceptions of China and Japan. The United States of America, Brazil, Nigeria, South Africa, the European Union, Germany, India, and Malaysia are Federations and liberal democracies where the principle of self-rule and shared rule is simultaneously combined. That is to say, they merge unity and diversity as an expression that recognises political identities in democratic coexistence. In that sense, federalism should be interpreted as an instrument for democratisation, the lack of a democratic culture usually being seen as an obstacle to such processes of federalisation.[48] Whatever the case might be, as Elazar pointed out, the federal spirit goes beyond the constitutionality of federalism.[49]

It is necessary to emphasise the multiplicity of federal models. As well as a model of dual vocation in which autonomous development of centres of power is

---

[46] Regarding the idea of privatising nationality as occurred with religion in Europe, see Bullain (2005).

[47] In January, 2011, the use of Basque, Catalan, Galician, or Valencian was authorised in the plenary sessions of the Senate. However, according to the leader of the PP, Mariano Rajoy: "working with simultaneous translation does not happen in a normal country. Languages are to understand each other, not to create problems". For his part, according to the socialist parliamentary spokesman in the Congress, Jose Antonio Alonso, who ruled out the possibility: "In the Congress we should speak the common language which is Spanish", as reported in 5 telecinco.es, 19-01-11: "Catalan, Basque and Galician in the Senate: Spanish in the corridors".

[48] Burgess (2006).

[49] Elazar (1994).

sought, other cooperative models also exist. The differences are marked and are dependent on different factors. Dual federalisms have, in general, led to a predominance of central power as has also normally occurred in cooperative systems. However, the alternative proposed in the present study has much to do with the variation of a dual, asymmetric federalism, which distinguishes between a common framework and another that is specific to certain territories and populations. This duality is justified by the existence of different political aims that are not necessarily restricted to different nationalities. Social options, depending on the social policies pursued or those most favourable to the wealthiest, also favour those possibilities linked to the options of dual federalism, in particular those Autonomous Communities that wish to implement neo-conservative models through privatisation.

The origin of Canada is based on a duality between French-speaking Quebec and English-speaking Ontario and was built around two core themes: autonomy of the provinces and the existence of two nations. In particular, recognition of Quebec as a "specific society" formed part of the evolution of the Canadian Federation during the second half of the twentieth century, and demand for autonomy has been the principle that has promoted the asymmetry of the Canadian model. However, in recent decades, Canada seems ever more concerned with other questions: waves of immigrants, rights of the indigenous population, or the role of the "new" Canada in the Canadian Federation. These questions are pushing the issue of Canada's relationship with Quebec to the background. Moreover, the economic crisis and ideological triumph of Friedman neo-capitalism is promoting centralisation and proving detrimental to regional autonomy. Likewise, the particular party system, with two completely different levels (provincial and federal), confer another special characteristic on the Canadian Federation.[50] In recent decades, growth towards the west and northwest, the great energy reserves of Alberta, and the role of the native and immigrant populations after the Second World War pose different perspectives. Multiculturalism seems to be an alternative to the original dual nationality. The Canadian Federation and federalism are torn between loyalty to the original model, interpreted as a contractual pact in Quebec, and adaptation to the new realities evident in English-speaking Canada.[51] Failure of constitutional reforms and the two secessionist referenda has given way to a guarantee-based model as regards the design of a framework for a process of independence. Thus, following the opinion of the Supreme Court, the so-called Clarity Act was passed according to which: "a constitutional obligation exists to negotiate if a secession referendum is won with a clear majority on a clear question".

The Canadian federal model has developed formulae that seek to guarantee autonomy of the provinces whilst also seeking to ensure federal government intervention. The so-called opt-out clauses enable the provinces to avail themselves of federal programmes or implement their own. A typical example is the Quebec

---

[50] A general reflection concerning Canadian federalism, in Simeon (2002).

[51] A general refection on Quebec and Canada, in Pelletier (2010).

Pensions Plan. It seeks to ensure, especially for Quebec, its freedom to develop its culture and social project. In the European Union, also, asymmetrical formulae have been employed in relation to such diverse questions as the Euro or the Schengen Area, making it possible for certain states that implement their own options to coexist with others that form part of a common system.

For its part, the United States system clearly demonstrates that few intergovernmental institutions have developed between the States whilst the Federation has, in contrast, increased its power since the 1930s. Neither the executive governments of the States nor their legislatures are organised to compete with associations and lobbies that operate to influence the Federal Authority. Over time, the federal model of the USA has also become one in which a growing number of federal actions are shifting the autonomy of the States towards mere tasks of execution and application.

Among the different federal experiments, asymmetrical federalism can be understood as a federalism of different levels. In the case of Spain, it could be reflected through one model that is common to all Autonomous Communities and another that is adapted to ensuring the specific political wishes of the majority in the Basque Country and Catalonia for self-government. With regard to a federal reform of the State, this could be undertaken by specifying the precise share of the competences in the constitutional text that, together with jurisdictional safeguards, accompanies others of a political or procedural nature, system of parliamentary alerts, principles of subsidiarity and proportionality, institutionalisation of bilateral State-Autonomous Community commissions for averting and solving conflicts, specificity clauses for particular matters concerning autonomic jurisdiction, etc. Furthermore, federal reform should integrate the Autonomous Communities in the constituent process and draw up a system of two lists: areas of central Government jurisdiction and concurrent competences of the central Government/Autonomous Communities, with a residual clause. In drawing up these lists, the accumulated experience and perspective of the twenty-first century (different to that envisaged by the constituent assembly of 1978) should be borne in mind.

As regards the question concerning whether a federation would solve the identity issue posed by Catalonia and the Basque country, the question should be answered, on the one hand, by Catalan and Basque citizens and, on the other, by Spanish citizens. The pact implies an agreement on coexistence in accordance with certain principles and procedures contained in a text. Given their electoral conduct, Basque and Catalan citizens appear to recognise a right to express their political will in relation to self-government, a will that is different to that of the majority of Spaniards. What exactly the desire for self-rule that they pursue might be and what agreements with the State and the European Union could be reached would have to be specified after a process of debate and negotiation. An agreement with the State would also depend on the interest of the Spanish citizens, represented in their institutions, in reaching one. The dominant political parties, PP and PSOE, would have to declare their intention to respect the majority wish of Basque and Catalan citizens represented in their institutions. For their part, the Basque and Catalan parties would have to declare their intentions and draw up and negotiate their proposals within the autonomic structure. Overcoming the present framework may require constitutional reform, and it might have to be accommodated via the First Additional Provision in the case of the Basque Country.[52]

The desire to apply a model of cooperative federalism based on Germany in order to diffuse the Basque and Catalan peculiarities is an undertaking that, up till now, has not succeeded.[53] However, in that uphill struggle that, for generations, Basque and Catalan nationalists have maintained with Spanish nationalism, the "solution" of the Autonomic State appears to have been left fatally discredited. The German cooperative model is not valid for responding to the Basque and Catalan specificities and their desire for self-government.

However, it seems unlikely that a federal solution will be accepted, even as a lesser evil, for Basque and Catalan nationalism. Experience of the post-war German federal model demonstrates that the federal power (Bund) has taken advantage of its normative and financial resources to impose itself on the autonomy of the Länders. The clauses favourable to federative power, such as "improving people's living conditions", "common tasks and cooperation", "authorisation of the Federation to adopt a law essential for maintaining legal or economic unity", "the conditions for federal adaptation or the different opinions in favour of federal legislation" have gradually limited the Länders' power to govern. Finally, they have even opted to limit the power of veto of the Bundesrat over federal legislation in exchange for recognising the Länders' possibility of diverging. The German federal model, although theoretically enabling the Länders to sign International Treaties with the authorisation of the State (Article 32.3), constitutes a possibility that has barely been used, given that the Länders acknowledge the unity of the federation and are subject to the dominance of party logic. Federal assimilation is also evidenced in the practice that accompanies the European competences that, although they recognise different degrees of enthusiasm for the participation of the Länders, does not pose serious political problems given the German party system.

Federalism can be understood as a type of marriage of convenience adapted to political realities in which more than one group are recognised as a nation and demand the power of self-rule. However, in Spain, federalism has been rejected on successive occasions. The Cadiz Parliament rejected it in 1812 for the bi-hemispherical monarchy. Neither has the project for a federal Constitution during the First Spanish Republic[54] been repeated since then. The idea, both in 1931, with

---

[52] In Spain the "foral" or charter-granted communities represent the existence of a specific framework, as the 1978 Constitution expressly recognises for the Basque Country and Navarre in the First Additional Provision and in the Second Temporary Provision. By means of these paths, some authors speculate about finding an agreement to the tangled problem of the Basque Country and Navarre in Spain.

[53] Arnold (2005), pp. 781–794.

[54] The project for a Federal Constitution during the First Spanish Republic was drawn up in 117 Articles divided into 17 Titles. In its first Article, it established the following: "The Spanish nation comprises the States of Upper Andalusia, Lower Andalusia, Aragon, Asturias, the Balearic Islands, the Canary Islands, New Castile, Old Castile, Catalonia, Cuba, Extremadura, Galicia,

the definition of Spain as an Integral State, and in 1978, when the Autonomous State was introduced, of transforming Spain into a federation failed to gain support. Neither can it be rigorously interpreted that the 1992 PP/PSOE Pacts regarding the Autonomic State or the statutory reforms in the 2000s, especially the New Catalan Statute, have brought about a federal model. The 1978 Constitution is an expression of the dominance of essentialist conceptions linked to Spanish nationalism. Article 2 (which is still in force) states that "The Constitution is founded on the indissoluble unity of the Spanish Nation, a common homeland indivisible to all Spaniards"—a declaration whose metaphysics refers to the National-Catholicism of the Franco dictatorship and its repercussion in the medieval Spain of the Catholic Monarchs. It would be difficult for a similar nationalist theology to justify appealing to a Habermasian constitutional patriotism as "progressives" and even certain "populists" have rhetorically sought to justify for years.

Whether federalism will find sufficient supporters in Spain remains to be seen. Up till now, Catalonia, and especially the PSC (Catalan Socialist Party), had been its principal champion, but the last elections have shown that electoral backing for the PSC has diminished significantly. Although during two successive legislatures the PSOE in Madrid and the PSC in Barcelona ruled, respectively, the Spanish and Catalan Governments did not move towards federalisation. However, while the PSC incorporated federalisation as part of its electoral manifesto, the PSOE merely flirted with the idea at the beginning of Zapatero's first term of office. The gloomy electoral future that seems to await both parties will probably weaken the prospect of federalism. Neither have Basque and Catalan nationalists, represented by the PNV and CiU, traditionally been in favour of federalisation, at least as regards an asymmetrical federalism that would reproduce the dominance of Spanish party logic over that of the federated institutions. Federalisation has even less backing among the pro-independence Basques of Bildu/Amaiur or among the Catalans of Esquerra Republicana. However, and perhaps paradoxically, an asymmetrical federalisation might be a compromise solution between pro-sovereignty Basque and Catalan political forces and Spanish nationalism.

The European Union not only provides the framework for developing self-government but also comprises a political sphere that makes territorial distribution of power between sub-state entities more complex.[55] An asymmetrical federal solution would have to integrate the European dimension of self-rule and recognise a specific status for the Basque Country and Catalonia within the EU. Such a framework could include, *inter alia*, agreements to integrate Basque and Catalan representatives within the Spanish Permanent Representation, the COREPER, and the Council and also to enable the Basque Country and Catalonia to become

Murcia, Navarre, Puerto Rico, Valencia, and the Basque Regions. The States will be able to conserve the present provinces or modify them, according to their territorial needs. These States would have "complete economic-administrative autonomy and all the political autonomy compatible with the existence of the Nation" as well as "the authority to award themselves a political constitution" (Articles 92 and 93).

[55] See Bullain (2006), pp. 11–48.

electoral districts in elections to the European Parliament or to adapt the provisions on subsidiarity and proportionality and link them to the Basque and Catalan Parliaments in the European decision-making process.

However, perhaps the alternative to a Basque and Catalan republic associated with a Spanish Federation within the framework of the EU is something that will not gain sufficient support either in the Basque Country or in Spain. The crisis and paradoxically also the prospect of the sovereignty referendum envisaged in Scotland[56] in the next few years, seem to be elements that will, contradictorily, influence the sovereignty processes that are already in motion in the Basque Country and Catalonia. In this political vein, the next autonomic elections in the Basque Country will be a key factor.[57] If, in those elections, the pro-sovereignty forces obtain a qualified parliamentary majority of around 60 %, it is highly likely that they will announce their intention to commence a debate to attain a new political status. It is still too soon to guess how the process of democratic redefinition of Basque self-rule will develop. Without doubt, it will shape the political life of the Basque Country and maintain a question mark over the future. The response of Spanish nationalism to that demand for self-government or the attitude that will prevail over the coming years are also unknown factors. There is still a long way to go. As a matter of fact parlamentary elections held recently in The Basque Country and Catalonia, in October and November 2012, has given broad mayorities to the pro-sovereignity forces. In the Basque Country, PNV and EH-Bildu obtained 27 and 21 seats, that is 48 out of 75, getting close to 2/3 of the representation. In Catalonia CiU obtained 50 seats, ERC, 21 and CUP 3, that is 74 in a Parliament of 135, an absolut mayority. Both parliaments express a clear will for a new political status. The parties that dominate the spanish parliament, Popular Party and PSOE, where they amont up to 3/4 of the seats, represent only 1/3 in both autonomous parliaments. The basque and catalan people has blowed a wistle for reforms. A new, long and hard transition is on its way. In the coming years a new status for the Basque Country and Catalonia in Spain and in the European Union will be a relevant political question of the agenda.

# References

Alberti Rovira, Enoch:"Las regiones en la nueva Unión Europea". Autonomies: 29/2003, 177–206
Arbós, X. (Coor.), Colino, C., Garcia Morales, M. J. and Parrado, S.: "Las relaciones interguber-
    namentales en el Estado autonómico. La posición de los actores". Barcelona: IEA, 2009.

---

[56] The Scottish First Minister and leader of the SNP, Alex Salmond, anticipates that the referendum will take place in the second half of the legislature: that is to say, between 2014 and 2016. With regard to the question, it could be similar to the following wording: "The Scottish Parliament should negotiate with the British Government, based on the proposals set out in the white paper, so that Scotland becomes a sovereign and independent state". The possible answers would be: "Yes, I agree" or "No, I disagree".

[57] Although foreseen for 2013, they are likely to be brought forward to 2012.

Arnold, Rainer: "Los conceptos fundamentales del federalismo alemán. ¿ ejemplo para la reforma española?" in "La España de las autonomías: reflexiones 25 años después", Barcelona: Bosch 2005, pages 781–794.

Astola, Jasone. "La actividad exterior de la CAPV", in Revista Vasca de Administración Pública 68/2004, pages 45–75.

Bullain, Iñigo: "Autonomy and the European Union", pages 343-356 in Suksi, Markku (ed.): "Autonomy: Applications and Implications". Kluwer Law International, 1998.

Bullain, Iñigo, "Revolucionarismo Patriótico. El Movimiento de Liberación Nacional Vasco. Origen, ideología, estrategia y organización". Madrid: Tecnos, 2011.

Bullain, Iñigo, "Regioak europear integrazioan": Basque Journal of Public Administration. 71/2005, pages 11–47.

Bullain, Iñigo, "Role and Prospects of the Spanish Self-governing Communities in Constitutions, Autonomies and the EU. Report of the Aland Islands Peace Institute, no. 3/2008, pages 19–41

Bullain, Iñigo: "25 urte Europan. Europear Batasuna eta Euskal Instituzioak" in Eleria 21/2011, pages 57-61.

Bullain, Iñigo. "Nantes o Westfalia?" El PAIS, 2/11/2005 (Basque Country edition).

Bullain, Iñigo. "Estatu-nazioa vs. Estatu europearra". Revista Vasca de Administración Pública. 75/2006, pages, 11-48.

Bullain, Iñigo: "The Basque Republic" in the Deia newspaper, 25/10/2011.

Burgess, Michael: "Comparative federalism: theory and practice". London, Routledge, 2006.

Castro Ruano, Jose Luis and Ugalde Zubiri, Alex. "La acción exterior del País Vasco (1980–2003)". Oñati: IVAP 2004.

Donaire Villa, Francisco Javier. "La Conferencia para asuntos relacionados con las comunidades europeas" in Autonomous Community Report, 2009, Barcelona: Instituto de Derecho Público 2010, pages 691–700.

Donaire Villa, Francisco Javier. Autonomous Community Report, 2009, p. 691.

Elazar, Daniel Judah (ed.): "Federal systems of the world: a handbook of federal, confederal and autonomy arrangements". London, Longman 1994.

Hrbek, Rudolf (ed.). "Political parties and federalism: an international comparison". Baden-Baden: Nomos Verlagsgesellschaft, 2004.

Olesti Rayo, Andreu: "El Tratado de Lisboa y su incidencis en las Comunidades Autónomas" in Autonomous Community Report 2009, pages 68–88.

Palomares Amat, Miquel: "La Participación del Parlamento de Cataluña en la aplicación y el control del principio de subsidiariedad", European Community Law Journal, no. 38/2011.

Pelletier, Benoit. "Une certain idée du Québec. Parcours d'un fédéraliste. De la réflexion à l'action". Quebec: Presses de l'Université Laval, 2010.

Pellisé, Cristina. "El Comité de las Regiones", Annual report on the Autonomous Communities, Aja, Eliseo (dir), 1999, pages 522–533.

Roig Molés, Eduard: "La Conferencia para asuntos relacionados con la Unión Europea en el año 2004". Autonomous Community Report 2004, pages 602–623.

Simeon, Richard. "Political Science and federalism: seven decades of scholarly engagement". Kingston: Queen's University, 2002.

Tajadura Tejada, J.: "Federalismo cooperativo y conferencias sectoriales. Marco normativo y propuestas de reforma". Navarre Law Journal, issue 49, 2010.

Roig, Eduard, p. 508, in: "La Conferencia para asuntos relacionados con la UE en el año 2000", in Autonomous Community Report, pages 503-519.

# Federalism and Democracy in the Basque Country

## The Spanish Federal Challenge

**Jule Goikoetxea**

This paper shows how the Basque political system, articulated in the *Law of the Historic Territories*, has checked the tendency that political and economic power has to centralize and concentrate by introducing an institutional distribution of these powers by territory and constitutionalizing them. It will be argued that this distinctive pattern of distributing power and political autonomy has led to a differentiated (Basque) federal democracy. This thesis will be developed by showing how the institutional system has determined a particular socio-economic structure and how both of these, in turn, have shaped specific democratic and federal practices and demands. A systematic analysis of the processes that have featured these practices and demands might clarify the conditions under which the antagonism between 'constitutionalists and nationalists' occurs. The inquiry into the political and socio-economic context in which this confrontation takes place could shed light on what federal arrangements would best nurture democratic governance of Spanish diversity—not only cultural but also political and territorial.

## Introduction

Following Franco's death in 1975, Spain entered a period of transition towards democracy that entailed an open-ended process of asymmetric decentralization under which, in 1979, the Basque Country (the Basque Autonomous Community) acquired its Statute of Autonomy.

'Basque Federal (or Quasi-Confederal) Structure' section describes the Basque federal structure, and 'Consequences of the Basque Federal System for Territorial and Social Cohesion' section attempts to explain its social and economic consequences for social and territorial cohesion. The next section explores the

J. Goikoetxea (✉)
St Edmund's College, University of Cambridge, Cambridge CB3 0BN, UK
e-mail: julegoikoetxea@cantab.net

A. López-Basaguren and L. Escajedo San Epifanio (eds.), *The Ways of Federalism in Western Countries and the Horizons of Territorial Autonomy in Spain*, Vol. 2, DOI 10.1007/978-3-642-27717-7_53, © Springer-Verlag Berlin Heidelberg 2013

consequences of this federal structure in terms of shaping not only specific political interests and demands but also a distinctive type of democracy. The paper concludes with a general reflection on the challenge Spain may face, in the twenty-first century, in accommodating not only different nationalities but divergent types of political systems within the same state.

There are not only many factors other than the political and institutional structure that determine social and territorial cohesion and the population's political interests and demands but also diversities of many kinds and many ways of governing them.

The main argument is that political-institutional diversity (whether this is based on a previously existing cultural diversity or otherwise) fosters socio-economic, cultural and territorial diversity, which in turn may (re)produce divergent political demands within the same state.

In line with this view, the only way Spain might have of democratically accommodating its diverse polities within an overarching political system that would allow each polity to maintain its fundamental integrity is either a federal or a confederal arrangement.

## Basque Federal (or Quasi-Confederal) Structure

The updated Basque *Foral* structure establishes a multilevel government based, on the one hand, on a territorial representation system articulated in the *Law of the Historic Territories* (LHT) and, on the other, on the Basque *Economic Agreement*, which sets up the pattern of relationship between the Spanish and the Basque systems of Public Finance.

It is said that the LHT is like a Basque internal constitution because it distributes the functions and competences of the public sector among different levels of Government (Gallastegui et al. 1986). This constitution may be considered a quasi confederal one that functions on the principle of subsidiarity. Its main characteristics are the equality and parity that it establishes among the three constituent Territories by means of the Parliamentary and the Territorial Finance systems.

### *The Parliamentary Representation System*

The system is articulated such that territorial representation is given greater importance than individual representation. Thus each Territory sends the same number of members to the Basque Parliament: Araba, with 313,819 inhabitants, sends 25 representatives; Bizkaia, with 1,152,658, sends 25; and Gipuzkoa, with 705,698, a further 25. In Araba, a candidate needs around 5,000 votes, while a Bizkaian candidate needs 20,000 to become a representative.

## The Territorial Finance System

The economic equality of the Territories is established by the so-called *Economic Agreement* (1981/2002), which endows the three Historic Territories of Araba, Bizkaia, and Gipuzkoa with powers to formulate, regulate, and collect 92 % of all taxes. After liquidation, each Territorial Government must deliver a part of the revenues collected to the Basque Government.

The second defining feature of the *Economic Agreement* is related to the obligation to pay a certain amount to the Spanish Treasury, which is referred to as the *Basque tax contribution* or 'cupo': each Territory pays 6.24 % of the general expenses of the Spanish state in areas for which it has not assumed responsibility (the army, diplomacy, etc.).

This, along with the fact that most of the competences are concurrent (Gallastegui et al. 1986), implies that Basque Public Institutions must operate by consensus (*pactismo*) in a complex but highly distributive system in which institutional and constitutionalized power (competences, functions, and resources) is subsidiarily distributed by territory.

Nonetheless, to claim that any causal relationship exists between this federal structure and levels of social and territorial cohesion, it will be necessary to show that economic-territorial autonomy (based on the Territorial Finance system) and political-territorial parity (based on the Representation system) tend to either increase or diminish territorial diversity/plurality and socio-economic equality.

# Consequences of the Basque Federal System for Territorial and Social Cohesion

Next we shall proceed to compare some of the major indicators of economic and social well-being of Spain. In the left-hand column of Table 1, it may be seen that only the Basque Country (BC) and Extremadura have the same rate of work activity amongst all their Territories and provinces, respectively.

What is remarkable, however, is that the active male population in some provinces (of Castilla La Mancha, Andalusia, etc.) reaches, on average, 31.27 points higher than the corresponding female figure, and in Aragón, Canarias, Catalonia, etc., it stands at an average of 19.2 points higher, while in the BC the difference is 13 points.[1]

Regarding the right-hand column, the interesting detail is that it is the capitals of each Autonomous Community (AC) that invariably (with the sole exception of Toledo) show the highest educational level. In Andalusia, for instance, the

---

[1] See Esping-Andersen (1990) and Huber and Stephens (2001) for the consequences that active participation by women in the labour force has in determining the socio-economic model and welfare regime.

**Table 1** Percentage of active population and of population with higher studies

| The active population. Percentage distribution | 2008 Men | 2008 Women | Percentage of population btw. 25 and 34 with higher studies | 2008 |
|---|---|---|---|---|
| **Total** | **57.86** | **42.14** | **Total** | 38.76 |
| **Andalucia** | **60.51** | **39.49** | **Andalucía** | **32.54** |
| Almeria | 61.83 | 38.17 | Almeria | **26.50** |
| Cádiz | 61.40 | 38.59 | Cádiz | 32.38 |
| Córdoba | 61.95 | 38.04 | Córdoba | 32.41 |
| Granada | 60.34 | 39.67 | Granada | 31.95 |
| Huelva | 60.75 | 39.27 | Huelva | 30.56 |
| *Jaén | **63.65** | **36.34** | Jaén | 30.78 |
| Málaga | **58.45** | **41.55** | Málaga | **26.15** |
| Sevilla | 59.58 | 40.43 | Sevilla | **42.17** |
| **Aragón** | **57.79** | **42.23** | **Aragón** | **42.02** |
| Huesca | 58.58 | 41.44 | Huesca | 38.39 |
| *Teruel | **59.55** | **40.49** | Teruel | **26.60** |
| Zaragoza | 57.34 | 42.67 | Zaragoza | **44.78** |
| **Asturias (Principado de)** | **56.20** | **43.79** | **Asturias (Principado de)** | **42.55** |
| **Balears (Illes)** | **57.02** | **42.97** | **Balears (Illes)** | **23.70** |
| **Canarias** | **58.56** | **41.44** | **Canarias** | **30.49** |
| *Las Palmas | **59.10** | **40.90** | Las Palmas | 28.72 |
| Santa Cruz de Tenerife | 57.96 | 42.04 | Santa Cruz de Tenerife | 32.65 |
| **Cantabria** | **57.85** | **42.16** | **Cantabria** | **45.97** |
| **Castilla León** | **59.87** | **40.13** | **Castilla León** | **42.72** |
| Ávila | 60.95 | 39.05 | Ávila | 36.70 |
| Burgos | 60.57 | 39.43 | Burgos | 42.65 |
| León | 58.57 | 41.42 | León | 40.07 |
| Palencia | **61.23** | **38.85** | Palencia | 46.38 |
| Salamanca | 60.58 | 39.40 | Salamanca | 41.61 |
| Segovia | 60.77 | 39.26 | Segovia | 36.84 |
| Soria | 59.82 | 40.12 | Soria | 41.96 |
| Valladolid | **58.12** | **41.88** | Valladolid | **49.01** |
| *Zamora | **63.34** | **36.70** | Zamora | **32.23** |
| **Castilla-La Mancha** | **62.15** | **37.48** | **Castilla-La Mancha** | **30.43** |
| Albacete | **58.47** | 41.52 | Albacete | 31.10 |
| Ciudad Real | 64.56 | 35.44 | Ciudad Real | 30.77 |
| *Cuenca | **65.66** | **34.37** | Cuenca | 30.23 |
| Guadalajara | 58.96 | 41.02 | Guadalajara | 32.08 |
| Toledo | 62.78 | 37.21 | Toledo | 29.31 |
| **Cataluña** | **56.22** | **43.79** | **Cataluña** | **39.20** |
| Barcelona | 55.53 | 44.47 | Barcelona | **42.12** |
| Girona | 58.20 | 41.80 | Girona | 31.09 |
| Lleida | 57.36 | 42.67 | Lleida | **30.44** |
| *Tarragona | **58.40** | **41.60** | Tarragona | 32.11 |
| **Comunitat Valenciana** | **58.10** | **41.90** | **Comunitat Valenciana** | **35.92** |
| *Alicante/Alacant | 58.35 | 41.65 | Alicante/Alacant | **29.46** |
| Castellón/Castelló | 57.73 | 42.26 | Castellón/Castelló | 34.64 |
| Valencia/Valéncia | 58.01 | 41.99 | Valencia/Valéncia | **40.22** |

(continued)

**Table 1** (continued)

| The active population. Percentage distribution | 2008 Men | 2008 Women | Percentage of population btw. 25 and 34 with higher studies | 2008 |
|---|---|---|---|---|
| **Extremadura** | **62.80** | **37.19** | **Extremadura** | **34.36** |
| *Badajoz | 62.92 | 37.08 | Badajoz | 34.29 |
| Cáceres | 62.60 | 37.38 | Cáceres | 34.52 |
| **Galicia** | **56.05** | **43.94** | **Galicia** | **43.51** |
| A Coruña | 55.86 | 44.13 | A Coruña | 47.95 |
| Lugo | 56.48 | 43.52 | Lugo | 42.42 |
| Ourense | 56.72 | 43.26 | Ourense | 37.80 |
| Pontevedra | 55.93 | 44.07 | Pontevedra | 40.18 |
| **Madrid (Comunidad de)** | **55.04** | **44.96** | **Madrid (Comunidad de)** | **47.79** |
| ***Murcia (Región de)** | **59.65** | **40.35** | ***Murcia (Región de)** | **30.13** |
| **Navarra (Comunidad Foral)** | **57.69** | **42.31** | **Navarra (Comunidad Foral)** | **47.98** |
| **Pais Vasco** | **56.57** | **43.43** | **Pais Vasco** | **57.72** |
| Álava | 56.81 | 43.18 | Álava | 60.29 |
| Guipúzcoa | 56.09 | 43.91 | Guipúzcoa | 61.96 |
| Vizcaya | 56.81 | 43.19 | Vizcaya | 54.72 |
| **Rioja (La)** | **59.41** | **40.59** | **Rioja (La)** | **37.86** |
| **Ceuta y Melilla** | **67.55** | **32.50** | **Ceuta y Melilla** | **27.85** |
| *Ceuta | 67.05 | 32.85 | | |
| *Melilla | 68.14 | 32.09 | | |

*Source:* INE (2011)

*ACs with high difference, Grey part is the Basque Country, Bold values at highest rates

difference between the capital, Seville, and Malaga is 16 points; in Catalonia, 12; etc. In contrast, in the BC there is only 7 points' difference, and furthermore the highest rate is found in Gipuzkoa, which is neither where the capital is nor the most populous territory.

At first glance, the figures point to a marked territorial and socio-economic inequality both between and within the ACs: between women and men, between provinces, and between the capital and the periphery. Is the more balanced state of the BC related to its federal structure, that is, to the economic autonomy and political parity of its Territories?

It may be suggested that this more balanced outcome in the distribution not only of the active population and of higher education but also of other social policies (Eustat and INE 2010) would have been otherwise had Bilbao (the most populous city, situated in Bizkaia) been the Capital of the BC (which is Gasteiz, in the least populous Territory). In this case, the mechanism of urban concentration/centralization would have meant that, within the space of a few years, several hundred thousand incomers would have migrated from the other two Territories—leading to what has happened in Spain: Madrid's population has increased by around 40 % and Barcelona's by around 20 % since democracy was established in 1979, and almost half of the Spanish population lives in the seven most populous provinces (INE and Inebase 2009).

From an analysis both of European varieties of capitalism (Kitschelt et al. 1999; Schmidt 2002; Hall and Soskice 2001) and of the distribution of population and

GDP across European regions (Eurostat Regional Yearbook 2009; Growing Regions Growing Europe 2007), one may draw the conclusion that policies of urban concentration/centralization are usually accompanied by a particular economic policy whereby most of the GVA comes from the (traditional) services sector rather than from industry (Huber and Stephens 2001: 225; Pierson 2001).

In the case of Spain, the main income within the services sector comes from tourism, while industry represents only 17 %. While the BC contributes 10.45 % of the Spanish industrial GDP with just 270,000 workers, tourism accounts for 10 % of the Spanish GDP (in 2008) but employs three million people (turismoa.euskadi.net, 2010). This disparity means that tourism has a very low added value, leading to Spain having an economic structure of low productivity (*España en cifras*, INE 2011; Goikoetxea 2011, unpublished). Nevertheless, having a more productive economic structure and a higher GDP helps but does not necessarily lead to greater social and territorial cohesion since Catalonia, for instance, also has high levels of GDP and productivity and, at the same time, marked social and territorial inequalities.[2]

Although the crisis of the 1980s and 1990s created a high level of unemployment in Spain, the industrial and technological restructuring in the BC was accompanied by a high demand for skilled labor, which required the Basque Government to ensure widespread access to higher education for all those living and working in Bizkaia, Araba, and Gipuzkoa, where 40 % of the population were, in the 1970s, Spanish immigrants.

Nowadays, the percentage of population with higher education is around 22 % in each Territory (Eustat 2011). This means that the restructuring of the BC's industrial network has entailed neither massive displacements nor depopulation of any Territory (Gomez et al. 2000), as may also be inferred from Table 2.

According to our thesis, this is a consequence of the political-institutional structure: each Territory's Parliament is made up of representatives elected by groups of towns. In this way, each Territory has preserved high levels of industry (and investment) in the towns and, hence, maintained the social structure of the BC, where 80 % of the population lives in towns.

Thus, the more balanced distributive outcome in the BC may be explained by the fact that the Territories of Araba and Gipuzkoa are not politically and economically subordinated to the Territory of Bizkaia. This means that neither are those who live and work in these Territories placed at a disadvantage with regard to social provisions, including higher education, vis-à-vis those who live in the most populous Territory, or the one with the highest economic activity—as happens in Spain.

The tables and the figures, alongside the information provided, suggest that even if the type of economic structure depends on the financial system, firm organization, and industrial and training systems (Kitschelt et al. 1999: 148), alongside particular party politics and economic and fiscal policies (Katzenstein 1985), territorial and

---

[2] Source: *Noticias de Gipuzkoa* (25-03-11); INE and BBVA-Ivie (2008); *España en cifras* (INE 2011: 32).

**Table 2** GVA by AC, municipality and sector (%) 2005–2006[a]

| Communities | Primary | Industry | Construct | Service |
|---|---|---|---|---|
| Basque Country | 1.0 | 29.8 | 8.9 | 60.3 |
| Catalonia (C) | 1.3 | 21.2 | 9.8 | 67.5 |
| Valencia (V) | 2.1 | 17.3 | 12 | 68.5 |
| Antzuola 2,169 (pop.) | 1.2 | 74.1 | 2.5 | 22.2 |
| Favara-V 2,118 | 3.9 | 10.8 | 18.3 | 64.8 |
| Ayala 2,635 | 8.4 | 45.2 | 3.6 | 42.8 |
| Hernani 19,000 | 0.6 | 51.9 | 5.4 | 42.1 |
| Tarrega-C 16,534 | 1.5 | 28.7 | 11.5 | 58.2 |
| Laudio 18,324 | 0.4 | 41.9 | 8.2 | 49.5 |
| Cardedeu-C 16,596 | 0.4 | 22.8 | 19.1 | 57.7 |
| Mungia 15,984 | 0.7 | 56.0 | 7.4 | 35.9 |
| Carlet-V 15,527 | 7.1 | 18.2 | 22.0 | 44.2 |

*Source:* Compiled by Goikoetxea (2011) with data from Eustat (2005), Idescat (2006), and IVE (2006)

[a]In grey are the Basque towns. Catalonia represents the average of the most industrialized ACs and Valencia represents the Spanish average

social cohesion are highly dependent upon who—i.e., which level of government— has the power to propose and implement such systems and policies (Huber and Stephens 2001: 126, 316), which in the BC are in the hands of the Basque Government, as well as the Territorial Governments and Parliaments of Bizkaia, Araba, and Gipuzkoa.

The Basque federal or quasi confederal structure has, through a parity representation of each Territory and the Territorial Finance systems and irrespective of the color of the government of the day, increased territorial plurality/diversity. This, as we have seen, entails the spreading out of production (and hence wealth) and well-being across the country and, consequently, leads to greater socio-economic equality.

Why does this apparently well-functioning federal system lead to political confrontation?

# Federal Versus Unitary Political Culture

## *The Blocking of the Statute of Autonomy of 1979*

The confrontation between the nationalists and the state-wide parties has been labeled by the latter as one of 'nationalists versus constitutionalists'. This labeling reflects the long-standing incompatibility between modern constitutional systems (based on the homogenization and centralization of powers) and the historical rights-based *Foral* regimes (based on differentiation and decentralization), whose best example is the Basque political structure (Herrero de Miñón 1998: 112). Closely related to this opposition is the incompatibility between the diverse patterns of relationship (either lateral or hierarchical) the BC does, or should, set up vis-à-vis the central state.

To see how this incompatibility arises, consider the 2009 negotiations for the fulfillment of the very Statute of Autonomy. After the Basque Nationalist Party (EAJ-PNV), the majority party, had for the past 20 years rejected the devolution of active labor market policies unless devolved in accordance with the *Foral* system (Article 41.1, Statute of Autonomy), the PSOE, pressed by the need to get its 2010 budget passed in Madrid, engaged once more with the EAJ-PNV on this matter. In the end, a deal was struck to devolve these policies according to the *Economic Agreement*; that is, the money to be paid by the state would have to be worked out by applying the Ministry of Work's 6.24 % share of the GDP for the fields to be devolved and offsetting it against the 'cupo' or the *Basque Tax Contribution* to the state.

In 2010, still with the PSOE's regional branch (the PSE) in the Basque Government, it was again the EAJ-PNV that negotiated the devolution of a further 20 competences. As may be inferred from this, in the Spanish two-party system, the government of the day needs the backing of the main nationalist parties—Basque (EAJ-PNV) or Catalan (CIU)—in order to govern Spain when the party in power is in the minority.

The Basque multiparty system fits into the consensus democracy model, where the parties are used to working by consensus (in broad multiparty coalitions) and by contractual entrenchment. However, in the majoritarian model in which Spain is placed with regard to the executives-parties dimension (Lipjhart 1999), the types of cooperation and the implementation of agreements are dependent upon the needs and interests of the majority party.

Therefore, it is plausible that constitutionalist parties should find it difficult to fulfill the Statute of 1979 since for the Statute to be fulfilled a symmetrical or lateral pattern of relationship between the BC and the central state/government would have to emerge (see the LHT, the Statute and the *Economic Agreement*) based on what Elazar, Burgess, and Gagnon call federal principles (autonomy, comity, contractual entrenchment, reciprocity, and self-determination).

Just as the Basque federal system subordinates neither Araba's nor Gipuzkoa's interests to Bizkaia's (see 'Basque Federal (or Quasi-Confederal) Structure' and

'Consequences of the Basque Federal System for Territorial and Social Cohesion' sections), nor are the BC's interests considered, by Basque nationalist parties, subordinate to those of Spanish governments (Herrero de Miñón 1998: 183). Nevertheless, constitutionalist parties, as the non-fulfillment of the Statute of Autonomy of 1979 shows, conceptualize the BC as a region of Spain and consider the BC's interests to be regional interests subordinate to Spanish national (central) ones (Lecours and Nootens 2009: 116–119).

One could argue that under this confrontation lies not only a divergent development of the democratic model established in 1980 but also an incompatible understanding of what 'self- and shared rule' means, or what 'self-government' refers to (Ordozgoiti 2010; Garaikoetxea 2002: 191). It may tentatively be said that an uneasy encounter is taking place between what we could provisionally call a Basque federal political culture and a highly decentralized but nevertheless unitary Spanish political culture.

## Self-Government Demands: Nationalist or Federal?

In a community where only 47 % of the population has parents who were both born in the BC while around 25 % is first-generation Spanish immigrants (Alvite 2000; Aranda 2004), the question is: Should the Basque Parliament's approval of a *New Statute of Free Association* (Project for the Reform of the Statute of Autonomy, 2004) be explained in terms of cultural identity or rather political practice?

---

Box 1. Summary of the Basque Project for the Reform of the Statute of Autonomy

- The Basque People's right of self-determination (Preliminary Heading, Art. 1);
- A relationship with the Spanish state based on 'free association' (Heading I);
- The Basque Judicial System (Heading II);
- Direct representation in Europe (Heading VI);
- Exclusive areas of competence of Basque Institutions (Heading IV, Arts. 46–51, 53, 54, 60): education, culture, language policy, social policy, health care system, economic policy, industry and commerce, agriculture, tourism, employment policies, tax system, financial Policies, housing, environment, natural resources, infrastructure, transport and public works, policing and public security, social security;
- Exclusive areas of competence of the Spanish state (Heading IV, Art. 45): Spanish nationality and immigration laws, Defence forces and the Army, Production, trading, use and possession of firearms and explosives, The Monetary and Customs system (non-EU), The Merchant Navy and Control of air space , Foreign policy (i.e. Diplomatic services).

After the rejection (without negotiation) of the *New Statute* by the Spanish Congress (2005), some scholars argued that it reached 'the ceiling of *autonomism*' since there was hardly any room left between the new level of autonomy demanded by the BC and the sovereignty of a current European state (Corcuera 2006; Tamayo 2008: 113–17). However, Spain shows that the divisibility of sovereignty has, so far, no foreseeable limits; although it does have far-reaching consequences for a state's level of success in claiming a monopoly over authoritative lawmaking, especially when divisibility includes self-rule but not shared rule (Moreno 2008: 142, 159–63), as the give and take between the intergovernmental and supranational institutions in the EU shows.

According to Tilly (2007), the degree of democratization depends on the degree to which the state can translate citizens' expressed demands into the transformation of social life. Nonetheless, the yielding of sovereignty implies giving up resources that states use not only to coerce but also to meet the needs and demands of their population, which in democratic societies include welfare and, hence, social and territorial cohesion.

Taking into account, on the one hand, the relatively high degree of both self-rule and cohesion in the BC ('Consequences of the Basque Federal System for Territorial and Social Cohesion' section) and, on the other, the Spanish state's failure to effectively translate some of the most politically relevant demands of Basque citizens (i.e., the Statute of 1979, the *New Statute* of 2004, etc.), it might be argued that despite the relatively low degree of shared rule, the Basque political system has, over the last 20 years, met the needs and demands of its population (to some degree at least) more successfully than the Spanish state has.

---

Box 2. Polls on Basque and Spanish governments

- 4 % would increase Spanish government's political power (Elzo 2001);
- b/n 60 % and 64 % wants the Basque self-government to be increased or developed;
- b/n 29 % and 36 % is towards an independent state;
- b/n 26 % and 29 % is towards a federal state (Euskobarometro 1999, 2011; CIS 2005, 2011);
- b/n 4 % and 11 % thinks that the Spanish government has contributed most to improving the BC (ibid; Bourne 2008);
- b/n 80 % and 90 % thinks that the Basque Self-government has contributed most (Euskobarometro 2008; CIS 2005).

---

Democracy building 'involves negotiated consent in the exercise of concentrated state power' (Tilly 2007: 58). In Spain, this process is determined by the ACs' particular institutional and political workings that concretize the meaning of those key categories (consent, equality, autonomy) that articulate not only nationalist but also federal-like practices and discourses, including government practice and political demands. Following this line of argument, the demand for a status of *Free Association* was effectively articulated (approved) not because the Basque community is a differentiated nationality (in the non-political sense of a pregiven cultural unit) but because it is also a federal political entity (constituted by *Freely Associated* Territories) that, due to its political and institutional functioning (which includes its polemical degree of both self- and shared rule), has shaped and most effectively met the needs/demands of its population, managing to uphold the claim to the monopoly of authoritative lawmaking more successfully than the Spanish state itself (see Box 2).

We have seen that the Basque federal system has led to a new pattern of distributing power and political autonomy, that is, to a distinctive Basque federal democracy, which in turn has shaped a particular set of nationalist demands that are barely distinguishable from democratic and federal demands to the extent that self-government-related demands (see Box 1) refer to the distribution of power and political autonomy.

## Conclusion

So far, our analysis illustrates that what is at stake is how much, and in which way, political power should be distributed; among which different political communities should it be distributed; and how, within the political community, this power will be shared.

This is why we propose that the aforementioned confrontation could be interpreted as taking place between two nationalities, but besides that, between two different democracies or demos-building projects.

The Basque federal structure, by facilitating not only the incorporation of second-generation immigrants into the middle class but also a more just distributive outcome for all those inhabiting the Basque territories ('Consequences of the Basque Federal System for Territorial and Social Cohesion' section), has led to the population's consolidation of strong federal-like territorial interests and identities ('Federal Versus Unitary Political Culture' section). Social and welfare policies have therefore been essential not simply for deepening the process of democratization but also for building a federal-like demos, since they have reinforced symbolic and intersubjective boundaries between the people living in these territories. These policies, which are not usually tied to the cultural and language issues traditionally associated with nationalist politics (Lecours and Nootens 2009), are in our current political context a relevant aspect of national identities. However, those conceptions in which national demands are systematically related to cultural identity rather than to political and institutional practices tend to split cultural identity from its territorial dimension, disconnecting nationalist demands from democratic and federal ones.

It may be concluded that the challenge Spain faces is a democratic, as well as a federal, challenge that might be reassessed not solely by how Spain accommodates national minorities by recognizing diverse identities but also, and above all, by how Spain builds political and socio-economic structures that facilitate social and territorial cohesion and, at the same time, political autonomy and territorial plurality/diversity.

The Basque case not only validates the integrative feature of the principle of territorial and political subsidiarity; it also shows that self- and shared rule, or 'federalization,' is not to be confused with decentralization.

# References

Alvite, P. (2000) La inmigración extranjera en el País Vasco. In: II Congreso sobre la Inmigración en España. Universidad del País Vasco, Leioa.

Aranda, J. (2004) La mezcla del pueblo vasco. Historia. Papeles de Ermua 6:145–80.

Bourne, A. K. (2008) The European Union and the accommodation of Basque difference in Spain. Manchester University Press, Manchester, 269 pp.

Centro de Investigaciones Sociológicas (2005, 2011). http://www.cis.es/cis/opencms/EN/index.html

Corcuera, J. (2006) The Autonomy of the Basque Country: Singularities. In: Fundación para la Libertad, 12 pp.

Elzo, J. (2001) Gipuzkoa 2020 - Reto 1: Sociedad Civil, La dimensión socio-cultural. www.gipuzkoa.net/g2020/docum/G2020-Sociedad-Elzo.es

Esping-Andersen, G. (1990) The Three Worlds of Welfare Capitalism. Princeton University Press, New Jersey, 248 pp.

Eurostat (2010), http://epp.eurostat.ec.europa.eu/portal/page/portal/eurostat/home/

Eurostat Regional Yearbook (2009) Statistical Book, European Communities, Luxemburg. http://epp.eurostat.ec.europa.eu/portal/page/portal/eurostat/home/

Euskal Erkidegoko Administrazio Publikoa (2011). http://www.euskadi.net/

Euskobarometro (1999, 2008, 2011). http://www.ehu.es/euskobarometro/

Eustat, Euskal Estatistika Erakundea (2011). http://en.eustat.es/idioma_c/indice.html#axzz1IYz5dbzq

Fundación BBVA- IVIE (2008) Competitividad de las regiones españolas, Ivie, Madrid.

Gallastegui, C. and Gallastegui, I. (1986) Un análisis económico de la Ley de Territorios Históricos. Eusko Ikaskuntza, San Sebastian, 79 pp.

Garaikoetxea, C. (2002) Euskadi: la transición inacabada. Planeta, Barcelona, 360 pp.

Gomez, M. and Etxebarria, G. (2000) Panorama of the Basque Country and its Competence for Self-Government. European Planning Studies 8, 4:521–35.

Growing Regions, Growing Europe (2007). European Communities, Luxemburg. http://ec.europa.eu/regional_policy/sources/docoffic/official/reports/cohesion4/pdf/4cr_en.pdf

Hall, P. A. and Soskice, D. (eds.) (2001) Varieties of capitalism: The Institutional Foundations of Comparative Advantage. Oxford University Press, Oxford, 540 pp.

Herrero de Miñón, M. (1998) Derechos históricos y constitución. Taurus Pensamiento, Madrid, 343 pp.

Huber, E. and Stephens, J. (2001) Development and crisis of the welfare state. University of Chicago Press, Chicago, 368 pp.

Idescat, Institut d'Estadística de Catalunya (2011). http://www.idescat.cat/en/

Ine, Instituto Nacional de Estadística (2011). http://www.ine.es/

Ive, Institut Valencià d'Estadística (2011). http://www.ive.es/

Katzenstein, P.J. (1985) Small states in world markets: industrial policy in Europe. Cornell University Press, Ithaca, 268 pp.

Kitschelt, H., Lange, P., Marks, G. and Stephens, J.D. (1999) Continuity and change in contemporary capitalism. Cambridge University Press, Cambridge, 527 pp.

Lecours, A. and Nootens, G. (eds.) (2009) Dominant Nationalism, Dominant Ethnicity: Identity, Federalism and Democracy. Peter Lang, Brussels, 336 pp.

Lipjhart, A. (1999) Patterns of Democracy: Governments Forms and Performance in Thirty-Six Countries. Yale University Press, London, 351 pp.

Moreno, L. (2008) La federalización de España. Siglo XXI, Madrid, 203 pp.

Ordozgoiti, K. (2010) El futuro nos pertenece. Alberdania, Irun, 300 pp.

Pierson, P. (2001) The new politics of the welfare state. Oxford University Press, Oxford, 519 pp.

Schmidt, V.A. (2002) The futures of European capitalism. Oxford University Press, Oxford, 357 pp.

Tamayo, V. (2008) Vasconia: la reivindicación política pendiente. Erein, Donostia, 314 pp.

Tilly, C. (2007) Democracy. Cambridge University Press, Cambridge, 234 pp.

# Fractal Federalism for Complex Societies: The Basque Case

Igor Filibi

*One preliminary version of this paper was presented at the International Conference "The ways of Federalism and the Horizons of the Spanish State of Autonomies", Bilbao 19–21 October 2011 (University of the Basque Country). The author is part of the Consolidated Research Team Parte Hartuz,* funded by the Basque Government.

## The Tension Between Unity and Diversity

Historically, different groups and territories have been integrated into larger units either by the sword or by a pact. The right of the conqueror was not a title that could be preserved with time, so another principle was to be used in order to give legitimacy to the ruler and his law. The many rights, alliances, unions, and results on the battlefields were configuring a complex mosaic of jurisdictions in Medieval Europe.

In that context, two main political principles arose. On the one hand, the principle of sovereignty was slowly but firmly designed and imposed in the favor of the great kings. Bodin (*The six books of the republic*, 1576) and Hobbes (*Leviathan*, 1651), among many others, were the masters of this ideology. They crafted the conceptual backbone of modern states. On the other hand, Bullinger (*The One and eternal testament or covenant of God*, 1534) and Althusius (*Politica methodice digesta*, 1603), among many others, elaborated a different concept, the federal principle, which defends the union of different peoples and territories into larger political bodies while maintaining their self-government and particular identity. Therefore, it is important to identify the tension between these two different political cornerstones because the first fostered and propelled the second.

I. Filibi (✉)
Department of International Relations, University of the Basque Country (UPV/EHU), Campus of Sarriena, Post Box 644, 48080 Bilbao, Spain
e-mail: igor.filibi@ehu.es

A. López-Basaguren and L. Escajedo San Epifanio (eds.), *The Ways of Federalism in Western Countries and the Horizons of Territorial Autonomy in Spain*, Vol. 2, DOI 10.1007/978-3-642-27717-7_54, © Springer-Verlag Berlin Heidelberg 2013

Many authors have highlighted this point, the correlation—sometimes the dialogue, many others the conflict—between both: (sovereign) state and federalism (Filibi 2007: pp. 73–75; Duclos 1968: p. 19; Duverger 1956: p. 73).

Recent centuries have shown how the state seems to have won the battle against federalism. The history of federalism has been that of "the progressive demise of the Althusian vision and its subversion by Bodin's paradigm of the state". Finally, "by the end of the 1800s, would-be federations had all turned into 'federal states'" (Nicolaïdis 2006: p. 64).

In any case, no trend is established forever, and in this sense Marks et al. (2008) have identified a new general trend in the world towards federalism, at least in the states that were more centralized by 1950 and have either higher levels of ethnic diversity or large populations, or both (Jeffery 2008: pp. 545–546). It must be said that by the end of World War II the two main superpowers, USA and USSR, were huge federal entities, and very soon the European Community was born following that federal pattern. From this point of view, that fact may be an indicator of some kind of historical turning point.

## The Architecture of Historical Orders

Throughout history, society has been organized into different institutional forms. It is interesting to observe that "these forms strongly reflect prevailing concepts of the legitimate relationship of the individual members of society to the prevailing conceptions of legitimate authority". So first, dynastic sovereignty; second, territorial sovereignty; and finally, national sovereignty have rebuilt the old state (Hall 1999: p. 50).

> Nations and the international nation-state system are now a natural feature of the international political landscape because they have a 'template' to work with. Political entities have enormous incentives to mould themselves into this landscape owing to the privileging of the state in the rules, or incentive structure, of the contemporary international system. However, this was not always so. Change in the international system occurs with changes in the collective identity of crucial social actors who collectively constitute the units from which the system is comprised (Hall 1999: 49).

In our opinion, it is this "template" that deserves more attention, although some considerations must be made first. This template or political model can be fully understood only within a more general theoretical framework. First of all, the legitimate institutional form acknowledged as the reference point in a concrete historical period constitutes a decision. This decision is essentially a political one or, more specifically an act of power because to choose this specific principle implies not choosing other different alternatives.

In other words, this decision about the model means a new starting point for that society. It is a very particular situation because one enters an ambiguous terrain. We are no longer within the clear and safe borders of the known world but facing an act of creation. In effect, once it has been decided who has the right to vote, in other words, once political body or the demos is clear, it is time to vote. However, who has decided who can or cannot vote? Who decides what concrete borders the new political community will have? It is crucial to observe that this key decision "cannot be resolved by the democratic process". By the same token, the authority to sign the American Declaration of Independence can only come after the document is signed. Derrida called this a "fabulous retroactivity", and Ricoeur termed it as a "virtual act". Thus, "for Ricoeur such virtual acts are crucial because they work to establish the ground from which the democratic order can be inaugurated; ground that can only be established retroactively". What is more, "this retroactive move is the only way that the political act of foundation, which cannot be authorized within or before the order it seeks to found, can acquire the semblance of legitimacy" (Doucet 2005: pp. 147–148).

Each different political principle of authority gives legitimacy and, as it has been said before, fosters its own reproduction because of the great incentives it offers to others to follow the general trend. So, within one particular order, there are clear rules of the game. Nonetheless, between one and the next principle or order, there is one moment of "openness" in which—even if not every option has a real chance of success—at least the final decision is not taken. This "undecidability" is one of the main features of "the political" (Zizek). Zizek summarizes the distinction made by Lefort and Laclau as one

> between "politics" as a separate social complex, a positively determined sub-system of social relations in interaction with other sub-systems (economy, forms of culture...) and the "Political" [*le politique*] as the moment of openness, of undecidability, when the very structuring principle of society, the fundamental form of social pact, is called into question – in short, the moment of global crisis overcome by the act of founding a "new harmony" (Edkins 1999: 3).

The distinction between "politics" and "the political" expresses this difference. "Politics" implies a narrow meaning, while "the political" refers to that initial moment in which the big decisions are made and the pure order is created. Mere "politics" will only try to legitimate that first decision[1] and establish clear rules and limits to the social sphere specialized in political decision-making. Politics is the realm of elections, political parties, the doings of government and parliament, etc. So an important corollary of this is that "the question of what counts as 'politics' (in the narrow sense) is part of 'the political' (in the broader sense)".[2] So as "the 'political' has to do with the establishment of that very social order which sets out a particular, historically specific account of what counts as politics it also defines

---

[1] "What is important about power is that it establishes a social order and a corresponding form of legitimacy. Power, for Lefort, does not 'exist' in any sort of naked form, before legitimation: rather, the ideological processes of legitimation produce certain representations of power" (Edkins 1999: p. 3).

[2] Similarly, Darby states that "what is political is itself a matter of politics", and "very often, what is not taken up as politics is that which threatens most. This is the zone of the not-yet-political" (Darby 2004: p. 30).

other areas of social life that are not politics".[3] In a similar vein, for Claude Lefort, "the political is concerned with the 'constitution of social space, of the form of society'. It is central to this process that the act of constitution is immediately concealed or hidden" (Edkins 1999: p. 2).

## Spaces and Scales

Henri Lefebvre stated that "(social) space is a (social) product" (Lefebvre 1974: p. 35). From the very beginning, the conflict is at the center of the stage. Not only does any social formation expresses itself spatially, but it also implies that if it does not, it will increasingly lose its identity, its name, its reality, until being blurred into another one (Lefebvre 1974: p. 65). From this point, Lefebvre elaborates a theoretical framework dealing with the different and interesting features of (social) space. One of the most intriguing of these features is its complexity. Properly speaking, there is not one singular space but multiple social spaces intertwined and superimposed. Every layer is intertwined with the rest, and only the whole thing makes sense, in other words, only this "millefeuille" [thousand leaves] is the single reality. Therefore, "le mondial n'abolit pas le local", the global does not abolish the local (Lefebvre 1974: pp. 103–104). This hypercomplexity of space explains why the local does not disappear, absorbed by the regional, national, or global, and why the global does not only include the national but also reconfigures it based on new divisions (Lefebvre 1974: pp. 105–106).

If this is true, the state as a "container" must be relativized. Nevertheless, the social sciences have not done this, but the contrary, because "...the new social sciences (economics, sociology, political science) used the territories of modern statehood to serve as a fixed and reliable *template* for their investigations into a wide range of phenomena. (...) In this way a largely implicit 'methodological nationalism' came to prevail in political and social thought" (Agnew 1998: p. 50, emphasis added[4]).

So globalization can be understood as a process of reconfiguration of the various social scales (Ferrero and Filibi 2004). Using multiscalar analytics allows us to see

---

[3] Zizek develops this argument elsewhere stating that "the political conflict itself involves a tension between the structured social body, where each part has its place, and the part of the no-part (...). For this reason, the very political struggle is never simply a rational debate between different interests but, simultaneously, a movement for the voice of those who do want to be heard and recognized as a legitimate participant". In other words, [those forgotten persons claim for] "their great right to be heard and recognized as an equal participant in the debate" (Zizek 2001: pp. 174–175). And defines the political as "the space of litigation where the excluded can protest the harm or grievance made to them" (Zizek 2001: p. 185).

[4] Here we can see one example of the power of the "template" associated to the current principle of legitimacy in a specific historical period, now the nation-state. A power of attraction that even "science" cannot avoid because of the incentives of grants, funding of research projects, academic hierarchy, *etc.*

that subnational processes and institutions are also critical sites for globalization, which diverges from the mainstream scholarship on the state of globalization (Sassen 2006).

## Spain: From a World Monarchy to a Nation-State?

After the French Revolution, the new national principle spread out across Europe and its colonies. It is necessary to observe that the ideal of the nation-state only requires an independent state with sovereignty over a territory; no specific territory is needed. This concrete territory does not come from the notion of state but of nation. At the same time, nationalism adapts itself to the existing state territory. For this reason, old empires became nations from one day to the next (White 2000: p. 23, 8–10). This was a clear application of the incentives Hall wrote about before. In his own words:

> Once constituted, a given system can provide (...) enormous incentives for a given society to reconstitute itself in conformity with the privileged institutional forms, and for its members to mould their identities and societal legitimating principles into collective identities and legitimating principles that are similarly privileged by these forms. Thus, in the age of nationalism, for example, societies organized along traditional, tribal or otherwise distinctly non-national forms, perhaps impelled by the norms, rules and principles of the national-sovereign state system not only to construct states (...) but also to construct nationalist movements and myths to legitimate their participation (see Conner 1992). (Hall 1999: 65–66)

This is exactly what happened with the Spanish monarchy, suddenly redefined as a nation following the French pattern. It is interesting to observe how the years previous to the Constitution of Cadiz (1812) saw the re-emergence of the foral tradition, with the Courts of the Kingdom of Aragon reunited after one century and a general revival of the old traditions of self-government in the various kingdoms that became by aggregation the Spanish Monarchy. In spite of the debate about on how to integrate this historical and institutional variety that informed the preliminary constitutional works, the final project of Constitution absolutely forgot this intent and established a clear centralized system, without any reference to that diversity of polities and identities. This centripetal trend has been constant throughout Iberian history. However, Bartolome Clavero highlighted how the Basque representatives were reluctant to swear that Constitution, which showed the frustration of that form of integration. The subsequent constitutional history to the present day only confirms this fact (Herrero de Miñón 2004: pp. 150–151).

In contrast with the French case, the Spanish monarchy had many problems to build a national state. For that reason, the Basques could maintain their particular institutions and political identity until the nineteenth century, when their Fueros [Basque old laws, expression of their self-government] were virtually dismantled. This process of centralization and abolition of the old Fueros was almost completed with the Spanish victory over the Carlist forces in 1876. As a result, the dismantling of the Basque self-government was closely related to a military defeat. However, not every Basque supported the Carlist army, so both Liberals and Carlists were equally punished by the Spanish central government, and this fact united the whole Basque people in one common cause in defense of their self-government. The Basques considered that it was an act of aggression of the central state to unilaterally abolish their self-government system based on a pact between the Basques and the Spanish Crown. Even those more loyal to Spain wanted their Fueros to be devolved. Ironically enough, the Spanish military victory over the Basque revolt created a political consensus—the so-called "Foral unanimity"—on the Basque self-government, which can be considered a starting point for a potent Basque prenationalist movement (De la Granja 1994: pp. 227–229).

Shortly afterwards, in part as a reaction against the long-standing Spanish centralism, the Basque Nationalist Party emerged around 1895 (Gibbons 1999: p. 275), in a context of accelerated industrialization (Rubiralta 1997: pp. 266–267). Hobsbawm emphasizes the link between the discontent because of the unilateral Spanish aggression to the Fueros and the emergence of the Basque nation. The new national movement was articulated remarkably fast. In fact, in 1894, less than 20 years after the end of the second Carlist War, Sabino Arana founded the Basque Nationalist Party. It is an exceptional case, as it got support from the masses in 1905 and made sweeping gains in the municipal elections of 1917–1919 (Hobsbawm 1992).

Finally, exactly as the Spanish state had reacted to the French nation-state, copying the new political template, the emergent Basque nationalism reacted to the Spanish pretension by claiming for its own symmetrical nation-state. This game of mirrors gives one interesting clue about how these models (templates) operate and are copied by others (Letamendia 2000). Nevertheless, this is not the whole story, as the Basque Nationalist Party initially proposed a confederate Basque state, something very different from the original French template. This shows how the template-copies dynamic must be completed with the centralist-federal one, something that has been detailed in this paper before.

The tension between the Spanish monarchy and the particular institutions of the Basque territories or those of the Crown of Aragon was ancient. The monarchical absolutism could discuss, and in fact did discuss, the practice of their self-government, but it did not question the principle of self-government itself of what was acknowledged as a distinct political reality. There are hundreds of proofs of this situation, for example, when José de Garmendia wrote in the proem to his *New Compilation of the Fueros of Guipuzcoa* (1696) that

> it was disposed in the kingdoms of Castile particular laws … in Aragon, Valencia and Catalonia [their peoples] are governed by their well-defended Fueros. In Navarre, even if it is incorporated into the Kingdom of Castile, the particular laws of that kingdom are maintained and conserved, being obeyed by all their inhabitants. With this same aim and motive the laws of the very noble and loyal province of Guipuzcoa were established (Herrero de Miñón 2004: 152-3).

In conclusion, this idea of the monarchy as the common government of a plurality of territories, coming from the Middle Ages, remained strong until the eighteenth century—one century later in the Basque territories— when the Hispanic Monarchy was abandoned in favor of the new Kingdom of Spain. The ideology behind the Nueva Planta decrees and later on the liberal constitutionalism combined to defeat the old way of plural Iberian integration and fostered the new centralization pattern. This old tension between centripetal and centrifugal trends remains in current Spain, as has been shown elsewhere (Lluch 1999: p. 17; Herrero de Miñón 2004: p. 157).

## Characterization of the Current Spanish State

Rokkan and Urwin (1983), after a systematic comparative work, constructed a theoretical framework with four categories to explain the main features of the diverse European states. Firstly, they identified the *unitary state*, characterized by overwhelming and unambiguous dominance of the center. This economic and political center, with its administrative structures and institutions, controls the entire territory. Secondly, we have the *union state*, which approximates the centralization and administrative standardization of the unitary state but with the strong difference of tolerating a degree of ethnic-cultural membership and preserving some degree of preexisting regional autonomy. *Mechanical federalism*, with its symmetrical accommodation imposed by the center, and *organic federalism*, stressing the voluntary association of several territories while retaining their specific institutional structures, complete Rokkan and Urwin's framework.

Following the categorization of Rokkan and Urwin, Spain is a Union State (Keating 2001a: p. 47). This implies that the Spanish political system can be seen as a tension between centralist and decentralist tendencies. Contrary to a common academic practice showing Spain as a (quasi) federal State, this system still has a number of important corrective mechanisms that privilege the powers of the center. Only one example will suffice for supporting this point: The central government has the right to stop every political or legal act coming from the Autonomous Communities—even those under exclusive autonomic powers—while awaiting final decision from the Constitutional Court (which may very well be delayed for months). In other words, the Spanish constitutional and political design starts with the presumption that power still remains in central hands, in spite of formal decentralization (which, in truth, is considerable in many aspects).

This means that Spain simultaneously shows features of several categories: firstly, some formal elements and main political culture are still very unitary/centralist; secondly, the main formal and emergent political culture elements are linked to the concept of union state; and thirdly, some residual, but very important, confederative elements (basically the constitutional distinction between nationalities and regions, the constitutional respect to the historical *Fueros*, and the quasi confederative economic and fiscal system of these territories).

This third confederative component needs to be developed a little more. It is important to note that the clear institutional and constitutional points we have just shown were introduced into the Spanish Constitution only after a bitter political struggle. It was not an obvious development of the state model (coming from a very strongly unitary model) but a hard conquest of the other nations, mainly the Basque and Catalan ones. They were not graceful concessions but an essential need, an absolute political minimum requirement for the new democracy to have an opportunity to start. Having said this, the distinction between formal/institutional and political culture domains is a key factor for the correct understanding of the Spanish political system. Backed with the legitimacy of the so-called "transition consensus", one of the main political myths of the nascent democracy, the successive Spanish governments have tried to erode the main decentralist factors. When it was impossible, they used the interpretation of the law in a very restrictive way (only slightly stopped by some important decisions of the constitutional court), and most important of all, the center has always tried to blur any qualitative differentiation between autonomous communities. This was one of the cornerstones of the entire model: the clear distinction between three nations—Catalonia, Basque Country/ Navarre,[5] and Galizia—and the rest of the State's regions.

In spite of this fact, the Spanish governments started to limit the scope of the emergent State of the Autonomies, trying to limit the impact of the autonomy of the three historical nations. In this way, after the frustrated coup d'état (1981), the two main Spanish parties at that time (center-conservative and socialist) used the coup to legitimate an agreement for the closing of the model, in the sense of limiting the expansive potential of the devolution process. The most important output of this state pact was the promulgation in 1982 of one constitutional-rank law [known by its acronym: LOAPA (*Ley Orgánica de Armonización del Proceso Autonómico*), pursuing the homogenization of the autonomic process]. The Basque government first and, later, several Basque and Catalan institutions appealed to the Constitutional Court, arguing it was an unconstitutional law because it strongly limited their autonomous powers and established the dilution of the political status of nationalities. The court ruled in favor of the claimants in 1983 but only declared some articles inactive, while most of the law and its spirit remained active.

In this context of direct confrontation between the center and the nationalities, the two main parties articulated one common discourse based on the idea that Spain had become one of the most decentralized political systems in the world, which was true only in part. Behind the devolved powers and their parallel amounts of money

---

[5] The division of the Basque Country into two communities was an important matter of debate. Finally it was decided, not without strong opposition of the Basque nationalist forces, to create two different Communities and to establish a clear constitutional disposition about the special bonds uniting both communities, even contemplating the possibility of reunification among them. It is important to remark that the Navarrese society was the only community who could not vote either on splitting from the Basque Country or on the political Statute of Autonomy, called *Amejoramiento del Fuero* (improvement of the old Fuero), so it was an elite-led initiative without any social debate or explicit support. As the territorial integrity of the Basque Country and Navarre is one of the main demands of nationalist forces, it is obvious that this move was very heavily politically charged and made with the approval (tacit or active) of the Spanish government, the main guarantee of the Autonomous Communities creation.

*conceded* from the central government to the autonomies, there was no real power in many cases because of the largely insufficient financial support. This fact configures a system in which autonomies are always dependent on the constant transfers of money, so the center can always control the policies of the Autonomous Communities (with the exception of the two *Foral* communities: the Basque Country and Navarre). For this reason, the central government still has the last say over the main strategic issues and core political powers and a privileged access to resources (via taxes).

Furthermore, this situation is supported by a still strong centralist and unitary political culture—very extended into the Spanish political elite and also into society after 40 long years of dictatorship—which widely legitimates this kind of politics. It is true that the ongoing political bargaining has changed this in some ways, but the tension between a formal quasi federal structure (strategically limited by serious corrective mechanisms) and a predominant unitary/centralist political culture still remains as the central feature of the Spanish political system. Perhaps it can be said that the previously unitary/centralist culture has increasingly become less central-istic, but the unitary vision of the state is still a powerful metaphor, both for the political elite as much as for a wide part of the Spanish society. Centralism has increasingly limited its force after 30 years of autonomous development, but even today whatever may affect or challenge unity (in very broad terms, not only linked to the risk of secession, we are thinking of different academic approaches to history or geography, of the use of every official language by central institutions, etc.) still legitimates fierce central counterattacks and exacerbates old, deep imperial-rooted ideas on unity and a strong Spanish nationalist concept.

Linked to the expansive devolution trend led by the three historical nations, it is interesting to observe how the "template" of those nationalities has been copied by most of the other Spanish regions in seeking more powers. In fact, even if their leaders and public opinions strongly make criticisms against the demands of Basque and Catalonian nations, once these have got them, many regions fiercely ask for the same. This situation has fostered an "emulation process", followed by a number of regions. This is a result of the use made by the new regional elites of the principle of equality invoked by the center. What's more, some of these regions have "activated" social and historical "latent" factors that have helped them become "real" political entities—less than nations but much more than mere political inventions. Some clear examples of this are Andalusia, Valencia, Aragon, or the Canary Islands. The social activation of their respective past as kingdoms, principalities, or colonies and the strong promotion of these identities have been a very successful tool for obtaining new powers. As a result of the importance of this mechanism, we have witnessed the emergence of several regional/nationalist parties, sometimes with great electoral success (Partido Andalucista, Chunta Aragonesista, Coalición Canaria, etc.), or of regional branches of Spanish statewide parties with strong regional consciousness and demands (for example, both Social-ist and Popular parties in Valencia).

This "emulation factor" fits with the new institutional theory findings over the autonomous functioning of institutions created by a political power, which may very well go far beyond any previous intended design (March and Olsen 1984). The main output of this emulation effect is the introduction of one expansive or centrifugal factor in the Spanish political system.

Both main parties (socialist and conservative) have made several attempts to reach an agreement between them in order to avoid this competitive and mutual-reinforcing trend towards (quantitative) decentralization, but with only limited success. They have been much more successful in according and implementing a common strategy to stop, or at least limit, the far more challenging nationalist (qualitative/recognition) demands.

There is a strong incentive between the two main parties taking turns in the central government and these regional interests to support a common strategy that widens the number and weight of the powers devolved while limiting the symbolic and recognition issues that might lead to proconfederative reaccommodation. To develop this informal arrangement, statewide parties act as the political interface between regional and central leaders and interests. The main difference among the three main statewide parties is the primacy of one or another type of the Rokkan/Urwin model:

a) The Conservative party is more unitary in its structure, expressing an internal coherence with its idea of a model of state.
b) The Socialist party has—mainly, but not always, because their discourse has oscillated with time—another idea of union, reflecting its internal tensions between more unitary factions (partly due to genuine Spanish national feelings and partly due to their interest in strong central redistributive powers towards less developed regions) and devolution-seeker factions (basically situated in the three nations' territories and the regions with stronger identities).
c) Finally, the ex-Communist/New Left party expresses in its discourse its own internal tensions and structure too. Formally composing a federation (almost a confederative organization, as happens with its Basque branch, which is a sovereign organization freely associated to the coalition), it demands a federal state. This is the compromise between three positions: firstly, a very unitary discourse (from the old communist structure), which was the official one until a few years ago but now losing weight because of the poor electoral success; secondly, a federal discourse from new left-wing sectors more open to formalizing the real social structure of Spain; and finally, a more confederative discourse, sensitive to national realities and demands, trying to recognize the plurinationality (Keating 2001b; Requejo and Caminal 2011) of the state while defending a federal arrangement based on the freely expressed will of every nation (supported mainly by the Basque and Catalan organizations).

Outside this Spanish-wide party system, there are several nationalist parties that challenge the idea of one Spanish "national" political system or unitary Spanish "nation". These actors are widely socially backed in two national societies: Basque Country and Catalonia, where there are both Basque and Catalan national party systems with their own agenda, political calendar (with their own electoral rhythms), and cleavages (national Basque or Catalan vs. Spanish, superimposed to the traditional left vs. right axis). This obvious social reality strongly demands its full recognition and that the Spanish State finally accepts the implications of the genuine national plurality that constitutes it.

All these facts show how Spanish polity is the result of a deep, long-standing tension over the unity-diversity issue. This explains the lack of coherence of the system, its trend towards asymmetry, as well as the delicate and fragile equilibrium of every arrangement, which is always, by definition, instable. This fits perfectly well with the great dynamism of the Spanish political system (with dynamism being the flip side of instability).

## The Basque Galaxy

When one looks at a current political map, Spain and France, each one highlighted in a different color, obviously appear to be two different societies. Maps have been very powerful tools in spreading a kind of "banal nationalism" (Billig 1999). If we turn to a geographical map, this separation becomes a question of pure common sense, since the Pyrenees—a mountain range of respectable height and breadth—appear once again to form a genuine natural frontier. However, a satellite photograph of the area reveals that the communicating valleys between the two sides of the frontier cross the range, uniting the north with the south in a natural way. This photographic evidence is supported by evidence that is much more solid: the existence of some cultures that spread out transversely. Two have survived until the present day: the Basque and Catalonian.

Basque culture, which has a transverse, cross-border character, emerged in the mountains of Navarre thousands of years ago and today still spreads out over seven territories, three to the north (Lapurdi, Behe Nafarroa, Zuberoa or Labourd, Basse Navarre, Soule), within the region of Aquitaine, and four to the south (Araba, Bizkaia, and Gipuzkoa, grouped in the Autonomous Community of the Basque Country, and Nafarroa/Navarre, which forms a separate Autonomous Community).

Historically, these territories have had clear and continuous links, as well as conflicts among themselves, configuring a very complex ensemble of both centripetal and centrifugal trends. It is precisely this whole range of ties and organizational patterns what will deserve more attention.

## *The Autonomous Community of the Basque Country*

At the end of the nineteenth century, the Spanish central government was eventually able to abolish the traditional relationship between the Basque territories and the Spanish polity. This brought about bad times for the Basques, who went through different dictatorships and policies of repression. With the end of Franco's dictatorship and the beginning of democratic times, the Basques got a certain degree of recognition and an important amount of devolved powers. That said, the current Basque Statute cannot be understood without relating it to Basque institutional history, that is to say, that "the Statute is the normative culmination of a historical process that begins in 1876; it attempts through a legal instrument to recover political identity, self-government and a particular right of integration in the state" (Caño 1997: p. 97). It can be said that the idea of the *Fueros*, fiercely defended by Basque nationalism until their introduction into the Spanish Constitution with the expression "*foral* rights", tries to guarantee the historical-national identity of the Basque people (Lucas Verdú 1986: p. 275).

This is the context for interpreting the present-day Basque political institutionalization, which starts in 1978, when the Spanish Constitution was approved following a complicated period of transition. The political model established is that of a state of autonomous communities, whose most outstanding characteristic is their openness or lack of definition (Torres Muro 1999: p. 17) since the Constitution barely says anything about which entities will accede to autonomy or what powers each community will have. This gives great relevance to the statutes of autonomy since they were to develop and specify the general principles.

On December 29th 1978, the autonomy statute project approved by the Basque deputies in Gernika, the symbolic town of Basque self-government, was sent to the Spanish parliament for discussion in a mixed commission of both parliaments. Negotiation took place basically outside the commission, between the Spanish president and the Basque president, which facilitated agreement facing the growing opposition of the more nationalist Spanish right-wing (*Vid.* for a more general view of the creation of Basque autonomy: Tamayo Salaberria 1994; his extensive and systematic bibliography on these key years of the Basque political institutionalization is also outstanding).

In 1979, the Spanish parliament approved the Basque Statute, and it was subsequently submitted to a referendum in the Basque Country, where it achieved broad support. Basically, the Statute creates a Basque political system with a parliament elected by the people and a central government for the three provinces. This is an essentially confederate system within which the Basque government has broad powers (education, health, police, etc.) but with the control of finances in the hands of the provincial political authorities, which gather taxes and then send a part to the Basque government and another part to the central state (the quantity agreed upon as payment for the share of common state services corresponding to the Basque Country).

It is, therefore, important to emphasize the agreed and consensual essence of the Basque Statute (Corcuera 1991: p. 146) based on agreement between the Basque society, led by the nationalist parties—above all, by the hegemonic *Partido Nacionalista Vasco* (Basque Nationalist party—PNV)—and the central state, led by the party that headed the government at the time, the *Unión de Centro Democrá tico* (Union of the Democratic Centre—UCD). This agreement-based nature is directly inspired by the Basque *foral* tradition, which, in a certain way, the democratic Constitution wished to recover. The basic pillar on which this nature was built was the Economic Agreement (*Concierto Económico*), an institution that replaced the *Fueros* following their abolition and guaranteed that the Basque institutions could fix and collect taxes and hand over a quantity previously agreed upon to the state (Azaola 1982). Thus, in spite of the state formally retaining its power to delimit the system of financing, the Basque Economic Agreement has been unanimously recognized by public opinion, the political class, and constitutional doctrine as an agreement between the Basque Country and the central state (Corcuera 1991: pp. 154–155). It is worth noting the specific importance held by this subject in the Basque Country—where it is a symbol of self-government (Uriarte 1999)—and the requirements of the autonomous agreement that is at the basis of the constitutional system. For this reason, any attack on this particular model of financing, which is practically equivalent to fiscal sovereignty, has been perceived as a threat to the true essence of the inclusion of the Basque Country in the state.

This mix of unitary defence of some common issues while remaining distinct political territories is not new at all. It is interesting to observe how the Basque territories of Bizkaia, Gipuzkoa, and Araba, "while firmly within the Castilian political orbit prior to the union of the crowns of Castilla and Aragon, made common cause in a largely successful defence of their fueros" (Douglas 2000: p. 69).

Following this spirit, the current Basque political system is a mix of some unitary elements (political orientation, symbols, representation of the community), some federal ones (most of them), and an important amount of confederate powers (fiscal, taxes).

## Navarre: A Kingdom Within a Kingdom

The question of Navarre is an especially virulent issue. For some, it is an integral part, in fact the historical core, of the Basque people. For others, it was a kingdom that was incorporated into the Castilian orbit and became a part of modern Spain. Spanish and Basque nationalisms have battled fiercely throughout history. In the same way, the union or political separation of the four Basque territories was the object of great political debate during the transition from Francoism to democracy. Finally, the Spanish central government opted to separate these territories into two different communities: the Basque Autonomous Community, formed by Alava, Bizkaia, and Gipuzkoa, and the *Foral* Community of Navarra. However, facing the constant demands of Basque nationalism and the close and evident links uniting these territories (from culture and language to history and types of law and institutions), a regulation was introduced in the Spanish Constitution envisaging their eventual union in the future. This question has given rise to numerous works denouncing their artificial separation and demanding union (Lasagabaster and Lazcano 1999; Sorauren 1998; Estornés Lasa 1981), as well as defending their *de facto* separation (Alli 1999; Landa El Busto 1999; Mina 1981). The attempt to consolidate this separation, in frontal opposition to the Basque nationalist theses, has found ideological expression through the articulation of a Navarrese regionalism allied to the Spanish nationalism of the state center (García-Sanz et al. 2002).

What is more interesting for us in this paper is the way Navarre was de facto annexed by Castile. In the fifteenth century, Aragon, Navarre, and Castile were European powers. When Fernando, prince of Aragon, and Isabel, princess of Castile, married, they created the political core of future Spain. Castile finished the *Reconquista*, reaching Granada exactly at the same time that three Castilian ships discovered America and started the Empire. The Iberian Peninsula was unified under Castilian rule, except for Portugal and Navarre, which remained free. Immediately after the death of Isabel, Fernando invaded Navarre with Castilian troops. He tried to incorporate Navarre into Aragon, but the Castilian Courts prevented it. Even though both Castile and Aragon were ruled by the same king, they remained different kingdoms, with their privative laws and institutions. So, Navarre was annexed by Castile—the real conqueror—but even the Law of War was not enough to finish with the law and institutions of the Kingdom of Navarre. For this reason, Navarre, even after its setbacks in the early sixteenth century, remained *a kingdom within a kingdom* (Bard 1982; Payne 1971) until it suffered a series of defeats (with consequent erosion of autonomy) during the Carlist Wars of the nineteenth century.

Present-day Navarre is a very special political community. Firstly, it maintains its historical continuity with the past in several important ways. On the one hand, the current statute of autonomy, named *Amejoramiento del Fuero* (Improved Fuero), clearly states its link with the old laws of the Kingdom of Navarre. On the other hand, this Fuero was not passed by the Navarrese people because, supposedly, it was nothing new but the simple technical adaptation to the new Spanish constitutional framework. So, in a very real sense, Navarre remains a kingdom within a kingdom. Secondly, the Navarrese people could not decide whether they wanted to constitute their autonomous community—as they finally did—or to join their Basque brothers to configure a common community. The decision was taken by the Spanish elites with the support of some Navarrese ones, in spite of great movements towards the reunification and the constitutional clause permitting to do this in the future. Thirdly, because of its foral feature, Navarre (like the Basque Country) has almost a total control over their taxes and fiscal capacity, which is the most important confederate element of the Spanish state.

## The French-Basque Country

In general, and due to economic backwardness and the absence of a broad working class, the French-Basque political system is dominated by the right and strongly conditioned by the political dynamic of the French State. Institutionally, the three little territories belonging to the French-Basque Country (Lapurdi/Labourd, Nafarroa Behera/Basse Navarre, and Zuberoa/Soule) are blurred within a huge

French Department and lack common political institutions or even a university of their own. They are only united in formal ways through the Chamber of Commerce, located in Bayonne.

In terms of identity, only a small sector of those holding a sense of Basque identity is linked to nationalism. However, during the 1990s, that small sector, very influential because of its connection with the cultural world, was able to articulate a broad movement of social support in favor of creating a Basque Department that would make regional development possible (Ahedo 2003). The advance of this thesis has made it possible to increase the electoral base of nationalism to almost 10 %.

One result of this increasing awareness, more pragmatic than ideological, has been an intensification of the contacts and collaboration with the Basque Country in Spain. A fruit of this increasing collaboration has been the emergence of new common projects of Cross-Border Cooperation like the project of Euro-Region, and some debates about the opportunity of seeking political autonomy like that of their brothers in the south. It is obvious that the institutional model of the Spanish Basque Country has become an inspiring "template" at hand to be studied.

# The European Polity

The study of the European integration process has been an increasingly difficult issue, at the same time, as the process itself was becoming more dense, sophisticated, and complex. On the one hand, classical theories in International Relations were challenged by the introduction of the Multi-Level Governance approach into EU studies, which "signifies the end of separate treatment of European and national politics" (Lenschow 2005: p. 56).

On the other hand, classical theories of Political Science had many problems to characterize the emergent European polity, particularly after the creation of the European Union in 1993. At first glance, the European Union is confederate, as well as federal (Moravcsik 2001, 2002; Elazar 2001), with the "community method" being "the dominant feature of EU governance" (Kohler-Koch and Rittberger 2006: p. 33).

However, if the focus is put on monetary issues, analysts observe that the structure of the European Central bank is "centralized and hierarchical", like no other area in the integration process (Kohler-Koch and Rittberger 2006: p. 33), and more independent of political control than any known national example (Herdegen 1998).

From a different point of view, "at least in normal times when no intergovernmental conferences take place, the EU very much looks like a state, and like a rather *unitary* one: it adopts public policies, different institutions execute these policies, legislate, and adjudicate, interest groups and political parties compete for influence and power, and so on" (Jachtenfuchs 2006: p. 162, emphasis added). This unitary trend is highlighted when comparing the evolution of competences in the EU and the US: "Both polities started with a low level of policy centralization. However, policy centralization occurred remarkably quickly in the EU compared to the US, and in some areas faster than others (Pollack 1995, 2000)" (Hix 2006: p. 143).

In conclusion, the European polity has unitary, federal, and confederate elements. It is the tension between them that gives its genuine atmosphere of uniqueness to the whole.

# Fractal Federalism

Fractals are structures that along different scales or levels repeat their patterns of organization, even if sometimes this same common trans-scalar pattern may not be easily observable. The usual example of fractal structure is the clouds in the sky. At first glance, they seem to be anarchical aggregations of water evaporations, but an in-depth analysis shows their extremely consistent and coherent replication of the same molecular organization pattern at every level of organization (scale).

By analogy, this paper proposes the notion of fractal federalism, which would be a mode of organization of different political levels, repeated in each one, structuring the whole. These and similar ideas are usual in the literature on European integration. It is generally accepted that the European integration is part of a wider process of state transformation and a unique process of polity building (Keating 2004). Several theories have tried to capture this fact, with the New Governance approach particularly influential. However, while these concepts try to express the uniqueness of the European integration process, the notion of fractal federalism shows that this kind of intertwining is a usual way of organizing complex societies. Therefore, what must be explained is how the opposite of this, namely the historical experience of the modern European state achieving immense success in imposing the notion of absolute and exclusive sovereignty, came about.

If this is true, one of the most interesting theoretical findings offered by European integration is its questioning of this absolute and exclusive sovereignty of the state, at the same time that it establishes a different legal order and promotes legal and constitutional pluralism (MacCormick 1999; Walker 1996, 1998). In this way, constitutionalism has been increasingly detached from its historical "container" (Ferrero and Filibi 2004), coming back paradoxically to premodern times, while the expression of "metaconstitutionalism" has been coined to name the domain where diverse constitutional visions meet each other and are negotiated (Walker 2002).

Furthermore, the European polity raises serious doubts about the old adage that democracy can only work in nationally homogeneous territories with a single identity. Interestingly enough, if Europe must work with several demoi or with none at all, this same argument can be properly applied to its member states (Keating 2004).

Today no one argues with the fact that for democracy to exist, it is essential to incorporate political levels with representatives elected by the people. There must be formal and informal ties linking the various levels in order to manage increasingly complex issues and improve public services and policies. Democracy is in fact trans-scalar, like it or not. So is political organization, at least, in certain cases. This is what has been shown in the case of the Basque Country, from the different historical territories to the European polity, through the Basque Autonomous Community and the Spanish state. Interestingly enough, it also happens if the starting point is Navarre—still a kingdom within a kingdom. It is the intertwining of unitary, federal, and confederate elements that unites the ensemble, the fractal principle configuring the trans-scalar reality of Europe.

As can be seen in this paper, this complexity of scales and political levels offers some common organizational patterns across them. Leaving aside the battle for the names, these ties can be considered federal, at least in spirit, if not all of them formally expressed. However, within federalism, which is always a process, there are tensions between unitary, federal, and confederate principles. It is precisely this mix of elements that would be the fractal pattern organizing European society, ranging from the local (*foral*) to the European scale, including the nation and state.

# References

Agnew, John (1998). *Geopolitics. Re-visioning world politics*. London and New York, Routledge.

Ahedo, Igor (2003). *Entre la frustración y la esperanza: políticas de desarrollo e institucionalización en Iparralde*. Oñati, IVAP.

Alli Aranguren, Juan-Cruz (1999). *Navarra, comunidad política diferenciada*. Burlada, Sahats.

Azaola, José Miguel de (1982), "Génesis del régimen de concierto económico para Álava, Guipúzcoa y Vizcaya", in: *First International Basque Conference in North America*. Fresno and Bilbao, California State University and la Gran Enciclopedia Vasca; pp. 45–82.

Bard, Rachel (1982). *Navarra. The durable kingdom*. Reno, University of Nevada Press.

Caño Moreno, Javier (1997). *Teoría institucional del Estatuto Vasco: concepción institucional e interpretación normativo-institucional del Estatuto de Autonomía del País Vasco*. Bilbao, Universidad de Deusto.

Corcuera, Javier (1991). *Política y derecho: la construcción de la autonomía vasca*. Madrid, Centro de Estudios Constitucionales.

Darby, Phillip (2004), "Pursuing the political: A post-colonial rethinking of Relations International", *Millenium*, Vol. 33, No. 1; pp. 1–32.

De la Granja, José Luis (1994), "Los orígenes del nacionalismo vasco", in: AA.VV. *Illes. Jornades de debat orígens i formació dels nacionalismes a Espanya*. Reus, Centre de Lectura de Reus.

Doucet, Marc G. (2005), "The democratic paradox and cosmopolitan democracy", *Millenium*, Vol. 34, No. 1; pp. 137–155.

Douglas, William (2000), "A Western perspective on an eastern interpretation of where north meets south: Pyrenean borderland cultures", in: Wilson, Thomas M. and Donnan, Hastings (eds.). *Border identities. Nation and state at international frontiers*. Cambridge, Cambridge University Press; pp. 62–95.

Duclos, Pierre (1968). *L'Être fédéraliste*. París, Librairie Générale de Droit et de Jurisprudence.

Duverger, Maurice (1956). *Droit constitutionnel et institutions politiques*. Paris, PUF.

Edkins, Jenny (1999). *Poststructuralism and International Relations: Bringing the political back in*. Boulder, Lynne Rienner.

Elazar, Daniel (2001), "The US and the EU: Models for their epochs", in: Nicolaïdis, K. and Howse, R. (eds.). *The federal vision: Legitimacy and levels of governance in the US and the EU*. Oxford, Oxford University Press; pp. 31–53.

Estornés Lasa, José (1981). *Navarra, lo que "NO" nos enseñaron*. Pamplona, Universidad Popular Leire.

Ferrero, Mariano and Filibi, Igor (2004), "Globalización, espacio, ciudadanía. Notas preliminares para una filosofía política de la sociedad mundial", *Revista de Investigaciones Políticas y Sociológicas*, Vol. 3, n° 1; pp. 7–24.

Filibi Igor (2007). *La Unión política como marco de resolución de los conflictos etnonacionales europeos: un enfoque comparado*. Bilbao, Servicio Editorial de la Universidad del País Vasco.

Flora, Peter (ed.) (1999). *State formation, nation-building and mass politics in Europe. The theory of Stein Rokkan*. Oxford, Oxford University Press.

García-Sanz Marcotegui, Angel; Iriarte López, Iñaki y Mikelarena Peña, Fernando (2002). *Historia del navarrismo (1841–1936)*. Pamplona, Universidad Pública de Navarra.

Gibbons, John (1999), "Spain. A semi-federal State?", en: MacIVER, Don (Ed.). *The politics of multinational States*. Houndmills…, Macmillan.

Hall, Rodney Bruce (1999), "Collective identity and epochal change in the international system", in: Yamamoto, Y. (ed.). *Globalism, regionalism and nationalism. Asia in search of its role in the twenty-first century*. Oxford, Blackwell; pp. 45–69.

Herdegen, M.J. (1998), "Price stability and budgetary restraints in the Economic and Monetary Union: The law as guardian of economic wisdom", *Common Market Law Review*, Vol. 35; pp. 9–32.

Herrero de Miñón, Miguel (2004), "El sentido histórico de la monarquía como forma de Estado (cómo sacar provecho del artículo 1.3 de la Constitución)", *Cuadernos de Historia del Derecho*, vol. extraordinario; pp. 147–161.

Hix, Simon (2006), "The European Union as a polity (I)", in: Jorgensen, K., Pollack, M.A., and Rosamond, B. (eds). *Handbook of European Union politics*. London, Sage; pp. 141–58.

Hobsbawm, Eric (1992). *Nations and nationalism since 1780. Programme, myth, reality*. Cambridge, Cambridge University Press.

Jachtenfuchs, (2006), "The European Union as a polity (II)", in: Jorgensen, K., Pollack, M.A., and Rosamond, B. (eds). *Handbook of European Union politics*. London, Sage; pp. 159–73.

Jeffery, Charlie (2008), "The challenge of territorial politics", *Policy & Politics*, Vol. 36, No 4; pp. 545–557.

Keating, Michael (2001a), "So many nations, so few states: territory and nationalism in the global era", in: Gagnon, Alain-G. and Tully, James (eds.). *Multinational democracies*. Cambridge University Press; pp. 39–64.

Keating, Michael (2001b). *Plurinational democracy. Stateless nations in a Post-Sovereignty Era*. Oxford, Oxford University Press.

Keating, Michael (2004), "European integration and the nationalities question", *Politics of Society*, Vol. 32, No. 2.

Kohler-Koch, Beate and Rittberger, Berthold (2006), "Review article: The 'governance turn' in EU studies", *Journal of Common Market Studies*, Vol. 44, Annual Review; pp. 27–49.

Landa El Busto, Luis (1999). *Historia de Navarra. Una identidad forjada a través de los siglos*. Pamplona, Gobierno de Navarra, Departamento de Educación y Cultura.

Lasagabaster Herrarte, Iñaki y Lazcano Brotóns, Iñigo (1999), "Derecho, política e historia en la autodeterminación de Euskal Herria", in: Gómez Uranga, Mikel *et al*. (Coords.). *Propuestas para un nuevo escenario. Democracia, cultura y cohesión social en Euskal Herria*. Bilbao, Fundación Manu Robles-Arangiz.

Lefebvre, Henri (1974). *La production de l'espace*. Paris, éditions anthropos.

Lenschow, A (2005), "Europeanization of public policy", in: Richardson, J. (ed.). *European Union. Power and policy-making*. London, Routledge.

Letamendia, Francisco (2000). *Game of mirrors: Centre-periphery national conflicts*. Ashgate.

Lluch, Ernest (1999), "Una visión de Aragón desde el exterior", *El Ebro. Revista aragonesista de pensamiento*, I-1; pp. 17–25.

Lucas Verdú, Pablo (1986), "Historicismo y positivismo ante la conceptualización de los derechos históricos vascos", in: *Jornadas de estudios sobre la actualización de los derechos históricos vascos*. Bilbao, Servicio Editorial de la Universidad del País Vasco; pp. 253–86.

MacCormick, Neil (2000). *Questioning sovereignty. Law, state and nation in the European commonwealth*. Oxford, Oxford University Press.

March, James G. and Olsen, Johan P. (1984), "The new institutionalism: Organizational factors in political life", *American Political Science Review*, Vol. 78, No. 3; pp. 734–749.

Mina Apat, María Cruz (1981). *Fueros y revolución liberal en Navarra*. Madrid, Alianza Editorial.

Moravcsik, Andrew (2001), "Federalism in the European Union: Rhetoric and reality", in: Nicolaïdis, K. and Howse, R. (eds.). *The federal vision: Legitimacy and levels of governance in the US and the EU*. Oxford, Oxford University Press; pp. 161–90.

Moravcsik, Andrew (2002), "In defence of the 'democratic deficit': Reassessing legitimacy in the European Union", *Journal of Common Market Studies*, Vol. 40, No. 4; pp. 603–24.

Payne, Stanley (1991), "Nationalism, regionalism and micronationalism", *Journal of Contemporary History*, Vol. 26, No. ¾; pp. 479–491.

Requejo, Ferrán and Caminal, Miguel (2011). *Federalism, plurinationality and democratic constitutionalism: Theory and cases*. London, Routledge.

Rokkan, Stein and Urwin, Derek (1983). *Economy, territory, identity: Politics of West European peripheries*. London, Sage.

Rubiralta, Fermí (1997). *El nuevo nacionalismo radical. Los casos gallego, catalán y vasco (1959–1973)*. Donostia, Tercera Prensa-Hirugarren Prentsa.

Sassen, Saskia (2006). *Territory, authority, rights: From medieval to global assemblages*. Princeton, Princeton University Press.

Sorauren, Mikel (1998). *Historia de Navarra, el Estado vasco*. Pamplona, Pamiela.

Tamayo Salaberria, Virginia (1994). *La autonomía vasca contemporánea. Foralidad y estatutismo 1975–1979*. Vitoria-Gasteiz, Instituto Vasco de Administraciones Públicas.

Torres Muro, Ignacio (1999). *Los Estatutos de autonomía*. Madrid, Centro de Estudios Políticos y Constitucionales.

Uriarte, Pedro Luis (1999), "El Concierto Económico es el elemento más consustancial de desarrollo de la autonomía vasca", *Euskonews & Media*, n° 51; pp. 7–16.

Walker, Neil (1996), "European constitutionalism and European integration", *Public Law*, summer; pp. 266–290.

Walker, Neil (1998), "Sovereignty and differentiated integration in the European Union", *European Law Journal*, Vol. 4, No. 4; pp. 355–388.

Walker, Neil (2002), "The idea of constitutional pluralism", *Modern Law Review*, Vol. 65, No. 3.

White, George W. (2000). *Nationalism and Territory. Constructing group identity in Southeastern Europe*. Lanham (Maryland, USA). . ., Rowman & Littlefield Publishers.

Zizek, Slavoj (2001), "Un alegato izquierdista contra el eurocentrismo", in: Mignolo, W. (comp.). *Capitalismo y geopolítica del conocimiento: el eurocentrismo y la filosofía de la liberación en el debate intelectual contemporáneo*. Buenos Aires, Signo; pp. 173–200.

# Diversity and 'Frontier Effect': The So-Called Shielding of the Basque Economic Agreement

Amelia Pascual Medrano

## The First Additional Provision of the Spanish Constitution as an Element of Regional Differentiating

The First Additional Provision (hereinafter referred to as AP) of the 1978 Spanish Constitution (hereinafter referred to as SC) stated that 'the Constitution protects and respects the historic rights of the territories with "fueros (local laws)"', adding, nevertheless, that 'The general updating of the "fueros" system shall be carried out, when appropriate, within the framework of the Constitution and of the Statutes of Autonomy".

This provision created the basis for the future definition of a complex factor of territorial differentiation. The Constitution employs the term 'historic rights' of the 'territories having "fueros" or local laws', which in fact created a special environment, even if not clearly specified, for certain territories (Navarre and the Basque provinces of Araba, Gipuzkoa, and Bizkaia) that had preserved certain local institutions or organizational schemes, the so-called fueros (local laws), over various unifying processes in previous centuries. In order to understand their present meaning, it is very significant to note, though, that the 'fueros' (local laws) have relied on the underlying assumption of a pact with the Crown since their creation in the fifteenth and sixteenth centuries and have maintained this assumption until the present time.

The constitutional acknowledgement of these misleading and vague 'historic rights' generated some intense political and juridical discussions in Spain. As a reflection of this, we should not forget the appropriate and yet classical quote from Manuel García Pelayo, later to become first President of the 'Tribunal Constitucional' (Spanish Constitutional Court, hereinafter referred to as CC), who

A. Pascual Medrano (✉)
Dpto. Derecho, Universidad de La Rioja, Edificio Quintiliano, C/ La cigüeña 60, Logroño 26004, Spain
e-mail: amelia.pascual@unirioja.es

A. López-Basaguren and L. Escajedo San Epifanio (eds.), *The Ways of Federalism in Western Countries and the Horizons of Territorial Autonomy in Spain*, Vol. 2, DOI 10.1007/978-3-642-27717-7_55, © Springer-Verlag Berlin Heidelberg 2013

in 1991 stated that 'This basic ambiguity is the first of many more still to come, it enables other theoretical and practical interpretations having potentially serious consequences, and above all, it provides a set of juridical reasons that can be employed, be it for far-reaching political strategies, be it to attain more modest ends –for example, to support the set up of a privileged environment in taxes or in some other field- but just as disturbing for the political system and the constitutional order presently in force' (García Pelayo 1991).

As a matter of fact, to include this peculiarity in our autonomous State represented, right from the start, some kind of a 'Pandora's Box' that, although meant to solve certain issues, could very well become the source of different and very harmful problems for a balanced development of the new Spanish regional organisation. Thus, it was easy to predict that it would be difficult for the rest of Autonomous Communities (hereinafter referred to as ACs) to accept a system with exceptions or peculiarities, specially when considering that it was a system that these same ACs could not use and that would often be regarded as being a real privilege or an inequality that no historic reasons could justify or make legal. Moreover, it is difficult to reject that the juridical logics behind a rational Constitution with legal application does not fit well with historic legal arguments, making possible the argument (Tajadura 2007) that the first AP is an example of an 'unconstitutional constitutional norm' (Bachof) as it challenges the principle of democracy.

However, it would not be fair to forget that, on the other hand, the social and political context did strongly advise for the acknowledgement of the local law element in the regional organization that the SC of 1978 had to design, if only to help to solve the issue of the integration of the Basque Country. Furthermore, certain writers (Herrero de Miñón) even regard the open interpretation of the first AP—in our view, incompatible with the present constitutional framework—as a solution for the so-called Basque problem.

At any rate, however, the bottom line is that, although including the first AP in the 1978 constitutional text did not make the main Basque political party (the Basque Nationalist Party) support it, this first AP undoubtedly was an element that contributed to the integration issue referred to above. Certainly, the problem seems to have really been in the particular development and practical workings of the contents of the first AP rather than in its constitutional acknowledgment, as the first AP also seems to warn against when it states that it has to be done strictly within constitutional limits (it is very significant that, when considering the Autonomous Community of Navarre, the local law regime has not generated any serious trouble: Rather the opposite to the Basque case, in Navarre, the local law regime has been an essential element of stability and integration all along).

The main objective of the present work is not to make a general analysis of this constitutional provision though, as it has already been made by Spanish analysts from several different points of view (See Castells 2007; Corcuera and García 2002; Herrero and Lluch 2000).

The objective of our work is not as far-reaching and is essentially aimed at the fact that, although from a juridical and political standpoint, we accept the differences established by the first AP, we believe that the establishment of the appropriate guarantees and instruments to prevent, compensate, or at least react against eventual harm caused by these constitutional peculiarities on other ACs— particularly on neighbouring ACs because of the 'frontier effect'—is an absolutely necessary and prudent demand. We have to bear in mind that these other ACs do not stand and cannot stand on equal grounds with the two local law ACs in certain matters, so it has nothing to do with the inequalities implied by the regular practice of the autonomy by different regional entities.

Adopting then this point of view, an example of just the opposite has been the process of 'blindaje del concierto económico vasco', which, apart from being dubiously constitutional, has reinforced the widespread feeling of unfairness and of being harmed among all other ACs, originally provoked by the special tax system of the Basque Country that is a consequence of the first AP.

## The Meaning of 'Blindaje del concierto económico vasco'

On the basis of the already mentioned first AP, the Autonomous Community of the Basque Country enjoys a peculiar institutional and competence organisation. Therefore, in this community the standard institutional structure to be found in any other autonomous community is combined with the specific one created in each of the three Historic Territories (Araba, Gipuzkoa and Bizkaia). In this respect, the Statute of Autonomy of the Basque Country acknowledges in its article 25.1 that 'the Basque Parliament exercises legislative power [...], without prejudice to the jurisdiction of the Institutions to which article 37 refers', that is, the 'local law institutions of the historic territories' (the 'Juntas Generales' and Province Councils). Specifically, article 41.1 of the Basque Statute states that 'the tax relations between the State and the Basque Country shall be regulated by the traditional system of the Economic Agreement or Conventions', adding in paragraph 2 that this Economic Agreement will respect, among others, the following principle: 'a) The competent Institutions of the Historic Territories may maintain, establish and regulate, within their own territory, the tax system'

Therefore, the 'Juntas Generales' of these territories are the exclusively competent institutions—momentarily forgetting about the limits of this competence—to create and regulate taxes based upon the constitutional acknowledgment of the 'historic rights' affecting these territories. Thus, along all these years, the 'Juntas Generales' of Araba, Gipuzkoa, and Bizkaia, within the legal framework of the Economic Agreement with the Spanish State (presently, the Law 12/2002 of the 23rd of May, through which the Economic Agreement with the Autonomous Community of the Basque Country is passed) have been defining the essential elements in the taxes of the Basque Country through the passing of various local rules. We must not forget that this procedure does not apply to the rest of ACs (Navarre excluded) that are forced to respect the ample competence of the State in taxes and consequently enjoy a rather restricted margin for internal decision in these matters.

This being the present state of affairs, the so-called shielding of the Basque Economic Agreement refers to the passing of a State legislative reform that makes the possibility to appeal against local tax laws—curiously enough only these—of the Historic Territories of Araba, Gipuzkoa, and Bizkaia depend on the constitutional jurisdiction on an exclusive basis (Organic Law 1/2010 of the 19th of February), excluding the direct or indirect appeal to the contentious-administrative jurisdiction.

In other words, laws that are statutory in the Spanish legal system, even if they are special and that until the passing of the law mentioned above could be appealed before the contentious-administrative jurisdiction by either the ACs or private individuals, can no longer be appealed in this way, so that all control over them is left to the CC, something that restricts greatly its procedure standing and parameters of control.

Likewise, this legal reform has brought up an additional issue for the constitutional jurisdiction to settle, namely, the 'conflict to defend the autonomy of the Historic Territories of the Basque Country based on local laws', although its specific features are beyond the scope of the present work.

## The Likely Unconstitutionality of the So-Called Shielding

The reform made by the Organic Law 1/2010 immediately raised serious doubts as to its constitutionality by an important part of the Spanish doctrine, doubts that we share. Following the appeals submitted by the ACs of Castilla-León and La Rioja, it is the CC that should settle these issues once and for all.

To summarize very briefly:

– Firstly, the reform mentioned above implies, firstly, that the unconstitutionality appeal and the submission for unconstitutionality before the CC against legal rules that, up to presently, were considered to have a statutory nature becomes a valid procedure, even if our Constitution restricts this procedure to laws and rules with law status [arts. 161.1 a) or 163 of the SC].

We have to consider that the local Basque tax rules show clear specific features. These local rules deal with matters that are constitutionally restricted to laws but are nevertheless considered to be compliant with the SC in this case. The resulting contrast with the tax system in the Autonomous Community of Navarre stands out, when considering how similar both systems are and that the tax system in Navarre is created by ordinary laws. The Spanish legal doctrine has underlined that, although local, these institutions that make these tax rules certainly have a peculiar and dual nature that some writers even consider parliamentary. Furthermore and in connection with this last remark, it has often been a matter of debate whether these rules would have to be regarded as singular rules, or even as rules with an effective status of law (in this respect, see Castells 2007).

However, and aside from what has just been said, in our present constitutional framework, the local Basque rules are not laws, and neither are they rules with a status of law. Even admitting all kinds of peculiarities in them, they have a statutory nature, and because of this, they have been subject all along to the contentious-administrative jurisdiction. In this respect, it is key to bear in mind that even the Basque Law of Historic Territories of the 25th of November 1983, in its article 6.2, solved this controversy by explicitly and exclusively restricting to the Basque Parliament the faculty of making rules with a status of law.

Based on all the above, in our opinion, and since we are dealing with rules not having the status of law, the so-called shielding of the Basque tax rules is difficult to harmonise with the present constitutional text. This difficulty is not diminished by the legal terms employed in this reform, which try to prevent an eventual unconstitutionality appeal by devising an *ad hoc* procedure following which the CC becomes the incumbent institution before which the jurisdictional institutions should lodge all appeals prior to court proceedings in relation with the Basque tax rules. Subsequently, the reform applies Title II of the Law of Unconstitutionality Appeals and Submissions (note the wording of the new fifth AP of the Organic Law of the CC).

- Secondly, the exception made by the Organic Law 1/2010, excluding all possibilities to lodge an appeal against the Basque tax rules (and not the rest) before ordinary courts, can hardly make sense with article 106.1 of the SC, which states that 'the The Courts control the power to issue regulations and to ensure that the rule of law prevails in administrative action, as well as to ensure that the latter is subordinated to the ends which justify it'. Moreover, this is a basic principle of the rule of law that, among others, implies no exceptions to the compliance with the law of all administrative institutions like the Basque 'Juntas Generales' and tries to eradicate all administrative areas not subject to court control. It is also possible to argue the violation of article 38.3 of the Statute of Autonomy of the Basque Country (which is a parameter of constitutionality), which states that 'the acts and agreements and rules and regulations emanating from the executive and administrative bodies of the Basque Parliament shall be open to appeal before the Administrative Law Courts'.

- Thirdly, the so-called shielding has rightly been criticised from the point of view of the fundamental right to effective legal protection for all citizens as expressed in article 24 of the SC, given the evident restriction in the access to appeals for citizens and institutions eventually affected by Basque tax rules. Likewise, criticism has come from the point of view of the control over these rules: This reform limits all control to the control of constitutionality because the legality control, characteristic in statutory rules, is eliminated.

# The Deepening of the Territory Differentiation and the Frontier Effect

The complex juridical issues resulting from this reform can only be wholly grasped if we start by reckoning with the fact that the ongoing exercise of the competence in taxes by the historic territories has been provoking continual trouble with bordering ACs. This is what has been referred to as the 'frontier effect'.

Since the 1990s, the tax authority of the Basque Tax Administrations has been creating a long and complex judiciary and political conflict with the bordering ACs, and especially with the Autonomous Community of La Rioja (hereinafter referred to as ACR). In fact, the Statute of Autonomy of this community reckons with the eventual damage originated by its border situation and explicitly states in article 46 that in order to define the income of the Autonomous Community, it will have to be taken into account, among other criteria, 'the correction of the unbalance created in La Rioja by the effects of the common borders with other territories'. From this standpoint, the ACR has repeatedly been staking its claims to economic compensations from the State and occasionally obtaining them (years 2002 and 2003).

Now then, aside from what has just been said above, and along this same period, the ACs bordering the Basque Country, and particularly the ACR, have been lodging appeals before the national and European jurisdictions (and often enough crowned by success) against a great deal of tax rules set by the Basque 'Juntas Generales'. In this respect, suffice it to remember the so-called the Basque tax break in 1993–1994 (10-year exemption from the corporation tax for newly created companies), the 'tax minibreak' of 1996 (progressive reduction in the taxable income in the corporation tax), the tax incentives valid until 1999 (45 % deduction in investments exceeding 15 million euros), or the various reductions on the standard State tax band passed by the 'Juntas Generales' of Araba, Gipuzkoa, and Bizkaia, which have been the main issue of conflict at jurisdictional courts.

Consequently, apart from the legal doctrine debates on the subject, the recently set restrictions to the available possibilities of appeal against these rules, leaving control over them exclusively to the CC, have obviously been perceived by institutions and by the general public from bordering ACs as a way to circumvent the most effective legal procedure that they had to diminish or prevent the damage and negative effects that may originate in the special tax system in the Basque Country. These negative effects, although arguable in terms of degree, are perceived as undoubtedly harmful by the vast majority of people, and from the point of view of the referred ACs and particularly from that of the ACR, this process has been a source of intense strain and frustration apart from provoking unanimous criticism from institutions, political parties, and society in general.

On the whole, the so-called shielding has only increased the feeling of territorial unfairness and of being harmed by the tax system in the Basque Country. As precisely explained by Solozábal, 'the episode of the tax rules 'shielding' means a strengthening of the local law system grafted on the constitution, unnecessarily underlining its juridical special character' (Solozábal 2010).

Since the mere existence of certain special status or territorial systems can be arguable or, perhaps, simply because they do exist, it makes little sense to restrict or deprive the legal system of the guarantees or procedures available to right any eventual abuse.

Last but in no way least, it is truly difficult to convince the affected parties of the rationality or of the reasons behind a legal reform that is generally regarded as nothing more than the political price paid to the Basque Nationalist Party for its parliamentary support to the 2010 General Budgets.

## Some Conclusions

Based upon all the explanations above, we can draw the following significant conclusions:

– Firstly, there are several well-founded reasons to maintain that the reform introduced by Organic Law 1/2010 is not in compliance with the SC, as it has repeatedly been argued by an important part of the specialised doctrine, so that this reform should not pass the constitutionality analysis that the CC will eventually perform.
– Secondly, it clearly seems not to be a timely reform. This reform has been associated with the obvious need of the central Government to gain momentary support in parliament, and this is too far away from the theoretical ideal of producing the rational arguments to convince the majority of parliament about the necessity or the benefits of such reform to our legal system.
– Thirdly, even if this reform argues in favour of the significance and importance of the Basque 'fueros' system and would apparently seem to back those points of view that, for various reasons, support the development of this system, all available evidence points to the continual appeals against Basque tax rules by the bordering ACs, and specially by the ACR, as the most evident reason for this reform.
– Lastly, the overall result is that the so-called shielding, far from easing the strain implied by territorial differentiation or asymmetry, has unnecessarily made it rise considerably.

The complex legal arguments backing this reform and the logical suspicion caused by these special elements peculiar to certain territorial entities forming a federal or almost federal state would appear to demand a great deal of prudence from those developing them. If the state model is not to be put under strain, there is little choice but to compensate all eventual harm arising for other territories. Additionally, far from restraining control, common sense would advise to extend the control procedures and instruments to prevent any abuse or deviations. This is exactly the opposite to what has been done in Spain with the so-called shielding resulting from the Organic Law 1/1020.

# References

Castells Arteche, J.M. (2007). El hecho diferencial de vasconia. Evidencias e incertidumbres. Fundación para el Estudio del Derecho Histórico y Autonómico de Vasconia, San Sebastián, España, 208 pp.

Corcuera Atienza, J. and García Herrera, M.A. (2002). La constitucionalización de los Derechos Históricos. Centro de Estudios Políticos y Constitucionales, Madrid, España, 127 pp.

Criado Gómez, J.M. (dir.) (2011). El blindaje de las normas forales vascas. Gobierno de La Rioja-Iustel, Madrid, España, 270 pp.

García Pelayo, M. (1991). Obras completas. Centro de Estudios Constitucionales, Madrid, España, 1991, 3379 pp.

Herrero de Miñón, M. y Lluch, E. (dirs.) (2000). Derechos históricos y constitucionalismo útil. Fundación BBVA, Madrid, España, 331 pp.

Pascual Medrano, A. (2010). La Comunidad Autónoma de La Rioja y el llamado blindaje del Concierto Económico Vasco. Revista General de Derecho Constitucional 9: 1–7.

Solozábal Echavarría, J.J. (2010). El blindaje foral en su hora. Comentario a la Ley Orgánica 1/2010. Revista Española de Derecho Constitucional 90: 11–28.

Tajadura Tejada, J. (2007). La inconstitucionalidad de los derechos históricos. Diario La Ley 6747: 1–9.

# Decentralization, Regional Parties, and Multilevel Governance in Spain

Bonnie N. Field

## Introduction

Minority governments in parliamentary systems have not been depicted with much favor. In academic circles, as Strøm (1990, p. 738) stated, the conventional wisdom associates minority cabinets "with political malaise, irrationality and poor performance". In the Spanish political context, on which this essay focuses, Popular Party (PP) opposition leader Mariano Rajoy accused Socialist Party (PSOE) prime ministerial candidate José Luis Rodríguez Zapatero of offering a "weak and unstable government" in 2004 (Diario de Sesiones 2004). Zapatero, without a Socialist majority, made his case to be elected prime minister without forming a coalition government and without an explicit legislative agreement with any particular party. However, these depictions of minority government are incomplete. There is substantial variation across minority governments with regard to performance. This paper seeks to identify factors that may help explain this variation.

The existing literature on minority parliamentary government draws our attention to key institutional, party system, and multilevel state characteristics as factors that may affect minority government performance. Regarding institutions, theorists hypothesize that certain parliamentary and legislative procedures (such as government control of the parliamentary agenda, the strength of parliamentary committees, voting procedures), executive decree powers, and investiture and censure rules (Helland 2004; Strøm 1990, pp. 110–111; Tsebelis 2002, pp. 98–99) can affect performance by strengthening or weakening the executive.

The performance of minority governments may also be facilitated or hindered by the governing party's spatial placement in the party system (Tsebelis 2002, pp. 97–98) and parliamentary arithmetic. A minority governing party that occupies the central position in the policy space, either the median position in a one-dimensional

B.N. Field (✉)
Department of Global Studies, Bentley University, 175 Forest Street, Waltham, MA 02452, USA
e-mail: bfield@bentley.edu

A. López-Basaguren and L. Escajedo San Epifanio (eds.), *The Ways of Federalism in Western Countries and the Horizons of Territorial Autonomy in Spain*, Vol. 2, DOI 10.1007/978-3-642-27717-7_56, © Springer-Verlag Berlin Heidelberg 2013

space or the core position (Schofield 1993) in a two-dimensional space, may still be able to govern effectively as no majority connected coalition can defeat it. The literature has drawn attention to the potential significance of shifting alliances (Field 2009; Green-Pedersen 2001; Strøm 1990, p. 97); shifting alliances (e.g., between parties on the left and the right) may increase the government's ability to get what it wants by negotiating on an *ad hoc* basis with the least expensive alliance partners. Additionally, theorists versed in the Spanish case suggest that in multi-level states, defined as states where political power resides at various territorial levels (e.g., in local, regional, national, and supranational governments), parties can exchange support across levels (Colomer and Martínez 1995; Hamann and Mershon 2008; Ştefuriuc 2009), which can impact governability (Field 2009).

As part of a larger project on the performance of minority governments, this paper builds on the latter literature by introducing a multilevel, territorial logic. It is based on the premise that in multilevel states parties can exchange support across state levels; deals do not exclusively need to be based on a compromise whereby, for example, two parties positioned at policy points seven and nine, respectively, pass a policy at compromise point eight. There can also be trade-offs based on giving one party what it wants on issue or level A, while another party gets what it wants on issue or level B. For example, the Catalan party Convergence and Union (CiU) can exchange the support of its national parliamentarians for a general budget bill proposed by the PP in exchange for the PP regional legislators in the Catalan parliament supporting a CiU-proposed regional budget.

Since Spain reinstituted democracy with the 1977 founding elections and the approval of a new democratic constitution in 1978, the Spanish state has experienced dramatic decentralization to 17 powerful regional governments. Additionally, Spain's political system is marked by the importance of regional or non-statewide parties. Regional parties present candidates for election in a limited number of territorially defined electoral districts, while national or statewide parties present candidates in all districts. Regional parties (or what are in some cases referred to as *nationalist* parties in the Spanish context) are significant in several of Spain's regional institutions, and a smaller set are also significant in Spain's national political institutions due to their ability to win seats in the national parliament. For stylistic purposes, this paper employs the terms *regional* and *national* parties. These regional parties are potential and actual allies of minority Spanish governments.

Using evidence from the minority government of Socialist Prime Minister Zapatero (March 2008–May 2011), this paper evaluates the effect of regional governing dynamics on a regional party's support for the national minority government. More specifically, it provides a preliminary test of whether the type of regional government cabinet to which a regional party belongs or whether it is in the opposition affects its support for a national minority government. Using a dataset of national parliamentary alliances and qualitative interviews, it finds support for the notion that the regional governing dynamics affect national minority governance; in particular, regional parties governing in minority at the regional level are the regional parties most likely to support a national minority government.

## The Spanish Case and Hypotheses

The Spanish national party system is two-dimensional, with left-right and center-periphery issues dominating and shaping political competition. National parliamentary elections frequently produce a situation in which no single party wins a majority of seats. In these minority situations, regional parties have been potential and real allies of the predominant national party, including the now defunct Union of the Democratic Center (UCD), the center-left PSOE, and the conservative PP. The typical Spanish pattern in minority situations is that the party with the largest number of seats forms a single-party minority government.[1] In fact, the frequency of national minority governments is a distinguishing characteristic of Spanish politics. Between 1977 and 2011, Spain had 11 governments at the national level, 7 or 64 % of which have been minority governments. This places Spain amongst the European countries with the highest frequency of minority governments (Field 2009). There have been no national coalition governments.

The analysis below is based on several attributes of regional parties that are derived from numerous interviews with regional party leaders: (1) They value governing at the regional level above governing at the national level (see also Reniu 2002); (2) They value governing in their region over other potential concessions; and (3) They value attaining some of their goals over no goals. There are multiple reasons a regional party may support (or not) a national minority government. Regional parties are minority parties and will have a difficult time attaining their goals without collaboration, there may simply be policy coincidence, national government proposals could be altered to accommodate regional parties' views, or there could be any number of side payments, including targeted regional investments, the devolution of state competences, influence over government appointments to key state bodies, and government concessions in separate policy arenas. In a multilevel state, the regional parliaments also confront situations where no single-party majority government is possible and therefore cross-party deals must be struck to form and maintain a government. Where regional parties are potential governing parties, national and regional parties may exchange support across levels to form, join or support a regional (or national) government.

Here I evaluate the proposition that the governing situation of a regional party at the regional level affects its incentives to support a national minority government. Any references to regional party in this analysis are to those that simultaneously hold seats in the national and respective regional parliaments. I identify four regional governing situations:

*Vulnerable*: regional party holds at least one cabinet position in a minority regional government that does not contain a cabinet member from the party governing in minority at the national level.

---

[1] A minority government comprises ministers from one or more political parties, and the governing party's or parties' parliamentarians hold less than an absolute majority of seats.

*Co-dependent*: regional party holds at least one cabinet position in a majority regional government that also contains a cabinet member from the party governing in minority at the national level.

*Incongruent*: regional party holds at least one cabinet position in a majority regional government that does not contain a cabinet member from the party governing in minority at the national level.

*Independent*: regional party does not hold a cabinet position in the regional government.

I test the hypothesis that regional parties in a *vulnerable* situation are the most likely to support the national government, followed in order by parties in *co-dependent*, *incongruent* and *independent* situations. The logic is that vulnerable parties may require the support of the sub-national branch of the national governing party to govern or alternatively may be able to govern less encumbered in exchange for offering its support to the national minority government. Co-dependent parties are in a co-dependent situation at the regional level. The national and regional parties depend on one another to maintain the regional government, and while this can at times be compatible with national-level adversarial relations, their regional co-dependence may facilitate national collaboration. In both situations, the national party governing in minority can trade its party's support in regional-level institutions or other side payments in exchange for regional parties' support in the national parliament in a classic *you-scratch-my-back*; *I'll-scratch-yours* strategy.

This suggests that national minority government performance may also be jeopardized if the incentives for regional parties to support the national minority government diminish. This occurs if the regional party does not require the support of the national governing party to govern at the regional level. The regional party can have a governing majority that does not include the national governing party (*incongruent*) or be in the opposition in its region (*independent*). Regional parties in an incongruent situation are not vulnerable or co-dependent; however, they are governing and directly capitalize on any regional side payments attained as a result of collaboration. Also, as *governing* regional parties, hostile interparty relations could manifest in hostile intergovernmental relations, making governing more difficult. Finally, while an independent regional party could certainly make its constituents and potential voters aware of the benefits the party attains in exchange for its support of a national minority government, since the regional party does not immediately administer these benefits, and is neither vulnerable or co-dependent, it is the least likely to support the national governing party. A logical corollary hypothesis, which cannot be tested here, is that regional parties that do not get or need support to govern in their respective region will require higher concessions in exchange for their support.

**Table 1** Election results, seats, Congress of Deputies, Spain, 2008

| National parties | Seats | Regional parties | Seats |
|---|---|---|---|
| PSOE | 169 | CiU | 10 |
| PP[a] | 154 | PNV | 6 |
| IU[b] | 1 | ERC | 3 |
| UPyD | 1 | CC | 2 |
| | | BNG | 2 |
| | | ICV[b] | 1 |
| | | NA-BAI | 1 |
| | | All parties | 350 |

*Sources*: Congreso de los Diputados, Ministerio del Interior
*Notes*: *PSOE* Partido Socialista Obrero Español, *PP* Partido Popular, *IU* Izquierda Unida, *UPyD* Unión, Progreso y Democracia, *CiU* Convergència i Unió, *PNV* Partido Nacionalista Vasco, *ERC* Esquerra Republicana de Catalunya, *CC* Coalición Canaria, *BNG* Bloque Nacionalista Galego, *ICV* Iniciativa per Catalunya Verds, *NA-BAI* Nafarroa Bai
[a]PP presented candidates jointly with UPN (Unión del Pueblo Navarro) in Navarre. See footnote 2
[b]IU and ICV presented candidates jointly in Catalonia. Here, the deputies are disaggregated

## The Empirical Test

In 2008, the PSOE, with sitting Prime Minister Zapatero repeating as its lead candidate, won the national general elections, though seven seats short of an absolute majority. Zapatero formed a single-party minority government. Eight regional parties gained representation in the Spanish national Congress of Deputies. On the left, they include the Catalan Republican Left (ERC), Initiative for Catalonia-Greens (ICV), Navarre Yes (NA-BAI), and the Galician Nationalist Block (BNG). ICV presented candidates jointly in the Catalonia region with the national leftist alliance United Left (IU). In Table 1, the seats are disaggregated into their respective parties. On the center-right, the Catalan Convergence and Union (CiU), the Basque Nationalist Party (PNV), the Canary Island Coalition (CC), and the Union of the Navarre People (UPN), not listed in the table, gained seats.[2]

I first evaluate regional party support for the national minority government using national parliamentary alliances. As an indicator, this study uses the Rice index of voting likeness (IVL) between each regional party and the governing PSOE in the national parliament. It is calculated as follows:

$$IVL = 100 - (A - B),$$

---

[2] UPN presented candidates jointly in Navarre with the PP and the two deputies elected on the joint list joined the PP parliamentary group. However, in November 2008 a UPN deputy abandoned the PP parliamentary group and joined the mixed group, which is an amalgam of parties individually too small to form a group according to the parliamentary rules. Subsequently, in May 2011, the UPN gained an additional parliamentary seat as a replacement for a deputy from Navarre. She also joined the mixed group. Therefore this study analyzes the voting behavior of the UPN deputies from the date they joined the mixed group.

"where $A$ = percentage of party group A voting pro on resolution X, $B$ = percentage of party group B voting pro on resolution X, and $(A-B)$ = absolute value of $A-B$. The IVL ranges between 0 (maximum disagreement) and 100 (maximum voting similarity). Average IVLs are calculated by summing up the IVLs on individual votes and then dividing the sum by the number of votes" (Raunio 1999, p. 201).

I use a new dataset of all plenary votes ($N = 1756$) cast in the Spanish Congress of Deputies between the beginning of the new government in March 2008 and through May 2011.[3] The votes include government and parliamentary bills and the sanctioning of the executive's decree laws. Individual legislator votes have been aggregated into yes, no, and abstention votes by party. If no member of a party voted, the corresponding number of votes on which the analysis is based is reduced.

The independent variable is the regional governing situation of each regional party (vulnerable, co-dependent, incongruent, or independent). A new government is coded when there is a change of regional premier, new elections, or a change in the party composition of the regional cabinet. The start date of a government is either the date of investiture of the regional premier or the official date of a new cabinet appointment that alters the partisan composition. The end of the government is the day prior to the beginning of the subsequent government.

Two analyses are performed. First, means are presented for the overall IVL of all regional parties according to their regional governing situation. Second, results are presented for each regional party to determine whether a change in their regional governing situation corresponds with a change of the IVL in the direction hypothesized. The governing situation of six of the eight regional parties changed during the period under study. In 2009, regional elections were held in the Basque Country and Galicia regions, altering the governing situations of the PNV and BNG. In the Basque Country, the PSOE negotiated the formation of a minority government under its control with the external support of the PP, thereby dislodging the minority coalition led by PNV. The PSOE and BNG had been governing jointly in a majority coalition in Galicia; however the PP won the regional election in 2009 and formed a new government. In October 2010, the majority governing coalition of CC and PP in the Canary Islands region collapsed and was replaced by a CC minority government. In November 2010, elections were held in the Catalonia region, altering the governing situation of CIU, ERC, and ICV. The tripartite majority coalition of PSC-PSOE (Socialist Party of Catalonia-Spanish Socialist Party),[4] ERC and ICV was replaced by a CiU minority government. The governing situation of NA-BAI remained constant; it did not have a cabinet seat in the regional government throughout the period. The governing situation of UPN also remained

---

[3] Prime Minister Zapatero announced parliamentary elections for November 20, 2011. Thirteen regional elections took place on May 22, 2011; however, no new governments had been formed by May 31.

[4] PSC–PSOE emerged out a fusion of various socialist parties, including the PSOE, during the Spanish transition. PSC is formally an independently registered party federated with the PSOE. There is no separate Catalan branch of the PSOE.

**Table 2** Index of voting likeness (IVL) with the Spanish Socialist Party (PSOE)

| Party | ALL | | PNV | | CIU | | CC | | BNG | |
|---|---|---|---|---|---|---|---|---|---|---|
| | Mean | N | Mean | N | Mean | N | Mean | N | Mean | N |
| Vulnerable | 77.6 | 2,478 | 98.5 | 372 | 83.6 | 154 | 96.4 | 587 | – | – |
| Co-dependent | 49.2 | 3,518 | – | – | – | – | – | – | 97.1 | 370 |
| Incongruent | 70.5 | 1,142 | – | – | – | – | 70.5 | 1,142 | – | – |
| Independent | 57.8 | 6,343 | 88.7 | 1,384 | 54.9 | 1,602 | – | – | 45.4 | 1,386 |
| Overall | 60.2 | 13,481 | 90.8 | 1,756 | 57.5 | 1,756 | 79.3 | 1,729 | 56.3 | 1,756 |

| Party | ERC | | ICV | | UPN | | NA-BAI | |
|---|---|---|---|---|---|---|---|---|
| | Mean | N | Mean | N | Mean | N | Mean | N |
| Vulnerable | – | – | – | – | 63.1 | 1,365 | – | – |
| Co-dependent | 43.1 | 1,600 | 44.0 | 1,548 | – | – | – | – |
| Incongruent | – | – | – | – | – | – | – | – |
| Independent | 73.0 | 136 | 68.8 | 154 | – | – | 42.9 | 1,681 |
| Overall | 45.4 | 1,736 | 46.3 | 1,702 | 63.1 | 1,365 | 42.9 | 1,681 |

*Notes*: $N$ = number of cases. A test of statistical significance was not performed as the distribution of IVL values is not normal

constant as it continually governed in minority, though initially as part of a minority coalition and subsequently alone.

# Findings

The first column of Table 2 presents the mean IVL for all regional parties in vulnerable, co-dependent, incongruent and independent governing situations. It is noteworthy that regional parties support the government quite frequently as indicated by the overall IVL of 60.2. Moving to the hypotheses, for all parties, does regional governing situation affect regional party support for the national minority government? If the hypotheses were correct, we would expect parties in a vulnerable situation to have the highest IVL, followed by parties in co-dependent, incongruent, and independent situations. The hypothesis that parties in a vulnerable situation are the most likely to support the governing party is supported by the data with the highest mean IVL of 77.6. While parties in an independent situation (57.8) vote with the governing party less than parties in incongruent situations (70.5), as predicted, the IVLs for co-dependent, incongruent, and independent are not in the expected order. Parties in a co-dependent situation (49.2) were the *least* likely to vote with the national governing party.

Turning to the data by party, the overall means indicate that the center-right regional parties (PNV, CiU, CC, UPN) provided substantially more support to the Zapatero government than the regional parties of the left (ERC, ICV, BNG, NA-BAI). The PSOE's most frequent allies were the PNV (90.8) and CC (79.3). In a chamber of 350 seats, the combination of PSOE, PNV and CC votes provided the government with an absolute majority of 177. Less frequently the government received the support of UPN (63.1), CiU (57.5), and BNG (56.3). In a dramatic contrast from the parliamentary politics of Zapatero's first government (2004–2008), the support of ICV and ERC less common, with IVL values of 46.3 and 45.4, respectively. NA-BAI was the party least likely to vote with the governing party (42.9). My study of voting patterns during the first Zapatero government demonstrated that CC voted most frequently with the PSOE followed by IU-ICV, BNG and ERC (Field 2009, p. 427).

Did a change of an individual party's regional governing situation change its behavior in the direction hypothesized? The mean IVLs provide some, though not consistent, support for the hypotheses. We also need to be cautious due to the small set of votes used to calculate some of the means. Of the six parties that changed governing situation during this period, four IVL values changed in the direction anticipated by the hypotheses (PNV, CiU, CC and BNG). However, the behavior of ERC and ICV, which moved from co-dependent to independent situations, is starkly contrary to the expectations.

An analysis of vulnerable situation by party adds additional support to the hypothesis that parties that are vulnerable regionally are most likely to support the national minority government. Two parties allow us to compare vulnerable to independent situations. When the PNV led a minority coalition government in the Basque Country, and needed additional support to pass its legislation and accomplish its governing priorities (*vulnerable*), its IVL in the Spanish Congress was 98.5. While still lending a tremendous degree of support to the governing Socialists in Madrid, its IVL score dropped approximately 10 points to 88.7 after losing the Basque government (*independent*). CiU only had an IVL of 54.9 when it was in opposition in Catalonia (*independent*). After regaining control of the Catalan government in 2010, yet in minority (*vulnerable*), its support for the national government increased dramatically to 83.6. In the case of CC, we can compare vulnerable to incongruent situations. While CC governed with the PP in the Canary Islands (*incongruent*), its IVL in Madrid was 70.5. Yet, when CC governed in minority (*vulnerable*), its IVL increased as expected to 96.4.

ERC, ICV, and BNG permit a comparison of co-dependent and independent situations. All three parties had governed in coalition with the Socialist Party at the regional level, in all cases the Socialists held the regional premiership. BNG's voting behavior lends support to the hypotheses; when it governed with the Socialist Party in Galicia its IVL was 97.1. However, after both parties lost the Galician government to the PP, BNG's IVL dropped dramatically to 45.4. However, strikingly, the voting behavior of ERC and ICV is the exact opposite of that predicted; their IVL scores were dramatically *lower* when they governed Catalonia with the Socialists (*co-dependent*) than when they found themselves in the opposition. ERC's IVL was 43.1 when in the government and 73.0 while in the opposition. ICV's IVL was 44.0 when in the government and 68.8 while in the opposition.

Qualitative evidence allows us to further explore these results and address other factors that may motivate alliance behavior. Taking into consideration both the party's aggregate level of support for the national minority government and the

changes depending on governing situation, CiU and BNG behaviors are most supportive of the hypotheses. Their support was comparatively low when they were in the opposition at the regional level and high when they were either in a vulnerable (CiU) or co-dependent (BNG) situation. The importance of governing situation is confirmed by interviews with deputies from the respective parties. Carles Campuzano, CiU deputy in the Spanish Congress since 1996, explains CiU Congressional behavior in terms of Catalan governing dynamics.[5] He emphasized that the limited support that CiU has provided to both Zapatero governments is due to losing the Catalan government to the tripartite coalition of PSC–PSOE, ERC, and ICV. His account emphasizes that the CiU national parliamentary group between 1980 and 2003 was another instrument of the CiU government in Catalonia. That changed when CiU lost control of the regional government. According to Campuzano, it is very difficult "to have any type of stable relationship" with the Spanish government when CiU is in opposition in Catalonia; very difficult to understand each other when in Catalonia the relationship is "confrontational"; very difficult to collaborate "when your specialty in Spanish politics has a lot to do with your party's role as defender of self-government and you are not in the government." He also emphasized that the dynamics of governance during periods of simultaneous minority governments in Catalonia and Spain follow a "logic of reciprocities"—that the party that guaranteed majorities in Madrid, in turn, has its majorities guaranteed in Catalonia.

While noting that policy distance matters, Francisco Xesús Jorquera, deputy and BNG party spokesperson in the Spanish Congress, also explained BNG's growing opposition to the PSOE national government, in part, in terms of regional governing dynamics[6]: "The first reason is the change of political context. We, during a good part of the last government and the beginning of this one, co-governed in Galicia with the Socialist Party. Well that was a scenario that facilitated that here in Madrid [i.e. national government] we could also reach agreements given that we were partners in Galicia. This scenario changed given that we...lost the last regional elections; now in Galicia there is a PP government. Upon this change of scenario, it made reaching agreements here in Madrid more difficult. But additionally there is a second factor and that is that we profoundly disagree with the policies this current government is developing, particularly in economic policy." Noteworthy, my prior work on the first Zapatero government found that regional governing situation explained parliamentary alliances better than ideological distance (Field 2009).

Regarding PNV and CC, their behavior changed in the expected direction with a change of regional governing situation; however, their aggregate high level of support for the national minority government while the PNV was in opposition in the Basque Country (*independent*) and CC was in an incongruent majority coalition with the PP in the Canary Islands requires further exploration. In a personal interview, PNV party President Iñigo Urkullu recognized that losing the Basque

---

[5] Interview with the author, 2011.
[6] Interview with the author, 2011.

government, after having won the 2009 regional elections, affected their disposition to support the Zapatero government.[7] However, a rational political analysis, consistent with the logic of this study, won out. In the PNV's analysis, a logical partner for the PSOE was CiU with ten seats, which would bring the government to an absolute majority. Cognizant of the government's weakness and of CiU's strategy of opposition to the Zapatero government, the PNV saw an opportunity to advance its goals. According to Urkullu, "...there was a space. The Popular Party doesn't enter to help the Socialist Party; Convergence and Union leaves the space free and we look for an opportunity." Their analysis was that the economic crisis in which Spain was engulfed affected everyone; elections would bring months of uncertainty; a PP government would likely implement very similar measures; and new elections could produce a majority PP government that would reduce the PNV's leverage. Therefore they saw a political opportunity to act responsibly and advance their political goals of attaining the transfer of competencies from the central to the Basque regional government. They determined that their best strategy, given the revealed strategies of the other parties, was to collaborate, despite being in opposition in the Basque Country.

Canary Island Coalition (CC) national deputy Ana María Oramas also recognized the importance of multilevel dynamics and lent particular credence to the importance of minority governance in the regions: "Normally the most comfortable is that you [regional party] govern in your autonomous community and the party that governs in Madrid [i.e. the national government] gives you parliamentary support, it doesn't enter the government, and in exchange you give them parliamentary support in Madrid."[8] But, she was quick to note that other governing scenarios do not preclude collaboration to advance the party's political agenda. Also, she calls our attention to the potential importance of regional dependence on the national government. The particular characteristics of the Canary Islands may make collaboration with the central government likely regardless of government type. Oramas emphasized the costs to the region of not collaborating with the central government. The Canary Islands, one of Europe's nine "outermost" regions, are a set of seven main islands located 2,000 km from Madrid. According to Oramas, the Canary Islands are unique because of their distance and isolation, which require special treatment in government policy.

As discussed above, the behavior of ERC and ICV run entirely contrary to the hypotheses presented here. Contextual factors may clearly matter. Representatives of both parties stressed negative prior experiences with the first Zapatero government with regard to the newly redacted Catalan regional government charter, referred to as a statute of autonomy, in 2005–2006. They highlighted Zapatero's reneging on his 2003 promise to defend any revised charter approved by the Catalan

---

[7] Interview with the author, 2011.

[8] Interview with the author, 2010.

parliament.[9] Other variables may matter. ERC and ICV had absolutely no prior history of governing at the regional level since the return of democracy in the mid-1970s. They are also leftist parties as opposed to PNV, CIU and CC, which are centrist parties. However, casting doubt on both variables, these characteristics also apply to BNG. An alterative explanation for their outlier behavior is that it may not be entirely accurate to code ERC and ICV as having governed in Catalonia with the party governing at the national level in Spain (PSOE). All interviewees were quick to point out that the Socialist Party of Catalonia (PSC–PSOE) is formally an independent party federated with the PSOE. It is subject to PSOE dictates regarding national strategy and in the national institutions, for example PSC deputies form part of the PSOE parliamentary groups in the Spanish parliament and are subject to PSOE party discipline. Yet, it has autonomy in its decisions in Catalonia.[10] Finally, three different Catalan regional parties gained representation in the national parliament. This makes Catalan dynamics distinct from any other region.

## Conclusions

The evidence from the Zapatero minority government (2008–2011) provides strong support for the hypothesis that regional parties that are governing in minority at the regional level are the regional parties most likely to support a national minority government. There is also support for the proposition that parties that are in the opposition at the regional level are less likely to support a minority national government than those governing regionally in an incongruent coalition or in minority. Though this may be subject to coding choices, there is no support for the hypothesis that regional parties governing in a regional coalition with the national governing party are more likely to support a national minority government than parties in incongruent and independent governing situations. Contrary to expectations, the findings indicate that they were the least likely to support the national minority government. All of these propositions need further testing in distinct national contexts and during additional periods of minority government in Spain.

The findings do suggest that regional governing dynamics can affect national minority government alliance patterns, which is an important finding. From the perspective of national government performance, certain regional dynamics, particularly when regional parties govern in minority in their respective region, may

---

[9] Personal interviews with Joan Ridao (ERC, 2009), Joan Tardá (ERC, 2010), Josep Lluis Carod Rovira (ERC 2011), and Joan Saura (ICV, 2011).

[10] According to the PSC website, "The PSC. . .is a sovereign party federated with the PSOE, and this makes it unique in the Spanish socialist context because, even though it participates in the federal organs [of the PSOE], it has its own legal identity, independent finances and it maintains total autonomy of action within the framework of Catalan politics" (Partido de los Socialistas de Catalunya 2011). Translated by the author.

provide more solid allies for a national minority government than others. It remains to be tested whether the *you-scratch-my-back*; *I'll-scratch-yours* strategy also limits the cost of concessions for the national minority government. The proposition that other regional governing dynamics can negatively affect national minority governments merits further research as these dynamics alter the balance of power between the national government and potential regional support parties.

**Acknowledgements** The author gratefully acknowledges the support of the Ministerio de Ciencia e Innovación, Gobierno de España (CSO2010-16337) and the Program for Cultural Cooperation between Spain's Ministry of Culture and United States Universities. The author thanks Kristin Anderson, Paige Roland, Teresa Sieiro, Maria Skaletsky, Lourdes Solana, Bayer Tumennasan and Steve Wuhs for their research assistance and advice; and the numerous politicians who generously agreed to be interviewed for this project.

# References

Colomer, J.M. and Martínez, F. (1995). The paradox of coalition trading. Journal of Theoretical Politics 7: 41–63.

Diario de Sesiones del Congreso de los Diputados. Pleno y Diputación Permanente, 15 April 2004, No. 2.

Field, B.N. (2009). Minority government and legislative politics in a multilevel state: Spain under Zapatero. South European Society and Politics 14: 417–434.

Green-Pedersen, C. (2001). Minority governments and party politics: the political and institutional background to the "Danish miracle". Journal of Public Policy 21: 53–70.

Hamann, K. and Mershon, C. (2008). Regional governments in Spain: exploring theories of government formation. In: Field, B.N. and Hamann, K. (eds.) Democracy and institutional development: Spain in comparative theoretical perspective. Palgrave Macmillan, Houndmills, UK and New York, USA, pp. 110–134.

Helland, l. (2004). Minority-rule budgeting under a de facto constructive vote of no confidence. Scandinavian Political Studies 27: 391–401.

Partido de los Socialistas de Catalunya (2011). La historia del socialismo catalán. Available at: http://www.socialistes.cat/pagina/historia/es

Raunio, T. (1999). The challenge of diversity: party cohesion in the European parliament. In: Bowler, S., Farrell, D. and Katz, R.S. (eds) Party discipline and parliamentary government. Ohio State University Press, Columbus, USA, pp. 189–207.

Reniu i Vilamala, J.M. (2002). La formación de gobiernos minoritarios en España, 1977–1996. Centro de Investigaciones Sociológicas, Madrid, Spain, 306 pp.

Schofield, N. (1993). Political competition and multiparty coalition governments. European Journal of Political Research 23: 1–33.

Ştefuriuc, I. (2009). Government formation in multi-level settings. Party Politics 15: 93–115.

Strøm, K. (1990). Minority government and majority rule. Cambridge University Press, Cambridge, UK, 293 pp.

Tsebelis, G. (2002). Veto players: how political institutions work. Princeton University Press, Princeton, USA, 320 pp.

# Autonomy or Independence: An Analysis of the 2010 Catalan Regional Election

Eric Guntermann

The election to the Parliament of Catalonia held on November 28th 2010 signaled the return to government of the conservative nationalist coalition Convergència i Unió (CiU). It also saw the emergence of new separatist parties Solidaritat Catalana per la Independència (SI) and Reagrupament Independentista (RI). Esquerra Republicana de Catalunya (ERC), which had been advocating independence for Catalonia since 1989, also participated in the election. At the same time, the nonnationalist Ciutadans-Partit de la Ciutadania (C's), which first ran in the 2006 regional election, retained its status as a minor party with parliamentary representation.

This election followed the June 2010 judgment by the Spanish Constitutional Tribunal that parts of the new regional autonomy statute adopted in 2006 were unconstitutional. This decision provoked a massive protest in the streets of Barcelona and seemed to be linked to a radicalization of the nationalist movement in Catalonia, with increasing demands for the independence of the region. There was also great dissatisfaction with the Spanish government's handling of intergovernmental relations, notably with respect to financial transfers to the regions. Moreover, the incumbent tripartite leftist coalition of the Partit dels Socialistes de Catalunya (PSC), Iniciativa per Catalunya Verds (ICV), and Esquerra Republicana had been widely criticized by the opposition, especially for its failures in defending Catalonia's self-government. Thus, this election is interesting not only because several parties challenged the current structure of the Spanish state but also because the short-term political context seemed to be favorable to these parties.

This paper uses the postelection survey conducted by the Centro de Investigaciones Sociológicas (CIS). It first shows that both long-term and short-term variables contribute to explaining Catalans' vote choice in 2010 but enduring predispositions have a more powerful impact than short-term evaluations of

E. Guntermann (✉)

Département de science politique, Canada Research Chair in Electoral Studies, Université de Montréal, C.P. 6128, succursale centre-ville, Montréal, QC, Canada H3C 3J7
e-mail: eric.guntermann@umontreal.ca

A. López-Basaguren and L. Escajedo San Epifanio (eds.), *The Ways of Federalism in Western Countries and the Horizons of Territorial Autonomy in Spain*, Vol. 2, DOI 10.1007/978-3-642-27717-7_57, © Springer-Verlag Berlin Heidelberg 2013

incumbent governments and of the economy. It then presents profiles of typical voters of the three most significant nationalist parties, CiU, ERC, and SI and of the nonnationalist C's. Too few people supported RI. It was, therefore, impossible to include it in the analysis. This paper ends with simulations showing that the nationalist vote of native Catalans is more resistant to changing evaluations of incumbent governments and of the economy than that of nonnative Catalans. This implies that the challenge posed to the Spanish State of the Autonomies by Catalan nationalism is relatively enduring regardless of the short-term political context.

## The Multistage Model of Nationalist Voting

The analysis presented here is based on the multistage model of voting widely used in election studies (Blais et al. 2002). This type of analysis identifies variables at different degrees of proximity to the vote. Those that are most distant, especially social background and values, are quite fixed in the long term. Others, such as evaluations of government performance and of the economy, change over time as the economic and political contexts vary. More distant variables can affect the vote both directly and via more proximate variables. The following figure shows a simplified representation of the model applied to nationalist voting in Catalonia. It shows the factors that are associated with voting for the nationalist coalition CiU (Fig. 1).

Other explanations of nationalist voting in Catalonia focus on spatial models either exclusively (e.g. Balcells i Ventura 2007) or in combination with some of the short-term variables analyzed here (e.g. Aguilar and Sánchez-Cuenca 2007). The analysis presented in this chapter presents a wider range of variables, from social background characteristics to leader evaluations, at varying degrees of proximity to the vote. Doing so allows us to explain a greater proportion of voting behavior in Catalonia. It also allows us to simulate changes in some of the variables, while keeping others fixed.

## Major Determinants of the Vote

To identify the variables that help explain nationalist voting in Catalonia, a series of multinomial logistic regressions were run, using vote as the dependent variable and adding variables that are progressively closer to the individual's voting decision. This allows us to determine which variables contribute to an explanation of nationalist voting at different levels of proximity to the vote.

The first level consists of social background variables. The most significant demographic influence on the nationalist vote is a Catalan voter's degree of nativeness. A variable was constructed combining respondents' answers to questions about whether they were born in Catalonia, whether their mother was

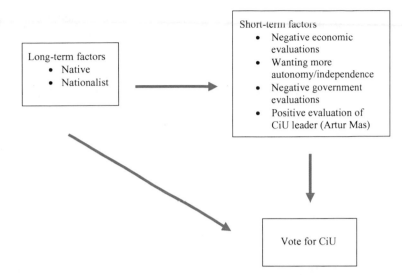

**Fig. 1** Simplified multistage model of Nationalist Vote Choice (for CiU)

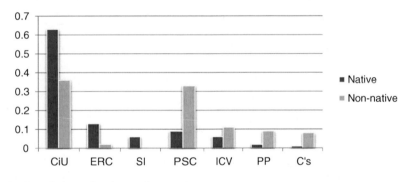

**Fig. 2** Vote choices of natives and nonnatives

born in the region, and whether their father was born there. Figure 2 displays the predicted vote choices of two ideal types. A native Catalan is someone who was born in Catalonia and whose mother and father were born there as well. A nonnative Catalan was born outside of Catalonia, as were his or her parents. As can be seen, nonnatives were significantly less likely to vote for CiU than natives, and their probabilities of voting for ERC and SI were practically nil. On the other hand, they were much more likely than native Catalans to vote for the nonnationalist Ciutadans. While it may be objected that native and nonnative are extreme categories that do not represent all Catalans, 36 % of Catalans are natives, as defined here, and 26 % of Catalans are nonnatives. In other words, these extreme categories include more than 60 % of the population. The other 40 % has interme- diate levels of support for the nationalist and nonnationalist parties. This initial

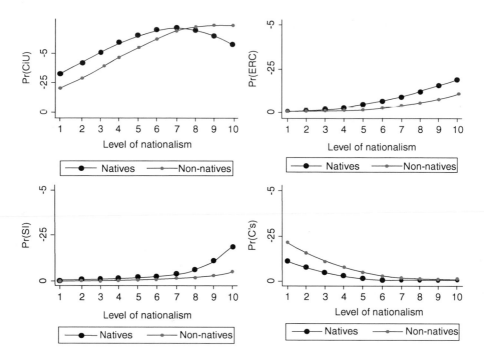

**Fig. 3** Impact of self-placement on scale of Nationalism

analysis has thus identified a major cleavage in Catalan society. Overall, this variable explains about 6 % of the variation in the vote.[1]

Once the influence of social background characteristics has been taken into account, Catalans' self-placement on a scale of nationalism running from one (low nationalism) to ten (high nationalism) adds significant explanatory power to our nationalist voting model. As can be seen in Fig. 3, voting for nationalist parties increases along with individuals' self-placement on the nationalism scale. However, natives are practically always more likely to vote for nationalist parties than do nonnatives. Moreover, support for the separatist Solidaritat is concentrated among the most extreme nationalists. Voting for the nonnationalist Ciutadans follows the opposite pattern. It decreases as the level of nationalism increases and is always higher among nonnatives. Respondents' subjective nationalism explains an additional 7 % of the vote in 2010.

Evaluations of the economy also had an independent impact on support for the nationalist parties. However, their impact was small, explaining only about 1 % of the vote. Negative evaluations of the Spanish economy, which were very common,

---

[1] Indicators of explained variance are all pseudo-$R^2$.

**Table 1** Typical voters of each party

| | |
|---|---|
| CiU | Native, high level of nationalism, negative evaluations of the Catalan and Spanish economies, preference for a state with more regional autonomy, negative evaluations of the Catalan and Spanish governments |
| ERC | Native, high level of nationalism, negative evaluation of the Catalan economy but neutral evaluation of the Spanish economy, negative evaluation of the Spanish government but neutral evaluation of the Catalan government |
| SI | Native, very high level of nationalism, negative evaluations of the Catalan and Spanish economies, negative evaluations of the Catalan and Spanish governments |
| C's | Nonnative, low level of nationalism, negative evaluation of the Catalan economy but neutral evaluation of the Spanish economy, neutral evaluations of the Catalan and Spanish governments |

benefitted CiU while hurting Ciutadans. Unfavorable evaluations of the Catalan economy, which were also quite common, helped CiU, ERC, and Ciutadans.[2]

Adding preferences regarding the form of the Spanish state to the model explains another 2 % of the vote. While the impact on the probability of supporting the nationalist coalition Convergència i Unió was negligible, separatist Esquerra republicana's support was strongest among those wanting at least more regional autonomy for autonomous communities in Spain, and Solidaritat's support was practically nonexistent among those who did not support independence for the regions of Spain. Support for Ciutadans was greatest among respondents preferring greater centralization.

Adding evaluations of the Spanish and Catalan governments allows us to explain an additional 1 % of the vote. The most significant influences on the vote in this category were evaluations of the central government's policies towards Catalonia's autonomy and of the regional government's handling of its own self-government. Respondents who rated the Spanish government's treatment of Catalonia's autonomy negatively were more likely to vote for CiU, ERC, and SI than those who had a neutral evaluation. Those who evaluated the Catalan government poorly on this issue were more likely to vote for CiU and SI but less likely to vote for ERC, which had been part of the previous governing coalition in Catalonia.

Finally, the short-term variables that seem to have the highest impact on the vote are evaluations of the leaders of the different parties. In fact, they explain almost as much of the vote as all the previous variables combined, about 31 %. Higher leader ratings are associated with higher probabilities of voting for the different parties. However, it is difficult to determine the direction of causality: Do people vote for a party because they like the leader, or do they like the leader of the party they vote for? Because these are not clearly causal variables, the rest of this paper will focus on the other variables we have identified.

The above findings allow us to identify typical voters for each party. Table 1 shows the values of each of the significant independent variables identified above that is associated with the highest probability of supporting each of the parties.

---

[2] It should be noted that, since evaluations of the economy and of government performance were overwhelmingly negative, positive and neutral evaluations were combined into one category "neutral".

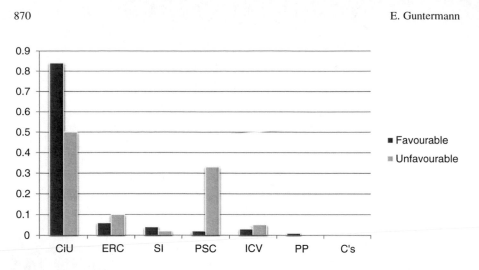

**Fig. 4** Vote probabilities for CIU given most and least favorable evaluations (natives). *Note*: Negative evaluations of the Catalan and Spanish governments and economies are favorable to CiU. The reverse are unfavorable

## Simulations

Using the model of nationalist voting presented above, it is possible to observe how the probabilities of voting for the different parties change when evaluations of the incumbent governments and of the economy change. The probability of natives and nonnatives voting for each party is shown when evaluations change from the most favorable for each party to the least favorable. For CiU, favorable evaluations are negative with respect to the governments and economies of both Catalonia and Spain. Figure 4 shows that the probability of voting for CiU declines among natives by about 34 % points when evaluations of the government and of the economy move from most favorable to least favorable for CiU. Meanwhile, support for the three left-wing parties that formed the previous governing coalition in Catalonia, including ERC, increases.

Figure 5 shows that support for CiU among nonnative Catalans declines by a similar 32 % points when evaluations go from being favorable to unfavorable for CiU, to the benefit of the Socialists. However, this decline represents a much more significant proportion of nonnatives' nationalist vote. In fact, unfavorable evaluations are associated with a probability of voting for CiU of less than 10 %. This means that most of nonnative Catalans' support for CiU is motivated by negative evaluations of the incumbent governments and of the economy.

Because so few respondents voted for the other parties discussed in this paper, it was impossible to conduct similar simulations for them. Nevertheless, the finding with respect to support for the moderate nationalist Convergència i Unió is intriguing. If its support is still relatively strong amongst native Catalans who have evaluations of the economy and of government that are all unfavorable to it, this suggests that its support is relatively firm, not being subject to changes in the

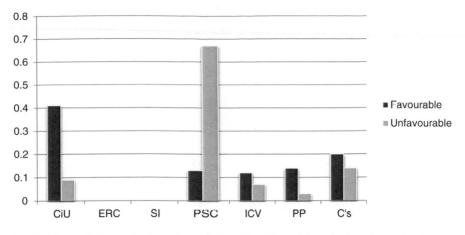

**Fig. 5** Vote probabilities for CIU given most and least favorable evaluations (nonnatives)

political and economic contexts. This suggests that any attempt to satisfy nationalists would be extremely difficult. If a significant amount of nationalist support comes from individuals who are highly committed to the party, it is unlikely that any change in policy, for example, would convince many of the native Catalans who voted for CiU to vote for another party that poses less of a challenge to the status quo. Therefore, any significant reduction in nationalist support could only be achieved by some major policy or institutional change that had an effect on how much people identify with Catalan nationalism.

# Conclusion

This paper has presented a multistage model of voting for nationalist parties, as well as for the nonnationalist Ciutadans-Partit de la Ciutadania in the 2010 election to the Parliament of Catalonia. It showed that the most powerful determinants of nationalist voting are, on the one hand, whether an individual and his or her parents were born in Catalonia and, on the other hand, how nationalistic an individual considers him or herself. Short-term factors, notably preferences regarding the future of the Spanish state and economic and governmental evaluations, also help explain voting in 2010, but their impact is much smaller. Simulations using this model show that much of the vote for CiU can be explained by negative short-term evaluations. Changing these to their most positive values decreases CiU's electoral support significantly. This paper has also identified two types of voters. Nonnative Catalans' support for CiU almost disappears when we simulate a context unfavorable to CiU, while native Catalans' propensity to support CiU remains relatively strong even when the context is not at all favorable for the nationalist coalition. This finding suggests that support for CiU among natives depends on their Catalan identity, as well as their evaluations of the political and economic context. Nonnatives' nationalist support is mostly motivated by short-term economic and political considerations. Therefore, it seems that the impact of the political and economic context on nationalist challenges to the Spanish state is relatively limited. Satisfying many of those who currently vote for nationalist parties would thus be a significant challenge.

# References

Aguilar, P. and Sánchez-Cuenca., I. (2007). ¿Gestión o Representación? Los determinantes del voto en contextos políticos complejos. Revista Española de Investigaciones Sociológicas 117: 61–86.

Balcells i Ventura, L. (2007). ¿Es el voto nacionalista un voto de proximidad o un voto de compensación? Una nueva aproximación "espacial" al voto en dos dimensiones. Revista Española de Ciencia Política 16: 61–88.

Blais, A., Gidengil, E., Nadeau, R. and Nevitte, N. (2002). *Anatomy of a Liberal Victory: Making Sense of the 2000 Canadian Election*. Broadview Press, Peterborough, Canada, 241 pp.

# The Role of Autonomous Communities in Euro-Regions and European Grouping of Territorial Cooperation Development (with Particular Reference to the Galician Case)

Santiago Roura

## Multilevel Governance and Intraregional and Cross-Border Cooperation

In my opinion, one of the reasons for the success of Federal Systems has been their ability to take different forms in accordance with the moment and the place in which this model of multilevel Governance has occurred. It is clear to me that there are as many similarities between the current different federal models as there are differences. However, all these formulas correspond to a common goal, which is what actually unites them and enables a unitary scientific treatment of the phenomenon, as is the case in this international conference: the structuring of multilevel constitutional systems of democratic and effective for citizenship Government. In fact, in the origin and development of American Federalism, as in other experiences, the allocation of powers between the different levels of territorial organizations has had much to do with the achievement of the best (i.e., most effective) solution. It has recently become common in Spain, with the pretext of the worldwide economic crisis, to discuss the size and budgetary consequences of the Autonomous Community model, in a way that projects the idea of an ineffective and inefficient Spanish Autonomous Community organization. Quite to the contrary, this paper aims to make clear how Statutes of Autonomy, as essential pieces of Spanish federalism, can play an important role in one of the forthcoming challenges for European territorial organization, namely that of cross-border and Euroregional cooperation formulas, insofar as these are able to provide long-awaited solutions for the specific demands of their citizens.

With the support of the Xunta de Galicia Research Project "Un novo Estatuto de Galicia: instrumento constitucional para o autogoberno útil" 10 PXB 101 255 PR.

S. Roura (✉)
Universidade da Coruña, Campus Elviña s/n, 15071-A Coruña, Spain
e-mail: santiago.roura.gomez@udc.es

A. López-Basaguren and L. Escajedo San Epifanio (eds.), *The Ways of Federalism in Western Countries and the Horizons of Territorial Autonomy in Spain*, Vol. 2, DOI 10.1007/978-3-642-27717-7_58, © Springer-Verlag Berlin Heidelberg 2013

The efficient and effective provision of public services concerning populations who live in areas close to intra-European borders requires the adoption of cooperative Euroregional solutions. In the case of Spain, insofar as these services are provided by the government of an Autonomous Community, its position in relation to this item is highly significant. I wish to present here how the different Statutes of Autonomy of some of the Spanish territories have addressed the question, and how an eventual reform of the Galician Statute could also address it.

Borders between European countries are good evidence of problems and solutions in the cooperative provision of public services, perhaps because citizens who live close to them are used to being subject to the jurisdiction of at least two, but often even more, States. In fact, the internal EU border areas have played, in my opinion, an important role in the translation of the idea of European integration, in the same sense in which K. Hesse used his notion of federal integration. Those who have on various occasions, crossed the borders that disappeared after the Schengen Treaty will know very well what kind of feeling I am referring to.

In Spanish Constitutional Law the question of cooperation between public subnational (regional or local) authorities belonging to two different EU members for the provision of public services must consider, first of all, the position of the Spanish State, Autonomous Communities, and Local Entities in relation to international relationships. As is well known, Article 149.1.3 of the Spanish Constitution allocates international relationships power under the jurisdiction of the Spanish Central State, so no decision in that item concerns Autonomous Community or local Authorities. However, the interpretation made by the Spanish Constitutional Court of this rule means that nowadays only the treaty-making power and the *ius legationis* (the capacity to establish embassies) remain with the competence of the Spanish State. As a result of this interpretation, Autonomous Communities have undertaken certain international actions intended to promote themselves before International Authorities [namely those of the European Union (EU)], establishing close relations with Spanish citizens living in other countries or descendants of them, providing services abroad, and even taking part in policy decision-making processes before the EU and other international institutions. These international activities of Spanish Autonomous Communities are explained by the widespread issues with international dimensions that they concern. That is why some Statutory Laws establish the international dimension of the exercise of political powers by Autonomous Communities, as we will show in this paper.

On the other hand, Spanish Local Entities have traditionally developed numerous relationships with local institutions of other countries, in accordance with their position in the range of subjects they implement. Nevertheless, and probably because of the uncontroversial political position of Spanish municipalities, article 87.2 of Spanish Basic Law of Local Governance allows local entities to create consortiums with other foreign local entities in order to provide public services they are concerned with within the frame of cross-border cooperation agreements.

This constitutional and legal framework we have briefly described must be considered in relation to the provisions of the European Council law concerning cross-border cooperation, namely the Treaty of Madrid of 1980, in force in Spain since 1990. Under this law, cross-border cooperation is open to Autonomous Communities and Municipalities if they have, according to their internal law, the power to implement policies related to the scope of the Treaty. Two International Conventions, the Bayonne Convention (in force in Spain since February 24th 1997) and the Valencia Convention (in force in Spain since January 30th 2004), have facilitated subsequent agreements between territorial entities of the French and Portuguese Republics and those of Spain. Under these two treaties, Spanish territorial entities (Municipalities, Autonomous Communities, and Provincial Councils) had subscribed (November 2010) 62 conventions of cross-border cooperation, even creating entities between the existing regional or/and local ones, invested with legal personality. The effectiveness that these conventions have made possible seems to me to be undeniable.

## In the Face of New Cooperative Formulas

Cities and city networks within the EU have gained an increasingly important role as a focus for the development of the Euroregions. The Conference of European Cross-Border and Interregional Cities Networks or the Euro-Cities (Twin Cities) defined as cities that grow together because of the synergies created from their proximity, are clear proof of this. However, the agents most closely involved in this matter have been demanding the adoption of more flexible ways to open what they call the second stage of cross-border cooperation. From that point of view, new cooperation must cover a wider range of issues, such as joint development, shared public services (education, health, etc.), and even joint territorial planning (transportation and communication networks, ICTs, and environmental protection).

The establishment of the INTERREG initiative, under the financial contribution of the European Regional Development Fund, served in the past as the main instrument for promoting regional cooperation inside the EU. Nowadays, there is a new formula, the European Grouping of Territorial Cooperation Development (EGTC), devised to respond to the request for these new forms, none exclusively under existing funding instruments. EGTC represents a new European legal regulation concerning cross-border cooperation, which some Euroregions are currently considering joining. The EU Parliament and the Council approved Regulation (EC) No 1082/2006 concerning EGTCs in order "to facilitate and promote cross-border, transnational and/or interregional cooperation (...) [and to] strengthen economic and social cohesion" (Art. 1.2). The most important and innovative characteristic of EGTCs is the mandatory legal personality they must acquire. EGTC is a new formula that could play an important role in conceiving and improving the kind of strategic cooperation to which we are referring. An EGTC must have members from at least two EU member States, with central, regional, or local Authorities and other entities governed by public law and associations consisting of bodies belonging to one or more of these categories being allowed to join it. In Spain, the Regulation has been developed by Real Decreto 37/2008 (January 18th).

The EGTC is created by a convention between its partners, which must be previously communicated to the authorities of the EU member States concerned, in accordance with constitutional rules, in order to certify its compliance with domestic law. The convention that forms the EGTC also defines its tasks, which will always be determined on the basis that all of them fall within the competence of every EGTC member under its national law. The convention creating the EGTC also establishes its internal organs, but an assembly made up of representatives from every member and a director (who will represent the EGTC and act on its behalf) is mandatory. According to Article 8.2(e) of Regulation (EC) No 1082/2006, the Convention shall specify the law applicable to the interpretation and enforcement of the convention itself, which shall be the law of the Member State where the EGTC has its registered office. This might create some problems because of the clearly transnational nature of EGTCs, and in my opinion, the regulation should probably have been more ambitious in order to avoid disharmony between EU members' national regulations.

The unique relevant limitation on the powers of an EGTC is its inability to exercise police and regulatory powers, justice, and foreign policy. The primary objective of an EGTC must be to implement cooperation programmes cofinanced by the European Regional Development Fund, the European Social Fund, and/or the Cohesion Fund, but it may also carry out other kinds of task, with or without EU financing.

Article 17 of Regulation (EC) No 1082/2006 ordered the EU Commission to prepare a report on the application of the Regulation by 1 August 2011 to be sent to the Parliament and the Council. On July 29th 2011, the EU Director General of Regional Policy presented that report, which includes some proposals for amendments and clarifications to the EGTC Regulation, in particular in order to simplify and accelerate procedures for the creation of EGTCs. The report denounces some practical difficulties it has identified, as in the case we have already referred to, in regard to the disharmony between national legal regulations. In particular, this occurs when some local bodies cannot be affected, according to their national law, by unlimited liability in their responsibility. Neither did the EGTC Regulation solve the question of the position of an EGTC with its principal office in one member State contracting, as a public entity, in another State. As we have said, private agents may not be EGTC members, and the Commission report also echoes a request to extend the possibilities of actual participation in EGTCs to private entities.

As the recent Commission Report has acknowledged, on behalf of EU institutions, the Committee of the Regions (CoR), representing regional and local Authorities, has promoted the creation of EGTCs. The CoR believes that EGTCs could contribute to redefine the concepts in Multi-level Governance, acting as laboratories of this kind of public policy-making system. In a similar sense, the Commission has recognized four examples of good practices in EGTC, of which I would highlight the EGTC "Hospital de la Cerdanya" created in April 2010 between the Autonomous Community of Catalonia, the French Ministry of Health, the Regional Agency for Hospitals in Languedoc-Roussillon, and others. It has to provide public health services to a population of around 30,000 persons and, in terms of budget, is the leading EGTC constituted to date. It is also a momentous experience because of the nature of the activities it carries out, namely the provision of public health services in a Franco-Spanish cross-border area.

## Legal Provisions Relating to Cooperation in Spanish Statutes of Autonomy

In the case of Spanish territorial structure, the Autonomous Communities' Fundamental Laws (Statutes of Autonomy) could also provide easier legal frameworks in order to extend the application of the EGTC cooperation formulas, as well as of other multilevel cooperative instruments. Such a possibility has already been explored by some Statute reforms, whilst others, as in the Galician case we herein consider, must wait until their Statutes of Autonomy can be modified in an interesting way.

The presence of international activity in Spanish Statutes of Autonomy is relatively frequent, especially after the first decade of this century. Previously, frequent mention was made (and still is) to the capacity of Autonomous Communities to be informed and to request the conclusion of international agreements relevant to their interests. Furthermore, the first Autonomous Communities' fundamental laws contained other references of international scope, such as the obligation to pay attention to the regional linguistic communities abroad (as, for instance, in Art. 6 of the Basque Country Statutory Law of 1979). Nevertheless, it has undoubtedly been the past decade that has revealed a major opportunity for a new regional legal framework for international subnational cooperation in Spain.

The 2006 Catalonian Statute of Autonomy refers to cross-border and intraregional cooperation in Art. 197. This article sets out a mandatory clause to the Regional Government (*Generalitat*) for promoting this kind of cooperation. In the case of Aragon, its Statute (Art. 98) proclaims the Community's cross-border nature and also the wish to promote interregional cooperation with other territories with shared interests, whilst similar declarations are included in Navarra's Fundamental Law (Art. 68 *bis*).

In my opinion, the most interesting legal framework for regional and local cross-border and interregional cooperation is set out in the Statutes of Autonomy of Extremadura, Castilla-Leon, and Andalusia. All of these Spanish Autonomous Communities share borders with Portugal and have previously worked intensely in the sphere of cooperative conventions, in particular between their Municipalities and those of the neighboring Portuguese Republic, many of which were signed, under the Treaty of Madrid, with the participation of the Regional Government. For this reason, these examples provide interesting material for a hypothetical reform of the Galician Statute of Autonomy.

We find just a single mention to the promotion of good neighborly relationships between Castilla-Leon and the cross-border Portuguese territories in Article 66 of the former's Statute of Autonomy. The Fundamental Laws of the Communities of Andalusia and Extremadura, however, go much further. That of Andalusia has a large number of articles dedicated to the external action of the Community. After setting out the usual reference to the maintenance of relationships with the European Regions with shared interests (Art. 239), Articles 246 and 247 refer to the applicable Constitutional, Regional and European legal framework in order to promote cooperation and to coordinate the external action of Andalusian public entities and Municipalities, in a sense that comes very close to the provisions contained in Regulation (EC) No 1082/2006 regarding the possible partners in an EGTC.

Finally, the Statute of Autonomy of Extremadura is, with regard to it being followed as an example in Galicia, the broadest Spanish regional legal framework for cross-border and interregional cooperation. In Extremadura, cooperation is not exclusively contained in articles specifically dedicated to the region's external action. The strategic vision of cooperative policies is revealed by the declaration set out in Article 7, which defines the aim of all regional public entities' public policies. Its paragraph 19 establishes, at the same level with other public policies that are considered essential for the proper development of the Community, that public entities of Extremadura shall "Promote all kind of relationships with Portugal, both by institutions and by society (...), under the principles of loyalty, respect for identities, mutual benefit and solidarity". This is why I submit that cross-border and interregional cooperation in the Statute of Extremadura has moved from a mere enunciation of regional powers towards a strategic vision, which involves regional public policy as a whole. It is also true that a static study of mere legal propositions cannot be considered conclusive because their subsequent application also needs to be taken into account. However, if regional public entities, in particular the Regional Government of Extremadura, behave as provided for in the Statute, we shall see a leading subnational political structure arise in the construction of a new age in Euroregional development. This, if confirmed by continuing practice, could become the key to a new understanding of Euroregional governance. The text of the Statute also specifies, in Article 71 "Cooperation with Portugal", a wide but not exhaustive list of nine different cooperative formulas that the Autonomous Community could use. I would like to emphasize letters c), d) and e) of Article 71 because they contain the basic structure of those characters that we used above to define the so-called second stage of interregional and cross-border cooperation, namely (1) the planning, negotiation, and execution of actions and programs shared with Portuguese organizations, whatever the source of funding; (2) the planning, negotiation, and execution of its own cross-border cooperation policy; and (3) the creation of joint agencies and services, whatever their nature, of common interest. No wider range of cooperative formulas is to be found in legal texts in Spain. So, if we agree on the importance of flexible cooperative formulas in the construction of a new strategic model of development, any attempt to maximize the possibilities of cooperation should begin with this starting point.

## The Case of Galicia

Galicia did not amend its Statute of Autonomy at the same time as all the Communities cited above. The Galician Statute has preserved the same text since 1981, and just two organic laws transferring competences to it, neither of which concerns cooperation, have been approved since then. However, Galicia has traditionally carried out an intense external activity, primarily because of the large number of Galician citizens and their descendants who are living abroad due to emigration. Article 7 of the Galician Statute has been the legal basis for the external action of the Galician Government (*Xunta*), which has been very intense in Latin American countries (namely Argentina, Venezuela, Brazil, and Uruguay) and in some European ones (namely Germany and Switzerland). The *Xunta* has carried out this kind of Government-to-person action through diverse legal formulas, such as public foundations, and until comparatively recently the Galician Government even had a Regional Ministry (*Consellería*) exclusively dedicated to this matter, although nowadays it enjoys a lesser status. I should add that the Spanish electoral legislation allows for an important, and sometimes overriding, influence of nonresidents' ballots. Nevertheless, in the absence of any mandatory fundamental legislation concerning cooperative interregional and cross-border cooperation, this issue in Galicia has depended on the willingness of the government in power at any given moment and, furthermore, on the work done by the local entities located along of the Spanish-Portuguese border. Both the EU INTERREG initiative and the Valencia Convention served as the financial instrument and the legal framework in order to conclude cooperative projects between Portugal and Galicia. In 1991, the Galicia-Northern Portugal Working Community was formally constituted, its founding members being the Galician Regional Government and the Portuguese Commission for Coordination and Regional Development of the North Region, with some municipalities joining at a later date. The Euroregion progressively acquired a growing importance, and the creation, in 1992, of the *Eixo Atlántico do Noroeste Peninsular* (Atlantic Axis of the Peninsular Northwest) was a milestone in the consolidation of one of the most active Euroregions of the 1990s. Although it enjoys the support of the Galician Regional Government, the *Eixo* is conceived of as an instrument of cooperation between local entities (12 founding municipalities, which have since increased to 34), and in the almost 20 years it has been active, its work has been characterized by the pursuit of effective cooperation with an increasing strategic vision, in permanent dialogue with the Regional Government and the European Commission.

After the comparative success of three different INTERREG Initiative Programmes affecting the Spanish-Portuguese cross-border area up to 2006, the EU Commission approved in 2007 (in force until 2013), under the financial coverage of the European Regional Development Fund, the Operational Programme for Cross-border Cooperation: Spain–Portugal, which affects a wide area of home to more than 10 % of the population of the Iberian Peninsula. The Region's priorities are cooperation and joint management for the improvement of

competitiveness and the promotion of employment, cooperation, and joint management in environment; cultural heritage and risk prevention; cooperation and joint
management in spatial planning and accessibility; cooperation and joint management for socio-economic and institutional integration; and technical assistance for
the process of cross-border cooperation. Twenty-seven different projects have been
approved to date under this Programme in the Galicia-Northern Portugal area.

In such a situation as we have briefly described, how could an amendment of the
Galician Statute help? We have noted above that the current text of the Statute of
Autonomy of Extremadura reveals the best statement of intentions to be found in
Spanish Regional Fundamental Laws. Accordingly, a hypothetical amendment
of the Galician Statute should follow the path blazed by the above-mentioned
example. As laws primarily binding Regional Governments, Statutes of Autonomy
have legal requirements directed at Regional Authorities. The latter have a large
number of powers involved, as we set out above, in providing public services in
which joint management and cross-border cooperation have demonstrated their
enormous potential. Some of these powers are joint with Local Authorities in a
multilevel Governance model with an extensive track record. Even if we take into
account some inefficient examples in cases in which concurrent powers have been
guilty of poor practices, the Spanish territorial structure, using both Regional and
Local Authorities, could serve again, as it has done over the last 30 years, as an
opportunity to solve real problems that affect cross-border and Euroregion citizens.
The joint management of a wide range of infrastructures already in place for
providing public services (health, water, waste treatment, transportation of people
and goods, culture, tourism, etc.) and, more particularly, the strategic planning of
future ones could be established more easily if, from its high position in the hierarchy
of Spanish Law, the Statute foresees the possibilities for Galician development that
cooperation involves.

Regrettably, Galician political parties have been unable to reach agreement over
the amendment of the Statute of Autonomy and in all probability will not come any
closer to doing so in the coming months or even during the whole parliamentary
term. Surely, there are worse consequences of this lack of agreement that concern
the powers and structure of Galician self-government. However, it is also true that
without specific legal provisions in the Galician Statute of Autonomy, cooperative
development formulas will struggle against legal barriers, wasting their strength,
which could be much more usefully employed in combating underdevelopment,
unemployment, lack of recourses, and other such problems. Now, that is what I call
inefficiency.

# Determining of Local Attributions on Sectorial Legislation in Spain

Cristina Zoco Zabala

**Abstract** The objective of this work is to explain the problems derived from statutory regulation of local attributions in the competencies of the Autonomous Communities (*Translator's note:* According to Article 143 of the 1978 Spanish Constitution, Autonomous Communities are territorial administrations composed of provinces with common historical, cultural, and economic characteristics. They are therefore entities similar—up to a certain point—to States in the United States and to the German *Länder*, albeit with considerable differences in terms of competencies with the aforementioned American and German entities and also with differences in competencies between the 17 existing Autonomous Communities) in Spain. Local autonomy is a concurrent competence that depends on it being attributed by the Spanish Central State, which in practice means that the development of its basic characteristics, in terms of listing the pertinent local attributions, is something that depends on the margin of intervention as established by the relevant Spanish Central State-level organs. Apart from its condition of being a concurrent competence, local autonomy is an institutional guarantee of minimum contents, recognised as a right but undefined as such in the Spanish Constitution. As a result, the *quantum* of Autonomous Community intervention in this matter is quite limited from a constitutional perspective. Since the competences of the Autonomous Communities are attributions determined by Statutes of Autonomy (according to article 147.2. of the Spanish Constitution), the proposal here is to regulate the local attributions of Autonomous-Community competences within the sectorial laws that regulate each matter. In this way, the rigid procedure of statutory reform is disconnected from the contingencies of the basic law to which, in any event, corresponds the determination of the margin of Autonomous Community intervention in the subject matter.

C. Zoco Zabala (✉)
Universidad Pública de Navarra, Campus Arrosadia, 31006 Pamplona, Spain
e-mail: cristina.zoco@unavarra.es

A. López-Basaguren and L. Escajedo San Epifanio (eds.), *The Ways of Federalism in Western Countries and the Horizons of Territorial Autonomy in Spain*, Vol. 2, DOI 10.1007/978-3-642-27717-7_59, © Springer-Verlag Berlin Heidelberg 2013

# Introduction

Recently, the Spanish Constitutional Court recognised the constitutionality of Article 84.2 of the Statute of Autonomy of Catalonia, as reformed in 2006, which articulates local faculties in Autonomous Community competencies (Constitutional Court Sentence 31/2010). The definition of local autonomy, as far as local attributions of Autonomous Community competencies is concerned, has been quite a novelty not only because a Statute of Autonomy—the basic institutional norm of an Autonomous Community with special approval and reform procedures—has for the first time ever assumed the regulation of this aspect of the matter of competencies. It was also a novelty because the Constitutional Court has limited the scope of what is basic in terms of local autonomy to the designation of competencies of local intervention without making reference to the functions of local entities in terms of Autonomous Community-level competencies. In this sense, it has not only determined that the statutory regulation of local attributions in Autonomous Community-level competencies is possible, as long as the framework established by the basic Spanish State-level legislation *ex* article 149.1.18 of the Spanish Constitution is respected; it has also expressed that in terms of local autonomy, State organs are to regulate the essential principles on State and local competencies, without expressly mentioning the functions that are susceptible of being under complete local intervention.

The jurisprudential delimitation of what is basic in local competencies is preceded by the repressed attempt by Spanish State-level legislators to define as a basic matter the faculties that are attributable to competencies that are susceptible of local intervention (Draft Project of the Basic Local Government and Administration Law, dated 3rd May 2006) both belonging to the State and to the Autonomous Community briefs. It would seem that it has been understood to be preferable that the determination of local faculties in competencies of sectorial attribution should be determined in the Autonomous Community level. However certainly desirable this may be in terms of guaranteeing the efficiency of public services and if the absence of a State-level definition allows for its determination in the Autonomous Community level, for various reasons questions are raised on whether such a definition should be made in the corresponding Statute of Autonomy.

First, because it is not possible to ignore that, as far as concurrent competencies are concerned, the ultimate decision on the *quantum* of Autonomous Community intervention in concurrent competencies corresponds to State-level organs. The delimitation of what is basic is also a State attribution, so the decision on whether the local faculties in Autonomous Community competencies is assimilated to the development of what is basic and thus also belongs to State-level organs. Inasmuch as the concrete articulation of concurrent competencies is a Central State attribution, the will of State organs to restrict any of the local faculties in Autonomous Community competencies or to define them in a contrary manner to what is foreseen in the sectorial level would determine the prevalence of the basic State-level legislation as against Autonomous Community-level legislation.

It is true that the delimitation of Autonomous Community regulation of non-basic content in terms of local autonomy does not leave room for uncontrolled State-level regulation of basic matters. However, the problem becomes more serious if we bear in mind that local autonomy, apart from being a concurrent competence, is an institutional guarantee of minimum levels. Such minimum levels are recognised but not defined as law in the Spanish Constitution, which makes it possible for the Spanish State-level legislator to restrict, to a greater extent, the margin of Autonomous Community intervention that is already limited not to essential but to minimum contents.

Regulating local attributions in Statutes of Autonomy would imply connecting the content of this basic institutional norm to the modifications established in the basic law. Also, article 147.2 d) of the Spanish Constitution regulates that the competencies assumed within the constitutional framework are to be part of the content of the Statutes of Autonomy, without referring to the concrete articulation thereof.

An intervention by State-level organs is necessary in order to limit, from a material perspective, the basic essential content of Autonomous Community competencies that are susceptible of local intervention or to assimilate the development of basic contents to the faculties of local entities. In terms of Autonomous Community rights, it is proposed that local attributions in Autonomous Community competencies are determined not in the Statutes of Autonomy, but in sectorial legislation that regulates each of the competencies susceptible of local intervention instead.

## Regulation of Local Attributions by Statutes of Autonomy

In general terms, reforms of Statutes of Autonomy have not developed the local attributions foreseen in the State-level basic norm, with the exception of the Catalan Statute. In comparison with other statute reforms that have based competencies of municipalities and even provinces on the basic Spanish State-level legislation and on the present or future law on local regime of the Autonomous Community,[1] the Catalan Statute has been a pioneering law in that it regulates, for the first time, functions in relation with Autonomous Community competences that municipalities may implement.[2]

---

[1] Articles 45.1 and 47.2 of the Statute of Autonomy of Castile-Leon (Spanish Organic Law 14/2007, dated 30th November), Article 64.1 *in fine* of the Statute of Autonomy of Valencia (Spanish Organic Law 1/2006, dated 10th April), Article 75.8 of the Statute of Autonomy of the Balearic Islands (Spanish Organic Law 1/2007, dated 28th February), and Article 46.1 b) of the LORAFNA (Spanish Organic Law 7/2010, dated 27th October).

[2] Article 84.2 of the Statute of Autonomy of Catalonia (Spanish Organic Law, 6/2006, dated 19th July).

The gradual assumption of competencies by the Autonomous Communities has pointed out not only the need for statutory reforms to award further guarantees to the exercise of local autonomy; it also establishes the need to determine the way in which competencies between Autonomous Communities and local entities are to be articulated in order to guarantee a degree of local autonomy, which is to be guaranteed in any case, and that best serves the purpose of efficiency in public proximity policies.

Before the statute reforms, juridical doctrine had pointed out that the Statutes of Autonomy had to assume the guarantee of local autonomy, gradually pushing aside the Basic Law on Local Regime, in terms of the determination of the local spheres of competency (Font and Llovet 2006). Therefore, it had been understood that the basic institutional norm of the Autonomous Communities had to contain a general declaration according to which municipalities are fully empowered to implement their initiatives, and serve the general interest, without any limit except that related to respecting the law and the competencies of other administrations (Carro 1999/ 2000).

Statute reforms have granted bigger guarantees to local autonomy. Thus, the Statute of Autonomy of Aragon has recurred to the principles of subsidiarity, proportionality, and differentiation, as criteria on which the activity of local entities is to be based.[3] The Statute of Autonomy of Catalonia has expressly referred to the application of the criterion of differentiation in terms of the laws that affect the juridical, organic, functional, competency, and financial regime of municipalities, and that principle is understood as the need for norms to take into account the various demographical, geographical, functional, organisational, dimensional characteristics and in terms of the management capacity such norms indeed have.[4]

With the exception of the Catalan statute, in general terms, the reformation of the Statutes of Autonomy has not brought about the local attributions foreseen in the national basic norm. The Catalan statute was pioneering in terms of regulating, for the first time ever, functions in relation with Autonomous Community competencies that the municipalities can implement,[5] if compared with other statutory reforms that have made reference to the competencies of municipalities and even of provinces that are established in the basic State legislation and in the present or future autonomous community-level legislation on local regime.[6]

---

[3] Article 85.1 of the Statute of Autonomy of Aragón (Spanish Organic Law 5/2007, dated 20th April).

[4] Article 88.1 of the Statute of Autonomy of Catalonia (Spanish Organic Law 5/2007, dated 20th April).

[5] Article 84.2 of the Statute of Autonomy of Catalonia (Spanish Organic Law, 6/2006, dated 19th July).

[6] Articles 45.1 and 47.2 of the Statute of Autonomy of Castile-Leon (Spanish Organic Law 14/ 2007, dated 30th November), Article 64.1 *in fine* of the Statute of Autonomy of Valencia (Spanish Organic Law 1/2006, dated 10th April), Article 75.8 of the Statute of Autonomy of the Balearic Islands (Spanish Organic Law 1/2007, dated 28th February), and Article 46.1 b) of the LORAFNA (Spanish Organic Law 7/2010, dated 27th October).

This regime expressly determines the functions that correspond to the municipalities in each of the competencies susceptible of local intervention while recognising at the same time that the competency of the Generalitat (the Catalan Autonomous Community government) in terms of local regime is to determine the restriction of the central State competency. Local entities are integrated, therefore, in the institutional framework of the Generalitat (Franch 2009).

Strictly speaking, statute reforms have awarded more protagonism to municipalities as the basic local entities and the fundamental instrument for the participation of the local community in public matters.[7] Several Statutes of Autonomy have recurred to a general clause on municipal competencies when establishing that such local entities have complete discretion for the exercise of their initiative in any matter that is not excluded from its competency or is attributed exclusively to other administrations or authorities[8]; in the same sense, it has been pointed out that the Statute guarantees the municipalities their own nucleus of competencies that is to be exercised with complete autonomy, respecting the Constitution and the Law.[9]

Only certain Statutes of Autonomy have mentioned the provinces or their functions, as a reminder of what is established in the Constitution and in the Basic Law on Local Regime for these local entities and in accordance with the autonomy the Constitution reserves for them.[10] In certain statute reforms, it has been expressly recognised that local competencies correspond solely to municipalities.[11] The omission of the provinces by other Statutes of Autonomy, ignores the functions that the Constitution establishes for them in its articles 137 and 141 (Salvador Crespo 2007).

---

[7] Article 82.1 of the Statute of Autonomy of Aragón (Spanish Organic Law 5/2007, dated 20th April), Article 75.1 of the Statute of Autonomy of the Balearic Islands (Spanish Organic Law 1/2007, dated 28th February).

[8] Article 75.5 of the Statute of Autonomy of the Balearic Islands (Spanish Organic Law 1/2007, dated 28th February).

[9] Article 92.1 of the Statute of Autonomy of Andalucía (Spanish Organic Law 2/2007, dated 19th March).

[10] Article 84 of the Statute of Autonomy of Aragón has appealed to the functions of the province in terms of cooperation, assistance, and providing of services to municipalities and districts mentioned in Article 36 of the Basic Law on Local Regime. Likewise, this is also the case of Article 66 of the Statute of Autonomy of Valencia. However, provinces are not mentioned as a local entity in the Statute of Autonomy of Catalonia (Spanish Organic Law 6/2006, dated 19th July), although Article 84.2 thereof makes reference, in general terms—to the competencies of "local governments", to express many of the matters of municipal competency regulated in Article 25.2 of the Basic Law on Local Regime.

[11] Article 45.2 of the Statute of Autonomy of Castilla-León (Spanish Organic Law 14/2007, dated 30th November).

# Local Autonomy: A Concurrent Competency Attributed by the Central State in Spain

The enumeration of local attributions in the competencies assumed by the Statute of Autonomy of Catalonia is an expression of the development of the basics in terms of local autonomy. However, it cannot be ignored that this assimilation of local attributions for the development of basic matters is continuously and necessarily connected to the margin of intervention allowed for under the basic State-level law, as a consequence of the competency entitlement attributed by the Constitution to State organs for the determination of the basic content of local autonomy (article 149.1.18 of the Spanish Constitution).

The determination of state competencies and those of the Autonomous Communities is initially carried out in the Constitution and in the Statutes of Autonomy, in such a manner that the regulation of the basic content reference to local autonomy corresponds to the Spanish State and the correlative development thereof corresponds to the Autonomous Communities. However, the concrete articulation of certain competencies is only achieved by means of the definition, by State organs, of the scope of application of their norms.

It is true that the competencies are of statutory attribution and are not attributed by legislative measures and that therefore those that are attributable to the State should not be understood as "competencies of the competencies", the mission of which is to separate scopes of sectorial norm intervention without restriction. However, all such considerations cannot conceal the fact that "the express determination of the basic or additional character of State Law produces a demarcation in competencies that is not an 'effect' but the objective, pure and simple, of the norm-producing capability of the State" (Jiménez et al. 2011).

The Constitutional Court has expressed the need to guarantee content for the development of basic matters when it points out that State competency attribution reference to the basic content of a matter may not be used to cut concurrent Autonomous Community competencies or to leave them devoid of content, from a constitutional perspective (Sentences of the Constitutional Court 69/1988 and 80/1998). Therefore, the Autonomous Communities are to have the necessary competencies to regulate what is not essential in that it does not affect general interests (Sentences of the Constitutional Court 32/1981, 1/1982).

In relation with local autonomy, there is a lack of explicit regulation from the state organs that establishes a demarcation between the content of basics in local intervention competencies, determining the development of local attributions for Autonomous Communities. Without doubt, the possibility that state legislators may restrict the development of basics expressed in the Autonomous Community sphere in terms of local attributions has not been ignored by the Constitutional Court in its Sentence 31/2010. Although it establishes that the enumeration of local faculties in Autonomous Community competencies constitutes a projection of the development of basics, it finally determines that this is possible within the framework of what is established in the basic State-level legislation. It is desirable that the basic content is reduced to essential principles and to the enumeration of local intervention competencies, but this depends on the state organs, as they are legitimated to connect the margin of intervention of Autonomous Community organs to the basic norms that may be adaptable depending on policies of a centripetal or centrifugal nature.

The second phase of local decentralisation started, at the national level, with the failed attempt to approve the draft Basic Law on Local Government and Administration, dated 3rd May 2006. In principle, this draft Law was to substitute Law 7/ 1985, dated 2nd April, still in force, regulating the Basics of the Local Regime. However, there was no agreement on what should regulate the future basic law in relation with the competencies that local entities should assume (Sánchez 2008). In the aforementioned draft Law, there was an extensive enumeration and definition of municipal competencies, in that, in contrast with article 25.2 of the Law on Basics of the Local Regime, local attributions corresponding to each of the matters susceptible of municipal intervention were explicitly enumerated.[12] Also provincial competencies on cooperation and economic and social assistance and cooperation (article 25.3 of the draft law) are established in a more generic fashion by article 36 of the Law on Basics of the Local Regime. The reason for this is that basic legislation is not part of the constitutional block, so that the delimitation of local attributions or the restriction of the State margin thereof is dependent, in any case, on constitutional determination.

# Local Autonomy: An Institutional Guarantee with a Minimum Content

The problem becomes more serious if it is necessary that local autonomy becomes, apart from a concurrent matter, a recognised institutional guarantee even though it is undefined as a right in the Constitution. A compulsory regulation of a minimum content, which is what the institutional guarantee of local autonomy consists of, means that local entities do not have the right to take matters of insufficient local autonomy as legally regulated before the Constitutional Court. It also means that

---

[12] Thus, for example, municipal competencies in terms of the historical and artistic heritage established by Article 25.2 e) of the Law on Basics of the Local Regime are completed with concrete attributions in Article 22.1 h) of the Draft Law on Local Government and Administration when it establishes that it is the municipalities who have to protect and conserve the municipal historical heritage and elaborate and approve special protection plans and catalogues. Reference to the provinces, Article 25.3 of the draft law determines the attributions of its specific functions of cooperation and economic, social, and technical assistance that is enunciated by Article 36 of the Law on Basics of the Local Regime. Among them, the juridical defence of the municipality, the formalities involved in the preparation of administrative matters, computer formats and the creation of computer networks, and the execution of works and provision of municipal services by the Town Council.

the state-level legislators are not obliged to assimilate, as a minimum content, regulation by the Autonomous Communities of local competencies.

Not even the limitations to local autonomy expressed in other laws different from that on the basics of the local regime have been considered violations of local autonomy, independently of the fact that the law on basics has a higher rank than other laws that have limited the *quantum* of the local entities' regulating power that other laws produced later on.

Constitutional Court jurisprudence, as guarantor of local autonomy, covered by the Constitution in defence of local autonomy, does not define local autonomy either as an institutional guarantee the outer limits of which are to be defined by national or autonomous community legislators in each of the competencies susceptible of local intervention. The Constitutional Court that decided on the first conflict of competencies formulated by the town of Ceuta did not produce a substantial change either in terms of the Constitutional Court jurisprudence on the meaning of a constitutionally guaranteed local autonomy (Constitutional Court Sentence 240/2006). Moreover, it could not have been otherwise since local autonomy does not imply a constitutional right to obtain exclusive competencies (Miguez 2002), and the fact that it is an institutional guarantee defers us to the decisions taken by ordinary legislators. Insofar as guaranteeing constitutional principles constitutes an essential component of the political juridical order, local autonomy is, in any case, a nucleus or redoubt that is not accessible for legislators,[13] but not even an obligation to extract the *quantum* of regulation power that it is going to defer to local entities.

## The Commitment to Insert Local Attributions in Sectorial Laws

The regulation of local attributions in the Statute of Autonomy of Catalonia has implied the recognition of the need to define local autonomy to guarantee a better efficiency of public administrations. A progressive assumption of competencies by Autonomous Communities requires, once more, the intervention by local entities in order to guarantee more efficiency in public services.

Juridical doctrine has postulated the need for Statutes of Autonomy to be interpretative norms and that on the basis thereof that determinations should be taken on the articulation of the respective competencies (Ortega 2006). However, it is questionable that such regulation should be contained in Statutes of Autonomy.

Firstly, only the autonomous community competencies and not the concrete articulation thereof are attributable to statutes of autonomy. Article 147.2 d) of the Spanish Constitution determines the competencies assumed by the Autonomous Community as contents of statutes of autonomy but makes no reference whatsoever to their concrete articulation.

---

[13] SSTC 32/1981; 46/1992; 40/1998, entre otras.

Another reason that justifies this statutory disconnection from the expression of local attributions is that statutes of autonomy are basic institutional norms by nature, which, from a formal perspective, implies a special reform procedure (Article 147.3 of the Spanish Constitution). A statutory delegation of the attributions in autonomous community competencies would imply connecting the rigid procedure of reform of the basic institutional norm to the feasibility of predictions that state organs may carry out on the margin of intervention of the autonomous community legislation, which are only limited by the inexistence of non-essential contents, which has not been defined.

The statutory expression of local faculties in autonomous community competencies connects statute modification to the contingencies of the basic law. This is the legal typology that integrates the constitutional block but, in contrast to other norms, is characterised by its elasticity, insofar as the delimitation of the scope of competence of Autonomous Communities is implemented in an indirect manner as a consequence of its content (Rubio Llorente: 2011).

Today, the basic law on local autonomy has not reached a consensus to express which local faculties are attributable to autonomous community competencies, but neither has it provided any freedom to autonomous community organs with which to determine such faculties.

The solution lies in the regulation of local functions in sectorial laws that regulate autonomous community competencies in terms of local intervention. This would imply leaving aside the rigid procedure of statute reform in case of inadequate development of basic contents to the state-level norms that cover such local interventions.

# References

Carro, J.L. (1999/2000). La cláusula de competencia municipal. Anuario del Gobierno Local, 1, 1999/2000: 37–60.

Font y Llovet, T. (2006). El régimen local en la reforma de los Estatutos de Autonomía. In: Font I Llovet, T. Ortega, L., Velasco, F. El régimen local en la reforma de los Estatutos de Autonomía, Centro de Estudios Políticos y Constitucionales, Madrid, España, pp. 11–39.

Franch, M. (2009). Existe-t-il des principes de répartition de compétences en Espagne?,. In : BRISSON, J.F. (ed.). Les transferts de compétences de l'État aux collectivités territoriales, L' Harmattan, Paris, pp. 39–44.

Jimenez, J. Duque, J.C. (2011) Legislación básica. In: Aragón Reyes, M., and Aguado, C. (eds.) Temas básicos de derecho constitucional. Organización general y territorial del Estado. Thomson Reuters, Cizur Menor, España, pp. 424–429.

Miguez, L. (2002). El sistema de las competencias locales ante el nuevo pacto local. Revista de Estudios de la Administración Local 289: 37–58.

Ortega, L. (2006). Legislación básica y Estatutos de Autonomía. In: Ortega, L. Solozábal, J.L., Arbós, X. Legislación básica y Estatutos de Autonomía. Centro de Estudios Políticos y Constitucionales, Madrid, España, pp. 1–103.

Rubio Llorente, F. (2011). Bloque de constitucionalidad. In: Aragón, M., Aguado, C. (eds.) Temas básicos de derecho constitucional. Constitución, Estado constitucional, partidos y elecciones y fuentes del derecho, Tomo I, Thomson Reuters, Cizur Menor, España, pp. 60–63.

Salvador, M. (2007). La autonomía provincial en el sistema constitucional español. Instituto Nacional de Administración Pública, Madrid, España, 495 pp.

Sánchez, A.J. (2008). Autonomía local y descentralización. Su naturaleza jurídica. Tirant lo Blanch, Valencia, España, 237 pp.

# The Governance of Metropolitan Areas: Problems and Alternatives in the Spanish Case

Joaquín Martín Cubas and Antonio Montiel Márquez

In federalist thinking, a constant is the tension in defining optimal levels of government, its territorial scope and functions. These questions are particularly difficult at the local level. This is where we find that the differences between various forms of structuring local governments are vast. This is the case from the point of view of their legal status. In Spain, for example, we find municipalities, provinces, island authorities, counties, metropolitan areas, communities, consortia, local entities below the municipal level and other juridical forms. However, it is also the case from the point of view of their socioeconomic characteristics. Thus, for instance, it is difficult to compare cities such as Madrid or Barcelona, with several million inhabitants, with those localities that do not even reach 100 residents.

Recently, this debate has gained some prominence in Spain. The economic crisis has forced cuts in government expenditures. In one way or another, with varying intensity, the main political parties have made proposals that would have the effect of removing some of the local authorities listed above. In particular, the most noteworthy proposals include the suppression of municipalities with fewer than 500 inhabitants and the elimination of Provincial Councils in a manner that is consistent with the Constitution of Spain.

This communication has been made under the research project "Environmental and Social Sustainability in metropolitan areas: the case of the metropolitan area of Valencia" (reference CSO2010 sub-6E06-20481) funded by the Ministry of Science and Innovation (Plan Nacional I + D + i 2008–2011). This article would not have been possible without the collaboration of Marcos Soler who kindly assisted us in the revision of the English translation. Marcos Soler is Director of Research and Strategic Initiatives for the Civilian Complaint Review Board (CCRB) and adjunct professor of government at the John Jay College of Criminal Justice in New York.

J. Martín Cubas (✉) • A. Montiel Márquez
Facultad de Derecho, Departamento de Derecho Constitucional y Ciencia Política, Universidad de Valencia, Avda. de los Naranjos s/n, 46071 Valencia, Spain
e-mail: joaquin.martin@uv.es; Antonio.Montiel@uv.es

A. López-Basaguren and L. Escajedo San Epifanio (eds.), *The Ways of Federalism in Western Countries and the Horizons of Territorial Autonomy in Spain*, Vol. 2, DOI 10.1007/978-3-642-27717-7_60, © Springer-Verlag Berlin Heidelberg 2013

None of these proposals addresses, however, the possibility of establishing metropolitan governments as a functional alternative to the current local and municipal structure. In our opinion, this state of affairs is paradoxical. Given their characteristics, metropolitan authorities provide the best conditions for real savings in public spending and greater efficiency in the management of certain public functions. The purpose is not to eliminate municipalities. First, this would be something difficult to fit in the constitutional structure. Second, metropolitan areas consist of municipalities. Third, from the point of view of identity politics, such an initiative is likely to find strong opposition. Rather, the objective is to explore the development of alternative forms of local authority. It is to move the management of many of traditional local functions from local bodies to the metropolitan authority. The reason is that the current management by municipal authorities multiplies bureaucracy, lacks coordination, and fails to generate cost-saving economies of scale in areas such as metropolitan transportation, water, or waste management.

In this paper, we aim to first, discuss the relevance of the notion of good governance within the government of metropolitan areas; second, describe the historical development of this political and administrative institutions in Spain; third, evaluate the current state of affairs on metropolitan areas and their governance from a legal perspective; fourth, assess models of metropolitan governance from a comparative perspective; fifth, analyze the situation of Spain's major metropolitan areas in the light of the foregoing considerations; and sixth, propose guidelines on metropolitan governance for the future of Spain.

## The Metropolitan Area as a Community of Interests

The *White Paper on European Governance* defines the term governance as the capability of societies to provide themselves with systems of representation, institutions, processes and social bodies as an instrument of democratic control, participation in decision-making, and collective responsibility. It is evident that large urban agglomerations and their metropolitan areas generate demands for governance. They demand answers that are to be conceived from the logic of a common interest. The goal is to maximize functionality and consistency, efficiency and effectiveness, and ultimately, the welfare of citizens.

For Joaquin Farinós, since the early 1980s, space and territory are two key factors in understanding governance. They are positioned as a strategic element of the first order that ensures the development and quality of life for residents. It leads to a new approach in making sense of the development of territories—one that is based on the notion of *government intelligence*. This is a new tool for managing information and knowledge at the service of good governance. If, in the past, the dimension of *policy* and *politics* were differentiated, they now come together. We argue that the current challenge is to *tailor public policy to the territory and not the opposite*. In Spain, however, urban planning and economic approaches that emphasize municipal or regional solutions rather than holistic approaches continue to dominate the debate. They fail to put the emphasis on territorial governance of a supramunicipal character. There are neither specific governmental institutions for our metropolitan areas nor territorial culture of the metropolitan area. At this juncture, many are the authors who have stressed the need to take "*neo-institutionalist* approaches, with greater presence of the public powers" (Farinós 2005, pp. 219–235).

From our perspective, the old and new contradictions and problems facing the major metropolitan areas compel us to think about the design of strategies and governments around the notion of a shared common good for a metropolitan area. However, to be sure, this does not mean that a territorial authority with responsibilities and powers must always be implemented. Thus, for instance, Bernard Jouve argues that, for a long time, the question of governance of the metropolis has been narrowly treated from an *institutional* perspective. This form of analysis looks for the streamlining of the administrative and political map of the metropolis. Yet, innovative ways of thinking about analysis and action have evolved very clearly in a different direction. His argument suggests that we can identify different types of metropolitan governance and, then, analyze their effects. At that point, we can determine whether or not these models have been able to establish causal links between modes of governance, economic competitiveness, and internal coherence. Furthermore, we see that the absence of an institutional form of authority can be the source of innovative forms of social mobilization (Jouve 2005: p. 89).

Institutional and noninstitutional innovative forms of metropolitan governance are not prevailing in Spain. In our country, traditional approaches continue to dominate urban and municipal economic planning. This is consistent with the style and culture of Spanish regional economic planning. Metropolitan strategic plans are infrequent. They deal rarely with metropolitan concerns. Their primary objective is not to address a sustainable development of the territory by bringing about a comprehensive rather than sectional approach (Farinós et al. 2005: p. 126). Furthermore, the most alarming aspect of the field of planning in Spain is the lack of innovation in thinking about our country's metropolitan areas.

## The History of Metropolitan Governance in Our Country (Spain)

In Spain, neither in the past nor in the present have we been able to fix indisputable objective criteria defining what a metropolitan area is from a functional point of view. The criteria that are normally used are population and the interdependence between the urban areas. However, from a juridical standpoint, it has been a constant, until the 1980s, the consideration of four major metropolitan areas, namely, Madrid, Barcelona, Valencia, and Bilbao. In any case, the definition of these areas as local authorities is very recent. It was not done until the 1970s. Prior to that point, they did not have that character. It was management by state-run agencies of certain functions or services. These agencies provided a venue for the involved municipalities to raise their concerns in a very limited fashion.

For example, for the purposes of urban planning, agencies were created in the *Gran Madrid* (1944), the *Gran Bilbao* (1945), and the *Gran Valencia* (1946). For the management of water, a body, *Canal Isabel II*, was created in 1851 for the Madrid area. In 1955, a similar body was created for the area of Barcelona. In the field of transportation, specific plans were approved for Madrid (1956) and Barcelona (1957). Finally, in 1963, in the area of Madrid, an autonomous state organ was established, the *Planning and Coordination Committee of the Metropolitan Area of Madrid* (COPLACO). The goal was to perform these functions.

In fact, the first metropolitan area established as a local government entity was the *Metropolitan Authority of Barcelona*. It was created by Decree Law of August 24, 1974. It preceded the setting of *metropolitan municipal authorities* under Law 41/1975 of November 19, 1975. The law was never implemented and was repealed in 1978. The reason was a twist of fate. The end of the Franco regime (franco dies on November 20, 1975) and the early days of the transition to democracy delayed the development of metropolitan governments. With the creation of a federalized government, which consists of *Comunidad Autonomas* (autonomous communities), for the regions and nationalities expressly recognized in the Constitution of 1978, the focus shifted towards the new political institutions—*the autonomous community*. The metropolitan areas were not even mentioned in the new Constitution, except for an indirect reference in Article 141.3: "different networks of municipalities, which are different, from the province can be set."

One has to wait for the approval of Law 7/1985 of April 2, 1985, which regulates the *Basis of Local Government*, to experience some revitalization of the idea of a metropolitan area. The law put forth three ideas. First, the law proclaims in Article 43.1 that the autonomous communities (after hearing from the central administration, municipalities, and provincial councils) can create, modify, and/or delete, by Law, metropolitan areas, according to the provisions of their Statutes. Second, metropolitan areas will consist of local governments and municipalities representing large urban centers. Two conditions applied. Economic and social linkages must exist among the population, and joint planning and coordination of certain services and public works is required. Finally, the legislation of each autonomous community determines the governance and management of the municipalities within the metropolitan area. It will also establish the economic and operational framework. This will ensure the participation of all municipalities in decision-making and the fair distribution of costs between them. It will also determine the allocation of services and public works within the metropolitan area.

The independence of the autonomous communities to regulate metropolitan areas resulted in various forms of government and different models of governance. For example, the Madrid metropolitan area, or at least the largest part, became an autonomous community. This gave it a government with broad powers. In the case of Barcelona, it is a true institutional metropolitan area since 1974. In the case of Valencia, in 1986, *Gran Valencia* was eliminated. At that time, Law 12/1986 of December 3, 1986, created the *Metropolitan Consell de l'Horta*. This is the governing body of the metropolitan area of Valencia. Finally, in the case of Bilbao and its area, the institution of *Gran Bilbao* was dismantled in 1980. There was no replacement. However, the *Consorcio Aguas del Gran Bilbao*, now called *Consorcio de Aguas Bilbao-Bizcaia*, continued to exist. It supplies water and sanitation services throughout the territory of Biscay. In addition, *Bilbao Metropoli-30* has been recently created representing a private association of public institutions involved in the ongoing strategic evaluation of the area.

The different paths taken conceal a fundamental problem common to all areas. This problem has been confirmed by the crisis and the demise of the two metropolitan areas that, in the strict sense of the term, were established in the 1980s. There are different analyses, but Rodríguez Álvarez has provided with the best compilation of reasons. As he notes, there were recurring problems for the institutionalization of metropolitan areas everywhere. They included fear of the municipalities in the periphery to be in a position of subordination to the central city or—the opposite of the previous phenomenon—fear from the central city; fear from the other levels of government, whether autonomous communities or the central state, in creating a political counterweight; the existence of different type of political majorities that were less inclined to political consensus with the municipalities they served; the possible existence of an imbalance in the development of the rest of the state; or an overly technocratic approach resulting in a subsequent distancing from the citizens, which created distrust towards the metropolitan governments (Rodríguez 2005).

It was precisely in the 1990s, partly for the reasons mentioned above, partly because metropolitan areas emerged as a kind of political counterpart to the respective regional governmental areas, that the metropolitan areas of Barcelona and Valencia were suppressed by the governments of Catalonia, first, and the Valencia. After that, they were replaced by single-purpose entities with a specialized form of management. In Barcelona (1987), the *Metropolitan Transport of Barcelona*, consisted of 18 municipalities, and the *Metropolitan Water Services and Waste Management*, which is later known as the M*etropolitan Municipalities of Environment*, grouped 32 municipalities. In Valencia (2001), the *Metropolitan Waste Treatment* consisted of 5 municipalities, and the *Metropolitan Water Services* consisted of 51 municipalities.

We would like to add that, in the case of Barcelona, about 30 municipalities created in 1988, following the abolition of the metropolitan area, the *Association of Municipalities of the Metropolitan Area of Barcelona*. Years later, in 2009, this group turned into a consortium. This was a voluntary association of municipalities with fewer functions than the previous authority. It could handle neither transportation nor water nor waste management. On the other side, the municipality of Barcelona laid out the design of a *Metropolitan Strategic Plan* with the involvement of 35 municipalities and many other political and social actors in the area.

This was the situation that Spanish cities faced at the turn of the century. With the change of government in 2004 and the push for reform of the statutes of autonomous communities, we saw the emergence of the current models of metropolitan governance in Spain. We explore them in the next section.

## The Regulatory Framework in Spain After the Reforms
## of the Statutes of the Autonomous Communities of 2006

The reforms of the Statutes of the autonomous communities occurred from 2005 to 2010. They dealt with new perspectives regarding the functional articulation of relations between different levels of government. It is therefore important to analyze the idea of a metropolitan area in light of these reforms.

The first reform to take place was the reform of the Statute of the autonomous community of Valencia. The previous 1982 Statute, which was approved by Law 5/1982 of July 1, 1982, regulated the then local government in Articles 44–47 of Title IV. It is appropriate to draw attention to short reference that is made the regulation of local governments, as it was also the case in the rest of statutes of autonomous communities of that time. The main objective of the various state legislators was to ensure the autonomy of the emerging communities from the central organs of state. Thus, the Statute of 1982 just defined some of the principles that were to guide the life of local entities in relation to the autonomous communities. Article 46.3 provided that "groups of metropolitan areas and counties are regulated by law of the Valencian Parliament to be approved under the same conditions as in the first paragraph", after the local authorities affected being consulted.

The reform of the Statute of the autonomous community of Valencia in 2006 has also affected the statutory regulation of local matters. It does so with less intensity than the evolution of social, political, and legal events permitted. In terms of new developments, this law includes the following novel aspects:

a) First is the mandate to the Valencian Parliament, as it is set in Article 63.4, to promote the creation of forms of association in order to improve the management of common interests and to ensure effective service delivery.
b) Also, the new statute, as did the old, in its Article 65 provides for the possibility of the creation of metropolitan areas, counties, and groups of counties. Their regulation is required by a law passed by two-thirds majority of Les Corts, after the local authorities affected by the proposed regulation being consulted. Regarding the requirement of a qualified majority, this seems consistent with the party system structure in Valencia. The goal is to achieve stability for these legal institutions. Paradoxically, the current law increases the difficulty of forming such entities, which is something that points in the opposite direction of the intent of the law.

A similar analysis applies to the rest of the statutory amendments that occurred since then. They devote virtually no attention to the notion of a metropolitan area. For example, in the case of Catalonia, there is only a reference to the metropolitan area in Article 93. As in the rest of the statutes of other communities, the article reiterates the point that the Catalan Parliament can, by law, set the creation, modification, and/or deletion of a metropolitan area, as well as the establishment of its legal system. In the case of Aragon, Article 81.2 of the new statute provides the only reference to the idea of metropolitan areas. It states that a law of the Parliament of Aragon regulates their creation, organization, and functions. In the case of Andalusia, it is Article 94 that refers to the possibility of a group of municipalities establishing a law to regulate the functions of metropolitan areas. In the case of Castilla-León, the only reference to the notion of a metropolitan area is limited to Article 52.1. The article states that the community of Castilla y León encourages association by autonomous local entities to protect and promote their common interests. These are poor regulations, and they do not bring innovation. In the vast majority of cases, they just copy the regulations adopted in the first period of the Spanish Constitutional process.

Contrary to the spirit of the statutory reforms, it is the case of Barcelona and its metropolitan area. A recent act of the Parliament of Catalonia seems to indicate a significant change in trend. The act is law 31/2010 of August 3, 2010, concerning the Metropolitan Area of Barcelona. This act creates an authority that will assume new powers, Powers that are currently exercised by the entities running metropolitan transportation, water, and waste treatment services. It also includes the current *Association of Municipalities*. Finally, it also incorporates a new urban planning function to comply with a new legislation by the Catalan Parliament concerning local planning. The adoption of Decree 175/2010, of November 23, 2010, which has created a Joint Commission between the Government of Catalonia and the representatives of the Metropolitan Area of Barcelona, calls for a rapid implementation of the provisions of the new law. The purpose is to propose the establishment of mechanisms for cooperation and collaboration regarding the implementation of the Law 31/2010 of August 3, 2010. Law 31/2010 regulates the scope of authority and functions of the Government of Catalonia. The feasibility of implementation of this is subject to changes in regional and municipal majorities that have occurred in recent elections.

## The Comparison of Metropolitan Governance Models

We have explored recent juridical and institutional developments in Spain in regard to the governance of metropolitan areas. We now turn to examine development in Europe and elsewhere concerning this matter. Our concern is to understand how metropolitan governments are structured from a comparative perspective. Jouve and Lefebre have identified five types of institutional settings in relation to the government of the metropolis:

1. *City-State*: cities whose regulation is largely due to the state. This is because either the city is geographically and politically fused with the state, as is the case in Singapore, or the state retains a central role in regulating urban politics, as it is the case of Britain and of the Netherlands. The main problems of these cities are, on the one hand, its reliance on national policy and, on the other hand, a

framework for action that is too rigid. In Spain, after the transition to democracy, the best examples of this model are the cities of Ceuta and Melilla.

2. *New Gargantuas*: metropolitan areas that are provided with a new common institutional authority. This is the case either through mergers or through the creation of new local entities that are superimposed on the existing metropolis. Good example of this type of configuration would be London, with the Greater London Authority, or Stuttgart, in Germany. The strength of this approach lies in the strong presence of local actors As a result, whenever these strong local actors are not present, as is the case in the metropolitan cities of Italy or the city-province of the Netherlands, the model has failed. In democratic Spain, the best example of this model was the establishment of the metropolitan authorities in the metropolitan areas of Barcelona and Valencia that ended in failure.

3. *Mesolevel of government*: cities in which the regional political and institutional authorities assume the role of a metropolitan institution. For example, this is the case for the cities of Madrid and Zurich. The model has clear advantages. It reduces institutional fragmentation, minimizes the impact of political checks, and balances and simplifies decision-making processes. The weakness is the potential for conflict between functional and institutional spheres within the metropolis. It results in a gap between policy-making organs and the public.

4. *Networked Governance*: cities in which the mode of aggregation does not pass through the creation of a particular institution. Rather, the process of aggregation works through the setting of alliances and agreements. They take place between various institutional levels and civil society for the purpose of meeting very specific needs. Current examples would be cities like Munich or Lyon. In Spain, only portions of Barcelona and Bilbao have gone down this path. The voluntary character of the agreement defines the very weakness of this type of governance.

5. *Defection and conflict*: cities that have not been able to generate mechanisms of aggregation at the metropolitan level. It does not necessarily mean a total absence of a dynamic metropolitan product of exhaustion. Rather, it implies that attempts to regulate the institutional nature have resulted in the defection of the dominant player. European examples could be Paris or Milan.

There is thus a wide diversity of forms of joint government—and nongovernment entities—within European metropolitan areas. Experience has shown that these formulas do not have the same consequences in terms of functionality and effectiveness in all cases.

## The Metropolitan Governance Models That Exist in Spain Today

The real process of "metropolization" does not cease in its gradual progress. From an empirical point of view, there are different criteria and therefore the results in terms of academic recognition and evaluation. In an Opinion adopted in 2004, ECO/120, The European Economic and Social Council identifies a total of 83

European metropolitan areas, including eight Spanish areas. In order of population (in thousands, period 1999–2003), they are the following: Madrid (4,709), Barcelona (3,950), Valencia (1,328), Sevilla (1,074), Malaga (868), Bilbao (735), Zaragoza (629), and Gijon-Oviedo (628). The Opinion uses as a reference the thresholds established by METREX (Network of European Metropolitan Regions and Areas).

From an academic perspective, other thresholds and criteria are available. They combine the criteria of population density, spatial interdependence, and functional relationships (basically, mobility residence/work). Based on these additional criteria, we identify up to 46 metropolitan areas in Spain. This form of analysis has been done in a broader research project, of which this paper is a part of. The algorithm used for analysis closely follows the conventional criteria used by the Office of Management and Budget (the *Office of Management and Budget*, 2000). However, it is adapted to the specific conditions of the Spanish urban system. According to the methodology applied in this research work, for example, the metropolitan area of Valencia now integrates 74 municipalities. For the purpose of this paper, for reasons of space and time, we only analyze the situation of the eight metropolitan areas identified by the European Economic and Social Council following the METREX thresholds.

The metropolitan area, as an alternative form of local government, is a territorial and functional reality. It has little translation to legal terms because the official data of the Spanish Ministry of Planning Policy shows that in Spain, there are only four metropolitan entities legally established. They are all of a sectorial nature, such as the cases described above for Barcelona and Valencia. To these institutional areas, we should add the case of the Madrid area. This is the formation of a functional city-region nearly coincident with the limits of a single-province, autonomous region.

Analyzing the evolution and current status of the remaining areas, the map is unclear and the routes are quirky. They have a common feature: in searching for solutions to common problems, these areas have used agencies or forms of action that avoided the creation of a comprehensive metropolitan authority. They opted for alternative solutions such as voluntary consortia and associations of variable "geometry" (as defined in terms of territorial boundaries, composition, and scope of authority).

In particular, we note that the issue of metropolitan transportation, one of the basic problems of metropolitan areas, has been largely addressed through the creation of consortia. Examples are Bilbao (1976), Barcelona (2007), Valencia (2000), Seville (2001), Malaga (2003), and Zaragoza (2007). Other sectorial policies such as housing have been addressed through the creation of a consortium. Instances are found in Seville (2007) and Barcelona (2007). This form of organization has extended to other unique cases such as the *Development Digital Terrestrial Television Local Public Consortium*. It applies to the county boundary of Torrent-TV 35, Valencia (2006).

These informal forms of association have also provided a useful remedy to deal with some problems affecting multiple localities and/or metropolitan areas. It is not uncommon for services as diverse as promoting local employment and economic development, social or other services related to culture or sport, to be managed by associations. This is a dynamic that could be more frequently adopted with the current financial crisis. It should be considered in the context of the reform of local government operated by Law 57/2003. The law set in place measures for the modernization of local government and sought to improve the regulation of the powers of municipalities.

In Spain, only the metropolitan areas of Barcelona and Valencia can be said to have come to enjoy a metropolitan government. Their experience seems to be living proof of the failure of the model designed by the legislation on local governments. Yet, the case of Barcelona is full of ambiguity. It is difficult to understand the road that takes from the abolition in 1987 of the Metropolitan Corporation that was established in 1974 to the recent creation of the Metropolitan Area of Barcelona in 2010. (The recently creation of the area was approved unanimously by all political groups present in the Parliament by the Law 31/2010 of August 3, 2010.)

## Conclusions on the Future of Metropolitan Governments in Spain

As we have seen, different Spanish metropolitan areas have faced, either voluntarily or involuntarily, in a different way, the manner in which they place themselves in the new network society. Some jurisdictions have real metropolitan governments. They adopt two possible models. In the case of Madrid, we have an autonomous community. In the case of Barcelona, we have a "pure" metropolitan area—which is of recent creation. Other jurisdictions do not have a government as such. However, they have a strong civil society that considers itself a metropolitan area. This civil society determines the fate of the government that it really exists. This is in the case of Bilbao. In other jurisdictions, they have sought solutions through contractual arrangements in the form of either associations or consortia. This is the case of Seville, Malaga, and Zaragoza, among others. However, the vast majority does not have any authority, albeit institutional or social, that functions in terms of a metropolitan government. The most severe case is the example of Valencia.

It is in this last situation—the example of Valencia—where we find the greater risks. It is a situation in which no specific government institutions have been articulated for a metropolitan area. It also a reality in which a territorial political culture, which is the basis for a metropolitan area, does not seem to exist. In this type of conditions, it is where the risk emerges for special interests to exert their power over the more general metropolitan area as a whole. In that respect, various authors highlight the need to take "*neo-institutionalist* approaches, with greater presence of public authorities" (Farinós 2005: p. 224). We need to adopt these changes because of the immensity of the socioeconomic changes. Once and for all, metropolitan governments must be adopted, even as we assume a variety of models and alternatives.

In short, we are faced with the usual lack of coordination and inefficiency of local and sectorial policies. This is exacerbated by the deep economic crisis resulting in the questioning of the legitimacy of much of the traditional public functions. It is a period in which we seem to be avoiding new approaches to strategic planning and the institutionalization of an agreed formula and flexible metropolitan governance. This scenario can only limit the implementation of a better approach in addressing the economic and social changes that are already taking place. We are losing a historic opportunity for the consolidation of a new local political system.

# References

Farinós, J. 2005. "Nuevas formas de gobernanza para el desarrollo sostenible del espacio relacional", *Eria* 67: 219–235.

Farinós, j. et al tri 2005. "Planes estratégicos territoriales de carácter supramunicipal", Boletín de la A.G.E. 39: 117–149.

Jouve, B. 2005. *Cuestiones sobre gobernanza urbana.* Barcelona: Fundación Carlos Pi i Sunyer.

Rodríguez Álvarez, J.M. 2005. "Las áreas metropolitanas en Europa: un análisis causal y tipológico". *Revista de Estudios de la Administración Local y* Autonómica: 298–299.

# The Advisable Coordination of the Autonomic Environmental Taxation as Reluctance to the Development of Fiscal Federalism

C.J. Borrero Moro

Approval of the "Ley Organica 3/2009" of the 18th of December and modification of the "Ley Organica 8/1980" of the 22nd of September, which concern the financing of the autonomic regions (LOFCA), reforms the regulation of the exercise of the financial system of the autonomic communities, modifying the article 6.3 LOFCA.

The reform of the article 6.3 LOFCA concerns the scope of the taxing power of the CCAA in creating its own taxes and establishes a fixed limit, in relationship with the local taxes, for the "taxable events", overriding the previous and conflictive edition.

The "Ley Organica 3/2009" has as basic axis of the reform, the increasing of the autonomy and of the responsibility of the fiscal space of the CCAA. A regulatory framework is proposed in which the possibilities of the CCAA's own environmental taxes are increased, coinciding with the need to increase the sources of public income for the deficitary CCAA.

However, the environmental taxes are essentially legal tools conducted to preserve the environment; an aim that needs to influence all the sources of pollution that affect the territory of the autonomic community, even though they are not established inside its territory. From there, the coordination of the environmental taxes is advisable in order to achieve full compliance of this objective, as stated in the article 156.1 CE.

C.J. Borrero Moro (✉)
Facultad de Derecho de la Universitat de València, Avda. de los Naranjos, s/n,
46071 Valencia, Spain
e-mail: borrero@uv.es

A. López-Basaguren and L. Escajedo San Epifanio (eds.), *The Ways of Federalism*
*in Western Countries and the Horizons of Territorial Autonomy in Spain*, Vol. 2,
DOI 10.1007/978-3-642-27717-7_61, © Springer-Verlag Berlin Heidelberg 2013

# In Search of Gold: The New Reform of the Autonomic Financial System in 2009

Approval of the organic law 3/2009 of 18th December, which modifies the organic law 8/1980 of 22nd September, regarding funding of the autonomic communities (referred to hereafter as LOFCA), as well as approval of the law 22/2009, of 18th December, which regulates the financial system of the autonomic communities of common regime and cities of autonomous status and modifies specific tax rules (referred to hereafter as LSFCA), has meant a new reform of the autonomic community financial system (referred to hereafter as CCAA) by modifying the base year (now 2007) of setting the global financial requirements of the CCAA, based upon the real population, qualified in terms of their aging, dispersion, area in which they live, insularity, or academic age, as well as regulation of the activity of the financial powers with regards to resources, recognised by the CCAA in article 157.1 of the Spanish Constitution (hereafter referred to as CE).

The seed for the already mentioned normative modification is the Agreement of the council for fiscal and financial policy 6/2009 of 15th of July, for reform of the financial system of the autonomic communities of common regime and cities with autonomous status (hereafter referred to as the Agreement). In effect, the Agreement defines as one of the main features, to the point of classifying it as the basic axis of the new of autonomic financial system, the increase in autonomy and of fiscal co-responsibility. For this, the participation (cession rates) of the CCAA in the main assigned taxes is also increased. The normative powers of the CCAA are increased in this way, both in the autonomy of the CCAA to determinate the level of taxation and in the weight of the tax resources as part of its total financing. These circumstances introduce an element of flexibility into the system and a capacity for adaptation to the evolution of resources and needs, which accentuates its stability. Thus, it reinforces another of the main axes that articulate the reform of the autonomic financial system: the improve of the dynamics and stability of the system and its capacity for adjustment to financial necessities.

In the framework of the strong political desire to increase the fiscal areas of the CCAA in the new autonomic financial system, the Agreement deals with the communities' own taxes in an epigraph named "Clarificacion del espacio de los tributos propios de las CCAA" (clarification of the taxable areas of the CCAA). This proposes revising article 6.3 LOFCA by fixing the limit of the CCAA for the creation of its own taxes in the "hecho imponible" (taxable event) of the local taxes and not in its tax base, as has happened up to now. This is based in the constitutional interpretation (in this case) of the meaning of tax base, contained in the old LOFCA article (Judgment of the constitutional court 289/2000). This aims to establish "an autonomous community fiscal system that is clearer in its local taxes, following a layout similar to that which exists for the State taxes". By giving a greater legal security, this reform will try to avoid, "the actual habitual constitutional conflicts", which despite repeated constitutional jurisprudence, has allowed contradictory interpretations to exist in both constitutional doctrine and in scientific literature (Borrero 2004, 2008).

Proposals for reform of the autonomic financial system were embodied in the legal reforms referred to as "*supra*". In fact, the organic law 3/2009 for the modification of LOFCA proposes (as explained in its preamble) to "introduce in the general legal framework of the financing of the autonomous regions and cities of autonomous status, the changes incorporated in the 6/2009 agreement", i.e., regulation of the financial powers exercised by the CCAA.

## The Necessary Coordination of the Financial Autonomy of the CCAA

This new arrangement of the autonomic fiscal system appears to be more in line with the true sense of financial autonomy (in our belief), as constitutionally recognised by the CCAA. It advances on the path of overcoming the image of "*Hacienda autonómica parasitaria*" (the state tax authority as a parasite on the autonomous regions), built on the system of state transfers that were at odds with the principle of financial autonomy. The overcoming of this situation required, according to the doctrine, making real the principle of fiscal co-responsibility as criteria for the planning of the autonomic financial system, in the sense of giving the CCAA more legal and political responsibility for their own citizens, by allowing the CCAA to determine the level of taxation required for financing its responsibilities. In effect, the complete principle of financial autonomy requires that the CCAA have a leading role in the management of the financial resources, which will allow the financing of the granted powers; assuming the responsibility for contributing to the resolution of the tax pressure already existing in its territory. The attainment of this objective requires an increase in the tributary resources of the CCAA, understood as those they already exercise, totally or partially, in their regulatory capacity.

However, the financial autonomy attributed to the CCAA is a limited power. The financial autonomy "is not defined in the constitution in absolute terms, but is subject to the limitations of the principles, which the same article 156.1 of the Spanish constitution proclaims as 'coordination with the state treasury and of solidarity among all the Spanish people'" (Judgment of the constitutional court 179/87/2). More precisely, in the scope of our work, the power of the CCAA for establishing and levying taxes needs to be exercised "in agreement with the constitution and the law" (article 133.2 CE). Specifically, the coordination of the state and autonomic treasuries is the responsibility of the state legislator, as presented in article 157.3 CE, which through constitutional law regulates the exercise of the financial powers of the CCAA (their own taxes, assigned taxes, participation in the state's income, etc.) (article 157.1 CE) through the establishment of the LOFCA. In this is defined the extension and limits of the financial autonomy of the CCAA (STC 179/1987/2); i.e. LOFCA fixes the "framework and limits in which that autonomy has to act" (STC 179/87/2). Certainly, the state legislator is responsible for establishing the legal parameters, based on those that will lead to the integration of the autonomic financial subsystems into the state financial system. As recognised by the constitutional court "the unquestionable existing connection between the articles 133.1, 149.1.14.a and 157.3 CE, which determine that the state is competent for regulating not only its own taxes, but also the general framework of the whole tax system and the defining of the autonomic community financial powers in respect of the state's own taxes" (Judgment 192/2000/6).

All this is understood to be principally of benefit in contributing to achieving a tributary system that makes it possible that the contribution of all towards maintaining public expenditure is in agreement with the idea of tributary justice (article 31.1 CE). This requires a "dose of inevitable homogeneity" in the regulation of the taxes "as an unavoidable requirement of the equality of the Spanish" (Judgments of the constitutional court 19/1987/4 and 135/1992/6) and the principle of economic capacity. This constitutional mandate requires the coordination of state, autonomic and local taxes, with the aim of guaranteeing the attainment of constitutional purposes, which include, among others, contributing to public expenses according to the economic capacity of each individual, and other purposes such as environmental protection.

All these function within the framework of the constitutional configuration of the financial autonomy as a pillar of the territorial organisation of the State, constitutionally recognised by the CCAA (articles 2, 137 and 156.1 CE) to which specific tributary resources are attributed (article 157.1 CE). Therefore, the state legislator will be able to regulate through constitutional law the exercise of the constitutionally given financial powers of the CCAA, but would not be able to suppress them, neither expressly nor tacitly, through the establishment of strict limits that would nullify the capacity of the CCAA to fully or partly establish its own tributary resources.

Within this framework, the tributory power of the CCAA is constitutionally recognised for establishing their own taxes (articles 156.1, 133.2 and 157.1.b CE). This power forms an inevitable part of the basic content of the tributary autonomy (article 157.1.b CE) and is an intrinsic part of it. Its exercise has resulted in the establishment of its own taxes with non-tax purposes, notably environmental, that are aimed at the execution of its powers and generate little economic resource for the CCAA. This tributary power for establishing its own environmental taxes can and, as we understand, should be globally regulated by the state legislation in the interest of making real the idea of constitutional justice, but must not be suppressed by the state legislator (article 157.3 CE). Any regulation should be of its practice not of its existence.

## The Necessary Coordination of the Spatial Aspect of the Taxable Event of the Autonomic Regions' Own Environmental Taxes

Since 1980, the regulation by the state legislator of the practice of the autonomic financial powers in the LOFCA, specifically in article 6.2, determines that in the face of the impossibility of the CCAA to establish its own taxes if they coincide with those already imposed by the state, it has been decided to favour taxes with non-taxable purpose, notably environmental taxes. This explains the number of autonomic environmental taxes established during recent years.

The environmental tax is one of the responses of the legislator to one of the main problems that currently exists in society: the environmental problem. The environmental tax is characterised by being aimed at environmental preservation. This is achieved through modulating behaviours (encouraging those favouring the environment and discouraging the opposite) and through generating public income to environmental expenses by charging the people who have caused them. This justifies the establishment of the tax as a legal technique for environmental intervention.

The seriousness of the environmental problem and the necessity of acting are the two most important purposes and require the technical coordination of the environmental tax, which is based fundamentally on the principle of "who pollutes, pays". The fairness in environmental tax matters is nowadays identified with the same principle of "who pollutes, pays". In consequence, this is the principle of tributary justice that basically shapes the environmental taxes, always respecting the principle of economic capacity.

In this way, the environmental taxes based on its technical coordination put the environmental costs on its creators, through the technique of taxing the polluting activity and internalising the environmental costs by a tributary levy. This circumstance materialises in the contribution of the polluters to the public costs, based on the principle of the cause of costs.

Contamination does not have borders, although the planet itself is a physical one. However, political borders change this fact, although in some cases this reality is difficult to perceive; for example, in the case of waste that appears in a rubbish dump in a specific territory.

In the composition of the spatial aspect of the objective element of the taxable event of the environmental taxes, the requirements of the principle "the polluter pays" have serious legal limitations. Thus, this principle imposes a particular composition of the budget of the environmental tax, aimed at taxing all the polluting activities (emissions, waste dumping, etc.) that are expected to be charged with the tax for polluting the territory, in our case, autonomic. It can therefore be seen that the power of the tax authority is limited to its territory. This means that it cannot apply a tax to those polluting activities that, even when they pollute in said form (emissions, waste dumping etc.) in the said territory, are not produced in this same territory, i.e. the source of contamination is not located in the area for which the autonomic law applies. For this reason, the environmental tax has been established and its efficiency developed.

The environmental effectiveness of certain environmental autonomic taxes is limited; especially those that attempt to influence the physical elements not totally within the area of effectiveness of the autonomic law (as happens with air or with water). Taking the case of a river that passes through different CCAAs, this cannot be fully environmentally protected by the establishment of an autonomic environmental tax that holds liable the polluting wastes in its community because, even though its own stretch would be less contaminated, if the autonomic community up-river does not establish an environmental tax, the river will be still polluted by the water coming from that community.

The same can be said of the polluting emissions in the atmosphere, and with more reason. This is the case with industries located in areas bordering other CCAAs. Certainly, these industries, which are the source of the contamination, are physically outside the autonomic communities affected by the contamination. But, the communities suffer the polluting effects and, as a consequence of the source not being located in the area regulated by these laws, are not able to apply the tributary rules. So, in this case there would be no possibility of applying the principle of "the polluter pays".

The solution, we believe, lies in the sphere of coordination between the state legislation of autonomous and state treasuries.


## The Italian Response: Fiscal Federalism

The reform of Title V, of part II of the Italian constitution (hereafter CI) created by the constitutional law of the 28 October of 2001, n.3, organises a constitutional text that is dedicated to the territorial distribution of financial power in Italia. This is referred to as fiscal federalism; i.e. organisation of the legal and political system characterised by the adoption of criteria to promote the financial autonomy of the sub-central entities (regions and municipalities). Financial autonomy has always existed in the sub-central entities disposed of sufficient and correct resources with respect to their attributed powers (Tosi and Giovanardi 2006), either through their own taxes or by the participation in income from the state taxes in the territories of the region (Alfano 2005).

A doctrinal and political debate is currently brewing about the scope of the Italian fiscal federalism. In this respect, the Italian constitution recognises the financial autonomy of the regions (article 119.1). Thus, they may have autonomic tributary resources and have the power to establish and collect their own taxes and income, according to the constitution and to the principles of coordination with the public treasury and the tax system, such as participation in the generation of state taxes in the respective territories (article 119.2) and in a sufficient mode (article 119.3 CI).

In this way, the tributary autonomy of the regions is limited by the principle of coordination, which consists of current legislation between state and the autonomous regions on the coordination of the public treasury and the tax laws. Therefore, legislative authority is given to the regions, within the framework of the fundamental principles fixed by the state (article 117.3 CI). Finally, the legislative power regarding any matter not expressly covered by the state legislation corresponds to the regions (article 114.4 CI).

In light of which, the regions have the legislative competence for establishing their own tributes because such matters are not covered by state jurisdiction (art. 117.4 CI) (Del Federico 2006), although the requirements of the constitutional principle of coordination of the global tributary system are derived from the state's legislative framework (articles 119.2 and 117.3 CI) (Tosi and Giovanardi 2006)

The state authority for coordinating the tributary system covers, therefore, its own regional taxes, although without specification because article 119 CI does not cover this matter either. In this way, the doctrine prefers that the legislator avoids regulation of every one of its taxes, but instead configures the structural elements of the possible taxes so that the regions can establish and implement the taxes as regional taxes (Del Federico 2006) in order to make real a tributary system that requires a minimum of homogeneity in regulation of the taxes (Sorrentino 2010). Meanwhile, the Italian constitutional court sustains that the coordination in such matters requires the establishment of fundamental principles to which the regional legislators must hold, as well as the determination of the structure of the tributary system, indicating precisely the options of the regions in relation to the type of tax and the characteristics of the region's own taxes (Judgment 37/2004).

This mandate for the coordination of the tributary system (included in article 119 CI) has taken form in law 42, of 5th May 2009, in which the fundamental principles of public financial coordination and of the tributary system are established. However, the law delegates to the government the issue of legislative decrees pertaining to the application of article 119 CI, with the aim of securing the financial autonomy of the regions through the fixing of these fundamental principles of coordination (article 2.1 of Law 42/2009). It is established as principle and guideline that these legislative decrees must give information about, for example, the following: with respect to the autonomous tax system (article 2.2.a), the rationality and coherence of each tax and of the tax system as a whole (article 2.2.c); with respect to the principle of economic capacity (article 2.2.1), the prohibition of double taxation in the same budget (article 2.2.o); the possibility to set their own regional taxes if they are not levied by the state (article 2.2.q). These make manifest the choice for cooperative federalism, as targeted by the doctrine (Alfano 2005; Del Federico 2006).

This is the narrative framework in which the environmental taxes should be analysed, especially in the local and regional context. It should be established in the state laws and attribute to the sub-central bodies the regulation of their payments and, eventually, of some quantitative elements (such as tax base and type of assessment) (Marchetti 2006) pertaining to those taxes that are characterised by having non-fiscal objectives, specifically environmental preservation, It should be remembered that the regions are recognised as having the exclusive authority for environmental guardianship in spite of its establishment as exclusive competence of the state legislation (article 117.2 CI). However, the constitutional court has realised an extensive interpretation of this and regards the environment as "materia transversal" (cross-cutting). As a result, they manifest various responsibilities, which can be regional or of the state, corresponding to the task of establishing the standards of uniform guardianship over all the national territory (Judgment n.407/2002 and n.96/2003) (Marchetti 2006).

Generally speaking, at the time of setting the requirements for coordination of the tributary system, both the guidelines and the doctrine are concerned with the results of the principle of economic capacity as a guarantee of the system's coverage (Cipollina 2009; Del Federico 2006). However, this special effort does not prevent part of the doctrine from emphasising the inefficiencies of the regional environmental taxes, as a consequence of the asymmetry between the dimension of the phenomenon of the contamination and the area of the tribute's application, especially in the framework of those environmental taxes that are applicable to polluting activities that are not connected to the territory; specifically, polluting emissions (Cipollina 2009; Alfano 2005). Thus, in this framework, a method of state environmental taxation is favoured, without discarding other forms of taxation (Alfano 2005).

This thesis now finds regulatory support in the fundamental principles of coordination, as fixed in the law 42/2009, which establishes as one of its principles the necessary rationality and coherence of each tax and of the tributary system as a whole.

## Solution Proposals

The decision to favour the full materialisation of the financial autonomy of the CCAA in our political system cannot ignore the constitutional requirements of making real, through coordination of the state and autonomic treasuries, the contribution to public expenses through a fair tributary system (article 31.1 CE). This fairness should be evident both in the contribution according to the economic capacity of each individual, as well as in the full preservation of the environment, for which the coordination of the autonomic tributary subsystems is vital.

This coordination is now described in the article 6 LOFCA, although it refers to the requirements of the principle of economic capacity. Now, we ask ourselves if it is necessary to extend these rules of coordination to issues such as those related to the spacial aspect of the objective element of the taxable event of the environmental taxes, especially those that tax the polluting emissions or waste that affect some CCAA. This would deal with the limits to the area over which the autonomic legal rules are effective and thus realise the purpose of the environmental tax in that the polluters assume the environmental costs,

These measures could consist of the establishment of a state environmental tax, on emissions or waste, of a framework character, which could be quantitatively substituted for the existing framework in those CCAA that opt for its establishment and would guarantee both the autonomy of the CCAA and permit them to fix, within reasonable limits, the quantitative aspect of the tax and the coordination of the tributary subsystems, with the final aim of full environmental preservation through environmental fiscality.

# References

ALFANO, R.: "L'applicazione di tributi ambientali nel nuovo contesto della finanza regionale", TributImpresa, núm. 3/2005.

BORRERO MORO, C.J.: *La materia imponible en los tributos extrafiscales. ¿Presupuesto de realización de la autonomía financiera?*, Aranzadi, 2004.

BORRERO MORO, C.J.: *El reparto de la materia imponible entre la Hacienda Autonómica y Local. Tirant lo Blanch, 2008.*

CIPOLLINA, S.: "Observazioni sulla fiscalità ambientale nella prospettiva del federalismo fiscales" RSFSF, núm. 4/I/2009.

DEL FEDERICO.L.: "L'autonomia tributaria delle regioni ed il principio di coordinamento de la finanza pubblica: CON IL PROGETTO Giorda bis verso l'attuazioni dell'art. 119", RDFSF, 2006, I, 1.

MARCHETTI, F.: "Ambiente (DIR. TRIB.), en *Dizionario di Diritto Pubblico, CASSESE, S. (dir.), Giuffrè, Milano, 2006, Vol. I.*

SORRENTINO, F.: "Coordinamento e principi costituzionali", RT núm. 6/2010.:

TOSI, L. y GIOVANARDI, A.: "FEDERALISMO (DIR. TRIB.), en *Dizionario di Diritto Pubbico, CASSESE, S. (dir.), Giuffrè, Milano, 2006, Vol. III.*